RECORDS OF CIVILIZATION

SOURCES AND STUDIES

Edited under the auspices of the
Department of History, Columbia University

GENERAL EDITOR: W. T. H. Jackson, Professor of German and History

PAST EDITORS

1915-1926

James T. Shotwell, Bryce Professor Emeritus of the
History of International Relations

1926-1953
Austin P. Evans, Late Professor of History

1953-1962
Jacques Barzun, Seth Low Professor of History

Number XI
The Sources for the Early History of Ireland:
Ecclesiastical

THE SOURCES FOR THE
EARLY HISTORY OF IRELAND:
Ecclesiastical

AN INTRODUCTION AND GUIDE

by

JAMES F. KENNEY

1966
OCTAGON BOOKS, INC.
New York

PATRI MEO

MARTIN KENNEY

SACRUM

Reprinted 1966
by special arrangement with Columbia University Press

OCTAGON BOOKS, INC.
175 FIFTH AVENUE
NEW YORK, N.Y. 10010

LIBRARY OF CONGRESS CATALOG CARD NUMBER 66-15998

Printed in U.S.A. by
NOBLE OFFSET PRINTERS, INC.
NEW YORK 3, N. Y.

EDITOR'S FOREWORD

THE primary object of this series is to bring easily within the reach of the inquiring reader certain treatises and documents which are of real importance for an understanding of the past. This aim is readily intelligible to anyone who has ever attempted to scratch beneath the surface in the investigation of any event, or who has endeavored to gain a little first-hand information about a people or an epoch. Many of us have neither the time nor the equipment to do this without the aid of translations and a certain amount of suggestion in the way of critical introduction and commentary.

In some fields of study there is also a lack of bibliographical guides which will lead the reader quickly and surely into his subject. In a few such cases the series attempts to make good this lack by including in its numbers works of bibliography. It is not the intention to publish here simple lists of books, but careful critical guides to the sources. To this group belongs the present work by Dr. Kenney.

The volume is timely. Within the last few years the study of Irish history has received new impetus, due, at least in part, to the events culminating in the establishment of the Irish Free State. But the materials for such study, especially for the early period of the history of Ireland, are widely scattered and difficult to find. There has been a real need of a guide, which the student might consult and in which he would find a critical evaluation of texts and literature. Into the making of the present volume Dr. Kenney has put much painstaking research, continued through a long period of years. The price of toil has won for him the right to speak. No labor has been spared to make the volume at once accurate and readable.

AUSTIN P. EVANS.

PREFACE TO 1966 REPRINT

James F. Kenney's book *Sources for the Early History of Ireland* (*Ecclesiastical*) not only established itself at once as an indispensable work of reference but marked an epoch in Hibernian studies. From its publication to the present day it has stimulated research on such a wide front as few books of this kind have ever done. Having been out of print for years, it is now issued as a reprint, incorporating a certain amount of revision.

The need of bringing Kenney's *Sources* up to date has been felt for some time. As far back as 1955, Jacques Barzun, as General Editor of the *Records of Civilization* series, approached the doyen in the field of early Irish history, Professor John Ryan, S.J., of University College Dublin, about a revision. The latter, owing to his many duties, had to decline, and suggested me. Being fully aware of the magnitude of the task, I did not accept without hesitation. I realized not only that this was a long-term project, especially for one who could give it only some portion of his working time and had to work singlehanded, but also that the publication of a new Kenney had better be postponed until a number of major enterprises, then at various stages of preparation or realization, were completed. That time has not yet come, and the amount of learned work bearing on the subject is steadily increasing. In the meantime I have done my best to take stock of the rich harvest that has been reaped so far, to keep a watchful eye on work in progress, to push ahead my own researches, and to encourage others engaged in similar pursuits.

When, in the autumn of 1964, I learned that Octagon Books was planning a reprint, I at once consulted the Columbia University Press, under whose license the reprint was to be issued, about the possibility of a preliminary revision at this stage. It was agreed that, while a full-scale revision was out of the question, one of limited scope was as feasible as it would be desirable.

For the present revision I have drawn on the following materials:

1. Corrections and additions made by Kenney himself in his hand copy.—This copy, along with all of Kenney's books, was bequeathed to University College Dublin and now forms part of its library. I am greatly indepted to the college librarian, Miss Ellen Power, for having placed this precious book at my unlimited disposal. Kenney's entries range from the marking of broken type to the addition of bibliographical references and the questioning of particular statements. In point of time, unfortunately, they do not go beyond 1931.

2. Reviews.—I have read carefully all the reviews of Kenney's book that have come to my notice. Four of the reviewers make substantial contributions to the subject in question: Dom L. Gougaud, O.S.B., in *RHE* XXVI (1930), 663–6; E. Gwynn in *EHR* XLVI (1931), 484–5; W. Levison in *Hist. Zs.* CXLV (1931–32), 580–2; and F. Lot in *Le Moyen Age*, 3d ser., XL (1930), 240–79. All criticism of detail by these and other reviewers has been taken into account; it has, of course, been impossible to take up issues of a more general nature such as those raised by F. Lot.

3. My own notes from learned literature up to 1931 (the year at which Kenney's revision stops).—For practical reasons, however, this limit has been exceeded in two directions. First, I have changed the form of Kenney's references to manuscript wherever it differs from the present shelfmark or catalogue number. I have neglected only such minor inconsistencies as RIA 13.P. 16 and RIA 13 P 16, or Bodl. Auct. III. 15 and Bodl.Auct.3.15 (the second form, in either instance, being that of the latest catalogue) because there can be no danger of confusion. Second, I have revised all datings of manuscripts in the light of recent research. The technique of reproduction here employed has made it impossible to give my reasons or to quote my authorities. In many instances the datings are those of Dr. E. A. Lowe's *Codices Latini Antiquiores*; others have been provided by Professor Bernhard Bischoff of Munich, privately as well as in his published work. For illuminated manuscripts I have consulted also the art historians, in particular Françoise Henry and Carl Nordenfalk; for biblical texts the Sigla volume of the Beuron *Vetus Latina*; and for liturgical manuscripts Klaus Gamber's *Codices Latini Laturgici*. In other instances the responsibility is entirely mine.

For technical reasons, only line corrections have been made in the actual text; the remainder has been gathered into Addenda, 1966, and Corrigenda, following upon the Addenda of the first edition.

It is hoped that this reissue of Kenney's *Sources* will be found to present the work purged of those minor blemishes which no pioneer can entirely avoid and which the author himself was most anxious to eliminate, and that it will play its part in the continued progress of studies in early Irish history along the lines laid down by Kenney (*Cath. Hist. Rev.* XVII, 1931, 1–9) thirty-five years ago.

                                                Ludwig Bieler

University College Dublin.

PREFACE

THE work of which the present volume is the first part is designed to serve as an introduction and guide to the study of the written sources for the early history of Ireland, so far as they have been made available in print. The period treated is that prior to the Anglo-Norman invasion, and terminates about A.D. 1170. The volume now published deals with the sources that have a character or associations predominantly ecclesiastical, and also with the references to Ireland that are found in the ancient writers of continental Europe and of Britain. It is hoped that a second volume may cover the Irish secular sources and such later foreign records as do not relate chiefly to ecclesiastical affairs. No absolute lines of division have, however, been drawn, either in time limits or in subject classification. The two volumes will, it is believed, constitute a fairly complete survey of the documentary—the word is used in its broadest sense — sources of early Irish history. An excellent guide to the archaeological sources is already provided by Dr. Mac-alister's *The Archaeology of Ireland*.

The scope of this survey has been made as broad as possible so as to cover all significant documents illustrative of old Irish life and civilisation. The sources listed are primarily those that can be consulted in printed editions, but notice has also been taken of some of the relatively few texts that are still confined to the manuscripts. Moreover, although the book is not a catalogue of manuscripts, some account is given of all important codices, written by Irish hands or under Irish influence within the period under consideration, of which facsimiles, analyses of the contents, or other descriptions have been published.

The normal treatment of each source is to give, first, the title and the date, or approximate date, followed by the *incipit* and *explicit* of the text; then a bibliographical paragraph, listing manuscripts and editions and the more valuable commentaries in books or periodicals; finally, a summary exposition of the character and significance of the document, and of the results of such noteworthy critical study as it may have received. From this scheme there are, of course, many divergences; especially in the treatment of foreign sources it has often seemed unnecessary to provide so full a critical apparatus. In the introductions, with their bibliographies, to the several chapters, sections, and subsections, an attempt has been made to present briefly the general characteristics and the historical settings of the various groups into which the sources have been classified.

The writer began his investigations into the historical records of Ireland when he was a graduate student at the University of Wisconsin in 1907–1908. The plan of the book took definite shape when he was at Columbia University in 1909–1910. The work was continued slowly through later years when the greater part of his time and energy had to be given to other tasks. In November, 1926, the manuscript of the present volume was placed in the hands of the printer. It was possible to make some slight changes in the text after it had reached the printer, but for the most part material that was either first published or first brought to the author's notice since that date has been treated in the *Addenda* at the end of the volume. To those *Addenda* the attention of the reader is directed.

It is a matter of regret that individual acknowledgment cannot here be made of the assistance that has been so fully and freely given by many scholars — historians and librarians — in both America and Europe. To five among them, however, the author feels that he must render explicit homage. To Dr. John L. Gerig, of Columbia University, under whom he studied Old and Middle Irish, he has appealed repeatedly for information and advice, and always with success. The late Kuno Meyer read a large part of the manuscript while it was still in relatively crude form. His kindly approbation is a treasured memory, and his suggestions and emendations have contributed materially to the making of the book. Father Paul Grosjean, S.J., of the Society of Bollandists, has shown an interest of the most helpful kind in the welfare of the work; to his keen observation, critical acumen and broad scholarship every section of it is indebted. The debt would have been still greater had it not been that the text was already in proof when it first came to his attention. Dr. James T. Shotwell, former editor of the series, has not only by counsel and criticism guided the author's efforts, but also by his own unflagging patience and enthusiasm kept him keyed to the task through long and difficult years. To him and his successor in the editor's chair it is due that the volume ever reached the stage where publication was possible, just as publication itself is due to the generosity of the Columbia University Press.

JAMES F. KENNEY.

TEDAVNET, OTTAWA, CANADA.
Lá Fhéile Pádraig, 1929.

CONTENTS

CONTENTS

MAPS
[At the End of the Volume]

ECCLESIASTICAL IRELAND IN THE EARLY MIDDLE AGES

EXTERNAL RELATIONS OF THE IRISH CHURCH IN THE EARLY MIDDLE AGES

ABBREVIATIONS

AA. SS. Boll. = *Acta Sanctorum* of the Bollandists [*cf*. p. 289 *infra*].
AA. SS. ex Cod. S. = *Acta Sanctorum ex Codice Salmanticensi* [*cf*. p. 304].
AB = Antiphonary of Bangor. *AB* = Warren's ed. [*cf*. pp. 706–7].
AC = Annals of Connacht.
ACL = *Archiv für celtische Lexicographie* [*cf*. p. 94].
AdeJ = Henri d'Arbois de Jubainville. AdeJ *Cat.* = *Essai d'un catalogue de la littérature épique de l'Irlande;* AdeJ *CLC* = *Cours de littérature celtique* [*cf*. pp. 92, 106].
AH = *Archivium Hibernicum* [*cf*. p. 94].
AHR = *American Historical Review* [*cf*. p. 93].
ALC = Annals of Loch Cé. *ALC* = Hennessy's ed. [*cf*. pp. 34, 104].
An. Boll. = *Analecta Bollandiana* [*cf*. p. 289].
An. hymn. = *Analecta hymnica medii aevi.* Blume *An. hymn.* LI = Clemens Blume *Die Hymnen des Thesaurus Hymnologicus H. A. Daniels* I [*cf*. p. 250].
Anec. = *Anecdota from Irish manuscripts* [*cf*. p. 104].
Anec. Oxon. = *Anecdota Oxoniensia* [*cf*. p. 72].
AU = Annals of Ulster. *AU* = ed. by Hennessy and MacCarthy [*cf*. pp. 23, 66].

BB = Book of Ballymote [*cf*. p. 24].
Bede *HE* = Bede's *Historia ecclesiastica gentis Anglorum* [*cf*. p. 230].
Bibl. hag. lat. = *Bibliotheca hagiographica latina* of the Bollandists; *Supp.* = *Supplementum* [*cf*. p. 288].
Bk. Fen. = Book of Fenagh [*cf*. p. 401].
Bk. Fer. = Book of Fermoy [*cf*. p. 24].
Bk. Lec. = Great Book of Lecan [*cf*. p. 25].
Bk. Lis. = Book of Lismore [*cf*. pp. 25, 308].
BM = British Museum, London.
BN = Bibliothèque nationale, Paris.
BNE = Charles Plummer *Bethada Náem nÉrenn Lives of Irish Saints* [*cf*. p. 290].
Bodl. = Bodleian Library, Oxford.
Bouquet = Martin Bouquet etc. *Rerum Gallicarum et Francicarum scriptores* [*cf*. p. 103].

CGG = J. H. Todd *Cogadh Gaedhel re Gallaibh The War of the Gaedhil with the Gaill* [*cf*. p. 104].
Cod. K. = Codex Kilkenniensis [*cf*. p. 305].
Cod. S. = Codex Salmanticensis [*cf*. p. 304].
Colgan *AA. SS.* = Colgan *Acta Sanctorum . . . Hiberniae; Tr. Thaum.* = *Triadis Thaumaturgae* [*cf*. pp. 41, 289].
Corp. SS. eccl. lat. = *Corpus scriptorum ecclesiasticorum latinorum* [*cf*. p. 104].
CS = Chronicum Scotorum. *CS* = Hennessy's ed. [*cf*. pp. 65, 104].

DNB = *Dictionary of National Biography* [*cf*. p. 105].

Duine *Memento* = F. Duine *Memento des sources hagiographiques de l'histoire de Bretagne* [*cf.* p. 170].

Eg. = Egerton MSS in the British Museum [*cf.* p. 90 n. 374].
EHR = *English Historical Review* [*cf.* p. 93].
EW = Ernst Windisch.

f., ff. = folio, folios.
Fél. Oeng. = Félire, or Calendar, of Oengus. *Fél. Oeng.*[1] = first ed. (Dublin 1880); *Fél. Oeng.*[2] = second ed. (London 1905) [*cf.* pp. 479–80].
Flower *Cat.* = R. Flower *Catalogue of Irish manuscripts in the British Museum* vol. II [*cf.* p. 90].
FM = Annals of the Four Masters. *FM* = O'Donovan's ed. [*cf.* pp. 43, 66].
3 Frags. = O'Donovan *Annals of Ireland Three Fragments* [*cf.* p. 45].

Hardy *Cat.* = T. D. Hardy *Descriptive catalogue of materials relating to the history of Great Britain and Ireland* [*cf.* p. 91].
Harl. = Harleian collection of MSS in the British Museum [*cf.* p. 88].
Hist. Zs. = *Historische Zeitschrift* [*cf.* p. 93].
HZ = Heinrich Zimmer.
H&S = Haddan and Stubbs *Councils and ecclesiastical documents relating to Great Britain and Ireland* [*cf.* p. 104].

IAS = Irish Archaeological Society [*cf.* p. 64].
IA&CS = Irish Archaeological and Celtic Society [*cf.* p. 64].
IER = *Irish Ecclesiastical Record* [*cf.* p. 94].
Ir. Sage: see RTh.
IT = *Irische Texte* [*cf.* p. 104].
ITS = Publications of the Irish Texts Society [*cf.* p. 81].

JTS = *Journal of Theological Studies* [*cf.* p. 93].

KM = Kuno Meyer.

LA = Liber Ardmachanus, Book of Armagh. *LA* = Gwynn's ed. [*cf.* p. 337].
Laud = Laud collection of MSS in the Bodleian Library [*cf.* p. 87]. Unless otherwise stated, the reference is to the "Miscellaneous" series.
LBr = Lebar Brecc, or Speckled Book [*cf.* p. 25].
LH = Liber Hymnorum. LH(F) = the Franciscan Convent MS; LH(T) = the Trinity College MS. *LH*[1] = Todd's ed. (1855–69); *LH*[2] = ed. by Bernard and Atkinson (1898) [*cf.* p. 716].
Lis. Lives = Whitley Stokes *Lives of saints from the Book of Lismore* [*cf.* p. 308].
LL = Lebar Laignech, or Book of Leinster [*cf.* p. 15].
LU = Lebar na hUidre, or Book of the Dun [Cow] [*cf.* p. 15].

Mabillon *AA. SS. o. s. B.* = *Acta Sanctorum ordinis sancti Benedicti* ed. J. Mabillon, etc. [*cf.* p. 289].
MacN = Eóin [John] MacNeill.
Manitius *Lat. Lit.* = Max Manitius *Geschichte der lateinischen Literatur des Mittelalters* [*cf.* p. 91].
Mart. = Martyrology. *Mart. Don.* = O'Donovan, Todd and Reeves *Martyrology of Donegal* [*cf.* p. 485].

MGH = Monumenta Germaniae Historica. The abbreviations for the several series are usually readily comprehensible; *SS* = the *Scriptores [rerum Germanicarum]* series begun by Pertz [*cf.* p. 103].

MHB = Monumenta Historica Britannica [*cf.* p. 104].

Migne *PG* = J. P. Migne *Patrologiae cursus completus Series graeca et orientalis*.

Migne *PL = Series latina* [*cf.* p. 104].

Moran *Essays* = P. F. Moran *Essays on the origin, doctrines and discipline of the early Irish Church* [*cf.* p. 109].

NA = Neues Archiv der Gessellschaft für ältere deutsche Geschichtskunde [*cf.* p. 93].

O'C = Eugene O'Curry, or Curry. O'C *MS Mat.* = *Lectures on the manuscript materials of ancient Irish history;* O'C *M&C = Manners and customs of the ancient Irish* [*cf.* pp. 92, 109].

O'D = John O'Donovan.

O'Grady *Cat.* = Standish H. O'Grady *Catalogue of Irish manuscripts in the British Museum* vol. I; O'Grady *SG = Silva Gadelica* [*cf.* pp. 90, 104].

OI = Old Irish.

PH = Robt. Atkinson *The passions and the homilies from Leabhar Breac* [*cf.* p. 740].

Proc. = Proceedings.

Rawl. = Rawlinson collection of MSS in the Bodleian Library [*cf.* p. 88].

RC = Revue Celtique [*cf.* p. 94].

Reeves *Ad.* = William Reeves *The Life of St. Columba by Adamnan* [*cf.* p. 430].

Rer. Hib. SS. = O'Conor *Rerum Hibernicarum scriptores veteres* [*cf.* p. 104].

RH = Revue Historique [*cf.* p. 93].

RHE = Revue d'histoire ecclésiastique [*cf.* p. 93].

RIA = Royal Irish Academy.

Roger *L'Enseignement* = M. Roger *L'Enseignement des lettres classiques d'Ausone à Alcuin* [*cf.* p. 106].

RS = Rolls Series [*cf.* p. 104].

RSAI = Royal Society of Antiquaries of Ireland.

RTh = Rudolf Thurneysen. RTh *Ir. Sage = Die irische Helden- und Königsage* [*cf.* p. 79].

s = saeculum, century.

Schmitz I = H. J. Schmitz *Die Bussbücher und die Bussdisciplin der Kirche;* Schmitz II = *Die Bussbücher und die kanonische Bussverfahren* [*cf.* p. 235].

SHR = Scottish Historical Review [*cf.* p. 94].

Skene *Picts and Scots* = W. F. Skene *Chronicles of the Picts, Chronicles of the Scots and other early memorials of Scottish history* [*cf.* p. 104].

SS = Scriptores, scriptorum, etc.; Sancti, sanctorum, etc.

Stowe = Stowe collection of MSS in the Royal Irish Academy [*cf.* p. 89].

TCD = Trinity College, Dublin.

Thes. Pal. = Stokes and Strachan *Thesaurus Palaeohibernicus* [*cf.* p. 104].

Tig. = Annals of Tigernach. *Tig.* = ed. by Whitley Stokes in the *Revue Celtique* [*cf.* p. 75].

Trans. = Transactions; translation, translated, etc.

ABBREVIATIONS

UJA = *Ulster Journal of Archaeology* [*cf.* p. 94].
Ussher *Sylloge* = Jas. Ussher *Veterum epistolarum Hibernicarum sylloge* [*cf.* p. 104].

Van der Essen *Étude* = L. Van der Essen *Étude critique et littéraire sur les vitae des saints mérovingiens de l'ancienne Belgique* [*cf.* p. 486].
Vat. = Vatican Library, Rome.
Vit. Trip. = Vita Tripartita, the Tripartite Life of St. Patrick. *Vit. Trip.* = ed. by Whitley Stokes [*cf.* pp. 104, 342].
VV. SS. Hib. = Plummer *Vitae Sanctorum Hiberniae* [*cf.* p. 290].

Warren *Lit.* = F. E. Warren *Liturgy and ritual of the Celtic Church* [*cf.* p. 684].
Wattenbach *DGQ* = W. Wattenbach *Deutschlands Geschichtsquellen im Mittelalter* [*cf.* p. 91].
WS = Whitley Stokes.

YBL = Yellow Book of Lecan [*cf.* p. 24].

Z = Johann Kaspar Zeuss. Z¹ = *Grammatica Celtica*, first ed. (1853); Z² = second ed. (1871) [*cf.* p. 95].
ZCP = *Zeitschrift für celtische Philologie* [*cf.* p. 94].
ZK = *Zeitschrift für Kirchengeschichte* [*cf.* p. 93].
Zs. = Zeitschrift.

In bibliographical references the number of the volume is usually indicated by Roman numerals, capitals; the number of the part, chapter, or section by Roman numerals, small; and the number of the page or column by Arabic numerals. Occasionally a suprascript Arabic numeral is used to indicate the number of the edition.

In dating, the following signs and abbreviations have been employed: *c* = "about"; *–in* = the beginning, and *–ex* = the end, of the century of which the number is given; the sign / = "or"; — signifies the whole period of which the first and last dates are given; and x, that the date in question falls somewhere within the period so indicated.

CHAPTER I

HISTORY IN IRELAND

I. The Early Records—Pre-Viking Period

The great majority of the written sources for the history of Ireland in the early middle ages are due to two sets of institutions, the monastic churches and the secular orders of learning. Although occasionally compositions in prose or verse may have been produced outside these specialised circles, it was only within them that the organisation and machinery existed to ensure the preservation of such texts.

Christianity came into Ireland in the fifth, or, quite probably, the fourth century. It brought with it the Latin language and the art of writing. Latin became the ecclesiastical language of Ireland as of the rest of western Europe, and seems to have been used as freely in Irish church circles as in those of lands where it was, in some form, the daily speech of the people. But in Ireland the speech of the people was Irish, and Irish was a language with both a national and a literary prestige. Although individual ecclesiastics may have occasionally displayed the scorn of their continental brethren for the vulgar tongue, the Church as a whole took Irish into its service in a spirit of liberal utilitarianism. The Latin system of writing was applied to Goidelic, and all through the middle ages Irish orthography retained marks of its origin in a society dominated by the Latin speech of foreign missionaries. Although Latin was the official language, employed in the great majority of formal documents, Irish was in constant use, especially for devotional, expository, and interpretative writings.

The following is a summary list of the chief classes of texts which were produced or preserved in the monasteries: (1) *acta sanctorum*, generally the Lives of founders of monasteries; also calendars, martyrologies, and like documents; (2) disciplinary regulations, including monastic rules, church canons, penitentials; (3) devotional compositions—hymns, prayers, religious poems, etc.; (4) homiletic literature;

(5) theological and philosophical compositions, especially works of
exegesis; (6) imaginative religious literature, including voyage and
vision tales and semi-apocryphal matter, to which may be added prophecies; (7) letters, charters, and other documents of a diplomatic character; (8) annals and chronicles. In addition there were the various
church and school books, the common heritage of Latin Christianity,
some of which acquired an Irish identity either by variations in the
text or by the attached commentary: (9) the Sacred Scriptures;
(10) apocrypha; (11) the writings of the Fathers and of other famous
churchmen; (12) liturgical books and documents; (13) works of Latin
classical authors, and possibly a few Greek texts; (14) treatises on
Latin grammar; (15) scientific texts, chiefly astronomical, computistical
and geographical writings.

Beside the ecclesiastical learning stood the secular.[1] In ancient
Gaul there were three orders of learning—the druids, the bards, and
those whom classical writers call *vates* [2]—and it is probable that in
pagan Ireland a similar organisation existed. In Christian times the
druids had disappeared, after a struggle against the new religion which
is celebrated in various hagiographical compositions. The bards
remained, although occupying an inferior status. The *vates* were represented by two bodies, the brehons, or jurisconsults, and the *filid*.[3] These
filid were the official *savants* and *littérateurs* of Ireland, to whom was
entrusted the care of the national traditions, literature and scholarship.

The separation of the functions of the brehon (*brithem, brethem,*
plur. *brithemin*) from those of the *fili* (plur. *filid*) had taken place, it
would appear, in pre-Christian times.[4] The brehon was not a judge;
in Ireland, as in other early societies, what we would call "the
administration of justice" as well as "the preservation of law
and order" was a function of the king. The brehon resembled
the Roman jurisconsult; he was the specialist who knew, preserved, and to some degree developed the law, to whom disputes and
difficulties were referred, and whose decision or opinion was usually
accepted as binding. He taught the law to his disciples, by whom his
interpretations and commentaries would be handed on from generation
to generation. The treatises now commonly known as the "Brehon

---

1 On the secular learning of ancient Ireland see especially AdeJ *CLC* I; also his "Les bardes en Irlande
et dans le pays de Galles" *RH* VIII (1878) 1–9.
2 The *word* survived in Irish as *fáith*, "prophet."
3 Believed to be from a root * *vel-*, "to see."
4 The memory of this separation is incorporated into the tale entitled *Immacallam in dá thuarad*, "Colloquy of the two sages."

Laws"—parts of them possibly as old as the sixth century—were the text-books of these ancient law schools. They were the only law records. There were no collections of case law or statute law. A small number of famous decisions—usually with legendary settings—are preserved in the text-books, but there was no official registration of judgments; and although formal legislation, of a kind and on rare occasions, took place, the terms of such enactments were simply handed down as part of the general *senchas*, history, of the nation.

The *filid* were a larger body than the brehons, with less specialised functions but a more developed organisation. They formed a close corporation, having a hierarchical order of dignities, a professional solidarity and *esprit de corps*, an esoteric teaching, including secret languages and cryptic writings, and an elaborate system of training recruits. According to legendary accounts they formed, in early ages, an itinerant fraternity, unrestrained by any ties or regulations, and wielding a tremendous power because of their prestige and the universal dread of their satire. So oppressive did they become by their increasing numbers, insolence and exactions that a national assembly was summoned to decree their banishment. This is localised at the *mórdáil*, or "grand convention," of Druim-Cetta, in 575, where, we are told, St. Colum-cille defended the *filid*, of whom he himself was one, with the result that they were not expelled, but reduced in numbers and given fixed appointments in the various states. In later times each *túath*, or state, seems to have had lands set apart for the support of an *ollam*, or *fili* of the highest rank, and perhaps for other members of the order; and their rights of travelling and refection, although retained, were limited by rule, as were also the rewards they might demand for panegyrical compositions. Each *fili* was expected to maintain and teach a number of pupils, and in some places there were large schools of *filidecht*, with a nation-wide reputation.

In the system of education of the *filid*, which originated in the days before the introduction of writing, memorisation and mental and oral exercises played a dominant part. At an early date, however, they took over from the ecclesiastics the method of writing the Irish language which these latter had evolved. This innovation Eóin MacNeill believes to be due to a certain Cenn-Faelad, who fought at the battle of Mag Roth (*anglice* Moira) in 637, and died in 679.[5] In literary style and ideals also the *filid* underwent "Latinist" influence, either ecclesiastical

---

[5] MacN "A Pioneer of Nations" *Studies* XI (Mar., Sept., 1922) 13–28, 435–46.

or secular. Most important was the influence on metrics: the majority of scholars agree that the classical system of Irish versification, which prevailed from the eighth to the seventeenth century, was in its origin based on the Latin versification of the later Roman empire. A most elaborate scheme of metre was built up by the Irish poets, and training in these metres formed a large part of the education of the *filid*, while the rank of members of the order was determined in part by the metres they were qualified and entitled to use. Such, and much else, was the technical side of *filidecht*, the lore of the *filid*. The other side, the knowledge to which this technique might be applied, included the bulk of the secular learning of the time, and especially what was known as *senchas* (stem *sen*, "old"), a word of wide significance, embracing history, both local and national, archaeology, myth, folk-lore, romance, topography, genealogy, and the customary rights, privileges and obligations of kings and states.

The following were the chief classes of texts composed or transmitted by the *filid:* (1) sagas or romances — in Irish *scéla* (sing. *scél*) — and poems on mythical, heroic or semi-historical subjects; (2) historical narratives and poems, often hardly to be distinguished from the preceding; (3) topographical matter, especially the *dindsenchas*—literally, "antiquities of fortified places"; (4) genealogies, regnal lists, and similar historical records; (5) official poetry, panegyrics, obituary eulogies, etc.; (6) texts relating to the customary duties and prerogatives of kings and peoples; (7) satire; (8) lyrical and miscellaneous poetry; (9) didactic, gnomic and proverbial literature; (10) charms, incantations, and other magical texts; (11) grammatical treatises, glossaries, works on metre; (12) translations and adaptations from foreign literatures.

Certain features of this source-material as a whole are worthy of note. First is the extent and importance of the secular sources. In them we have the productions of the mind of an early mediaeval people practically unmodified by ecclesiastical control. Nothing similar to the organised secular learning and literature of Ireland existed elsewhere in contemporary western Europe. This literature presents to us not only the thought and life of the society from which it immediately sprang, but also, because of the fact that a considerable portion of it consists of evidently well-preserved traditions of an older age, extraordinarily interesting reflections from primitive, pre-Christian, pre-Roman stages in the development of European culture. In Ireland, thanks to her freedom from Roman domination, to the absence of anti-national bias in her Church, to the existence of a powerful body of *literati* specially devoted to the perpetuation of the ancient tradition, and to the relatively early application of writing to the vernacular language, we have sources of the highest value to the student of the proto-history either of Europe or of mankind.

Second is the almost complete absence of official archives and diplomatic documents. No doubt the present dearth of these is in part due to the calamities which overtook all the literature and records of Ireland. Documents that had no literary or religious appeal, that had value only as evidence of official acts or of material rights and privileges, would fare particularly ill through the accumulated disasters of six centuries which wiped out and rendered a thing of naught the whole ancient social and political system of the country. For example: the only extant charters of earlier date than the twelfth century owe their preservation to the chance that they were entered on the blank pages of that wonderful art treasure, the Book of Kells. Nevertheless it is certain that if early Irish *diplomata* do not exist to-day the chief reason is that they never did exist in quantity. This was in part due to the antecedent history of the country and to the generally simple character of its society and government. Ireland did not share that tradition of the use of written records for administrative and other official purposes which all the states that were heirs of the Roman empire in some degree inherited. It was also in part due to certain special peculiarities of the Irish political system. One such was the nature of the state, or *túath*, a comparatively small community of people inhabiting a quite limited extent of territory—there were about one hundred of these *túatha* in the ninth and tenth centuries.[6] The Irish *túath* resembled in several respects the Greek πόλις: there was a similar limitation to such size as made government a matter of personal relationship for each citizen; a similar sanctity arising from a long historic or mythical antiquity; and a similar general popular respect for local autonomy. The autonomy of each *túath*—which did not necessarily imply exemption from the rendering of military service or the payment of tribute to the king of another state—was one of the broad principles of old Irish polity. The Irish mind—like the Greek—did not grasp, or, at any rate, did not approve the idea of a wide territorial sovereignty involving the need of an administrative machinery and a clerical service standing between the ruler and the people. Another Irish peculiarity militating against the growth of a clerical service and its complement, a body of

[6] MacN *Phases of Irish History* (1919) 274; *Celtic Ireland* (1921) 73 *sqq.*

official archives, was the character of the kingship. The king, ordinarily, attended to his duties in person. He succeeded not by inheritance but by election, and he was expected to retire when physical or mental disabilities rendered him incapable of performing his functions. No minor and no manifestly incompetent adult occupied an Irish throne, with the result that there was neither such opportunity nor such incentive for the development of an administrative bureaucracy attached to the court as existed in other lands. Finally, Church and State were more clearly separated in Ireland than elsewhere in Christian Europe. On the Continent, and even in Anglo-Saxon England, when the king needed the assistance of men of learning he could turn only to the bishops and abbots of his kingdom and the chaplains of his household, all of whom had received through the Church something of the Roman tradition of the use of the written record. In Ireland his brehon and his *ollam* stood beside the king, in whom he had counsellors with a long tradition of service;—in which, however, the written record did not play a part. Only very rarely do we hear of a churchman holding the position of a king's minister; and, of course, even in the Church in Ireland the Empire tradition was weak.

A third noteworthy feature of these old Irish sources is their essentially national character. They are, with but few and partial exceptions, sources for the history of Ireland as a whole, and it is evident that their authors had in view an audience from all Ireland. Particularism in things political may have been as pronounced in Hibernia as in Hellas, but Irish civilisation showed less local divergences than did Hellenic. In things spiritual and intellectual Ireland was one. Neither in the Old Irish nor in the Middle Irish period of the language are there any notable signs of dialectical distinctions. Likewise no cleavage appears in religion, law, literature, social and political customs. Local diversities there were, of course, but subject to an unified whole. Church, brehons, *filid*, bards, all were national institutions, the members of which travelled freely from school to school and from state to state, and show in all their writings their appreciation, consciously or unconsciously expressed, that the culture of which they were part was the common and distinct heritage of the whole Irish people.

In addition to the sources of Irish origin there are those of foreign origin. These consist of (1) references to Ireland in works by foreign writers; (2) *acta sanctorum* and other records of Irishmen abroad; and (3) the writings of these expatriated Gaels, writings which covered much the same range of subjects as those produced in the monasteries at home. These form a very considerable and very valuable body of documents. The whole expansion movement of the Irish Church from the sixth to the twelfth century is one of the important phases of mediaeval Irish history. The fact worthy of special note here, however, is that, because of the immeasurably better preservation of early documents on the continent of Europe than in Ireland, we have far more material relating to individual careers among these exiles than to those of their contemporaries, a thousand times more numerous, who remained at home. It is to the manuscript collections of Europe that we must go for really first-rate biographical material regarding Irishmen of leading in the religious and intellectual world of the early middle ages, and it is in the writings of these men, trained in Ireland but working abroad, that we find the most important examples extant to-day of some of those classes of sources listed above as the products of the monastic schools of Erin.

II. The Early Records—Post-Viking Period

The onslaught of the Norse sea-kings was the next great movement, after the introduction of Christianity, to affect seriously Irish life and civilisation. These freebooters began their attacks in 795, and continued to be a constant menace for more than two centuries. The history of the struggle cannot here be even sketched. It must be sufficient to indicate the chief features of the war: in its first stage, which lasted through much of the ninth century, it consisted of pillaging descents on the coast, with raids inland which penetrated deeper and deeper until all parts of the island were being harassed, but with the enemy usually sailing home before the winter storms began; in the second stage, permanent settlements were made at strategic havens, which served as bases for plundering forays into the interior and for more or less continuous efforts at the subjugation of the neighboring states; in the third stage great expeditions were from time to time assembled from the far-flung sea-empire of the Scandinavians and directed to attempts at conquest on a large scale. The characteristics of each of these stages, however, persisted into those which followed. In the second stage the Hiberno-Norse towns of Dublin, Waterford and Limerick were founded—Dublin perhaps as early as 841, Waterford and Limerick not later than the first quarter of the tenth century. In the third stage the greatest of the northern invasions met decisive defeat

at the battle of Clontarf (Clúain-tarbh, "Bull Meadow") in 1014.
Thereafter the Northmen seem to have abandoned hope of subjugating
Ireland,[7] and their settlements tended more and more to accept the
status of principalities within the Irish polity.

It is necessary now to consider some of the effects of this long struggle with a strange and heathen foe.

In the first place, Ireland was involved in a whole new set of international relations. The activities of the Scandinavians extended from
Greenland in the west to Constantinople in the east. Their settlements
in Ireland, and particularly Dublin, became important maritime centres,
well known throughout northern and western Europe. They were
traders as well as robbers; in the eleventh and twelfth centuries the
greater part of the foreign commerce of Ireland was in their hands,
and there is no doubt of their trading extensively with the Irish even
before Clontarf. Friendly intercourse between Irish and Norse had
not been uncommon. Many Irish, either freely or of compulsion,
amalgamated with the invaders. Irish blood formed a not inconsiderable element in the colonisation of Iceland. The Norse settlers in
Ireland were in time Christianised and partially Hibernicised. And
when, partly under Irish influence, a great Norse literature arose in
the eleventh and twelfth centuries, it produced a long series of compositions which serve as sources for the history of the war in Ireland
and for the careers of the Hiberno-Norse in the Scottish isles and in
Iceland.

Less satisfactory were the effects on the Irish Church and on the
scholarship which had flourished under its protection. Throughout the
whole struggle, but more especially in its earlier phases, the monasteries were peculiarly the objectives of the enemy's attacks. They
were numerous, easily accessible, capable of offering little resistance, and
usually sources of considerable booty. A large portion of the record
of the war in the Irish chronicles is a record of the plundering and
destruction of churches. We hear of Armagh being sacked nine or ten
times, Clonmacnois ten or eleven times, Kells five times, Glendalough
four times, Lismore perhaps six times, Kildare some sixteen or seventeen times. Only the more important churches are, in general, noticed
by the annals, and of these the story is meagre and probably incomplete.
The Irish themselves in this as in other respects acquired anti-religious

---

[7] There were threats of danger, such as the expedition which the Norwegian king Magnus "Barefoot"
led in 1103, but they passed away without materialisation.

habits from contact with their enemies. Attacks on churches, while not unknown, had been rare before the ninth century; in the tenth and eleventh they became not infrequent episodes in inter-state hostilities. An evil result to religion and learning from all this was inevitable. It is possible that the Irish Church would in any event have entered on a period of decline; the damage it received from the foreigners undoubtedly hastened the movement of dissolution and secularisation by which a majority of the old monasteries either disappeared entirely as religious institutions or were perpetuated only by a single priest or a few anchorites. Nevertheless many of the churches came safely through the ordeal, and a few of the larger, notably Armagh, Clonmacnois, Derry and Lismore, seem to have grown in power and importance.

The fate of the manuscripts belonging to these ancient monasteries is a subject of special interest. The historical saga *Cogadh Gaedhel re Gallaibh,* "War of the Irish with the Foreigners," speaks of "the burning and the drowning of their writings and their books in each church and in each sanctuary where they were, by the spoilers, from first to last."[8] Whether the invaders displayed any peculiar enmity to books or not, the destruction of a monastery would usually involve the destruction of its library. There is no doubt that the Viking ravages are responsible for only a part of the present dearth of ancient Irish manuscripts; that large numbers which escaped the torch of the sea-kings perished in later times of trouble. But be that as it may, the fact remains that only some ten manuscripts of older date than the year 1000 have survived on Irish soil.[9] On the other hand, of the books which Irish emigrants carried with them to foreign lands well over fifty, complete or fragmentary, are still extant.[10]

It is difficult now to determine the remoter history of many of the Irish manuscripts in foreign libraries. Manuscripts were left, doubtless, wherever Irish monks went, and they were ubiquitous in western Europe. Lindisfarne must have had codices from Ireland, or, what

---

[8] Ed. Todd, RS (1867) 138–9.

[9] The Cathach, or Psalter of Colum-cille; Codex Usserianus I; Book of Durrow; Book of Mulling (embodying at least two distinct MSS); Book of Dimma; Domnach Airgid; Book of Kells; Book of Armagh; and Garland of Howth, or Codex Usserianus II. *Cf.* nos. 453–8, 467, 471, 474, 477.

[10] Walther Schultze listed 117 Irish MSS, older than the eleventh century, in continental libraries (*Centralblatt für Bibliothekswesen,* July 1889, pp. 287–96). He professes to give only a partial list of Paris MSS, and does not enumerate any in the Vatican or, of course, in British libraries. But some of those named by him are not now classed as Irish. W.'M. Lindsay, in the appendix to his *Notae Latinae* (1915), lists 32 Irish MSS, 38 insular MSS (some of which, doubtless, are Irish), and several continental MSS copied from Irish originals, all preserved in foreign countries and all believed to be of date earlier than A.D. 850. Moreover, with but a few exceptions, MSS in majuscule script were omitted by Lindsay.—It is probable that some of these distinctively Irish MSS were written abroad by Irish scribes, but this does not seriously affect the argument.

to all intents was the same, from Iona. On the Continent *Perrona Scottorum*, Irish monastery in Picardy, to-day Péronne, probably had many Irish books before it was sacked by the Northmen in 880. Brittany and Tours may also have served as *entrepôts* for Irish manuscripts. The chief collections, however, and three of the greatest monastic libraries in Europe, came to be at Bobbio, St. Gall, and Reichenau. Bobbio, founded by the Irish saint, Columbanus, in 614, was a favorite resort of Irish ecclesiastics for centuries. So, too, was St. Gall, which, although not founded until the eighth century, had its origin as a church in the cell built there by another Irish saint, Gall, who was a companion of Columbanus. Reichenau, on an island in the lake of Constance, had not the same historical or sentimental attractions for Irishmen, but there is evidence that actual association was quite intimate, and that its library received donations from Irish monks.[11] The most important accession of Irish books to Reichenau was, however, perhaps due to the fact that for a time it sheltered the library of St. Gall. In the year 925 an incursion of the Magyars led the monks of St. Gall to remove their books to Reichenau for safe-keeping. When the danger had passed and St. Gall was re-established, the same number of codices was brought back, we are told, from Reichenau, but not in all cases the identical volumes.[12] It resulted that thereafter some of the Reichenau manuscripts were of St. Gall provenance.

At home in Ireland the churches that survived the Viking storm experienced, in the eleventh and twelfth centuries, important religious and intellectual developments. Two dominating and, in some of their phases, antagonistic movements may be distinguished. One was the movement towards uniformity with the continental Church and towards religious reform in accordance with Cluniac ideals: this culminated in the introduction of the Cistercian and other foreign religious orders, and in the substitution of an episcopal administrative system and a territorial organisation for the old Irish monastic organisation. It also paved the way, if it did not afford the occasion, for the Anglo-Norman invasion. The other movement was nationalist in character, and perhaps part of a general national reaction following on the Norse attacks. It showed itself in the expansion of the Irish at the expense of the Latin language in ecclesiastical usage, in the devotion of the clergy to the national literature and history, and in the elaborate study of the antiquities of the national Church.

---

[11] *Cf.* pp. 86, 518, 550, 668, 675, 677 *infra*.
[12] Ekkehard *Casus St. Galli* (no. 411 *infra*): *MGH SS* II 105.

The chief note of the intellectual life of this era is the amalgamation of secular and religious learning. Such a note was already struck, in the ninth or early tenth century, in that epic of the old Irish Church, the "Voyage of St. Brendan." Though based to a large degree on Gaelic sources it is written in Latin—perhaps the last notable Hiberno-Latin literary production. Characteristic of the succeeding centuries are the saints' Lives in Irish, many of them translations from Latin; the Irish dramatic poems put in the mouths of famous saints, as Columcille and Moling; the Irish homilies, largely adopted or translated from Latin; the extensive commentaries in Irish on ancient religious texts. The shifting of emphasis from Latin to Irish is indicated by the appearance of *fer léiginn* ("man of reading," lecturer, master of studies) in place of *scriba* as the designation of the head of the intellectual activities of the monastery.[13]

It may be noted here that at a synod of the clergy of all Ireland, held at Cloenad (Clane, in Kildare), in 1162, it was decreed "that no one should be a *fer léiginn* in a monastic church in Ireland unless he were an alumnus of Armagh."[14] In furtherance of this policy of making Armagh the national university Ruadri hÚa Conchobuir (Rory O'Connor), king of Ireland, in 1169 "gave ten cows each year from himself and from every king after him till doomsday to the *fer léiginn* of Armagh, in honor of Patrick, to give lectures to students of Ireland and Scotland."[15]

The obituary notice of the man who was at this time head of the school of Armagh is given in 1174: "Flann Úa Gormain, *árd-fer-léiginn* [chief *f. l.*] of Armagh and of all Ireland, a learned man, distinguished in divine and human wisdom, after having spent twenty-one years in study among the Franks and Saxons, and twenty years directing the schools of Ireland, died peacefully on the 13th of the Kalends of April [March 20], the Wednesday before Easter, in the seventieth year of his age."[16]

The first prominent example of ecclesiastical interest in secular literature is that of the bishop—if he was bishop—Cormac mac Cuilennáin, who became king of Munster, and was slain in 908. He is reputed to have been the author or compiler of *Sanas Cormaic*, "Cormac's Glossary," a dictionary of Irish words unusual or obsolete in

[13] In AU the ordinary use of the term *scriba* seems to end with 932, when the obit of Fer-domnach mac Flannacáin, scribe of Clonard, is recorded. Exceptional later occurrences are under 989 — Dunchad úa Braen, of Clonmacnois; 1006 — Airmedach mac Coscraich, of Armagh; and 1098 — "Mael-Isu úa Stuir, scriba philosophiae Mumunensium, immo omnium Scotorum." In this last entry, however, the title seems to have a different signification. The title *fer léiginn* is applied first in 879 to one Mochta, of Armagh, who was, doubtless, the same man as the *scriba* of that name whose obit is given in 898. *Cf.* art. "Scribhneoir" in Smith and Cheetham *Dict. Christ. Antiq.*

[14] AU.   [15] AU.   [16] AU.

his time; of the earlier version of *Leabhar na gCeart*, or the "Book of Rights" of the kings of Ireland; and of the lost *Saltair Caissil*, the "Psalter of Cashel," apparently a collection of texts on historical, genealogical, and allied subjects. Other churchmen whom we know to have been interested in secular lore were Flann mac Máil-Máedóc (d. 977), *airchinnech* or official head [17] of the church of Glenn Uisen; Eochaid úa Flainn, or Flannacáin (d. 1004), *airchinnech* of one of the institutions at Armagh and of the church of Clúain-Fiachna (Clonfeacle near Dungannon), described as "a *súi* [sage] in *filidecht* and *senchus*," a large number of whose poems on the history of pagan Ireland have survived; Flann *Mainistrech* (d. 1056), *fer léiginn* of Mainister-Buiti (Buite's monastery, Monasterboice), the subject-matter of whose extant poems is entirely within the province of the *filid*; Dub-dá-Leithe, *fer léiginn* of Armagh, 1046–1049, and head of that monastery, 1049–1064, who was compiler of the book known by his name; Máel-Muire mac Céilechair of Clonmacnois (d. 1106), one of the scribes of the codex known as *Lebor na hUidre*, or "Book of the Dun [Cow]"; Gilla-Comáin úa Congalaig, *fer léiginn* of Roscommon (d. 1135); [18] Aed mac Crimthainn, abbot of Tír-dá-glas [Terryglass], compiler of the Book of Leinster; and his friend, Finn mac Gormáin, bishop of Kildare, who died in 1160. [19] Dub-dá-Leithe of Armagh and Tigernach úa Broín (d. 1088), *airchinnech* of Clonmacnois, are known also as chroniclers, theirs being almost the only names preserved from those of the many who must have helped to compile our annalistic records. [20]

The attacks of the Northmen did not cause as much harm to secular learning as to ecclesiastical. Doubtless they did check for a time the activities of the *filid* and their schools, causing something like a break in the literary history, with the result that critics now draw a line between pre-Viking and post-Viking texts. The ultimate effect, however, seems to have been rather stimulating: the national revival which developed out of two centuries of alternate disaster and triumph showed itself in a rejuvenated literature and scholarship. Noteworthy features of this intellectual renaissance were that amalgamation of secular and religious interests to which reference has just been made; growth of a patriotic-historical mentality; development of the impulse to the compilation and conservation of the national antiquities; and a revolution in saga-composition which changed completely the subject-matter of the chief field of popular literature.

[17] *Airchinnech (anglice erenagh)*, "head," "leader," "superior," is the name which in the post-Viking period was most frequently applied to the head of a monastic church. The *airchinnech* seems to have held the same position as the earlier *abbas*. Probably the change is another instance of that shifting from Latin to Irish in ecclesiastical usage which has been noticed in connection with *scriba* and *fer léiginn*, but perhaps also the associations of the title *abbas* were such as to make its use seem incongruous when the position was becoming more or less secularised.

[18] *Cf.* O'Grady *Cat.* 94; RTh *Ir. Sage* 16.

[19] It is possible, in view of the extensive secularisation of the monastic churches, that some of these men had no ecclesiastical associations beyond the fact that they drew a living from the monastic property.

[20] MacN believes that Sinlán, or Mo-Sinu, moccu Mín (d. 607–Tig.), abbot of Bangor, was the author of an Irish continuation of Eusebius, coming down to 607, and that about 712 an "Old Irish Chronicle" was compiled, on which all our present annals were based. *Cf. Ériu* VII (1913) 30 *sqq*; MacN *Celtic Ireland* (1923) 28.

The amalgamation of religious with secular intellectual interests is seen in the recasting of the national history. When Christianity arrived in Ireland, bringing in its train the Bible, Eusebius, Orosius, Isidore, etc., Irishmen began to learn world history as taught by the early mediaeval Church. There inevitably followed the impulse to fit their own Irish past into this scheme of history, and to pour their myths, traditions, sagas, genealogies, into an orderly historical mould. Apparently as early as the seventh century churchmen, such as Mo-Sinu moccu Mín, and *filid*, such as Cenn-Faelad, were attempting to elucidate, with the help of the Old Testament and Orosius, the origins of the Irish people, and, with the help of Eusebius and other chroniclers, to set up a chronological scheme of their later history. But it was not until the ninth, and especially the tenth, eleventh and twelfth centuries, that this historical impulse acquired full momentum. Then many of the *filid* seem to have turned their energies almost entirely to the task of transmuting the national folk-lore into a harmonised history. A twelfth-century text declares that "he is no *fili* who does not synchronise and harmonise all the sagas."[21]

Only a few shadowy names, such as Adna, Ferceirtne, Torna *éces*, Dallán Forgaill, Senchán Torpéist, Cenn-Faelad, Rumann, remain of the *filid* prior to the ninth century. But thereafter there is a long list, many of whose compositions can be read to-day: Máel-Muru of Othain, or Fahan, near Derry (d. 887), called "king-*fili* of Ireland"; Flannacán mac Cellaig of Brega, who was, doubtless, the king of Brega of that name slain by the Norse in 896; Flann mac Lonáin (d. 896 or 918), called the Vergil of Ireland; Cormac mac Cuilennáin (d. 908), of whom mention has been made; Cormacán *éces* mac Máele-Brigte (d. 946); Cináed úa hArtacáin (d. 975), called *príméces Érenn*, perhaps about equivalent to "dean of the scholars of Ireland"; Flann mac Máil-Máedóc (d. 977); Erard mac Coisse (d. 990),[22] to whom the same title is given; Eochaid úa Flainn, or Flainnacáin, (d. 1004), who also has been mentioned previously; Mac Liag (d. 1016), *ollam* to Brian *bóroimhe*; Cúan úa Lothcháin (d. 1024), *príméces Érenn*; Flann *Mainistrech* (d. 1056), previously mentioned; Eochaid *eolach* ["the learned"] úa Círín, who seems to have been associated with Flann and possibly was his successor at Monasterboice; Gilla-Coemáin (d. 1072); Gilla-Mo-Dutu of Dam-Inis (Devenish), who was writing in 1147;[23] Gilla-in-Choimded úa Cormaic; Gilla-na-naomh úa Duinn (d. 1160), *fer léiginn* of Inis Clothrann (in Loch Ree); and many others of lesser fame. Almost all the compositions of these men are either panegyrics of their contemporaries or attempts at the reconstruction of past history. Máel-Muru, Cinaed úa hArtacáin, Eochaid úa Flainn, Cúan úa Lothcháin, Flann *Mainistrech* and Gilla-Coemáin appear to have been the most active in the work of "synchro-

---

[21] O'C *MS Mat.* 593.

[22] So AU and Tig.: FM give the obit of an Erard mac Coisse in 1023. *Cf.* O. Bergin *Ériu* IX (1923) 175.

[23] So RTh *Ir. Sage* 46; KM identifies him with a Gilla-Mo-Dutu úa Casaide (d. 1143)—*Primer of Irish Metrics* (1909) 43; *Fianaigecht* (Dublin, 1910) p. xxix.

nising and harmonising," and they may be classed as the chief of what Eóin MacNeill aptly designates "the synthetic historians."

"The work," says MacNeill, "of dating and correlating the national legends and traditions was possibly carried out under their direction. At all events, it was they who summarised the results, and on whose authority those results were accepted by later writers as genuine history. So far as their history refers to pre-Christian times, it is partly fabricated, and partly made up of mythology, legend, and epic narrative, arranged under an arbitrary chronology."[24]

The chief objects these men had in view were to provide the Irish people with an antiquity equal to that of the Hebrews and the empires of the East, and the principal families, states and institutions of their own time with a long and heroic past. In particular, the high-kingship of Ireland, theoretically localised at Tara, and the kingship of Munster, at Cashel, sovereignties that appear in reality to have arisen quite late in the pagan era, were endowed with an elaborate and venerable history. To serve the needs of this pseudo-history the old Irish mythology was worked over until it is hardly recognisable. The *Lebor Gabála*, or "Book of Takings" (*i.e.*, the successive occupations of Ireland by the various races that were fabled to have inhabited it), completed this syncretistic movement by gathering into one narrative the story of Ireland and the Irish from Noah to Ruadri hÚa Conchobuir, a narrative into which were incorporated many of the poems of the later *filid*. In its final form the *Lebor Gabála* dates from about 1168.

Essentially part of the same growth of historical consciousness was the impulse to the conservation in permanent written collections of the old legends, literature and records. Since all earlier secular manuscripts have disappeared, it is to these compilations of the twelfth and later centuries that we owe almost all our Old Irish non-ecclesiastical texts. Whether the compilers of the earlier of these bulky codices had in mind the repairing of the damage wrought by external and internal wars, or not, it is certain that the practice was continued in later centuries with the motive of saving from destruction amid contemporary disasters the records of the nation's antiquities. Through so much of Ireland's story the primary duty of the historian has been to gather up the fragments, lest they be lost!

The oldest secular manuscript of which we have genuine knowledge was the *Cín* [25] *Dromma-Snechta*, the "Book of Drumsnat" (in Monaghan), which may have been

---

[24] MacN *Celtic Ireland* (Dublin 1921) 40. See the whole chap. iii, "The Irish Synthetic Historians."
[25] *Cín*, Lat. *quinio*: the arrangement of the vellum sheets in gatherings of five was a favorite with the Irish book-makers, whence the word came to have the general signification of "codex."

as old as the first half of the eighth century. It is now lost, but extensive transcriptions were made from it in the later middle ages, by means of which Thurneysen has ingeniously reconstructed a large part of its contents.[26] These seem to have been chiefly, or entirely, old saga texts. The *Saltair Caissil*, or "Psalter of Cashel," compiled about the beginning of the tenth century by Cormac mac Cuilennáin, contained genealogical texts, the original version of the "Book of Rights," and other semi-historical matter. It was still in existence in 1453, when portions of it were copied into the manuscript Laud 610 of the Bodleian Library. In the "Book of Dub-dá-Leithe," written at Armagh about 1050, there were, we know, annalistic records and saga texts.[27] Other lost books of which we meet the names in extant manuscripts are the "Yellow Book of Slane," the "Short Book," the "Books of Monasterboice," the *Duanaire*, or "Poem-Book," of Flann mac Lonáin, the "Books of Eochaid úa Flannacáin." [28] The oldest surviving codex of this kind is the *Lebor na hUidre*, or, in later orthography, *Leabhar na hUidhri*,[29] "Book of the Dun [Cow]," originally transcribed at Clonmacnois about A.D. 1100. About the same time as the *Lebor na hUidre*, and probably also at Clonmacnois, was written the oldest section of the Bodleian manuscript now known as "Rawlinson B. 502," the section containing the so-called "Fragment I of the Annals of Tigernach." The largest section of Rawlinson B. 502, a very important collection of secular and religious texts, dates from about 1120.[30] The *Lebor Laignech*, or *Leabhar Laighneach*,[31] "Book of Leinster," is the third great *bibliotheca* of Irish texts, antedating the Norman invasion, that has survived to our time. As already stated, it was compiled by Aed mac Crimthainn, abbot of Tír-dá-glas, the bulk of it before 1161, with some additions later in the century. It is a beautiful example of calligraphy, and contains much valuable material, but unfortunately the scribe was careless and inaccurate in copying his documents.

It has been said that one of the features of the post-Viking renaissance was a change in the subject-matter of the saga literature. The "sagas," "romances," "stories"—the Irish word was *scéla*—fall into various groups according to the subjects of which they treat—"mythological cycle," "Ulster" or "Cú-Chulainn cycle," "Tara cycle," etc. The majority of these sagas had their origin in pre-Norse times, but are now represented by versions composed in the tenth, eleventh or twelfth century and inserted in the great manuscript tomes compiled then or later. One set of stories, dealing with the *fianna* (sing. *fian*), bands of professional soldiers who formed an element in ancient Irish

---

[26] "Zu irischen Handschriften und Literaturdenkmälern" (Berlin 1912) 23 *sqq.*; *Ir. Sage* 15–8.

[27] *Cf. AU*, Index; RTh *Ir. Sage* 378.

[28] *Cf.* O'C *MS Mat.* 8–23: Some of the books he mentions were of later date than the 12th century, and some have been identified since his time. See also O'D "The lost and missing Irish manuscripts" *UJA* IX (1861) 16–28.

[29] (LU): MS in RIA, 23. E. 25, 67 ff., vellum. Published in facs. by RIA in 1870. *Cf.* R. I. Best "Notes on the script of Lebor na hUidre" *Ériu* VI (1912) 161–74.

[30] Bodl. Rawl. B. 502, in two vellum sections, of 12 and 70 ff. respectively, with 2 additional strips of vellum at end. Published in facs. by the Clarendon Press in 1909, under the editorship of KM.

[31] (LL): TCD 1339 (H. 2. 18). Eleven leaves are in the Franciscan Convent, Dublin. Published in facs. by RIA, 1880. TCD 1428 (L. 5. 20) is a copy by O'C, made in 1852, as far as p. 115 of the facs.; it is more accurate than the facs., and parts of the MS that are now illegible could then be read.

society, had only a few representatives in the seventh, eighth and ninth centuries. But a certain *fian* chieftain, Find úa Báiscne, or Find mac Umaill, later Finn mac Cumaill, grew in literary importance until, in the tenth, eleventh and twelfth centuries, a vast cycle of stories relating to this hero, to his son, the poet Oisín (the "Ossian" of Macpherson), and to other members of his *fian*, appeared and spread over Ireland and Gaelic Scotland. From the twelfth century on these stories continued to multiply and to oust from circulation the older sagas. The causes of this development are obscure; possibly it had some connection with the contemporaneous rise to prominence of the bards, hitherto overshadowed by the *filid*.

III. Transmission of the Records—Later Middle Ages

The Norman invasion may be dated from 1170, when the expedition of Richard de Clare, Earl of Pembroke, landed at Waterford. This event marked the opening of an armed struggle which continued without cessation till the beginning of the seventeenth century, and, with intermissions rather than cessation, till the complete consolidation of the English conquest at the end of that century. This war had throughout certain general characteristics the recognition of which is important. In the first place, it was, on the side of the aggressors, a war for private plunder. Almost all the enemy leaders, and undoubtedly a large proportion of their followers, fought either to win or to retain the lands and chattels of the Irish. This, to be sure, is not a state of affairs elsewhere unknown, in mediaeval or even in modern times, but nowhere else in Christendom has the principle of *Vae Victis* been applied so long, so thoroughly, or with such "entail of blood and tears," as in Ireland. Secondly, it was a war between widely divergent and apparently incompatible civilisations. The charges of moral depravity levelled at the Irish throughout were in part the normal accompaniment of wars of aggression—'in ancient as in modern times charges of this kind mean but one thing, that those accused are in possession of lands which their accusers wish to obtain'—but also in part the outcome of a genuine inability to see good in a culture which had developed along distinct lines from those of the half-Roman, half-barbarian feudal society of the remainder of western Europe. Thirdly, it was an internal war maintained by a foreign power. Prior to the sixteenth century England was not strong enough, while supporting her commitments elsewhere, to conquer Ireland, but she was strong enough to maintain a firm foothold there, to keep a constant stream of new adventurers pouring in, and to prevent a national accommodation between the invaders and the native inhabitants. In France the Normans became Frenchmen, in England Englishmen, in Italy Italians, in Scotland Scotsmen, but in Ireland, although becoming Irish in manner of living, they were able neither to establish an independent kingdom of their own nor to coalesce in allegiance to an Irish kingdom. So went forward this five-centuries war of attrition, constantly renewed and constantly re-embittered. Through such a Phlegethon the history of the old independent Ireland had to be salvaged.

At the first onset the Normans met with extraordinary success— success paralleled, however, by their earlier triumphs in England and in the Sicilies. The Normans—the name includes the whole crowd of French-speaking military adventurers who, having made themselves dominant in England and southern Wales, were now turning to the neighboring island—were superior to the Irish in military equipment, in the science of warfare, and in political knowledge and craft. They were especially superior in the art of fortification, and their success was largely due to their castle-building. On the Irish side the central political power broke almost at the first impact. The local states, the *túatha*, proved of tougher fibre, and strongest of all in throwing back the attack was the national civilisation. But by the middle of the thirteenth century the invaders were in control of fully half—and that the more valuable half—of the island.

Towards the end of the thirteenth century the tide began to flow in favor of the Irish. Slowly the English frontier shrank back until, by the middle of the fifteenth century, "the Pale" of English dominion had been reduced to a strip of territory about twenty miles wide running from Dublin to Dundalk, with a small extension inland along the Liffey. Beyond this, and still nominally of English allegiance, were a number of walled towns and a few powerful families that retained their ancient conquests by becoming practically Irish. Outside the towns and the Pale the Anglo-Normans almost everywhere adopted the Irish language,[32] laws, customs and mode of living, and even within those bounds the process of assimilation had, in the fifteenth century, made great headway. The triumph of Irish civilisation was greater than that of Irish arms.

[32] *Cf*. Edmund Curtis "The spoken languages of mediaeval Ireland" *Studies* VIII (July 1919) 234–54

The Anglo-Norman invasion sealed the fate of the old Irish monastic churches. The invaders plundered and demolished them without compunction. Armagh, which had suffered severely from fires in 1179 and 1189, was plundered in 1184 by "the foreigners of Meath," in 1185 by Philip of Worcester, the English king's representative, and in 1189 by a famous adventurer, John de Courci. Thereafter the monastery and the incipient university[33] fell into decay: the last *fer léiginn*, Martin Úa Brolaigh, "arch-sage of all the Gael," died in 1188. Derry —now the head of the churches of Colum-cille in Ireland—had been reconstructed and enlarged in 1162-64, and maintained its dignity till the end of the century. Finally in 1196 or 1197 De Courci penetrated to it on one of his raids, and in 1198 he repeated the exploit. In 1212 or 1213 the church was again sacked, this time by plunderers from Galloway and the Isles of Scotland. In 1220 we hear for the last time of the appointment of a *fer léiginn* at Derry.[34] It is probable that few or no organised monastic communities of the old order persisted much after this date. Moreover, the keen and persistent efforts of Normans and English to seize for their own candidates all Irish bishoprics and other worth-while benefices destroyed the possibility that the new ecclesiastical system which the Irish reformers of the twelfth century had set up might at once take the place of the old monasticism in spiritual and cultural leadership.

Already before the coming of the Anglo-Normans the reform party had introduced the continental religious orders. To the friendship between Máel-Máedhóc Úa Morgair, known as St. Malachy, and St. Bernard of Clairvaux it was due that Cistercians from that house formed the advance guard.[35] Contemporaneously communities of Augustinian or Regular Canons were being established. A century later the Dominican and Franciscan friars arrived. They were brought in by the Anglo-Normans, but later became thoroughly Irish, and among the chief ministers to the spiritual needs of the people.

In their origins these communities made a clean break with the old traditions of the country. In time, however, they too came into that

---

[33] Armagh, as the seat of the primate, continued to be an ecclesiastical centre of importance. In 1462 AU has the entry: "Thomas Cusin, the Master of Law who was the best that was in Ireland in his time, was in Armagh and kept a school this year." No university, however, arose in mediaeval Ireland. Such ecclesiastical students as desired higher education had to go to the English and continental schools; from the former they were excluded by acts of parliament at the beginning of the fifteenth century. *Cf.* Alice Stopford Green *The Making of Ireland and its Undoing* (London 1908) 265-304, where a list of Irish students at Oxford is given.
[34] AU.
[35] The first foundation was Mellifont, near Drogheda, in 1142. *Cf.* p. 767 *infra.*

inheritance. It was probably for them that the great majority of the redactions now extant of the Latin Lives of Irish saints were prepared. The example was set by the Life of Patrick compiled about 1185 by Jocelin, one of the community of English monks whom John de Courci had established on the ruins of the Irish church of Down.

We have a few manuscript collections of saints' Lives which appear to have been lectionaries used in some of these religious houses in the era of the Irish revival: the *Codex Insulensis*,[36] of the thirteenth or fourteenth century, which probably belonged to Saints' Island, Loch Ree; *Codex Salmanticensis*,[37] a fourteenth-century volume, the original home of which is not known; and *Codex Kilkenniensis*, extant in two transcripts [38] of about the year 1400, also of unknown origin. That historical and hagiographical work was carried on at Saints' Island, Loch Ree, is known from the obituary notice of Augustin Mag Radoigh, or Magradin, one of the continuators of the so-called Annals of Tigernach, who died in 1405: "one of the canons of Saints' Island [*oilén-na-naom*], a sage [*saoi*] during his lifetime in divine and worldly wisdom, in literature, in antiquities, and in various other sciences; and *ollam* of oratory of western Europe;—the man who compiled this book and many other books, both Lives of Saints and historical records."[39] The oldest copy of *Codex Insulensis*, however, appears to have been written before Magradin's time.

But it was mainly to secular scholarship that the transmission through the later middle ages of the old Irish records and traditions was due. The learned classes, like all others of the Irish polity, staggered under the early blows of the Normans, but with the Irish revival came back into their own, and by the fifteenth century were once more flourishing. In these later ages we find that the old distinction between bards and *filid* has broken down: the bards have come forward to a position of equality, and in fact, the *filid* as a distinct order gradually disappear, and the word *fili* assumes a connotation almost the same as the English "poet." The chief men of learning in the various states are now usually designated as *ollam* in one or other of the several fields of scholarship: in *brethemnas* (jurisprudence), in *senchus* (history), in *bairdne*, *filidecht* or *dán* (literature, poetry, art), in *leges* (medicine). It is certain, however, that the training for any of these professions was not narrow: even the legal and medical books frequently contain much literary or historical matter.[40]

---

[36] Bodl. Rawl. B. 485; there is an ancient copy, Rawl. B. 505; and a seventeenth-century copy in the Franciscan Convent, Merchants Quay, Dublin. *Cf.* pp. 306–7 *infra*.

[37] Brussels Bibl. roy. 7672–4. *Cf.* pp. 304–5 *inf*,*a*.

[38] Dublin, Primate Marsh's Library V. 3. 4; TCD 175 (E. 3. 11). *Cf.* pp. 305–6 *infra*.

[39] Tig. 1405: O'C *MS Mat.* 74, 529.

[40] Some aspects of the intellectual life of Ireland in the later middle ages are examined by E. C. Quiggin, "Prolegomena to the study of the later Irish bards 1200-1500" *Proc. Brit. Acad.* V [read 1911; also printed separately].

One of the features of the Irish social system was the hereditary transmission in particular families of dignities, offices, professions and trades. This resulted mainly from the fact that in each *túath* special lands were set apart for the benefit of such positions or callings. From the thirteenth to the sixteenth century almost all the prominent *savants* and *literati* were members of these families.

The following are some of the more famous names:
Mac Aedhagáin (MacEgan): brehons in Connacht, Breifne (Leitrim-Cavan), West-meath, Offaley, Desmond, and northern Tipperary, where they kept a celebrated law school.[41] *Mac an Bháird* (Macaward, Ward): bards, said to be originally of Galway, but later found also in Donegal, Sligo and Air-gialla (Monaghan-Armagh). *Mac an Chrósain*: poets to the O'Moores of Leix. *Mac an Gobann* (McGowan): historians to the O'Kennedys of Ormond. *Mac an Legha* (McKinlay): physicians. *Mac Beatha* (McBeth, McVeagh): physicians who settled in Scotland. *Mac Bruaidedha* (MacBrody): poets in Clare.[42] *Mac Con-Midhe* (MacNamee): poets, one branch with the O'Neills of Tyrone and Clandeboy, another in Sligo. *Mac Craith* or *Mag Craith* (McGrath, Magrath): hereditary *comarbai* of St. Dá-Beócc, or Dabeog, at Termonn-MagCraith in Donegal; branches of the family were poets and historians in Thomond and Ormond.[43] *Mac Cruitin* (MacCurtin): of Thomond. *Mac Duinnt-shléibhe* (MacDonlevy): physicians of Ulster. *Mac Eochadha* (MacKeogh): poets of Leinster. *Mac Fir-Bisigh* (MacFirbis): historians at Lecan in Sligo. *Mag Fhlann-chadha*: brehons of Ossory. *Mac Rithbeartaigh* (MacRifferty): poets of Fermanagh. *Úa an Cháinte*: poets of Cork. *Úa Breislen* (O'Breslen): one branch princes of Fanad in Donegal; another, holding the position of *airchinnig* in Fermanagh, became brehons there. *Úa Caiside* (O'Cassidy): physicians in Fermanagh. *Úa Callanáin* (O'Callanan): physicians in southern Munster. *Úa Cianáin* (O'Keenan): *airchinnig* of Clain-Inis (Cleenish)[44] in Loch Erne, and historians in Fermanagh and Air-gialla. *Úa Cléirigh* (O'Clery): of Tirawley in Mayo: one branch settled in Donegal.[45] *Úa Clumháin* (O'Cluane): poets of Mayo and Sligo. *Úa Cobhthaigh*: (O'Coffey): churchmen and poets in Ulster, Offaley and Westmeath. *Úa Coindlis*: historians. *Úa Cuirnín*: historians of Breifne. *Úa Dálaigh* (O'Daly): the most prolific of the bardic families, with branches in many parts of Ireland.[46] *Úa Deoradháin* (O'Doran): brehons in southern Leinster. *Úa Domnalláin* (O'Donolan, O'Donnellan): poets to the O'Conors and MacWilliams in Connacht. *Úa Duibdábhoireann* (O'Davoren): brehons in Corcomroe and Burren, Clare.[47] *Úa Duibgennáin* (O'Duigenan): *airchinnig* of Kilro-nan, near Boyle, and, later, historians.[48] *Úa Duinnín* (O'Dinneen): historians to the

---

[41] *Cf. ALI* I introd. p. xxxiv; Martin J. Blake "Two Irish Brehon scripts: with notes on the MacEgan Family" *Galway Archaeol. and Hist. Soc. Journal* VI (1909) 1–8.
[42] O'Grady *Cat.* 342.
[43] *Cf. AU* 1287 (p. 379), 1290 (p. 385), 1395, 1471, 1496, etc.
[44] The Úa Corcráin family, *littérateurs*, were also connected with Cleenish.
[45] *Cf.* O'D *Genealogies, Tribes and Customs of Hy-Fiachrach* (Dublin 1844) 72 *sqq.*; FM index *s. v.*; Denis Murphy (ed.) *Beatha Aodha Ruaidh ui Dhomhnaill The Life of Hugh Roe O'Donnell* [by Lugaid O'Clery] (Dublin 1893).
[46] *Cf.* O'D in *The Tribes of Ireland* (Dublin 1852); O'Grady *Cat.* 343.
[47] *Cf.* Geo. U. Macnamara "The O'Davorens of Cahermacnaughton, Burren, Co. Clare," *North Munster Archaeol. Soc. Journ.* II (1912) 63–93, 149–64.
[48] *Cf. ALC* introd.; P. Walsh *IER* April 1921 pp. 225–35.

MacCarthys. *Úa hEichthighern* (O'Ahiarn, Aherne): physicians. *Úa hEoghusa* (O'Hosey, O'Hussey): poets to the Maguires. *Úa Ferghussa* (O'Fergus): physicians to the O'Malleys of Iar-Umhall, in Mayo. *Úa Fialáin* (O'Phelan):[49] *airchinnig* of Bohoe, near Enniskillen, and poets in Fermanagh. *Úa Gnímh* (O'Gnive, Agnew): poets to the O'Neills. *Úa hIcidhe* (O'Hickey): physicians of Thomond. *Úa hIfearnáin* (O'Heffernan): bards in Tipperary and Kilkenny. *Úa Leighin* (O'Leyne): physicians. *Úa Luinín* (O'Luinin): *airchinnig* of Arda in Fermanagh, and, later, *littérateurs* and physicians. *Úa Máil-Conaire* (O'Mulconry, Conroy): historians to the O'Conors and other families of Connacht. *Úa Rígh-Bhárdáin* (O'Riordan): bards and historians of Éle (parts of Offaley and Tipperary). *Úa Ruanadha* (O'Roney): poets of Down. *Úa Sgingín*: historians of Donegal. *Úa hUiginn* (O'Higgin): poets, originally of Fermanagh.[50]

Unfortunately there is no good description of the bardic or other secular schools prior to the sixteenth century, but there are accounts of gatherings of the learned at the courts of the ruling princes. Some of these were on a huge scale.

The seventeenth-century translation of the lost Annals of Clonmacnois has this entry under 1351: "William o'Donogh Moyneagh o'Kelly[51] inuited all the Irish Poets, Brehons, bards, harpers, Gamesters or common kearoghs, Jesters, & others of theire kind of Ireland to his house upon Christmas this yeare, where euery one of them was well used dureing Christmas holy Dayes, & gaue contentment to each of them at the tyme of theire Departure, soe as euery one was well pleased and extolled William for his bounty, one of which assembly composed certaine Irish verses in commendation of William and his house which began thus: *Filidh Ereann go haointeach* &c." The poet was Gofraidh *fionn* Ó Dálaigh,[52] of the O'Dalys of southern Munster, and the poem runs in part as follows: "The poets [*fílid*] of Ireland to one house to-night; it will not be niggardly; what poet has he not snatched from sorrow — the master of the house into which they come! . . . Many coming to the son of Donnchadh from the north, no less from the south, an assembly of scholars: a billeting from west and east, a company seeking for cattle. There will be brehons of legal judgments, there will be druids and poets [*fílid*] of worth, there will be in his dwelling the authors of Ireland, they who compose the battle rolls. The musicians of Ireland — vast the flock — the followers of all public arts, the flood of companies, side by side — the assemblage of all is at one house. . . . The poets [*aos dána*] of the Irish land are prepared to seek O'Kelly. A mighty company is approaching his house, an avenue of peaked hostels is in readiness for them. Hard by that — pleasant is the aspect — a separate street has been appointed by William for the musicians that they may be ready to perform before him. The historians of comely Ireland, it is a gathering of a mighty host, the company is in the town; where is the street of the historians?

---

49 Not to be confused with the princely family of the Dési (Waterford), *Úa Faoláin*.

50 *Cf.* E. C. Quiggin "Prolegomena to the study of the later Irish bards " *Proc. Brit. Acad.* V (1911; also separate print) 15–16, and *passim*; Eleanor Knott (ed.) *Poems of Tadhg Dall O'Higgin* (ITS XXII) (London 1922) introd.

51 Uilliam, son of Donnchadh *Muimnech* Úa Ceallaigh, died in 1381. Donnchadh *Muimnech* ("the Munsterman," because he had been fostered there) had died in 1307: hence, no doubt, this annalist regarded Uilliam as his grandson (*o* instead of *mac*).

52 Ob. 1387.

The fair, generous-hearted host has another spacious avenue of white houses for the retinues and the jugglers." The poem then goes on to describe the great stone castle of O'Kelly, rising above the "white city" erected for his guests; and the beauty and wealth of the surrounding country, which the Úi Maine once more occupy, since O'Kelly has expelled the foreigners.[53]

Just a century later, in the year 1451, another collection of annals, extant only in the translation which An Dubhaltach Mac Fir-Bhisigh made in 1666, has the following: "A gracious yeare this yeare was, though the glory and solace of the Irish was sett by, the Glory of heauen was amplyfied and extolled therin, and although this is a yeare of grace or to with the Roman Church, it is an ungratious, and vnglorious yeare to all the Learned in Irland, both philosophers, poets, guests, strangers, religious persons, souldiers, mendicant or poore orders, and to all manner and sorts of the poore in Irland also; for the generall support of their maintainances decease, to wit Margarett daughter to Thady O-Carole King of Ely, O-Conner ffaly Calwaghs wife,[54] a woman that never refused any man in the world for any thing that shee might command, onely besides her own body. It is shee that twice in one yeare proclaimed to, and comonly invited, (.i. in the darke dayes of the yeare) [55] to wit, on the feast day of Dasinchell [56] in Killaichy [57] all persons both Irish and Scotish or rather Albians, to two generall feasts of bestowing both meate and moneyes with all other manner of guifts, wherinto gathered to receue gifts the matter of two thousand and seauen hundred persons, besides gamsters and poore men, as it was recorded in a Roll to that purpose, and that account was made thus, ut vidimus (viz.) the Chieftaine of each famelie of the Learned Irish, was by Gilla-na-naomh mac AEgans hand writen in that Roll, the chiefe Judg to O-Conner and his adherents, and kinsmen, so that the aforesaid number of 2700 was listed in that Roll with the arts of Dan or poetry, musick and Antiquitie. And Maelyn O-Maelconry [58] one of the chiefe learned of Connaght, was the first writen in that Roll and first payed and dieted or sett to super, and those of his name after him, and so forth, every one, as he was payed, he was writen in that Roll, for feare of mistake, and sett downe to eate afterwards, and Margarett on the garretts of the greate church of Da Sinceall clad in cloath of gold, her deerest friends about her, her clergy and Judges too, Calwagh himselfe being on horseback by the churchs outward side, to the end, that all things might be done orderly, and each one serued successiuely; and first of all she gave two chalices of gold as offerings that day on the Altar to God Almighty, and she also caused to nurse or foster two young orphans. But so it was, we never saw, nor heard neither the like of that day, nor comparable to its glory and solace. And she gaue the second inviting proclamation (to every one that came not that day) on the feast

[53] Adapted from the ed. and trans.by E. Knott, Ériu V (1911) 50–69.

[54] Margaret's father, Tadhg Úa Cerbhaill (O'Carroll), prince of Éle, who was killed at the battle of Callan, 1407 (when, according to the English accounts, the sun stood still while the Lord Deputy rode six miles to the battlefield), and her husband, an Calbach Úa Conchobuir (O'Conor), prince of Offaley, who died in 1458, were two of the most famous of Irish leaders in the long border warfare with the English Pale. A bardic eulogy of Úa Conchobuir, ed. and trans. by Osborn Bergin, is published in Studies IX (July 1920) 416–20.

[55] The year was 1433: "a summer of famine came this year, namely, the Summer of Slight Recognition, for no one recognised relative or friend, because of the greatness of the famine" (AU).

[56] March 26.

[57] Cell-Achid, now Killeigh, about 4 miles S. E. of Tullamore, was one of the principal churches of Offaley. The two (dá) Sinchells were abbots of Cell-Achid.

[58] Maelin Úa Máil-Conaire, "ollam in history of the Síl Muiredaigh and head of dignity and honor of Ireland in his time," who died in 1441 (AU).

day of the Assumpõn [59] of our blessed Lady Mary in haruest at, or in Rath-Imayn.[60] And so we haue been informed, that that second day in Rath-Imayn, was nothing inferiour to the first day, and she was the onely woman that has made most of preparing high-wayes, and erecting bridges, churches and mass-bookes, and of all manner of things profittable to serue God, and her soule, and not that onely, but while the world stands, her very many gifts to the Irish and Scotish Nations shall never be numbered." [61]

These hereditary scholars, in so far as they gave attention to the past, were chiefly copyists and annotators of the older records. Exception should be made of three men who stand out as historians of some importance: Seán *mór* Úa Dubhagáin (O'Dugan) (d. 1372), "chief historian of Ireland," *ollam* of Úi Máine, and author of treatises on history, genealogy, chronology and topography; Gilla-na-náemh Úa Huidhrin (d. 1420), author of a supplement to a topographical poem by Úa Dubhagáin and, it is said, of some synchronistic studies; and Cathal Mac Maghnusa Mag Uidhir (or, MacManus Maguire) (d. 1498) "*biatach* [62] over Seanadh [an island in Upper Loch Erne] and canon choral in Armagh and in the bishopric of Clogher and dean over Loch Erne and parson of Inis-Cain in Loch Erne,"[63] who was the compiler of the very valuable Annals of Ulster. But for the most part the immediate importance to us of these men of the later middle ages is for their work as scribes.

The work of the scribes varied greatly in calligraphy and in accuracy. Although abundant material is available, little scientific study has yet been given to the palaeography of this period. With regard to their characteristics as copyists, it must be kept in mind that the scribes always felt at liberty to edit their texts by changing the verbal forms or even reshaping the matter. In transcribing older texts the language was often modified to bring it nearer to contemporary speech, but, as the scribes were trained antiquarians, proud of their attainments, they never entirely modernised the texts, and sometimes they deliberately introduced archaic or pseudo-archaic forms to give an air of learning to their writings.[64] A large proportion of texts of this "Middle Irish" period are of such type: the language was an artificial product of the *savants*, standing between genuine Old Irish and the contemporary spoken language, which approximated to modern Irish. It is usually

---

[59] August 15.
[60] Now Rathangan in Kildare.
[61] *Miscellany of the IAS* (Dublin 1846) 227–8.
[62] A tenant who held his holding on condition of supplying food to the king's retainers.
[63] AU.
[64] *Cf.* KM *Hibernica Minora* (Oxford 1894) pp. vii–x.

possible for the investigator to detect and reconstruct the Old Irish text
from its Middle Irish setting: in poetry, where metre and rime either
preserved the older forms or made manifest their loss, the reconstruction can be effected with considerable assurance.

Of the manuscript *bibliothecae* written during this period the following are among
the most important, or those to which the student will find most frequent reference:
Stowe D. IV. 2:[65] written in the year 1300 in Cell-Chormaic, now Frankford, Offalley.
H. 2.15a:[66] a fourteenth-century manuscript, in the main, although parts were written
about 1237 "in the house of Cían Mac an Gabann in Ormond." A note entered in
1350 by Aed Mac Aedhagáin (who died in 1359) says that it was the property of
his father Conchobar, and in 1575 it was at Muilenn-Dúna-Daigre (Duniry, on the
Galway side of the Shannon), one of the seats of the MacEgans. It is the oldest
surviving brehon manuscript. *Leabhar Úi Máine*:[67] the "Book of the O'Kellys,"
written between 1360 and 1427; the older part is said to have been written by that
Seán *mór* Úa Dubhagáin of whom notice has been taken above. Another scribe was
Faelán Mac an Gobhann (d. 1423),[68] who wrote for archbishop Muirchertach O'Kelly
(d. 1407)[69]. *The Yellow Book of Lecan*:[70] consists of seventeen distinct sections —
independent manuscripts or fragments — united by the modern binder: one of these,
the original "Yellow Book," seems to have belonged to the Mac Fir-Bisigh family,
but has no date; another was written by Gilla-Iosa, son of Donchad *mór* Mac Fir-
Bisigh, in 1380; another by Murchad Ó Cuindlis, writing in 1398-9 in Muscrige-
Treithirne (barony Clanwilliam, Tipperary); another by Aed Ó Duibhdábhoireann
et al., written at a house of the MacEgans at Pairc in Galway in 1408; another by a
scribe who calls himself Gilla-Padraig *Albanach* ("the Scotsman"), writing at Loch
Tethead (Loch O'Gara, near Boyle) in 1413; another by Donchadh son of Gilla-na-
náem Úa Duinnín for Fingín O'Mahony at Rossbrinn in Cork, in 1465; another
by Seanchán son of Máel-Muire Úa Máil-Conaire in 1473; and another by Iolland
and Torna Úa Máil-Conaire in 1572. *The Book of Ballymote*:[71] written by Solam
O'Droma, Robert MacSheehy, and Magnus O'Duigenan, pupils of a certain Domnal
MacEgan, in the year 1400 or a little later. MacEgan seems to have sold it to
MacDonogh, lord of Ballymote; and in 1522 it was purchased by Aed *óg* O'Donnell,
prince of Tír-Conaill, for one hundred and forty milch cows. *The Book of Fermoy*:[72]
the greater part of the present volume belonged to the Norman-Irish Roches of Fermoy

---

[65] RIA. *Cf.* KM in *RC* VI (1884) 173; *Merugud Uilix maicc Leirtis* (London 1886) p. v.

[66] TCD 1316 (H. 2. 15a) *s* XIV, vellum.

[67] RIA Stowe D. ii. 1. Described by E. O'Reilly in *Trans. Hiberno-Celtic Soc.* I (1820) 1 *sqq.* (partly
reprinted *Journ. Galway Archaeological and Historical Soc.* IV (1905-6) xi 92-6). Also by KM in *ACL*
II iii (1903) 138-46. *Cf.* C. Plummer *Irish Litanies* (London 1915) p. xiii.

[68] FM.

[69] AC in *ALC* II 123. As O'Kelly is called "bishop," it is probable that this part of the MS was written between 1378, when he was consecrated bishop of Clonfert, and 1394, when he became archbishop of
Tuam.

[70] (YBL): TCD 1318 (H. 2. 16) *s* XIV-XV, 958 cols., vellum. Published in facs. by RIA in 1896,
but the facs. is unsatisfactory: *cf. ZCP* I (1897) 493-6; XII 432-4.

[71] (BB): RIA 23. P. 12 *s* XIV/XV, 550 pp., vellum. Published in facs. by RIA in 1887; the ed.,
although far superior to that of YBL, is not very good. One page is reproduced in *Facs. Nat. MSS. Ire.*
III (1879) pl. xxv.

[72] RIA, 23. E. 29, *s* XIV/XV, 129 ff., vellum. *Cf.* J. H. Todd "Descriptive Catalogue of the Book of
Fermoy" *RIA Irish MSS Series* I pt. I (Dublin 1873).

and was written at the end of the fourteenth or in the fifteenth century; attached
are fragments of medical treatises that probably belonged to the O'Hickeys. *Leabhar
Breac* [*"Speckled Book"*], *Leabhar Mór Dúna-Daighre* [*"Great Book of Duniry"*][73]:
this volume, the contents of which are chiefly religious, was compiled by one of the
MacEgans of Muscrige-Tíre, in northern Tipperary, in or before 1411; by the middle
of the sixteenth century it was in the hands of a branch of the family established
at Dún-Daighre [Duniry]. *The Great Book of Lecan*:[74] the greater part of this codex
was written at Lecan in Sligo by Gilla-Ísa Mac Fir-Bisigh in 1416; other scribes were
Adam Úa Cuirnín and Murchadh *riabhach* Úa Cuindlis. *Liber Flavus Fergusiorum*:[75]
compiled in the fifteenth century — by an unprofessional scribe, says O'Curry: the
dates 1437 and 1446 are found on its pages. At one place the following note is to be
read: "Seán Úa Conchobair put these small matters into Gaelic and Donnchad Úa
Máel-Chonaire wrote them at Lios Aedain in Ciarraighe Airde, in the house of Ruaidri
Úa hUiginn,[76] in great haste; and I implore mercy of Christ." This note, however,
is believed to have been copied from an earlier exemplar. The book is first known
as the property of Dr. John Fergus, or O'Fergus, a well-known Dublin physician and
collector of manuscripts, who died in 1761. *Saltair of MacRichard, Laud 610*:[77]
compiled in 1453 by Seán *buide* Úa Cléirigh and others, in Kilnamanagh, county
Kilkenny, for Edmund Mac Richard, head of a Hibernicised branch of the Butlers
of Ormond. The Saltair of Cashel, the Book of Cong, the Book of Rahan and the
Yellow Book of Ferns, none of which is now known to exist, were used in its compilation. In 1462 Mac Richard was taken prisoner by the Earl of Desmond; for his
ransom he handed over this book, and also the "Book of Carrick," which may be
the British Museum Additional MS. 30512, written about the same time, at Carrick-
on-Suir, by Uilliam Mac an Lega.[78] *The Book of Lismore*:[79] written in the later part
of the fifteenth century by Angus O'Callanan, a friar named Ó Bruadhacháin, and
apparently at least one other scribe, for Finghín Mac Carthaigh *riabhach* (d. 1505)
and his wife Catherine, daughter of Thomas, Earl of Desmond. Hence it is sometimes called "the Book of MacCarthy Reagh." The now lost "Book of Monasterboice" is mentioned as one of its sources. *Rawlinson B. 512*:[80] written in 1500 and
earlier by Dubthach Ó Duibgennáin for the cousin of a Conchobar Ó Máil-Chonaire.

[73] (LBr): RIA 23. P. 16 + 23. H. ij, s XIV/XV, 280 pp., vellum. Published in facs. by RIA in 1876.
Two pages are reproduced in *Facs. Nat. MSS. Ire.* III pls. xxviii, xxx. *Cf. PH* 36-40.

[74] RIA 23. P. 2 s XV, 302 ff., vellum. *Cf.* O'C *MS Mat.* 192. One page is reproduced in *Facs. Nat.
MSS. Ire.* III pl. xlvi.

[75] RIA, 23. O. 48, s XV, 92 ff., vellum. *Cf.* O'C *MS Mat.* 76n., 531-3; E. Gwynn *Proc. RIA* XXVI
(1906-7) C 15-41; *BNE* I p. xxiv.

[76] FM give the deaths of these three men, or of men of similar names, in 1391, 1404 and 1425, respectively.

[77] Bodl. Laud 610, s XV, 146 ff., vellum. *Cf.* J. H. Todd *Proc. RIA* II (1842) 336-45; O'D *Book
of Rights* (Dublin 1847) pp. xxviii-xxxiii. One page is reproduced in *Facs. Nat. MSS. Ire.*III (1879) pl.
xlvii.

[78] Such is the opinion of Robin Flower, *Ériu* IX i (1921) 65. It has been known as the "Book of the
O'Mulconrys." WS gives a list of its chief contents, *RC* XXVIII (1907) 308-9. See now Flower
Cat. 470 sqq.

[79] MS, the property of the Duke of Devonshire, which is, or was, in Lismore Castle, Waterford: s XV,
197 ff., vellum. *Cf.* O'C *MS Mat.* 196-200; *Lis. Lives* introd.; O'Grady *SG* II (1892) p. x n. 2. There
is a facs. of one page in *Facs. Nat. MSS. Ire.* III (1879) pl. lvii. RIA has two MS copies, one by Michael
O'Longan, the other by O'C.

[80] Bodl. Rawl. B. 512 s XV; 154 ff., vellum. Description by WS *Vit. Trip.* I (1887) pp. xiv-xlv,
supplemented in *The Academy* XXXIII (1888) 191-2, and by KM *Hibernica Minora* (Oxford 1894)
39-85.

Egerton 1782:[81] a collection of distinct sections, for the most part written in or about 1517, by members of the family of Ó Máil-Chonaire, and at Clúain-Plocáin [82] in Roscommon. A note, dated Poll-in-Móintigh (Poulmounty in Carlow), 1419, was, probably, copied from an exemplar. *Harleian 5280:*[83] copied in the first half of the sixteenth century by An Gilla-Riabach, son of Tuathal, son of Tadhg *cam* Úa Cléirigh, a scribe who was somewhat ignorant and careless, but who made an important selection of documents.—There are also several important law codices compiled in the fifteenth century.[84]

IV. TRANSMISSION OF THE RECORDS—THE ENGLISH CONQUEST

In the year 1500 English rule in Ireland—to be distinguished from the rule of the great Anglo-Irish nobles—hardly extended thirty miles from Dublin. In 1603 the English king's writ ran undisputed from Malin Headland to Cape Clear. By 1700 every trace of the old Irish states and of their political and legal systems had disappeared; the ownership of the entire property of the nation had passed to the alien invaders—with the exception of a minute fraction retained by men of Irish blood at the price of national apostasy; practically the whole Irish people had been, or were on the eve of being, deprived of all political and civil rights except such as must of necessity be left to a servile population; and, as far as physical and economic power could make it so, the fate of that population, individually and collectively, was at the mercy of its conquerors.

In the fifteenth century the standards of life in Ireland had been, in a broad survey, but little lower than those of England. But in the field of political development Ireland was inferior. She had done nothing to create a centralised government or a nation-wide political organisation of any kind, and but little to produce a disciplined morale capable of meeting a national crisis. The penalty for this weakness had now to be paid.

With the end of the Hundred Years' War and the Wars of the Roses, and the increase in national wealth in the sixteenth century, the English monarchy was able to turn greater resources than ever before into the struggle against the Irish. At the same time the development of fire-

---

[81] BM Eg. 1782 s XV/XVI, 125 ff., vellum. *Cf.* ZCP IV (1903) 31–2; *Ériu* IX (1921) 62; Flower *Cat.* 259 sqq.   [82] *Cf.* Flower *op. cit.* 261.

[83] BM Harl. 5280 s XVI, 66 ff., vellum. *Cf.* KM *Hibernica Minora* pp. v–vi; Flower *Cat.* pp. xxxii, 298 sqq.

[84] TCD 1387 (H. 5. 15); TCD 1433 (E. 3. 5); RIA 23. P. 3, part; and parts of Bodl. Rawl. B. 487, and 506.

arms rendered the English armies as much superior to those of the Irish states as had been the Norman invaders of the twelfth century. In the consciousness of this accession of strength Henry VIII assumed the title of "King of Ireland" in 1541 and inaugurated a definite policy towards Ireland, a policy of "reduction" through "politic practices" combined with force, and of "reformation," that is, Anglicisation, partly by conciliation of the princely families and the education of their sons in England, and partly by the confiscation of portions of Irish land to be converted into English "plantations." The policy broke down because of the fierce resistance of the Irish to both Anglicisation and confiscation, and because of the uncontrollable rapacity of the "adventurers" who were the instruments of its execution. In Elizabeth's reign the struggle drifted into a naked war of conquest, with the "extirpation" of the Irish, or at least their expulsion from large sections of their country, coming more and more into serious consideration. It was war such as Ireland had never experienced before, war in which all possible horror was systematically applied to the civilian population. Organised learning and literature went down in this common welter of blood and ruin.

But no high-spirited nation acquiesces in its subjugation by a foreign conqueror. The determination of the Irish sooner or later to reverse the decision of the Elizabethan wars has been the most important underlying factor in the nation's subsequent political history.

The aftermath and completion of the conquest must be briefly sketched. Aedh Ó Néill, prince of Tír-Eoghain—called by the English Hugh, Earl of Tyrone—last of the Irish leaders, submitted on March 31, 1603. Already Queen Elizabeth was dead and the Tudors had been succeeded by the Stuarts. Followed the political and judicial organisation of Ireland on English lines; the huge confiscations by legal chicanery; the "plantation" of Ulster and, less thoroughly, of Leinster; the insurrection of 1641, the Confederation of Kilkenny, the Cromwellian conquest—another war of extermination in which about half the population of the island perished;[85] Cromwell's confiscations and "settlement"; the "restoration" of Charles II, and the practical confirmation of the Cromwellians; the Catholic administration of James II; and, finally, the third, or Williamite, conquest, confiscation, and "settlement." Each of the three conquests was followed by the emigration, in thousands, of the Irish fighting men and upper classes, so that for some generations Europe rather than Ireland became the more conspicuous field of activity of the Irish genius.

[85] *Cf.* W. F. T. Butler *Confiscation in Irish History* (Dublin and London 1917; 2nd ed. 1918) 116.

One new factor in the relations of Irish and English in this epoch must be noticed. England became Protestant, Ireland remained Catholic. That the Gaelic population should repudiate all association with the creed of their enemies is not surprising, but it is more noteworthy that so also did the great majority of the Anglo-Irish of the towns and the Pale,the descendants of the earlier Norman and English invaders. The new line of cleavage had serious results. Europe, and particularly Britain, became obsessed with religious fanaticism to a degree almost unthinkable. So the English people and their agents in Ireland were wonderfully encouraged in the execution of a policy of rigor towards the Irish. To their victims' natal depravity of being Irishmen was added the baptismal infection of being Papists. War in Ireland was in a better cause than war against the Red Indian: it was war against the veritable representatives of Popery and Antichrist. On the other hand, the new issue gradually forced the old Anglo-Irish, willy-nilly, into the national camp. They shared in the Confederation of Kilkenny, making possible its political organisation and stultifying its military action. To them, and to the influences of continental Catholicism, was largely due the linking up of Irish national aspirations with the fortunes of the house of Stuart.[86] And in the end they were brayed in the common mortar of defeat, confiscation and penal laws.

There were further important results on the Irish side from the religious issue. At home, the bards, hitherto the instruments for maintaining patriotism and morale, were now reinforced by the clergy, and particularly by the friars. Abroad, the Irish for the first time received European sympathy in their struggle against England. The religious and intellectual aspects of this sympathy are important here. It made possible the erection of those Irish colleges at the chief centres of learning in Catholic Europe where for two centuries was maintained the ecclesiastical, and in some degree the secular, scholarship of Ireland.

The Irish students attending continental universities had, doubtless, increased in numbers as the English government's attack on the monasteries and other ecclesiastical bodies progressed. For a time schools arose and flourished in the Irish towns—in Dublin, Kilkenny, Wexford, Waterford, Cork, Limerick and Galway—but towards the end of the century these were either suppressed or converted into instruments of

---

[86] It is to be borne in mind, however, that, in comparison with the age which preceded and that which followed, the reigns of Charles II and James II were, for the mass of the Irish people, a period of relative freedom and comfort. *Cf.* Geo. O'Brien *The Economic History of Ireland in the Sevententh Century* (Dublin 1919).

proselytism.[87] The school maintained by the Lynches in Galway, which seems to have been that most frequented by the Gaelic Irish, was the last to fall: it was suppressed in 1615.[88] The training of recruits for the priesthood, and the higher education, in the learning of Europe, of such of the Irish youth as wished to obtain it without forswearing their national and religious convictions, became entirely dependent on continental institutions.

The more important colleges of secular ecclesiastics were those founded at Alcalá about 1590; Salamanca, 1592; Lisbon, 1593; Douai, 1594; Antwerp, 1600–1604; Bordeaux, 1603; Santiago da Compostella, 1605; Paris, 1605; Rouen, about the same time; Lille and Tournai, each 1607 or earlier; Seville, 1612; Louvain, 1624; Rome, 1628; Madrid, 1629; Toulouse, 1659, or earlier; Nantes, 1680. The majority of these colleges were suppressed about the time of the French Revolution, and were not revived, but those of Rome and Salamanca still flourish. Of the regular orders the Irish Franciscans had colleges at Lisbon, Louvain, Rome, Paris, Boulay in Lorraine, Prague, Vielun in Poland, and elsewhere; [89] the Dominicans at Rome, Louvain and Lisbon; [90] and after 1682 the Benedictine nuns a house at Ypres. The Jesuits established a college at Poitiers in 1674, and for a time exercised control over the secular colleges of Rome, Lisbon, Salamanca and Seville.[91]

[87] Cf. A. S. Green The Making of Ireland and its Undoing (London 1908) 364 sqq.

[88] Roderic O'Flaherty (ed. Jas. Hardiman) A Chorographical Description of West or h-Iar Connaught (IAS: Dublin 1846) 34–5, 214 sqq. Also T. Corcoran State Policy in Irish Education (Dublin 1916) 65.

[89] Some documents relating to the Irish Franciscans on the continent and their connections with Ireland are to be found in the Franciscan Convent, Merchants Quay, Dublin. Cf. Hist. MSS Commission, 16th Report: Franciscan Manuscripts [Cd. 2867] (1906).

[90] Founded, or rather the foundation completed, by the famous diplomat Daniel O'Daly (1595–1662), author of a history of the Geraldines of Desmond. Cf. Cath. Encycl.

[91] For these Irish colleges on the continent of Europe cf. A. Bellesheim Geschichte der katholischen Kirche in Irland II (Mainz 1891) 216 sqq., 314 sqq., 360 sqq., etc.; J. Healy Maynooth College Centenary History (Dublin 1895) 51–86; Victor Tourneur Esquisse d'une histoire des études celtiques (Liége 1905); A. S. Green The Making of Ireland and its Undoing (London 1908) 439–58; Patrick Boyle "Irish Colleges on the Continent" Cath. Encycl. On particular localities: ALCALA: IER VIII (1872) 307, IX (1873)545–7. SALAMANCA: IER IX 1–5, 137–42; The Month LXVIII (1890) 85; Denis J. O'Doherty and Amalio Huarte "Students of the Irish College Salamanca" AH II (1913) 1–36, III (1914) 87–112, IV (1915) 1–58, 96–130. LISBON: IER VIII 308–13; The Month LXVIII 514. DOUAI: IER IX 261–72; L. Dancoisne Histoire des établissements religieux Britanniques fondés à Douai avant la révolution française (Douai 1889), esp. 88–91. ANTWERP: Principium ac progressus collegii pastoralis Hibernorum (Antwerp 1680); J. Laenen Het iersch college te Antwerpen (extract from Bijdragen tot de geschiedenis) (Baesrode 1922), BORDEAUX: Bertrand Histoire des séminaires de Bordeaux et de Bazas (Bordeaux 1894); Boyle "The Irish college at Bordeaux 1603–1794" IER 4th ser. XXII (1907) 127–45; Caraman "Recherches sur l'ancienne église Notre-Dame-de-la-Place, à Bordeaux, et sur ses diverses appellations" Rev. historique de Bordeaux et du département de la Gironde July-Aug. 1912. PARIS: IER 4th ser. XI (1902) 193–210, 432–50, XIV (1903) 24–45, XV (1904) 48–73, XXI (1907) 285–99 [cf. also "Lord Iveagh and other Irish officers, students at the Collège des Grassins in Paris, 1684–1710" X (1901) 385 sqq.]; Boyle The Irish College in Paris (1578–1905) with a brief sketch of the other Irish colleges in France (London and Dublin 1905). SEVILLE: IER VIII (1872) 307–8, 465–73, IX (1873) 208–21. LOUVAIN: Historical Works of Nicholas French, Bishop of Ferns . . with an introduction containing notices . . of the Irish colleges of Louvain (Duffy's Library of Ireland: Dublin 1846); O'C MS Mat. 644 sq.; V. De Buck "L'Archéologie irlandaise au couvent de St-Antoine de Padoue à Louvain" Études religieuses historiques et littéraires de la Compagnie de Jésus XXII (1869) 409–37, 586–603 [also separately]; "The Franciscan college of St. Anthony of Padua at Louvain" IER VII (1871) 31–43; J. Gilbert Append. to 4th Report Hist. MSS. Comm. (1874) 599–613; Denis Murphy "The college of the Irish Franciscans at Louvain" Jour. RSAI

The Tudor movement of aggression included an assault on the secular as well as on the ecclesiastical supports of Irish culture. Hitherto the invaders, as a general rule, had not shown any peculiar enmity towards the learned classes. An exception was Sir John Talbot, the famous military leader of the end of the Hundred Years' War, who as Lord Justice in 1415 "despoiled many of the poets of Ireland, to wit, Úa Dálaigh of Meath and Aedh óg Mac Eochadha and Muirgis Úa Dálaigh."[92] But in the sixteenth century the promoters of the composite policy of Anglicisation and subjugation early realised that the learned and literary classes were among the most vigorous champions of Irish culture and independence, or, as Spenser and his fellows preferred to phrase it, "such lycentious partes as these, tending for the most parte to the hurte of the English, or mayntenaunce of theyre owne lewde libertye."[93] Robert Cowley in the reign of Henry VIII wrote:

"Harpers, rhymers, Irish chroniclers, bards, and isshallyn commonly go with praises to gentlemen in the English Pale, praising in rhymes, otherwise called *danes*, their extortions, robberies, and abuses, as valiantness, which rejoiceth them in that their evil doings, and procure a talent of Irish disposition and conversation in them, which is likewise convenient to be expelled."[94]

Perhaps the most complete example of this propaganda against the Irish *literati* is the production of an English apothecary named Thomas Smyth, who was writing in Dublin in 1561:

"The thirde sorte is called the Aeosdan,[95] which is to saye in English, the bards, or the rimine sepctes; and these people be very hurtfull to the comonwhealle, for they chifflie mayntayne the rebells; and, further, they do cause them that would be true, to be rebelious theves, extorcioners, murtherers, ravners, yea and worse if it were possible. Their furst practisse is, if they se anye younge man discended of the septs of Ose or Max, and have half a dowsen aboute him, then will they make him a Rime, wherein they will commend his father and his aunchetours, nowmbrying howe many heades they have cut of, howe many townes they have burned, and howe many virgins they

5th ser. II (1898) 237–50; Brendan Jennings "The return of the Irish Franciscans to Louvain 1606–1925" *Studies* Sept. 1925 pp. 451–8. ROME: P. F. Moran *Memoir of the Ven. Oliver Plunkett* (Dublin 1861); M. O'Riordan "Irish College in Rome" *Cath. Encycl.* MADRID: *IER* IX 544–5. TOULOUSE: Pagny *Mémoires historiques et chronologiques sur les séminaires établis dans la ville de Toulouse* (Toulouse 1852); Boyle "The Irish seminary at Toulouse" *AH* I (1912) 122–47. NANTES: Patrick Hurley "A Bishop of Cork and the Irish at Nantes" *Dublin Review* CX (1892) 38–51, 351–62. PRAGUE: Green *op. cit.* 454–8; R. J. Kelly "The Irish Franciscans at Prague" *Journ. RSAI* LII ii (1922) 169–74.

[92] *AU.*

[93] Edmund Spenser *A View of the Present State of Ireland*, written in or before 1598, but first published by Ware in 1633.

[94] Quoted in *Calendar of Carew Manuscripts* II (1868) p. xxix n.; Alice Stopford Green *The Making of Ireland and its Undoing* (London 1908) 373.

[95] *Aes dáno* (sometimes *aes dán*), "people having a trade, profession or art," especially "poets."

have defloured,[96] howe many notable murthers they have done, and in the ende they will compare them to Aniball, or Scipio, or Hercules, or some other famous person; wherewithall the pore foole runs madde, and thinkes indede it is so. Then will he gather a sorte of rackells to him, and other he most geat him a Proficer, who shall tell him howe he shall spede (as he thinkes). Then will he geat him lurking to a syde of a woode, and ther keepith him close til morninge; and when it is daye light, then will they go to the poore vilages, not sparinge to distroye young infants, aged people; and if the women be ever so great with childe, her they will kill; burninge the houses and corne, and ransackinge of the poore cottes. They will then drive all the kine and plowe horses, with all other cattell, and drive them awaye. Then muste they have a bagpipe bloinge afore them; and if any of theis cattell fortune to waxe wearie or faynt, they will kill them, rather than it sholde do the honeur's goode. . . . And when he is in a safe place, they will fall to the devision of the spoile, accordinge to the dyscresion of the captin. . . . Now comes the Rymer that made the Ryme, with his Rakry.[97] The Rakry is he that shall utter the ryme; and the Rymer himself sitts by with the captain verie proudlye. He brings with him also his Harper, who please all the while that the raker sings the ryme. Also he hath his Barde, which is a kinde of folise fellowe; who also must have a horse geven him; the harper must have a new safern shurte, and a mantell, and a hacnaye; and the rakry must have xx or xxx kine, and the Rymer himself horse and harnes with a nag to ride on, a silver goblett, a pair of bedes of corall, with buttons of silver; and this, with more, they loke for to have, for reducinge distruxione of the Comenwealth, and to the blasfemye of God; and this is the best thinge, that ye Rymers causith them to do."[98]

In 1549, by statutes made at Limerick by the king's commissioners, it was ordained "that no poet or any other person hereafter shall make or compose any poems or anything which is called 'auran' to any person, except to the King, on pain of forfeiting all his goods, and imprisonment, at the pleasure of the King or his Deputy"; [99] and in 1571 Sir John Perrot, Lord President of Munster, directed by ordinance "all carroughes, bards, rhymers and common idle men and women wthin this province making rhymes, bringing of messages, and common players at cards, to be spoiled of all their goods and chattels, and to be put in the next stocks, there to remain till they shall find sufficient surety to leave that wicked thrade of life, and to fall to other occupation."[100]

Of the fate of individual men of learning not much is known. No institution survived to treasure their martyrology, but it may well have carried as many names as that of the priests and friars. Among the noteworthy victims were Tadhg Ó Cobhthaigh (O'Coffey), "chief preceptor of Ireland and Scotland," who was imprisoned and threatened with death in 1546, but escaped;[101] Eoghan *ruadh* Mac an Bháird and Muiris *ballach* Ó Clérigh, "skilled men in history and in poetry," hanged by the Anglicising Earl of Thomond in 1572;[101] Donnchadh *an tSneachta*

---

[96] So far as the Irish poetry of the sixteenth century has been made available for examination, it is, compared with other contemporary literatures, remarkably free from sexual licentiousness.

[97] *Recaire*, a professional elocutionist.

[98] Smyth's "Information for Ireland", 5 May, 1561: *UJA* VI (1858) 166-7.

[99] *Calendar of the Carew Manuscripts* I (1867) 214-5.

[100] *Ibid.* 410.

[101] FM.

("of the snow") Mac Craith, of Galbally, Aherlow, hanged by the President of Munster about 1597;[102] Cúchonnacht Ó Cianáin—brother of Tadhg who accompanied O'Neill and O'Donnell to the Continent in 1607 and wrote the history of that flight [103] — who was racked in Dublin on June 26, 1615, and hanged at Derry a few weeks later.[104] Of the three best-known writers of Ulster at the close of the sixteenth century we have no information as to the fate of Eochaidh Ó hEoghasa (O'Hosey or O'Hussey); Eoghan *ruadh* Mac an Bháird died quietly at an advanced age in 1609;[105] and Tadhg *dall* Ó hUiginn was murdered in 1617 or earlier by some plundering Irish soldiers whom he had satirised.[106] Aonghus *ruadh* O Dálaigh, called Aonghus *na n-aor*, "of the satires," was, according to tradition, murdered in the house of O'Meagher of Ikerrin while making, at the instigation of government agents, a tour through the country lampooning the former princely families in their poverty and humiliation.[107] Some certainly went over to the English. Patrick and John Mac Crossan, of a family of hereditary bards to the O'Moores of Leix, adopted the name Crosbie and passed themselves as of English blood. John became Protestant bishop of Ardfert and Aghadoe in Kerry, while Patrick received extensive grants in Leix and also in Kerry, whither, in 1608-9, he transplanted as his tenants those of his former masters, the O'Moores and their allies, who had survived the fifty years' guerrilla warfare against the English planters of Leix.[108] The great majority of the learned families, however, went the way of their patrons into submission and ultimately the helot's *status*.[109]

The letters of Sir John Davies, attorney-general in Ireland under James I, to Sir William Cecil, in the years following the pacification of 1603, although written by a prejudiced foreigner with only a superficial

---

[102] Philip O'Sullivan Beare *Historiae Catholicae Iberniae Compendium* (Lisbon 1621) tom. II lib. IV cap. xxii; *Pacata Hibernia. Cf. Proc. RIA* XXXVI (1922) C vi 103-4.

[103] *AH* II *sqq.*

[104] *Proc. RIA* XXXVI (1922) C vi 117-8. The hanging propensities of Sidney, Drury, Fitton, Carew and other officials of the sixteenth century were remarkable. In 1580 the Earl of Clanrickarde in a statement of his services wrote: "I did within one towelmonethes hang my own sonne, my brotheres sonn, my cousayne germaynes sonn, and one of the Captayns of my galleglasses, besides fiuftie of my owne followers that bare armoure and weapone, wiche the Archbusshopp of tuame, the busshopp of clownferte and the whole corporatione of the towne of gallwey may wittness." State Papers relating to Ireland, Reign of Elizabeth, vol. LXVI, no. 4, quoted by O'Grady, *Cat.* 375.

[105] FM.

[106] O'Grady *Cat.* 407-8, 439-42.

[107] *The Tribes of Ireland: a satire, by Aenghus O'Daly: with poetical translation by the late James Clarence Mangan: together with an historical account of the family of O'Daly: and an introduction to the history of satire in Ireland,* by John O'Donovan (Dublin 1852). *Cf.* O'Grady *Cat.* 443-5.

[108] Lord Walter FitzGerald "Notes on the Family of Patrick Crosbie" *Jour. RSAI* LIII ii (1923) 133-50.

[109] See the valuable study by Thos. F. O'Rahilly, "Irish Poets, Historians, and Judges in English Documents, 1538-1615" *Proc. RIA* XXXVI (1922) C vi 86-120.

understanding of the country he was helping to govern, contain matter of much interest, part of which may be quoted:

"From Monaghan we went [110] the first night to the ruins of the abbey of Clonays, where we camped; and passing from thence through ways almost impassable for our carriages by reason of the woods and bogs, we came the second night after to the southside of Lougherne, and pitched our tents over against the island of Devenish, a place being prepared for the holding of our sessions for Fermanagh, in the ruins of an abbey there. [An examination was made into the land system of the district, which examination was left in Davies' charge while the lord deputy went on to Bally-shannon. It was found that there were fifty-one and a half "ballibetaghs " [111] of land "chargeable with McGuire's rent, and other contributions of the country," and in addition certain free lands.] Touching the free land, we found them to be of three kinds. 1. Church-land, or termon-lands, as the Irish call it. 2. The mensal land of McGuire. 3. Lands given to certain septs privileged among the Irish, viz., the lands of the chroniclers, rimers and galloglasses. The church-land was either monastery land, corbe-land, or Erenach's-land; for it did not appear unto us that the bishop had any land in demesne, but certain mensal duties of the corbes and Erenachs; neither did we find that the parsons and vicars had any glebe land at all in this country. For monastery-land, we found not other than that which belonged to the abbey of Lisgoole, which doth not exceed the quantity of two ballibetaghs, and lieth for the most part in the barony of Clanawley. But the lands belonging to the corbes and Erenachs are of a far greater quantity, and are found in every barrony. [Here follows a statement of results of his enquiries from "one of the best learned vicars in all the country, and one that had been a Brehon, and had some skill in the civil and canon laws," and from others, regarding the significance of the terms "corbe" and "erenach."]

"Touching McGuire's mensal lands, which were free from all common charges and contributions of the country, because they yielded a large proportion of butter and meal, and other provisions, for McGuire's table, albeit the jury and other inhabitants did set forth these mensal lands in certainty, which lying in several baronies did not in quantity exceed four ballibetaghs, the greatest thereof being in the possession of one McManus and his sept; yet touching the certainties of the duties or provisions unto McGuire out of these mensal lands, they referred themselves to an old parchment roll, which they called an indenture, remaining in the hands of one O'Brislan,[112] a chronicler, and principal brehon of that country: whereupon O'Brislan was sent for, who lived not far from the camp, who was so aged and decrepid as he was scarce able to repair unto us; when he was come, we demanded of him a sight of that ancient roll, wherein, as we were informed, not only the certainty of McGuire's mensal duties did appear, but also the particular rents and other services which were answered to McGuire out of every part of the country. The old man, seeming to be much troubled with this demand, made answer, that he had such a roll in his keeping before the

[110] This letter, written in 1606, describes a visitation by the Lord Deputy to the newly created counties of Monaghan, Fermanagh and Cavan.
[111] In Monaghan this was estimated by Davies to contain 960 English acres, but he seems to think that in Fermanagh it was a measure of much larger extent. In origin it was the *baile*, demesne, of a *biatach*. *Cf.* p. 23 n. 62 *supra*.
[112] Úa Breislen. *Cf.* p. 20 *supra*. In the other eds. of this letter the name is given, incorrectly, as "O'Bristan."

wars, but that in the late rebellion it was burned among others of his papers and books by certain English soldiers. We were told by some that were present, that this was not true; for they affirmed that they had seen the roll in his hands since the wars. Thereupon, my lord chancellor being then present with us (for he did not accompany my lord deputy to Ballyshannon, but staid behind in the camp) did minister an oath unto him, and gave him a very serious charge to inform us truly what was become of the roll. The poor old man, fetching a deep sigh, confessed that he knew where the roll was, but that it was dearer to him than his life, and therefore he would never deliver it out of his hands, unless my lord chancellor would take the like oath, that the roll should be restored to him again: my lord chancellor smiling gave him his hand and his word, that he should have the roll re-delivered unto him, if he would suffer us to take a view and a copy thereof. And thereupon the old brehon drew the roll out of his bosom, where he did continually bear it about him. It was not very large, but it was written on both sides in a fair Irish character; howbeit, some part of the writing was worn and defaced with time and ill keeping. We caused it forthwith to be translated into English, and then we perceived how many vessels of butter, and how many measures of meal, and how many porks, and other such gross duties did arise unto McGuire out of his mensal lands; . . . albeit Hugh McGuire, that was slain in Munster, were indeed a valiant rebel, and the stoutest that ever was of his name, notwithstanding generally the natives of this country are reputed the worst swordsmen of the north, being rather inclined to be scholars or husbandmen, than to be kerne, or men of action, as they term rebels in this kingdom; . . . . Concerning the free-land of the third kind, namely, such land as is possessed by the Irish officers of this country, viz., Chroniclers, galloglasses, and rimers, the entire quantity, if it were laid down together, as it is scattered in sundry baronies, doth well nigh make two ballibetaghs, and no more; which land (in respect of the persons that merit no respect, but rather discountenance from the state, for they are enemies to the English government,) may perhaps be thought meet to be added to the demesne lands of the chief lords."[113]

Through the terrors and disasters of the sixteenth century the bards, historians and brehons kept constantly at the task of compiling and copying manuscripts. Although individually not of as great importance as some of the codices of earlier ages, many manuscripts of the sixteenth and the first half of the seventeenth century have much value for old Irish history: transcripts made later than the middle of the seventeenth century are, with a few exceptions, worth but little for this particular study.

Of strictly historical works the most important of which we have information was the Annals of the O'Duigenans of Kilronan, which, according to the Four Masters, came down to the year 1563. This no longer exists, but it appears to have formed the basis for what are now known as the "Annals of Connacht," written by the O'Mulconrys for the O'Conors, and the "Annals of Loch Cé," written for (and in

[113] The letter has been printed several times (e.g., in *Ireland under Elizabeth and James the First*, ed. by Henry Morley (London 1890) 343–80): it is here quoted from Chas. Vallancey's *Collectanea de Rebus Hibernicis* I (Dublin 1770) 131–74, which in some respe c^t seems to be the best text.

part by) Brian MacDermot, lord of Moylurg (d. 1592), by scribes of the O'Duigenans, about 1580–88. There are several important brehon codices of the sixteenth century: the Trinity College manuscripts 1336 (H. 3. 17) — made up of originally distinct sections, written wholly or chiefly by MacEgans, though part belonged to an Edmond O'Doran and later — in 1666 — to Duald MacFirbis; 1337 (H. 3. 18) — various legal and miscellaneous sections, the legal believed to have belonged to the MacEgans, written at their castle of the Park, near Tuam, and elsewhere; later they were in the possession of Agnew, or Ó Gnímh, of Ulster; and 1363 (H. 4. 22) — also consisting of several distinct sections, of which those of a legal character were written by Cosnamach Mac Aedhagáin and other scribes, probably of his school;[114] Royal Irish Academy 23. Q. 6; British Museum Egerton 88 and 90; Cotton Nero A. VII, written by Matha Ó Luinín in 1571; and Harleian 432. The manuscript Egerton 88 was written about 1564–9 by Domhnall Ó Duibhdábhoirenn (Donall O'Davoren) and others, his assistants or pupils, chiefly at the MacEgan castle of the Park. Its many *marginalia* throw interesting side-lights on the lives of the scribes: their sufferings and difficulties, the war which was going on around them, and the jokes and jibes — perhaps eighty *per cent.* of them no longer intelligible — in which they sought amusement.[115]

We meet now for the first time with some descriptions in detail of Irish schools—unfortunately from foreign or anti-national sources. Edmund Campion, who wrote his *History of Ireland* in 1571, has the following passage—repeated in part by his friend Richard Stanyhurst in his *Description of Ireland*:[116]

"One office in the house of great men is a taleteller, who bringeth his Lord on sleepe with tales vaine and frivolous, whereunto the number give sooth and credence. So light they are in beleeving whatsoever is with any countenance of gravitie affirmed by their Superiours, whom they esteeme and honour, that a lewd Prelate within these few yeares needy of money, was able to perswade his parish: That S. Patricke in striving with S. Peter to let an Irish Galloglass into Heaven, had his head broken with the keyes, for whose reliefe he obtained a Collection.[117]

"Without either precepte or observation of congruity they speake Latine like a vulgar language, learned in their common Schools of Leach-craft and Law, whereat they begin Children, and hold on sixteene or twentie yeares conning by roate the Aphorismes of *Hypocrates*, and the Civil Institutions, and a few other parings of those two faculties. I have seene them where they kept Schoole, ten in some one chamber, groveling upon couches of straw, their Bookes at their noses, themselves lying flatte prostrate, and so to chaunte out their lessons by peece-meale, being the most part lustie fellowes of twenty-five yeares and upwards.

"Other Lawyers they have, liable to certaine families which after the custome of the country determine and judge causes. These consider of wrongs offered and received

---

114 Scholars of this name are mentioned by *FM* in 1422 and 1529. It is quite possible that the MS is of the fifteenth century.

115 O'Grady *Cat.* 85–141. The *marginalia* are given *in extenso. Cf.* G. U. Macnamara *North Munster Archaeological Journal* II 149 *sqq.*

116 *Cf.* p. 46 *infra.*

117 Campion, if the first, was certainly not the last alien whose condescending pity for the gullibility of the "natives" has been the prelude to his own undoing.

among their neighbours, be it murder or felony, or trespasse, all is redeemed by com-position, (except the grudge of parties seeke revenge:) and the time they have from spoyling and proyning they lightly bestow in parling about such matters. The Breighoon (so they call this kind of Lawyer) sitteth him downe on a banke, the Lordes and gentlemen at variance round about him and then they proceede."[118]

More detailed is the description of the schools of poetry given by the editor of *Memoirs of the Right Honourable the Marquis of Clanricarde*, first published in London in 1722.[119] The conditions depicted must have been of the seventeenth century, when the confiscations had taken away the lands of the poets:

"Concerning the poetical seminary, or school . . . it was open only to such as were descended of poets, and reputed within their tribes: And so was it with all the schools of that kind in the nation, being equal to the number of families, that followed the said calling: But some more or less frequented for the difference of professors, con-veniency, with other reasons, and seldom any come but from remote parts, to be at a distance from relations, and other acquaintance, that might interrupt his study. The qualifications first requir'd, were reading well, writing the mother-tongue, and a strong memory. It was likewise necessary the place shou'd be in the solitary recess of a garden, or within a sept or inclosure, far out of the reach of any noise, which an intercourse of people might otherwise occasion. The structure was a snug, low hut, and beds in it at convenient distances, each within a small apartment, without much furniture of any kind, save only a table, some seats, and a conveniency for cloaths to hang upon. No windows to let in the day, nor any light at all us'd but that of candles, and these brought in at a proper season only. The students upon thorough examination being first divided into classes; wherein a regard was had to every ones age, genius and the schooling had before, if any at all; or otherwise. The professors, (one or more as there was occasion) gave a subject suitable to the capacity of each class, determining the number of rhimes, and clearing what was to be chiefly observ'd therein as to syllables, quartans, concord, correspondence, termination, and union, each of which were restrain'd by peculiar rules. The said subject (either one or more as aforesaid) having been given over night, they work'd it apart each by himself upon his own bed, the whole next day in the dark, till at a certain hour in the night, lights being brought in, they committed it to writing. Being afterwards dress'd and come together into a large room, where the masters waited, each scholar gave in his performance, which being corrected, or approv'd of (according as it requir'd) either the same or fresh subjects were given against the next day. This part being over, the students went to their meal, which was then serv'd up; and so after some time spent in conversation, and other diversions, each retir'd to his rest, to be ready for the business of the next morning. Every Saturday, and on the eves of festival days, they broke up, and dispers'd themselves among the gentlemen and rich farmers of the country, by whom they were very well entertain'd, and much made of, till

118 *A Historie of Ireland, Written in the Yeare 1571* — By Edmund Campion, *sometime fellow of St. John's Colledge, in Oxford:* In Sir James Ware's *The Historie of Ireland, collected by three learned authors* (Dublin 1633). Reprint in *Ancient Irish Histories* (Dublin 1809). The work was edited and published in Holinshed's *Chronicles* (London 1577).

119 I quote from the Dublin, 1744, reprint, pp. cvii–cix.

they thought fit to take their leaves, in order to reassume their study. Nor was the people satisfied with affording this hospitality alone; they sent in by turns every week from far and near, liquors, and all manner of provision towards the subsistence of the academy; so that the chief poet was at little or no charges, but on the contrary got very well by it, besides the presents made him by the students, upon their first coming, which was always at Michaelmas; and from thence to the 25th of March, during the cold season of the year only, did that close study last. At that time the scholars broke up, and repair'd each to his own country, with an attestation of his behaviour and capacity, from the chief professor, to those that sent him."[120]

The period of peace if not security which followed on the conquest of 1603 was marked by an extraordinary outburst of literary and scholarly activity. The survivors of the learned orders seized the occasion to gather up once more the national treasures. Their work was a conscious appeal from a doomed civilisation against the oblivion which it saw approaching. They realised that extinction was hovering over the story of Ireland's national past, and that the prejudices of English historians were like to write her epitaph. "There is, indeed, hardly to be found in the history of literature a more pathetic tale than that of the way in which Colgan and his fellow workers strove, amid poverty, and persecution, and exile, to save the remains of their country's antiquities from destruction."[121]

From the ecclesiastical refugees on the continent came the prime impulse to this historical movement. There the interest in religious antiquities and hagiology was strong: the works of Surius and Baronius had but recently been completed, that of the Bollandists was just commencing. Henry Fitz Simon (1566 or 1569–1643 or 1645),[122] a native of Dublin who became a Jesuit and a famous protagonist of Catholicity in its Irish struggles, published in 1611 a *Catalogus praecipuorum sanctorum Hiberniae*, the beginning of Irish hagiological publication. Luke Wadding[123] (1588–1657), a native of Waterford, educated at home, and at Lisbon, Salamanca, and other centres of learning abroad, became

---

[120] On the schools, see also O. Bergin "Bardic Poetry" *Ivernian Journal* V no. xix, and Daniel Corkery *The Hidden Ireland* (Dublin 1925) 59–89. Though there is no description of the schools from the Irish side, there are numberless tributes to learning and literature.

"Pleasant the scholar's life	O'er him the strongest lord
When his books surround him;	Rules not as prince or king;
'Tis clear to ye, O people,	For him no Church's dues,
No better is in Ireland.	Nor fines nor early rising."

—From an anonymous poem, probably of the seventeenth century, quoted by Corkery, *op. cit.* 79.

[121] *VV. SS. Hib.* I p. x n. 3.

[122] See Edmund Hogan, ed. of his *Words of comfort to persecuted Catholics* (Dublin 1881); and *Distinguished Irishmen of the sixteenth century* (Dublin 1894) 198–310. Also *DNB* and *Cath. Encycl.*

[123] See articles in *DNB* and *Cath. Encycl.*, and references there given; also G. Cleary *Father Luke Wadding and St. Isidore's College, Rome* (Rome 1925).

one of the foremost scholars of Europe. He founded the Irish Franciscan College of St. Isidore at Rome, and, among his many voluminous undertakings, planned a history of Ireland, which, however, he was compelled to abandon. Another Waterford man, and a relative of Wadding, Peter Lombard[124] (c. 1555–1625), who, after attending Westminster school and the university of Oxford, attained fame as a scholar at Louvain and Rome and was appointed by the Pope archbishop of Armagh, wrote a controversial work on Irish history entitled *De regno Hiberniae sanctorum insulae commentarius*.[125] Lombard, who never returned to Ireland, had as administrator of his diocese David Rothe[126] (1573–1650),˙of Kilkenny, afterwards bishop of Ossory, who had been educated at Douai and Salamanca. Rothe's first published work, the *Analecta Sacra*,[127] was an account of the recent persecutions of his co-religionists in Ireland, but he projected, and labored at during a great part of his life, an ecclesiastical history of the country and a work entitled *Hierographiae sacrae insulae Hiberniae lineamenta*, a compilation of ecclesiastical and secular antiquities. The second at least of these was ready for publication at the time of his death, which took place in Kilkenny a few weeks after that city had been captured by Cromwell. A friend and co-worker of Rothe's was Thomas Messingham,[128] rector of the Irish College in Paris, who in 1624 published the first printed collection of the *acta* of Irish saints, *Florilegium insulae sanctorum*. Stephen White[129] (1574–1646) of Clonmel, perhaps a relative of Thomas White, founder of the Irish College of Salamanca, was educated at that institution, became a Jesuit, and taught at Ingolstadt, Dilingen, and elsewhere in southern Germany. His antiquarian researches earned him a high reputation: he worked especially to recover the records and vindicate the Irish character of the "Scotti" who played such a prominent part in early mediaeval Europe.

It happened that a number of members of the old families of hereditary *literati* had joined the order of St. Francis and become associated with the College of St. Anthony at Louvain in the Spanish Nether-

---

124 Renehan *Irish Archbishops* (Dublin 1861); Stuart (ed. Coleman) *Historical Memoirs of Armagh* (Dublin 1900); *DNB*.

125 First published at Louvain in 1632; re-edited at Dublin by P. F. Moran in 1868.

126 C. P. Meehan *The Rise and Fall of the Irish Franciscan Monasteries and Memoirs of the Irish Hierarchy* (Dublin 1872, and later eds.); P. F. Moran *Spicilegium Ossoriense* (Dublin 1874–84); *DNB*.

127There seems to have been an edition of the first part in 1616 or earlier: the complete work was issued at Cologne 1617–19. A new ed. was published by Moran in 1884.

128 Not much is known regarding Messingham. *Cf.* Patrick Boyle *The Irish College in Paris* (London and Dublin 1905); *Cath. Encycl.*

129 W. Reeves "Memoir of Stephen White" *Proc. RIA* VIII (1861) 29–38; E. Hogan "Life of Father Stephen White, S. J." *Waterford Archaeological Journal* III (1897); *DNB*. White's *Apologia pro Hibernia adversus Cambri calumnias* was published with notes, etc., by Matthew Kelly (Dublin 1849).

lands.[130] The college was founded by Flaithri Ó Máil-Chonaire, called also Florence Conroy[131] (1560-1629), of the Connacht family of historians, who became provincial of his order and archbishop of Tuam. Among the inmates were Aedh Mac Cathmhaoil, or Hugh MacCaghwell[132] (1571-1626)—native of Down and friend of Aedh Ó Néill of Tír-Eoghain—who, after studying at Salamanca, joined the Franciscans and was appointed guardian or superior of St. Anthony's; Aedh Mac an Bháird, or Hugh Ward[133] (1590-1635), of a Tír-Conaill family of historians, also a graduate of Salamanca, and MacCaghwell's successor at Louvain; Máel-Brigde or Gilla-Brigde Ó hEoghasa, otherwise Bonaventura O'Hosey or O'Hussey[134] (d. 1614), of a Fir-Manach family of bards, educated at Douai but one of the original community of St. Anthony's, of which he was guardian at his death—he is said to have borne among his brethren a high reputation for his knowledge of Irish literature and antiquities; John Colgan[135] (1592-1658), of the family Ó Colgáin, holders of the office of *airchinnech* of Domnach-mór, or Donaghmore, in Inis-Eoghain,[136] educated under MacCaghwell at Louvain; Antony Hickey[137] (1586-1641), of the Thomond family of Ó hIcidh, pupil and colleague of MacCaghwell and Ward at Louvain, and later collaborator with Luke Wadding at Rome; Tadhg, or, in religion, Micheál Ó Cléirigh—Michael O'Clery[138]—who, after being trained to the historical profession hereditary in his family,[139] became a lay brother at Louvain; Christopher, in religion Patrick, Fleming[140] (1599-1631), of the Anglo-Irish kindred of the barons of Slane, who, educated at Douai, became a Franciscan at Louvain in 1617. These men undertook to make Louvain an asylum of Irish culture. Hugh Ward, with the assistance of his colleagues in the college, and with the encouragement of Luke Wadding at Rome and of Rosweyde and the

[130] On the historical work of the Irish Franciscans at Louvain see articles by De Buck, Gilbert and Murphy cited *supra*, p. 29; also *IER* VII (1871) 31-43, 56-77, 193-216, 268-89, and Tourneur *Esquisse d'une histoire des études celtiques* (Liége 1905). A thorough study of the subject is a *desideratum* of Irish history. *Cf.* M. Esposito *Proc. RIA* XXXII (1913) C v 80 n.

[131] *DNB; Cath. Encycl.;* and references there given.

[132] *Ibid.*

[133] *Ibid.* Also *IER* VII (1871) 56-77.

[134] *Ibid.;* also O'Grady *Cat.* 407 n.; *Studies* VII (June 1918) 279; Flower *Cat.* pp. xxvii, 27 *sq.*

[135] Reeves's memoir on Colgan in *UJA* I (1853); C. P. Meehan *The Rise and Fall of the Irish Franciscan Monasteries and Memoirs of the Irish Hierarchy* (Dublin 1877); Doherty *Inis-Owen and Tirconnell, being some account of antiquities and writers of the county of Donegal* (Dublin 1895) 49-52, 71-106; *Cath. Encycl. s. n.*

[136] O'Grady *Cat.* 342 n.

[137] *DNB; Cath. Encycl.;* and references there given.

[138] O'C *MS Mat.* 142-78; *DNB;* Tourneur *Esquisse d'une histoire des études celtiques* (Liége 1905).

[139] It would appear from the preface to his *Glossary* that O'Clery studied under Baothghalach *ruadh* Mac Aedhagáin, and perhaps Seán Ó Máil-Chonaire and Flann Mac Aedhagáin.

[140] *IER* VII (1871) 193-216; *DNB; Cath. Encycl.;* and references; also R. J. Kelly "The Irish Franciscans at Prague" *Jour. RSAI* LII ii (1922).

other early Bollandists in the Netherlands, drew up a plan for a *Thesaurus Antiquitatum Hibernicarum*, civil as well as religious. The work thereon was executed under the general direction of Ward, and, after his death, of Colgan.[141]

The first object was to collect at Louvain as many as possible of the historical sources, either originals or transcripts. For this purpose communications were opened with all persons likely to be of assistance. Stephen White sent copies of several important manuscripts discovered by him in German and Swiss monasteries. Of the members of the order, Patrick Fleming and another friar named Brendan O'Conor were deputed to gather material in Europe. Some of Fleming's letters to Ward in connection with the undertaking have been preserved.[142] An important collection of documents regarding Columbanus, some of them copied in the monastery of Bobbio, was left by him in Flanders when, in November, 1630, he was sent to Prague as head of the Irish Franciscan College in that city. He never resumed his hagiological investigations: in the course of the Thirty Years' War a Protestant army under the Elector of Saxony advanced against Prague in the autumn of 1631, and Father Fleming, fleeing from the city, was murdered by some peasants on 7 November.

The chief work, however, had to be done in Ireland, and thither went Brother Michael O'Clery, charged with the task of making exact transcripts of all the manuscripts in the Irish language, bearing on religious history, that he could discover.[143] He remained in Ireland continuously, or with but short intervals of absence, from 1626 to 1642. His industry was enormous: many of his manuscripts survive, and from the colophons added to them, if collected, a fairly complete record of his work could be constructed. He made his headquarters with the friars of Donegal in their establishment on the river Drowse, between the present counties of Donegal and Leitrim, whither they seem to have removed after the destruction of their house at Donegal during the Elizabethan wars. His brother Máel-Muire, or, in religion, Bernardin O'Clery was superior of this community. There the manuscripts Michael collected or transcribed were assembled, and there he made fair second copies of many documents.

---

141 *Cf.* Plummer *VV. SS. Hib.* I (1910) pp. x–xi, xviii–xix.

142 *IER* VII (1871) 56–77, 193–216.

143 Other men helped in the collection, and perhaps in the transcription of texts. The Stowe MS RIA A. 4. 1, a collection of saints' Lives copied in 1627 by Domnall Ó Duinnín for Francis Ó Mathgamna (O'Mahony), Franciscan Provincial in Cork, was, doubtless, intended to serve the same undertaking. *Cf.* p. 309 *infra*. On O'Mahony, see the *Franciscan Tertiary* III ii (Mar. 1897) and Plummer *Misc. hag. Hib.* (1925) 157 n.

The White, Fleming, O'Clery and other collections gradually came together at Louvain, where remained the tasks of collating, translating into Latin, annotating, and editing for the press. Ward on his death left several treatises prepared for publication, the majority of them designed to form part of the "prolegomena." Colgan carried on the editorial work, and in 1645 and 1647 published at Louvain the third and second volumes of the whole design. The third volume, issued in 1645, is entitled *Acta Sanctorum . . . . Hiberniae . . . . tomus primus*, and includes Lives of the Irish saints whose festivals fall within the months January, February and March; the second volume, *Triadis Thaumaturgae*, contains documents relating to the three great saints, Patrick, Brigit and Colum-cille.

Michael O'Clery had died a few months before the 1645 volume appeared, and, whether because his loss interfered with the treatment of the Irish texts, or because the Cromwellian conquest destroyed all hope of further literary and financial help from Ireland,[144] Colgan proceeded no further with publication. He died in 1658, leaving in manuscript three treatises on the early Irish saints of the continent of Europe.[145] Thomas O'Sherin, one of his disciples, published Ward's *Acta S. Rumoldi* in 1662, and Fleming's *Collectanea sacra* in 1667.

But the Louvain movement had had a development on Irish soil which has overshadowed it in fame. O'Clery, trained historian of the Irish schools, evidently found the work of exact transcription, to which he was bound by his instructions, very irksome,[146] scrupulously conscientious though he was in its performance. He obtained permission to devote part of his time to works in Irish after the manner of the old historical schools, and for this purpose associated with himself several of the still surviving professional historians. The first of their compilations is the *Réim Rioghraide*, "Succession of Kings," work on which was begun in 1624: it was carried out at the expense of Toirdhelbhach, or Turlough, Mag Cochláin, of the old ruling family of Delbna (bar. Garrycastle, co. Offalley), and the final writing seems [147] to have been finished on November 4, 1630, in the Franciscan friary of Ath-

---

[144] Hugh O'Reilly, archbishop of Armagh, had borne a large part of the expense of publishing the *Acta Sanctorum* volume, and Thomas Fleming, archbishop of Dublin, of *Triadis Thaumaturgae*.

[145] In the Bibl. roy., Brussels, and the Franciscan Convent, Merchants Quay, Dublin, are many writings connected with the work at Louvain. W. Reeves has edited, *Proc. RIA* VI 372–5, a "Catalogus actuum sanctorum quae MS habentur ordine mensium et dierum," covering the months April to December, evidently a draft for the unpublished vols. of the *Acta Sanctorum*.

[146] *Cf.* Plummer *BNE* I p. xiii.

[147] *Cf.* p. 44 *infra*, n. 159.

lone.[148] It was designed to assist the work at Louvain by giving a list of the successive kings of Ireland, and the genealogies of the saints descended from them.[148a]

The following is extracted from the preface:

"Upon its having been observed by certain parties of the true order [149] of St. Francis that the holiness and righteousness of their mother and nurse, Ireland, had perceptibly diminished, through not having the lives, wonders and miracles of her saints disseminated within her, nor yet made known in other kingdoms, the counsel they adopted was to send from them into Ireland a poor Friar Minor of their own, the Observantine, Order, Micheál Ó Cléirigh (a chronicler by descent and education), in order to collect into one place all the books of authority in which he could discover anything that related to the sanctity of her saints, with their pedigrees and genealogies. Upon the arrival of the aforesaid friar, he searched through every part of Ireland in which he had heard that there was a good or even a bad book, so that he spent four full years in transcribing and procuring the matters that related to the saints of Ireland. However, though great his labor and his hardships, he was able to find but a few out of the many of them, because strangers had carried off the principal books of Ireland into remote and unknown foreign countries and nations, so that they have left her but an insignificant part of her books. After what the aforesaid friar could find had been collected to one place, what he thought of and decided to do was this, to bring together in one place three persons whom he should consider most suitable to finish the work he had undertaken (with the consent of his superiors), for the purpose of examining all the collections that he had made. These were Ferfeasa Ó Máil-Chonaire, of Baile Úi Máil-Chonaire, county Roscommon; Cú-cóigcriche Ó Cléirigh,[150] of Baile Úi Cléirigh, county Donegal; and Cú-cóigcriche Ó Duibgennáin, of Baile Coille Foghair [Castlefore], county Leitrim."[151]

Meanwhile Michael O'Clery had been at work on his *Félire na naomh nÉrennach*, or "Calendar of the saints of Ireland," last and largest of the Irish calendars, which, according to the colophon at the end of the manuscript, was completed April 19, 1630. "In the Convent of Friars of Donegal it was begun and finished." Hence the work is generally known as the "Martyrology of Donegal."

The next work to which O'Clery and his three colleagues devoted themselves was a new edition of the *Leabhar Gabhála*, "Book of Takings,"

---

[148] Or, rather, at Coill-an-Iubhair on Loch Ree, whither the friars of Athlone had withdrawn in this age of persecution.

[148a] Published by Paul Walsh *Genealogiae regum et sanctorum Hiberniae* (Dublin 1918) [also in *AH* V, VI].

[149] The brethren of the strict observance (distinguished from the conventuals), who had been declared the true order of St. Francis in 1517.

[150] Son of Lugaidh O'Clery, who was third cousin of Michael O'Clery, head of his house, and author of various poems and of a "Life of Aodh *ruadh* O'Donnell" (published by the Rev. Denis Murphy, Dublin 1893). Cú-cóigcriche, after losing his paternal estates, migrated to Mayo, where he died in 1664, bequeathing his books to his sons. *Cf.* O'C *MS Mat.* 178–80, 560–9; *DNB.*

[151] Adapted from the trans. in O'C *MS Mat.* 165–6.

or early settlements, of Ireland.[152] In 1631 this was carried out under the patronage of Brian *ruadh* Mag Uidhir (Maguire), baron of Enniskillen, and with the assistance of his historian, Gilla-Patraic Ó Luinín, at the Franciscan house of Lisgoole on Loch Erne. Then the four men turned to their *magnum opus*, a new compilation of the national annals. For this work O'Clery obtained the patronage of Fearghal Ó Gadhra, or Feral O'Gara, of Coolavin, in Sligo, and the hospitality of the friars of Donegal, in whose convent it was accomplished between January 22, 1632, and August 10, 1636. Some assistance was received from Muiris, son of Torna Ó Máil-Chonaire, and from Conaire Ó Clérigh, brother of Michael. On its conclusion O'Clery obtained testimonials to the work from the friars of Donegal, from four members of the Irish episcopacy, and from two of the hereditary *savants*, Flann Mac Aedhagáin of the MacEgans of Tipperary, and Conchobur Mac Bruaidedha, or Conor MacBrody, of Clare. Colgan, in the introduction to the *Acta Sanctorum Hiberniae*, after telling the story of this great production, gives it the title "Annals of the Four Masters," by which it has ever since been known.[153]

After O'Clery's return to Louvain he published, in 1643, *Foclóir nó Sanasán nua*, "A New Vocabulary or Glossary" of difficult or obsolete Irish words.[154] This was the only one of his compositions to be printed during his life-time.[155]

Contemporary with O'Clery and his colleagues were other workers in Irish history. Finghín Mag Carthaigh *riabhach*, the MacCarthy Reagh, held a prisoner in London from 1601 till his death about 1640, wrote in English a history of Ireland to the Norman invasion.[156] Conall Mag Eochagáin,[157] of Liss-Maighne (Lismoyny, bar. Moycashel, co. Westmeath), "one by whom are prized and preserved the ancient monuments of our ancestors, one who is the industrious collecting bee of everything that belongs to the honor and history of the descendants of Milesius and of Lugaidh, son of Ith, both lay and ecclesiastical, as far

---

[152] *Cf.* p. 14 *supra.*

[153] *Cf. IER* VII (1871) 268–89.

[154] He refers to the following authorities: of the preceding generation Baothghalach *ruadh* Mac Aedhagáin, Lúghaidh Ó Cléirigh, Torna Ó Máil-Chonaire, Maelseachlainn *modartha* ("the moody") Ó Máil-Chonaire, and Seán Ó Máil-Chonaire, the last, apparently, recently deceased; and Flann, son of Cairbre Mac Aedhagáin, living.

[155] It was republished, with trans., by A. W. K. Miller *RC* IV (1880) 349–428, V (1881) 1–69; and this ed. is collated with the original by WS *ACL* I iii (1899) 348–59. *Cf.* E. J. Gwynn *Hermathena* XIV (1907) 464–80, XV (1909) 389–96.

[156] Daniel MacCarthy *Life and Letters of Florence MacCarthy Reagh* (London 1867); *DNB*; O'Grady *Cat.* 61–2.

[157] *DNB.*

as he could find them," translated into English in 1627, for his "brother,"[158] Toirdhelbhach Mag Cochláin — him to whom the Four Masters dedicated the *Réim Rioghraide* — the annals now designated "Annals of Clonmacnois," and so preserved for us that compilation.[159]

More important was the work of the priest Seathrún Céitinn, or Geoffrey Keating,[160] of an old Hiberno-Norman family in Tipperary, who was educated at Bordeaux. In 1633 or 1634 he completed his *Foras Feasa ar Éirinn*, "Elements of the History of Ireland," covering the period to the coming of Henry II. This, the first comprehensive history of Ireland written in the Irish language, is drawn faithfully and uncritically from ancient sources many of which have since perished. Besides the contrast in form — a history in place of a chronicle — it differs in two noteworthy respects from the "Annals of the Four Masters": it is controversial in design and setting, the author avowing his object to be the refutation of the calumnies against Ireland put forth by her enemies, while the "Annals" were produced in a spirit of historical detachment;[161] and, while the work of the Four Masters is dry and formal, and written in the archaic diction of the schools, Keating's is composed in an interesting style, and in the best modern Irish, for which, indeed, it has established the standard. It attained great popularity, and circulated extensively in manuscript copies, many of the earliest and best of which are due to Seán son of Torna and other members of the Ó Máil-Chonaire family.

The most prominent figure in the next generation after Keating and the Four Masters was An Dubhaltach Mac Fir-Bhisigh, or Duald Mac Firbis,[162] of the well-known Sligo family of historians. According to Eugene O'Curry,[163] he received his training at the school of the Mac

---

158 Foster-brother, or brother-in-law, or perhaps simply kinsman.

159 It would seem that in 1644 the Franciscan friar Paul Ó Colla, while stopping in Mageoghegan's house, copied the *Réim Rioghraide* and various other Irish works in the library. This, at least, is the interpretation I give to the rather obscure introduction to one copy of that composition, as published by O'C, *MS Mat.* 163–4, 548–50.

160 *DNB* and references there given.

161 Although not impeccable, O'Clery and his colleagues have, on the whole, maintained the fine tradition of impartiality of the schools of *senchas*. "It is noteworthy that Irish annalists, and even poets, show much impartiality in recording their enemies' successes as well as their own; even when there is some natural expression of regret the facts are not garbled or palliated, often they are stated quite impassively. Not so with English historians, and especially with writers of state papers: these latter, living in chronic dread of a penurious yet exacting sovereign's displeasure, exaggerate their smallest achievements and water down their losses; where the mishap has been too considerable for that, they seek to muffle it up in excuses and with calling of bad names." O'Grady *Cat.* 506 n. 1.

162 O'D *Genealogies, Tribes and Customs of Hy-Fiachrach* (Dublin 1844) pp. vi–xii; O'C *MS Mat.* 121–8; *CS* pp. xiv–xxv, where a list of his writings is given; *DNB*.

163 *Loc. cit.*

Egans in Ormond and at that kept by Donall O'Davoren in Burren, Clare, but the second part, at least, of this statement is improbable.[164] During the period of the Catholic Confederation he taught in Galway in the school which John Lynch, probably son of the former master, Alexander Lynch, had re-opened.[165] In 1643 he copied for Lynch "Three Fragments of Annals of Ireland," from a book belonging to Nehemias MacEgan, of Ormond, and in 1650 he completed, in "the College of St. Nicholas in Galway," his most famous composition, the Book of Genealogies, the largest of all the collections of Irish pedigrees. The Cromwellian conquest ended the school at Galway, but Mac Fir-Bhisigh found employment with Sir James Ware from about 1655[166] to Ware's death in 1666, doing historical hackwork. As Ware had no knowledge of Irish, it is probable that a large part of his researches were dependent on the assistance of Mac Fir-Bhisigh. The latter has left a considerable number of works, including a treatise on Irish authors, a list of bishops and bishoprics, a collection of glossaries, a martyrology, some poems, and transcripts and translations of older texts. His last years were spent in poverty in his native Sligo, where he was murdered by one of the new foreign aristocracy in 1670. He was the last great antiquary trained in the old Irish schools.

His friend John Lynch[167] (1599?-1673?) fled from Galway to France, where he ended his days. In 1662 he published, under the title *Cambrensis Eversus*, a well-known historical defense of Ireland against the aspersions of Giraldus Cambrensis and later enemies.

The old Irish learning was rapidly breaking down. Mac Fir-Bhisigh says that in his time only three or four persons understood the language of the ancient law tracts.[168] His pupil at Galway, Roderic O'Flaherty[169]

[164] O'Grady *Cat.* 134-5. The report of his education with the MacEgans seems to come from Charles O'Conor of Belanagare: Ledwich *Antiquities of Ireland* 2nd ed. (Dublin 1804) 303.

[165] Considerable efforts were put forth at this time to revive Irish education. Rory O'Moore, organiser of the insurrection of 1641, wrote on Sept. 20, 1642, to Father Hugh de Bourgo at Brussels: "If we may, before Flan MacEgan dies, we will see an Irish school opened, and therefore would wish heartily that these learned and religious fathers in Louvain would come over in haste with their monuments (?) and an Irish and Latin press."—Quoted by Douglas Hyde, *Literary History of Ireland* 615.

[166] W. M. Hennessy states that "there are two tracts compiled by MacFirbis in 1655 — one a catalogue of Irish bishops, preserved in the British Museum [n. Cod. Clarend. tom. 68; Ayscough, 4799; Plut. cxv. E.], in each of which he states that it was drawn up for his friend and patron, Ware."—*CS.* As Ware was in France from 1649 to 1651, and in London from 1651 to 1660, it is probable that MacFirbis had made his acquaintance before 1649.

[167] Matthew Kelly (ed.) *Cambrensis Eversus* (Celtic Soc.: Dublin 1848-52); *DNB.*

[168] Quoted by Hennessy, *CS* p. xxv. Thady O'Roddy, writing about 1700, says: "I have several volumes that none in the world now can peruse, though within 20 yeares there lived three or four that could read and understand them all, but left none behinde absolutely perfect in all them books, by reason

(1629–1718), member of a princely family of the west, collected a number of old manuscripts and published a Latin work on Irish history, *Ogygia seu rerum Hibernicarum chronologia.*[170] To a considerable knowledge of the annals he added a propensity for unrestrained theorising: with him originated the hypothesis of the Phoenician origin of the Irish people, so popular with eighteenth-century writers, and perhaps not yet extinct. He also wrote a defense of *Ogygia* against its critics [171] and a topographical description of his native country, West or Iar Connacht.[172] His friend Tadhg Ó Rodaighe, or Thady O'Roddy,[173] of the family of *comharbai* of the church of Fenagh in Leitrim, who became a lawyer of prominence in the reign of James II, shared O'Flaherty's enthusiastic and uncritical attitude towards Irish history, and made a large collection of ancient manuscripts. Both O'Flaherty and O'Roddy lived to an extreme old age and saw the Williamite conquest and the beginning of the penal laws.[174]

In the second half of the sixteenth century several writers sprung from England or from the English colony in Ireland — Campion, Stanyhurst, Hooker, Hanmer, and others — turned their attention to Irish history. Ignorance and prejudice, however, render their works of little importance except for contemporary affairs. Edmund Campion [175] (1540–1581), an Oxford scholar who came to Ireland as a tutor in 1569, wrote, in 1571, the history of the country to 1509 for the collection of chronicles which Raphael Holinshed published in London in 1577.[176] His friend Richard Stanyhurst [177] (1547–1618), a Dublin man, contributed an account of the reign of Henry VIII and a "Description of Ireland." The second edition of Holinshed's *Chronicles*, brought out in

that they lost the estates they had to uphold their publique teaching, and that the nobility of the Irish line, who would encourage and support their posterity, lost all their estates too, so that the antiquaryes posterity were forced to follow husbandry, etc., to get their bread, for want of patrons to support them." *Miscellany of the IAS* (Dublin 1846) 123.

169 *DNB.*

170 London 1685. A trans. by the Rev. Jas. Hely was published in Dublin, 1793.

171 *Ogygia Vindicated*, published in Dublin in 1775 by Charles O'Conor.

172 *A Chorographical Description of West or h-Iar Connaught, written A.D. 1684. Edited by* . . . James Hardiman (IAS: Dublin 1846).

173 J. H. Todd "Autograph Letter of Thady O'Roddy" *Miscellany of the IAS* (Dublin 1846) 112–25; Flower *Cat.* pp. xxviii, 52–3.

174 Dr. Thomas Molyneux, brother of William Molyneux of political fame, writes as follows in a diary of a visit to Connacht in April, 1709: "Wednesday, 21st.—I went to vizit old Flaherty, who lives, very old, in a miserable condition at Park, some 3 hours west of Galway, in Hiar or West-Connaught. I expected to have seen here some old Irish manuscripts, but his ill fortune has stripp'd him of these as well as his other goods, so that he has nothing now left but some few of his own writing, and a few old rummish books of history printed."—*Miscellany of the IAS* 171.

175 *DNB* and *Cath. Encycl.*, and references there given.

176 *Cf.* p. 36 *supra.*

177 *DNB* and *Cath. Encycl.*

1586-7, had as one of its editors John Hooker [178] (1526-1601?), who had been solicitor in Ireland to a particularly predatory English adventurer, Sir Peter Carew: he added a translation of Giraldus Cambrensis, and a sketch of Irish history from 1547 to 1587. Dr. Meredith Hanmer [179] (1543-1604) was an English clergyman of doubtful reputation who, coming to Ireland, fared remarkably well in the acquisition of church livings and spent his leisure in writing a chronicle of the country. Campion and Stanyhurst both later became Catholics: Campion died on the scaffold at Tyburn, and Stanyhurst lived for nearly forty years in exile on the continent, where he published *De rebus in Hibernia gestis* (1584), a history of Ireland to the time of Henry II, and *De vita sancti Patricii* (1587), both of them credulous, uncritical compositions.

In 1591 the English government established the university for Ireland which had long been proposed. This University of Trinity College, Dublin, was opened in 1593 and became the seat of higher education for the English colony in Ireland and its Church.[180]

During the seventeenth century the English colony in Ireland and its new university produced two scholars whose work in Irish history is worthy of remembrance. A nephew of Richard Stanyhurst and native of Dublin, James Ussher (1581-1656), who in 1625 became archbishop of Armagh under the new establishment, was one of the first students enrolled in Trinity College, with which institution he maintained close relations throughout his life. Among his voluminous writings are several treating, in whole or in part, of Irish Church-history: they are marked by a strong polemical tone, but also by deep erudition.[181] It

[178] *DNB.*

[179] *Ibid.*

[180] J. W. Stubbs *The History of the University of Dublin from its foundation to the end of the eighteenth century* (Dublin 1889); *The Book of Trinity College, Dublin, 1591-1891* (Belfast 1892); W. M. Dixon *History of Trinity College* (Dublin 1902); J. P. Mahaffy *An Epoch in Irish history: Trinity College, Dublin, its foundation and early fortunes, 1591-1660* (London 1903). For the general history of the governmental educational policy in Ireland see T. Corcoran *State Policy in Irish Education A.D. 1536 to 1816* (Dublin 1916).

[181] These are: (1) "Of the Original and First Institution of Corbes, Herenaches, and Termon Lands" (1609), first published in full in Vallancey's *Collectanea de Rebus Hibernicis* I (Dublin 1770); (2) *A Discourse of the Religion anciently professed by the Irish and British* (Dublin 1631); (3) *Veterum Epistolarum Hibernicarum Sylloge* (Dublin 1632); (4) *Britannicarum Ecclesiarum Antiquitates* (Dublin 1639). His collected works, with a biography, were published by C. R. Elrington and J. H. Todd, *The Whole Works of the Most Rev. James Ussher, D.D.* 17 vols. (Dublin 1847-1864). *Cf.* also *DNB.*

Ussher could be charmingly frank in regard to his historical methods: "Although my principal intention in this discourse was to produce such evidences as might shew the agreement that was betwixt our ancestors and us [*i.e.*, those of his own persuasion] in matter of religion, and to leave the instances which might be alleged for the contrary to them unto whom the maintaining of that part did properly belong: yet I have upon occasion touched upon that part also, and brought to light some things which I met withal in such hidden antiquities, as in all likelihood would not have come unto their notice without my discovery. [He then refers to the MSS of the collection of Sir Robert Cotton, which are indicated in his list of sources, in order that others may consult them:] my intention herein being to deal fairly, and not to desire the

is pleasing to note that in the field of scholarship Ussher maintained friendly relations with men like David Rothe, Stephen White, and Conall Mageoghegan, for whose religious ideals he felt the greatest repugnance. One of Ussher's pupils was Sir James Ware (1594-1666), son of an English official who came over in 1588 and rose to the post of auditor general, to which position the son succeeded. Ware followed Ussher's example in scholarly tastes and principles, but far surpassed him in sympathy. He devoted his life to investigations in Irish history, collected a library of old manuscripts, and published a series of valuable compilations.[182] To him is mainly due the introduction of Irish history as a subject of scholarly interest to the English-speaking world. In the eighteenth century his compositions, which were in Latin, were translated into English and expanded by his grand-daughter's husband, Walter Harris,[183] a man who, however, fell short of Ware's standards both in scholarship and in impartiality.

V. Ascendancy, Anglicisation, Emancipation

With the surrender of Limerick on October 3, 1691, to the forces of William of Orange the conquest of Ireland initiated by Henry VIII was finally consummated. The policy of the conquerors had now two aims: first, to maintain this "dependence" of Ireland on England; and, secondly, to maintain in Ireland the "ascendancy" of the new foreign aristocracy which had been "planted" in the country and enriched with more than nine-tenths of its landed wealth. This was the practical purpose of the "penal laws." Ostensibly that code was enacted for "the extirpation of Popery"—the aspirations of zealots were thus satisfied, and the approval of a fanatical public opinion assured. But actually nothing was less desired than the conversion of the body of the Irish people to Protestantism. The real design was to deprive them of all power which might come from the possession of property, education, political rights, social or official position, even special industrial skill — to reduce them into a helpless, hopeless mass

concealing of any thing that may tend to the true discovery of the state of former times, whether it may seem to make for me or against me."—Note "To the Reader," appended to the discourse on "The Religion professed by the ancient Irish," *Whole Works* IV 376-7.

    182 *Archiepiscoporum Casseliensium et Tuamensium vitae* (Dublin 1623); *De praesulibus Lageniae* (Dublin 1628); *De scriptoribus Hiberniae* (Dublin 1639); *De Hibernia et antiquitatibus ejus disquisitiones* (London 1654; 2nd ed. 1658); *S. Patricio adscripta opuscula* (London 1656); *Venerabilis Bedae epistolae duae* (Dublin 1664); *Rerum Hibernicarum annales* [1485-1558] (Dublin 1664); *De praesulibus Hiberniae commentarius* (Dublin 1665). He also reprinted Campion's *History of Ireland*, the chronicles of Hanmer and Marlborough, and Spenser's *View of Ireland*. For Ware's Life, see Harris's ed., and *DNB*.
    183 *The Whole Works of Sir James Ware concerning Ireland* 3 vols. (Dublin 1739-64).

of ignorant agricultural helots.[184] 'It was not merely the persecution of a religion, it was an attempt to degrade and demoralise a whole nation.'[185] Chance and design had combined in Ireland to identify "Papist" with "Irishman." Hence the blows feigned to be directed against a menacing world-power called "Popery" actually fell on the prostrate bodies of the Irish people. "It was," to adopt the words of Edmund Burke, "a complete system, full of coherence and consistency, well digested and well composed in all its parts. It was a machine of wise and elaborate contrivance, and as well fitted for the oppression, impoverishment and degradation of a people, and the debasement in them of human nature itself, as ever proceeded from the perverted ingenuity of man."[186]

While the colonial aristocracy in Ireland was at one with the British Government in the policy of maintaining "Protestant Ascendancy," the same unanimity might not have been expected in the primary object which that government held in view, the "dependence" of Ireland, colonial and "native" alike, on England. Nevertheless to the middle of the eighteenth century the planters acquiesced and even cooperated in a series of measures whereby their political and judicial subjection to Britain was specifically enforced, and their manufactures and commerce in large part destroyed in order to promote those of their "mother country." But in the second half of that century opposition began to develop. Two generations had passed in peace, and the victors' fear of a revolt of the conquered was beginning to abate. Also, the grandsons and great-grandsons of the planters were commencing to consider themselves Irishmen and to resent their subordination to the inhabitants of Britain. The result was a successful movement for legislative independence; an independence, however, which lasted less than a score of years, when it was destroyed by the Act of Union which joined Ireland and Britain politically as one country, the United Kingdom of Great Britain and Ireland.

The long upward struggle of the Irish people from their Egyptian bondage began in the third quarter of the eighteenth century. Repeal of practically all the penalties based specifically on religion was gradu-

---

[184] On the penal laws see Scully *Penal Laws* (Dublin 1812); G. de Beaumont *L'Irlande, sociale, politique, et religieuse* I (Paris 1839); Jas. Bryce (ed.) *Two Centuries of Irish History* (London 1888); W. E. H. Lecky *History of Ireland in the Eighteenth Century* (London 1892). The statutes themselves should, of course, be read.   [185] Lecky, as paraphrased by Paul-Dubois.

[186] Letter to Sir Hercules Langrishe, 3 Jan. 1792. Burke's many articles relating to the Penal Code will be found conveniently collected in Matthew Arnold's *Letters Speeches and Tracts on Irish Affairs by Edmund Burke* (London 1881).

ally obtained between 1771 and 1829. We are here particularly interested in the field of education. In 1782 Catholics were permitted by law to establish schools, although until 1792 a licence had to be obtained in each case from the Protestant bishop. The concession came in time to meet the crisis caused by the closing of almost all the Irish colleges on the Continent during the French Revolution. Carlow College was founded in 1793, Navan in 1802, Clongowes in 1814, St. Jarlath's, Tuam, in 1817. Maynooth College, designed particularly for the education of the priesthood, was established by act of Parliament in 1795, and received a governmental endowment until 1869. In 1831 the government created a "national," although not a compulsory, system of primary education, and in the seventies subsidised, and to some degree organised, secondary education. In 1793 Catholics were made eligible for degrees in Trinity College, a licence but little utilised. In 1845 Queen's Colleges were set up at Belfast, Cork and Galway, and in 1850 incorporated into the Queen's University. This university was abolished in 1879 and the Royal University, an examining, not teaching, body, created. Such make-shifts were finally abandoned in 1908, when an act was passed establishing the National University of Ireland. A Catholic University had been opened in Dublin in 1854, but lack of official recognition and other difficulties checked its career, although its "University College" persisted through the era of the Royal University to become the principal college of the National institution.

The winning of economic liberty and political power involved a more desperate struggle. The first serious effort, inspired by the American and French revolutions, was trampled out in blood in 1798. But it was only the beginning. "The history of Ireland in the nineteenth century is that of a great and slow revolution, at once political and social, by which the English Garrison, the sovereign minority, tends to lose its privileges and to return to the ranks, while the majority, the subject people, gradually free themselves and resume their natural rights."[187] Agrarian reform began in 1870, when the first effective restrictions were placed on landlord power, and culminated in 1903, when facilities were provided by which the Irish people are buying back the land of their forefathers. In 1793 Catholics were admitted to the franchise, and in 1829 to seats in the parliament of the United Kingdom, concessions which became of real consequence only with the more democratic extension of the voting power. Not until 1898 was local government taken out of the hands of the oligarchy and given to the

---

[187] L. Paul-Dubois (trans. T. M. Kettle) *Contemporary Ireland* (Dublin 1911) 91.

people, and only in 1921 did the longest and hardest contest, that for national independence, achieve essential victory.

Thus exactly one hundred and fifty years have elapsed between the first breach in the penal code and the day when the Irish people stood forth once more as — with a semi-autonomous "Pale" in the North — masters in their own land. Weighed by the difficulties overcome, it has been a wonderful triumph. Yet there are qualifications to this verdict. The main successes have been achieved, not by peaceful conciliation but by agitation culminating in physical violence or revolt, coercion, and wide-spread suffering, conditions not at all conducive to the development of learning and culture. Also, while the nation has on one road been toiling painfully to victory, on another it has been slipping constantly towards defeat. Henry VIII's policy of Anglicisation at length became effective in the nineteenth century, when the Irish people themselves sacrificed the greater part of their remaining inheritance from their ancient civilisation.

Official statistics are not available, but from what evidence we possess it seems certain that at the beginning of the nineteenth century more than half the population of Ireland spoke Irish as their mother-tongue.[188] Once the penal barriers which had isolated the subject people in the eighteenth century were broken down it was inevitable that Irish would tend to succumb to English, the speech of the dominant class in every walk of life. The decline of Irish was hastened by the facts that it was abandoned by almost all the political leaders of the people from O'Connell onwards; that the Catholic clergy in general encouraged English,— partly, it is said, for the curious reason that Irish was being used for proselytising purposes by certain anti-Catholic institutions, chiefly, we may believe, because they believed themselves to be thereby bettering the material condition of their people and promoting the power and influence of the Church; and that the "National" school system, accepted by the leaders of the Irish people because in general it did not attack their religion, was absolutely a system of Anglicisation, from which the Irish language and Irish history were rigidly excluded. Then came the great famine of 1846-7, when 729,000 people died of hunger;[189] the wholesale evictions, known as "the great clearances"— 482,000 families were evicted between 1849 and 1882;[190] and the emigration movement —

---

[188] *Cf.* Douglas Hyde *A Literary History of Ireland* (London 1899) chap. xliv "The history of Irish as a spoken language."

[189] T. W. Grimshaw, Registrar-General, in *Facts and Figures about Ireland* (Dublin 1893), gives the number 729,033. In addition, some 200,000, it is estimated, of those who fled perished on the emigrant ships or immediately after landing in America.

[190] Mulhall *Dictionary of Statistics* (London 1886) 175. Of these, 119,000 obtained reinstatement sooner or later.

between 1846 and 1901 some 4,976,462 persons emigrated;[191] — all of which have affected the Irish-speaking districts with disproportionate severity. From 1851 we have the census records as to the number of persons who spoke Irish only and both Irish and English:

	Irish Only	Irish and English	Total Population
1851	319,602	1,204,684	6,552,385
1861	163,275	942,261	5,798,967
1871	103,562	714,313	5,412,377
1881	64,167	885,765	5,174,836
1891	38,192	642,053	4,704,750
1901	20,953	620,189	4,458,775
1911	16,870	565,576	4,390,219

To turn now to the fortunes of literature and learning, and especially of history: Although the seventeenth century had seen the slaughter or exile of the greater part of the old Irish aristocracy — including the families of hereditary savants — the ablest and most vigorous stock in the nation, and had reduced the remnants to the lot of the peasant, the intellectual life of the Irish people in the eighteenth century was not as depressed as might be expected. The "wild geese"[192] and the smugglers kept open communication with the Continent, where in every land the exiles and their children had risen to positions of honor and power. Even in the darkest days the Irish colleges kept the Church at home at least partially supplied with clergymen of good classical education. At home the professional schools had disappeared with the professional families, but "hedge schools" braved the penalties of the penal code to keep alive some fragments of scholarship. A House-of-Lords report on the "State of Popery" in 1731 gives the number of "popish schools" as 549;[193] the report is not quite complete, and undoubtedly many schools escaped the notice of the inquisitors. Moreover the peasantry had in their own language resources of culture undreamed of by the speakers of English. The penal days were a period

---

[191] Paul-Dubois (trans. T. M. Kettle) *Contemporary Ireland* (Dublin 1911) 352–4, and references there given.

[192] Name given to the Irishmen who emigrated to enter the Irish brigade in the French military service.

[193] *AH* I (1912) 10–27, II (1913) 108–56, III (1914) 124–59, IV (1915) 131–77. Conditions varied much in different districts. The bishop of Derry reported: "There are not any Popish schools; sometimes a straggling schoolmaster sets up in some of ye mountainous parts of some parishes, but upon being threatened, as they constantly are, with a warrant, or a presentment by ye Churchwardens, they generally think proper to withdraw." On the other hand, the archbishop of Tuam wrote: "I have an account of 32 schools taught by Papists in the several parts of this diocese; Diverse of whom teach Latin and Philosophy, and some of them Divinity, in order to qualifie young men for their Priesthood: And many Papists keep Tutors in their houses, who privately teach not only the youth of the family, but others of the Neighbourhood who report to them. There being scarce a Papist who will send his Child to a Protestant School even to learn his Grammar, or so much as to read." *Ibid.* I 17; III 126–7.

of high literary productivity, especially in poetry, wherein by a complete revolution a new and popular style of versification was substituted for the ancient classical metres. A long series of writers, men sprung from the people, kept the torch of Gaelic literature burning from the collapse of the old bardic families until well into the nineteenth century. The names of a few may be mentioned, poets who, in mastery of technique and in wealth of literary and historical allusion, those two touchstones of an old and solid intellectual culture, can be placed side by side with the best that the contemporary literatures of France and England can produce, but who, to the great world of wealth and ease and freedom and power, then, and even now, were but so many unknown heads in a mob of starving and stupid boors: Egan O'Rahilly (c 1670-1726), of the neighborhood of Killarney, in spirit an aristocrat "to the manor born," who after the Williamite conquest dragged out a poverty-stricken existence in west Munster; Séamus *dall* Mac Cúarta (d. 1732), wanderer in northern and north-central Ireland; Pierce Fitzgerald (1700-1791), of Ballykineally, county Cork, who in anguish of soul saved the last remnant of his ancestral lands by accepting the religion of the foreigner; John O'Twomey (1706-1775), innkeeper at Croom, and, later, farm-yard help; Brian Merriman (c 1747-1805), of Clare, small farmer and "teacher of Mathematics"; and three who show the inevitable reaction to despair, Denis MacNamara "the Red" (1715-1810), Owen Roe O'Sullivan (1748-1784), and Andrew MacGrath, wandering school-teachers and day-laborers, but also reckless, though penniless, roisterers.[194]

The "Courts of Poetry," which assembled occasionally or periodically, took, in some measure, the place of the defunct bardic schools in the maintenance of the traditional standards of literature and of an organisation of learning.[195] Scribes by laborious copying of manuscripts and shanachies by oral transmission kept alive the old poems and romances. The shanachie (*seanchaidhe*) was the representative of the mediaeval historian, now become purely a story-teller. Patrick W. Joyce, writing in 1879, gives a brief sketch of the last stage of this institution:

"The ancient institution of professional story-telling held its ground both in Ireland and in Scotland down to a very recent period; and it is questionable if it be even yet quite extinct. Within my own memory, this sort of entertainment was quite usual among the farming classes of the south of Ireland. The family and workmen, and any neighbours that chose to drop in, would sit round the kitchen fire after the day's work — or perhaps gather in a barn on a summer or autumn evening — to listen to

[194] An excellent account of the lives and works of these eighteenth-century peasant *literati* can be read in that remarkable book, *The Hidden Ireland*, by Daniel Corkery (Dublin 1925). See also Flower *Cat.*, *passim*. A considerable portion of their poetry has been published.

[195] Corkery *op. cit.* 90-125.

some local shanachie reciting one of his innumerable Gaelic tales. The story-teller never chose his own words — he always had the story by heart, and recited the words from memory, often gliding into a sort of recitative in poetical passages, or when he came to some favourite grandiose description abounding in high-sounding alliterative adjectives. And very interesting it was to mark the rapt attention of the audience, and to hear their excited exclamations when the speaker came to relate some mighty combat, some great exploit of the hero, or some other striking incident."[196]

Something of this traditional culture has continued unbroken in communities where the daily speech is Irish.

On the Continent text-books of the Irish language began to appear for the use of students. Francis O'Molloy (d. c 1684), a survivor of the famous company of Irish Franciscan scholars, and the successor of Luke Wadding as head of St. Isidore's, published at Rome in 1677 the first Irish grammar in print.[197] Francis Walsh, of the same order, lector jubilate in divinity at St. Anthony's, Louvain, compiled a manuscript dictionary in 1706 and a grammar in 1713;[198] Aodh MacCruitín, a bard, published a grammar at Louvain in 1728, and, in conjunction with a priest, Conor O'Begley, an English-Irish dictionary at Paris, 1732;[199] Andrew Donlevy (1694-?), prefect of the Irish College at Paris, prefixed a grammar to his Irish catechism published there in 1742;[200] and John O'Brien (d. 1769), bishop of Cloyne, published the first Irish-English dictionary at the same place in 1768.[201] In 1765 O'Brien and John O'Mulconry, or Conry, had compiled in France the so-called "Dublin Annals of Innisfallen."[202] The Abbé Mageoghegan (1702-1764), sprung from the Westmeath family to which the translator of the Annals of Clonmacnois had belonged, educated at the Irish College in Paris, and appointed for a time chaplain to the Irish brigade in the service of France, was the author of a history of Ireland which still deserves some attention.[203] In addition to Colgan, Lynch and other printed sources he made considerable use of the Great Book of Lecan, at that time in France.

Of the hundreds of scribes, the majority farmers and laborers who in their scanty leisure copied their country's records and literature, the names of only a few can be mentioned: Seán Ó Neachtain, or O'Naghton (d. 1729), and his son, Tadhg or Teig [204] (1671- c 1749), of Meath and Dublin, two of the most voluminous and most

196 P. W. Joyce *Old Celtic Romances* (London 1879) Preface.

197 *Grammatica Latino-Hibernica, nunc compendiata* (Rome 1677). The prosody, which is still of interest and value, was published, Latin text and trans., by Tomás Ó Flannghaile (Dublin 1908). *Cf. Cath. Encycl. s. v.* "Molloy."

198 *Cf.* Abbott and Gwynn *Cat. Ir. MSS. TCD* (1921) 123; O'Grady *Cat.* 167.

199 *The Elements of the Irish Language, grammatically explained in English* (Louvain 1728); *The English-Irish Dictionary. An Focloir Bearla Gaoidheilge* (Paris 1732). *Cf.* Douglas Hyde *Literary History of Ireland* 599.

200 *An Teagasg Criosduidhe* (Paris 1742; 2nd ed. Dublin 1822; 3rd ed. Dublin 1848).

201 *Focalóir Gaoidhilge-Sax-Bhéarla or An Irish-English Dictionary* (Paris 1768; 2nd ed. Dublin 1832). *Cf. DNB;* T. Ó Donnchadha *Dánta Sheáin Úi Mhurchadha* (Dublin 1907) pp. xxix, xxxix.

202 *TCD* 1281 (H. 1. 7). *Cf.* Abbott and Gwynn *Cat. Ir. MSS TCD* (1921) 16, 64.

203 L'abbé Jacques Mageoghegan *Histoire de l'Irlande ancienne et moderne* 3 vols. (Paris 1758, 1762, 1763). The work is dedicated to the Irish Brigade. Trans. by Patrick O'Kelly (Dublin 1831-2); with continuation by John Mitchell (New York 1868). On Mageoghegan see *Biographie universelle Michaud*, 2nd ed. XXVI 33.

204 A poem by Tadhg, giving a list of 26 Irish literary men residing in Dublin about 1726-9, is printed by T. F. O'Rahilly in *Gadelica* I (Dublin 1912-3) 156-62.—On the work of the O'Neachtains, and some others of these scribes, consult the index to Abbott and Gwynn *Cat. Ir. MSS TCD* (1921) and Flower *Cat.* 88 *sqq*, 98 *sqq*. Seán came originally from Roscommon.

learned writers of their time—Tadhg prepared an extensive Irish-English dictionary;[205] Aindrias Mac Cruitín, or Andrew MacCurtin, of Enistymon, Clare, "one of the best, if not the very best, Irish scholar of his day";[206] Dermot O'Conor, author of a poor translation of Keating's history;[207] John *clárach* MacDonnell [208] (1691–1754) — poet, scribe, and author of a history of Ireland, now lost — president of the Court of Poetry which assembled regularly at either Rath Luirc (Charleville), in Cork, or the neighboring Bruree, in Limerick county; Seán Ó Murchadha, or John Murphy [209] (1700–1762), of Raheenagh, near Blarney, county Cork, a poet and a good and prolific scribe, last head of the Court of Poetry of Whitechurch, itself sprung from the ancient bardic school of Blarney; Hugh O'Daly, an industrious but careless copyist who seems to have been at work between 1720 and 1760 — he worked for Dr. Francis Stoughton Sullivan, fellow of Trinity College from 1738 until his death in 1766, who from that stronghold of ascendancy displayed a zeal for Irish literature in one of its darkest hours; Aodh Ó Maol-Bhuaidh, or Hugh O'Molloy, a good scribe who was writing for Dr. O'Fergus in 1734–5; Muirís, or Maurice, O'Gorman, a scribe of the second half of the century from whom we have a large number of not very accurate manuscripts; Muirís O'Conor,[210] a shipwright of Cork — where he was writing in 1778–82 — who had been a pupil of John Murphy of Raheenagh; Michael O'Longan, of the second half of the eighteenth century, his sons Michael and Peter, and his grandsons Peter, Paul and Joseph, a family of accomplished penmen, of whom Joseph (d. 1880) was the last professional Irish scribe;[211] Denis O'Flynn, a grocer of Cork, early in the nineteenth century, "a professed, but very indifferent, Irish scholar";[212] Eoghan Caomhánach, or Eugene Kavanagh,[213] a country schoolmaster in Limerick and Clare at the same period, and his brother Thomas, of the city of Limerick; John Collins [214] (1754–1817) of Myross in Carbery, schoolmaster, scholar and poet, who began an English-Irish dictionary and a history of Ireland in Irish.

In general, the work of these eighteenth and nineteenth-century scribes, although important for texts of the modern period, is of little value for those of the early middle ages. They had no real understanding of Old Irish—although in some cases a certain amount of traditional knowledge—and frequently corrupted the texts they did not comprehend, either through inaccuracies or through ignorant attempts at emendation and modernisation. Nevertheless it is probable that with the growth of knowledge of the language in all its periods it will be possible to make greater use of such modern corrupt texts.

[205] TCD 1290 (H. 1. 16), said to have been compiled 1734–49. *Cf.* Hyde *Literary History of Ireland* 597–9.

[206] O'C *MS Mat.* 234.

[207] *The General History of Ireland* . . . (Dublin 1723; also London 1723; 2nd ed. Westminster 1726; 3rd ed. London 1732; 4th ed. London 1738; 5th ed. Dublin 1809). *Cf.* Flower *Cat.* 36, 39, 174.

[208] Hyde *Literary History of Ireland* 600–1; Corkery *The Hidden Ireland* 257–61.

[209] O'Grady *Cat.* 515; Corkery *op. cit.* 112–5; Flower *Cat.* 385. Some of his poems have been edited by Prof. Tadhg Ó Donnchadha, *op. cit.*

[210] O'Grady *Cat.* 34 *sqq*; Flower *Cat.* 48, 377, 385, 622–3.

[211] *Cf.* HZ in *Sitzungsberichte d. k. preuss. Akad. d. Wissensch.* 1910 LI 1091 n. 2.

[212] O'C *MS Mat.* 196; *cf.* O'Grady *Cat.* 563.

[213] O'Grady *Cat.* 630, 664.

[214] Corkery *op. cit.* 298–302; P. Ó hAnnracháin *Gaelic Journal* XVIII 261,300; Flower *Cat.* 233. Information regarding many other scribes will be found in Flower *Cat.*

A few men of Irish blood were still in a position to collect manuscripts and, in a small way, to promote Irish researches. John Conry, of the ancient family of Ó Máil-Chonaire, was living in Dublin in 1724, when he had "great numbers of our Historico-Poetical Composures," including what are now known as the Annals of Ulster, the Annals of Loch Cé, and the Annals of the Four Masters, "and (being a perfect Master of their Language and *Prosodia*) knows how to make the best use of them." [215] Dr. John Fergus, or O'Fergus [216] (d. 1761), a well-known Dublin physician, a member, doubtless, of the Mayo family of hereditary medical men bearing this name, made a large collection of Irish manuscripts, including some that had belonged to Conry. Even of more prominence was his friend Charles O'Conor [217] (1710-1791) of Belanagare, county Roscommon, first leader in the constitutional struggle for the civil and religious liberties of the Irish people, who was the most valuable servant Irish history had in the eighteenth century. He was of the family of the O'Conor Don, but only a small portion of the ancestral property was saved for him.[218] He received his education from several Irish priests and scholars, including Toirrdhealbhach Ó Cearbhalláin, or Turlough Carolan (d. 1738), the famous harper, but chiefly from his maternal uncle, Thaddeus Francis O'Rourke, bishop of Killala, who, although he had been chaplain and secretary to Prince Eugene of Savoy, was in Ireland pursued by the priest-hunters and died as a result of exposure while fleeing from arrest. O'Conor obtained from Bishop O'Rourke the autograph copy of the Annals of the Four Masters, which he had brought back from the Continent, where it had been presented to him by Colonel O'Gara, descendant of Fergal O'Gara, the patron of that compilation. From an uncle of his mother he received some of the manuscripts of Roderic O'Flaherty. He devoted himself throughout life to the encouragement of students of literature and history, and to the collection and transcription of old books. "I wish to save as many as I can of the ancient manuscripts of Ireland from the

---

215 Bishop Nicholson *The Irish Historical Library* (Dublin 1724) 243-6, where a partial list of Conry's MSS is given.

216 *Cf.* p. 25 *supra*; also Sir John Gilbert in *Irish Quarterly Review*, 1853, p. 610 n.; Abbott and Gwynn *Cat. Ir. MSS TCD* (1921) pp. xii-xiv.

217 *Gentleman's Magazine* Aug. 1791 p. 776; the Rev. Chas. O'Conor *Memoirs of the life and writings of the late Charles O'Conor, of Belenagare, Esq., M. R. I. A.* vol. I (Dublin [1796]) [all published; the author destroyed the MS of the second vol., and so far as possible suppressed the first]; J. T. Gilbert in *8th Report Hist. MSS Comm.* (1881) 442-92; J. J. Kelly "Charles O'Conor of Belanagare" *IER* 3rd ser. III (1882) 731-8, IV (1883) 226-34, 573-83, V (1884) 235-42, 786-95, VI (1885) 560-71; The O'Conor Don *The O'Conors of Connaught* (Dublin 1891); *DNB*.

218 Even this moderate competence was much reduced when his youngest brother became a Protestant and on that ground filed a claim to the Belanagare estate. Charles was compelled to compound with him by a large money payment.

wreck which has overwhelmed everything that once belonged to us." He did much careful investigation into Irish history, but his published dissertations are marred by the influence of the theories of O'Flaherty.[219]

A contemporary of O'Conor was Dr. Sylvester O'Halloran [220] (1728–1807), of Limerick, who, having studied at the medical schools of Paris and Leyden, attained to a great reputation as a physician and surgeon; his *History of Ireland*, published in 1774, is of importance now only as marking the beginning of such publications in the English language by writers of Irish origin.[221]

In the world of European letters, throughout the eighteenth century, the history and literature of Ireland were, in general, unknown and ignored; by the majority of English speakers, both in England and in Ireland, they were regarded with contempt. The first great influence in breaking down this barrier of ignorance and prejudice was the pseudo-Ossianic poems published by the Scotsman James Macpherson, in 1760–3.[222] In the "Romantic Movement," of which he was one of the chief fore-runners, the literatures of Ireland, Scotland and Wales gradually came into their due honor. "The arrival of James Macpherson marks a great moment in the history of Celtic literature. It was the signal for a general resurrection. It would seem as if he sounded the trumpet, and the graves of ancient manuscripts were opened, the books were read, and the dead were judged out of the things that were written in them."[223]

Several writers, predecessors or contemporaries of Macpherson, were preparing the way for this new interest in ancient Ireland. Most important was Edward Lhuyd, or Llwyd (1660–1709), a Welshman, keeper of the Ashmolean Museum, who travelled extensively in Wales, Scotland, Ireland and Brittany. While in Ireland in 1700 he made the acquaintance of Roderic O'Flaherty, Thady O'Roddy, and other antiquarians, and collected many manuscripts. The first and only volume of his *Archaeologia Britannica*, published in 1707, contained lexicographical and other philological matter regarding the Irish, Welsh,

---

[219] *Dissertations on the Ancient History of Ireland* (Dublin 1753); 2nd ed., with remarks on Macpherson's *Ossian*, 1766. Three essays "On the History of Ireland during the times of heathenism" were published in Vallancey's *Collectanea*. The introduction and other editorial matter which he added to O'Flaherty's *Ogygia Vindicated*, published by him at Dublin in 1775, are of value, and contain information regarding both O'Flaherty and An Dubhaltach Mac Fir-Bhisigh.

[220] *DNB.*

[221] O'Halloran also published *Insula Sacra* (1770), *An Introduction to the study of the history and antiquities of Ireland* (1772), and *Ierne Defended* (1774), essays asserting the validity of the ancient Irish records and urging their preservation.

[222] *Fragments of Ancient Poetry collected in the Highlands* (Edinburgh 1760); *Fingal* (London 1761); *Temora* (London 1763).

[223] Dr. Magnus MacLean, quoted by MacN, *Phases of Irish History* (Dublin 1919) 8.

Cornish and Breton languages, and was the first work to establish for the reading public the kinship of these as being all "Celtic" tongues. The doctrine of the relationship of the early inhabitants of the British Isles with the Celts and Gauls of classical authors had been advanced first, apparently, by the well-known Scottish scholar, George Buchanan (1506-1582), in his *History of Scotland* published in 1582, but his argument seems to have attracted little attention.[224] But since Lhuyd's time the Celtic family of peoples has received recognition from scholars and, gradually, from the general public.

The *Irish Historical Library*,[225] by William Nicholson, bishop of Derry, and the *Bibliotheca Britannico-Hibernica* [226] of the English antiquarian, Thomas Tanner, were important in their time and still have interest for the investigator in bibliography. Mervyn Archdall (1723-1791), a native of Dublin, descendant of an Elizabethan settler, spent his life in antiquarian researches the result of which was his *Monasticon Hibernicum* [227]— a rather poor imitation of Dugdale's great English work — which has still some value. Two other Dublin men who also, like Archdall, were graduates of Trinity College and clergymen of the established Church of Ireland, devoted themselves to Irish history: Thomas Leland (1722-1785), author of a *History of Ireland* [228] published in 1773, and Edward Ledwich (1738-1823), who assisted Archdall and Vallancey, wrote a book of his own on Irish antiquities,[229] and edited another by the English antiquarian Francis Grose.[230] The ignorance and the combination of childish scepticism and childish credulity in these authors leave their works of no value except as milestones in the history of Irish historiography.

A further and more important milestone is marked by the works of Charles Vallancey [231] (1721-1812), who, in his collection of treatises entitled *Collectanea de Rebus Hibernicis*, for the first time published texts and translations of early Irish literary and historical sources. Vallancey was an English military engineer of French Protestant parentage,

224 *Cf.* MacN "The Re-Discovery of the Celts" *Irish Review* Dec. 1913 pp. 522-32.

225 *The Irish Historical Library. Pointing at most of the authors and records in print and manuscript, which may be serviceable to the compilers of a general history of Ireland*, by William, Lord Bishop of Derry (Dublin 1724).

226 Ed. by David Wilkins (London 1748).

227 *Cf.* p. 109 *infra*.

228 *History of Ireland from the Invasion of Henry II, with a preliminary discourse on the ancient state of that kingdom* 3 vols. (Dublin 1773; 3rd ed. 1774).

229 *Antiquities of Ireland* 2 vols. (Dublin 1790; 2nd ed. 1794-6).

230 *Antiquities of Ireland* 2 vols. (London 1791-5). The plates which illustrate the works of Ledwich and Grose are important as records of the then appearance of the antiquities.

231 *Cf. DNB.* His publications include *An Essay on the antiquity of the Irish language, being a collation of the Irish with the Punic language* (Dublin 1772); *A Grammar of the Iberno-Celtic, or Irish Language* (Dublin 1773; 2nd ed. 1782); (ed.) *Collectanea de Rebus Hibernicis* 6 vols. (Dublin 1770-1804).

who came to Ireland in 1762, remained there the rest of his life, rose to the rank of general, and devoted his spare time and energies to the Irish language, literature and history. The Irish speakers whom he engaged to assist him seem to have been but indifferent scholars, and his own contributions consisted of shallow theorising: his works, indeed, are examples of a considerable class which appeared in the eighteenth and nineteenth centuries, composed in almost entire ignorance of the original sources and founded on various imaginative theories, such as the identity of the Irish with the Phoenicians or the Chalmucks or the American Indians. Nevertheless Vallancey's enthusiasm, and the prestige which his position imparted, contributed very much to the advancement of Irish studies. Coeval with his publications were two others, containing translations of Irish texts, in which the fruits of the movement inaugurated by James Macpherson are clearly seen — *Historical Memoirs of the Irish Bards*,[232] by Joseph C. Walker, and *Reliques of Irish Poetry*,[233] by Charlotte Brooke.

The "Romantic Movement," the relaxation of the penal laws, the growth of an Irish national sentiment among the British colonists in Ireland, the influence of Vallancey and his friends, all made possible the development of a genuine movement for the rehabilitation of native Irish scholarship. In 1772 the "Dublin Society" had appointed a committee to make enquiries on Irish antiquities; the committee soon disappeared, but a few of its members cooperated with Vallancey in bringing out his *Collectanea*. About 1782 a little society, chiefly of Trinity College men, was formed which met weekly for the reading of essays. "Anxious to make their labours redound to the honour and advantage of their country they formed a plan more extensive, and admitting such additional names only as might add dignity to their new institution, or by their publications had given sure ground to hope advantage from their labours, became the founders of the Royal Irish Academy."[234] The first volume of *Transactions* appeared in 1787. The Royal Irish Academy, by its consistent encouragement of literary and historical research and by its collection of manuscripts and antiquities has per-

---

[232] Dublin 1786.

[233] Dublin 1789.

[234] From Preface to Vol. I of the *Transactions*. The members included the Rev. Mervyn Archdall, Sir Joseph Banks, John Talbot Dillon, Baron of the Holy Roman Empire, Charles O'Conor of Belanagare. Sylvester O'Halloran, Archibald Hamilton Rowan, Col. Charles Vallancey, the Rev. Thomas Leland, Richard Lovel Edgeworth, and many of the leading statesmen of the day, as William Conyngham, Isaac Corry, John Philpot Curran, Denis Daly, Henry Flood, John Forbes, John Forster, Henry Grattan, John Hely Hutchinson, Sir Lucius O'Brien, George Ogle, Laurence Parsons, Charles Francis Sheridan, Arthur Wolfe, John Wolfe and Barry Yelverton. Among those subsequently admitted were the Marquess of Antrim, the Earl of Moira, John Monck Mason, Arthur Browne, Dr. Whitley Stokes, the Rev. Edward Ledwich, Dr. William Drennan, Dr. William James McNeven, the Rev. James Whitelaw.

formed a service for national scholarship of incalculable value.[235]

In Dublin in the last years of the eighteenth century and the beginning of the nineteenth there was a considerable group of workers on Irish history and literature. Among these were, besides Vallancey and Ledwich, Theophilus O'Flanagan, the brothers William and Charles Haliday, Edward O'Reilly, Dr. John Lanigan, James Hardiman and Sir William Betham. O'Flanagan, William Haliday, O'Reilly, Lanigan and Father Paul O'Brien,[236] professor of Irish at Maynooth, were associated in founding the "Gaelic Society of Dublin," the earliest of organisations intended to protect the interests of the Irish language. It remained in existence long enough to publish, in 1808, one volume of *Transactions*, in which O'Flanagan edited several Irish texts. William Haliday [237] (1788-1812), a Dublin solicitor, learned Irish, published an Irish grammar [238] and the first volume of an edition, with translation, of Keating's History,[239] and at the time of his death was collecting materials for an Irish dictionary. His brother Charles [240] (1789-1866), a merchant, was no linguist, but he made a hobby of investigations into the early history of Dublin, especially under Norse rule.[241] Edward O'Reilly (d. 1829), of the O'Reillys of Cavan, came to Dublin about 1790, obtained William Haliday's lexicographical notes, and in 1817 published an Irish-English dictionary,[242] much the best which had till then appeared. In 1818 another short-lived Irish-language association, the "Iberno-Celtic Society," was formed, and O'Reilly was appointed secretary; its only publication was his catalogue of Irish writers,[243] a very important piece of investigation. He also contributed treatises on Irish subjects, valuable in their time, to the *Transactions* of the Royal Irish Academy.[244]   The Rev. Dr. Lanigan [245] (1758-1825), another

[235] The *Transactions* of the Academy were published from 1787 to 1907; another series, the *Proceedings*, begun in 1836, is in progress. *Cf.* p. 94 *infra*.

[236] *Cf.* "A Biographical Sketch of the Rev. Paul O'Brien" *Irish Magazine and Monthly Asylum for Neglected Biography* III (Dublin 1810) 30-2. He was the author of *A Practical Grammar of the Irish Language* (Dublin 1809) and of several Irish poems, one of which has been edited by J. H. Lloyd, *Gaelic Journal* X (1899) 28-9.

[237] *DNB*.

[238] *Uraicecht na Gaedhilge A Grammar of the Gaelic Language* (Dublin 1808). The introduction is signed "E.O'C," *i.e.*, Edmond O'Connell, a name adopted by Haliday in some of his Irish work, it is said because of the prejudice then existing against the Irish language.

[239] Dublin 1811.

[240] *DNB*.

[241] His papers on this subject were collected and edited, after his death, by John P. Prendergast: *The Scandinavian Kingdom of Dublin* (Dublin 1881; 2nd ed. 1884).

[242] *An Irish-English Dictionary* (Dublin 1817; 2nd ed. 1821; 3rd ed., by O'D, 1864). *Cf.* p. 96 *infra*.

[243] *Transactions of the Iberno-Celtic Society for 1820* vol. I part I (Dublin 1820).

[244] "An Essay on the nature and influence of the ancient Irish institutes, commonly called Brehon Laws" *Trans. RIA* XIV (1825) 141-226; Essay on the authenticity of the poems of Ossian, *ibid.* XVI pt. I, "Polite Literature" 163-336.

[245] *DNB*; *Cath. Encycl.* XVI.

member of this Dublin group, the son of a schoolmaster of Cashel who was of the Úi Langacháin of Úi Cuanach, or Coonagh, in Limerick and Tipperary, had received a scholarship in the Irish College in Rome, taken a brilliant course there, and become professor of ecclesiastical history and Hebrew in the University of Padua. At the Napoleonic invasion of 1796 he left Padua and returned to Ireland. Some aspersions cast on his orthodoxy caused him to resign an appointment as professor at Maynooth, and in 1799 he was, at the suggestion of Vallancey, made assistant librarian and foreign correspondent of the Royal Dublin Society. He was a leading figure in the little group of Irish scholars now growing up in Dublin. He became the Lingard of Irish church history, and his monumental work on that subject [246] remains of value: it was in part inspired by a desire to refute the mistakes of Ussher, Archdall, and especially Ledwich.

Another figure prominent in Dublin antiquarian circles in the early nineteenth century was that of Sir William Betham [247] (1779-1853), an Englishman who obtained appointments in the Irish records and heraldry offices, and ultimately became Ulster King of Arms. He was a most enthusiastic but superficial student of Irish antiquities, a kind of second Vallancey whose pet theory was the identity of the Irish language with Etruscan and of both with Phoenician.[248] When the Royal Irish Academy awarded a medal to George Petrie's scholarly investigation of the history of the round towers, in which no recognition had been accorded Betham's vagaries, the latter, although he had been an energetic worker for the Academy, resigned and attempted to bring official restraint against that body.

Meanwhile in England this development of Irish studies had produced the first important publication of historical sources since the days of the Franciscans of Louvain.

The Rev. Dr. Charles O'Conor [249] (1764-1828), grandson of Charles O'Conor of Belanagare, was educated at Rome, became a priest, and in 1798 was appointed chaplain to the Marchioness of Buckingham. He was also given charge of the famous library at Stowe, near Buckingham, the property of Richard Grenville, afterwards Duke of Buckingham

246 Cf. p. 109 infra.   247 DNB.
248 His chief publications on Irish history and literature are: Irish Antiquarian Researches, 2 vols. (Dublin 1827); The Gael and Cymbri, or an inquiry into the origin and history of the Irish, Scots, Britons and Gauls, and of the Caledonians, Picts, Welsh, Cornish and Bretons (1834); Etruria Celtica: Etruscan literature and antiquities investigated and the language of that people compared and identified with the Iberno-Celtic, and both shown to be Phoenician (1842); and several papers read before the RIA.
249 The O'Conor Don The O'Conors of Connaught (Dublin 1891); DNB and references there given; also "The Rev. Chas. O'Conor and the Marquis of Buckingham "Irish Magazine and Monthly Asylum for Neglected Biography V (Dublin 1812) 406-7, 418.

and Chandos. In it he placed the magnificent collection of Irish manuscripts made by his grandfather. From these manuscripts, and from others in the Bodleian Library, the British Museum, and elsewhere, he edited his *Rerum Hibernicarum Scriptores Veteres,* published in four volumes [250] at the charge of the Duke of Buckingham. O'Conor's knowledge of the Irish language and of Irish history was inadequate, and both his texts and his translations are filled with errors, but he made available to the public, in some form, a most important body of historical sources, and in the case of the Annals of Boyle and of Innisfallen his text remains still the only one in print. He also began the vindication of Ireland's title to those many and important early Irish manuscripts in European libraries which continental scholars in the days of Irish national eclipse had been classifying as Anglo-Saxon.[251] A catalogue of the Stowe manuscripts prepared by him remains the best printed description of this collection, which is now in the Royal Irish Academy.[252]

In addition to Sir William Betham the Irish Records Office provided employment for another historical student who forms a link between the days of O'Conor and Lanigan and those of Petrie, O'Donovan and O'Curry. James Hardiman [253] (*c* 1790–1855) was sprung from a family named O'Hartigan which had contrived to keep a small estate in Mayo. He studied law in Dublin, was appointed sub-commissioner of public records, became an active member of the Iberno-Celtic Society and of the Royal Irish Academy, and carried on the work, now well under way, of publishing Irish historical texts.[254] He ended his days as librarian of the new Queen's College, Galway.

An elaborate survey of Ireland was inaugurated by the British ordnance department in the second quarter of the nineteenth century. Captain, afterwards Sir, Thomas Aiskew Larcom, who was appointed director of the Ordnance Survey in 1828, planned to have the maps of each county accompanied by memoirs describing in detail its economic condition and resources and its historical antiquities, including archaeo-

[250] Buckingham 1814, 1825, 1826, 1826. *Cf.* p. 104 *infra.*
[251] There was some excuse for this. Irish and English script in the early middle ages were so closely related that even now it is occasionally doubtful to which of the islands a MS should be assigned. Many of these MSS are, of course, loaded with Irish glosses, but before the nineteenth century few scholars who came in contact with them were acquainted with either Irish or Anglo-Saxon.
[252] *Cf.* p. 89 n. 372 *infra.*
[253] *DNB.*
[254] The following are his chief publications: *The History of the Town of Galway* (Dublin 1820); "Ancient Irish deeds and writings chiefly relating to landed property from the twelfth to the seventeenth century" *Trans. RIA* XV (1826) Antiq. 3–95; *Irish Minstrelsy, or Bardic Remains of Ireland* 2 vols. (London 1831); ed. of the Statute of Kilkenny, for the IAS, 1843, and of O'Flaherty's *Description of hIar-Connacht,* for the same, 1846; besides official publications for the Record Commissioners.

logical monuments, place names and local legends. It was a magnificent historical enterprise, and the first official recognition on a notable scale of Irish national antiquities. In 1833 George Petrie was placed in charge of the antiquities section. Petrie [255] (1789-1866) was the son of a Dublin portrait-painter of Scottish ancestry, and himself began life as an artist. He produced many drawings of antiquarian monuments for book-illustration, and became so interested in archaeology that he made it his life work. In 1828 he became a member of the Royal Irish Academy, to the museum and library of which he rendered important services, and in 1832-3 he contributed archaeological articles to the *Dublin Penny Journal*, a periodical devoted to national lore which was edited by a patriotic *littérateur*, Caesar Otway.[256] For the survey he gathered around him a committee of men soon to be famous in the Irish world of letters—John O'Donovan, Eugene O'Curry, W. F. Wakeman,[257] and the brilliant but erratic James Clarence Mangan.[258] They entered on their work with enthusiasm: one accompanied the surveyors in the field, reporting on the archaeological remains, place-names, and local legends, the others collected all possible information regarding the history of the district being covered, and met regularly at Petrie's house to co-ordinate their material. O'Donovan did the major part of the field work, while to O'Curry was chiefly entrusted the task of conducting investigations in the ancient manuscripts in the libraries of Ireland and England.[259] After only one of the proposed memoirs [260] had been published the government, in 1839, ordered this part of the work stopped on the alleged ground of expense. Protests were so strong that a commission of inquiry was appointed, which in 1843 recommended resumption, but without result.

[255] William Stokes *The Life and Labours in art and archaeology of George Petrie, LL.D.* (London 1868) an interesting and important book.   [256] *DNB*.   [257] *Cf.* p. 102.

[258] O'Donoghue *Life of J. C. Mangan* (1897).

[259] O'C tells the following story of Thomas Moore, the poet, author of a *History of Ireland*: "In the year 1839, during one of his last visits to the land of his birth, he, in company with his old and attached friend, Dr. Petrie, favoured me with quite an unexpected visit at the Royal Irish Academy, then in Grafton Street. I was at that period employed on the ordnance survey of Ireland; and, at the time of his visit, happened to have before me, on my desk, the Books of Ballymote and Lecain, the *Leabhar Breac*, The Annals of the Four Masters, and many other ancient books, for historical research and reference. I had never before seen Moore, and after a brief introduction and explanation of my occupation by Dr. Petrie, and seeing the formidable array of so many dark and time-worn volumes by which I was surrounded, he looked a little disconcerted, but after a while plucked up courage to open the Book of Ballymote, and ask what it was. Dr. Petrie and myself then entered into a short explanation of the history and character of the books then present, as well as of ancient Gaedhlic documents in general. Moore listened with great attention, alternately scanning the books and myself; and then asked me, in a serious tone, if I understood them, and how I had learned to do so. Having satisfied him upon these points, he turned to Dr. Petrie, and said: 'Petrie, those huge tomes could not have been written by fools or for any foolish purpose. I never knew anything about them before, and I had no right to have undertaken the History of Ireland.'" *MS Mat.* 154.

[260] [Col. Colby] *Ordnance Survey of the County of Londonderry Vol. I Memoir of the City and North Western Liberties of Londonderry, Parish of Templemore* (Dublin 1837).

"From a review of the official objections to the continuance of the work," says William Stokes in his *Life of Petrie*,[261] "and from considering the tenor of some of the questions put by the Commissioners of Inquiry, . . . it seems as if some strong, though concealed, influence had been brought to bear on the Government in reference to the danger of re-opening questions of Irish local history. These one-sided views prevailed, and the great undertaking, so earnestly desired by all who wished for the future prosperity and happiness of the country, was finally given up."[262]

The survey had, however, given Petrie, O'Donovan and O'Curry the unique knowledge and experience on which their future careers were based. Petrie's "History and Antiquities of Tara Hill,"[263] read before the Royal Irish Academy in April and May, 1837, was to have been a portion of the memoir on Meath. His "Inquiry into the Origin and Uses of the Round Towers of Ireland,"[264] re-issued as *The Ecclesiastical Architecture of Ireland*,[265] was published by the Academy in 1845. During 1842 he edited the *Irish Penny Journal*, of character similar to the *Dublin Penny Journal*; in 1855 he published a collection of Irish music;[266] and at his death he left unpublished an essay on the "Military Architecture of Ireland"[267] and a gathering of Christian inscriptions in Irish. This last was afterwards edited by Miss Margaret Stokes.[268]

The work of O'Donovan and O'Curry was henceforth more fully connected with the written sources. About 1840 a great era of publication commenced: this was carried on almost entirely either by the various historical societies or by the government. Of the societies the most important was the Irish Archaeological Society, organised in 1840 largely by the energy of Dr. James H. Todd, of Trinity College, who wished to provide a medium through which the labors of O'Donovan and the new generation of Irish scholars could be given to the public. In 1845 the Celtic Society, similar in scope, was formed, and in 1853 the two bodies united as the Irish Archaeological and Celtic Society. A long series of Irish texts was issued by these organisations, the majority relating to Ireland before the Norman invasion, and all well edited. The Ossianic Society, founded in 1853, had for its object the publication of literary pieces from the Ossianic, or Finn, cycle of poems and

---

[261] *Life and Labours in art and archaeology of George Petrie* 108.
[262] Some 468 large volumes of material had been collected. The greater part, including O'D's field-letters, is now in the RIA library; the remainder is still in the Ordnance Survey office.
[263] *Trans. RIA* XVIII (1837) 25–206.
[264] *Trans. RIA* XX (1845).
[265] *Cf.* p. 103 *infra*.
[266] *The Petrie Collection of the ancient Music of Ireland* I (Dublin 1855), II [incomplete] (1882).
[267] Now in RIA.
[268] Dublin, 1872–8. *Cf.* p. 103 *infra*.

sagas: it issued six volumes before it suspended activities in 1861. The Irish Archaeological and Celtic Society practically came to an end about the same time, although some volumes bearing its name appeared later. The death of William Elliot Hudson, generous patron of all this movement, in 1853, of O'Donovan in 1861, and of O'Curry in 1862, and the demoralisation of the national spirit in the years following the famine, explain the outcome. One society which persevered was the Kilkenny Archaeological Society, established by James Graves and J. G. A. Prim in 1849: it became successively the Kilkenny and South-East of Ireland Archaeological Society (1855), the Royal Historical and Archaeological Society of Ireland (1869), and the Royal Society of Antiquaries of Ireland (1890). The Royal Irish Academy continued to publish important historical papers in its Proceedings and Transactions; in its "Irish Manuscripts Series" and "Todd Lecture Series" it printed many valuable texts; and furthermore, and most usefully, it issued facsimile editions of several of the great mediaeval codices— *Lebar na hUidre* (1870), *Leabhar Breac* (1872-6), *Book of Leinster* (1880), *Book of Ballymote* (1887), and *Yellow Book of Lecan* (1896).[269]

To complete the record of facsimile editions of the Irish mediaeval *bibliothecae* it may be added here that in 1909 the Oxford University Press so published the codex *Rawlinson B. 502.*

Under government auspices a considerable number of historical documents, edited with various degrees of excellence, have been published. In 1869 the Master of the Rolls, London, issued the *Appendix A*, and supplements, prepared by Charles Purton Cooper about 1835, to an intended report on Rymer's *Foedera*: it contained facsimiles of pages from many Irish manuscripts in continental libraries and in the British Museum. In 1874-84 the Master of the Rolls in Ireland published *Facsimiles of National Manuscripts of Ireland*, in five bulky parts, edited by Sir John T. Gilbert.[270] In the series *Rerum Britannicarum Medii Ævi Scriptores, or Chronicles and Memorials of Great Britain and Ireland during the Middle Ages*, published under the direction of the Master of the Rolls, and commonly known as the Rolls Series,[271] have appeared the *Chronicum Scotorum*, edited by W. M. Hennessy (1866), *Cogadh Gaedhel re Gallaibh — The War of the Gaedhil with the Gaill*, edited by

[269] The first three are lithographs from exact transcripts made by Joseph O'Longan, the last two from photographs of the original pages. The last is a very poor reproduction.
[270] Cf. p. 99 infra. Sir Samuel Ferguson (1810–1886), deputy keeper of the public records, and Sir John Thomas Gilbert (1829–1898), secretary of the public record office, both did much to promote all Irish historical studies. Cf. Mary C. Ferguson *Sir Samuel Ferguson in the Ireland of his day* 2 vols. (London 1896); Rosa M. Gilbert *Life of Sir John T. Gilbert* (London 1905).
[271] Cf. p. 104 infra.

J. H. Todd (1867), *The Annals of Loch Cé*, edited by W. M. Hennessy (1871), and *The Tripartite Life of Patrick*, edited by Whitley Stokes (1887). Under the direction of the Commissioners for Publishing the Ancient Laws and Institutes of Ireland, appointed in 1852, the greater part of those laws have been published in six volumes (1865-1901), of which the last is a glossary; and under the direction of the Council of the Royal Irish Academy *The Annals of Ulster* were published, edited by W. M. Hennessy and B. MacCarthy (1887-1901).

O'Donovan, O'Curry, and their contemporaries were the last representatives of the old Gaelic scholarship of Ireland. Their lives saw the famine, the clearances, and the beginning of the great emigration, the triple calamity which almost destroyed Gaelic-speaking Ireland and broke the continuity of its cultural tradition. Later Irish scholars either have had to learn the national language as a foreign tongue, or, if they have possessed a speaking knowledge, they have lacked that traditional learning which scribe and bard and shanachie and hedge-schoolmaster succeeded in preserving until the middle of the nineteenth century. Fortunately that traditional learning survived long enough to clasp hands with the new science of philology and the renovated science of history coming in from the universities of modern Europe.

John O'Donovan [272] (1806-1861) was the son of a Kilkenny farmer and descended from an ancient princely family of south Munster. From his father and his uncle he received his early instruction in Irish history and literature, and he was given a certain amount of classical training in a Latin school in Dublin. In 1826 he obtained employment in the record office,[273] and in 1832 in the ordnance survey. From the cessation of his work in the survey until his death a constant stream of publications came from his pen, chiefly editions and translations of texts, with very valuable historical, topographical and literary annotations. His *Grammar of the Irish Language* [274] was the best of its kind prior to the application of the principles of comparative philology, and contains a useful sketch of the work of earlier grammarians. But the book on which his fame especially rests is the magnificent edition of *The Annals of the Four Masters*, brought out by the patriotic Dublin publisher, George Smith, in the years 1848-51. In 1852 O'Donovan received an appointment under the Brehon Law Commission which he held till his death; and he also was appointed professor of Celtic in Queen's College,

[272] [Henry Dixon] "John O'Donovan" *An Leabharlann* II (Dublin 1906) 1-39; *DNB*; *Cath. Encycl.*
[273] Apparently he had previously done scribal work for Hardiman.
[274] *A Grammar of the Irish Language, published for the use of the senior classes in the College of St. Columba* (Dublin 1845).

Belfast. In knowledge of the contents of the manuscripts O'Donovan fell short only of O'Curry, while in topographical lore and in sanity of judgment, breadth of scholarship, sympathy towards new ideas and discoveries, and critical acumen he surpassed all his Irish-speaking contemporaries.

Eoghan Ó Comhraidhe, or Eugene O'Curry[275] (1794-1862), was the son of a poor farmer of Dunaha, near Carrigaholt, Clare, a man, however, who had a good knowledge of Irish literature and of the traditional learning of the people. It is possible that the boy received instruction also from Peter O'Connell,[276] one of the most remarkable of the forgotten scholars of the early nineteenth century. Compelled to leave his farm during the agricultural distress of 1815, O'Curry found work in Limerick and, later, in Dublin, whither he was brought by the publisher Smith. In 1834 he was appointed to the ordnance survey. In 1852 he was employed by the Brehon Law Commission, and in 1855 was appointed to the chair of Irish history and archaeology in the newly established Catholic University of Ireland. The fruits of his professorship were two works that are still of high value, *Lectures on the Manuscript Materials of Ancient Irish History* and *Lectures on the Manners and Customs of the Ancient Irish*,[277] both published at the expense of the University. The importance of O'Curry's lectures results from his unrivalled knowledge of the sources, acquired through his almost superhuman labors in transcribing and cataloguing manuscripts: the inferences and conclusions which he himself draws have to be treated with caution, for his critical sense was inferior to his patriotic enthusiasm.

Others of the last representatives of native Gaelic scholarship were Owen Connellan[278] (1800-1869), son of a Sligo farmer, scribe of the Royal Irish Academy, Irish historiographer to George IV and William IV, professor of Irish in Queen's College, Cork, and author of a trans-

[275] *Irish Monthly Magazine* April 1874; Sarah Atkinson "Eugene O'Curry" in *Essays*, new ed. (Dublin 1896) 1-26; Rev. Timothy Lee "Eugene O'Curry" *Limerick Field Club Journal* I (1897-1900) i 26-31, ii 1-11, II (1903) 177-89; *DNB*; *Cath. Encycl.*

[276] O'C says only that O'Connell was a welcome guest at his father's house, and that his brother Malachi O'Curry was O'Connell's pupil. Peter O'Connell (c 1743-1824), a native of Carne, near Kilrush, Clare, and a hedge-schoolmaster, seems to have had a better knowledge of OI than any of his contemporaries. About 1785 he began work on an Irish-English dictionary. He visited Charles O'Conor of Belanagare, and spent some time in his house. From about 1812 to 1819 he was given a home and all possible assistance by a Dr. O'Reardon of Limerick. At the end they quarrelled and O'Connell returned to Carne and died. His nephew attempted to get Daniel O'Connell "the Liberator" to assist in publishing the book, but, according to O'C, was told "that his uncle was an old fool to have spent so much of his life on so useless a work." Hardiman later obtained possession of the MS and sold it to the BM, where it is numbered Egerton 83. There is a copy in TCD 1396 (H. 5. 25). O'Grady expresses a very high opinion of O'Connell's knowledge, pointing out that he was acquainted with the "infixed pronoun" of OI, commonly considered to be a discovery of Zeuss.—O'Grady *Cat.* 160-5; *DNB*.

[277] *Cf.* pp. 92, 109 *infra*.

[278] *DNB*.

lation of part of the Annals of the Four Masters [279] and of other editions and treatises; John O'Beirne Crowe and Brian O'Looney, scribes and editors of texts; William Maunsell Hennessy [280] (1829-1889), a native of Kerry who became assistant deputy keeper of the public records in Dublin and a not unworthy follower of O'Donovan in history and topography; and Standish Hayes O'Grady [281] (1832-1915), son of Admiral O'Grady, of Erinagh House, Castleconnell, on the Shannon, and descendant of the ruling family of Cenél nDúngaile, who, a member of the first council of the Ossianic Society in 1853, lived to become the Nestor of an entirely new generation of Irish students.

The names of two clergymen of the established Church of Ireland should be mentioned with those of Petrie, O'Curry and O'Donovan in any account of the revival of Irish historical studies in the nineteenth century. James Henthorn Todd (1805-1869), who was associated with Trinity College, Dublin, almost all his life either as pupil, teacher or official, and was honorary secretary of the Royal Irish Academy, 1847-55, and president, 1856-60, worked both within and without those institutions to promote Irish scholarship. He was actuated in particular by two motives, that of raising the standard of learning in the Church of Ireland, and that of improving the character of Irish historical studies. He published many historical articles, editions of several documents, and one important piece of historical research, a *Life of St. Patrick*.[282] William Reeves [283] (1815-1892), who became bishop of Down, Connor and Dromore in 1886, was less the organiser and less the controversialist than Todd, but his superior in pure scholarship. Of his many important productions in ecclesiastical history only one can be noticed here, his remarkable edition of Adamnán's *Life of St. Columba*.[284]

A few other works should be mentioned: the three volumes on *Celtic Scotland* [285] by the Scotsman, William Forbes Skene (1809-1892), in which much attention is given to Irish affairs, especially ecclesiastical; the archaeological studies [286] of Margaret Stokes (1832-1900),

279 *The Annals of Ireland, translated from the original Irish of the Four Masters* (Dublin 1846). It covers the years 1171 to 1616.
280 *DNB*.
281 Eleanor Hull "Standish Hayes O'Grady: a personal reminiscence" *Studies* Mar. 1916 pp. 96-103; *RC* XXXVII (1917-9) 415-7. *Cf.* also the memoir in vol. II of *Cat. of Irish MSS in BM* (1926).
282 Dublin, 1864. *Cf.* pp. 109, 320 *infra*, also *DNB*.
283 Mary C. Ferguson *Life of the Right Rev. William Reeves, D.D.* (Dublin 1893).
284 Irish Archaeological and Celtic Society, Dublin — Bannatyne Club, Edinburgh 1857. *Cf.* p. 430, *infra*.
285 *Cf.* p. 108 *infra*.
286 *Cf.* p. 103 *infra*. She edited Petrie's *Christian inscriptions in the Irish language* (Dublin 1872-8),

sister of Whitley Stokes; and the detailed and careful, but uncritical, *Social history of ancient Ireland* [287] by Patrick Weston Joyce (1827–1914).

Much of the historical writing in Ireland during the nineteenth century has been vitiated by the abnormal political and other prejudices which have prevailed. In history these have reacted in much the same manner as that which the following paragraph describes for the associated field of archaeology:

"It may be said that there are two kinds of meddlers in Irish archaeology, and it is hard to tell which of them is more mischievous. The first kind (who are ardent members of one political party) are full of the glories of Brian the Brave, and of that dreamland time when Ireland, as one of their own poets has said, was peopled by a race "taller than Roman spears" — a condition of things that could not be brought about, save by an epidemic of acromegaly or some similar disease! The other kind (who are rampant members of the opposite political party) are forever chortling over the savagery of the country down to the time of Queen Elizabeth, the evidence for human sacrifices, people going about without any clothes on, and so forth. As is usually the case, there is an element of truth in both ways of interpreting the evidence; but the exaggerations on both sides are so great that the truth is completely hidden."[288]

VI. MODERN SCHOLARSHIP AND THE GAELIC REVIVAL

THE application of the methods of natural science to the study of language has had results of a far-reaching kind both for linguistics and for history. The most extensive use of this science of comparative philology has been in connection with the family of languages variously designated as Indo-European, Indo-Germanic, or Aryan. It was in the second half of the eighteenth century, when a few European scholars began to study Sanskrit as others had long been studying Latin and Greek, that the relationship between these three languages, and between them and the other languages of Europe, began to be recognised. The scientific basis for the comparative study of these languages was first laid down in 1816 and 1819 respectively by the works of two German scholars, *Über das Conjugationsystem der Sanskritsprache* by Franz Bopp (1791–1863), and *Deutsche Grammatik* by Jacob Ludwig Carl Grimm (1785–1863). These men and their successors have carried on the work so successfully that the history of almost every Indo-

and Lord Dunraven's *Notes on Irish architecture* (London 1875), and was herself the author of *Early Christian architecture in Ireland* (London 1878), *Early Christian art in Ireland* (London 1887), *Six months in the Apennines* (London 1892), and *Three months in the forests of France* (London 1895).

287 *Cf.* p. 109 *infra.*

288 R. A. S. Macalister *Ireland in Pre-Celtic Times* (Dublin and London 1921) 6–7.

European language and of a vast number of the words and formations of those languages has been investigated in detail.[289]

In no other field has the application of the methods of comparative philology brought a greater relative increase of knowledge than in that of Celtic studies. Since the time of Lhuyd the existence of a Celtic group of languages had been admitted; but the general opinion long was that it lay outside the Indo-European domain, and no attempt was made to control the theorising of the Vallanceys and Bethams.[290] Scientific study began with the monographs of a French philologist, Adolphe Pictet, in 1837,[291] and the German, Bopp, in 1838.[292] They established definitely that Celtic belonged to the Indo-European family.

It was not until 1853, however, when the epoch-making *Grammatica Celtica* of Johann Kaspar Zeuss appeared, that clear light was thrown on the subject of Celtic philology. Zeuss (1806-1856), a native of Vogtendorf in Upper Franconia, became a student and teacher of history of remarkable erudition. In his study of early German history he came to the conclusion that a knowledge of ancient Celtic was a necessity, and to acquire it turned to the earliest literary remains of the Celtic languages, especially Old Irish. He was encouraged by his friend, Franz Mone (1796-1871), an extraordinarily industrious historian who was a somewhat over-enthusiastic Celtophile. Old Irish was still a sealed book to all but a few Irishmen like O'Curry and O'Donovan, and their knowledge was not based on any comprehensive understanding of linguistic laws, and, as regards the earliest texts, was quite limited. Zeuss knew no Irish and never met an Irish speaker, but he had received the best training of the time in the principles of philology and the methods of research. He visited the manuscript collections of Carlsruhe, Darmstadt, Heidelberg, Würzburg, St. Gall, Milan and London, and, chiefly by the intensive study of those Old Irish glosses on Latin texts which he made famous, he was able to create the science of Celtic — and Irish — philology. Zeuss had exhausted his

289 See A. Meillet *Introduction à l'étude comparative des langues indo-européennes* 6th ed. (Paris 1924).

290 In 1786 Sir William Jones, President of the Bengal Society, in his "third anniversary discourse" delivered before that Society in Calcutta, had expressed the opinion that Gothic and Celtic, as well as Greek and Latin, were related to Sanskrit.—*Asiatic Researches, or Transactions of the Society instituted in Bengal* . . . I (Calcutta, 1788; reprint London, 1799), 422–3. The same idea was developed by an English physician and anthropologist, James Cowles Prichard, in his *Eastern Origin of the Celtic Nations*, which appeared in 1831. Neither Jones nor Prichard, however, attracted much attention from students of philology.

291 *De l'affinité des langues celtiques avec le sanscrit* (Paris 1837).

292 Read before the Berlin Academy as "Über die celtischen Sprachen vom Gesichtspunkte der vergleichenden Sprachforschung"; published in the following year under the title *Die celtischen Sprachen in ihrem Verhältnisse zum Sanskrit, Zend, Griechischen, Lateinischen, Germanischen, Litthauischen und Slawischen* (Berlin 1839).

physical strength, and his death followed quickly; but his work was done: the scholars who have come after have only followed the lines that he laid down.[293]

European students of philology welcomed the new subject of study. In Irish they found a language which in linguistic interest and in its contributions to the elucidation of Indo-European origins rivalled Latin, Greek and Sanskrit. From the time of Zeuss to the present Old and Middle Irish have received unremitting attention for reasons primarily philological; but for the historian the practical result has been that he can now use the sources in Irish almost as freely as those in Latin.[294]

In 1870 the *Revue Celtique*,[295] the first journal dedicated exclusively to Celtic subjects, was established in Paris by Henri Gaidoz, director at the École des Hautes Études. From its appearance it has been the most important of all learned periodicals for the student in any field of Celtic learning. Gaidoz was personally more interested in folk-lore and primitive literature than in philology, and in 1877 he and Eugène Rolland founded *Mélusine*, a journal devoted to those subjects, in which Irish material has from time to time been published. Henri Gaidoz still lives, sole and honored survivor of the founders of the science of Celtic philology.

In 1896 a second periodical to serve students of Celtic was founded, the *Zeitschrift für celtische Philologie*,[296] edited by Kuno Meyer and Ludwig Christian Stern. In 1898 the *Archiv für celtische Lexicographie*[296] appeared, under the direction of Whitley Stokes and Kuno

[293] *Cf.* Chr. W. Glück "Erinnerung an Kaspar Zeuss" *Gelehrte Anzeigen* nos. 61, 62 (Munich 1857); *UJA* VII; Edw. Schröder in *Allgemeine deutsche Biographie* XLV (1899) 132–6; L. C. Stern (ed.) "Briefe von J. K. Zeuss an Chr. W. Glück" *ZCP* III (1901) 334–76; Henri Gaidoz *Pour le centenaire de Gaspar Zeuss fondateur de la philologie celtique* (Paris 1906); Ernst Kuhn *Johann Kaspar Zeuss zum hundertjährigen Gedächtnis* (Munich 1906); Anton Dürrwächter "Johann Kaspar Zeuss" *Historisches Jahrbuch* XXVII (1906); "Die bamberger Centenarfeier zum Gedächtnis an Johann Kaspar Zeuss" *ZCP* VI (1908) 195–227.—WS's punning quotation may be recalled: Ζεὺς ἀρχή, Ζεὺς μέσσα, Διὸς δ'ἐκ πάντα τέτυκται. *Three Irish Glossaries* (London 1862) p. lxxv.

[294] The following works, *inter multa*, may be consulted for the history of Celtic studies: EW "Keltische Sprachen," in J. S. Ersch and J. G. Gruber (ed. August Leskien) *Allgemeine Encyklopädie der Wissenschaften und Künste*, 2nd sect., pt. XXXV (Leipsic 1884) 132–80; RTh "Celtic Philology 1880–1886" *Philol. Soc. Trans.* 1885–6 pp. 386–93; Victor Tourneur *Esquisse d'une histoire des études celtiques* (*Bibl. de la Faculté de Philosophie et Lettres de l'Univ. de Liège* fasc. xv) (Liége 1905); G. Dottin "Les études celtiques depuis 1900" *Rev. des études anciennes* XII ii (1910); J. Loth "Les études celtiques; leur état présent; leur avenir" *Rev. internationale de l'enseignement* 1911, and "Les études celtiques et leur importance" *Rev. hebdomadaire* 20 Sept. 1919; A. Meillet "La linguistique," and G. Dottin "La philologie celtique," in *La science française* II (Paris 1915) 117–24, 189–95; J. L. Gerig "Celtic Studies in the United States" *Columbia University Quarterly* XIX i (Dec. 1916) 30–43. Dr. Gerig's articles on "Philology" in *The New International Year-Book*, beginning with 1910, give a brief list of the annual publications on Celtic philology and allied subjects. In order to follow more minutely the development of Celtic and Irish studies it is, of course, necessary to consult carefully the various periodicals, especially *RC*.

[295] *Cf.* p. 94 *infra*.

[296] Halle a. S.: published by Max Niemeyer. *Cf.* p. 94 *infra*.

Meyer; it ceased publication in 1907. Other periodicals of interest to students of early Irish are the *Gaelic Journal*, published in Dublin from 1882 to 1909, the *Celtic Review*, which began publication in Edinburgh in 1904, and *Ériu*, published at irregular intervals since 1904 by the School of Irish Learning, Dublin. It should be mentioned that during the eighties and early nineties of the last century *The Academy*, published weekly in London, was a favorite medium for communications of Irish and Celtic scholars, and its files should be consulted by any person wishing to trace the history of their labors.

The early students of Celtic philology gave their attention chiefly to the glosses and the small number of other Irish texts to be found in the oldest manuscripts. A second edition of the *Grammatica Celtica*, by Hermann Ebel, successor of Bopp in the chair of comparative philology at Berlin, appeared in 1871. Other noteworthy monuments in the progress of these studies were the *Goidilica* of Whitley Stokes in 1866,[297] with a second edition, *Goidelica*, in 1872;[298] Count Constantino Nigra's edition of the Turin glosses in 1869,[299] and his description of the St. Gall glosses in 1872;[300] G. I. Ascoli's publication of the Milan and St. Gall glosses, 1878-89;[301] and Heinrich Zimmer's *Glossae Hibernicae*, 1881.[302] Finally came the great *Thesaurus Palaeohibernicus*[303] of Whitley Stokes and John Strachan, containing practically all the Irish texts which on purely manuscript evidence can be dated before the year 1000.

From the glosses the students of philology worked their way into the general literature of Old and Middle Irish, preserved chiefly in those great *bibliothecae* compiled in the twelfth and later centuries. Thus this field, which had been and was being attacked by O'Donovan, O'Curry, Hennessy, O'Grady and others from the basis of an intimate knowledge of modern Irish, was now invaded from the opposite quarter of linguistic science and Indo-European philology. The first important collection was the *Irische Texte* of Ernst Windisch and Whitley Stokes, in four volumes,[304] with an *Extra-Band* containing Windisch's edition of the famous saga, the *Táin Bó Cúalnge*.[305] Other notable collections of texts were the *Todd Lecture Series* of the Royal Irish Academy, already noticed; the *Anecdota Oxoniensia*, in which the Clarendon

297 Calcutta: privately printed.
298 London.
299 *Glossae hibernicae veteres Codicis Taurinensis* (Paris 1869).
300 *Reliquie Celtiche Il manoscritto irlandese di S. Gallo* (Turin 1872).
301 *Archivio Glottologico Italiano* vols. V and VI: *Il Codice irlandese dell' Ambrosiana* (Rome).
302 Berlin. A supplement was published in 1886.
303 2 vols. (London 1901, 1903). There is a supplement by WS (Halle a. S. 1910).
304 Leipsic: 1880; 1884, 1887; 1891, 1897; 1900, 1909.
305 Leipsic 1905.

Press issued beautiful editions of several important Irish documents; the publications of the Henry Bradshaw Society, which include Irish liturgical texts, some written in Irish, others in Latin; the works of the Irish Texts Society; and the *Anecdota from Irish Manuscripts*,[306] edited by Kuno Meyer and several Irish scholars.

Grammatical and lexicographical publications make available the linguistic results of these studies. The first scientific grammar of Old Irish was the *Kurzgefasste Irische Grammatik* of Windisch, issued in 1879.[307] Later noteworthy works are the the the *Old-Irish Paradigms* of Strachan,[308] a very useful booklet; the *Grammaire du Vieil-Irlandais* of Joseph Vendryes;[309] Rudolf Thurneysen's *Handbuch des Alt-Irischen*,[310] the recognised chief authority, but a work of difficulty for readers who are not specialists in philology; F. W. O'Connell's *Grammar of Old Irish*;[311] and Julius Pokorny's *Concise Old Irish Grammar*.[312] Georges Dottin's *Manuel d'Irlandais moyen*[313] is the only important work in its field, and in that of the comparative grammar of Celtic there is only one notable book since Zeuss and Ebel, the *Vergleichende Grammatik der keltischen Sprachen* of Holger Pedersen.[314] For the general grammar of the Indo-European languages the standard work is the second edition of Karl Brugmann's *Grundriss der vergleichenden Grammatik der indogermanischen Sprachen*,[315] in which the Celtic sections were revised by Thurneysen. In lexicography the situation is less satisfactory. We have only the older, unscientific dictionaries of O'Reilly and O'Donovan, and the special vocabularies added to particular publications, of which the most useful are the *Indices* to the second edition of *Grammatica Celtica*,[316] Windisch's "Wörterbuch" in the first volume of *Irische Texte*, Ascoli's *Glossario*[317] and the "Glossary" to Atkinson's *The Passions and the Homilies from Leabhar Breac*.[318] Kuno Meyer's "Contributions to Irish Lexicography," in the *Archiv für celtische Lexicographie*, cover in a somewhat desultory fashion words having initial letters from A to Dn. For many years the Royal Irish Acad-

[306] *Cf.* p. 104 *infra*.
[307] Leipsic. There are two Eng. trans.: by Norman Moore (Cambridge 1882) and the Rev. Jas. P. Mac Swiney (Dublin 1883).
[308] Dublin, The School of Irish Learning, 1905; and later eds.
[309] Paris 1908.
[310] 2 pts. Heidelberg 1909.
[311] Belfast 1912.
[312] See p. 96 *infra* for this and other publications by Pokorny.
[313] 2 vols. Paris 1913.
[314] 2 vols. Göttingen 1909, 1913.
[315] *Cf.* p. 95 *infra*.
[316] By B. Güterbok and RTh: *cf.* p. 96 *infra*.
[317] *Cf.* p. 96 *infra*.
[318] RIA Todd Lect. Ser. II (Dublin 1887).

emy has been making preparations for the publication of an exhaustive
Irish dictionary, the fruit of endowments by William Elliot Hudson,
the patron of the Irish Archaeological, Celtic and Ossianic Societies, and
the Rev. Maxwell Close, patron of the *Gaelic Journal.* Robert Atkinson, Kuno Meyer and Carl Marstrander were successively appointed
editors, and in August, 1913, the last brought out one fascicule,[319] from
D to *Degóir,* but since then publication has been suspended.

To interests purely linguistic there came gradually to be added an
appreciation of the value of Irish sources from the points of view of
literature, of history, and of the whole group of sociological studies.
In the work of what may be called the second generation of Celtic
scholars — such men as Whitley Stokes, Ernst Windisch, Henri d'Arbois
de Jubainville, Sir John Rhŷs, Heinrich Zimmer, Kuno Meyer, Rudolf
Thurneysen — this development can be clearly traced.

Whitley Stokes (1830–1909) was the greatest scholar in philology
that Ireland has produced, and the only one that may be ranked with
the most famous of continental savants. He was the son of Dr. William
Stokes, the friend and biographer of George Petrie, and was the grandson of that Dr. Whitley Stokes who was one of the early members of
the Royal Irish Academy. After being graduated from Trinity College he studied law, and from 1856 to 1862 practised in London. From
1862 to 1882 he was in India, where he won enduring fame by his vast
work in draughting and codifying Indian laws and rules of procedure.
His chief interest, however, was in linguistic studies, for which he had
a natural genius. He had begun the study of Celtic philology in 1848,
and in those early years was encouraged and assisted by O'Donovan,
O'Curry, and Rudolf T. Siegfried, afterwards professor of Sanskrit and
Comparative Philology in Trinity, who had been trained in the schools
of Germany. Even during his sojourn in India Stokes published several important philological works, but from 1882 until his death his
whole energies were given to Celtic studies. His most original contributions to knowledge were in the field of pure philology — such as, for
example, his *Urkeltischer Sprachschatz,*[320] a dictionary of primitive
Celtic — but his best known and most important work was the editing
and translation of Irish texts. His achievement was prodigious: of
the Old and Middle Irish literature now available in scholarly editions
and translations a much larger portion is due to him than to any one
other man. He did not attempt the reconstruction of critical texts:
believing that in Irish the time for that had not yet come, he limited

[319] *Cf.* p. 96 *infra.*   [320] *Cf.* p. 95 *infra.*

himself to diplomatic editions, with rectification only of purely scribal errors. His intimate knowledge, both literary and philological, of the English language gives his translations from Irish to English an accuracy, felicity and conciseness that have never been surpassed. His standards of scholarship were austere and his criticisms had a rigor and acerbity that often gave needless pain and offense.[321] His attacks were directed especially against Dr. Bartholomew MacCarthy, editor of the *Annals of Ulster* and of other historical and religious documents, Professor Zimmer, and Professor Atkinson, and some of his comments on their publications are brilliant examples of trenchant criticism. They struck back with vigor, and, although Stokes was seldom worsted in a philological argument, in other respects chinks were sometimes found in his armor. He naturally disliked the uncritical enthusiasms of O'Curry and the patriotic school of Irish writers, and was inclined, in reaction against them, to assign unduly late dates to Irish texts and to belittle the worth of their style and content. In his later years, however, he came more into accord with other scholars on these subjects. He was deeply interested in folklore and primitive law and religion, and his intimate knowledge of the literature, customs and traditions of the East helped his commentary on Irish texts. Nevertheless, from the point of view strictly of the historian, his editorial work is often unsatisfactory: indeed, his edition of the *Annals of Tigernach* [322] is an example of how bad a botch a good philological scholar can make of an important historical document. But Stokes had no more exacting critic than himself: the student should always consult the extensive *addenda* and *corrigenda* which are usually appended to his publications. On occasion he would, after hurling back the attacks of a critic, proceed to give the *coup-de-grâce* by pointing out the errors that his critic might have, but did not, discover in his work. And the controversies in which he was a protagonist had the good effect of holding Celtic studies on a high plane of efficiency.[323]

Ernst Windisch (1844–1918) was an excellent type of the German university scholar. A graduate of Leipsic, he began teaching there in 1869, became extra-ordinary professor in 1871, professor at Heidelberg

---

[321] That kindly old gentleman, Joseph O'Longan, suffered keenly because of the harsh criticism made by Stokes of the RIA facsimile eds. of LU and LBr, the lithographic plates of which were prepared from O'Longan's transcripts. (WS *Remarks on the Facsimiles published by the Royal Irish Academy* (Simla 1875)). How comparatively trifling were the mistakes of the transcripts was made clear when, this last of the professional scribes having passed beyond the reach of praise or blame, the Academy undertook to publish facsimiles of BB and YBL by direct photographic process.

[322] *RC* XVI–XVIII (1895–7). *Cf.* MacN in *Ériu* VII pt. i (1913).

[323] Rev. Richard Henebry "Whitley Stokes" [including a list of his principal works prepared by Miss A.M. Stokes] *Celtic Review* VI no. xxi (July 15, 1909) 65–85; KM *Proc. of the Brit. Acad.* IV (1909–10) 363–7; R. I. Best "Bibliography of the Publications of Whitley Stokes" *ZCP* VIII (1912) 351–406.

in 1873, at Strasburg in 1875,[324] and in 1877 ordinary professor of Sanskrit at Leipsic, where he remained for the rest of his life. In 1870-71, while in London and Dublin, he made the acquaintance of Standish Hayes O'Grady and Whitley Stokes, and became interested in Celtic. Mention has been made of his Irish grammar and of the *Irische Texte*, including his "Wörterbuch" and his great edition of the *Táin Bó Cúalnge*: by these and many minor works he laid the foundations for the study of Irish literature. In his later years he too felt the drift towards history, as is indicated by his volume on early Britain, *Das keltische Britannien bis zu Kaiser Arthur.*[325]

Marie-Henri d'Arbois de Jubainville (1827-1910) was a graduate of the École des Chartes and was in charge of the departmental archives of Aube prior to his retirement in 1880. His historical interests attracted him to the study of the primitive inhabitants of France and Europe, and through this he came to concentrate on Celtic languages, literature, law and social history. In 1882 he was appointed to the newly founded chair of Celtic at the Collège de France, and in 1886 he succeeded Gaidoz in the direction of the *Revue Celtique*. Through these two positions he exercised a remarkable influence on the development of Celtic and Irish studies. Among the abundant published fruits of his activities mention should be made specially of the *Essai d'un catalogue de la littérature épique de l'Irlande*[326] — next important guide to Irish sources after O'Curry's *Manuscript Materials* — and the twelve volumes of his *Cours de littérature celtique*,[327] in which he gives particular attention to the use of this literature as sources for social history. He was the first scholar trained in the best modern historical methods to write extensively on early Ireland.[328]

Of the few English scholars in Celtic the best known was Robert Atkinson (1839-1908), who, although a native of Gateshead, was educated at Trinity College, Dublin, and passed his whole career in Ireland, where he was professor of Comparative Philology and Sanskrit at Trin-

---

[324] In this year he gave the first university course ever offered in Celtic. In the following year Gaidoz gave a course at the École pratique des Hautes Études.

[325] Leipsic 1912.—*Cf.* J. Vendryes *RC* XXXVII iv (1917-9) 420-5; KM *ZCP* XIII i (1919) 148-50; Eleanor Knott *Studies* VIII no. xxx (June 1919) 264-7.

[326] Paris 1883. *Cf.* p. 92 *infra*. It was partly the result of a mission to the British Isles which he undertook on behalf of the department of public instruction in France to report on Irish MSS. *Cf.* "Rapport sur une mission littéraire dans les Isles Britanniques" *Archives des missions scientifiques et littéraires* 3 sér. X (1883). G. Dottin published a supplement to the *Essai* in *RC* XXXIII (1912).

[327] *Cf.* p. 106 *infra*. Some portions were contributed by other authors.

[328] *Cf.* *RC* XXXI (1910) 1-3, 527; XXXII (1911) 453-74; Ferdinand Lot *RH* CIV 229-33 (mai 1910); Émile Chénon *Bulletin de la Société nationale des Antiquaires de France*, 1912; A. Morel-Fatio *Acad. des Inscriptions et Belles-Lettres, séance du 13 juin 1913*, and *Bibl. de l'École des Chartes*, Sept.-Dec. 1913.

ity from 1871 to 1907, and president of the Royal Irish Academy from 1901 to 1906.[329] From the Celtic divisions of Britain — Wales, the Isle of Man, and especially Scotland — have come many students of their ancestral languages. The colleague of Stokes in the compilation of the *Thesaurus Palaeohibernicus*, and of Meyer in the foundation of the School of Irish Learning, was John Strachan (1862–1907), a native of Keith, a graduate of Aberdeen and Cambridge, and a pupil of Thurneysen, who became professor of Greek and Comparative Philology at the University of Manchester, where he had courses in Celtic established.[330] Better known to the general public was Sir John Rhŷs (1840–1915), a native of Cardiganshire whose chief interest was in the lore of his kinsfolk, the Welsh people. He published one paper of *Studies in Early Irish History*,[331] stimulating if not convincing, and his investigations in Celtic mythology and folk-lore, in early British history, and in Celtic epigraphy all have a more or less close connection with Ireland. Much of his work is marked by theorising of a risky order: indeed, Rhŷs was a kind of Welsh Zimmer, but without Zimmer's extraordinary resourcefulness, and also without his irascibility.[332]

Heinrich Zimmer (1851–1910) was, much more than Stokes, the Ishmael of Celtic studies, whose hand was against every man's. A pupil of Windisch, one of his early essays was a severe and largely unjustified attack on his master's "Wörterbuch."[333] He was, however, a man of remarkably keen and vigorous mentality, who has left a strong impress on the subjects of both Celtic philology and Irish history. Although a teacher of linguistics, and ending his days as professor of Celtic philology at the university of Berlin, the bent of his mind was more towards history, and his most striking productions were historical or semi-historical in character. Among the best known of these is his article on "The Celtic Church in Britain and Ireland," contributed to the third edition of the *Realencyklopädie für protestantische Theologie und Kirche*,[334] which by its characterisation of the mission of St. Patrick aroused a long controversy. Some of his published monographs were designed to form parts of a large history of the Celtic world that had been in part mapped out at the time of his death.[335] His historical

[329] *Proc. RIA* XXVII sect. C (1908–9).
[330] KM *Ériu* III (1907) 202–6; Rev. Geo. Calder *Celtic Review* IV no. xiv (Oct. 15, 1907) 188–91; RTh *Indogerm. Forschungen* XXII, *Anzeiger* 79–80 (1908).
[331] *Cf.* p. 109 *infra*.
[332] *Cf.* *RC* XXXVI iii–iv (1915–6) 418–22; also H. Gaidoz in *Rev. internationale de l'enseignement* Jan. 15, Feb. 15, 1916.
[333] *Keltische Studien, Erstes Heft: "Irische Texte mit Wörterbuch von E. Windisch"* (Berlin 1881). *Cf. Göttingische gelehrte Anzeigen* 1882 pp. 673–736; *RC* V (1882) 255–65.
[334] *Cf.* pp. 107, 157, 310, 320 *sqq. infra*.
[335] *Cf.* KM "Aus dem Nachlass Heinrich Zimmers" *ZCP* IX (1913) 87 *sqq.*

writings are marked by daring hypotheses and by brilliant ingenuity in the massing of evidence in their support: his theories have seldom been approved in full by the sober judgment of other scholars, but their effect in both stimulating and clarifying Irish historical investigation has been most valuable.[336]

Kuno Meyer (1858-1919), another pupil of Windisch, succeeded Zimmer in the chair of Celtic at Berlin after having been for twenty-seven years, from 1884 to 1911, lecturer or professor in the department of Teutonic languages in University College, Liverpool. At Liverpool he was well placed for pursuing his Celtic studies. He spent much of his spare time in going over the great Irish manuscript collections in Dublin, Oxford and London. In Dublin he was one of the founders, and the first director, of the School of Irish Learning, and editor of its journal, *Ériu*. His resignation from these positions, in December, 1914, was accepted by the governors and trustees of the School in a resolution expressive of their appreciation of the signal services he had rendered in the promotion of Irish scholarship.[337] He alone since Zeuss left behind a body of disciples, the scholars who to-day are continuing the work of Zeuss on Irish soil. In the extent and quality of his work as editor and translator he rivalled Whitley Stokes. In the annals of philology he will hardly be ranked as high as Stokes, in spite of the magnitude and importance of his lexicographical studies. It was by his appreciation of Irish as a great historical literature that Meyer broke advance ground. He was largely the discoverer of the *literature* of early Irish: in the vast debris where others had seen only the crude, if rich, products of the primitive folkmind he perceived gem after gem of individual worth and high artistic finish, while his mastery of both English and German enabled him to convey this appreciation to the non-Irish world. In the last years of his life particularly his chief interest was in the collection and interpretation of the scattered fragments of early Irish poetry.[338]

If Kuno Meyer was the apostle of the literary criticism of Old Irish, Rudolf Thurneysen, some time professor of Sanskrit and Comparative Philology at the University of Freiburg-im-Breisgau, and, later, at that of Bonn, is the pioneer of its "higher textual" criticism.

[336] *Cf.* J. Vendryes *RC* XXXI (1910) 410–2; *Journal of the Welsh Bibliographical Society* I ii (Aberystwith 1911) 48–55 [bibliography; *cf.* *ZCP* VIII (1912) 593–4]; Wilhelm Schulze "Gedächtnisrede auf Heinrich Zimmer" *Abhandl. d. kgl. preuss. Akad. d. Wissenschaften* 1911.
[337] *Ériu* VIII i (1915) "Report."
[338] *Cf.* J. Vendryes *RC* XXXVII iv (1917–9) 425–8; Julius Pokorny *ZCP* XIII ii (1920) 283–5; Wilhelm Schulze *Studies* IX no. xxxiv (June 1920) 291–7; Douglas Hyde *ibid.* 297–9; R. I. B [est] *Ériu* IX ii (1923) 181–6; id. "Bibliography of the Publications of Kuno Meyer" *ZCP* XV (1924) 1–65.

He and Joseph Loth of Paris, are the only members of the second generation of Celtic scholars who are still actively engaged in Celtic research.[339] His early activities were chiefly in the field of grammar, but he has gradually turned to the study of the saga texts and the investigation of early Irish literary history. These later studies are culminating in his great work, *Die irische Helden- und Königsage*, of which the first two parts, in one volume, were published in 1921,[340] "with the assistance of the Irish language department of Dáil Éireann." It is a study of the saga texts, their origins, interrelationships, development and manner of transmission, and is a worthy successor in our day to the productions of O'Curry and d'Arbois de Jubainville.

Meanwhile in Ireland itself a revolution had begun which was destined to have far-reaching effects on national scholarship as well as on the national life. This was that reaction against Anglicisation and reversion towards Gaelic culture which is known as the Gaelic Revival, and which has manifested itself chiefly, but by no means exclusively, in the resumption, by a considerable section of the nation, of Irish speech. Forerunners in the Gaelic movement were the Society for the Preservation of the Irish Language, founded in 1876, and the Gaelic Union, in 1878, but the body through which it has done its real work has been the Gaelic League. The Gaelic League was founded in 1893 by Douglas Hyde,[341] Father Eugene O'Growney, T. O'Neill Russell, David Comyn, Eóin MacNeill, and a few others. The enthusiasm, ability and energy of Hyde were peculiarly responsible for the outcome. The founding of the League signalised the inauguration of a nation-wide organisation and of nation-wide propaganda. The remarkable success achieved and the remarkable developments which have followed that success make the event epoch-marking. Starting slowly, the movement gradually acquired tremendous impetus. Almost all nationalist and a considerable section of unionist Ireland was swept into sympathetic support if not practical cooperation. The movement took on a character of inspiration and self-sacrificing devotion that was almost religious. Although the League limited its own action to the revival of the Gaelic language and culture, it provided inspiration and training for the majority of the leaders of *Sinn Féin*, the Irish Volunteers, the Irish Republican Army, *Dáil Éireann*, and the other elements that produced the political revolution culminating in the establish-

---

[339] *Cf.* J. Vendryes in *RC* XXXIX (1922) 360: "Moins téméraire que Zimmer, dont les hardiesses ont souvent quelque chose de désordonné, moins timide que Windisch, dont l'érudition prudente reste trop abritée derrière les faits, M. Thurneysen réalise le type complet que ses deux devanciers faisaient seulement désirer: il est aujourd'hui sans conteste le maître des études de philologie irlandaise."

[340] Halle a. S.

[341] Diarmid Ó Cobhthaigh *Douglas Hyde* (Dublin and London 1917).

ment of *Saorstát Éireann*, and it gave to the Irish people as a whole the mentality that made possible the work of those organisations. In the first number of *The Irish Volunteer*, February 7, 1914, Padraic Pearse, who had been editor of the Gaelic League's organ, *An Claidheamh Soluis*, and was to be president of the Irish Republic of Easter Week, 1916, wrote as follows:

"The Irish Revolution really began when the seven proto-Gaelic Leaguers met in O'Connell street. Their deed in 1893 made our deed of 1913 possible. The germ of all future Irish history was in that back room. . . . Whatever happens to the Gaelic League it has left its mark upon Irish history and the things that will be dreamt of and attempted in the new Ireland by the men and the sons of the men that went to school to the Gaelic League will be dreamt of and attempted — yea, and accomplished — just because the Gaelic League has made them possible."

One of the chief practical objects for which the League worked was the firm establishment of Irish in the educational curriculum. This meant primarily the study of modern Irish, but also, in the more advanced grades, of the older Irish literature. Against this programme strong opposition was offered, notably by Robert Atkinson, who, almost alone among the adversaries of Irish, possessed some knowledge of the subject. Already in the introduction to the facsimile edition of the Yellow Book of Lecan, in 1896, he had set forth his opinions on mediaeval Irish literature:

'There are so many repetitions of certain tales, there is so much of mere metrical sawdust and technical scaffolding, so many pages taken up with genealogical fact and speculation, such an amount of problematical scriptural history taken usually from any source but the Bible itself, that the whole mass, when sifted, furnishes in reality but a very small quantity of what may be called imaginative literature. And even of this remainder, one feels how little of it is informed by the 'shaping spirit of imagination.' . . . No conception of history seems to have taken hold of the Irish mind. The monks write annals, carefully no doubt, but baldly, and there is practically no trace of anything like contemporary history. . . . Hence, in all the enormous mass of Irish manuscripts preserved, there is absolutely nothing that in the faintest degree rivals the splendour of the vernacular literature of the Middle Ages. . . . Whatever be the value of these pages from the side of folk-lore in its widest sense, their value as literature is but small; it is from the point of view of linguistic study chiefly that students will continue to pore over them. For educational purposes, save in this limited sense, they are wholly unsuited. They do not often sin by grossness of speech, and probably never by licentiousness of thought, but there is an utter absence of any elevation of thought or dignity about them. Their details are often curious and interesting; but the severance from the great movements of the world, and the complete seclusion from the current of the ideas that were destined to shape and animate modern civilisation, led naturally and inevitably to the elaboration of mere form, and the later poets aided the impoverishment by trammelling themselves with metrical difficulties which have no parallel in other literatures, and which transformed Irish poetry into an arena for the development of enormous technical dexterity, in which the expression of freely expanding thought was the last element to be considered."

It has seemed well to present thus fully the heaviest onslaught which has ever been made on old Irish literature. Before the Intermediate Education Commission of 1898-9 Atkinson repeated and enlarged on his criticism.[342] The Gaelic League countered by securing the testimony of Zimmer, Windisch, Stern, Pedersen, Dottin, Rhŷs, York Powell, and other scholars in repudiation of Atkinson's attack and in vindication of the worth of Irish literature.

When the National University was established the Gaelic League had another struggle to secure the recognition of Irish as a compulsory subject for matriculation and in the general course. The League was successful, and Dublin, through the University and the School of Irish Learning, has become the great centre of Irish scholarship. In the University, Douglas Hyde was given charge of the department of Modern Irish, Osborn Bergin of Old Irish, R. A. S. Macalister of Celtic Archaeology, and Eóin MacNeill of Early Irish History. The appointment of MacNeill was a deserved recognition of one who has done more than any other to place the story of pre-Norman Ireland on a basis of sound historical criticism. He began the work of demolition and reconstruction in a series of papers on pre-Christian Ireland contributed to the *New Ireland Review* in 1905-1907 — some of the theories advanced are no longer tenable — and has continued it by many contributions to periodicals and to the proceedings of learned societies, and by two publications of greater bulk, *Phases of Irish History* and *Celtic Ireland*.[343] MacNeill has also edited several collections of Irish texts.

In 1898 the Irish Texts Society was founded, with headquarters in London. Its object was to take up again the work of publishing systematically Irish texts, as this had formerly been attempted by the Irish Archaeological, Celtic and Ossianic Societies. A long series of volumes, chiefly of late mediaeval and modern documents, now stands to its credit. Some of these, as, for example, the four volumes containing the first complete edition of Keating's *History of Ireland*,[344] are of much historical importance.

[342] *Intermediate Education (Ireland) Commission, Appendix to the Final Report*, Part I (Dublin 1899) [C.-9512] 637-45. He declared that, among the published ancient Irish texts, "it would be difficult to find a book in which there was not some passage so silly or so indecent as to give you a shock from which you would not recover during the rest of your life." Under cross-examination, Atkinson added that "all folklore is at the bottom abominable." It was only from the point of view of philology, and, apparently, in some degree, of history, that he would admit Irish to have value.

[343] *Cf.* p. 108 *infra.*   [344] London 1902, 1908, 1908, 1914.

Abroad the study of Celtic philology and linguistics, and, in a lesser degree, of Irish literature and history, is maintained by a new generation of scholars in the great centres of European learning. A few out of many names may here be mentioned, those which the student is likely most frequently to encounter: Foremost are Joseph Loth, of the Collège de France, who succeeded d'Arbois de Jubainville as editor of the *Revue Celtique*; and his collaborators, two men who are the outstanding figures of what may be called the third generation of Celtic scholars, Georges Dottin, Dean of the University of Rennes, and Joseph Vendryes, professor in the University of Paris. In Germany, Julius Pokorny has succeeded Kuno Meyer as Professor of Celtic in the University of Berlin and editor of the *Zeitschrift für celtische Philologie*. Alexander Bugge and Carl Marstrander, in Oslo, have brought a national interest to their studies of the ancient relationships of Irish and Norse.

Extended attention has been given to the development of Irish-language studies because the movement within the last seventy-five years that is of outstanding importance for the Irish historian is the opening up of the sources written in Irish. Less space need be devoted to the work on Latin sources. These, of course, have always been decipherable, and they have long received some attention from European scholars, one part because of their interest to Church historians, another because, being records or writings of Irishmen residing on the Continent of Europe, they have importance for the history of France, Belgium, Germany, Switzerland or Italy. Thus it is that documents of Irish provenance have received a share of attention in such publications as the *Acta Sanctorum* of the Bollandists, the *Monumenta Germaniae Historica* of the Gesellschaft für ältere deutsche Geschichtskunde, the *Patrologiae Latinae Cursus Completus* of the abbé J. P. Migne.[345] But of systematic work on Irish sources as such there has been relatively little. Mario Esposito has made a valuable beginning of the cataloguing of Latin documents and of the manuscripts in which they are to be found.[346] The foundations of Hiberno-Latin palaeography have been laid by Ludwig Traube and W. M. Lindsay,[347] this last of the University of St. Andrews. To Ludwig Traube (1861–1907), the great mediaevalist of Munich, Ireland owes much, both for his investigations in Latin literature and script of Irish origin, and in the history of Irish writers in early mediaeval Europe, and for the inspiration he has given others to carry on similar studies.[348] Another investigator of palaeography whose

---

[345] *Cf.* pp. 289, 103–4 *infra.*　　　　[346] *Cf.* pp. 85, 92 *infra.*　　　　[347] *Cf.* pp. 97–8 *infra.*

[348] *Cf.* his *O Roma nobilis* (Munich 1891) and his eds. of mediaeval Latin poetry in *MGH*. The first vol. of *Quellen und Untersuchungen zur lateinischen Philologie des Mittelalters* of which Traube was editor, contains S. Hellmann's *Sedulius Scottus* and E. K. Rand's *Johannes Scottus* (Munich 1906). *Cf.* pp. 530, 553, 570 *infra.*

scholarship receives international recognition, Luigi Schiaparelli, of Florence, Italy, has recently given attention to early Irish writing.[349]

In the field of hagiography considerable work has been done. In 1888 [350] the very important *Codex Salmanticensis* was published through the munificence of the Marquess of Bute and under the editorship of two Bollandist scholars, Charles De Smedt and Joseph De Backer. Separate texts have been published by Patrick F. Moran (afterwards archbishop of Sydney and cardinal), J. T. Fowler, Newport J. D. White, J. B. Bury, Hugh Jackson Lawlor, R. A. S. Macalister, and many others. Finally Charles Plummer, of Corpus Christi College, Oxford, has brought out two great collections, *Vitae Sanctorum Hiberniae* [351] and *Bethada Náem nÉrenn* [352] which contain scholarly editions of practically all the more important Lives of Irish saints, both those in Latin and those in Irish, that are not elsewhere available in print. In the future roll of the founders of Irish historical scholarship Dr. Plummer's name will stand beside those of Michael O'Clery and John Colgan. His some-time disciple, Father Paul Grosjean, has for the first time brought within the circle of the great Bollandist Society a specialist's proficiency *in rebus Hibernicis*.

In other classes of sources besides the hagiographical a certain amount of valuable publication work has been done, the details of which must be passed over. It would not be right to close, however, without mentioning the magnificent edition of the *Book of Armagh* — a manuscript partly biblical, partly hagiographical — begun by William Reeves and completed by John Gwynn, which was published in 1913 by the Royal Irish Academy.

Such is an outline of what has been accomplished by modern scholarship towards the publication of the sources of early Irish history. In constructive historical work much less can be recorded. The important task hitherto has been to get the sources into print in trustworthy editions. The labors of analysis and synthesis will follow in due time. A beginning can be found in the writings of d'Arbois de Jubainville, Heinrich Zimmer, and Eóin MacNeill, of which mention has already been made; in the studies on St. Patrick of the late J. B. Bury, Regius Professor at Cambridge, formerly of Trinity College, Dublin, who approached the subject from a long mastery of Roman imperial history, and those of S. Czarnowski, from the point of view of the latest French sociological school;[353] in the exceedingly valuable treatises on Church history by Dom Louis Gougaud; and in a considerable number of other works,

---

[349] *Cf.* pp. 97–8 *infra.*   [350] Edinburgh and London.   [351] 2 vols. Oxford 1910.
[352] 2 vols. Oxford 1922. Three more Irish Lives are printed in his *Miscellanea Hagiographica Hibernica* (Brussels 1925), which has also a useful "Catalogue."   [353] *Cf.* pp. 320–1 *infra.*

chiefly contributions to periodicals and to Society transactions. Noteworthy also is the appearance of a few very useful aids to the historical student, the fruits of arduous labors on the part of their compilers: *Onomasticon Goedelicum*,[354] an index of Irish geographical names, by Edmund I. Hogan (1831–1917),[355] long professor of Irish Language and History in University College, Dublin; *Alt-Celtischer Sprachschatz*,[356] by Alfred Holder (d. 1916), librarian at Carlsruhe, a similar index of Celtic geographical and personal names in ancient and early mediaeval times; and the indispensable *Bibliography*[357] prepared by R. I. Best, of the National Library of Ireland.

Irish historical work is not as yet well organised. There is no Irish historical association. The Royal Society of Antiquaries, the Royal Irish Academy, and the various local archaeological societies but partially supply its want. So too the need of an Irish historical review is not adequately met by the occasional articles and generally excellent reviews of historical publications which appear in *Studies*, a quarterly edited by a committee drawn from the faculty of the National University. Trained historical workers are few. But the nation which has maintained its devotion to history from the days of the pagan *filid* through centuries of stress and disaster will not fail in this duty in the generation which at last beholds its *fáinne an lae*.[358]

VII. The Chief Collections of Manuscripts

There are two broad classes of manuscripts in which the student of early Irish history is interested, those written by Irishmen and those which, though written by foreigners, contain copies of Irish documents or of sources having some relation to Ireland. The second class is, in general, simply part of the mass of European manuscripts and has no corporate Irish history. There is, however, such a history attached to many of the collections of codices of strictly Irish origin.

Irish manuscripts are to be found in almost all the great European collections of early mediaeval written books. The Irish monks must have left their books in the monasteries and churches here and there

[354] Dublin and London 1910.
[355] *Cf. RC* XXXVII iv (1917–19) 418–9. Dr. Hogan's fruitful services to both history and linguistics during more than a quarter of a century preceding the founding of the National University demand special recognition. [356] *Cf.* p. 96 *infra.* [357] *Cf.* p. 92 *infra.*
[358] *Studies* XIII, June 1924, pp. 177–200, contains a proposal by Eóin MacNeill.— with discussion by others — that the celebration in 1932 of the fifteenth centenary of the coming of St. Patrick include the creation of a permanent foundation for the publication of the *Monumenta Hiberniae*, the historical records of Ireland.

through all those parts of western Europe which they frequented, and to a degree these books have shared the vicissitude of other mediaeval codices until the surviving remnants found themselves in the present great depositories. The fate of the Irish codices was undoubtedly a little harder than that of others: being written in insular script and frequently glossed with notes in the Irish language, both of which were either obscure or unintelligible to the later middle ages, they were much more likely to be cut up for book-bindings or otherwise destroyed.[359]

Of the monastic libraries the richest in Irish materials were, as has been said, those of the famous monasteries of Bobbio, St. Gall and Reichenau. A large proportion of the very early writings of Irish origin which we have to-day are known to have belonged to one or other of these three houses.

The library of Bobbio, an especially rich quarry for the humanists of the fifteenth and later centuries, has been entirely scattered.[360] The following are the principal depôts which are known to contain Bobbio manuscripts: (1) The Biblioteca Ambrosiana at Milan, for which its founder, Cardinal Federico Borromeo, about 1606 obtained from Bobbio some eighty-six volumes. (2) The Vatican Library in Rome: in 1618, under Pope Paul V, it received a collection of books from Bobbio that now forms nos. 5748-5776 of the *Codices Vaticani Latini*. (3) The Biblioteca Nazionale of the University of Turin, where were gathered seventy-one volumes, the residuum of the library of Bobbio. Unfortunately these were destroyed or seriously damaged in the fire at the university on January 26, 1904.[361] (4) The royal library at Turin contains a few items from Bobbio. (5) In the Biblioteca Nazionale at Naples there are also a small number of Bobbio codices.

[359] There is no recent and comprehensive study of the Irish MSS in Europe. See Walther Schultze in *Centralblatt für Bibliothekswesen*, July 1889, pp. 287-96; Mario Esposito "Hiberno-Latin Manuscripts in the libraries of Switzerland," *Proc. RIA* XXVIII C iii (1910), XXX C i (1912).

[360] *Cf.* A. Peyron *M. Tulli Ciceronis orationum . . . fragmenta inedita* (Turin and Stuttgart 1824; also Leipsic 1825) pp. iii-xxvii "De bibliotheca Bobiensi commentatio," also pp. 1-62; A. Reifferscheid *Bibliotheca patrum latinorum Italica* I (1865) 415 *sqq*, II (1871) 3-139, 298 *sqq*; Th. Gottlieb "Über Handschriften aus Bobbio" *Centralblatt für Bibliothekswesen* IV (1887) 142-463, 568; O. von Gebhardt "Ein Bücherfund in Bobbio" *ibid.* V (1888) 343-64, 383-431, 538; O. Seebass "Handschriften von Bobbio in den vatikanischen und ambrosianischen Bibliotheken" *ibid.* XIII (1896) 1 *sqq*, 57 *sqq*; A. Ratti *Le ultime vicende della Biblioteca e dell' Archivio di S. Columbano* (Milan 1901); A. Wilmart "Bobbio (Manuscrits de)" *Dict. d'archéol. chrét. et de liturgie* II pt. I (1910) 935-9; R. Beer "Bemerkungen über den ältesten Handschriftenbestand des Klosters Bobbio" *Sitzungsb. d. k. Akad. d. Wissensch. in Wien* philos.-hist. Cl. 1911 no. xi.

[361] G. Ottino *I Codici Bobbiesi della Biblioteca nazionale di Torino* (Turin 1890); G. de Sanctis, C. Cipolla, C. Frasi "Inventario dei codici superstiti greci e latini antichi della Biblioteca nazionale di Torino," *Rivista di filol.* XXXII (1904) 385 *sqq*; I. Quareschi *Della pergamena con osservazioni ed esperienze sul ricupero e sul ristauro di codici danneggiati negli incendi e notize storiche* (1905); C. Cipolla *Codici Bobbiesi della Biblioteca nazionale di Torino con illustrazione: Collezione paleografica Bobbiese* (Milan 1907 — in progress). See also Léon Dorez "L'Incendie de la bibliothèque nationale de Turin" *Rev. des. bibliothèques* Jan.-April 1904; C. Bourgin "L'Incendie de la bibliothèque nationale et universitaire de Turin" *Bibl. de l'école des chartes* Jan.-June 1904.

(6) Several Naples manuscripts, long in the Hof-bibliothek, Vienna, were returned after the World War. (7) The Doria-Pamphili collection at Rome. (8) In the Bibliothèque Nationale, Paris, there are two manuscripts which the French scholar, Mabillon, carried off from Bobbio in 1686. (9) There are said to be Bobbio codices in the libraries at Florence, at Wolfenbüttel, and in the Escurial, Madrid.

The monastery of St. Gall and its library were fully as famous as those of Bobbio. In St. Gall, however, the monastic library, or Stifts-bibliothek, still exists as a distinct institution, although the monastery was suppressed in 1798.[362] This library, though it contains some 1725 manuscript volumes, of which a large number date from the early middle ages, is far from representing the old abbey collection in its integrity. That collection suffered heavy losses at the hands of the theologians who attended the Councils of Constance (1414-1418) and Basel (1431-1443), of the Italian humanists, who obtained access to the library about the same time and carried off many rare classical manuscripts, and of the Calvinist forces in the religious wars, not only in the sixteenth century but especially in 1712, when most of the manuscripts were taken to Zürich, Berne and other places, whence only a portion of them was recovered.

The monastery of Reichenau was closed in 1757 and its property was secularised in 1802. The bulk of the manuscripts were removed to the Hof- und Landesbibliothek at Carlsruhe, where they now form a very valuable collection.[363] A considerable number, however, had been scattered — some were carried off by the last monks who occupied the institution — and the librarian, Alfred Holder, states that there are Reichenau manuscripts at Heidelberg, Donaueschingen, Cologne, Munich, Stuttgart, Trèves, Wolfenbüttel, St. Paul in Carinthia, Vienna, Einsiedeln, Engelberg, St. Gall, Schaffhausen, Zürich, Rome, Paris, Brussels, Leyden, London, Oxford, Cambridge, and in the Phillipps collection at Cheltenham.[364]

Perhaps some of the *Schottenklöster*, or Irish monasteries, established in southern Germany in the tenth, eleventh and twelfth centuries, may have had libraries of Irish books represented now by a few volumes in the German university libraries, in the Vatican, and elsewhere. But the next important library of Irish manuscripts, situated on the Continent of Europe, of which we have definite knowledge, was that which the Irish Franciscans, Ward, Colgan, O'Clery and their confrères, col-

[362] *Cf.* the works by Weidmann, Hogan, Clark and Scherrer noticed p. 594 *infra*.
[363] There is an excellent catalogue by Alfred Holder, *Die Reichenauer Handschriften* vols. I–III (Leipsic 1906, 1914, 1918) [sect. V–VII of *Die Handschriften der grossherzoglich badischen Hof- und Landesbibliothek in Karlsruhe*]. Holder died Jan. 12, 1916, and the third vol. was completed by Karl Preisandanz.
[364] *Ibid.* I p. viii.

lected in the college of St. Anthony at Louvain in the first half of the seventeenth century. This collection remained at Louvain until 1797, when, following the occupation of the Netherlands by the forces of revolutionary France, the college of St. Anthony was suppressed. We do not know the story of the library's vicissitudes during the next few years, but they must have been somewhat similar to those of the library of the Bollandists at Tongerloo.[365] It seems certain that a considerable number of codices were lost or destroyed. But when the revival of Irish historical interests led, in the second quarter of the nineteenth century, to investigation it was found that one part of the Louvain library — presumably the volumes which the Franciscans succeeded in removing from the Netherlands at the time of the French invasion — was in the old Irish Franciscan college of St. Isidore in Rome, and another part was at Brussels in the Burgundian Library, now the Bibliothèque royale, where it still remains.[366] In 1872, after the annexation of Rome to the kingdom of Italy, the manuscripts at St. Isidore's were brought back to Ireland and deposited in the Franciscan Convent on Merchants Quay, Dublin.[367]

In Ireland itself fate decreed that practically none of the collections of the old Irish monasteries, or of the religious houses of the later middle ages, or of the secular learned families, should survive in Irish hands. It is to the foreigner who happened to take an interest in Irish antiquities that we owe the preservation of the bulk of our manuscripts.

The first of these of note was George Carew, Earl of Totnes (1555–1629), President of Munster from 1600 to 1603, and, like his brother, Sir Peter, an obnoxious representative of the Elizabethan conquerors. He made a gift, or bequest, of five codices to Trinity College, Dublin, and thereby laid the foundation of what is to-day, for the historian, perhaps the most important of Irish manuscript libraries. The bulk of Carew's manuscripts passed to Sir Thomas Stafford, who edited his *Pacata Hibernia*, and from him to Archbishop Laud, and are now either in the Lambeth library or in the Laud collection in the Bodleian. Trinity received a much larger accession in the library of Archbishop

---

[365] Cf. Ch. De Smedt "Bollandists" *Cath. Encycl.*; H. Delehaye *A travers trois siècles L'Oeuvre des Bollandistes* (Brussels 1920) 179 *sqq.*

[366] S. H. Bindon "On the Manuscripts relating to Ireland in the Burgundian Library at Brussels" *Proc. RIA* III (1844) 477–502; O'C *MS Mat.* 644–8; WS "Notes of a Philological Tour III Belgium" *Academy* XXX (1886) 246–7; KM "Irish MSS at Brussels" *ibid.* XLIV (1893) 298–9, 324. There is a good catalogue of the Bibliothèque royale by J. Van den Gheyn, *Catalogue des manuscrits de la Bibliothèque royale de Belgique:* the Irish manuscripts are treated in the following volumes: I "Ecriture sainte et liturgie" (Brussels 1901) 318–21 [martyrologies]; V "Histoire-Hagiographie" (1905) 381–9 [Lives of saints in Irish, by V. Tourneur]; VII "Histoire des Pays" (1907) 45–50 [Ireland].

[367] John T. Gilbert "The Manuscripts of the former college of Irish Franciscans, Louvain" *Fourth Report of the Royal Commission on Historical Manuscripts* Pt. I (London 1874) 599–613 [this catalogue is brief, incomplete, and not entirely accurate].

Ussher. Among the Irish volumes were, it is reasonably certain, the Book of Kells, the Book of Durrow, Codex Usserianus I, the Garland of Howth, the Trinity Liber Hymnorum, the Book of Ballymote and the Great Book of Lecan.[368] This library, after some strange vicissitudes, was purchased for Trinity in 1657 by the officers and men of Cromwell's army in Ireland and was placed in the college in 1666.[369]

It was to the next great Anglo-Irish scholar, Sir James Ware, and to his co-worker, An Dubhaltach Mac Fir-Bhisigh, that the Irish collections in the British Museum and in the Bodleian Library, Oxford, ultimately owe their beginnings. Ware's own library was large and important, but to it was added the far more valuable collection of Mac Fir-Bhisigh, who, it is said, left the majority of his manuscripts with Ware's son when he returned to Sligo after his patron's death, and did not live to reclaim them. In 1786 this son, Robert Ware, sold all the manuscripts to the Earl of Clarendon, then Lord Lieutenant of Ireland. From Clarendon they passed, on his death, to the great collection of the Duke of Chandos, a collection which, after the death of the Duke, was again, in 1746, scattered by public auction. Dr. Milles, Dean of Exeter, purchased a large number and deposited them in the British Museum, where they form the Clarendon collection. Another extensive section, including several of the most valuable Irish codices, was acquired by Dr. Rawlinson, who bequeathed them to St. John's College, Oxford. Thence — as the Rawlinson collection — they were transferred to the Bodleian. The subsequent history of other codices, sold in smaller lots, has not been traced.

In England the famous collector Sir Robert Cotton (1570–1631) picked up many Irish items, chiefly Latin documents, in company with his other acquisitions from the scattered remains of the monastic libraries. In 1731 the Cottonian collection suffered severely from fire. About this time what is now the Harleian collection in the British Museum was being gathered together by Robert Harley, Earl of Oxford, and his son. They secured many Irish items, including part of the Stafford collection and one important volume which had been stolen from the king's library, Paris, by Jean Aymon.[370]

[368] The Great Book of Lecan was removed to France at or about the time of the Williamite invasion, and subsequently placed in the Irish College at Paris. The Book of Ballymote was lost from Trinity between 1720 and 1742. Both these books are now in the RIA.

[369] Ussher's library was in Drogheda during the siege of 1641; was removed to Chester, and in 1643 to Chelsea College; was confiscated by the English House of Commons, but later restored, less some volumes lost; was with Ussher in London 1647–1656; was removed to Dublin after its purchase, but detained in Dublin Castle by Cromwell's orders; and was finally assigned to Trinity by the Irish House of Commons in 1661. Cf. Urwick Early History of Trinity College (London 1892) 90; The Book of Trinity College, Dublin (Belfast 1892) 148–51; H. J. Lawlor Proc. RIA ser. III vol. VI (1900) 216–64.

[370] BM Harl. 1802.

A large number of very valuable Irish manuscripts were acquired by Edward Lhuyd during his Celtic investigations. These were purchased after his death by Sir John Sebright, whose heir, Sir Thomas, presented them, and others, to Trinity College, Dublin, in 1786. They form the most important group among the "Irish" manuscripts of that Library: among them are the two great codices, the Book of Leinster and the Yellow Book of Lecan. Other eighteenth century accessions to Trinity were the manuscripts of John Stearne, Bishop of Clogher; those of Dr. Francis Stoughton Sullivan; several of the more valuable of those which had belonged to Dr. John Fergus; and also several from the collection of Col. Vallancey. During the nineteenth century the library of Trinity acquired many individual manuscripts, chiefly through the initiative of Dr. Todd. Noteworthy were the Book of Dimma, purchased from Sir William Betham in 1836, and the Book of Armagh, purchased in 1854 from Dr. Reeves. The Book of Mulling had been placed in the library towards the end of the eighteenth century by its last owner, Kavanagh of Borris Idrone.[371]

The other principal manuscript library in Ireland is that of the Royal Irish Academy. It naturally contains a larger proportion of items which are modern in both date and subject-matter. The Academy acquired, during the nineteenth century, all or the larger portion of the collections of Edward O'Reilly, Sir William Betham, and the Dublin book-dealers Hodges and Smith (which included the library of the Chevalier O'Gorman). On historical grounds the most important acquisition, however, was the Stowe collection. This consisted of the greater part of the manuscripts of Charles O'Conor of Belanagare, which had been taken to Stowe by Dr. Charles O'Conor when he became librarian. In 1849 all the Stowe manuscripts were offered for sale by auction, but before the day of the sale they were purchased by the Earl of Ashburnham by private contract. In 1883 they were acquired by the British government, which deposited the Irish manuscripts in the library of the Royal Irish Academy and the others in the British Museum.[372] Important individual acquisitions by the Academy include

---

[371] The librarian, Dr. T. K. Abbott, published a *Catalogue of the manuscripts in the library of Trinity College, Dublin* (Dublin and London 1900). The treatment of the Latin MSS appears somewhat superficial, and has been severely criticised by Mario Esposito (*Rev. des bibliothèques* XXIII (1913) 374). The sections on the Irish MSS, based on a text prepared by O'D, have been superseded by the *Catalogue of the Irish manuscripts in the library of Trinity College, Dublin* (Dublin and London 1921), begun by Dr. Abbott and completed by E. J. Gwynn. There is a short description of the library, by Sir J. T. Gilbert, in *4th Report Hist. MSS Comm.*, but it is now of little interest.

[372] There are three catalogues of the Stowe collection: Dr. Chas. O'Conor *Bibliotheca MS. Stowensis A descriptive catalogue of the manuscripts in the Stowe Library* I (Buckingham 1818) (pt. II Irish MSS pp. 21–232, and index); *Catalogue of the important collection of manuscripts from Stowe, which will be sold by auction by Messrs. S. Leigh Sotheby and Co. — on Monday, 11th of June, 1849 —* (London 1849); *Eighth*

the Book of Ballymote, presented by the Chevalier O'Gorman in 1785; the Great Book of Lecan, presented in 1787 by the Irish College in Paris; the Leabhar Breac, purchased in 1789 from its owner; the O'Gara presentation copy of the Annals of the Four Masters — once in the possession of Charles O'Conor — received from George Petrie in 1831; the *Cathach* of St. Colum-cille, deposited in 1843; the *Domnach Airgid* manuscript, obtained in 1847; the Book of Fermoy, purchased by Dr. Todd at the sale of the collection of William Monck Mason in 1858; and the *Liber Flavus Fergusiorum*, deposited in 1875 by its owner, who had inherited it from the daughter of Dr. John Fergus.[373]

In Great Britain the most important collections of manuscripts of "early Irish" interest are in the British Museum, London, the Bodleian Library, Oxford, and the National Library of Scotland, Edinburgh. Mention has already been made of the Cottonian, Clarendon and Harleian collections in the British Museum; scattered through the other collections also are many codices of Irish origin or association.[374] The Bodleian contains a few such in addition to those of the Laud and the Rawlinson series.[375] Because of the ancient cultural relationships of the two countries, the Gaelic manuscripts of the National Library of Scotland, formerly known as the Advocates' Library, are of great importance for the history and literature of Ireland as well as for those of Scotland. The bulk of this collection was brought together in the middle and second half of the nineteenth century through the efforts of William F. Skene, who induced the Highland Society of London and several Scottish owners to deposit their Gaelic manuscripts in the Advocates' Library, to which he bequeathed his own collection.[376]

Report of the Royal Commission on Historical Manuscripts (1881) Appendix III 1–110, and index. None of them is quite satisfactory.

[373] In the library of RIA there are extensive MS catalogues and indices to the older portion of the collection, prepared by O'C, O'Longan and O'Beirne Crowe. Thos. F. O'Rahilly is preparing for publication a complete catalogue, of which a first fasciculus, 130 pp., has been issued (Dublin and London 1926).

[374] There is a *Catalogue of Irish Manuscripts in the British Museum*, vol. I by Standish H. O'Grady, vol. II by Robin Flower (London 1926). A third volume, containing general introduction and index, is promised. Pp. 1–672 of vol. I were printed off, and sold as loose sheets since 1892; it is this portion only that has been used throughout his work by the present writer. Older general catalogues are available for various collections, of which the following contain items of Irish interest: the King's, or Royal (1734), Cottonian (1802), Harleian (1808–12), Arundel and Burney (1834–40), Additional and Egerton (1843–).

[375] *Catalogi codicum manuscriptorum Bibliothecae Bodleianae* pt. II fasc. I, by H. O. Coxe (Oxford 1858) 432–3, 443; pt. V fasc. I, by W. D. Macray (1862) 695–734 (Ir. MSS of the Laud and Rawlinson collections). See also J. H. Todd "On the Irish MSS in the Bodleian Library, Oxford" *Proc. RIA* V (1851) 162–77. *A summary catalogue of western manuscripts in the Bodleian Library*, by F. Madan and H. H. E. Craster, is in course of publication.

[376] There is an excellent catalogue by Donald MacKinnon: *A descriptive catalogue of Gaelic manuscripts in the Advocates' Library, Edinburgh, and elsewhere in Scotland* (Edinburgh 1912). See also Chas. Graves "On Irish MSS in the possession of the Highland and Agricultural Soc. of Scotland" *Proc. RIA* IV (1847) 255–60; H. Gaidoz "Les manuscrits irlandais d'Édimbourg" *RC* VI (1883) 109–14; KM "The Irish MSS at Edinburgh" *Academy* XXVI (1884) 344.

GENERAL BIBLIOGRAPHY

1. Guides and Bibliographies

(a) WORKS ON GENERAL EUROPEAN HISTORY: Ernst Bernheim *Lehrbuch der historischen Methode und der Geschichtsphilosophie* 5th and 6th ed. (Leipsic 1908) [besides being the best treatise on historical method, contains valuable directions for the study of mediaeval history]. — L. J. Paetow *Guide to the study of medieval history for students, teachers and libraries* (Berkeley, California, 1917) [the best work of this kind, at least in English]. — August Potthast *Bibliotheca historica medii aevi — Wegweiser durch die Geschichtswerke des europäischen Mittelalters bis 1500* 2nd ed. 2 vols. (Berlin 1896) [the standard catalogue of mediaeval historical sources, with bibliographical references; so much material has appeared since 1896 that a new ed. is required]. — Ulysse Chevalier *Répertoire des sources historiques du moyen âge:* I *Bio-bibliographie* 2nd ed. 2 vols. (Paris 1905-7), II *Topo-bibliographie* 2 vols. (Montbéliard 1894-1903) [a great compilation, but needing careful revision]. — Adolf Ebert *Allgemeine Geschichte der Literatur des Mittelalters im Abendlande* 3 vols. (Leipsic 1874-87; 2nd ed., vol. I, 1889): Fr. trans. by J. Aymeric and J. Condamin, 3 vols. (Paris 1883-9) [extends to about A.D. 1000: an important treatise which, however, gives little attention to Irish literature]. — Max Manitius *Geschichte der lateinischen Literatur des Mittelalters* (*Handbuch der Klassischen Altertums-Wissenschaft*, edited by Iwan von Müller, Robert von Pöhlmann, Walter Otto, vol. IX pt. ii) 2 vols. (Munich 1911-23) [a most important and useful work, the first to give fair consideration to Hiberno-Latin writings]. — C. V. Langlois *Manuel de bibliographie historique* 2nd ed. (Paris 1901-4) [a good bibliography of bibliographies]. — *Jahresberichte der Geschichtswissenschaft im Auftrage der historischen Gesellschaft zu Berlin* 1878-1913 (Berlin 1880-1916) [an annual publication containing extensive and careful bibliographies of special topics and of countries: useful for continental history, but Ireland is almost entirely ignored]. — *Theologischer Jahresbericht* (Freiburg i. Br., Brunswick 1882-) [renders a similar service for ecclesiastical history].

(b) WORKS ON FRANCE AND GERMANY: Gabriel Monod *Bibliographie de l'histoire de France* (Paris 1888). — Auguste Molinier *Les sources de l'histoire de France* 6 vols. (Paris 1901-6) [vols. I–II cover the period to 1180, V contains a general introduction, and VI an index; this work and the following are descriptive and critical catalogues of the sources, many of which have Irish interests]. — Wilhelm Wattenbach *Deutschlands Geschichtsquellen im Mittelalter bis zur Mitte des dreizehnten Jahrhunderts* 7th ed. by Ernst Dümmler I (Stuttgart, Berlin 1904). — Dahlmann-Waitz *Quellenkunde der deutschen Geschichte* 8th ed. by Paul Heere (Leipsic 1912) [bibliographies; the mediaeval portion, by Hofmeister, is especially good].

(c) WORKS ON THE BRITISH ISLES: Thomas Duffus Hardy *Descriptive catalogue of materials relating to the history of Great Britain and Ireland to the end of the reign of Henry VII* 4 vols. (RS: London 1862-71) [the author had but little understanding of Irish history: the work has some value, especially for the MSS, the long synopses of some *vitae sanctorum*, and the lists of printed materials in the appendix to vol. I, including, *e.g.*, analyses of the contents of the rare works of Messingham and Colgan]. — Charles Gross *The sources and literature of English history from the earliest times to about 1485* 2nd ed. (London, etc. 1915) [includes Irish history, but inadequately, and with some errors].

(d) WORKS ON IRELAND — GENERAL: New York Public Library *List of works relating to Ireland, the Irish language and literature* (New York 1905).

(e) IRELAND — THE LATIN SOURCES: Mario Esposito "A bibliography of the Latin writers of mediaeval Ireland" *Studies* II (Dec. 1913) 495–521 [very important: there are preliminary studies in *Hermathena* XIV (1907) 519–29, XV (1909) 335–64, XVI (1910–1) 77–99, and in *The Irish Theological Quarterly* IV (1909) 57–65 (by Gougaud) and 181–5; *cf.* p. 82 *supra*].

(f) IRELAND — THE IRISH SOURCES: Edward O'Reilly "A chronological account of nearly four hundred Irish writers . . . . with a descriptive catalogue of such of their works as are still extant" *Trans. of the Iberno-Celtic Society for 1820* I pt. i [still of value, but must be controlled by later knowledge: *cf.* p. 60 *supra*]. — Eugene O'Curry *Lectures on the manuscript materials of ancient Irish history* (Dublin 1861; re-issue 1873) [uncritical, but containing much valuable information: *cf.* p. 67 *supra*]. — H. d'Arbois de Jubainville *Essai d'un catalogue de la littérature épique de l'Irlande précédé d'une étude sur les manuscrits en langue irlandaise conservés dans les Iles Britanniques et sur le continent* (Paris 1883) [valuable: *cf.* p. 76 *supra*; also KM "Addenda" *RC* VI (1883) 187–8; WS *Academy* XXIV (1883) 435–6; HZ *Göttingische gelehrte Anzeigen* 1887 pp. 153–99]. — Georges Dottin "Supplément à l'Essai d'un catalogue de la littérature épique de l'Irlande" *RC* XXXIII (1912) 1–40; "Notes bibliographiques sur l'ancienne littérature chrétienne de l'Irlande" *Rev. d'hist. et de litt. religieuses* V (1900) 162–7; "La littérature gaélique de l'Irlande" *Rev. de synthèse historique* III (1901) 60–97) [valuable summary: Eng. trans., privately printed, by Jos. Dunn, Washington, D. C.]. — Eleanor Hull *A Text Book of Irish literature* 2 vols. (Dublin 1906–8) [convenient treatise, with but little *apparatus criticus*]. — National Library of Ireland *Bibliography of Irish philology and of printed Irish literature* [by Richard Irvine Best] (Dublin 1913) [a book that is, above all, indispensable to the student of Irish history: *cf.* p. 84 *supra*].

(g) CATALOGUES OF MANUSCRIPTS: The works of Potthast, Hardy, O'C and AdeJ, noticed above, give much information regarding MSS. Whitley Stokes "Notes of a philological tour: I France, II Switzerland, III Belgium" *Academy* XXX (1886) 209–10, 227–8, 246–7 [*re* MSS containing Irish texts or glosses]. — Walther Schultze "Die Bedeutung der iroschottischen Mönche für die Erhaltung und Fortpflanzung der mittelalterlichen Wissenschaft 3. Irische Handschriften auf dem Continent" *Centralblatt für Bibliothekswesen* VI (July 1889) 281–98 [first attempt at a complete list — except as regards Vat. and BN — but with some omissions, and the inclusion of MSS not now regarded as Irish]. — Mario Esposito "Hiberno-Latin Manuscripts in the libraries of Switzerland" *Proc. RIA* XXVIII C. iii (1910) 62–95, XXX C. i (1912) 1–14 [MSS containing Hiberno-Latin texts]. — H. Omont "Catalogue des MSS celtiques et basques de la Bibliothèque nationale" *RC* XI (1890) 389–433. For other individual libraries, see pp. 84–90 *supra*.

2. Periodicals, Publications of Societies, etc.

The *Year-Book of the scientific and learned societies of Great Britain and Ireland* (London 1884–), and the *Bibliographie générale des travaux historiques et archéologiques publiés par les sociétés savantes de la France* (Paris 1888–1918) [to 1900; supplements to 1910].

(a) JOURNALS AND REVIEWS, GENERAL HISTORY: The *Revue Historique* (Paris 1876–), *Revue des questions historiques* (Paris 1866–), *Historische Zeitschrift* (Munich, Berlin 1859–), *English Historical Review* (London 1886–) and *American Historical Review* (New York 1895–) all maintain a high standard of scholarship, and treat extensively of general history as well as of that of their particular countries. *History* (London 1912–), a later and smaller publication, is of similar character. The *Revue critique d'histoire et de littérature* (Paris 1866–), *Revue de synthèse historique* (Paris 1900–), *Moyen Âge* (Paris 1888–), *Speculum, A Journal of mediaeval studies* (Cambridge, Mass. 1926–), and *Zeitschrift für deutsches Altertum und deutsche Litteratur* (Leipsic 1841–) are important but more specialised periodicals. The *Historisches Jahrbuch* (Munich 1880–) and *Historische Vierteljahrschrift* (Leipsic 1898–) have especial value because of the vast number of reviews or notices of publications which their pages contain; the *Neues Archiv der Gesellschaft für ältere deutsche Geschichtskunde* (Hanover, etc. 1876–) (in succession to the *Archiv*, 1820–74) has, besides reviews, specialised studies of problems in mediaeval history, a considerable number of which have in some way connection with Irish subjects; the *Bibliothèque de l'École des chartes* (Paris 1839–) gives particular attention to works on the technical side of history — palaeography, chronology, historical method, etc. — and to bibliography. The *Centralblatt für Bibliothekswesen* (Leipsic 1884–) and *Revue des bibliothèques* (Paris 1890–) are important for the history and location of manuscripts. Mythology, popular literature, folk-lore, etc., are treated in *Mélusine* (Paris 1878–1901) (*cf.* p. 71 *supra*) and *Folk-lore* (London 1890–). Since the establishment of a chair of Celtic at Berlin the *Sitzungsberichte der [königlich] preussischen Akademie der Wissenschaften* have contained many papers relating to Ireland.

(b) RELIGIOUS AND ECCLESIASTICAL — GENERAL: The most important for general church history are the *Zeitschrift für Kirchengeschichte* (Gotha 1877–) and the *Revue d'histoire ecclésiastique* (Louvain 1900–); the latter is particularly useful because of its extensive bibliographies, reviews, and chronicle of historical news. Excellent bibliographical articles appear from time to time in the *Theologische Rundschau* (Tübingen, Leipsic 1897–). The *Revue de l'histoire de religions* (Paris 1880–), *Revue d'histoire et de littérature religieuses* (Paris 1896–), *Revue Bénédictine* (Abbaye de Maredsous, Belgium 1884–), *Journal of Theological Studies* (Oxford 1899–), and *Dublin Review* (Dublin, London 1836–) — this last a Catholic more than an Irish publication — will also be found of interest.

(c) PHILOLOGY — GENERAL: *Zeitschrift für vergleichende Sprachforschung* (Berlin 1852–). — *Beiträge zur Kunde der indogermanischen Sprachen* (Göttingen 1877–1907; then amalgamated with preceding). — *Indogermanische Forschungen* (Strasburg, Berlin, Leipsic, 1892–). — *Transactions of the Philological Society, London* (1859–). — *The American Journal of Philology* (Baltimore 1880–).

(d) CELTICA; SCOTLAND; WALES; BRITTANY: The most important periodical is the *Revue Celtique* (Paris 1870–) [*cf.* p. 71 *supra*]. Of equally high scholarship, but less useful as a guide to contemporary literature, is the *Zeitschrift für celtische Philologie* (Halle a. S. 1897–) [*cf.* p. 71 *supra*]. — *Archiv für celtische Lexicographie* (Halle a. S. 1898–1907) [*cf.* p. 71 *supra*]. — *Scottish Historical Review* (Glasgow 1903–1928).— *Proceedings of the Society of Antiquaries of Scotland* (1852–). — *Celtic Magazine* (Inverness 1876–88). — *Celtic Review* (Edinburgh 1904–1916). — *Archaeologia Cambrensis* (London 1846–). — *Y Cymmrodor* (London 1877–). — *Trans. of the Hon. Soc. of Cymmrodorion* (London 1894–). — *Revue de Bretagne* (Nantes 1857–). — *Annales de Bretagne* (Rennes 1886–).

(e) IRELAND: *The Ulster Journal of Archaeology* (Belfast 1853–62, 1896–1915). — *Studies An Irish Quarterly Review* (Dublin 1912–) [devoted to all fields of scholarship: *cf.* p. 84 *supra*]. — *Ériu The Journal of the School of Irish Learning, Dublin* (Dublin 1904–) [treats of Irish philology and literature, and only incidentally of history; maintains a high standard; has no reviews or news notes: *cf.* p. 72 *supra*]. — *The Irish Ecclesiastical Record* (Dublin 1865–) has published much material, both primary and secondary, for the early history of Ireland. — *The Gaelic Journal Irisleabhar na Gaedhilge* (Dublin 1882–1909), although devoted mainly to language topics and contemporary affairs, occasionally included matter of interest on early history. — The Royal Irish Academy [*cf.* pp. 59, 65 *supra*] has two chief series of publications, the *Transactions* (Dublin 1786–1907) and the *Proceedings* (1836–): both contain a large quantity of Irish historical matter. In the "Irish Manuscript Series" there is one issue (1880) in the *Transactions* and two (1889, 1890) in the *Proceedings*. There is also the "Todd Lecture Series," vols. I–XI, XIII–XVII (1889–1924), almost entirely composed of editions of Irish texts. — There are 22 vols. of publications of the Irish Archaeological Society [after 1853 the Irish Archaeological and Celtic Society] (Dublin 1841–80); 6 of the Celtic Society (Dublin 1847–55) [merged with the preceding in 1853]; and 6 of the Ossianic Society (Dublin 1854–61) [*cf.* pp. 64–5 *supra*]. — The *Journal of the Royal Society of Antiquaries of Ireland* (Dublin 1890–) was originally (1849) the *Transactions of the Kilkenny Archaeological Society*, next the *Proceedings and Transactions*, and, later, the *Journal, of the Kilkenny and South-East of Ireland Archaeological Society;* and afterwards (1868) the *Journal of the* [1869–89 *Royal*] *Historical and Archaeological Association of Ireland*. This body has also published several separate works. [*Cf.* p. 65 *supra*.] — The publications of the Irish Texts Society (London 1899–) [*cf.* p. 81 *supra*]. — *Archivium Hibernicum or Irish Historical Records* (Maynooth, Dublin 1912–), chiefly, but not exclusively, sources for the history of the Catholic Church in Ireland. — There are also a large number of local archaeological and historical societies, whose publications occasionally contain articles of more than provincial interest. Noteworthy are the *Journals* of the Co. Louth Archaeological Society (Dundalk 1904–); the Waterford and South-East of Ireland Archaeological Society (Waterford 1895–); the Cork Archaeological Society (Cork 1892–); the Ivernian Society (Cork 1908–); the North Munster Archaeological Society (1908–) [earlier the Limerick Field Club (Limerick 1897–1908)]; the Galway Archaeological and Historical Society (Dublin 1900–).

3. Auxiliary Sciences — Philology

The study of language has two interests for the historian: first, it provides him with the instrument for deciphering certain historical records; and, secondly, in itself it provides him with historical records, for the speech of a people and the evidence of its evolution constitute veritable sources for the history of that people. From both these points of view interest will be found in these three books: A. Meillet *Linguistique historique et linguistique générale* (Paris 1921); Jos. Vendryes *Le langage Introduction linguistique à l'histoire* (Paris 1921); and Edward Sapir *Language An introduction to the study of speech* (New York 1921). — See sect. 2 above for periodicals; also Best's *Bibliography* for fuller lists up to 1913.

(a) INDO-EUROPEAN PHILOLOGY: The best treatise on the general structure of the Indo-European languages is the second edition, brought out with the collaboration of Berthold Delbrück, of Karl Brugmann's *Grundriss der vergleichenden Grammatik der indogermanischen Sprachen* (Strasburg 1897–1916). Of the first ed. (1886–93) there is a trans. by Jos. Wright, R. Seymour Conway and W. H. D. Rouse, *Elements of the comparative grammar of the Indo-Germanic languages* 5 vols. (London 1891–5), but the second ed. of the original is preferable [*cf.* p. 73 *supra*]. A. Meillet's *Introduction à l'étude comparative des langues indo-européennes* (Paris 1903; 6th ed. 1924) and *Les dialectes indo-européens* (Paris 1908) should also be consulted. — For the evidence as to primitive vocabularies, see August Fick's *Vergleichendes Wörterbuch der indogermanischen Sprachen*, 4th ed. by Adalbert Bezzenberger, A. Fick and Whitley Stokes (Göttingen 1894): Part II is the *Urkeltischer Sprachschatz* of Whitley Stokes, trans. by Bezzenberger: there are additions and corrections by WS, *Beiträge zur Kunde der indogermanischen Sprachen* XXI (1896) 122–37, XXIII (1897) 41–65, 321; and by J. Loth, *RC* XVII (1896) 434–43, XVIII (1897) 89–99, XX (1899) 344–55 [*cf.* p. 74 *supra*].

(b) LATIN: Interesting essays on some aspects of mediaeval Latin philology are contained in the following publications: Ludwig Traube (ed. Franz Boll) *Vorlesungen und Abhandlungen* II: *Einleitung in die lateinische Philologie des Mittelalters*, ed. Paul Lehmann (Munich 1911); Paul Lehmann *Vom Mittelalter und von der lateinischen Philologie des Mittelalters* (*Quellen u. Untersuchungen z. lat. Philol. d. Mittelalters* V i (Munich 1914); "Aufgaben und Anregungen der lateinischen Philologie des Mittelalters" *Sitzungsberichte d. bay. Akad. d. Wissensch. philos.-philol. u. hist. Kl.* 1918 no. viii. There is no good dictionary of mediaeval Latin, but a very valuable glossary of peculiar and technical terms is that of Du Cange, *Glossarium mediæ et infimae Latinitatis* 3 vols. (Paris 1678); ed. by the Benedictines and Pierre Carpentier, 10 vols. (Paris 1733–66); by G. A. L. Henschel, 7 vols. (Paris 1840–50) [best ed.]; and by Léopold Fabre, 10 vols. (Niort 1883–7). An international committee with headquarters in Paris has undertaken the preparation of a mediaeval Latin dictionary, and, in connection with the preliminary work, is publishing a periodical, the *Bulletin Du Cange* (Paris 1924–).

(c) CELTIC: Johann Kaspar Zeuss *Grammatica Celtica: e monumentis vetustis tam Hibernicae linguae quam Britannicae dialecti Cambricae Cornicae Armoricae nec non e Gallicae priscae reliquiis* 2 vols. (Leipsic 1853); 2nd ed. by H. Ebel (Berlin 1871) [*cf.* p. 70 *supra*]. — Ernst Windisch, "Keltische Sprachen" *Allgemeine Encyklopädie der Wissenschaften und Künste*, by J. S. Ersch and J. G. Gruber (ed. August Leskien), 2nd sect. XXXV (Leipsic 1884) 132–80 [*cf*. p. 71 n. *supra*]; anda nother article with the same title in G. Gröber's *Grundriss der romanischen Philologie* I (Strasburg 1888) 283–312, 2nd ed. (1904) 371–404. — Henri d'Arbois de Jubainville's *Eléments de la grammaire celtique* (Paris 1903) is a brief, clear and simple exposition, but deals with Old Irish much more than with primitive Celtic. — The standard work of reference is Holger Pedersen *Vergleichende Grammatik der keltischen Sprachen* 2 vols. (Göttingen 1909, 1913) [*cf*. p. 73 *supra*]. — Georges Dottin *La langue gauloise* (Paris 1920), although limited geographically to France, is the best survey of the ancient continental Celtic [*cf*. J. Vendryes *RC* XXXVIII (1920–1) 179–85; J. Loth *Revue archéologique* XIII 108–19]. — Alfred Holder *Altceltischer Sprachschatz* 21 parts, in 2 vols. and 5 extra sections (Leipsic 1896–1913): this work of vast and painstaking labor was designed to give all ancient and early mediaeval occurrences of Celtic words, and words of whose Celtic origin there is even a possibility: with the *Urkeltischer Sprachschatz* of WS and the vocabulary of Gaulish given by Dottin it provides a very complete survey of Celtic words.

(d) IRISH: John Strachan *Old-Irish Paradigms* (Dublin 1905, 2nd ed. 1909). — Jos. Vendryes *Grammaire du vieil irlandais* (Paris 1908) [especially valuable for syntax; *cf*. HZ *Deutsche Literaturzeitung* XXX (1909) 289–94; O. J. Bergin *ZCP* VII (1910) 512–6]. — Rudolph Thurneysen *Handbuch des Alt-Irischen* 2 parts (Heidelberg 1909) [the most important work on O-I grammar: *cf*. J. Vendryes *RC* XXXI (1910) 100–4; H. Pedersen *Göttingische gelehrte Anzeigen* Jahrg. CLXXIV i (1912) 19–48]. — F. W. O'Connell *A Grammar of Old Irish* (Belfast 1912) [*cf*. J. Pokorny *ZCP* X (1915) 449–52]. — Julius Pokorny *A concise Old Irish Grammar and Reader* pt. I [all published] (Halle a. S. and Dublin 1914) [*cf*. *RC* XXXIV (1913) 237–9, XXXV (1914) 247–8]; *A Historical Reader of Old Irish* (Halle 1923); and *Altirische Grammatik (Sammlung Göschen)* (Berlin and Leipsic 1925). — G. Dottin *Manuel d'irlandais moyen* 2 vols. (Paris 1913) [*cf*. J. Vendryes *RC* XXXV (1914) 92–6. On all these works *cf*. pp. 72–3 *supra*. Pokorny's *Reader* will afford to the student who is not a specialist in linguistics a convenient survey of the historical development of O-I.] — There is no dictionary of Old or Middle Irish; the student has to do as best he may with several incomplete compilations, the glossaries added to various published texts, and a few dictionaries of the modern language: Edward O'Reilly (ed. John O'Donovan) *An Irish-English Dictionary* new ed., with supplement (Dublin 1864) [an uncritical gathering of middle and modern Irish words and forms; *cf*. p. 60 *supra*]. — Rev. Patrick S. Dinneen *Foclóir Gaedhilge agus Béarla An Irish-English Dictionary* (Dublin 1904; new ed. in the press) [the best dictionary of modern Irish]. — Ernst Windisch *Irische Texte mit Wörterbuch* [vol. I] (Leipsic 1880). — B. Guterbock, R. Thurneysen *Indices glossarum et vocabulorum Hibernicorum quae in Grammaticae Celticae editione altera explanantur* (Leipsic 1881) [a very useful glossarial index to Z²]. — Robt. Atkinson *The Passions and the Homilies from Leabhar Breac . . . and glossary* (RIA Todd Lecture Ser. II) (Dublin 1887) [this work has been severely criticised — *cf*. p. 740 *infra* — nevertheless it is a helpful compilation]. — Graziadio I. Ascoli *Il Codice Irlandese dell' Ambrosiana*: III *Illustrazioni* a *Glossario dell' antico Irlandese* (Turin 1888–1907) [incomplete]. — Kuno Meyer " Contributions to Irish lexicography " Supplement to *ACL* I–III (1898–1907) [covers words with initial letters A–Dn]. — *Dictionary of the Irish language based mainly on Old and Middle Irish materials Published by the Royal Irish Academy under the editorship of* Carl J. S. Marstrander, fasc. I (Dublin 1913) [*D — Degóir*]. — On these books see pp. 73–4 *supra*.

4. Auxiliary Sciences — Palaeography and Diplomatics

There are three classes of evidence by which Irish writing of the mediaeval period may be distinguished: (i) palaeography proper, the manner in which the letters are formed and are joined to each other; (ii) abbreviations; (iii) orthography of Latin words. It is only with regard to abbreviations that, thanks chiefly to Traube and Lindsay, a good foundation has been laid for the study of Irish script of the early middle ages. On the palaeography of the codices written in Irish in the later middle ages practically nothing has been done. Some of the older grammars contain lists of scribal abbreviations, for the most part inherited from the Hiberno-Latin *scriptoria* of the earlier period.

(a) PALAEOGRAPHY, GENERAL: R. L. Poole "The teaching of palaeography and diplomatic" in *Essays on the teaching of history* (Cambridge 1901) 11–30 [a good introduction].—Hubert Nelis *L'Écriture et les scribes* (Brussels 1918) [a bibliography of palaeography]. — Wilhelm Wattenbach *Das Schriftwesen im Mittelalter* (Leipsic 1871; 4th ed. 1904). — Lecoy de la Marche "L'art d'écrire et les calligraphes" *Rev. des quest. hist.* 1884. — Paoli Cesare *Programma scolastico di paleografia latina e di diplomatica* (Florence 1883–98). — Maurice Prou *Manuel de paléographie* (Paris 1890; 4th ed. 1924). — E. H. J. Reusens *Eléments de paléographie* (Louvain 1891; new ed. 1899). — Ludwig Traube *Nomina sacra Versuch einer Geschichte der christlichen Kurzung (Quellen u. Untersuchungen z. lat. Philol. d. Mittelalters* II) (Munich 1907) [intended to be the first vol. of a history of Latin abbreviations, but this part only was completed, and that by a race against death]; (ed. Franz Boll, *Vorlesungen und Abhandlungen* I:) *Zur Paläographie und Handschriftenkunde*, ed. Paul Lehmann (Munich 1909) [a history of palaeography, of MSS and of libraries]. — Franz Steffens *Lateinische Paläographie*, 2nd ed. (Trèves 1909) [Fr. trans. by Remi Coulon, *Paléographie latine* (Trèves 1910)]. — B. Bretholz *Lateinische Paläographie* 2nd ed. (Leipsic 1912). — E. M. Thompson *An introduction to Greek and Latin palaeography* (Oxford 1912) [an enlarged ed. of his *Handbook of Greek and Latin palaeography*, first published in 1893; there is a short section on Irish writing]. — Adriano Cappelli *Lexicon abbreviaturarum* (Milan 1899; revised ed. 1912). — W. M. Lindsay *Notae Latinae An account of abbreviations in Latin MSS. of the early minuscule period (c. 700–850)* (Cambridge 1914) [a monumental work, based on an examination of every minuscule MS recognised as of the eighth cent., and of a large number of the first half of the ninth: adequate attention is given to Irish MSS]. — A. Mentz *Geschichte der griechisch-römischen Schrift bis zur Erfindung des Buchdrucks* (Leipsic 1920). — Luigi Schiaparelli *La scrittura latina nell' età romana (Note paleografiche) Avviamento allo studio della scrittura latina nel medioevo* (Como 1921) [valuable: is really a systematic re-editing of Paoli Cesare's book]; *Avviamento allo studio delle abbreviature latine nel medioevo* (Florence 1926). — All these works give some notice to Irish script, or at least to the Anglo-Saxon and continental scripts which were formed under its influence.

(b) PALAEOGRAPHY, IRISH: Ludwig Traube *Perrona Scottorum Ein Beitrag zur Ueberlieferungsgeschichte und zur Palaeographie des Mittelalters* (Munich 1900); also in *Sitzungsb. d. philos.-philol. u. d. hist. Cl. d. kgl. bayer. Akad. d. Wissensch.* 1900 Heft IV, and, with the exception of the study of the abbreviations of *noster*, in Franz Boll's *Vorlesungen und Abhandlungen von Ludwig Traube* III (ed. S. Brandt) (Munich 1920) 96–119 [important: has notes on the history of Irish palaeography]. — W. M.

Lindsay "The Bobbio scriptorium: its early minuscule abbreviations" *Centralblatt für Bibliothekswesen* XXVI (1909) 293–306; *Early Irish minuscule script* (*St. Andrews University publications* VI) (Oxford 1910) [very important]; "Irish cursive script" *ZCP* IX (1913) 301–8, 2 pls. — Luigi Schiaparelli "Note paleografiche Intorno all' origine e ad alcuni caratteri della scrittura e del sistema abbreviativo irlandese" *Archivio Storico Italiano* anno LXXIV vol. II disp. 3a, 4a, 1916 (Florence 1917) pp. 3–126 [very important].

(c) ILLUMINATIONS: The illuminations of manuscripts belong primarily rather to the archaeological section of historical sources than to that of written records. But they also serve, like the script and the abbreviations, as valuable means of determining the provenance of the manuscripts. In this, as in other respects, Irish illumination is particularly important. — Waagen "Die Miniaturmalerei in Irland" *Deutsches Kunstblatt* 1850. — Ferdinand Keller "Bilder und Schriftzüge in den irischen Manuscripten der schweizerischen Bibliotheken" *Mittheilungen der antiquarischen Gesellschaft in Zürich* VII iii (Zürich 1851); trans. by W. Reeves "Early Irish Calligraphy — Illuminations and fac-similes from Irish manuscripts in the libraries of Switzerland" *UJA* VIII (1860) 210–30, 291–308 [important: with Z completed the vindication, begun by Dr. Chas. O'Conor, of Ireland's claim to MSS previously classed as Saxon [1]]. — W. Wattenbach *Zeitschrift für christliche Archäologie und Kunst* 1856 pp. 21–49. — J. O. Westwood "On the distinctive character of the various styles of ornamentation employed by the early British, Anglo-Saxon and Irish artists" *Archaeological Journal* X (London 1853) 275–301. — F. M. Unger "La miniature irlandaise, son origine et son développement" *RC* I (1870) 9–26. — Eugène Müntz "Recherches sur l'origine des ornements connus sous le nom d'entrelacs" *RC* III (1878) 243–5; "La miniature irlandaise et anglo-saxonne au IXe siècle" *Études iconographiques et archéologiques sur le moyen âge* (Paris 1887). — Margaret Stokes *Early Christian art in Ireland* (London 1887, reprint 1894) 6–52. — Franz Friedrich Leitschuh *Geschichte der karolingischen Malerei Ihr Bilderkreis und seine Quellen* (Berlin 1894). — Johan Adolf Bruun *An enquiry into the art of the illuminated manuscripts of the middle ages* pt. I *Celtic illuminated manuscripts* (Edinburgh 1897) [very valuable]. — Bernhard Salin *Die altgermanische Thierornamentik* (Stockholm 1904) chap. V "Die angelsächsische und die irländische Thierornamentik." — Leprieur "La peinture en Occident du Ve au Xe siècle en dehors de l'Italie" in André Michel *Histoire de l'art depuis les premiers temps chrétiens jusqu'à nos jours* I (Paris 1905). — J. Strzygowski in *Neue Jahrbücher für das klassische Alterthum, Geschichte und deutsche Literatur* Jahrg. VIII Heft i (1905); (trans. O. M. Dalton, H. J. Braunholtz) *The Origin of Christian Church Art New facts and principles of research* (Oxford, London 1923) [the author advances a new theory of the oriental, and especially Armenian, origin of western mediaeval, including Irish, art]. — J. Romilly Allen *Celtic Art in Pagan and Christian times* (London [1904]). — Stephan Beissel *Geschichte der Evangelienbücher in der ersten Hälfte des Mittelalters* (Freiburg i. B. 1906). — Baldwin Brown "Art (Celtic)" in Hastings *Encyclopaedia of Religion and Ethics* II (1909). — H. Leclercq "Celtique (Art)" *Dict. d'archéol. chrét. et de liturgie* II ii (1910). — J. A. Herbert *Illuminated manuscripts* (London 1911).—L. Gougaud "L'Art celtique chrétien" *Rev. de l'art chrét.* LXII (1911). — L. Bréhier *L'Art chrétien Son développement iconographique des origines à nos jours* (Paris 1918). — Jean Ebersolt "Miniatures irlandaises à sujets iconographiques" *Rev. archéol.* XIII (1921) 1–6.

[1] *Cf.* Traube *Perrona Scottorum* 470–6, 529–32.

(d) FACSIMILES: A list of facsimiles of Irish manuscripts, practically exhaustive to date, is given by Dom Louis Gougaud, "Répertoire des facsimilés des manuscrits irlandais" *RC* XXXIV i (1913) 14–37, XXXV iv (1914) 415–30, XXXVIII i (1920) 1–14. Reference should be made to this for individual reproductions. The following are the more important collections: Charles Purton Cooper *Appendix A* (*B. C. D. E. Supplement to Appendix A*) [appendices to a report on Rymer's *Foedera*, intended to have been made to the Commissioners on Public Records (London 1835–6?)], issued by the Master of the Rolls, 1869 [contains poor facsimile plates of pages of many important Irish MSS].— Joseph B. Silvestre *Paléographie universelle Collection de facsimilés d'écritures de tous les peuples et de tous les temps*, 4 vols. (Paris 1841); trans. by Sir Frederick Madden, *Universal Palaeography* 4 vols. (London 1850).— J. O. Westwood *Palaeographia sacra pictoria Being a series of illustrations of the ancient versions of the Bible* (London 1843–5); *Facsimiles of miniatures and ornaments in Anglo-Saxon and Irish manuscripts* (London 1868).—*Facsimiles of manuscripts and inscriptions* 3 vols. (The Palaeographical Soc., London 1873–83); 2nd ser. 2 vols. (1884–94); indexes (1901); *Facsimiles of ancient manuscripts* (The New Palaeographical Soc., London 1903–) [there is an *Index to facsimiles in the Palaeographical Society publications*, by L. R. Dean (Princeton, Univ. Lib. 1914)].— J. T. Gilbert *Facsimiles of national manuscripts of Ireland, selected and edited under the direction of the Rt. Hon. Edward Sullivan* 4 vols. in 5 (Dublin 1874–84).— Anton Chroust *Monumenta palaeographica Denkmäler der Schreibkunst des Mittelalters* 1st ser. 3 vols. (Munich 1902–6), 2nd ser. 24 pts. (1909–17).— Stanford F. N. Robinson *Celtic illuminative art in the gospel books of Durrow, Lindisfarne and Kells* (Dublin 1908).

(e) DIPLOMATICS: There is no work dealing with the diplomatic features of early Irish documents. The best general treatise is Arthur Giry *Manuel de diplomatique* (Paris 1894); new ed., not revised, in 2 vols. (1925). Many of the works on palaeography contain some information on diplomatics.

5. *Auxiliary Sciences — Chronology*

See Giry's *Manuel*, bk. ii. There is a review of the literature in *Mittheilungen des Instituts für oesterreichische Geschichtsforschung* XXV (1904) 338–51. The best special works on the theory and history of chronology are: Ludwig Ideler *Handbuch der Chronologie* 2 vols. (Berlin 1825–6; 2nd ed. Breslau 1883) [the *Lehrbuch der Chronologie* (Berlin 1831) is an abridgment].— Franz Rühl *Chronologie des Mittelalters und Neuzeit* (Berlin 1897).— P. Marichal "Calendrier solaire, julien et grégorien" *Bibl. de l'École des chartes* Sept.-Oct. 1905.— F. K. Ginzel *Handbuch der mathematischen und technischen Chronologie* 3 vols. (Leipsic 1906–14).— A subject of importance is discussed by R. L. Poole, "The beginning of the year in the middle ages" *Proc. Brit. Acad.*, 1922. For the ecclesiastical calendar see K. A. H. Kellner *Heortologie oder Das Kirchenjahr und die Heiligenfeste in ihrer geschichtlichen Entwicklung* (Freiburg 1901; 2nd ed. 1906); trans.: *Heortology A history of the Christian festivals from their origin to the present day* (London 1908). Irish chronology is treated in B. MacCarthy *The Codex Palatino-Vaticanus no. 830* (RIA Todd Lect. Ser. III) (Dublin 1892) 341–95, and his "Introduction" to *AU*, IV (1901) [*cf. ZCP* IV (1903) 332–8]. Calendar tables will be found in Robert Schram *Kalendariographische und chronologische Tafeln* (Leipsic 1908). — For lists of historical dates by which events may be located the best works are: *L'Art de vérifier les dates* (Paris 1750; 3rd ed. 1783–7; 4th ed., 44 vols.,

1818–44). — [J. M. J. L.] de Mas Latrie *Trésor de chronologie* (Paris 1889). — A. M. H. J. Stokvis *Manuel d'histoire, de généalogie, et de chronologie de tous les états du globe* 3 vols. (Leyden 1888–93).

6. Auxiliary Sciences — Geography and Topography

W. Fitzgerald *The historical geography of early Ireland* (London [1926]) [introductory]. There are, of course, many descriptive geographical works on Ireland. Useful for the ordinary purposes of the historian is the series, *The Provinces of Ireland*, ed. Geo. Fletcher: — *Ireland* (Cambridge 1922), *Ulster* (1921), *Leinster* (1922), *Munster* (1921), *Connaught* (1922). For the historical geography of Europe see Joachim Lelewel *Géographie du moyen-âge, accompagnée d'atlas* 5 vols. (Brussels 1852–7), and E. A. Freeman *The historical geography of Europe* 2 vols. (London 1881; 3rd ed. by J. B. Bury, 1903). Irish names of places are treated in P. Power *The place-names of Decies* (London 1907) [chiefly Co. Waterford]; P. W. Joyce *The origin and history of Irish names of places* new ed. 3 vols. (Dublin 1910–12–13); and Edmund Hogan *Onomasticon Goedelicum locorum et tribuum Hiberniae et Scotiae An index, with indentifications, to the Gaelic names of places and tribes* (Dublin, London 1910). This last, although a pioneer, not a final, work, has great value: it gives very full references to the sources. There are several short treatises in periodicals and society proceedings. Holder's *Altceltischer Sprachschatz* [p. 96 *supra*] renders a similar service for early occurrences of Celtic place-names throughout Europe. For Latin and other mediaeval names of places see *Dictionnaire de géographie ancienne et moderne par un bibliophile* [Pierre Deschamps] (Paris 1870), and J. G. Th. Graesse *Orbis latinus oder Verzeichnis der wichtigsten lateinischen Orts- und Ländernamen*, 2nd ed. by Friedrich Benedict (Berlin 1909). There is no good historical atlas of Ireland; the best general atlases are Karl von Spruner (ed. Theodor Menke) *Historischgeographischer Handatlas* 3rd ed. (1880); Gustav Droysen *Allgemeiner historischer Handatlas* (Leipsic 1886); R.L. Poole (ed.) *Historical atlas of modern Europe from the decline of the Roman Empire* (Oxford 1902); W. R. Shepherd *Historical Atlas* (New York 1911; 6th ed. 1927). Irish associations with mediaeval France give importance to the excellent *Atlas historique de la France* of Auguste Longnon (Paris 1885–9). The best modern maps of Ireland are those of the Ordnance Survey; there are also the "New Reduced Ordnance Survey Maps" of J. G. Bartholomew, one inch to four miles.

7. Archaeology and Anthropology

Archaeology, which every year is becoming in itself a more important and more extensive science, is, from the historian's point of view, a subdivision of history. It is the study of the material records of the past, and is generally considered to include inscriptions. The present work deals only with written sources, but in the practical task of historical investigation and exposition the archaeological and the written records must be used side by side. A list is given of a few important books which may serve to introduce the student to the subject. — In a lesser degree the above remarks apply also to anthropology, which in some of its phases is a section of history, but, in another aspect, a larger whole of which history is a part. — For periodicals and societies, see pp. 93–4 *supra*.

(a) ANTHROPOLOGY: One of the best volumes, especially for the student who is not a specialist, is A. L. Kroeber *Anthropology* (New York [1923]); of value also are Eduard

Meyer "Elemente der Anthropologie" *Geschichte des Altertums* 3rd ed. I pt. i (Stuttgart, Berlin 1910); J. Fleure *The Peoples of Europe* (London 1923); and Eug. Pittard *Les races et l'histoire* (Paris 1924). Older works that may still be consulted are W. Z. Ripley *The Races of Europe* 1 vol. and supp. (bibliog.) (New York, etc. 1899; new ed. London 1913); and Joseph Deniker *Les races et les peuples de la terre* (Paris 1900), trans. *The Races of Man An outline of anthropology and ethnography* (London 1900).

(b) PRIMITIVE EUROPEAN ARCHAEOLOGY: Interesting, though over-enthusiastic, expositions of the methods and results of what is called "prehistory" [2] are found in two articles by Camille Jullian in the *Revue bleue* (Paris) of Dec. 14, 1907, and Jan. 16 and 30, 1909: "Plaidoyer pour la préhistoire" and "L'héritage des temps primitifs." — Excellent treatises based mainly on archaeology are: James Geikie *The antiquity of man in Europe* (London 1914). — Carl Schuchhardt *Alteuropa in seiner Kultur- und Stilentwicklung* (Strasburg, Berlin 1919). — M. C. Burkitt *Pre-History A study of early cultures in Europe and the Mediterranean basin* (London 1921). — R. A. S. Macalister *A Text-Book of European archaeology*: I *The palaeolithic period* (Cambridge 1921) [the succeeding volume will have more relationship with Irish history]. — Marcellin Boule *Les hommes fossiles Éléments de paléontologie humaine* 2nd ed. (Paris 1923); trans. Jessie Elliot Ritchie and James Ritchie (London 1923). — Geo. Grant MacCurdy *Human Origins A manual of prehistory* 2 vols. (New York and London 1924). — Jacques de Morgan *Pre-Historic Man A general outline of prehistory* (London 1924). More closely connected with our subject are the following: Joseph Déchelette "L'Archéologie celtique en Europe" *Rev. de synthèse historique* III (1901) 30–59 [bibliography]; *Manuel d'archéologie préhistorique celtique et gallo-romaine* 4 vols. (Paris 1908, 1910, 1913, 1914) [covers only the "prehistoric" and "Celtic" periods: for Déchelette was killed on the field of battle, Oct. 6, 1914. The work is really a comprehensive treatise on the early history of western Europe, with extensive references to the literature. Irish matters are not treated at length, but the student of Irish history will find it indispensable for comparative study and for the general background. *Cf.* C. Jullian "L'époque de La Tène" *Journ. des Savants* (Jan. 1915), a review of part of the work, and "Joseph Déchelette" *Rev. des études anciennes* XVI (Oct.–Dec. 1914), an obituary notice.] — Harold Peake *The Bronze Age and the Celtic World* (London 1922) [interesting, but containing some dubious theory; the study of the distribution of sword types is important].

(c) THE CELTS: The following works, which relate, for the most part, to a comparatively late period of proto-history, that when Celtic-speaking peoples dominated western Europe, make use of archaeological evidence, but depend chiefly on anthropological (*i.e.*, linguistic), and literary (*i.e.*, Greco-Latin): Otto Schrader *Sprachvergleichung und Urgeschichte* (Jena 1883); 3rd ed. 3 vols. (1906–7) [has much value for the history that is based on linguistics; there is a trans. by F. B. Jevons, *Prehistoric antiquities of the Aryan peoples* (London 1890), but the last German ed. should be used]; *Reallexicon der indogermanischen Altertumskunde, Grundzüge einer Kultur- und Völkergeschichte Alteuropas*, 2nd ed. by A. Nehring, 2 vols. (Berlin, Leipsic 1917–23). — H. Hirt *Die Indogermanen, ihre Verbreitung, ihre Urheimat, und ihre Kultur* 2 vols. (Strasburg

---

[2] A number of workers in archaeology and a vast crowd of popular writers have combined to force this inaccurate and illogical word into use. The term "proto-history," although an abomination to the eye, would logically be less objectionable as a designation of all that period of human history that lies before written records.

1905, 1907). — D'Arbois de Jubainville *Les premiers habitants de l'Europe d'après les écrivains de l'antiquité et les travaux des linguistes* (Paris 1874), 2nd ed. 2 vols. (1889–94) [a standard work; 2nd ed. gives extensive quotations from sources: *cf.* Gaidoz *Revue critique* 6 mai 1876; Babelon *Bibl. de l'école des chartes* L 584–6; Lot *ibid.* LV 148–55]. — Georges Dottin *Les anciens peuples de l'Europe* (Paris 1917) [good; *cf.* J. Loth *RC* XXVII (1917–9) 358–60]; *Manuel pour servir à l'étude de l'antiquité celtique* (Paris 1906; 2nd ed. 1915) [an excellent introduction with abundant references to sources and literature; *cf.* J. Loth in *Annales de Bretagne* XXII i (Nov. 1906)]. — A. Bertrand and S. Reinach *Les Celtes dans les vallées du Pô et du Danube* (Paris 1894) [a very important study of the early history of the Celts; some of the conclusions are no longer tenable]. — D'Arbois de Jubainville *Les Celtes depuis les temps les plus anciens jusqu'en l'an 100 avant notre ère* (Paris 1904) [clear, popular exposition, with considerable discussion of the evidence]. — Niese " Galli," in Pauly and Wissowa *Realencyclopädie der classischen Altertumswissenschaft* VII (Stuttgart 1912) 610–39. — Fustel de Coulanges (ed. C. Jullian) *La Gaule romaine* 3rd ed. (Paris 1891). — Bloch *Les origines, la Gaule indépendante et la Gaule romaine* (vol. I of Lavisse's *Histoire de France*) (Paris 1900). — Camille Jullian *Histoire de la Gaule: I Les invasions gauloises et la colonisation grecque* (Paris 1908), II *La Gaule indépendante* (Paris 1908), III *La conquête romaine et les premières invasions germaniques* (Paris 1910) [continued in 3 more vols.; a work characterised by remarkable detailed knowledge of the sources, both archaeological and literary, and ingenuity in coordinating them, and in applying them to the reconstruction of the past]. — [Sir] John Rhŷs "The early ethnology of the British Isles" (Rhind Lectures) *Scottish Review* XV 233–52; XVI 30–47, 240–56; XVII 60–82, 332–49; XVIII 120–43 (1890–1). — T. R. Holmes *Ancient Britain and the invasions of Caesar* (Oxford 1907) [includes an important study on the primitive inhabitants of Britain].

(d) IRELAND — PRIMITIVE TIMES. See the book by J. Romilly Allen noticed p. 98 *supra*. — John Cooke (ed.) *Wakeman's Handbook of Irish Antiquities* (Dublin, etc. 1903) [a convenient summary, treating also of the mediaeval period; does not give the historical setting. This is the 3rd ed. of *Archaeologia Hiberniae*, by W. F. Wakeman, first published in 1848. *Cf.* p. 63 *supra*.] — W. G. Wood-Martin *Pagan Ireland A handbook of Irish pre-Christian antiquities* (London, etc. 1895) [contains a good bibliography]. — Sir William R. W. Wilde *Descriptive catalogue of the antiquities in the museum of the Royal Irish Academy* (Dublin 1857–62) [includes early mediaeval objects]. — George Coffey *New Grange (Brugh na Boinne) and other incised tumuli in Ireland : the influence of Crete and the Ægean in the extreme west of Europe in early times* (Dublin 1912); *The Bronze Age in Ireland* (Dublin 1913). — W. G. Wood-Martin *The lake dwellings of Ireland, or, ancient lacustrine habitations of Ireland, commonly called crannogs* (Dublin 1886). — Thomas Johnson Westropp "The ancient forts of Ireland: being a contribution towards our knowledge of their types, affinities, and structural features" *Trans. RIA* XXXI (1902) pt. xiv 579–730 [supplement in *Proc. RIA* XXIV C (1904) xv 267–76. Westropp did a vast amount of valuable work in the survey of the forts and other field antiquities, the results of which are to be found in the publications of RIA and RSAI.] — R. A. S. Macalister *Ireland in pre-Celtic times* (Dublin and London 1921) [the best single work on Irish archaeology of the stone and bronze periods; *cf.* MacN *Studies* Dec. 1922 pp. 632–4]. — Because of the close relationship, archaeologically, between Scotland and Ireland, the very good study by Joseph Anderson, *Scotland in Pagan times* (Edinburgh 1883, 1886), is useful for Irish history.

(e) IRELAND — EARLY MIDDLE AGES: R. R. Brash (ed. G. M. Atkinson) *Ogam inscribed monuments of the Gaedhil in the British islands* (London 1879). — R. A. S. Macalister *Studies in Irish epigraphy* 3 vols. (London 1897, 1902, 1907) [the best collection of ogam inscriptions]. — Geo. Petrie (ed. Margaret Stokes) *Christian inscriptions in the Irish language from the earliest known to the end of the twelfth century* 2 vols. (Dublin 1872–8) [*cf*. p. 64 *supra*; the collection is neither complete nor entirely trustworthy, but contains many inscriptions now lost]. — H. Gaidoz "Notice sur les inscriptions latines de l'Irlande" *Mélanges publiés par la section historique et philologique de l'École des hautes études* (Paris 1878) 121–35. — R. A. S. Macalister *The memorial slabs of Clonmacnois* (Dublin 1909). — Henry O'Neill *Illustrations of the most interesting of the sculptured crosses of ancient Ireland* (London 1857). — Margaret Stokes *The high crosses of Castledermot and Durrow with an introduction on the high crosses of Ireland* (Dublin 1898). — Geo. Petrie *The ecclesiastical architecture of Ireland anterior to the Anglo-Norman invasion, comprising an essay on the origin and uses of the round towers of Ireland* (Dublin 1845) [appeared first in *Trans. RIA* XX: *cf*. p. 64 *supra*]. — E. R. W. Wyndham-Quin, third Earl of Dunraven (ed. Margaret Stokes) *Notes on Irish architecture* 2 vols. (London 1875–7) [valuable]. — Margaret Stokes *Early Christian architecture in Ireland* (London 1878). — Arthur C. Champneys *Irish ecclesiastical architecture with some notice of similar or related work in England, Scotland and elsewhere* (London 1910) [good]. — Margaret Stokes *Early Christian art in Ireland* (London 1887; reprint 1894). — Geo. Coffey *Guide to the Celtic antiquities of the Christian period preserved in the National Museum, Dublin* (Dublin, London 1909; 2nd ed. 1910). — See also Jos. Anderson *Scotland in early Christian times* (Edinburgh 1881) [*cf*. p. 102 *supra*]. Also the works on "Illumination" under *Palaeography* pp. 98–9 *supra*, especially the articles by Brown, Leclercq and Gougaud.

8. Collections of Sources

The following list contains the names of collections which the student of early Irish history will encounter most frequently. For more extensive lists see Potthast, Gross and other guides noticed in sect. 1 of this bibliography. *Acta sanctorum*, liturgical texts, and other special collections are noticed at the head of the chapters or sections dealing with these particular subjects.

(a) GENERAL EUROPEAN: Henricus Canisius *Antiquae lectionis tomus Ius* [2, etc.] *in quo . . . antiqua monumenta ad historiam mediae aetatis illustrandam . . . nunc primum e mss. codd. edita et notis illustrata* 6 vols. (Ingolstadt 1601–4); 2nd ed. by Jacobus Basnage, *Thesaurus monumentorum ecclesiasticorum et historicorum, sive Henrici Canisii Lectiones antiquae . . .* 7 vols. in 3, 4 or 5 (Antwerp [Amsterdam] 1725). — Lucas d'Achery *Spicilegium sive collectio veterum aliquot scriptorum . . .* 13 vols. (Paris 1655–77; 2nd ed. of vols. I–II, 1665); new ed. by L. F. J. de la Barre, Steph. Baluze, Edm. Martène, 3 vols. (Paris 1723). — Edm. Martène and Ursinus Durand *Thesaurus novus anecdotorum seu Collectio monumentorum* 5 vols. (Paris 1717); *Veterum scriptorum et monumentorum historicorum . . . amplissima collectio* 9 vols. (Paris 1724–33). — Martin Bouquet, etc. *Rerum Gallicarum et Francicarum scriptores Recueil des historiens des Gaules et de la France* 23 vols. (Paris 1738–1876); new ed. by Leopold Delisle (1869–1894). — J. D. Mansi *Sacrorum conciliorum nova et amplissima collectio* (Florence, Venice 1759–98). — *Monumenta Germaniae historica* (Hanover, Berlin 1826–   ). [This scholarly collection is, with the possible exception of Migne

PL, the most useful of all the general compilations of sources. It is divided into five series — *Scriptores*, *Leges*, *Diplomata*, *Epistolae* and *Antiquitates* — and many sub-series. The divisions to which most frequent reference must be made are the sub-series *Auctores antiquissimi*, *Scriptores rerum Merovingicarum*, and *Scriptores* [*rerum Germanicarum*] ed. G. H. Pertz, of the series *Scriptores*; the series *Epistolae*; and the *Poetae latini* of the series *Antiquitates*. *NA* — *cf.* p. 93 *supra* — is published by the same society as the *Monumenta*.] — J. P. Migne *Patrologiae Latinae* tomus I-CCXXI (Paris 1844-64) [an extraordinarily extensive and very useful publication, composed almost entirely, however, of typographically poor reprints of older, and often imperfect, texts). — *Corpus scriptorum ecclesiasticorum latinorum* (Vienna 1866-   ) [good editions of early Church writers]. — *Collection de textes pour servir à l'étude et à l'enseignement de l'histoire* (Paris 1886-   ) [sources for early French history].

(b) IRELAND, GREAT BRITAIN: James Ussher *Veterum epistolarum Hibernicarum sylloge* (Dublin 1632); also in *Whole Works* IV 383-572 [*cf.* p. 47 *supra*]. — Charles O'Conor *Rerum Hibernicarum scriptores veteres* 4 vols. (Buckingham, 1814-25-26-26) [*cf.* p. 62 *supra*: contains, besides extracts from Latin and Greek authors and several historical 'poems, the annals of Tigernach, Inisfallen, Boyle, the Four Masters, and Ulster, in whole or in part]. — *Monumenta historica Britannica*: I [all published] *Extending to the Norman conquest* ed. Henry Petrie, John Sharpe, T. D. Hardy ([London] 1848) [contains extracts from Greek and Roman writers; inscriptions; and various historical works to 1066, including Gildas, Nennius, Bede, the Anglo-Saxon Chronicle, Asser, Florence of Worcester, Simeon of Durham, Henry of Huntingdon, Gaimar, the Annales Cambriae and the Brut y Tywysogion]. — *Rerum Britannicarum medii aevi scriptores, or Chronicles and memorials of Great Britain and Ireland during the middle ages, Published . . . under the direction of the Master of the Rolls* (London 1850-96) [the "Rolls Series": *cf.* p. 65 *supra*: the publications of chief interest for early Irish history are the *Brut y Tywysogion* (1860); *Annales Cambriae* (1860); *Giraldi Cambrensis opera* 8 vols. (1861-91); *Anglo-Saxon Chronicle* 2 vols. (1861); Hardy's *Descriptive Catalogue* 3 vols. in 4 (1862-71) [*cf.* p. 91 *supra*]; *Chronicum Scotorum* (1866); *War of the Gaedhil with the Gaill* (1867); *Willelmus Malmesbiriensis* (1870; 1887-9); *Annals of Loch Cé* (1871); *Henrici Huntindunensis Historia* (1879); *Historians of the Church of York* 2 vols. (1879-86); *Symeon of Durham* 2 vols. (1882-5); *Eadmeri Historia novorum* (1884); *Icelandic Sagas* 2 vols. (1887); *Tripartite Life of St. Patrick* 2 vols. (1887)]. — William F. Skene *Chronicles of the Picts, chronicles of the Scots, and other early memorials of Scottish history* (Edinburgh 1867). — A. W. Haddan and William Stubbs *Councils and ecclesiastical documents relating to Great Britain and Ireland* 3 vols. in 4 (Oxford 1869-73-78-71) [vol. II pt. ii (1878) contains early Irish documents: the death of Haddan prevented final revision of this section, which is imperfect, and also inferior in scholarship to the remainder of the work]. — Ernst Windisch and Whitley Stokes *Irische Texte* 4 vols. in 7 (Leipsic 1880-4-7, 1891-7, 1900-9) [*cf.* pp. 72, 76 *supra*]. — Standish Hayes O'Grady *Silva Gadelica A collection of tales in Irish with extracts illustrating persons and places* 2 vols. (London 1892). — Whitley Stokes and John Strachan *Thesaurus Palaeohibernicus A collection of Old-Irish glosses, scholia, prose and verse* 2 vols. (Cambridge 1901-3); *Supplement* (Halle a. S. 1910) [*cf.* p. 72 *supra*; also *ZCP* V (1905) 505-21, 575-8]. — O. J. Bergin, R. I. Best, Kuno Meyer, J. G. O'Keeffe *Anecdota from Irish manuscripts* 5 vols. (Halle a. S., Dublin 1907-8-10-12-13) [*cf.* p. 73 *supra*]. — Alan Orr Anderson *Early sources of Scottish history* 2 vols. (Edinburgh 1922) [extracts arranged chronologically, with trans.; good bibliog.].

9. Works for Historical Reference

(a) ENCYCLOPAEDIAS AND ENCYCLOPAEDIC DICTIONARIES: A few articles in the general encyclopaedias, such as Ersch and Gruber's *Allgemeine Encyklopädie der Wissenschaften und Künste*, the *Grande Encyclopédie*, and the *Encyclopaedia Britannica*, 11th ed., will be found useful, but the most important works of this kind are in the domain of religious and ecclesiastical affairs. The *Encyclopaedia of Religion and Ethics*, edited by James Hastings, 12 vols. (Edinburgh 1908–22), contains many articles on Celtic and Irish religion, both pagan and Christian. The *Dictionary of Christian antiquities* of William Smith and Samuel Cheetham, 2 vols. (London 1875–80), and the *Dictionary of Christian biography, literature, sects and doctrines*, of William Smith and H. Wace (London 1877–87; abridged ed. by Henry Wace and W. C. Piercy, 1911), are still useful. Of great value are the *Realencyklopädie für protestantische Theologie und Kirche* of J. J. Herzog, in the carefully revised 3rd ed. by A. Hauck, 24 vols. (Leipsic 1896–1913), and the *Kirchenlexikon oder Encyclopädie der katholischen Theologie und ihre Hilfswissenschaften*, 2nd ed. by Hergenröther and Kauler, 12 vols. and index (Freiburg 1882–1901). *The Catholic Encyclopedia*, edited by C. G. Herbermann *et al.*, 16 vols. and Supplement (New York [1907–14, 1922]) is of uneven character, some of the articles, especially those by continental European scholars, being of high merit; the treatment of many of the Irish topics is unsatisfactory. — The following two works, which are in progress, are magnificent monuments of contemporary French scholarship and have a very practical value for the student of Irish history: *Dictionnaire d'archéologie chrétienne et de liturgie*, ed. Dom Fernand Cabrol (Paris 1903–); and *Dictionnaire d'histoire et de géographie ecclésiastiques*, ed. A. Baudrillart, A. Vogt and U. Rouzies (Paris 1909–).

(b) BIOGRAPHIES AND GENEALOGIES: The best biographical compilation is the *Dictionary of National Biography*, ed. Leslie Stephen and Sidney Lee, 63 vols. (London 1885–1900); supp. 3 vols. (1901); index and epitome (1903); errata (1904); new ed. 22 vols. (1908–9); 2nd supp. 3 vols. (1912); index and epitome (1913). Its biographies of early Irish personages, though fairly full, show usually only elementary criticism. The *Dictionary of Christian biography* [cf. sub-sec. (a) *supra*] also contains a number of articles on Irish subjects, as does Thomas Wright's *Biographia Britannica literaria* 2 vols. (London 1842–6). A. Webb *Compendium of Irish biography* (Dublin 1878) is the chief Irish biographical dictionary: it is quite incomplete, both in subjects and in treatment. J. O'Hart *Irish Pedigrees* 2 vols. (Dublin 1876–8) is the principal treatise on Irish genealogy. It makes no attempt at critical reconstruction of the ancient lists.

(c) HISTORY OF EUROPE, GENERAL: The *History of Medieval Europe*, by Lynn Thorndike (under the editorship of Jas. T. Shotwell) (Boston, etc. 1917); *The Middle Ages 395–1272*, by Dana Carleton Munro (New York 1921); and the *Histoire de l'Europe au moyen âge 395–1270*, by Charles Bémont and Gabriel Monod, new ed. (Paris 1921), may be mentioned as excellent brief surveys of mediaeval history, without derogation to the many other good short manuals which are available. Of larger treatises the most useful are, probably, the *Histoire générale*, ed. E. Lavisse and A. Rambaud (Paris 1893–1901), of which the first three volumes relate to the mediaeval era; the *Histoire de France*, ed. E. Lavisse (Paris 1900–11); and *The Cambridge Mediaeval History*, ed. J. B. Bury, of which 4 vols. have appeared (London, New York 1911–). For the study in detail of any period the most useful collections are the *Jahrbücher der*

deutschen Geschichte by various German scholars under the auspices of the Bavarian
Academy of Sciences (Berlin, Leipsic 1866–   ), and G. Richter *Annalen der deutschen
Geschichte im Mittelalter* 3 vols. (Halle 1873–98), a condensation of the *Jahrbücher.*
None of these works gives any special attention to Irish history. Of more direct
interest to the student of that subject are, for one or another reason, various treatises
on special topics, of which the following may be mentioned: H. O. Taylor *The classical
heritage of the middle ages* (London 1901). — Sir John Edwin Sandys *A history of
classical scholarship:* I *From the sixth century B.C. to the end of the middle ages* (Cambridge 1903; 3rd ed. 1921) [treats the Irish evidence with some fulness]. — M. Roger
L'enseignement des lettres classiques d'Ausone à Alcuin (Paris 1905) [also devotes considerable space to Ireland]. — R. L. Poole *Illustrations of the history of mediaeval
thought and learning* (London 1884; 2nd ed. 1920). — W. P. Ker *The Dark Ages*
(vol. I of *Periods of European Literature,* ed. Saintsbury) (Edinburgh, London 1904).
— C. R. Beazley *The dawn of modern geography* 3 vols. (London 1897–1906). — Fridtjof Nansen (trans. Arthur G. Chater) *In Northern Mists Arctic exploration in early
times* 2 vols. (London 1911). — See also the works of Ebert and Manitius noticed
above, p. 91.

(d) CHURCH HISTORY, GENERAL: Charles De Smedt *Introductio generalis ad historiam
ecclesiasticam critice tractandam* (Ghent, etc., 1876) [the chief "introduction" devoted
solely to this field; has valuable bibliographies of the older literature]. — W. E.
Collins *The study of ecclesiastical history* (London 1903) [brief but valuable]. — Peter
Guilday *An introduction to Church history* (London, St. Louis 1925). — Caesar Baronius *Annales ecclesiastici a Christo nato ad annum 1198* 12 vols. (Rome 1599–93);
there are several continuations, and also later eds., the most important being that by
Mansi, 38 vols. (Lucca 1738–59), and that by Theiner, 37 vols. (Bar-le-Duc and Paris
1864–83) [this work has been the foundation for all subsequent church history, and
remains, in spite of many defects, a compilation of importance for reference purposes].
— Louis Sébastien Le Nain de Tillemont *Mémoires pour servir à l'histoire ecclésiastique
des six premiers siècles* 16 vols. (Paris 1693, etc.; 2nd ed. 1700, etc.) [a famous work
of erudition; the only purely Irish topic treated is St. Patrick]. — J. Alzog *Universal-
geschichte der Kirche* (Mainz 1840), 10th ed. by F. X. Kraus (1882); trans. from 9th
ed. by F. J. Pabisch and T. S. Byrne, *Manual of universal Church History* 4 vols.
(Dublin 1889–1902). — Wilhelm Moeller *Lehrbuch der Kirchengeschichte* 3 vols.
(Freiburg 1889–94); later eds. by Hans von Schubert (1897–1907); trans. by Andrew
Rutherford and J. H. Freese, *History of the Christian Church* 3 vols. (London, etc.
1893–1900), 2nd ed. of vol. I (1898). — Karl Müller *Kirchengeschichte* 2 vols. (Freiburg 1892–7; new ed. Tübingen 1916, etc.) — Joseph Hergenröther *Handbuch der
allgemeinen Kirchengeschichte,* 5th ed. by J. P. Kirsch, 4 vols. (Freiburg i. B. 1911–
3–5–7). — Karl Heussi *Kompendium der Kirchengeschichte* 4th ed. (Tübingen 1919).
— F. X. Funk (ed. K. Bihlmeyer) *Lehrbuch der Kirchengeschichte* 7th ed. (Paderborn
1921): Eng. trans. from 4th ed. by L. Cappadelta (London, St. Louis 1910). — Albert
Hauck *Kirchengeschichte Deutschlands* 5 pts. (Leipsic 1887–1920; 4th ed. of vol. I,
1904) [of great value]. — Hans von Schubert *Geschichte der christlichen Kirche im
Frühmittelalter* (Tübingen 1917–21) [sixth to ninth centuries, inclusive]. Of the above,
Baronius, Tillemont, Alzog, Hergenröther and Funk wrote from the Catholic point
of view, Moeller, Müller, Heussi, Hauck and Schubert from the Protestant, but all
maintain a high standard of scholarship.

(e) CELTICA; THE BRITISH ISLES: H. d'Arbois de Jubainville (ed.) *Cours de littérature
celtique* 12 vols. (Paris 1883–1902): I *Introduction à l'étude de la littérature celtique,*

by the ed. (1883); II *Le cycle mythologique irlandais et la mythologie celtique*, by the ed. (1884) [trans. R. I. Best *The Irish mythological cycle and Celtic mythology* (Dublin, London 1903)]; III–IV *Les Mabinogion*, by J. Loth (1889); V *L'épopée celtique en Irlande*, by the ed., with several collaborators (1892); VI *La civilisation des Celtes et celle de l'épopée homérique*, by the ed. (1889); VII–VIII *Études sur le droit celtique*, by the ed. (1895); IX–XI *La métrique galloise*, by J. Loth (1900-2); XII *Principaux auteurs de l'antiquité à consulter sur l'histoire des Celtes* (1902) [AdeJ]'s work is most attractive and important, but should be used with certain precautions: his primary motive was to reconstruct the antiquities of Celtic Gaul, which he attempted to do partly by the direct study of the Irish literary sources, partly by comparing these with Greek and Roman records: he was too much prepossessed by ideas drawn from the classics, and too prone to press the identity of Irish, British and Gallic customs and institutions, and their analogy with those of Greece and Rome]; *La famille celtique: étude de droit comparatif* (Paris 1906); *Les druides et les dieux à formes d'animaux* (Paris 1906). — E. C. Quiggin "Celt" (Languages, Literature) *Encycl. Britannica* 11th ed. — Heinrich Zimmer, Kuno Meyer, Ludwig Christian Stern "Die keltischen Literaturen" in *Die romanischen Literaturen und Sprachen mit Einschluss des Keltischen* (Paul Hinneberg's *Die Kultur der Gegenwart* Teil I Abteilung XI i) (Berlin and Leipsic 1909) 1-137. — G. Dottin *Les littératures celtiques (Collection Payot)* (Paris 1924) [small but comprehensive]. — Sir John Rhŷs *Origin and growth of religion as illustrated by Celtic heathendom (Hibbert Lectures 1886)* (London 1888). — Sir E. Anwyl *Celtic religion in pre-Christian times* (London 1906). — John Arnott MacCulloch *The religion of the ancient Celts* (Edinburgh 1911); *Celtic Mythology (Mythology of all nations III)* (Boston 1918). — Geo. Henderson *Survivals in belief among the Celts* (Glasgow 1911). — Eóin MacNeill *Celtic religion* (Cath. Truth Soc., London).

Sir John Rhŷs *Celtic Britain* (London 1884; 4th ed. 1908) [interesting, but to be used with caution: *cf.* pp. 77, 111]. — Ernst Windisch *Das keltische Brittannien bis zu Kaiser Arthur* (Leipsic 1912) [topical treatment; *cf.* p. 76 *supra*; also *RC* XXXIV (1913) 207-10]. — J. W. Jeudwine *The first twelve centuries of British story* (London 1912) [follows unconventional lines; uses Irish sources].

The following works ostensibly deal with the "Celtic" Church in the British Isles as a whole; but, because the sources are chiefly Irish, they are, in the main, treatises on the early Irish Church: Jas. Ussher *A Discourse of the religion anciently professed by the Irish and British* (Dublin 1631); also in *Whole Works* IV 235-381; *Britannicarum ecclesiarum antiquitates* (Dublin 1639); in *Whole Works* V-VI [*cf.* p. 47 *supra*; Ussher was influenced by controversial preoccupations, but he was a scholar well versed, for his time, in Irish antiquities, and his writings are worthy of consideration; he made use of some manuscripts that have since been lost]. — C. W. Schoell *De ecclesiasticae Britonum Scotorumque historiae fontibus* (Berlin 1851) [of value, though marred by confessional prepossessions]. — Friedrich Loofs *Antiquae Britonum Scotorumque ecclesiae quales fuerint mores, quae ratio credendi, quae controversiae cum Romana ecclesia causa atque vis* (Leipsic and London 1882) [work of merit]. — Heinrich Zimmer "Keltische Kirche in Britannien und Irland" *Realencyklopädie f. prot. Theol. u. Kirche* 3rd ed. X (1901) 204 *sqq*; (trans. A. Meyer) *The Celtic Church in Britain and Ireland* (London 1902) [*cf.* p. 77 *supra*; important; brief and topical; a radical and iconoclastic study that has inspired much controversy; *cf.* H. Williams "Heinrich Zimmer on the history of the Celtic Church" *ZCP* IV (1903) 527-74; J. Gwynn *LA* pp. xcvii-c]. — Louis Gougaud *Les Chrétientés celtiques* (Paris 1911) [a compact and comprehensive little manual, indispensable to every student of early Irish history; has excellent bibliographies; *cf.* J. Loth *RC* XXXII (1911) 488–94].

(f) SCOTLAND: WALES; BRITTANY; ENGLAND: William Forbes Skene *Celtic Scotland: a history of ancient Alban:* I *History and Ethnology* (Edinburgh 1876, 2nd ed. 1886), II *Church and Culture* (1877, 1887), III *Land and People* (1880, 1890) [*cf.* p. 68 *supra*; gives much attention both to early Britain and to Ireland, and, in spite of imperfections and errors, is worthy of careful consultation]. — Alphons Bellesheim, *Geschichte der katholischen Kirche in Schottland* 2 vols. (Mainz 1883): trans. D. O. Hunter Blair *History of the Catholic Church in Scotland* 4 vols. (Edinburgh 1887–90). — John Dowden *The Celtic Church in Scotland* (London 1894). Ferdinand Walter *Das alte Wales Ein Beitrag zur Völker-, Rechts-, und Kirchenge-schichte* (Bonn 1859). — Frederic Seebohm *The tribal system in Wales* (London, etc. 1895; 2nd ed. 1904). — Sir John Rhŷs and David Brynmor-Jones *The Welsh People* (London 1900; 5th imp. 1909) [the early mediaeval period is treated in broad lines only]. — John Edward Lloyd *A history of Wales from the earliest times to the Edwardian conquest* 2 vols. (London 1911; 2nd ed. 1912) [an excellent work]. Arthur Le Moyne de La Borderie *Histoire de Bretagne* 3 vols. (Rennes and Paris 1896-8-9) [widely informing but somewhat uncritical; there is a continuation by Barthélemy Pocquet for the later middle ages and modern times]. Chas. I. Elton *Origins of English history* (London 1882; 2nd ed. 1890) [valuable, especially for the literary sources]. — Frederic Seebohm *Tribal custom in Anglo-Saxon law* (London, etc. 1902; reprint 1911). — Thomas Hodgkin *The history of England from the earliest times to the Norman conquest* (London, etc. 1906). — Charles W. C. Oman *England before the Norman conquest* (London [1910]). — G. B. Adams *The history of England from the Norman conquest to the death of John (1066–1216)* (London, etc. 1905). — H. W. C. Davis *England under the Normans and Angevins 1066–1272* (London [1905]). — William Bright *Chapters of early English Church history* (Oxford 1878; 3rd ed. 1897) [gives considerable attention to the Celtic Church]. — William Hunt *The English Church* A.D. *597–1066* (London 1899). — W. R. W. Stephens *The English Church 1066–1272* (London 1901). — H. D. Traill (ed.) *Social England A record of the progress of the people in religion, laws, learning, arts, industry, commerce, science, literature and manners* 6 vols. (London, etc. 1894-7; illustrated and revised ed. 1901-4).

(g) IRELAND: There are few good histories of Ireland: even some that are fairly satisfactory for modern times fail in their treatment of the early middle ages. A brief but very good German compendium is Julius Pokorny's *Irland* (Gotha 1916), in Perthes' *Kleine Völker- und Länderkunde*. Patrick Weston Joyce *A short history of Ireland to 1608* (London etc., 1893; new imp. 1911), is one of the best of the older works. It has been re-issued, without the revision which it should have received, as *A history of Gaelic Ireland from the earliest times to 1608* (1925). *Irish Nationality*, by Alice Stopford Green, in the "Home University Library," is an impressionist sketch, bringing out well some salient features of the nation's story. Of similar character, but with much greater detail, is her *History of the Irish State to 1014* (London 1925), which is a valuable general sketch of the early mediaeval period. — Artur Ua Clerigh *History of Ireland to Henry II* (London 1908) is a work of originality containing some acute observations amid much ill-founded speculation. The best studies covering the early middle ages are *Phases of Irish history* (Dublin 1919) and *Celtic Ireland* (Dublin, London 1921), both by Eóin MacNeill, but the former is a series of

lectures, popular and in places sketchy, and the latter a collection of essays on special topics (*cf.* p. 81 *supra*). See also "Ireland: Early History," by E. C. Quiggin, *Encycl. Brit.* 11th ed. XIV (1910) 756–70; and "Irlande," by F. Lot, in the *Grande Encyclopédie*. Two papers dealing, one with the beginning, the other with the end of our period, which attempt, not too successfully, to apply the principles of criticism to the Irish records, are Sir John Rhŷs "Studies in early Irish history" *Proc. Brit. Acad.* I (1903–4) 21–80 (*cf.* p. 77 *supra*), and Standish O'Grady "The last kings of Ireland" *EHR* IV (1889) 286–303. The following works relate to special fields: Eugene O'Curry (ed. W. K. Sullivan) *On the manners and customs of the ancient Irish* 3 vols. (London 1873) [*cf.* p. 67 *supra*, and *RC* II (1874) 260–4, III (1876) 31–9, 90–101: a vast collection of material; Sullivan's contributions should be treated with special caution]. — W. G. Wood-Martin *Traces of the elder faiths of Ireland, a folk-lore sketch* 2 vols. (London 1902). — P. W. Joyce *A social history of ancient Ireland* 2 vols. (London 1903) [*cf.* p. 69 *supra*; another important collection, generally trustworthy as to facts but showing only elementary criticism]. — Douglas Hyde *A literary history of Ireland from the earliest times to the present day* (London 1899: also later reprints) [popular]. — Also the work by Eleanor Hull noticed p. 92 *supra*.
Mervyn Archdall [3] *Monasticon Hibernicum; or an history of the abbies, priories, and other religious houses in Ireland* (Dublin 1786); re-edited in part by P. F. Moran 2 vols. (Dublin 1873–6) [*cf.* p. 58 *supra*]. — John Lanigan *An ecclesiastical history of Ireland from the first introduction of Christianity . . to the beginning of the thirteenth century* 4 vols. (Dublin 1822; 2nd ed. 1829) [*cf.* p. 61 *supra*; a work of old scholarship, based on the Latin sources]. — J. H. Todd *St. Patrick, Apostle of Ireland . . . with an introductory dissertation on some early usages of the Church in Ireland . . .* (Dublin 1864) [this introduction is very important, but Todd was influenced by Protestant preconceptions]. — P. F. Moran *Essays on the origins, doctrines and discipline of the early Irish Church* (Dublin 1864) [uses much original material, but is propaganda for the Catholic interpretation]. — Carl J. Greith *Geschichte der altirischen Kirche* (Freiburg i. B. 1867) [also from the Catholic point of view]. — Alphons Bellesheim *Geschichte der katholischen Kirche in Irland von der Einführung des Christenthums bis auf die Gegenwart* 2 vols. (Mainz 1890–1) [on the whole good, but see a severe criticism by B. MacCarthy in *The Academy* 23 Aug. 1890 p. 153]. — Geo. T. Stokes *Ireland and the Celtic Church A history of Ireland from St. Patrick to the English conquest in 1172* (London 1886); 6th ed. by H. J. Lawlor (1907) [popular and attractive, but filled with erroneous views and mistakes of fact; Lawlor, whose ed. alone should be used, offers a mild antidote to the more glaring errors]. — John Salmon *The ancient Irish Church as a witness to Catholic doctrine* (Dublin 1897) [although controversial in design, has a scholarly basis]. — F. Kattenbusch "Irland in der Kirchengeschichte," *Theologische Studien u. Kritiken* XCIII 1 Jan. 1921 (Gotha) 1–53.

---

[3] The works of Ware (*cf.* p. 48 *supra*) are now of little value except occasionally for special investigations.

CHAPTER II

IRELAND IN THE ANCIENT WORLD

To about A.D. 700

THE earliest written sources for the history of Ireland are the occasional statements and allusions to be found in the ancient authors of Carthage, Greece and Rome. The evidence offered by these writers, and by those of what may be called the succession states of the Roman Empire, down to the end of the seventh century, will now be considered. From the seventh century, records in some abundance have been bequeathed to us by Ireland herself, and, on the other hand, the relations between Ireland and the Continent took on thereafter, as a result of ecclesiastical connection, a new character.

First, however, it seems well to give, as background and setting, a summary appreciation of what archaeology and anthropology can tell us regarding the position of Ireland and the Irish people in this ancient world.

I. PROLEGOMENA — IRELAND AND THE IRISH BEFORE WRITTEN HISTORY

Bibliography

The books on anthropology and archaeology listed on pp. 100–3 *supra*; also those on Indo-European and Celtic philology on pp. 95–6.
O. Montelius "The chronology of the British Bronze Age" *Proc. Brit. Acad.* 1909 pp. 97 *sqq.*—Geo. Coffey "Origins of prehistoric ornament in Ireland" *Journ. RSAI* XXV 37 *sqq*; "Archaeological evidence for the intercourse of Gaul with Ireland before the first century" *Proc. RIA* XXVIII C iv (1910).—O. G. S. C. Crawford "The distribution of early bronze age settlements in Britain" *Geographical Journ.* Aug., Sept. 1912 [important also for early trade relations of Ireland].—J. Loth "La première apparition des Celtes dans l'Ile de Bretagne et en Gaule" *RC* XXXVIII (1920–1) 259–88.— E. C. R. Armstrong "The La Tène period in Ireland" *Journ. RSAI* LIII i (1923) 1–33.
Sir John Rhŷs "The Celts and other Aryans of the P and Q groups" *Trans. Philol. Soc.* 1891–4 pp. 104–31 [a brief statement of Rhŷs's theory as to the settlement of the

British Isles]; "Celtae and Galli" *Proc. Brit. Acad.* II (1905).—E. Zupitza "Kelten und Gallier " *ZCP* IV (1903) 1–22.—HZ "Auf welchem Wege kamen die Goidelen vom Kontinent nach Irland?" *Abhandl. d. k. preuss. Akad. d. Wissensch.* 1912 [also in separate print; the greater part a criticism of portions of Rhŷs's *Celtic Britain* (p. 107 *supra*); *cf. RC* XXXIII (1912) 384–7].—Cecile O'Rahilly *Ireland and Wales* (London etc. 1924) 1–34 "Goidels and Brythons."

The earliest traces of the existence of man in Ireland belong to that intermediary period between the palaeolithic or "Old Stone" age and the neolithic or "New Stone" age to which some archaeologists give the designation mesolithic. During much of the "Old Stone" age of human history — the epoch when chipped stone implements were the characteristic products of man's handicraft — Ireland seems to have been largely or entirely covered with a glacial cap. It is possible that, as the glaciers disappeared, men of at least the later palaeolithic era made their way thither with the fauna that have since prevailed, and evidences of their presence may yet be found. It is noteworthy that within the time of recorded history there have been apparent certain phenomena in Irish life pointing to the former existence there of a race of people resembling in culture the Eskimos.[1] If such were the case, they were doubtless a stranded fragment of an ancient sub-glacial race, but they may, of course, have been in the neolithic stage of culture. Ireland possesses in abundance archaeological remains of the "New Stone" age — when the characteristic implements were of polished stone — and of the bronze age which was its successor.

Archaeologists are chary of fixing dates for the palaeolithic and neolithic periods. It is certain, however, that the mesolithic culture, and the presence of human life in Ireland, must precede the bronze age by several thousands of years: 10 000 × 6000 B.C. is, perhaps, a not unreasonable approximate location for the era of transition from the "Old" to the "New" stone culture. For the bronze age we are offered more precise estimates: Déchelette gave the limits for western Europe as 2500 to 900 B.C., and for northern Europe and the British Isles 2500 to 500, including in this a preliminary "copper" period coming down, perhaps, to 1900;[2] Coffey, with whom Macalister agrees, thought that for Ireland the copper age goes back hardly as far as Déchelette suggests, and put the limits of the true bronze age as 1800 × 1500 to about

---

[1] J. Pokorny " Beiträge zur ältesten Geschichte Irlands" *ZCP* XI (1917) 189–204, XII (1918) 195–231; D. MacRitchie " Earth-houses and their occupants " *Proc. Soc. of Antiquaries of Scotland* LI (1917) 178–97.

[2] J. Déchelette *Manuel* II i (1910) 105–7, ii (1913) 555, 588, iii (1914) table at end.

350 B.C.[3] Ireland has always — by reason of her geographical position — lagged a little behind in the movements which have spread over continental Europe. Her isolation, however, may easily be exaggerated, for the period before the use of writing as well as for that since: from the years when the great forests succeeded the post-glacial steppes down to comparatively recent times the easiest and the most frequented way of communication was the sea, or rather the sea-coast, and Ireland's maritime position is most favorable. The archaeological evidence indicates that in the greater part of both neolithic and bronze ages she was in the full current of West-European culture, and maintained relatively close intercourse with other lands, particularly on the one side with Scotland and the Scandinavian countries, and on the other with north-western France and the coasts of the Spanish peninsula.[4] Recently some anthropologists have been attempting to distinguish a special variety of neolithic culture, called heliolithic, "Sunstone," because associated with sun-worship and the erection of megalithic monuments, which was spread over the borders of the Atlantic, from the British Isles to about equatorial Africa, those of the Mediterranean Sea and the Indian Ocean, the East Indies, eastern Asia, Polynesia and even the Pacific slope of America.[5] This hypothesis may be regarded with some scepticism, but the point of interest here is that the monumental remains which are one of its strongest foundations are practically as numerous in Ireland, at one extreme of the "culture area," as anywhere throughout its extent.

What peoples inhabited Ireland during these long centuries we do not know. There was ample time for the migration and coalescence of innumerable tribes and races. When at length clear information begins to be available we find the inhabitants a Celtic people, that is to say, a people speaking a Celtic language and possessing a social system and culture resembling those of the other Celtic-speaking peoples of Europe. Nevertheless all the evidence indicates, and all the anthropologists agree, that the oldest inhabitants were not Celts, that the Celts appeared, at the earliest, not before the bronze age. It is also accepted that the original Celtic-speaking peoples of Ireland were invaders, obtaining, doubtless very gradually, the dominance through-

---

[3] G. Coffey *The bronze age in Ireland* (Dublin 1913); R. A. S. Macalister *Ireland in Pre-Celtic times* (Dublin 1921).
[4] Déchelette *op. cit.* II i 12, 28, 92–3, 349, and *passim*.
[5] See G. Elliot Smith *Migrations of early culture* (Manchester, London, etc. 1915). Also, for a more restricted interpretation, J. Déchelette " Une nouvelle interprétation des gravures de New-Grange et de Garr'inis " *L'Anthropologie* 1912 p. 29; H. Breuil " Les pétroglyphes d'Irlande " *Rev. archéologique* 5th ser. XIII (1921 I) 75–8.

out the island which resulted in the universal adoption of their language by the older inhabitants, who, it may be, then formed, and still form, the largest blood-strain in the population.[6]

The Celtic language-family is one in the group of language-families to which philologists give the name of Indo-European, Indo-Germanic, or Aryan. Other families of the group are Italic, Greek, Teutonic, Slavonic, and the Asiatic languages Armenian, Zend, Sanscrit, and their descendants. The languages of all these families, although each has developed along its own lines out of all recognition by its brethren except through the eyes of science, are fundamentally similar in structure, and must be used by people following fundamentally similar ways of thinking. It cannot be too often insisted that identity or relationship in language does not imply, either now or at any period in the past, identity or relationship in blood, but it is obvious that such relationship does testify to long and intimate past association in actual living. Hence it is certain that at some time in the dim neolithic past there was a people living together in a somewhat well-marked-off society and conversing together in a common speech, the speech from which have sprung all the Indo-European tongues of later ages. Philology can even reconstruct part of their vocabulary, and from it history can determine something of the manner of life they led, and the type of culture they had evolved.[7] The habitat of these primitive Aryans cannot be fixed with certainty, but scholars of the present day incline to place it either in south-eastern Europe, to the north and north-west of the Black Sea, or in west-central Asia. In time, as a result of the development of linguistic differentiations caused, or accentuated, by the spreading out of the people, the primitive language split into the ancestral tongues of the several language-families already named. This must have taken place, at the latest, in early bronze times, for we have

---

[6] Anthropologists distinguish, on the basis of *physical* characterististics, three prevailing human types in Europe, extending laterally across the continent: a northern, or " Nordic," stock, fair and " long-headed;" a central, or " Alpine," dark and " broad-headed;" and a southern, or " Mediterranean," still darker and " long-headed." The British Isles show a mixture of the three stocks. Only very slight anthropological *data* regarding the population of Ireland is available, but it seems to indicate that, as compared with Britain, the " Nordic " element is slightly greater, the " Alpine " and the " Mediterranean " slightly less. Documentary evidence shows that in early mediaeval times the dominant class in Ireland, who, probably, were largely the descendants of the Celtic-speaking invaders, described themselves as having the physical characteristics of the " Nordic " type, while they described the subject peoples, whom we may believe to have sprung chiefly from the pre-Celtic inhabitants, as having those of the " Mediterranean " type. *Cf.* Macalister *Ireland in Pre-Celtic times* (1921) 30–51. However, it is doubtful whether a common linguistic stock formed also a common physical type in the days of the Celtic expansion any more than to-day.

[7] Fick *Vergleichendes Wörterbuch der indogermanischen Sprachen* (Göttingen 1873) [*résumé* in AdeJ *Les premiers habitants de l'Europe* I (Paris 1889) 101; to be modified by later investigations]; also the works by Schrader and Hirt cited p. 101 *supra*.

evidence that by 1400 B.C. Aryans were well established in Asia and had developed their own distinctive religious system.[8] If the Hittites of eastern Asia Minor spoke, as is now generally believed, an Indo-European language, we have Aryans in Asia at a still earlier date.

The Celtic-speaking peoples moved westward, probably in close association with the Italic speakers until these branched off and made their way into the peninsula which has since been their home.[9] The linguistic peculiarities which differentiated the Celts from the other Indo-European groups — some of which undoubtedly developed after the separation of those groups — have been determined by philological research: noteworthy among them was the weakening [10] and disappearance of the sound of "p" at the beginning of words and between vowels, from which it results, for example, that the word which appears in Latin as *pater* and in English as *father* is in Irish *athair*. This Celtic-speaking people must have remained together as a fairly closely-knit society for a long period of time, during which they developed a quite elaborate civilization. The evidence, as in the case of their predecessors, the primitive Aryans, lies in part in their vocabulary, a vocabulary of which about 2250 words have been identified.[11]

Probably by the time at which we hear of Aryans in Asia the Celts had become well established in the table-land of central Europe, occupying the whole or large parts of what are now east-central France, Switzerland, Baden, Würtemberg, Bavaria, Austria and Bohemia.[12]

---

[8] The Tell-el-Amarna tablets, and more particularly records discovered at Boghaz-Keui in Cappadocia, have shown that in the fifteenth and fourteenth centuries B.C. the kings of the Mitani people, who dwelt in the upper valley of the Euphrates, worshipped among their gods Mitra, Varuna, Indra and the Nåsatyas. *Cf.* Eduard Meyer " Das erste Auftreten der Arier in der Geschichte " *Sitz. d. k. preuss. Akad. d. Wissensch.* 1908 I; *L'Anthropologie* 1908 p. 314, 1910 p. 160; *Revue des Études Ethnographiques et Sociologiques* 1908 p. 301. The question arises whether the gods mentioned, who are well-known Indian divinities, represent a western extension of an already distinct Indian culture, or whether they are Asiatic Aryan prototypes of their later Indian namesakes, and represent a stage when Indo-Iranians had long broken away from the Furopean Aryans, but had not themselves yet split into their two chief divisions. The former hypothesis is supported by H. Jacobi *Journ. of the Roy. Asiatic Soc.* 1909 pp. 721 *sqq*, 1910 pp. 456 *sqq*, and Sten Konow *The Aryan Gods of the Mitani People* (*Publications of the Indian Institute of the Royal Frederik University* I i) (Christiania 1921). If correct, it probably pushes the date of cleavage among the Aryans back to a much earlier epoch. *Cf.* also H. R. Hall " The Hittites and Egypt," in W. H. Buckler and W. M. Calder (eds.) *Anatolian Studies presented to Sir William Mitchell Ramsay* (Manchester, London, etc. 1923) 165-85.

[9] For a brief statement of the characteristics that are peculiar to Celtic and Italic, and mark them off from the other families, see art. " Latin " in *Encycl. Brit.*, 11th ed. For more extensive treatment see A. Meillet *Les dialectes indo-européens* (Paris 1908) 31-9; W. Christ in *K. Akad. d. Wissensch. zu München, Sitz. d. philos.-philol. u. d. hist. Kl.* 1906 Heft II; A. Walde *Über älteste sprachliche Beziehungen zwischen Kelten und Italikern* (Innsbruck 1917); J. Vendryes *RC* XLII (1925) 379-90.

[10] G. Dottin *La langue gauloise* (1920) 307.

[11] WS *Urkeltischer Sprachschatz: cf.* p. 95 *supra*. Holder in his *Alt-celtischer Sprachschatz* lists over thirty thousand words, but some of these are probably not Celtic, and the great majority are place-names, in which a quite small number of roots are used over and over again.

[12] For the conclusions very summarily presented in these paragraphs detailed references cannot be

Apparently they were in the lower Rhine country, and Belgium also, at an early date, but whether before or after the end of the bronze age is not very clear. About 900 B.C. the knowledge of the working of iron came into central Europe from the south, and ushered in a period of power and prosperity for the Celts. Their country was rich in iron ore, and they themselves seem to have developed remarkable mechanical skill. The culture of the iron age north of the Mediterranean lands, although it spread beyond the bounds of Celtica, was dominated by the Celts.[13] This iron age is divided into two main epochs, and these again into several subdivisions, for which an approximate chronology can be fixed. The "First Age of Iron," or Hallstatt epoch — so named from a site [14] in upper Austria where extensive remains have been found — dates from 900 to 500 B.C., and includes Hallstatt I, 900–700, and Hallstatt II, 700–500; the "Second Age of Iron" or La Tène epoch — La Tène is a site on lake Neuchâtel in Switzerland — covers the period from 500 B.C. to the Christian era, and includes La Tène I, 500–300, La Tène II, 300–100, and La Tène III, the last century before Christ. This is the archaeological chronology for the times which saw the expansion of the Celts over a large part of the ancient world, followed by their almost complete subjugation by the Romans and the Germans.[15]

The pre-Celtic inhabitants of western Europe of whom we hear from Greek writers were the Ligurians and the Iberians.[16] The Ligurians in Roman times were a small people living around the Gulf of Genoa, but before the coming of the Celts they certainly held southern France east of the Rhone, and perhaps extended north and west. The Iberians in the later period are found mingled with Celts in Spain and Portugal, and it seems fairly well established that they had at cne time occupied the south of France from the Rhone to the Bay of Biscay. For the British Isles some have identified the pre-Celtic peoples as Ligurians.[17] Others, especially

given, but through the bibliography the reader will be able to locate many of the most important special studies.

[13] See, e.g., AdeJ " Les témoignages linguistiques de la civilisation commune aux Celtes et aux Germains pendant le Ve et le IVe siècle avant J-C." *Rev. archéol.* 3rd ser. XVII 187–214; Dottin *Manuel pour servir à l'étude de l'antiquité celtique* (1915) 420 *sqq*, and works there noticed.

[14] Some scholars consider Hallstatt itself a foundation of the Illyrians — from whom, probably, the Celts learned the use of iron — others assign it to the Sigynnes, an obscure Mid-European people who seem to have been absorbed by the Celts.

[15] See Léon Joulin " La protohistoire de l'Europe barbare d'après les découvertes archéologiques récentes" *Rev. archéologique* Nov.-Dec. 1923.

[16] See Déchelette *Manuel* II i 6–28.

[17] So AdeJ and Camille Jullian. *Cf.* Jullian " Survivances géographiques " *Revue des études anciennes* VIII (1906) July–Sept. Now Jullian believes that the Ligurians were not Pre-Celts but Proto-Celts, identical with the Italo-Celtic people when they were still united: " Notes gallo-romaines " lxxii, lxxiv, lxxvii *Rev. des études anciennes* Oct.-Dec. 1916, April–June 1917, Jan.-March 1918; and in Dottin *La langue gauloise* (Paris 1920) pp. xii–xiii.

English writers, have long been accustomed to speak of them, more particularly in connection with Ireland, as Iberians. In recent times quite an elaborate theory has been built up from this basis: the Iberians, who would be represented to-day by the Basques of the western Pyrenees, would be one of the branches of a dark-skinned Mediterranean race, which included also the Berbers of North Africa, the ancient Egyptians, and the Minoan-Mycenaean peoples of the Aegean, a race to which would be due the old heliolithic culture. Sir John Rhŷs, who did so much to promote Celtic studies in Great Britain, was an advocate of the Iberian theory, and expended much labor in an effort to show that the ancient speech of the British Isles was related to Basque.[18] But the whole subject is still quite nebulous, and the questions still remain open whether the Iberians were a race of such antiquity,[19] whether the Basques had any ethnic or linguistic affinity with them, and whether either had any association with Ireland or Britain.

For the more important phases of the expansion movement of the Celts precise dates can in some cases be given, derived from Greek and Latin records. To the south-east they were advancing into the Balkan peninsula in the fourth century B.C., making a treaty with Alexander the Great in 335, raiding into Greece in 279, and soon after crossing to Asia Minor, where they seized the country henceforth known as Galatia;[20] to the south they occupied northern Italy about 390. To the west and south-west they expanded over France, Britain, Ireland and the Spanish peninsula. Spain seems to have been entered before 450 and the Mediterranean coast of France between 350 and 220.[21] It may have been under pressure from the Germans, who hitherto, it would appear, dwelt in the region of the Baltic, that these Celtic migrations took place. Henceforth the old home of the Celts in central Europe was occupied by mixed German and Celtic peoples, with the Germans more and more predominating and pressing southward and westward against Celts and Romans. One of these Germano-Celtic peoples, the

---

[18] See, e.g., his " The inscriptions and language of the northern Picts " Proc. Soc. Antiq. Scot. XXVI.

[19] Jullian holds that the Iberians were not a race of ancient date, but a state created in the valley of the Ebro towards the sixth century B.C., which received its name from that river: Revue des études anciennes 1903 p. 383. Other important studies on the Iberians are Déchelette " Chronologie préhistorique de la péninsule ibérique " Revue archéologique 4th ser. XII (1908 II) 219–65, 390–415, XIII (1909 I) 15–38; Philippon Les Ibères, étude d'archéologie et de linguistique (1909).

[20] It is now generally accepted that the terms Celtae and Galli or Galatae were originally equally applicable to the whole Celtic people. Some Celticists, however, have seen in these names the manifestation of a two-fold division. Cf. Dottin Manuel (2nd ed. 1915) 12 sqq; Déchelette Manuel II ii (1913) 560 n. Julius Caesar appears to have been the first to limit Gallia to the region between the Rhine and the Pyrenees.

[21] As early as 368 Celts were serving as mercenaries in the army of Syracuse, and we hear of them in this capacity repeatedly down to the Christian era. Cf. Dottin Manuel (2nd ed. 1915) 257 sq.

Belgae, had settled in Belgium and north-eastern France well before 103 B.C., and before 55 B.C. also in parts of the coast districts of England and perhaps of Ireland, in all cases dispossessing earlier Celts.[22]

The date of the advent of the Celts in Ireland can not, on this showing, be closely fixed. Archaeological testimony is to the effect that — except for sporadic occurrences — the earliest type of "iron" culture in northern and western France is Hallstatt II (700–500),[23] and in the British Isles the end of La Tène I (350?–300). As it is hardly possible that a Celtic people could have made any great migration after 900 without bringing iron, the conclusion is that their invasion of Britain and Ireland took place either before 900 or about 350 B.C.[24]

The Celts in these two islands were quite sharply distinguished from each other in language. One of the chief distinctions was, in the terms of the philologists, that the Gaelic, or Goidelic, speech of Ireland retained the original Indo-European q^u (modified to $c = k$ by the time a written literature appeared) while the Briton, or Brythonic, changed it to p. Thus the word for "son" is in Irish *mac* (in the ogam inscriptions *maqu*), in Welsh *map*, later *ap*; for "head" Irish has *cend*, later *cenn, ceann*, Welsh *penn*. The Gallic of ancient Gaul, so far as can be determined from its scanty remains, seems to have been, for the most part, in agreement with Brythonic in this respect.[25] It might seem probable that the division into "Q" peoples and "P" peoples was the result of the remote position of the Irish Celts, but the fact that the same cleavage is found in the Italic languages (Latin belongs to the "Q" division, Osco-Umbrian to that of "P") suggests that it may go back to the very beginnings of Celtic history, and that the Goidelic speakers were a distinctive branch of the Celts before they left central Europe.

[22] On these relations of Celts and Germans, see MacN *Phases of Irish history* (Dublin 1919) 15–25, 52–60. On the Celtic migrations in general see Müllenhoff *Deutsche Altertumskunde* II 247 *sqq*; Niese "Zur Geschichte der keltischen Wanderungen" *Zeitschrift f. deutsche Litteratur* 1898 pp. 129 sqq. *Cf.* also AdeJ "Les Celtes en Espagne" *RC* 1893 pp. 357 *sqq*; "Conquête par les Gaulois de la région située entre le Rhin et l'Atlantique, au nord des Pyrénées" *ibid.* 1903 pp. 162 *sqq*.

[23] G. Radet "La Gaule primitive et archaïque" *Journ. des savants* 1908, April–May, puts the Celtic invasion of Gaul in the 8th century.

[24] Loth (*op. cit.* in bibliog. p. 110), mainly on the risky interpretation of certain archaeological and anthropological evidence, argues for the beginning of the Bronze Age, 2000–1500 B.C., as the date of the Celtic invasion of western Gaul and the British Isles. His argument shows a tendency to identify anthropological "race" with linguistic stock, and also largely ignores the Irish evidence. In Britain at the beginning of the Bronze Age a new people become prominent in the archaeological records, "round-heads" who bury their dead in "round barrows." These Loth would identify with the Celts. The Britons of the stone ages were "long-heads" and were buried in "long barrows." But in Ireland, where there is no doubt of the presence of large numbers of both Celts and Pre-Celts, there were, on the one hand, no "long barrows," and, on the other, to judge from the scanty evidence, very few "round-heads."

[25] Dottin *La langue gauloise* (1920) 98. There may be traces of "Q" peoples in Gaul. *Cf.* also Rhŷs "Celtae and Galli" *Proc. Brit. Acad.* II (1905); H. Pedersen *Vergleichende Grammatik* I (1909) 4.

The theory has been held by H. d'Arbois de Jubainville, Sir John Rhŷs, and others, that the Goidels crossed the channel at an early date, in the bronze age or before 800 B.C., and overran first Britain and then Ireland. Later the Brythons (who, according to d'Arbois de Jubainville were identical with the Belgae and came in the second century B.C., but according to others preceded the Belgae by 300 years or more) followed in the same path and conquered the Goidels in Britain, but not in Ireland.[26] Rhŷs thought that there were still considerable bodies of Goidels in the west of Britain at the time of Julius Caesar, but this certainly is not attested, and there is no clear testimony to the presence of Goidelic peoples at any time in the greater part of Britain. Coffey and Zimmer, with whom Windisch agreed, maintained that the Goidels came to Ireland not by way of Britain but directly from western France. The Brythonic invasion of Britain may, of course, have been contemporaneous. Some such view, it would seem, must be held by all who place the advent of the Celts in the British Isles as late as 350 B.C.

II. PHOENICIANS AND GREEKS

Bibliography

The majority of the items in the following bibliography will be found to relate also to the succeeding section.

John Dalton "Essay on the ancient history, religion, learning, arts and government of Ireland" *Trans. RIA* XVI ii (1831) 1–379 [of value only for the references to foreign sources].—AdeJ *Principaux auteurs de l'antiquité à consulter sur l'histoire des Celtes depuis les temps les plus anciens jusqu' au règne de Théodore Ier* (*CLC* XII) (Paris 1902) [an excellent guide, in which the Irish student can find much of value for his special subject].

The following six works contain extracts from the ancient Greek and Latin authors: Martin Bouquet *Recueil des historiens des Gaules* I (1738; new ed. 1869) [*cf*. p. 103 *supra;* this collection, and that by Cougny, are designed to cover only matter relating to Gaul, but of necessity many passages of Irish interest are included].—*Rer. Hib. SS.* I (1814) [the only collection relating peculiarly to Ireland, but incomplete and anti-quated].—*MHB* (1848) *Excerpta* [contains almost all passages of classical writings which refer to the British Isles, with trans. of those in Greek].—Edmond Cougny (the last vol. by Henri Lebègue) Ταλλικῶν συγγραφεῖς ἑλληνικοί *Extraits des auteurs grecs concernant la géographie et l'histoire des Gaules* 6 vols. (Soc. de l'hist. de France: Paris 1878–92) [Greek texts *in extenso*, with Fr. trans.; *cf. RC* April 1893]. — Holder

---

[26] A somewhat similar view has been maintained recently by Peake, chiefly on anthropological and archaeological grounds. But the most original evidence he develops, that from the different types of swords, favors the view that in the later Celtic period there was an important settlement in Ireland of people who did not enter Britain.

Alt-celtischer Sprachschatz II *s. v.* " Iveriu " [*cf.* p. 96 *supra*; extracts are given only so far as to indicate the use of the word]. — W. Dinan *Monumenta historica Celtica Notices of the Celts in the writings of the Greek and Latin authors from the tenth century, B.C., to the fifth century, A.D., arranged chronologically, with translations*, etc. I (London 1911) [this vol., all that has appeared, ends with Poseidonius; the chronological arrangement and the fullness of the extracts and trans. make the work very useful; it attempts to assign to each author all quotations from his works — otherwise lost — to be found in later writings. *Cf. RC* XXXIII (1912) 108–11.]

Wilhelm von Christ (ed. Wilhelm Schmid) *Geschichte der griechischen Literatur* (in Iwan von Müller's *Handbuch der klassischen Altertums-Wissenschaft*) Part I *Klassische Periode* (6th ed. Munich 1912–1920); Part II *Die nachklassische Periode—Erste Hälfte: Von 320 vor Christus bis 100 nach Christus* (5th ed. Munich 1911); *Zweite Hälfte: Von 100 bis 530 nach Christus* (5th ed. Munich 1913) [careful summaries and bibliographies of the Greek authors].

The majority of the allusions to Ireland and other countries of northern and north-western Europe in the writings of the ancients have value chiefly as indicating the geographical knowledge and opinions of the time. Hence they are studied with some care in the larger histories of geography, of which the following may be noticed: F. A. Ukert *Geographie der Griechen und Römer von den frühesten Zeiten bis auf Ptolemäus* 3 vols. in 2 (Weimar 1816–46) [exhaustive in its time, and still of value]. —E. H. Bunbury *A History of Ancient Geography among the Greeks and Romans from the earliest ages to the fall of the Roman Empire* 2 vols. (London 1879). — Hugo Berger *Geschichte der wissenschaftlichen Erdkunde der Griechen* 4 vols. (Leipsic 1887–1893; new ed. 1903). — H. F. Tozer *History of Ancient Geography* (Cambridge 1897). — AdeJ "L'Ile Prétanique" *RC* XIII (1892) 398–403, 519. — Louis Gougaud "Les noms anciens des îles britanniques " *Revue des quest. hist.* LXXXIII (1907) 537–47.

Eleanor Hull "Observations of classical writers on the habits of the Celtic nations, as illustrated from Irish records " *Celtic Review* III (1906) no. ix 62–76, no. x 138–54. — MacN *Phases of Irish history* (Dublin 1919) 133–60 "Greek and Latin writers on pre-Christian Ireland " [popular survey, with some trans.]. See also the books and papers by Nansen, Elton, Rhŷs and Windisch listed on pp. 106–8 *supra*.

The earliest writings now known in which information is to be found regarding the north and west of Europe are due to the Phoenicians and the Greeks. The Phoenicians in their time must have produced a literature of historical and geographical importance, but it has resulted from the disasters that befell the race, particularly the destruction of their great western imperial city of Carthage, that only a few fragments — in Greek and Latin versions — survive. Our inheritance from the Greeks is much more ample, but it too is only a fraction of what once existed.

These early documents have the interest due to their antiquity, but intrinsically their value (and this applies also to the productions of Roman imperial times) is, for the Irish historian, very slight. The references to Ireland and north-western Europe are, for the most part, meagre and obscure, written down by authors who had no personal knowledge of the subject and only rudimentary ideas of criticism. Furthermore, it is often difficult to determine the true date and origin of these passages. The ancient writers, like their mediaeval successors, culled freely from those who had gone before, and seldom gave any indication of either the source or the extent of their borrowings. Even when the borrowing is acknowledged, it may be impossible to discover just how much of the text is due to the earlier author, or how accurately his statements have been reproduced.

The Phoenicians were a Semitic people, closely akin to the Hebrews, who, from their cities along the Syrian coast, had, even in the second millennium before Christ, extended their commercial activities over the entire Mediterranean sea, and out into the Atlantic ocean. After the decline of Minoan Crete, perhaps about 1200 B.C., their maritime power was practically undisputed for five hundred years. Colonies were established at strategical points throughout the Mediterranean and commerce built up with the bordering countries, notably with Tartessus, or "Tarshish," the southern part of the Spanish peninsula.[27] About 1100 B.C., according to tradition, Cadiz (Semitic *Gader*, "fortress") was built, perhaps as a basis for the tin trade with Britain. Carthage (Semitic *Kart-hadshat*, "new city") was founded towards the end of the ninth century, and grew steadily in wealth and power until it attained to the hegemony of all the Phoenician settlements and the rule of a commercial and military empire which disputed with Greeks and Romans the dominion of the ancient world. To a Carthaginian mariner we owe the first written source for Irish history.

1. The Periplus of Himilco *s* VI B.C.(?)

EDS: A. Holder *Rufi Festi Avieni Carmina* (1887) 144–71. — *Rev. des études anciennes* VIII (1906) pl. vii–x [facs. of portion of original ed. of Avienus relating to Gaul]. — Adolf Schulten *Rufi Festi Avieni Ora Maritima* (Berlin 1922). COMM: W. Christ *Avien und ältesten Nachrichten über Iberien und die Westküste Europa's* (*Abhandl. d. philos.-philol. Cl. d. k. bayer. Akad. d. Wissensch.* XI) (Munich 1866). — H. Gaidoz " Du prétendu nom d'Ile Sacrée anciennement donné à l'Irlande " RC II 351. — K. Müllenhoff *Deutsche Altertumskunde* 2nd ed. I (Berlin 1890) 73–210 [complete analysis of text]. — F. Marx " Aviens Ora maritima " *Rheinisches Museum für Philologie* new ser. L (Frankfurt-am-Main 1895) 321–47. — C. Jullian " Himilcon et Pythéas " *Journ. des savants* III (1905) 95-8. — Antonio Blazquez y Delgado-Aquilera *El periplo de Himilcon* (Madrid 1909). — Geo. Bonsor " Tartessos " *Boletin de la real Academia de la Historia* LXXVIII (June 1921) 515 *sqq* [suggests that Himilco's

---

[27] *Cf.* Victor Bérard *Les Phéniciens et l'Odyssée* 2 vols. (Paris 1902, 1903); Adolf Schulten *Tartessos: ein Beitrag zur ältesten Geschichte des Westens* (Hamburg 1922).

"Oestrymnides," "Sacred Island," and "Island of the Albiones" were really small islands off the south coast of Portugal].

Himilco was a Carthaginian who was sent, some time in the sixth, or perhaps fifth, century before our era, to make explorations along the western coast of Europe. He wrote an account of his discoveries, apparently a kind of periplus. Pliny, who speaks of Himilco and his voyage,[28] does not seem to have been acquainted with his writings, but they were rendered into a Greek version [29] which formed one of the sources of the *Ora maritima* of Rufius Festus Avienus. Avienus was a high official of the later Roman Empire — in A.D. 366 he was proconsul of Africa, and in 372 of Achaia — who occupied his leisure time in writing various poems, among them this description in archaic terms of the coast of Europe, based on Himilco and other ancient authors. All the versions of Himilco — Phoenician, Greek and Latin — are now lost, but before the disappearance of the last manuscript of the text of Avienus a fragment of 4015 of his lines got itself printed in Vienna in 1488. This printed text, even as representing the poem of Avienus, is corrupt — in places hardly intelligible — and the narrative of its antecedents is sufficient to give warning how very far removed it must be from the veritable report of Himilco the Carthaginian. The portion of the description of the western coast which is believed to depend ultimately on that report is not long.

"Here is the city of Gadir, formerly called Tartessus; here are the Pillars of stubborn Hercules,[30] Abila and Calpe (that to the left of the land mentioned, next to Libya, is Abila); they groan under the hard north wind, but stand fixed in their place. And here rises the head of the mountain chain (an older age called it Oestrymnis) [31] whose whole lofty and rocky mass runs chiefly towards the warm south wind. Under the head of this range the Oestrymnic gulf opens before the inhabitants, in which stand the Oestrymnides islands, widely scattered, and rich in minerals, tin and lead. Here is a vigorous people, proud in spirit, skilful at their work. Zeal for business displays itself on all the hills, and in their famous skiffs they sail widely over the turbid gulf, and the abyss of the monster-infested ocean. These people have no knowledge of building ships of pine; they do not follow the common practice of shaping barks from fir; but — a thing to marvel at — they always construct their ships of skins sewn together, and often in a hide speed over the vast deep.[32] From thence it is a two days' voyage to the Sacred Island [33] (so the ancients called it). This lies amid the waves, abounding in verdure, and the race of the Hierni [33] dwell there, wide spread. Next after it extends the island of the Albiones.[34] The Tartesii were accus-

[28] *Historia naturalis* II lxvii, clxix.
[29] Probably by a Massaliote of the 5th century, in the opinion of Müllenhoff: *op. cit.* I 202.
[30] Now Straits of Gibraltar.
[31] Avienus is the only source for this name. It may have denoted the Bay of Biscay, and the Oestrymnides were the islands which Greek writers designated Cassiterides. *Cf. infra.*
[32] If this passage be derived from Himilco, it gives a recorded history of twenty-four centuries for the *currach*, or coracle, still in use on the Irish coasts. The existence of the *currach* is one of the evidences advanced for the former presence of an Eskimo-like people in Ireland. *Cf.* p. 111 n. *supra.*
[33] Both these names go back to the ancient Irish *Everjī Iverni* (*cf.* the notes on Ptolemy, p. 133 *infra*). In the Greek version the designation of the island had, no doubt, the stem form ιϝερ-, becoming ιερ-, which was interpreted as cognate with ἱερός = Lat. *sacer*. So, as has been said, Ireland's title "Holy Island" rests ultimately on a mistaken etymology. If these names were found in Himilco we have here further evidence of their pre-Celtic character. But we must always reckon with the suspicion that they may be due to Avienus, who was writing two centuries after Ptolemy.
[34] *Alba*, the Irish name for Britain up to the tenth century or later (afterwards it was restricted to

tomed to trade as far as the limits of the Oestrumnides, as were also the Carthaginian colonists, and a multitude, sailing between the Pillars of Hercules, used to visit these waters. Himilco the Phoenician declares that, as he himself had proved by sailing thither, this voyage can scarcely be accomplished in four months, such lack is there of breezes to propel the ship, so sluggish lies the water of the lazy sea. He adds that much sea-weed is found over the waves, which often like a thicket retards the ship. He says, nevertheless, that the ocean-bed is not of great depth, and is covered with only a small amount of water; that the wild creatures of the sea meet one constantly on every side and that the monsters swim among the languid, slowly moving ships.[35] Whoever dares to push his ship beyond the Oestrymnic isles into the waters where under the northern constellation the air grows rigid reaches the land of the Ligurians, now uninhabited; for the bands of the Celts have long wasted it with many a battle.[36] The Ligurians, defeated — as fate often brings about — came to these regions, which they hold amid the rough thickets. Thick in these parts lie rock, stern cliffs, and mountains threatening the sky. Within such bounds the fugitive race long led a timid life, withdrawn from the waves; for because of the ancient danger they feared the sea. Afterwards repose and peace, when security had strengthened their courage, induced them to come down from their mountain lairs and descend again to the coast lands."

The trade in tin was the lure which drew the Phoenicians to the western coasts of Europe.[37] Tin, to be used as an alloy of copper in the manufacture of bronze, was a metal of supreme industrial importance before the discovery of iron, and tin, unlike copper, was not widely distributed. If south-eastern Asia be excluded — and there is no good reason to believe that tin was carried thence in quantity to the Mediterranean world — the only extensive deposits of the mineral were in Cornwall. There were also some mines in Spain and in Brittany, which districts may have been grouped with Cornwall in the general designation of "the Tin Islands," the *Cassiterides*. Whether the Phoenicians sailed regularly as far as Cornwall we cannot be certain, but it seems a fair inference from Avienus that before Himilco's time they frequently went at least as far as some district on the Bay of Biscay. But whoever may have been the intermediaries, the tin route to the Mediterranean, at least till Roman times, was from Cornwall to Brittany and thence along the coasts of France and Spain to the Straits of

what is now Scotland), seems to be derived from a primitive * *Albiō*, * *Albionos*, which was represented in early Greek texts as 'Αλβίων or 'Αλουίων. See EW *Das keltische Brittannien* (Leipsic 1912) 3.

[35] These are travellers' tales, widely scattered through ancient literature. As a matter of fact, the Bay of Biscay was a whale resort, and parts of the French coast have wide expanses of shallow water.

[36] This would suggest that in Himilco's time the Celts had attained the western sea-board only in the neighborhood of the North Sea — perhaps around the mouth of the Rhine. But we cannot be certain who are meant by " Celts."

[37] Sir Christopher Hawkins *Observations on the tin trade of the ancients* (London 1811); Geo. Smith *The Cassiterides* (London 1863); L. Siret " Les Cassitérides et l'empire colonial des Phéniciens " *L'Anthropologie* XIX (1908) 129-65, XX (1909) 129, 283, XXI (1910) 281; Déchelette *Manuel* II pt. I 94-8; Cary in *Journal of Hellenic Studies* XLIV pt. II (1924).

Gibraltar. This was also the chief way of communication between Ireland and the Continent:[38] access from Cornwall to Ireland was easy, and Ireland, although she did not produce tin, seems to have been the chief source of gold for western Europe in the bronze age.[39] Doubtless to the circuitous nature of the route, together with the reticence of the traders who controlled the trade, is due the surprising geographical errors of the ancient writers. Until long after the Roman conquest of Britain the *Cassiterides* were not regarded as in any way connected with that country, but were located off the coast of Spain, while Ireland was represented as lying between Spain and Britain.[40]

Associated with the tin trade is the first hazardous inference regarding the history of the British Isles which some scholars have thought to wrest from the literature of the Greeks. The Greek-speaking branch of the Aryans, who had moved down into the Aegean basin in the second millennium before Christ and amalgamated with the older Minoan-Mycenaean peoples, produced the first European literature. In the *Iliad* of Homer, the oldest monument of that literature, the word κασσίτερος, the Greek designation of tin, occurs several times.[41] Salomon Reinach, d'Arbois de Jubainville, and other scholars have seen in κασσίτερος a word of Celtic origin, and have inferred that the name was derived from the same locality as the substance, and, therefore, that Cornwall and Britain were occupied by a Celtic-speaking people at the time of the composition of the *Iliad*.[42] This was formerly the principal argument advanced for a Celtic invasion of the British Isles in the ninth century B. C. or earlier. The line of evidence, it will be seen, is very slight to span so many centuries: the problem, even if correctly stated, might be solved by discovering that an early tin route to the Greeks led through Celtic lands. But the initial proposition is by no means established. Julius Pokorny has made quite improbable the Celtic origin of the word κασσίτερος.[43]

The first Greek writer to mention the Celts—so far as extant sources

---

[38] *Cf.* the articles by Coffey and HZ noted in Bibliography *supra*.

[39] Coffey " Distribution of gold *lunulae* in Ireland and N. W. Europe" *Proc. RIA* XXVII C 251; Déchelette *Manuel* II pt. I 349, pt. II 562–4; Armstrong " Clare find of 1854 " *Journ. RSAI* XLVII (1917) 21; Macalister *Ireland in Pre-Celtic times* (1921) 118–21.

[40] *Cf.* J. Loth *RC* XXXV 291–2.

[41] XI ll. 24–5, 34–5, XVIII 474–5, 574, 613, XX 269–72, XXI 592–3, XXIII 503–4, 561–2.

[42] S. Reinach " L'étain celtique" *L'Anthropologie* III (1892) 275–81; " Un nouveau texte sur l'origine du commerce de l'étain " *ibid*. X (1899) 397–409; *Revue archéologique* 3rd ser. XX 262; *Académie des inscriptions et belles-lettres, Comptes-rendus des séances* 4th ser. XX 154; AdeJ *CLC* XII (1902) 4–9; *Les celtes depuis les temps les plus anciens* (1904) 19–21; Holder *Alt-celtischer Sprachschatz* I 824–34; Déchelette *Manuel* II pt. I (1910) 97.

[43] " Griechisch κασσίτερος, ' Zinn ' " *ZCP* IX (1913) 164–5; XII (1918) 305–6.

show—was Hecataeus of Miletus (540–475 ?),[44] a fragment of whose geographical work describes Massalia, now Marseilles, as "a city of Liguria, near Celtica, a colony of the Phocaeans"; and the first to allude to the British Isles—under the name *Cassiterides*—was Herodotus of Halicarnassus (*c* 484–425). "Concerning the western extremities of Europe," says he, "I am not able to speak with certainty . . . nor have I knowledge of the existence of Cassiterides islands from which tin is brought to us."[45] Herodotus was, for his time, a man of wide knowledge, good judgment, and scholarly curiosity. He was comparatively well informed as to all the countries of the eastern Mediterranean, from Sicily and Cyrenaica to Persia. His confession of ignorance and scepticism makes it certain that in the fifth century no knowledge of the British Isles—beyond this vague report of the *Cassiterides*—had reached the Greek intellectual world.

More positive are the statements of Herodotus regarding the beginnings of Hellenic maritime activity in the western Mediterranean.[46] From the eighth century the Greeks had been extending their trade and their colonies over the Mediterranean and the Black Sea, but it was not till the latter part of the seventh century that they penetrated beyond Sicily and Italy. "These Phocaeans were the first of the Hellenes who made long voyages, and these are they who discovered the Adriatic and Tyrsenia [Etruria] and Iberia and Tartessus."[47] Apparently about 600 B.C. Massalia, or Marseilles, was founded,[48] a city which has continued almost ever since to be an important commercial centre. From Massalia went out the second recorded expedition sent to explore the western coasts of Europe.

2. Pytheas: Concerning the Ocean *c* 330 x 300 B.C.

There is an extensive literature regarding Pytheas, of which only a few items can be noticed here. ED: C. Müller *Geographi graeci minores* I (Paris 1855) pp. cxxxv, 561 *sqq.* COMM: Joachim Lelewel *Pytheas und die Geographie seiner Zeit* (Berlin 1831); also Fr. trans. (Paris 1836). — K. Müllenhoff *Deutsche Altertumskunde* 2nd ed. I

[44] Quoted in an abridgment of Stephen of Byzantium (*fl. c* A.D. 500). The fragments of Hecataeus are collected in Müller *Fragmenta historicorum graecorum* (Paris 1841) I 1–31, IV 623, 627.
[45] Herod. III cxv. *Cf.* Camille Jullian "Les Celtes chez Hérodote" *Rev. des études anciennes* VII (1905) Oct.–Dec.
[46] Ernst Maas "Die Griechen in Südgallien" *Jahreshefte des österreichischen archäologischen Instituts in Wien* IX (Vienna 1906) 139–82, X (1907) 85–117.
[47] Herod. I clxiii. Quoted in G. W. Botsford and E. G. Sihler *Hellenic Civilization* (New York 1915) 128. *Cf.* C. Jullian " Ulysse et les Phocéens, à propos de la fondation de Marseille " *Rev. des études anciennes* 1905 Jan.–March; Clerc "Les premières explorations phocéennes dans la Méditerranée occidentale " *ibid.*, pp. 329 *sqq.*
[48] Déchelette *Manuel* II pt. II 580–7.

(Berlin 1890) 211–497. — Gustav Hergt *Die Nordlandfahrt des Pytheas* (Halle 1893) [dissertation]. — C. R. Markham " Pytheas, the discoverer of Britain " *Geographical Journal* I (London 1893). — F. Mathias *Pytheas von Massilia und die ältesten Nachrichten von den Germanen* (Königl. Luisensgymnasium Berlin: Programm no. 62–1901; no. 64–1902). — C. Jullian "Himilcon et Pythéas" *Journ. des savants* III (1905) 95–8. — Victor Chapot "Albion remota" *Rev. des études grecques* 1919 vol. XXXII (1921) 66–78.

About the time of the death of Aristotle (322 B.C.) a citizen of Massalia named Pytheas published a work "Concerning the Ocean" (περὶ τοῦ ὠκεανοῦ) in which he gave a narrative of one or more voyages which he had made to northern Europe. This, one of the most important geographical works of antiquity, has not survived, but some idea of its contents can be obtained from quotations or allusions in Polybius, Diodorus Siculus, Strabo, Pomponius Mela, Pliny, Geminus and Cleomedes.[49] Polybius and Strabo were hostile critics — Strabo did not hesitate to brand Pytheas as an impostor — but modern scholars have rehabilitated the reputation of the Massaliote. It would seem that Pytheas sailed from the Straits of Gibraltar along the coast as far as Ushant; that he circumnavigated Britain; that from its northern extremity he crossed the sea to a region he called Thule — the Shetlands or, more probably, Scandinavia; and that he also explored the continental coast as far as Jutland, and possibly into the Baltic. The expedition bore the character of a scientific exploration: in addition to his geographical and anthropological notes, Pytheas made what were, for his time, elaborate astronomical observations.   In the scanty fragments we possess Pytheas does not mention Ireland, although he claims to have visited all parts of Britain; one element in his text has, however, an immediate interest for the Irish historian. It is established that the designation applied by him to Britain, or the British Isles, was πρετανική, or νῆσοί πρετανικαι. This is almost identical with the Welsh *Ynys Prydyn*, or *Priten*, and is the " P " form of * *Qriten-*, from which comes *Cruthen, Cruithnech*, the Goidelic name of the people whom later Latin writers call Picts.[50]   Testimony may be seen in this that the Picts were the principal inhabitants of Britain in the fourth century B.C. Pytheas distinguished *Pretanica* from *Celtica:* he says that the promontory of *Cantion* (Kent), which he seems to have reached by crossing from about Ushant (declared to be " Celtic," not " Iberic ") to Cornwall and then voyaging along the south coast of Britain, was several days' sail from *Celtica*.[51]

Pytheas was a contemporary of Alexander the Great, whose conquests created the political foundation for that reign of Greek culture

---

[49] Some of these appear not to have known the work of Pytheas at first hand, but through intermediaries, as Eratosthenes, Hipparchus and Timaeus.

[50] AdeJ "L'Ile Prétanique" *RC* XIII (1892) 398–403, 519; EW *Das keltische Brittannien* (1912) 5–6; J. Loth *RC* XXXVIII (1920–1) 280–1. This does not prove that the Picts were Celts of the " P " group; the Massaliotes doubtless obtained the name through Gallic or Hispanic informants.

[51] Their designation by a word of Celtic provenance is no proof that the inhabitants of Britain at the time were Celts.   See preceding note.   On the other hand no importance need attach to the distinction from *Celtica:* this word was often used as the equivalent of Caesar's *Gallia*, and, in any case, ancient nomenclature did not always respect modern scientific boundaries in either linguistics or ethnology.   In spite of the large amount of ink which has been expended on the subject, the problem of the linguistic relations of the Picts has not been solved.   It still remains probable, but by no means certain, that they were a Celtic-speaking people.

in the world of the eastern Mediterranean which is termed by historians the Hellenistic age. It witnessed the beginning of organised and state-supported scholarship, especially at Alexandria in Egypt. Unfortunately the writings of the scholars of this epoch have, for the most part, disappeared, except for a few fragments. The loss of the writings of Timaeus [52] (c 350–c 260 B.C.), a Sicilian historian residing at Athens, who is believed to have devoted considerable space to the movements of the Celts; of Eratosthenes [53] (273–192), third librarian of Alexandria; and of Hipparchus [54] (fl. c 161–126), astronomer at Rhodes, whose geographical works embodied information derived from Pytheas and other sources no longer known, is particularly unfortunate for the history of the north and west. From Polybius [55] (c 198–c 120) much more has been transmitted. He was a Greek of rank and culture who, having been carried to Rome as a hostage, lived on terms of intimacy with the leaders of the Roman aristocracy. His *Histories* are the record of the Roman conquest of the Mediterranean world, and of the beginnings of Roman imperial rule. He travelled extensively — in Libya, Iberia, Gaul, and on the western ocean — but knew nothing of northern Europe beyond Narbonne, and declares that others who pretend to write of those regions relate nothing but fables. He is a source of interest for Celtic history, but the only Celtic people of whom he had intimate knowledge were the Cisalpine Gauls. He barely mentions the British Isles, and notices Pytheas, in whom, however, he puts no trust. The ignorance of Polybius in the second century, as that of Herodotus in the fifth, is evidence that Ireland, as also Britain, still remained *terra incognita* to the enlightened public opinion of the Mediterranean basin.

The *Histories* of Polybius were continued by Poseidonius [56] (c 135–c 45), a native of Apamea in Syria, who became the foremost Stoic philosopher of his time and the founder of a famous school at Rhodes.

---

[52] C. Müller *Fragmenta historicorum graecorum* (Paris 1841) I 193–233, IV 625 *sq*, 640 *sq*.   *Cf.* J. Geffcken "Timaios' Geographie des Westens" in Kiessling and Wilamowitz-Möllendorf *Philologische Untersuchungen* XIII (1892).

[53] H. Berger *Die geographischen Fragmente des Eratosthenes* (Leipsic 1880). — A. Thalamas *La Géographie d'Ératosthène*; *Étude bibliographique de la géographie d'Ératosthène* (Versailles, Paris 1922). — *Cf.* G. W. Botsford and E. G. Sihler *Hellenic Civilization* (*Records of Civilization*) (New York 1915) 635 *sqq*.

[54] H. Berger *Die geographischen Fragmente des Hipparch* (Leipsic 1869); *Erdkunde der Griechen* III (1891) 130 *sqq*.

[55] *Cf.* Botsford and Sihler *Hellenic Civilization* (1915) 646–56; J. T. Shotwell *Introduction to the history of history* (*Records of Civilization*) (New York 1922) 191–201. Of the forty books of the *Histories*, the first five and some sections of others have survived.

[56] Bake *Posidonii Rhodii reliquiae* (Leyden 1819); Müller *Fragmenta historicorum graecorum* III 245–96. *Cf.* R. Scheppig *De Posidonio Apamensi rerum gentium terrarum scriptore* (Berlin 1870); Müllenhoff *Deutsche Altertumskunde* II (2nd ed. 1890) 145; Karl Reinhardt *Poseidonius* (Munich 1921); Maurice Croiset *Journ. des savants* July–Aug. 1922, pp. 145–52.

He travelled extensively, visiting Gades (Cadiz) and other parts of Spain and Gaul, and wrote voluminously on all manner of topics. His historical and geographical works, almost entirely lost, appear to have contained the fullest account given by any of the ancient writers of the manners and customs of the Celts: fortunately it seems certain that large extracts from these descriptions have been transmitted to us, embedded in the treatises of later authors, especially Caesar, Diodorus Siculus, and Strabo. Some critics think that Strabo's description of Ireland was derived mainly from Poseidonius.

Timagenes, believed to be a native of Syria educated at Alexandria, who came to Rome in 55 B.C., also wrote extensively on the Celts, and may have treated of the British Isles.[57] His works in their original form have disappeared, but Ammianus Marcellinus made free use of them in his description of the Gauls.[58]

3. Diodorus Siculus: Historical Library c 60 x 20 B.C.

Special bibliographies have been omitted in the cases of this and certain other well-known classical texts.—Although Diodorus, like Timagenes, was a contemporary of Julius Caesar and Augustus, his writings may better be considered with those of the Alexandrian age, from which they are, largely, a compilation. He was a Greek, a native of Agyrium in Sicily, and prepared a general history (βιβλιοθήκη ἱστορική) of the world in forty books, bringing the story down to Caesar's conquest of Gaul. It is made up of excerpts from older authors, and includes several important passages regarding the Celts, for the most part extracted, it would appear, from Poseidonius. Among these are descriptions of certain customs of which remarkable parallels are found in the life depicted in the heroic sagas of Ireland.[59] The only reference to Ireland is a probable allusion to cannibalism there: "It is said that some of them [the 'Galatae' bordering on Scythia] eat men, as do also the Britons who inhabit the region called Ireland."[60] Diodorus gives two accounts of the tin trade, for which before his time a new route had been opened up. One is in connection with his description of Britain, the other of the Cassiterides. The tin was carried " to the opposite coast of Gaul, and thence conveyed on horses by the merchants through the intervening Celtic land to the people of Massilia and to the city called Narbonne."[61]

[57] Müller *Fragmenta historicorum graecorum* (Paris 1841) III 317–23. *Cf.* Hirschfeld "Timagenes und die gallische Wandersage" *Sitzungsb. d. k. preuss. Akad. d. Wissensch.* 1894 XIX pp. 331 *sqq*; Th. Reinach " Timagène, Josèphe et la géographie de la Gaule " *Rev. des études anciennes* VIII (April–June 1906).

[58] No. 13 *infra*.

[59] See the art. by Eleanor Hull noted in Bibliography.

[60] τὴν ὀνομαζομένην Ἴριν: V xxxii. The form is peculiar, but there can be little doubt that it is a variant of the name of Ireland.

[61] V xxxviii; *cf.* xxi, xxii, where the overland journey is said to have taken thirty days. These passages are believed to be derived from Timaeus.

III. THE ROMAN EMPIRE

Bibliography

To the works listed in the preceding section are to be added the following: W. S. Teuffel (ed. Wilhelm Kroll and Franz Skutsch) *Geschichte der römischen Literatur:* vol. II *Die Literatur von 31 vor Christus bis 96 nach Christus;* vol. III *Die Literatur von 96 nach Christus bis zum Ausgange des Altertums* (Leipsic and Berlin 1910, 1913). Trans. from the 5th German ed.: Geo. C. W. Warr *Teuffel's History of Roman literature revised and enlarged by Ludwig Schwabe:* vol. I *The republican period;* vol. II *The imperial period* (London 1891, 1892) [of similar character, in its field, to Christ's book on Greek literature]. — Otto Bardenhewer (trans. Thos. J. Shahan) *Patrology: the lives and works of the Fathers of the Church* (Freiburg i. B. and St. Louis, Mo., 1908); *Geschichte der altchristlichen Literatur* 2nd ed. 3 vols. (Freiburg i. B. 1913-14-12). — J. Tixeront *A Handbook of Patrology* (London 1920). — P. de Labriolle *Histoire de la littérature latine chrétienne* (Paris 1920) and trans. H. Wilson *History and literature of Christianity from Tertullian to Boethius* (London) [these works render a like service for the early Christian writers]. See also Holder *op. cit.* p. 96 *supra s. v.* " Scotti," etc., " Atecotti."
T. Rice Holmes *Ancient Britain and the invasions of Julius Caesar* (Oxford 1907) [a work of much value for the early history of the British Isles].

The political union of the Mediterranean world, foreshadowed for a time by the career of Alexander of Macedon, was accomplished by Rome, a city-state of the Latins, one of the divisions of the Italic-speaking peoples. The first time the name of this little city seems to have been heard through that world was when, about 390 B.C., it was sacked by a raiding party of the Celts who were then moving south into Italy from over the Alps. Two centuries later Rome had conquered and consolidated Italy and, by the successive defeats of Carthage, Macedonia and Syria, disposed of the only powers capable of disputing seriously her supremacy. Rather more than another century and a half were taken up in completing the conquests in detail, and in the organisation of the new world-empire. Then, from 30 B.C., began a period of more than four centuries during which Greco-Latin civilisation enjoyed comparative peace and prosperity throughout the Mediterranean basin and hinterlands, under the political autocracy of the "imperator," the commander-in-chief of the legions, at Rome.

The triumph of Rome involved the destruction of Celtic independence. Cisalpine Gaul was conquered in 222 B.C., the Spanish peninsula by 206 (in both cases there were subsequent insurrections), Narbonnese Gaul by 120, the remainder of Transalpine Gaul in 58-51, the central table-land between the Alps, the Rhine and the Danube in

15 B.C.–A.D. 9, and Britain, to the foot of the Scottish Highlands, during the period A.D. 43–85. Almost everywhere the triumph of the Latin civilisation and the Latin language followed that of the Roman arms. In Britain alone did enough of the old Celtic polity persist to reassert itself after the collapse of the imperial power.

Ireland was the only Celtic land where the Roman eagles never flew. She alone carried down into the Christian middle ages the political, social and cultural traditions of central and western Europe unbroken by the impact of the Mediterranean civilisation. And she alone stood outside both the official and the unofficial knowledge of the Roman world. For three hundred and sixty years — that is to say, for a longer period than has now elapsed since the first permanent English and French settlements on the American continent — the Romans remained in practically unbroken occupation of Britain. Yet it is surprising and disappointing how slight is the information they have left us regarding their next-door neighbor of all these centuries. The most important sources are the geographers, who carried on the Alexandrian tradition, but even of them only one, Ptolemy, offers any precise and detailed description of the western island.

4. Caius Julius Caesar: Notes on the Gallic War   c 58–50 B.C.

Caius Julius Caesar, conqueror of Transalpine Gaul and first Roman to invade Britain, published, either during or immediately after his campaigns, a series of notes on his military achievements, *Commentarii de bello Gallico*, which have much historical value. To the seeker after information regarding the character of the countries and their inhabitants, however, the work is of little help. Caesar must have had at his command first-hand knowledge of the Celtic peoples with whom he came in contact that would be of priceless value to the modern student. But he was too busy with practical affairs, it would seem, to investigate or record such matters at any length. Even the descriptions given by him of Gaul and Britain and their inhabitants seem to have been largely " cribbed " from Polybius and Poseidonius. In the section devoted to Britain Caesar makes, quite casually, his only reference to Ireland: " The second [side of Britain] looks towards Spain and the west. In this direction is Hibernia, smaller by half, as is thought, than Britain, but at the same distance as the passage from Gaul to Britain."[62] We here meet with the name *Hibernia* for the first time, a modification of ιϜερια under the influence, doubtless, of a false analogy with the latin *hibernus*, " wintry."

Caesar's account [63] of his maritime war with the Veneti and other tribes of north-

---

[62] *Lib.* V *cap*. xiii. The theory has recently been advanced that this whole description of Britain is an interpolation by a later writer. *Cf.* A. Klotz *Cäsarstudien, nebst einer Analyse der Strabonischen Beschreibung von Gallien und Britannien* (Leipsic 1910).
[63] *Lib.* III.

western Gaul has importance because of its testimony to the maritime enterprise [64] of those peoples dwelling on the main line of communication between the Continent, south-west Britain, and Ireland.

The Roman elegiac poet Sextus Propertius, in a poem written about 23 B.C., makes a passing allusion to the "Hiberni" among other savage peoples: "Hibernique Getae, pictoque Britannia curru "—IV iii 7.

5. Strabo: Geography A.D. 17–23

Strabo, a Greek of Pontus, was born about 63 B.C. He travelled extensively in the East, lived at Rome for some time, but seems to have been no farther west than Etruria. His Geography, published in seventeen books, was the first attempt to produce a general descriptive treatise on the subject. His chief sources were Eratosthenes and other Greek writers of the Alexandrian school. For Gaul and Britain, however, he seems to have made considerable use of Poseidonius. The view has been recently advanced that for this section of his work he derived his information from Timagenes, whose text, now lost, depended on Caesar, Artemidorus, of Ephesus (first century B.C.), and Poseidonius.[65] Book III is devoted to Spain and the Cassiterides, Book IV to Transalpine Gaul and the British Isles. There are several references to Ierne ('Ιέρνη), or Ireland, and descriptions which, though the fullest up to this date, are by no means flattering to our Goidelic ancestors or their country.

" There are other small islands around Britain, and one of great extent, Ierne, lying parallel to it towards the north — long, or rather, wide; concerning which we have nothing positive to say, further than that its inhabitants are more savage than the Britons, feed on human flesh and are enormous eaters. They deem it commendable to devour their deceased fathers, as well as openly to be connected not only with other women but also with their own mothers and sisters. But we relate these things, perhaps, without having trustworthy authorities." In attacking the statements of Pytheas regarding Thule he declares that " such persons as have seen the Bretannic Ierne say nothing of Thule." Elsewhere he adds that the farthest sea-voyage from Celtica towards the north was said, among men of his time, to be that to Ierne, which was situated beyond Britain and was barely habitable on account of the cold. And again: " Writers of the present time have nothing to say of anything beyond Ierne, which is just north of Britain. The natives are wholly savage and lead a wretched existence because of the cold. In my opinion it is there that the limits of the habitable earth should be fixed."

An obscure geographer named Isidore, a native of Charax on the Tigris, seems to have been a contemporary of Strabo. Only a small fragment of his work survives: in it he mentions the British islands, Albion and Ierne. Ed. in C. Müller *Geographi graeci minores* I 244–56.

---

[64] *Cf.* Serre *Les marines de guerre de l'antiquité* (Paris 1891) 313.
[65] Klotz *op. cit.*

6. Pomponius Mela: Description of the World   c A.D. 43

Pomponius Mela, the first Latin geographer, was a native of southern Spain. His work (De situ orbis libri tres) is, for the most part, a mere compendium of earlier writings in Greek, but it is evident that he knew the west better than his predecessors. He gives a somewhat fabulous account of Ireland.

" Beyond Britain is Iuverna, of almost the same extent, but in shape oblong, with an equal length of coast on either side. The climate is unfavorable for the ripening of grain, but so luxuriant is the herbage, in quality both nutritious and savoury, that the cattle eat their fill in a small part of the day, and, if they were not restrained from feeding, would, by eating too long, burst. The inhabitants are rude and more ignorant of every virtue than other races, being even devoid of 'all sense of duty (pietas)." [66]

7. Caius Plinius Secundus: Natural History   A.D. 77-79

Pliny the Elder was born in A.D. 23 and died in 79. His Historia naturalis, surviving in thirty-seven books, is a curious encyclopaedic but uncritical compilation, said to be drawn from over two thousand written sources. Pomponius Mela was one of his chief authorities for geographical knowledge. The first seven books treat of geography: in Book IV are a few references to " Hibernia." Elsewhere he gives us some information regarding the Celts of Gaul and the druids.

8. Pseudo-Aristotle: Concerning the World   s I/II

EDS: Bekker's Aristotle (Berlin 1831) I 391-401. — Didot's ed. of Aristotle III 630. —C. Wachsmuth and O. Hense Joannes Stobaeus (Eclogae Physicae I 31). TRANS: E. S. Forster (Oxford 1914). COMM: W. Capelle Neue Jahrbücher XV (1905) 529-68.

This treatise on the world (περὶ κόσμου) takes the form of a letter ostensibly addressed by the Greek philosopher Aristotle to Alexander the Great. It is probably a popular exposition based on certain works of Poseidonius and written in the first or second century after Christ. Mention is made in it of the Bretannic Isles, Albion and Ierne.

9. Publius Cornelius Tacitus: Life of Agricola   A.D. 97-8

Little is known of the life of Tacitus, usually regarded as the greatest of Roman historians, beyond the facts that he belonged to the nobility, was a son-in-law of one

---

[66] Mela III vi 53. Sir John Rhŷs has called attention to another passage in Mela which may preserve the name of Ireland. The Greek hero Hercules, having obtained the cows of Geryon in Spain, is attacked while passing through Liguria by two giants, Albiona and Beryon, whom he slays. These may be corruptions of the words Albion and Iberion representing Britain and Ireland. Mela II 78; cf. Rhŷs Celtic Britain 204-5. — On Irish knowledge of Mela in the early middle ages see Manitius Lat. Lit. I 677-8.

of the ablest administrators of the Roman state, Cnaeus Julius Agricola, and became a lawyer of prominence, and a member of the literary circle under the Emperor Trajan which included Suetonius and the Younger Pliny. Though his writings cannot be regarded as absolutely trustworthy, his subject matter was weighed with more than usual care.

The *Agricola* is an account, somewhat idealised, of the life of his father-in-law, who was governor of Britain from A.D. 78 to 86. Tacitus doubtless had first-hand information for this work. A brief and, in parts, obscure, but interesting description of Ireland is given, the conquest of which was under consideration by Agricola.

" In the fifth year [A.D. 83] Agricola crossed over on the first ship and by many successful battles subdued peoples who were till then unknown. He assembled his forces in that part of Britain which looks towards Ireland, in a spirit of anticipation of the future rather than because of any apprehension of danger. For Ireland, lying midway between Britain and Spain, and also convenient to the Gallic Sea, would have united them by extensive mutual intercourse into a very powerful section of the empire. In area it is less than Britain, but exceeds the islands of the Mediterranean. The soil and climate and the character and civilisation of the people, do not differ much from Britain. The interior parts are little known, but through commercial intercourse and the merchants there is better knowledge of the harbors and approaches.[67] Agricola had received one of their petty kings, expelled in a local struggle, and, under the guise of friendship, retained him to be made use of should the opportunity offer.[68] I have often heard Agricola say that Ireland could be invaded and conquered with one legion and a moderate number of auxiliaries. The result would be of advantage even with reference to the coercion of Britain, if Roman arms were to be seen everywhere and independence, so to speak, swept from the horizon." [69]

Contemporary with Tacitus was the satirist Juvenal (c A.D. 60–c 140) who, in what is probably an allusion to the conquests of Agricola, mentions Ireland under the form *Iuuerna*.[70] Perhaps of about the same era is the metrical " Description of the habitable world " (περιήγησις τῆς οἰκουμένης), attributed to a certain Dionysius, which speaks of islands " the birth-place of tin " and of two Britannic islands.[71]

10. Claudius Ptolemaeus: Geography c A.D. 130 × 180

EDS: C. F. A. Nobbe 3 vols. (Leipsic 1843; another ed. 1881). — Carl Müller and C. T. Fischer 2 vols. (Paris 1883, 1901) [in Firmin-Didot's *Bibliotheca graecorum*

[67] This is the reading now generally accepted. Another would make the harbors and approaches of Ireland better known than those of Britain.
[68] This is the first individual Irishman to appear on the pages of history.
[69] *Agricola cap.* xxiv. In Tacitus *Annals, lib.* XII *cap.* xxxii, there is a casual reference to *Hibernia*.
[70] " We have advanced our arms beyond the shores of Iuuerna, and the Orcades lately conquered, and the Britons who are satisfied with brief nights." *Sat.* II 159–62. The satire may have been written not long after A.D. 84, when the fleet of Agricola subdued the Orcades, but can hardly have been published before 100.
[71] C. Müller *Geographici graeci minores* II 102–458. See vv. 563, 566. A Latin version of this poem, prepared by Priscian in the fifth century, seems to have been known in mediaeval Ireland. *Cf.* p. 683 *infra*.

scriptorum]. — J. L. Heiberg 2 vols. (Leipsic 1898, 1907). Comm: Henry Bradley
" Ptolemy's geography of the British Isles " *Archaeologia* XLVIII (1885). — A. E.
Nordenskiöld *Facsimile Atlas* (Stockholm 1889) 1–32 [with maps]. — T. G. Rylands
Geography of Ptolemy elucidated (Dublin 1893). — G. H. Orpen " Ptolemy's map of
Ireland " *Journ. RSAI* 5th ser. IV (1894) 115. — MacN in *New Ireland Rev.* Sept.
1906. — G. Schütte *Scottish Geographical Magazine* XXX (1914) 57, 294, 617. —
J. Pokorny " Spuren von Germanen im alten Irland vor der Wikingerzeit " *ZCP* XI
(1917) 169–88; " *Érainn, Dárin(n)e* und die *Iverni* und *Darini* des Ptolemäus "
ibid. XII (1918) 323–57. — Ed. Norden *Janus* 1921 I 182 *sq.*

Ptolemy, the celebrated mathematician, astronomer and geographer of Alexandria,
lived in the second century. His recorded astronomical observations date from
A.D. 127 to 151, and it is said that he survived to the time of the Emperor
Marcus Aurelius (161–180). His interests were primarily mathematical and
astronomical, and he attempted to follow a system of mathematical accuracy
in his " Geographical Guide." This is in eight books, and contains a discussion of geographical problems, but the greater part consists of a series of tables of
the different countries, in which rivers, capes, tribes, towns, etc., are located by degrees
of latitude and longitude. These tables cover the twenty-six fields into which he
systematically divided the surface of the known world, and are obviously guides
for cartographers. They were, no doubt, used in the construction of his own maps,
which, there is reason to believe, are well represented by the twenty-seven charts
(one of the world as a whole) now to be seen in the manuscripts and early printed
editions. The scientific form of his work is deceptive: in reality, Ptolemy had accurate
astronomical *data* for the location of only a few places; all the others were located
by means of information on which, we would say, no reliance could be placed in scientific work, — itineraries, travellers' tales, reports derived from merchants, etc. Much
of the material on which he drew seems to have been amassed by a certain Marinus
of Tyre, a geographical writer who must have lived not long before himself. Ptolemy
freely acknowledges the deficiencies of his material. But, imperfect as may have
been his knowledge, it was superior to that of any of his predecessors. The *Pax
Romana* and the consequent development of trade and intercourse were the probable
causes of this advance.

The first of Ptolemy's twenty-six tables covers the British Isles. The description of
Ireland [72] here given is by far the most complete and detailed to be found among
all Greek and Roman writers, and is the earliest source for Irish history of really
first-rate importance. Some of the localities and peoples mentioned by him have
been identified with probability, a few with certainty.[73]

———————

Lucius Apuleius was a younger contemporary of Ptolemy, but his treatise *De Mundo*
displays no scientific prepossessions. He is mentioned here only because he himself

———

[72] Ἰουερνίας νῆσου Πρεττανικῆς. The same root seems to be found in several local place-names
given by Ptolemy. The primitive form was probably *everjo*, from which came Irish *Ériu*, Welsh *Iwerddon*,
Greek Ἰέρνη (for Ἰφέρνη), Ἰουέρνοι, and Latin *Hiberio, Iuberna, Hibernia*. The hypothesis has been
advanced that the name is identical with that of the people *Éraing*, or *Érnai*, who at a later time dwelt
in Munster, but Pokorny argues strongly to the contrary (*op. cit.*). He thinks that the original meaning
was " height," " hill " (*cf. ZCP* XV 197–203). *Cf.* p. 121 n. 33 *supra.*

[73] In Book I chap. xi sect. 7 Ptolemy refers to the exaggerated length assigned to Ireland by an otherwise unknown Philemon, on the basis of reports from merchants, and to the criticism thereof by Marinus
of Tyre.

names " the two Britains, Albion and Ibernia . . . situated on the confines of the Celts." [74] Another contemporary was Aelius Aristides (129-189), also called Theodorus, a Greek sophist, who in his *Egyptian Oration*, a rhetorical composition, speaks of a great island opposite the Iberians, by which he may have meant one of the British Isles.[75]

11. Caius Julius Solinus: Collection of Matters of Note (*Collectanea rerum memorabilium*) c A.D. 253 X 268 (?)

ED: Theodor Mommsen C. *Iulii Solini collectanea iterum recensuit* (Berlin 1895).

Mommsen assigns this treatise of marvels to the reigns of Valerian and Gallienus. It is, for the most part, a compilation from Pliny's *Natural History* and Pomponius Mela. It was through the intermediary of Solinus that Martianus Capella, Isidore of Seville and other later writers derived much of their knowledge of Pliny. Solinus gives us a famous description of Ireland and its inhabitants, evidently in part imaginary, but containing some curiously accurate details. Mommsen, however, believes that the text as we have it has been edited by an Irishman, perhaps in the fifth century.

"Britain is surrounded by many important islands. Of these Ireland, which approaches nearest to it in size, is savage in respect of the rude customs of its inhabitants, but on the other hand so rich in herbage that, were it not that the cattle are at times removed from pasture, the satisfaction of their appetites would become dangerous for them.[76] In that land there are no snakes, birds are few, and the people are inhospitable and warlike. The victors in battle drink the blood of the slain and smear it on their faces. No distinction is made by them between the moral and the immoral [*fas ac nefas*]. [Whenever a mother has brought forth a male child, she places the first bit of food on her husband's sword, and with the sword's point gently introduces this omen-giving nutriment into the mouth of the little one, and with the vows of her clan prays that not otherwise than in war and in the midst of arms he shall meet his death. Those who have a taste for luxury decorate the handles of their swords with the tusks of the sea-monsters, which shine with the brightness of ivory: for the peculiar pride of the men is in the brightness of their arms.][77] No bees have ever been there; and if sand or pebbles brought from thence be sprinkled among beehives, the swarms will abandon the combs. The sea lying between Ireland and Britain is stormy and restless during the whole year, and can be navigated only for a very few days. The natives sail in boats of wickerwork covered with the hides of oxen. When the voyage is delayed by any kind of storm, those wishing to sail abstain from food. Those who have made a trustworthy reckoning have estimated the width of the channel at one hundred and twenty miles." [78]

[74] *De Mundo* vi, vii.
[75] Eds.: Dindorf (1829); Keil (1898). "Neither can you hear the fishermen at Gadeira, nor those who cross over to that great island opposite the Iberians, asserting that the outer sea is tranquil. Although expeditions of all kinds perpetually pass into it, and return at convenient seasons. Thousands also of nobles and private persons frequently go over thither."
[76] *Cf.* no. 6.
[77] A later interpolation.
[78] *Cap.* xxii. — Slight allusions to Ireland in two other works of the third or fourth century may be here noted: *Iverio* in the *Itinerarium provinciarum Antonini Augusti* (ed. Gustav Parthey and Moritz

The decline of Roman power in the fourth century was accompanied by an influx of barbarian peoples from across the frontiers. To those who came from Ireland the Romans gave the name *Scotti*, a name which was to become the normal Latin designation of the people of Ireland from the fifth to the eleventh century.[79] The records speak chiefly of the ravages committed by these early *Scotti* in Britain,[80] but they were at the same time making permanent settlements on the western coast, and some of them, it seems probable, were entering the Roman service as auxiliary troops.[81] The occasional appearance of *Scottus*, *Scottius*, and, in a few cases, *Hibernus*, in Latin inscriptions on the continent of Europe indicates that a certain number of Irish were filtering into the cosmopolitan population of the Roman Empire.[82]

12. Eumenius: Panegyrics   A.D. 296, 310

EDS: Migne *PL* VIII 619–54. — E. Bährens *Panegyrici veteres* (Leipsic 1874) 117 *sqq*. *Cf*. S. Brandt "Beiträge zur Kritik der gallischen Panegyriker" *Rheinisches Museum* XXXVIII 603–11.

Eumenius was a native of Autun in Gaul. In the panegyrics offered by him and his fellow rhetoricians of Gaul to Constantius Chlorus and Constantine the Great are many references to Britain and at least two to Ireland and its inhabitants. In a panegyric addressed to Constantius Chlorus after his victory in 296 over a military leader named Allectus, who had maintained a position in Britain independent of the imperial authority, the Picts and the *Hiberni* are for the first time found associated together as enemies of the Britons.[83] " The British race, still rude and accustomed to the hostility of only the half-naked Picts and Irish, yielded easily to Roman arms and standards, so that almost the only thing for which on that expedition fame should be awarded Caesar is that he had sailed across the Ocean."   In another panegyric in praise of Constantine, dating from 310, we find the statement: "After so many glorious exploits he disdained to seize, — I shall not say the woods and swamps of

---

Pinder: Berlin 1848) [*cf*. Raven " The British Section of Antonine's Itinerary " *The Antiquary* XXXVI–XL (1900–4)], a " road guide " of the Roman Empire which, originating with one of the Antonines, in its present form preserves a text probably of the reign of Diocletian (284–305); 'Ιέρνις in the *Argonautica* of Pseudo-Orpheus, vv. 1171, 1186 [ed. J. W. Schneider (1803), E. Abel *Orphica* (1885); *cf*. Christ (ed. Schmid) *Geschichte der griechischen Literatur* Teil II, Zweite Hälfte (Munich 1913)], which is now usually assigned to the second half of the fourth century.

[79] The etymology of *Scottus* is uncertain. MacN, with whom Pokorny agrees, associates it with the Irish verb *scothaim*, which signifies a rapid cutting or striking movement. *Scottus* would, on this view, mean " raider," or " reaver." *Cf*. *Phases of Irish History* 145. On the application of the word *cf*. Skene *Celtic Scotland* I 2–5 and nn.; Plummer *Baedae opera historica* II 11–12; Holder *Alt-celtischer Sprachschatz* II 1406–18.

[80] J. B. Bury, *Life of St. Patrick* 325–31, gives an analysis of the information regarding these attacks. See also Vendryes *De hibernicis vocabulis* (Paris 1902) 14–9.

[81] *Cf*., in addition to the matter below, the Irish saga *Aided Dathi*, and Bury, *op. cit*. 354.

[82] *Cf*. Holder *cp. cit*. III, 1413–4. But it must be remembered that *Scottus* was a proper name in Continental Celtic. *Cf*. *RC* XLI 56.

[83] *Eumenii Panegyrici Constantio Caesari cap*. xi.

the Caledonians and other Picts, but — the neighboring Ireland, the distant Thule, even the Islands of the Blest, if such there are." [84]

13. Ammianus Marcellinus: History c A.D. 380–391

Ammianus Marcellinus was a native of Antioch, a soldier of the imperial body-guard, who served under the Emperor Julian against the Parthians, and afterwards wrote a history, in thirty-one books, of the Empire from A.D. 96 to 378. The first thirteen books are lost, with the result that we have only the narrative of the last twenty-five years. This, which deals almost exclusively with the wars between Romans and barbarians, seems based on personal observations or the reports of eye-witnesses and is regarded very favorably by historical critics. He gives some account of the attacks made on Britain about A.D. 360, and the victories of the elder Theodosius, who pacified the province in 368 and 369. The invaders were the " Picti," " Atacotti," " Scotti," " Franci " and " Saxones." We here meet with the terms " Atacotti " and " Scotti " for the first time. [85]

In a panegyric of the Emperor Theodosius, composed in 389, a certain Pacatus Drepanius alludes to his father's victories in Britain and to " the Scot driven back to his native swamps." — E. Bährens Panegyrici latini (Leipsic 1874) no. xii p. 275 (cap. v). The Chronicon imperiale (MGH Auct. ant. IX 646–62) under A.D. 382 says that Maximus, at that time ruler of Britain, afterwards candidate for the imperial purple, " vigorously defeated the invading Picts and Scots."

14. Claudius Claudianus: Poems c A.D. 396–403

Claudian was a native of Alexandria, born about 365. He came to Rome in 395, and made himself the warm partisan of Stilicho, the administrator of the West under the emperor Honorius. The few allusions in his poems constitute the only contemporary sources for the last years of Roman military administration in Britain, and the struggles with the " Scotti " and other enemies which those wars witnessed.

References to the Irish are to be found in the following passages: *Panegyric on the third consulship of the Emperor Honorius* (A.D. 396) vv. 51–8; *Panegyric on the fourth*

---

[84] *Eumenii Panegyrici Constantio Augusto cap.* vii.

[85] In the *De Bello Judaico*, a Latin version, abridged and expanded with much freedom, of the " Jewish Wars " of Josephus, there is in the added material a reference to the operations of Theodosius in Britain in 368–9, in which " Scotia " is said to tremble at the power of the Romans. This work passes under the name of " Hegesippus," which, however, appears to be only a scribal corruption for " Iosippus." It was prepared within the period 370–400, and is considered by some scholars to be the work of St. Ambrose (*cf.* Otto Scholz *Die Hegesippus-Ambrosius Frage:* Königshutte 1913). In any case it is possible that here, instead of in Ammianus, we have the earliest occurrence of *Scotia* [*Scottia, Scottus*]. Ed: C. F. Weber and J. Caesar (Marburg 1864); *cf. Cath. Encycl. s.v.* " Hegesippus." — The *Atacotti* or *Atecotti*, who are associated in Latin writings of this period with the *Scotti* and *Picti*, have not been identified, nor is it certain whether they came from Ireland or from North Britain. *Cf.* Skene *Celtic Scotland* I 99–106; MaçN *Phases of Irish History* 148–9.

consulship of Honorius (398) vv. 28-33; *On the consulship of Stilicho* (400) II vv. 250-5; *On the Gothic War* (402) vv. 416-8; *Epithalamium to Palladius* vv. 88-91.

15. Notitia dignitatum et administrationum orientis et occidentis
c A.D. 400

EDS: E. Böcking (Bonn 1839-53). — O. Seeck (Berlin 1876). TRANS: Fairley in *Translations and Reprints from the Original Sources of European History* (published by the Department of History, University of Pennsylvania, Philadelphia) VI no. iv (1899) [extracts].

This is a kind of official almanac of the Roman Empire, dating from about the beginning of the fifth century, though some portions of it seem of an earlier period. The British section shows the military organisation in that island. In the section on Gaul five bodies of Attacotts are represented as serving there in the Roman army: " Atecotti seniores," " Atecotti iuniores," " Honoriani Atecotti seniores," " Honoriani Atecotti iuniores," " Atecotti iuniores Gallicani." In the eastern half of the empire there was another body known simply as " Atecotti." The epithet " Honoriani " probably indicates that these corps were enlisted under the emperor Honorius, who succeeded Theodosius in 395.[86]

16. Symmachus: Epistola II A.D. 393

ED: O. Seeck *MGH Auctores antiquissimi* VI (Berlin 1883) 65 [ed. of *Symmachi Epistolae*]. *Cf. MHB Excerpta* p. xcvii.

Symmachus was a prominent member of the Roman nobility at the close of the fourth century, and a champion of the old pagan order. In a letter to his brother Flavian he makes a passing allusion to Irish dogs, " Scottici canes," used for public amusements: " . . . as has been shown by the offering of seven Irish dogs; which on the day of the prelude so astonished Rome that it was thought they must have been brought in iron cages."

17. St. Jerome (Hieronymus) *fl. c* A.D. 370-420

St. Jerome was born in Dalmatia about A.D. 340. He received a good education and travelled extensively. He was in Gaul 366-370, in Syria and Constantinople 374-381, in Rome 382-385, and in Bethlehem and its neighborhood 386-420. His works are very extensive; but, like many of the writers of his age, he showed a strong tendency to rhetorical exaggeration and also to wholesale transcription from the writings of his predecessors. Because of their relationship in one form or another with Irish historical questions the following are worthy of particular note here: (1) his revision of the Latin version of the New Testament and translation from the Hebrew of the Old Testament, the two forming the so-called " Vulgate " text which became the

---

[86] The *Honoriani* were, doubtless, the same as the *Honoriaci*, barbarian auxiliaries who, according to Orosius (VII xl), were sent from Gaul to Spain in 408.

accepted version of the mediaeval Church; — this work was carried out at intervals between the years 384 and 405;[87] (2) commentaries on various parts of the Bible, begun about the same time as his edition of the text, and continued until his death;[88] (3) translation, and continuation to 378, of the Chronicle of Eusebius (a chronicle from the Creation to A.D. 325 prepared by Eusebius, bishop of Caesarea); this work came to serve as a model for the chroniclers of the middle ages.[89]

During his sojourn in Gaul Jerome had an opportunity of learning something of the Irish enemy, then beginning to attract the attention of imperial Rome. In his tract *Adversus Jovinianum*, written about 393, he asserts that he had seen Scots, — or Attacots — who were cannibals of particularly revolting tastes. " Why should I speak of other peoples when I myself as a young man saw in Gaul the Scots,[90] a British race, feeding on human flesh?[91] — and when they come upon herds of swine or cattle in the woods, they usually cut off the buttocks of the shepherds and their wives, and their breasts, and regard these as their only dainties. The Scots have no separate wives, but, as if they read Plato's Republic and were following Cato's example, no woman among them is the wife of one particular man. According to the desires of each, they take their pleasures like the beasts of the field." [92] A letter *Ad Oceanum*, dating from about 400, repeats the statement as to Irish matrimonial relationships.[93]

Jerome's testimony as to the Irish origin of Pelagius will be considered later, in connection with the beginnings of Christianity in Ireland.[94]

There is a brief, uncomplimentary reference to the " Scottus " by Jerome's contemporary, Aurelius Clemens Prudentius, a Spanish Christian, in his poem *Apotheosis*, v. 216, written about 390. Ed: A. Dressel (Leipsic 1860).

To conclude this section three geographical compilations of late but uncertain date may be noticed: The *Periplus of the Outer Sea* (Περίπλους τῆς ἔξω θαλάσσης),[95] by Marcianus (c 400) of Heraclea in Pontus, a work depending ultimately on Ptolemy, has a summary description of Ireland, denominated 'Ιουερνία. The *Outlines of Geography* (Γεωγραφίας ὑποτύπωσις)[96] of Agathemer, gives Ireland — under the same form of the name — a location opposite and parallel to Spain. Stephen of Byzantium, who perhaps lived as late as the sixth century, in his *Nations* ('Εθνικά),[97] a geographical dictionary, made an extensive gathering of matter from older authors. It survives only in a late and poor abridgment, in which the names 'Ιέρνη, 'Ιουερνία and Ιουερνή are given without indication that they designate the same land.

[87] *Cf*. pp. 626 *sqq infra*.   [88] *Cf*. pp. 659 *sqq infra*.   [89] *Cf*. p. 165 *infra*.
[90] Variant reading " Attacots." Doubtless the persons referred to were either captives from the campaign of Theodosius or auxiliaries enrolled in the Roman army.
[91] " Viderim Scotos . . . humanis vesci carnibus."
[92] *Adv. Jovin. lib.* II *cap.* vii; Migne *PL* XXIII 335.
[93] *Ep*. lxix. — Migne *PL* XXII 653-64; *Corp. SS. Eccles. Lat.* LIV 678-700. Mention is made of the Irish races, who knew not Moses or the prophets, in the epistle *Ad Ctesiphontem*. — Migne *PL* XXII 1157.
[94] *Cf*. no. 26.
[95] C. Müller *Geographi graeci minores* I pp. cxxix, 515-73.
[96] *Ibid*. II pp. xlii *sqq*, 471-511.
[97] Westermann (Leipsic 1825); Meineke (Berlin 1849).

IV. GAUL AND SPAIN

Bibliography

S. Dill *Roman society in the last century of the empire* 2nd ed. (London 1899). — T. R. Glover *Life and letters in the fourth century* (Cambridge 1901). — Fustel de Coulanges *Les institutions de l'ancienne France:* I *La Gaule romaine;* II *L'Invasion germanique* (Paris 1891). — C. Jullian *Histoire de Bordeaux* (Bordeaux 1895); *Ausone et Bordeaux, Études sur les derniers temps de la Gaule romaine* (Bordeaux 1895). — Labroue *L'École de Périgueux au Ve siècle* (Paris 1903). — Roger *L'Enseignement* (1905). — Theodore Haarhoff *Schools of Gaul: a study of pagan and Christian education in the last century of the western empire* (London, etc. 1920). — E. Norden *Die antike Kunstprosa vom VI Jahrhundert vor Christus bis in die Zeit der Renaissance* 2 vols. (Leipsic 1898; 3rd ed. 1918) [includes a minute study of the Latin rhetorical style, in vogue especially in Gaul]. HZ " Über direkte Handelsverbindungen Westgalliens mit Irland im Altertum und frühen Mittelalter " 5 parts *Sitz. d. k. preuss. Akad. d. Wissensch.* (1909) pp. 363-400, 430-76, 543-613; (1910) pp. 1031-1119 [very important, although some arguments are far-fetched and others erroneous]. — KM *Learning in Ireland in the fifth century and the transmission of letters* (Dublin 1913) [also very important].

One of the last of the many important contributions made by Heinrich Zimmer to Irish history was an exhaustive study of the texts bearing on direct trade relations between Ireland and West Gaul in ancient times and the early middle ages. He has made it clear from both native and foreign sources that a trade considerable for its time was maintained for many centuries between Ireland and the western coast of Gaul — Brittany and the mouths of the rivers Loire and Garonne. The most important article of this commerce was wine, which Ireland could not produce, but used in large quantities.[98] This route was, as we have seen,[99] a very ancient one, going back to the bronze and neolithic ages. As a result Gaul, and Spain, which lay only a little further along the route and was in ancient times in close cultural association with south-western Gaul, had a dominant share in the transmission of European influences to Ireland.[100]

Spain, as it was the oldest Roman conquest, outside the bounds of modern Italy, was, at least in its southern and eastern parts, the most

---

[98] See, besides HZ, *op. cit.*, J. Vendryes " Les vins de Gaule en Irlande et l'expression *fín aicneta* " *RC* XXXVIII (1920) 19-24.

[99] *Cf.* pp. 122 *sqq supra.*

[100] To the fact that Ireland's principal foreign relations were with western Gaul must it be due that *Gall* became the Irish equivalent of " foreigner." In later times it was used to designate the Norsemen, and, still later, the English.

completely Latinized.   The schools and the writers of Spain became, under the emperors, indistinguishable from those of Italy.   In Gaul, although the Romanising process began much later, it was almost as complete.   In some districts the Celtic language persisted into the fifth century and possibly till much later, [101] but the nobility and a large part of the town-dwellers adopted Latin and the Roman culture within two or three generations of the conquest by Caesar, and the bulk of the population followed their lead during the first century of the Christian era.   The Roman government encouraged the movement, especially by the establishment and maintenance of schools, to which the Gallic upper classes eagerly sent their children.   Thus it came about that during the second, third and fourth centuries Italy, Spain and Gaul formed practically one people, enjoying and developing a common civilisation.

In the fourth century learning and letters still flourished in western Gaul, public schools were maintained in Poitiers, Vesuna or Périgueux, Angoulême, Toulouse, probably Auch, and, most important of all, Bordigala, the modern Bordeaux.   There were, doubtless, other public schools, no contemporary references to which happen to survive, and there were many private schools.   The courses of study, under the broad designations of grammar and rhetoric, embraced a very wide range of literature and philosophy.   The schools were secular, independent of the Church, and although many of the teachers, *grammatici* and *rhetorici*, were Christians, the instruction imparted was of the pagan tradition.

With the fifth century came collapse.   The Roman defences on the Rhine crumbled, and various Germanic tribes began to move into Gaul, sometimes wandering through the country, pillaging as they went, sometimes seizing a district and settling down as rulers.   A horde of Alans, Sueves and Vandals crossed the Rhine in 406, about 413 the Burgundians and the Visigoths came in, and by 430 the Huns, the greatest terror of all, were pressing on the eastern frontiers.   In 451 came a huge invasion of these Huns, who swept the country as far as Orleans, until driven back by the union of Romans and Goths.   Under such conditions public order and the machinery of civilised society broke down.   In some of the southern and central districts the Roman public administration maintained itself with difficulty till about 485, but by the end of the century the whole of Gaul was dominated by three barbarian peoples, the Franks in the north and centre, the Burgundians in the south-east, and the Visigoths, who also held Spain, in the south-west.   Under the Visigoths, whose rule

101 Cf. Dottin *La Langue gauloise* (Paris 1920) 68–71.

extended over such former centres of learning as Toulouse, Poitiers and Bordeaux, more encouragement or tolerance seems to have been accorded learning than under the other barbarians, but all south-western Gaul was taken from them by the Franks in 507.

These conditions were disastrous for letters and learning. None of the public schools seems to have survived the second decade of the fifth century, and little more is heard of private schools. Nevertheless the writings of Sidonius Apollinaris (430–484),[102] bishop of the Arverni, the modern Auvergne, show us a cultivated society maintaining a brave face in the midst of disintegration, and play-acting at literature whilst the flood of barbarism was rising steadily to engulf it.

These conditions are of interest to the student of Irish affairs because it was chiefly in the fourth and fifth centuries that Roman civilisation made its way into Ireland. And the more we learn about letters in early mediaeval Ireland the more probable it appears to be that the literary ideals and practices of Gaul in the last era of Roman dominion and the first epoch of barbarian rule exercised a powerful influence on the formation of Irish vernacular literature.

18. Orosius: *Historiae adversum paganos* c A.D. 417

Orosius was a Christian priest of Spain who accepted from St. Augustine the task of showing, in opposition to the adherents of paganism, that the calamities of his time were neither unusual nor a proof of the anger of the gods at the spread of the new religion of Christianity. To his survey of human history from this point of view he prefixed a geographical essay, evidently adopted from some other work. Portions of the same treatise are preserved in the fragments of an obscure writer named Julius Honorius, and in various geographical collections which seem to have been based on his work. It contains a brief but somewhat important description of Ireland.

" And inasmuch as there are islands in the ocean, called Britain and Ireland (*Hibernia*), which are situated opposite the Gauls in the direction of Spain, they will be described briefly . . . . The island of Ireland, situated between Britain and Spain, is of greater extent from south to north. Its nearer regions bordering on the Cantabrian ocean look across, from the north-west, a wide expanse towards Brigantia, a city of Galicia, which faces them from the south. This is true in particular of the headland where the mouth of the river Scena is located, and where the Velabri and Luceni dwell.[103] Ireland is nearer to Britain, than which it is smaller in extent but of greater value because of the favorable character of its climate and soil. It is inhabited by

---

[102] In a panegyric of about 455, addressed to his father-in-law, the Emperor Avitus, he refers casually to past Roman successes in Britain over Irish, Saxons and Picts. Eds: Migne *PL* LVIII; Luetjohann *MGH Auctores antiq.* VIII (1887). Trans: O. M. Dalton *The Letters of Sidonius* (Oxford 1915).
[103] *Cf.* p. 144 *infra.*

the tribes of the Scots. Quite near to Ireland is the island of Mevania, also of considerable extent and of fertile soil. It likewise is inhabited by tribes of Scots."[104]

The writings of Orosius were studied in Ireland as well as elsewhere in mediaeval Europe, and Eóin MacNeill has shown that they had an influence on the shaping of the " Milesian " legend of the origin of the Gaelic people.[105]

19. The Leyden Glossary

MS: Leyden Voss. Lat. F. 70 (s XII) f. 79. ED: Lucian Müller *Neue Jahrbücher für Philologie und Pädagogik* XCIII (1866) 389. COMM: Roger *L'Enseignement* (1905) 203. — HZ *ZCP* IX (1913) 118–9. — KM *Learning in Ireland in the fifth century* (1913).

A Leyden manuscript contains a glossary, entitled *Quaedam excerpta utilium verborum*, in which appears, abruptly and without relation to its setting, a short note on the barbarian invasions of Gaul. This reads as follows:

"The Huns, who are the offspring of an infamous union, i.e., of demons, after they had found their way by the guidance of a hind through the Maeotic marshes, attacked the Goths, whom they terrified exceedingly because of the unlooked-for horror which they inspired.[106] From them the devastation of the whole empire took its beginning, and it was completed by Huns and Vandals,[107] Goths and Alans, at whose devastation all the learned men on this side of the sea took flight, and in transmarine parts, namely, in Ireland [108] and wherever they betook themselves, brought about a very great increase of learning to the inhabitants of those regions."

It is reasonably certain that the original of this extract was written in Gaul in the sixth or seventh century [109] and represents a tradition then held regarding the decline of learning on the continent and its advance in Ireland. It is the only reference among our scanty sources to the flight of a portion of the upper classes across the western sea to escape the barbarian terror, but that such a movement took place in at least a small measure would be, in view of the general situation, a not unnatural inference. It was made by d'Arbois de Jubainville,[110] who, seemingly, never heard of the Leyden document. But the words of the text point to an exodus on a considerable scale, and have been accepted as evidence thereof by Zimmer and Meyer, who see in it the explanation of much that is otherwise obscure in early Irish history. Among specific facts which derive a peculiar significance in the light of this record are the following: (1) the occurrence of the word " Bordgal " — the Irish form of *Burdigala*, Bordeaux — as a place-name in Westmeath and in Kilkenny, and also as a common noun in the

[104] *Lib.* I *cap.* ii.
[105] *Phases of Irish History* 90–5.
[106] This opening sentence is based on the *History of the Goths*, by Jordanis, written in 551; or, possibly on one of his sources, now lost. According to Mommsen, *MGH Auct. antiq.* V i (1882) p. xlv, all our copies of this work of Jordanis go back to an Irish exemplar. *Cf.* Manitius *Lat. Lit.* I 214.
[107] *Guandalis.* The form shows that the writer belonged to a Romance-speaking people.
[108] *Hiberia.* This form is used by Columbanus, and agrees closely with the *Hiberio* of Patricius. *Cf.* p. 167 *infra.*
[109] HZ assigned it to the second half of the sixth century.
[110] *RC* XXI 339; XIX 73.

sense of " meeting-place, place of assembly "; [111] (2) the implication in the *Confession of Patricius* — a contemporary of these Gallic *émigrés* — of the presence in Ireland of a body of scholars well educated in the Latin tongue who regarded with scorn the illiteracy of the saint and even questioned the legitimacy of his mission; [112] (3) the Irish origin of the *Hisperica Famina*; [113] (4) the traces in early Irish writings of the influence of late Gallo-Latin literature.[114]

20. Virgilius Maro *grammaticus*

EDS: A. Mai *Classici auctores* V i [and *Append. ad opera* 113, 151]. — J. Huemer *Virgili grammatici opera* (Leipsic 1886); "Die Epitomae des Grammatikus Virgilius nach dem Fragmentum Vindobonense 19556" *Sitzungsberichte d. kais. Akad. d. Wissensch. z. Wien* IC (1882) 509–59 [a 9th cent. fragment of 5 leaves, originally from Salzburg]. — Th. Stangl *Virgiliana* (Munich 1891) [supplement to Huemer's ed.; *cf. Wochenschrift für klassische Philologie* 1890]. COMM: Stowasser *Zeitschrift für österr. Gymn.* XXXIV 211, 511, XXXVIII 122. — A. Ernault *De Virgilio Marone grammatico Tolosano* (Paris 1886). — Roger *L'Enseignement* (1905) 110–26. — J. E. Sandys *History of classical scholarship* 3rd ed. I (Cambridge 1921) 450, 665. — HZ " Über direkte Handelsverbindungen Westgalliens mit Irland: 4 Der Gascogner *Virgilius Maro grammaticus* in Irland " *Sitz. d. k. preuss. Akad. d. Wissensch.* 1910 no. LI 1031–98 [*cf.* J. Vendryes *RC* XXXII 130 *sqq*]. — Manitius *Lat. Lit.* I (1911) 119–27. — HZ (ed. KM) *ZCP* IX (1913) 117–20. — KM *Learning in Ireland in the fifth century* (Dublin 1913). — Geo. Calder *Auraicept na nÉces* (Edinburgh 1917) pp. xl–xlv. — L. Wiener *Contributions towards a history of Arabico-Gothic culture* I (New York 1917) [eccentric criticism; gives considerable attention to Maro].

The last of the ancient *grammatici* of Gaul, and the one whose associations with Ireland are most marked, was the curious and obscure writer known as Virgilius Maro. Of his date all that is known is that he was a contemporary of Ennodius (474–521), bishop of Pavia, by whom he was ridiculed as a *fatuus homullus*, arrogating to himself a sacred name.[115] He has been called a citizen of Toulouse,[116] and also a Spaniard;[117] his writings, which show that he regarded himself as a Gaul, contain allusions to Bigorre, Ate near Limoges, and Carca in Spain. It seems, therefore, that he lived in south-western Gaul, under the rule of the Visigoths, and perhaps of their conquerors the Franks, in the first or second generation after the death of Sidonius Apollinaris. His surviving writings consist of twelve *epitomae*, treating of " wisdom, the letter,

[111] *Cf.* KM *Betha Colmáin maic Lúacháin* (*Todd Lecture Series* XXII) (Dublin 1911) 116; *Miscellanea Hibernica* (*University of Illinois Studies in Language and Literature* II iv) (Nov. 1916) 34.
[112] *Cf.* pp. 165–9. In one passage he addresses these *rhetorici* directly: White's ed. sect. 13. It is just possible, however, that the persons Patricius had in mind were not residents of Ireland.
[113] No. 84.
[114] Hardly a beginning has been made in the investigation of this important problem. *Cf.* KM *Learning in Ireland in the fifth century.*
[115] *ZCP* IX 118. HZ was the first to recognise the significance of this passage of Ennodius. Before his discovery Virgil was generally regarded as posterior to Isidore of Seville, because of certain supposed borrowings of etymologies from the latter. KM (*Learning in Ireland* 22) shows that, while the etymologies are the same, the language is different, suggesting that both drew from matter commonly taught in the schools of Gaul and Spain.
[116] By Abbo of Fleury, writing about 980. Mai *Auct. class.* V 349 n. 1.
[117] The Milan MS. M 79.

syllables, composition of metres, the noun, the pronoun, quality of the verb, six other accidents of the verb, the remaining parts of speech, the breaking up of words (*de scinderatione fonorum*), the etymological relationships of some nouns (?), the grammarians' catalogue," and eight *epistolae*, dealing with the parts of speech. Virgil and his circle represent a stage later than that of Sidonius in the decay of classical letters: disappearance of the soul has been followed by disintegration of the form; play-acting at literature has degenerated into puerilities and mummery. Virgil displays little acquaintance with the classical Latin authors, but his work is filled with the barbarisms — adopted, some consciously, some unconsciously — of contemporary Gallo-Latin speech, and with the childish inventions of himself or his fellow grammarians. He and they were interested above all in enigmatic language and writing, and his description of the " twelve kinds of Latin," and of what he designates *scinderatio fonorum*, illustrates some of the processes of cryptic composition then in vogue. These include the substitution of strange or fabricated words for those in normal use, the abbreviation of words, the omission, addition and rearrangement of words, syllables and letters, and other like devices.[118] Such absurdities are not the only signs in Virgil of the early-mediaeval idiosyncrasy; in him are witnessed also the preposterous importance attached to inconsequential problems, the delight in dialectics, the use of the catechetical form of exposition, the uncritical acceptance of authority, which were to characterise the intellectual life of succeeding centuries. Nevertheless, if we could accept Virgil's statements at their face value we should find therein testimony to a strong, if misdirected, interest in letters in south-western Gaul about the year 500. His works are filled with references to contemporary *littérateurs*, their writings and their schools — all, except for him, to-day unknown. But their fantastic names, improbable geographical distribution, and *bizarre* conduct give to the whole the appearance of *extravaganza*. Yet it seems impossible that the setting of Virgil's works is entirely the product of his imagination. Perhaps the most probable explanation is that there was, in south-western Gaul and in Spain, in the second generation after the Visigothic conquest and the Hun terror had shattered the already crumbling antique culture and sent many of its chief exponents in flight across the sea, a circle of would-be devotees of letters, who took themselves very seriously and went through the forms of perpetuating, in a kind of local academy, the ancient glories of Roman civilisation.[119]

Virgil's works have three main associations with Irish history: (1) They show some acquaintance with Ireland. Kuno Meyer noted about forty names which he considered to be of Celtic origin, one at least of which he regarded as Irish — " Bregandus Lugenicus " (that is, Bregand of the Luceni, a people mentioned by Orosius [120]). Virgil had sufficient knowledge of the Irish language to observe its peculiarity of placing the verb at the beginning of the sentence. (2) Virgil's writings have been preserved only through Irish intermediaries. His editor, Huemer, points out that the orthographical blunders common to all the manuscripts indicate that they depend on an archetype which was written in Irish script. (3) His writings must have had considerable vogue in Ireland. They were used by the Hiberno-Latin grammarians

---

[118] These, and the following, statements regarding Virgil cannot here be illustrated in detail. The student who has not the opportunity, or the patience, to work through the original will find an illuminating exposition in either Roger or Manitius.

[119] Paul Lehmann, in *Die Parodie im Mittelalter* (Munich 1922), suggests that the whole work may be a parody on the grammatical schools.

[120] *Cf.* p. 141 *supra*.

Malsachanus, Cruindmelus and Clemens Scottus, and in the Hibernensis collection of canons.[121] His influence shows itself chiefly, however, in works in the Irish language, and in this connection has been examined with some care by Heinrich Zimmer, Kuno Meyer and George Calder. Zimmer, reviewing the evidences of Virgil's Irish connection, was led to postulate that the grammarian himself migrated to Ireland, where he is to be identified with the "Ferchertne fili" who holds a noteworthy position in the beginnings of Irish literature and grammar. Zimmer based this identification on an equation of the two names which has not met the approval of other scholars.[122]

21. Ethicus Ister: *Cosmographia*

EDS: D'Avezac *Ethicus et les ouvrages cosmographiques intitulés de ce nom* (*Mém. présentés par divers savants à l'Acad. des inscr. et belles lettres* 1st ser. II) (Paris 1852). — H. Wuttke *Die Kosmographie des Istrier Aithikos* (Leipsic 1853). — C. Pertz *De cosmographia Ethici libri tres* (Berlin 1853). — Riese *Geographi latini minores* (Heilbronn 1878). — Krusch *MGH SS rer. merov.* VII (Hanover, Leipsic 1920) 517-27 [gives only the text on the origin of the Franks, but has a valuable introd.]. COMM: H. Wuttke *Die Echtheit des Auszugs aus der Cosmographie des Æthicus geprüft* (Leipsic 1854). — Kunstmann *Münchener gel. Anzeigen* 1854 p. 249. — C. L. Roth *Heidelberger Jahrbb.* 1854 pp. 270-7, 1855 pp. 100-6. — A. von Gutschmid "Über Ursprung und Abfassungszeit der Kosmographie des Ethicus" *Kleine Schriften* V (Leipsic 1894) 418 *sqq.* — Charles Müller in Hoefer's *Nouvelle biographie générale* XVI (Paris 1856). — Manitius *Lat. Lit.* I (1911) 229-34 [gives references to other works]. — G. Dottin "Le philosophe Aethicus et les Celtes insulaires" *Rev. des études anciennes* April-June 1923.

This *Cosmography*, written in barbarous Latin, professes to be an abridged translation of a Greek account of the wonderful travels of Ethicus, or Aethicus,[123] Ister ("the Istrian Philosopher"). The translator gives his own name as Hieronymus, and makes a deliberate attempt to masquerade as St. Jerome. It is practically certain that there never was a Greek original: if the present text really was derived from an earlier, the work of the "translator" consisted in deciphering the cryptic writing of Ethicus, whose alphabet, a mixture of Latin, Greek, Hebrew, and other elements, is given at the end of the treatise. The work was, apparently, very popular in the ninth and tenth centuries, and it probably had considerable influence on the geographical ideas of the time. The opening sections contain an account of the creation and a description of the universe. Then follow the travels of Ethicus: from Taprobane (Ceylon) across Asia and Africa to Spain; thence to Ireland, Britain, Thule and Germany; and then again to the east, to Asia Minor, Greece, Armenia. Among the Irish Ethicus spent much time "turning over their books," but was not favorably impressed by what he saw and requited the hospitality of his hosts by calling them

---

[121] Nos. 360, 361, 344, 82.

[122] HZ thought that "Fili" was the equivalent of "Virgilius," name of the preeminent "fili" of Latin literature, and that "fer-certne," "man of art," was to be equated with "grammaticus." The hypothesis is far-fetched, and philologists regard "Ferchertne" as a genuine compound, of the type designated *bahuvrîhi*, having the meaning "one possessing a man's, or a manly, art or trade."

[123] *Aethicus* is a Merovingian variation of *ethicus*, a synonym in late Latin for *philosophus*.

bad names.[124] This is testimony to the fame of the books of Ireland in the *milieu* in which the author lived, for one of his devices is to represent the vast superiority of the wisdom of Ethicus to that encountered in each important centre of learning, such as Spain and Greece, that he visited.

It is evident that the author's travels were actually executed—with his finger over a contemporary *mappemonde*. He made use of matter which is found also in Solinus, Justin, Orosius, and Isidore of Seville, and wove into this a whole tissue of absurdities derived from popular fable or from his own imagination. Both the language and the content of the work suggest Merovingian Gaul as the place of composition. It displays, but in a more barbarous form, the same grandiloquent make-believe and puerile pseudo-scholarship which characterise Virgilius Maro.[125] The date of composition is placed by Gutschmid between the time of Alcimus Avitus (died *c* 518), whom Ethicus quotes, and that of the so-called "first continuator" of the Chronicle of Fredegarius (*c* 742), by whom he is quoted. [126] Krusch, on the other hand, denies that Ethicus is quoted in Fredegarius, and regards him as a contemporary of the "continuator." It is usually stated that he must have been later than about 630, because of the use made of the *Etymologies* of Isidore, but so much of the material which went into that compilation seems to have already been in existence that the argument cannot be pressed. The description given of the " Turks " supports a late date, although this people was known by name to Pomponius Mela.

22. Isidore of Seville

Eds: Arevalo 7 vols. (Rome 1797–1803) [the *Etymologiae* in vols. III, IV]. — Migne *PL* LXXXI-LXXXIV [*Etymologiae* in LXXXII]. — W. M. Lindsay (Oxford 1911) [the *Etymologiae*]. Trans: Ernest Brehaut *An Encyclopedist of the Dark Ages Isidore of Seville* (New York 1912) [account of Isidore and his writings, with summaries and extensive translations]. Comm: H. Schwartz *Observations criticae in Isidori Hispaliensis Origenes* (Hirschberg 1895). — Roger *L'Enseignement* (1905) 195–201. — Manitius *Lat. Lit.* I (1911) 52–70 [with references to other works]. — C. H. Beeson *Isidor-Studien* (Traube's *Quellen u. Untersuchungen zur lat. Philologie des Mittelalters*) (Munich 1913).

In Spain under the Visigoths more of the old classical learning and culture seems to have survived than in any of the other barbarian kingdoms.[127] The most famous representative of this Spanish civilisation of the sixth and seventh centuries was Isidore (*c* 560–636), who succeeded his brother as bishop of Seville in 599 or 600 and played a prominent rôle in the history of the peninsula. He wrote voluminously on all manner of sacred and secular subjects, and his works had a great influence on

---

124 Hiberniam properavit, et in ea aliquandiu commoratus est; eorumque volumina revolvens, appellavit eos idiomochos vel idiotistas, id est imperitos laboratores vel incultos doctores, et pro nihilo eos ducens ait: Mundi fines terminare et Hiberniam pervenire, onerosus est labor, sed nulla facultas: honorem nimium incutit, sed ad utilitatem non proficit; imperitos enim habet cultores et instructores, destitutos habet habitatores. — D'Avezac *op. cit.* 469.

125 Ethicus shows what may be a trace of the influence of Maro: *cf.* Krusch *op. cit.* 520.

126 We have a reference to a copy of the text made in 754. *Cf.* Manitius *Lat. Lit.* I 233. On the question of the dates of the " Fredegarius " *cf.* p. 205 *infra*.

127 *Cf.* Bourret *L'École chrétienne de Séville sous la monarchie des Visigoths* (Paris 1855).

the scholarship of western Europe, including Ireland, throughout the middle ages. They are for the most part compilations from older writings, and, in the midst of much that is fantastic and absurd, preserve a considerable amount of the debris of ancient learning. His most important compilation was the *Etymologiae*, or *Origines*, which became a kind of encyclopaedia for the early middle ages. It contains a few references to Ireland and the Irish.

Further evidence of the relations between Gaul and Ireland from the fourth to the seventh century will be considered in connection with the Christianising of Ireland and the subsequent expansion of Irish Christianity to the Continent.[128]

V. BRITAIN

Bibliography

Emil Hübner " Das römische Heer in Britannien " *Hermes* XVI (Berlin 1881) 513–84 [an excellent account of Roman administration; see also his *Römische Herrschaft in Westeuropa* (Berlin 1890) 3–68]. — F. J. Haverfield *The Romanization of Roman Britain* (London 1905; 4th ed. rev. by Geo. Macdonald, Oxford 1923); (ed. Geo. Macdonald) *The Roman Occupation of Britain* (Oxford and London 1924); " Ancient Rome and Ireland" *EHR* XXVIII (1912) 1–12 [on archaeological grounds concludes that intercourse between the two was slight]. — Theodore Mommsen (ed. Haverfield) *Provinces of the Roman Empire* 2 vols. (London 1909). — François Sagot *La Bretagne romaine* (Paris 1911) [gives some attention to the Irish invasions; *cf.* RC XXXV 109–14]. — E. Foord *The last age of Roman Britain* (London 1925).
The books by Elton, Rhŷs, EW, Walter, Rhŷs and Brynmor-Jones, Lloyd, Le Moyne de la Borderie, and Skene noticed on pp. 107–8 *supra*. Also the following papers by Rhŷs: " Early Irish Conquests of Wales and Dumnonia " *Proc. RSAI* ser. V vol. I (1890–1) 642 *sqq*; " The Goidels in Wales " *Archaeologia Cambrensis* 1895 pp. 18–39; " Goidelic words in Brythonic " *ibid.* 264–302. — HZ *Nennius Vindicatus Über Entstehung, Geschichte und Quellen der Historia Brittonum* (Berlin 1893) [this work, characterised by the author's usual learning and untrustworthy brilliance, also, *more suo*, covers the field of British-Welsh history much more widely than might be expected; *cf.* the exposition by RTh in *Le Moyen Âge* 1894, 1895, 1896]. See also the studies by HZ listed in the preceding section. — KM " Early relations between Gael and Brython " *Trans. Hon. Soc. of Cymmrodorion* 1895–6 (London 1897) 55–86 [important]. — J. Loth " Bretons insulaires en Irlande " *RC* XVIII (1897) 304–9. — Cecile O'Rahilly *Ireland and Wales* (London, etc. 1924) 35–67. — J. Loth *L'Émigration bretonne en Armorique du Ve au VIIe siècle de notre ère* (Paris 1883) [important]. — F. Lot *Mélanges d'histoire bretonne* (Paris 1907) [important].

The extent of Romanisation in Britain is less clear than in Gaul, and is, indeed, a subject of controversy among historians.[129] It has,

---

[128] *Cf.* especially pp. 157–209.
[129] Haverfield was the chief advocate of the theory of extensive Romanisation.

however, no great interest for the student of Irish history, for Roman Britain, as we have seen, seems not to have exercised much influence on Ireland. It is in connection with the conversion of Ireland to Christianity, a subject to be considered later, that Britain becomes of importance.

In the days of the Roman occupation the relations of the two countries, so far as reported to us, consisted chiefly of hostile descents made on Britain by the *Scotti* from Ireland. Such raids took place before 296, and about 343, 360–369, and 382–390. They were associated with attacks made by the *Picti*, "the painted people," from the northern part of the island beyond the Roman Wall, and by the *Saxones*, Germans from across the North Sea. In 402 and 407 the Roman troops were withdrawn to the Continent, and in 409 the Emperor Honorius directed the cities of Britain to look after their own defense. Before long the britons had overthrown the Roman civil government. Irish traditions tell us that Niall "of the Nine Hostages," king of Ireland, was killed on the English Channel in 405, and that his successor, Nath-Í or Dathi, who died in 428, also led an expedition overseas. Gildas, the earliest British source, says that the attacks of the Scots continued until 446. It is noteworthy that from this date we hear but little of plundering expeditions sent out from Ireland. Possibly the progress of Christianity, expecially over the central and northern parts of the country, may explain the change.

In the fourth and fifth centuries large Goidelic settlements existed on the western coast of Britain. Their extent is in part indicated by the distribution of ogam stones, which, with the exception of a few among the Picts of Scotland, are all of Irish or Goidelic origin.[130]   Sir John Rhŷs maintained that, with some exceptions, these peoples were the remnants of the Goidels who, in his theory, preceded the Brythons in the occupation of Britain. This theory remains dubious, and, although certain archaeological evidence suggests an earlier date, the literary sources [131] support the view that the Goidelic settlements in the west of Britain of which we have positive knowledge came from Ireland subsequently to Ptolemy's time. Their establishment was part of the "Scottic" invasions of Britain.[132]   An account of one such migration from Ireland to South Wales towards the end of the third century is contained in the

---

[130] There are 13 of these stones in Pembrokeshire, 12 in the remainder of South Wales, 1 in North Wales, 5 in Cornwall and Devon, and 1 in Hampshire. — Rhŷs *Journ. RSAI* 1902 p. 1.

[131] *Cf.* the criticism by HZ noticed above, p. 111.

[132] *Cf.* the art. by A. D. Passmore on the Wansdyke, which cuts off the south-west of England and is believed to have been built against the Scots and Picts: *The Antiquaries' Journal* IV i (London Jan. 1924).

Irish tale *Indarba inna nDési,* the "Expulsion of the Dési," of which there is partial corroboration in Welsh sources. Another Irish text bearing on this subject is found in the *Glossary* of Cormac mac Cuilennáin (d. 908) and elsewhere, and was regarded by Kuno Meyer as of older date than Cormac. It is an explanation of the Irish name *Mugéme:*

" *Mug-éme, i.e.* 'slave of hilt,' was the name of the first lap-dog in Ireland. Coirpre Musc first brought one into Ireland out of the land of the Britons. For at that time great was the power of the Gaels over the Britons. They had divided Britain among them into estates, and each knew his friends' abode. And the Gael used to dwell to the east of the sea not less than in Ireland, and their dwellings and royal forts were built there. Hence is said Dind Tradui, *i.e.,* Dún Tredui, *i.e.,* the triple fosse of Crimthann the Great, son of Fidach, King of Ireland and Britain as far as the English Channel. And hence is Glastonbury of the Gael, a monastery on the Brue. . . . And there also, in the lands of the Cornish Britons, stands Dind map Lethan, *i.e.* the fort of the sons of Liathán, for *mac* [son] is the same as *map* in British. Thus every kindred divided on that side, for its property on the east was equal to that on the west, and they long continued in that power, even after the coming of Patrick."

Coirpre Musc is represented to have been son of Conaire, king of Ireland, whom the old Irish chronologists placed in the middle of the second century. Crimthann, however, was the immediate predecessor of Niall "of the Nine Hostages," and is said to have reigned 366–379. The sons of Liethan are mentioned at a later date, in the *Historia Britonum* ascribed to Nennius, as settled in South Wales.

It would seem from all the evidence that by the beginning of the fifth century Goidels from Ireland were established in North Wales, South Wales, and the Cornish peninsula. The settlement in Argyll, which was to persist and give name and dynasty and culture to the kingdom of Scotland, was probably effected at the same time: Patricius's *Letter against Coroticus* [133] implies its existence in the middle of the century.

If the *Scotti* then ceased their attacks on Britain, not so the *Saxones.* These, and their compatriots the Angles and the Jutes, augmented their aggressions after the withdrawal of the Roman troops until the movement became a wholesale migration, part of the general *Völkerwanderung* of the Germanic peoples in western Europe. But while the provincials on the Continent offered little or no resistance to the barbarian invaders after the collapse of the imperial military organisation, the Britons fought desperately and were only gradually pressed back towards the western coast. It resulted that for some five centuries Britain south of

[133] No. 29.

Pictland was occupied on the east by a series of Germanic communities [134] and on the west by a hostile array of Celtic principalities. Of the latter, Cornwall in the south finally succumbed in the ninth century, Cumbria in the north in the tenth, while Wales in the centre maintained a condition of independence or semi-independence till beyond the period of which the present work treats.

It is necessary to notice two further results of the westward movement of the Britons before the invading Saxons. One was the transmarine migration of some of these Britons, who in the middle and second half of the fifth [135] and in the sixth century crossed the channel and established themselves in that western peninsula of Gaul which has ever since borne the name of Brittany.[136] The other was that the Goidelic communities of the Welsh and Cornish peninsulas disappeared in the sixth and seventh centuries, either expelled, as may have been the case in North Wales,[137] or submerged and absorbed, as would appear to have been elsewhere their fate. With Ireland, however, the relations of these Celtic buffer-states which stood between her and the Teutonic conquerors of the Roman West seem henceforth to have been fairly intimate and friendly.

23. Gildas: *De excidio et conquestu Britanniae*

EDS: Jos. Stephenson (Eng. Hist. Soc.: London 1838) [poor]. — Migne *PL* LXIX 329-92 [reprint of preceding]. — *MHB* (1848) 1-46. — H&S I (1869) 44-107 [omits the "Historia"]. — Mommsen *MGH Auct. Antiq.* XIII (*Chron. min.* III i) (1894) 1-85. — Hugh Williams *Gildas: The Ruin of Britain* (*Cymmrodorion Record Ser.* 3) (Hon. Soc. of Cymmrodorion: London 1899) [text, trans.]. — For other eds., see Hardy, Potthast, Gross. COMM: R. A. Lipsius in Ersch and Gruber *Allgem. Encykl.* I lxvii 231. — A. de la Borderie " La date de la naissance de Gildas " *RC* VI (1883) 1-13; *Études hist. bretonnes* 1st ser.: *L'historien et le prophète des Bretons: Gildas et Merlin* (Paris, etc. 1884) [*cf.* Duchesne *Bulletin critique* 15 Jan. 1885 p. 25]. — The works by J. Loth, HZ and F. Lot cited p. 147 *supra.* — F. Seebohm *The tribal system in Wales*

---

[134] This is, of course, stated as a generalisation without prejudice to the much-discussed question how far a subject Briton population may have survived under the rule of the conquerors.

[135] A certain Mansuetus, designated " bishop of the Britons," was at a council held at Tours in 461. — Mansi VII 947. It may be noted that F. Lot advanced a theory, which has not obtained much favor, that the Britons migrated to Armorica in the fourth century as a result of the attacks of the Irish. *Bibl. de l'École des Chartes* LXI (1900) 547-9.

[136] Some of the clergy, at least, of the Britons, passed on to Galicia in Spain, where we hear of British bishops in the sixth and seventh centuries, and of an episcopal see of Britonia till the end of the ninth century. — H&S II 92-101; Fita " Concilio Ovetense del año 900? Texto inedito " *Boletin de la Real Academia de la Historia* XXXVIII (1901) 113-33.

[137] Some think that North Wales was recovered by the Britons before or early in the fifth century. — HZ *Nennius Vindicatus* 92; J. Loth *RC* XXXIX (1922) 78. Cunedda and his sons, the leaders of this British movement into North Wales, seem to have come from beyond the Wall of Hadrian, probably because of Pictish, and perhaps Irish, pressure following the withdrawal of the Roman legionaries.

2nd ed. (London, etc. 1904) 186 *sqq.* — J. Fonssagrives *St Gildas de Ruis et la société bretonne au VIe siècle* (Paris 1908). — Baring-Gould and Fisher *British Saints* III (1911) 81–130. — Manitius *Lat. Lit.* I (1911) 208–10. — André Oheix *Notes sur la vie de S. Gildas* (Nantes 1913). — F. Duine *Memento* 27–31. — R. Thurneysen "Zum Geburtsjahr des Gildas" *ZCP* XIV (1923) 13–5. — On the position of Gildas in literature see Roger *L'Enseignement* 223–7, 251 *sqq*; Jenkinson *Hisperica Famina* (Cambridge 1908) pp. xix–xxii. — For the controversy as to the date and authorship of the present text, see the following: Alfred Anscombe *St. Gildas of Ruys and Irish regal chronology of the sixth century* (London 1893), and arts. in *The Academy* 1895 Sept.–Nov. pp. 206, 251, 318, 411; in reply, E. W. B. Nicholson *ibid.* pp. 297, 364; W. H. Stevenson *ibid.* pp. 340, 522; *An. Boll.* XIII 175–6. See also arts. by Anscombe and Nicholson noticed under no. 24, and esp. *ZCP* VIII 148–50. A. W. Wade-Evans "Notes on the Excidium Britanniae" *Celtic Review* I (1905) 289–92; "The Ruin of Britannia" *ibid.* II (1905) 46–58, 126–35; and further arts. *ibid.* Jan. 1913, Aug. 1913, April 1914, Nov. 1915 and June 1916; "The Scotti and Picti in the Excidium Britanniae" *Archaeologia Cambrensis* 6th ser. X (1910) 449–56; "The Saxones in the Excidium Britanniae" *ibid.* XI (1911) 170–83; "The chronology of Arthur" *Y Cymmrodor* XXII (1910) 125–49; "The year of the reception of the Saxones" and "Some insular sources of the Excidium Britanniae" *ibid.* XXVII (1917) 26–69; "Gildas and modern professors" *ibid.* XXXI (1921) 60–80. In reply, E. W. B. Nicholson "The Ruin of History" *Celtic Review* II (1906) 369–80.

The "book" or "epistle" of Gildas "Concerning the ruin and conquest of Britain" is the earliest literary source, of native origin, for the history of Britain. It consists of a prologue (chaps. i–ii), a sketch of British history (iii–xxvii), and a denunciation of the evil lives of the author's contemporaries, especially clergy and kings. It is written in a vein of moral indignation reminiscent of the Hebrew prophets, and in a style that is heavy, incoherent and often well-nigh unintelligible. It shows, however, a certain straining after literary art and some echoes of earlier Latin literature. The style and vocabulary are slightly suggestive of those of the *Hisperica Famina.*[138] There are extensive quotations from the Scriptures, quotations that offer interesting evidence as to the biblical versions then in use in Britain.[139] In all these literary characteristics the whole work displays a marked homogeneity.

Two passages bear on the date of composition. (1) In chap. xxvi an obscure reference is made to the battle of "Badon mount," which Gildas associates in some way with the date of his birth.[140] This battle was fought, according to the *Annales Cambriae,* in A.D. 516.[141] (2) One of the kings whom Gildas upbraids is Maglocunus, or Maelgwyn, whose death is placed by the *Annales Cambriae* in 547. Thus it would seem that the *De Excidio* was written within the period 516–547, but the interpretation of Gildas's phrases is so uncertain, and the chronology of the *Annales* so untrustworthy, that no inference therefrom can be regarded with confidence.

Some of the older editors of Gildas divided this text, which they agreed to be of his

[138] No. 84.
[139] *Cf.* p. 625 *infra.*
[140] The words are variously interpreted as meaning that the author was writing in the forty-fourth year after the battle, which occurred in the year of his birth; that he was born in the same year as the battle, the forty-fourth after some unnamed event, perhaps the coming of the Saxons; or that he was in the forty-fourth year of his age when it was fought.
[141] They give a second battle of Badon in 665.

authorship, into two compositions, the *Historia* and the *Epistola*. Mommsen and Williams, however, and the majority of historians of the present day, look on it as one integral production. On the other hand Anscombe and Wade-Evans not only divide it into two distinct works, but maintain that the *Historia* section, chaps. i (or ii) to xxvii, was not written by Gildas, but by some unknown Welshman about the year 655 (Anscombe) or 700 (Wade-Evans).[142] This theory has not been received with much favor; it solves some difficulties, but ignores, or creates, others, and involves so many forced hypotheses and emendations of texts — for the ramifications are extraordinarily wide — that it needs must arouse scepticism. It should be noted that these two critics assign the *Epistola* section (chaps. xxviii-cx, and perhaps i), which they regard as the work of the true Gildas, to a date about A.D. 500.

The historical section of the *De Excidio* is a vague, often unintelligible, sketch which has value as a record only because of the want of anything better. It treats chiefly of the period of the breakdown of Roman power in Britain, and of the struggle between Britons and Anglo-Saxons which followed. For the reason just stated it is a source of considerable importance for the attacks of the Irish on Britain in the fourth and fifth centuries.[143] The jeremiad against contemporary social, moral and religious conditions has interest because it seems probable that just then Britain was exercising a special religious influence on Ireland.

For other writings attributed to Gildas see nos. 82, 100 and p. 239; for his Life, no. 34.

24. Nennius: The *Historia Britonum*

Eds: Jos. Stevenson (Eng. Hist. Soc.: London 1838). — San-Marte [Albert Schultz] (Berlin 1844). — *MHB* (1845) 47 *sqq.* — Mommsen *MGH Auct. antiq.* XIII (*Chronica minora* III i) (1894) 111-222 [best ed.: rev. RTh *ZCP* I 157-68; F. Lot *Moyen Âge* VIII (1895) 177-84, IX 25-36]. — L. Duchesne *RC* XV (1894) 174-97 [only ed. of earliest text]. TRANS: J. A. Giles (London 1841); and in *Bohn's Antiquarian Library* (1848). COMM: C. W. Schoell *De ecclesiasticae Britonum Scotorumque historiae fontibus* (Berlin 1851) 29-37. — W. F. Skene *The four ancient books of Wales* I (Edinburgh 1868) 37-41. — Arthur de la Borderie *L'Historia Britonum attribuée à Nennius et l'Historia Britannica avant Geoffroi de Monmouth* (Paris and London 1883). — G. Heeger *Über die Trojanersage der Britten* (Munich 1886) 19-60. — WS *The Academy* May 7, 1887, p. 325. — HZ *Nennius Vindicatus* (Berlin 1893) [*cf.* p. 147 *supra*: very valuable, but some of the conclusions are too hazardous, and the oldest version is neglected; *cf. The Academy* Aug. 12, 19, 1893; *Folklore* IV 380-6; *RC* XV 126-9,— by AdeJ — and XVI 1-5,— by Duchesne; *Zs f. deut. Philologie* XXVIII (1895) 80-113,— by RTh: very important]; *NA* XIX (1894) 436-43, 667. — Mommsen "Die Historia Brittonum und König Lucius" *NA* XIX (1894) 283-93. — L. Traube *ibid.* XXIV 721 *sqq.* — A. Anscombe "The identification of 'Libine Abas Iae' in the Historia Brittonum" *ZCP* I (1897) 274-6. — E. W. B. Nicholson "Filius Urbagen" *ibid.* III (1901) 104-11. — V. H. Friedel "Les vers de Pseudo-Nennius" *ibid.* III 112-22, 515. — Manitius *Lat. Lit.* I (1911) 240-2 [good summary]. — F. Lot

---

[142] Although Anscombe and Wade-Evans agree in the initial proposition of their theory, they differ appreciably in its development.

[143] Bury *St. Patrick* 330-1 gives a brief equation of the statements of Gildas with the Roman evidence and the Irish traditions.

in *Mélanges d'histoire offerts à M. Charles Bémont* (Paris 1913) 1–19 [important; *cf.* *RC* XXXVII (1917–9) 406–8]. — A. G. van Hamel in J. Hoops *Reallexicon der germanischen Altertumskunde* III (Strasburg 1915–6) 302–5. — F. Liebermann " Nennius the author of the Historia Brittonum " in A. G. Little and F. M. Powicke (eds.) *Essays in mediaeval history presented to Thomas Frederick Tout* (Manchester 1925) 25–44 [important]. — Max Förster " War Nennius ein Ire? " *Heinrich-Finke-Festschrift* (Marburg 1925) 36–42. *Cf.* also the articles on chronology by RTh in Kölbing's *Englische Studien* XXII (1896) 163–79, by Anscombe in *ZCP* III 492–514, VI 339–94, VII 419–38, *Ériu* III 117–34, and by Nicholson in *ZCP* VI 439–53, VIII 121–50. These constitute a further phase of the controversy noticed in no. 23.

THE IRISH VERSION (*Leabhar Breathnach*). MSS: LU pp. 3–4 [a fragment]. — BB 203–11. — RIA Bk. Lec. [has 2 copies; leaves belonging to this codex are in TCD 1319 (H. 2. 17) pp. 172 *sqq*]. — RIA Leabhar Húi Maine ff. 91–4. — TCD 1336 (H. 3. 17) *s* XV/XVI cols. 806 *sqq*. EDS: J. H. Todd and Algernon Herbert *Leabhar Breathnach annso sis The Irish version of the Historia Brittonum of Nennius* (IAS: Dublin 1848) [with trans.]. — E. Hogan *The Irish Nennius from L. na Huidre* (RIA Todd Lect. Ser. VI) (Dublin 1895) [with trans.; also the fragments of the Irish version of the *Sex Aetates mundi* which precede Nennius in LU. *Cf.* *ZCP* I 169 *sqq*.]. LAT. TRANS.: HZ in Mommsen's ed.

The *Historia Britonum*, preserved in many varying texts, is the result, it has generally been thought, of a long process of compilation. The investigation of its evolution has produced an extensive literature, but only a brief summary of the results obtained and theories advanced can here be given.

The extant versions may be classified as follows:

I The shortest redaction, that of the 9th or 10th (11th, Nicholson) century Chartres MS, No. 98. The title as read by Nicholson is " Beginning of excerpts Discoveries of the son of Urbagen with regard to the Book of St. Germanus, and the origin and genealogy of the Britons." Thurneysen and Nicholson identify Urbagen with a British King Urbgen, slain *c* 572–9, and his son with a certain Run map Urbgen who is said to have baptized the Northumbrians *c* 627, and may be the same man as Paulinus, bishop of York.[144] A chronological note points to the year 750, in connection with which there is a reference to Slebine, abbot of Iona *c* 752–767.[145] The

---

[144] *Annales Cambriae* 626: " Etguin baptizatus est, et Run filius Urbgen baptizauit eum." Plummer (*Ven. Baedae opera historica* II 100–1) considers the story a fable, designed to claim for the British Church a principal share in the evangelisation of Northumbria. Paulinus was sent from Rome by Gregory in 601 to assist Augustine. It is possible — nothing more — that he was a Briton by origin, chosen for the Northumbrian mission because of some personal or family relationship with King Edwin. Edwin had been an exile from Northumbria from soon after his father's death in 588 until he himself overthrew Ethelfrid in 616 or 617. According to Welsh tradition (*Myvyrian Archaiology* II 17 triad 81) part of this time he spent at the court of Cadvan, king of Gwynedd — perhaps until he was forced to flee as a result of Ethelfrid's great victory over the Britons at Chester in 616 or a little earlier. However, on overthrowing Ethelfrid, Edwin continued the policy of aggression in North Wales and reduced Anglesey and Man.

[145] As emended by Nicholson *ZCP* III 107: sicut [S]libine abas Iae Inripum ciuitate inuenit uel reperit. Inripum = Ripon (*cf.* Plummer *Baedae opera historica* II 103–4; Bede uses this very form in *Hist. Eccles.* III xxv, V xix): Nicholson suggests that Slebine went there to see the pastoral staff given by Columba to Kentigern, which was kept in St. Wilfrid's church at Ripon. — Reeves *Ad.* 324; p. xc of the 1874 ed.

text ends imperfect. It is possible that it once included eighth-century versions of other *excerpta* besides the " discoveries " of the son of Urbagen.

II a. The most extensive redaction: its best exemplar is in the British Museum Harleian MS 3859. The work is anonymous. It bears the date 831. b. An abbreviated edition of the same text, with some slight additional matter. Here the treatise is attributed to Gildas, but, like the preceding, it bears the date 831. c. The same shorter recension, but with still more additions. The preamble runs: " I, Nennius, disciple of Elvodug, have taken care to copy some excerpts, which the people of Britain in their stupidity had thrown away, for they had no knowledge, and the learned men of that island of Britain had made no records in their books. Now I have collected everything which I found, both from the annals of the Romans and from the chronicles of the holy Fathers, that is, Jerome, Eusebius, Isidore, Prosper, and from the annals of the Irish and the Saxons, and from the tradition of the elders of our people. Many learned men and scribes have attempted to write this out, but for some reason or other they left it more obscure . . . ." Elbodug, bishop of Guenedota, who was instrumental in bringing about the adoption of the Roman Easter in Wales, died, according to the *Annales Cambriae*, in 809. The *computus* dated 831 is, here also, prefixed to the *Historia*, but it has a continuation written apparently in 910.

III This is the Harleian text (except in two sections), but with slight variations and considerable omissions. The Vatican MS *Reginensis* 964 opens "Beginning of the *Historia Britonum*, edited by the anchorite Marcus, a holy bishop of that nation." The date of this version is given as 945. The compiler seems to have been an Englishman. He may have used a version by Marcus, or the *incipit* may be simply a guess based on the Life of Germanus by Heiric of Auxerre.[146]

IV The Irish translation, ascribed to Gilla-Coemáin, who died in 1072. It is based on the Nennius redaction (II c), but with considerable modifications. Zimmer expressed the opinion that it preserved the order of subjects in the composition of Nennius with more fidelity than do the surviving Latin copies. The several Irish texts, however, differ considerably among themselves.

The *Historia Britonum* (using the term to designate the source under consideration as a whole) is made up of a series of distinct documents, the majority of which are themselves composite in character: 1 The preface of Nennius [found in the versions II c and IV]. 2 Some verses by Nennius [II c]. 3 The *Computus* and *De sex aetatibus mundi* (I, II a, b, c, III). 4 *Historia Britonum* proper: i description of Britain; ii legend of Brutus the Trojan; iii the different settlements in Ireland, " as the wisest men of the Irish told me " (II c adds " No established account of the origin of the Irish is given "): Zimmer considered this of peculiar importance as the only pre-Norse version of the *Leabhar Gabhála*, or Book of the Settlements of Ireland; iv genealogy of the sons of Noah; v Roman conquest of Britain; vi legend of the Christian king Lucius; vii the attacks of the Picts and Scots, and the end of Roman rule; viii the story of Vortigern and the coming of the Saxons; ix legend of Germanus of Auxerre, who visited Britain in 429 and *c* 445 to suppress the Pelagian heresy; [147] x legend of Ambrosius; xi genealogy of Vortigern's descendants. [This part is to be found in all versions, though the order and extent varies: I has only subsections i, ii, iv, v, viii, ix; the MS ends imperfect here, and we do not know what were the contents of the

---

[146] *Cf.* no. 407.   [147] *Cf.* pp. 163-4.

remainder of this version.] 5 *Vita Patricii*, based on the documents in the *Liber Ardmachanus;*[148] but showing a few variations [II a, b, c, III; IV considered the subject-matter sufficiently well known to Irishmen]. 6 List of King Arthur's battles [II a, b, c, III, IV: precedes 5 in III]. 7 Genealogies of Saxon kings, and a North-umbrian or Cumbrian tract on the history of the English kingdoms, dating apparently from A.D. 679: it contains the earliest reference to the British conquest of the Irish settlements in Wales [II a]. 8 *Compuĺus* [II a]. 9 *Annales Cambriae* [one MS of II a]. 10 Welsh genealogies [*ibid.*]. 11 List of British cities [II a, b, c, III, IV]. 12 List of the wonders of Britain [II, IV].

The nucleus of the compilation was, doubtless, a legend of Germanus, and, perhaps, of the Saxon invasion.[149]   To this were added the Brut legend, material from Gildas and Bede, the Arthurian, the Saxon, and the Irish documents, etc.   The whole was worked over by Nennius in the ninth century. — In the opinion of Liebermann, however, Nennius was the original author of the compilation, by whom its various elements were first brought together. — A new edition of this compilation, made about 910, passed into Ireland and was used by Gilla-Coemáin.   Zimmer believed that the work had been known under the name of Nennius to Cormac mac Cuilennáin (d. 908).[150]   It should be added that Van Hamel and Liebermann have advanced the — very doubtful — hypothesis that Nennius himself was Irish.

In some late and generally quite fabulous hagiographical texts of Wales and Brittany there are a few passages which appear to relate to early Irish settlements in Britain. In the *Cognatio de Brychan*[151] — an account of Brychan, reputed royal progenitor of a vast family, embracing many of the Welsh saints, which formed one of the " Three Saintly Tribes of Britain " — it is said that his father was Anlach, son of Coronac, king of Ireland.   Brychan's companion and confessor, Brynach, was in Welsh legends called " Gwyddel," that is, Goidel, or Irishman.[152]   In the Life of St. Carantoc,[153] or Carannog, who had an extensive cult in both Wales and Brittany, there is an explicit allusion to the Irish invasions: " In those times the Irish conquered Britain for thirty years; the names of their leaders were Briscus, Thuihaius, Machleus, Anpa-cus."   The same Life also speaks of an Irish conquest of Cardigan: " Keredic held Kerediciaun, i.e., Keredigan, and it was named from him.   And after he had held it, the Irish came and fought with them and seized all the districts."

---

[148] *Cf.* pp. 329-39.
[149] F. Lot, *op. cit.*, argues that the account of the Saxon invasion and of Vortigern was taken from Bede.
[150] *NA* XIX 436. *Cf.* pp. 11-13 *supra*.
[151] Ed: A. W. Wade-Evans *Y Cymmrodor* XIX (1906) 24-37 [with trans.]. *Cf.* Baring-Gould and Fisher *Lives of the British Saints* I 303-21; A. Anscombe *ACL* I 516 *sqq.*
[152] *Nova Legenda Anglie*, ed. Horstman (Oxford 1901) I 114-8, gives an epitome of a Life of Brynach, or Bernacus, which may be of the tenth century. *Cf.* Baring-Gould and Fisher *op. cit.* I 321-7.
[153] *AA. SS. Boll.* Maii III 585-7; Rees *Lives of the Cambro-British Saints* (Llandovery 1853) 97-101 [corr. by KM *Y Cymmrodor* XIII (1900) 84]; S. Baring-Gould *Y Cymmrodor* XV (1902) 88-99.

CHAPTER III

THE IRISH CHURCH IN THE "CELTIC" PERIOD

Fourth to Seventh Century

THE predominant institution of western Europe during the early middle ages was the Christian Church. In the centuries following the disintegration of the Roman Empire, when organised secular states hardly existed, the Church maintained with reference to all Christians a position not unlike that of the modern state towards its subjects. It exercised not only spiritual but also a vast amount of secular power. Its clergy formed a corporate body of, comparatively, high training and intelligence, segregated, organised, undying, which carried on its mission unbroken through century after century of political instability. Its organisation was perfected in the midst of the Roman Empire, when the Roman administrative system which it largely imitated was still working unimpaired, and was preserved through later ages when more or less short-lived barbarian principalities were aping in childish fashion the imperial power they had replaced.

Fundamentally, the Church in Ireland was one with the Church in the remainder of western Europe. The mental processes and the *Weltanschauung* of the ecclesiastic who looked out from Armagh or Clonmacnois or Innisfallen were not essentially different from those of him whose centre of vision was Canterbury or Reims or Cologne. But in many important aspects, and particularly those of organisation and of relationship with the secular powers, the Church in Ireland presented a marked variation from that on the Continent. These divergences were the occasion, in their own times, of friction culminating in accusations of heresy, and, in modern days, of belief in the former existence of a more or less distinct entity designated the "Celtic Church." The term includes the Churches of other Celtic lands—where, as the rather scanty evidence seems to indicate, a similar ecclesiastical organisation existed—but the representative Celtic Church is the ancient Church of Ireland.

The assimilation of this ancient Irish ecclesiastical system to that of the rest of western Christianity had three chief phases: (1) the adoption of the Roman Easter and the development of closer relations with the Continent in the seventh century; (2) the introduction, in the twelfth, of a territorial episcopal organisation and of the continental religious orders; and (3), in the sixteenth, the English conquest, the Protestant establishment, and the Catholic reorganisation.

In the present chapter consideration will be given to the chief contemporary sources for Irish church history in that early, "Celtic," era which terminated with the first of these movements towards conformity; and also to some foreign sources of subsequent date, the treatment of which at this place seems most convenient. Certain classes of sources are, however, reserved for later chapters: (1) hagiographical texts, together with the vast mass of historico-legendary matter regarding early saints and churches, are examined in the two chapters following; (2) it has also seemed best to bring together, in chapter VII, all the biblical and all the liturgical sources, including other documents of the sixth and seventh centuries which have a biblical or a liturgical aspect.

I. THE COMING OF THE FAITH

Bibliography

See the works listed on pp. 106–109 *supra*. Special notice should be taken of the following: HZ *Pelagius in Irland* (Berlin 1901); (trans. A. Meyer) *The Celtic Church in Britain and Ireland* (London 1902) [*cf.* pp. 77, 107 *supra*]; " Beiträge zur Erklärung altirischer Texte der kirchlichen und Profanliteratur 1, 2" *Sitzungsb. d. k. preuss. Akad. d. Wissensch.* philos.-hist. Cl. 1908 xlix 1100–1130; "Über direkte Handelsverbindungen Westgalliens mit Irland im Altertum und frühen Mittelalter. 3. Galliens Anteil an Irlands Christianisierung im 4/5 Jahrhundert und altirischer Bildung " *ibid.* 1909 xx–xxi 543–613. — J. B. Bury *The Life of St. Patrick and his place in history* (London 1905). — KM *Learning in Ireland in the fifth century and the transmission of letters* (Dublin 1913). — M. P. Boisannade *Les relations entre l'Aquitaine, le Poitou et l'Irlande du Ve au IXe siècle* (Poitiers 1917) [extract from *Bulletin de la Soc. des Antiquaires de l'Ouest* IV (1917); see a valuable rev. in *RC* XXXVIII (1920) pp. 71–5].

The beginnings of Christianity in western Europe are obscure. It was probably introduced by immigrants from the countries of the eastern Mediterranean who spread over all the Roman world and were especially numerous in southern Gaul.[1] By A.D. 177 a church of

---

[1] *Cf.* H. Leclercq " Colonies d'Orientaux en Occident " *Dict. d'archéol. chrét. et de liturgie* III ii 2266–77.

considerable size existed at Lyons, a church which seems to have been bound in close relationship to that of Smyrna in Asia.[2] During the next two centuries the new religion obtained a firm foothold in most of the cities of Gaul and Spain, and even entered Britain.[3] In 314 a great council of the clergy of Gaul was assembled at Arles, where were present five ecclesiastics from Britain, including three bishops, Eborius of York, Restitutus of London, and Adelfius, perhaps of Colchester.[4]

In western and north-western Gaul there were, by 314, bishops' sees at Bordeaux and at Rouen. If not at this date then very soon after there was a bishopric at Tours on the Loire, and at latest by 350 another at Poitiers, on a tributary of the Loire. Hilary, bishop of Poitiers from about 353 to 368, and his disciple, Martin, bishop of Tours from about 371 to about 399–403, were two of the great churchmen of the fourth century. Martin was celebrated for his missionary activities. By his time the majority of the townsfolk seem to have become Christian, but the villagers and country people, the *pagani*, adhered to the old beliefs: to their conversion Martin especially devoted himself.[5]

Martin was also a protagonist of monasticism, just then being introduced into western Europe from Egypt. About 361 he began the monastery of Ligugé near Poitiers, and after he became bishop of Tours he set up near that city another monastery which came to be known as "the greater monastery," *maius monasterium*, hence Marmoutier. Here he made his home, apparently exercising the double functions of abbot and bishop. Two thousand monks, it was said, attended his funeral. About the time of his death a monastery was founded on the island of Lérins,[6] in the Mediterranean sea off the south coast of Gaul, which during the next century became even more famous than

---

[2] Some 48 persons suffered martyrdom at this time. *Cf.* Eusebius *Ecclesiastical History* V. Pothinus, first bishop, and his successor, Irenaeus, were both of Asia and seem to have been sent to Gaul by Polycarp of Smyrna.

[3] From certain passages in Tertullian and Origen it seems certain that Christianity had reached Britain by the beginning of the third century. These extracts can be seen conveniently in H&S I 3.

[4] H&S I 7. *Cf.* Harnack *Mission und Ausbreitung des Christentums* II (1906) 233; S. N. Miller *EHR* XLII (1927) 79–80.

[5] On Martin see art. by Léon Clugnet in *Cath. Encycl.* IX, and works listed there: also the iconoclastic treatise by E. Ch. Babut *St. Martin de Tours* (Paris [1912]) (extract from *Rev. d'hist. et de litt. relig.* 1910–12) [*cf. RH* CXII (1913) 338–9; *Hist. Zs* CXV (1916) 606–8]; Hippolyte Delehaye " Saint Martin et Sulpice Sévère " *An. Boll.* XXXVIII (1920) 5–136; Marc Bloch " Saint Martin de Tours, à propos d'une polémique " *Rev. d'hist. et de litt. relig.* VII (1921) 44–57; Camille Jullian " Remarques critiques sur la vie et l'oeuvre de saint Martin": "Notes gallo-romaines" xciii–xcviii *Rev. des études anciennes* 1922–1923. Memoirs of Martin were compiled by his younger contemporary, Sulpicius Severus: *cf.* p. 668 *infra*.

[6] See Besse " Premiers monastères de la Gaule méridionale " *Rev. des quest. hist.*, 1902; J. B. Bury *Life of St. Patrick* (London 1905) 294–6; Henri Moris *L'Abbaye de Lérins: histoire et monuments* (Paris 1909) [*cf. RH* CIV (July 1910) 398].

Martin's foundations. From it were sent out many of the leading ecclesiastics of Gaul, and to it came disciples from the greater part of the Christian West, including at least one man from Britain, Faustus, who was abbot from 432 to 450 or later, and afterwards bishop of Riez.

We know that monasticism was well rooted in Britain by the sixth century.[7] The earliest foundation as to which there is a definite tradition was *Candida Casa*, the "White House" (now Whithern in Wigtownshire, Scotland): the tradition as preserved by Bede[8] is that it was built by Nynias (Ninian), a Briton who, having studied at Rome, had become the apostle of the southern Picts, and that the church, built of stone, an unusual thing among the Britons, was dedicated to St. Martin. A twelfth-century Life by Ailred, abbot of Rievaulx, in Yorkshire, adds that Nynias visited Martin at Tours, obtained masons there, and afterwards, while his church was under construction, received news of Martin's death.[9] It seems a safe inference from these traditions that this monastic establishment among the Picts of Galloway about A.D. 400 sprang from the work of Martin in western Gaul.

Ireland, it is reasonable to believe, must have received Christianity from western Gaul and Britain in the fourth and early fifth century. The record is hazy, yet there are facts and considerations, some of which have been elaborated with great wealth of argument by Heinrich Zimmer, that seem to give at least the broad outlines of the story of the coming of the Christian faith. The more important heads of this evidence may be summarised as follows: (1) the commercial relations between Ireland and western Gaul; (2) the wars and settlements of the Irish—*Scotti*—in Britain, their relations, as foes or as auxiliaries, with the Roman army, and the consequent associations with Christians and introduction of Christian captives into Ireland; (3) the peculiar veneration accorded to St. Martin in the early Irish Church;[10] (4) similar, though slighter, evidence of the honor accorded to Ninian and the

---

[7] Victricius, bishop of Rouen from about 380 to about 408, a friend of Martin of Tours and, like him a zealous missionary and a promoter of monasticism, visited Britain about 395, but there is no explicit record of his introducing the monastic movement. *Cf.* Vacandard *Saint Victrice*; A. Anscombe " St. Victricius of Rouen and St. Patrick " *Ériu* VII (1913) 13–7.

[8] *Hist. Eccles.* III iv. See Plummer's ed.

[9] The *Vita* by Ailred is in A. P. Forbes *Lives of St. Ninian and St. Kentigern* (*Historians of Scotland* V) (Edinburgh 1874) and in W. M. Metcalfe (ed.) *Pinkerton's Lives of the Scottish Saints* I (Paisley 1889). *Cf.* J. Mackinnon *Ninian und sein Einfluss auf die Ausbreitung des Christenthums in Nord-Britannien* (Heidelberg 1891); Karl Strecker " Zu den Quellen für das Leben des hl. Ninian " *NA* XLIII (1920) 1–26) [*cf. An. Boll.* XL (1922) fasc. iii–iv]. Strecker believes that Ailred used as a source a Latin poem similar to the *Miracula Nyssiae episcopi* in *MGH Poetae latini aev. Carol.* IV fasc. 2–3 (Berlin 1923) 943–62.

[10] To this, and to the question of heresies in Ireland, HZ has given particular attention. *Cf.* pp. 270, 324, 348; also *RC* XXXVIII (1920–1) 72–4, 337.

monastery of *Candida Casa*;[11] (5) the traces in Ireland of those heresies —Arianism, Priscillianism, Pelagianism—which flourished in western Europe in the fourth and early fifth centuries;[12] (6) the testimony, previously considered, to an *émigré* movement from Gaul to Ireland in the fifth century.[13] There is also certain linguistic evidence which is undoubtedly important if it can be correctly interpreted. Old Irish has several words of Latin origin and of Christian religious significance which show by their modifications that they were derived not directly from Latin but through the medium of British speech.[14] The inference is that the Irish people learned these words from British Christians. Zimmer at one time thought that they afforded testimony to the gradual conversion of Ireland by Britons in the fourth century; but perhaps they are due, as Bury suggested,[15] to the intercourse between Goidels and Brythons in the Irish settlements of western Britain; or, more probably, to a movement of British churchmen into Ireland in the fifth and sixth centuries.

There remain to be considered a certain number of positive records.

25. Mansuetus of Toul

(a) *Vita, auctore Adsone*: A.D. 974 x 992. EDS: Martène and Durand *Thesaurus novus anecdotorum* (Paris 1717) III 1013-24 [prologue only]. — Calmet *Histoire de Lorraine* I (Nancy 1728, 2nd ed. 1745) p. xxvii and " Preuves " 83-106. — *AA. SS. Boll.* Sept. I 637-51. — Migne *PL* CXXXVII 619-44. *Cf. MGH SS* IV 509-14. COMM: Ussher *Whole Works* VI 294-9. — Todd *St. Patrick* (1864) 193-4. — H&S II pt. ii 289. — KM *Learning in Ireland in the fifth century* (Dublin 1913) 23. — Manitius *Lat. Lit.* II (1923) 432-42. (b) *Gesta episcoporum Tullensium*: c A.D. 1107. EDS: Martène and

---

[11] *Candida Casa* was known in Ireland as " the great monastery " and there is much legendary matter regarding its associations with Ireland. Ninian was honored in the martyrologies under the hypocoristic form Mo-Ninn or Moinenn. *Cf.* Skene *Celtic Scotland* II (Edinburgh 1887) 46-9. An Irish Life of Ninian, now lost, declared that he passed into Ireland and died there, after founding the church of Clúain-Conaire (Cloncurry, in northern Kildare). *Cf.* Ussher *Britannicarum ecclesiarum antiquitates* xv in *Whole Works* VI 209; Colgan *AA. SS. Hib.* 438; *AA. SS. Boll.* Sept. V 318-28. The story may be the result of the fame to which *Candida Casa* attained.

[12] *Cf.* the writings of HZ listed above. The evidence for Arianism and Priscillianism in Ireland is very slight. Pelagianism, however, is on a different footing: Pelagius was quoted in Irish exegetical MSS three centuries after his death. It may be noted that after Priscillian had been put to death by the imperial pretender Maximus in 385 some of his followers were banished to the Scilly Islands in the next year. Passage thence to Ireland would have been easy. *Cf.* Sulpicius Severus *Chronica* II li (in Migne *PL* XX and *Corp. SS. eccles. lat.* I (Vienna 1866)).

[13] *Cf.* pp. 142 *sqq supra*.

[14] B. G. Güterbock *Bemerkungen über die lateinischen Lehnwörter im Irischen* (Leipsic 1882) 92 *sqq*; HZ *The Celtic Church in Britain and Ireland* (London 1902) 24-7. *E.g.* ā survived in Irish, but changed to ō in British: but for Lat. *trinitāt(is)*, *altāre*, Irish has *trindóit*, *altóir*. HZ's claim that the borrowings must have been made before the first half of the fifth century is dubious. *Cf. Ir. Theol. Quarterly* I (1906) 58-62.

[15] *Life of St. Patrick* 351.

Durand *ibid.* 991–1091. — Calmet *ibid.* — Waitz *MGH SS* VIII 631–48. — Migne *PL* CLVII 447–76.

The earliest Christian to whom an Irish origin is explicitly assigned was a Mansuetus [16] who, according to tradition, was the first bishop of Toul, in north-eastern France. It would appear that he flourished about the middle of the fourth century, although legend said that he was a disciple of St. Peter. His biography as we have it was written by Adso (*c* 920–92), abbot of Montier-en-Der, a well-known ecclesiastical author, and an abridgment was inserted into the "History of the bishops of Toul" prepared in the twelfth century. There were earlier versions of both the Life and the History, and Adso appears to have derived his information regarding the saint's origin from a written source.[17] Nevertheless we may doubt the Irish birth as well as the Petrine mission of Mansuetus, and believe the tradition to be testimony rather to the mediaeval fame of Ireland's saints and missionaries than to the antiquity of her Christianity.[18]

26. Pelagius

Cf. the various Church histories and encyclopaedias; especially A. Harnack *Lehrbuch der Dogmengeschichte* 4th ed. (Tübingen 1909–10), trans. N. Buchanan *History of Dogma* (London 1896–9, Boston 1897–1900), Loofs in *Realencyklopädie für protestantische Theologie und Kirche*, 3rd ed. XV (Leipsic 1904) 744 *sqq*, and Pohle in *Cath. Encycl.* XI 604–8.— Also: Todd *St. Patrick* (1864) 189–93. — H&S I 15–16, II 290. — HZ *Pelagius in Irland* (Berlin 1901), esp. 13 *sqq*; *Sitzungsb. d. k. preuss. Akad. d. Wissensch.* 1909 XX 553 n. 1. — Bury "The Origin of Pelagius" *Hermathena* XIII (1904) 26–35. — Roger *L'Enseignement* (1905) 214–5. — Bruckner *Quellen zur Geschichte des pelagianischen Streites* (Tübingen 1906) [also in Gebhardt and Harnack *Texte und Untersuchungen* XV iii (Leipsic 1906)]. — A. Souter "Pelagius' doctrine in relation to his early life" *Expositor* 8th ser. IX (London 1915) 180–2. — *Cf.* no. 17 and pp. 661 *sqq infra.*

In the writings of St. Jerome are to be found the first contemporary references to an Irishman who was also a Christian, even though, in Jerome's opinion, a miscreant.

The prologue to the first book of the *Commentary on Jeremiah*, composed about 415–6, has the statement: "An ignorant calumniator has recently broken forth, who thinks

---

[16] This was the Latinisation of the Irish name *Fethgno: cf. Mart. Don.* (1864) 417.

[17] Ea tempestate, ut scripturae documento percepimus, quidam sanctae indolis fuerat adolescens, nomine Mansuetus, ex transmarinis partibus nobilium quidem Scotorum clara progenie genitus.— Migne *PL* CXXXVII 621 D.

[18] So the metrical prologue of Adso's Life:

> Inclyta Mansueti claris natalibus orti
> progenies titulis fulsit in orbe suis.
> Insula Christicolas gestabat Hibernia gentes,
> unde genus traxit et satus inde fuit.

Adso, who was educated at Columban's monastery of Luxeuil, would be quite familiar with these ideas.

that my Commentaries on the Epistle of Paul to the Ephesians ought to be condemned . . . and this most stupid fellow, heavy with Irish porridge,[19] does not remember that we have said in that very work," etc. The prologue to the third book of the same commentary, referring to the malicious activities of the devil, proceeds: " Although silent himself, he does his barking through an Alpine [20] dog, huge and corpulent, who can rave more with his claws than with his teeth: for he has his lineage of the Irish race, from the neighborhood of the Britons.[21] In accordance with the fables of the poets he, another Cerberus, must be struck down with a spiritual club in order that, with his master Pluto, he may keep eternal silence."

It seems reasonably certain that this unnamed " calumniator " was the heresiarch Pelagius, into the controversy with whom Jerome had by this time entered.[22] There is, however, the difficulty that his other adversaries, Orosius,[23] Augustine,[24] and Marius Mercator,[25] and his younger contemporary, Prosper of Aquitaine,[26] all describe Pelagius as a Briton. Various solutions have been proposed: (1) the Irishman of Jerome's attacks was not Pelagius but his chief disciple, Caelestius; (2) Pelagius was a Briton, and Jerome's application of the — to him — opprobrious epithet Scottus [27] had that freedom from ethnological accuracy which characterised vituperative literature then as now; (3) Pelagius was Irish, but born in one of the Goidelic settlements in Britain,[28] or (4) educated in a British monastery;[29] (5) the term Brito, Britannus, may have been used in a broad sense to designate any person from what Greek geographers still named αἱ πρετανικαὶ νῆσοι.[30]

If Pelagius was an Irishman he must rank in fame with those mediaeval emigrants, Columbanus and Johannes Eriugena. He was a monk, though not a priest, and a man of considerable intellectual power: he was able to defend himself successfully in the Greek tongue before a council of the province of Jerusalem, held at Diospolis in 415, while his accuser, Orosius, had to employ an interpreter.[31] This knowledge of Greek, however, was acquired only after he himself had become a resident of the East.[32] He went to Rome not later than A.D. 400, perhaps as early as 384;[33] in 411, after the raid of Alaric, he passed

---

19 " Scotorum pultibus praegravatus."

20 " Albinum " or " Alpinum ": the significance is not clear; Vallarsi, the editor of St. Jerome, associated it with Albion, Ἀλβίων, the Irish name of Britain.

21 " Habet enim progeniem Scoticae gentis de Britannorum vicinia." The opinion of Ussher (Whole Works V 253-4) and Williams that Jerome is speaking, not of the devil but of Pelagius, and that his disciple Caelestius is the dog of Irish breed, seems far-fetched if not impossible. Apart from this there is less reason to believe Caelestius an Irishman than Pelagius. Todd and especially Bury develop the interpretation here given.

22 In 415 by his Epistola ad Ctesiphontem and Dialogus contra Pelagianos (Migne PL XXIII 495 sqq).

23 Liber apologeticus contra Pelagium de arbitrii libertate (c A.D. 415): Migne PL XXXI 1173-1212; Zangemeister Corp. SS. Eccl. Lat. V (Vienna 1882) i.

24 Epistola clxxxvi (417): Migne PL XXXIII 816.

25 Commonitorium adversus haeresim Pelagii et Caelesti (c 418): Migne PL XLVIII 109-72.

26 De Ingratis (c 429): Migne PL LI 94. Cf. no. 28 infra.

27 Cf. p. 138 supra.   28 So Bury.   29 HZ in Pelagius in Irland.   30 HZ in his later treatise.

31 Augustine: Migne PL XLIV 322.

32 Cf. H. J. Chapman " Pélage et le texte de s. Paul " RHE XVIII (1922) 469-81, esp. 472-4.

33 Cf. Gougaud Chrétientés celtiques (1911) 34.

on to Asia by way of North Africa. In the East he lived chiefly at Jerusalem till 418, after which date he disappears from history. He never took a position of open defiance of ecclesiastical authority, and was very successful in defending his suspected doctrines on grace and free will.

Of his writings only a few letters, some fragments of longer works, and the *Commentaries on the Epistles of St. Paul*, written at Rome before the sack of that city by Alaric in 410, survive. The preservation of this last in the schools of Ireland is one of the interesting phases of the history of ancient Irish learning, as its recovery is one of the remarkable achievements of present-day patristic scholarship.[34]

27. Germanus of Auxerre

Vita auctore Constantio (c 480–5) EDS: B. Mombritius *Sanctuarium* (Milan c 1480) I 319 *sqq* [the best of the older printed texts]. — Surius *De probatis sanctorum historiis* (2nd ed.) 30 Jul. IV 358–69. — *AA. SS. Boll.* 31 Jul. VII 200–21. — Duru *Bibliothèque historique de l'Yonne* I (Auxerre 1850) 47–89. — Narbey *Étude critique sur la vie de s. Germain d'Auxerre* (Paris 1884) [all these contain the heavily interpolated version]. — W. Levison *MGH SS. rer. Merov.* VII i (1919) 225–83 [best ed.]. COMM: Levison *NA* XXIX i (1903) 97–175. — S. Baring-Gould "The Life of S. Germanus by Constantius" *Y Cymmrodor* XVII (1903) 65–81; and the reply of J. Loth " Le prétendu s. Germain armoricain " *Annales de Bretagne* April 1905. — Bury *St. Patrick* (1905) 247–8, 297. For the Life by Heiric of Auxerre, see no. 407 *infra*. *Cf.* also KM *Learning in Ireland in the fifth century* (Dublin 1913) 23–4.

Germanus (c 380–c 448) was a native of Auxerre who, after receiving the best secular education of the time at Arles, Lyons and Rome, became one of the imperial administrators of the Gauls. Amator, bishop of Auxerre, won him to the religious life, and on Amator's death in 418 he became bishop of Auxerre and one of the leading ecclesiastics of Gaul. His Life was written by Constantius, a priest of Lyons who had known him, but who was a contemporary and friend of Sidonius Apollinaris.[35] Constantius tells the story of the two missions of Germanus to Britain to combat the Pelagian heresy, probably in 429, when he was accompanied by Lupus, bishop of Troyes, formerly a monk of Lérins, and in 447, when he had with him Severus, bishop of Trèves. These visits of Germanus made a profound impression in Britain: it would seem that there was an ancient British biography which formed one of the sources of the *Historia Britonum*, or Nennius.[36] Perhaps his British mission brought him into relations with Ireland, for in an appendix to a metrical version of his Life, prepared by Heiric of Auxerre in the ninth century he is said to have had an Irish

---

[34] Dr. Alexander Souter has published an ed. *Cf.* p. 661 *infra*.
[35] The text of the usual editions has been much altered: *cf.* Levison *op. cit.*; *Bibliotheca hagiographica latina Boll.* I 515 no. 3453, II 1354.
[36] *Cf.* no. 24 *supra*.

disciple named Michomeri.[37] There are, however, traces of Irishmen at Auxerre before this: a certain Corcodemus, mentioned by Constantius as at Auxerre in the third century, is assumed by Zimmer, solely on the basis of the name, to have been Irish; and there is some slight evidence of an ancient Irish tradition that Iserninus, the fellow bishop of Patricius, was at Auxerre under both Amator and Germanus.[38] Patricius himself, who was, of course, a Briton, was commonly represented as a disciple of Germanus.

28. Prosper of Aquitaine

Epitoma Chronicon (A.D. 425–55); *Contra Collatorem* (*c* A.D. 433): EDS: Migne *PL* LI [complete works]. — Mommsen *MGH Auct. Antiq.* IX (*Chronica Minora* I) 353–499. For other eds. of the *Chronicon* and the older literature see Potthast. COMM: Holder-Egger " Die Chronik Prospers von Aquitanien" *NA* I (1876) 15–90, 327–34. — L. Valentin *St. Prosper d'Aquitaine* (Toulouse 1900).—Otto Bardenhewer *Patrologie* 3rd ed. (Freiburg i. B. 1910) and trans. Thos. J. Shahan *Patrology* (Freiburg i. B. and St. Louis 1908). On the later history of Pelagianism, and on Semipelagianism: Caspari *Briefe, Abhandlungen und Predigten aus den zwei letzten Jahrhunderten der kirklichen Alterthums* (Christiania 1890). — Pohle in *Cath. Encycl.* XI, XIII.

Constantius's Life of Germanus was written long after its subject's death, and by an author more interested in miracle than in history. But in the writings of Prosper of Aquitaine we have records contemporary with the events they narrate, by a man who was active in the public ecclesiastical life of the time.

The teaching of Pelagius had inaugurated a vast discussion throughout the Christian Church on the subjects of grace, free will and predestination, in which advocates of each of the different points of view were found to be widely scattered. St. Augustine, bishop of Hippo in North Africa, was the great opponent of Pelagianism, and carried his doctrine of the all-importance of divine grace so far as to give offence to many who were themselves Anti-Pelagians. Especially among the monks of Lérins and its daughter monasteries, and among the clergy which Lérins had given to the dioceses of Gaul, did an Anti-Augustinian party arise. Its leaders were Faustus of Lérins and John Cassian (*c* 360–*c* 435), principal western exponent of monasticism, who from Lérins had founded the monastery of Marseilles. Prosper of Aquitaine (*c* 390–*c* 465), a layman of good education, and apparently a resident of Marseilles, first appears on the scene in 428 or 429 by a letter he wrote

---

[37] KM suggests *Míchomairle*. Heiric also speaks of St. Patrick as a disciple of Germanus, but this information was derived from Irish sources. No. 407 *infra*.

[38] Bury *St. Patrick* 348–9.

to Augustine describing this situation in southern Gaul. For the remainder of his life he was a warm partisan of the Augustinian teaching. In 431 he visited Rome in connection with the controversy, and about 433 or 434 he published a direct attack on Cassian, entitled *Liber contra Collatorem*. In 434, or, in the opinion of others, 440, he removed to Rome, where, it is said, he obtained a position in the papal chancery. His most important historical work, the *Chronicon*, was a revision of Jerome's chronicle, with a continuation from 378 to his own time: there seem to have been three editions, the first to 433, the second to 445, and the third to 455.

The following excerpts from the writings of Prosper are of interest: *Chronicon*, A.D. 429: " The Pelagian Agricola, son of the Pelagian bishop Severianus, corrupts the churches of Britain by the propagation of his doctrine. But at the instigation of the deacon Palladius, Pope Celestine sends Germanus, bishop of Auxerre, in his stead, who overthrows the heretics and guides the Britons to the Catholic faith." [39]   431: " To the Irish believing in Christ Palladius, having been ordained by Pope Celestine, is sent as first bishop." [40]   *Contra Collatorem* xxi: " With no less care did [Celestine] free the British Isles from that same disease [Pelagianism] . . . and by ordaining a bishop for the Irish, whilst he strove to keep the Roman island Catholic, he also made the barbarous island Christian." [41]

Of Palladius or his Irish mission we have no further authentic record.

29. Patricius

(1) *Confessio*: Ego Patricius peccator, rusticissimus . . . et haec est confessio mea antequam moriar.
(2) *Epistola*: Patricius peccator indoctus scilicet.—Hiberione . . sani efficiantur hic et in aeternum. Pax Patri et Filio et Spiritui Sancto. Amen.

MSS: LA *s* IX ff. 22–24ᵛ [*confessio* only; imperfect].—BN lat. 17626 *s* X ff. 72 *sqq*; —Arras Bibl pub. 450 *s* XII ff. 50ᵛ–52ᵛ [imperfect; formerly of the monastery of St. Vaast, Arras].—BM Cotton. Nero E. I *c* A.D. 1000 ff. 169ᵛ *sqq*.—Bodl. Fell 4 *s* XI *ex* ff. 158–64; Fell 3 *s* XII² ff. 7–11ᵛ [these two MSS formerly belonged to Salisbury cathedral].—Rouen Bibl. pub. 1391 (U.39) *s* XI/XII ff. 157ᵛ–9 [*confessio* only; imperfect.

---

[39] Constantius says that the orthodox Britons appealed to the churches of Gaul, and that Germanus and Lupus were sent by a Gallic council.

[40] " Ad Scottos in Christum credentes ordinatus a papa Caelestino Palladius primus episcopus mittitur." As Prosper was in Rome this year, and published his Chronicle in 433, this is a remarkably good historical source.

[41] "et ordinato Scottis episcopo dum Romanam insulam studet servare catholicam fecit etiam barbaram christianam." There need be no contradiction between this and the preceding extract: the natural implication in *Scottos in Christum credentes* is not that all or a majority of the Irish were Christians, but a sufficient number to justify the appointment of a bishop; and that in *fecit barbaram christianam* is not that Celestine inaugurated an overwhelmingly successful missionary enterprise, but that — a well-known ecclesiastical manner of speech — by erecting an episcopate in a new country he had brought it within the pale of the official Christian world. For this reason it is not impossible that Prosper knew in 433 or 434, what later Irish legend declared, that Palladius had failed and died within a few months after his arrival in Ireland; but his words certainly make this improbable.

formerly of Jumièges]. Eds: Ware *S. Patricio adscripta opuscula* (London 1656). — Andreas Denis *AA. SS. Boll.* 17 Mar. II 530 *sqq* [based on St. Vaast MS, but with emendations, some of value]. — A. Gallandius *Bibl. vet. patrum* X (Venice 1774) 159 *sqq.* — *Rer. Hib. SS.* I (1814) pp. cvii *sqq.* — Betham *Irish Antiquarian Researches* II (Dublin 1827) Append. [*Confessio*, LA text; poor]. — J. L. Villanueva *Sancti Patricii synodi canones opuscula et scriptorum quae supersunt fragmenta* (Dublin 1835) [Boll. text with variants from Ware]. — Migne *PL* LIII 801–18 [from Gallandius]. — H&S II pt. II 296 *sqq* [poor]. — Gilbert *Facs. Nat. MSS. Ire.* II App. III A-M pl. lii. — *Vit. Trip.* II (London 1887) 357–80 [LA and Cotton]. — Newport J. D. White "Libri sancti Patricii: the Latin writings of St. Patrick" *Proc. RIA* XXV C vii (1905) 201–326 [good critical text, with trans. and notes]; "The Paris manuscript of St. Patrick's Latin writings" *ibid.* xi 542–52 [study of the MS, giving its variant readings]; *Libri Sancti Patricii* (S. P. C. K.: London 1918) [revised text]. — J. Healy *The Life and Writings of St. Patrick* (Dublin 1905) [has a good trans.]. — Gwynn *LA* (1913). Trans: M. F. Cusack *Life of St. Patrick* (London, etc. 1871). — Sir Samuel Ferguson "On the Patrician documents" *Trans. RIA* XXVII *Pol. Lit. & Antiq.* (1885) 70 *sqq* [see also *Proc. RIA* 2nd ser. *Pol. Lit. & Antiq.* II 1–3, 15–16, 205–8]. — C. H. H. Wright *The Writings of Patrick* (*Christian Classics Series* VI) (Religious Tract Soc.: London 1889). — T. Olden *Epistles and hymns of St. Patrick* (London 1889). — White *Translation of the Latin writings of St. Patrick* (S. P. C. K.: London 1918); *St. Patrick, his Writings and Life* (S. P. C. K.: London 1920). — G. Dottin *Les Livres de s. Patrice* (Paris 1909). Comm: See the works cited pp. 319–21, especially Robert, HZ and Bury. — Tillemont *Mémoires pour servir à l'histoire ecclésiastique* XVI (Paris 1712) 455–61. — J. von Pflugk-Harttung "Die Schriften S. Patricks" *Neue Heidelberger Jahrbücher* III i (1893) 71–87 [against the authenticity of the *Confessio*; described by Bury as "a piece of extraordinarily bad criticism"; cf. Hyde *Literary History of Ireland* 112 n. 2]. — F. Kattenbusch *Das apostolische Symbol* I (Leipsic 1894) 188, 212 *sq*, 395. — J. Haussleiter *Göttingische gelehrte Anzeiger* May 1898 pp. 369–71 [these two on the relation of the creed of Patricius to Victorinus of Pettau]. — E. W. B. Nicholson *The Academy* May 11, 1895. — Glover *Classical Review* X (1896) 39 [on the word "heliam"]. — Roger *L'Enseignement* (1905) 220–2 [on the Latinity of Patricius]. — F. R. Montgomery Hitchcock "The Creeds of SS. Irenaeus and Patrick" *Hermathena* XIV (Dublin 1907) 168 [studies the declaration of faith given in the *Confessio*]; *Irenaeus of Lugdunum* (Cambridge 1914) 348 *sqq*; *St. Patrick and his Gallic friends* (London 1916) [describes, *inter al.*, the leading ecclesiastics of Gaul in the early fifth century, and attempts to trace a literary relationship with them in the writings of Patrick]. — Alfred Anscombe "St. Victricius of Rouen and St. Patrick" *Ériu* VII (1913) 13–7. — M. Esposito "Notes on the Latin writings of St Patrick" *JTS* XIX (July 1918) 342–6. — MacN "Silva Focluti" *Proc. RIA* XXXVI C xiv (1923) 249–55 [an acute piece of textual and historical criticism].

After Prosper of Aquitaine the next contemporary records of the conversion of the Irish are two documents written in Ireland itself by a bishop named Patricius. This Patricius, according to the Irish annals, came to Ireland in A.D. 432 and died in 461.

The authenticity of the two compositions attributed to him is now generally accepted. It is probable, however, that the texts, even as restored by the best critical scholarship, are quite faulty.[42]

What the author calls his *Confession* is a kind of *apologia pro vita sua*, written as a general justification of his mission to Ireland and his manner of life there, against accusations of ignorance, incompetence, presumption, and even self-seeking, which would seem to have been current, perhaps both in Ireland and abroad.[43] Accordingly he gives an exposition of his religious experiences, emphasising especially the supernatural communications which he believed himself to have received, the whole tending to demonstrate that his mission was of divine inspiration and executed by divine grace.[44] Only occasionally and incidentally does he refer to events of his active life. Moreover, the document is marred by an exasperating incoherence which leaves the meaning constantly in doubt.

The *Confession* was composed in Ireland (*Hiberione*), and in the writer's " old age " — " this is my confession before I die." It was intended for his " brethren," " kinsfolk," " fellow-servants," — primarily the clergy and monks [45] who formed his immediate following, but also, it would seem, his relatives and ecclesiastical friends abroad.[46] Ireland and the Irish are spoken of in an objective way that forces the conclusion that Patricius did not think of himself as addressing Irishmen: it would appear, however, that in Ireland, as in other missionary countries, the Christian population was regarded as a distinct people, *plebs Domini*, separated from the *Hibernae gentes*.

The facts regarding the career of Patricius which may be elicited from the *Confession* can be summarised as follows: He was born in Britain, at a place which has not been identified, of a family of some local importance; when about sixteen years of age he was taken captive and carried into Ireland " with many thousands of persons," doubtless

[42] There are several large gaps in the LA copy, the oldest, of the *Confession*. White suggests that somes leaves of the exemplar had been lost. If so, the *Epistle* may also have disappeared. It is not copied, but the title, " *Incipiunt libri* sancti Patricii episcopi," prefixed to the *Confession*, indicates that the *Epistle* had also formed part of the exemplar. Bury and Gwynn believed that the scribe of LA omitted sections of his text. It is much more probable that, if omissions were deliberately made, they were due to the scribe of the exemplar. That seems to have been a very old text which, though in reality a poor copy, had come to be regarded as an autograph of Patricius.

[43] Among his critics were men of education, designated " rhetoricians." It is not clear from the context whether they were residents of Ireland or not: there is, perhaps, a suggestion of proximity in the contemptuous expression used. *Cf.* pp. 142-3 *supra*. — Patricius freely admits his lack of literary education.

[44] The author was not a theologian, but he shows the unconscious influence of Anti-Pelagian controversy. His declaration of faith, however, resembles that of Pelagius. It seems to be related to eastern creeds, and especially to that in an ancient commentary attributed to Victorinus of Pettau, a martyr in the Diocletian persecution. See the books and articles by Kattenbusch, Haussleiter, Esposito and Hitchcock noted above; also S. Czarnowski *Le Culte des héros — Saint Patrick* (Paris 1919) 40-2, and August Hahn (ed. Ludwig Hahn) *Bibliothek der Symbole und Glaubensregeln der alten Kirche*, 3rd ed. (Breslau 1897), as referred to by Czarnowski.

[45] The author was a promoter of monasticism, and apparently had been a monk himself.

[46] At one place he speaks as though making a report to Britons on the state of their countrymen in Ireland. He testifies that these are very numerous, some of them slaves, but the majority, it would appear, free. The *Epistle* also shows closer association between Patricius and his clergy on the one hand and the clergy of Britain on the other than might have been expected.

on the occasion of one of the attacks of the " Scotti " on Britain; for six years he served as a herdsman, for part if not for the entire time in the neighborhood of *Silua Uluti*, the " Wood of the Ulaid," now Killultagh, east of Loch Neagh;[47] then he made his escape to a port some two hundred (Roman) miles distant — it must have been on the southern coast — from which he sailed on a ship carrying a cargo of dogs,[48] apparently to south-western Gaul.[49]   After a few years he returned to Britain and there received what he believed to be a supernatural call to come back to the Irish.   He became a deacon and at length, in spite of opposition, was consecrated bishop and sent on the mission to Ireland.   At a later time some of his ecclesiastical seniors brought charges against him, apparently aiming at his degradation, but were frustrated.[50]   His mission in Ireland, of which some interesting details are given, was most successful,[51] but he lived in poverty and danger and in readiness for martyrdom.   He would have liked to revisit his relations in Britain and his ecclesiastical brethren in Gaul, which he regarded as his spiritual home,[52] but duty required that he remain with the people entrusted to his charge.

The *Epistle* is a document very similar in thought and language to the *Confession*, but more coherent.   The soldiers — regarded as Roman citizens — of a ruler in North Britain named Coroticus,[53] in alliance and perhaps in company with "Scotti" [54] and "Picti," [55] had made a raid into Ireland and fallen on a company of newly-baptized converts, killing many and carrying off others to be sold as slaves.   Patricius writes to certain subjects of Coroticus, no doubt clergy, denouncing the crime and demanding the excommunication of those guilty.   The same tone of self-justification against ill-defined accusations pervades this document as the *Confession*.

---

[47] This identification, after Patrician students had been at fault for more than twelve centuries, is due to Dr. MacNeill.

[48] *Cf.* T. Olden *The Church of Ireland* (London 1892) 16-18, App. B; Bury *St. Patrick* 340-1.

[49] Gaul is not mentioned, but the inference is natural.

[50] Possibly allusion is made to this event in AU 441: " Patrick the bishop was approved in the Catholic faith."

[51] He was particularly impressed by the fact that it had been granted to him "in the last times" to be a witness to the accomplishment of prophecy, that the Gospel had been "preached to the limit beyond which no man dwells."   His words, however, are not inconsistent with the view that in parts of Ireland Christianity had been introduced before his time.

[52] That Patricius had received his religious training in Gaul, and probably in a monastery, can be fairly inferred from his words.   The Biblical quotations which he uses abundantly are, according to White in his edition, mainly Old Latin, but with a mixture of Vulgate forms: such a confusion would accord with a Gallic education in the first third of the fifth century.   In a few phrases his work recalls that of Irenaeus of Lyons.

[53] He has been identified with a "Ceretic guletic" who, according to Welsh genealogies, was fifth in the upward line from Rodercus or Rhydderch who ruled at Ail-Cluith (Dumbarton) towards the end of the sixth century.   *Cf.* Skene *Celtic Scotland* I 157-8; HZ *Celtic Church* 54; Bury *St. Patrick* 314-5.

[54] This may be evidence that " Scotti " were by now settled in northern Britain.

[55] The Picts are designated " apostates ": they probably were Southern Picts and had fallen away since their conversion by Ninian.

Was Patricius identical with the Palladius of Prosper of Aquitaine? That there was an ancient supposition or tradition to this effect is a probable inference from a statement in the *Book of Armagh* that Palladius was also called Patricius.[56] Several modern scholars, notably Heinrich Zimmer, have been of this opinion, but the majority have opposed the identification.

30. Patricius, Auxilius and Iserninus: Circular Letter

Gratias agimus Deo patri et filio et spiritui sancto. Presbiteris et diaconibus et omni clero Patricius Auxilius Isserninus episcopi salutem. Satius nobis negligentes . . . abbate vagulus debet vindicari.

MSS: Cambridge Corpus Christi College 279 *s* IX² [formerly of Worcester cathedral; written in France (Tours?)]; 298 *s* XV [imperfect]. EDS: Spelman *Concilia* I (London 1639) 52. — Ware *S. Patricio adscripta opuscula* (London 1656) 42–6. — Migne *PL* LIII 823–6. — H&S II pt. II (1878) 328–31. — H. T. Bruns *Canones apostolorum et conciliorum veterum selecti* (Berlin 1839) II 301. COMM: Todd *St. Patrick* (1864) 485–8. — Wasserschleben *Die irische Kanonensammlung* 2nd ed. (Leipsic 1885) p. 1. — Henry Bradshaw *The Early Collection of Canons known as the Hibernensis* (Cambridge 1893). — Bury *St. Patrick* (1905) 166–8, 233–45 [valuable]. — J. T. MacNeill *RC* XXXIX iii-iv (1922) 259–60.

This document, usually entitled "Synodus Patricii," is in reality a joint letter to the clergy of Ireland from the bishops Patricius, Auxilius and Iserninus. Its authenticity has frequently been denied, but Bury has made out a good case in its favor. As a whole it has every appearance of being what it purports to be; and, even if the objections to certain passages should be made good, the possibility of interpolation is so great that the character of the major part of the text would not thereby be impugned. The fact that fourteen of its canons are ascribed to Patricius in the *Collectio Hibernensis*, compiled about the end of the seventh century, is evidence of weight in its favor. In any event, it must be a record from the very early days of the Irish Church.

Auxilius and Iserninus were contemporaries of Patricius who have escaped in some degree the activities of the myth-makers. They are noticed in the annals: they were sent into Ireland as bishops to assist Patricius in 439, and died in 459 and 468, respectively.[57] The name of Auxilius is commemorated in the church of Cell-Usailli, or

---

[56] Paladius episcopus primo mittitur, qui Patricius alio nomine appelabatur. — *LA* f. 16. The entry, in the opinion of Gwynn, was due to the scribe Fer-domnach himself, not copied from an older record.— Bury, *St. Patrick*, 343, suggests a different explanation. Schoell *De ecclesiasticae Britonum Scotorumque historiae fontibus* (1851) 77; Loofs *Antiquae Britonum Scotorumque ecclesiae quales fuerint mores* (1882) 51; O'Brien *IER* Aug. 1887 pp. 723–31; W. J. D. Croke *ibid.* Nov. 1902 pp. 442–50; HZ *Celtic Church in Britain and Ireland* 35 *sqq*; De la Lande de Calan "Saint Patrice et Palladius" *Rev. de Bretagne* Nov. 1910.

[57] AU 439: Secundus [Secundinus], Auxilius et Serninus mituntur et episcopi ipsi in Hiberniam in auxilium Patricii. — 459: Auxilius episcopus quieuit. — 468: Iserninus episcopus moritur. From a

Auxili, now Killossy or Killashee, near Naas. To Iserninus, whose Irish name is given as Fith, are ascribed the foundations of Cell-Chuilind (Kilcullen) in Kildare and Áth-Fithot (Ahade) in Carlow.

The legislation here enacted has considerable interest. It is intended for a Church not yet fully organised, among a people still in part pagan. It consists of a series of separate practical regulations applying evidently to special abuses. The following points may be noted: a married clergy is recognised; the Roman tonsure is enjoined;[58] clerics are assumed to be inmates of religious houses; the bishop has some administrative importance, though, on a strict interpretation, it may not be great; rules are laid down to govern the collection of money for the ransom of captives; alms must not be accepted from pagans; Christians must not consult witches and soothsayers or believe that there is a witch in a mirror [crystal?]; the penitential sentences to be imposed are comparatively light.[59] An interesting regulation provides that no cleric who has come "from the Britains" without bringing proper credentials shall be permitted to perform the priestly duties.[60] It is probable that Christian Ireland in the fifth and sixth centuries received many British religious refugees fleeing before the Teutonic invasion of Britain, just as continental Europe in the ninth century received Irish churchmen who were fugitives from the Viking assault, and that in the one case as in the other special measures had to be taken to maintain ecclesiastical discipline.

For the traditional records of the foundations of Irish Christianity, as gathered together in the seventh and later centuries, see pp. 309 *sqq*; for the beginnings of Hiberno-Latin literature, pp. 250 *sqq*.

II. EARLY RELATIONS WITH BRITISH CHRISTIANITY

Bibliography

GUIDES: F. Duine *Memento des sources hagiographiques de l'histoire de Bretagne — Première partie Les fondateurs et les primitifs* (Rennes 1918); also in *Mémoires de la Soc. archéol. d'Ille-et-Vilaine* XLVI [very useful]. — The works by Hardy and the Bollandists noticed on pp. 91, 288. COLLECTIONS: *Nova Legenda Anglie* [*cf*. p. 307 *infra*]. — W. J. Rees *Lives of the Cambro-British Saints* (Llandovery 1853) [see emendations by KM *Y Cymmrodor* XIII (1900) 76–96]. — H&S I, II i. COMPILATIONS: Albert Le Grand *Les Vies des saints de la Bretagne Armorique* (1636; last ed., Quimper and Paris 1901) [contains much material on Breton hagiography otherwise lost]. —

passage in the Life of Patrick by Muir-chú it appears that there was an early tradition that Patricius, Auxilius and Iserninus had received minor orders together from Bishop Amator of Auxerre. See Bury *St. Patrick* 347–9.

[58] This provision, seeming to imply the seventh century opposition of the Irish to the Roman tonsure, has been regarded with peculiar suspicion. See Bury's remarks.

[59] MacNeill, *loc. cit.*, points out that the type of penance here implied corresponds, so far as can be determined, more with that of the early Church than with that of the Church in Ireland in the era of the penitential books. *Cf.* pp. 235 *sqq infra*.

[60] Clericus qui de Britanis ad nos ueniat sine epistola etsi habitet in plebe non licitum ministrare.

Guy Alexis Lobineau *Les Vies des saints de Bretagne* (Rennes 1725). — La Borderie *Histoire de Bretagne* [*cf.* p. 108 *supra*: the first vol. is mainly a modernisation of Le Grand]. — Sabine Baring-Gould and John Fisher *The Lives of the British Saints* 4 vols. (London 1907–13) [extensive but uncritical]. COMMENTARIES: Hugh Williams " Some aspects of the Christian Church in Wales during the fifth and sixth centuries " *Trans. Soc. of Cymmrodorion* 1893–4 (London 1895) 55–132; *Christianity in early Britain* (Oxford 1912). — Roger *L'Enseignement* 202–37. — J. Loth *Les Noms des saints bretons* (Paris 1910). — Jacques Chevalier *Essai sur la formation de la nationalité et les réveils religieux du pays de Galles, des origines à la fin du VIe siècle* (Paris 1923) [has an extensive, but hazardous, treatment of religious conditions in Wales]. — Cecile O'Rahilly *Ireland and Wales* (London etc. 1924) 48–59. — See also the works by Skene, HZ, KM, J. Loth, F. Lot, L. Gougaud noticed on pp. 147, 107, and, in general, sect. v of chap. II.

From the days of Prosper of Aquitaine and Germanus of Auxerre to those of Columbanus of Luxeuil and Augustine of Canterbury there is little record of association between the Church on the continent of Europe and the Church in the British Isles. When contact was renewed at the beginning of the seventh century the Irish and the Britons were found to have certain peculiarities of ecclesiastical organisation and religious practice which marked them off from their continental brethren and which have led some modern writers to designate them " the Celtic Church." Whether the homogeneity of British and Irish Christianity was such as to justify this designation or not, it is certain that they were in agreement on the main heads of dissension with the continental or Roman Church, and that during those one hundred and fifty years of obscurity when the Church in Ireland developed its ecclesiastical system, its closest and almost its only foreign relations were with the Christian Britons, both those who maintained their principalities along the eastern border of the Irish sea and those who had crossed the channel to found a colony in north-western Gaul, since known as Brittany. Beyond these Celtic buffer states lay a wall of more or less antipathetic Teutonic kingdoms, pagan or semi-Christian in religion.

We have seen that in the fourth and fifth centuries Irish settlements were established on the west coast of Britain; that there is linguistic testimony to a powerful Brythonic influence on the beginnings of Irish Christianity; that the writings of Patricius indicate the presence of a considerable British population in Ireland and close relations between the missionaries in Ireland and the British Church; that the occurrence of an exodus to Ireland of Britons, especially of the clergy and learned classes, as a result of the Anglo-Saxon invasion, is a not unreasonable hypothesis; and, finally, that the monastery of *Candida Casa* holds a place of importance in Irish religious tradition.[61] The later legends retained the memory of some early British missionaries, such as Cairnech of Tulén (Dulane near Kells), Mél of Árd-achad (Ardagh), Lommán of Trim, Mochta of Lugmad (Louth), but for the most part their history was either eclipsed by the fame of the great church-founders of the sixth century or absorbed by the Patrick Legend. In the sixth century some of the British saints, in particular Gildas, are said to have visited Ireland, and several Irish churchmen, including Buite mac Brónaigh, Finnian of Clonard, Máedóc of Ferns, and Brendan of Clonfert, to have studied, or at least sojourned, in Britain. The curious *Catalogue of the Saints of Ireland* [62] (which includes Britons among the groups of saints of the first order) states that the saints of the second order (*c* A.D. 544–598) " received a mass from bishop David, and Gildas and Docus,[63] the Britons." The penitential books, which will be considered later,[64] witness at least to the close association of the Irish and British Churches in the sixth century, and, indeed, to the influence of the British on the Irish. Basing their opinion partly on a statement in the late Life of Gildas, some historians have hypothecated a pagan reaction in Ireland after the time of Patricius, and the restoration of Christianity by British effort. The theory seems improbable, and is strongly opposed by Heinrich Zimmer and Dom Louis Gougaud. It is probable, however, that there was a development of monasticism on a large scale in western Britain towards the end of the fifth and in the sixth century, and that it had an intimate relationship with the similar and contemporary movement in Ireland.

Germanus of Auxerre is said to have ordained Iltut, or Iltud,[65] " egregius magister Britannorum," founder of the famous monastic school of Llan-Iltut — identified with Llantwit — and reputed teacher of many of the British saints, including Cadoc, David, Samson, Paulus Aurelianus and Gildas. It seems certain, in any case, that Iltud was one of the principal pioneers of Celtic monasticism. Cadoc, who, according to another tradition, was the master, not the disciple, of Iltud,

61 Énda of Aran (no. 164), Finnian of Moville (no. 183), Tighernach of Clones (no. 179) and Eoghan of Ardstraw (no. 193) are said to have been alumni of that school.

62 No. 271.

63 Under 473 AU have the entry " Rest of the holy bishop Doccus, abbot of the Britons." Many have thought that Cadoc was meant, but there is evidence that there was a Doccus, Dochou, or Docwinn, an early saint of Wales. *Cf.* Loth in *RC* XXXV iii (1914) 292–3, XXXIX iii-iv (1922) 329–30; Duine *Memento* (1918) 122.

64 *Infra*, sect. vi.

65 The *Vita Iltuti* is late and of little value, but the saint is mentioned in the Life of Samson and other good sources. *Cf.* Gougaud *Chrétientés celtiques* 66; Duine *Memento* 127–31. His association with Germanus is hardly possible, but the report indicates the position he held in tradition.

founded the monastic church of Llan-Carvan; David that of Menevia, now St. David's; Dubric,[66] or his disciple Teilo,[67] that of Llan-Dâv or Llandaff; and Kentigern[68] that of St. Asaph. Tradition is obscure as to the foundation of Bangor Iscoed, on the river Dee, which, it would seem from Bede's testimony,[69] was in the seventh century the most important of the Welsh churches. Across the channel, in Brittany, Dol was founded by Samson, Landévennec by Guénolé, Alet by Malo,[70] Léon by Paulus Aurelianus, Trécor by Tutwal, Saint-Brieuc by Brioc, or Brieuc.[71] These are the names of only a few of those monastic churches which among the Britons took the place of episcopal cities.

The Welsh, Cornish and Breton *acta sanctorum* are even less satis-factory as historical sources than those of Ireland. Only one of these texts has any claim to be older than the ninth century, and the majority are not older than the twelfth. While some of the later Lives appear to contain an element of genuine traditions, others seem to have been invented out of whole cloth, with their only bases the names of the saints and the fact of the dedication to them of certain churches. Nevertheless it is on these unpromising documents that we are chiefly dependent for what we know of the early relations of Irish and British Christianity.

31. St. Samson of Dol

Vita s. Samsonis. EDS: (i) Mabillon *AA. SS. o. s. B. s.* I 165–86. — *AA. SS. Boll.* Jul. VI 568–93 [the reprint of 1868 is poor]. — Robt. Fawtier *La vie de saint Samson*: *essai de critique hagiographique (Bibliothèque de l'École des Hautes Études)* (Paris 1912) [rev. by Duine *Annales de Bretagne* XXVIII (1913) iii 332–56; also *RH* CXVI (1914) 74; and the controversial articles noticed below]. (ii) Plaine *An. Boll.* VI (1887) 77– 150 [*cf.* XII 56–7]; also separately, *La très ancienne vie inédite de s. Samson* (Paris 1887). (iii — *Vita metrica*) Extracts in *An. Boll.* and Plaine, *loc. cit.*, and La Borderie *Histoire de Bretagne* I (Rennes 1896) 264, 562–3. (iv) Extracts in Plaine, *loc. cit.* (v) W. J. Rees *The Liber Llandavensis* (Llandovery 1840) 8–25. — J. G. Evans and John Rhŷs *The Text of the Book of Llan Dâv* (Oxford 1893). TRANS: T. Taylor

---

[66] Dubric seems to have been a personage of importance, although his *vita* is of little value. *Cf.* Duine *Memento* 125.

[67] *Cf.* Duine *op. cit.* 133–6.

[68] Founder of the church of Glasgow, who is said to have come south during a period of pagan reaction in Strathclyde. There are several versions of his Life, published as follows: (1) Before 1164: Co:mo Innes *Registrum Episcopatus Glasguensis* I (Edinburgh 1843) pp. lxxviii–lxxxvi; Forbes *Lives of S. Ninian and S. Kentigern* (Edinburgh 1874); Metcalfe ed. of Pinkerton's *Lives of the Scottish Saints* II (Paisley 1889) 99–109. (2) By Jocelin of Furness *c* 1185: Metcalfe *loc. cit.* 1–96. (3) Abridgment of preceding: *Nova Legenda Anglie* ed. Horstman II 114–27; *AA. SS. Boll.* 13 Jan. I 815–25. *Cf.* A. O. Anderson *Early sources of Scottish history* I (Edinburgh, etc. 1922) 126–40.

[69] Bede *HE* II ii.

[70] *Cf.* no. 205 *infra.*

[71] *Cf.* Duine *Memento* 61–3, 84–6; Baring-Gould and Fisher *British Saints* IV 271–4, I 288–301.

(S. P. C. K.) (London 1925) [i]. Сомм: L. Duchesne *Catalogues épiscopaux de la province de Tours* (Paris 1890); *Fastes épiscopaux de l'ancienne Gaule* 2nd ed. II (Paris 1910) 381 n., III (1915) 229. — F. Duine *S. Samson et sa légende* (Paris 1900) [reprint from *Hermine* Dec. 1899 *sqq*]; "Culte de s. Samson à la fin du Xe siècle" *Annales de Bretagne* April 1902; *Les Saints de Bretagne: s. Samson* (Rennes 1909); *Histoire civile et politique de Dol* (Paris 1911) 229–34 [reprint from *Hermine* 1907–11]; *Les Saints de Domnonée* (Rennes 1913) 5 *sqq*; *Origines Bretonnes Études des sources — Questions d'hagiographie et vie de S. Samson* (Paris 1914) [contains a careful study of the language of the first Life]; *Le schisme breton* [reprint from *Annales de Bretagne* Nov. 1915]; *La Métropole de Bretagne* (Paris 1916) 41–2, 123 n; *Memento* 31–5. — *Y Cymmrodor* XI 127. — *Annuaire de l'École pratique des Hautes Études*, 1910–11, pp. 117–9 [*re* the MSS]. — Baring-Gould and Fisher *British Saints* IV (1913) 130–70 A considerable controversial literature has grown out of Fawtier's ed. of *Vita* I: Duine "La Vie de s. Samson à propos d'un ouvrage récent" *Annales de Bretagne* April 1913 pp. 332–56; J. Loth "La Vie la plus ancienne de s. Samson de Dol, d'après des travaux récents" *RC* XXXV (1914) 269–300; Fawtier "Saint Samson, abbé de Dol" *Annales de Bretagne* XXXV (1922) ii; Duine "S. Samson, évêque de Dol" *ibid.* XXXV 171–86 [all these have also been printed separately]; Loth "La Vie la plus ancienne de St. Samson de Dol" *RC* XXXIX (1922) 301–33, XL (1923) 1–50. — F. C. Burkitt *JTS* XXVII (1925) 42–57 [assigns a late date to text I].

Of Samson of Dol, one of the most famous saints of Brittany, there are five biographies, the first four by clerics of Dol: the primitive *vita;* the second, a literary recasting of the first, with some additions, made in the second half of the ninth century; a metrical Life, based on the second, probably of the end of the ninth or beginning of the tenth century;[72] a Life by Baldricus, or Baudry, archbishop of Dol, (d. 1130), also based on the second; and the Welsh version of the primitive Life, in the *Book of Llan-Dâv*, compiled about 1132.

Fawtier, editor of the *vita prima*, maintains that it is not older than the end of the eighth, or, more probably, the beginning of the ninth century, and that the author knew nothing of his hero except that he had come from Britain and had founded Dol and Pental.[73] On the other hand, La Borderie had assigned the Life to about 610–615,[74] and Duine and Loth have argued strongly in favor of this date. If they are right the Life assumes a peculiar importance, for it marks the beginning — at least as regards extant texts — of Celtic hagiography. It is noteworthy, moreover, that two of the earliest Irish *vitae sanctorum*, the Life of Brigit by Cogitosus and that of Patrick by Muir-chú, show certain striking verbal resemblances to this Life of Samson.[75]

---

[72] Duine suggests that the author was a certain Radbod of Dol.

[73] On the lower Seine, in the country of the Franks. It was for some time a dependency of Dol.

[74] The superficial evidence is that the author claims to have obtained his information from a Life written by the deacon Henoc, cousin and companion of the saint, and, orally, from Henoc's nephew and other credible witnesses. The abbé Duine finds that the chief literary influences shown by the text are of the Bible, Gregory the Great, Sulpicius Severus, Jerome and Cassian, and that there is no reminiscence of a work of later date than A.D. 600. — *Origines bretonnes* 26 *sqq.*

[75] In the prologues to the three texts. It is possible that all drew from a common source. Part of the common phraseology seems to come ultimately from Cassian's *Collationes*, preface to Leontius. Duine, however, suggests that there may have been literary manuals containing turns of expression for the use of the monks in composing *vitae sanctorum*. *RC* XXXV (1914) 299 n.

Samson was, undoubtedly, a historical personage. It is reasonably probable that he was the Samson who was present at a synod held at Paris some time between 556 and 573. Duine thinks that the synod met about 563 and that Samson died about 565. According to the primitive *vita* he was a native of Wales and in early life went to Ireland with some Irish scholars — *peritissimi Scotti* — who were returning from Rome. In Ireland he lived for a time in *arx Etri*, no doubt Dún Étair, surmounting Benn Étair, or Howth Headland.[76] This seems to have been a well-known landing-place for travellers from Britain. One of the Irish monasteries, we are told, put itself under his charge.

The text of the primitive *Vita Samsonis* is debased, and no attempt has been made at a critical restoration. Such restoration and further critical study of the text are desirable for the investigation both of the origins of Celtic hagiography and of the early history of the insular churches.

32. Winwaloeus or Guénolé — Life by Wrdisten *c* A.D. 880

EDS: *AA. SS. Boll.* 3 Mar. I 256–61 [incomplete]. — C. De Smedt *An. Boll.* VII (1888) 172–249 [with a metrical *vita* appended]. — La Borderie *Cartulaire de l'abbaye de Landévenec* (Rennes 1888). COMM: La Borderie *Annales de Bretagne* IV (1888) 295–364; *Histoire de Bretagne* I, II *passim.* —F. M. Luzel *La vie de St Gwennolé* (Quimper 1889). — J. Loth " Landévennec et s. Guénolé " *Annales de Bretagne* April 1893 pp. 488 *sqq.* — Le Nestour " Vie de s. Guénolé " *RC* XV (1894) 246–71. — Latouche *Mélanges d'histoire de Cornouaille* (Paris 1911). — R. Fawtier *Une rédaction inédite de la vie de s. Guénolé* (Rome 1912). — Duine *Les Saints de Domnonée* (Rennes 1913); " Note sur la vita Winwaloei " *Annales de Bretagne* April 1913 p. 355, Nov. 1915 p. 443; *Memento* 40–8 [with further bibliography]. — Baring-Gould and Fisher *Lives of the British Saints* IV (1913) 353–62. — Donatien De Bruyne " Notes sur les vies de s. Guénolé et de s. Idunet " *Bull. de la soc. archéol. du Finistère* 1916 pp. 173–83 [*cf.* *Annal. de Bret.* Jan. 1918 pp. 180–1].

Situated in the peninsula of Crozon, on the southern side of the bay which forms to the north the famous harbor of Brest, Landévennec was one of the most important of Breton monasteries. It had been founded in the fifth or sixth century by a Saint Winwaloe — modified in French to Guénolé — whose name in hypocoristic form, after the fashion so well known in Irish hagiology, it retained: Landévennec — *Lan-Towennoc = Lann To-Winn-oc*. Landévennec was a stronghold of Celtic custom. When the Carlovingian emperor Louis the Pious, having conquered the Breton prince Mourman, or Morvan, was attempting to force ecclesiastical as well as political conformity on Brittany, it was to Matmonoch, abbot of Landévennec, that he primarily addressed his order of 818 enjoining on all the Breton clergy the abandonment of Irish practices and the adoption of the Roman tonsure and the rule of St. Benedict.[77] Landévennec, however, seems to have continued to maintain associations with Ireland and with Celtic Britain.[78]

---

[76] So identified by R. I. Best: *cf. RC* XXXV 288.

[77] *Vita Winwaloei* II xii; also Bouquet *Recueil des historiens des Gaules et de la France* VI 328, (new ed. Paris 1870) 513–4; H&S II 79. *Cf.* Bernhard Simpson *Jahrbücher des frankischen Reichs unter Ludwig dem Frommen* I (*Jahrbücher der deutschen Geschichte* VI i) (Leipsic 1874) 128–36; Duine *Memento* 183–4.

[78] *Cf.* Gougaud *Chrétientés celtiques* 123.

About 880 the abbot Wrdisten wrote a Life of the founder. He made use of an earlier *vita*, but it was probably not older than the beginning of the century. Wrdisten's composition has little value for the period of which it professes to treat. His statement, for example, that Winwaloe had wished to associate himself with St. Patrick has no importance for the history of those two men, but it does show the respect in which Patrick was held at Landévennec in the ninth century. Wrdisten makes it the occasion for a brief notice of Patrick's career, based on the Life by Muir-chú. Some interesting light is thrown also on the commercial and other relations between Ireland and the west of Brittany.[79] It has the positive statement that Britons fleeing from the Saxon invaders took refuge among the Irish as well as on the Continent.

33. St. Paulus Aurelianus or Pol Aurélien — Life by Wrmonoc
A.D. 884

EDS: F. Plaine *An. Boll.* I (1882) 208–58.—C. Cuissard *RC* V(1883) 413–60 [*cf. An. Boll.* II 191–4]. COMM: Rhŷs "Goidelic words in Brythonic" *Archaeologia Cambrensis* 5th ser. XII (1895) 300–1. — La Borderie *Histoire de Bretagne* I *passim.* — G. Guenin "L'Évangélisation du Finistère au VIe siècle" *Bull. de la Soc. académique de Brest* 2nd ser. XXXII (1906–7) 29–82. — L. Duchesne *Fastes épiscopaux de l'ancienne Gaule* II (2nd ed. Paris 1910) 380–1. — Baring-Gould and Fisher *British Saints* IV (1913) 75–86. — Duine *Memento* 58–61 [with bibliography].

The abbot Wrdisten had under him at Landévennec a monk named Wrmonoc who followed his master's example in hagiography by writing a Life of Paulus Aurelianus, first bishop of the neighboring church of Léon. He made use of an older biography, but it does not seem to have been of any great antiquity. Paulus Aurelianus, or Pol Aurélien, said to have been a disciple of Iltud, had come from Wales to this western extremity of Armorica in the sixth century and founded several churches. Wrmonoc preserves the names of some of his companions and gives evidence that the Irish custom — *more gentis transmarinae* — of giving hypocoristic names to the inmates of monastic churches was followed in this part of Brittany.[80] Such, at least, is Zimmer's opinion, but it is by no means certain that this usage, extensively as it was practised in Ireland, was not equally of British provenance.[81]

34. Gildas — Life (1) by a Monk of Ruys; (2) by Caradoc of Llan-Carvan

EDS: (1) John à Bosco in *Bibliotheca Floriacensis* (Lyons 1608) 429–63 [imperfect]. — *AA. SS. Boll.* Jan. II 952–67. — Colgan *AA. SS.* (1645) 181–7 [excerpts]. — Mabillon *AA. SS. o. s. B.* I (1668) 138–52 [fuller text]. — Bouquet III 449–51, IX 136, X 337–8. — J. A. Giles *Vitae quorumdam Anglo-Saxonum* (Caxton Society: London 1854)

---

[79] *Vita Winwaloei* I xviii, xix. There is an allusion to this document in Jocelin's Life of Patrick, *AA. SS. Boll.* Mar. II 577 n. 159.

[80] "Quonoco quem alii sub additamento more gentis transmarinae Toquonocum uocant."

[81] HZ "Zur Personennamenbildung in Irischen" *Zs. f. vergleichende Sprachforschung* XXXII (1891) 153–246, esp. 180–9; *Nennius Vindicatus* (1893) 258–9. — J. Loth "Landévennec et s. Guénolé" *Annales de Bretagne* VIII (1892–3) 488–91; *RC* XXXII 488–94. See p. 305 n. 54 *infra.*

315–48. — Mommsen *MGH Auct. Ant.* XIII (*Chronica minora* III pt. I) (1894) 91–106. — Williams *Gildas: The Ruin of Britain*, etc. (*Cymmrodorion Record Series* no. 3) (London 1899) 317–389 [text, trans.]. — F. Lot *Mélanges d'histoire bretonne* (Paris 1907) 207–83, 431–73 [also in *Annales de Bretagne* XXV (1909–10) 348–65, 493–519: text, valuable introd.]. (2) Jos. Stephenson (London 1838). — San Marte (= A. Schulz) *Nennius und Gildas* (Berlin 1844) 116–24. — Mommsen *op. cit.* 107–10. — Williams *op. cit.* 390–413. *Cf.* J. Armitage Robinson " The Lives of St. Cungar and St. Gildas " *JTS* XXIII (1921) 15–22. COMM: See no. 23.

Of the association of Gildas, reputed author of the *De excidio et conquestu Britanniae*,[82] with Ireland, and of the high regard in which he was held by the Irish, there is excellent testimony. Columbanus, in a letter to Pope Gregory the Great[83] written about A.D. 600, says that a certain Vennianus (doubtless either Finnian of Magh-Bile or Finnian of Clúain-Iráird) consulted Gildas on a question of monastic discipline. And in the Irish collection of canons,[84] compiled probably towards the end of the seventh century, Gildas is quoted extensively as an authority side by side with Holy Scripture and the Fathers of the Church.

Other early authors who mention Gildas are Bede, who uses his work for the history of the Anglo-Saxon invasion of Britain; a compiler of the *Historia Britonum;* Alcuin; and Wrdisten and Wrmonoc of Landévennec. The *Annales Cambriae* mention his voyage to Ireland in 565 and his death in 570. The Annals of Ulster also assign his obit to 570, but the entry looks like a comparatively late insertion, derived, doubtless, from the last-mentioned source.[85]

Our earliest Life of Gildas was written in the eleventh century by a monk of Ruys, a monastery in Brittany which claimed the saint as its founder. Ferdinand Lot, who has carefully studied the subject, is of the opinion that it was written *c* 1060–1067 by Vitalis, abbot of Ruys since 1038. The author may have had earlier sources for the part treating of the career of Gildas in the British Isles, but that relating to Armorica seems wholly fictitious. It is quite probable that the saint never went to the Continent. Williams believes that the *vita* proper, as distinguished from the chapters on the history of Ruys appended to it, was written in the ninth century, perhaps at Fleury from materials brought from Brittany when the monks fled before the Norsemen. Lot thinks that the primitive Life originated in South Wales.

Gildas, we are told, was a native of Arecluta (Strat-Clut or Strathclyde); was educated under St. Iltud and, later, in Ireland; returned to preach to the heathen in North Britain, whence he corresponded with St. Brigit; again visited Ireland; and, when returning from a pilgrimage to Rome, settled in Armorica. He made his second

[82] No. 23. [83] No. 42 (i). [84] No. 82.
[85] *Gildas obiit.* In Irish *ld* became *ll* about the middle of the ninth century.

journey to Ireland on the invitation of King Anmericus, who promised to observe his teaching in all things if he would come and restore ecclesiastical order in his kingdom, for almost everybody in the island had abandoned the Catholic faith. Gildas travelled through all the districts of Ireland, rebuilding the churches, instructing the clergy in the Catholic faith, re-asserting the dogma of the Trinity, and repairing the damages wrought by heretics. As a result, the Church and the Catholic faith flourished and the country rejoiced in having such a patron.

So the Life. Its " Anmericus " is, undoubtedly, Ainmire, who, according to the Annals of Ulster, ruled as árd-rí, or high king, from 566 to 569, or, alternative dates, 573 to 576.[86] Whether the monk of Ruys had any genuine information regarding conditions in Ireland at this time, or not, it is certain that the story of degeneration and revival is, at least, exaggerated.

The second *vita* is ascribed, probably correctly, to Caradoc of Llan-Carvan (d. *c* 1150), a fellow-worker of Geoffrey of Monmouth and William of Malmesbury. The narrative is much modified by late legendary matter such as the Arthurian romances, and by the contemporary literary campaign for the exaltation of Glastonbury. It makes Gildas, during part of his sojourn in Ireland, a teacher at Armagh.

35. St. David — Life by Rhygyfarch   *c* A.D. 1090

Eds: Wharton *Anglia Sacra* II 645–7 [incomplete]. — *AA. SS. Boll.* Mar. I 41–6 [epitome]. — Rees *Cambro-British Saints* 117–43 [cf. *Y Cymmrodor* XIII (1900) 85]. — Colgan *AA. SS.* 425–9. — *Nova Legenda Anglie* (ed. Horstman, Oxford 1901) I 254–63 [these two are abridgments]. — A. W. Wade-Evans " Rhygyvarch's Life of St. David " *Y Cymmrodor* XXIV (1913) 1–73 [text, trans.: cf. *An. Boll.* XXXVIII (1920) 221–2]. Trans: Wade-Evans *Life of St. David* (London 1923). Comm: Hardy *Cat.* I pt. II 118–24. — E. W. B. Nicholson *ZCP* VI (1908) 447 *sqq.* — Baring-Gould and Fisher *British Saints* II 285–322. — Duine *Memento* 123–5 [with bibliography].

Standing out into St. George's channel from the present county of Pembroke is the promontory known as St. David's Headland, the extreme western point of the mainland of Wales. Nearby is the port of St. David's, in mediaeval Latin *Menevia*, old Welsh *Moniu*, later *Mynyw*, Irish *Muine*. This southern peninsula of Wales, known in early mediaeval times by the names Demet and Dyfed, had been one of the chief districts of Irish settlement in Britain in the fourth and fifth centuries, and here a distinctive Goidelic population seems to have persisted longest. Moniu, called in the *Annales Cambriae* " Moniu De[s]orum," Moniu of the *Dési*,[87] was naturally the chief centre of

---

[86] A. Anscombe argues that the true dates were 548 to 551. See his *St. Gildas of Ruys and Irish regal chronology* (1893) and *ZCP* VI (1908) 363.

[87] J. Loth *RC* XXXVII iv (1919) 315–6. *Cf.* p. 149 *supra*.

communication between Wales and Ireland, and there are several references in the *acta sanctorum* to the presence there of Irish ecclesiastics.

The founder of the monastic church at Moniu was Dewi, a name to which the Latinists gave the Hebraic form David. There are no early records for the life of David. The town and church of Moniu or Menevia were sacked repeatedly by the Norsemen, and few if any of the local archives can have escaped.

The earliest Life was written about 1090 by Rhygyfarch (Ricemarchus), son of Sulien, bishop of St. David's. He and his father were prominent in public affairs in the eleventh century, and had intimate associations with Ireland.[88] The *Life of David* was a piece of propaganda in favor of the claims of St. David's to the rank of an archiepiscopal see and of metropolis of Wales. The author claims to have made use of ancient sources, but it is evident that he had little material except oral traditions and ballads. St. David, however, held a position in mediaeval Wales similar to that of St. Patrick in Ireland, St. Samson in Brittany and St. Martin in France, and popular tradition was, no doubt, abundant. In Ireland, too, David enjoyed a great celebrity. He is represented to have been in close association with the clergy of Ireland. His disciple, Donnóc or Modomnóc, introduced the first bees into that country.[89] Another story tells of the saint winning over to repentance an Irish freebooter named Boia, ruler of Moniu, whose pagan wife thereupon offered human sacrifice to her gods, the *siddi*.[90] If the legend had an historical origin, Boia was probably the local Goidelic chieftain.

The *Annales Cambriae* give what seems to be an obituary notice of David under 601. William of Malmesbury assigned his death to 546. The *data* afforded by Rhygyfarch point to 544, of which a variant, correct or erroneous, was 547.[91]

For the Penitential attributed to David, see p. 239 *infra*.

36. St. Cadoc of Llan-Carvan — Life by Lifris

EDS: Rees *Cambro-British Saints* 22–96 [corrections by KM *Y Cymmrodor* XIII (1900) 77–84]. — *Nova Legenda Anglie* (ed. Carl Horstman, Oxford 1901) I 167–73 [epitome]. There are other versions in *AA. SS. Boll.* Jan. III 217–20; Colgan *AA. SS.* 158–61. *Cf.* Hardy *Cat.* I pt. I 147–9. COMM: Newell *Archaeologia Cambrensis* 5th ser. X (1893) 334–5. — Rhŷs *ibid.* XII (1895) 278. — Plaine *Bull. de la Soc. archéol. du Finistère* XXVII (1901) 128–30. — De Calan " Essai sur la chronologie des rois et des saints de la Bretagne insulaire " *Associat. Bret. Congrès* 1912 [for Cadoc, pp. 214

---

[88] *Cf. Archaeologia Cambrensis* I (1846) 117–25; Lloyd *History of Wales* II 459–61; Lawlor *Psalter and Martyrology of Ricemarch* I pp. ix *sqq.*

[89] *Cf.* Giraldus Cambrensis *Topogr. Hib.* I vi; O'D *Banquet of Dun na nGedh and Battle of Magh Rath* (1842) 34; *Fél. Oeng.*² 60, 75, 113; Plummer *Misc. hag. Hib.* (1925) Cat. no. 152.

[90] The *síde*, or *des síde*, of Irish mythology and folk-lore.

[91] *Cf.* Nicholson, *op. cit.* Perhaps the David, bishop of Armagh and legate of all Ireland, whose name appears in AU 551, owes his existence to some old textual corruption of an obituary notice of the Welsh saint.

sqq]. — Baring-Gould and Fisher *British Saints* II 14-42, III 132-3. — Duine *Memento* 115-8 [with bibliography].

The earliest extant Life of Cadoc was written by a cleric named Lifris, who flourished at the end of the eleventh century, if, as seems probable, he was the son of Bishop Herwald of Llandaff, who died in 1104. It is a fabulous composition, but doubtless reflects the ideas and traditions of Cadoc's monastery of Llan-Carvan. Cadoc's mother is said to have been of Irish descent; he himself was trained by an Irish hermit named Meuthi; and he also went to the schools of Ireland, especially Lismore, " until he had acquired the complete knowledge of the West." Many disciples accompanied him on his return, among them Finnian (of Clonard),[92] MacMoil and Gnauan. Mention is also made of a skilful Irish wood-worker named Liuguri (= Lóiguire), whose fellow laborers killed him in jealousy. — MacMoil and Finnian are named in a collection of alleged records of donations made to Cadoc and his monastery.[93]

37. British Legends of Saints who went to Ireland

(1) CARANTOC. EDS: *AA. SS. Boll.* 16 Mai. III 583-7. — Rees *Cambro-British Saints* 97 *sqq.* — *Nova Legenda Anglie* ed. Horstman I (Oxford 1901) 177-9. —S. Baring-Gould *Y Cymmrodor* XV (1902) 88-99. *Cf.* Hardy *Cat.* I i 46-7; Duine *Memento* 118-9. He is said to have followed Patrick to Ireland, and is identified with the St. Cairnech, or Carnech (*i.e.*, the " Cornishman "), of Irish tradition. *Cf.* p. 352 *infra.* (2) CYBI, KEBIUS. EDS: Rees *op. cit.* 183-8 [corrections by KM *Y Cymmrodor* XIII (1900) 87-8]. — *Nova Legenda Anglie* II 100-2. COMM: Baring-Gould *Y Cymmrodor* XIV (1901) 86-95. — Baring-Gould and Fisher *British Saints* 202-15. He lived under St. Énda at Aran. (3) ETHBIN, EGBIN, EDIUNET. EDS: Surius *De probatis sanctorum historiis* Oct. IV (Cologne 1617) 307 *sqq.* — *AA. SS. Boll.* Oct. VIII 474-8. — *Nova Legenda Anglie* I 368-9. COMM: La Borderie *Cartulaire de Landévenec* (Rennes 1888) 137-41. — Donatien De Bruyne " La Vie de s. Idunet " *Bull. de la Soc. archéol. du Finistère* 1916 pp. 178-9. — Duine *op. cit.* 87-9. A disciple of Winwaloe who ended his life in Ireland, at the " silua Nectensis." The Life is by a monk of Landévennec, perhaps of the eleventh century. (4) GUÉNAËL. ED: *AA. SS. Boll.* Nov. I 669-79. COMM: Baring-Gould and Fisher *op. cit.* III 172-81. — Duine *op. cit.* 38-40 [with bibliography]. He was the successor of Winwaloe at Landévennec, and is said to have founded a monastery in Ireland. The Life is of the ninth or tenth century. (5) MACHAN. *Cf.* A. P. Forbes *Kalendars of Scottish Saints* (Edinburgh 1872) 380-1. (6) PADARN, PATERN. EDS: Rees *op. cit.* 188-97 [corrections by KM *loc. cit.* 88]. — *AA. SS. Boll.* Apr. II 377-81. — *Nova Legenda Anglie* II 274-8. COMM: Hardy *op. cit.* I pt. I 129-30. — Duchesne *RC* XIV (1893) 238-40. — Phillimore *Y Cymmrodor* XI 128. — Lot " Caradoc et s. Patern " *Romania* XXVIII (1899) 568 *sqq.* — Duine *op. cit.* 69-70 [with bibliography]. He and his father, Peran, lived for a time in Ireland. The Life, a Breton composition of the second half of the eleventh century, seems to have absorbed an earlier Welsh text. (7) PETROC. EDS: *Nova Legenda Anglie* II 317-20. — *AA. SS. Boll.* Jun. I 399-402. COMM: Baring-Gould and Fisher *op. cit.* IV 94-

---

[92] We are told that the monks of Clonard, through veneration for the memory of Cadoc, would honorably receive any of his clergy, and make him as one of their heirs.

[93] Frederick Seebohm *The Tribal System in Wales* (2nd ed. London, etc. 1904) 205 *sqq.*

103. — Duine *op. cit.* 132–3 [with bibliography]. He spent twenty years studying in Ireland.

38. Legends of Irish Saints in Britain and Brittany

(1) BREACA. *Cf.* Lucy Toulmin Smith (ed.) *Itinerary of John Leland* I (London 1907) 187; Baring-Gould and Fisher *British Saints* I 229–32. Leland in the sixteenth century made extracts from a Life kept at Breage Church, Cornwall. She was an Irishwoman who came to Cornwall with Senan and many other saints. (2) BRIAC. *Cf.* Albert le Grand *Les Vies des saints de la Bretagne* (ed. of 1901) 714; La Borderie *Histoire de Bretagne* I 359–61; Baring-Gould and Fisher *op. cit.* I 262–4. Son of an Ulster prince, he became a disciple of St. Tugdual in Wales, founded the monastery of Bourbriac in Brittany, and made a voyage to Rome. (3) BUDOC. *Cf.* Lucy Toulmin Smith *op. cit.* I 196–7; Baring-Gould and Fisher *op. cit.* 329–37; Duine *Saints de Domnonée* (1912) 20–31, 50; *Memento* 65–6 [with bibliography]. A pan-British saint who is localised in Pembroke, Devon, Cornwall and Brittany, and who, according to some traditions, was Irish. (4) CAST. *Cf.* Duine *Memento* 94–5. (5) EFFLAM. ED: La Borderie *Annales de Bretagne* VII (1892) 279–312. *Cf.* Duine *op. cit.* 89. An Irish prince who went to Armorica. The Life is of the twelfth century. (6) FEOCK. *Cf.* Albert le Grand *op. cit.*; Baring-Gould and Fisher *op. cit.* III 4–9. His name, in many variations, is found in the legends, church dedications and place names of Cornwall and Brittany. Le Grand's Life makes him an archbishop of Armagh who floated to Brittany on a stone. (7) FINGAR (GUIGNER) and PIALA (CIARA). EDS: (i) Messingham *Florilegium insulae sanctorum* (Paris 1624) 210–8. — Colgan *AA. SS.* (Louvain 1645) 387–90. — *AA. SS. Boll.* Mar. III 456–9. — G. Gerberon (ed.) *Anselmi Cantuariensis opera* (2nd ed. Paris 1721) I 508, II 703. — Migne *PL* CLIX 325–34. (ii) Albert le Grand *op. cit.* COMM: Baring-Gould and Fisher *op. cit.* III 24–30, 267–9. — Duine *op. cit.* 126–7, 155–6. Children of an Irish king, they were banished for accepting the teaching of St. Patrick, and went to Brittany and later to Cornwall, where they were murdered. They were followed to Cornwall by St. Hia. The Life was by a monk named Anselm, perhaps of St. Michael's Mount, Cornwall. Another Life was extracted by Le Grand from Breton *legendaria*. (8) LEUTIERN. *Cf.* Duine *op. cit.* 149 and references there given. A Breton saint who has been identified as an Irishman, Lughtiern. (9) MAUDETUS, MAUDEZ, MAWES. EDS: La Borderie *Mém. de la Soc. d'émulation des Côtes-du-Nord* XXVIII (1890) 198–266 [also separately 1891]. — U. Robert *Vie de S. Maudé* (1889). COMM: Y. M. Lucas " Le culte de s. Maudet et de s. Rion " *Rev. hist. de l'Ouest* (Vannes 1893) [and separately]. — Baring-Gould and Fisher *op. cit.* III 441–9. — Duine *op. cit.* 97–8. An Irish saint who went to Brittany, where many dedications attest his fame, as does the place-name, St. Mawes, in Cornwall. The earliest Life — fragmentary — may be of the eleventh century. (10) MENULFUS, MENORE. EDS: Labbe *Novae bibliothecae* II (Paris 1657) 433–4. — *AA. SS. Boll.* 12 Jul. III 307–8. COMM: Duine *op. cit.* 81–2. He went to Armorica, and thence to Rome, and founded St. Menoux in Bourges. (11) NINNOCA. EDS: L. Maitre and P. de Berthou *Cartulaire de l'abbaye de Sainte-Croix de Quimperlé* 15–27, 2nd ed. 55–68. — *AA. SS. Boll.* Jun. I 408–11 [partial]. COMM: Molinier *Sources de l'histoire de France* I no. 403. — Duine *op. cit.* 101. (12) OSMANNA. EDS: *AA. SS. Boll.* Sept. III 417–25. Plaine " Ste Osmanne, patronne de Féricy-en-Brie " *Rev. de Champagne et de Brie* and separately (1892) [*cf. An. Boll.* XII (1893) 314]. —

Nova Legenda Anglie ed. Horstman II (1901) 237–9. (13) RONAN, RENAN. ED: De Smedt *Catalogus codicum hagiographicorum B. N. Paris.* I (Brussels 1889) 438–58. FR. TRANS.: *Bull. de la Soc. archéol. du Finistère* XVI (1889) 263 *sqq.* COMM: Duchesne *Bull. critique* XI (1890) 124–5. — Baring-Gould and Fisher *op. cit.* IV 120–5. — Duine *op. cit.* 102–3 [with bibliography]. —L. Gougaud *RC* XXXIX (1922) 220; *Gaelic pioneers of Christianity* (1923) 137–8. (14) SEZNIUS, SEZNY. *Cf.* Albert le Grand *op. cit.* 391–3; Colgan *op. cit.* 477; Baring-Gould and Fisher *op. cit.* IV 199; Duine *op. cit* 104. He went to Brittany. Colgan wished to identify him with Iserninus. (15) TATHEUS, TATHAN. EDS: Rees *Cambro-British Saints* (1853) 255–64 [corrections by KM *Y Cymmrodor* XIII (1900) 93]. — H. Idris Bell *Vita S. Tathei and Buched Seint Y Katrin* (Welsh MSS. Soc.: Bangor 1909). — *Nova Legenda Anglie* ed. Horstman II (1901) 361–3. COMM: Baring-Gould and Fisher *op. cit.* IV 211–4. He went to Wales and became teacher of Cadoc. (16) TENENANUS, TINIDORUS. *Cf.* Le Grand *op. cit.* 307; *AA. SS. Boll.* Jul. IV 179–80; La Borderie *Hist. de Bretagne* I (1896) 496; Baring-Gould and Fisher *op. cit.* IV 244–9, 293–6; Duine *op. cit.* 78–9. Of Léon in Brittany, said by some to have been of Irish birth, by others, of Irish education. (17) VOUGAY, VIO. *Cf.* Le Grand *op. cit.* 222; Duine *op. cit.* 107. An archbishop who went to Brittany.

These texts are of late date and fabulous character. Yet they do witness to a wide and deep tradition of the early association of the Irish and British churches. The probability, on other grounds, of a movement of British ecclesiastics into Ireland in the fifth and sixth centuries has been mentioned. For the stories of the presence of Irish clerics in Brythonic lands there are also credible explanations: some may have gone to seek the teaching and the discipline of the British monasteries; others to dwell with their kindred in those Goidelic settlements which still existed in some districts of Wales and Cornwall in the early sixth century; and others under the influence of that idea of religious exile which became so powerful in the following centuries. Some legends of Irish saints in Britain — notably Senan and Ciarán (Cornish " Piran ")[94] — must have had their origin solely in church dedications. Such dedications are particularly numerous at the extreme western point of Cornwall, where, doubtless, there was a Goidelic population.

The works of Geoffrey of Monmouth and William of Malmesbury also have some interest for early Hiberno-British religious relations.

[94] *Cf.* nos. 157, 124.

III. RENEWAL OF INTERCOURSE WITH CONTINENTAL EUROPE —
ST. COLUMBANUS

Bibliography

See the works listed on pp. 486–7 *infra*, especially those by Gougaud. — Margaret
Stokes *Six months in the Apennines, or a pilgrimage in search of vestiges of the Irish
saints in Italy* (London 1892); *Three months in the forests of France A pilgrimage in
search of vestiges of the Irish saints in France* (London 1895) [travel-letters by a student
of history and art; interesting though uncritical].

It is highly probable that a considerable amount of intercourse
was maintained between Ireland and western Gaul even in the Visigothic and early Frankish eras. Wine was to be bought and sold no
matter who took toll in Aquitaine. Doubtless a few ecclesiastics made
their way to Tours or even to Rome, and others, journeying to Brittany,
passed thence into the Frankish dominions. Of some of these, memories
lingered in the legends of later days. But so far as our records indicate,
permanent intellectual contact between Irish and continental Christianity was resumed only when Columbanus and his companions, some
Irish, some Britons, established themselves in eastern Gaul towards
the close of the sixth century. In Columbanus, too, we meet the
first Irishman whose own words survive in sufficient number to show
what manner of man he was.

39. Associates of St. Remi of Reims

(a) FLODOARD: *Historiarum ecclesiae Remensis libri IV* (A.D. 948). EDS: Geo. Col-
venerius (Douai 1617). — Bouquet VIII. — Migne *PL* CXXXV 27–406. — Lejeune
2 vols. (Reims 1854) [with Fr. trans.]. — J. Heller and G. Waitz *MGH SS* XIII
(1881) 409–599. (b) *Vita s. Gibriani.* ED: *AA. SS. Boll.* Mai. II 301–2, 3rd ed.
610–40. (c) *Vita s. Tresani.* EDS: Colgan *AA. SS.* 271–3. — *AA. SS. Boll.* Febr. II
53–5. COMM: *Histoire littéraire de la France* IV (1738) 193. — L. Paris *Légende de s.
Trésain d'Avenay avec l'histoire de son église* (Paris 1844). (d) *Vita s. Amandi.*
ED: *AA. SS. Boll.* Jun. III 106–7.

St. Remigius, or Remi, archbishop of Reims, who died in 532, was the most prominent
ecclesiastic of Gaul in his time. In 496 he received Clovis, king of the Franks, into the
Church. He is said to have been friendly to " pilgrims," and there are legends regarding several Irish saints who settled in his diocese. The most reputable witness is
Flodoard (894–966), a canon of the cathedral church at Reims who wrote extensively
on local and general history. In his *History of the Church of Reims* [95] he recounts the

[95] *Lib.* IV *cap.* ix.

translation to that edifice of the relics of St. Gibrianus, from whom the village of St. Gibrien, near Châlons-sur-Marne, takes its name. Gibrian was, he proceeds, one of a party of seven brothers and three sisters — Gibrian, Helan, Tressan, German, Veran, Abran and Petran, and Francla, Portia and Promptia —who came from Ireland to Reims and were allowed by Remi to settle on the banks of the river Marne. The same legend is given in the *vita* of Gibrian, and in that of Tressan, reputed founder of the church of Avenay, south of Reims, which are late and fabulous compositions, perhaps of the tenth or eleventh century. The shadowy St. Breaca of Cornwall was associated with this group of religious, and church-dedications in Cornwall and Brittany seem to show that they, or their legend, were well known in those countries.[96]

There is also a legend of an Irish pilgrim named Amandus, who, returning from Italy through Gaul, was granted land at Beaumont, near Reims, by Remi and Clovis, and there built a hermitage.

An eleventh or more probably twelfth or thirteenth-century text tells the story of St. Germanus, a bishop, who suffered martyrdom near Amiens apparently in the fifth century. The Life, which is quite untrustworthy, represents him as having come from *Scotia*, which to the author may have meant Scotland; but it is probable that either the older legend represented the saint as a " Scottus," an Irishman, or else that the biographer gave him a Scottish origin because of the traditional fame of the " Scotti." EDS: Labbe *Bibl. nova* I 716–23. — *AA. SS. Boll.* 2 Mai. I 261–70; *cf.* VII 549–51. COMM: Tillemont *Mémoires de l'hist. ecclés.* XV (1711) 28–9. — *Hist. lit. de la France* VII (1746) 151. — E. A. Pape *Vie de s. Germain l'Ecossais* (Amiens 1856). — J. Corblet *Hagiographie du diocèse d'Amiens* II (Paris 1870) 488–522.

Of similar apocryphal character are, probably, the statements in their Lives which attribute an Irish origin to two saints whose careers are placed in the sixth century, Ursus or Ours, patron of Aosta, and Praecordius or Précord, a hermit at Vesly-sur-Aisne. *Vita Ursi*: ED: *AA. SS. Boll.* I Feb. I 97–8, 937–9; 3rd ed. 945–6. *Vita Praecordii* (A.D. 932 x 942): EDS: Colgan *AA. SS.* 230–2. — *AA. SS. Boll.* 1 Feb. I 196–8. *Cf.* the Bollandists' *Bibl. hag. lat.* no. 1006.

40. St. Frediano of Lucca

(i) Beatus igitur Fridianus, sicut prisci catholici tradiderunt, ex Hibernia Scotiae insula . . . in his aquis moriatur. Quod usque in hodiernum diem ita esse probatum est. (ii) Summae Trinitati . . . Beatus igitur . . . Lucana decoratur. Veneremur ergo. . . . (iii) Sanctus ergo Fridianus . . . altare constituit. In quo loco multa exuberant beneficia. . . . (iv) Sanctus igitur Fridianus, mente pius. . . sibi adhaerere, qui vivit etc.

EDS: Colgan *AA. SS.* 633–51 (Vitae i, iii, & iv). *Cf.* [Augustinus Ticinensis] *Elucidarium christianarum religionum* (Brixie 1511) ff. xlvii–xlix; Ughelli *Italia Sacra* I

---

[96] *Cf.* Baring-Gould and Fisher *British Saints* I 105–7, 229–32, III 80–1, 253–4. These authors identify them with the sons of Goll whom St. Ailbe is said to have left in a monastery on the continent (Cod. S. 244). A German mac Guill is commemorated in the Irish martyrologies. Abran and the Cornish Kevern are identified with the Achebranus of *Domesday Book* — " Canonici sancti Achebrani tenent Lan-Achebran et tenebant tempore regis Eduardi " — and the Aed Cobran of the Irish martyrologies. All this is farfetched, and the last identification, at least, linguistically impossible. See *RC* XLVII i–ii 160–3.

794 *sqq*; G. Fanucchi *Vita di S. Frediano* (Lucca 1870); *An. Boll.* XI (1892) 262–3 [excerpts from Vita ii]; Margaret Stokes *Six Months in the Apennines* (1892) 20–49; Seebass *ZK* XIV (1894) 437–8; A. Poncelet *Cat. cod. hagiogr. lat. bibl. Romanarum* (Brussels 1909) 145, 243; *Cat. cod. hag. lat. bibl. Vaticanae* (Brussels 1910) 49, 194, 466.

St. Frediano was bishop of Lucca in northern Tuscany *c* 560–588. His reality is vouched for by a passage in the *Dialogues* of Pope Gregory the Great,[97] written before 604 (the date of that Pope's death), in which he describes a miracle performed by Frediano in turning the river Serchio near Lucca from its former course. The miracle is related also in the Lives. These are late compositions, the earliest being posterior to 1171. They state that Frediano was an Irishman, the son of a king of the Ulaid, who came to live as a hermit near Lucca and was induced to accept the bishopric. He is identified with Finnian of Moville,[98] some incidents of whose life are attached to Frediano, and the identification has been accepted by Colgan, Margaret Stokes, and other modern writers. No solid justification thereof seems to exist.

41. St. Cathaldus of Tarentum

[Io. Bapt. de Algoritiis] *Officium B. Cataldi archiepiscopi Tarentini de eius vita, miraculis, canonizatione, ac translatione* (1555) [contains a short account of his life]. *Cf.* Colgan *AA. SS.* 542–62; *AA. SS. Boll.* Mai. II 570–8 (ed. 1866: 568–77); Ughelli *Italia sacra* IX 121; Moroni *Vita e miracoli di s. Cataldo vescovo, protettore principale della città di Taranto* (Naples 1779); Montalembert *Les moines d'Occident* III (Paris 1868) 316; Lo Jodice *Memorie storiche di san Cataldo, vescovo e confessore* (Bologna 1879).

St. Cathaldus, bishop of Tarentum in the seventh century and subsequently patron of the city, is an important figure in south Italian religious legend. Of his existence there can be no doubt, but the circumstantial account of his career given in late sources, which makes him an Irishman, a monk of Lismore who went on a pilgrimage to the Holy Land, and, returning, stopped at Tarentum to win the people from their evil living, is manifestly fictitious. Nevertheless the ascription of an Irish origin to so prominent a personage in a region so remote from Ireland and from the usual resorts of Irish emigrants is noteworthy.

---

[97] *Dial. lib.* III *cap.* ix: Migne *PL* LXXVII 233–6. A document of the year 680 making mention of the monastery of San Frediano in Lucca is said to be still extant in the archiepiscopal archives of that city: *cf.* M. Stokes, *loc. cit.*

[98] *Cf.* no. 183.

COLUMBANUS

Bibliography

Patrick Fleming *Collectanea sacra seu S. Columbani Hiberni abbatis . . . necnon aliorum aliquot è Veteri itidem Scotiâ seu Hiberniâ antiquorum sanctorum acta & opuscula . . . per V. A. P. F. Thomam Sirinum . . . recens castigata & aucta* (Louvain 1667) [a rare and valuable collection: *cf.* p. 40 *supra*]. — Benedeto Rossetti *Bobbio illustrato* (Turin 1795). — A. Digot "St Colomban et Luxeuil" *L'Austrasie* 1840. — Antonio Gianelli *Vita di s. Colombano abate, i¹landese, protettore della città e diocesi di Bobbio* (Turin 1844; 2nd ed. 1894). — Bertacchi *Monografia di Bobbio* (Pinerolo 1859). — P. J. Moran *Essays* (1864) 268–70, 276–96. — C. J. Greith *Die heiligen Glaubensboten Kolumban und Gall und ihre Stellung in der Urgeschichte St. Gallens* (St. Gall 1865). — J. A. Zimmerman *Die Heiligen Columban und Gallus nach ihrem Leben und Wirken geschildert* (St. Gall 1866). — G. Hertel "Über des heiligen Columba Leben und Schriften, besonders über seine Klosterregel" *Zs. f. d. hist. Theologie* XLV (Gotha 1875) 396–454; "Anmerkung zur Geschichte Columba's" *ZK* III (1879) 145–50. — B. MacCarthy *IER* V (1884) 771 [on date of Columbanus's death]. — Godefroi Kurth "La reine Brunehaut" *Rev. des questions hist.* L (Paris 1891) 5–79. — H. Baumont *Étude historique sur l'abbaye de Luxeuil (590–1790)* (Luxeuil 1895). — A. Hauck *Kirchengeschichte Deutschlands* 2nd ed. I (1898) 251–302 [important]. — O. Seebass "Columba der Jüngere" *Realencykl. f. prot. Theologie u. Kirche* 3rd ed. III (1898) 241–7 [important: the author is the foremost student of the history of Columbanus]. — G. Bonet-Maury "S. Colomban et la fondation des monastères irlandaises en Brie au VIIᵉ siècle" *RH* LXXXIII (1903) 277–99 [*cf. Atti del Congresso internazionale di scienze storiche* VIII (Rome 1905) 123–9]. — Thos. J. Shahan "Saint Columbanus at Luxeuil" *Amer. Cath. Quart. Rev.* Jan. 1902. — C. W. Bispham *Columban, saint, monk, and missionary, A.D. 539–615* (New York 1903). — J. J. Dunn "Irish monks on the continent — St. Columban, St. Gall" *Cath. University Bulletin* X (Washington 1904) 307–28. — Eug. Martin *St. Colomban* (Paris 1905; 3rd ed. 1921) [in the series *Les Saints*; a work of good scholarship]. — Gougaud "Un point obscur de l'itinéraire de s. Colomban venant en Gaule" *Annales de Bretagne* XXII (1906–7) 327–43; Eng. trans. *Celtic Review* V (Oct. 1908) 171–85 [argument, in opposition to Krusch, that Columbanus went to Gaul by way of insular, not continental, Britain; see, for the other view, HZ *Sitzungsb. d. k. preuss. Akad. d. Wissensch.* 1909 xiv 391–400]; "Colomban (Archéologie de saint)" *Dict. d'archéol. chrét. et de liturgie* III pt. II (1914) 2196; *RC* XXXIX (1922) 211–4 and *Gaelic pioneers of Christianity* (Dublin 1923) 121–6 [the cult of Columban and Gall in Europe]. — Geo. Metlake (J. J. Laux) *The Life and writings of St. Columban 545–615* (Philadelphia 1914). — Johann Joseph Laux *Der hl. Kolumban, sein Leben und seine Schriften* (Freiburg i. Br. 1919). — Helena Concannon *The Life of St. Columban* (Cath. Truth Soc.: Dublin 1915); "St. Columban, apostle of peace and penance" *Studies* IV (Dec. 1915) 513–26; "The date of St. Columban's birth" *ibid.* VIII (Mar. 1919) 59–66 [reply to Aubrey Gwynn *ibid.* VII (Sept. 1918) 474–84]. — Dr. J. J. O'Gorman *St. Columban* (Ottawa, privately printed, 1915). — Dom Placido Lugnano "San Colombano, monaco e scrittore" *Rivista storica benedittina* XI (Rome 1916) 5–46 [also separately]. — D. Cambiaso "San Colombano, sua opera e suo culto in Liguria" *Rivista diocesana Genovese* VI (1916) 121–5. — G. Domenici "San Colombano (543–

615) " *Civiltà Cattolica* 1916. — " San Colombano, il testo della ' Regula monachorum,' dell' ' Ordo de vita et actione monachorum ' e dell' ' Oratio ' " *Rivista storica benedittina* XI (Rome 1920) 185–202. — O. Celi " Cimeli Bobbiesi " *Civiltà Cattolica* 1923 [also separately]. RELIGIOUS INFLUENCE: Ch. Fred. Weiss *Die kirchlichen Exemptionen der Klöster von ihrer Entstehung bis zur gregorianisch-cluniacensischen Zeit* (Basel 1893). — A. Malnory *Quid Luxovienses monachi discipuli S. Columbani ad regulam monasteriorum atque ad communem ecclesiae profectum contulerint* (Paris 1894) [valuable]. — E. Vacandard " Le pouvoir des clefs et la confession " *Rev. du clergé français* (1899) 147 *sqq.* — A. Hüfner " Das Rechtsinstitut der klösterlichen Exemtion in der abendländischen Kirche " *Archiv f. kath. Kirchenrecht* LXXXVI (1906) 302–18. *Cf.* sects. iv and vi *infra.* LITERARY: *Histoire littéraire de la France* III 505–25, 603–8. — T. Wright *Biographia Britannica literaria* I (London 1842) 142–63. — Adolf Ebert *Allgemeine Geschichte der Literatur des Mittelalters* I (1889) 617–22. — Roger *L'Enseignement* 230–2, 406–15. — Manitius *Lat. Lit.* I 181–7 [valuable; see also *NA* XXXII (1907) 661].

The two Irishmen who had the greatest influence on the course of development of west-European civilisation in the middle ages were two namesakes and contemporaries of the sixth century, Columba of Iona and Columba, or, as he is now usually designated, Columbanus, of Luxeuil and Bobbio.

Columbanus was born in Leinster — *Lagenorum terra* [99] — about A.D. 530 x 545. After some preliminary religious training he entered the monastery of Bendchor (Bangor) in Ulidia, then recently founded by St. Comgall.[100]   In 590, or perhaps a little earlier, he set out with twelve companions " on his pilgrimage " and proceeded by way of Britain — insular or continental — and western Gaul to Burgundy. Of those best years of his life, fifty or thereabout, spent in his native land, we know almost nothing. The history of Columbanus begins when he was already past the prime of life, and seeking, doubtless, a place of exile and retirement to spend his old age in undisturbed penance and devotion.[101]

[99] By this time the territory of the Lagin had been reduced to the bounds it retained through the remainder of our period, approximately those of the present ecclesiastical province of Dublin (from which, probably, the diocese of Ossory should be excluded).   See map of Ireland in *Cath. Encycl.* VIII.

[100] No. 189 *infra.* I use the term Ulidia to designate the north-eastern province of Ireland, consisting of Antrim and Down and some adjacent districts. *Cf.* p. 322 *infra.*

[101] This is based on the generally received interpretation of the evidence, in which the most important fact is the statement of the author's age found in the poetic epistle to Fidolius, no. 42 x *infra.* Should we reject the Columban authorship of that composition, and fall back on Jonas's Life, we find it stated that Columban was thirty (or twenty) years of age at the time of his migration. (*Cap.* iv. There is MS authority for both readings, the better being for " twenty ": but the terms of Jonas's narrative make it probable that he wrote " thirty.")   He is said to have come to eastern Gaul in the time of King Sigibert, but undoubtedly Jonas, whose notions of Frankish history were of the haziest, thought that this king, who really died in 575, was still living more than fifteen years later.   Jonas states (*cap.* xx) that the expulsion of the saint from Burgundy — which, on the evidence he gives, must be dated in 610 — took place in the twentieth year of his sojourn.   According to his biographer, therefore, Columban was born in 559, 560, or 561, and settled in Gaul in 590 or 591.   See the arts. by Gwynn and Concannon given above.

The first retreat of the pilgrims was at Annegray, in a forest district forming the present department of Haute-Saône. Two other religious colonies were later established in the neighborhood, at Luxeuil, which became the principal monastery, and at Fontaine. Columbanus and his monks soon became objects of interest to the surrounding country, disciples flocked to the new establishments, and all were quickly involved in the ecclesiastical and political life of Merovingian Gaul. The controversies over the celebration of Easter and the monastic discipline, over the morality of bishops and kings, followed, till Theoderich, or Thierry, king of Burgundy, sent his officer to escort the troublesome foreigner to the western coast, there to be placed on board ship for Ireland. The final instructions were not carried out, and Columbanus passed from Nantes to the courts of the two other Frankish kings, Clothaire of Neustria and Theodebert of Austrasia. Next he proceeded up the Rhine to the present Switzerland, whence, after some attempt to teach the gospel to the pagan inhabitants, he crossed the Alps and was received at Milan with warm welcome by Agilulf and Theodelinda, king and queen of the Lombards. By them he was granted the tract of land in a valley of the Apennines, south of Milan towards the Gulf of Genoa, where he established his celebrated monastery of Bobbio and found his final resting place.[102]

The influence of Columbanus on the historical development of western Europe may be summarised under four heads. (1) He gave an extraordinary impetus and a special direction to the growth of monasticism. So many founders of religious houses in seventh-century Gaul drew their inspiration from Luxeuil that the hagiographers came in time to send almost every saintly hero to that centre,[103] just as their Irish brethren made each sixth-century Irish saint a disciple of Finnian of Clonard. The Rule of Columbanus was widely accepted and long retained, even in many monasteries where the Rule of St. Benedict was adopted by its side. Moreover Columbanus, by insisting on the custom of his country which allowed no control by bishops over the administration of the monasteries, began that movement for monastic exemptions which played so large a part in mediaeval Church history. (2) His introduction of the Penitential and of frequent private confession wrought a revolution in the penance-discipline of continental Europe. In his work among the people he seems to have been above all an apostle

---

[102] We have still the texts of two charters (Migne *PL* LXXX 321–3), the first of which purports to be the grant of Bobbio to Columbanus, made by King Agilulf in 598 (!), and the second a grant of the monastery made by Columbanus to the Pope. Neither is regarded as authentic.

[103] *Cf.* Roger *L'Enseignement* 406–8.

of penance. (3) It is probable that he rendered important service for the preservation of classical culture. It is true that direct evidence is slight. Strict religious utilitarianism was the keynote of his work, and the advancement of secular learning in the Vosges or the Apennines does not seem to have entered into his plans. But a certain promotion of letters must have been a by-product from the example and labors of a man of such literary training and tastes as Columbanus. He has the appearance of a product of the Gaul of Sidonius Apollinaris dropped into the Gaul of Gregory of Tours. His foundation of Bobbio became in later centuries a great storehouse of ancient literature. (4) He inaugurated that long struggle between the Celtic and the Roman ecclesiastical system in which the Synod of Whitby and the "Bull" of Adrian IV were but episodes.

42. The Letters of Columbanus

MSS: The following contain one or more letters; the folio reference is given under each separate epistle; the reference symbols within the brackets are those of Gundlach: (B) Berlin Staatsbibl. Diez B Sant. 66 s VIII. — (S1) St. Gall Stiftsbibl. 273 s IX pp. 38–49; (S2) 899 s X pp. 109–11; (M) 1346 s XVII [transcribed by Metzler " ex manuscripto codice monasterii Bobbiensis litteris Hibernicis confecto "]. — (Z) Zürich Stadtbibl. C. 78 (451) s IX/X [cf. E. Bährens Poetae latini minores III (Leipsic 1881) 103 sqq; V (1883) 262]. — (T) Turin Bibl. nazionale G. V. 38 s X in. — (P1) BN lat. 16361 s XII; (P2) lat. 8303 s X. — (M1) Munich Staatsbibl. 6404 s X; (M2) 17208 s XII. — (V) Vienna Nat. Bibl. 806 (Theol. 434) s XII. EDS: Exact references are given under each epistle: (1) Melchior Goldast Paraeneticorum veterum pars I (1604) passim. — (2) Ussher Sylloge (1632). — (3) Fleming Collectanea sacra (Louvain 1667) 108–64. — (4) Bibliotheca maxima veterum patrum (Leyden 1677) XII 24–32. — (5) Andreas Gallandius Bibliotheca veterum patrum XII (Venice 1778) 345–60. — (6) Rossetti Bobbio illustrato (Turin 1795) II 89 sqq. — (7) Migne PL LXXX 259–96. — (8) Bruno Krusch " Chronologisches aus Handschriften " NA X (1885) 83–8. — (9) W. Gundlach MGH Epistolae III (1892) 154–90 [best ed.]. COMM: P. Leyser Historia poetarum et poematum medii aevi (Halle 1721) 176–81. — Ampère Histoire littéraire de la France avant Charlemagne (Paris 1870) II 398–410. — Krusch NA IX (1884) 144–7. — Huemer Wiener Studien VI (1884) 324 sqq [on the poems of Columbanus]. — Manitius " Zu spätern lateinischen Dichtern " Rheinisches Museum XLIV (1889) 552; Geschichte der christlich-lateinischen Poesie bis zur Mitte des 8. Jahrhunderts (Stuttgart 1891) 390–4. — Gundlach " Über die Columban-Briefe " NA XV (1890) 499–526. — O. Seebass " Über die Handschriften der Sermonen und Briefe Columbas von Luxeuil " ibid. XVII (1892) 245–59. — Gundlach " Zu den Colomban-Briefen Eine Entgegnung " ibid. 425–9 [a reply to Seebass]. — B. MacCarthy AU IV (1901) pp. cxxvii–cxxxiii. — Roger L'Enseignement 230–2. — Schanz Geschichte der römischen Litteratur III (2nd ed. 1905) 38.

Gundlach, the latest editor of the Epistles of Columbanus, publishes the texts of eleven letters, one at least of which is probably not authentic.

Of the others, six are in prose, five of them having a close connection with his religious work in Gaul and Italy, and four are poems sent to his personal friends for their pleasure and edification. The letters in prose, though treating of the affairs of a foreign land, have a peculiar interest to Irish historians in being part of the very small legacy of original documents which has escaped the annihilation that waited on almost all the records of the early Church in Ireland. Those dealing with the Easter question are, indeed, our only sources from the Irish Celtic side in that famous controversy. The poetical epistles are valuable chiefly as first-hand evidence regarding the character of the literary training in the schools of sixth-century Ireland.[104] The literary excellence which they display is so remarkable for the time of Columbanus, and their tone in such contrast to that of the somewhat dour churchman felt in most of his purely ecclesiastical writings, that the accuracy of their ascription to the saint has sometimes been questioned.[105]

The prose writings of Columbanus are characterised, as might be expected from their subject-matter, by considerable rhetorical vigor, but not in especial degree by grace of style. The language in the main is the customary ecclesiastical Latin of the early middle ages, but there are some evidences of more classical influences.[106] His compositions in verse, however, display remarkable skill in language, purity of style, and versatility of ideas. Both prose and verse show in marked degree the mediaeval delight in moralising and in gnomic quotations. Gundlach indicates the passages in which he finds quotations or reminiscences of other authors. Some of the parallels seem questionable, but enough remain to give us a respectful appreciation of the extent of Columbanus's studies. As might be expected, he was deeply versed in the Scriptures, especially the Psalms, the didactic books, and the New Testament; he also had some acquaintance with the works of Eusebius, Jerome, the early Christian poets Sedulius, Dracontius and Ausonius, and his own contemporaries Gildas, Fortunatus and Gregory the Great. Among pagan authors Vergil and Horace are his great favorites, but it seems probable that he was directly

---

104 It has been suggested that Columbanus acquired his classical lore on the Continent. This is improbable. If, as is generally accepted, he came to Gaul in 590 or very shortly before, he was then about fifty years old. A man without previous literary training does not at that age learn to compose Adonic or hexameter verse, nor does he acquire an intimate knowledge of Horace and Vergil — especially a man leading the life of a Columbanus in the Gaul of the Merovingians.

105 Cf. Hertel Zs. f. d. hist. Theol. XLV 396 sqq; Seebass Realencykl. f. prot. Theol.³ IV 245; Hauck Kirchengesch. Deutschl.³ I 600. Gundlach (NA XV 514 sqq) defends their authenticity.

106 Also of the influence of the Hisperica Famina: NA XXXV 654 no. 382. Cf. pp. 255-8.

acquainted with the writings of Ovid, Prudentius and Juvenal, perhaps of Statius, Persius, Juvencus, Lucan and others. But it must always be remembered that the knowledge of classical authors displayed by mediaeval writers may have been derived through the works of intermediaries, which either have perished or have not as yet been examined from such a point of view. There is no basis in his writings for the opinion sometimes expressed that Columbanus had a good first-hand knowledge of Greek and Hebrew.

(i) To Pope Gregory the Great A.D. 600

Domino sancto et in Christo Patri, Romanae . . . Gratia tibi et pax a Deo . . . quae illum reprehendit.

MS: M p. 109. EDS: (3) 157; (4) 31; (5) 345; (6) 89; (7) 259; (9) 156. Also Mansi *Sacrorum conciliorum nova et amplissima collectio* X 206–9. *Cf.* Krusch *MGH SS. rer. merov.* IV 5–7.

This letter, a product of the saint's conflict with the bishops of Gaul, is an important document for the Paschal Controversy. It is a vindication, and demand for approbation, of the Irish system of determining Easter. " Know that by our teachers and the old Irish philosophers and computists most skilled in making calculations, Victorius [the author of the Victorian paschal cycle] not alone was not accepted, but was thought worthy of derision or pity rather than of authority." It also asks advice as to the attitude to be observed towards simoniacal and adulterous bishops — the lax married episcopate of Merovingian Gaul; and as to the treatment of monks who, fired with unrestrained zeal, abandoned their monasteries to seek (*more Hibernico?*) the life of hermits in the wilds.[107]

(ii) To a Gallic episcopal synod c A.D. 603

Dominis sanctis et in Christo Patribus . . . Gratias ago Deo meo . . . quique et fratres.

MS: M p. 77. EDS: (3) 113; (4) 24; (5) 347; (6) 99; (7) 264; (9) 160. *Cf. MGH SS. rer. merov.* III 620; Hertel " Anmerkung zur Geschichte Columbas " *ZK* III 145–50; *NA* IX 146, XV 510.

In the year 603 a synod was held at Chalons-sur Saône,[108] at that time capital of Burgundy, and it is probable that it was to the ecclesiastics there assembled that Columbanus addressed this letter. It contains some condescending admonishments to the recipients, a defense of his life and practices, and a plea that he be left undisturbed to follow the custom of his nation in the celebration of Easter. The statement, " I have now been permitted to live among you twelve years," points to 590 or 591 as the date of the saint's arrival in eastern Gaul.

---

[107] About this time Gregory, in a letter to Conon, abbot of the now venerable monastery of Lérins, commends to him "our son Columbus the presbyter," *i.e.*, possibly, Columbanus.—Epist. xi 12: Migne *PL* LXXVII 1126.

[108] *Pseudo-Fredegarius ad ann.* 603, 607. *Cf.* no. 49.

(iii) To the Pope (Sabinian?) *c* A.D. 604

Domino sancto et in Christo apostolico Patri . . . Iam diu omnes . . . edoctos a patribus, iudicantes.

MS: M p. 74. EDS: (3) 110; (4) 24; (5) 349; (6) 111; (7) 269; (9) 164.

The date of this epistle is uncertain, but the probability seems to be that it was written in 604.[109] Columbanus asks the Pope to approve the Irish method of determining Easter, in opposition to the Gauls and their "improbato synodo." The tone, however, is not so self-confident and domineering as that employed in the letter to Gregory.

(iv) To his monks A.D. 610

Dulcissimis suis filiis . . . Pax vobis sicut Dominus . . . ut Deo vivam.

MS: M p. 60. EDS: (3) 131; (4) 26; (5) 349; (6) 114; (7) 270; (9) 165.

On the orders of King Thierry of Burgundy, given ostensibly because of Columbanus's firm adherence to his Celtic rules of discipline, the saint and his Irish and British companions were in the year 610 conveyed to Nantes at the mouth of the Loire, there to be placed on board a ship trading with Ireland. This letter was written when the ship was on the point of sailing. It gives directions as to the government of the community left behind, and the policy to be pursued, and urges the monks to stand fast to their rule, but to conduct themselves with prudence. The document affords us an interesting view of the tenderer side of its author's nature.

(v) To Pope Boniface IV A.D. 612 x 613

Pulcherrimo omnium totius Europae . . . Quis poterit glaber . . . omnibus sanctis hic et in aet. s. s.

MS: M p. 88. EDS: (3) 138; (4) 28; (5) 351; (6) 125; (7) 274; (9) 170. *Cf.* Krusch *MGH SS. rer. merov.* IV 12; M. V. Hay "Columbanus and Rome" *RC* XXXVIII iv (1920-1) 315-8.

When Columbanus arrived at the court of King Agilulf at Milan he found northern Italy in religious anarchy. The king and his Lombards were Arians; the queen and the subject population to some degree in antagonism to the Church at Rome and in the East, as a result of the condemnation of the "Three Chapters"[110] at the Second Council of Constantinople, 553. Columbanus was warned against the Pope as a man of heretical tendencies, including, rather extraordinarily, Nestorianism. The Irish missionary, who may have known and regarded with favor some of the works of Theodore of Mopsuestia, earliest of the writers of the "Three Chapters," but probably had little comprehension of the real character of the controversy, conceived it his duty to write this epistle to Pope Boniface, sharply urging — in the midst of much obsequious language — that he clear himself from suspicion by a declaration of faith before a church synod.

---

109 *Cf.* Krusch *MGH SS. rer. merov.* IV 8; Gundlach *MGH Epistolae* III 164; Martin *St. Colomban* 93n.
110 The "Three Chapters" was a term which came to be applied to certain writings of Theodore of Mopsuestia (d. 428; *cf.* pp. 664-6), Theodoret of Cyrus (d. 457), and Ibas of Edessa (d. 457), having Nestorian tendencies. The Emperor Justinian used his influence to have them condemned at the Second Council of Constantinople, and, by means which bore the appearance of compulsion, obtained the assent cf Pope Vigilius. The Catholics of northern Italy, incensed at what they deemed a surrender to the imperial power, broke off relations with the See of Rome and accused the Popes of heresy.

" For," he justified his boldness, " we are the disciples of Sts. Peter and Paul and of all the disciples who by the Holy Spirit wrote the divine canon — we, all the Irish, dwellers at the ends of the earth, who accept nothing beyond the evangelical and apostolical teaching. No one of us has been a heretic, no one a Jew, no one a schismatic;[111] but the Catholic faith, just as it was first transmitted from you, to wit, the successors of the holy apostles, is maintained unchanged." And, a little later: " For we, as I have said before, are bound to the chair of St. Peter: for, although Rome is great and famous, through that chair only is it great and renowned with us." It is because of the two apostles, Peter and Paul, that " Rome is head of the churches of the world, saving the singular prerogative of the place of resurrection of the Lord."[112] Here we have an echo of the Irish ecclesiastical system with the great importance attached by it to each saint's " place of resurrection."[113]

(vi) To Pope Boniface IV c A.D. 612 x 615

De sollempnitatibus et sabbatis et neomeniis . . . temporis otium exigunt. Ora pro me, venerabilis papa.

MS: P1 p. 288. — Vat. 642 f. 89. EDS: (8); (9) 177; also in Vallarsi *Sancti Hieronymi Epistolae* 1114-20; Migne *PL* XXII 1220. *Cf.* Seebass " Über dem Verfasser eines in Cod. Paris. 16361 aufgefundenen Briefs, über die christlichen Feste " *ZK* XIV (1894) 93-7; Krusch *MGH SS. rer. merov.* IV 201; Martin *St. Colomban* 160.

It is possible that this report regarding the observance of the Church festivals was, as Bruno Krusch at first believed, written by Columbanus at the request of Pope Boniface. The probability, however, is very slight, and Krusch himself has since come to the opposite opinion. If by Columbanus, it seems to show that in his last years he abandoned the Celtic Easter.

(vii) To a young man A.D. 590 x 615

Cum iam de moribus . . . rapiunt regnum caelorum.

MSS: T f. 126; M p. 70. EDS: (3) 77; (4) 19; (5) 342; (6) 69; (7) 256; (9) 190.

A letter written to some unknown young man who served as " ministrum " — probably " secretary " — to Columbanus. It appears probable that this is one of many letters written by him in the years following his removal from Luxeuil to his disciples left behind in that monastery.

(viii) To Hunaldus c A.D. 612 x 615

Casibus innumeris decurrunt tempora vitae. . . . Omne quod est nimium semper vitare memento. 17 ll. The initial letters spell the words " Columbanus Hunaldo."

MSS: S1 p. 38; S2 p. 109; P2 f. 18; M1 f. 50; M2 f. 69; V f. 55. EDS: (1) 47; (2); (3) 167; (4) 33; (5) 357; (7) 285; (9) 182. Also in Sirmond *Opera varia* II 655.

---

[111] Perhaps Columban had in mind the charges of heresy and of Judaising — in the paschal reckoning — that were frequently made against the Irish Church; but it is more probable that the passage is simply a boast of " one hundred per cent." orthodoxy, without any *arrière-pensée*.

[112] R. L. Ramsay, *ZCP* VIII 450, points out that this same passage makes an application of certain quotations from the psalms similar to that found in the commentary attributed to Columban. *Cf.* no. 47.

[113] *Cf.* p. 292 *infra*.

This acrostic in hexameters is an exhortation to despise the pleasures of the world and seek eternal happiness.

(ix) To Sethus *c* A.D. 612 x 615

Suscipe, Sethe, libens et perlege mente serena. . . . Tempora sic habeas optatae longa senectae. 76 ll.

MSS: S1 p. 38; S2 p. 109; P2 f. 18; M1 f. 50; M2 f. 69; V f. 55. EDS: (1) 48; (2); (3) 168; (4) 33; (5) 357; (7) 285; (9) 183. Also in Fabricius *Poetarum eccl. opera* 779; Canisius *Antiquae lectionis* I app. 10; Sirmond *Opera varia* II 655.

Another set of hexameter verses on the vanities of this life and the duty of following Christ. This poem is thickly strewn with reminiscences of the classics; many lines towards the end are taken bodily from the works of the African Christian poet Dracontius, who wrote towards the end of the fifth century.

(x) To Fidolius A.D. 612 x 615

Columbanus Fidolio fratri suo. Accipe queso. . . . Regnat in aevum. (l. 159). . . . Vive, vale laetus tristisque memento senectae. (l. 165).

MSS: B p. 277; S1 p. 45; S2 p. 111; P2 f. 19ᵛ; BM Harley 3091 *s* IX f. 141ʳ⁻ᵛ. EDS: (1) 52; (2); (3) 170; (4) 34; (5) 360; (6) 82; (7) 291; (9) 186.

This, the most famous of the poems of Columbanus and that which gives us the best expression of his literary tastes and skill, consists of 159 Adonic lines and six hexameters. It is addressed to his " brother " Fidolius, who is said to be a frequent correspondent. It consists of a discourse, in a manner quite Horatian, on the evils that flow from gold and the wisdom of discarding cares. Fidolius is instructed as to how similar verse should be composed. The hexameters at the end give the poet's age: " Nunc ad olympiadis ter senae venimus annos." Literally, this would mean that he was from sixty-nine to seventy-two years of age at the time. Mabillon and Krusch,[114] however, believe that Columbanus used " olympias " as the equivalent of " lustrum," and hence that he was from eighty-six to ninety years old. He must have been born not later than 545, perhaps some fifteen years earlier.[115]

(xi) To a young man *c* A.D. 590 x 615

Mundus iste transibit . . . a mundis videbitur. 120 ll.

MSS: Z f. 159. EDS: (1) 146; (2); (3) 180; (4) 36; (5) 356; (6) 145; (7) 283, 293; (9) 188. — Blume *An. hymn.* LI (1908) 352–6.

An exhortation on the familiar theme of the vanities of human life and the call of the life eternal. The rime and rhythm suggest that it was one of those compositions intended for singing to which Jonas alludes.[116] Unlike the preceding poems, which are classical in structure, this is a pure example of Hiberno-Latin versification, based on rhythm, rime and alliteration. The fact suggests a doubt as to Columban author-

---

[114] Mabillon *Annales o. s. Benedicti* I 308; Krusch *MGH SS. rer. merov.* IV 13. But see Martin *St. Colomban* 12n.

[115] *Cf.* p. 187 n. 101 *supra*.

[116] *Vita Columbani* etc. *lib.* I *cap.* iii *ex.*

ship. The immature character of the riming system of the poem argues, however, for an early date, perhaps contemporary with Columbanus.

43. Minor Literary Works attributed to Columbanus

(i) *Celeuma — Carmen navale*

En siluis caesa fluctu meat acta carina. . . . . Uestra, uiri, Christum memorans mens personet heia! 24 ll.

MS: Leyden: Vossianus Graecus Q. 7 *s* X ff. 40ᵛ–41. ED: E. Dümmler *NA* VI (1881) 190–1. *Cf.* W. Gundlach *NA* XV (1890) 514; B. Krusch *MGH SS. rer. merov.* IV (1902) 19; *Zs. f. deutsches Alterthum* N.F. V 144; Bährens *Anal. Catull.* 77; Peiper *Rheinisches Museum* XXXII 523.

This boat-song is now generally assigned to Columbanus. In the manuscript the beginning of the author's name has been cut off and only the letters " banus " remain. The refrain is borrowed from an older Latin boat-song. Krusch suggests that the date is 611, or thereabouts, when Columbanus's mind was fresh from his experiences on the Rhine.

(ii) *Columbani monosticha*

Haec praecepta legat devotus, et impleat actu . . . Diligit hic natum, virga qui corripit illum. 205 ll.

MSS: Basel Universitätsbibl. F III 15 e *s* IX f. 50. — St. Gall Stiftsbibl. 197 *s* X pp. 281–9; 198 *s* X pp. 141–9. — Rome Vat. Palat. lat. 243 *s* X f. 62. — BM Cotton. Cleopatra C. VIII *s* X ex f. 34ᵛ. — BN lat. 8303 *s* X ff. 23–4. — Leyden B. P. L. 190 *s* XI ff. 30ᵛ–34ᵛ. — Munich Staatsbibl. 408 *s* XI f. 83; 8092 *s* XI f. 38ᵛ. — Cambridge Univ. Lib. Gg. V. 35 *s* XI ff. 412ᵛ–5ᵛ. EDS: Migne *PL* LXXX 287–91; Dümmler *MGH Poet. lat. aevi Carol.* I (1881) 164 *sqq*, 275–81. — COMM: E. Baehrens *Poetae latini minores* III (1879) 213, 240. — Peiper *MGH Auct. antiq.* VI pt. II pp. liii, lxxii. — Gundlach *NA* XV (1890) 519–21. — Huemer *Wiener Studien* VI 324. — Manitius *Lat. Lit.* I 183–6. — L. Bellanger in *Rev. de Gascogne* April 1904. — A. Streib in *Münchener Museum* II 343–64.

The authenticity of the manuscript tradition which ascribes this collection of "praecepta vivendi " to Columbanus is doubtful. Dümmler and Streib assign it to Alcuin. The style and subject-matter harmonise with the other remains of Columbanus. The work is a collection of moralising precepts in metre, largely drawn from earlier sources. More than a fourth of the whole is said to be derived from the *Disticha Catonis*, now lost; large contributions are taken from the favorite authorities of Columbanus; a new source is Orientius, a Christian Gallic poet of the fifth century.

(iii) *De saltu lunae*

De lunari motatione . . . amittere videtur.

MSS: St. Gall Stiftsbibl. 250 *s* IX pp. 112–4. — Zürich Kantonsbibl. C 176 *s* XI ff. 174ᵛ–5ᵛ. — Munich Staatsbibl. lat. 14569 *s* XI ff. 26–8. ED: Gabriel Meier *Jahresbericht über die Lehr- und Erziehungs-Anstalt des Benediktiner-Stiftes Maria-Einsiedeln* 1886–7 p. 30. *Cf.* B. Krusch *MGH SS. rer. merov.* IV 20.

This short tract has been traditionally attributed to Columbanus, but Krusch believes that it is not earlier than the end of the eighth or beginning of the ninth century.

(iv) *In mulieres*

Omnis mente pius . . gaudia longa dedit. 4 ll.

ED: Migne *PL* LXXX 294.

This quatrain, which forms a satirical attack on women, has been included among the writings of Columbanus, but is not now regarded as his composition.

44. Sermons of Columbanus

(i) [De Deo Uno et Trino.] Instructionis valde necessariae . . . ad se ducat, donante D.n. J. C., cui cum P. et S. s. est gloria in s. s. (ii) [De mortificatione vitiorum et acquisitione virtutum.] Divinae profunditatis . . . cum Dei gratia praestabit, per D. n. J. C., cui est h. et g. et v. in s. s.   Amen. (iii) [Qualiter monachus Deo placere debet.] Quid in mundo . . . Verax enim est D. n. J. C., cui h. et g. in s. s.   Amen. (iv) [Quod in praesenti vita laborandum, ut in futura quiescamus.] Omnis disciplina . . . in aeterna saecula haereamus saeculorum.   Amen.   (v) [Quod praesens vita non sit dicenda vita, sed via.] O tu, vita, . . . haeredes efficiamur, donante D. n. J. C., cui g. in s. s.   Amen. (vi) [Praesentem vitam similem esse umbrae.] Donante Domino . . . feramus ad Dominum, praestante D. n. J. C., cui gloria in s. s. Amen. (vii) [De coecitate hominis, qui neglecto spiritu inservit corpori.] O te caecam . . . pauperes pro Christo sunt! cui g. in s. s.   Amen. (viii) [Quod ad coelestem patriam, viae praesentis finem, festinandum sit.] Ecce nunc de fine . . . regnantem Dominum n. J. C., cui g. in s. s.   Amen. (ix) [De extremo judicio.] Adhuc de fine . . . dignetur eripere per D. n. J. C., cui g. in s. s.   Amen. (x) [De terribili venturi Judicis ira declinanda.] Multum nobis de fine . . . praestare dignetur, qui cum P. semper et S. s. est unus Deus in s. s.   Amen. (xi) [De dilectione spirituali.] Moyses in lege . . . et caritatis Deus, cui g. in s. s.   Amen. (xii) [De compunctione et vigilantia qua Judicis adventus expectandus est.] Compunctionis necessariae . . . ex parte possit, te donante D. n. J. C., cui g. in s. s.   Amen. (xiii) [De fonte vivo Christo Jesu adeundo et potando.] Quotidianae experientiae . . . vulnerare dignetur, cui cum P. et cum S. s. unitas in s. s.   Amen. (xiv) [Varia spiritualis vitae documenta.] Cum iam de moribus . . . rapiunt regnum coelorum. (xv) [De fervore serviendi Deo.] In Ecclesia Dei . . . judex Christus, qui est super omnia benedictus in s. s.   Amen. (xvi) [De homine misero, quid est, aut quid erit?] Cogita non quid es . . . si nihil accepisses. (xvii) [De octo vitiis principalibus.] Octo sunt vitia . . . Dei timorem vincuntur.

MSS: Zürich Zentralbibl. Rh. hist. 28 *s* IX. — St. Gall Stiftsbibl. 915 *s* X/XI pp. 167–9 [these MSS contain no. v]. — St. Gall Stiftsbibl. 1346 *s* XVII [*cf.* p. 189 *supra*]. — Turin Bibl. nazionale G. V. 38 *s* X *in.* ff. 90ᵛ–128; G. VII. 16 *s* IX² ff. 13ᵛ–62ᵛ [these 2 MSS formerly were at Bobbio]. — Vat. Regin. lat. 140 *s* IX/X ff. 78 *sqq.* — BN lat. 17188. *Cf.* Esposito *Proc. RIA* XXVIII sect. C no. 3 p. 71. EDS: Ussher *Sylloge* iii [v only]. — Fleming *Collectanea sacra* (1667). — *Bibl. max. vet. patrum* (Leyden 1677) XII 8–23. — Gallandius *Bibl. vet. patrum* XII (Venice 1788). — Rossetti *Bobbio illustrato* II. — Migne *PL* LXXX 229–60. — O. Seebass *ZK* XIV (1894) 76–97 [iii, xi, xvi, xvii only]. COMM: A. Hauck *Zs. f. kirchlichen Wissenschaft und kirchliches Leben* (Leipsic 1885) 357–64. — O. Seebass " Über die sogennanten Instructiones Columbani " *ZK* XIII (1892) 513–34 [an important study on the question of authorship]; " Über die Handschriften der Sermonen und Briefe Columbas von Luxeuil " *NA* XVII (1892) 245–59; " Über die beiden Columbá Handschriften der Nationalbibliothek in Turin " *ibid.* XXI (1896) 739–46.

No less than seventeen texts of sermons or homilies exist which have been attributed to Columbanus. It is quite certain, however, that the majority of these do not belong to him. The German church-historian Hauck pointed out that a certain

Faustus who is eulogised in the second of the sermons enumerated above was in all probability the Briton of that name who came to Gaul in the fifth century, becoming abbot of Lérins and bishop of Riez, and that most of the sermons were, doubtless, by one of his disciples. His British relationships might account for the association of compositions from his entourage with those of Columbanus. For Dr. Seebass, with whom Hauck agrees, has shown that four of the homilies in the collection offer good indications of being veritable productions of the Irish saint. These four are found together in a MS from the old library of Fleury-sur-Loire under the title of *Ordo Sancti Columbani, abbatis, de vita et actione monachorum*. They are the sixteenth, third, seventeenth, and eleventh of Migne's edition, and may be discourses addressed by the saint to his monks which he afterwards edited to serve as a " rule of life."

45. Rule of Columbanus

I. The *Regula Monachorum*

Primo omnium docemur . . . dicente Moysi: audi Israel et caetera. [Sect. ix ends: qui me misit, Patris.]

MSS: Turin Bibl. nazionale G. V. 38 *s* X *in.* ff. 80ᵛ-90; G. VII. 16 *s* IX² ff. 2-13ᵛ [these 2 are Bobbio MSS]. — St. Gall Stiftsbibl. 915 *s* X/XI pp. 154-67. — Zürich Zentralbibl. Rh. hist. 28 *s* IX [from Reichenau]. — Munich Staatsbibl. lat. 14949 (Em. w. 6) *s* XV. — Cologne Stadtarchiv 231 *s* XV. — BN lat. 10879 *s* X/XI. — Berlin Staatsbibl. Meermann Collection Phillipps MS 1747 *s* XI [these 2 MSS have extracts only; see *ZK* XV 369]. EDS: Melchior Goldast *Paraeneticorum veterum* pars I (1604) 166-80. — Messingham *Florilegium* (1624) 403-7. — Fleming *Collectanea sacra* (1667). — Holsten *Codex regularum* (Rome 1661, 3rd ed. Augsburg 1759). — *Bibl. max. vet. patrum* (Leyden 1677) XII 3-5. — Andreas Gallandius *Bibl. vet. patrum* XII (Venice 1778). — Migne *PL* LXXX 209-16. — O. Seebass *ZK* XV (1895) 366-86. COMM: G. Hertel " Über des h. Columba Leben und Schriften, besonders über seine Klosterregel " *Zs. f. d. histor. Theologie* (Gotha 1875) 396-454. — Seebass *Über Columba von Luxeuils Klosterregel und Bussbuch* (Dresden 1883) [Dissertation]; *ZK* VIII (1886) 459-65. — W. C. Bishop " A Service Book of the Seventh Century " [Antiphonary of Bangor] *Church Quarterly Rev.* XXXVII (1893-4) 337-63. — A. Malnory *op. cit.* (p. 187 *supra*). — *NA* XVII (1891) 243 *sqq.* — O. Seebass " Über die beiden Columba-Handschriften der Nationalbibliothek in Turin " *ibid.* XXI (1896) 739-46. — *AB* II (1895) pp. xii-xvi. — G. Morin " Explication d'un passage de la règle de s. Colomban relatif à l'office des moines celtiques " *Rev. Bénédictine* (Maredsous 1895) XII 200-2. — L. Gougaud *ibid.* XXV (1908) 183-4. — Krusch *MGH SS. rer. merov.* IV 14-17. — T. Roche *Ir. Theol. Quarterly* XIII (1918) 220-32.

The *Regula monachorum* is divided into ten short chapters: (i) *De oboedientia;* (ii) *De taciturnitate;* (iii) *De cibo et potu;* (iv) *De cupiditate calcanda;* (v) *De vanitate calcanda;* (vi) *De castitate;* (vii) *De cursu* [*psalmorum*]; (viii) *De discretione;* (ix) *De mortificatione;* (x) *De perfectione monachi.* This last chapter is an extract from St. Jerome not found in all the manuscripts of the Rule.[117] No reasonable doubt

[117] *Hieronymi Epistolae* CXXV (Ad Rusticum monachum) no. 15.—Migne *PL* XXII col. 1080-1.

exists that the rest of the document, except in points of detail, is the work of Columbanus.

Although written for the use of continental institutions, we may feel certain that the Rule, like its author, is a true product of the Irish Church. It is the only monastic rule of Irish origin, written in the Latin language, which still survives, and is the earliest and most inform-ing of all the rules which can be regarded as Irish. It must bear the impress both of the powerful personality of Columbanus himself, and of the peculiar circumstances in which he was placed in Gaul,— the tendency from both these influences being towards the rigorous and the puritanical,— but there can be little doubt that fundamentally the Rule implanted at Luxeuil was a reproduction of the famous Rule of Bangor, celebrated in the Antiphonary of that church.[118]

Like other Irish rules, that of Columbanus forms a "Mirror of Perfection" for the guidance of cenobites in the spiritual life rather than a collection of practical regulations for the organisation and admin-istration of the monastic institution, and as a result is disappointing to the student who is interested in these aspects of the Irish Church. But it does throw considerable light on the external life of the monks, while as to the spirit of the Church in which Columbanus was moulded its testimony is clear and decisive. Acceptance with unflinching logic of the precepts of Christ as preserved in the New Testament is its essential characteristic. A severity seemingly greater than human nature could endure results: absolute obedience to the will of the "senior," heavy and unremitting toil, mortification of the flesh to a degree that might be expected to impair the physical strength, are some of its impositions. Regulations regarding the frequent exercises of devotion are specific, though not always entirely intelligible, and have considerable value for the study of the Irish liturgy.

II. The *Regula Coenobialis*

Diuersitas culparum diuersitates penitentiae . . . x diebus peniteat in pane et aqua. [So the first, or shorter recension; the second continues to:] nunquam decidente in aeuum.

MSS: (i) St. Gall Stiftsbibl. 915 s X/XI pp. 170–84. — Munich Staatsbibl. lat. 14949 s XV. — Vienna Nationalbibl. lat. 1550 s XII/XIII ff. 74^v–79^v; lat. 3878 s XV ff. 173–5^v. (ii) Cologne Stadtarchiv 231 s XV. EDS: Fleming *Collectanea sacra* (1667). — *Bibl. max. vet. patrum* (Leyden 1677) XII 6–8. — Andreas Gallandius *Bibl. vet. patrum* XII (Venice 1778). — Holsten *Codex regularum* (Rome 1661; 3rd ed. Augs-

---

118 *Cf.* p. 265.

burg 1759). — Migne *PL* LXXX 216-24 [this and the preceding have 2nd recension]. — O. Seebass *ZK* XVII (1897) 215-34. Comm: As in preceding. Also Seebass " Regelbuch Benedikts von Aniane " *ZK* XV (1895) 244-60; *ibid.* XVI 464-70; " Über die sogen. Regula coenobialis Columbani und die mit dem Pönitential Columbas verbundenen kleineren Zusätze " *ibid.* XVIII (1898) 58-76. — Hauck *Kirchengeschichte Deutschlands* I 257 and n.

The *Regula Coenobialis* is a list, in fifteen sections, of punishments to be undergone by the monks for various sins and offences. In one text of St. Benedict of Aniane it appears as chapter X of the *Regula Monachorum,* and manifestly it is complementary to that treatise. There are two recensions, a shorter and a longer. Seebass and some others believe that only the first nine sections of the short recension formed part of the original *Regula:* the latter part uses technical expressions different from those employed by Columbanus.[119] This opinion is not approved by all scholars, but the tradition of the text lends some weight to it. Donatus, bishop of Besançon in the seventh century, made extensive use of the *Regula Coenobialis* in preparing a rule for religious women,[120] but his excerpts run parallel only to the first nine sections. This work is, obviously, closely related to the Penitentials. It may well be that even in the earliest form to which we can now restore it, it had been modified and interpolated from other Irish documents of that class. In the manuscripts it is sometimes described as *Regula patrum* (or *fratrum*) *Hybernensium.*

Benedict of Aniane (d. 821), of whom mention has just been made, was the compiler of a *Codex regularum,*[121] a collection of monastic rules. The Rule of Columbanus is included, but with considerable modifications, among them the introduction of those technical terms found in the later sections of the *Regula Coenobialis.* There is also an anonymous rule for nuns,[122] which Seebass, in opposition to Krusch, believes to be the final section of the Rule of Columbanus.

46. Penitential of Columbanus

[A] Poenitentia vera est . . . juste vivat. [B] Diversitas culparum . . . salutis compaginem.

MSS: Turin Bibl. nazionale G. V. 38 *s* X *in.* ff. 125-30ᵛ; G. VII. 16 *s* IX² ff. 62ᵛ-70ᵛ. Eds: Fleming *Collectanea sacra* (1667). — *Bibl. max. vet. patrum* (Leyden 1677) XII 21 *sqq.* — Migne *PL* LXXX 223-30. — Wasserschleben *Die Bussordnungen der abendländischen Kirche* (Halle 1851) 353-60, *cf.* 12, 52-7. — Schmitz I (1883) 588-602 [*cf.* Schmitz II (1898) 146-53]. — O. Seebass *ZK* XIV (1894) 430-48. Comm: O. Seebass *Über Columba von Luxeuils Klosterregel und Bussbuch* (Dresden 1883); " Zu Columba von Luxeuils Klosterregel und Bussbuch " *ZK* VIII (1886) 459-65; " Über

---

[119] " Pater " and " senior " disappear; " abbas " and " oeconomus " are introduced; " percussiones " takes the place of " verbera." However, Seebass suggests that this latter part really belongs to the Penitential of Columban. *Cf.* bibliog. *supra,* and *Über Columba von Luxeuils Klosterregel u. Bussbuch* 49.

[120] Published by Holsten *Codex Regularum* (1759) VI 377 *sqq* (*cap.* xxiii-xxxiv).

[121] MSS: Munich Staatsbibl. lat. 12118 *s* IX [so Seebass in *ZK* XL 132; Manitius *Lat. Lit.* I 90 gives the no. 28118; the *Catalog. codicum lat. bibl. reg. Monacensis* lists neither]. — Cologne Stadtarchiv theol. 231 *s* XV. Eds: L. Holsten *op. cit.*

[122] O. Seebass *ZK* XVI (1896) 464-70. Comm: Seebass " Über das Regelbuch Benedikts von Aniane " *ZK* XV (1895) 244-60, XVIII (1898) 59 *sqq;* " Ein Beitrag zur Rekonstruktion des Regel Columbas des Jungeren " *ibid.* XL (1922) 132-7. — Br. Krusch *MGH SS. rer. Merov.* IV 15 *sqq.*

die sogen. Regula coenobialis Columbani und die mit dem Pönitential Columbas verbundenen kleineren Zusätze " *ibid.* XVIII (1898) 58–76; *NA* XVII (1892) 245 *sqq*; " Über die beiden Columba-Handschriften der Nationalbibliothek in Turin " *ibid.* XXI (1896) 739–46. — Hauck *Kirchengeschichte Deutschlands* I (2nd ed. Leipsic 1898) 262 *sqq.* — Schmitz *Archiv für katholisches Kirchenrecht* XLIX 3 *sqq*; LI 3 *sqq*; LIX 209 *sqq*; LXXI 436 *sqq.* — A. Malnory *op. cit.* (p. 187 *supra*) 70 *sqq.* — Geo. Metlake " Saint Columban and the penitential discipline " *The Ecclesiastical Rev.* (Philadelphia) Dec. 1913 pp. 663–73. — O. D. Watkins *A history of penance* II (London 1920) 612–21. — J. T. MacNeill *RC* XXXIX (1922) 277–88. *Cf.* pp. 235 *sqq infra.*

The majority of scholars accept as authentic the main portion of the *Paenitentiale Columbani,* or *Liber S. Columbani abbatis de paenitentiarum mensura taxanda.* Such is the opinion of Seebass and MacNeill, and, less emphatically, of Wasserschleben. The argument of Schmitz in favor of an eighth-century origin was strongly opposed by Seebass. However, the Columban authorship, though probable, is hardly beyond dispute; and, in any case, the work may contain considerable interpolations.

The text falls into two divisions, sections 1–12 and 13–42, originally, it would seem, independent treatises. The second offers the stronger evidence of Columban authorship, but the first, too, may be the saint's composition, or may have been brought by him from Ireland. To the second division Seebass would add the latter part of Columban's *Regula Coenobialis.*

The Penitential, like the Monastic Rule, is a document based on earlier Irish ecclesiastical legislation, but probably stamped with the personality of Columbanus. Many passages, it is clear, correspond with regulations to be found in the Penitential of Vinniaus. The spirit of the treatise is logical and severe — though not more so than that of the Monastic Rule — but it displays considerable intelligence, good judgment and sense of justice and of proportion. Historically, it is a piece of religious legislation of remarkable significance: it marks the introduction of frequent private confession and of the later system of church-penance into the early Gallic Church.

It will be necessary to refer to this document again in the section treating of Penitentials.[123]

47. Commentary on the Psalms attributed to Columbanus

Psalterium romae dudum . . . Primum psalmum quidem in ioas . . . per omnes sonos [   ] laudem domini reson[   ]t.

MSS: Milan Bibl. Ambrosiana C. 301 inf. *s* VIII/IX. — Turin Bibl. Nazionale F. IV 1 fasc. 5–6 *s* VIII/IX [fragment from ps. xiii 12 to xvi 15]. *Cf.* p. 665 *infra.* EDS: Muratori *Antiquitates Italicae* III 857 *sqq.* — Vallarsi *Hieronymi opera* VII. — Migne *PL* XXVI 863–1378. — G. I. Ascoli *Il Codice Irlandese dell' Ambrosiana: Archivio glottologico Italiano* V (Rome 1878) 1–610 [careful reproduction of the text of C. 301 inf.]. Comm: A. Peyron *Ciceronis orationum fragmenta inedita* I (1824) 188–9. — Z² p. xxi. — Nigra *RC* I 60 *sqq.* — Geo. T. Stokes " Columbanus and his Teaching " *The Expositor* X (1889) 136–50. — A. Ceriani *Rendiconti di R. Istituto Lombardo* XXIX (1896) 406–8. — G. Mercati *Riv. Bibl. Ital.* I (May 25, 1896) 95; *Atti di R. Accad. di Scienze di Torino* XXXI (1896) 655–76; *Rendiconti di R. Istituto Lombardo* XXXI (1898) 1046–52; " Varia Sacra " *Studi e Testi* XI (Rome 1903) 91 *sqq* [important, especially the last]. — S. R. Driver *The Academy* L 82 (Aug. 1, 1896). — Jos. Offord, Jr. *ibid.* L 100 (Aug. 8, 1896). — *Thes. Pal.* I pp. xiv-xxi. — Krusch *MGH SS. Rer. Merov.* IV 18–19. — R. L. Ramsay " Theodore of Mopsuestia and St. Columban on the Psalms," " Theodore of Mopsuestia in England and Ireland " *ZCP* VIII (1912) 421–97 [two valuable studies].

Columbanus, who undoubtedly was much interested in the exposition of the Holy Scriptures, is said by Jonas [124] to have composed, while yet a young man in Ireland, a commentary on the Psalms. What were regarded as copies of a commentary by the saint existed at St. Gall and Bobbio in the ninth and tenth centuries, according to the old catalogues of those monastic libraries.[125] But when Fleming, in the seventeenth century, made a search for this work, he could find no traces of it. A century later, however, Muratori found and published what he believed to be the veritable commentary. This is in the ninth-century Bobbio manuscript now known as C. 301 inf. of the Ambrosian Library at Milan. The commentary escaped the notice of earlier investigators because, being preceded by a letter of St. Jerome, it had been catalogued as his work. Succeeding scholars, such as Peyron, Zeuss and Nigra, approved of Muratori's opinion as to the authorship. Krusch took the opposite view, but from evidence which the discoveries of Mercati, of which he seems to have been ignorant, and of Ramsay render inapplicable. Mercati was the first to point out that the work is really derived from the celebrated commentary in Greek by Theodore of Mopsuestia, of " Three Chapters " fame.[126] He believed that, because of its vigorous Latinity, it must date back to the fifth century, and, while admitting the possibility, doubted the probability of Irish authorship. If, however, the commentary is only a summary and adaptation of a fuller translation, as is indicated below, arguments based on literary style have little force. Ramsay favors Columban authorship; but the attribution must still be regarded as questionable. The suggestion would be enticing that Columbanus wrote the commentary after coming into friendly association with the " Three Chapters " heretics in north-

---

[124] *Vita* I *cap.* iii.
[125] G. Becker *Catalogi bibliothecarum antiqui* 48 no. 229, 67 nos. 216–7. *Cf.* pp. 599, 516 *infra.*
[126] *Cf.* p. 192 *supra.*

ern Italy, and left his codex in Bobbio. But the exemplar of C. 301 inf. was, almost beyond doubt, a manuscript written in Ireland itself; and the Latin text of this exemplar had descended through enough copies to become considerably corrupted.

This commentary is derived from that by Theodore, though apparently not directly, but through a fuller version of which the Bobbio manuscripts have preserved some fragments.[127] It is much condensed and abbreviated, but for the most part retains fairly accurately the ideas of the original. The object of most of the modifications and excisions is to tone down and reconcile with orthodox teaching the more heretically-inclined passages of Theodore's work.

Something further should be said here of the MS C. 301 inf. and the O-I glosses which it carries. EDS of glosses: C. Nigra *RC* I (1870) 60–84. — *Z²* pp. xxi *sqq.* — WS *Goidelica* ² (1872) 17 *sqq.* [All these are partial eds.] — Ascoli's ed. as above. — *Thes. Pal.* I (1901) pp. xiv–xxi, 7–483, *Supplement* (1910) 1–34. [These have the glosses complete.] COMM: Ascoli *Note Irlandesi concernenti in especie il Codice Ambrosiano* [extract from *Rendiconti del R. Istituto Lombardo* Jan.-Feb. 1883] (Milan 1883); *R. Istituto Lombardo* 16 June 1887 (Milan 1887) 113–28. — J. Strachan *RC* XVIII (1897) 212–35, XIX (1898) 62–6; *ZCP* I (1897) 7–16, IV (1903) 48–71. — WS *Zs. f. vergl. Sprachforschung* XXXVII (1901) 251–2. — Chr. Sarauw *Irske Studier* (Copenhagen 1900) 138 *sqq* [all these treat of linguistic topics]. — W. M. Lindsay " The Bobbio Scriptorium; its early minuscule abbreviations " *Centralblatt für Bibliothekswesen* XXVI (1909) 392–6; *Early Irish minuscule script* (Oxford 1910).

SCRIPT: Irish minuscule: authorities differ in the dating from the eighth to the first half or middle of the ninth century. Certain archaic abbreviations, unfamiliar and in some cases unintelligible to the scribe, are preserved, which date from, at latest, the seventh century. The scribe was somewhat ignorant and very careless. CONTENTS: (1) Two Irish poems, partly illegible, and obscure in meaning (*Thes. Pal.* II 291–2: text, trans.). (2) Jerome's preface to the Psalter (Vallarsi's ed. X 106). (3) The prologue *David filius Iessae* (*Bedae opera omnia* (Cologne 1612) VIII 308). (4) Jerome's *Prologus ad Sopronium* (cited in part in *Contra Ruffinum* Vallarsi II 525–6). (5) Extracts from the Latin trans. of the commentary of Theodore of Mopsuestia (ff. 4–13). (6) The commentary on the whole psalter, ascribed to Columbanus (ff. 14–146). GLOSSES: These are added to sects. 2, 3 and 6 of the contents as listed above. They form an extensive collection of early language records dating from the end of the eighth or beginning of the ninth century. The majority, and probably all, are copied from an earlier MS. Allusion is made to two Irish authorities, Coirbre and Máil-gaimrid.[128] COLOPHON: " The end. Amen. Diarmait has written it. Pray for that sinner." This may, however, have been the colophon to the exemplar of the commentary here used. COMMENT: It appears probable that this codex was written at Bobbio, but, as regards the text ascribed to Columbanus, from an exemplar of Irish origin, in which the date of

---

127 *Cf.* no. 515.

128 Persons of these names are mentioned in the St. Gall Priscian. *Cf.* p. 675 *infra.* A Máel-gaimrid, abbot of Bangor, died in 839, and a Coirpre, abbot of Trim, in 846.

the Latin text was very early,[129] but the glosses were added about A.D. 800. The MS does not throw light on the question of Columban's authorship, but it does testify to the minute study of the commentary in Ireland.

48. Life of Columbanus by Jonas   c A.D. 639 x 642

[Preface] Dominis eximiis et sacri culminis regimine decoratis religionisque copia fultis Waldeberto et Boboleno patribus Ionas peccator. Memini me ante hoc . . . Deo dicati aeterno. Amen. [Book I] Incipiunt capitula . . . . Incipit liber primus . . . . Rutilantem atque eximio fulgore . . . [In *cap.* ii are the following verses: Columbanus etenim qui et Columba, Ortus Hibernia insula . . . carens bella nationum. 1 + 19 ll.] . . . pollent presole Christo, cui est g. per o. s. s. Amen. Incipiunt versus in eius festivitate ad mensam canendi. Clare sacerdos, clues . . . et omnia futura. 60 ll. Hymnum subdidi, quem eius in transitu praecipiatis canere, quia primus, quem vobis nuper transmisi, eius virtutes non continet. Nostris sollemnis saeculis . . . Et nunc et in perpetuum. 36 ll. [Book II] Incipiunt capitula . . . Incipit liber secundus . . . Cumque ergo venerabilis Columba . . . patratas virtutes non credit.

MSS: Krusch in his eds. lists 130, of which some are incomplete. Even the more important MSS are too numerous to be catalogued here: the student may consult the eds. by Krusch and Lawlor's monograph. EDS: Boninus Mombritius *Sanctuarium sive Vitae Sanctorum* (Milan c 1475) I 207-9 [excerpts]. — *Nova Legenda Anglie* (1st ed. London 1516; ed. C. Horstman, Oxford 1901 I 206-16) [condensed]. — *Opera venerabilis Bedae* III (Basel 1563) 275-305 [*lib.* I, and parts of *lib.* II elsewhere; also the Cologne ed. 1613]. — Surius *De probatis sanctorum historiis* VI (Cologne 1575) 484-505 [*lib.* I]; II (1571) and IV (1573) [parts of *lib.* II; also later eds.; the text was so emended as to be of little value]. — Vincentius Barralis *Chronologia sanctorum et aliorum virorum illustrium ac abbatum sacrae insulae Lerinensis* (Lyons 1613) II 83-110 [*lib.* I], I 97-101 [part of *lib.* II; text of Surius]. — Messingham *Florilegium* (Paris 1624) 219-39 [the Bedan text]. — Fleming *Collectanea sacra* (Louvain 1667) 211-42 [*lib.* I]. — Mabillon *AA. SS. o. s. B.* II (Paris 1669) 5-29 [*lib.* I, and *lib.* II distributed through vol.]. — Rossetti *Bobbio illustrato* (Turin 1795) I 13-51 [*lib.* I], III 5-24 [part of *lib.* II]. — Migne *PL* LXXXVII 1011-84 [reprint of Mabillon]. — Bruno Krusch *MGH SS. rer. merov.* IV (1902) 1-152, VII ii (1920) 822-7 [text critically restored, with valuable *apparatus criticus*]; *SS. rer. Ger. in usum scholarum: Ionae Vitae Sanctorum Columbani, Vedastis, Iohannis* (Hanover and Leipsic 1905) [best ed.: introd. is a scholarly study]. On the poems in the text see Mone *Lateinische Hymnen des Mittelalters* III (1855) 255; Daniel *Thesaurus Hymnologicus* V (1856) 371; *Catalogus Codicum Hagiographicorum Bibliothecae Regiae Bruxellensis* pars I tom. II (1889) 12 [*cf.* Mario Esposito "Hiberno-Latin MSS in the Libraries of Switzerland" *Proc. RIA* XXVIII (1910) Sect. C no. iii 70-1]. TRANS: Dana C. Munro *Translations and Reprints from the original sources of European History published by the Department of History of the University of Pennsylvania* vol. II no. 7 (Philadelphia 1899) [from Migne's text, now superseded by that of Krusch]. COMM: *Histoire littéraire de la France* III 603-8. — Adolf Ebert *Allgemeine Geschichte der Literatur des Mittelalters* I (2nd ed. 1889) 650-1. — Otto Seebass " Jonas von Bobbio " *Realencykl. f. prot. Theologie u. Kirche* IX (Leipsic 1901) 340-1. — Wattenbach *DGQ* I (7th ed. Berlin 1904) 133. — Krusch *Mitth. d. Instituts f. österreich. Geschichtsforsch.* XIV 437 [deals with the language of Jonas]. — The Rev. H. J. Lawlor " The Manuscripts of the Vita S. Columbani " *Trans. RIA* XXXII Sect. C (1902-4) 1-132 [valuable textual criticism, with a fine set of photographic plates of MSS]. — Krusch

---

[129] Nevertheless the text had become corrupted in many places.

" Eine englische Studie über die Handschriften der Vita Columbani " *NA* XXIX 445 *sqq* [further critical study of MSS].

Jonas, author of the *Vita Columbani*, was born in Susa, a town at the foot of the Alps in north-western Italy. In 618, probably within three years of the death of Columbanus, he entered the monastery of Bobbio. There he must have been on intimate terms with many of the saint's companions and disciples. He served as secretary to the second and third abbots, Athala (615–*c* 626) and Bertulf (*c* 626–640), and seems to have been a close personal friend of Bertulf. He also had some opportunities of conversation with Eustasius (d. 629), who had succeeded Columbanus at Luxeuil, and with St. Gall. Jonas spent his later life in missionary work among the Franks in northern Gaul, where he died in 659, after having been raised to the dignity of abbot.

On the occasion of a visit which Jonas paid to Bobbio, probably about 639, he undertook, at the command of Bertulf and the request of the monks, to compile a Life of their founder. The work cannot have been completed until two or three years later: it is dedicated to Walde-bert, who followed Eustasius as abbot of Luxeuil, and to Bobolenus, Bertulf's successor at Bobbio. The first book deals with the life of Columbanus; the second with the careers of Athala, Eustasius and Bertulf, and with miracles performed at Evoriacas (now Faremoutiers, a short distance east of Paris), a convent established under the influence of Luxeuil, and at Bobbio. Three poems are introduced into the text, but two at least of these are probably not by Jonas, but by some Irish writer. The Latinity of Jonas is comparatively pure, and he was acquainted with Livy and Vergil: his chief models, however, were Saints' Lives by Sulpicius Severus and other earlier hagiographers.

Jonas was very well qualified for his task: besides what he may have heard from Athala, Eustasius and Gall, he had the testimony, at first or second hand, of many other eye-witnesses of incidents in the life of Columbanus, some of whom he mentions by name. Consequently his composition is one of the best historical sources of its age and kind: and yet those limitations of time and genus result in much that is unsatisfactory. There is an especial dearth of definite information in the early chapters, treating of the saint's life in Ireland and his first years in Gaul; probably few recollections of those periods survived among the contemporaries of Jonas.[130]

---

[130] There is a metrical Life of Columbanus by Flodoard (see no. 39 *supra*) beginning " Diversae Hesperia

In the second book Jonas treats of events within the period of his own maturity. It is the story, in part, of the fortunes, during the generation immediately following the death of their founder, of the Irish religious establishments in eastern France and northern Italy. Particularly noteworthy is the account of the Synod of Mâcon,[131] at which Agrestius, at one time notary to King Thierry of Burgundy and afterwards for a time an inmate of Luxeuil, attacked the Celtic customs of that abbey.[132]

49. Chronicle of Fredegarius

EDS: Gabriel Monod " Études critiques sur les sources de l'histoire Mérovingienne" Part II " Compilation dite de Frédégaire " *Bibl. de l'École pratique des hautes études* fasc. LXIII (Paris 1885). — Bruno Krusch *MGH SS. rer. Merov.* II (1888) 18–168. FRENCH TRANS: Guizot *Collection des mémoires relatifs à l'histoire de France* II (Paris 1823). Relating to this work there is a large and important literature which cannot here be catalogued. *Cf.* Potthast I (1896) 468–9; Molinier *Les Sources de l'histoire de France* I (1901) 63–5; Wattenbach *DGQ* I 114 *sqq*; Max Manitius *Lat. Lit.* I (1911) 223–7. *Cf.* also Godefroi Kurth " La reine Brunehaut " *Rev. des quest. hist.* L (Paris 1891) 5–79; F. Lot " Encore la chronique du Pseudo-Frédégaire " *RH* CXV (1914) 305–37, and works there mentioned.

This famous source for Frankish history is commonly referred to as Pseudo-Fredegarius. The author's name is not known; the appellation " Fredegarius " was first given him in 1579. The work consists of five parts, of which the first three and the fifth are compilations from various earlier writers, and the fourth a chronicle for the period 584–642, prepared in the first half of the seventh century by one or more hands, Burgundian or Austrasian. It has been suggested that the earlier part of the chronicle was written at Luxeuil by Agrestius, the former notary of King Thierry, but this seems improbable. Some account is given of the career of Columbanus in Burgundy and particularly of his relations with the court. The greater part of Jonas's *Vita Columbani cap.* xviii–xx is incorporated into Fredegarius IV *cap.* xxxvi. It gives us an early and independent redaction of a portion of Jonas, valuable for purposes of textual criticism. The chronicle has also some value for the subsequent fortunes of Luxeuil and its offshoots.[133]

patriae radiante nitescunt." It is published in Mabillon *AA. SS. o. s. B.* II 30–40; Migne *PL* CXXXV 869–82. As a source for the career of Columbanus it adds nothing to Jonas.

[131] *Cap.* ix, x.

[132] *Cf.* Warren *Liturgy of the Celtic Church* 96.

[133] Many references to Columbanus and Gall are found in the Life of St. Magnus (Messingham *Florilegium* 296–317; *AA. SS. Boll.* Sept. II 735–59). It is alleged that Magnus was Gall's companion and successor, and that the Life was written by his own disciple Theodore. In reality it seems to be a production of a later age, in its earliest form composed after the translation of the saint's remains in 851. The statements regarding Columbanus and Gall, when not drawn from Jonas, are wholly imaginative. *Cf.* Meyer von Knonau *Realencykl. f. prot. Theologie u. Kirche* XII (1903) 75–6; Wattenbach *DGQ* (6th ed.) I 284, II 66, 492.

50. St. Gall

(i) The Oldest Life c A.D. 771 [134]

[Imperfect] usque dum venies . . . nonaginta et quinque. Incipiunt signa. . . . Audiens autem . . . perspicue videtur.

MS: Fragment in Zürich State Archives C. VI. 1. EDS: Emil Egli *NA* XXI (1896) 361–71. — Bruno Krusch *MGH SS. rer. Merov.* IV (1902) 251–6. *Cf.* J. M. Clark *The Abbey of St. Gall* (Cambridge 1926) 27–8.

Only a small fragment of this Life is now extant, but it would seem to have been the source of all the later biographies of the saint. Clark, differing from Krusch, thinks that the author was an Irishman, but the evidence *pro* or *con* is very slight.

(ii) Life by Wettinus A.D. 816 x 824

[Prologue] Cum mundus per inania vertatur volitando. . . . Sancti acta stilo merear recitare volante. The initial letters form the acrostic " Cozberto patri VVettinus verba salutis."] I Fuit vir nobilitate pollens . . . ero in ore tuo. II Fama nempe . . . adoretur, regnans c. P. et S. s. in s. s. Amen.

MS: St. Gall Stiftsbibl. 553 *s* IX / X pp. 166–227. EDS: Ildephonsus ab Arx *MGH SS.* II (Hanover 1829) 1–21 [21–31 contain *lib.* II of Walahfrid's recension]. — *AA. SS. Boll.* Oct. VII (1869) 856–95 [895–909 continuation as preceding]. — G. Meyer von Knonau *Mittheilungen zur vaterländischen Geschichte* XII (St. Gall 1870) 1–93, 140–7 [also reprinted]. — E. Dümmler *MGH Poetae Lat. Aevi Carol.* II (Berlin 1884) 476–7 [*cf.* 701; metrical introd. only]. — Bruno Krusch *MGH SS. rer. Merov.* IV (1902) 256–80 [excellent ed.]. GERM. TRANS: A. Potthast *Geschichtschreiber der deutschen Vorzeit s.* VIII, vol. I (Berlin 1857) [2nd ed. Leipsic 1888]. — Ernest Götzinger *Das Leben des heiligen Gallus* (St. Gall 1896).

A certain Gozbert was abbot of the monastery of St. Gall from 816 to 837. He was most energetic in improving the status of the institution placed under his charge, and, amongst other things, laid the foundations of the monastic library which became one of the most famous of the early middle ages. No doubt Gozbert, to obtain a Life of the patron saint, written in the literary style approved of the ninth century, applied to Wetti or Wettinus (d. 824), monk and teacher in the monastery of Reichenau in the Lake of Constance, then one of the chief centres of learning in western Europe. The language of the old Life is, however, purer and simpler than that of its improvement by Wettinus. The identity of the author of this second version was determined only in the last century by the elucidation of the acrostic contained in the prologue.

(iii) Life by Walahfrid Strabo c A.D. 833

[Prologue] Nisi me sanctarum . . . conservare dignetur. Amen. O pater, O patris proles, O Spiritus alme. . . . Quod nocet, evellat, quod iuvat, amplificet. 8 ll. I Cum praeclara sanctissimi . . . comprehendenda reservet. II Meritis beatissimi . . . mentem offendant. Oratio Walahfridi. Obsecramus itaque . . . implorare digneris. Amen.

MSS: Very numerous. See Krusch's ed. for a list. EDS: Mombritius *Sanctuarium sive Vitae Sanctorum* (Milan c 1480) I 311–2 [imperfect]. — Surius *De probatis sanc-*

---

[134] Clark says about 745.

torum historiis V (Cologne 1574) 807–39. — Messingham *Florilegium* (Paris 1624) 255–94 [reprint of Surius]. — Melchior H. Goldastus *Alamannicarum rerum scriptores* I ii (Frankfort 1606) 233–76. — Mabillon *AA. SS. o. s. B.* II (Paris 1660) 227–68 [poor text]. — Migne *PL* CXIV 975–1030 [Mabillon's text]. — Robert Thuli *Mittheilungen zur vaterländischen Geschichte* XXIV (St. Gall 1890) 1–75. — Krusch *MGH SS. rer. Merov.* IV (Hanover and Leipsic 1902) 280–337, VII pt. II (1920) 834–5 [excellent critical edition, with valuable preface]. COMM: [On Walahfrid Strabo see no. 358.] Rettberg *Observationes ad vitam sancti Galli spectantes* (Marburg 1842) [Programm]. — Carl J. Greith *Der heilige Gallus, der Apostel Alemanniens und seine Glaubenslehre gegenüber den Deutschkirchlern und ihren Irrthümern* (St. Gall 1845); *Die heiligen Glaubensboten Kolumban und Gall und ihre Stellung in der Urgeschichte St Gallens Zur Widerlegung der Wyler-Chronik und des Nachtrags* (St. Gall 1865); *Geschichte der altirischen Kirche* (Freiburg i. Br. 1867) 244–5. — Sickel " St. Gallen unter den ersten Karolingern " *Mittheilungen zur vaterländischen Geschichte* (St. Gall 1865) 1–21. — J. A. Zimmermann *Die heiligen Kolumban und Gallus nach ihrem Leben und Wirken geschildert* (St. Gall 1866). — G. Meyer von Knonau " Das Leben und die Wunder des h. Gallus " *St. Gallische Geschichtsquellen* I (1870) pp. xiii–xxv; *Mittheilungen zur vaterländischen Geschichte* XIII (1872) 239–43; XVI (1877) 470–1. — G. von Wyss " Der Tuggensee " *Anzeiger für Schweizerische Geschichte* N. F. XX (1889). — Emil Egli *Kirchengeschichte der Schweiz* (Zürich 1893) 56–8. — L. Knappert " La vie de s. Gall et le paganisme germanique " *Rev. de l'hist. des religions* XXIX (1894) 259–95 [cf. *An. Boll.* XIV 339]. — Hauck *Kirchengeschichte Deutschlands* I² (1898) 327–8. — Wattenbach *DGQ* I⁷ 133–4.

It is probable that the inferiority of the edition by Wettinus was soon recognised by Abbot Gozbert, and that he again sought an editor from the school of Reichenau, this time selecting a young man, but one already famous for his learning. Walahfrid Strabo wrote his Life of St. Gall probably in 833 or 834, and dedicated it to Gozbert. The work is a new redaction, the first book from the older *Vita*, the second from a treatise on the miracles of the saint by the younger Gozbert, nephew of the abbot.

(iv) Metrical Life *c* A.D. 850

Promissi memor ecce. . . . Sol qui multifluo distinguit lumine mundum. . . . Et memoris, quas ipse deus custodiat. Amen. 1808 ll.

MS: St. Gall Stiftsbibl. 587 *s* XIV. ED: E. Dümmler *MGH Poet. lat. aevi Carol.* II (Berlin 1884) 428–73. *Cf.* Manitius *NA* XXXII (1907) 674.

This is a version of Walahfrid's Life, in hexameter verse, written by an unknown monk of St. Gall at the request of the younger Gozbert.

(v) Life by Notker Balbulus A.D. 885

MS: St. Gall Stiftsbibl. 395 *s* XV. EDS: Canisius *Lectionis antiquae* V 790–2 [partial]. — Weidmann *Geschichte der Stiftsbibliothek von St. Gallen* (1841) 483–93. — Karl Strecker *MGH Poet. lat. aevi Carolini* IV fasc. ii–iii (1923) 1093–1108. COMM: Wattenbach *DGQ* ⁶ (1893) I 270. — Manitius *Lat. Lit.* I (1911) 366–7. — P. von Winterfeld *NA* XXVII (1902) 744–51, XXVIII (1903) 63–76. — Strecker *ibid.* XXXVIII (1913) 59–93 [important].

Notker Balbulus (*c* 840–912), a monk and teacher at St. Gall,[135] was the author of a metrical Life of the patron, of which only some fragments remain. It took in part the form of a dialogue between Notker and a certain Hartmann, who became abbot.

(vi) Genealogy of St. Gall

Ista sunt ergo. . . . Fuit ergo in Scottia vir venerabilis nomine Unuchun . . . omnia recognoscis.

MS: St. Gall Stiftsbibliothek 553 *s* X *in* p. 163. — Erlangen Universitätsbibl. 237 f. 95 [*cf.* Clark *The Abbey of St Gall* (Cambridge 1926) 22]. EDS: Ildephonsus ab Arx *MGH SS.* II (1829) 34. — Krusch *MGH SS. rer. Merov.* IV (1902) 241.

This document contains genealogies of Gall and Brigit after the usual manner of Irish hagiography. They seem to have been obtained by the monks of St. Gall from certain " venerabiles Scotti."

Of St. Gall little trustworthy information is preserved beyond what Jonas tells us in the *Vita Columbani*, that he was one of Columban's Irish companions who accompanied him throughout his continental career until he set out for Italy; then Gall remained behind in Switzerland, teaching the pagan and semi-pagan peoples and leading the life of a hermit. Jonas talked with him about Columbanus several times, and it would seem that Gall lived into the second quarter of the seventh century. The Lives contain a vast amount of legendary material, some of which may have a basis in fact.[136]

51. Life of St. Deicolus of Lure *c* A.D. 965

(i) Qui sanae mentis [Cum omnium . . .] Cum beati monarches atque auriga . . . ut lampas emicat.
(ii) Qui se mundumque . . . Cum monarches . . . si tantum discipuli.

MSS: Brussels Bibl. roy. 7569. — BM Addit. 21917 *s* X. — BN lat. 16734. EDS: (i) Colgan *AA. SS.* 115–27. — *AA. SS. Boll.* Jan. II 199–210, 3rd ed. 564–74. — *MGH SS* XV pt. II 675–82 [partial]. (ii) Mabillon *AA. SS. o. s. B.* *s* II 102–16, 2nd ed. 95–108. COMM: I. G. Eccardus *Origines . . . familiae Habsburgo-Austriacae* (Leipsic 1721) 159–68. — *Histoire littéraire de la France* VI 410–1. — L. Besson *Mémoire historique sur l'abbaye et la ville de Lure* (Besançon 1846). — Wattenbach *DGQ*[6] I 116 n. 2.

Deicolus, Desle or Diey, was, according to tradition, one of the Irishmen who accompanied Columbanus to Luxeuil. When his master was expelled in 610 Deicolus accompanied him, but soon became too ill to continue the journey. Left behind, he built a hermitage in the valley of the Oignon in Burgundy, which in time became the great abbey of Lure. A monk of Lure wrote his Life more than three hundred years later. It has very little historical value.

---

[135] *Cf.* pp. 596–7.
[136] To Gall have been attributed, erroneously, a letter to a certain Bishop Desiderius (Ussher *Sylloge* no. x), and a sermon (Migne *PL* LXXXVII 13–26).

52. Life of St. Roding by Richard of St. Vannes *s* XI

Beatus Chraudingus Scotorum prosapia exortus . . . sepulcri deponunt locum; ubi praesentibus et futuris . . . . Amen.

EDS: H. Menard *Martyrologium sanctorum ordinis divi Benedicti* (Paris 1629) 910–9. — Mabillon *AA. SS. o. s. B. s* IV pt. ii 531–6. — *AA. SS. Boll.* Sept. V 513–7. COMM: Didiot *Saint Rouin et son pèlerinage* (Verdun 1872). — Hauck *Kirchengeschichte Deutschlands* (Leipsic 1904) I 303.

St. Chrauding, Roding, or Rouin, is said to have been an Irishman, a companion of St. Columbanus and St. Gall, who became abbot of Beaulieu in the Argonne. The earliest Life is by Richard, abbot of St. Vannes in Verdun, who died in 1046.

53. Life of St. Walaricus, or Valery *s* XI

EDS: *AA. SS. Boll.* April. I 14–23. — Mabillon *AA. SS. o. s. B.* II 76 *sqq* (2nd ed. 70), III ii 628 (568), IV i 556–7 (546–7). — Krusch *MGH SS. rer. Merov.* IV (1902) 157–75, VII ii (1920) 827.

St. Valery (d. *c* 622), abbot of Leuconay, or Leucone, in Picardy, is said to have spent some time at Luxeuil. His Life, written in the eleventh century, was based on the work of a certain Abbot Ragimbert in the seventh. It gives us some little additional information regarding Columbanus, but the value of this is problematical.

References to Columbanus, based chiefly if not entirely on Jonas, are to be found also in the Life of St. Salaberga (or Sadalberga) (d. *c* 665) — foundress of the abbey of St. John at Laon — written in the seventh or eighth century,[137] and in the Life of St. Audomar, or Omer (d. *c* 667) — a monk of Luxeuil who became bishop of Thérouanne — written at the end of the eighth or early in the ninth century.[138] Bercharius (d. 685), abbot of Hautvilliers and Montier-en-Der, was another monk of Luxeuil. His Life — as we have it, rewritten by Adso of Montier-en-Der in the tenth century — testifies to the tradition of the Columban influence in Gaul: " And now what place, what city does not rejoice in having for its ruler a bishop or an abbot trained in the discipline of that holy man? For it is certain that by the virtue of his authority, almost the whole of the land of the Franks has been for the first time properly furnished with regular institutions." [139]

------

[137] Best ed. by Krusch *MGH SS. rer. Merov.* V (1910) 40–66, VII pt. II (1920) 844–5. Others in Mabillon *AA. SS. o. s. B.* II (1669) 421–32; *AA. SS. Boll.* Sept. VI (1757) 516–30; Migne *PL* CLVI 1223–38. *Cf. Hist. littéraire de la France* III (1735) 636–7; XI (1739) 136–7; M. Büdinger *Sitzungsber. d. Wiener Akad. d. Wissensch.* XXIII (Vienna 1857) 372–83. It is one of the sources for the statement that many Gallic cloisters in the seventh century used conjointly the rules of Columbanus and Benedict. *Cap.* vii.

[138] Best ed. *MGH loc. cit.* 729 *sqq.* Others in Mabillon *loc. cit.* 559–65; *AA. SS. Boll.* 9 Sept. III 384–403; Ghesquière *AA. SS. Belgii* III (1785) 598 *sqq*; Migne *PL* CXLVII 1179–90. *Cf. Hist. lit. de la France* IV (1738) 48–9; Drival *La vie de s. Omer* (Boulogne 1852).

[139] Quoted in O. D. Watkins *A history of penance* II (1920) 626–7. *Cf.* p. 161 *supra*.

IV. The Paschal Controversy

Bibliography

GENERAL: Moran *Essays* (1864) 80–160 [*cf*. p. 109 *supra*]. — Skene *Celtic Scotland* II (1877; 1887) chap. iv. — Bright *Early Eng. Church History* (1878; 3rd ed. 1897). — Gougaud *Chrétientés celtiques* (1911) 175–211. — Daniel Rock *Did the early Church of Ireland acknowledge the Pope's supremacy?* (London 1844). TIME RECKONING; PASCHAL RECKONING: *Cf*. pp. 99–100 *supra*. Also Varin *Mémoire sur les causes de la dissidence entre l'Église bretonne et l'Église romaine à la célébration de la fête de Pâques* (*Mémoires présentés par divers savants à l'Académie des inscriptions et belles-lettres* I sér. V ii) (1858) [useful]. — *Dict. Christ. Antiq.* I (1875) *s. v.* "Easter." — Bruno Krusch *Studien zur christlichmittelalterlichen Chronologie Der 84-jährige Oster-cyclus und seine Quellen* (Leipsic 1880); " Die Einführung des griechischen Paschal-ritus im Abendlande " *NA* IX (1884) 99–169; *Prooemium* to ed. of Jonas *Vita Co-lumbani, MGH SS. rer. Merov.* IV (1902) 5–6. — Bernard MacCarthy *op. cit.* p. 99 *supra* [the most important treatment in Eng., but MacCarthy's conclusions are not entirely acceptable]. — C. Plummer (ed.) *Ven. Baedae opera historica* II (1896) 348–54: " Excursus on the paschal controversy and tonsure " [good; neglects tech-nicalities]. — Joseph Schmid *Die Osterfestberechnung auf den britischen Inseln* (Ratis-bon 1904); *Die Osterfestberechnung in der abendländischen Kirche bis zum Ende des viii Jahrhunderts* (Freiburg i. Br. 1907). — E. Schwartz *Christliche und jüdische Oster-tafeln* (*Abhandl. d. k. Gesellsch. d. Wissensch. z. Göttingen*, philol.-hist. Kl., N. F. VIII) (1905) [valuable for the general subject]. — Bury *St. Patrick* (1905) 371–4 " Patrick's Paschal Table." — " Comput paschal " *Dict. d'archéol. chrét. et de liturgie*. — H. Koch " Pascha in der ältesten Kirche " *Zs. f. wissenschaftliche Theologie* LV (Leipsic 1914) 289–313. — P. Corssen " Das Osterfest " *Neue Jahrbucher* XX (1917) 170 *sqq*. — R. L. Poole " The earliest use of the Easter cycle of Dionysius " *EHR* XXXIII (Jan., April 1918) 57–62, 210–3. — M. A. Power " Nisan fourteenth and fifteenth in Gospel and Talmud " *Amer. Journ. of Theol.* XXIV (1920) 252–76. — F. E. Bright-man " The Quartodeciman Question "*JTS* XXV no. xcix (April 1924). THE TON-SURE: Du Cange *Glossarium s. v.* "Tonsura." — Clerc " En quoi la tonsure irlandaise différait-elle de la forme générale des tonsures? " *Trav. acad. Reims* XXXI (1861) 191–9. — John Dowden "An examination of original documents on the question of the form of the Celtic tonsure " *Proc. Soc. of Antiquaries of Scotland* 1895–6 pp. 325–37. — " Tonsur " *Realencykl. f. prot. Theol. u. Kirche* 3rd ed. X (1901) 204 *sqq*. — Ph. Gobillot " Sur la tonsure chrétienne " *RHE* XXI (1925) 399–454 [has very little on the Celtic tonsure]. HERETICAL TENDENCIES: The works by HZ listed on p. 157 *supra*. Also F. C. Conybeare " The character of the heresy of the early British Church " *Trans. Soc. Cymmrodorion* 1897–8 pp. 84–117 [argues that the British and Irish Churches did not recognise, or, at any rate, emphasise, the doctrine of the Trinity, especially in the formula of baptism: the evidence offered is inconclusive]. LITURGY, ETC.: See pp. 683 *sqq infra*.

In the first stage of the controversy between Celtic and continental Christianity, a stage that began with the mission of Columbanus in

Gaul and continued into the eighth century, there were many points of friction: tonsure, liturgy, method of administering baptism, method of episcopal ordination, the whole system of church organisation and discipline. But the subject which was made the gauge of battle was the method of determining the date of Easter.

In Christian world-history the two supreme events were the death and the resurrection of the Saviour. The anniversary of the resurrection, the Pasch [140] of the Greek and Latin world, the Easter of later Teutonic-speaking peoples, became the great central festival of the Christian year, from which most of the feasts and seasons of the Church were calculated backward and forward. The determination of the date of the paschal festival was, therefore, a matter of great practical importance to the Church, and want of uniformity might occasion not only much inconvenience but also serious scandal. Yet this determination of the paschal date was not a simple calculation. Such it might have been had the record of Christ's passion been Roman, assigning it to a definite day in the solar year according to the calendar of Julius Caesar. But Jesus lived in the kingdom of the Jews, and died on the Jewish festival of the Passover, or the day immediately following, and the peculiarities of the Jewish calendar made it impossible to equate this with a Julian date. Moreover, for both historical and mystical reasons it was important that the annual commemoration of the passion and the resurrection should be in some degree kept associated with the date of the Passover. The Jewish Passover was celebrated on the fourteenth day [141] of the month Nisan, that is, the day of the full moon of the first lunar month of the spring, in which the first-fruits of corn became available for offering to Jehovah. The Jews employed a lunar calendar, with a mean year of 354 days. This was kept roughly consistent with the true lunar periods by the occasional addition or subtraction of a day, and with the solar seasons by the insertion from time to time of an intercalary month. These adjustments were made arbitrarily by the Sanhedrin, which thereby insured that Nisan would fall when the lambs and the first fruits would be ready for the sacrifice. In time it became the rule that Nisan should be that lunar month of which the full moon fell on or came first after the vernal equinox.

It is probable that the primitive Christians kept the Pasch on the

---

[140] πάσχα, Lat. *pascha*, was taken over from the Aramaic form of the Hebrew *pesach*, " passover." The Irish, hearing the word from Christian Britons, and knowing that Brythonic *p* = Goidelic *k*, rendered it *casc*.

[141] The lunar day began at nightfall. The paschal meal was prepared towards the end of the fourteenth of the moon, and eaten at the beginning of the fifteenth.

14th of Nisan as determined by the Jewish authorities, and regarded it as the anniversary of the crucifixion. But they also observed the first of every seven days, the Jewish week, as a holy day in commemoration of the resurrection. It would seem that gradually a shifting of emphasis took place until in the second century it was generally accepted that the great annual solemnity of the Pasch was the commemoration not of the crucifixion but of the resurrection. Accordingly the majority of Christians celebrated the Pasch not on the 14th of Nisan but on the Sunday which fell on, or first after, that date. The churches of the Roman province of Asia, however, followed the older custom, keeping the Pasch on the 14th of Nisan, whatever the day of the week. The controversy became acute towards the end of the second century, and the observants of the 14th of Nisan, hence called Quartodecimans, were finally excommunicated.

With the world extension of the Christian Church and the overthrow of the Jewish state, Christians began to break away from dependence on the calendar of the Jews. The rules of computation adopted by the various Christian communities were not identical, and divergences resulted. The Council of Arles, in 314, and, seemingly, the Council of Nicaea, in 325, ruled that Easter must be celebrated throughout the world on the same day. Uniformity was to be obtained by the acceptance of the principle that paschal dating should depend, in the ultimate test, on ecclesiastical authority, and by the practical expedient of leaving to the Church of Alexandria, chief centre of science, the duty of determining the date of each coming Easter and communicating it to the rest of the world.

Nevertheless, irregularities continued, and the gradual disintegration of organised society, as Roman imperial power declined, made communication and control difficult. This decentralisation was chiefly responsible for the disagreement between the Irish and British Churches on the one side and the continental on the other. Christianity entered the British Isles in the third and fourth centuries, bringing with it methods of paschal computation then in vogue. In the sixth and seventh centuries, when communication with continental churches became more free after the long interruption of the barbarian invasions, it was found that the insular Christians were employing, and venerating almost as sacred dogma, a system of Easter-reckoning which on the Continent had passed from memory.

The problem presented to the Christian computist may be summarised as follows: (1) To determine the date of the vernal equinox, and from it the first lunar month of spring, for this month was held to be that of which the fourteenth day, the full moon, fell on or after the equinox. But because the Julian year of 365 days with an extra day every four years was slightly longer than the true astronomical year,[142] the actual, as distinguished from the calendar, equinox was slowly moving back towards the beginning of the calendar year. (2) To decide what day of this lunar month should be the beginning of the paschal term, the period of seven days the Sunday falling within which was to be Easter. This allowance of seven days was necessary because, the lunar month not being a multiple of the week, the incidence of the Sundays in any lunar month would vary from year to year. Actually, three different days were adopted in different systems, the 14th, the 15th, and the 16th.[143] (3) To discover, for each particular year, what were the dates, in the Julian solar calendar, of these seven days of the paschal term, and which of them was Sunday. (4) To decide whether any *terminus ad quem* should be fixed in the solar calendar, beyond which Easter should not go. The early Roman church maintained for a time what was known as " the Petrine tradition " — because believed to have been laid down by St. Peter — the rule that Easter must not fall before March 25 nor after April 21. The limit of March 25 was connected with the dating of the equinox, but that of April 21 constituted another distinct restriction on paschal reckoning. When the other rules gave a date later than April 21 they were ignored and the feast celebrated on the preceding Sunday.

For practical purposes the task that ecclesiastical computists set themselves was the construction either of a table of Easter dates for a certain number of future years, or of such a table for a cycle of years that would repeat itself indefinitely. The technique of the paschal cycles is abstruse and their history obscure. The perfect cycle would be the least common multiple of week, lunar month and solar year; at the end of such a period the co-incidence of solar, lunar and week time would be the same as at the beginning, and the yearly dates of a festival such as Easter, having fixed relationships to all three elements, would proceed to repeat themselves. If the Julian estimate of the solar

---

[142] Estimated by astronomers at present as being 365.2422 days.

[143] As has been said, the oldest custom set the paschal term from the fourteenth to the twentieth. Others, perhaps influenced by the texts (*e.g. Exodus* xii 18) which fixed the seven days of unleavened bread from the evening of the fourteenth day to the evening of the twenty-first, set the Easter term as fifteenth to twenty-first. According to another argument, since Christ died on Friday, the fourteenth, and rose on Sunday, the sixteenth, the term should be sixteenth to twenty-second.

year [144] and the modified Metonic of the lunar month [145] be accepted as accurate, the least common multiple of solar year and week is twenty-eight years, of solar year and lunar month nineteen years, and of all three five hundred and thirty-two years, which last period would form a perfect paschal cycle. However, there was no such universally accepted lunar calendar as the Julian for solar time, and the different Easter cycles achieved the obvious synchronism of solar and lunar periods and the approximate agreement of calendar and true lunar time by modifying the lunar calendar. The modification consisted in the location of the *saltus lunae*, the " moon's leap," that is, the occasional dropping of a day from a lunar month, and this distribution of the *saltus lunae* constituted one of the chief technical distinctions between the different cycles.

Eastern paschal tables were generally based on a nineteen-year cycle. Such were the paschal cycle of Anatolius, bishop of Laodicea, who died in A.D. 283; the *Festal Letters* of Athanasius, bishop of Alexandria, belonging to the period 328 to 373;[146] the paschal letters of Cyril, patriarch of Alexandria, for the years 414 to 442, and his paschal table for the period 437 to 531; and the paschal table, continuing the last, which Dionysius, a Scythian monk in Rome, drew up in 525 for 532 to 626.[147] Early computists in the West did not use the Metonic cycle; instead they employed a luni-solar cycle of 84 years. It would seem, however, that the Popes usually accepted the decision of the church of Alexandria, unless it was at variance with the " Petrine tradition." Such variance occurred twice in the pontificate of Leo the Great, in 444 and in 455, and was, each time, the occasion of an epistolary discussion with the Egyptian patriarch. The Pope yielded, but his archdeacon, Hilary, who succeeded him as Pope in 461, commissioned an Aquitanian scholar named Victorius to draw up a new paschal table. This Victorius did in 457, producing a 532-year table, from A.D. 28 to 559, which could be used as a cycle. He indicated the divergences, comparatively

---

[144] 365.25 days.

[145] In 432 B.C. the Athenian astronomer Meton estimated that 235 lunar months equaled 19 solar years. He drew up a calendar in which 125 lunar months were of 30 days each, and 110 were of 29 days. As modified to synchronise with the Julian calendar, the mean lunar year was of 354.25 days, with seven intercalary months inserted in every 19 years, six of 30 days, and one of 29 days. The true lunar month is estimated as 29.530588 days. There is an error of approximately three days in four hundred years in the Julian reckoning (rectified in the Gregorian calendar), and of one day in about three hundred and twenty years in the modified Metonic.

[146] The last letter extant is for 348, but the *Chronicon Athanasianum*, an index to the letters, runs from 328 to 373.

[147] On the Dionysian paschal writings see J. W. Jan *Historia cycli Dionysiani* (Wittenberg 1718); Migne *PL* LXVII 453–520; *AU* IV pp. lv–lvii.

few, of the Alexandrine Easters from his, in order that the Pope might in these cases make the decision. The Victorian system was adopted in the West and maintained in Gaul until the eighth century, and at Rome apparently until some time between 640 and 664,[148] when it was replaced by the Alexandrine as expounded by Dionysius.

The antagonists of the Irish in the paschal controversy were, up till about 664, adherents of the Victorian system,— after that date, of the Alexandrine. The dispute turned on four points: (1) The date of the equinox. The Irish placed it on March 25, as it would seem to have stood in the first year of Caesar's reformed calendar, 46 B.C. But because of the inaccuracy of that calendar [149] it had, in the seventh century, fallen back to about March 19. The continental churches, placing it on March 21, were nearer to being correct. (2) The Irish paschal terms were the fourteenth to twentieth of the lunar month, the Victorian the sixteenth to the twenty-second, the Alexandrine the fifteenth to the twenty-first. Because the Celts celebrated Easter on the fourteenth, if that happened to be Sunday, they were denounced as Quartodecimans, although the distinction between them and the true Quartodecimans is manifest. (3) The Irish cycle was of eighty-four years, but its details are not certain.[150] Paschal tables of continental origin, based on a cycle of eighty-four years, have survived, but they were governed by different paschal terms and seem to have differed slightly in technique. Dr. MacCarthy, basing his work chiefly on the *Munich Computus*, has attempted to reconstruct the Irish cycle.[151] It is commonly assumed that the same cycle was in use in western Christendom in the third and early fourth centuries, but the evidence is not clear. (4) The Irish adhered to the " Petrine tradition " restricting Easter to the period March 25–April 21, but the Roman partisans of the seventh century regarded the " tradition " with as little respect as had the Alexandrines of the fifth.

The history of the Easter controversy may now be briefly sketched. In the sixth century, as we learn from certain fabrications of Celtic and probably of Irish origin, the Churches of Ireland and Britain became aware of the discrepancy between their paschal dating and that accepted elsewhere. About A.D. 600 the controversy was sharply opened by the

---

[148] See R. L. Poole, *op. cit.*; MacCarthy *AU* IV p. cxlv.

[149] P. 214 n. 145 *supra*.

[150] If MacCarthy's theory is correct, this period made an apparently perfect cycle, but there would be a discrepancy of about 30 hours between the true and the cyclic lunar time at the end of the eighty-four years.

[151] *AU* IV pp. lxxvi *sqq*.

mission of Columbanus in Gaul.   In or about 632 many of the southern Irish accepted the Victorian system.   The northern ecclesiastics stood by the old customs, and a certain amount of bitterness must have entered the struggle on Irish soil if, as seems a probable guess, the expulsion of St. Carthach from his monastery of Raithin at Eastertide, 636, was due to his acceptance of the new teaching.[152]   The " Romans " formed a recognised party in the Irish Church for the remainder of the century,[153] and their efforts to win over the northern Irish seem to have had a marked influence on the country's ecclesiastical history.[154]   In England the dispute between Irish and Roman missionaries came to a head at the synod of Whitby in 664: the Irish lost, and subsequently withdrew to Iona and Ireland.   In 685 and 688 Adamnán, the successor of Columba of Iona, visited Northumbria and was induced to adopt the Roman Easter.   His monks in North Britain refused to follow him, but towards the end of the century he crossed to Ireland and persuaded the northern Irish to conform.   In 716 part at least of the monks of Iona were won over by Egbert, an English bishop long resident in Ireland.   A schism which broke out about this time in the Columban community may have originated in disagreement on the paschal question.[155]   Soon after 710 Nectan, king of the Picts, conformed to Roman custom, and in 717 expelled the still recalcitrant Columban clergy from his dominions.[156]   Cornwall abandoned the Celtic Easter about the beginning of this century, but Wales not until its second half.

The chief specific subject of controversy between Celt and continental ecclesiastic, after the paschal dating, was the form of the tonsure. The earliest Christian tonsure, practised probably in the fourth century, consisted in shaving the entire head.[157]   In the sixth century we meet for the first time with the Roman tonsure, which consisted in shaving the top of the head, leaving a circular band of hair in the form of a crown.   In the seventh century this Roman tonsure came into conflict with the Celtic.   The Roman party, who traced their own usage to St. Peter, attributed that of their rivals to his opponent, Simon Magus, and, with that curious absence of historical criticism which characterised the time, the Celts never seem to have thought to question the gratuitous fiction.   What the Celtic tonsure really was we cannot be certain, but the probability seems to lie between two suggestions: either the front of the head, from a line joining the ears, was completely

[152] Cf. p. 451 infra.   [153] Cf. p. 249 infra.   [154] Cf. p. 325.
[155] Skene Celtic Scotland II 175-8, 278-88.   [156] Cf. p. 425.
[157] This may have been the appearance of the head to which the druids' prophecy alluded. Cf. p. 344.

shaved, or it was shaved to form a half crown, thus differing from the full crown of the Roman practice.

54. Paschal Fabrications

(i) ACTS OF THE COUNCIL OF CAESAREA. EDS: Migne *PL* XC 607–10. — Krusch *Der 84-jährige Ostercyclus* (Leipsic 1880) 302–10. COMM: Burn *Facsimiles of the Creeds* (Henry Bradshaw Soc. XXXVI) (London 1909) 3–4, 27–8, 43–4 [*re* MS, Berne Stadtbibliothek 645]. — MacCarthy *AU* IV pp. cxv–cxvii. (ii) TRACTATE OF ATHANASIUS. ED: Krusch *op. cit.* 328–36. COMM: MacCarthy *op. cit.* pp. cxvii–cxviii. (iii) ANATOLIUS: ON PASCHAL RECKONING. EDS: Bucherius *De doctrina temporum* 439–41. — Gallandius *Bibliotheca veterum patrum* III (Venice 1767). — Migne *PG* X 209–22. — Krusch *op. cit.* 311–27. COMM: Ideler *Handbuch der Chronologie* 229–30, 297–8. — *Dict. Christ. Antiq.* I 593–4. — A. Anscombe " The Paschal Canon attributed to Anatolius " *EHR* X 515–35. — Turner *ibid.* 708. — MacCarthy *op. cit.* pp. cxviii–cxxvii. (iv) EPISTLE OF CYRIL. EDS: Petavius *De doctrina temporum* (Venice 1757) I 114 *sqq*, II 503 *sqq*. — Krusch *op. cit.* 101–9, 344–9. COMM: MacCarthy *op. cit.* pp. cxxxiv *sq*.

In relation to the controversy over paschal reckoning there are extant a series of forgeries, believed by scholars to be of insular, and probably of Irish, origin. (1) The *Acts of the Council of Caesarea*, held at Caesarea in Palestine about A.D. 197 in connecnection with the Quartodeciman controversy. The genuine *acts* were lost. The date, place and motive of the forgery are uncertain. The prevalent opinion is that it was of Celtic origin, and designed to promote a modification of the 84-year cycle to bring it into agreement with the Victorian.[158] (2) The *Tractate of Athanasius of Alexandria on the paschal system*. It professes to be a composition of the famous Alexandrian bishop, expounding the preceding *Acts*. In reality it seems to have been a fabrication of the sixth century,[159] having a similar object in view to that of the *Acts*. (3) The *Book on Paschal Reckoning by Anatolius of Laodicea*, purporting to be the text of the lost paschal cycle that he composed.[160] It was quoted as authoritative by Columbanus, by Cummian, and by Colman and Wilfrid at Whitby.[161] Bede alone seems to have suspected its authenticity.[162] It was forged perhaps with the intention of discrediting the decemnovennal cycle of Easters which it purports to expound, and of supporting the Celtic system in opposition to the Victorian.[163] (4) The *Epistle of Cyril of Alexandria*, based on a scribal error in a copy of the authentic letter which he sent to the Council of Carthage in 419, declaring the date of Easter for 420. The paschal *data* of the forgery agree with those of the Alexandrine Easter of 607, and it was probably composed in 606 in support of the Alexandrine cycle.

---

[158] Bede accepted the *Acts* as genuine. — *De temp. rat.* xlvii. So did Marianus Scottus, who reproduced the text *in toto* in the first book of his chronicle. *Cf. RIA Todd Lect. Ser.* III 8.

[159] MacCarthy, on very slight grounds, suggested the date A.D. 546.

[160] Eusebius *Hist. Eccles.* VII xxxii; Rufinus VII xxviii.

[161] Bede *Hist. Eccles.* III xxv.

[162] *Epistola ad Wicredam: Opera* (ed. Giles) I (1843) 161.

[163] MacCarthy suggested the date 556.

55. Sinlan moccu Min d. 610

MS: Würzburg Universitätsbibl. M. p. th. f. 61 s VIII² f. 29. EDS: Georg Schepss *Die ältesten Evangelienhandschriften der Wurzbürger Universitätsbibliothek* (Würzburg 1887). — WS " Hibernica " *Zs. f. vergleichende Sprachforschung* XXXI 232–55. — MacCarthy *AU* IV pp. cxxxiii *sq* [*cf.* II 104 n.]. — *Thes. Pal.* II (1903) 285. COMM: Sanday " Byzantine influence in Ireland " *Academy*, Sept. 1, 1888, pp. 137–8.

In an eighth-century (Irish?) gospel of St. Matthew at Würzburg [164] is the following note in Latin, written probably in the ninth century: " Mo-Sinu maccu Min, scribe and abbot of Bangor, was the first of the Irish who learned by rote the computus from a certain learned Greek. Afterwards Mo-Cuaroc maccu Neth Semon [*ms: maccumin semon*], whom the Romans [165] styled doctor of the whole world, a pupil of the aforesaid scribe, in the island called Crannach of Downpatrick,[166] set this knowledge down in writing, lest it should slip from memory."

Both these men are known from other sources. Mo-Sinu moccu Min [167] is identified in the *Martyrology of Tallaght* with Sillán, abbot of Bangor. As Sinlan,[168] " famous teacher of the world," he is commemorated in the hymn in memory of the abbots, preserved in the *Antiphonary of Bangor*.[169] His obit is given by the Annals of Ulster in 610. He was probably third abbot of Bangor. Mo-Chuaróc moccu Neth Semon is commemorated in the *Félire* of Oengus on February 9, where a note says that he was known also as Crónan, and as Mo-Chuaróc " the Wise " (*lit.* " of the Wisdom ") and Mo-Chuaróc of the *None*, this last because of a change in the observation of the canonical hours which he introduced. He was patron of Cell-Cuaráin, or Kilcoran, near Youghal, in his native country, for, though a pupil in the North, he was, as his name indicates, of the Semuine [170] of the Dési.

The note, we may believe, records an introduction of the Alexandrine paschal cycle into Ireland. It is probable that Mo-Chuaróc was one of the early champions of the Roman party in the South.

For the letters of Columbanus relating to the paschal controversy in Gaul, see no. 42.

56. Letter from Bishops Laurentius, Mellitus, and Justus, to the bishops and abbots of Ireland A.D. 605 x 617

Bede *Historia Ecclesiastica Gentis Anglorum* II iv [the best ed. is Plummer *Venerabilis Baedae opera historica* (Oxford 1896) I 87–8, II 82–3]. Printed separately in Ussher *Sylloge* no. vii.

---

[164] No. 462 *infra*.

[165] Doubtless the Romanising party in the Irish Easter controversy. The note is obviously copied from an older document.

[166] Cranny Island, in the s. w. arm of Strangford Loch. *Crannach* = " place of trees," " wooded."

[167] The people-name is uncertain. Lugbeus and Lugneus mocu Min are mentioned by Adamnán as disciples of Columba.

[168] Perhaps the correct form of the name was Silnan. *Cf. Thes. Pal.* II 277, 282.

[169] *Cf.* p. 265 *infra*.

[170] The Semonrige or Semmuine, *i.e.*, people of rivets, belonged to the coppermining district of the Dési in what is now Waterford. *Cf.* MacN *Proc. RIA* XXIX (1911) C iv 81.

Albinus, who succeeded Hadrian as abbot of the Monastery of Sts. Peter and Paul at Canterbury in 709 or 710, and died 732 x 734, was the person at whose instigation Bede undertook to write his *Ecclesiastical History*.[171] Through the agency of Nothelm, a priest of London, afterwards archbishop of Canterbury (735–739/740), he sent Bede copies of documents from the records of Canterbury, among which, doubtless, was this epistle. It was written by Laurentius, archbishop of Canterbury, and his suffragans, Mellitus, then bishop of London, and Justus, bishop of Rochester, probably about the year 608. The only certain knowledge, however, which we have regarding the date is that it was within the episcopate of Laurentius, who succeeded Augustine, 604 x 610, and died Feb. 2, 619, and before Mellitus and Justus withdrew to Gaul, about the beginning of 618.

Unfortunately, Bede has not given us the body of the letter, which has peculiar interest as the earliest document in the campaign to bring Irish Christianity into conformity with Roman. The introductory paragraphs which he reproduces do not suggest a conciliatory spirit on either side. The Italian bishops relate how they have learned from Bishop Dagan and Abbot Columbanus, who came into Britain and the Gauls respectively, that the Irish are no better than the Britons in the observation of the customs of the universal Church. Dagan even refused to eat under the same roof with the writers.[172]

Columbanus had been in Gaul, and probably involved in controversies with the Gallic bishops, since before the Italian mission set out for England.[173] The missionaries, in their several journeys back and forth, from Rome to Canterbury, would assuredly hear of him, if they did not meet the saint in person. Dagan was probably the Bishop Degan, or Dagan, of Ath-Dagain,[174] who is said, in the Life of Molua of Clonfert-Molua,[175] to have visited Rome in the time of Gregory the Great.[176] Perhaps too he should be identified with Bishop Dagan of Inber-Daele (now Ennereilly, about four miles north-east of Arklow, co. Wicklow) who died in 639, according to the annals, and is commemorated on September 13 in the martyrologies.[177]

---

[171] Plummer's ed. I 1.

[172] No explanation has been offered for this fanaticism at such an early stage in the controversy. Perhaps Dagan was influenced by the nationalist prejudices of the Britons, whom he may have visited first, but, if so, why did he enter Saxon-land?

[173] *Cf.* pp. 186–205.

[174] Not identified.

[175] *AA. SS. ex Cod. Salm.* 285–6; *cf.* no. 191.

[176] Gregory died in 604, and Molua in 609 (AU). The story, therefore, may be authentic, although Gregory is a stock name for the Pope in Irish legends relating to saints of any date. If Dagan journeyed across Anglo-Saxon Britain to Kent, it is the first recorded instance of an Irish ecclesiastic doing so, and was a result, doubtless, of the conversion in 597 of Ethelbert of Kent, over-king of England south of the Humber.

[177] CS, FM; Fél. Oeng., Mart. Don.

57. Letter from Cummian to Segene, abbot of Iona, and Beccan, a recluse A.D. 632/633 (?)

MS: Taken by Ussher from a MS of the Cotton collection, now lost. EDS: Ussher *Sylloge* no. xi. — Migne *PL* LXXXVII 969 *sqq. Cf.* MacCarthy *AU* IV pp. cxxxv-cxlv; Roger *L'Enseignement* 258.

Segene, fourth successor of Columba, was abbot of Iona 623–652. His correspondent, Cummian, was probably, as MacCarthy suggests, abbot of Durrow, one of the chief foundations of Columba in Ireland. This letter is the only important controversial document written in Ireland regarding the paschal question that we still possess. The text is evidently much corrupted.

The Venerable Bede, in his *Ecclesiastical History of the English People,*[178] says that Pope Honorius I, who ruled from 625 to 638, sent a letter to the Irish in which he exhorted them " not to consider their small number, situated at the ends of the earth, wiser than all the churches of Christ, ancient and modern, throughout the world; and not to celebrate a different Easter, contrary to the paschal calculations, and the synodical decrees of the bishops of the whole world." How much of this is Honorius, how much Bede, we do not know,[179] but it is probable that the epistle from the Pope brought on the crisis in southern Ireland which is described by Cummian.

He says that in the year in which the 532-year cycle began to be adopted by the Irish he kept silent, and made a careful study of the subject.[180] After his year of study he consulted his elders, the successors of Bishop Ailbe,[181] Queran of Clúain,[182] Brendan,[183] Nessan [184] and Lugid,[185] who assembled, either in person or by deputy, in Mag-Léna.[186] This, perhaps, was a council held in the neighborhood of Durrow at the instance of its abbot. The decision was to celebrate Easter the following year with the universal Church; but, Cummian proceeds, " soon after there arose a certain whited wall, pretending to maintain the tradition of the elders, who in place of union caused disunion and in part made void what was promised: him, as I hope, the Lord shall smite

In nomine divino Dei . . . in Christo salutem: Verba excusationis meae . . . sine inquietudine liberare dignetur. Amen, amen.

178 II xix.

179 Part of Cummian's text sounds like an echo of Bede's: " Which are the conventicles of perverse doctrines [who eat not the flesh of the lamb, but of the dragon], the Hebrews, Greeks, Latins and Egyptians, who are united together in the observance of the chief solemnities, or the particle of Britons and Irish, who are almost the ultimate limits of the world? . . . What more derogatory can be thought of Mother Church than to say: Rome is in error, Jerusalem is in error, Alexandria is in error, Antioch is in error: the Irish and Britons alone have true wisdom? "

180 Bede tells us (*Hist. eccles.* III *cap.* iii) that already before the time of Aidan of Lindisfarne (635–51) the southern Irish, in deference to papal admonition, had conformed on the Easter question.

181 Ailbe of Emly: *cf.* no. 122.

182 Ciarán of Clonmacnois. *Cf.* no. 166 and p. 117.

183 Probably Brendan of Birr.

184 Probably Nassán of Mungairit (Mungret, 3 miles s. w. of Limerick).

185 Molua of Clúain-ferta-Molua. *Cf.* no. 191.

186 A plain in Offaley, around Durrow.

in what way it shall please Him." Then,[187] in accordance with the synodal decree that major causes should be referred to the chief of cities,[188] they sent men known to be wise and humble, as children to their mother, some of whom arrived in Rome and returned in the third year.   They reported that at Rome they had been in the same lodging house with a Greek, a Hebrew, a Scythian and an Egyptian, and also in St. Peter's for Easter (when the Irish date differed by a whole month), and these told them that the same date was observed throughout the rest of the world.   Moreover, the trustworthiness of these strangers was proved by the miracles wrought by the relics they brought.

The greater part of the epistle is taken up with arguments in favor of the Victorian paschal system, and with a plea, in part quite harsh in tone, for uniformity with the rest of Christendom.   Most interesting is his enumeration, among the cycles at variance with the Irish, of " that which St. Patrick, our father (*noster papa*), brought and made, in which Easter is observed from the fourteenth to the twenty-first [189] of the moon, and the equinox on March 21."   This is one of the earliest, if not the earliest, allusion to Patrick extant, and is the only definite testimony that he introduced a paschal system differing from that of the later Celtic Church.

During Segene's abbacy the only years in which a month separated the Roman and Irish Easters were — if the usual restoration of the Irish system be correct — 631 and 642, the Victorian and Alexandrine being on March 24, the Irish on April 21. As 642 seems too late, it would appear that the Irish envoys were in Rome in 631. We may, then, advance this tentative chronology: epistle of Pope Honorius written, 628; arrived in Ireland, 628/629; synod of Mag-Léna, 629/630; delegates set out, 630; in Rome, 631; returned 632; letter of Cummian 632/633.

58. Letter from John, the Pope-Elect, and the Clergy of Rome, to the Clergy of northern Ireland Aug. 3 x Dec. 24, A.D. 640

Bede *Hist. Eccles.* II xix [best ed. Plummer *Venerabilis Baedae opera historica* (Oxford 1896) I 122–4, II 112–4].   Separately in Ussher *Sylloge* no. ix.

The same Nothelm who brought Bede information regarding the early history of Canterbury afterwards made a journey to Rome and obtained, by permission of Pope Gregory II, who had been papal librarian, copies of various documents relating to the history of Christianity in the British Isles.   Probably one of these documents was the present letter, of which Bede gives two extracts.

---

[187] It is probable that the council in Mag-Ailbe, of which we are told in the Life of Fintan, or Munnu, of Taghmon (*cf.* pp. 449–50), was held about the same time.   Unless, indeed, it was held after the return of the envoys from Rome, of whom Lasrian of Leighlin, called " apostolic delegate," might have been one. If the two conferences could be regarded as closely associated we might identify Munnu himself as the " whited wall."

[188] The reference is probably to the canon (xx. 5. b) of the *Hibernensis* collection, ascribed there to Patrick and in *Liber Angueli* (*cf.* p. 337) to Patrick, Auxilius, Iserninus and Benignus: " If any disputes shall arise in this island, let them be referred to the apostolic see."

[189] These are the paschal limits of the spurious *Acts of Caesarea* (no. 54 (i) *supra*).   It is quite possible, however, that we have to do with a scribal error in copying the numerals.

This letter was signed by the Pope-Elect, afterwards John IV, and by the archpriest, the chief notary, and the counsellor of the Roman See.[190] It must have been written between August 2, 640, date of the burial of Pope Severinus, and December 25, when John IV was consecrated, and was in reply to a communication from certain Irish prelates which arrived at Rome during the pontificate of Severinus,[191] probably shortly before his death. We may infer that a synod of the Irish clergy who still adhered to the Celtic Easter had been held in 639 or early in 640, at which it was decided to consult once more the Papal See. The ecclesiastics to whom the document is addressed were, doubtless, those by whom the original missive from Ireland was signed. They were the abbots of the great monasteries of Armagh, Clonard, Clonmacnois, Moville and Iona, and some others, more difficult of identification.[192]

The text as given by Bede runs in part as follows: " The letters which envoys brought to Pope Severinus of holy memory, and the questions which they contained, were, at his death, left without an answer. In order that a matter of such importance should not be left longer in obscurity, we opened them and found that some of your province, in opposition to the orthodox faith, are striving to revive a new heresy out of an old. In the darkness of ignorance they reject our Easter, on which Christ was sacrificed, and contend that it should be celebrated on the fourteenth moon with the Jews." Bede omits what follows regarding the manner of keeping Easter, and resumes his report thus: " This also we have learned, that the poison of the Pelagian heresy again springs up among you. We exhort you that such venomous and superstitious wickedness be put away utterly from your minds," etc.

It is remarkable that neither here, nor in the letter of Laurentius, Mellitus and Justus, nor in that of Pope Honorius, does Bede quote the

---

[190] The archpriest, the archdeacon (in this case perhaps John himself) and the chief notary administered the papal see during an interregnum.

[191] Severinus was elected in 638, but the Emperor's confirmation was not obtained until 640. He was consecrated May 28 of that year.

[192] " Tomiano, Columbano, Cromano, Dinnao, et Baithano episcopis; Cromano, Erniano, Laistrano, Scellano, et Segeno presbyteris; Sarano ceterisque doctoribus seu abbatibus Scottis." " Tomiano " — Tommene, bishop and abbot of Armagh, 623–661 (AU). The position of this name indicates that some kind of primacy was accorded to Armagh. " Columbano " — probably Colman moccu Telduib, bishop and abbot of Clonard, who died in 654. We may infer from the story of Mo-Chutu of Raithin (no. 235) that he was a leader of the Celtic party. " Cromano " — perhaps Bishop Cronan of Nen-druim, now Inishmahee, in Strangford Loch, who died in 643. " Dinnao " — perhaps Dimma *dubh* of Connor, whose obit is under 659. " Baithano " — Baetan moccu Cormaicc, abbot of Clonmacnois, died 664. " Cromano " — may be Cronan of Moville, co. Down, who died in 650. " Erniano " — possibly the " Ernanus presbyter " of the third order of Irish saints (*cf*. no. 271), who may have been Ernan of Tory Island (*cf*. Reeves *Ad*. 238, 279). " Laistrano " — Colgan suggested Laissen mac Nesca, of Árd-mic-Nesca (Holywood on Belfast Loch); — perhaps Mac Laisre, abbot of Bangor, who died in 646, although it is possible that Bangor had already conformed (*cf*. no. 55). " Scellano " — doubtfully equated with Bishop Sillan of Devenish, whose obit is given by CS in 655; in 640 he might not yet have attained episcopal rank. " Segeno " — Segene, abbot of Iona, died 652. " Sarano " — Sárán úa Critáin, patron of Tech-Sáráin, or Tisaran, near Banagher, died 662.

essential part of the text, that in which the paschal rules were laid down. This gives reason to suspect that the paschal system they expounded was not the Alexandrine but the Victorian. The perplexity that would thereby be caused to Bede, to whom the infallibility of the Alexandrine rules was an article of faith,[193] can be well imagined.

For the paschal controversy in England, see the next section; and for the activity of Adamnán in northern Ireland, see no. 81.

59. The Munich *Computus*

MS: Munich Staatsbibl. lat. 14,456 (Em. E. 72) s IX ff. 8-46. *Cf.* MacCarthy *AU* IV pp. lxvii–lxxxi, clxxviii–clxxx.

A Munich manuscript, formerly belonging to the monastery of St. Emmeram in Ratisbon, contains a *computus*, of Irish origin, having considerable interest. It was probably brought to Ratisbon by some Irish " pilgrim," and there copied into the present codex. The date of composition was 718: some Victorian paschal computations of 689 are incorporated. The date is not without suggestiveness. It was in 716, according to the Annals of Ulster, that the paschal system was changed in Iona. The chief object of the work seems to have been to explain the Alexandrine nineteen-year cycle, but many subjects connected with time-reckoning are touched. Among these is the old paschal cycle of eighty-four years. For this it is our most important source, and the principal basis for MacCarthy's reconstruction. Among works cited or used were the spurious compositions, *Acts of Caesarea*, Anatolius, and *Epistle of Cyril*, and the *De mirabilibus sacrae scripturae* of the Irish Augustine.[194]

60. Acts of a Council at Rome A.D. 721

EDS: *Conciliorum omnium generalium et provincialium collectio regia* XVII (Paris 1644) 299–305. — Labbe *Sacrosancta concilia* (Paris 1672) VI 1458. — Mansi *Sacrorum conciliorum nova et amplissima collectio* XII (Florence 1766) 261–6. — H&S II pt. i 7, 116. *Cf.* Skene *Celtic Scotland* II 232–3.

The signatures to these acts of a council held at Rome by Pope Gregory II include the names of " Sedulius episcopus Britanniae de genere Scottorum " and " Fergustus episcopus Scotiae Pictus." [195] Literally, this means that Sedulius came from Britain, Fergustus [196] from Ireland. It is a fair guess, however, that they were members of the community of St. Columba, and that their presence at Rome was a result of the conformance of a dominant party at Iona to the Roman Easter in 716.

[193] He was deceived, no doubt, by the misrepresentation of Dionysius, to the effect that the decemnovennal cycle had been prescribed by the Council of Nicaea. *Cf.* MacCarthy *op. cit.* pp. lvi–lvii.
[194] *Cf.* nos. 54, 104.
[195] The same names are subscribed to the acts of a synod held by Pope Gregory III in 731. These acts, however, are known to be spurious. *Cf.* Dümmler *MGH Epistolae* III (1892) 704-7, 723-4.
[196] There was a Scottish tradition of a Fergus, or Fergusianus, who, after being for many years a bishop in Ireland, went to Scotland, where he founded churches and converted barbarians. *Cf.* Wynton's *Chronicle* V xiii; Forbes *Kalendars of Scottish saints* 336.

V. The English Mission

Bibliography

The works by Skene, Hodgkin, Oman, Bright, and Hunt noticed on p. 108 *supra*; also *MHB*, H&S, and Roger *L'Enseignement.* — P. F. Moran *Irish saints in Great Britain* (Dublin 1879). — A. C. Fryer *Aidan, the Apostle of England* (London 1902). — A. W. Ward and A. R. Waller (eds.) *Cambridge History of English Literature.*

In 563 St. Columba, or Colum-cille, left Ireland with twelve companions and founded a monastery on the island of Hii, or Iona, off the coast of Argyll. It became one of the most important of Irish churches, and the centre of Irish religious influence in northern Britain. From it Columba and his disciples went out to convert the Picts in what is now known as the Highlands of Scotland, and from it, after Columba's death, went forth the mission which Christianised the English of Northumbria, that is, the present southern Scotland and northern England. Oswald, son of a king of Northumbria, had found refuge among the Irish—probably in their settlements in Argyll, and perhaps at Iona—when his father fell in battle and the throne had been seized by his enemy. In exile Oswald embraced the Christian religion, and when, in 635, he recovered his kingdom, he at once applied to Iona for Christian clergy. Bishop Aidan [197] was sent in response to the request, who founded the monastic church of Lindisfarne,[198] an island off the coast of Northumberland, whence he, and his successors, Finan and Colmán,[199] completed the conversion of the Northumbrians, and even began that of the Mercians, in the centre of England, and of the East Saxons, in Essex. The Irish Church seemed about to extend its influence over the whole English people. But at this point came the clash with the adherents of the Roman mission which Augustine, sent by Pope Gregory, had founded in Kent. The Easter controversy culminated in the Synod of Whitby in 664, where Oswiu, king of Northumbria, abandoned the Irish for the Roman side, and Irish religious predominance in England came to an end. As a body, the Irish missionaries were defeated and expelled, though their influence, exercised through the

---

[197] There is no early Life of Aidan (d. 651); all we know of him is derived from Bede. *Cf.* Hardy *Cat.* I i 246–7.

[198] *Cf.* William Dugdale *Monasticon Anglicanum* (reprint of 1846) I 219–52. — P. Anderson Graham *Lindisfarne or Holy Island* (London 1920).

[199] Of Finan (d. 661), the "Apostle of Mercia," and of Colmán the only important notices are in Bede and in the Breviary of Aberdeen (p. 484 *infra*).

presence of individual priests and teachers in England, and the education of Anglo-Saxon youths in Ireland, continued long after the conference at Whitby and the ostensible triumph of the Roman party.

From the point of view of world history the most momentous achievement of the Irish people was the Christianising of their Pictish and Anglo-Saxon neighbors. For the conversion of the Picts the chief source is Adamnán's *Life of St. Columba*, which will be considered later with other *acta sanctorum*. For the conversion of the English, the writings of Venerable Bede and certain of his compatriots afford the most valuable testimony. These, too, are the important sources for this first great conflict between the two rival ecclesiastical systems of western Europe. For, although on the immediate point of controversy, the Easter question, the Irish at home were already conforming when the struggle was keenest in England, the Roman organisation movement waited four centuries more before crossing the Irish Sea.

61. St. Cuthbert

(i) LIFE BY AN UNKNOWN AUTHOR, A.D. 698 x 705. EDS: *AA. SS. Boll.* Mar. III 117–24. — Jos. Stevenson *Venerabilis Bedae opera historica minora* (Eng. Hist. Soc.: London 1841) 259–84. TRANS: W. Forbes-Leith *The Life of St. Cuthbert, written anonymously about A.D. 700* (Edinburgh 1888). (ii) METRICAL LIFE BY BEDE, c 700 x 705. EDS: Mabillon *AA. SS. o. s. B.* II 915–37. — J. Smith *Bedae opera* (Cambridge 1722) 267–91. — Stevenson *op. cit.* 1–43. — Migne *PL* XCIV 575–96. (iii) PROSE LIFE BY BEDE, c 720. EDS: *AA. SS. Boll.* Mar. III 97–116. — Mabillon *op. cit.* II 877–915. — Colgan *AA. SS.* 659–703. — J. Smith *op. cit.* 227–64. — Stevenson *op. cit.* 45–137. — J. A. Giles *Venerabilis Bedae opera* IV (London 1843) 202–357. (iv) LIBELLUS DE ORTU S. CUTHBERTI DE HISTORIIS HYBERNENSIUM EXCERPTUS ET TRANSLATUS s XII/XIII. ED: Jas. Raine *Miscellanea biographica* (Surtees Soc.: London, etc. 1838). *Cf. AA. SS. Boll.* Mar. III 95–6; Hardy *Cat.* I 310–3. (v) DE S. CUTHBERTO [compilation]. ED: *Nova Legenda Anglie*, ed. C. Horstman (Oxford 1901) I 216–43. — COMM: Chas. Eyre *The history of St. Cuthbert* (London 1849; 3rd ed. 1887). — Reeves *Ad.* 296–7. — Moran *Irish Saints in Great Britain* (Dublin 1879). — Skene *Celtic Scotland* II 205. — Geo. Phillips *Ushaw Magazine* II (June 1892) 176–201 [*cf. An. Boll.* XIII 59–60].

Melrose was one of the monastic churches founded by the monks of Lindisfarne. Its abbot was Eata, an English boy whom Aidan, when he first came to Lindisfarne, had received as a student. In 651, or very soon after, Cuthbert, or Cudberct, entered Melrose. He and Eata were, naturally, followers of the Irish church customs, but after the Synod of Whitby they adhered to the Roman order. Cuthbert was appointed bishop of Lindisfarne in 684, and died in 687. The early Lives have considerable interest because of the pictures they offer of the Irish Church in Northumbria, and of the conditions in the midst of which the Easter controversy raged. The late text, *Libellus de ortu*, tells an elaborate story of the Irish origin of the saint. There is no reason to place any credit in this fiction, but it may preserve the substance of Irish legends of the twelfth century.[200]

62. Aldhelm

(i) WORKS. EDS: J. A. Giles (*Patres Ecclesiae Anglicanae*) (Oxford 1844). — Migne *PL* LXXXIX 63–314 [reprint of last]. — R. Ehwald *MGH Auct. ant.* XV iii (1919). — Ussher *Sylloge* (*Whole Works* IV 448–53) [Letter to Eahfrid]. — Mai *Classici Auctores* V [Letter to Acircius]. — Jaffé *Bibl. Rer. Germ.* III: *Monumenta Moguntina* (Berlin 1866) 24–31 [letter to Gerontius]. (ii) LIFE by Faricius. EDS: Giles and Migne *loc. cit.* — *AA. SS. Boll.* 25 Mai. VI 84–93. (iii) LIFE by William of Malmesbury. EDS: *AA. SS. Boll. ibid.* 79–83. — Mabillon *AA. SS. o. s. B.* IV i 726–33. — Migne *PL* CLXXIX. — N.E.S.A. Hamilton *Willelmi Malmesbiriensis De gestis pontificum Anglorum* (*RS:* London 1870) 332–443. COMM: Thos. Wright *Biographia Britannica literaria* I (1842) 209–22. — Leo Bönhoff *Aldhelm von Malmesbury, ein Beitrag zur Angelsächsischen Kirchengeschichte* (*Inaug. Diss.*) (Dresden 1894). — HZ *Zs. f. deutsches Alterthum* XXXII 202 [as to the date of the letter to Eahfrid]. — L. Traube *Perrona Scottorum* (1900) 477 *sqq* [relations of Aldhelm with Cellanus of Péronne; see also *Hermes* XXIV 648 *re* the letter to Acircius]. — G. F. Browne *Aldhelm* (London 1902). — Manitius *Lat. Lit.* I (1911) 134–41 [see also *Sitzungsberichte d. kaiserl. Akademie d. Wissenschaften in Wien:* phil.-hist. Klasse CXII (1886) 535 *sqq re* Aldhelm's knowledge of earlier writers]. — D. Mazzoni " Aldhelmiana Studio critico letterario su Aldhelmo di Sherborne " *Rivista storica benedittina* 1915 [also separately, Rome 1916].

Aldhelm (*c* 640–709), abbot of Malmesbury and bishop of Sherborne, the first Anglo-Saxon man of letters, represents the combined influence of the Irish and the Roman religious movements operating in England in the seventh century. He received his early education at Malmesbury from the founder of that monastery, an Irishman named Máel-dubh or Máel-dún,[201] but afterwards he studied at Canterbury under the Hellenised African, Abbot Hadrian, who accompanied Archbishop Theodore from Rome to England. The knowledge of the classics displayed in Aldhelm's writings is, therefore, of especial interest, though we cannot determine how much of it came to him through Irish channels.

Four of his compositions have a more direct association with Irish history. (1) For the letter to Cellanus, see no. 306 below. (2) The letter to Acircius,[202] of about 695,

---

[200] The Life by Bede, *cap.* xxiv, contains some important information regarding Aldfrid, prince and afterwards king of Northumbria, who spent some time in study in Ireland and at Iona. *Cf.* Plummer's ed. II 263.

[201] *Cf.* Plummer *Baedae opera historica* II 310–1. Bede uses the form " Maildufus," which is sometimes anglicised Meildulf, as if containing the A.-S. termination -*wulf*. The place name " Maldubia civitas," or " Maildubi byrig," became — apparently as a result of false analogy with " Ealdelmesburg " (Aldhelm's borough), used of the same place — " Mealdelmes burg," " Mealmes byri," and " Malmesbury."

[202] *Epistola ad Acircium, sive Liber de septenario, de metris, aenigmatibus ac pedum regulis.*

treating of metrical composition, was addressed to Aldfrid, king of Northumbria (685–705), who had himself received an Irish education, perhaps both in Ireland and in Iona. (3) The letter to Eahfrid [203] — who had lately returned from Ireland, where he had lived six years — complains of the large numbers who frequent the schools of that island though they could obtain competent masters in England. Grammar, geometry, physics, and the allegorical interpretation of Scripture, are mentioned as subjects of study in the Irish schools. This epistle is written in extraordinarily obscure and involved diction and style, resembling those of the *Hisperica Famina*. If the latter are of Irish origin, this may be a conscious imitation, designed to demonstrate the quality of the author's literary training. (4) The letter to Gerontius, or Geraint, king of Cornwall, written in 705 in support of the Roman Easter and the Roman tonsure, is a document of some value for the study of that controversy.

The earliest Life of Aldhelm was written by Faricius (d. 1117), an Italian, physician to Henry I of England, a monk of Malmesbury, and afterwards abbot of Abingdon. He made use of earlier sources, Anglo-Saxon and Latin. William of Malmesbury also compiled a Life of Aldhelm, based on Faricius and some texts now lost.[204]

63. Letter to Aldhelm A.D. 680 X 705

Domino Sancto, sapientissimo. . . . Dum te praestantem . . . gratia custodire dignetur.

MS: Vienna Nationalbibl. 751 (Theol. 259) *s* IX f. 25. ED: N. Serarius *Epistolae s. Bonifaci* (Mainz 1605) xli; and many later eds. of Boniface's letters, notably, Migne *PL* LXXXIX 96; Dümmler *MGH Epistolae* III (1892) 237. — Ussher *Sylloge*. — J. A. Giles *Aldelmi opera* (Oxford 1844) 98.

This letter, written to Aldhelm by "an Irishman, name unknown," is found in one of the manuscript collections of the letters of St. Boniface. Possibly, but not probably, it is the letter written by an Irish prince named Artuil to which William of Malmesbury refers. Neither is the suggestion that it is by Cellanus, abbot of Péronne,[205] likely to be true. The letter praises Aldhelm's learning, and asks that the writer be taken as a pupil.

64. The Abbots Ceolfrid and Cynefrid

Historia abbatum by an unknown author A.D. 717 X 733

EDS: Jos. Stevenson *Ven. Bedae opera historica minora* (Eng. Hist. Soc.: London 1841). — J. A. Giles *Ven. Bedae opera* VI (London 1843) 416–32. — Chas. Plummer

---

[203] He has been identified with King Aldfrid; with Eadfrid, bishop of Lindisfarne (d. 721); with Bishop Egbert (*cf.* p. 216 *supra*); with Alfrith, an envoy of Wilfrid of York; and with Echfrid, abbot of Glastonbury 719–729.

[204] One of Aldhelm's disciples was Aethilwald, who became king of Mercia, 716–757. He has left a considerable amount of Latin verse which shows the influence of Hiberno-Latin versification. *Cf.* Manitius *Lat. Lit.* I 141-2, W. Meyer *Nachrichten v. d. kgl. Gesellsch. d. Wissensch. z. Göttingen* philol.-hist. Kl. 1916 pp. 628-44. Ed. by R. Ehwald *MGH Auct. ant.* XV iii 519-37.

[205] *Cf.* no. 306.

Ven. Baedae opera historica (Oxford 1896) I pp. cxl *sq*, 388–404, II 371–7. TRANS: D. S. Boutflower *Life of the Abbot Ceolfrid* (Sunderland 1912).

Some unknown monk of Wearmouth and Jarrow wrote a Life of Ceolfrid, abbot of those monasteries from 688/689 to 716, which was used by Bede in his History of the Abbots of the same houses. The opening paragraphs tell how Ceolfrid's brother Cynefrid, abbot of Gilling, resigned his office shortly before 660 and retired to Ireland to devote himself to prayer and the study of the Scriptures. There he died soon after of the plague, along with other Englishmen of noble rank who had preceded him to Ireland with the same object of studying the Scriptures.[206]

65. Theodore of Tarsus — Penitential

EDS: Wasserschleben *Die Bussordnungen der abendländischen Kirche* (Halle 1851) 182–219. — H&S III 173–213 [from the oldest and best MS]. — Schmitz I (1883) 524–59; II (1898) 543–89. — Finsterwalder [see Addenda] 239–334. COMM: Watkins *History of Penance* (London 1920) II 649–53. — J. T. MacNeill *RC* XXXIX iii–iv (1922) 293–6. — Oakley *English Penitential Discipline and Anglo-Saxon Law* (New York 1923) 105 *sqq* and *passim*. See bibliog. of sect. vi *infra*.

In the year of the synod of Whitby, 664, the see of Canterbury, founded by the Roman missionary Augustine, became vacant. The king of Northumbria, now joined to the Roman party, and the king of Kent sent a priest named Wighard to Rome to be consecrated bishop. Wighard died before this could be done, and Pope Vitalian chose Theodore (*c* 602–690), a Greek monk of Tarsus in Cilicia, then residing in Rome, for the office. Theodore arrived in England in 669 and spent the remainder of his life in performing the duties of primate, especially in eradicating traces of the Irish system and in organising the English Church on the Roman model.

The so-called *Penitential of Theodore* is generally regarded as authentic. It professes to be a document addressed to all English Catholics by an anonymous *discipulus Umbrensium*, perhaps a cleric from some other part of England who was sojourning in some Northumbrian monastery, and to be made up, for the most part, of the decisions which Theodore gave to questions propounded by a priest named Eoda, " of blessed memory." Eoda, it would seem, based his interrogations on a certain *Scottorum libellus*, " little book of the Irish," doubtless a penitential handbook which had been used by the Irish missionaries in Northumbria,[207] and Theodore sometimes increased, sometimes lessened, the penances therein prescribed.

---

[206] Strictly interpreted, the narrative points to 661 as about the date of his death. A freer interpretation is, however, quite possible, and it is natural to conclude that the occasion was the great pestilence of 664.

[207] Through this handbook, no doubt, came Theodore's borrowings from the Welsh and Irish canons and from the penitentials of David, Gildas and Vinnian. It certainly contained part, if not the whole, of the *Canones Hibernenses* (no. 78). *Cf.* MacNeill, *loc. cit.*

This whole story, and, indeed, the use of a penitential, a custom, it appears, of Celtic origin,[208] indicates the persistence of Irish influences, even while the text itself is devoted to their denunciation. In the chapter treating of heretics,[209] the only heresies specifically mentioned are, holding wrong belief regarding the Trinity, and keeping the Pasch with the Jews on the fourteenth moon.[210] In a special chapter [211] it is provided that " they who have been ordained by Irish or British bishops, who in regard to Easter or the tonsure are not Catholics, are not united to the Church, but shall be again confirmed with the imposition of hands by a Catholic bishop "; churches consecrated by them shall be exorcized and re-consecrated; neither confirmation nor communion shall be given to them unless they conform; and all of those races, and any others who have doubts regarding their own baptism, shall be re-baptized.

The later English penitentials, such as those assigned, rightly or wrongly, to Bede and to Egbert, bishop of York, are witnesses to the persistence of this Irish penitential impulse.[212]

66. Wilfrid of York — Life by Eddius A.D. 711 X 731

EDS: Mabillon *AA. SS. o. s. B. s.* IV i append. 661–722; *cf.* IV ii 550–3. — J. A. Giles *Vitae quorundam Anglo-Saxonum* (Caxton Soc.: London 1854) 198–277. — Jas. Raine *Historians of the church of York* (RS: London 1879) 1–103. — W. Levison *MGH SS. rer. Merov.* VI (1913) 163–263 [with valuable introduction]. COMM: Wright *Biographia Britannica literaria* I (1842) 164–84, 229–30. — B. W. Wells " Eddi's Life of Wilfrid " *EHR* VI (1891) 535–50. — Manitius *Lat. Lit.* II 497–501.

After Bede's *Ecclesiastical History* this is the principal source for the Easter controversy in England. Wilfrid (634–709) was the great protagonist of the Roman party and their spokesman at the synod of Whitby in 664. The author of the Life, Aeddi, or Eddius, also named Stephen, was a chorister of Kent whom Wilfrid called to Northumbria to teach sacred music. He wrote the Life at the request of Bishop Acca of Hexham, some time between 711 and the date of publication of Bede's *History*. His narrative supplements that of Bede, with which it does not always agree. He gives a much briefer report of the decisive disputation at Whitby.[213]

---

[208] See sect. vi *infra.* On the anomaly of Theodore, implacable opponent of the Irish ecclesiastical system, accepting *in toto* the Irish penitential system, see Watkins, *loc. cit.*

[209] I v.

[210] MS " xix," undoubtedly a slip. — This is said to be contrary to the Council of Nicaea, further evidence that the acerbity against the Celts resulted from the falsification of Dionysius. *Cf.* p. 223 *supra.*

[211] II ix.

[212] *Cf.* Oakley *op cit.* 117 *sqq*; J. T. MacNeill *loc. cit.* 296–7.

[213] For other Lives of Wilfrid see Potthast and the Bollandists' *Bibl. hag. lat.*; for his relations with Dagobert II of Austrasia see pp. 496–8 *infra.*

67. The Venerable Bede

EDS: Folio eds. of Bede's works were issued at Basel, 1563, and at Cologne, 1612 and 1688. Ed. in 12 vols., by J. A. Giles, with trans. of historical works, London, 1843–4: reprint in Migne *PL* XC–XCV. Eds. of *Hist. Eccl.*: John Smith (Cambridge 1722) [good]. — Jos. Stevenson (Eng. Hist. Soc.: London 1838). — *MHB* (1848) 103–289. — G. H. Moberly (Oxford 1869; reprint 1881). — J. E. B. Mayor and J. R. Lumby (Cambridge 1878; 3rd ed. 1881) [bks. III–IV of *Hist. Eccl.* only; has trans. of Ebert's account of Bede]. — Alfred Holder (Freiburg i. Br. 1882; 2nd ed. 1890). — Chas. Plummer 2 vols. (Oxford 1896) [best ed.; especially valuable for students of Irish history]. TRANS: Jos. Stevenson *The Church Historians of England* I (London 1853). — Lewis Gidley (London 1870). — [L. C. Jane] in *Temple Classics*. — A. M. Sellar (London 1907; revised ed. 1912). — In *Everyman's Library*. COMM: C. W. Schoell *De ecclesiasticae Britonum Scotorumque historiae fontibus* (Berlin 1851) 20–8. — Adolf Ebert *Geschichte der Literatur des Mittelalters* I (Leipsic 1874) 595–611, 2nd ed. (1889) 634–50. — Karl Werner *Beda der Ehrwürdige und seine Zeit* (Vienna 1875; 2nd ed. 1881). — Plaine *Revue Anglo-Rom.* III (1896) 49–96 [*cf. An. Boll.* XVI 201–2]. — Roger *L'Enseignement* 304–10. — Manitius "Zu Aldhelm und Beda" *Sitzungsber. d. kaiserl. Akad. d. Wissensch. in Wien* phil.-hist. Kl. CXII (1886) 535 *sqq*; *Lat. Lit.* 70–87. — J. Hoops *Reallexikon d. germ. Altertumskunde* I (Strasburg 1911) 189–203. — G. F. Browne *The Venerable Bede* (London 1919). For further bibliog. see Potthast, Chevalier and Gross.

Bede the Venerable was born in 672 or 673, entered the monastery of Jarrow [214] in Northumbria when seven years old, and died there in 735. His life seems to have been devoted entirely to study, teaching and writing. The founder of the monastery, Benedict Biscop, had collected a good library, and Bede's works may be said to sum up all the learning of his time. To us the most important of these is the *Ecclesiastical History of the English Nation*, completed in A.D. 731. It is the one supremely valuable source for the history of England, secular as well as religious, from 597 to the date of its completion. Bede used, with a care and good judgment remarkable for his time, numerous records now entirely lost, and, for much of his subject-matter, had the testimony of eye-witnesses either at first or second hand. The whole he has woven into a clear and comprehensive narrative immeasurably superior to the ordinary annalistic records of the early middle ages.

The importance of his work for the history of Ireland — the Greater Ireland of the seventh century — scarcely needs to be indicated. The subject of his story is the establishment and organisation of Christianity in the English kingdoms, but the plot that lies at its centre is the struggle between the Irish and the Roman forms of church discipline for control

---

[214] *Cf.* R. B. Hepple " The monastery school of Jarrow " *History* VII (1922, July) 92–102.

of the British Isles. He gives a quite extensive report,[215] doubtless in part his own creation, of the arguments used by both sides in the synod of Streanaeshalch, or Whitby, in 664, when King Oswiu of Northumbria declared for the Roman Easter. Bede is plainly a partisan — at times a bitter partisan — of the Roman order, but his sanity and broadness of sympathy are too manifest to make his testimony thereby suspect. Indeed it is probable that in the matter of personalities, apart from principles, Bede's sympathies were with the Irish more than with the Roman clergy. In his monastery of Jarrow he was in the midst of a country whose inhabitants, in the generation just preceding his own, had been turned from heathenism to Christianity by Celtic missionary monks from Ireland and Iona.

The information Bede gives us, directly or indirectly, regarding Ireland and men of Irish birth [216] or training, is not only peculiarly precious but also very considerable in amount. It is evident that intercourse in his day between the two countries was constant. His quotations from episcopal and papal letters to Ireland,[217] his testimony as to the Irish schools,[218] his references to the Anglo-Saxon ecclesiastics in Ireland and their organisation of the mission to Frisia,[219] his account of St. Fursa and the " Vision of Fursa," the earliest example of this type of Christian Irish literature,[220] his story of Adamnán and the description of the Holy Places written by that saint,[221] are some of the passages of especial interest and value.

The other historical writings of Bede are the metrical *Vita Cudbercti*, written before 705, the prose *Vita* [222] of the same saint, about 720, and the *History of the Abbots of Wearmouth and Jarrow*, some time after 716. His chronological treatises, *De Temporibus*,[223] of 703, *De Ratione Bissexti*, before 725, and *De Temporum Ratione*,[223] of

---

[215] *Lib.* III *cap.* xxv.

[216] As Columba, Aidan, Finan, Colmán, Ronan, Fursa, Foillan, Ultán, Gobbán, Dicul, companion of Fursa, Dicul of Bosham, Diuma, Ceollach, Máel-dubh, Adamnán of Hii and Adamnán of Coldingham.

[217] *Cf.* nos. 56, 58. The letter from ⁀eolfrid, abbot of Wearmouth and Jarrow (*cf.* no. 64), to Nechtan, king of the Picts, written about 710 to confirm him in his adhesion to Roman discipline on the questions of Easter and the tonsure, has not been given a separate notice, but is worthy of especial attention from the Irish historical student. It is the fullest controversial statement giving the Roman side in the dispute. Although in Ceolfrid's name, there is little doubt that it was drawn up by Bede himself, to whose chronological studies, *De Temporibus*, and *De Temporum Ratione*, it bears a striking resemblance. It also contains an interesting report of a conversation between Ceolfrid and Adamnán of Hii, on the occasion of one of Adamnán's visits to Northumbria, when Bede himself may have seen the famous Irishman.

[218] *Lib.* III *cap.* xxvii.

[219] Of these were Egbert, Ethelwin, Ethelhun, Wilbrord, Tuda, Ceadda, Wictbert, Hygbald, the two Hewalds, and Haemgils. *Cf.* especially *lib.* V *cap.* ix, x.

[220] *Lib.* III *cap.* xix. *Cf.* no. 296.

[221] *Lib.* V *cap.* xv–xvii. *Cf.* no. 112.

[222] *Cf.* no. 61.

[223] Sometimes designated the *Chronica minora* and *maiora*.

725, have some interest to students of the paschal question, as has also the *Epistola ad Wicredam de aequinoctia vernali*, of uncertain date. Reference is made elsewhere to the *Penitential*,[224] the authenticity of which is doubtful.

Bede composed a martyrology, but as published [225] it represents a text which had received a great augmentation, apparently in France towards the end of the eighth century.[226] It is this version that notices St. Patrick: the original contained no Irish saint.

The greater part of the works of Bede seem to have been known in Ireland soon after they appeared. An Old Irish translation, or rather epitome, of the *Ecclesiastical History* was composed in the ninth century.[227] There is also an Anglo-Saxon version,[228] attributed to King Alfred, which, it may be remarked, omits all notice of the synod of Whitby and in other ways shows special sympathy for the Irish Church.[229]

68. St. Willibrord — Life by Alcuin c A.D. 782 × 797

EDS: Surius *Vitae SS* 7 Nov. VI 127–37. — Canisius *Lectionis antiquae* VI 351–64 [ed. Basnage II i 457–71]. — Mabillon *AA. SS. o. s. B. s.* III i 603–29. — Duchesne *Alcuini opera* III (Paris 1617) 1433–62. — Migne *PL* CI 693–724. — Wattenbach in Jaffé *Bibliotheca rerum Germanicarum* VI (*Monumenta Alcuiniana*) (Berlin 1873) 35–79. — Dümmler *MGH Poet. lat. aevi Carol.* I (Berlin 1881) 207–20 [bk. II only]. — *AA. SS. Boll.* Nov. III (1910) 435–57. — Levison *MGH SS. rer. Merov.* VII (1920).

Among the writings of Alcuin is a prose Life of St. Willibrord, the apostle of the Frisians, which is accompanied by an abridgment thereof in verse, and a homily treating of the same saint. It was written at the request of Beornred, archbishop of Sens, who was also abbot of Echternach.

Willibrord, or Wilbrord (d. 738 or 739), who was given the name Clement at his consecration to the episcopacy by Pope Sergius, was the

---

[224] *Cf.* p. 229.

[225] The best ed. is *AA. SS. Boll.* Mar. II.

[226] *Cf.* H. Quentin *Martyrologes historiques du moyen âge* (Paris 1908) chap. ii; " Bède le Vénérable " *Dict. d'archéol. chrét. et de liturgie* II pt. I (1910) 636–41 [résumé of preceding].

[227] MS: Bodl. Laud 610 ff. 89ᵛ–92ᵛ. EDS: O. J. Bergin in *Anec.* III (Halle 1910) 63–76 [text]. — E. G. Cox in *Studies . . . in celebration of the seventieth birthday of J. M. Hart* (New York 1910) 122–78 [reprint, with introd. and trans.; *cf. RC* XXXII (1911) 222]. *Cf.* KM *ZCP* II (1899) 321–2 [with text of introduction].

[228] EDS: T. Miller *The Old English version of Bede's Ecclesiastical History*, 2 pts. (Early English Text Soc.: London 1890, 1898) [with trans.]. — J. Schipper in C. W. M. Grein's *Bibliothek der Angelsächsischen Prosa* IV (Leipsic 1899).

[229] Bede mentions (*Hist. Eccl.* IV xxiii) a certain Begu as a nun in the monastery of Hackness, which was under the rule of Hilda, abbess of Streanaeshalch (at or near Whitby, where the synod of 664 was held). At Hilda's death, in 680, Begu had been thirty years in religion. In a twelfth-century *Vita Begae* she is identified (probably solely because of the similarity of name) with a Bega, daughter of an Irish king, who fled to England. The Life is largely, or wholly, fictitious. EDS: *AA. SS. Boll.* Sept. II 694–700 [the "lections" from the *Breviary of Aberdeen*]. — G. C. Tomlinson *The Life and Miracles of Saint Bega* (Carlisle 1842) [text, trans.]

most noteworthy of that group of English ecclesiastics who, while residing in Ireland, received the impulse to undertake missionary labors among the heathen of the European continent. It was by direction of Egbert,[230] an Englishman who would seem to have held an eminent position in the religious life of Ireland at the end of the seventh and beginning of the eighth century, that he and his companions [231] set out, in 690, for Frisia, which was to be the scene of their missionary labors. There Willibrord became founder of the monastery of Epternach or Echternach and bishop of Utrecht.

The earliest references to Willibrord are in Bede's *Ecclesiastical History*, bk. V, chaps. x, xi,[232] written while Willibrord was still living. Soon after his death a Life was written by an Irish monk, but this is not extant.[233] It was probably used by Alcuin in the present work. Alcuin testifies as to the condition of learning in Ireland at this time. Willibrord went there "because he heard that scholarship flourished in Ireland." [234] He was then twenty years of age, having been an inmate of the monastery of Ripon from childhood. He spent twelve years in Ireland before undertaking the mission to the Continent. In Frisia he had the support of the Pope, of Pipin, duke of the Franks, and, in his later years, of St. Boniface. An Irish *evangeliarium* said to have belonged to him is now at Paris.[235]

69. The Calendar and Martyrology of Willibrord s VIII in

MS: BN lat. 10837. EDS: *Calendar:* H. A. Wilson *The Calendar of St. Willibrord* (The Henry Bradshaw Soc.: London 1918) [with facs., including one page of martyrology]. *Martyrology:* G. B. de Rossi and L. Duchesne " Martyrologium Hieronymianum " *AA. SS. Boll.* Nov. II — *New Palaeographical Society Facsimiles* pl. 183.

This volume, which was found at Trèves by Rosweyde, the projector of the Bollandists' undertaking, is made up as follows: (1) ff. 1 and 45, fly-leaves from much later books; (2) ff. 2–33, containing the martyrology; (3) ff. 34–41, the calendar, the paschal cycle A.D. 703–721, and, in another hand, the paschal cycles 722–740, 741–759; (4) ff. 42–3, containing, in later script, a horologium, a mass for the vigil of the Ascension, and the paschal cycles 760–778, 779–798; (5) f. 44, in a distinct but early script, the paschal cycle 684–702. The martyrology and the calendar were originally separate, but were united in the first half of the eighth century.

These books were probably in the possession of Willibrord. In the case of the martyrology there is no conclusive evidence, but an autobiographical note of the year

---

[230] *Cf.* Bede *Hist. Eccl. lib.* III *cap.* xxvii, V ix, x, xxii. Also p. 216 *supra*, p. 246 *infra*.

[231] One of these was Adalbert (Æthelberht), who settled at Egmond in North Holland (*Annales Xantenses* 690, 694 in *MGH SS* II 220). Another, Suidbert, founded a monastery on the island of Kaiserwerth in the river Rhine (Bede *Hist. Eccles.* V xi).

[232] *Cf.* no. 67.

[233] *MGH SS* XXIII 11.

[234] *Cap.* iv " quia in Hibernia scholasticam eruditionem viguisse audivit."

[235] On Alcuin *cf.* no. 340. On other sources relating to Willibrord *cf.* arts. by A. Poncelet in *An. Boll.* 1903 iv, 1906 i, ii, 1907 i. On the *evangeliarium cf.* no. 460.

728 in the margin of f. 39ᵛ of the calendar was almost certainly written by the saint himself. They are in English semi-uncial and minuscule of the early eighth century, and the facsimiles will show the student how closely English and Irish script were related. It has been suggested that the calendar was written in Ireland, but this is improbable, except as regards the single f. 44. The remainder of the volume was written at Echternach, the martyrology by a certain Laurentius [236] whose name appears on Echternach documents of 704, 710 and 717. Internal evidence seems to show that the calendar was written within the period 703–709,[237] the martyrology perhaps a little later.

The evidence of Irish influence is less than might be expected, although there are some traces of kinship with the *Félire Oengusso*.[238] The only Irish saints noticed in the calendar are Brigit, Patrick, and Columba, all in the original script, and among the additions, Aidan.

70. Ethelwulf: Poem A.D. 802 x 819 (?)

MSS: BM Cotton. Tiberius D iv *s* X *ex* ff. 309–21 [damaged by fire]. — Bodl. 163 *s* XI ff. 209ᵛ–26ᵛ. — Cambridge Univ. Ff. 1.27 *s* XIII pp. 203–15. EDS: Mabillon *AA. SS. o. s. B.* IV ii 304–21. — Dümmler *MGH Poet. lat. aevi Carol.* I 583–604. COMM: Hardy *Cat.* I ii 509–11. — L. Traube *Karolingische Dichtungen* I (Berlin 1888) 1–37. — Manitius *Lat. Lit.* I 552.

Ethelwulf, or Aedilvulf, was, we are told, a monk of Lindisfarne, and the Egbert, or Ecgbercht, to whom his poem or series of poems is addressed, the bishop of that see who ruled from 802 to 819. Besides the *praefatiuncula*, an address to Egbert, there are twenty-three sections, the first and last in distichs, the others in hexameters. The story runs that Osred, king of Northumbria (705–716/717) compelled many persons, among them a nobleman named Eanmund, to enter the religious life. Eanmund obtained rules for a monastery from Egfrid, bishop of Lindisfarne (698–721), and Egbert in Ireland (doubtless the bishop of that name who inaugurated the Frisian mission and later won the monks of Iona to the Roman Easter, dying in 729), and, in accordance with their directions, built a church in honor of St. Peter. The history of this monastic church is given down to the writer's time; from some of the expressions used it might seem that he himself was abbot. Some persons whom the author describes appear to have been Irish, as Ultan [238A] the scribe and Cuicuin the smith. The location of the church is not given, but it has generally been assumed that it was in the neighborhood of Lindisfarne. Might it have been one of the English establishments in Ireland?

71. Council of Celchyth A.D. 816

EDS: Spelman *Concilia* I 327. — Wilkins *Concilia* I 169–71. — H&S III 579–85. COMM: E. Bishop *Liturgica historica* (Oxford 1918) 172.

---

[236] It is at least possible that Laurentius was an Irish follower of the English missionaries to Frisia.
[237] There are many additions, but perhaps none later than 728.
[238] No. 272.
[238A] In *LH* 2 II 107 he is identified with Ultán of Árd-mBreccain (*cf.* p. 329 *infra*). This seems impossible.

This council of the bishops of the province of Canterbury was held under Wulfred, archbishop of Canterbury, and Cenulf, king of Mercia. In its acts it directed that no one "of Irish race" should be permitted to perform any ecclesiastical functions, "because we cannot be certain whence they come and whether they have been ordained by anyone," and because "we should scorn to receive the holy rites from foreign peoples who have no organisation under a metropolitan nor any [hierarchical] dignity." [239]

Further evidence of the close relations between Ireland and the early English Church can be found in the remains of Anglo-Saxon art, especially the script and the ornamentation of manuscripts; in the exchange of books; in the Irish texts and "symptoms" found in English devotional, liturgical and biblical volumes; and in the testimony of certain texts to be considered later, as, e.g. the *Anglo-Saxon Chronicle*.

VI. ECCLESIASTICAL LEGISLATION — CANONS AND PENITENTIALS

Bibliography

EDS. OF PENITENTIALS: F. W. H. Wasserschleben *Die Bussordnungen der abendländischen Kirche* (Halle 1851) [good ed.]. — H. J. Schmitz *Die Bussbücher und die Bussdisciplin der Kirche* (Mainz 1883); II *Die Bussbücher und das kanonische Bussverfahren* (Düsseldorf 1898) [for the theory advanced in these works, see below; on the methods, cf. B. Albers *Archiv für katholisches Kirchenrecht* LXXXI (1901): they are very useful because of the great number of texts and of variants that they give]. COMM: GENERAL: The apposite articles in Smith and Cheetham *Dict. Christ. Antiq.*; Hergenröther and Kauler *Kirchenlexikon oder Encyclopädie der katholischen Theologie;* Herzog and Hauck *Realencyklopädie für protestantische Theologie u. Kirche;* Vacant and Mangenot *Dictionnaire de théologie catholique.* — Fr. Maasen *Geschichte der Quellen u. der Literatur des kanonischen Rechts* (Gratz 1870). — Edg. Loening *Geschichte des deutschen Kirchenrechts* (Strasburg 1878) [see below for his theory of penance]. — A. Tardif *Histoire des sources du droit canonique* (Paris 1887). — Scherer *Handbuch des Kirchenrechts* (Gratz 1898). — A. Harnack *Lehrbuch der Dogmengeschichte* 4th ed. (Tübingen 1909-10). — Gougaud *Les Chrétientés celtiques* 267-78 [good summary account of Celtic canon law]. — J. B. Sägmüller *Lehrbuch des katholischen Kirchenrechts* 3rd ed. (Freiburg i. B. 1914) [has excellent bibliographies]. ON PENANCE: D. Petavius *De poenitentia vetere in ecc. ratione diatriba* (Paris 1624). — Morin *Commentarius hist. de disciplina in admin. sacram. poenitentiae* (Paris 1651) [two early studies that are still of value]. — A. Boudinhon "Sur l'histoire de la pénitence" *Rev. d'hist. et de litt. relig.* II (1897) 496 sqq. — H. C. Lea *History of auricular confession* (Philadelphia 1898) [important, though now becoming antiquated]. — Vacandard "Le Pouvoir des clefs" *Rev. du clergé français* 1898-9. — G. Rauschen *Eucharistie u. Busssakrament in den ersten sechs Jahrhunderten der Kirche* (Freiburg i.

[239] *Cap.* v. The text seems to be corrupt.

B. 1903; Eng. trans. 1908; Fr. trans. 1910). — M. J. O'Donnell *Penance in the early Church* (Dublin 1908). — E. J. Hanna " Penance " *Cath. Encycl.* [*cf.* Oakley, *op. cit. infra*, 210]. — O. D. Watkins *History of Penance* 2 vols. (London 1920) [valuable: vol. II " The western Church from 450 to 1215 " gives much attention to Irish and British sources]. ON THE PENITENTIALS: Schmitz *Archiv für katholisches Kirchenrecht* LI (1884) 25 *sqq*. — Paul Fournier " Études sur les pénitentiels " *Rev. d'hist. et de litt. relig.* VI (1901) 289 *sqq*; VII (1902) 59 *sqq*, 121 *sqq*; VIII (1903) 528 *sqq*; IX (1904) 97 *sqq* [a very valuable series of articles]. — J. T. MacNeill " The Celtic Penitentials " *RC* XXXIX (1922) 257–300, XL (1923) 51–103, 320–41 [the most important study of the origin and character of Irish penitentials]. — T. P. Oakley *English Penitential Discipline and Anglo-Saxon Law in their joint influence* (New York 1923) [gives considerable attention to Irish and British sources; presents the results of the latest critical scholarship]. ON THE CANONICAL COLLECTIONS: Ballerini *De antiquis collectionibus et collectoribus canonum* in Migne *PL* LVI. — Jules Besson " Canons, Collections of ancient " *Cath. Encycl.* [useful for the general field, but not for the Irish]. — See also the manuals of canon law listed *supra*, and the bibliog. of no. 82 *infra*.

The mediaeval priest needed to have at hand and be able to use a considerable number of books. He required such books as he must use in the ritual of the Church, the service of the mass and the administration of the other sacraments; and in the observance of the canonical hours. All these we shall consider later in connection with the liturgical remains of the Irish Church. As has been seen, he had to have a computus, a book containing the table for the contemporary Easter cycle, directions for its use, and instructions for drawing up the tables of future cycles. In connection with the liturgical services, and with the other duties of his office, he had need of part at least of the biblical books — the psalter, the gospels, the epistles. Of these also the surviving Irish copies will later be considered. To know the rights and the obligations, both of himself and of those committed to his spiritual care, he must be able to consult a compilation of canon law. And he came to find it extremely useful, in administering the sacrament of penance, to have available a penitential, a little book containing a schedule of the expiatory works to be imposed for the various sins for which penitents might wish to make atonement.[240]

In the history of the production of penitentials and of books of canons the Irish Church has an important place. Irish " pilgrims " and missionaries carried Irish penitentials and Irish canonical collections with them to foreign lands. Perhaps foreign students returning

---

[240] Bishop Haito of Basel, in a *capitulare* issued 806 x 823, directs that priests must know the following: sacramentarium, lectionarium, antiphonarium, baptisterium, computus, penitential-canon, psalterium. *Cf.* Schmitz I 165.

from the Irish schools brought back with them such books. Abroad these Irish handbooks found great favor. They were transmitted from one church to another, copied and re-copied, modified and expanded according to new conditions and new ideas, until they had produced a quite considerable mass of religious literature. The books used by the Irish clergy at home have, for the most part, perished, but through the copies and adaptations made by their English and continental admirers we have been able to recover many of these ancient documents.

Church legislation was enacted in Ireland, as elsewhere, by synods of bishops and abbots. It is possible, or even probable, that, as Fournier asserts,[241] the legislative machine functioned less efficiently in the Irish than in the continental Church. But councils were held and their acts were recorded, even though these have, with one or two exceptions, been lost. A portion of this legislation has been preserved through being incorporated into the compilation of canon law known as the *Hibernensis*, which, as has been said, was copied many times in continental manuscripts.

In early mediaeval Ireland, likewise, legislation was frequently half-secular, half-ecclesiastical, in its origin as well as in its application. Such were the injunctions to which the general term *cáin*, "law, rule," was given a peculiar application.

" These are the four *cána* of Ireland," says the commentary to *Félire Oengusso*: [242] " Patrick's law (*cáin Patraic*), not to kill the clergy; and Adamnán's law, not to kill women; Dáire's law, not to kill cattle; and the law of Sunday, not to transgress thereon."

There were, however, more than four *cána*. The annalists, with whom *lex* seems undoubtedly to be equated with *cáin*, mention from time to time the enforcement of the " laws " of many saints.[243] It would seem that the Irish legal mind, with its strict sense of obligation, held that, in return for the social benefits resultant from each of these " laws," the populace was bound to make payments to the saint who was its author, in the person of his " heir," the abbot of his monastic church. Hence it is probable that the chief feature of many of these enforcements, or promulgations, of " laws " was the levying of a cess.

[241] *RC* XXX (1909) 228-9.
[242] WS *Fél. Oeng.*² 211. This is the text of the MS Laud 610. A similar note in the Franciscan LH makes Dáire's law " not to steal cattle."
[243] *Cf. AU*, index *s. v.* " Law."

There are separate texts of only two of these *cána*, the "Law of Adamnán" and the " Sunday Law." Of these, the " Sunday Law " belongs to the ninth century, and will be considered later.[244]

Two other classes of texts have, to a degree, the character of ecclesiastical law: (1) The monastic rules. These will be noticed in the following chapters, dealing with the several Irish churches or church-leagues, their records and traditions. (2) The Brehon law tracts which treat of ecclesiastical matters. They are part of the secular law, bearing the impress of its principles and its methods, and must be regarded in that setting, but they are of very great importance for the understanding of the organisation, discipline and customs of the Irish Church.

To turn now to the penitential books. A system of penitential discipline had, of course, been enforced in the Christian Church from primitive times. The characteristic of this discipline was the public exclusion, more or less complete and for varying periods of time, of the penitents from the religious services. This system of public penance was less rigorously enforced in western Europe than in the East, and it is doubtful whether it was ever observed in the British Isles. In the seventh century a new [245] penitential system appeared in continental Europe, and, although meeting with some opposition, acquired wide and lasting vogue. It was penance imposed privately by the confessor and performed privately by the penitent, penance of which the essential was prayer, mortification and good works, the amount being proportioned to the number and character of the sins in accordance with a fixed tariff set down in the penitential book. It is the opinion of the majority of historians, in particular of Wasserschleben and Fournier, to whom the elucidation of this phase of penitential history is largely due, that this discipline and the penitential books associated with it had their origin in the Celtic Churches of the British Isles, passed by way of Irish missionaries to the Anglo-Saxons, and then by way of both Irish and Anglo-Saxons, notably Columban and his disciples, to the Continent.

Opposition to the theory has come principally from Mgr. H. J. Schmitz, who has given a lifetime to the study of the penitentials.

---

[244] No. 270.

[245] It is possible that private penance, subordinate to the public system and without the use of elaborate penitential tables, may have existed from ancient times. So argues, *e.g.*, H. Brewer " Die kirchliche Privatbusse im christlichen Altertum" *Zs f. kath. Theologie* XLV (1921) [also separately]. — The word "penance" has two significations which should be distinguished: (1) as the equivalent of "sacrament of penance," the whole sacramental process by which the sinner might be restored to grace; (2) more restrictedly, the acts by which he might give expression to his penitence and offer some spiritual satisfaction for his transgressions. Unless the context indicates otherwise, it is in this narrower sense that the word is here used.

Taking a Catholic view-point, he has seen in the propositions of Wasserschleben but another phase of a centuries-old attempt on the part of Protestant historians, for propaganda purposes, to establish the existence of an ancient evangelical, independent-of-Rome Church, arising from the British Isles and spreading over the Frankish empire. For him, the origin of the penitentials was Roman. The facts that the actual manuscripts of the penitentials are comparatively late and chiefly continental, and that the same regulations are found repeated over and over again with no direct clue as to which is the primary text, which the borrowed, makes it difficult for any but the expert to reach an opinion in such a controversy. The other experts, Catholic and Protestant, have, however, been practically unanimous in rejecting Schmitz's arguments and accepting the hypothesis outlined above of a Celtic origin of the penitentials.

A subsidiary controversy has arisen out of the theory of Loening that private penance was originally a purely monastic practice which the Irish and Anglo-Saxon missionaries extended to the lay world.[246] Be that as it may, it seems certain that one of the features of the strict and enthusiastic Irish monastic Church of the sixth and seventh centuries which contrasted with the more lax Christianity of the Continent was the emphasis laid on confession and works of penance.

It would seem that the earliest penitentials were compiled in the British Church. Extant texts are the Penitential of David (*Excerpta quaedam de libro Davidis*), the penitential canons ascribed to the synods of Brevi (*Sinodus Aquilonalis Britanniae*) and of the Grove of Victory (*Sinodus Luci Victoriae*),[247] believed to have been held in the time of St. David and perhaps under his influence, and the Penitential of Gildas (*Prefatio Gildae de Penitentia*).[248] The Penitential of Gildas, and part at least of that of David, were designed for the use of monks and priests.

---

[246] Loening *op. cit.* II 468 *sqq*; Malnory *Quid Luxovienses monachi discipuli S. Columbani ad regulam monasteriorum atque ad communem ecclesiae profectum contulerint* (Paris 1894) 62 *sqq*. For the other side, *cf.* L. Duchesne *Bulletin critique* IV (1883) 366; Batiffol *Études d'histoire et de théologie positive* 1st ser. (Paris 1902) 193–4.

[247] These three texts, as also the *Prefatio Gildae*, are in BN lat. 3182 *s* XI. Eds: Martène and Durand *Thesaurus novus anecdotorum* IV (Paris 1717) 9–10. — Migne *PL* XCVI 1317–9. — Wasserschleben *Bussordnungen* 101–4. — Moran *Essays* (Dublin 1864) 267–8 [in part]. — Schmitz I 492–4. — H&S I 116. — Hugh Williams *Gildas* (London 1899) 286–8. *Cf.* Watkins *op. cit.* 588 *sqq*; Oakley *op. cit.* 33–7; J. T. MacNeill *loc. cit.* 274–7. The text of the Penitential of David may be made up of extracts from a larger book.

[248] MS: See preceding note. Eds: Martène and Durand *op. cit.* IV 7–8. — Migne *PL* XCVI 1315–7. — Wasserschleben *op. cit.* 105–8. — H&S I 113–5. — Schmitz I 494–7. — Williams *op. cit.* 272–85 [with trans.]. *Cf.* Mommsen *MGH Auct. ant.* XIII (*Chron. Min.* III) (1894) 89–90; Henry Bradshaw *Collected Papers* (Cambridge 1889) 417; Watkins *loc. cit.*; Oakley *loc. cit.*; MacNeill *loc. cit.* 265. Some critics think that the document is of later date than Gildas.

Doubtless the development of penitential discipline and the penitential books in Ireland was due to the influence of British ecclesiastics, especially of David and Gildas. There are grounds for believing that the extant British penitentials have been transmitted through Irish copies.[249]

For the Synod, or rather Circular Letter, of the bishops Patricius, Auxilius and Isernius, see no. 30 *supra;* for an alleged Synod of Patricius, Auxilius, Secundinus and Benignus, no. 130 *infra.*

---

72. The Penitential of Vinnian

Poenitentiale Vinniai. [In nomine Dei . . . .] Si quis in corde suo . . . donec penitentia expleatur. Finit Deo gratias. Haec, amantissimi fratres . . . hominibus facinora.

MSS: BN lat. 12021 *s* IX [formerly St. Germain 121: at one time belonged to Corbie; was written by a scribe Arbedoc for his abbot Haelhucar, both Bretons]. — Vienna lat. 2233 *c* A.D. 800 f. 25. — St. Gall Stiftsbibl. 150 *s* IX pp. 365–77 [incomplete]. — BN lat. 3182 [formerly Bigot. 89] *s* X² [*cf.* pp. 239, 241–50.] EDS: D'Achéry *Spicilegium* I (1655) 491. — Martène and Durand *Thesaurus novus anecdotorum* IV (Paris 1717) 1 *sqq.* — Wasserschleben *Die Bussordnungen* 10–11, 108–19. — Moran *Essays* (1864) append. [extracts]. — Schmitz I (1888) 497–509. COMM: Seebass *ZK* XIV (1894) 435–7. — Watkins *History of Penance* I 609–12. — Oakley *English Penitential Discipline* 40–1. — J. T. MacNeill *RC* XXXIX (1922) 266–74.

The author of this penitential, Vinniaus, or, as it is quoted in the *Collectio Canonum Hibernensis*, Vinnianus, is, doubtless, the same person as the "Vennianus auctor" who, according to Columban, consulted Gildas on a question of discipline.[250] In Irish, initial V was replaced by F about the beginning of the seventh century, so the word is the well-known Irish name, Finnio, Finnian or Findian. There is absolutely no evidence for identification, but almost all scholars have assumed that the author was one of the two great saints, Finnian of Clúain-Iráird (Clonard) and Finnian of Mag-Bile (Moville).[251] Wasserschleben and MacNeill favor Finnian of Clonard, Schmitz and Seebass, in his later period, Finnian of Moville. The legends of the residence of Finnian of Clonard in Britain and of his association with Gildas are too precarious to be given much trust, but there must be some foundation for his reputation as head of the great religious movement of sixth-century Ireland, and, if so, this is such a document as we might expect him to have composed.

---

[249] The MS BN lat. 3182 contains the only extant copy of these documents. The whole contents of this codex, which seems to have been written at Fécamp in Normandy, are of Irish origin. *Cf.* Maassen *op. cit.* 786. — There is a document, sometimes designated *Canones Wallici*, which has some relationship with the penitentials. It is a collection of secular laws, of Welsh origin but showing Goidelic influences, perhaps from a part of Wales where a Goidelic population still lived. H&S date it 550 x 650. MSS: BN lat. 3182; BN lat. 12021 *s* IX. Eds: Martène and Durand *op. cit.* IV 13 *sqq;* Wasserschleben *op. cit.* 124 *sqq;* H&S I 127–37; Williams *op. cit.* II 286 *sqq.* *Cf.* Oakley *op. cit.* 37; MacNeill *loc. cit.* 288–90.

[250] The fact that the Penitential of Columban draws very extensively on that of Vinniaus makes this the more probable.

[251] *Cf.* nos. 165, 183.

The Penitential of Vinnian holds an important position in the history of penitential literature. It makes use of the Bible, and perhaps of Cassian and some early Irish canons, but in the main is either original or based on sources not now known. The author says that he followed the sense of the Scriptures and the opinion of certain very learned men. The text, apart from some general provisions, falls into two large sections, the one dealing with the sins of clerics, the other of the laity. It is, of its kind, comprehensive, discriminating and precise, qualities by which it may have earned its strong influence on later compilations.

For the Penitential of Columban, see no. 46.

73. The Penitential of Cummean

Incipit prologus de medicinae salutaris animarum. . . . Finitus est hic liber scriptus a Comminiano.

MS: Vat. Palat. lat. 485 ff. 101ᵛ–7ᵛ. ED: J. Zettinger *Archiv f. kath. Kirchenrecht* LXXXII (1902) 501–40. COMM: Oakley *English Penitential Discipline and Anglo-Saxon Law* (1923) 30.

Of penitentials of purely Irish origin the next in point of time after Vinnian and Columban, and in some respects the most important of all, is that which bears the name of Cummean. Zettinger, who was the first to distinguish the genuine text from the later, perhaps continental, compilation which had previously been known as Cummean's,[252] dates it about the middle of the seventh century. This would synchronise with the career of St. Cuimine *fota* (d. 662),[253] whom the Old-Irish Penitential[254] quotes as author of a penitential treatise.

74. The *Paenitentiale Bigotianum*

Hieronymus vir memoriae ecclesiae pastores . . . ab occultis meis munda me Domine.

MS: BN lat. 3182 (formerly Bigot. 89) *s* X² pp. 286–99 [*cf*. p. 240 n. 249 *supra*]. EDS: Martène and Durand *Thesaurus novus anecdotorum* IV (Paris 1717) 22–30 [partial]. — Wasserschleben *Die Bussordnungen* (1851) 441–60. — Schmitz I (1883) 705–11 [analysis only]. COMM: E. J. Gwynn *Ériu* VII ii (1914) 129. — J. T. MacNeill *RC* XXXIX iii–iv (1922) 298.

The *Paenitentiale Bigotianum* takes its name from the former library-designation of the manuscript in which it is found, a well-known collection of penitential and canonical documents of Irish origin or association. It is closely related to the Penitential of Cummean and to the Old-Irish Penitential edited by Gwynn, and in date probably lies between them, that is, at the end of the seventh or in the eighth century. It has usually been classed as a continental penitential of Irish derivation, but there seems no good reason for not classifying it as an original Irish production, which its character and manuscript connections suggest. It has two noteworthy features: (1) There is a preface giving a schedule of commutations by which long penances may be changed into shorter and more severe terms, or into money payments. (2)

---

[252] No. 77.   [253] *Cf*. pp. 420–1 *infra*.   [254] No. 75.

Sins and their penances are classified under the headings of the "eight principal vices" of John Cassian, whose complete list of the sins arising therefrom is quoted in the introduction.

For the Penitential of Theodore, see no. 65.

75. Old-Irish Penitential

Conaemdetar sruithe Érenn a ríaglaib . . . .

MSS: LBr s XV *in* p. 186 [fragment]. — RIA 23 P 3 A.D. 1467 [255] ff. 15 *sq* [prefaces]. — RIA 3 B 23 s XV [256] ff. 16–28 [the entire penitential, but imperfect at beginning and end]. — Bodl. Rawl. B. 512 s XV ff. 39–40^v [prefaces]. — Cheltenham MS s XV pp. 47–8 [*cf.* WS *Fél. Oeng.*[2] p. ix]. EDS: KM *ZCP* III (1901) 24–8 [Rawl. B. 512, text only]. — E. J. Gwynn " An Irish Penitential " *Ériu* VII ii (1914) 121–95 [text, trans., comm. and glossary: *cf.* John MacErlean *Studies* Mar. 1915 p. 154; KM *Miscellanea Hibernica* (*Univ. of Illinois Studies in Language and Literature* II iv) (Nov. 1916) 39]. COMM: J. T. MacNeill *RC* XXXIX iii–iv (1922) 298.

" The venerable of Ireland have drawn up from the rules of the Scriptures a penitential for the annulling and remedying of every sin, both small and great. For the eight chief virtues, with their subdivisions, have been appointed to cure and heal the eight chief vices, with whatsoever springs therefrom." So begins the only penitential in the Irish language as yet published. It is divided into eight sections, corresponding with the eight principal sins, and each section is preceded by a preface. These prefaces have been gathered together in several manuscripts to form a separate text, a kind of homily on the deadly sins.

The extant versions go back to an archetype, a small volume, perhaps a *quinio*, or gathering of five sheets, which was already in a dilapidated condition when the first of these copies was made. It was probably an old penitential book that had been long in use.

The chief sources of the compilation seem to be the *Paenitentiale Bigotianum*, with which it has a peculiar kinship, Cummean and Theodore. These two authors are mentioned by name. The language is badly corrupted by late transcribers, but sufficient old forms remain to indicate that the piece must be at least as old as about the year 800. MacErlean points out that the presence of ante-Hieronymian scriptural readings is evidence of the antiquity of some at least of the contents. The penitential was intended chiefly for monastic use, although some provision is made for penitents in the world.

76. Old-Irish Treatise on Commutations

Arra tesairgne anma a ifurnd . . . .

MSS: RIA 3 B 23 s XV ff. 13–16. — Bodl. Rawl. B 512 s XV ff. 42^v–4. — EDS: KM *RC* XV (1894) 485–98 [text of Rawl. B 512; trans.]. — E. J. Gwynn *Ériu* V (1911) 45–8 [collation of 3 B 23 with KM's text].

---

[255] The scribe was Uilliam Mac an Lega. *Cf. Ériu* VII ii 126.

[256] Written by Tadg Úa Rig-bardáin (O'Riordan), whom we know to have been writing another MS in 1473. *Cf. Proc. RIA* XXIX C (1911) 115.

The Old-Irish word *arra* signifies "equivalent, substitution." Hence it, and the Latin derivative *arreum*, were applied to those commutations by which penances of longer duration were converted into others of brief space but great severity. The present text contains a list of such commutations. On linguistic and other grounds it is assigned to the eighth century.

77. The Penitential of Pseudo-Cummian

Diversitas culparum diversitatem facit poenitentiarum. . . . Et de remediis vulnerum. . . . [Different explicits are found in the several MSS.]

MSS: Numerous. See Wasserschleben and especially Schmitz II; also Holder *Die Reichenauer Handschriften* (Leipsic 1906) 256, and Esposito *Proc. RIA* XXVIII C iii 76. EDS: Fleming *Collectanea sacra* (1667). — *Bibl. max. vet. patrum* XII (Leyden 1677) 41–5. — Migne *PL* LXXXVII 977–98 [this and the preceding are reprints of Fleming]. — Wasserschleben *Die Bussordnungen* (1851) 61, 460–93. — Schmitz I (1883) 602–53. — Schmitz II (1898) 581–644 [with elaborate *apparatus criticus*]. COMM: J. T. MacNeill *RC* XXXIX iii–iv (1922) 297. — Oakley *English Penitential Discipline and Anglo-Saxon Law* (1923) [see index].

The penitential which, until Zettinger published the genuine text in 1902, was known as Cummean's, is a composite production,[257] drawn from the true Penitential of Cummean, the *Bigotianum*, the Penitential of Theodore, that of Gildas, that of Columbanus, and some others. It is found in a great number of copies, the majority of them showing each its own variations, additions and omissions. This Pseudo-Cummean is the form in which the Irish penitentials attained their greatest popularity in Europe. It seems to have been compiled on the Continent in the ninth century.

A considerable amount of Irish influence is found in many other penitential texts preserved in continental manuscripts and themselves probably of continental origin. To the seventh or early eighth century belong the so-called *Paenitentiale Romanum*,[258] the *Paenitentiale Bobiense*[259] and the *Paenitentiale Parisiense*,[260] all of which drew their inspiration and in large part their contents from the penitential of Columbanus. Of the ninth century are the *Penitential of Thirty-Five Chapters*, or *Paenitentiale Capitula Judiciorum*,[261] which in some respects is nearer the genuine Penitential of Cummean than is Pseudo-Cummean, and the *St. Gall Tripartite Penitential*,[262] the third division of which professes to be derived entirely from Cummean. Even what Schmitz designates the *Paenitentiale Valicellanum* I,[263] which is to him the representative early Roman penitential, displays Irish (Vinnian), Welsh and Anglo-

---

257 Several MSS have the title *Excarpsus de aliis pluribus poenitentialibus et canonibus*.
258 Wasserschleben *op. cit.* 360 *sqq*; Schmitz II 290–300. *Cf.* Watkins *History of Penance* II 682–30, 708–10.
259 Wasserschleben *op. cit.* 407 *sqq*; Schmitz II 322–6. *Cf.* p. 692 *infra*.
260 Wasserschleben *op. cit.* 412 *sqq*; Schmitz II 326–30.
261 Wasserschleben *op. cit.* 505–26; Schmitz II 204–51.
262 Schmitz II 175–88.
263 Schmitz I 239 *sqq*.

Saxon features.[264] The predominant influence in the later continental penitentials was the Penitential of Theodore.

78. Canones Hibernenses

MSS: BN lat. 12021 s IX. — BN lat. 3182 s X². EDS: Martène and Durant *Thesaurus novus anecdotorum* IV (Paris 1717) [Titles I–III, VI]. — Mansi *Sacrorum conciliorum nova et amplissima collectio* (Florence 1759, etc.; Paris 1901, etc.) XII 142 [Title V]. — Wasserschleben *Die Bussordnungen* (1851) 136–44 [complete text]. — Moran *Essays* (1864) 271-4 [partial: from Wasserschleben]. — *Thes. Pal.* II (1903) 38 [the glosses on BN 12021]. COMM: Bellesheim *Geschichte d. kath. Kirche in Irland* I (1890) 191; *Archiv f. kath. Kirchenrecht* LIV 467. — P. Fournier *RC* XXX 227-8, 232-3. — Frederic Seebohm *Tribal Custom in Anglo-Saxon Law* (London, etc. 1911) 100-5. — J. T. MacNeill *RC* XXXIX iii-iv (1922) 260-4. — Oakley *English Penitential Discipline and Anglo-Saxon Law* (1923) 38-40, 69 *sqq.*

The group of canons to which the title *Canones Hibernenses* has been attached appears to be an early attempt at putting together a collection for ecclesiastical use. It is at least as old as the eighth century, and probably considerably older than the *Collectio Canonum Hibernensis*. It falls into six divisions, or titles, some and perhaps all of which had been independent entities with a still earlier history of their own. However, there is only internal evidence from which to form conclusions. Title I is *De disputatione Hibernensis sinodi S. Gregorii Nasaseni sermo de innumerabilibus peccatis incipit:* the significance of neither of these headings is apparent, for the contents are simply twenty-four penitential canons of rather severe character. We meet here, perhaps for the first time, with provision for payments, in the normal secular unit of value, the female slave, Latin *ancilla*, Irish *cumhal*. No. II is *De arreis incipit*. It treats of commutations, the substitution of shorter and more severe, for longer penances, and is related to the Old-Irish treatise on the same subject.[265] No. III, *Sinodus Hibernensis decrevit*, is a list of punishments and mulcts to be imposed for offences to ecclesiastical personages. For some of these penalties a saying attributed to Patrick, possibly a later addition, permits the substitution of penance. Title IV, *De jectione*, treats of evictions and refusals to succor the helpless, especially ecclesiastics; title V, *De canibus sinodus sapientium*, contains purely secular regulations regarding dogs; and title VI, *Item sinodus sapientia* [sic] *de decimis disputant*, deals with tithes and first-fruits.

All, except no. II, profess to be acts of synods. Nos. III to VI have secular affiliations, and were probably passed in a joint assembly, or assemblies, at which clergy and laity were present, such as that which enacted *Cáin Adamnáin*.

They should be studied in connection with the Brehon Laws. Interesting is the curious acceptance, in both, of the Hebraic dispensation regarding tithes and first-fruits. Title II is probably later than the others, but it is doubtful if any of these canons can be of date later than the first half of the seventh century.

---

[264] F. H. P. Hinschius *System des katholischen Kirchenrechts* V 92; J. T. MacNeill *RC* XXXIX iii-iv (1922) 298-300.
[265] No. 76.

79. Pseudo-Patrician Synod: *Synodus II Patricii*

De eo quod mandastis . . . peccator judicandus est. Finit Patricii synodus. 31 canons.

EDS: Spelman *Concilia* I (London 1639) 55–9. — Wilkins *Concilia* I (London 1737) 4–6. — Ware *S. Patricio adscripta opuscula* (London 1656) 31–9. — Migne *PL* LIII 817–22. — H&S II ii (1878) 333–8. COMM: Bury *St. Patrick* (1905) 237.

This collection of ecclesiastical canons has been traditionally ascribed to St. Patrick. Critics, however, are unanimous in rejecting the ascription, among other reasons because one canon (xxvii) is in opposition to a passage in the *Confession* of Patricius, in which the saint approves of maidens entering the religious life in opposition to the wishes of their fathers. An important fact is that twelve of these canons are quoted in various manuscripts of the *Collectio Canonum Hibernensis*, and only one, in one manuscript, has the name of Patricius attached. The majority are attributed to *synodus Romana*, or *Romani*. It may be presumed that we have here the acts of some council of the pro-Roman clergy of the seventh century.[266]

80. Canones Adomnani

Marina animalia ad littora cadentia . . . pelles in usus varios habebimus. Finiunt haec judicia.

MSS: Orleans Bibl. de la ville 221 (formerly 193) *s* VIII/IX [once belonged to monastery of Fleury; contains Breton glosses and was written by a Breton scribe, Junobrus]. — Bodl. Hatton 42 *s* IX. — BN lat. 12021 *s* IX. — BN lat. 3182 *s* X². — BM Cotton. Otho E. XIII *s* X *in.* ff. 141ᵛ–143ᵛ. — Dublin Marsh's Library Z. 3. 1. 14 [copy of Otho E. XIII]. EDS: D'Achéry *Spicilegium* IX 490–1 [attributed to Theodore]. — Martène and Durand *Thesaurus novus anecdotorum* IV (Paris 1717) II, 18–9 [partial]. — Wasserschleben *Die Bussordnungen* (1851) 120–3. — Migne *PL* LXXXVIII 815 *sqq*, XCVI 1319, 1324–5. — Robertson *Ecclesiae Scoticanae Statuta* 229–30 [Martène and Durand, collated with the Cotton text]. — H&S II i 111–4 [from Wasserschleben, with emendations]. COMM: J. T. MacNeill *RC* XXXIX iii–iv (1922) 293.

This collection of twenty canons, almost entirely alimentary regulations, is attributed in the manuscripts to Adamnán. There is no other evidence. In the Haddan and Stubbs edition it is suggested that they were enacted by some Irish synod under the influence of Adamnán — a pure guess. They treat chiefly of the animal foods that may, or may not, be eaten.

81. Law of Adamnán (*Cáin Adamnáin*)

Cóic amsira ría ngein Críst. i. ó Ádam co dílinn . . . dia mbé túarasndal bansgál.

MSS: Bodl. Rawl. B 512 ff. 48–51ᵛ (the ff. 31–52 form a distinct section of the codex, and date from *s* XV). — Brussels Bibl. roy. 2324–40 pp. 76–85, copied in 1627 by Michael Úa Clerigh from a MS written by his cousin Cú-mumhan mac Tuathail Í Clerigh. The O'Clery MS, and probably the Rawlinson, goes back to a certain old book of the monastery of Raphoe — of which Adamnán was patron — which seems to have contained a collection of documents relating to Adamnán. ED: KM

---

[266] In Migne *PL* LIII 823, 827 will be found other canons attributed to Patrick.

Cáin Adamnáin An Old-Irish Treatise on the Law of Adamnan (Anec. Oxon. Med. &
Mod. Ser. XII) (Oxford 1905) [text, trans., notes, etc.; corrigenda in *ACL* III (1906)
108]. *Cf.* KM in *Festschrift Ernst Windisch* (Leipsic 1914) " Eine verschollene Artur-
saga " [*cf. RC* XXXVII iv (1919) 370].

This is a historical tract describing the origin and the provisions of
the Law of Adamnán. It was written in the ninth century, probably,
but embodies documents, notably the list of personages who approved
the enactment, which have every appearance of being survivals, linguistically modified, from the end of the seventh or beginning of the
eighth century. According to the annals, Adamnán promulgated his
" Law," known as the " Law of the Innocents," in 697.

The text describes the circumstances which led up to the assembly
at Birr of the ecclesiastics and the secular rulers of Ireland, where
Adamnán published his "Law" for the amelioration of the condition of
women, particularly their exemption from military service, and the
protection of children and clerics.

As elsewhere, *cáin* means not only a law, but also the dues which should be paid in
acknowledgment of the benefits derived from the law. So the tract sets forth the
tributes to be paid to Adamnán, and to his successors, because of what he had done
for women.[267]

Then follows what clearly was an independent treatise on the same subject.[268] It
resembles an amalgamation of a penitential and a Brehon Law tract. Very severe
ecclesiastical penances for the killing of a woman are laid down, and there are long
enactments, in the manner of the Brehon code, regarding punishments and compensa-
tions for slaying, or injuring, women, children, or clerical students.

The list of persons present at the assembly, which is incorporated into the first part
of our text, is an historical document of much interest. It may have been somewhat
corrupted, but a large number of the names can be identified with those of persons
living at the time, and it would not seem that the presence of any constitutes a real
anachronism. The joint meeting of the clergy of the south, and of such supporters of
the Roman Easter as Adamnán, Coeddi and Ecgberct, with some of the leading northern ecclesiastics, makes it probable that these last had become reconciled to the new
paschal system — if the reconciliation was not effected at this very assembly.[269]
Noteworthy also is the mention of the presence of those two promoters of the *paruchia
Patricii* and the Patrick Legend, Aed of Sletty and Muir-chú maccu Machthéni.
This may lend support to Zimmer's theory that the development of Patrick's story
in the seventh century was in reality one phase of the campaign to win the northern
Irish to conformity with Rome on the paschal question.[270]

---

[267] FM gives in 929 the death of Caencomhrac mac Máel-Uidhir, abbot and bishop of Derry and *maor*,
i.e., collector, of the Cáin Adamnáin.

[268] Incipit sententia angeli Adomnano: — Adamnanus post xiiii annos hanc legem . . . secundum
iudicium huius legis. Ista est sententia angeli Adomnano.

[269] *Cf.* pp. 216, 432 and Bede *Hist. Eccles.* V xv.   [270] *Cf.* pp. 325 *sqq.*

82. Collectio Canonum Hibernensis

Praefatio. Synodicorum exemplarium innumerositatem conspiciens . . . . Episcopus nomen a graeco ductum . . . aquas fideles legem Dei videlicet accepisse. [Wasserschleben's text.] The number of books varies in the MSS from 64 to 69.

MSS: A Recension: St. Gall Stiftsbibl. 243 s IX [by a scribe named Eadberct, perhaps an Englishman]. — Cambrai 679 (619) A.D. 763 x 790 [transcribed for Albericus, bishop of Cambrai and Arras during this period, from an Irish original; ends incomplete]. — Orleans Bibl. de la ville 221 (formerly 193) s VIII/IX. — Cologne Dombibl. 210 s VIII [formerly 2178, and earlier Darmstadt 127; ends at same place as Cambrai MS]. — BN lat. 12021 s IX ff. 33–127. — BM Cotton. Otho E. XIII s X in. [formerly of St. Augustine's, Canterbury]. — BN lat. 3182 s X² pp. 19–160 [see p. 240 n. 249 supra]. — Chartres Bibl. de la ville 127 s XI ff. 2–75 [this and the following copy end at the same place as the Cambrai and Cologne MSS; neither shows any Irish features]. — Tours Bibl. de la ville 556 s XI. — B Recension: Carlsruhe Landesbibl. Cod. Augiensis XVIII c A.D. 806 ff. 75–90 [incomplete at beginning and end]. — Rome Lib. of S. Maria Valicella XVIII s X ff. 58–136 [renders Patricius as "Paterius" and Gildas as " Gelasius "]. — Bodl. Hatton 42 s IX [belonged to Canterbury and, earlier, to Glastonbury]. Eds: D'Achéry Spicilegium IV 232 sqq, 2nd ed. I 492 sqq. — Martène and Durand Thesaurus novus anecdotorum IV (Paris 1717) 1 sqq. — Migne PL XCVI 1281–1308, 1311–4 [these are partial eds.]. — Wasserschleben Die irische Kanonensammlung (Giessen 1874; [271] 2nd ed. Leipsic 1885) [the A Recension; an excellent ed. in its time, but a new treatment is needed]. Comm: Maassen Geschichte der Quellen u. der Literatur des kanonischen Rechts I (Gratz 1870) passim. — H. Bradshaw The early collection of canons known as the Hibernensis: two unfinished papers (Cambridge 1893) [valuable, although some statements and deductions are unacceptable]. — Paul Fournier " De l'influence de la collection irlandaise sur la formation des collections canoniques " Nouvelle rev. historique de droit français et étranger XXIII (1899) 27–8 [valuable study of the MS evidence]. — Bury St. Patrick (1905) 235–9. — S. Hellmann Sedulius Scottus (Munich 1906) [cf. p. 553 infra]. — J. T. MacNeill RC XXXIX iii–iv (1922) 290–3. — On the authorship of the collection see the following: WS Academy July 14, Dec. 1, 1888. — B. MacCarthy ibid. Nov. 3, 1888. — E. W. Nicholson " The Origin of the ' Hibernian ' Collection of Canons " ZCP III (1901) 99–103. — RTh "Zur irischen Kanonensammlung" ibid. VI (1908) 1–5 [cf. 556].

Beginning at latest with the fourth century there had appeared in the Christian Church a series of collections of canons, that is, ecclesiastical laws and regulations, drawn chiefly from the acts of councils and the epistles of the hierarchy, in particular of the Popes. One of the most important of these collections was made early in the sixth century by that Scythian monk, Dionysius, whose paschal table has been mentioned in connection with the Easter controversy, but there were many others. Most influential for a time was the " Hibernian Collection," Collectio Hibernensis, which appeared in Gaul in the eighth century,

---

[271] This first ed. was almost entirely destroyed by fire.

and during the next four hundred years was not only itself used widely in western Europe, but also drawn on extensively, as a source and as a model, by the compilers of other codes.

The spread of the *Hibernensis*, as of the Irish penitentials, must in part reflect the expansion movement of Irish Christianity. Irish monks travelling abroad, foreign monks returning from a visit to the Irish monasteries, took the book with them. Notably in Brittany was it received and copied, and an important group of the extant manuscripts are of Breton origin. Henry Bradshaw argued that Brittany was the chief, if not the sole, route by which the work entered the Continent, but his case is overstated. Once introduced to continental churchmen, however, the collection was welcomed on its merits. It came at a time when a reform movement in morals and discipline was under way in Gaul, and, with all its peculiarities, it emphasised points which were dear to the reformers: the independence of the clergy from secular control; the condemnation of simony; the right of intervention of the papal see; the indissolubility of marriage. Moreover, its method of arrangement and its comprehensiveness made an appeal to practical minds. Some of the continental compilations had attempted a logical arrangement, but the majority gave in succession the full texts of each synod and each decretal, the order, if any, being chronological. Such codes were inconvenient for use in determining particular questions that might arise. But the Irish compilation was not a *corpus* of historico-legal documents; it was a reference book on the teaching of the Church with regard to practical matters of administration, discipline, and the care of souls, classified under some sixty-five main headings, and many sub-headings. To each title were attached applicable decrees and judgments, drawn not only from conciliar and other legislation, but also, in accord with the object of the work, from the writings of the saints and the Fathers of the Church, and especially from the Holy Scriptures. The fact that little method can be discerned in the arrangement of the topics was a less serious objection then than it would be to-day.

There has never been any reasonable doubt that the *Hibernensis* was of Irish origin.[272] As a result of the joint contributions of several scholars it has been possible, through the elucidation of a colophon that the Breton scribe copied, inaccurately, from his original into one of our manuscripts, to determine the names of the compilers.[273]

---

[272] Loofs, *Antiquae Britonum Scotorumque ecclesiae* (1882) 76, assigned it to Northumbria, and Nürnberger, "Die Würzburger Handschrift (Mp. th. qu. 31 s VIII) der irischen Canonensammlung" *Archiv f. kath. Kirchenrecht* LX (1888) 33 *sqq*, thought the author was St. Boniface, both on very flimsy grounds.

[273] The text, in BN lat. 12021, is: " Hucusq; nuben & cucuiminiae. & du rinis." (1) Bradshaw in

They were Rubin of Dair-Inis, a monastery on an island in the Blackwater river not far from Youghal, who in his obituary notice of 725 is designated " Rubin mac Connadh, scribe of Munster," [274] and Cú-Chuimne of Iona, called " the wise," who died in 747.[274] Cú-Chuimne is reputed author of an extant Latin hymn,[275] the introduction to which in the Liber Hymnorum professes to give some details regarding his life and his relations with Adamnán.

It has long been recognised that there are two main recensions of the collection, but the relations between them have never been adequately investigated. It is not certain, even, which is the older.[276] In one, the latest author cited is Theodore, in the other, Adamnán.

The ultimate sources from which the work is compiled may be classified thus: (1) The Old and the New Testament. Interesting is the extensive use made of the former, and the inculcation of such customs as cities of refuge and the jubilee year. (2) Foreign synods. (3) Papal decretals — few, and never with this attribution. (4) Foreign authors: Origen, Jerome, Augustine, Isidore, Clement, Gregory the Great, Gregory Nazianzene, Basil, Lactantius, Ambrose, Eucherius, Martin (Sulpicius Severus), Theophilus, (Rufinus), Orosius, (Gennadius), Faustus, Pelagius, Cassian, Dionysius; and certain writings, *Life of the Monks, Lives of the Fathers,* etc. (5) Irish synods. Not only the canons attributed to *synodus Hibernensis,* but also many of those having the reference simply *synodus,* or *synodus Romana,* appear to be drawn from the acts of Irish councils. Bury's suggestion that the *Romani,* or *synodus Romana,* of these entries designated the pro-Roman party in the Irish Church of the seventh century, is now generally accepted. (6) Insular authors: Patricius, Gildas, Vinnian, Theodore, Adamnán. The sources of many of the quotations are not given, and some of those given are incorrect.[277]

Hellmann has pointed out that among the writings of Sedulius Scottus two collections of excerpts [278] paralleling those in the *Collectio canonum Hibernensis* are to be found, another in a Cambridge codex,[279] and a fourth, in his opinion, in a Cologne manuscript.[280] He argues that behind these there was originally a large " Collection of Sentences " made, or at least in use, in Ireland, which, by selection, addition, and re-arrangement, was turned into a code of canon law.

1885 suggested that the last name was Dair-Inis: he thought the second last was that of Cummean, the compiler of the penitential. (2) In 1888 WS proposed " Ruben " for " nuben " (already so given by Wasserschleben), and recognised the name of Cú-Chuimne in the second last word. (3) MacCarthy in the same year identified " Ruben " as " Rubin mac Connadh." (4) Nicholson in 1900 detected in the scribal " cu-cuiminiae " the words " Cú-Chuimne Iae," *i.e.* of Ia, or Iona. (5) Finally in 1907 RTh called attention to the significance of a common O–I order of related words: ABba where we would have ABab; and rendered the colophon " Hucusque Ruben & Cú-Cuimine Iae & Durinis " as " So far Rubin of Dair-Inis and Cú-Chuimne of Iona."

[274] AU.

[275] No. 98.

[276] Hellmann maintains that the B recension, which Wasserschleben and Bradshaw considered more recent, is really the older.

[277] It does not follow that the author is in error. The text may have been copied, or re-enacted, in the source which he mentions.

[278] *Cf.* pp. 566–8 *infra.*

[279] Corpus Christi Coll. 279 s IX/X. On this MS see Wasserschleben *Die irische Kanonensammlung* pp. xxii *sqq.* The extracts from Gildas which it professes to give are published in H&S I 108–13 and Hugh Williams *Gildas* (1899) 255–71.

[280] Dombibl. 210: *cf.* bibliog. *supra.*

In any case, it seems certain that the book was composed early in the eighth century by members of the " Roman " section of the Irish clergy.

83. Liber ex lege Moysi

MSS: Cambridge Corpus Christi Coll. 279 *s* IX². — Orleans Bibl. de la ville 221 *s* VIII/IX pp. 1-15. — BM Cotton. Otho E. XIII *s* X *in.* [on this and the preceding *cf.* no. 80 *supra*]. — BN lat. 3182 *s* X² pp. 1-12 [arrangement incorrect; from Fécamp]. COMM: Paul Fournier " Le Liber ex Lege Moysi et les tendances bibliques du droit canonique irlandais " *RC* XXX (1909) 221-34 [*cf. Bull. de l'Acad. des inscriptions et belles-lettres* 14 May, 1909].

This is a compilation of canons composed entirely of texts drawn from the Pentateuch. It has not been published, but has been described quite fully by Fournier. His belief is that it was prepared in Ireland in the eighth century and that copies were in use on the Continent towards the end of that century or, at latest, in the ninth.

VII. The Beginnings of Christian Literature

Bibliography

GENERAL: Manitius *Lat. Lit.* — Roger *L'Enseignement.* — L. Gougaud *Les Chrétientés celtiques* (Paris 1911). HYMNS: The chief guide to hymns is Ulysse Chevalier's *Repertorium hymnologicum Catalogue des chants, hymnes, proses, séquences, tropes en usage dans l'église latine depuis les origines jusqu'à nos jours* 6 vols. (Brussels 1889-1920) [*cf.* a criticism by C. Blume *Repertorium repertorii* (Leipsic 1901)]. There are many general collections of Latin hymns, among which may be noted: Georg Cassander *Hymni ecclesiastici* (Cologne 1556), also in his *Opera* (Paris 1616); Thomasius (Tommasi; pseudonym: Josephus Carus) *Psalterium . . . et hymnarium atque orationale* (Rome 1683); Angelo Mai *Hymni inediti vel qui certe in B. Thomasii collectione desiderantur* in *Nova patrum bibliotheca* (Rome 1852); H. A. Daniel *Thesaurus hymnologicus sive hymnorum canticorum sequentiarum . . . collectio amplissima* 5 vols. (Halle 1841; Leipsic 1844-46-55-56); Franz J. Mone *Lateinische Hymnen des Mittelalters* 3 vols. (Freiburg i. Br. 1853-5); A. S. Walpole *Early Latin Hymns* (Cambridge 1922). The largest and best of the older compilations are those of Daniel and Mone. The whole field is being covered by the *Analecta hymnica medii aevi*, ed. by Guido M. Dreves, Clemens Blume and H. M. Bannister (Leipsic 1886-). In this series vol. LI (1908) pt. II contains *Hymnodia Hiberno-Celtica saeculi V-IX*, ed. by C. Blume, in which are given good eds. of almost all early Hiberno-Latin hymns and versified prayers. For eds. of AB and LH see pp. 706-7, 716 *infra*. General commentaries, etc.: John Julian *A dictionary of hymnology* (London 1892; rev. ed. 1907). — "Kirchenlied" *Realencykl. f. prot. Theologie u. Kirche.* — Blume "Hymnody and hymnology" *Cath. Encycl.* — G. M. Dreves "Hymns (Latin Christian)" Hastings's *Encycl. of religion and ethics* VII (1915) 16-25. — E. Hull "Hymns (Irish Christian)" *ibid.* 25-8. — "Hymnes" *Dict. d'archéol. chrét. et de liturgie.* — Kayser *Beiträge zur Geschichte und*

Erklärung der ältesten Kirchenhymnen (Paderborn 1881-6). — Max Manitius *Geschichte der christlich-lateinischen Poesie bis zur Mitte des 8. Jahrhunderts* (Stuttgart 1891). — Chevalier *Poésie liturgique du moyen âge* (Paris, Lyons 1893). — G.M. Dreves *Die Kirche der Lateiner in ihren Liedern* (Kempten 1908). In 1897 Blume and Dreves began at Leipsic the publication of their *Hymnologische Beiträge*, to contain critical articles in hymnology. The general theories on versification of Wilhelm Meyer (aus Speyer) are presented in his *Gesammelte Abhandlungen zur mittellateinischen Rhythmik* (Berlin 1905), and his special studies of Hiberno-Latin verse in " Die Verskunst der Iren in rythmischen lateinischen Gedichten " *Nachrichten v. d. kgl. Gesellschaft d. Wissenschaften z. Göttingen* philol.-hist. Kl. 1916 pp. 605-44. LORICAE: E. Hull " The ancient hymn-charms of Ireland " *Folk-Lore* XXI iv (1910). — L. Gougaud " Étude sur les *loricae* celtiques et sur les prières qui s'en rapprochent " *Bull. d'ancienne litt. et d'archéol. chrétiennes* I (1911) 265-81, II (1912) 33-41, 101-27, gives a list, with bibliographies and commentary. [*Cf. RC* XXXIII (1912) 477-8.]

Irish Christianity, it has been reiterated several times, was an extension of the Christianity of western Europe, especially of Gaul and Britain, in the fourth and fifth centuries. To that Christianity Hebrew was the sacred language of the fore-running dispensation, and a great reverence for Hebrew, and perhaps some slight knowledge of it, passed into Ireland. But the home of Christianity, the centre of its power and its greatest activity, was the Hellenised East; Greek was the language of its Scriptures and of almost all its older literature; and Greek-speaking travellers and settlers had been the founders of, and perhaps still formed an important element in, the Church of the West. Greek must have come to Ireland with Christianity, and the freedom with which Greek words and phrases are used in the earliest Christian literature of the island evidences a practical familiarity with the language. Some Irishmen of the ninth century and later made a parade of their — often very slight — knowledge of Greek, but this note of affectation does not seem to touch the Hellenic elements of the oldest religious writings. The dominant language of the West, however, was Latin, and Latin of necessity became the prevailing language of the western Church and of its establishment in Ireland. In Ireland it had, in some small measure, a rival in the native language: the significance of the admission of Irish to ecclesiastical service has already been noticed.[281]

It is possible that there was, in fifth- and sixth-century Ireland, a certain number of people, Christians but not clerics, who, perhaps sprung from fugitives from the barbarian invasions of Gaul and Britain, preserved for a time the language and literary traditions of the Roman world. The *Hisperica Famina* may be a relic of their activities. But

[281] *Cf.* p. 1 *supra.*

the bulk of the early Christian literature is ecclesiastical in both content and origin. It consists of devotional prose and verse, especially hymns, and of hagiographic, didactic and exegetical compositions, also in prose and verse. The hymns, though falling far behind the great literature of continental Europe, have real worth and interest.

Although singing had formed part of Christian devotions apparently from the earliest times, the composition of hymns seems to date only from the fourth century. The first Latin hymn-writer of whom we hear was that Hilary, bishop of Poitiers, who has been mentioned as one of the dominant figures of the Gallic Church at the time of the beginnings of Christianity in Ireland. The only hymn of his preserved intact is that in praise of Christ which begins

> Hymnum dicat turba fratrum,
> hymnum cantus personet,
> Christo regi concinnantes
> laudes demus debitas.[282]

It may have been written for the " brethren " who had gathered around Hilary's friend and disciple, Martin, at Ligugé, close to Poitiers, but this is not a necessary interpretation. We can conjecture further that through the channel of Martin's monasteries it came to the monasteries of Ireland. Certain it is that it was highly regarded and extensively used in Ireland: it holds a place of honor in the Antiphonary of Bangor and the Liber Hymnorum, and there are several references in mediaeval Irish documents to its popularity and its virtues. This hymn seems to have been preserved only through Irish sources.[283] It is a fine example of early hymnography. The metre is the *versus popularis*, the trochaic tetrameter catalectic which enjoyed extraordinary popularity throughout the Latin world of the Roman Empire. Such was the metre of the song of Caesar's legionaries which Suetonius has recorded:

> " Caesar Gallias subegit,
> Nicomedes Caesarem,
> Ecce Caesar nunc triumphat
> qui subegit Gallias."

---

282 W. Meyer denied the authorship of Hilary of Poitiers. — *Nachrichten v. d. k. Gesellsch. d. Wissensch. z. Göttingen* philol.-hist. Kl. 1909 p. 423.

283 MSS: Turin Bibl. nazionale F. IV. 1 frag. 9 s VII. — AB s VII ff. 3–4ᵛ. — Gotha I 75 pt. I s VIII. — St. Gall Stiftsbibl. 2 s VIII. — Cambridge Univ. Lib. Ll. I. 10 (Bk. of Cerne: *cf.* no. 578) s VIII/IX ff. 84–5ᵛ. — St. Gall Stiftsbibl. 577 s IX/X. — LH (T) s XI ff. 6ᵛ–8. — LH (F) s XI pp. 20–2. — BN lat. 9488 s XI ff. 75–6. — Brussels Bibl. roy. 3132 (207–8) s XIII. Eds: Cassander *Hymni ecclesiastici* (Cologne 1556); also *Opera* (Paris 1616) 149, 186 [MS not now known]. — Daniel *Thesaurus hymnologicus* I (Halle 1841) 191 [Cassander's text; there are other secondary eds.]. — The eds. of AB, the Turin Liturgical Fragment (no. 569), the Bk. of Cerne and LH. — Blume *An. Hymn.* LI (1908) 264–71. — Walpole *Early Latin Hymns* (1922) 1–15. *Cf.* A. J. Mason " The first Latin Christian poet " *JTS* V (1904).

This type of verse, and probably this very hymn, had an important influence not only on Hiberno-Latin versification, but also on that in the Irish language.

The other chief popular measure of the Latin world was the iambic dimeter, which was used by the greatest of early hymn-writers, St. Ambrose of Milan, and by his imitators. In the Irish manuscripts there is one hymn, *Ignis creator igneus*,[284] written in this metre and in accordance with classical rules.

The classical metres, which were based on quantity — that is, they were formed by a fixed succession of long and short syllables — were always, at least among the Latins, confined to the learned in their appeal. With the break-up of the old civilisation in the fourth, fifth and sixth centuries this appeal declined and almost disappeared. Popular song, Latin and barbarian, was based on a succession of voice-stresses: it is said to be rhythmical instead of being quantitative. The best of the early hymns attained their popularity by the skill with which the long quantity and the heavy stress were made to agree in incidence. But as time went on quantity was abandoned and all religious poems designed for singing became purely rhythmical. The earliest continental writer to produce such poems is believed to be Auspicius, bishop of Toul, who died about 478.

The history of Latin poetry in Ireland is more obscure than on the Continent, but we have the evidence that there did arise a flourishing hymnody in the early Irish Church. This Hiberno-Latin versification has a character of its own, the nature of which has been investigated to some extent, especially by Wilhelm Meyer: quantity is ignored, but the different measures are constructed in imitation of quantitative metres; the fixed elements of each measure are the number of syllables in each line, or half-line, and the rhythmical cadence of the endings of line and half-line (as the lines are all short, the rhythm of these endings dominates that of the whole poem); rime, assonance and alliteration are important, but not essential, ornaments. The subject of the influence of native prosody on this Latin verse is not clear.[285] Meyer held that there was none: that not only the rhythmical measures but

---

[284] No. 89 (i).

[285] Prof. Thos. FitzHugh, of the University of Virginia, has published a series of " Bulletins of the School of Latin " of that university in which he advances a theory of the evolution of European verse in opposition to that commonly held. He denies that Hiberno-Latin versification was derived from classical models: its basis was the natural Latin rhythm, revived by Irish speakers using a similar rhythm. See especially Bulletin No. 9 *The Indoeuropean Superstress and the evolution of verse* (Charlottesville 1917), and No. 10 *The Old-Latin and Old-Irish Monuments of verse* (1919).

also rime, assonance, and even alliteration were derived from foreign models. There is no doubt, however, that all these received a remarkable development in the hands of Irish verse-makers. Blume is, in a degree, right in his assertion that the progress of rime was so constant that it may be taken as a criterion of date.

From writing hymns in Latin ecclesiastics turned to writing them in Irish. Here, too, the dating is doubtful, but the beginning of such composition cannot be later than the seventh century and may be as early as the sixth. It is probable that some kind of verse-material on Patrick was made use of by Tírechán and Muir-chú,[286] while Adamnán speaks [287] of the singing of Irish hymns in honor of Columba as though it were a well-established custom. To the work of these Latin-trained clerics who sought to give the people a devotional literature in their own tongue was due the first application of writing to the Irish language, and the beginning of the whole written Irish literature. The early compositions in Irish were of two kinds, those called *retoric*, prose in periods of irregular length, but balanced, rhythmical, and alliterative, a form which was, perhaps, derived from the Latin rhetoricians of western Gaul,[288] and poems in regular measures which imitated those of the Latin hymns.

Some of the texts usually designated hymns were probably intended to serve simply as versified prayers. Such were those litany-like prayers called *loricae*, " breast-plates," supplications for protection against evil, which had a remarkable vogue in mediaeval Ireland. In these strange pieces the ideas and the *formulae* of pagan incantations were converted to the use of Christian devotion. Some genuine hymns were in popular usage treated as *loricae* and equipped with magical properties in forestalling physical dangers.

In the present section will be noticed — with the exceptions to be mentioned — so much of the early Christian literature of Ireland as we have good reasons for believing was produced down to the time of Adamnán and his contemporaries, that is, to the beginning of the eighth century, and as has not, like the writings of Columbanus, been already catalogued. It is possible that considerable material not here included really belongs to this period. On the dating of many pieces nothing very positive can be said. The Irish manuscripts, with the exception of the Antiphonary of Bangor and some fragments, are of later date,

---

[286] *Cf.* pp. 331, 333 *infra.* [287] *Vita Columbae* I i.
[288] So KM *Learning in Ireland in the fifth century* (Dublin 1913) 13 *sqq.*

some of them far later. Also several continental and English manuscripts, notably the Book of Nunnaminster and the Book of Cerne, contain matter that appears to be of Irish origin and quite ancient, but in the present state of the evidence it seems better to leave consideration thereof to a later chapter, where a general review will be made of all the liturgical and devotional material.

Hagiography also will receive a separate treatment, and for it the very important hagiographical productions of the seventh century will be reserved.

84. The *Hisperica Famina*

(A-Text) Ampla pectoralem suscitat uernia cauernam . . . fabulosam exprimunaccole soriam. Hisperica: finiunt famina. AMHN.

MSS: Luxemburg 89 *s* IX [4 leaves formerly bound with other MSS; came from the monastery of Echternach]. — BN lat. 11411 ff. 99–100 [belonged to same original codex as Luxemburg 89]; ff. 101–2 *s* IX [believed to have belonged to the abbey of St. Victor at Paris at the beginning of the 16th century]. — Vat. Regin. lat. 81 *s* IX/X [once belonged to Paul Petau of Orleans; the only complete, or apparently complete, text]. Eds: Angelo Mai *Classici auctores ex codicibus vaticanis* V 479–500 [the Vatican text]. — Migne *PL* XC 1185 *sqq* [reprint]. — F. Mone *Die gallische Sprache* (Carlsruhe 1851) 76 [the Luxemburg fragment]; *Pub. de la sect. hist. de l'Institut de Luxembourg* XXIV (1869) 311 *sqq* [reprint, with facs.]. — John Rhŷs " The Luxembourg Folio " *RC* I (1872) 346–75 [corrections in *RC* XIII 248 *sqq*]. — J. M. Stowasser " Incerti auctoris Hisperica famina " *Dreizehnter Jahresbericht über das k. k. Franz-Josef-Gymnasium in Wien* (Vienna 1887) [Vatican text]. — HZ " Neue Fragmente von Hisperica famina " *Nachrichten d. k. Gesellschaft d. Wissensch. zu Göttingen* philol.-hist. Kl. 1895 Heft II 117–65 [identified the Luxemburg and Paris fragments as from the same MS]. — F. J. H. Jenkinson *The Hisperica Famina* (Cambridge 1908) [contains all the texts]. Comm: P. Geyer " Die Hisperica Famina " *Archiv für lateinische Lexicographie und Grammatik* II (1885) 255–66 [argues for Spain as the country of origin]. — J. M. Stowasser " Zu den Hisperica Famina " *ibid.* III (1886) 168–76. — RTh *ibid.* 546–8. — J. M. Stowasser "Das Luxemburger-Pergamen" *Wiener Studien* (*Zs. f. classische Philol.*) IX (1887) 116 *sqq*, 309–22. — H. Bradshaw *Collected Papers* (Cambridge 1889) 463, 468–9. — HZ *Nennius Vindicatus* (Berlin 1893) 291–336. — Robinson Ellis " Notes on MSS of Catullus and Hisperica Famina " *Hermathena* XII (1902) 22–4; " On the Hisperica Famina " *Journ. of Philol.* XXVIII (1903). — Roger *L'Enseignement* (1905) 238–56 [valuable]. — HZ *Sitzungsb. d. k. preuss. Akad. d. Wissensch.* 1910 LI 1119. — Manitius *Lat. Lit.* I (1911) 156–9. — W. Meyer *Nachrichten v. d. k. Gesellsch. d. Wissensch. zu Göttingen* 1916 p. 623.

In certain manuscripts of the ninth and tenth centuries are found fragments of a composition, or series of compositions, of curious Latinity, to which the title *Hisperica Famina* — " Western Sayings " — is given.

The most extensive of the four surviving versions [289] seems to be the modified copy of a very ancient, and possibly Irish, exemplar. All the manuscripts give indications suggesting an ultimate origin in Ireland or Britain. The Latin of these texts is so strange as to form practically a secret language, reminiscent of the cryptic *formulae* of Virgilius Maro. In fact, the *Hisperica Famina* must have been the product of a literary society dominated by fancies similar to those in which that Gallic grammarian delighted.[290] In form these texts consist of short rhythmical lines of simple structure, each line normally, though not invariably, constituting a clause or sentence. To the vocabulary, a thing *sui generis*, is chiefly due the obscurity of meaning. The less usual word is substituted for that in normal use, the familar word is given a meaning not elsewhere recognised. Other elements in this extraordinary vocabulary are: poetical words; words from late Lat;n or from the spoken language; words derived from ecclesiastical writings; words borrowed from Greek and Hebrew; a large number of words specially invented by attaching unusual suffixes to known Latin stems; [291] a few words of unknown origin.

In content the Hisperic writings seem to be made up of a series of composition exercises on various subjects, loosely strung together. Jenkinson gives the following summary of the principal text: " 1–48. Glorification of the rhetors or *sophiae arcatores* and their school, and of the speaker himself as a match for any of his contemporaries. 49–86. A would-be scholar, a grazier, who has mistaken his vocation, is recommended to go home to his family, where confusion reigns in his absence. 87–115. The superiority of the speaker's Latin is illustrated by similes. 116–132. The connexion of this passage with what precedes is not clear. It describes the faults which writers of Latin are liable to commit. 133–357. A day, from sunrise to sunset, and its occupations are described. (133–177 the awakening of nature, 178–189 of the rural population, 190–221 of the school: 222–302 midday; a walk and a meal, provided by *possessores*, who have to be addressed in Irish, about which there is some difficulty as the scholars may only talk Latin: [292] 303–357 sunset; another meal, apparently provided by inhabitants of the town; then the scholars turn in, some to sleep, and others to sit up.)" Here follow a number of short sections on various subjects: 358–380 de caelo: 381–425 de mari: 426–451 de igne: 452–476 de campo (*or* de

---

[289] Jenkinson distinguishes these as A, the text of the Vat. MS; B, that of the Echternach MS; C, represented only by a series of glossed words in this MS; and D, the text of the St. Victor codex.

[290] There is, however, no trace of the actual use of any of Maro's *formulae*. The only works which offer indications of a possible direct influence on the Hisperic compositions are the *Nuptiae* of Martianus Capella and *Hermeneumata* of Pseudo-Dositheus.

[291] As -*men* for nouns and -*eus* for adjectives.

[292] Non (nam) ausonica me subligat catena
Ob hoc scottigenum haud cripitundo eulogium. Ll. 273–4.

The B, or Echternach, text, reads:

Nam strictus romani tenoris me septricat nexus
Nec scotigenum aperto forcipe pompo seriem. Ll. 67–8.

terra): 477–496 de uento: 497–512 de plurimis (the point of this is not clear . . .): 513–530 de taberna (apparently a book-chest): 531–546 de tabula (a tablet): 547–560 de oratorio: 561–570 de oratione [the text of a prayer, of unusual perspicuity]: 571–612 de gesta re [an essay in narration: the story of a hunt, a meal, and an encounter with robbers].[293]

There are several other documents, all known or believed to have been composed in the British Isles, which in style and vocabulary show, or seem to show, relationship with the *Hisperica Famina*. Most closely related are the *Lorica* of Gildas (or Laidcend),[294] the *Rubisca*,[295] and the St. Omer Hymn;[296] of more remote association the *De excidio Britanniae* of Gildas;[297] *Altus Prosator* ascribed to Columba;[298] some of the writings of Columbanus;[299] the metrical *De laude virginum* and especially the *Epistola ad Eahfridum* of Aldhelm;[300] the *Lorica* of Leyden;[301] the Cambridge Juvencus;[302] and the work of Lios monocus, a British writer of the ninth century.[303] This evidence, with that of the manuscripts, points to Ireland or Britain as the place of composition of the *Hisperica Famina*. The internal evidence is strongly in favor of Ireland: the scene is laid in a land where the inhabitants speak Irish.[304] Of scholars who have considered the question, Mai, Bradshaw, Stowasser and Jenkinson declare for an Irish origin. Zimmer in his earlier works advocated a location in south-western Britain, influenced in part, it would seem, by a misinterpretation of the textual reference to the Irish language. But in his last pronouncement on the subject, Zimmer declared the *Hisperica Famina* to be the production of some of those fugitive *littérateurs* from Gaul who had found in Ireland a place of refuge from the barbarian invasions.

It seems probable that there arose in Ireland in the fifth and sixth centuries a literary society which perpetuated for a time the Latin and Greek learning of Gaul in the last years of the Roman Empire, and that the Hisperic texts represent one of the lines of activity of that society. They may be the oldest writings of Irish provenance extant, with the exception of the compositions of Patricius. They appear to be of Christian origin, but are so secular in tone that they should not be ascribed to those monastic institutions which were introduced into Ireland in the fourth or fifth century, and in the sixth achieved such an extraordinary development. With more probability may they be assigned to that society of letters, whatever it was, which produced the rhetoricians who scorned the rustic speech of Patricius.[305] We can understand how such a society, no longer reinforced from Gaul, Spain,

---

[293] In this section only does the B Text differ entirely from that of the Vatican. B gives an account of a sea voyage.

[294] No. 100.   [295] No. 85.   [296] No. 86.   [297] No. 23.   [298] No. 91 (i).

[299] Pp. 190 *sqq.*   [300] No. 62.   [301] P. 272.   [302] No. 530.

[303] *Cf.* Manitius *Lat. Lit.* I 600–1. Ed. in *MGH Poet. lat. aevi Carol.* IV i (1899) 276–95.

[304] *Cf.* also, of the evening meal obtained in the town:

> Farriosas sennosis motibus corrosimus crustellas
> Quibus lita scottigeni pululauit conditura olei. A 298–9.

Perhaps part of southern Wales was Goidelic-speaking in the fifth and sixth centuries.

[305] *Cf.* p. 167 *supra.*

or Britain, would disappear in the Ireland of the sixth and seventh centuries, leaving only indirect traces of its influence in the religious writings of the monastic churches and in the vernacular literature of the schools of the *filid*.

85. The *Rubisca*

[Introductory quatrain] Parce domine digna narranti . . . . [Text] Amica aue habilis bonus . . . misero mihi domine parce. In all, 96 ll.

MS: Cambridge Univ. Lib. Gg. V. 35 *s* XI [by an English scribe: it was at Canterbury in the 13th cent.]. ED: F. J. H. Jenkinson *The Hisperica Famina* (Cambridge 1908) pp. xxiii, 55–9. *Cf.* Manitius *Lat. Lit.* 160.

This is an alphabetical religious poem, divided into riming quatrains. Jenkinson says: " It is presumably of Irish origin, and, though obscure of diction, metrically excellent. Obscure it undoubtedly is, owing partly to the extraordinary way in which the words are shaken into their places to suit the metre." It seems to be related to the Hisperic compositions, and contains, besides many curious and unusual Latin terms, several Greek and a few Hebrew words. The author's name appears to be represented as Olimbrianus.[306]

86. The St. Omer Hymn

Adelphus adelpha meter . . . pro redemptione antrophon. 66 ll.

MSS: St. Omer 666 *s* X [from the monastery of St. Bertin, and believed to have been listed in a 12th cent. catalogue as "Iuvenci libri III "]: G. Becker *Catalogi bibliothecarum antiqui* (Bonn 1885) no. 77: 132–4]. — Cambridge Univ. Lib. Gg. V. 35 *s* XI [*cf.* no. 85]. EDS: Bethmann *Zs. f. deutsches Alterthum* V 206. — J. M. Stowasser " De quarto quodam Scoticae latinitatis specimine " *Fünfzehnter Jahresbericht über das k. k. Franz-Josef-Gymnasium* (Vienna 1889). — RTh *RC* XI 86. — F. J. H. Jenkinson *The Hisperica Famina* (Cambridge 1908) pp. xxiii *sq*, 61–4. COMM: HZ *Nennius Vindicatus* (Berlin 1893) 309–11. — Manitius *Lat. Lit.* I 160.

This devotional composition is an alphabetical poem in riming triplets, with lines of seven or eight syllables. Its vocabulary is a mixture of Greek written in Roman characters, and of Hisperic and classical Latin words. It seems to be related to the *Rubisca*, which it immediately follows in the Cambridge manuscript. Some Breton or British glosses appear in the St. Omer copy. The text was already much corrupted before being written in either codex.

87. Hymn of Secundinus in honor of Patricius

Audite, omnes amantes Deum, sancta merita. . . . Cum apostolis regnabit sanctus super Israhel. 23 double quatrains.

MSS: AB *s* VII ff. 13ᵛ–5ᵛ. — LH (T) *s* XI ff. 1–2ᵛ. — LH (F) *s* XI pp. 12–4. — LBr *s* XIV p. 238 (of facs.). EDS: Colgan *Tr. Thaum.* (1647) 210. — Ware *S. Patricio*

[306] L. 78.

adscripta opuscula (London 1656) 146–50. — Muratori *Anecdota Ambrosiana* IV (Padua 1713) 127–59; *Opera omnia* XI iii (Arezzo 1770). — Andreas Gallandius *Bibl. vet. patrum* X 183 [Ware's text]. — J. L. Villanueva *S. Patricii . . . opuscula* (Dublin 1835) App. ii 307 *sqq.* — Migne *PL* LIII 837–40 [from Ware], LXXII 590–2 [from Muratori]. — Daniel *Thesaurus hymnologicus* IV (Leipsic 1855) 91 [from Muratori]. — *LH* ¹ I (1855) 7–53 [with text and trans. of LBr introd.]. — H&S II ii (1878) 324–7 [from *LH* ¹]. — O'Laverty *Historical account of the diocese of Down and Connor* II (Dublin 1884) 120, append. pp. xx–xxii [with trans.]. — *Vit. Trip.* (1887) I pp. cix *sq*, II 382–401, 669 [with text and trans. of LH (F) and LBr introd.]. — *AB* I (1893) [facs.], II (1895) 14–16, 48–55 [excellent ed. of oldest text]. — *LH* ² (1898) I 2–13, II 3–7, 99–106. — Blume *An. Hymn.* LI (1908) 340–6 [good ed.]. — G. F. Hamilton (of Moylough, co. Galway) (1918) [with trans.]. TRANS: Graves *Catholic Layman* II liv (Dublin, Dec. 1853) 134 *sqq.* — Olden *Epistles and hymn of St. Patrick* (London 1889) [reprint of preceding]. — Atkinson *Celtic Review* II vii (Jan. 1906) 242–5. COMM: Manitius *Geschichte der christlich-lateinischen Poesie bis zur Mitte des acht Jahrhunderts* (Stuttgart 1891) 221, 238–40. — Burkitt *JTS* III (1902) 95. — Bury *St. Patrick* (1905) 246–7. — A. Anscombe " The Longobardic origin of St. Sechnall " *Ériu* IV 74–90. — S. Czarnowski *Le Culte des héros — St. Patrick* (Paris 1919) 30–1.

The earliest copy of this hymn is that of the Antiphonary of Bangor (A.D. 680 x 691), written when it was already of considerable antiquity. The title is " Ymnum sancti patrici magister [307] scotorum "; and " the hymn of St. Patrick " seems to have been the name by which it was generally known in the early Irish Church. It was, no doubt, the " hymn composed concerning thee " mention of which Muir-chú,[308] writing about 670x700, puts into the mouth of the angel Victor, and also was " his hymn," the continual singing of which, according to a note in the Book of Armagh,[309] was one of Patrick's four-fold honors.[310]

St. Secundinus, or Sechnall, is said to be the author. The earliest statement seems to be in the *Félire* of Oengus, of about A.D. 800: " A stream of wisdom with splendour, Sechnall diadem of our lords, has chanted a melody — noble profit! — a praise of Patrick of Armagh."[311] There is a fantastic story of the circumstances in which the hymn was composed, to be found in the Tripartite Life of Patrick and in the prefaces attached to the Franciscan *Liber Hymnorum* and *Lebar Breac* copies.

---

[307] A scribal slip.

[308] LA 8. Some passages in Muir-chú, and in later developments of the Patrick legend, seem to have been elaborated from simple statements or phrases in the hymn: *cf. AB* II 50; *LH* ² II 101, 105.

[309] LA 16.

[310] The last three stanzas form part of a liturgical office inscribed in the Bk. of Mulling (*cf.* no. 562) about the end of the eighth or beginning of the ninth century.

[311] Nov. 27. WS trans.

Secundinus, according to the annals, came to Ireland with Auxilius and Iserninus in 438 or 439, and died in 447. Tírechán names him among Patrick's bishops. He was honored as the founder of the church of Domnach-Sechnaill (Dunshaughlin) in Meath,[312] and at Armagh his name occurred in the diptychs immediately after that of Patrick.[313] It is probable that he was one of several missionaries from Gaul who came to Ireland in the fifth century.[314]

The hymn is alphabetical (*i.e.*, the stanzas begin with the successive letters of the alphabet). The measure resembles that of the *Hymnum dicat* of Hilary of Poitiers, from which it differs by being rhythmical instead of quantitative. Between the two lies the gap that separates classical from mediaeval verse-making. Although rime is absent and alliteration rare and perhaps fortuitous, the characteristic Hiberno-Latin rhythm seems too well developed for a date as early as 447 or 461. A fifth-century origin is not, however, impossible.

The contents are not biographical, nor even thaumaturgical,[315] but consist almost entirely of somewhat extravagant praises of Patricius because of his virtues and of his labors in preaching the Gospel. The present tense is used, as though the subject of the poem were still alive. Yet it is hardly probable that such a panegyric would be written of a living man.[316] The use of the present may be a dramatic expedient on the part of the author, such as is frequently met with in later Irish hagiographical poems. But this composition may well be both " the first hymn made in Ireland " [317] and the beginning of the Patrick Legend.

88. Hymn of St. Camelacus

Audite bonum exemplum. . . . Cum sancto Elizaro [Lazaro]. 24 ll.

MS: AB *s* VII f. 17ᵛ. EDS: The eds. of AB [*cf.* p. 706 *infra*]. — Moran *Essays* (1864) 326 [*cf.* p. 109 *supra*]. — Blume *An. Hymn.* LI (1908) 321.

Camelacus was one of the saints of the primitive Irish Church whose fame has been lost both to history and to legend. As " Camulacus " he is named by Tírechán in

---

[312] Máel-Sechlainn, euphonised from Máel-Sechnaill, became a favorite name with the southern Úi Néill, the principal family of Meath.

[313] *Cf.* H. J. Lawlor and R. I. Best " The ancient list of the coarbs of Patrick " *Proc. RIA* XXXV C ix (1919).

[314] Nechtan, Usaille (Auxilius) and Sechnall (Secundinus) all bear in Irish documents the clan name " moccu Baird." Such a name could hardly have been applied later than about A.D. 700, when the " moccu " formula was dropped. The later Irish explanation (it is applied to Sechnall in a quatrain ascribed to Eochaid úa Flannacáin, d. 1004) is that the people to whom it referred were the "Longo-Bardi," who first entered Italy in 568. The Irish cannot have had much association with them until Columbanus founded Bobbio in 612 (or thereabouts). According to the legend, Patrick's sister Lupait (sometimes the name is given as Darerca, and sometimes as Liamain) married Restitutus a Lombard, and their children included, with others, the three just mentioned. The story is much confused.

[315] If stanza 8 had been written in the later middle ages it would be interpreted as an allusion to the stigmata of the Lord; as it is, it probably is only a reminiscence of St. Paul *Gal.* vi 17. There are many such scriptural reminiscences.

[316] Czarnowski (p. 31 n. 2) argues that the designation of Patricius as " testis Domini fidelis " is evidence that he was no longer living.

[317] So the prefaces.

his list of Patrick's bishops;[318] and the same writer relates that Patrick came into Tethbe (part of Westmeath and Longford): " sending Camulacus Commiensium [319] into Mag Cuini he pointed out to him with his finger from the crest of Granard a place [to establish himself], namely, the church of Raithin." [320] Camelacus is not noticed in the earlier calendars, but in the Martyrology of Donegal we have under November 3 " Caomlach ó Raithin."

The hymn is in the same metre as *Audite omnes amantes*. With two exceptions the lines — instead of the stanzas — begin with the letters of the alphabet in regular succession. It is undoubtedly of Irish, and apparently of very early, composition — sixth or perhaps fifth century. The subject-matter is praise of the life and virtues of the saint, who has been called to his heavenly reward.

89. Early devotional hymns

(i) Ignis creator igneus . . . quaerat securis pennulis. 8 stanzas, followed by a 9th, a doxology: Gloria patri . . . in sempiterna saecula. (ii) Spiritus divinae lucis gloriae. . . . In una substantia, Respice in me, Domine. 10 stanzas of unequal length, each with refrain, Respice, etc. (iii) Sacratissimi martyres summi Dei. . . . Trinitati cum sanctis dicamus: Alleluia. 9 stanzas. (iv) Precamur patrem . . . miserere, Domine. 42 quatrains. (v) Sancti, venite . . . iudicare homines. 11 quatrains.

MSS: (i) AB *s* VII f. 11. — Turin Bibl. nazionale universitaria G. v. 38 *s* X *in.* [Bobbio MS]. (ii) Turin Bibl. naz. univ. F. iv. 1 *s* VII [Bobbio MS]. — AB f. 13. — BN lat. 9488 ff. 75–6 *s* XI [in Irish hand]. (iii) AB ff. 12ᵛ–3. (iv) AB ff. 4ᵛ–6ᵛ. (v) AB ff. 10ᵛ–1. EDS: (i–v) Eds. of AB [*cf.* p. 706 *infra*]. Also: (i) Daniel *Thesaurus hymnologicus* IV (1855) 77. — Blume *An. Hymn.* LI (1908) 296–7. — Walpole *Early Latin hymns* (1922) 346–9. *Cf.* Mercati *Studi e testi* XII (1904) 25; Wilhelm Meyer *Nachrichten v. d. kgl. Gesellsch. d. Wissensch. z. Göttingen* philol.-hist. Kl. 1916 p. 625. (ii) W. Meyer *op. cit.* philol.-hist. Kl. 1903 p. 196 [Turin text]. — Bannister *JTS* IX (1908) 425 [variants of Paris text]. (iii) Daniel *loc. cit.* 88 [from Muratori]. — Blume *loc. cit.* 313–4. (iv) Daniel *loc. cit.* 31 [from Muratori]. — Blume *loc. cit.* 271–5. (v) Daniel *op. cit.* I 193, IV 109. — *LH* ¹ 43–4. — Moran *Essays* (1864) 165. — E. H. Bickersteth *Hymnal Companion* revised ed. (London 1880) no. 383. — J. M. Neale *Hymns ancient and modern* no. 313; new ed. (1904) no. 269; revised ed. (1909). — Blume *loc. cit.* 298–9. — Walpole *op. cit.* 344–6. TRANS: (v) J. O'Laverty *Historical account of the diocese of Down and Connor* II (Dublin 1884) 117, App. p. xvi n. [the former a prose trans., the latter metrical, by Denis Florence McCarthy; McCarthy's trans. is also in Gaffney *The ancient Irish Church*, and MacIlwaine *Lyra Hibernica sacra*]. — Atkinson *Celtic Review* V no. 18 (Oct. 15, 1908) 111–2 [metrical].

These anonymous hymns are of early date — fifth or sixth, certainly not later than the seventh, century — and probably of Irish origin. They are found in the seventh-century Antiphonary of Bangor, and their other manuscript tradition seems to be Irish.

[318] LA 9ᵛ.
[319] This epithet occurs in the hymn with the form " cumiensis." Its significance has not been determined.
[320] LA 11. Rathan, in Offalley, became later the church of St. Mo-Chuta. *Cf.* no. 234.

(i) *Ignis creator igneus* has, in the Antiphonary of Bangor, the title " Hymn when the candle is blessed ": the allusion appears to be to the blessing of the paschal candle on Easter eve. The custom of a paschal fire (though perhaps not that of the paschal candle) seems to have been of Irish, or British, origin, and to have been spread over Europe by the Irish and English missionaries.[321] This hymn may also have been used at the *lucernarium*, the lighting of the candles at the evening office known later as vespers. The metre is the classical iambic dimeter, quantitative, not rhythmical, for which reason Wilhelm Meyer asserted that it was not of Irish origin. It is at least possible, however, that there were clerics in Ireland as well as on the Continent in the fifth or sixth century who could write simple classical verse. A considerable antiquity is indicated by both form and language: although alliteration is used with some skill, there is no rime.

(ii) *Spiritus divinae lucis* is a rhythmical prose adaptation of the language of the creeds. At Bangor, and perhaps throughout Ireland, it was chanted at matins on Sunday.

(iii) *Sacratissimi martyres* is an eulogy of the martyrs in the form of a prayer to Christ, and, according to the Antiphonary of Bangor, was sung " on the festival of martyrs or on Saturday at matins." Because the early Irish Church had no martyrs, editors have thought that this hymn was an importation from Gaul or Spain. This is possible, but it may be noted that the expressions are general in character, without anything suggesting special local application, and that the cult of the martyrs seems to have flourished in the primitive Church in Ireland, which was only an extension of West Gallic and British Christendom. The verse-form of the piece is unique: it is quite different from all other examples of Hiberno-Latin versification. The lines are not broken into half-lines, and there is irregularity in the number of syllables in each line but regularity in the recurrence of the accent. Wilhelm Meyer has shown that it was written probably in imitation of some Greek hymn.[322]

(iv) *Precamur patrem* is a long hymn which Blume thinks to have been formed from the union of at least three distinct compositions. It is a prayer to God, with references to the history of the Pentateuch and of the Gospel. The rubric of the Antiphonary of Bangor gives the title "Hymn of the Apostles, as some say," doubtless indicating a tradition that it was of apostolic authorship. It is a curious example of versification: the rime is occasional and irregular.[323] It is probably of early origin, not later than the sixth century; some commentators have considered it to be an adaptation from a Greek original.[324]

(v) *Sancti venite* is, perhaps, the best known of the early Irish hymns. It is a communion hymn, noteworthy for the unequivocal character of its eucharistic doctrine, and for its — to barbarian ears — grace and vigor. The rubric of the Antiphonary of Bangor designates it " Hymn when the priests (*sacerdotes*) communicate "; the *Lebor Breac* preface to *Audite omnes amantes* (no. 87) says that it was sung by angels at the church of Sechnall when Patrick visited him, " wherefore from that time forward this hymn is sung in Ireland when one goes to Christ's Body."[325] It is in the same metre as *Precamur patrem*, and seems undoubtedly to be of Irish origin.

[321] L. Duchesne *Origines du culte chrétien* 5th ed. (Paris 1920) 263 *sqq.*
[322] *Op. cit.* philol.-hist. Kl. 1916 pp. 612–6.   [323] *Cf.* W. Meyer, *loc. cit.* 621–2.
[324] *Cf.* Julian *Dict. of Hymnology* 642.   [325] *Vit. Trip.* II 396–7.

90. Hymn of Mugint

Parce, Domine, parce populo tuo . . . redime nos propter nomen tuum.

MSS: LH (T) f. 4. — LH (F) p. 19. EDS: *LH* ¹ I (1855) 94–120. — *LH* ² (1898) I 22–4, II 11, 112–13.

The so-called Hymn of St. Mugint is a prayer in rhythmical prose, an interesting imitation of the penitential psalms. It is a supplication to the Lord to spare His people and His *civitas* — probably " monastery " — from threatening dangers, and has the tone of having been composed for a special occasion. What that was we do not know, and the *Liber Hymnorum* preface is of no help. It would seem that all that was known of Mugint was a legend of his attempt to kill Finnian of Mag-Bile at Candida Casa, or Whitherne, monastery, an attempt which recoiled on his own head.[326] The writer of the preface made a fatuous attempt to link the composition of the "hymn" with this legend. The legend, however, has some importance, especially as embodying a tradition of early Irish associations with Whitherne.[327]

91. Hymns attributed to Colum-cille

(i) Altus prosator, uetustus. . . . A saeculis in saecula. 23 stanzas, 139 ll. (ii) In te Christe credentium. . . . Deus in adiutorium. . . . Recto vado itinere. 8 quatrains, of which the first is, probably, a refrain. Christus lorica militum . . . Christus redemptor gentium. . . . In sempiterna saecula. A couplet, perhaps refrain, and 6 quatrains. (iii) Noli pater indulgere. . . . Auri ponitur gemma. 6 stanzas, irregular.

MSS: (i) LH (T) [stanzas 14–21, ll. 80–127, missing through loss of a leaf]. — LH (F) pp. 2–8. — LBr *s* XIV p. 237 [stanzas A–H only. These 3 MSS have prefaces in Irish, the two LH practically identical; prose arguments to each stanza; and glosses. LH (T) and LBr are heavily glossed.] — Milan Bibl. Ambrosiana M. 32 sup. *s* IX [Bobbio MS]. — Montpellier School of Medicine 218 *s* IX. — Orleans Bibl. de la ville 169 (146) *s* IX/X pp. 300–8 [from Fleury]. — Munich Staatsbibl. lat. 18665 *s* X/XI ff. 229–39 [formerly Tegernsee 665. These 4 MSS have texts of a similar type, neither preface nor arguments, and only a few glosses: they attach the poem to the *Vita contemplativa* ascribed, incorrectly, to Prosper of Aquitaine.] (ii) LH (T) f. 13. — LH (F) p. 9. (iii) LH (T) ff. 13ᵛ–4. — LH (F) p. 10. Also in O'Donnell's Life of Colum-cille (no. 221). EDS: (i) Colgan *Tr. Thaum.* (1647) 473. — *LH* ¹ pt. II (1869) 201–51. — Reifferscheid *Sitzungsb. d. philos.-hist. Kl. d. Wiener Akad.* LXVII 544–9 (*Bibl. patr. lat. ital.* II 80) [catalogue of Ambrosian Library: text of Milan MS]. — A. Boucherie " Hymne abécédaire contre les antitrinitaires " *Rev. des langues romaines* VII (1875) 12–26 [Montpellier text, Fr. trans.; *cf. ibid.* 3rd ser. VIII (1882) 293]. — Ch. Cuissard *RC* V (1881) 205–12, 396, 507 [Orleans text]. — John, Marquess of Bute *The Altus of St. Columba edited with a prose paraphrase and notes* (1882) [based on *LH* ¹ ed.]. — Gilbert *Facs. Nat. MSS. Ire.* IV (1884) App. xxi [LH (F)]. — *LH* ² (1898) I 62–83, II pp. xxvi–xxix, 23-6, 140–69. — Blume *An. Hymn.* LI (1908) 275–83. TRANS: Dowden *The Celtic Church in Scotland* (S. P. C. K.: London 1894) [free metrical rendering by the Rev. A. Mitchell]. — MacGregor *St. Columba* (1897). *Cf.* Burkitt *JTS* III (1902) 95; Roger *L'Enseignement* (1905) 230, 254–5; *ZCP* XII iii

[326] The same legend appears in Lives of Frigidianus (identified with Finnian) in Colgan *AA. SS.* 633 *sqq.* *Cf.* pp. 184, 391.

[327] *Cf.* p. 160 *supra.*

(1918) 434. (ii) Colgan *op. cit.* 475. — *LH* ¹ pt. II 252–8. — *LH* ² I 84–6, II pp. xxiii *sq*, 27, 169–71. — Blume *loc. cit.* 283–6. TRANS: Mitchell *Scottish Standard Bearer* June 1897; MacGregor *op. cit.* (iii) Colgan *op. cit.* 397, 476. — *LH* ¹ II 259–63. — *LH* ² I 87–9, II pp. xxiv *sq*, 28, 171–2. — Blume *loc. cit.* 286–8. — Henebry's ed. of O'Donnell's Life of Colum-cille *ZCP* IV (1903) 292–3, and the ed. by O'Kelleher and Schoepperle (Urbana, Ill. 1918) 66. TRANS: MacGregor *op. cit.*

Of literary compositions by the great Columba of Iona (d. 597) his biographer, Adamnán,[328] makes no mention, but many poems, both in Latin and in Irish — the great majority undoubtedly apocryphal — have been ascribed to him by legend of more or less antiquity.[329] For his authorship of the Latin hymn commonly designated the *Altus* there is an ancient tradition,[330] and with that hymn are linked, in the Irish manuscripts, two others, *In te Christe credentium* and *Noli Pater.* All three have antiphons and other additions indicating liturgical use.

(i) *Altus prosator* is a kind of early "Paradise Lost." The subject is the "great argument" of Christian cosmogony: the nature of the Godhead; the creation of the orders of angels; the fall of Lucifer; the creation of the universe; the seduction of Adam and Eve and second fall of the devil;[331] the nature of the world, and of the infernal regions; the giving of the Law to Moses; the terrors of the Judgment Day (the hymn is not unworthy as a precursor of the great *Dies Irae*); the fate of the wicked and of the good. Curiously, there are only two slight references to the Redemption, and there is some basis for the alleged criticism of Pope Gregory the Great that the poem's praise of the Trinity is indirect rather than direct; but in general the theology is that of the early middle ages, in a setting of mediaeval lore of the supernatural world, here ultimately derived, in the main, from the *Celestial Hierarchy* of Pseudo-Dionysius [332] and the Jewish *apocryphon* known as the *Book of Henoch.* It is an alphabetical poem, in rhythmical metre with end-rimes but without regard to quantity.[333] The style, though rude and "barbarian," apparently "Celtic," is vigorous, and the grammar is not incorrect. There are reminiscences of the Bible, the *apocrypha*, and the *Hisperica Famina:* the version of Scripture familiar to the author was some form of the Old Latin. On this evidence we may, with reasonable probability, regard the *Altus* as a genuine production of the saint of Iona.[334] The Irish prefaces, recording

---

[328] No. 214.

[329] *Cf.* no. 220.

[330] Found in the prefaces to the hymn, and in the later Lives of the saint. There are not many references to the *Altus* elsewhere: the most important are in the legend of Máel-Suthain úa Cerbhaill (no. 620) and the *Mesca Coluim-cille* (no. 220 xliv), both probably of late date.

[331] The glossators explain that Satan fell first from heaven to earth, and, after the tempting of man, from earth to hell.

[332] *Cf.* no. 386.

[333] The stanzas are of 6 (or 12) lines each, except the first, which has 7 (or 14). It looks as though this may have been altered in the interest of orthodoxy. Hraban Maur knew the stanza as we have it.

[334] The continental MSS, which evidently depend on an ultimate common exemplar, attach the hymn to a treatise ascribed to Prosper of Aquitaine (no. 28), but believed by some to be by Julianus Pomerius (*c* A.D. 500). It is certain that neither Prosper nor Pomerius was the author. — A large part of the hymn, from a text of this continental type, was incorporated by Hraban Maur (*cf.* pp. 549–50) into his poem *De fide catholica. Cf.* Migne *PL* CXII 1610; E. Dümmler *MGH Poetae latini* II (1884) 197.

opinions of the tenth or eleventh century, give several accounts of the occasion of composition. One statement is that the hymn was sent to " Gregory " in return for his gifts, a cross called " the Great Gem " and the " Hymns of the Week." [335]

(ii) *In te Christe credentium* is a jingling composition, having no resemblance either in form or in substance to the *Altus*. Prefaces to both represent it as composed by Columba in response to Pope Gregory's criticism of that hymn. It is probably of Irish origin, but of a date much later than Columba's. It falls into two parts, and Blume seems to be right in printing these as two poems, with associated antiphons and responses.

(iii) *Noli Pater* also is a composite production: the first part may be as old as the time of Colum-cille and, perhaps, his composition; the second (*Benedictus in saecula*) [336] seems to be a later poem, written in honor of St. John the Baptist, which became associated with the first because both were regarded as *loricae* against fire and lightning; and the last two parts are antiphons.

92. Hymns of the Monastery of Bangor

(i) [Introductory stanza] Recordemur iustitiae . . . [Refrain] Quem Deus ad aetherea . . . Audite πάντες τὰ ἔργα . . . Reddetur merces condigne. 23 stanzas. (ii) Benchuir bona regula . . . Sine fine mansura. 10 quatrains. (iii) Sancta sanctorum opera . . . Regnantem in saecula. 6 stanzas. [Refrain] Quos convocavit Dominus . . .

MS: AB ff. 15^v-17^v (i), 30 (ii), 36^v (iii). EDS: The eds. of AB. Also: (i) Moran *Essays* (1864) 323-5. — Blume *An. Hymn.* LI (1908) 321-4. (ii) Moran *op. cit.* 166. — Blume *op. cit.* 356-7. TRANS: Reeves *UJA* I 175. — J. O'Laverty *Historical account of the diocese of Down and Connor* II (Dublin 1884) 44. (iii) Moran *op. cit.* 326. — *Thes. Pal.* II (1903) 282. — Blume *op. cit.* 357-8. TRANS: Reeves *loc. cit.* — O'Laverty *op. cit.* 45.

These three hymns are found only in the ancient manuscript of the monastery of Bend-chor, or Bangor, on Belfast Loch, a manuscript now known as the Antiphonary of Bangor. The first is an impersonal panegyric of an anonymous saint, whom the rubric and refrain identify as Comgall, founder of Bangor; the second an exaltation of Bangor and its monastic rule; and the third a commemoration of the early abbots of that church. It is probable that they were written at Bangor — although the first may have been adopted from elsewhere — and in the period between 602, when Comgall died, and 691, date of death of the abbot Cronán, who was living when the third hymn was composed. They have certain similarities in versification, especially the trick of ending successive lines with the same letter or letters. Apparently they belong to the time when end-rime was being developed in Hiberno-Latin verse.

---

[335] *Cf.* p. 715 *infra.*

[336] This and the following antiphon appear to be part of the liturgical office in the Book of Mulling (no. 562).

(i) *Audite πάντες τὰ ἔργα* follows, in the Antiphonary of Bangor, immediately on the hymn of Secundinus, *Audite omnes amantes*, which it resembles in form and in the colorless character of its eulogy. The stanzas begin with the successive letters of the alphabet, and within each stanza there is a more or less elaborate scheme of agreement in initial and final letters. As a Latin composition it is quite inferior to *Audite omnes amantes*.

(ii) *Benchuir bona regula* gives no concrete historical information regarding the monastery (here designated by the Irish word *munther*, "family") of Bangor. It has, however, peculiar interest as an example of versification: the rime, the alliteration, and the distribution of the rhythmical accent are all curious and noteworthy.[337]

(iii) *Sancta sanctorum opera*, which has as rubrical title [*In*] *memoriam abbatum nostrorum*, is another *tour-de-force* of Hiberno-Latin versification. It embodies, however, some historical information, for it professes to give the names of the first fifteen abbots of Bangor. These were, it is probable, taken from the diptychs read in the mass at Bangor, an hypothesis which may account for the presence of the third name, Aedeus, which is otherwise unknown as that of an abbot of Bangor.[338] The last abbot mentioned is Cronán, who ruled from 680 to 691. In referring to him the tense changes to the present, indicating that the poem was composed within this period. We thus get one of the few fairly definite dates in early Irish literary history.

93. Hymn of Cuimíne *fota* in honor of the Apostles

Celebra Iuda . . . spiritu cum [h]agio. 22 stanzas.

MSS: LH (T) ff. 3–4. — LH (F) pp. 17–8. EDS: *LH* [1] I (1855) 71–93. — *LH* [2] (1898) I 16–21, II pp. xix–xxi, 9–10, 108–12. — Blume *An. Hymn.* LI (1908) 308–11.

The saints named in this eulogy of the "apostles" are Peter, Paul, Andrew, James, John, Philip, Bartholomew, Thomas, Matthew, James, Thaddeus, Simon, Mathias, Mark, Luke, Patrick, Stephen. The stanza devoted to Patrick is probably an interpolation, and a scholium suggests that such also may be those to Mark and Luke. The hymn is mentioned in the liturgical office of the ninth century (?) in the Book of Mulling.[339] In structure, rime, alliteration and rhythm it is of Irish character, being of the same form as *Precamur patrem*. Its "Irish" characteristics are so well developed that it can hardly be of earlier date than the seventh century. There is, therefore, nothing to cast doubt on the tradition, given in the preface, which ascribes the authorship to Cuimíne *fota*, "the tall" (591 or 592–662). Cummain, Cummene, or Cuimíne *fota* was one of the successors of Brendan of Clonfert. There is no Life of him, but he is prominent in legend.[340] A story of his incestuous origin is given in the preface,[341] and elsewhere.[342]

---

[337] *Cf.* W. Meyer *Nachrichten v. d. kgl. Gesellsch. d. Wissensch. z. Göttingen* philol.-hist. Kl. 1916 pp. 611–2.

[338] *Cf.* p. 697 *infra*; also Lawlor and Best *Proc. RIA* XXXV C (1919) 335–6. They identify Aedeus with Aedach mac Daill whose obit is given by AU in 608. More probably he was the "Aedán, anchorite of Bangor," who died in 610.

[339] *Cf.* no. 562.

[340] *Cf.* pp. 420–1.

[341] This contains several Irish verses.

[342] *Cf.* WS *Fél. Oeng.*[2] 242–3. Some of these stories may have had their origin in records coming

94. Hymns in honor of St. Peter

(i) Sanctus Petrus, apostolus . . . cantemus in perpetuum. 6 stanzas. (ii) Audite, fratres, famina . . . in angelorum editis. 23 stanzas. Refrain: Assint nobis sublimia Sancti Petri suffragia.

MSS: (i) Carlsruhe Landesbibl. Cod. Augiensis CXCV *s* IX *in* f. 47 [follows *Cantemus in omni die; cf.* pp. 269, 670 *infra*]. (ii) *Ibid.* Cod. Augiensis CCXXI *s* VIII *ex* f. 190 [precedes *In trinitate spes mea; cf.* pp. 269, 393]. EDS: (i) Mone *Lateinische Hymnen* III (Freiburg 1855) 74. — Moran *Essays* (1864) 86–7 [has trans.]. — Blume *An. Hymn.* LI (1908) 349. (ii) Mone *op. cit.* 68–70. — Moran *op. cit.* 81–5 [with trans.]. — Blume *op. cit.* 347–9.

Both these anonymous hymns in honor of St. Peter are undoubtedly of Irish origin and of fairly ancient date.

(i) *Sanctus Petrus apostolus* is a simple and somewhat pleasing poem in which rime and alliteration are used adventitiously. It has an appearance of antiquity, but the date Blume suggests, the first half of the sixth century, may be too early.

(ii) *Audite fratres famina* is an alphabetical poem showing that extensive use of rime and alliteration that characterises the developed Hiberno-Latin versification. It is evident, however, that the poet was not fully master of his instrument. There are many scribal errors in our text: apparently the eighth-century Frankish copyist could not fully decipher his Irish *Vorlage*. The hymn may be assigned to the eighth or, more probably, the seventh century.

95. Hymns in honor of Brigit

(i) Xristus in nostra insula . . ut sol in caeli culmine. 3 stanzas. (ii) Alta audite τὰ ἔργα . . . saecla in aula regia. 12 stanzas. (iii) Brigit bé bithmaith . . . ronsóira Brigit. 6 stanzas.

MSS: (i) Vat. Palat. lat. 482 *c* A.D. 1071 [from Trèves]. — LH (T) ff. 2ᵛ–3. — LH (F) p. 16. (ii) Basel Universitätsbibl. A. vii. 3 *s* IX [*cf.* pp. 557, 713]. (iii) LH (T) ff. 16–7ᵛ. — LH (F) pp. 38–9. — Bodl. Laud Misc. 615 *s* XV/XVI p. 113. — Bk. Lis. *s* XV f. 16ᵛ. EDS: (i) Colgan *Tr. Thaum.* (1647) 542 [at end of *Vita Tertia* of Brigit; *cf.* no. 151]. — *LH* ¹ I (1855) 54. — *LH* ² (1898) I 14–15, II pp. xxix *sq*, 8, 106–8. — Blume *An. Hymn.* LI (1908) 317–9. *Cf.* H. J. Lawlor *Chapters on the Book of Mulling* (Edinburgh 1897) 162–5. (ii) F. Mone *Lateinische Hymnen* III (1855) 241. — A. P. Forbes *Liber ecclesie beati Terrenani de Arbuthnott* (Burntisland 1864) p. xlii. — Blume *op. cit.* 319–20. (iii) WS *Goidilica* (Calcutta 1866), 2nd ed. *Goidelica* (London 1872) 133–5. — *IT* I (1880) 24–5. — Lis. *Lives* (1890) 51–2, 198–9, 332–4. — *LH* ² (1898) I 107–11, II pp. xxxiii *sq*, 37–9, 187–9. — *Thes. Pal.* II (1903) pp. xxxviii, 323–6. — T. FitzHugh *Old-Latin and Old-Irish monuments of verse* (Charlottesville, Va. 1919) 76–7. Trans. in all eds. except *IT* and FitzHugh. *Cf.* J. Pokorny *ZCP* IX (1913) 337–8.

These hymns are simple eulogies of the saint, having no biographical value.

down from a pagan social order the rules of consanguinity of which were incomprehensible and abhorrent to Christian minds. In an exogamous matrilinear society the marriage of father and daughter might be quite permissible.

(i) Three stanzas beginning with the last three letters of the alphabet, respectively. Another stanza, beginning *Audite virginis laudes*, accompanies them, but cannot belong to the same poem, for it is in a different metre. The three stanzas may be all that remain of an once complete alphabetical hymn, or they may constitute the entire hymn, such a composition arising from the common custom of reciting only the last three stanzas of long religious poems. The versification is Irish, and suggests a seventh or eighth-century date. The Irish preface makes three guesses at the authorship — Ninnid " of the Pure Hand," a legendary contemporary of the saint; Fíacc of Slébte; [343] and Ultán of Árd-mBrecáin (Ardbraccan in Meath).[344] Ultán, who died in 657, may have been the author, but it is probable that his name was used because of the tradition that he wrote a Life of Brigit.[345]

(ii) In the Irish psalter at Basel [346] there is entered, in a hand of the ninth or early tenth century, several texts which formed, perhaps, a liturgical office.[347] Following a hymn (*Cantemus in omni die*) and a collect in honor of Mary is the hymn *Alta audite* τὰ ἔργα, and immediately after it the entry "item χρs in nostra insola que uocatur." This last must refer to the hymn just considered, which the scribe, it is evident, regarded as well known. *Alta audite* is an alphabetical hymn: the full lines begin with the successive letters and end in *-ia* or *-ea*, in one case *-a*, while within the full line the first half-line always ends in *-a*. Such devices confirm the Irish authorship, which is probably fairly early.[348]

(iii) *Brigit bé* may be the oldest of the extant hymns in the Irish language. On linguistic grounds it can be assigned to the seventh century. The *Liber Hymnorum* preface (which has some value for the history of the legend of Brigit) makes five suggestions as to authorship: (1) Colum-cille; (2) Broccán *clóen;* [349] (3) three members of Brigit's community; (4) Brendan the Navigator; (5) Ultán of Árd-mBrecáin. If any consideration were to be paid these guesses, the claims of Broccán and Ultán would seem strongest; and the poem is now usually referred to as " Ultán's Hymn." It is an invocation and extravagant eulogy of Brigit, who is described as " my saint of Leinster-men," " one of the columns of the realm with Patrick the pre-eminent," " golden sparkling flame," " dazzling resplendent sun," " the branch with blossoms," and — carrying to extreme the well-known comparison with the Blessed Virgin — " the mother of Jesus." The versification is elaborate and skilful, and the hymn ranks high as an example of Irish poetic art.

96. Evening Hymn

In pace Christi dormiam . . . in sempiterno gaudio. 7 stanzas. LBr has another half-stanza, ending: . . . uocem Deum laudantium.

MSS: BM Harl. 7653 s VIII/IX f. 7 [*cf.* p. 718]. — LBr f. 148. Eds: *Vit. Trip.* I (1887) p. cxv. — *AB* II (1895) 86, 95. — Blume *An. Hymn.* LI (1908) 295-6.

This evening prayer in verse is markedly Irish both in versification — end rime and alliteration are abundantly, though not very artistically, used — and in matter.

---

[343] *Cf.* p. 340.   [344] *Cf.* pp. 325-9.
[345] *Cf.* pp. 357, 362.   [346] *Cf.* no. 364 (iv).   [347] *Cf.* p. 714.

[348] It may be noted that the hymn contains two references to Patricius, and is perhaps the earliest document to bring him and Brigit into association.

[349] *Cf.* no. 148.

Invocations are addressed to the seven patriarchs (whoever they may be), the angels, the apostles, the prophets and the martyrs, and by name to Enoch and Elias, John the Baptist, Patricius and " Ciricius." This last seems to be St. Cyriacus, one of the Diocletian martyrs. The presence of his name is one of many little traces of a strong cult of martyrs in the early Irish Church.[350]

97. Hymn of Colmán mac Mur-chon

In trinitate spes mea . . . in uno consilio. 11 stanzas, the last a version of the doxology.

MSS: Carlsruhe Landesbibl. Cod. Augiensis CCXXI s VIII ex ff. 190ᵛ-1 [cf. pp. 267, 393]. — LH (T) f. 8. — LH (F) p. 22. EDS: Mone Lateinische Hymnen I (1853) 450. — Daniel Thesaurus hymnologicus IV (1855) 105-6. — LH ¹ II (1869) 165-70. — Dreves An. Hymn. XIV (1893) 85-6. — LH ² (1898) I 43-5, II pp. xv-xvi, 19, 132-4. — Blume An. Hymn. LI (1908) 330-1. TRANS: D. F. MacCarthy in O'Laverty Historical account of the diocese of Down and Connor II (Dublin 1884) 18.

This invocation of the archangel Michael is a fine example of Hiberno-Latin versification, with rich trisyllabic rimes and frequent use of assonances, alliterations and harmonies. The basis of its form is that of Hilary's Hymnum dicat, but the treatment is entirely Irish. Dr. Bernard [351] identifies it with one of the items in the liturgical office [352] in the Book of Mulling, and with the " Michael's hymn " of the similar office in the eleventh-century " Second Vision of Adamnán."[353]

The identification of the author is of interest. The preface in the Liber Hymnorum tells a story of three sons of an otherwise unknown Mur-chú of Connacht,[354] a story which seems to be pure guesswork. The only Colmán mac Mur-chon mentioned in the annals was abbot of Magh-Bile (Moville, co. Down) and died in 736. Mur-chú or Muir-chú (" Sea-Hound ") is not a common name: the only known person of this designation who could be identified with the father of Abbot Colmán is the Muir-chú, protégé of Aed of Slébte, who wrote a Life of Patrick.[355]

The hymn seems to have passed into use on the Continent. There is a revised version which retains the form and to a large extent the ideas and the vocabulary, but changes the persons of the verbs from first singular to plural.[356]

98. Hymn of Cú-chuimne

Cantemus in omni die . . . litteris caelestibus. 13 quatrains.

MSS: Carlsruhe Landesbibl. Cod. Augiensis CCXXI s VIII f. 1ᵛ [cf. p. 267]; Cod. Augiensis CXCV s IX in f. 47 [cf. p. 669; this folio is a cover, not originally part of the codex, but of about the same date and in Irish script]. — Basel Universitätsbibl.

---

[350] Cf. AB II 91-2; Fél. Oeng.² 140, 150-1, 212-3.
[351] LH ² I p. xxiii.   [352] No. 562.   [353] No. 627.
[354] For a possible explanation of this localisation, see p. 332 n. 129 infra.
[355] Cf. pp. 331-4 infra.
[356] Unitas in trinitate . . . laus et iubilatio, 13 stanzas, the last a doxology. MSS: Vienna National Lib. 4089 A.D. 1460.— Salzburg St. Peter's b. VII. 10B, A.D. 1470.— Munich Staatsbibl. lat. 20020 A.D. 1470; 20001 A.D. 1476; 19824 A.D. 1490. Ed: Blume An. Hymn. LI (1908) 332-3.

A. vii. 3 *s* IX f. 2 [*cf.* pp. 557, 713]. — LH (T) f. 6. — LH (F) p. 30. Eds: Mone *Lateinische Hymnen* II (1855) 383–6. — Daniel *Thesaurus hymnologicus* IV (1855) 86–7. — A. P. Forbes *Liber ecclesie beati Terrenani de Arbuthnott* (Burntisland 1864) p. xli. — Moran *Essays* (1864) 225–7. — *LH* ¹ II (1869) 137–47. — *LH* ² (1898) I 32–4, II pp. xvi *sq*, 17, 123–5. — Blume *An. Hymn.* LI (1908) 305–7. Trans: *IER* I 204.

This is considered to be the finest example extant of Hiberno-Latin versification. It is of the same form as, and closely resembles, the Hymn of Colmán mac Mur-chon, but shows even greater technical skill. There is consistent use of Irish internal rime. The hymn was evidently written for singing, and testifies to the devotion to the Blessed Virgin Mary in the Irish Church of the eighth century. It is ascribed to Cú-chuimne (" Hound of Memory "?), who is, doubtless, identical with the " Cu-cuimne sapiens " whose obit is given by the Annals of Ulster under 747. This man, as has been seen,[357] was probably one of the compilers of the *Hibernensis* collection of canons, and a monk of Iona. Two ancient quatrains, in Irish, are attached to his name, and seem to contain all the information the writer of the preface in the *Liber Hymnorum* possessed. In the Annals of Ulster both are said to be by Cú-chuimne's nurse, in the *Liber Hymnorum* the first is ascribed to Adamnán, the second, as a reply, to Cú-chuimne. Their gist appears to be that, having abandoned his studies for a life of vice, he later repented and became a sage.[358]

99. Hymn of Oengus mac Tipraite

Martine, te deprecor . . . deprecare, Martine. 6 stanzas.

MSS: LH (T) ff. 8ᵛ–9. — LH (F) p. 23. Eds: *LH* ¹ II (1869) 171–6. — *LH* ² (1898) I 46–8, II pp. xvii–xix, 20, 134–5. — Blume *An. Hymn.* LI (1908) 328–9.

This somewhat obscure hymn is another noteworthy example of Hiberno-Latin verse as well as of early Irish devotion to Martin of Tours. The versification resembles that of *Benchuir bona regula*. It is attributed to Oengus mac Tipraite, who, according to the Annals of Ulster, was abbot of Clúain-fota [-Baitan-Aba] (Clonfad, bar. Farbill, 5½ miles s. e. of Mullingar), and died in 746. The *Liber Hymnorum* preface tells a story according to which he composed the poem on the occasion of a visitation of Adamnán in Ireland, a statement which suggests the year 692 or 697. The story is probably fictitious, designed to explain the magical virtues popularly ascribed to the hymn.

100. The *Lorica* of Gildas

Suffragare, trinitatis unitas . . . Laetus vehar regni refrigeria. 92 ll.

MSS: BM Harl. 2965 (Bk. of Nunnaminster) *s* VIII ff. 38–40. — Cambridge Univ. Lib. Ll. I. 10 (Bk. of Cerne) *s* IX *in.* ff. 43–4ᵛ. — Cologne Dombibl. 106 (*cf.* no. 572) *s* IX ff. 62 *sqq.* — Verona Chapter Lib. LXVIII (64) *s* X ff. 32 *sqq* [*cf.* Reifferscheid

---

[357] *Cf.* p. 249 *supra.*
[358] Perhaps because of this tradition, Cú-chuimne is not mentioned in the older martyrologies. In that of Gorman he is commemorated on Oct. 7.

Bibl. patr. Ital. I 10]. — BM Harl. 585 *s* X ff. 152 *sqq.* — LBr *s* XIV f. 111. — Vienna Nationalbibl. 11857 *s* XVI [in close agreement with Cologne MS; *cf.* Denis *Cat. codd. theol. Vindob.* I iii 2932, where some verses are published]. EDS: Mone *Lateinische Hymnen* I (1853) 367–70 [Cologne text; reprinted by Bartsch *Zs. f. roman. Philol.* II 213]. — Daniel *Thesaurus hymnologicus* IV (1855) 111, 364 [Mone's and the Vienna text]. — WS *Irish Glosses* (IAS: Dublin 1860) 133 *sqq* [LBr text]. — O. Cockayne *Lechdoms, Wortcunning and Starcraft of early England* (RS: London 1864) pp. lxviii, lxxiii–lxxv [Cerne text, with some variants]. — W. de Gray Birch *An ancient manuscript . . . formerly belonging to . . . Nunnaminster* (Hampshire Record Soc.: London, Winchester 1889) 90–5, 120–8. — HZ *Nennius vindicatus* (Berlin 1893) 299–311, 337–40 [Cologne text; *cf.* RTh *Zs. f. deut. Philologie* XXVIII 111–2]. — *LH* ² (1898) I 206–10, II 242–4. — H. Williams *Gildae De excidio Britanniae* (Hon. Soc. of Cymmrodorion: London 1899) 289–313 [with trans.]. — A. B. Kuypers *The Book of Cerne* (Cambridge 1902) 85–8. — Blume *An. Hymn.* LI (1908) 358–64. — F. J. H. Jenkinson *The Hisperica Famina* (Cambridge 1908) pp. xxii, 50–4. COMM: HZ *Nachrichten des k. Gesellschaft der Wissensch. zu Göttingen* 1895 Heft 2. — Roger *L'Enseignement* (1905) 239, 241, 250–5. — L. Gougaud " Le témoignage des manuscrits sur l'oeuvre du moine Lathcen" *RC* XXX (1909) 44. — Manitius *Lat. Lit.* I (1911) 159, 210. — Strecker *MGH Poetae latini* IV 618.

This metrical prayer or hymn is probably the oldest of those invocations to which the term *lorica*, "breast-plate," is applied. The idea was derived from various biblical texts, particularly *Ephes.* vi 11 and I *Thessal.* v 8: the actual word *lorica* is used twice in the present composition. The prayer falls into three parts: an invocation of the Trinity and of the heavenly powers for protection against dangers and enemies; an enumeration of the parts of the body that are to be safeguarded; and a second similar enumeration, with constant repetition of the petition for protection. It is not impossible that the three sections were of separate origin. Like all the *loricae* and much of the other devotional literature of the Irish, the piece is curious and bizarre in both its ideas and its vocabulary. Many Greek terms are used, and there are several words found elsewhere only in the *Hisperica Famina*. Undoubtedly there is a real relationship between these two works. The *lorica*, however, for all its peculiarities, is not a Hisperic composition.[359]

All the older manuscripts [360] put this text under the name, variously spelled, of a certain Laid-cend, who was, no doubt, he who made an abridgment of Gregory the Great's commentary on the Book of Job, and who died in 661.[361] Only in the preface

---

[359] It seems probable that Aldhelm, part of whose works shows kinship to the *Hisperica Famina*, knew also the *Lorica*. *Cf.* Jenkinson *op. cit.* p. xxii.

[360] Bk. of Nunnaminster: " Hanc luricam Lodgen in anno periculoso constituit." — Bk. of Cerne: " hanc luricam loding cantauit ter in omne die." — Cologne MS: " hymnus quem Lathacan scotigena fecit." — Verona MS: " Lorica Ladcini sapientis."

[361] *Cf.* no. 106. See also KM *Über die älteste irische Dichtung* I (*Abhandl. d. k. preuss. Akad. d. Wissensch.* 1913 phil.-hist. Cl. vi) 15 n. 2; *Bruchstücke der älteren Lyrik Irlands* (*ibid.* 1919 vii) 40.

in the fourteenth-century *Leabhar Breac* is it affirmed that " Gillus [Gildas] made this *lorica* " and that " Laid-cend . . . brought it into the island of Ireland and carried it to the altar of the holy bishop Patrick." [362] Stokes, Zimmer (at the time when he held the theory, afterwards abandoned, that the *Hisperica Famina* were of British origin), Bernard and Williams accepted the truth of this tradition, while it was denied by Thurneysen and Strecker. Form and content are not incompatible with either authorship, although the character of the versification and the developed scheme of the heavenly hierarchy favor a seventh-century date.[363] But as we know little of the history of Hiberno-Latin, and nothing of that of early Cambro-Latin versification, the verse-form affords poor ground on which to base a judgment.[364]

The so-called " *Lorica* of Leyden " appears to be in reality a love incantation, modeled on and to some extent using the language of the *Lorica* of Gildas. There is a similar lengthy enumeration of the parts of the body. It is found in the MS Leyden Universiteitsbibl. Voss. Q. 2 f. 60, *s* IX *ex*, which is a cover taken from some other MS, Lindsay thinks the same as Berne C 219 frag. 4. Lindsay gives the script as Welsh of the end of the ninth century (*Notae Latinae* 459; *ZCP* I 361). The text has been published by V. H. Freidel *ZCP* II (1899) 64-72, and by H. Williams *Cymmrodorion Record Series* no. III (London 1899) 293-4. It runs " Domine exaudi [Ps. ci] usque in finem. descendat meus amor . . . N. pro amore meo." There is a bare possibility that it is Irish, even though found only in a Welsh manuscript.

101. Patrick's *Lorica*

Atomriug indiu niurt trén togairm trindóit . . . in dúleman dail. Domini est salus . . . sit semper nobiscum. Amen.

MSS: LH (T) *s* XI f. 19ᵛ. — BM Egerton 93 f. 19 [O'C says written in 1477]. — Bodl. Rawl. B 512 *s* XV *ex* f. 7 [this is the Vit. Trip. text]. Eds: Geo. Petrie in " The history and antiquities of Tara hill " *Trans. RIA* XVIII (1837) 57-67 [ed. and trans. by O'D from LH]. — WS *Goidilica* (Calcutta 1866); 2nd ed. *Goidelica* (London 1872) 150-1. — J. O'B. Crowe *Hist. and Archaeol. Assoc. of Ire. Journal* 3rd ser. I (1869) 285-307. — H&S II ii (1878) 320-3 [from WS and Todd]. — *IT* I (1880) 52-8 [text

---

[362] The MS text makes Laid-cend (d. 661) come from Gildas (d. 570). HZ amends it so as to remove this difficulty.

[363] It is worthy of note that the particular rhythmical measure in which the "*Lorica* of Gildas " is written seems to be found elsewhere only in the *Kanon Evangeliorum* of Aileran "the wise" (no. 107 ii), a paraphrase of the *Carmen paschale* of Sedulius (no. 108), and a " traveller's prayer " which the ninth-century MS attributes to Gildas. The prayer has the appearance of being an early religious piece In Hiberno-Latin verse (which may be, for anything we know to the contrary, also Britanno-Latin). Apart from the metre it shows no peculiar relationship either with the *lorica* or with the prose writings of Gildas. The MS contains a collection of devotional pieces, the compilation of which has been attributed to Alcuin:— Oratio Gildae pro itineris et navigii prosperitate. Dei patris festinare maximum . . . usque loci destinati [imperfect]: 20 stanzas, of which 2 imperfect. MS: BN lat. 1153 *s* IX 1st half, f. 95ᵛ. Eds: In the *Officia per ferias* in the eds. of Alcuin's works by Duchesne (Quercetanus) (1617), and by Froben (1777), vol. II; also Migne *PL* CI 607. — Wilhelm Meyer " Gildae oratio rythmica " *Nachrichten v. d. kgl. Gesellsch. d. Wissensch. z. Göttingen* philol.-hist. Kl. 1912 pp. 48-108.

[364] Some have seen in the " mortalitas huius anni," against which protection is asked, an allusion to the great pestilence mentioned in the *Annales Cambriae* in 547 and in AU 549. But epidemics were of such frequent occurrence that any such localisation is uncertain.

only]. — [Rev. A. Cameron] *Scottish Celtic Rev.* I (1881–5) 49–61, 305–7. — *Vit. Trip.* (1887) I 48–53. — *LH* ² (1898) I 133–6, II pp. lvii *sq*, 49–51, 208–12. — *Thes. Pal.* II (1903) pp. xl, 354–8, *Suppl.* (1910) 80 [best ed.]. TRANS: In all eds. except *IT*. Also: WS *Saturday Review* 5 Sept. 1857. — J. H. Todd *St. Patrick* (Dublin 1864) 426–9. — C. H. H. Wright *The writings of Patrick* (London [1889]) 109 *sqq* [metrical trans. by J. C. Mangan, J. J. Murphy, and Mrs. C. F. Alexander]. — Thos. Olden *Epistles and hymn of St. Patrick* (London 1889, 3rd ed. 1894). — G. Dottin *Les livres de s. Patrice* (Paris [1909]) 54–7 [Fr. trans.]. — KM *Selections from ancient Irish poetry* (London 1911) 25–7. — N. J. D. White *St. Patrick his life and writings* (London 1920) 61–7 [the *LH* ² trans. with emendations by E. J. Gwynn and others]. COMM: J. B. Bury *St. Patrick* (London 1905) 246. — *Cf.* also Gougaud " Étude sur les *loricae* " as noted p. 251 *supra.* — E. Knott *Ériu* VII (1914) 239 [*cf. RC* XXXVI (1915) 227; J. Mac-Erlean *Studies* Mar. 1915 p. 155].

The prayer known as " Patrick's *Lorica*," and also as *Fáeth Fiada*, " Deer's Cry," is among the most interesting relics of early Irish Christianity. Although in Irish, it shows a fuller assimilation of the incantation-form to the Christian idea than does the *Lorica* of Gildas. At the same time it presents in a remarkable way the attitude of mind of a primitive Christian believer, probably monk, to whom paganism and the superstitions sprung from it were a very real terror. It is written in *retoric* — periodical, rhythmical and alliterative prose — and in imitation of early secular and perhaps pagan compositions.

It is a morning hymn or prayer:

> " I arise to-day
> in a mighty strength, invocation of the Trinity;
> belief in Threeness;
> confession of Oneness;
> towards the Creator." [365]

There follow similar passages in which mention is made of events in the life of Christ, of the orders of angels and saints, of some of the principal objects and phenomena of nature, and of the various aspects of God's protecting care.

> " I summon to-day all these powers for my protection
> against every cruel merciless power that may oppose my body and my soul;
> against incantations of false prophets;
> against black laws of heathendom;
> against false laws of heretics; .
> against encompassment of idolatry;
> against spells of women and smiths and druids; [366]
> against every knowledge that corrupts [?] man's body and soul."

[365] Trans. adapted from those listed above.

[366] Text: " fri brichtu ban *ocus* gobann *ocus* druad." The druid, or magician, medicine-man, and the *gobann*, or smith, especially the *gobann saor*, play important parts in early Irish myth and folk-lore. The magic character of the smith is not unknown to other European literatures.

Then comes an invocation of Christ's presence in all acts of the day, followed, in conclusion, by a repetition of the opening paragraph.

The name of Patrick has been associated with this prayer from a fairly early date if, as is most probable, allusion is made to it in a note in the early ninth-century Book of Armagh, where the last of the fourfold honors due to the saint is said to be " canticum eius scotticum semper canere." [367] In the preface to the *lorica* in the eleventh-century *Liber Hymnorum* it receives a definite place in the Patrick legend: Patrick sang it when he had to pass through the ambuscades set by King Loeguire, and as a result he and his companions took on the appearance of wild deer, and his little disciple Benignus, or Benén, that of a fawn. Muir-chú, writing his Life of Patrick, tells the legend of the deer, but does not mention the *lorica;* nor, apparently, did the original text of the *Vita Tripartita*, written at the end of the ninth century. [368] But to the deer story must be due the Irish title, *fáeth fiada*, " deer's cry," which seems to be a modification of *fóid fiada*, technical term applied to those charms of druids and *filid* which produced invisibility. [369]

The silence of Muir-chú need not mean that he did not know of the prayer, or of its ascription to Patrick. There is nothing, however, in the text itself to suggest authorship by the fifth-century bishop Patricius, and the language forms, although, no doubt, great allowance must be made for modernisation, are, as they stand, not older than the eighth century. [370]

102. Nimíne's Prayer

Admuinemmar nóeb Patraicc . . . Patraicc prímapstail.

MSS: LH (T) ff. 16^v-7. — LH (F) p. 38. EDS: WS *Goidelica* (London 1872). — *IT* I (1880) 23–4, 322. — *Vit. Trip.* II (1887) 426–7. — *LH*² (1898) I 105–6, II pp. xlix–l, 36, 187. — *Thes. Pal.* II (1903) pp. xxxviii, 322. Trans. in all eds. except *IT*.

This short prayer in Irish is addressed to " holy Patrick, Ireland's chief apostle," who " baptized heathen," " warred against druids," and " purified Ireland's meadowlands." It is another of the ancient Irish *retorics*, irregular and unrimed, but rhythmical and alliterative compositions, and shows considerable poetic grace and feeling. The manuscripts attribute the poem to Nimíne, or Nindíne, *éces*, or to Fiacc of Slébte. Of Nindíne little is known. He is mentioned in the Annals of Tigernach under A.D. 621, and a quatrain attributed to him is quoted in the notes to the Calendar of Oengus. [371] Legend associated him with the saintly nun Moninna, [372] doubtless only

---

[367] *Cf.* p. 334 *infra. LA* f. 16.

[368] As it now stands, the *lorica* is included in full, but it has the appearance of being an interpolation.

[369] The course of evolution may have been as follows: A play began on the sound relationship of *Benén* and *bennán*, " the male calf of a cow or deer." This gave occasion for a version of the folk-lore *motif* of metamorphosis into deer. Then the *lorica*, already called *fóid fiada*, probably because it resembled in form the " invisibility charms," got itself attached to the legend and became known as *fáeth fiada*, " deer's cry."

[370] KM *Selections from ancient Irish poetry* 112. — There may possibly be a reminiscence of the *lorica* in the Milan glosses (early ninth century). *Cf.* p. 202 *supra*, and *Thes. Pal.* II p. xl.

[371] *Fél. Óeng.*² 258–9.

[372] *Ibid.* 166–7. *Cf.* no. 160.

because of the similarity of names. It is not impossible that Nindíne was the author: the language forms are not of earlier date than about A.D. 700, but the text might have been modified from an older version.

On the Latin translation of the commentary on the Psalms composed by Theodore of Mopsuestia, a translation which, it is possible, was made in Ireland in the sixth century, see no. 515.

103. Verses of a certain Irishman on the Alphabet

A. Principium uocis ueterumque inuentio mira. . . . Saepe etiam sibilans inter dentes morientum. 69 ll.

MSS: Leyden Universiteitsbibl. Voss. Lat. Q. 33 s X f. 176. — BM Reg. 12 C. xxiii s X. — Chartres 55 s X f. 1. — BN 2773 s X/XI f. 108ᵛ; 5001 s X/XI f. 23. — Cambridge Univ. Lib. Gg. V. 35 s XI f. 381. — Brussels Bibl. roy. 10615–729 s XII f. 194ᵛ; 9799–809 s XII f. 137ᵛ. — Leyden Univ. Lib. B.P.L. 190 s XI f. 35 [fragm.]. EDS: Thos. Wright and J. O. Halliwell Reliquiae antiquae (London 1845) I 164 sq [the Cambridge MS]. — L. Müller Rheinisches Museum new ser. XX (Frankfort 1865) 357–74 [Leyden MS], XXII 500 [collation of the Leyden fragment]. — W. Wagner ibid. XXII 630 [collation of BM MS]. — E. Grosse ibid. XXIV 615 sqq [collation of Brussels MSS]. — J. Klein ibid. XXXI 465–8 [collation of BN 2773 and Cambridge MS]. — H. Omont Bibl. de l'École des chartes XLII 431–40 [with the scholia of the Chartres MS]. — E. Baehrens Poetae latini minores V (Leipsic 1883) 375–8. COMM: Manitius Geschichte der christlich-lateinischen Poesie bis zur Mitte des 8. Jahrhunderts (Stuttgart 1891) 484, 504; Lat. Lit. I (1911) 190–2.

The title which the manuscripts give to this rather widely distributed poem is Versus cuiusdam Scotti de alfabeto. It consists of 23 stanzas of three hexameters each, devoted to riddling notices of the successive letters of the alphabet. In some manuscripts the stanzas for Y and Z are missing. The poet shows a knowledge of the Greek and Hebrew letters and their use. It seems probable that he wrote in Ireland about the middle of the seventh century. To the Chartres copy of the poem there is attached an explanatory commentary, as far as R, which, in the opinion of Manitius, was composed by the author.

104. The Irish Augustine: De mirabilibus sacrae scripturae A.D. 655

Venerandissimis urbium et monasteriorum episcopis et presbyteris, maxime Carthaginensium, Augustinus per omnia subjectus, optabilem in Christo salutem. Beatissimi, dum adhuc viveret, patris mei Eusebii . . .

MSS: Those of late date are quite numerous: see Esposito in Proc. RIA. — Bodl. Rawl. C 153 s XII ff. 1–42. — Rouen Bibl. publ. 665 (A. 453) ff. 67–102ᵛ. — Troyes Bibl. publ. 280 s XII sect. ii. — Oxford Balliol Coll. 229 s XII ex ff. 57–79ᵛ. — BN 1956 s XII ex sect. v. EDS: The older eds. of St. Augustine: e.g. the Benedictine ed. (Paris 1679–1700) III pt. II App. 1–32; the reprint by Gaume (Paris 1836–39) III pt. II 2716 sqq; Migne PL XXXV 2149–200. COMM: Wm. Reeves " On Augustin, Irish writer of the seventh century " Proc. RIA VII 514–22 [read June 10, 1861]. — B. MacCarthy The Codex Palatino-Vaticanus No. 830 (RIA Todd Lect. Ser. III) (Dublin 1892) 365–7, 393–4. — G. T. Stokes Ireland and the Celtic Church 6th ed.

(Dublin 1907) 221–4. — L. Gougaud *Les Chrétientés celtiques* (Paris 1911) 256–7. — Mario Esposito *Studies* II (1913, Dec.) 515; *Proc. RIA* XXXV (1919) C 189–207.

With the writings of the great Augustine of Hippo there has been preserved and published a treatise on the wonders of Holy Scripture which is certainly the composition of an Irish ecclesiastic of the seventh century. Either the author adopted the Latin form "Augustinus" or some later scribe, with or without intent to deceive, modified the name he used into that of the famous Father of the Church. The name, in any case, insured the preservation of the work. We have no other evidence as to the person and career of Augustinus. He appears to have been an inmate of a monastery in south-central Ireland. His treatise is addressed to "the very reverend bishops and priests of the cities and monasteries, especially of Carthage" — a name substituted, we may believe, by a continental scribe for that of an Irish monastery, possibly Clonmacnois.[373] Mention is made of the author's spiritual father, "Eusebius," and of two of his religious brothers or teachers, "Bathanus" and "Manchianus." These are Latinised forms of the not uncommon Irish names Baetan or Baedan and Mainchine or Manchén. From another passage we learn that Manchianus, or Manichaeus, died in 652, which indicates that the person meant was Manchén, abbot of Men-droichet (now Mundrehid, near Borris-in-Ossory, Leix), whose obit is recorded in the annals under that year.[374] Bathanus was probably Baetan moccu Cormaicc (that is, one would suppose, of the Dál Cormaic of Leinster — but the Chronicon Scottorum says he was of the Conmaicne Mara, of Connemara), abbot of Clonmacnois, who died in the great plague of 664. Eusebius has not been identified.

Incidentally in his commentary [375] on one of the famous miracles of the Old Testament the author lets us know the year in which he was writing. Treating of the statement in the Book of Joshua that the sun and moon stood still, he points out that the simultaneous suspension of motion was necessary if chronology was not to be disturbed. He tells us that the sun and moon return to the same relative position after every cycle of 532 years, and gives an outline of the progress of these cycles from the creation down through scriptural history. The eleventh cycle came down to "our times," and in its final year Manchan, with many wise men of the Irish, died; the

---

[373] "Carthaginensium" replacing "Cluanensium." This suggestion, made by Lanigan, is discounted by the usually sane Reeves, who postulates the existence of an Irish monastic colony at Carthage, and, *ex hypothesi*, the dedication to them of this work produced in central Ireland!

[374] To him we may owe the commentary many extracts from which, distinguished by the letters M, MA, or MAN, are entered in the Gospels of Máel-Brigte (no. 483). He had, however, a contemporary, Manchan of Liath-Manchain (now Lemanaghan, Offalley) who died in 665. *Cf.* Jas. Graves *Journ. Roy. Hist. & Arch. Soc. Ire.* 4th ser. III 134–50.

[375] *Lib.* II *cap.* iv.

current year was the third of the twelfth cycle, which the chronological *data* indicate as 655. The cycle employed, as also certain minor peculiarities, make it clear that Augustinus had before him the paschal treatise of Victorius of Aquitaine.[376]

The Irish Augustine's study of the miraculous in Holy Scripture is divided into three books, of which the first treats of the Law, to the death of Moses, the second of the Prophets, being the remainder of the Old Testament, and the third of the New Testament. His thesis is, for the time, a somewhat rationalistic one: that God ceased from the work of *creatio*, creation, on the seventh day of Genesis, and that the " work " which He is sometimes said to be doing thereafter [377] is that of *gubernatio*, governing. Hence no miracle can involve new creation: it is only the calling forth of some principle which normally lies hidden in the depths of nature. On this basis he attempts to explain the wonderful events recorded in Holy Writ: the metamorphosis, for example, of Lot's wife was merely the abnormal development of the salt element which is present in every human body. The reasoning is often childlike, but it is a childishness which has a note of curious originality.

Augustinus evidently had a good knowledge of patristic literature, which he uses extensively, though generally without naming the source. Considerable information of interest to the student of Irish history can be extracted from his work. He excludes from the canon of Scripture the story of Bel and the Dragon and the two Books of Macchabees.[378] He treats at some length the problem of tides.[379] He gives, in connection with his discussion of the deluge, the earliest list of wild animals in Ireland. Islands, he says, are formed by the action of the sea in separating them from the mainland, instances of which action were known to old men then living.

" This shows that those wild animals which are enclosed within the confines of islands were not brought there by human agency, but, manifestly, were to be found at that separation of the islands from the continent. Who, for example, brought wolves, deer, wild hogs, foxes, badgers, hares, and *sesquivoli* [whatever that ἅπαξ λεγόμενον may mean] to Ireland? " [380]

The literary style of the work seems good; it shows no contamination from the *Hisperica Famina* type of Latinity. Augustinus, though differing widely in thought and diction from Cogitosus, was worthy to rank as a Latinist with that pioneer hagiographer.[381]

105. Commentary on the Catholic Epistles

Incipit commentarius epistolae Iacobi; Septem tubae quae fuerunt . . . susceptor sanctificationis est.

MS: Carlsruhe Landesbibl. Cod. Augiensis CCXXXIII *s* IX ff. 1–40^{v}. COMM: A. Holder *Die Reichenauer Handschiften* I (Leipsic 1906) 531–2; " Altirische Namen

---

[376] We know, from Columbanus, that the Irish were acquainted with his system in the sixth century, and from Cummian that it had been adopted by many of the southern Irish more than twenty years before the date of Augustine's composition.

[377] *E.g.* John v 17.   [378] II xxxiv.

[379] II iv. He applies to spring and neap tides the terms *malina* and *ledo*, used later in Bede's *De Natura Rerum*.

[380] I xx.

[381] The work is quoted. under the title " Compotus sancti Augustini," in the Munich Computus of 718 (no. 59), extant in a ninth-century copy.

im Reichenauer Codex CCXXXIII " *ACL* III iv (1907) 266–7. — Alex. Souter " The Commentary of Pelagius on the Epistles of Paul " *Proc. Brit. Acad.* 1905–6. — Mario Esposito " A seventh-century commentary on the Catholic Epistles " *JTS* XXI (July 1920) 316–8.

This Reichenau manuscript [382] was written on the Continent, but perhaps, in this portion, from an Irish *Vorlage*. It contains Irish contractions and possibly one Irish word. The Commentary on the Catholic Epistles which forms this first section was composed in Ireland, to all appearances in the second half of the seventh century. Holder described it as having a Priscillian character, apparently because it contains the so-called *Comma Iohanninum*, the passage in I John v 7–8 which is wanting in the majority of the manuscripts.

The earlier authorities mentioned by the compiler include Jerome, Augustine, Pelagius,[383] Gregory and Eucherius (of Lérins — bishop of Lyons *c* 434–449); and, of Irish writers, Breccán, Bercán mac Aido, Manchian " doctor noster," Lodcen, Lath and Bannbán. Some of these have not been identified, but it is probable that Manchian was Manchén, abbot of Men-droichet (d. 652),[384] Lodcen and Lath was Laidcend mac Baith Bannaig (d. 661),[385] and Bannbán was Banbán *oscach*, or *sapiens*, scribe of Cell-dara (d. 685 or 686).[386] If Manchén was his teacher the author wrote in the middle or second half of the seventh century, and may, as Esposito suggested, be identical with the Irish Augustine.[387]

106. Laid-cend: *Egloga de Moralibus Job* [388]

MSS: Leningrad (St. Petersburg) National Lib. lat. F. 1. 7 *s* VIII. — Carlsruhe Landesbibl. Cod. Aug. CXXXIV *s* IX ff. 1–127 [the entire codex]. — Munich Staatsbibl. 16053 *s* XI. ED: Mario Esposito *Hermathena* XVII (1912) 104–6 [opening sentences only]. COMM: L. Gougaud " Le témoinage des manuscrits sur l'oeuvre du moine Lathcen " *RC* XXX (1909) 37–46 [a statement of all that is known of Laid-cend]. — Dom A. Staerk *Les manuscrits latines du Ve au XIIIe siècle conservés à la bibliothèque impériale de St.-Pétersbourg* I (1910) 39–41. — Manitius *Lat. Lit.* I (1911) 99–100, II (1923) 796.

Of the writings of Gregory the Great none was more popular in Ireland — as elsewhere in mediaeval Europe — than the *Moralia*, a great commentary on the Book of Job.[389] In Ireland an abridgment, consisting largely of excerpts, of this work was prepared in the century following its appearance by a certain Laid-cend, or Lathcen, who has been mentioned previously as a reputed author of the so-called " *Lorica* of Gildas." [390] He seems to have been a monk of Clonfert-Molua.[391] His death is recorded in the Annals of Ulster under the year 661, where he is called " Laidhgen the

---

[382] It is mentioned in the catalogue of Reichenau prepared by Reginbertus (d. 846). *Cf.* Becker *Catalogi bibliothecarum antiqui* (Bonn 1885) 22 no. x 16.

[383] Commentary on the Pauline Epistles: Ephes. vi 14.

[384] *Cf.* p. 276 *supra*.   [385] *Cf.* nos. 100, 106.   [386] AU, Tig., 3 Frags.   [387] No. 104.

[388] The title in the Petersburg MS is *Egloga quam scripsit Lathcen filius Baith de moralibus Iob quas Gregorius fecit.*

[389] *Cf.* pp. 644, 667, 673.   [390] No. 100.

[391] In *Fél. Oeng.* he is commemorated on January 12: " Christ's mysteries Laidcenn son of Baeth *bannach* interpreted." A marginal note adds: " Of Clúain-ferta-Molua was Laidgenn. " *Fél. Oeng.*[2] 35, 42–3.

wise, son of Baeth *bannach.*" Reference to his compilation is made by Notker Balbulus,[392] and also in two manuscripts of the ninth century.[393]

107. Aileran

(i) *Interpretatio mystica progenitorum domini Jesu Christi* [394]

In Nativitate Sanctae Genitricis Ipsius Legenda. Oportunum videtur de nominibus genealogiae dom-
inicae . . . exemplis sacrae scripturae asseruimus. Item Moralis Explanatio eorundem nominum ab
eodem compilata. Oportunum quoque nunc videtur ut eiusdem genealogiae nomina . . . in Azor
[Assur] ut adiuvante Domino. . . . [So the St. Gall MS, which ends incomplete. The Vienna MS ends:]
. . . et electis in Domino conveniat.

MSS: St. Gall Stiftsbibl. 433 *s* IX pp. 685–706 [incomplete; *cf. Proc. RIA* XXVIII
(1910) C 73]. — Carlsruhe Landesbibl. Cod. Augiensis CCXLIX *s* X/XI ff. 80ᵛ–94
[ends at same words as preceding]. — Vienna Nationalbibl. 740 [Cod. membr. theol.
CIX; *cf.* Denis *Codices mss. theol. bibl. Palatinae Vindobonensis* I pt. I (1795) 294]. —
Berlin Staatsbibl. Meerm. 56 [formerly Phillipps 1660] *s* X [these two MSS contain
the *Collectaneum in Mattheum* of Sedulius Scottus, in which he gives Aileran's work,
slightly abridged]. Eds: Patrick Fleming *Collectanea sacra* (Louvain 1667) 182–92
[St. Gall text]. — *Bibl. max. vet. patrum* (Leyden 1677) XII 37 *sqq.* — Migne *PL*
LXXX 327–42 [this and the preceding give Fleming's text]. — Chas. MacDonnell
Proc. RIA VII (1861) C 369–71 [description of Vienna MS and text of concluding
lines, wanting in others]. Comm: Roger *L'Enseignement* 258. — M. Esposito *Studies*
I (1912) 671 [as to Aileran's alleged knowledge of Greek]; *ibid.* II (1913) 499. — Von
Dobschütz *Ein Bücherkleinod* 15–7 [from the *Jahresbericht der schlesischen Gesell-
schaft für vaterländische Cultur: Evangelisch-theologische Sektion* 1913].

Aileran *sapiens* — Aileran the Wise — or Airerán *a n-écnai* — Airerán
of the wisdom — died, according to the annals, in the great plague of
665. In the Calendar of Oengus he is commemorated both on August
11 and on December 29. He is noticed several times in the late marginal
notes attached to that text; according to one, he was *fer léighinn* of
Clúain-Iraird (Clonard); another says he was of Tech-Aireráin in Meath,
and " lector " of Clonard, or in Clondalk·n, or abbot of Tamlachta.[395]

Another of these notes purports to give a prophecy of his regarding that
famous plague, the fear of which took such a hold on the minds of Irishmen in the early middle ages, the " Broom out of Fánad."

" Two alehouses shall be in one rath side by side: he that shall go out of one house
into the other will not find anyone before him alive in the house into which he shall

392 *Notatio de illustribus viris qui ex intentione sacras scripturas exponebant* ed. Dümmler *Das formelbuch
d. Bisch. Salomo* III 67: " excerptum Ladkeni Hiberniensis inquire." *Cf.* Manitius *Lat. Lit.* I 358–9.

393 Reichenau: Becker *Catalagi bibliothecarum antiqui* (1885) xv 150 [*cf.* Holder *Die Reichenauer
Handschriften* I p. viii] — perhaps the present Carlsruhe MS; Murbach Strassb. Phil. Vers. 270, 231 ("Liber
eglogarum Ladcen filii Baith ") (Manitius *Lat. Lit.* I 100).

394 Vienna MS: *Tipicus ac tropologicus Jesu Christi genealogiae intellectus quem sanctus Aileranus Scottorum sapientissimus exposuit.*

395 *Fél. Oeng.* 2 184–5, 263. The last is a mistake of some kind.

go, and afterwards he will not find anyone alive in the house out of which he shall have come, such will be the swiftness with which the broom shall come out of Fanait."[396]

Whatever faith may be placed in these rather dubious sources, certain it is that Aileran was the author of a treatise in scriptural interpretation which is one of the few surviving products of old Irish exegesis. It is an interpretation of the names which appear in the genealogy of Christ as given in the Gospel of Matthew, setting forth the allegorical and mystical signification of the words. Some students have thought to find in this treatise evidence of a wide acquaintance on Aileran's part with patristic literature in Latin and even in Greek. But the work seems to be merely an adaptation from Jerome's " Book of Hebrew Names." It offers testimony to the early prevalence in the Irish schools of the allegorical methods of scriptural exposition. Comparison may profitably be made between it and the more rationalistic writings of Aileran's contemporary, the Irish Augustine.[397]

(ii) *Kanon Evangeliorum*

In nomine divino trino atque uno. Quam in primo speciosa quadriga. . . . Nonagies loqui atque septies.

MSS: Harburg (Bavaria) Öttingen-Wallersteinsche Bibl. [Evangeliarium, no. 459 *infra*] f. 1ᵛ. — Poitiers Bibl. de la ville 17 *s* VIII/IX f. 26. — Bodl. Add. C. 144 f. 69. — Zürich Zentralbibl. C. 68 f. 2 [written in Germany *c* 879; afterwards belonged to St. Gall]. Eds: Du Chesne *Alcuini opera* (Paris 1617) 1686 [from MS in monastery of St. Bertinus near St. Omer, now lost]. — Frobenius *Alcuini opera* (Ratisbon 1777) II pt. I 204 [reprint]. — Migne *PL* CI 729. — Dom Pitra *Spicilegium Solesmense* III (1855) 407-8. — Bartsch *Zs. f. roman. Philol.* II (1878) 216-7. — Dümmler *Anzeiger f. Kunde d. deutsch. Vorzeit* XXVI (1879) 80 *sqq.* — M. Esposito *Proc. RIA* XXX (1912) C 2-5. — W. Meyer *Nachrichten d. k. Gesellsch. d. Wissensch. z. Göttingen* philol.-hist. Kl. 1912 I 63-7. Comm: W. Meyer *Sitzungsb. d. k. bayer. Akad. philos.-philol. Kl.* 1882 I 91. — Manitius *Geschichte der christlich-lateinischen Poesie bis zur Mitte des 8. Jahrh.* (1891) 481 [studies on the metre]. — Dom De Bruyne *Rev. Bénédictine* XXIX (1912) 339-40 [investigation as to authorship].

In many Latin and Greek manuscripts the gospels are divided into a large number of sections — about 1165 — which are attributed, perhaps wrongly, to Ammonius of Alexandria (who in the first half of the third century composed a harmony of the gospels) and are known as " Ammonian sections." The church historian Eusebius drew up ten tables (κανόνες) in which he placed in parallel columns the numbers of the sections common to four, three, or two gospels, and those found in only one. These " Eusebian canons " were very popular with mediaeval, including Irish, biblical students; they are prefixed to many Irish gospel-books.[398] The present poem sets

[396] *Ibid.* 190-1.

[397] *Cf.* no. 104. A work entitled *Rethorica Alerani*, which possibly may have been a grammatical composition of Aileran, was, in the twelfth century, in the monastic library of St. Florian, near Linz. *Cf.* Manitius *Lat. Lit.* I 10; Czerny *Die Bibliothek des Chorherrnstifts St. Florian* (Linz 1874) 235.

[398] *Cf.* J. Armitage Robinson *The times of St. Dunstan* (Oxford 1923) 171 *sqq.*

forth in riming Latin verse the number of agreements found by the canons to exist between the different gospels. It seems to have been known fairly widely on the Continent in the early middle ages. In modern times it has been found of interest to students of mediaeval Latin versification; the measure is the same as that of the so-called " *Lorica* of Gildas." [399] But it is only recently that the identity of the author with Aileran the Wise has been established.

108. Paraphrase of the *Carmen paschale* of Sedulius

Genitorem nati atque filium . . . Moysi rub [ends imperfect]. 26 ll.

MS: BN 9347 *s* IX f. 4 [written at Reims]. Ed: W. Meyer " Rythmische Paraphrase des Sedulius von einem Iren " *Nachrichten v. d. k. Gesellsch. d. Wissensch. z. Göttingen* philol.-hist. Kl. 1917 iv 594–6.

The *Carmen paschale* of the fifth-century Christian poet Sedulius was known in Ireland. A fragment of a versified paraphrase of that poem — it covers bk. I vv. 103–31 — is attributed by the editor, Wilhelm Meyer, to an Irish or, less probably, an English author. He bases his conclusion on the versification, which is that of the *Lorica* of Gildas.[400]

109. De duodecim abusivis saeculi

Duodecim abusiva sunt saeculi, hoc est: sapiens sine operibus. . . . Primus abusionis gradus est . . . ne sine nobis Christus esse incipiat in futuro.

MSS: Hellmann divides them into 3 groups: (1) Zürich Zentralbibl. Rh. 95 1st pt. *s* IX/X pp. 3–38. — Berlin Staatsbibl. Phill. 1691 *s* XII. — Oxford New College 140 *s* XIII. — BN lat. 1651 *s* XIII. — BN lat. 2155 *s* XIII/XIV. (2) St. Gall Stiftsbibl. 277 *s* IX. — Berne Stadtbibl. 618 *s* XI/XII. (3) St. Omer Bibl. pub. 267 *s* IX [insular script]. — St. Gall Stiftsbibl. 89 *s* IX. — Metz Bibl. de la ville 138 *s* XII. There are many others. Eds: In the older eds. of Augustine and Cyprian. Also Ware *S. Patricio adscripta opuscula* (London 1656). — J. L. Villanueva *S. Patricii . . . opuscula* (Dublin 1835). — Migne *PL* IV 947–60, XL 649 *sqq.* — W. Hartel *Cypriani opera omnia (Corp. script. eccles. lat.* III) pt. iii (Vienna 1871) 152 *sqq.* — Siegmund Hellmann *Pseudo-Cyprianus De XII abusivis saeculi* (Harnack and Schmidt *Texte u. Untersuchungen z. Geschichte d. altchristlichen Literatur* XXXIV i) (Leipsic 1909). Comm: J. B. Bury *St. Patrick* (London 1905) 245. — Gougaud *Les Chrétientés celtiques* (Paris 1911) 282. — Manitius *Lat. Lit.* I 107–8, II 796.

The treatise *De duodecim abusivis*, or *abusionibus*, *saeculi* is a discussion of public morals under the headings of the following twelve evils: the wise man without works; the old man without religion; the youth without obedience; the rich man without alms-giving; the woman without modesty; the nobleman without virtue; the Christian who is quarrelsome; the poor man who is proud; the king who is unjust;

the bishop who neglects his duties; the populace without discipl ne; the nation without law. In both the turn of thought and the form it is characteristically Irish, and would be immediately recognised as such by any person familiar with the secular gnomic literature of the Irish language. The literary style is of that rhetorical type which, it has been suggested, Ireland received from West Gaul: the majority of the sentences are divided into balanced periods, more or less rhythmical and with occasional riming endings. There is a certain amount of concrete information and original thought that may have value for Irish social and intellectual history, but for the most part the actual ideas, apart from their presentation, are, like those of other mediaeval works on morals, abstract and traditional.

The treatise shows the use of the Vulgate version of the Bible, of the Rule of St. Benedict, and of the *Etymologiae* of Isidore, or, perhaps, some source adopted by Isidore. This indicates that it cannot have been written much before A.D. 600, probably not before 630. On the other hand a long extract is taken from it in the *Hibernensis* collection of canons,[401] evidence that it must date from before 725. As the *Hibernensis* credits the quotation, impossibly, to St. Patrick, we may conclude that the work was then of considerable antiquity. It should, perhaps, be assigned to about 630 x 650.

The author, apparently, drew on certain material also used by the compilers of the *Hibernensis* — probably that early " Collection of Sentences " which was known to Sedulius Scottus.[402]

After the *Hibernensis*, the next allusion to the *De abusivis* is in a letter which one Cathuulfus, or Kathvulf — we may presume that he was an Englishman — wrote to Charles the Great about 775.[403] Here, too, the attribution is to Patrick. It was also used by the compiler, probably Irish, of the pseudo-Bedan *Kollektaneum*,[404] and by Sedulius Scottus.[405] Meanwhile the tract had passed to the Continent, where it met ecclesiastical favor. It was quoted by a Paris synod in 829,[406] by Jonas, bishop of Orleans, in 834,[407] by a council at Metz in 859,[408] and in several of the writings of the famous Hincmar of Reims.[409] It was attributed to Cyprian of Carthage,[410] to Augustine of Hippo,[411] to Isidore of Seville,[412] and under these famous names its future was assured. More than fifty manuscript copies are known to exist.

The section which especially interested these continental students was that discussing the *rex iniquus*, and it can be said that the unknown Irish author made a real contribution to the development of European political theory.

---

[401] Ed. Wasserschleben, *lib.* XXV, p. 77. *Cf.* no. 82.
[402] *Cf.* pp. 249, 566.   [403] *MGH Epp.* IV 502 *sqq.*   [404] *Cf.* no. 541.
[405] *Cf.* p. 554 *infra.*   [406] Mansi XIV 575.   [407] Migne *PL* CVI 288.
[408] *MGH Cap. reg. Fr.* II 444.
[409] Migne *PL* CXXV 626, 662, 769 *sq*, 772, 835, 850 *sq*, 991 *sq*, 997, 1009, 1012. *Cf.* Hellmann's ed. p. 17.
[410] The Paris synod.
[411] Cat. of the lib. of St. Riquier in 831: Becker *Catalogi bibliothecarum antiqui* (Bonn 1885) no. xi 40.
[412] Cat. of the lib. of Murbach shortly after 840: Migne *PL* LXXXI 624.

110. De tribus habitaculis

Tria sunt sub omnipotentis Dei manu habitacula . . . laudabunt Deum omnipotentem, benignum et misericordem: cui h. et g. et n. et per o. s. s. Amen.

EDS: The Benedictine ed. *Opera S. Augustini* VI append. 159 *sqq.* — Migne *PL* XL 991-8, LIII 831-8. COMM: L. Gougaud *Les Chrétientés celtiques* (Paris 1911) 282.

Another work formerly attributed to Patrick, and still regarded as of Irish provenance, is the theological tract on heaven, earth and hell, entitled *De tribus habitaculis*, or *De triplici habitaculo*, of which no modern study has been published. Ussher used it as evidence against any belief in purgatory in the ancient Irish Church, but seems to have been doubtful of its Patrician authorship.[413] The Latinity of the piece is very good.

111. The Cambrai Homily

[Restored text] De donis non recipiendis . . . insce inso asber ar féda ĩsu . . . nos-comalnnamar . . non recipiendis.

MS: Cambrai 619 A.D. 763 x 790 [414] ff. 37-8. FACS: C. P. Cooper *Appendix A to a Report on Rymer's Foedera* (London 1835 ?; issued 1869). EDS: Z² 1004. — Bethmann and O'C in Adolphe Tardif " Fragment d'homélie en langue celtique " *Bibl. de l'École des chartes* 3rd ser. III (1852) 193-202 [with Eng. and Fr. trans.]. — H. Wasserschleben *Die irische Kanonensammlung* (Giessen 1874) 83-4. — HZ *Glossae Hibernicae* (Berlin 1881) pp. xix *sq*, 213-7 [original and restored text]. — *Thes. Pal.* II (1903) pp. xxvi, 244-7 [original and restored text, trans.; *cf. Supplement* (1910) 75]. COMM: L. Gougaud " Les conceptions du martyre chez les Irlandais " *Rev. Bénédictine* 1907 no. 3.

In the Irish manuscript from which a continental scribe copied the *Collectio Canonum Hibernensis* [415] for Albericus, bishop of Cambrai 763-790, there must have been inserted by chance a stray leaf or two containing a fragment of a sermon in Irish. The scribe, faithful but unintelligent, copied on without a break, so that we pass from the Latin canons to the Irish homily, and back again, with no indication of change. There has thus been preserved to us one of the oldest pieces of continuous Irish prose. Philological authorities date it from the second half of the seventh or the beginning of the eighth century. It is an interesting expression of early Irish religious ideas, notably of the conception of three kinds of martyrdom.

ADAMNÁN

Bibliography

Thos. Wright *Biographia Britannica literaria Anglo-Saxon period* (London 1842) 201-6. — Paul Geyer *Adamnanus, Abt von Jona* I Teil *Sein Leben Seine Quellen Sein Verhältnis zu Pseudoeucherius de locis sanctis Seine Sprache* (*Programm z. d. Jahresberichte d. k. h. Gymnasiums bei St. Anna in Augsburg*) (Augsburg 1895); *Adamnanus* II Teil *Die handschriftliche Überlieferung der Schrift De locis sanctis* (*Programm d. k. h. Gymnasiums in Erlangen*) (Erlangen 1897) [valuable]. — Hahn in the Hauck-Herzog

---

[413] *Whole Works* IV 265.   [414] *Cf.* p. 247 *supra.*   [415] No. 82.

Realencyklopädie f. prot. Theologie u. Kirche I (1896) 166 *sq.* — Manitius *Lat. Lit.* I 236-9, II 799 [good; see also *NA* XXXII (1907) 659-60]. — Also the bibliographies to the following: no. 80 *Canones Adomnani*; no. 81 *Cáin Adamnáin*; no. 214 Adamnán's Life of Columba; no. 224 Life of Adamnán; no. 226 Vision of Adamnán. The most important of the books there listed is Reeves *Ad.*

The representative of the pre-eighth-century Irish Church who by his writings is best known to-day is Adamnán, ninth abbot of Iona. Something has been said of him above, in connection with the canons and the law, or *cáin*, which bear his name. Like all the early abbots of Iona, he was of the family known as the Cenél Conaill, and a kinsman of the founder, St. Columba: his great-grandfather was Columba's first cousin. He was born about 624, became abbot in 679, and died in 704. The outlines of his life can be drawn from sound historical sources — his own writings, the statements of his younger contemporary, Bede, and the Irish annals.

In his own age Adamnán was an eminent ecclesiastical statesman. In 684 the coast of Meath had been ravaged by Beart, an officer of King Ecgfrid of Northumbria.[416] In the following year Ecgfrid was slain by the Picts, and Aldfrid, who had been educated at Iona and perhaps in Ireland, succeeded. In 686, apparently, Adamnán visited the new king, whom, no doubt, he already knew.[417] He obtained the release of sixty prisoners taken by Beart, and brought them back to Ireland. Two years later he again journeyed to the Northumbrian court.[418] On one of these occasions he was won over to the Roman party in the Easter controversy by certain English ecclesiastics, among them Ceolfrid, abbot of Jarrow.[419] It is probable that he thereupon became one of the principal agents in securing the adhesion of the northern Irish, but of his own monks of Iona he failed to win more than a minority. He was in Ireland in 692, and again in 697, and probably remained for a considerable time. On the second occasion, according to the records, he obtained the promulgation of " The Law of the Innocents," or *Cáin Adamnáin*.

Of Adamnán's writings, the most important is the Life of Columba, which will be considered in Chapter V.

---

[416] Irish annals; Anglo-Saxon Chron.; Bede *Hist. Eccl.* IV xxvi. The motive for this apparently wanton outrage has never been disclosed. It is suggested that it was because the Irish harbored Aldfrid. Athough Aldfrid's exile may have been not entirely voluntary, and it is probable that he spent some time in Ireland, in this year, according to the anonymous Life of Cuthbert, he was in Iona.

[417] Aldfrid is called " the famous scholar, Adamnán's pupil " in *3 Frags.* 111.

[418] *Cf.* p. 431 *infra.*

[419] Bede *Hist. Eccl.* V xxi.

112. Adamnán: *De Locis Sanctis*

Praefatio. Arculfus sanctus episcopus gente Gallus. . . . I. De situ Hierusalem nunc quaedam scri-
benda sunt. . . . II. In huius nostri secundi libelli exordio de situ Bethlem. . . . III. Arculfus saepe
memoratus ab Alexandria reuersus . . . Christum iudicem saeculorum exorare non neglegat.

MSS: Geyer arranges them in three families, as follows: (i) Vienna Nationalbibl.
[formerly Bibl. Caesar. Palat.] lat. 458 *s* X ff. 1–26 [formerly Salzburg no. 174; has
plans]. — Vienna *ibid.* lat. 609 *s* XIII ff. 1ᵛ–9 [formerly "hist. eccles. 154"; fragment;
has plans]. — BN lat. 13048 *s* IX ff. 1–28 [St. Germain lat. 844, earlier 665; formerly
of Corbie; has plans, and an O-I gloss]. — BM Cotton. Tiber. D. v. pt. II *s* XIV
ff. 78–92ᵛ [badly damaged by fire; *cf.* Reeves *Ad.* p. lviii n.]. (ii) Zürich Zentralbibl.
Rh. 73 *s* IX¹ ff. 2–28 [*cf.* Mario Esposito *Proc. RIA* XXVIII C 81–3, who accepts the
identification of this with a MS given by Walahfrid Strabo to Reginbert, scribe at
Reichenau, before 842 — *cf.* G. Becker *Catalogi bibliothecarum antiqui* (Bonn 1885)
p. 23 no. 30; but Geyer, *Adamnanus* II 17–9, favors a 10th cent. date. Contains
an O-I gloss.] — Berne Stadtbibl. 582 *s* X ff. 1–46 [*cf.* M. Esposito *Proc. RIA* XXX
C 8; Geyer *op. cit.* 20–2, who considers it a copy of the preceding]. — St. Gall Stiftsbibl. 320 *s* XII/XIII pp. 254–84. — Königswart Bibl. des Fürsten Metternich 20 H
39 *s* XII *ex* ff. 1–23. — Carlsruhe Landesbibl. Cod. Augiensis CXXIX *s* IX/X f. 10
[extract, with plan]. — (iii) Brussels Bibl. roy. 2921–2 *s* IX ff. 1–52ᵛ. — Munich Staatsbibl. lat. 19150 *s* X [from Tegernsee; extract]. — Vat. Regin. lat. 618 *s* XV ff. 105–44.
— Berlin Staatsbibl. lat. oct. 32 *s* XV ff. 47–83. — Vat Vat. lat. 636 A *s* XIII
ff. 79ᵛ.–99. — BN lat. 12943 *s* XI ff. 95 *sq* [frag.]. — Laon Bibl. municipale 92 *s* IX
[frag.]. — Périgord, MS 37 of Cadouin abbey libr. *s* XII [frag.]. EDS: Jacobus
Gretser *Adamnani Scotihiberni de situ terrae sanctae* (Ingolstadt 1619); also in *Opera* IV
(Ratisbon 1734) 239–79 [from a lost or unidentified MS]. — Mabillon *AA. SS. o. s. B.*
III ii (1672) 499–522 [from a Vatican and the Corbie MS]. — Migne *PL* LXXXVIII
779–814. — Delpit *Essai sur les anciens pélerinages à Jérusalem* (Paris 1870) 260–
361. — Tobler and Molinier *Itinera Hierosolymitana et descriptiones terrae sanctae* I
(Geneva 1879) pp. xxx *sqq*, 139–210, 238–40, 392–418 [good ed.]. — Paul Geyer
Corp. SS. Eccl. Lat. XXXIX (Vienna etc. 1898) pp. xxx *sqq*, 219–97 [best ed.]. TRANS
ENG: Wright *Early travels in Palestine* (London 1848). — Jas. Rose Macpherson
Pilgrims' Text Soc. Pub. X (London 1889). FR.: A. Baron *Voyage à la Terre Sainte
de l'évêque français Arculphe* (Limoges 1869). GERM. trans. by P. Mickley. COMM:
Halm *Sitzungsb. d. k. Akad. in Wien* phil.-hist. Cl. L (1865) 112, 117, 136. — R. Röh-
richt *Bibliotheca geographica Palaestinae* (1890) 12–4. — Beazley *Dawn of modern
geography* I (1897) 518–9, II (1901) 131–40. — Geyer *op. cit.* p. 283 *supra* [II 54–66
has extracts from text]. — Heisenberg *Grabeskirche und Apostelkirche* I (1908) 130,
175, 192. — *Byzantinische Zs.* IV 338 *sqq*; X 704 *sqq*. — C. Mommert *Golgatha und
das heilige Grab* 212 *sqq*.

A Gallic bishop named Arculf was, while returning from a pilgrimage to the Holy
Land, shipwrecked on the west coast of Britain. He came to Iona, and was there
hospitably entertained by Adamnán. Adamnán, a biblical scholar and possibly
already contemplating the writing of a treatise on the Holy Places, questioned his
visitor and made notes — apparently on the wax tablets inherited from classical civilisation — of the answers. From these notes the work *De Locis Sanctis*, was composed. It treats not only of Palestine, but also of Alexandria, Tyre, Crete, Constantinople and Sicily. It shows Adamnán in a very favorable light. He exercised such
control over his guest's reports as the resources of his library permitted. Among the

authors consulted for confirmation or comparison mention is made of Jerome, Sulpicius Severus, and the so-called Hegesippus.[420]

The story of Arculf's pilgrimage has primary interest as one of the earliest narratives of a journey from the West to Palestine and the Levant. But it has also a very real value as illustrating the interests and scholarship of an Irish monk dwelling in a small island off the Scottish coast in the latter part of the seventh century.

Adamnán presented his book to his friend King Aldfrid of Northumbria on one of his visits to that monarch. It thus passed into Anglo-Saxon monasteries and became the basis of Bede's composition on the same subject.[421] It was probably conveyed to the Continent through both Irish and Anglo-Saxon channels. There it enjoyed considerable popularity, as is evidenced by the large number of copies known to have existed in the early middle ages.[422]

113. Commentary on Vergil attributed to Adamnán

MSS: BN lat. 11308 *s* IX ff. 16 *sqq.* — Berne Stadtbibl. 167 *s* IX/X ff. 6ᵛ-214ᵛ [works of Vergil as well as commentaries]; 172 *s* X [MS said to be originally from Fleury]. — BN lat. 7960 *s* X ff. 1 *sqq.* — Florence Bibl. Laurent. Plut. XLV Cod. 14 *s* X ff. 2 *sqq* [said to be of French origin; the colophon to the first series of excerpts from Philargyrus seems to contain a Latin rendering — *Fatosus* — of the name of the Irish scribe, which may have been *Toicthech*]. — Leyden Voss. Lat. F. 79 *s* X. EDS: Of scholia: G. Thilo *Rheinische Museum* N. F. XV (1860) 132 *sqq.* — H. Hagen *Jahrbücher für classische Philologie* Vierter Suppl. Bd., Heft 5 (1867) 690 *sqq* [" Scholia Bernensia "]; *Servii Grammatici qui feruntur in Vergilii carmina commentarii* III fasc. ii *Appendix Serviana* (Leipsic 1902) 1–189 [" Explanatio Junii Philargyrii grammatici in Bucolica "]. EDS: Of Irish glosses: HZ *Glossarum Hibernicarum Supplementum* (Berlin 1886) 5 [all but one reprinted from Thilo]. — WS *The Academy* Jan. 17, 1891; April 15, 1893; July 21, 28, 1894. — WS *Zs. f. vergleichende Sprachforschung* XXXIII (1893) 62–86, 313–5; *Trans. Philol. Soc.* 1893 pp. 308–26 [these two articles contain the glosses of Laurent. Plut. XLV Cod. 14]; *RC* XIV (1893) 226–37 [glosses of BN lat. 7960], XVI 123. — *Thes. Pal.* II (1903) pp. xvii, 46–8. COMM: H. Hagen *Catalogus codicum Bernensium* (Berne 1875) 234, 237. — Em. Thomas *Essai sur Servius et son commentaire sur Vergile* (Paris 1879) 275 *sqq.* — Conington and Nettleship *The Works of Vergil* I (5th ed. London 1898) pp. xcvii–xcix. — Teuffel *Geschichte der römischen Literatur* (3rd ed.) 472, 13. — AdeJ *RC* XXI (1900) 111. — RTh *ZCP* III (1901) 52–4 [date of glosses]. — Roger *L'Enseignement* (1905) 262–3, 266–7. — Manitius *Lat. Lit.* I (1911) 239. — Mario Esposito *Proc. RIA* XXX C i (1912) 6.

There are on the continent of Europe several manuscripts containing commentaries on Vergil's Bucolics and Georgics which evidently depend originally on Irish compilations. They differ considerably among themselves both in extent and character, but all consist, in the main, of excerpts taken from earlier scholiasts. From the

---

[420] *Cf.* p. 136 *supra.*

[421] *Bedae Opera* ed. Giles IV 402–42. The epitome in *Hist. Eccles.* V *cap.* xv-xvii, is extracted, not from Adamnán, but from Bede's own book.

[422] There is a treatise *De locis sanctis* ascribed to one Eucherius. Geyer has shown that this is not, as has sometimes been assumed, a source of Adamnán's work, but is, itself, based on Bede.

Berne manuscripts have been published the " Scholia Bernensia," well known to Vergilian scholars, while from those of Paris and Florence has been reconstructed the " Explanatio Junii Philargyrii grammatici in Bucolica." The manuscripts contain two series of excerpts from this treatise, one older than the other. All the texts contain many very old glosses in the Irish language. Thurneysen, from a study of the glosses of two manuscripts,[423] would assign them to the end of the seventh century, or not much later. The glosses in their present form are, however, very corrupt, as all our copies were written in the ninth and tenth centuries by continental scribes who knew no Irish. It seems probable, indeed, that the immediate archetypes of these manuscripts also were written on the Continent by men ignorant of the Irish language.

The most plausible explanation of these facts is that some Irish scholar towards the end of the seventh century edited a collection of scholia on the Bucolics and Georgics, that more or less modified transcripts of his book were made by his disciples or others, and that several copies derived from these passed to the Continent at the time of the great migration of Irish scholars in the ninth century, and thereafter into the hands of continental scribes.[424] But be that as it may, the texts offer good evidence that Vergil was studied in Ireland in the seventh century.

Who was the original compiler? His name is apparently preserved as Adananus [425] or Adannanus.[426] An Irish scholar Adananus of the end of the seventh century would be a contemporary of Adamnanus of Hii, who, we know from his *Vita Columbae*, had some knowledge of Vergil.[427] The supposition is not far fetched that the two men were identical.

The superscription to the *scholia* on the Georgics in the Berne codices contains the statement: " I have collected all this from the commentaries of the Romans, namely Titus Gallus and Gaudentius and especially Junius Philargyrius of Milan."[428] Our texts, then, contain extracts from the works of these late Roman commentators — some of them from Philargyrius alone. But Adananus, or Adamnán, added considerable matter of his own — illustrations from Latin, Irish, and occasionally Greek; references to at least Plautus and Suetonius; grammatical, historical and archaeological information of that half childish, semi-encyclopaedic type so dear to the early Middle Ages. In especial, he expanded his sources continually with Christian allegory.

---

[423] BN lat. 7960, Laurent. Plut. XLV Cod. 14.
[424] Thilo *Rhein. Mus.* N.F. XV 132; Manitius *Lat. Lit.* I 239.
[425] BN lat. 11308 f. 23.
[426] BN lat. 7960 ff. 5, 36–7.
[427] Cf. p. 433 *infra*.
[428] Haec omnia de commentariis Romanorum congregavi id est Titi Galli et Gaudentii et maxime Iunilii Flagrii [= Iunii Filargirii = I. Philargyrii] Mediolanensis.

CHAPTER IV

THE MONASTIC CHURCHES, THEIR FOUNDERS AND TRA-
DITIONS — PART I: THE PRIMITIVE FOUNDATIONS

Bibliography

See the works and periodicals on church history noticed at pp. 93, 106, 109 *supra*.

ON MONASTICISM IN GENERAL: Lucas Holstenius, or Holste *Codex regularum monasticarum* 3 pts. (Rome 1661); new ed. 6 vols. (Augsburg 1759). — Adolf Harnack *Das Mönchtum, seine Ideale und seine Geschichte* (Giessen 1895); trans. by C. R. Gillett *Monasticism: its ideals and its history* (New York 1895). — Otto Zöckler *Askese und Mönchthum* 2nd ed. 2 vols. (Frankfort 1897). — Grützmacher " Mönchtum " *Realencykl. f. prot. Theologie u. Kirche* XIII. — U. Berlière *L'ordre monastique des origines au XIIe siècle* 2nd ed. (Paris 1921). — Lina Eckenstein *Woman under monasticism A.D. 500–1500* (Cambridge 1896). — Mention should also be made of the huge work of the Comte de Montalembert *Les moines d'occident depuis s. Benoit jusqu'à s. Bernard* 7 vols. (Paris 1860–77); trans.: *The Monks of the West* 7 vols. (Edinburgh, etc. 1861–79); another ed., 6 vols. (London, etc. 1896): much space is given to Irish monasteries and Irish saints, but the matter is mainly uncritical eulogy. ON IRISH MONASTICISM AND MONASTERIES: Notes to W. Reeves *Life of St. Columba . . . by Adamnan* (Dublin 1857). — W. F. Skene *Celtic Scotland* vol. II (Edinburgh 1877; 2nd ed. 1887). — H. Concannon *The Life of St. Columban A study of ancient Irish monastic life* (Dublin 1915). — J. P. Rushe *A Second Thebaid: a popular account of the ancient monasteries of Ireland* (Dublin 1905) is uncritical, while John Healy *Insula sanctorum et doctorum or Ireland's ancient schools and scholars* (Dublin 1890; 4th ed. 1902) is a quite untrustworthy combination of romance and pseudo-criticism. The only attempt at a historical survey of the several monasteries is Mervyn Archdall *Monasticon Hibernicum* (Dublin 1786), in part re-edited by P. F. Moran, 2 vols. (Dublin 1873–6). For the material character of the monastic churches see the sections devoted to the subject in the works and periodicals on archaeology listed on pp. 94, 103 *supra*, particularly those of ·Petrie, Margaret Stokes, Dunraven and Champneys; also H. J. Lawlor *Chapters on the Book of Mulling* (Edinburgh 1897) 167–85; W. F. Wakeman *Survey of antiquarian remains on Inismurray* RSAI extra vol. for 1892 (London, etc. 1893); and H. C. Lawlor *The monastery of Saint Mochaoi of Nendrum* (Belfast 1925).

IRISH MONASTIC RULES: L. Gougaud "Inventaire des régles monastiques irlandaises" *Revue Bénédictine* XXV (1908) 167–84, 321–33; and his *Chrétientés celtiques* (Paris 1911) 85–8.

GUIDES to the *acta sanctorum*: Potthast *Bibliotheca historica* [*cf.* p. 91] II 1131–1646 has an useful list, with bibliography. — *Bibliotheca hagiographica latina antiquae et*

288

mediae aetatis ediderunt Socii Bollandiani 2 vols. (Brussels 1898–1901). *Supplementum* (1911): a full bibliography of hagiographical texts in Latin, giving *incipit* and *desinit* of each; the Lives of each saint are arranged according to date of composition, or dependence on each other. Hardy *Cat.* gives notices, with lists of MSS, of many Lives of Irish saints. The most valuable guide to Irish texts only is Plummer's " tentative " list in his *Miscellanea hagiographica*, noticed below. There is one important periodical devoted to hagiology, the Bollandist Fathers' *Analecta Bollandiana* (Brussels, Paris, Geneva 1882–, in process).

GENERAL COLLECTIONS OF TEXTS: Laurentius Surius *De probatis sanctorum historiis* 6 vols. (Cologne 1570–5); 2nd ed. 7 vols. (1576–81); 3rd ed. 12 vols. (1618); new ed. *Historiae seu vitae sanctorum* 13 vols. (Turin 1875–80): the most important collection prior to that of the Bollandists, but inferior to their work because of poor texts and of editorial alterations. *Cf.* P. Holt " Die Sammlung von Heiligenleben des Laurentius Surius " *NA* XLIV (1922) 341–64. — *Acta sanctorum quotquot toto orbe coluntur* (Antwerp, Brussels, Tongerloo, 1643–, in process): this, the most important of all hagiographical collections, has been edited by John Bollandus and his successors in the Society of Jesus, known as the Bollandists; 65 vols. have been published embracing the saints, in the order of their festivals in the calendar, through Nov. 10. There were partial reprints, differing slightly in division and pagination of some vols., at Venice (1739–70) and Paris (1863–75). The work has always, but especially in the later volumes, maintained a high standard of scholarship; the Lives of Irish saints, however, are, on the whole, not up to the mark of others.[1] — Luc d'Achery, Jean Mabillon, Theod. Ruinart *Acta sanctorum ordinis s. Benedicti in saeculorum classes distributa —* saeculum I–VI 9 vols. (Paris 1668–1701; 2nd ed. Venice 1733–40): not confined strictly to members of the Benedictine order; Mabillon included some Irish saints.[2]

IRISH COLLECTIONS: For Capgrave's *Nova Legenda Anglie* see p. 307 *infra.* — Thomas Messingham *Florilegium Insulae Sanctorum seu vitae et acta sanctorum Hiberniae quibus accesserunt s. Patricii Purgatorium aliaque monumenta* (Paris 1624): has now only an antiquarian interest; an introductory essay by David Rothe on the ancient names of Ireland is followed by texts relating to various saints: a list of contents is given in Hardy *Cat.* I pt. II 844–5. — John Colgan *Acta Sanctorum veteris et maioris Scotiae, seu Hiberniae, sanctorum insulae . . . tomus primus, qui de sacris Hiberniae antiquitatibus est tertius, Januarium, Februarium, et Martium complectens* (Louvain 1645); *Triadis Thaumaturgae seu divorum Patricii Columbae et Brigidae, trium veteris et maioris Scotiae, seu Hiberniae, sanctorum insulae, communium patronorum acta . . . tomus secundus sacrarum eiusdem insulae antiquitatum, nunc primum in lucem prodiens* (Louvain 1647): Colgan's was long the most important publication of Irish *acta*, and even yet is very valuable, containing documents not printed elsewhere. It is, as the titles indicate incomplete. The texts are often unsatisfactory, partly because of liberties taken therewith by the editor. Lives in the Irish language are reproduced in Latin translations, or paraphrases. Both vols. are very rare. A list of contents can be seen in Hardy *Cat.* I pt. II 750–2.— For Fleming's *Collectanea sacra* see p. 186 *supra.*— WS *Three Mid-*

---

[1] Such reservation does not, of course, apply to the editions by Father Grosjean in tom. IV of November. — On the work of the Bollandists see art. "Bollandists," by Ch. De Smedt, *Cath. Encyl.*, and H. Delehaye *À travers trois siècles L'œuvre des Bollandistes 1615–1915* (Brussels 1920; trans.: Princeton 1922) [has useful bibliographical guide].

[2] See Dom Paul Denis *Dom Mabillon et sa méthode historique Mémoire justificatif sur son édition des Acta sanctorum o. s. B.* (Paris 1910).

dle Irish homilies on the Lives of Saints Patrick, Brigit and Columba (Calcutta 1877 — 100 copies privately printed). — For the *Acta sanctorum ex codice Salmanticensi* see p. 304 *infra;* for *Lis. Lives* p. 308 *infra.* — Charles Plummer *Vitae Sanctorum Hiberniae* 2 vols. (Oxford 1910): the most valuable of recent contributions to Irish hagiology. It contains a careful edition of 34 Latin Lives, of which 13 were hitherto unpublished, a scholarly introduction, and useful indices. The *addenda* and *corrigenda* should be noted. The introductory dissertation on Irish hagiography is the best we have. It is open to criticism chiefly in its over-emphasis of mythological influences: attributes of " fire-deities " and " water-deities " are discovered as direct survivals in what seem to be nothing but the stock supernatural trappings of the hagiographer. *Cf. An. Boll.* 1910, no. 3; J. Vendryes *RC* XXXII (1911) 104–6. — Idem *Bethada náem nÉrenn Lives of Irish Saints* 2 vols. (Oxford 1922): a collection of Irish texts, with trans., paralleling the preceding in form and treatment; 17 documents, all but two previously unpublished. *Cf. London Times Literary Supplement* Jan. 25, 1923 p. 59; P. Walsh *Studies* XII (1923) 148–51. — Idem *Miscellanea hagiographica Hibernica Vitae adhuc ineditae sanctorum* (Bollandists' *Subsidia hagiographica* XIV) (Brussels 1925): contains, besides minor texts, an exceedingly valuable " tentative catalogue of Irish hagiography."

MODERN BIOGRAPHICAL COLLECTIONS: John O'Hanlon *Lives of the Irish Saints* 10 vols. (Dublin 1875–1903): this work, to be completed in twelve volumes, was left unfinished at the death of the author. He has gathered together and presented in English garb practically all the information obtainable from every source regarding the saints of Ireland. The introduction gives a detailed account of the history and materials of Irish hagiology. The note of edification pervades the work, and the historical criticism displayed is only of an elementary character. — For *Lives of the British Saints,* by Baring-Gould and Fisher, which contains a few Irish saints, see p. 171 *supra.*

CRITICAL STUDIES of the *acta sanctorum* in general: C. A. Bernoulli *Die Heiligen der Merowinger* (Tübingen 1900): an important study of continental hagiography, 5th to 8th century. — Hippolyte Delehaye *Les légendes hagiographiques* (Brussels 1905; 2nd ed. 1906); part in *Rev. des questions historiques* LXXIV (1903) 56–122; trans. by V. M. Crawford *The legends of the saints, an introduction to hagiography* (London and New York 1907). — Heinrich Günter *Legenden-Studien* (Cologne 1906); *Die christliche Legende des Abendlandes* (Heidelberg 1910). These studies, of which that by the learned Bollandist, Father Delehaye, will be found most useful, treat of the general development of the saint-legend in mediaeval western Europe. Such general studies constitute a necessary setting for the more particular examination of Irish legend, such as is offered by Plummer. — See also the art. " Sanctus," by Delehaye, *An. Boll.* 1909, no. 2. — L. Zoepf *Das Heiligenleben im 10. Jahrhundert* (Leipsic, Berlin 1908). — For the theory that the cult of the saints sprang from that of the pagan gods: E. Lucius (ed. G. Anrich) *Die Anfänge des Heiligenkults in der christlichen Kirche* (Tübingen 1904), and trans. by E. Jeanmaire *Les origines du culte des saints* (Paris 1908); P. Saintyves *Les saints successeurs des dieux* (Paris 1907); *Le discernement du miracle* (Paris 1909). And for the contrary opinion: V. Ernoni " Les commencements du culte des saints " *Rev. des questions historiques* Jan. 1907; E. Vacandard *Études de critique et d'histoire religieuse* 3rd ser. (Paris 1912). — G. H. Gerould *Saints' legends* (Boston, New York 1916) is a popular survey of the subject. IRISH TOPICS: Edmund Hogan *The Latin Lives of the Saints as aids towards the translation of Irish texts and the production of an Irish dictionary* (RIA Todd Lecture Series V: Dublin

1894): primarily of philological interest, but useful for the historical student of the Lives. — L. Gougaud "Les conceptions du martyre chez les Irlandais" *Rev. Bénédictine* 1907 no. 3; also his *Chrétientés celtiques* (Paris 1911) 60–3 " Valeur des Vies de saints celtiques." — For Czarnowski *Le culte des héros — St. Patrick* see p. 320 *infra*.

In the fourth and fifth centuries the Christian Church in western Europe was organised along the main lines which have since generally prevailed.   The chief depository both of the sacerdotal functions and of the ecclesiastical jurisdiction was the bishop, *episcopus;* the centre of administration was the city where his residence, chair, *cathedra*, stood, and its limits the boundaries of his province or *dioecesis;* and his auxiliaries in the work of serving the churches and ministering to the people were the priests, *presbyteri*, to some of whom, it would seem, special districts for their labors, *parochiae*, were beginning to be assigned. Such a system was, no doubt, that in the minds of those who, in 431, sent Palladius " as first bishop to the Irish believing in Christ," [3] and in the mind of Patricius when he wrote " I am a bishop, appointed by God, in Ireland." [4]

It is not till the middle and second half of the seventh century, perhaps three hundred years after the introduction of Christianity, that our sources begin to give us a serviceable picture of the Irish ecclesiastical system.   Then and for the next four centuries the organisation of the Irish Church differed radically from that just described.

Monasticism was the basis of the Irish system.   Every important Irish church was a monastic church; that is, it was the church of a little walled village whose dwellers were monks or nuns living under ecclesiastical discipline and ministering to the spiritual needs of the surrounding people.   Doubtless there were churches to which no such community was attached, but they seem generally to have belonged to one of two classes — the solitary oratory where a hermit priest led a life of rigorous asceticism (such a hermitage sometimes, through the advent of disciples, grew into a large monastery and the single anchorite became the canonised founder of a great community), or the chapel dependent on a monastery, to the *familia* of which its ministrant was regarded as belonging. Administration and coercive power, a power autocratic and far-reaching, were in the hands of the abbot.[5]   The bishop retained his prerogatives of highest ecclesiastical dignity and his sacramental func-

[3] *Cf.* p. 165 *supra.*
[4] The Epistle. No. 29.
[5] The word *abbatia*, designating the office of abbot, is believed to have originated in Ireland. *Cf.* K. Blume " Abbatia Ein Beitrag zur Geschichte der kirchlichen Rechtsprache " *Kirchenrechtl. Abhandlungen hrsg. von* U. Stutz, Heft 83 (Stuttgart 1914).

tions, but not, unless he were also abbot, the administrative jurisdiction.[6] In secular law [7] and popular regard the abbot's authority was based on the fact that he was the heir, *comarba*, of the holy man who had founded the monastery. To him belonged by inheritance all the property, powers, dues and privileges which had been or should have been accorded to the founder. He was chosen from the blood-relations of the founder, unless they failed to provide a qualified candidate.[8] If the same saint had founded several churches these formed a league or congregation, *paruchia*, under the rule of the abbot of the mother-church, usually the place of the saint's " resurrection," that is, where his body was buried. The monks of all the churches of his *paruchia* made up the saint's *familia*, or *muinter*. The *paruchia* was not a territorial unit, for the monastic churches composing it might be widely scattered. Nevertheless there was a tendency towards territorial ecclesiastical divisions arising from the desire of each secular state, *túath*, for some autonomy in religious matters. The saint of the chief mother-church within a *túath* became the patron of that *túath*, and the interests of monastery and state would naturally become closely related. But there was no great sectionalism in Irish religion; the influence of the *comarbai* of the more famous saints, such as Patrick of Armagh, Columci'le of Iona, Ciarán of Clonmacnois, Finnian of Clonard, Comgall of Bangor, Brendan of Clonfert, Maedóc of Ferns, was nation-wide. In the Irish world these abbots played the rôle that on the Continent was assumed by the archbishops of Reims, Trèves, Mayence or Cologne.

How did this peculiar church organisation come to exist? It has been stated [9] as probable that the monastic movement entered Ireland almost as soon as Christianity itself, coming from the monasteries of Tours and Lérins in Gaul, and from Candida Casa in Britain. The bishop Patricius favored the coenobitic life, which he himself would seem to have experienced in Gaul. But it was as bishop that he did his work in Ireland, and the evidence appears to show that in the first era of Irish church history the administration was episcopal and the majority of the churches were not monastic. When we examine the Irish ecclesiastical system of the eighth century and later we find that almost all the great ruling churches and congregations of churches attributed their

---

[6] It is possible that a kind of *fainéant* episcopal jurisdiction survived over some churches or districts that the monastic system had not absorbed.

[7] The secular law-tracts, the so-called " Brehon Laws," contain much valuable matter regarding the ecclesiastical system.

[8] In such case the choice passed to the family who owned the land from which the site of the monastery had been granted.

[9] *Cf.* pp. 158 *sqq supra.*

foundation to saints of the sixth and seventh centuries. With a few exceptions, such as Armagh, which would appear to have adopted a monastic polity in the sixth century, and Kildare and Saigir, which perhaps were monasteries from their inception, the primitive churches have dropped into insignificance, so that it is impossible to tell what was their *status*. It would seem, therefore, that something like a revolution was wrought in the Irish Church in the sixth century, and that it was the work of the famous saints of that era. British influences may have helped the movement, for it has been seen that David, Gildas, Cadoc, and their contemporaries had close relations with Ireland and that they appear to have been promoters of a similar monastic movement.[10]

The decisive reason for the dominance of monasticism in Ireland was, we may be sure, the enthusiasm with which the early Irish Christians embraced the coenobitical life and the ideals of asceticism. This it was that provided inmates, sometimes in thousands, for all the monasteries, and, as the spirit of asceticism grew, sent Irish anchorites to seek hermitages on the islands of the Irish and Scottish coasts or overseas in foreign lands.

The old Irish monastic churches have disappeared, leaving only the slightest material traces of their existence. Their records have, for the most part, gone with them. Only one important class of such documents has been preserved in quantity, those *memoranda*, traditions and legends of their founders and famous men which form the Irish *acta sanctorum*. With them may be associated a few other texts, such as lists of abbots, lists of church dues, and monastic rules.

These biographies and other *acta* of saints make up one of the most extensive classes of material relating, *ex prima facie*, to the early history of Ireland. Their magnitude, and the fact that for so much of the past they are the only records, give them importance, but their character is such that they may be used only with special precautions.

The majority of the *acta sanctorum* as now extant are considerably removed from the texts kept in the ancient churches: they are available to us only in large collections compiled in the thirteenth, fourteenth, fifteenth, and even sixteenth and seventeenth centuries. The popularity in later mediaeval Europe of Lives of the Saints as reading matter, especially during the holy offices of the Church and in the monastic

---

[10] *Cf.* pp. 170 *sqq supra.*

refectories, had caused the preparation of many books of *Legenda*, "things to be read," made up of such Lives, either abridged or *in extenso*. The most famous collection was the *Legenda Aurea* of Jacopo de Voragine, archbishop of Genoa (d. *c* 1298). In England, in the first half of the fourteenth century, John of Tynemouth prepared his *Sanctilogium Angliae, Walliae, Scotiae, et Hiberniae*, in which he included several Lives of Irish saints. Certainly in that century, probably in the preceding, the same impulse was producing Irish *legendaria*. In them the national and antiquarian note, apparent in John of Tynemouth, was still more manifest: their folios were reserved, almost exclusively, for native saints.[11] Irish collections of Latin Lives were produced primarily for devotional purposes in the houses of the European religious orders that had taken the places of the old Irish monasteries and themselves in time become Hibernicised, but there is good reason to believe that the motive of recording the country's ancient glories was not wanting to the compilers. Of the Lives in the Irish language a considerable number are found in the *bibliothecae* of miscellaneous antiquities written in the secular schools. The most extensive gathering of saints' Lives in Irish was made by that "poor brother of the order of St. Francis," Michael O'Clery, in whom religious and national motives united so strongly at a time when friar and antiquarian alike had fallen on evil days.

The collections give us fairly faithful reproductions of the individual *vitae* on which they were based. Some of the Latin Lives were abridged for lectionary purposes, and almost all were, in some degree, edited. The methods of compilers differed, but it is clear that certain of them deliberately suppressed details considered irrelevant or unedifying, and interpolated explanatory or devotional padding. In preparing literature for the inmates of the houses of the new congregations much matter which was familiar to the monks of the old Celtic churches had to be either omitted or explained. Nevertheless, it is broadly true that there is available the substance of the individual Latin Lives as they were known in the thirteenth century, and of the Irish as they were known in the fourteenth, fifteenth, or sixteenth.

These individual *vitae*, some of which have come down through independent channels, were themselves late compositions. The Latin documents, as a general rule, represent an earlier tradition than the Irish,[12]

---

[11] Cod. S. contains a Life of Catharine of Alexandria, and the Cod. K. collection Lives of Louis of Toulouse and Anthony of Padua. There is a Life of David in *Cod. Insulensis*, where its presence is due, doubtless, to his associations with Ireland.

[12] The contrary opinion is held by the Rev. P. Power, ed. of the Lives of Déclán and Mo-Chuda, *ITS*

but even they are of the post-Viking age.[13] Linguistic tests cannot be applied to Latin documents as to Irish, but the available evidence indicates in nearly every case that the redaction is of the tenth, eleventh, or later centuries. Not a hagiographical *manuscript* of the pre-Viking age exists in Ireland, except the Book of Armagh [14] — which, perhaps, was venerated as a relic too sacred for a copyist's use. And — apart from the contents of that manuscript — of the considerable number of early Lives of Patrick, Brigit and Columba, only the Tripartite Life [15] of Patrick, written at the very end of the ninth century, survived in a *manuscript tradition* on Irish soil. We owe the others to the fact that copies passed at an early date to Britain or the Continent. The documents relating to these saints which Irish manuscript compilations of later centuries offer are Jocelin's Life of Patrick (after 1186), the Life of Brigit by Laurence of Durham (d. 1154), a *Vita Columbae* of possibly the tenth century, and several biographical homilies in Middle Irish.[16]

The historical student, then, has before him, in the main, Lives of the saints of the fifth, sixth and seventh centuries as, with a few exceptions, they were written in the eleventh, twelfth, thirteenth — perhaps in a few cases the tenth. Some of these — as the Life of Colmán mac Lúacháin—were compositions then written down for the first time.[17] But more frequently the available text is the last of a series of redactions. For Patrick so many of these have been saved that it is possible to trace the genealogical tree of the latest biography with considerable precision. Though other saints were not so fortunate, traces of dependence on, or actual survivals from, older Lives of the ninth, eighth, even seventh, century, are not infrequent. For some—as for Brendan of Clonfert— late versions are available in sufficient numbers to invite the restoration, by the methods of comparative criticism, of a *vita*, perhaps not the earliest, but certainly early in date and dominating in influence. In other Lives the workmanship has been crude to such a degree that a serviceable distribution of the contents into their principal *strata* should be possible.[18] Nevertheless it remains "very difficult to distinguish in a saint's Life that which belongs to the first text and that which has

---

XVI (1914). Bury thinks that there were early Irish texts on Patrick: *cf.* p. 331 *infra*. There are, of course, Latin translations of Irish Lives as well as Irish translations of Latin, but the translations in all cases seem to be comparatively late.

[13] So HZ *Göttingische gelehrte Anzeigen* March 1891.

[14] No. 131.   [15] No. 135.

[16] *Cf.* nos. 140, 151 (iv), 217, 218, 136, 152, 215.   [17] *Cf.* pp. 454–5.

[18] Evidence of the composite character of the Lives is plentiful. We frequently find an anecdote repeated, two, three, or four times, a slight modification of the circumstances concealing the identity from the hagiographer.

been added one hundred or two hundred years later,"[19] and, although critical analysis of the *acta* should still yield important results for Irish history, there obviously is much we would like it to do which the nature of the materials makes impossible.

To such fragmentary survivals of primitive compositions as can be distinguished in these later Lives are to be added a few early *acta* which have been handed down intact through other channels. From the seventh century we have the Life of Columbanus by Jonas [20] (a foreign production having little direct relationship to the Church in Ireland), the Life of Brigit by Cogitosus, the Lives of Columba by Cuimíne Ailbe and Adamnán, the works on Patrick by Tírechán and Muir-chú [21] and the Life of Fursa.[22] Several documents on the same personages emanated from the eighth and ninth centuries.[23] The whole constitutes a not inconsiderable mass of ancient Irish hagiography. But even these are far from being contemporary records. The Lives of Columbanus and Fursa come nearest to that class. Cuimíne wrote fully fifty years after the death of Columba, Cogitosus more than one hundred after the annalists' obit for Brigit, Tírechán at least two hundred and ten years after Patrick. A Life of Ita contains portions of a biography which may have been written within a century of her death.[24] But the bulk even of these relatively few early *acta* date from two hundred years or more after the epochs of which they profess to treat.

They are not, therefore, first-rate sources for those epochs. In an age when historical criticism was so defective, when the importance of objective truth and the difficulty of securing it were so little appreciated, when subjective ideas received such a free rein, trustworthy testimony could not be given by the writer far removed in time from the events he narrated. Moreover, in Ireland there were other causes besides the lapse of time to spread a gap between the saints and their biographers. One was the great plague of 664-5, which so decimated the monastic population that it must have occasioned an appreciable break in the ecclesiastical traditions; and the other was the paschal controversy, which raged with considerable bitterness through much of the seventh century and, as the Romanising party triumphed, may have resulted in the repudiation and disappearance of many of the records, oral and written, of the churches.

[19] Fustel de Coulanges.
[20] No. 48.
[22] No. 296. Probably not composed in Ireland.
[24] *Cf.* p. 390 *infra.*

[21] Nos. 147, 213, 214, 127, 128.
[23] *Cf.* nos. 129, 130, 132-135, 148, 149, 151.

Also, the literary tradition weighed heavily on the hagiographer. The Bible, especially the Pentateuch and the Gospels; John Cassian's *Institutes*, describing the life of the monks of Egypt; the Latin Life of St. Anthony; the Life of St. Martin by Sulpicius Severus; some of the writings of Jerome and of Gregory the Great — these seem to have been authorities which the monastic writer felt obliged to use for both phraseology and subject-matter. It may well be that many other continental *vitae sanctorum* were known in the Irish monasteries. Indeed, contemporary Irish and continental *acta* are compositions of the same class, with much less distinction between them than is at times alleged.

One contribution of high value the author of a saint's Life did make to the materials of history: the environment, both material and spiritual, in which he placed his story. Just because this was composed of the unconsidered incidentals, not the essentials, and because author and reader alike lacked the historical imagination, it forms, usually, a true picture of the hagiographer's own age. It is of the social conditions of that age, its ideas, customs and manner of living, that the historian will find authentic record in the Lives of the saints.

Primarily, the *acta sanctorum* are sources for the times in which they were written and revised, not for those in which their heroes flourished. The editorial work found in the last revisions gives the point of view of ecclesiastics and antiquarians in the later middle ages; the texts which they used, and which can be approximately restored, are, in general, monuments of the Celtic monasteries of the tenth, eleventh and twelfth centuries; and the primitive documents which survive, either imbedded in these or independently, are contemporary records of those of the seventh, eighth and ninth centuries. The writings of Cogitosus, Cuimíne, Tírechán, Adamnán and Muir-chú form an exceedingly valuable set of sources for the study of the eccesiatical system, the monastic churches, and the social and religious life of the seventh century.

Also, the *acta* are first-hand sources for the history of the legends and cults of the saints. When several successive redactions of the same *vita* are available, it is possible to trace from age to age the development of the saint's story in monastic tradition or folk legend. The evolution of the Patrick Legend is the most noteworthy example. Very frequently, in Christian hagiology as in pagan mythology, the legend follows the cult. The saint's story was shaped by the institution in which he was peculiarly venerated. Almost always the first edition of a saint's Life, and commonly the subsequent redactions, were produced in the monastery which he himself founded and where his relics were exposed to honor.

Already in Christian Europe, at the time of the introduction of the faith into Ireland, the custom whereby each community gave religious honor to its martyrs, early bishops, and former members eminent for sanctity, was well established. In the monastery the founder, naturally, was held in special veneration. Undoubtedly this custom passed to Ireland. She had no martyrs, and her bishops, as such, made little impression on the historical imagination of a monastic church. But the whole system of ecclesiastical organisation made the founder of the monastic church, or of the *paruchia*, the person whose memory must be honored and virtues extolled.[25] The development of the cult of relics in the seventh and eighth centuries, possibly as a result of closer associations with continental Christianity, helped the canonisation of the great church-founders. Not having those of martyrs, the Irish monks began to enshrine and display the relics of their first abbots.[26] The possession of a *vita* to accompany, explain and enhance the relics would then become most important. The saints whom Irish hagiography canonised were, almost all, founders of monastic churches, and the importance of each is, commonly, in proportion to the subsequent fame of his chief foundation.

An Irish *vita sancti* is, then, a panegyric of its patron and founder produced in a monastic church many years after his decease. Its character is determined by its origin. To the Irish Lives, even more than to the Gallic, may be applied the words of Fustel de Coulanges: " To say that they were composed for the edification of the faithful is not entirely correct. More often it was to demonstrate the sanctity of their subject, and to make known his worth as a saint, in the interest of the church or monastery which claimed him as patron. The biography, like the legend, was explanatory of the relics which the monastery

---

[25] Early Irish church calendars, giving the saints' festival days, have not survived, but many such must have preceded such a compilation as Fél. Oeng. (no. 272). Many of the Lives, though not, perhaps, in their earliest redactions, took the form of homilies for the feast days.

[26] The cult of relics on the Continent began with the relics of the martyrs. The earliest Irish word for " relics " was *martre*. From many entries in the annals it is evident that in the eighth century the relics of native saints assumed much prominence in the religious economy of the country. His relics, however, may not have been the holy man's bones. The objects we usually hear of are his book, his bell, his *bacall*, or staff. *Cf*. HZ " Keltische Kirche " in *Realencyclopädie f. prot. Theologie u. Kirche* X (3rd ed. 1901); trans. A. Meyer *The Celtic Church in Britain and Ireland* (London 1902) 119–29. The evidence seems to be constrained to the purposes of HZ's theories. The annalistic *commotatio reliquiarum*, " transfer of relics," is assumed to mean the disinterment of the saint's remains; this may be the meaning, but more probably the word signified the solemn carrying of the relics through the country.

possessed, and which made its fortune."[27]   More than that, it explained the church's position in the *paruchia*, its relations with other churches, and its claims to tribute from the secular population.   In many of the older and fuller texts, narratives of church foundations are plentiful and historically important, for, although in special cases these were, doubtless, pious fictions designed to extend the bounds of the *paruchia*,[28] in general they must have been based on genuine traditions.   In connection with church foundations it was particularly important to record any grants made or obligations incurred by the local state.   Their *acta sanctorum* were the charters of the early Irish churches.   Other passages told of the alliances which different saints made with each other, to be perpetuated, of course, in their communities.   And the association of the saints did not end here.   It seems to have been the ambition of each church to bring its patron into relationship with as many as possible of the famous early ecclesiastics, regardless of chronology.   The result was a huge syncretistic system in which almost all the celebrated founders of churches were brought together, as masters, disciples, fellow-pupils, or intimate friends, or through the medium of prophecy, baptism or blessing, in one great confraternity under the ultimate headship of Patrick. — The main interest of the hagiographer, however, was in thaumaturgy: for the essential proof of an individual's sanctity was his power to work miracles.   Each community must be able to demonstrate that its patron was, in this respect, inferior to none other.[29]   There cannot be the slightest doubt that the monastic hagiographers themselves provided a large portion of the anecdotes of the miraculous set forth in their compositions, in the pious belief, perhaps, that a saint must necessarily have performed such wonder-works.[30] Yet their miracles were not the pure product of their imaginations.   The pages of Holy Writ, the Lives of other saints, were the sources, and the same miracle is made to do service for saint after saint with an extraordinary default of originality.[31]   At times there is a superficial occasion for such borrowings, as in several instances where two saints have the

---

[27] *Histoire des institutions politiques de l'ancienne France, La monarchie franque* (Paris 1888) 9.   The whole passage, which has much interest for Irish hagiology, is quoted in *Lis. Lives* pp. xci *sq.*

[28] *Cf.* p. 344 *infra.*

[29] *Cf.* p. 454 *infra.*

[30] *Cf.* the words of Agnellus of Ravenna, writing, about 840, the history of the bishops of that see: " Lest there should be gaps in our account of the succession of bishops, by the help of your prayers [he says, addressing his brethren], I have composed the lives of them all; and I do not think I have told falsehood herein, for they were all men of prayer, and chaste, and lovers of almsgiving, and fishers of men."   Trans. by Edmund Bishop in *Liturgica historica* (Oxford 1918) 377.

[31] There is one case, that of the Life of Bishop Mac Cuilinn of Lusca, where the *acta* of one saint (Bairre of Cork) have been taken over as a whole and appropriated to another.   But this is quite unusual.   *Cf.* Plummer *Misc. hag. Hib. Cat.* no. 276.

same name. But in general the practice is not plagiarism so much as the exercise of an equal right to draw on a common stock of hagiographical lore.[32]

What materials were used by the earliest biographers of the saints? They give few indications of having possessed written records. Perhaps in some cases, as in that of Patrick, authentic documents from the saint's own hand or that of a contemporary still existed. But in general the written sources seem to have been of the most meagre kind: the diptychs read at the mass; lists of abbots and abbesses, which the churches kept from a very early date;[33] the calendars, in which the festival days of the founder and others held in special honor by the community were entered, for yearly celebration;[34] the paschal tables on which, from year to year, important events, especially the deaths of eminent ecclesiastics, were noted — and the annals which grew out of these;[35] probably occasionally a collection of notes regarding church foundations, the bounds of land grants, and such matters.[36] The bulk of the information available to these biographers, removed one, two, or more centuries from their heroes, came by oral transmission — monastic tradition or popular legend.

[32] Duine has put the case very well thus: " Les *miracula* en hagiographie sont un peu comme les *exempla* en prédication: il est souvent impossible de dire qui les a mis le premier en cours; *miracula* et *exempla* appartiennent à tout le monde et chacun les approprie à un sujet spécial."—*Memento* 57.

[33] *Cf.* pp. 368–9.   [34] *Cf.* pp. 480 *sqq.*

[35] *Cf.* pp. 213 *sqq.* One of the peculiarities of the records regarding many of the early saints is the great ages to which they are said to have lived, ranging from over one hundred to over four hundred years. These statements are found occasionally in the Lives, but usually in the annals and calendars. The only attempt at a solution is that of Alfred Anscombe, " The great ages assigned to certain Irish saints " *Ériu* V (1911) 1–6. He suggests that the number given as the saint's age was in reality the date of his death in a chronology no longer understood when our present texts were written down, and that the reason of this ignorance was because the tables of the old paschal cycles had been destroyed when the Irish churches conformed to the Roman Easter. The hypothesis is plausible, but when Anscombe proceeds in an attempt to show from particular cases that the lost chronology was in the " era of Diocletian," or " era of the martyrs," in which the year one began August 29, A.D. 284, and that its dates were written in Greek numerals, he is not so convincing. — The repeated association of these statements as to ages with others giving the saints' feast-days makes it probable that the sources from which the entries were copied and erroneously expanded were the church calendars. These entries would be of some such form as this: " Kal. Jun. — Obit N—— anno clxxx." The annal reference may have been to some commonly accepted era, or it may have been to some other record in the monastery, *i.e.*, most probably, the paschal table. The paschal table, in the margins of which notable events were jotted down, might begin with the first year of an 84-year cycle (as to the customary incidence of which, we have no knowledge), or, later, one of 532 or 19 years, but it might begin at some other year. With our present information, therefore, we cannot postulate uniformity in the chronological records of the different monasteries. — The old paschal tables would, of course, be either deliberately destroyed or cast aside and allowed to disappear when the new Easter was adopted, but the calendars of saints' days would remain as serviceable as ever, and be retained.

[36] This seems to have been the nature of the contents of the Book of Ultán, and of other documents which Tírechán may have consulted. *Cf.* pp. 330–1 *infra.* Some, and perhaps all, of the monasteries kept a *lebar sochair*, a " book of emoluments," in which were recorded the claims of the monastery to rents and payments. (*Cf. BNE* I p. xxxv.) It was drawn on by the hagiographer, especially in the later middle ages, and in some cases, as in that of St. Caillín (p. 401), seems to have been the basis for the greater part of the saint's story.

Genuine monastic tradition, when it existed, was a source of considerable authority. It was subject, undoubtedly — and in a greater degree — to all the influences which warped the written work of the monastic hagiographer. But it was the tradition of a permanent corporate community whose members, in intelligence and literary education, must have been higher — in some cases far higher — than the mass of the population. The most favorable example of monastic tradition embodied in a *vita* is Adamnán's Life of Colum-cille. Not only is this a source of extraordinary value for contemporary conditions, but its statements of fact regarding the past seem, so far as they can be tested, to be remarkably accurate. But monastic tradition was always contaminated in some degree by what we may distinguish as popular legend. The churchmen were from the people and, in general, lived in the midst of the people. Even the greater part of the " monks " were, in the majority of Irish monasteries during the period when the *acta sanctorum* developed, a secular population, dwelling on church lands under the jurisdiction of the abbot.[37]

Legend, whether in the less adulterated form of certain Lives in the Irish language,[38] or with ecclesiastical modifications, is a main source of hagiography. Legend belongs to the realm of folk-lore, where the transmission of facts is exceedingly erratic. The folk mind sometimes retains the record of an event with extraordinary accuracy from generation to generation, sometimes within a few years distorts it beyond recognition. It is a medium that cannot be trusted. Yet we may say that, as a rule, folk-lore transmutes the personality which appeals to it — and the saint is such — into something different, something associated with a world of wonder and make-believe and primitive ethics, created out of the people's oldest and most elementary ideas.[39]

The mind of the Irish people during the early Christian era was, fundamentally, the product of countless ages of paganism. The popular legends moulded under a pagan, or semi-pagan, attitude of mind contained a large amalgam of "magic" and "superstition," those survivals of primitive religion. So far, therefore, as the *acta sanctorum* depend on popular legend they are, in some degree, records of primitive religious ideas and practices. Irish paganism seems to have consisted of a lower *stratum*, deep and wide, of magical belief and practice, and, super-

[37] *Cf.* p. 747 *infra.*   [38] *E. g., Geinemain Molling ocus a Bhethae*, no. 249.
[39] It is often difficult to determine whether the basic element in a miracle story or other anecdote of a saint has originated in a folk-lore *conte* or in the biblical or other source of the hagiographer's literary tradition.

imposed thereon, an upper section of mythology. Myth and magic were ejected from their positions of supremacy by the coming of Christianity, but the evidence does not indicate that the sphere of operation of either was extensively diminished.

The influence of pure mythology on the saint's legends seems not to have been great. The Christian voyage literature and probably some elements of the vision literature depend on mythological antecedents, but, except in the cases of Brigit and a few others,[40] there is little indication that attributes of individual deities were transferred to individual saints.[41] The Irish saints assuredly are not the successors of Lug and Nuadu and Oengus and the Dagda.

Nevertheless the myths, and that very considerable mass of heroic romance which was pervaded by mythology, prepared the ground for the spread of the legends of the saints. To the Irish people the saints were the heroes of the new order. Emain and Tara had passed away, but Armagh and Kildare were to endure forever. The contrast was felt and stated, not only in the late Ossianic literature, but also in compositions of far earlier date.[42] The glories of the warriors of a pagan civilisation were eclipsed by those of the Christian wonder-workers. It is possible also that the heroic sagas, besides constituting a secular tradition which invited emulation, suggested in some degree the forms of the new literature. In a late stage of the evolution of the vitae whole passages were taken over, practically intact, from secular romances,[43] but this was when ama'gamation had replaced rivalry in the relations of the two literatures.

In the content of Christian legend magical lore is far more prevalent than mythological. Temporal success and spiritual favors and even eternal salvation are made to depend on material agencies which at bottom are examples of " sympathetic " or " contagious " magic. The army of the Dési will always be victorious if, before going to battle, they march around Déclán's stone.[44] Any person who dies resting on the hide of the dun cow of Ciarán will be saved.[45] All who are buried in the churchyards of a long list of saints are assured of salvation.[46] In the legend of Caillín we learn that those who are buried in another neighboring parish are certain of damnation.[47]

---

[40] Cf. pp. 312, 314, 357, 364 infra.
[41] So good an authority as Dr. Plummer holds the opposite opinion. Cf. p. 290 supra.
[42] Cf. the hymn of Fíacc (no. 132), the poem "Hail Brigit," (ed. KM, Halle and Dublin 1912), and the prologue of Fél. Oeng. (no. 272).
[43] Cf. pp. 313, 411. [44] Cf. p. 313 infra. [45] Cf. p. 379 infra. [46] Cf. p. 376 infra.
[47] Cf. p. 400 infra. Many of the objects, such as holy wells, which are said to have received certain

Saintship itself was, to the popular mind, a concept of the magical order. Its essential characteristic was not moral goodness but the possession of that mysterious power which works miracles. The " sanctifying grace " of the legendary saint neither arose from habitual virtue nor resulted primarily in holiness; it was the Christianised counterpart of the magic potency of the druid. The saint's birth was, almost always, heralded and accompanied by supernatural phenomena, and his infancy and childhood were signalised by wonder-works. In his maturity he becomes the Christian " medicine-man," differing from his pagan rivals by superior power and a better cause. Sometimes he practises extraordinary austerities, paralleling those of the Hindu fakir and the American sun-dancer.[48] He fasts to obtain the power of compulsion over others, even the Deity.[49] His *bacall* and bell are his instruments of supernatural power, hymns and psalms serve him as incantations.[50] His numerous *facbála*, " leavings," that is, blessings and curses left on persons, places and things, continue to operate for centuries after his death. Indeed, to many an Irish saint, as pictured by the legends, might be applied what the poem attributed to Cuimmín Condeire says of Rúadán, " he loved cursing."[51]

These atavistic conceptions, dominating the folk-legends and influencing more or less the hagiographers, are much more prominent in some texts than in others. Those of the ninth to twelfth centuries are, in general, richer in pagan survivals than the compositions of earlier ages. This may indicate a relapse towards paganism — it certainly accompanies a decline in the number, size and intellectual standards of the monastic churches. But it is likewise possible that it results from the fuller acceptance of Christianity by the people. Christian legend has become the property of a larger circle, and has been debased accordingly. There are other indications that the post-Viking age witnessed a syncretism of the spiritual and the secular in Ireland such as had not been possible in earlier centuries.

To sum up, the Lives of the saints are sources of very great importance for Irish *Kulturgeschichte* — the monastic life and ideals, social conditions, the workings of the folk mind. They also usually reveal

virtues through the blessings of the saints, doubtless had magical potency in pagan days, and were thus brought within the pale of Christianity.

[48] There can be no doubt, however, that asceticism was actually carried to extreme lengths by the religious of the seventh and eighth centuries. *Cf.* L. Gougaud *Dévotions et pratiques ascétiques du moyen âge* (Paris 1925).

[49] *Cf.* p. 464 *infra.*

[50] *Cf.* the pictures of Patrick, and of Rúadán and his companions, before Tara, nos. 141 (ii), 184 *infra.*

[51] *Cf.* no. 274.

something of the character and history of the monastic churches from which they respectively sprang. But the amount of trustworthy information they give regarding the saints of whom they treat is, comparatively, slight. It is exceptional that, as in the case of Colum-cille, any considerable quantity of genuine historical and biographical matter survived. Nevertheless, with due precautions taken, we may extract from them a composite picture, having some fidelity, of the men and women who were the organisers of the old Irish Church and the leaders of a truly remarkable religious movement.[52]

I. Manuscript Collections of *Acta Sanctorum*

114. *Codex Salmanticensis*

MS: Brussels Bibl. roy. 7672–4 *s* XIV. Ed: *Acta Sanctorum Hiberniae ex Codice Salmanticensi nunc primum integre edita opera Caroli De Smedt et Josephi De Backer e Soc. Jesu, hagiographorum Bollandianorum; Auctore et sumptus largiente Joanne Patricio Marchione Bothae* (Edinburgh and London 1888) [" The edition is far from perfect; it suffers from the fact that the editors have no acquaintance with the Irish language, a knowledge of which is absolutely necessary for an editor even of Latin lives of Irish saints. The work was severely criticised by Zimmer. . . . Still, it is not difficult for an Irish scholar to correct the mistakes of the editors, and with all its shortcomings the edition does make the MS. available for students of Irish matters in a convenient form." — Plummer *VV. SS.* I p. ix n. 3.] Comm: S. H. Bindon *Proc. RIA* 1st Series III 496–9 [a description of the MS, not entirely accurate]. — HZ *Göttingische gelehrte Anzeigen* March 1891 [a severe criticism of *AA. SS. ex Cod. S.*, but also an interesting examination thereof. *Cf. An. Boll.* XI (1892); *RC* XII 393–7.] — *VV. SS. Hib.* I pp. ix, xi, xxii [summary description of MS and contents].

This is a folio volume which formerly belonged to the Irish College of Salamanca. It now consists of 175 leaves, but a considerable section at the beginning, and some leaves through the MS, are missing. The first folio is numbered 48. The volume was written in Ireland in the fourteenth century. The only scribal note is at the end of the Life of St. Cuanna, f. 219: "The blessing of Cuanna and of the saints who made their covenant with him on the soul of the man who translated this Life from Irish into Latin, i.e. Brother John MacKerñ [? MacTiernan] of Oriel." A later hand has

---

[52] One of the peculiarities of Irish hagiography was the importance attached to genealogy. The strong aristocratic sentiment of the Irish people and the care given to the preservation of the genealogies of all the great ones of the secular world naturally resulted in the preservation, or invention, of noble pedigrees for the saints. The rule by which the first claim to succession as *comarba* of the saint lay with his blood relations gave such records an importance also in the ecclesiastical world. Doubtless many of the royal origins assigned are well founded — the same stock provided the lay and the ecclesiastical leaders of the people; but a large part of the pedigrees are fictions, serving the double purpose of proving that the saint was of " good blood " and of providing the secular kin with famous representatives in the kingdom of heaven as well as in that of earth. True or fictitious, however, they are all sources for the study of the matter and methods of the old genealogists.

added "Also may the soul of Brother Dermot O'Donohue [53] rest in peace." Of the history of the MS in Ireland and Salamanca we know nothing. About 1620 or 1625 it was obtained from Father Thomas Bryan, then Rector of the College of Salamanca, for the hagiographical library which Father Heribert Rosweyde, the founder of the work of the Bollandists, was collecting. It remained in the library of the Bollandists until their organisation was suppressed during the French Revolution, when, after an interval of some years, it was deposited in the Burgundian Library, which is now the Royal Library of Brussels.

The compiler of the *Codex Salmanticensis* does not seem to have followed any predetermined plan, but to have copied the different *vitae* as they came to hand. Consequently these are of diverse character: some are extensive and valuable texts, others meagre epitomes; some are of early date, some of quite late composition. As a rule the Lives in the beginning of the volume are of greater antiquity and more value than those in the later part. The compilation as a whole, compared with other collections of Irish *acta sanctorum*, represents an earlier stage of development. This is shown both by the primitive character of much of the subject-matter and by the early forms of many of the Irish names of persons and places.

The Irish saints, Lives of whom are to be found in the codex, are: Brigit, Fursa, Brendan of Clonfert (2), Ciarán of Clúain, Darerca or Monenna, Finnian of Clonard, Tigernach, Fintan of Duleng, Ailbe, Mo-Lúa of Clonfertmulloe (2), Fintan of Clonenagh, Finan of Kinnity, Rúadán, Aed mac Bricc, Cainnech, Fintan or Munnu, Colmán Ela, Columba of Terryglass, Máedóc, Abbán, Cronan of Roscrea, Malachy, Laurence O'Toole, Flannan, Senán, Comgall of Bangor, Carthach or Mo-Chuta, Mo-Laise of Leighlin, Mac Cairthinn, Ciarán of Saigir, Moling, Colmán of Dromore, Coemgen, Colum-cille, Baithene, Dega, Mochta, Eoghan of Ardstraw, and Mac Nisse. There are also fragments regarding Colum-cille, Brendan, Cuannatheus and Mochulleus.[54]

115. The *Codex Kilkenniensis* Collection

MSS: Dublin Primate Marsh's Library Z. 3. 1. 5 (formerly V. 3. 4) *c* A.D. 1400. — TCD 175 (E. 3. 11) *c* A.D. 1400. *Cf.* Reeves *Proc. RIA* Jan. 1875; *VV. SS. Hib.* I pp. xi–xiv.

In Primate Marsh's Library, Dublin, and the Library of Trinity College, Dublin, are two manuscript collections of Irish hagiography which are closely related to each other.

---

[53] Norman Moore suggested that this should be read "Dermot from Theaghlach Dhunchadha," *i.e.*, the present barony of Tullyhunco, Cavan, the seat of the MacTiernans. — *EHR* July 1911 p. 563.

[54] It is noteworthy how many of the Irish saints are known not by the true form of their names but by modifications giving familiar, endearing, what are designated "hypocoristic" forms. The extensive use of familiar, "pet" or "nick" names seems to have been a characteristic of Irish society from the time of the earliest records until the present day. Primitive Celtic, and, indeed, Indo-European proper names were usually, but not always, true compounds, in which two stems were united to form one whole: *e.g.* Gallic *Divo-genos*, Greek Διογενής, "God-begotten." The hypocoristic appellations were usually formed by dropping the second element and either declining, or adding a suffix to, the first. The practice was adopted and extended by the Irish Christians in designating the saints: to the first stem were added both prefixes and suffixes, the prefixes usually *mo-*, "my," or *to-*, *do-*, "thy," and the suffix usually the diminutive of affection, *-óc. Cf.* AdeJ *CLC* VI 172–7; Dottin *Manuel pour servir à l'étude de l'antiquité celtique* (1915) 120–1; HZ "Zur Personennamenbildung in Irischen" *Zs. f. vergleichende Sprachforschung* XXXII (1891) 153–246; KM "Zur keltischen Wortkunde" no. 33 *Sitzungsb. d. k. preuss. Akad. d. Wissensch.* 1912 LI, no. 92 *ibid.* 1914 XXI; Marstrander *RC* XXXVI (1915–6) 360–1.

They seem to have been transcripts of the same original, and both to have been copied about the beginning of the fifteenth century. Both — but especially the Trinity College volume — are badly mutilated, but each to a very large extent supplies the deficiencies of the other. They contain Lives, in whole or in part, of Flannan, Columba, Máedóc, Brendan, Coemgen, Moling, Fintan, Senán, Mo-Choem-óc, Finan, Rúadán, Cronan, Comgall, Carthach, Déclán, Ciarán of Saigir, Ita, Mo-Lúa, Laurence O'Toole, Cainnech, Munnu, Colmán Ela, Bairre, Aed mac Bricc, Ailbe, Abbán, Ciarán of Clúain, and Malachy. The collection " represents a literary recension of earlier materials fairly evenly carried out. Things likely to cause difficulty or scandal are toned down or omitted, and style and matter are more homogeneous than in " Codex Salmanticensis.[55]

The volume in Marsh's Library was, as has been proved by Reeves, the Codex Armachanus from which Fleming printed several Lives in his Collectanea sacra. Plummer has argued further — what was denied by Reeves — that the same manuscript, or a copy of it, was the Codex Kilkenniensis to which Colgan refers so frequently and from which he printed eight Lives. Both the manuscripts were used by Ussher, and that in Marsh's Library probably also by Ware.[56]

116. The Codex Insulensis Collection

MSS: Bodl. Rawlinson B 485 s XIII[1]; Rawlinson B 505 s XIV[1]. — Dublin Franciscan convent, Merchants Quay, A 24 A.D. 1627. Designated by Plummer R[1], R[2], F, respectively. Cf. Plummer " On two collections of Latin Lives of Irish Saints in the Bodleian Library " ZCP V (1905) 429–54; VV. SS. Hib. I pp. xv–xxiii.

The first of these manuscripts, R[1], is a small folio, written in a contracted hand, with many abbreviations. It now contains 160 folios; 19 leaves have been lost in the body of the codex, and probably 24 at the end. The second manuscript, R[2], is a large folio, consisting of 221 leaves, which include at the end 10 leaves containing a copy of Fél. Oeng., bound up with the rest in the sixteenth or seventeenth century. The third, F, is a folio of 304 pages. It is reasonably certain that F is a copy of R[2], and R[2] of R[1]. F is one of the manuscripts formerly belonging to the Irish College of Louvain which were in Colgan's library when he died. A colophon at the end states that it was copied by John Goolde, Warden of the Franciscan Convent of Cashel, from a transcript of a very old manuscript belonging to Inis-na-náom [Isle of Saints] on Loch Ree. This must be the Codex Insulensis, Codex Inisensis, Codex Insulae Sanctorum, or Codex Lochriuensis to which Colgan frequently refers. The inference is that R[2] belonged to the monastery of Inis-na-náomh, Loch Ree. The two Bodleian manuscripts had been part of the collection of Sir James Ware.[57] Marginalia in R[2] indicate that during the sixteenth and early seventeenth centuries it was the property of members of the O'Farrell and Moriarty families, who dwelt in Longford near Loch Ree. Perhaps it passed to them in the time of Flaithbertach úi Fergaill, prior

---

[55] VV. SS. Hib. I p. xxii.

[56] In St. Patrick's College, Maynooth, there is a 17th-cent. MS containing Latin Lives of Irish saints of the Cod. K. recension, but much modified by editing. It purports to have been copied by Thomas Arthur in 1627 from an old vellum MS belonging to Ussher, who, we know, used a hagiographical collection of the Cod. K. type, probably Cod. K. itself. The Maynooth MS has not been used by hagiologists. Cf. Plummer Miscellanea hagiographica Hibernica (Brussels 1925) 178.

[57] Cf. p. 88 supra.

of Saints' Island, who died, according to an entry, in 1504. Another entry indicates that the name of the scribe was Matthew O'Dwyer. It was written, it would seem, for lectionary purposes in the monastery; the contractions of R¹ were expanded, and the Lives were re-arranged according to the order of the saints' festivals in the calendar. R¹ was in the sixteenth century in the possession of the Dillon family. Its earlier history is obscure, but probably it too belonged to the monastery of Saints' Island.

It should be noted that R², when it served as *Vorlage* for F, and R¹ when it rendered a similar service for R², were more nearly intact than they are to-day. Hence all three MSS are of value in restoring the original texts.

The Lives of Irish saints to be found in this collection are those of Patrick, Columba, Baithene, Fursa, Moling, Colmán of Dromore, Finnian of Clonard, Berach, Brigit, Brendan of Clonfert, Ciarán of Clúain, Mo-Laise of Devenish, Aed mac Bricc, Énda, Gerald, Féchín, Mo-Chúa of Timahoe (erroneously designated in the manuscripts " of Balla"), Tigernach, Bairre, Munnu of Taghmon, Laurence O'Toole, Cainnech, Colmán Ela, Columba of Terryglass, Finan *cam*, Rúadán, Fintan of Clonenagh, Samthann, Comgall of Bangor, Máedóc, Flannan, Ailbe, Ciarán of Saigir, Senán, Ita, Coemgen, Mo-Lúa of Clonfertmulloe, and Buite. The recension is the same as that of *Codex Salmanticensis* in the Lives of Baithene, Moling, Colmán of Dromore, Munnu of Taghmon, Comgall of Bangor, Ciarán of Saigir, Senán, Coemgen, Mo-Lúa of Clonfertmulloe, and Tigernach. In the cases of Fursa and Columba of Terryglass the differences are very slight.

On the whole, this collection represents a later stage in the evolution of hagiography than *Codex Salmanticensis* or even *Codex Kilkenniensis* — although this statement is not true in the case of every individual Life. The influences governing alterations are homiletic — simplification and edification. Texts are abbreviated, unsatisfactory material is expurgated, names of persons and places and unusual Irish expressions are omitted, explanatory notes and pious reflections are interpolated, and in some cases distinct documents are conflated to give one narrative.

117. John of Tynemouth's *Sanctilogium*

MS: BM Cotton Tiberius E 1 *c* A.D. 1325×1350 [written in St. Albans; much damaged by the fire in the Cotton Library in 1731. There are several MSS of a later recension of the collection.] EDS: *Nova Legenda Anglie* (London 1516; reprinted 1527). — Carl Horstman *Nova Legenda Anglie: As collected by John of Tynemouth, John Capgrave, and others, and first printed, with New Lives, by Wynkyn de Worde a. d. m d x u i Now re-edited with fresh material from MS. and printed sources* 2 vols. (Oxford 1901) [a scholarly edition].

One of the priories dependent on the great English abbey of St. Albans was that of Tynemouth, on the north-east coast of England, on the other side of the Tyne from Bede's Jarrow. From about 1315 to about 1325 the vicar was a certain John, who, doubtless, was a Benedictine monk, an inmate of the priory. This John of Tynemouth was a voluminous writer, or, rather, compiler of records. Horstman has shown that it is probable that he was summoned to the mother house of St. Albans, was made historiographer, and died there of the Black Death in 1348 or 1349.

At some time during his career John of Tynemouth prepared a " Sanctilogium Angliae, Walliae, Scotiae, et Hiberniae," a collection of abridged Lives of saints of these countries, arranged in the order of the calendar, of which only one copy now survives. John obtained his materials in part, doubtless, by research in the library of St. Albans, but also in part by extensive travels in England and Wales. There is no reason to believe that he ever visited Ireland. His *vitae* of Irish saints were found in British monasteries — several, probably, at Glastonbury. He was a careful worker, who, for the most part, made use of good texts, and performed his task of abridgment, often very slight, with accuracy and discrimination.[58]

In the fifteenth century John's collection was re-edited, perhaps by John Capgrave, Augustinian scholar and hagiographer, to whom later ages attributed the whole work. The Lives were re-arranged in alphabetical order, and some of the subsidiary matter appended by John of Tynemouth was omitted. The collection thus reconstructed was, with further omissions and the addition of fifteen new Lives, printed in 1516 by Wynkyn de Worde.

The *Sanctilogium* contained Lives of the following Irish saints: Fursa, Brigit, Aiduus (Máedóc of Ferns), Piran (Ciarán of Saigir), Patrick (also texts of Patrick's Purgatory and of Tundal), Patern, Indract, Brendan, Columba, Modwenna, Fiacre, Osmanna, Foillan, Malachy, Benignus, Maxentia, Columban, Thatheus, and Finan (Finian of Magh-Bile). The published *Legenda* added Kilian and Wyro, and a Life of Ita ascribed to John is to be found in the MS Bodl. 240. The collection also contains records of many of those British, Scottish and English saints who were more or less closely connected with Irish history.

118. The Book of Lismore

ED: Whitley Stokes *Lives of Saints from the Book of Lismore* (*Anec. Oxon.*, Mediaeval and Modern Ser. V) (Oxford 1890) [the introd. contains a description of the MS and its contents which, though described by the ed. as " very incomplete," is the best in print; there is also an analysis of the information regarding social conditions to be found in the Lives, similar to that prefaced to *Vit. Trip. Cf.* criticisms and replies in *IER* 3rd ser. XII (1891) 147–58, *The Academy* XXXVII (1890) 286–7, 303–4, 321, XXXIX (1891) 90–1, 114–5, 138–9, 188, 305.] COMM: J. H. Todd *Proc. RIA* I (1840) 449–50, 458–9 [description of MS]. — John Windele " The Book of MacCarthy Reagh " *Journ. Kilkenny etc. Archaeol. Assoc.* n. s. I (1858) 370–8. — O'C *MS Mat.* 196–200. — O'Grady *SG* II (1892) p. x n. 2.

The Book of Lismore is a vellum manuscript of 197 leaves, now much mutilated, kept at Lismore Castle, co. Waterford, where it was discovered in 1814 by some workmen when repairing the building. It had been in Timoleague Abbey in 1629, when it was seen by Michael O'Clery. It was compiled in the latter half of the fifteenth century by several scribes, among them an Angus O'Callanan and a friar named O'Buagachain, for Finghín MacCarthaigh *Riabhach* and his wife Catherine, daughter of Thomas, eighth Earl of Desmond. Hence it has sometimes been called " The Book of MacCarthy Reagh." It was compiled from the Book of Monasterboice

---

[58] John produced other hagiographical works, nearly all of which are lost. A few *vitae* ascribed to him are preserved in the MS Bodl. 240, a volume written at Bury St. Edmunds in the last quarter of the fourteenth century.

and other older manuscripts now lost. The contents include Lives in Irish — several in the form of homilies — of Patrick, Colum-cille, Brigit, Senán, Finnian of Clonard, Find-chú of Brigown, Brendan of Clonfert, Ciarán of Clúain, and Mo-Chúa of Balla; many religious anecdotes and legends; and a considerable mass of secular material.

119. The O'Clery Collections

MSS: Brussels Bibl. roy. 2324-40 and 4190-200. COMM: S. H. Bindon " On the MSS relating to Ireland in the Burgundian Library at Brussels " *Proc. RIA* III (1844) 477-502 [a descriptive catalogue of considerable value]. — KM " Irish MSS at Brussels " *The Academy* XLIV (1893) 298-9, 324 [description of 2324-40 and 4190-200]. — J. Van den Gheyn *Catalogue des manuscrits de la Bibliothèque Royale de Belgique* V *Histoire-Hagiographie* (Brussels 1905) 381-9: V. Tourneur " Vies de Saints en irlandais." — *BNE* I pp. xii-xiv.

These two manuscript volumes, of 356 and 281 paper folios, respectively, are gatherings of the transcripts of older texts, almost all in Irish, made by Michael O'Clery in Ireland and transmitted to Ward, Colgan, and the other Irish antiquarians at Louvain.[59] The dates of transcription entered in MS 2324-40 run from 1627 to 1635, and those in MS 4190-200 from 1627 to 1634. They are mainly, but not entirely, made up of hagiographical matter.

120. The O'Dinneen Collection

MS: RIA A. 4. 1 (Stowe 9) A.D. 1627. COMM: The Stowe catalogues (*cf*. p. 89 *supra*). — *VV. SS. Hib.* I pp. xxv, xxvi. — *BNE* I p. xii.

This is a paper manuscript of 300 pages, much injured by damp and in some parts illegible. It was copied by Domnall Ó Duinnín at Cork in September, 1627, for Francis Ó Mathgamna (O'Mahony), Provincial of the Friars Minor, and, as previously suggested,[60] may have been intended for the use of the Irish scholars at Louvain. If so, it probably never reached them, for a note entered in 1766 says that it then belonged to Charles O'Conor of Belanagare. Of the sixteen Lives it contains fifteen seem to have been taken from a vellum codex in the possession of Ó Duinnín, from which Michael O'Clery also made some transcripts, and the last, that of Rúadán, from some other source.

II. ANCIENT CHURCHES OF SOUTHERN IRELAND

Bibliography

See the *Bibliography* to Chapter III sect. i; also P. J. O'Donnell " The Christian episcopate in Ireland before St. Patrick " *Amer. Eccles. Rev.* LVIII (1918) 258-74.

In the preceding chapter some notice has been given of a few foreign texts which testify to the presence of Christianity in Ireland before the

---

[59] *Cf*. pp. 38-41 *supra*.   [60] P. 40 *supra*.

coming of the bishop Patricius. The Irish legends on the same subject will now be considered.

Among the churches and peoples of the South, where the earliest traces of Christianity would naturally be expected, there were several traditions of such a pre-Patrician introduction of the faith. The Corcu Loegde, or Dáirine, who occupied a territory on the south-west coast which in the later middle ages corresponded approximately with the present diocese of Ross, but in earlier times was of greater extent, probably at least from Cork harbor to Kenmare bay, asserted that it was among them that " the cross was believed in first in Ireland." [61] Saints whose Lives, still extant, represent them as teaching the Christian religion before the coming of Patrick, were Déclán of Ardmore, on the coast of Waterford; Ailbe of Emly, chief church of ancient Munster; Ciarán of Saigir, in the old kingdom of the Osraige; and Abbán of Moyarney and Killabban, among the Lagin, or Leinstermen. Associated with them is Ibar of Beg-Eri island, in Wexford harbor, of whom no Life survives. The story told by these Lives is, briefly, that Ibar, Ciarán, Déclán and Ailbe were elder contemporaries of St. Patrick, who preceded him in the work of converting the south of Ireland; and that, on Patrick's arrival in Munster, they acknowledged, but only after some controversy, his superior authority. But, apart from these *vitae* and a few stray traditions associated with the same saints, the epic of Ireland's conversion made Patrick the one great apostle; hagiographers, martyrologists and annalists represent Ibar and his companions as disciples of Patrick or contemporaries of his successors.

All these Lives are, in their present form, quite late, but they cannot fairly be dismissed, as they are by Todd and Bury, as " so full of contradictions and inconsistencies that they are useless for historical purposes." The contradictions and inconsistencies are not greater than those found in the majority of Irish *acta sanctorum*. On the other hand, there is no good reason for giving them the amount of credence that appears to have been given by Zimmer. This was, however, only part of his general theory, which nothing at our disposal can be deemed to substantiate:

" Ireland was, therefore, about 431, a Christian country, as Christian as Roman Britain before the Saxons and Angles overflowed it, as Christian as Gaul in the days of Ausonius, Martin of Tours, Sulpicius Severus and Germanus of Auxerre." [62]

[61] MacN *Phases of Irish history* (Dublin 1919) 162; *Fél. Oeng.*[2] 88–9.
[62] *Sitzungsb. d. k. preuss. Akad. d. Wissensch.* 1909 p. 550.

Zimmer believed that the saints in question lived in the fourth century, and he even assigned dates: " 320–350 as the *floruit* of Ibar, and 330–350 as the period within which the others were born, Declan between 330 and 340, Ciaran about 350." [63]   Later Irish legend drew their story into the orbit of its great hero, Patrick.

Todd, Baring-Gould and Fisher, and others, have, on the contrary, maintained that the pre-Patrician careers of these men were due to inventions of Munstermen in the eleventh and twelfth centuries, who sought a claim to more or less ecclesiastical independence of Armagh at a time when the Irish Church was being reorganised on a territorial and episcopal basis, and when Munster was making a bid for the political hegemony of the island.

To the student of hagiography it must seem fairly certain that the later stage in the evolution of these *acta* was the reconciliation with the Patrick Legend, not the independence of it.   Indeed the independence in mission, if not the antecedence in date, with reference to St. Patrick, seems so much of the essence of the Lives, that we cannot feel much hesitation in denying that it could be due to interpolations of the eleventh or twelfth century.   It seems safe to assume that this independence was present, implicitly or explicitly, in the popular and monastic traditions of the eighth century or earlier which lay behind the earliest written *acta*.   But those traditions were already several centuries removed from pre-Patrician Christianity.   The only safe general deduction is that before the great development of the Patrick Legend there were local legends in various parts of southern Ireland telling of the Christianising of those districts by saints who knew not Patrick.

Becc-Ériu, Beg-Éire

Becc-Ériu ("Little Ireland "), or Beggery island, in Wexford harbor,[64] was the site of a church of which mention is occasionally made in early mediaeval sources.   Its foundation was attributed to a Bishop Ibar, or Iubar, whose relics were still there when the passage regarding him in the *Codex Salmanticensis* Life of Abbán [65] was written.[66]   No Life

---

[63] KM *Learning in Ireland in the fifth century* (Dublin 1913) 25.   The only basis for this chronology seems to be the doubtful identification of Hilary, teacher of Ailbe, with Hilary of Poitiers, and that still more doubtful of Ibar with Eborius of York (*cf.* p. 158 *supra*).

[64] The island is now attached to the mainland.   It was also known as Inis-Fáil.

[65] *AA. SS. ex Cod. S.* 509–10.

[66] In the ninth century, when the question was of little immediate consequence, for the Norsemen held the islands of Wexford harbor, Armagh laid claim to this church: " In thirties and forties are the churches which [Cremthann, king of Leinster] gave to Patrick in the east of Leinster and in Úi-Censelaig, including

of Ibar exists [67] — the Northmen plundered Beg-Éire in 813 [68] and, doubtless, on other occasions, and any *acta* in the monastery may have been lost — but there is much about him in the Lives of the other pre-Patrician saints, and in calendars and annals. He is represented as the most obdurate of these saints in opposing Patrick's demand for their submission.

Zimmer identified Ibar with that Eburius, or Eborius, bishop of York, who attended the Council of Arles in 316; [69] afterwards, we are to assume, he went as missionary to south-east Ireland. The scorn with which this fantastic guess-work, if emanating from another man, would have been treated by Zimmer, can be imagined.

On the other hand, R. A. S. Macalister advances a mythological explanation, believing that the island was a pagan sanctuary of a divine *ibar*, the Irish name for " yew-tree ":

" Of the servant of Christ who founded and laboured in the church of Beg Éire, and who now enjoys his reward, nothing is known. For it is clear that the few facts recorded of him belong, not to him, but to his pagan predecessors. His very name is forgotten; that of the sacred yew-tree (*ibar*) of the island has been substituted. Another island in Wexford Harbour had a sacred oak-tree upon it, from which it derived the name *Dair-inis*, ' Oak Island.' Probably Beg-Éire had an alternative name analagous to this, *Inis Ibair*, ' island of the yew-tree.' In time this was understood to mean ' Island of Ibar,' interpreted as referring to the forgotten founder of the monastery. . . . Let it be clearly understood that the historicity of these saints is not in question. That is amply attested by the existence of the ruins of the religious houses associated with them. But their names have suffered the usual fate of names handed down by tradition, and have become confused with other names which by reason of a much longer history, stretching far back into the unknown abysses of pagan ages, had made a deeper impression on popular memory." [70]

ÁRD-MÓR (ARDMORE)

About sixty miles south-west of Wexford and Beg-Éire, on the coast of Waterford near Youghal harbor, is the rather notable promontory of Árd-mór, or Ardmore. The Life of Déclán, perhaps enshrining a geological fact, says that it was an island until the saint attached it to the mainland. Here are a cathedral and a round tower, built, or rebuilt, in the twelfth century, and a much older, primitive church known as

---

. . . Inis-Fáil, wherein are Mo-Chon-óc and Mo-Chat-óc. Erdit and Agustin are in the lesser island, and since it was taken by the pagans their shrines are in Slébte." *Vit. Trip.* I 192–3.

[67] There is a short account, beginning " Ep. Ibar, tri bliadna trichat," in LL 371. *Cf.* Plummer *Miscellanea hagiographica Hibernica* Cat. nos. 143, 266.

[68] FM.   [69] *Cf.* p. 158 *supra*.   [70] *Proc. RIA* XXXIV (1919) C 340.

" Déclán's House." Árd-mór and Liss-mór [71] were the principal
religious centres of the Munster branch of the Dési, a people who, according to tradition, were expelled from central Ireland in the third or
fourth century and settled, part in what is now Waterford county, part
across the channel in Pembrokeshire.[72]

121. Life of St. Déclán

(i) [Latin] Beatissimus episcopus Declanus . . . omni tempore per eum fiunt, prestante D. n. J. C.,
cui est h. g. atque p. cum D. P. in unitate S. S. in s. s.. Amen. (ii) [Irish] Beatissimus . . . i. an tespoc
naemhta re nabartar . . . agus do cuaid in áentadh an Athar agus an Mheic agus an Spirait Naoimh in
saecula saeculorum, Amen. Finis.

MSS: (i) Cod. K. ff. 101 sqq. — TCD 175 s XIV ex ff. 66–71 [both slightly mutilated].
(ii) Brussels Bibl. roy. 4190–200 s XVII ff. 171–93 [copied by O'Clery in 1629 from a
book of Eochaidh úi Ifernain the date of which was 1582]. — RIA 23 M 50 s XVIII
pp. 109–20 [by John Murphy of Raheenagh,[73] dated 1740]. — RIA 24 L 11 A.D. 1758
f. 22 [imperfect]. — Dublin King's Inns 19.[74] EDS: (i) AA. SS. Boll. Jul. V 590–
608 [from an O'Clery MS at Louvain collated with a MS of St. Isidore's, Rome; poor
text]. — VV. SS. Hib. I pp. lx–lxii, II 32–59. (ii) P. Power ITS XVI (1914).

Déclán was the founder of Árd-mór and the patron of the Dési. His labors are represented as being within the territory of the Dési or their immediate neighborhood —
except once, when he visited the ancestral home of the race in Meath. An old dictum
incorporated into the Life declares: " Let Déclán be the Patrick of the Dési, let the
Dési be with Déclán till doom."[75] His Life, of which the Irish version seems to be a
translation of the Latin, has considerable interest. It is a composite production: the
final redaction cannot be much older than the twelfth century, but there seem to be
various strata of older material of which it is a loose amalgamation.[76] The introductory sections are taken over bodily from the secular sagas, especially from Tochomlod
na nDéssi, Aided Meidbe, and Ferchuitred Medba. Yet the compiler was, it would seem,
an ecclesiastic of Árd-mór.

IMBLECH-IBAIR (EMLY)

In east-central Munster, about fifty miles directly inland from
Árd-mór and some ten miles west of the present town of Tipperary, is
Imblech-ibair, anglicised Emly. It was, almost certainly, a holy place
in pagan times, for the name seems to mean " the umbilicus [77] of the
[sacred] yew-tree." An alternative designation was Medón-Mairtine,

[71] Cf. p. 451 infra.   [72] Cf. p. 149 supra.   [73] Cf. p. 55 supra.
[74] There is also a copy in the collection of Dr. Douglas Hyde.
[75] Also published in Ussher Whole Works VI 428; Z² 961; Thes. Pal. II 297. — Déclán still has an
extraordinary hold on the popular piety of eastern Munster. His " pattern " at Ardmore is " the most
noted celebration of its kind in Ireland." Cf. Power op. cit. p. xxi.
[76] The text appears to say that it is an abbreviation of a longer vita (cap. 38); also there are allusions
to " old writings " containing information about Déclán (cap. 15).
[77] See J. Loth "L'omphalos chez les Celtes" Rev. des études anciennes July–Sept. 1915 pp. 193–206,
where, however, this particular instance is not noticed.

" centre of the Mairtine." [78]　The Mairtine were a people anciently of considerable importance, of whom little is heard after about A.D. 845, when they suffered heavily from the Norsemen.[79]　In early Christian times they were, perhaps, vassals to the Cashel branch of the Eoghanacht race, the dominant people of Munster, who conquered Cashel and the surrounding district probably at the time of the Dési settlement immediately to the south.[80]　There can be little doubt that it was to the control and support of the Eoghanacht that Emly owed its rank as chief church of Munster.

122. Life of St. Ailbe

(i) Albeus sanctus episcopus, sanctorum virorum Munnensium. . . . Suavia carmina canentium migravit ad D. n. I. C., cui h. est et g. in s. s. Amen. (iii) Albeus episcopus virorum Momenencium . . . suauia carmina, etc. (iv) Bai rí for Ara Cliach . . . 7 rugad a anam maille re hainglib, 7c.

MSS: (i) Cod. S. ff. 90–4^v. (ii) Bodl. Rawl. B 505 s XIV ff. 130–5. — Dublin Franciscan Convent A 24 pp.111 sqq. — BM Addit. 4788 s XVII ff. 72 sqq [one of Ware's transcripts; these 2 MSS are copies of Rawl. B. 505]. (iii) Cod. K. ff. 135 $bis sqq$ [mutilated]. — TCD 175 s XIV ex ff. 132–5. (iv) RIA A. 4. 1 (Stowe 9) s XVII pp. 97–119. — Brussels Bibl. roy. 2324–40 s XVII ff. 139–46 [these 2 are copies of the same original, an abbreviated Ir. trans. of iii]. EDS: (i) AA. SS. ex Cod. S. 235–60. (iii) VV. SS. Hib. I pp. xxviii–xxxi, clxxxiii, 46–64. (iv) Fáinne Fionn Irish Rosary XVI (1912). Cf. AA. SS. Boll. Sept. IV 26–31; Baring-Gould and Fisher Lives of the British Saints I (1907) 128–36.

Ailbe, founder of Imblech-ibair, was honored as patron saint of Munster, and his vita shows a desire to set him over against, even while acknowledging his subordination to, Patrick. He is " virorum Mummensium preses, Ybernie insule alter Patricius."[81] The dictum already quoted regarding Déclán says " Let humble Ailbe be the Patrick of Munster."[82]　The Life is a composite production. It seems certain not only that Emly had been a pagan sanctuary, but that Ailbe himself had a mythological forerunner who contributed part of his legend and perhaps his name. The saint is the son of Ol-chú, " Great Hound," is cared for when a baby by a she-wolf, and in after life protects his savage foster-mother.[83]　Now Ailbe was the name of the divine hound of Mac Dá-thó, from which the great plain of Mag-Ailbe in central Leinster was said to take its name.[84]

The Life is certainly late, and very artificial. It can hardly be assigned to a date earlier than the twelfth century. Nor is there anything to indicate that it represents

[78] Bk. Lis. 172b, 176a. Cf. Hogan Onomasticon Goedelicum (Dublin 1910) 537.
[79] CGG 14–5, 226–7.
[80] MacN Proc. RIA XXIX C (1911) 73 n. 5.
[81] Original text of Cod. S., later additions being omitted.
[82] P. 313 supra.
[83] On lycanthropy in Ireland see Geo. Henderson Survivals in belief among the Celts (Glasgow 1911) 170–3.
[84] Scél mucci maic Dá-thó. — Lia Ailbe, " Stone of Ailbe," " chief monument of Magh-Bregh," which fell and was broken up in 999, seems to have been a menhir dedicated to this divinity. — It is to be noted also that the saint Mac Creiche (p. 384 infra) is represented to have been the son of an Ailbe (elsewhere confused with our saint) who is called " the war-dog of Slíab-Crot." Plummer Misc. hag. Hib. 33, 73.

a redaction of a much earlier text.   Unlike so many Irish *acta sanctorum*, it shows no evidence of being based on a narrative preserved by the saint's own monastic family. Some points of interest may be noted.   The infant when rescued from the she-wolf is given to British slaves, according to one text Christians, to be raised.   The story of the saint's visit to Rome took two forms, in one of which he went to Bishop Hilary, in the other to Pope Clement.[85]   Zimmer believed that the Hilary who gave his name to the story was the bishop of Poitiers (350–368).[86]   The account of the submission to Patrick is made very brief.   On the other hand, a tale is introduced to show that Imar, or Ibar, though older than Ailbe, received a divine command to acknowledge his precedence.

123. The Rule of Ailbe

[O'Neill's text] Apair dam fri mac Saráin . . . fri hEogan atabera.   70 stanzas.

MSS: Brussels Bibl. roy. 5100–4 p. 24 [O'Clery MS]. — RIA 23 N 11 pp. 186 *sq*. — RIA 23 P 3 A.D. 1467 [part missing].   — TCD 1136 [19th-century copy from last two]. Eds: Jos. O'Neill *Ériu* III (1907) 92–115 [text, trans.; *cf. ibid.* VI 111].   Trans: W. M. Hennessy and Brian O'Looney *IER* VIII (1871) 178–90.   Comm: L. Gougaud *Rev. Bénédictine* XXV (April 1908) 173–8.

The title of this metrical monastic rule is *Riagol Ailbi Imlecha oc tinchosc Eogain mic Saráin*, "Rule of Ailbe of Imlech for the instruction of Eogan mac Saráin."[87]   The opening words are: "Say for me to the son of Sarán, heavy is the burden he takes," and the close, "Thou shalt recite it, thou shalt write it, in Clúain-Cóiláin — thou shalt say them to Eogan."   One of the stanzas begins: "A command to thee from Ailbe." From this it has been assumed that the verses were the composition of Ailbe, addressed to Eogan, head of a neighboring monastery called Clúain-Cóiláin, and (for which there seems no authority) successor of Ailbe at Imblech-ibair.   The language is Old Irish: that is, the text must have been written within the period A.D. 700–950.   The metrical form makes impossible the supposition that it is the modernisation of an earlier composition.   Authorship by Ailbe is, therefore, out of the question.

Variations in the metre show that many stanzas from other compositions have been interpolated into the poem.   These generally contain practical directions for the monastic life; they all are of very early date.   It is a reasonable hypothesis that the poem was written originally by, or rather at the command of, the *comarba* of Ailbe at Emly to Eogan on the occasion of his elevation to the headship of Clúain-Cóiláin, and contained moral exhortations and some account of the customs and practices of his own monastery.   In later times an attempt was made to expand this into a monastic rule by incorporating extracts from other somewhat similar sources.   In offering definite illustrations of monastic life and organisation it is the best of the Irish rules.

[85] The Life of Déclán amalgamates the two versions more completely: "eodem tempore sanctus Albeus erat Romae multis annis in discipulatu sancti Hilarii episcopi, ex cuius iussione atque rogatu a beato Papa Albeus ordinatus est episcopus."

[86] KM *Learning in Ireland in the Fifth Century* 25.

[87] He is mentioned in the *Martyrology of Donegal*, Mar. 15.

SAIGIR (SEIRKEIRAN)

Between Leinster and Munster lay the very ancient kingdom of
the Osseirge, later Osraige, the boundaries of which in the early middle
ages corresponded with those of the present diocese of Ossory, but in
pre-Christian times extended westward at least to the Suir river. Their
patron saint was Ciarán,[88] whose monastic church was at the north-
western corner of their dominion, at Saigir,[89] now Seirkeiran, four and
a half miles south-east of Birr, in Offaley.

124. Life of Ciarán of Saigir

(i) [BNE ii] Tareis an scriptuir diadha do legadh . . . n'díligther cadhus 7 onoir per infinita s. s. Amen.
[Cap.] Beatus autem Piranus qui a quibusdam Keranus . . . et a Mousehole vigintiquinque. (ii) [VV.
SS. Hib.] Beatissimus episcopus Kyaranus Hybernie sanctorum primogenitus . . . migrauerunt ad Christi
regnum. Cui est h. et g. cum D. P. et S. S. in s. s. Amen. [BNE i] Baoi fer amhra a nOsraighibh i. do
Dhal mBirn . . . naoim Chiarain go riseam uile an aontoigh sin. In s. s. Amen. [SG.] Beatissimus . . .
primogenitus. i. is é an tesbog Ciarán saighre . . . ris dochum flaithis dé. (iii) [Cod. S.] Beatus pontifex
Keranus, Hibernorum primogenitus . . . mereamur aulam eterne hereditatis.

MSS: (i) Brussels Bibl. roy. 4190–200 s XVII ff. 144–53ᵛ [copied by O'Clery from a
transcript of a book belonging to Eochaidh O'Heffernan, an Irish trans. of a Latin text
resembling, if not identical with, Capgrave's source]. (ii) Cod. K. ff. 106ᵛ–9ᵛ. — RIA
A. 4.1 (Stowe 9) s XVII pp. 222–43 [abbreviated Irish trans. of a related text]. —
BM Egerton 112 A.D. 1780–2 ff. 513–20 [an 18th cent. Irish trans. of this text: MS
written by Maurice O'Conor, ship-carpenter of Cork, perhaps from a copy, said to be
RIA 23 M. 50, made by his tutor, John Murphy of Raheenagh; — there are also other
MSS of this trans.: see Plummer *Misc. hag. Hib.* Cat. no. 20]. (iii) Cod. S. ff. 197–9.
— Bodl. Rawl. B 505 ff. 199–201. — Dublin Franciscan MS pp. 237–44. EDS: (i)
BNE I pp. xxv–xxvii, 113–24, II 109–20, 339–41 [text, trans.]. — *Nova Legenda Anglie*
(ed. Horstman, Oxford 1901) II 320–7 [Plummer regards it as probably an epitome of the
source of which the Brussels MS is a trans.]. (ii) Colgan *AA. SS.* 458–68 [modified
text]. — *VV. SS. Hib.* I pp. li–liv, 217–33. — *BNE* I p. xxv, 103–12, II 99–108, 338–9
[Stowe text, trans.].—O'Grady *SG* I 1–16, II 1–17 [text of Eg. 112, trans.].—Mulcahy
Life of St. Kiaran the Elder of Seir (Dublin 1895) [same text]. (iii) Colgan *AA. SS.*
467–9. — *AA. SS. Boll.* Mart. I 389–99 [Cod. S. text with extracts from Cod. K.].
— *AA. SS. ex Cod. S.* 805–18. COMM: John Hogan *St. Ciaran, Patron of Ossory*
(Kilkenny 1876) [has trans. of an Irish text of ii]. — O'Hanlon [*op. cit.* p. 290 *supra*]
III 115 *sqq.* — Baring-Gould and Fisher *Lives of the British Saints* II 119–38.

The recensions of the Life of Ciarán differ considerably in details, but all appear to
go back to one original, a work of considerable antiquity. It was evidently composed
at Saigir by a monk of Ciarán's community. The miracles bear the monastic stamp —
they are numerous and wonderful enough to secure the saint against comparison with

---

[88] Called Sean-Chiarán, "Old Ciarán," or Ciarán Saigre, to distinguish him from Ciarán of Clonmacnois. — *Cf. 3 Frags.* 190–1, where the Osraige are represented as relying on Ciarán for victory over the
Leinstermen, who trusted in Brigit.
[89] Saigir may have been a pagan sanctuary: it is said that a perpetual fire was kept burning there.
Cf. p. 380 *infra*.

the patron of any rival church or people — and there is local coloring which indicates a date when Saigir was still a flourishing community. The irascible temper displayed by Ciarán in some of the episodes wherein his miraculous power is displayed to the destruction of his adversaries is in marked contrast to the galaxy of Christian virtues with which some later redactor has concluded the Life.

Ciarán was, we are told, of the Osraige on his father's side, but on his mother's of the Corcu Loegde, who, as has been seen,[90] claimed to be the first in Ireland to receive Christianity. He was " the first-born of the saints of Ireland," and his position was regularised in the Patrick Legend by a journey to Italy, when Patrick sent him back to Ireland as his precursor. The idea of the " precursor " may have influenced the legend: Ciarán is a western " John the Baptist " who wears the skins of wild animals and eats but the simplest food. He founds his church in a forest wilderness, and the Irish love of animate nature may have added the story that the animals were his first monks: " Now a boar, a fox, a badger, a wolf and a deer with her fawn came humbly to him and served him in all obedience. But one day blessed Ciarán's fox stole his sandals, and wishing to eat them carried them off with him to his old dwelling-place. Then Ciarán sent the badger into the woods to look for the fox and the sandals. The badger went to the fox's den, and finding him there bit his ears and his tail with his teeth, and pulled his hair sharply. Then the fox, following the badger, with the sandals unharmed, came at the ninth hour to St. Ciarán, who said to him ' Why have you done such a wrong, and not endured the want of food and drink? ' But the fox doing penance fasted for three days. . . ." [91]

The stories of the saint's migration to Cornwall are probably due to traditions brought over by travellers or settlers from the south-east of Ireland. There are, however, some indications that his name was associated with the Voyage literature.[92]

125. Senadh Saighri: The Synod of Saigir

Slúaiged la Donchad mac Flaind . . . otá sin anall fós. Contains the poem: Muinter Donnchaid móir meic Cealdaigh . . . sinne a muinter. 7 quatrains.

MS: RIA Stowe D IV 2 f. 51. EDS: KM Gaelic Journal IV (1892) 106–7 [with trans.]; ZCP XII (1918) 290–1. The story is given in Keating's History: Dinneen's ed. III 216–21.

One of the public characters of ill repute in mediaeval Ireland was the crossán, a kind of jester or buffoon. In the law tract Egerton 90 a section on " mouth-crime " begins: " It is ' mouth-crime ' for one to eat that which is stolen, to prompt crosáns, or to proclaim aloud, i.e. to betray."[93] The name of such satiric or scurrilous compositions, partly in prose and partly in verse, was crossán(t)acht. It would seem that the evolution of the crossán was the Irish counterpart of a process not unusual elsewhere in mediaeval Europe. The crossán was the cross-bearer in religious processions, whose position gave him licence to lampoon the by-standers, especially those

[90] P. 310 supra.

[91] Nova Legenda Anglie.

[92] A note in Fél. Oeng.[2] 90 mentions Imarce (?) Ciaráin, " Ciarán's Journey," as a wonderful illuminated manuscript, the work of one Cairnech Moel, Ciarán's scribe, and still existing at Saigir in the writer's time. A Litany (no. 586) invokes " The fifteen men who went with Ciarán of Saigher."

[93] O'Grady Cat. 78. Cf. ZCP II 582, VII 287.

under the displeasure of the Church. In time the name came to signify a class of scurrilous buffoons whose attacks were directed against all classes, perhaps especially the clergy. The present story was, doubtless, composed in retaliation. It localises at Saigir the first appearance of *crossáns:* they were devils who came thither and chanted the poem here given over the new grave of Donnchad, son of Cellach, king of Osraige.[94] From them certain men learned *crossántacht.*

MAG-ARNAIDE (MOYARNEY) AND CELL-ABBÁIN (KILLABBAN)

To the eastward of the Osraige, and occupying the south-east of Ireland from Dublin Bay to Waterford harbor, lay the dominions of the Lagin, or Leinstermen. Their patron saint was Brigit of Kildare, but their apostle, to whom they ascribed their conversion, was Abbán mocu Corbmaic.[95] In primitive times the Lagin seem to have formed two kingdoms, Lagin Tuath-Gabair, or North Leinster, which at one time extended over Meath to the Boyne river, and Lagin Des-Gabair, or South Leinster. Eóin MacNeill thinks the dividing line was a ridge in southern Kildare, known as Gabair Lagen.[96] Each division had its church which claimed Abbán as founder: for the south, Mag-Arnaide, Moyarney, near New Ross, a short distance up the Barrow from its mouth, and for the north Cell-Abbáin, Killabban, much farther up the river, in the barony of Ballyadams, Leix.

126. Life of St. Abbán

(i) In occidentali plaga tocius orbis . . . [Plummer believes this a later addition, and the earlier text to have begun: Fuit vir vite venerabilis, Abbanus nomine . . .] . . . ab hoste maligno eripias, adiuuante dilecto Filio tuo, I. C. D. n. Qui tecum v., et r., in unitate S. s., D. per o. s. s. Amen. (ii) In occidentali plaga orbis . . . ad gaudia perducas eterna: qui v. et r. per infinita s. s. Amen. (iii) Ro gabh rí oirdnidhe cennus for Laighnibh . . . connaigset fair, 7 ceilebrait iaramh.

MSS: (i) Cod. K. ff. 138ᵛ–44ᵛ. — TCD 175 ff. 135 *sq* [opening sections only]. (ii) Cod. S. ff. 140–7. (iii) RIA A. 4.1 (Stowe 9) pp. 205–21. — Brussels Bibl. roy. 2324 40 *c* A.D. 1629 ff. 146ᵛ–50ᵛ. EDS: (i) Colgan *AA. SS.* 610 *sqq.* — *AA. SS. Boll.* Oct. XII 270–93. — *VV. SS. Hib.* I pp. xxiii–xxvi, 3–33. (ii) *AA. SS. ex Cod. S.* 505–40.[97] (iii) O'C *M&C* III 44 [one chapter]. — *BNE* I pp. xiv–xv, 3–10, II 3–10, 323–4.

The Life of Abbán has considerable interest. All the recensions are late, but contain much early material. Recension I seems to represent the last stage in the develop-

---

[94] D. 976. There is a chronological difficulty, for it is represented to have been in the time of the high-king Donnchad, son of Flann, who died in 944.

[95] This means that he was a member of the Dál Corbmaic, one of the four *prímsloinnte*, or " chief names," of the Leinstermen. *Cf.* MacN *Proc. RIA* XXIX C iv (1911) 76. The writer of the Latin Life, however, made him a son of Cormac, thereby showing that he did not understand the meaning of " mocu," and regarded it as equivalent to " mac." This would indicate a date of composition not earlier that the second half of the eighth century.

[96] *Proc. RIA ibid.* 91; *Phases of Irish history* (Dublin 1919) 107–8.

[97] By a misreading the name is rendered Albanus throughout.

ment of the *vita;* II is a transcript, slightly condensed and edited, made from that text, at an earlier stage in its evolution. Neither is far removed from the common exemplar, which may have been an edition prepared in the twelfth or thirteenth century for one of the new religious houses. Behind it lay a text which had been used for lectionary or homiletic purposes at Mag-Arnaide. Recension III is a late Irish translation, probably abbreviated, of a Latin version not much removed from the other two. The original text was written in Moyarney by a man who believed himself to have a personal relationship with the saint. After speaking of the conversion of a king who had murderous intentions towards Abbán, and of his son, he adds: " And the holy man said to him: ' Your son will beget sons and daughters and from his seed will be rulers and dignitaries of my [monastic] city, wherein I myself shall depart from this world to the kingdom of heaven.' And so it came about. Now I, who have gathered together and written out the Life of the most blessed father Abbán, am á descendant of that very son, whom St. Abbán baptized and of whom he prophesied." [98] This, perhaps, means that the author was abbot of Moyarney.

There is nothing to indicate with precision the time of compilation. The material used cannot have taken its given form earlier than the middle of the eighth century; on the other hand there is no indication of any of the effects of the Norse inroads. Perhaps the first half of the ninth century might be accepted as an approximate date.

III. Árd-Macha (Armagh), the *Paruchia Patricii*, and the Patrick Legend

Bibliography

All general works on Irish history, particularly ecclesiastical history. *Cf.* pp. 107–9 *supra.*

Armagh: H[ugo] M[acMahon] *Jus primatiale Armacanum in omnes archiepiscopos, episcopos et universum clerum totius regni Hiberniae* ([Dublin] 1728). — Jas. Stuart *Historical memoirs of the city of Armagh* (Newry, etc. 1819); new ed. by Ambrose Coleman (Dublin 1900). — Robert King *A memoir introductory to the early history of the primacy of Armagh* 2nd ed. (Armagh 1854). — Wm. Reeves *The ancient churches of Armagh* (Lusk 1860). — H. Irgens " Armagh " *Dict. d'hist. et de géogr. ecclés.* IV pt. I (1925) 253–60.

Patrick and the Patrick Legend: See the works noticed on pp. 165–6. Betham's ed. of Tírechán, Muir-chú, and some of the minor LA documents has now interest only as an historical curiosity. Much the same may be said of Richard Stanihurst *De vita sancti Patricii Hiberniae apostoli libri II* (Antwerp 1587) [*cf.* p. 47 *supra*]; Richard Archedekin *Vitae et miraculorum sancti Patricii, Hiberniae apostoli, epitome* (Louvain 1671); R. S. Nicholson *St. Patrick, apostle of Ireland in the third century* (Dublin 1864); and, indeed, the majority of the works listed, *e.g.,* in Chevalier's *Répertoire.* — John Colgan *Triadis Thaumaturgae* (1647) [*cf.* pp. 41, 289: this cele-

---

[98] Cod. K. text, *cap.* xxvi Cod S. reads: " Unde compilator vite huius nepos illius filii fui*r*."

brated work contains the texts of seven Lives of St. Patrick, some of which have never been reprinted. Colgan's editorial work, though not of the standard demanded at the present day, has formed the basis for all Patrician scholarship.] — Still of some value is the study of several of the Lives in Ussher's *Britannicarum ecclesiarum antiquitates* (Dublin 1639) [*cf.* p. 47]. — James Henthorn Todd *St. Patrick Apostle of Ireland A memoir of his life and mission with an introductory dissertation on some early usages of the Church in Ireland, and its historical position from the establishment of the English colony to the present day* (Dublin 1864) [*cf.* pp. 68, 109: this is the only Life of St. Patrick, in English, prior to Bury's epoch-making work, which demands the serious attention of the modern scholar. It is marked by much erudition and critical insight, but the author's confessional bias is quite pronounced.] — M. F. Cusack *Life of St. Patrick* (London 1871) [has value by reason of the trans. of original documents and the notes contributed by William Hennessy]. — John Francis Shearman *Loca Patriciana: an identification of localities, chiefly in Leinster, visited by St. Patrick and his assistant missionaries and of some contemporary kings and chieftains With an essay on the three Patricks, Palladius, Sen Patrick and Patrick mac Calphurn, apostles in Ireland in the fifth century* (Dublin and London 1879, 2nd ed. 1882) [reprinted from the *Journal of the Kilkenny Archaeological Society*; contains much interesting information, but the critical treatment of the material is crude]. — Benjamin Robert *Étude critique sur la vie & l'œuvre de Saint Patrick — Thèse présentée à la Faculté de Théologie protestante de Paris* (Paris 1883) [the next publication after Todd's book which is still of real value to the student of the history of Patrick; there is a good survey of the majority of the sources]. — Whitley Stokes *The Tripartite Life of Patrick, with other documents relating to that saint* 2 vols. (RS: London 1887) [a very useful ed. of the more important documents relating to Patrick, including all those from LA; the editor has prefixed an analysis of the material regarding social conditions which can be found in the texts. The *addenda* and *corrigenda* should be consulted. *Cf.* p. 342 *infra*.] — Zimmer's " Keltische Kirche " (1901) [*cf.* p. 107 *supra*] advanced a radical and daring hypothesis regarding Patrick and his legend, the occasion of the principal recent Patrician controversy: the majority of the critics have rejected his main contentions. In " Über direkte Handelsverbindungen Westgalliens mit Irland " (1909) [*cf.* p. 139 *supra*] Zimmer re-states his theory, with some modifications.— T. J. Shahan *St. Patrick in history* (New York 1904). — J. B. Bury *The life of St. Patrick and his place in history* (London 1905) [*cf.* F. E. Warren *EHR* XXI (April 1906) 347. Bury's work is one of the few modern studies in early Irish history having high merit. Of special value are the appendices, particularly the sections devoted to a critical examination of the sources. In contradistinction to the iconoclasm of HZ, Bury is over-lenient towards the received tradition. See also his " Sources of the early Patrician documents " *EHR* XIX (July 1904) 493 *sqq*] — John Healy *The life and writings of St. Patrick* (Dublin 1905) [may be described as representing the final stage in the evolution of the Patrick Legend: all the traditional material is gathered together and harmonised into a connected narrative. The original documents and very good trans. which are published in the appendices give the book some value.] — L'abbé Riguet *Saint Patrice* (*Les Saints:* Paris 1911) [a good work of *vulgarisation*, based in large part on Bury]. — S. Czarnowski *Le culte des héros et ses conditions sociales — Saint Patrick héros national de l'Irlande* (Paris 1919) [there is a long preface by H. Hubert, who has an article of similar tenor in *Rev. de l'hist. des religions* July–Aug. 1914, May–June 1915; see reviews *ibid.* VII (1921) 134–5; *Études* CLXII (Paris 1920) 573–81; *RC* XXXVIII (1920–1) 332–8. This is the only exten-

sive study of the Patrick Legend as such, and is a contribution of the highest importance: the sociological ideas of the Durkheim school are combined with an extensive
and minute knowledge of the Patrician sources, but also with the absence of a genuine
understanding of the deeper factors of Irish history, and with an academic readiness
to fit the facts to the theory.] — For the very important eds. of LA documents by
Hogan and Gwynn see no. 131. Some special studies should also be noticed: Geo.
Petrie " Tara Hill " [cf. p. 64; treats of the legends of Patrick at Tara]. — J. W.
Hanna An enquiry into the true landing place of St. Patrick in Ulster (Downpatrick
1858). — AdeJ " Saint Patrice et Sen Patrice " RC IX (1888) 111–7; cf. XXII (1901)
335–6. — WS " St. Patrick's doctrines " The Academy XXXIV (1888) 26, 54–5, 104. —
T. Olden " On the burial-place of St. Patrick " Proc. RIA 3rd ser. II 655–66 (read
Feb. 27, 1893) [interesting, but following lines now generally regarded as untrust-
worthy]. — F. E. Warren " The Stowe Missal and St. Patrick " The Academy XLVI
(1894) 304–5. — Roger L'Enseignement (1905) 216–23. — Edmund MacClure British
place names in their historical setting (London 1910) 129 sqq [re the birthplace of Pat-
rick]. — KM Sitzungsb. d. k. preuss. Akad. d. Wissensch. philos.-hist. Cl. 1914 pp.
635–9. — L. Gougaud RC XXXIX (1922) 201–2; Gaelic pioneers of Christianity
(Dublin 1923) 101 sqq [devotion to St. Patrick on the Continent of Europe].

From the beginning of recorded history to the end of Irish independence the centre, north and west of Ireland were dominated by a
group of families known as Dál Cuinn, " division of Conn "; and from
at least the beginning of the fifth to the beginning of the eleventh century one branch of this group also held the over-kingship of the whole
island. The same eponym is found in Leth Cuinn, " Conn's Half,"
a name for the northern half of Ireland, and in Connachta, whence is
derived the name of the province of Connacht. Connachta appears
to have been the designation, of great antiquity, of the free and ruling
people of the West, from the Shannon river to the sea. Dál Cuinn was
probably a term of much later, but still very ancient, origin, applied to
the dynastic family, or families, of the Connachta.

The reconstruction of Irish political history prior to the fifth century
is very precarious, but there seems good ground for assuming that in
the third or early fourth century Dál Cuinn crossed the Shannon and
gradually wrested from the northern Lagin, and probably from the
Ulaid, who anciently dominated the north of Ireland, much of the
present counties of Longford, Westmeath and Meath, including four
famous hill-sanctuaries, Uisnech (near Ballymore), Tlachtga (Hill of
Ward, near Athboy), Tailtiu (Telltown, between Kells and Navan), and
Temair (Tara). A new kingdom of the " mid-lands," Míde (Meath),
was established, with its royal fortress at Tara. Eventually the rulers
of Tara asserted suzerainty over all Ireland. One of the results of the
consolidation of the kingdom of Míde was the migration of the Dési to

Waterford and to Wales; another was a condition of latent or open hostility between Dál Cuinn and the Lagin, which continued at least into the eighth century. By 515, however, according to the chronicles, the control of the Lagin over southern Meath, and probably also over the greater part of the present Offalley, came definitely to an end, and the province of Leinster was reduced to the bounds which it retained till the Norman invasion.

If we may trust the ancient epic romances, a similar antagonism had existed since before the Christian era, between the Connachta and the Ulaid. In the fourth century, perhaps contemporaneously with the attack on the northern Lagin, but probably later, another branch of Dál Cuinn entered southern Ulster, overthrew the Ulaid and captured their capital fortress of Emain-Macha, the remains of which, now known as Navan Fort, can still be seen about two miles west of Armagh. The conquered territories included the greater part of what are now the counties of Fermanagh, Monaghan, Armagh, Tyrone and Derry, and were known as *Air-gíalla*, " the eastern subjects " (*i.e.*, from the point of view of Connacht). Henceforth they were ruled by princes, petty kings, of the Dál Cuinn, but it is not certain whether, as in Míde, a single large kingdom was organised.

At the end of the fourth and beginning of the fifth century the king of Tara was a certain Níall, surnamed *nói-gíallach*, " of the nine hostages," who, if his personal power and energy are reflected in the fecundity and aggressiveness of his offspring, must have been a personality of extraordinary domination. He is the first *árd-rí*, " high king," of Ireland, as to whose existence there can be no reasonable doubt. Of his eight or more sons the majority founded families in Míde or its neighborhood, which in later times were known collectively as the Southern Úi Néill, but three, Conall Gulban, Eogan and Énda, made a new conquest in what is now Donegal and northern Sligo, over peoples who, doubtless, had in earlier ages been vassals of the Ulaid. The new kingdom was known as *in Fochla, in Tuaiscert* (both phrases mean " the North "), or Ailech (from a famous fortress of this name, on Loch Swilly). These Northern Úi Néill thrived greatly, conquered what is now Derry and Tyrone from the Air-gíalla and the Dál Araide, and in the eighth or ninth century imposed their suzerainty over the kings of Air-gíalla.

Of the old province, or " fifth," of the Ulaid all that remained unconquered by Dál Cuinn was a small section in the north-east, comprising the present counties of Antrim and Down and portions of Louth and, for a time, of Tyrone. The three principal *túatha*, or states, in this section were that of the remnant of the Ulaid, in southern Down, that of Dál Araide, who were Cruitne, or Picts, in northern Down and southern Antrim, and that of Dál Riada, in northern Antrim.

The high-kingship of Ireland was held for six hundred years, from about 404 to 1002, by the descendants of Níall *nói-gíallach* and his brothers. From 482 or 483 it was held exclusively by Níall's own offspring, the Úi Néill, and from 734 was shared in alternate succession between the northern and southern branches of the family. The whole is a noteworthy evidence of the stability of the Irish political system in the early middle ages.

This sketch of the political *status* and history of central, northern and western Ireland will serve as a background to the history of the churches of the same regions. It has been seen how some of the chief peoples of the South, Corcu Loedge, Dési, Eoganacht, Osraige and Lagin, preserved traditions of the introduction of Christianity and of its first Irish apostles. For the north-eastern residue of the old province of Ulidia, and for the wide dominions of Dál Cuinn, there was a tradition of only one apostle, that bishop Patricius the direct sources for whose history have been considered in the preceding chapter. When the time came to compile the stories and exalt the fame of the founders of the Irish Church, it was inevitable that the apostle of Leth Cuinn should win some such position of predominance in the ecclesiastical legend as Dál Cuinn held in the national polity and, it may be added, as the records of Dál Cuinn hold in the surviving sources of early mediaeval history.

Patricius labored in Ireland from 432 to 461. The base of his mission, it is a fair inference from his writings, was the province of Ulidia in the north-east, but his statements also imply, what would in any case be a natural hypothesis, that he travelled extensively through the dominions of Dál Cuinn, and in particular to the western coasts of Ulster and Connacht.

The churches he founded we know only by tradition. That he fixed his episcopal see at Árd-Macha, or Armagh, close to the ruins of the ancient Ulaid capital of Emain-Macha, is probable. The universal acquiescence in Armagh's claims, the fitness of the location for a missionary working out from the neighboring Ulaid and seeking a suitable centre of operations in the territory of Dál Cuinn, and the appeal that would be made by the prestige of Emain-Macha, which in the time of Patricius must have outshone Tara in historical fame somewhat as Rome outshone Constantinople, are considerations that confirm the tradition. No doubt some others also of the many churches which after ages called his were actually founded by the saint.

Patricius died in 461. His name was kept in honor in the diptychs of the church of Armagh; the entries in the annals show that some records of him and his disciples were preserved in calendars and paschal tables; he was invoked in a colophon to the Book of Durrow which may preserve the words of Columba of Iona; Cummian's paschal epistle of about 632 refers to his Easter reckoning; Ultán of Árd-mBrecáin (d. 657) had a book containing early *memorabilia* regarding him; the so-called Hymn of Secundinus in his praise was probably written in the fifth or sixth century; and it seems certain that there was, at least throughout Leth Cuinn, considerable popular and traditional knowledge of the saint, and a number of distinct legends preserved in prose and verse. Patricius was not entirely forgotten, but such evidence as we have regarding the two hundred years following his death seems to show that his memory had slipped into the background of old and far-off things. Neither Columbanus, nor Jonas the biographer of Columbanus, nor Cogitosus in his Life of Brigit alludes to him in any way. Adamnán and Bede, to whom were peculiarly available the earlier records of Irish and English Christianity, make no mention of Patricius in their great historical works.[99] Zimmer has shown that, on Adamnán's testimony, the position in the commemoration in the mass, as celebrated by Colum-cille, which, had the Patrick Legend been accepted, it might be expected would be held by the name of Patrick, was occupied by that of Martin of Tours, and that likewise Martin's name is found where Patrick's would be looked for in an obituary notice of Colum-cille, written, Zimmer thought, just after that saint's death, by an Irishman in Gaul.[100]

In the meanwhile, as has been seen, the great saints of the sixth century arose, founded their monastic churches and congregations, and wrought a revolution in Irish ecclesiastical polity. With the seventh century came the historical spirit. Cogitosus and Cuimíne, perhaps drawing their inspiration from overseas, began Irish hagiography with Lives of Brigit and Colum-cille. Clerics of Patrician churches under-

---

[99] In the second preface to his Life of Columba — which possibly may be of later composition than the rest of the work — Adamnán alludes to St. Mochta of a disciple of " the holy bishop Patricius."
[100] *Sitzungsberichte d. kgl. preuss. Akad. d. Wissensch.* ('1909) pp. 595 *sqq* 584 *sqq*. But see Br. Krusch *NA* XXXV 275.

took to collect the records of their patron, now known in Irish as Pát-raic.[101]   In their handling the story grew to a vast legend of a great St. Patrick, apostle of all Ireland and hero of her conversion to the Faith.

The two sources of primary importance for the history of the forma-tion of the Patrick story are, so far as available evidence shows, the notes of Bishop Tírechán, compiled about 675, and the Life by Muir-chú moccu Machthéni, written, in part at least, before 700.   Curiously, both these documents had their points of origin in south-central Ireland. Tírechán, a Connachtman, began his work under the inspiration of Bishop Ultán of Árd-mBrecáin in Meath, and Muir-chú, who was possibly a native of Armagh, wrote his Life "at the dictation," or, perhaps, only by order of, Bishop Aed of Slébte (Sletty), in the present Leix, one of the chief churches of Leinster.   It is probable that Tírechán and Muir-chú were sent, according to the Irish custom, to these two churches for fosterage, that is, education.   Therefore, the first two men known to have given attention to the recording of the acts of Patrick were Ultán (d. 657) and Aed (d. 700).   As has been noted, Patrick had been men-tioned in the Paschal Epistle [102] written about 632 by Cummian, a prominent southern Irish ecclesiastic, who may have been abbot of Durrow, in Offaley.

It is worthy of remark that all the men associated with our earliest documentary products of the Patrick Legend were residents of that section of the island which, early in the seventh century, conformed with Rome on the Easter question, and three of them, Cummian, Aed and Muir-chú, are known to have been members of the Romanising party. Whether we accept or not Zimmer's theory that the Patrick Legend in its entirety was an invention of these seventh-century advocates of a closer union with continental Christianity, we can regard it as quite natural that they should feel an especial interest in the exaltation of the saint who had come as an apostle therefrom to Ireland.[103]

---

[101] To his Irish contemporaries Patricius was known as *Quadriga, Quotirche,* or some similar form (becom-ing later *Cothraige*), which was really a Goidelic (Q-language) rendition of what they no doubt thought to be a Brythonic (P-language) word.   But in the seventh century this equation was forgotten, the Patricius of the Latin documents was Hibernicised *Pátraic,* and absurd etymologies were advanced for *Cothraige.* The fact indicates that there was not any really strong and continuous historical tradition, linking the age of the saint with that of the hagiographers. — There were ancient peoples' names in the forms Catraige, Cathraige, Cotrige, Cothraige, which appeared as place-names in various parts of Ireland.   It is possible that the career of Patrick was occasionally eked out by the deliberate or unconscious confusion of these forms with Cothraige = Patricius.

[102] *Cf.* no. 57.

[103] The law treatises contain early matter relating to Patrick.   The preface to the *Senchus mór,* probably of the eighth century, and the *Córus Béscna,* which may be of the second half of the seventh, are the most important.   *Cf.* MacN in Mrs. A. S. Green *History of the Irish State to 1014* (1925) 107 *sqq.*

Because of the relatively large number of stages at which it has left permanent records, the Patrick Legend has a special interest as an example of the development of the *acta* of a mediaeval saint. It shows very clearly not only the manner of this development but also some of the motives, religious and secular, lying behind it. Two main sets of motives were, first, local or national pride in the patron saint and the desire to bring as many places, persons and peoples as possible into relationship with him; and second, the honor and the interests of the ecclesiastical organisation with which the saint was associated.

The *paruchia Patricii*, that league of monastic churches which regarded Patrick as founder and patron, and especially the head thereof, the church of Armagh, found in the cultivation of the Patrick Legend both prestige and profit. The abbots of Armagh, *comarbai* of Patrick, came to formulate claims, on behalf both of themselves and of their subordinate churches, against the Irish people in general, and in particular against those peoples who, according to the accepted traditions, owed their conversion or the foundation of their local churches—hence members of the *paruchia Patricii*—immediately to the great apostle.

The first evidence in the annals of the use of the Patrick Legend to further the financial interests of Armagh seems to be in 734, when, apparently, certain relics said to have been donated to that church by its founder were carried into other districts to promote the payment of tribute to Patrick. From this date on, the *comarbai* of Armagh from time to time "went on circuit" in all parts of the country, carrying these relics to stimulate the generosity of the people. Later the collection of the Patrick tribute, "Patrick's pence," was better organised, and a permanent steward, called *maer* or *equonimus* (*oeconomus*), was established in each of several districts to superintend the work. The first mention in the Annals of Ulster of such an official is in 814. The Patrician document known as the *Liber Angeli*,[104] "Book of the Angel," is manifestly connected with the early stages of the imposition of the Patrick tribute. A curious product of its later development is the poem interpolated, about the year 995, into *Leabhar na gCeart*, which makes Patrick convert the Norsemen of Dublin — not founded till four centuries after his time — and declares his successor at Armagh to be in consequence entitled to tribute in gold from them.

Early in the ninth century the church of Armagh produced what appears to have been an "official edition" of many of the more impor-

---

[104] No. 130.

tant records and memoranda regarding Patrick then known, an edition still preserved to us in the Patrician section of the *Liber Ardmachanus*, "Book of Armagh." [105] The compiler, Fer-domnach, died in 846; we know that he had been working under the supervision of the abbot of Armagh in 807. The records which he copied or indexed were being collected, he tells us, right down to his own day, thanks to the diligence of Patrick's "heirs." They were, it would appear, made use of especially as material for sermons, and towards the end of the century were amalgamated, along with other matter, into that great repertoire of the Patrick Legend, the collection of homilies known as the *Vita Tripartita*,[106] which is, in many respects, "rather a plea for the privileges of the primatial see than a eulogy of the apostle of Ireland."[107]

Lives of St. Patrick in the line of descent of the Patrick Legend continued to be written throughout the middle ages and down to the present day. In the secular literature its influence made Patrick a central character in a new mythopoeic movement, expressed chiefly in the Ossianic poems and sagas. But the Tripartite Life really marks the culmination of the hagiographic movement for the exaltation of Patrick.

Several solutions have been proposed for the problems which this mass of legend, when examined as sources for the career and personality of the saint, presents.

One is to accept the Patrick of legend as, with some obviously necessary modifications, the Patrick of history. Another has been to reject Patrick entirely as a pure fable. Todd accepted the historical character and apostolical importance of the saint, and found an anti-Roman and "evangelical" character in his work and teachings. Zimmer, whose studies on the Patrick Legend excited unusual interest, asserted that Ireland at the coming of Patrick was already a Christian country; that Patrick, who was identical with Palladius,[108] was sent to Ireland to

---

[105] *Cf.* pp. 337-9.   [106] *Cf.* p. 342.

[107] Dr. B. MacCarthy, in *Trans. RIA* XXXIX 185. A note attached at a later date, as it would seem, to the Tripartite Life, professes to give a list of the persons who narrated the miracles of Patrick: " These are the miracles which the elders of Ireland declared, and connected with a thread of narration. Colum-cille, son of Fedlimid, first declared Patrick's miracles and composed them. [Then] Ultán mocu Chonchobair, Adamnán ua Tinni, Elerán the Wise, Ciarán of Belach-Dúin, Bishop Ermedach of Clochar, Colmán Uamach, Priest Collait of Druim-Roilgech." (*Vit. Trip.* I 60, 256.) According to AU, Colum-cille died in 595 or 601, Ultán in 657 or 663, Elerán or Aileran in 665, Adamnán in 704, Colmán Uamach, a scribe of Armagh, in 725, and Ciarán of Belach-Dúin (now Castlekeeran, Meath) in 775. Ultán is the only one of these whom we know on no other authority to have helped preserve the traditions of Patrick. The association of Colum-cille, Aileran and Adamnán with the work is probably legendary; Colum-cille was said to have enshrined Patrick's relics in 553, but this story seems to be one of the later offshoots of the Patrick Legend.

[108] *Cf.* pp. 165, 169 *supra*.

exterminate Pelagianism; that his activity was confined to Wicklow and adjoining regions, and had no significant influence on the Irish Church; and that the Patrick of legend was created by the Romanising ecclesiastics of the seventh century, partly to provide Ireland with a national apostle such as Colum-cille, Aidan and Augustine were to Pictland, Northumbria, and South England, and partly to help win over the recalcitrant to the Roman side. Bury, who approached the subject as a phase of the expansion of Roman influences beyond the bounds of the Roman Empire, made a very thorough, though perhaps over-credulous, examination of the sources, and produced something like a scientific recasting of the main features of the traditional story, accepting both the saint's general pre-eminence and much of the record of his local activities. Finally to Czarnowski, who looks at the subject from the point of view of the sociological and anthropological sciences, the Patrick Legend is predominantly neither the corrupted tradition of a genuine historical record nor the pious invention of an ecclesiastical institution; it is the product of the workings of the folk-mind seeking the creation of a national "hero."

In connection with the use of the Patrician documents as sources for the history of the churches of the *paruchia Patricii* certain facts may be noted: (1) The legends used by the earliest compilers, Tírechán, Muirchú and Fer-domnach, were popular rather than ecclesiastical in character; "the arguments . . . were created by popular imagination, and suggested by the motives of 'folklore.'" [109]   In later Lives more use was made of the usual hagiographic miracles and other devices, but throughout its course the Patrick Legend shows less evidence of a monastic *origin* than the Lives of any other prominent Irish saint. The effects of ecclesiastical *handling* are, of course, quite manifest, notably of the preconception of a parallelism between Patrick and Moses. (2) The traditions of local churches, churches of little importance alongside the foundations of Colum-cille, Finnian, Ciarán, Brendan, etc., were the other chief sources of the seventh and eighth-century historians of Patrick. A few of these traditions were of some length, but the majority consisted of little more than the name of the first priest or bishop: his identification as a disciple of Patrick often looks like an assumption of the hagiographer. (3) Armagh seems to have played but a slight part in the beginnings of Patrician hagiography, which took its rise in Meath and in Slébte, north-west Leinster. Tírechán barely mentions Armagh, and seems to imply that the "heirs of Patrick," no doubt its abbots, were

109 Bury *St. Patrick* 267.

remiss in their duties. The evidence of the annals and other sources suggests that Armagh, although first in rank among the churches of northern Ireland,[110] did not attain the foremost position in size and importance before the eighth century. (4) Nor is there evidence of the existence in the seventh century of any organisation binding together the Patrician churches, such as from the first united the churches of the *paruchia* of Colum-cille. The first step in the effective organisation of the *paruchia Patricii* seems to have been taken when Bishop Aed of Slébte went to Armagh, within the period 661–88, and offered "his kin and his church to Patrick forever."[111]

Can it be that the churches, especially of the territory of Dál Cuinn and of Ulidia, that dated from the early days of Christianity and in many cases may not have been of monastic character, found themselves in an unsatisfactory position as a result of the rise of the monasteries and church-leagues of the sixth century, and that the early stages of the development of the Patrick Legend were in part the product of a movement to unite all these older churches, under the headship of Armagh, into a *paruchia* such as that of Colum-cille, on the basis of an assumption, largely fictitious, that they all owed their foundation to Patrick, first apostle and greatest of the saints of Ireland?

127. Tírechán's Memoir c A.D. 670 x 700

Tírechán episcopus haec scripsit ex ore uel libro Ultani episcopi cuius ipse alumpnus uel discipulus fuit.[112] Inueni iiii nomina . . . petram Coithrigi hi Caissiul.

MS: LA ff. 9–15ᵛ. EDS: Hogan *An. Boll.* II (1883) 35–68. — *Vit. Trip.* (1887) II 300–31. — *Thes. Pal.* II (1903) 261–9 [only passages containing Irish names and words; *cf.* ZCP I 348]. — *LA* (1913) pp. xliii–lxvii, cclxxxii–cclxxxvii, 17–31, 453–5. COMM: Robert *Étude critique* (1883) 46–8. — HZ "Keltische Beitrᵽge" III 77, 79: *Zs. f. deut. Altertum* XXXV (1891). — Bury " Tírechan's Memoir of St. Patrick " *EHR* April 1902 pp. 235 *sqq;* " Itinerary of Patrick in Connaught " *Proc. RIA* XXIV C (1903) 153–68; *Life of St. Patrick* (1905) 248–51, 358–60.

Tírechán was a bishop, a native of Tír-Amolngid (Tirawley, co. Mayo), who had been a disciple of Bishop Ultán moccu Conchobuir.[113] Presumably he had studied under Ultán at his church of Árd-mBrecáin (Ardbraccan) near Navan in Meath. The memoir was written after the death of Ultán (657, or, perhaps, 663) and soon after the great plague which ravaged Ireland in 664–8,[114] that is, probably in the seventies

---

[110] See no. 58.   [111] *Cf.* p. 335 *infra*.   [112] Probably due to a scribe.   [113] *Cf.* pp. 268, 325.

[114] He accuses the " familia Clono " (Clúain-maccu-Nóis, Clonmacnois, probably), " because since the last epidemic they hold by force many of Patrick's places." (*LA* 23 a 8.)

of that century. It forms a clear exemplification of the interests of the *paruchia Patricii* at work in the shaping of the Patrick Legend, and an excellent illustration of a saint's *acta* in the making. It is a collection of *memoranda* regarding Patrick gathered evidently from widely scattered sources, the majority being notices of church foundations. This is the raw material on which the hagiographer could, later, work; and, more important, served the very practical purpose of providing the successors of Patrick with a list of Patrician foundations from which they could claim allegiance.

Tírechán began his memoir with some extracts regarding Patrick from a book which had been in the possession of his master Ultán,[115] and some information which that teacher had given him by word of mouth. We do not know the extent of these sources, but it cannot have been very great: they gave a brief account of Patrick's early life, and perhaps part of the narrative of his labours in Meath and the list (obtained from a written source) of bishops and priests ordained by him. But the plan of Tírechán's work expanded as he proceeded. Perhaps on his own initiative — he found some reason for considering himself a hereditary member of Patrick's congregation [116] — perhaps at the instigation of the Patrician clergy, and the Romanising party of southern Ireland, he undertook to collect such records as could be discovered of the work of Patrick, more especially in Meath and in his native province of Connacht. A fictitious journey of the saint from Tara to North Connacht and back through Ulster to Meath — a journey impossible to reconcile with the actual narratives recorded — was used as the thread to connect these *memoranda*. With this setting the remaining Meath traditions were put down, and then probably Tírechán set out to collect material in Connacht: the first part of his work was written in Meath (" in the territories of the Húi Néill "), but the second in Connacht, and it is certain that he personally visited some, if not all, of the localities of which he speaks.

The second part of the memoir, addressed, it would appear, to the Patrician communities in Meath, begins as follows: " All the things of which I have written from the beginning of this book are known to you, for they have taken place in your country — unless an exception be made of a few matters which I learned as a reward of my industry, from many *seniores* and from that Bishop Ultán moccu Conchubuir who fostered me.[117] But my heart is troubled within me through love of Patrick, for I see with what hatred the renegades and robbers [or, defamers, satirists] and soldiers of Ireland [118] regard Patrick's *paruchia*, in that they have taken away from him what was his and they are in fear, since, if the heir of Patrick were to demand his *paruchia*, he could recover as such almost the whole island."

---

115 It must have been from Ultán's book that he obtained the date of Patrick's death: " a passione Christi . . . anni ccccxxxiii " (MS ccccxxxvi), a date which shows that this material had not yet undergone the editing which later placed the event in 493. *Cf.* Bury *Life of St. Patrick* 382-4.

116 After relating how Endeus, son of Amolngid (*a quo* Tír-Amolngid, Tír-Amhalghaidh, Tirawley) dedicated his share of his father's patrimony to God and Patrick, he adds: " For this reason, some say, we are Patrick's servants to the present day " (*LA* 20 b 27).

117 It is evident throughout that Tírechán assumes in his readers familiarity with some general story of St. Patrick's career.

118 " dissertores et archiclocos et milites Hiberniae." *Cf. Vit. Trip.* II 312; *The Academy* Jan. 5, 1884 p. 13; Bury *EHR* (1902) p. 703.

The basis of the whole work was clearly local traditions gathered from the people or from the *seniores* of the monastic churches.[119] Bury has pushed the argument for the use by Tírechán of written sources as far as it is possible to do so, but at most these cannot have been extensive. It is quite probable, however, that the local legends were in some cases in fairly elaborate form: the idyllic story of the conversion of Loígaire's daughters has been shown by Bury with probability to be the Latin rendering of an Irish poetical source.[120]

The memoir ends abruptly: perhaps the last leaf of the original exemplar was lost; perhaps Tírechán had expected to gather further material. The copy used by the scribe of the Book of Armagh must have been at least one remove from the autograph. Dr. Gwynn found that on its first leaf were entered a passage omitted in the body of the memoir, and the *Dicta Patricii*.

128. The Life of Patrick by Muir-chú *c* A.D. 680 x 700

[LA f. 20: Preface; table of contents of Book I] Quoniam quidem, mi domine Aido . . . Coirthech regem Aloo. Haec pauca de sancti Patricii peritia et uirtutibus Muirchu maccu Machtheni, dictante Aiduo Slebtiensis ciuitatis episcopo, conscripsit. [*Vita*] Patricius qui et Sochet [LA f. 2 *sqq* (f. 1 missing) sibi in Hibernica] . . . fructum felicissimum obtinent. Finit. Amen. [Portauit Patricius . . . in Gallis inuenit.]

MSS: LA ff. 2–8ᵛ, 20. — Brussels Bibl. roy. 64 [from Wirzburg] *s* XI ff. 299 *sqq*. EDS: Hogan *An. Boll.* I (1882) 531–83 [also separately]. — *Vit. Trip.* (1887) II 269–300, 494–8. — *Thes. Pal.* II (1903) 45, 259–61 [only passages containing Irish names and words; *cf.* ZCP I 347–8]. — LA (1913) pp. xvii–xlii, cclxxxi *sq*, 3–16, 39–40, 442–52. TRANS: Albert Barry *Life of St. Patrick by Muirchu maccu Machtheni* (Dublin 1895). — N. J. D. White *St. Patrick His Writings and Life* (London, New York 1920) 68–109, 121–37. — COMM: Chas. Graves *Proc. RIA* VIII (1864) 269–71. — Robert *Étude critique* (1883) 41–5. — Bury " The oldest Life of St. Patrick " *The Guardian* Nov. 20, 27, 1901; " The tradition of Muirchu's text " *Hermathena* XIII no. xxviii (1902); " Sources of the early Patrician documents " *EHR* July 1904; *Life of St. Patrick* (1905) 255–63, 266–8. — Roger *L'Enseignement* (1905) 258–9. — P. Walsh *Irish Theological Quarterly* XVI (April 1921) pp. 177 *sqq*.

Muir-chú ["sea-hound"] moccu Machthéni was, it is a probable inference from his name, a member of the Túath Mochtaine,[121] a people who dwelt in Mag-Macha, the plain surrounding and extending south and east from Árd-Macha, Armagh. If so, he was, no doubt, also a member of the ecclesiastical family of Armagh. He alludes to the hagiographical work of his father Cogitosus,[122] who must have been the

---

[119] *Cf. e.g.* the story of Patrick's founding the church of Ath-Brón in Meath: "He left in it three brothers and one sister. These are their names: Cathaceus, Cathurus, Catneus, and their sister Catnea, who milked the wild does, as old people told me." LA f. 10 b.

[120] It is to be remembered, however, that the introduction of periodised, rhythmical passages into narrative Latin prose was quite in the tradition of literary style. *Cf.* p. 282 *supra*.

[121] Hogan *Onomasticon* 652; MacN *Proc. RIA* XXIX C (1911) 79; XXXVII C (1926) 122 n.

[122] " Coguitosi," Graves' emendation of the MS " cognito si." — *Op. cit.* in bibliog. It has been suggested that *Cogitosus* was a Latinisation of the people-name *moccu Machthéni*, by a fancied association with the Irish verb *machtnaigim*, " I wonder at," but such a translation, and such a method of forming a personal name in Latin, are alike highly improbable.

Cogitosus to whom we owe a Life of St. Brigit.[123]   It is probable that
" spiritual father " rather than " father in the flesh " is meant, for it is
reasonable to suppose that Cogitosus was a native of Leinster; nevertheless it is not impossible that Cogitosus was originally of Armagh, for,
at least at a slightly later date, there were friendly relations between
Patrick's church at Armagh and Brigit's at Kildare.[124]   Muir-chú
wrote his Life of Patrick (or, possibly, only the first book thereof) at the
command — a note says " dictation," but this may be the entry of a
later scribe — of Bishop Aed of Slébte (Sletty, in Leix), who is usually
identified with the anchorite Aed who died in A.D. 700.[125]   Both Aed
and Muir-chú attended Adamnán's synod in 697, at which, it seems
likely, the northern ecclesiastics were induced to conform to the Roman
Easter.[126]   During the rule of Bishop Ségene of Armagh, 662–688, Aed
had officially incorporated the church of Slébte in the *paruchia Patricii*,[127]
and it was, doubtless, after, and as a result of, this union that Muir-chú
became associated with Aed.   A further credible hypothesis is, as has
been mentioned previously,[128] that Muir-chú was the father of the Colmán mac Mur-chon, abbot of Mag-Bile (Moville, co. Down) who died in
736.   There is one other possible early allusion to our author: a Muir-chú
is commemorated in the Martyrology of Oengus on June 8, and the notes
— which are, of course, of later date — designate him as moccu Machthéni and say that his church was Cell Mur-chon, which Colgan locates
near Wicklow.[129]

Thus there appear to have been personal associations between Muir-
chú and Armagh, Sletty, Wicklow and Down, traditions from each of
which he incorporated into his work.[130]

Muir-chú's preface is interesting, although the Latin is turgid and obscure: " Foras-
much as,[131] my Lord Aed, many have taken in hand to set forth in order a narration
according to what has been delivered to them by their fathers and those who at the

123 No. 147.   124 *Cf.* pp 337, 358 *infra.*   125 AU.
126 *Cf.* no. 81.   The appearance of Muir-chú's name in the document indicates that at this time he
was something more than a youthful disciple of Aed.
127 *Cf.* p. 335 *infra.*
128 *Cf.* no. 97.   Also M. Esposito *Proc. RIA* XXX C (1912) 323.
129 *AA. SS.* 465 and n. 31.   A commentator whose note is preserved in the LBr copy of Fél. Oeng. (and
another, or the same, in the Franciscan copy) says that he does not know where was Muir-chú's church.
Another places it in the territory of the Úi Faeláin, probably in Kildare.   A note in the Laud 610 copy
says that it was among the Úi Ailella.   There were many families of this name, of which the best known
dwelt in Tír-Ailella, Tirerill, Sligo.   Perhaps for this reason the author of the preface to Colmán mac Mur-
chon's hymn (no. 97) says that Colmán was the son of Muir-chú of Connacht.   But there was also an
Úi Ailella family among the Fotharta, of whom one division was located in Wicklow.
130 It may be that we owe the account of Patrick's first landing in Wicklow to the fact that Muir-chú's
own church was there, and the whole story of his journey from Wicklow to Down and Antrim, and back
again to Meath, to a similar voyage made by the hagiographer.

beginning were ministers of the word, but because of the difficulty of the narrative and the different opinions and many doubts of many people never arrived at one definite line of history; so, unless I deceive myself, I, — to use that proverb of ours, 'as boys are led into the amphitheatre,'[132] — have led my boyish skiff with its unskilled oar into this deep and dangerous gulf of sacred narrative, with its mounds of waves surging wildly amidst the sharpest rocks fixed in uncharted waters, a gulf hitherto entered and occupied by no boats except only that of my father Cogitosus. However, not to seem to make much of little, I shall undertake to set forth, though tediously and unmethodically, these few out of the many acts of St. Patrick, — for my skill is slight, my sources are vague,[133] my memory frail, my intelligence dulled, my language barbarous, but my intentions are most dutiful and I am obeying your kind, holy and just command."[134]

Muir-chú's work forms the basis of all subsequent Patrician biography, yet we can easily see, after due allowance is made for the author's rhetoric, that the information on which he based it was, even to the mind of a seventh-century hagiographer, uncertain and unsatisfactory. At the same time he makes it clear, both from this and other passages, that he had some written sources.[135] Bury and others have shown that for the period of the saint's life anterior to his arrival in Ireland Muir-chú used a source, or sources, which included, or was based on, the Confession, with the addition of a fairly sober narrative of his career in Gaul.[136] He has pointed out also that with the beginning of the mission in Ireland a considerable legendary element enters into the narrative, that Muir-chú, like Tírechán, translated some Irish poetical records, and that in some cases he and Tírechán have used identical sources.

Muir-chú gives us two connected narratives that have the form of biography. The first, embracing chapters i–xxii of the first book, relates Patrick's early life and the mission to Ireland up to the point where, on the occasion of the first Easter, he confronts and overthrows the assembled powers of paganism at Tara.[137] With the triumph of Christianity, culminating in the conversion of the árd-rí Loigaíre,[138] this section comes to a close. The second, forming chapters iv–xiv of the second book, tells of his death and of the contest between the Úi Néill and the eastern Air-gíalla on the one side, and the Ulaid on the other, for possession of his body.[139] The

---

[131] Muir-chú adopts the opening words of St. Luke's Gospel.

[132] Perhaps the Irish word was *aonach*.

[133] " incertis auctoribus ": Bury thinks the meaning may be " anonymous."

[134] A trans. of this preface is given in Todd's *St. Patrick* 402.

[135] *Cf.* " post vero miracula tanta quae alibi scripta sunt et quae ore fideli mundus celebrat " LA f. 8 a.

[136] One piece of evidence shows that part of this information was at some time transmitted through the medium of the Irish language. Patrick is said to have been sent by Germanus of Auxerre to be ordained " ab Amatho rege." HZ (*Nennius Vindicatus* 122–3) has shown that this must be a re-Latinising of the Irish Amatorig, which in turn would be the equivalent for Amator, the well-known predecessor of Germanus in the see of Auxerre, who died about 418. Probably there is a confusion between the ordination of Patrick as deacon and as bishop. Bury notes the fruitful results of the mistake in the development of the Patrick Legend. " Later compilers divided *Amatho rege*. — In *Tripartite Life* (p. 34) we get a further step in the evolution; the bishop appears as Amatho rí Románach (King of the Romans); and the final stage is reached when Patrick is ordained *coram Teodosio imperatore*." — *Life of St. Patrick* 347 n. 3.

[137] The Tara episode is more extravagant and more ecclesiastical in character than the other legends used by Muir-chú. It seems to have been influenced by the parallel of Moses before Pharaoh. It is possible also that the prominence given to Easter reflects the controversy on the observance of that festival in Muir-chú's Ireland.

[138] Tírechán preserves the undoubtedly accurate tradition that Loigaire remained a pagan.

[139] *Cf.* Bury *St. Patrick* 208–10, 380–2.

remaining chapters of the two books treat of isolated miracles and other episodes.[140]

Two short notes are added to Muir-chú's text in the Book of Armagh, one describing the articles which Patrick took with him across the river Shannon, the other giving his age. This last information is said to have been found by a certain Constans among the Gauls. These notes are not by Muir-chú, but were probably found by Fer-domnach on the last page of his manuscript of that author.

129. Additions to Tírechán's Memoir

MS: LA ff. 9, 15^v-19. EDS: Todd *St. Patrick* (1864) 257-62 [text, trans. of portion *re* Trim; *cf.* 149-54]. — Hogan *An. Boll.* II (1883) 213-38. — *Vit. Trip.* (1887) II 301, 331-51. — *Thes. Pal.* II (1903) pp. xiii, 238-43, 269-71, and App. II [text, trans. of O–I portions]. — *LA* pp. lxvii-lxxv, cclxxxvii *sq*, 17, 31-37, 456-64. COMM: Robert *Étude critique* 44, 48-9, 74. — Jenkinson *The Academy* Aug. 11, 1888. — Bury *St. Patrick* 228-33, 252-5.

In the Book of Armagh the scribe Fer-domnach has added to the Memoir of Tírechán a considerable number of other records relating to Patrick:

I The *Dicta Patricii*, apparently found by Fer-domnach written on the first page of his exemplar of Tírechán. They are three in number, and were evidently regarded as habitual sayings of Patrick: (i) An allusion to the saint's journey in Gaul, Italy, and the islands of the Tyrrhene sea.[141] (ii) An extract from the epistle against Coroticus (no. 29). (iii) An admonition for the use of the liturgical *formulae* " Kyrie eleison," " Christe eleison." [142]

II A collection of notes appended to Tírechán: (i) The three petitions of Patrick for the Irish. (ii) Patrick's age and the periods of his life.' (iii) Comparison between Patrick and Moses. (iv) The contest for his body, and Colum-cille's discovery of his grave. (v) The mission of Palladius. (vi) Patrick's four honors.[143] Gwynn shows that there is reason to believe that the first of these sections was found by Fer-domnach entered on his copy of Tírechán, and that he himself inserted the others.

III A collection of records in Irish, in continuation of Tírechán's work, gathered by the abbots of Armagh, and translated wholly or partially into Latin. The linguistic evidence points to the early eighth century as the date of composition of the greater part.[144] Fer-domnach introduces them thus: " The beginning of a few other records, discovered in recent times and now to be set forth in due order: through the care of his

---

[140] Bury's investigation of the early MS tradition of Muir-chú's text is of importance in any minute study of this source.

[141] A similar sentence is given by Tírechán with the comment " as he himself said in the commemoration of his labors," whatever may have been meant by that. The whole passage seems to be from the book of Ultán.

[142] The *Kyrie* did not come to Rome before the fifth century, nor to Gaul before the sixth; the *Christe* took its origin in Rome in the sixth. It may be that the third *dictum* was originally " Deo gratias," and was expanded in the seventh century by a member of the Romanising party. *Cf. Cath. Encycl. s. v.* " Kyrie eleison "; E. Bishop *Liturgica historica* (Oxford 1918) 116-36.

[143] The 3rd and 4th call for the continual singing of his " ymnum " and his " canticum scotticum," doubtless the Hymn of Secundinus (no. 87) and the *Lorica* (no. 101).

[144] *Cf.* T. Ó Máille *The language of the Annals of Ulster* (Manchester 1910) 109 n. 5.

heirs and their diligent regard for his sanctity, these are being collected even to the present day for the honor and praise of the Lord and to preserve the kindly memory of Patrick." This material is divided into three sections, distinguished graphically by the scribe. (i) A notice of the founding of the church of Trim, and a list of the spiritual and lay successors of the founder. It must have been prepared, and, doubtless, transmitted from Trim to Armagh, in the latter part of the eighth century. (ii) Six records of grants of land and churches made to Patrick, in Connacht. (iii) Four Leinster records, treating of Bishop Iserninus (*cf.* p. 169), of Fíacc of Slébte (*cf.* nos. 132, 141 iv), of the foundation of Slébte, and of its subsequent dedication to Armagh by Bishop Aed. Aed visited Armagh during the time of Bishop Ségene (661–688), and we may presume that the preceding Leinster notices were then brought to the Patrician capital. A successor of Aed, Conchadh, made a similar visit to Ségene's successor, Fland Febla (688–715).

Fer-domnach evidently believed that with this his enterprise was finished, for he adds: " Here end these few items imperfectly written in Irish not because I was not able to express them in the Rôman tongue, but·because these stories can be understood with difficulty even in their own Irish. But if on the other hand they had been rendered into Latin, one would have been not only uncertain as to their meaning but even ignorant as to what he had read or what language he was pronouncing, by reason of the multitude of untranslatable Irish names." There follow four rude hexameters in which the scribe asks the prayers of his readers.

IV But a mass of further documents must have come to his attention, for there follows a long list of memoranda and catchwords, very much abbreviated and written in the scribe's smallest script, forming a kind of inventory of Patrician material. This must have been a miscellaneous collection, and included records parallel to some of those used by Tírechán in his second book. The collection was retained at Armagh, for much of it has been incorporated into the Tripartite Life (no. 135). On linguistic grounds the memoranda, and probably the records to which they form catchwords, cannot, in the setting given, be dated much earlier than Fer-domnach's time.

130. The Book of the Angel

[Patricio sancto episcopo . . .] Quondam itaque sanctus Patricius de Alti Mache . . . ualde eiusdem libros conscripserunt. [Fundamentum orationis — dominatu in mea erit.]

MS: LA ff. 20ᵛ-2. EDS: Hogan *IER* 3rd ser. VII 845–53; *Vita Sancti Patricii* II (Brussels 1889). — *Vit. Trip.* II (1887) 352–6. — *LA* pp. lxxv–lxxviii, cclxxxviii *sq*, 40–3. COMM: *The Academy* July 7, 14, 21, 1888. — HZ *Celtic Church* 83, 96, 126–7. — Bury *St. Patrick* 287.

Early Irish records contain many references to a *Lex Patricii, Cáin Pátraic,* or Law of Patrick, and to its enforcement, at various times, in different parts of the country. The earliest allusion thereto in the Annals of Ulster is under the year 734: " Transfer of the relics of Peter and Paul and Patrick, to enforce the law." [145] Under 737 we read: " The Law of

---

[145] Commotatio martirum Peter ocus Phoil ocus Phatraicc ad legem perficiendam." Certain relics of the two apostles, according to Tírechán, were brought from Rome in Patrick's time (LA f. 9). " Com-

Patrick held Ireland "; under 767 simply " Lex Patricii "; 783 " The promulgation of the Law of Patrick in Crúachne [the plain of Rathcrogan, Roscommon] by Dub-dá-leithi [abbot of Árd-Macha] and by Tipraite son of Tadhg [king of Connacht], " etc. What the nature of the Law of Patrick was is nowhere clearly explained. Keating describes the *Cáin Pádraig* as one of the four laws of Ireland, its provision being " not to kill clerics." [146] Elsewhere the title seems to be applied to the *Senchus Mór*, the largest section of the so-called " Brehon Laws." Some texts of the secular law on the relationships of Church and people are designated *Ríagail Pátraic*, " Rule of Patrick." But a comparison of all the information available makes it reasonably certain that the " Laws " of various saints — for there are many others besides that of Patrick — while they might include moral and social injunctions, commonly imposed also the payment of some pecuniary or other tribute to the saint's successor and representative.[147] We may, therefore, conclude that the Law of Patrick, or, at least, one version of it, is preserved to us in the " Book of the Angel."

The *Liber Angeli* [148] consists of two parts, an introduction from which the name is derived, and a code of decrees regarding the rights and dignity of the *paruchia Patricii* and the church of Árd-Macha. This second part may date back to 734; the introduction cannot be much anterior to Fer-domnach's own period, though possibly it is based on an old Armagh tradition. The work is a very interesting source for Irish church organisation. The second part defines the supremacy of Árd-Macha throughout Ireland and its relationships with other churches; [149] the rights to refection for himself and his retinue possessed by its abbot; [150] the penalties for dishonoring the " insig-

---

motatio " here probably means the carrying of the relics from Armagh through the districts where the " law " was to be enforced.

    [146] Ed. Dinneen III 107.   [147] *Cf.* p. 246 *supra.*
    [148] In Fer-domnach's orthography, " Liber Angueli."
    [149] After asserting the pre-eminence of Armagh, and the superiority of its head over all other abbots, provision is made that every free church and *civitas* of episcopal rank, and every place called *Dominicus*, should be in the special society of the pontiff Patrick and of the heir of his see of Armagh. — The monastic churches which arose in the sixth and seventh centuries most frequently bore the designation *cell*, perhaps from the saintly hermit's *cella* around which each grew up. The terms *domnach* (from *dominicus*, or, in continental usage, *dominicum* — see Du Cange *s. v.*), and, less frequently, *ecclas* (from *ecclesia*) and *tempall* (from *templum*) seem to have been more usually applied to the older churches, antecedent to the monastic movement of the sixth century; they were probably founded as churches, not monasteries, at a time when the continental episcopal organisation still persisted in Ireland, and, perhaps, in the majority of cases never became monasteries. If the hypothesis advanced in the introduction to the present section is well founded, it is probable that the decree here under consideration meant the assertion by Armagh of direct jurisdiction over all churches which were independent of the various monastic congregations of the sixth and later centuries, of all churches which were, or had been, bishops' sees, and of all churches which, by bearing the designation *domnach*, indicated that they were ancient non-monastic foundations. It may be noted that, although *domnach* enters very extensively into Irish place-names, and many churches so named are mentioned in the early Patrician documents, very few such are noticed in the annals for the eighth and later centuries, and only two seem to have been of any special importance, Domnach-Pátraicc (Donaghpatrick, Meath) and Domnach-Sechnaill (Dunshaughlin, Meath).
    [150] The *Liber Angeli* makes no mention of direct payments to Armagh, but the claims it sets up would

nia " of Patrick; the rights of legal jurisdiction possessed by the abbot; and the conditions under which an appeal should be made to the " Chair of Peter." Some of these decrees, or perhaps only the last, are said to have been enacted by Auxilius, Patrick, Secundinus and Benignus. The introduction relates the colloquy between Patrick and an angel who announces a great extension of the " terminus " of Árd-Macha, and the granting to him of all the tribes of the Irish as his *paruchia*. Then follow statements by Patrick on the duties and claims of himself and his successors, and certain explanations as to the religious organisation of the people of Árd-Macha.

Appended to the *Liber Angeli* are two notes, one apparently recording certain liturgical regulations at Árd-Macha, the other recognising the sovereignty of Brigit within her own province.

131. *Liber Ardmachanus:* Book of Armagh

N. B. This section gives special attention only to the Patrician division of LA; for a description of the two other portions *cf.* nos. 474, 523, 560.

EDS: Wm. Betham *Irish Antiquarian Researches* 2 vols. (Dublin 1827) [Pt. II has a description of the MS, text and trans. of the Patrician documents, all now of no value, and several fair facs. pls. See also his art. in *The Christian Examiner* 3rd ser. III (1836) 308 *sqq.*] — Edmund Hogan *Vita Sancti Patricii* (Brussels 1882) [also in *An. Boll.* I (1882) 531–85, II (1883) 35–68, 213–38; contains Muir-chú, Tírechán, and the *Additamenta*]; Part II (Brussels 1889) [*Liber Angeli* and *Confessio;* not in *An. Boll.* Portions of the two vols. were reprinted in his *Outlines of the Grammar of Old Irish* (Dublin 1900).] — *Vit. Trip.* (1887) I pp. xc–xcix, II 269–375 [Patrician documents]. — *Thes. Pal.* I (1900) 494–8, II (1903) pp. xiii–xvii, 45, 259–71 [Irish passages, words and glosses]. — John Gwynn *Liber Ardmachanus The Book of Armagh edited with introduction and appendices* (RIA: Dublin 1913) [an excellent ed. of the whole MS, " paginatim, lineatim, verbatim, literatim," with very valuable introductory chapters: it is one of the monuments of contemporary Irish scholarship]. — FACS: *Facs. Nat. MSS. Ire.* I (Dublin 1874) pp. xiv *sqq*, pls. xxv–xxix. — For others see Gougaud *RC* XXXIV (1913) 29–30. — COMM: *Rer. Hib. SS.* I (1813) [the *epistola nuncupatoria* gives Lhwyd's *memorandum*]. — Chas. Graves *Proc. RIA* III (1846) 316–24, 356–9 [a very valuable paper, setting forth the evidence on which the date of the MS was determined]. — Wm. Reeves " On the Book of Armagh " *ibid.* 3rd ser. II 77–99. — W. M. Lindsay *Early Irish minuscule script* (Oxford 1910) 24–30, pl. ix [palaeographical description].

The most important historical manuscript of Ireland prior to the twelfth century, and, in one of its sections, the only collection of the *acta* of a saint actually compiled and written down in his own monastic church in the ages of faith, that has survived to our day, is the Book of Armagh, *Liber Ardmachanus*.

It is a small volume, measuring 7¾ inches by 5¼, and consisting originally of 222 leaves of vellum. Folios 1 and 41–44 are now missing. There are three main divisions of

imply these and it is clear from the annals that the promulgation of the Law of Patrick was accompanied, or followed, by the payment of dues.

the codex: 1 The Patrician Documents, occupying ff. 1–24; 2 The New Testament, ff. 25–191; 3 The Life of St. Martin of Tours by Sulpicius Severus, ff. 192–222.

The calligraphy — Irish minuscule — which is of very fine character, is of the same hand throughout. It varies considerably, however, in different parts, a variation due to the greater or less degree of care taken by the writer or the supervisor. These changes in the character of the handwriting, as well as the arrangement of the folios as shown above, make it probable that originally several of the divisions of the book were separate codices. If so, they must have been bound together at a — comparatively — early date, for the outer leaves of the main and subordinate divisions, with one exception, have not the appearance of exposure which long existence as separate volumes would be likely to produce. The exception is the section containing the Pauline Epistles, the first page of which is much defaced: it is possible that this was, originally, the first part of the collection.

The date and the scribe were, in modern times, unknown, until determined by the Rev. Charles Graves (afterwards Bishop of Limerick), in a brilliant paper read before the Royal Irish Academy in 1846. The manuscript had been traditionally honored as the autograph of Patrick, and, doubtless to remove evidence which might tend to lessen its sanctity, several subscriptions added at various places by the scribe had been wholly or partially erased. Two of these (ff. 215, 221) can, however, still be read: "Pro Ferdomnacho ores." Dr. Graves succeeded in partially restoring one of the obliterated colophons (f. 53ᵛ); with the substitution of Latin characters for the Greek [151] which the scribe occasionally affected, it runs

> F DOMNACH HUNC LIB
> E RUM . . . E DICTANTE
> R TORBACH HEREDE PAT
> RICII SCRIPSIT

i.e., "Fer-domnach wrote this book . . . at the dictation of Torbach, Heir of Patrick." The "death of Torbach, a scribe, abbot of Armagh," is recorded by the Annals of Ulster in 808, and that of "Fer-domnach, a wise man and excellent scribe of Armagh" in 846.[152] Some of the lists of the successors of Patrick give Torbach as abbot for one year,[153] and Colgan states that his memorial day, that is, the day of his death, was July 16.[154] Another entry, made, like that quoted above, at the end of St. Matthew's Gospel, states that the Gospel was finished on the feast of Matthew, September 21. It follows that this portion of the book was written in 807. A marginal entry confirms this dating. Opposite the passage of St. Mark's Gospel giving Christ's prophecy of the miseries at the destruction of Jerusalem (Mark xiii 20, f. 65ᵛ) is the word "Cellach." Cellach was abbot of Iona 802–815: in 806 his monastery of Iona was sacked by the Northmen and the inmates slain, but he himself fled to Ireland, where in the following year he established the headquarters of the Columban community at Kells.[155]

---

[151] Fer-domnach's knowledge of Greek seems to have been limited to a not wholly accurate acquaintance with the letters of the alphabet. *Cf. LA* pp. cxxiv *sq.*

[152] There is said to be a pedigree of a Fer-domnach in the Book of Lecan, which represents him as 23rd in descent from Conaire *mór*. On the basis of the received chronology this would place him in the ninth century. — *Proc. RIA* III 322.

[153] *Cf. Vit. Trip.* II 547.

[154] *Tr. Thaum.* 294.

[155] *Cf.* pp. 425, 445 *infra*, also Skene *Celtic Scotland* II 291.

By an examination of the script Gwynn came to the conclusion that the order of transcription was as follows: (1) Pauline Epistles; (2) Catholic Epistles and Apocalypse; (3) Muir-chú (lacking preface and table of *capita* of first book), Tírechán, and the *additamenta* to Tírechán (pp. 334–5 *supra*), to f. 18^v b; (4) the omitted preface and *capita* of Muir-chú, *Liber Angeli, Confessio Patricii*, ff. 20–4; (5) the catch-word notes of *memoranda* collected at Armagh, ff. 18^v–19^v (p. 335 *supra*): it is possible that these were entered before the last-mentioned texts, but more probable that they were written on a space left blank; (6) Gospels, of about the same period as the *Liber Angeli* and *Confessio;* (7) Acts; (8) Life of St. Martin, possibly earlier than Acts.

The earliest external reference to the Book of Armagh is that preserved by the Four Masters under 937: " A case (*cumhdach*) was provided for the *Canóin Pátraicc* by Donnchadh, son of Flann, King of Ireland." The name *Canóin Pátraicc*, or *Phádraig*, by which the codex was henceforth generally known, indicates that already the Patrician documents and New Testament were united into one volume.

In 1004 Brian *boroimhe* visited Armagh, and had entered in a blank space of the manuscript a confirmation of the privileges claimed by the clergy of that church.[156]

At some unknown date the hereditary office of " Steward of the Canon " (*Maor na Canóine*) was created for the safe-keeping of the book. From the office this family took the name Mac Maoir, Mac Moyre, Muire or Wyre. At the time of the Plantation of Ulster they lost their lands, but retained the book until 1680, when the last steward, Florence Mac Moyre, pledged it for five pounds on the eve of his departure for London to give perjured evidence against the venerable Oliver Plunket, archbishop of Armagh, who, as a result of the trial, was condemned, and put to death in 1681. Mac Moyre, whose signature is to be seen in the manuscript (f. 105^v), was never able to recover it.

In 1707 Edward Lhwyd noted that the Book of Armagh was in the possession of Arthur Brownlow, of Lurgan (co. Armagh). Lhwyd has left an interesting memorandum regarding the codex and its traditions. In 1846 the Rev. Francis Brownlow, fifth in succession to Arthur Brownlow, deposited it in the library of the Royal Irish Academy, where it was studied with such good results by Dr. Graves. In 1853 it was offered for sale, and purchased by Dr. William Reeves, from whom it was obtained in the following year by Archbishop Beresford, of Armagh, for the library of Trinity College. The manuscript, however, was left at the disposal of Dr. Reeves until his proposed edition of it should be published. Reeves died in 1892, leaving the task still incomplete. The Royal Irish Academy then entrusted the undertaking to Dr. John Gwynn, by whom the work of publication was brought to completion in 1913.

132. Fíacc's Hymn

Génair Patraicc i nNemthur . . . ba sén gaire i ngénair

MSS: LH(T) ff. 15–16. — LH(F) pp. 36–8. EDS: Colgan *Tr. Thaum.* (1647) 1–10 [text, Lat. trans.]. — *Rer. Hib. SS.* I (1814) pp. 88, xc–cv. — H. Leo *Commentatio de carmine vetusto Hibernico in S. Patricii laudem* (Halle a. Saale 1845). — [MacCarthy]

---

[156] *Cf.* no. 144.

IER IV (1868) 269–93 [text, trans.]. — WS *Goidilica* (Calcutta 1866); *Goidelica* (London 1872) 126–8 [T text, trans.]. — H&S II ii 356–61 [reprint of preceding]. — *Facs. Nat. MSS. Ire.* I (1874) pls. xxxii–xxxiv [facs., letterpress, trans., of T]. — *IT* I (1880) 10–22, 321–2 [T text, variants from F]. — HZ *Keltische Studien* II (Berlin 1884) 160–85 [text given in connection with a metrical study]. — *Vit. Trip.* (1887) II 402–27 [F text, trans.]. — *LH*² (1898) I 96–104, II pp. xl–xlix, 31–5, 175–87 [T, F texts, trans.]. — *Thes. Pal.* II (1903) pp. xxxvii *sq*, 307–21 [critical text, trans.]. — Thos. FitzHugh *Italico-Keltic accent and rhythm* (Charlottesville, Va., 1909) 33 *sqq* [of metrical interest only]. TRANS: Ferguson *Trans. RIA* XXVII 105. — COMM: *LH*¹ II (1869) 287–304. — Loofs *Antiquae Britonum Scotorumque ecclesiae quales fuerunt mores* (Leipsic 1882) 44. — Robert *Étude critique* (1883) 49–54. — RTh *RC* VI 326–36 [includes a criticism of HZ's ed.]. — *Lis. Lives* (1890) 293. — Bury *St. Patrick* (1905) 263–6. — HZ " Beiträge zur Erklärung altirischer Texte der Kirchlichen u. Profanliteratur " *Sitzungsb. d. kgl. preuss. Akad. d. Wissensch.* 1908 no. xlix pp. 1100–1130 [studies in the interpretation of certain significant words; *cf. RC* XXXIII (1912) 94–5].

The church of Slébte, of which mention has been made several times,[157] attributed its foundation to a Bishop Fíacc, who, according to legend, was a disciple of a *fili* named Dubthach moccu Lugir, and a convert of Patrick. Slébte was united to the *paruchia Patricii* in 662 x 688, and the legend must have been either a cause, or a justification, of the union. From Slébte, doubtless, came the poem *Génair Patraicc*, to which Fíacc's name is attached, a metrical biography of Patrick and one of the earliest hymns in the Irish language.[158] The theory of a Slébte origin is supported by the close relationship between the subject-matter of the poem and Muir-chú's Life. Other sources, too, were used, including some known to Tírechán. The terms *scéla*, "tales" and *lini*, "writings," indicate that the author was acquainted with both oral and written material. The Patrick Legend exhibits here some development from the stage represented by Muir-chú: there is now a second Patrick and the miracles and penances are of a more extreme form.

Internal evidence and language tests imply that the hymn was composed in the eighth century. Some interpolations have been made in it, but while Zimmer, Atkinson and Bury believe these to be extensive, Stokes, Strachan and Thurneysen regard them as but slight. The linguistic forms prove that the interpolations, if there are such, cannot be later than the early ninth century.

A careful study of the poem reveals considerable matter of historical interest. It is one of the few documents that identify the *sídi* with the gods of pagan Ireland.[159] Reference is made to the desolation of Tara and Emain-Macha, to Éber and Érimón as progenitors of the Irish, and to the virtue of Patrick's *Lorica*.[160]

The extensive commentaries added to the poem are probably of the eleventh century. They represent the Patrick Legend in full growth.

[157] *Cf.* pp. 332–5 *supra*.

[158] The literary character assigned to Fíacc may be due, as Gwynn has suggested, to the existence of this and other versified traditions at Slébte.

[159] In Tírechán's account of the conversion of Loigaire's daughters it is stated that Patrick and his companions were taken for " uiros side aut deorum terrenorum." (*LA* 23 a 22.)

[160] *Cf.* no. 101.

133. Colgan's Second and Fourth Lives of Patrick

(V2) *Vita Patricii secunda apud Colgan*

Natus est igitur in illo oppido . . . de semine tuo in aeternum.

MSS: St. Omer 716 *s* XI vol. II ff. 155–9. Colgan used MSS from St. Hubert in the Ardennes, now lost, and Aulne-sur-Sambre, Belgium, now Brussels Bibl. roy. II. 1124 *s* XIV. ED: Colgan *Tr. Thaum.* (1647) 11–20. COMM: Robert *Étude critique* 54–6. — Bury "The tradition of Muir-chú's text" *Hermathena* XIII no. xxviii (1902); *St. Patrick* 268–9.

(V4) *Vita Patricii quarta apud Colgan*

Incipit praefatis de eo quod . . . Quidam Santum Patricium ex Judaeis . . . in hodiernum diem conferuntur.

MSS: BM Add. 19890 *s* XII *in.* [*cf.* Esposito *JTS* XIX 346], from Aulne-sur-Sambre. ED: Colgan *op. cit.* 35–50 [without preface]. COMM: Robert *op. cit.* 57–8. — Bury *loc. cit.*

These two Lives, which are very closely related, date from the eighth or ninth century. V2 was written by an Irishman, V4, which is somewhat more prolix than the other, by a man ignorant of Irish. V2 covers only the period embraced in Muir-chú's Book I. Both devote considerable attention to the family relations and childhood miracles of Patrick. Bury's studies of the two Lives led him to the following conclusion: Neither depends on the other, but both on a common source (W), the tenor of which can be almost mechanically reconstructed. W was sometimes a free paraphrase, sometimes a close copy of Muir-chú, and included material of other origin. Some of the independent documents used by W must have gone back to an early age, perhaps to the sixth century.[161] W was probably the earliest document which made Patrick visit Pope Celestine before setting out for Ireland.

134. Colgan's Third Life of Patrick

Patricius qui uocatur et Succet . . . Cui h. et g. et u. et p. in s. s. amen.

MSS: Bodl. 285 *s* XII/XIII ff. 143–9. — Cambridge Univ. Lib. Ff. 1.27.21 *s* XIII *ex* ff. 101–10. — TCD 171 *s* XIII ff. 19–28ᵛ. EDS: Colgan *Tr. Thaum.* (1647) 21–34 [based on a MS of the monastery of Biburg in Bavaria, now Munich Univ. Lib. 2⁰ 312 *s* XII²: has accretions at beginning and end from V2 and V4]. — *Nova Legenda Anglie* (ed. Horstman, Oxford 1901) 279–92 [abridgment]. — Bury " A Life of St. Patrick (Colgan's Tertia Vita) " *Trans. RIA* XXXII C (1902–4) 199–262 [restoration of the text from the Oxford, Cambridge and Dublin MSS]. COMM: Robert *Étude critique* (1884) 56–7. — Bury *Life of St. Patrick* (1905) 272–3.

This anonymous Life has come down to us in two recensions, both of which, as Bury has shown, were written in south-west Britain, where they received some interpolations. The two recensions depend on a common original written by an Irishman in Ireland, probably in the second half of the ninth century. In the main the Life is

---

161 Instead of *Cothraige*, the Goidelic form of " Patricius " which Tírechán has preserved, it gives us the still older *Quadriga* or *Quotirche*. *Cf.* p. 325 *supra*.

based on Muir-chú, Tírechán and the Confession, but there is new material, part of which appears in the Tripartite Life and had been noted in the *additamenta* to Tírechán, There are also additions which are found only here. The new matter, for the most part, consists of accounts of extravagant miracles, some evidently based on, but surpassing, the miracle-narratives of the Gospels. Other *motifs* lying behind these additions are the establishment of a connection with Rome and Pope Celestine, and with Martin of Tours; the working out of the analogy between Patrick and Moses; explaining the origin of the relic known as the " Staff of Jesus "; satisfying the desires of all localities to have some share in the glory of the great apostle; and developing the latent possibilities of the earlier records. We here meet with the story of the destruction of the idol Crom Cruaich, a story which received afterwards very full development.[162]

135. The Tripartite Life of Patrick *c* A.D. 895 x 900

Populus qui sedebat in tenebris uidit lucem magnam i. in popal deissid i ndorchaib. . . . [Rawl. B. 512] perfruitur in presentia Trinitatis, P. et F. et S. S. Alme trocairi, et reliqua. [Eg. 93 arranges the last paragraphs somewhat differently.]

MSS: BM Eg. 93 ff. 1–18ᵛ [written by Domnall *Albanach* O'Troightigh in 1477]. — Bodl. Rawl. B. 512 *s* XV ff. 5–30. — TCD 1337 (H. 3.18) pp. 520–8 [extracts]. All the MSS are imperfect in some sections, for which we are dependent on Colgan's Latin version. Colgan used three MSS, none of which is now known to exist. EDS: Colgan *Tr. Thaum.* (1647) 117–88 [professes to give a Latin version of the Irish parts, and to retain most of the original Latin; but his work is not a commensurate trans., but rather resembles a paraphrase; his text represents a different tradition from that of the extant MSS]. — *Vit. Trip.* I (1887) [introd., text, trans.; a good ed., but not final; it is neither diplomatic nor critical, in the technical meanings of these terms (WS rightly believed that the time had not yet come for the critical reconstruction of Old and early Middle Irish texts); gives for the most part the Rawlinson text, which seems on the whole to be inferior to the Egerton. Corrigenda, review, criticisms and replies *re* this ed. are to be found in *The Academy* XXXIII (1888) 191–2, 424–5, 447–9, XXXIV (1888) 10–11, 73, 138–9, 172–3, 354–5, XXXVI (1889) 25, 88, 221–2, 238–9, 256.] — " Glossed extracts from the Tripartite Life of St. Patrick H. 3.18 " *ACL* III (1905) 8–38, 56. TRANS: Cusack *Life of St. Patrick* (London 1870) 371–502 [partial trans. by W. M. Hennessy]. COMM: Robert *Étude critique* 58–60. — B. Mac-Carthy " The Tripartite Life of St. Patrick: new textual studies " *Trans. RIA* XXIX (1887–1892: read Jan. 14, 1889) 183–206 [includes a severe, but in some respects not unfounded, criticism of the ed. by WS]. — F. Lot " La date de la Vie Tripartite de s. Patrice " *Annales de Bretagne* (1896) 360–1. — Bury *Life of St. Patrick* 269–72. — *LA* pp. lxxii–lxxv, 458–64. — Kathleen Mulchrone " Die Abfassungszeit und Über-lieferung der Vita Tripartita " *ZCP* XVI (1926) 1–94 [very valuable].

The first of the four-fold honors which, according to a note in the Book of Armagh,[163] were to be paid to Patrick by the monasteries and churches of all Ireland was " the celebration, during three days and three nights in mid-spring, with every kind of good food except flesh,[164]

---

[162] *Cf.* Vit. Trip. (no. 135) and the Dinnsenchas.
[163] LA f. 16. *Cf.* p. 334 *supra.*   [164] Since March 17 falls in Lent.

of the festival of his ' falling asleep.' " There can be little doubt that the so-called Tripartite Life, forming, as it does, three homilies with appropriate texts and setting, was intended to provide sermons, or the material of sermons, for the three days of the celebration. The homiletical character of the three parts is, however, only formal: the first part contains some structural unity,[165] the other two, none. In the second and third the homiletical introduction and conclusion are simply fastened onto a string of Patrician anecdotes, disconnected, or bound together merely by a loose, illogical geographical sequence. The text is in Irish, but with numerous, and in some cases quite lengthy, Latin passages interspersed.

Our manuscripts are of the fifteenth century, and are filled with textual modifications and corruptions. Enough early forms are preserved, nevertheless, to suggest the end of the ninth or beginning of the tenth century as the time of composition.[166] It is obvious, however, that a work serving the purpose which seems to have been served by the *Vita Tripartita* would be peculiarly liable to constant modification of its linguistic character — as, indeed, also of its subject-matter. There is internal evidence pointing to the last years of the ninth century as the date when the subject-matter assumed approximately its present form. " Twenty-seven kings," we are told, " of the race of Ailill and Oengus ruled in Cashel under a crozier until the time of Cenn-Gécán." [167] This Cenn-Gécán was deposed, according to the Annals of Ulster, in 901; the last preceding king of Cashel, of whom mention is made, died in 895. It would seem probable that the author was writing between those dates.[168] No allusion to events later than the year 900 is discoverable.

---

[165] It is possible that the first part is, in substance, an earlier composition than the other two. *Cf.* Bury, *loc. cit.*

[166] *Cf.* Tomás Ó Máille *Ériu* VI 3 n. 1, 85 n. 2. He points out that it contains a form of the article which occurs for the last time in AU in 892. WS had assigned it to the eleventh century, but in the earlier period of his Celtic studies he commonly gave to early Irish documents a later date than was accepted by other philologists, or by himself in after years.

[167] *Vit. Trip.* I 196-7.

[168] There are other allusions having value in dating the work. Nuada, abbot of Armagh, is said (*ibid.* 82) to have released certain churches from a tribute they had paid since Patrick's time. The obit of this Nuada, who, according to the lists of Patrick's successors, ruled three years, is given by AU in 812. The capture of Inis-Bec by the Northmen is mentioned (192), an event which happened in 819. Reference is made to Fedilmid of Cashel, who died, according to AU, in 847, Conchobar of Tara, died 832 or 833, and Gaithin of Leix, whose son is mentioned by AU under 867 and 870 (194). Speaking of the fulfilment of a prophecy, the author declares: " Quod probavimus, when Connacán, son of Colmán, son of Níall *Frossach*, came into the land with an army " (174). Connacán was killed in 855: the form of words implies that the event had occurred within living memory. An angel is made to promise Patrick " that the Saxons should not dwell in Ireland, by consent or perforce, so long as I abide in heaven " (117). WS thinks this indicates a date posterior to 871, when the Norsemen brought a multitude of English captives to Ireland, but the argument does not seem very strong. Finally, mention is made of a *Céle Dé*

The Tripartite Life shows the evolution of the Patrick Legend nearly completed. Only minor elaborations have since taken place. In general form and character — the topographical basis, the loose stringing together of material of the most miscellaneous kind and origin, the free way in which historical facts and personages, legendary heroes, place names, tribal fortunes, proverbs, local folklore are all brought into association with the central theme — it resembles some of the later developments of the secular cycles of romances, in particular the *Acallamh na Senórach*.[169] It is based chiefly on Muir-chú, Tírechán, and the other Patrician documents transcribed or indexed in the Book of Armagh. The additions to these sources are for the most part of folklore or mythopoeic character. But it is clear that behind the compilation as a whole lay the same ecclesiastical purpose as behind the work of Tírechán and Fer-domnach and those " heirs of Patrick " to whom Fer-domnach makes reference.[170]

The compiler is careful to make note of all churches founded by Patrick and his disciples, of all grants made to them, and of any special claims the saint has on the allegiance of particular peoples. He also occasionally notices cases where churches which in his opinion should form part of the *paruchia Patricii* have passed under the control of other ecclesiastical organisations.

It should be added that the Tripartite Life is a valuable source for social history.

Incorporated into the Tripartite Life are several quatrains and longer metrical compositions, apparently of independent origin. The following are the more important:

(a) Ticfa táilcend . . . . The druids' prophecy of Patrick. *Vit. Trip.* I 34–5. Also in *scholia* to Fíacc's Hymn (no. 132): *LH*[2] I 100, II 181–2; and in abridged versions of the Tripartite Life (no. 136): WS *Three Middle-Irish Homilies; Vit. Trip.* II 448–9; *Lis. Lives* 9, 157; *Anec.* III 33. A Latin trans. is given by Muir-chú, and another in Colgan's Second and Fourth Lives (no. 133). It must have been already old when Muir-chú wrote at the end of the seventh century, and is an interesting survival of pagan propaganda; but probably as a prophecy it is *ex post facto;* it may not refer to Patricius in particular; and its origin can hardly be as early as the first half of the fifth century.

(b) Uarán gar . . . . Patrick's address to a well. *Vit. Trip.* I 106–7.

(c) A fir há. . . . Patrick's address to his tooth. Also LL 353; Bodl. Laud 610 f. 74. EDS: *Vit. Trip.* I 140–1; KM *ZCP* X 41.

(d) Mo bennacht forsna túatha . . . . Blessing of Cenél nEogain by Patrick and Brigit. Also in the LBr and Bk. Lis. homilies. EDS: *Vit. Trip.* I 154–5, II 480–1; *Lis. Lives* 11, 159.

(e) Orulae Coathraigi cáin for Érinn uaig . . . . Verses on the *Cáin Pátraicc* (*cf.* p. 335): *Vit. Trip.* I 212–5.

(f) Bendacht for firu Muman . . . Patrick's blessing of Munster. Also in the

among the companions of Patrick (198): on the beginnings of this title, *cf.* pp. 470–1 *infra.* A list of authors who narrated the miracles of Patrick is given (*cf.* p. 327 *supra*), but from the position this holds in the MSS it would appear to be a later addition, not part of the original text.

169 O'Grady *SG;* WS *IT* IV i.

170 *Cf.* p. 335 *supra.* The work gives considerable evidence of the late but vigorous campaign of Armagh to secure jurisdiction in Munster: *e. g.,* " No one is King of Cashel until the *comarba* of Patrick instals him and confers ecclesiastical rank upon him." — *Vit. Trip.* I 196–7.

three homilies. EDS: *Vit. Trip.* I 216-7, II 470-1; *Lis. Lives* 16, 164; *Anec.* III 41-2. TRANS: KM *Selections from ancient Irish poetry* (1911) 29.

136. Abridged Versions of the Tripartite Life

Populus qui sedebat in tenebris. . . . Ailim trocaire, etc.

MSS: LBr *s* XV *in* pp. 24-9. — Bk. Lis. *s* XV ff. 1, 3-7. — BN Fonds celt. et basq. 1 (formerly Ancien fons 8175[1]) ff. 74-6ᵛ [*cf. Proc. RIA* III (1846) 223-8; *RC* XI 399; *Vit. Trip.* I pp. lvii-lxi].[171] — Dublin King's Inns 10 *s* XV ff. 17-9 [illegible at beginning and imperfect at end]. — Liber Flavus Fergusiorum *s* XV ff. 29-30ᵛ (or I pt. iii f. 5) [copy of preceding, according to Miss Mulchrone]. — RIA Reeves 42 pp. 91-102. — Brussels Bibl. roy. 2324-40 *s* XVII ff. 13-23. — RIA C. iv. 3 (Stowe 38) pp. 233 *sqq*; 23 A 15 pp. 323-55. — TCD 1285 (H. 1. 11) A.D. 1752 ff. 95ᵛ-106ᵛ EDS: WS *Three Middle-Irish Homilies on the Lives of Saints Patrick, Brigit, and Columba* (Calcutta 1877) 2-47; *Vit. Trip.* (1887) I p. cxiii, II 428-89 [from LBr; with trans.; *cf. RC* XXXIII 95]. — *Lis. Lives* (1890) 1-19, 149-67, 293-9 [with trans.]. — R. I. Best *Anec.* III (1910) 29-42 [the King's Inns text]. COMM: Alfred Anscombe " The Pedigree of Patrick " *Ériu* VI 117 *sqq.* — Plummer *Misc. hag. Hib.* (1925) Cat. no. 59. — Kathleen Mulchrone " Die Abfassungszeit und Überlieferung der Vita Tripartita " *ZCP* XVI i (1926) 1-94 [studies the relationships of the first five of the above MS texts; important].

In the later middle ages the most popular form of the Life of Patrick in Irish was as an abridgment of the Tripartite Life in a single homily. Several such versions exist, closely resembling each other. They help to restore parts of the Tripartite now lost, and they also contain some new material.[172] The following scheme represents the conclusions of Kathleen Mulchrone from her studies of the tradition of the Tripartite Life:

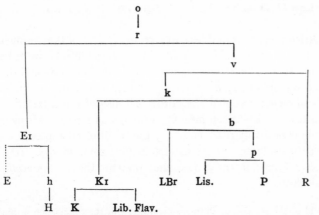

E, R = the Egerton and Rawlinson copies of Vit. Trip.; H = the TCD H. 3. 18 extracts; K = the King's Inns copy; P = the BN celt. et basq. I 38 version. E1 and K1 represent the respective MSS when in a better state of preservation than at present. Dark-face letters indicate revised, *i.e.*, abridged, versions. The original text is represented by o, and r stands for the earliest exemplar which it is possible to restore critically, a text probably of the ninth century.

---

[171] WS and Plummer class this as a collection of fragments of Vit. Trip.

[172] *E. g.* Patrick's pedigree, found also in the notes to Fíacc's Hymn (no. 132), in a poem attributed to Flann *Mainistrech* in *FM* 432; and in LL 347a, LBr 13b, BB 215 col. 5, 229 col. 5.

137. Patrick's Household A.D. 927 X 936

Is iatso in cethrur ar xx bói i nn-urd la Pátraic . . . rí dá chóiced Muman ocus rl.

MSS: LL 353 d. — LBr *s* XIV pp. 23, 220 b. — BB 215, 225. — BM Eg. 93 *s* XV f. 18ᵛ [follows Vit. Trip.]. EDS: Colgan *Tr. Thaum.* (1647) 167 [Lat. trans.]. — *Vit. Trip.* I 264–7, II 574.

The Patrick Legend as it developed took note of many persons, members of Patrick's household, who performed various services for him; as, for example, his " strong man " or champion, his charioteer, his smiths. In the present document a list of these is given. A note at the end of the Egerton text says: " And that is the number that should be in Joseph's company, and it is the number that should be at the king of Cashel's table down from the time of Feidlimid son of Crimthann, king of the two provinces of Munster, etc." This probably indicates that the text — or at least this version of it — was written in the time of Joseph, abbot of Armagh, who, according to the Annals of Ulster, died in 936.[173]

138. Loigaire's conversion and death (*Comthoth Loegairi co cretim ocus a aided*)

Bai comthinol fer nErend hi Temraig in amsir Lóegaire maic Néill . . . ocus is airi conaitechsom a adnacul and.

MSS: LU pp. 117–8. — TCD 1336 (H. 3. 17) and 1337 (H. 3. 18) Petrie's text — ed. and trans. by O'D — is from a preface to the law-tract *Senchas Mór*]. EDS: Petrie "History and antiquities of Tara Hill" *Trans. RIA* XVIII (1837) 71–8 [extract]. — Chas. Plummer *RC* VI 162–72 (LU). — *Vit. Trip.* (1887) II 562–7 (LU). All eds. have trans.

This Irish prose text professes to give an account of the arrangements for re-casting the national laws and polity, entered into between Patrick and the new religion on the one side, and the *árd-rí* Loígaire and the men of Ireland on the other, when these last had, under the compulsion of Patrick's miracles, accepted the faith; and also of the occasion of Loigaire's death. It has much interest, although as a record of the events in question it probably represents only the traditions accepted some four or five centuries later. It seems certain that some of these traditions came down from an early date and present the metamorphosis of historical truth.

We are told of the murder of Patrick's charioteer; of the commission of nine that revised *filidecht ocus brethemnas ocus recht* (perhaps " learning and jurisprudence and principles of equity," but the words have a definite, though broad, technical significa- tion [174]); and of the fate of Loigaire, who was killed by the sureties he had given the Lagin (Leinstermen), " to wit, Sun and Moon, Water and Air, Day and Night,

---

[173] A metrical version of this list is contained in Bk. Lec. 44ᵛ and is printed therefrom in *FM* 448.
[174] *Cf.* p. 4 *supra.* There follows a passage of importance regarding social rights and *status*.

Sea and Land," when, breaking his word, he attempted to exact from Leinster the *bóraime* (tribute). Afterwards Loígaire's body was brought from the south, and he was buried with shield and spear in the outer south-easterly dyke of Loígaire's royal *rath* in Tara, and his face was to the south towards the Lagin, fighting against them, for all his life he had been a foe to the Lagin."

139. Life of Patrick by Probus *s* IX x XI

Santus Patricius, qui et Sochet uocabatur, Brito fuit . . . non ad seditionem istorum populorum pro-fuit. [Then follows a postscript by the author:] Ecce habes frater Pauline, a me humili Probo . . . euasisse supplicium: praestante D. n. I. C., qui cum P. et S. s. v. D. per o. s. s. Amen.

EDS: *Opera Bedae* (Basel 1563) III 311–34. — *Venerabilis Bedae Opera . . . omnia* (Cologne 1688) 225 *sqq.* — Colgan *Tr. Thaum.* (1647) 51–63. COMM: Robert *Étude critique* 62–5. — Bury " The Tradition of Muirchu's Text " *Hermathena* XIII no. xxviii (1902) 183; *St. Patrick* (1905) 273–7. — L. Gougaud *Irish Theological Quarterly* Jan. 1909 p. 64.

Some ancient editor of the works of the Venerable Bede, induced by an error to which we have no longer the key, was led to interpret the name " Probus " as an adjective and to include this Life of Patrick among the compositions of the Monk of Jarrow. A Patrician document which otherwise would have been lost was thereby preserved to us.

The author, Probus, and his " Frater Paulinus," to whom the work is addressed, have not been identified. Probus appears to have been an Irishman; if he wrote in Ireland, he probably belonged to Armagh or some other Patrician community, but it is quite probable that he wrote on the Continent. The date may reasonably be placed in the tenth century. There is a prophesy that Patrick will baptize " Scotiam atque Britaniam, Angliam et Normanniam caeterasque gentes insulanorum," which, if not an interpolation, would point to the eleventh, or late tenth century.[175] In the main Probus follows the text of Muir-chú's Life very closely. He has, however, made some surprising variations and additions.

140. Life of Patrick by Jocelin of Furnes A.D. 1185/1186

Plurimorum propositum erat et studium . . . scripta incendio deleta sunt.

EDS: Messingham *Florilegium* (1624) 1–85. — Colgan *Tr. Thaum.* (1647) 64–116. — *AA. SS. Boll.* Mart. II 536–77. COMM: *Facs. of Nat. MSS.* II pl. lxxxvi, p. liii. — Robert *Étude critique* 61–2. — Bury *St. Patrick* 279.[176]

The best known of the mediaeval Latin Lives of St. Patrick was written by Jocelin, one of the " black monks " whom the Norman John de Courci brought from Furnes

---

[175] Colgan took " Normanniam " to signify Gallic Normandy, but it is much more probable that the reference is to Scandinavian settlements in the British Isles. This passage possibly marks the beginning of the campaign to win for Armagh jurisdiction over the Scandinavian Christians in Dublin and other Norse towns. — If the passage be an interpolation the author of the *vita* might be the priest Probus who died at Mainz in 859. *Cf.* p. 551 *infra.*

[176] There is a modern Irish trans. of this Life, beginning: A mbaile darab ainm Tiburnia. *Cf.* Plummer *Misc. hag. Hib.* Cat. no. 61.

in Lancashire and established at Down after he had effected a military lodgment in that district. As it falls beyond the period embraced in the present work, and does not appear to have made use of any earlier sources not now preserved, no extended notice need here be given to it.

There is a short Latin Life, unpublished, in Bodl. Laud Misc. 315 *s* XIII *ex* ff. 100ᵛ-1. *Cf.* Plummer *Misc. hag. Hib.* Cat. no. 292. — For the Life in "Nennius" *cf.* no. 24, and Bury *St. Patrick* 277-9.

141. Minor texts relating to Patrick

(i) Poem on Patrick's bell

Mo chean duit a chluicc blaith bind. . . . A ri na salm rit mo chean. 8 quatrains; originally ended with 5th.

MS: Bodl. Laud 615 p. 119. ED: Wm. Reeves " On the Bell of St. Patrick, called the Clog an Edachta " *Trans. RIA* XXVII 1-30 (read Nov. 9, 1863) [the poem is on pp. 4-5: text, trans.].[177]

(ii) Story of Patrick and Loegaire's wife and son — The Michaelmas Sheep

(A recension) Fechtus tainic Patraic cu Temruig . . . (B recension) Dia mboi conflicht mór . . .

MSS: A: Bk. Lis. f. 44. — Bodl. Rawl. B 512 f. 143. — BM Egerton 92 f. 30 d. — RIA 23 M 50 *s* XVIII p. 166. B: Edinburgh Nat. Lib. Gael. XXVI f. 2. — Rawl. B 512 f. 108. — Dublin King's Inns 14 f. 3. — BM Addit. 30512 f. 10. — TCD 1285 (H. 1. 11) f. 114 [copy of preceding]. ED: *Vit. Trip.* (1887) II 556-9 [with trans.; B recension from Rawl. B 512].

(iii) History of the Martinmas Pig

(*Senchus Muici féili Martain*) Martan is é tuc . . . manach Pátraic hé.

MS: Bodl. Rawl. B 512 *s* XIV/XV f. 108ᵛ.— Liber Flavus Fergusiorum I pt. i f. 12 d. ED: *Vit. Trip.* (1887) II 560-1 [text, trans.].

(iv) How Sechnall and Patrick saved Fíacc from death

Feacht n-aile luidh Seachnall . . . .

MS: Cheltenham MS of Fél. Oeng. p. 46 [*cf. Fél. Oeng.*² p. x]. ED: KM *ZCP* VIII (1912) 106-7 [text only].

---

[177] There is a poem on a bell of Patrick in the *Book of Fenagh*, ed. Hennessy and Kelly (1875) 236-49: " Beir a Chaillin clog na righ . . ." *Cf.* p. 401 *infra.*

(v) Patrick's Blessing of Ireland

Patricius benedictionem pro habitatoribus Hibernia[e] insola[e] deidit, conid adbeart Pátraic andso. Beandacht Dé foraib uili fearaib Érenn . . . is mó ebert ós bithbeandacht. Bend.

MS: Bk. Lec. f. 191ᵛ. EDS: O'D *The Book of Rights* (Celtic Soc.: Dublin 1847) 234–5 [with trans.]. — KM *ZCP* VIII (1912) 560 [text].

(vi) Poem on the Leinstermen, ascribed to Patrick

Cumma lem etir . . . a bein, is cumma. 15 stanzas.

MS: Brussels Bibl. roy. 5100–4, p. 49. ED: KM *ZCP* VIII 110–1 [text].

(vii) Hymn in praise of Patrick

Ecce fulget clarissima Patricii sollempnitas . . . qui suae dono gratiae misertus est Hiberniae amen. 22 ll.

MSS: LH(T) f. 32 [in later hand than the bulk of the codex]. — TCD 80 (B. 1. 5: Antiphonary of Kilmoone) s XV f. 122 [part of an office for St. Patrick's Day]. EDS: Thos. Messingham *Officia SS. Patricii, Columbae, Brigidae, et aliorum quorundam Hiberniae sanctorum ex ueteribus membranis et manuscriptis breuiariis desumpta* (Paris 1620) [in the office for the translation of the relics of Patrick, Brigit and Colum-cille]. — Colgan *Tr. Thaum.* (1647) 189. — Dreves *An. hymn.* XIX 233. — Wright *Writings of Patrick* (1889) 39. — *LH²* (1898) I 160, II 222. — Blume *An. hymn.* LI (1908) 346–7.

(viii) Poem on the ascetic practices of Patrick

Trí caoca salm luaidter lib . . . is dol i cionn a chaecat. 7 stanzas, with heading and postscript in prose.

MS: BM Egerton 138 A.D. 1807 f. 36ᵛ. ED: O'Grady *Cat.* 637–9 [with trans.; poor].

(ix) Old Irish poem on Patrick

Pátraicc Macha mártai Gáidil . . . légenn Pátraic. 13 stanzas.

MS: RIA B. iv. 2 (Stowe 23) A.D. 1628 f. 143. ED: KM *ACL* III iv (1907) 303.

There are many minor texts relating to Patrick. Several are Middle-Irish poems which profess to be compositions, usually prophetical, of the fifth-century missionary. Of the documents entered above, the first, written in Middle-Irish, purports to have been addressed by Colum-cille to Patrick's bell [178] on the occasion which is described as follows by the Annals of Ulster under 553:

" Thus I find in the Book of Cuanu, viz.: — The relics of Patrick were placed in a shrine, at the end of three score years after Patrick's death, by Colum-cille. Three splendid *minna* were found in the tomb, to wit, his goblet, and the Angel's Gospel, and the Bell of the Testament. This is how the Angel distributed the treasures for Colum-cille, viz.: — the goblet to Down, and the Bell of the Testament to Armagh

---

[178] *Cf.* Coffey *Guide to the Celtic antiquities of the Christian period preserved in the National Museum, Dublin* (Dublin 1909) 47–9.

and the Angel's Gospel to Colum-cille himself. The reason it is called the Angel's Gospel is, because it is from the Angel's hand Colum-cille received it."

This entry is in Middle Irish, but may be an eleventh-century translation from the original Latin. The whole passage, however, is suspect.

The second and third texts are legends designed to account for certain customs of the feasts of Michaelmas and Martinmas. The first of the two is also a source of some interest for the Irish practice of " fasting on " an adversary.

For other anecdotes related to Patrick *cf.* Plummer *Misc. hag. Hib.* Cat. nos. 158–72.

142. The Companions and Disciples of Patrick

(i) Life of St. Benignus, or Benén, of Árd-Macha

[Lat.] Sanctus enim Benignus, in regimine . . . et laudes et gratie ab omnibus deo et sancto eius referuntur. [Ir.] Qui perseuerauerit ad finem . . . in secula seculorum. Amen.

MSS: BM Cotton. Tiberius E I A.D. 1325×1350 [Lat.].—Brussels Bibl. roy. 4190–200 ff. 210-9. Eds: Colgan *Tr. Thaum.* 203 [extracts from Ir.]. — *Nova Legenda Anglie* ed. Horstman (Oxford 1901) I 112-4 [Lat.]. — *AA. SS. Boll.* 9 Nov. IV 145-88 [all texts]. *Cf. An. Boll.* XLIII (1925) 241-60.

(ii) Life of St. Mochta of Lughmadh (Louth)

Apostolicus pontifex Mocteus, ortus de Britannia . . . resurrecturus in gloria Christi, cui c. P. et S. s. est h. et g. in s. s. Amen.

MS: Cod. S. 213ᵛ-5ᵛ. Eds: Colgan *AA. SS.* 729 *sqq.* — *AA. SS. Boll.* Aug. III 736-47. — *AA. SS. ex Cod. S.* 903-14.

(iii) Life of Bishop Mac Cairthinn of Clochar (Clogher)

[Imperfect] Die quodam sanctum magistrum . . . viri sui ad tempus supervixit.

MS: Cod. S. ff. 217ᵛ-21 [*recte* 218]. Eds: *AA. SS. Boll.* Sept. I 662-6. — *AA. SS. ex* 209-10. — *AA. SS. ex Cod. S.* 799-804.

(iv) Life of Bishop Mac Nisse of Condere (Connor)

3° Nonas Septembris. Incipit vita sancti Macnissi episcopi. Hodie, fratres dilectissimi, beatus Engus, qui vulgo dicitur filius Macnisse [*sic*] . . . fulsit meritis preclaris, ad laudem ejus qui c. P. et S. s. v. et r. in s. s. Amen. Explicit vita Sancti Engula [*sic*] qui et Mac Nessi dicitur.

MS: Cod. S. ff. 217ᵛ-21 [*recté* 218]. Eds: *AA. SS. Boll.* Sept. I 662-6. — *AA. SS. ex Cod. S.* 925-30.

(v) Text regarding St. Cairnech

Gabas Sarran rigi mBretan . . .

EDS: J. H. Todd and Algernon Herbert *The Irish version of the Historia Britonum of Nennius* (IAS: Dublin 1848) 178–93. — W. F. Skene *Chronicles of the Picts . . . Scots* (Edinburgh 1867) 52–6. *Cf. Fél. Oeng.*[2] 132–3, 244–7, 406, and references there given; Baring-Gould and Fisher *Lives of the British Saints* II 61 *sqq*; Plummer *Misc. hag. Hib.* Cat. nos. 94–5.

Very few Lives of the companions and disciples of Patrick who are mentioned in his Legend have come down to us. Even such important personages as Secundinus and Fíacc have left no separate *acta*. Moreover, the Lives that have survived are late and not of much value.

(i) Benignus is well known to the Patrick Legend as the saint's first Irish disciple and his successor in the see of Armagh.[179] His Latin Life, an abridgment by John of Tynemouth of a larger work, is a curious product of the Glastonbury off-shoot of the Patrick Legend. He is made to follow Patrick to Glastonbury, where he dies.

(ii) Adamnán, in the second preface to his Life of St. Columba, written towards the end of the seventh century, quotes, " on the testimony of experienced men of old," the prophecy regarding Columba delivered by " a certain British pilgrim, a holy man, a disciple of the holy bishop Patrick, Mochta by name." It is probable, however, that the references in the annals and calendars represent a much earlier record, although the date, 535 or thereabouts, with which his death is equated, must, if he was a disciple of Patrick, be erroneous.[180] His *vita* is late, and much abbreviated. He was honored as the founder of the church of Lugmadh (Louth),[181] a place which bore the name of the god Lug.

(iii) Mac Cairthinn (the name is probably not a patronymic but a personal name of pagan origin, " son," *i.e.*, devotee, " of rowan-tree " [182]) was honored as an early bishop and founder of the church of Clochar (Clogher, Tyrone). He was taken into the Patrick Legend as Patrick's " strong man," or body-guard, and the Tripartite Life tells an attractive story of his assignment by Patrick to Clochar.[183] That place

---

[179] *Cf.* LA f. 9ᵛ a. Also p. 274 *supra*.

[180] *Cf. Ériu* V (1911) 4. — AU 535 " Dormitatio Muchti discipuli Patricii XIII Kl. septembris "; one MS adds, " sic ipse scripsit in epistola sua, Mauchteus peccator prespiter, sancti Patricii discipulus, in Domino salutem." Under 471 AU attribute to a Mauchteus, or Mochtae, information regarding a raid by Saxons in Ireland. The entry would appear to be derived from the Book of Cuanu.

[181] The sixteenth-century English writer John Bale identified Mochta with Bachiarius, the author of a confession of faith written early in the fifth century, and was followed by many later writers. There seems to have been earlier references to Bachiarius as a Briton, an Irishman, a disciple of St. Patrick, and Bale or some predecessor perhaps tried to reconcile part of these statements by equating him with Mochta. Any association of Bachiarius with either Britain or Ireland is improbable. *Cf.* Fritzsche *ZK* XVII (1896–7) 211–5; Künstle *Antipriscilliana* (1905) 46, 163–7; M. H. MacInerny " St. Mochta and Bachiarius " *IER* 1923 [also printed separately]. Curiously, the only ancient MS of the *Fides Bachiarii* — Milan Bibl. Ambrosiana O. 212 sup. *c* A.D. 700 — is in an Irish hand, though possibly written at Bobbio. *Cf.* no. 520 *infra*. — In LL 361 and LBr 94 there is a quatrain on the number of disciples Mochta had at Lugmadh: printed in MacCarthy *Cod. Palatino-Vaticanus 830* (Dublin 1892) 116.

[182] *Cf.* MacN *Proc. RIA* XXVII C (1909) 366.

[183] *Vit. Trip.* I 175–8. — Tírechán mentions a " filius Cairtin," maternal uncle of Brigit, who was in

seems to have been a pagan shrine,[184] and perhaps Mac Cairthinn was the man who turned it to Christian service. The extant Life is only a fragment, and, apparently, a late composition.[185]

(iv) Mac Nisse, reputed founder of Condere (Connor, Antrim), derived his name from his mother Ness, following a custom of which there are other traces among the Picts of Down and Antrim. The extant Life is late — perhaps prepared for monks of the diocese of Connor after the Norman invasion — but is probably an abbreviation of an older text. The statement that Mac Nisse was baptized by Patrick might be correct, but the earliest Patrician documents do not mention him. The *Tripartite Life* says he read psalms with Patrick, and this story seems to be noted among the *memoranda* entered by Fer-domnach in the Book of Armagh. The Life also makes him foretell to Patrick the founding of Lann-Ela by Colmán Ela, thus giving an early sanction to the close relationship which in later times existed between the two churches, Connor and Lann-Ela.

(v) Cairnech, " the Cornishman," is a hazy and ubiquitous personage of whom there are many notices but not much clear information. Two or more Cairnechs have been postulated to solve some of the difficulties: one, from Cornwall, was founder of Tulén (Dulane, near Kells) in Meath; another, a member of the Dál Araide, labored in Ulster; etc. In the fairly old tale of Loígaire's Conversion and Death.[186] and the preface to the *Senchus mór*, Cairnech is associated with Patrick and Benignus on the commission which, we are told, revised the Irish laws. A Cairnech, apparently the same, is connected with the *árd-rí* Muirchertach mac Erca [187] (d. 534 or 536 [188]), whose death he is represented as foretelling, in a poem beginning " Is om oman ar in ben." [189] In one of the topographical poems of the fourteenth-century *savant* Seán *mór* Úa Dubhagáin [190] mention is made of a body of Welshmen living in Meath and known as *Comthinól Chairnig*, " Cairnech's Congregation." [191]

143. List of Patrick's Successors

MSS: LL *c* A.D. 1160 + f. 21. — YBL *s* XIV/XV p. 327 c. — LBr *s* XIV p. 220. — Bodl. Laud 610 A.D. 1453 f. 115 [said to be from the Saltair Caisil: is part of a set of synchronistic tables where lists of the monarchs of Ireland and of various provincial

charge of the church of Ráith-Dallbrónig, somewhere in Meath (LA f. 11), and in the *Additamenta* to Tírechán we read of a " filius Cairthin " who made a grant of land in Sligo or Leitrim to Patrick (LA f. 17), and is perhaps the same person as the " macc Cairthin " who, the Tripartite Life says, was placed in the church of Domnach-Mór-Maige-Tochair (in Inishowen, co. Donegal) (*Vit. Trip.* I 156-7). One of the families of the Air-gíalla was the Úi Maicc Cairthinn, whose eponymous ancestor must have been about contemporary with Patricius. *Cf.* MacN *Proc. RIA* XXIX C (1911) 85.

[184] *Cf. Fél. Oeng.*[2] 186-7.

[185] In the later martyrologies Mac Cairthinn is curiously identified with Fer-dá-crich, abbot of Dair-inis, who died in 747 (AU). The mistake seems to have arisen through taking as the place-name the word *clochar*, " assembly," which is used in the quatrain for August 15, the festival of Fer-dá-crich, in Fél. Oeng. — On the Clogher relic called the *Domnach Airgid* see no. 467.

[186] No. 138.

[187] *Cf.* " Aided Muirchertaig maic Erca," *RC* XXIII (1902) 395-437.

[188] AU.

[189] Eds: O'D in Geo. Petrie " Tara Hill " *Trans. RIA* XVIII (1837) 120-1; CS anno 531; Tig. anno 534.

[190] *Cf.* p. 23 *supra.*

[191] O'D *The topographical poems of John O'Dubhagain* 51.

kings are also given]. EDS: Colgan *Tr. Thaum.* 292 [the Saltair Caisil list has five names subsequent to last in Laud].— Todd *St. Patrick* (1864) 173–83 [the four lists, giving names, and trans. only of additional matter]. — *Vit. Trip.* (1887) II 542–9 [LL and LBr texts, with trans.; also Laud text]. — KM *ZCP* IX (1913) 478–9, 481–2 [Laud text]. — H. J. Lawlor and R. I. Best *Proc. RIA* XXXV C ix (1919) 316–62 [reconstructed list, with extracts from the annals and other sources, and a valuable commentary; text of LL in appendix].

There are four lists in manuscript of the *comarbai,* or *comarbada,* the " heirs " — that is, successors — of Patrick, the bishops or abbots of Armagh. They all go back to an ultimate source in the diptychs [192] read in the mass at Armagh. The Laud 610 text ends with Máel-Muire (d. 1020), and Colgan's version with Domnall (d. 1105); Lebor Breac also with Domnall; the Yellow Book of Lecan with Gilla-meic-Liac (d. 1174); and the Book of Leinster with Tommaltach (d. 1201), although as originally entered in that manuscript the last name seems to have been Cellach (d. 1129).

The list, with the attached notes, is of considerable value for the history both of Armagh and of Ireland. It lends support to the following outline of the fortunes of the primatial church: Till about the middle of the sixth century Armagh was an episcopal see; then it became a monastic church, but during the next two centuries the abbots occasionally held also the office of bishop; this ceased about the middle of the eighth century, and during the following hundred years the abbacy was repeatedly the object of a struggle between rival factions, apparently chiefly the neighboring ruling families of the Air-gíalla; the struggle ended with the triumph of the family Úi Sinaich, who dwelt in the district around Armagh, and from the middle of the tenth to the first half of the twelfth century one of their branches held the abbacy in hereditary succession, the incumbents being, almost all, laymen. In the twelfth century came the reform movement and the restoration of the episcopacy.

144. Confirmation of the claims of Árd-Macha by Brian *bóroimhe*
A.D. 1004

Sanctus patrius iens . . . omnibus regibus maceriae.

MS: LA f. 16ᵛ. EDS: *Vit. Trip.* II 336. — LA pp. ciii, 32.

Brian *bóroimhe,* " of the tribute," head of the Dál gCais of northern Munster, after freeing his people from the domination of the Danes of Limerick and making himself

---

[192] This, as the latest editors point out, accounts for the presence in the list of Secundinus, who died, according to the other records, before Patricius.

king of Munster, forced the *árd-rí* of all Ireland, Máel-Sechlainn of Meath, to abdicate in his favor in 1002. Thus was broken a dynastic succession which had lasted more than six centuries. In 1004 Brian made a royal progress around Ireland, stopping for a week at Armagh and placing a gold ring of twenty ounces on Patrick's altar.[193] It was then, doubtless, that he had this entry made on a blank space in the Book of Armagh:

" Saint Patrick, when going to heaven, ordered that the whole fruit of his labor, as well of baptism and of causes as of alms, should be paid to the apostolic city which in Irish is named Ardd-Macha. So I have found in the books of the Irish. I, namely, Calvus Perennis,[194] have written in the sight of Brian, emperor of the Irish,[195] and what I have written he has confirmed for all the kings of Cashel."

145. Poem in praise of Bishop Aed and other officials of the church of Árd-Macha A.D. 1032 x 1049

Úasalepscop Éirenn Aodh . . . beóil i mbí séis aifrinn úais. 33 quatrains.

MS: RIA B. iv. 2 (Stowe 23) A.D. 1628 ff. 142–3^v [by Michael O'Clery]. ED: KM *ACL* III iv (1907) 306–8 [text only].

Aed mac Cróngillae húa Farréith became bishop at Armagh in 1032.[196] The then abbot, Amalgaid, is mentioned in the poem, which must have been written before his death in 1049.[196] Dub-dá-Leithe, the *fer léiginn*, succeeded as abbot in 1049, and Aed became *fer léiginn*, which position he held till his death in 1056.

To complete the legends of the church of Árd-Macha mention should be made of a curious story of a devil named Caincuile who visited the monastery to observe the sins of the monks: Caincuile. i. demon bái inn-Ardmacha . . .   MS: Edinburgh Nat. Lib. of Scotland XXVI (Kilbride 22). ED: KM *Anec.* III (1910) 7–8.

146. St. Patrick's Purgatory

TEXT OF HENRY OF SALTREY: Messingham *Florilegium* 86–109. — Colgan *Tr. Thaum.* 273–89. — Migne *PL* CLXXX 975–1004. GENERAL WORKS: Thos. Wright *St. Patrick's Purgatory, an essay on the legends of purgatory, hell and paradise current during the middle ages* (London 1844). — S. Eckleben *Die älteste Schilderung vom Fegefeuer des heil. Patricius* (Halle 1885). — G. Ph. Knapp *The legend of St. Patrick's Purgatory: its later literary history* (dissertation) (Baltimore 1900). — Ph. de Félice *L'autre monde* (Paris 1906) [cf. *ZCP* VI 254]. — H. Delehaye *An. Boll.* XXVII (1908) 36–40. — O'Connor *St. Patrick's Purgatory, Lough Derg* 3rd ed. (Dublin 1910). — G. Dottin Introd. to ed. of " Louis Eunius " *Annales de Bretagne* XXVI (1910–1)

---

[193] AU.
[194] Trans. of the name of Máel-Suthain, *anmchara*, or confessor, of Brian. *Cf.* no. 620.
[195] " imperatoris scotorum."
[196] AU.

781 *sqq.* — St. John D. Seymour *St. Patrick's Purgatory* (Dundalk [1918]). The literature is extensive. — For Irish versions see Plummer *Misc. hag. Hib.* Cat. no. 172.

An important division of the Christian literature of Ireland was that composed of voyage or vision tales, in which were given narrative descriptions either of an earthly paradise or of the several parts of the other world. These sprang more or less directly from the old pagan literature and folk-lore which described the over-seas, or sometimes subterranean, dwellings of immortal beings, but under Christian influences became a distinct and elaborate literary *genre*. The most famous of these stories were the " Vision of Fursa " and the " Voyage of Brendan," but several of the great churches or church-leagues developed each its own legend of wonderful voyage or supernatural vision. It is somewhat strange that this element did not enter into the official Patrick Legend; but it is probable that some local tradition of a visit by Patrick to the other world lay behind the belief and practices of St. Patrick's Purgatory. For when the " vision " element did come to influence the Patrick cult it did not take the form of a romance of the long ago, but that of the stark reality of the present, that any Christian having the proper dispositions might, under the patronage of St. Patrick, himself behold and even experience the horrors of purgatory and hell.

St. Patrick's Purgatory — one of the renowned places of pilgrimage of Europe in the later middle ages — was, and is,[197] on an island in Loch Derg in southern Donegal. There had been an ancient monastery here under the patronage of, perhaps founded by, St. Da-Bhe-óc; but it had, apparently, ceased to exist before the twelfth century, when, during the reform movement,[198] an establishment was made of Augustinian canons. There is no positive evidence as to the " Purgatory " during the period of which the present work treats, but it seems certain that the belief and practices had made their appearance before 1170.

The following are the earliest sources: (1) It is said that David *Scottus* [199] of Würzburg wrote, about 1120, a book *De purgatorio Patritii*. The book, if it ever existed, cannot now be found. (2) Jocelin, in his Life of Patrick (no. 140), refers to the Purgatory and the custom of visiting it, but places it on Croagh-Patrick, in Mayo. (3) Giraldus Cambrensis, writing about 1186-7, gives a description of the Purgatory,[200] which he evidently had heard of as on Loch Derg, " a lake in Ulster." (4) A Cistercian monk of Saltrey, in Huntingdon (who signs himself " Fr. H.," which Matthew Paris expanded as " Henricus "), wrote, apparently about 1190, an account of the

---

[197] It is still an important place of pilgrimage and penance, although the " cave " of the visions and the practices connected with it have long since disappeared.

[198] *Cf.* pp. 745 *sqq infra.*   [199] *Cf.* no. 448 *infra.*   [200] *Top. Hib.* II v.

visit to the Purgatory, and the visions seen by, a knight named Owen, a follower of the English king Stephen. The date was 1153. Later Owen was companion of a certain Gilbert, for a time a monk of Louth, but later, it is said about 1157-9, become abbot of Basingwerk in Flintshire. From Gilbert's report Henry of Saltrey wrote down his narrative. The story became very popular, and there are many later versions and translations. Of these, and of the numerous texts referring to subsequent pilgrimages to the Purgatory, notice need not here be taken.

IV. CELL-DARA (KILDARE) AND ST. BRIGIT

Bibliography

Colgan Tr. Thaum. [cf. pp. 41, 289 supra]. — Hardy Cat. I pt. i 105-16 [list of MSS]. — Lina Eckenstein Woman under monasticism, A. D. 500-1500 (Cambridge 1896) [has some notice of the mythological element in the Brigit legends]. — Douglas Hyde A Literary History of Ireland (London 1899) 56-65 [popular]. — Mary Bateson "The origin and early history of double monasteries" Trans. Roy. Hist. Soc. n. s. XIII (London 1899) 137-98 [a few remarks on the monastery of Kildare]. — Mario Esposito " On the earliest Latin Life of St. Brigid of Kildare " Proc. RIA XXX C (Dublin 1912) 307-26 [cf. p. 359 infra]. — L. Gougaud RC XXXIX (1922) 203-7, 356; Gaelic pioneers of Christianity (Dublin 1923) 105-12 [devotion to St. Brigit in continental Europe]. — L. Pfleger " Le culte d'une sainte irlandaise en Alsace: Ste Brigide " Bull. ecclés. de Strasbourg XLII (1923) 51-5.

In the seventh century there stood in the valley of the Liffey, in the midst of the territory of the Lagin, or Leinstermen, an important and peculiar monastery known as Cell-dara, the " Church of the Oak." The ancient oak tree from which it took its name is said to have survived to the tenth century. Cell-dara (now modified into Kildare) was a double monastery, one part of it being for women, the other for men. The church, one of unusual size and ornamentation, was divided by a screen into two parts, one for the nuns, the other for the monks. Under the high altar were preserved the remains of the foundress of the church, Brigit, or Brigid, and of the bishop, Conlaed, to whom she entrusted the sacerdotal functions of the community. Tradition and custom alike, however, assigned the predominant position to Brigit and the abbesses who succeeded her: according to some accounts, the abbot of the men's community was appointed by the abbess. One of the noteworthy duties of the nuns was to tend, after the manner of Vestal Virgins, the sacred fire which burned perpetually in the monastery.

Some time about the middle of the seventh century the community of Cell-dara asked a certain Cogitosus to write a Life of their patroness and foundress. The composition which he produced forms the basis of Brigitine hagiography.

There is no evidence of a strong historical tradition behind the *acta* of Brigit, such as undoubtedly did lie behind those of Patrick and especially of Colum-cille. Cogitosus, living probably within a century of the alleged date of her death,[201] could give very little of her personal history. What he does offer us is a series of narratives of the saint's wonder works, preserved traditionally, no doubt, by the community of Cell-dara, but based ultimately in large part on popular legends, myths and folk-lore.[202]

Brigit is one of the Irish saints as to whose relationship with a pagan divinity there can be little doubt. Certain aspects of her character and career must be based on the myth or the ritual of a goddess, probably a goddess associated with a fire cult.

" Brigit (cp. Skr. *bhargas*) was born at sunrise neither within nor without a house, was bathed in milk, her breath revives the dead, a house in which she is staying flames up to heaven, cow-dung blazes before her, oil is poured on her head; she is fed from the milk of a white, red-eared cow; a fiery pillar rises over her head; sun rays support her wet cloak; she remains a virgin; and she was one of the two mothers of Christ the Anointed. She has, according to Giraldus Cambrensis, a perpetual ashless fire watched by twenty nuns, of whom herself was one, blown by fans or bellows only, and surrounded by a hedge within which no male could enter."[203]

It may be added that her feast-day, February 1, corresponds with *Imbolc*, one of the four great festivals of the pagan year. Still more conclusive is the fact that Brigit was the name of an Irish, and, indeed, a Pan-Celtic, deity.[204] From Cormac's Glossary we would infer that there was a trinity of Brigits, and that the name came to be applied to any goddess.

" Brigit, i.e., a learned woman, daughter of the Dagda. That is Brigit woman of learning, i.e., a goddess whom *filid* [205] worshipped. For her protecting care was very

---

[201] AU 524, 526, 528. Unless there is other evidence to support them, little attention need be paid to the annalistic dates of the very early saints.

[202] Tírechán (*cf.* no. 127) mentions Brigit twice: Patrick is said to have founded a church in Ráith-Dallbrónig, which was held by Bishop Mac Cairtin, maternal uncle of Brigit; and another in Mag-Teloch, where Brigit received the veil from the hands of MacCaille. The Lives represent Brigit's mother as daughter of Dallbrónach. MacCaille was a bishop of the early Irish Church, whose obit is given by AU in 480; later tradition seems to make him a layman. — Tírechán was a disciple of Ultán of Ardbraccan (*cf.* pp. 329-30), who was a contemporary of Cogitosus and, according to tradition, likewise a collector of records regarding Brigit.

[203] WS Preface to *Three Middle Irish Homilies*.

[204] *Cf.* RC VII 398; [Sir] John Rhŷs *Lectures on the origin and growth of religion as illustrated by Celtic Heathendom* (*The Hibbert Lectures for 1886*) (London 1888) 74-6; AdeJ *Le cycle mythologique irlandais*, trans. R. I. Best *The Irish mythological cycle* (Dublin, London 1903) 81-4. In British inscriptions the goddess appears as *Brigantia*.

[205] *Cf.* p. 3 *supra*.

great and very wonderful. So they call her goddess of poets. Her sisters were Brigit woman of healing and Brigit woman of smith-work, daughters of the Dagda, from whose names among all the Irish a goddess used to be called Brigit." [206]

It is noteworthy that the saint has taken over some of the attributes here assigned to the goddesses. She is in especial the patron of poets and men of learning.

It is almost equally probable that Cell-dara was a pagan sanctuary before it became a Christian monastery. The oak from which it took its name must have been a sacred tree, and the perpetual fire described by Cambrensis an inheritance from heathen ritual.

" There was doubtless here, in pagan times, a college of priestesses who tended a perpetual fire, and who . . . honoured the fire-goddess Brigid, this divinity being immanent in the sacred sun-oak which gave to the place the name that it still bears. Probably the head of the college was regarded as an incarnation of the goddess, and so bore her name. . . . But one of the succession came under Christian influence, and, embracing the Faith of the Cross, she accomplished the tremendous feat of converting the pagan sanctuary into a Christian religious house — a work in its way far more wonderful than the miracles with which her biographers credit her. It is no detraction from the honour due to her for this achievement, that she could not quite rid the establishment over which she presided of all its pagan vestiges. . . . And though it is probable that she herself changed the official name 'Brigid' which hitherto she had borne (for no Christian lady would willingly continue to bear a name so heathenish while paganism was still a force), it was too deeply rooted in the folk-memory, and continued to be used locally to designate her." [207]

Such is R. A. S. Macalister's plausible explanation of the amalgamation of pagan goddess and Christian saint displayed so strikingly in the Brigitine legend. In popular favor Brigit grew to a *status* inferior only to that of Patrick: she was in especial the patroness of the Lagin, but in devotion to her all Ireland joined. " She is the Prophetess of Christ, she is the Queen of the South, she is the Mary of the Gael." [208]

Cell-dara remained one of the chief Irish monastic churches down to the Norman invasion, when Giraldus Cambrensis visited it, and left us an interesting description.[209] The annals give considerable lists of abbesses, or *comarbai* of Brigit, and abbots. According to Cogitosus, Brigit's *paruchia* extended over the whole of Ireland, but we hear little of subordinate monasteries. There was a church dedicated to Brigit in Armagh, and the Patrician clergy showed themselves particularly favorable to the Brigitine community.[210]

---

[206] *Sanas Cormaic: Anecdota from Irish MSS* IV 15.   [207] *Proc. RIA* XXXIV C (1919) 340-1.
[208] *Lis. Lives* 51, 198.   [209] *Top. Hib. cap.* xxxiv–xxxvi.   [210] *Cf.* p. 337 *supra.*

147. Life of Brigit by Cogitosus s VII

[Prologue] Cogitis me, fratres, ut sanctae et beatae memoriae Brigidae. . . . [Vita] Sancta itaque Brigida, quam Deus praescivit . . . veniam peto a fratribus et lectoribus haec legentibus. . . . Orate pro me Cogitoso nepote culpabili haedo . . . pacem evangelicam sectantes exaudiat.

MSS: Very numerous: see the lists, with descriptive matter, given by Esposito, *op. cit. infra;* also *Bibl. hag. lat.* of the Bollandists I 217. Almost all the codices are large collections of *vitae sanctorum* — in which the Life of Brigit forms one — from continental monasteries. None is of Irish origin. EDS: Boninus Mombritius *Sanctuarium seu Vitae sanctorum* (Milan *c* 1480) I ff. 144-6ᵛ; 2nd ed. (Paris 1910) I 257-61, *cf.* pp. x, 633 [abridgment]. — Canisius *Antiquae lectionis* (Ingoldstadt 1604) V ii 623-41; 2nd ed. by Basnage (Antwerp-Amsterdam 1725) I 413-24. — Surius *De probatis sanctorum historiis* (4th ed. Cologne 1618) II 21-5. — Messingham *Florilegium* (Paris 1624) 189-200 [text of Canisius]. — Colgan *Tr. Thaum.* 518-26. — *AA. SS. Boll.* Feb. I (1658) 135-41 [best ed.]. — Migne *PL* LXXII 775-90 [reprint of Basnage]. COMM: *Trans. RIA* XX 195-205. — Mario Esposito " On the earliest Latin Life of St. Brigid of Kildare " *Proc. RIA* XXX C (1912) 307-26 [a valuable study].

Muir-chú moccu Machthéni, author of the earliest Life of Patrick, speaks of that work as a novel experiment, undertaken hitherto only by his father, Coguitosus, or Cogitosus.[211] There can be little doubt that the man to whom he referred was the author of this Life of Brigit. Muir-chú was probably an Ulsterman, but he spent much of his life in northern Leinster, in the neighborhood of Kildare, and Cogitosus must have been personally familiar with, and interested in, that church. Whether he was Muir-chú's spiritual father, or father in the flesh, we do not know, but the former is more probable.[212] One manuscript [213] has the *explicit* " Orate pro me cogitoso nepote culpabili haedo," which suggests that Cogitosus was of the Úi hAedo (nepos haedo = úa hAedo), perhaps of Leinster,[214] and, if so, probably not related in blood to Muir-chú. A Cogitosus is noticed under April 18 in the *Martyrology of Tallaght* and the *Martyrology of Gorman.*[215]

There is a noticeable similarity between the preface of Muir-chú's work and the prologue and concluding paragraph of that by Cogitosus, and between both these and the introductory sections of the *Vita s. Samsonis,*[216] which, if composed in Brittany early in the seventh century, is our earliest extant example of Celtic hagiography. Cogitosus, we may suppose, wrote about the middle of the same century. We cannot be certain what was the new movement which, according to Muir-chú, he inaugurated; perhaps it was the preparation of connected biographical narratives in the place of popular legends and disconnected *acta* and *memorabilia.*[217]

---

211 *Cf.* no. 128 *supra.*   212 *Cf.* p. 332 *supra.*   213 Bibl. Vallicelliana XXI.
214 *Cf.* ZCP IX 187.   215 Nos. 273, 275.   216 *Cf.* p. 174 *supra.*
217 Bury believed the innovation to be the use of Latin instead of Irish as the language of hagiography (*St. Patrick* 256, 266). *Cf.* p. 300 *supra.*

It is evident that Cogitosus was able to find little genuine biographical material regarding Brigit. His Life is a succession of miracle narratives, of interest in themselves for the information they convey regarding the life of the times, the people, the animals, tame and wild, etc., but telling us nothing of the career of the historical Brigit. The chief personage associated with Brigit is Conlaed, who served as bishop in her church of Cell-dara and, like herself, was buried under the altar. Noteworthy, and doubtless an evidence of the antiquity of the Life, is the fact that no mention is made of Patrick. The most valuable portion of the work of Cogitosus is the description of the monastic church at Kildare, with its elaborate ornamentation and the provision made for the accommodation of the religious of both sexes whom it served as a place of worship. The description, we may be certain, is of the days of Cogitosus, not of those of Brigit.

For early hymns in honor of Brigit see no. 95; for a genealogy of Brigit, associated with that of St. Gall, no. 50 (vi).

148. Broccán's Hymn " Ní car Brigit "

Ní car Brigit búadach bith . . . fora fóessam dún díb línaib. 53 stanzas; the original ending was at the 47th, with a repetition of the opening words.
[Antiphon] Sanctae Brigtae uirgo sacratissima in Christo domino fuit fidelissima. Amen.

MSS: LH(T) ff. 17–9. — LH(F) pp. 39–42. EDS: Colgan *Tr. Thaum.* 515–20 [with Lat. trans.]. — WS *Goidilica* (Calcutta 1866); 2nd ed. *Goidelica* (London 1872) [text, trans.]. — [B. MacCarthy?] *IER* IV (1868) 220–37 [text, Lat. trans.]. — *IT* I (1880) 25–49, 322–4 [text, with illustrative extracts from Cogitosus and the LBr Life]. — *LH²* (1898) I 112–28, II pp. l–lvi, 40–6, 189–205 [text, trans., notes]. — *Thes. Pal.* II (1903) pp. xxxviii *sq*, 327–49 [collated text, trans.].

The preface ascribes this hymn to Broccán *clóen* (" the squinting "), who is said to have been a disciple of Ultán of Árd-mBrecáin and to have written it in the time of Lugaid, son of Loigaire, king of Ireland, two statements obviously irreconcilable. Broccán's obit is given as of Sept. 17, 650. But the linguistic evidence, after allowance is made for scribal emendations, shows that the text which we have cannot be older than the ninth century. It is, in fact, probably the latest of the older Irish hymns. As the metrical form, however, is irregular and often incorrect, there is no guarantee that our poem has not been greatly altered from an original and earlier form. In subject-matter the poem follows very closely the Life by Cogitosus, and was certainly based thereon. It is, however, rather a string of allusions to stories of miracles — as if well known — than a narrative.

The preface and notes added to the hymn contain much interesting matter, some of which is to be found in the Latin Lives, the *Félire Oengusso*, etc.[218]

149. Poem in praise of Brigit

Brigit búadach . . . bethad beó. 2 stanzas; probably incomplete.

MSS: LL p. 38; BB; TCD 1308 (H. 2. 12 no. 8). Quotation in the treatise on versification having the title " Do aistib ind aircetail i coitchinn indso." EDS: RTh *IT*

---

[218] *E.g.* the procuring of Brigit's Rule from the submarine city of Plea (*cf. RC* XLII 403–4); the ascetic practices of Coemgen of Glendaloch; the charm for the blessing of a kitchen, given also, with variations, in the Bk. Lis. Life and in BM Egerton 161 f. 123 (*cf.* O'Grady *Cat.* 624).

III (1891) 71. — KM. " Bruchstücke der älteren Lyrik Irlands," *Ahhandl. d. preuss. Akad. d. Wissensch.* 1919 phil.-hist. Kl. vii (Berlin 1919) 23 no. li [with Germ. trans.].

150. List of nuns of Brigit

Brigitae sanctae subiectae erant omnes hae virgines sanctae, quarum loca et nomina enumerabimus Cainer ingen Chruthecháin . . . Cellan i n-Achud Aeda.

MS: LL 353 col. 2. ED: *Lis. Lives* 336.

This document purports to give a list of nuns subject to Brigit, and of their churches. It is probably the counterpart in the history of Kildare of many of the Patrician documents in that of Armagh, and represents an attempt to claim as followers of Brigit the reputed founders of the older monasteries for women, and thereby to bring those churches within the *paruchia* of Kildare.

151. Later Lives of Brigit in Latin

(i) Life in verse attributed to Chilienus, or Coelan

[Prol. I] Christe Dei virtus, splendor, sapientia. . . . [Prol. II] Quisquis in hoc hominum. . . . [Prol. III] Finibus occiduis describitur optima tellus. . . . Has ego Donatus virtutes sanguine Scottus. . . . [Praesul ego dictus Donatus sanguine Scottus . . .] . . . Cernere post obitum mereamur pace futura. [Vita] Quadam namque die genitrix dum forte sedebat. . . . Multis, ut fertur, vicinis atque puellis [incomplete].

MS: Monte Cassino 232 *s* XI. EDS: Colgan *Tr. Thaum.* 582–99. — *AA. SS. Boll.* Feb. I 141–55. — Bandinius *Bibl. Leopoldina Laurentiana* I 567–8 [prologue by Donatus]. *Cf. Boll. Bibl. hagiographica latina* nos. 1458, 1459, and *Supplementum*; Margaret Stokes *Six Months in the Apennines* (London 1892) 237–8 [trans. of prologue by Donatus].

(ii) Life attributed to Animosus, or Anmchad

[Prol.] Tribus iam, fratres mei, meus mea. . . . [Vita] Fuit gloriosus rex in Hibernia nomine Feidlimidh . . . Igitur sacrosancta et gloriosissima virgo Brigida migravit de hac vita Kal. feb. . . .

EDS: Colgan *Tr. Thaum.* 546–67. — *AA. SS. Boll.* Feb. I 155–71.

(iii) Colgan's third Life

Fuit quidam vir nobilis, Laginensis genere, Dubtachus . . . collocata, nunc gaudia cum Christo possidet sempiterna: cui cum D. P. et s. S. manet h. et l. et g. per cuncta s. s. Amen. [Epitome] Vir quidam in Hibernia, genere Laginensis, Dubtacus . . . et circa annum domini quingentesimum octavumdecimum kalendis februarii migravit ad dominum.[219]

MSS: Cambrai Bibl. communale 857. — Bodl. Rawl. B 485 f. 62; Rawl. B 505 f. 184. EDS: Colgan *Tr. Thaum.* 527–42. — *AA. SS. Boll.* Feb. I 118–34. Epitome: *Nova Legenda Anglie* ff. 48ᵛ–50ᵛ; ed. Horstman (1901) I 153–60. — Surius *De probatis sanctorum historiis* I (Cologne 1570) 782–5; 3rd ed. (1618) II 19–20; new ed. (1875) II 42–7. — Messingham *Florilegium* (1624) 206 *sqq.*

[219] There is an unpublished Irish Life which professes to be a trans. of this epitome: Ase ionad a rugad an oig beannaighti glormar . . . . *Cf.* Plummer *Misc. hag. Hib.* Cat. no. 13.

(iv) Life by Laurence of Durham

[Epistola Laurentii ad Ethelredum] Licet inexplicabili quodam laberintho. . . . [Vita] Fructificante in diversis ubique terrarum nationibuś. . . . Decessit autem venerabilis Brigida prima die mensis februarii . . . vita, gaudium et gloria sanctorum omnium, per o. s. s. Amen.

MSS: Bodl. Laud Misc. 668 (1052) s XII ff. 106 sqq. — Oxford Balliol College CCXXVI s XIII ff. 86–94. — Cod. S. ff. 48–62ᵛ [beginning missing]. EDS: Colgan Tr. Thaum. 567–82. — AA. SS. ex Cod. S. 1–76. Cf. Thos. Wright Biographia Britannica literaria II (London 1846) 160–6 [re Laurence of Durham].

(i) This versified Life was attributed by Colgan to Coelan of Inis-celtra (d. c 750), but almost certainly it is of later date. One of the prologues is by Donatus, bishop of Fiesole [220] (826 x 877), and Mario Esposito suggests that he may be author of the entire Life.[221] This prologue begins with a description of Ireland, probably based on old classical models. Ultán, Aileran, and Animosus [222] are spoken of as earlier writers on the subject of the virtues of Brigit.

(ii) Of Animosus, or Anmchad, nothing is definitely known. Todd suggested that he was a bishop of Kildare who died about 980.[223] The Life is extensive, containing much detail, and is of value for the study of Irish social conditions. There is a gap in the text — according to Colgan, from chap. xii to chap. xxxiv.

(iii) Colgan's third Life was ascribed by him to Ultán of Árd-mBrecáin. Legend said that Brigit's mother, the bondsmaid Broicsech, was the daughter of Dallbrónach of the Dál Conchobair in Meath, the same race of which Ultán was a member. The Life may be fairly early. It is a loose and prolix document.

(iv) This Life was written by Laurence, monk and prior of Durham, who died in 1154. It is a lengthy work, giving expanded accounts of the various miracles, of which it, like the other Lives of Brigit, is mainly composed.

152. Lives of Brigit in Irish

(i) Hi sunt qui sequuntur Agnum. . . . Ailim trocaire etc.

MSS: LBr pp. 61–6. — Bk. Lis. ff. 11–7. — BN Fonds celt. et basq. 1 s XIV x XVI ff. 76–81. — Brussels Bibl. roy. 2324–40 s XVII ff. 24–30; 4190–200 ff. 6–30. — Bk. Lec. f. 166 [last sect. of Life]. — Dublin King's Inns 14 f. 3 [as preceding]. EDS: WS Three Middle-Irish homilies (Calcutta 1877) [with trans.]; "A Parallel" RC III (1878) 443–4 [text, trans. of story of Brigit and Breccan]; Lis. Lives (1890) 34–53, 182–200, 318–36 [with trans.]. — KM ZCP XII (1918) 293–4 [Lecan text].

(ii) [Imperfect] . . . miracula uulgata sunt. Laae nand . . . uentum sedauit. [Appended is a series of anecdotes similar to those in the LH notes to Ni car Brigit (no. 148); cf. Plummer Misc. hag. Hib. Cat. nos. 12, 86]

MS: Bodl. Rawl. B 512 ff. 31–6. ED: Lis. Lives 319–31 [extracts].

---

220 Cf. no. 421.

221 Hermathena XVI 330.

222 Possibly this is the emendation of a scribe for the "Cogitosus" of Donatus.

223 FM. Cf. Todd St. Patrick 108. If Donatus, in the prologue to the preceding Life, really wrote "Animosus," this hagiographer must have lived at least as early as the middle of the ninth century.

Life (i) is of the later middle ages; it apparently is a translation of an abridged version of Colgan's third Life. Life (ii) is probably not later than the ninth century, cf. R. I. Best ZCP XVII (1927–28) 397; it possibly testifies to an earlier stratum of the legend.[224]

153. Poem ascribed to Brigit

Robad maith lem corm-lind mór . . . 7 quatrains.

MS: Brussels Bibl. roy. 5100–4 p. 33. ED: O'C MS Mat. 616 [with trans.].

A not unpleasing devotional poem, but the opening line, which may have had a mystical significance — " I should like a great lake of ale for the King of Kings " — gave occasion for Stokes's sneer that God was regarded as a soma-quaffing Indra.[225]

154. Dialogue between Patrick and Brigit

A Brigit a naem ingen . . . 5 quatrains.

MSS: Brussels Bibl. roy. 5100–4 p. 48. — Vat. Palatin. 830 f. 148 [2 quats.]. EDS: Z² 961 [from Vat. MS]. — WS Zs. f. vergl. Sprachf. XXXI (1890) 252–3 [with trans.] — B. MacCarthy Codex Palatino-Vaticanus 830 (RIA Todd Lect. Ser. III) (Dublin. 1892) 20 [Vat. text].

Among the poems ascribed to Moling (cf. p. 463 infra) are two addressed to Brigit, one in the tract on the Bóroma (O'Grady SG I 389) and the other in the " Birth of Moling and his Life " (no. 249) chap. xvi. — For other anecdotes related to Brigit cf. Plummer Misc. hag. Hib. Cat. nos. 83, 86–8.

155. Later Hymns in honor of Brigit

(i) Phoebi diem fert orbita plenum decoris gratia . . . uni substantialiter trinoque personaliter amen. 18 ll.

MS: LH (T) f. 32 [the MS is of the 11th cent., but this hymn has been added in a later hand]. EDS: Dreves An. hymn. XIX 98 [cf. ibid. LI 320]. — LH² (1898) I 161, II 223.

(ii) Brigidae nomen habet, gemino et diademate fulget. . . . Ad Dominum semper mitte beata preces. 14 ll.

MSS: Rome Bibl. Corsiniana 777 s XIII f. 51. — Cambrai Bibl. communale 857. — Vat. lat. 6075 A.D. 1601 f. 71. — Rome Bibl. Vallicelliana H 25 s XVI/XVII f. 50ᵛ. — Rome Biblioteca Alessandrina della Reale Universitá 91 s XVII f. 501. EDS: Colgan Tr. Thaum. (1647) 542. — LH¹ 64. — Kelly Martyrology of Tallagh (Dublin 1857) 188–9.

These two hymns seem to be of late date and not of Irish authorship. At least they do not show the peculiarities of Hiberno-Latin versification. Nevertheless Colgan ascribed the second to Ultán of Árd-mBrecáin.

---

[224] Several of the legends regarding Brigit are incorporated into the notes of the Calendar of Oengus on February 1, her feast-day.

[225] Martyrology of Gorman.

156. Aed *dub*, abbot of Cell-dara

A bráthair . . . . 2 stanzas, ends incomplete.

MS: LL 316, 388.   ED: KM *ZCP* IX (1913) 458–60 [with trans. and commentary].

The beginning of a poem on a bishop Aed *dub* mac Colmáin, of the royal line of the
Lagin, who was abbot of Cell-dara and died in 639.

V. INIS-CATHAIG (INISCATHY, SCATTERY ISLAND) AND ST. SENÁN

It has been observed that certain of the saints who belong to that
dim backward of time which saw the beginnings of Irish Christianity —
Ibar, Brigit, Ailbe, perhaps Mac Cairthinn — appear to have taken each
the name and something of the legends and cult of a pagan deity.   In
the same company should be placed Senán, who from the island known
as Inis-Cathaig (Scattery Island, about a mile from Kilrush) ruled the
waters of the great river Sinann,[226] now the Shannon.   In pagan days
Senán was, we may believe, a river-god, to whom, as to Neptune, the
horse was sacred, and a slayer of monsters, at whose sanctuary on Inis-
Cathaig was told the legend of his killing, or driving away, the dragon-
like creature Cathach.   It is probable that his cult was particularly
strongly established among the Corcu Baiscinn, a sea-faring people who
dwelt in the southwestern section of the present Clare, between the
Shannon and the Atlantic.   In Christian times Senán was founder of the
church of Inis-Cathaig; patron of the Corcu Baiscinn, and of the Úi
Fidgente, the ruling kindreds of the territory on the southern side of the
estuary of the Shannon; and a saint whose cult, spread by these peoples,
was to be found in Wales, Cornwall and Brittany.   As in the cases of
Ibar and Brigit, Macalister offers the hypothesis that the saint was the
Christian hermit who turned Inis-Cathaig from a pagan to a Christian
shrine, but whose name and fame ultimately fell captive to those of the
god whom he overthrew.[227]

157. Life of St. Senán

(i) Senanus ex nobilibus procreatur parentibus . . . plura facit miracula per infinita secula.   Amen .
(ii) Sanctus Senanus Episcopus eo tempore, quo Patricius . . . per S. Senanum post mortem patrata
miracula sufficiant.   (iii) [Irish] Mirabilis Deus in sanctis suis et caetera.   In Spirut naob. . . Ailim
trócaire Dhe tre impidi Senáin co roisem in aentuidh-sin.   In s. s.   Amen.   This Life opens in the form
of a homily, but immediately turns to a narrative of the saint's career.

MSS: (i) Cod. S. ff. 186–8 *bis* [imperfect]. — Cod. K. ff. 76^V *sqq*. — Bodl. Rawl. B 505
ff. 201 *sqq*.   (iii) Bk. Lis. ff. 17–23. — Bodl. Laud 610 ff. 1–5 [imperfect]. — BN

---

226 The two names are not of the same origin.   227 *Proc. RIA* XXXIV C (1919) 340.

Fonds celt. et basq. 1 ff. 33–8. — Brussels Bibl. roy. 2324–40 ff. 226–41. — RIA A. iv. 1 (Stowe 9) s XVII pp. 244–77. — BM Egerton 91 ff. 52–6; Egerton 180 ff. 86–103 [from RIA A. iv. 1]. Eds: (i) Colgan *AA. SS.* 512 [602]–27. — *AA. SS. Boll.* Mart. I 760–8. — *AA. SS. ex Cod. S.* 735–58. (ii) Colgan *AA. SS.* 530 [630]–7. — *AA. SS. Boll.* Mart. I 769–78. (iii) *Lis. Lives* 54–74, 201–21, 337–41 [text, trans., notes]. There is a Life in the Breviary of Léon, and another, a compilation, in Albert le Grand *Les Vies des Saints de la Bretagne.* Cf. Baring-Gould and Fisher *Lives of the British Saints* IV (1913) 182–94.

The several versions of Senán's Life differ considerably in content. The metrical Latin version is probably the oldest, but it seems to be a monastic composition having no very direct connection with Inis-Cathaig. On the other hand the Irish Life, which, though quite fabulous, is also very interesting, seems to depend directly on legends of the lower Shannon, and probably on a Life written at Inis-Cathaig when that was still a flourishing monastery, that is, not later than the tenth century. The imposing array of miracles, the list of famous saints with whom the subject of the Life is brought into contact, and the records of church foundations made by him, all indicate an origin in a monastery of his community.

The extraordinary inconsistencies of the chronological setting may reflect the absence of historical *data:* Senán is, while still in his mother's womb, foretold by Patrick [228] (d. 461); he succeeds Maedóc (d. 626 [229]) as abbot of Ferns; he makes a league with Martin of Tours (d. 397 x 403); he associates with various Irish saints of the middle and second half of the sixth century; and he dies on the same day as David of Wales (544 x 547, or 601 [230]). But the hagiographers were capable of a wonderful recklessness in these matters, even when dealing with saints whose records were well founded.

The establishment of many different churches by Senán is recorded: they represent, doubtless, the *paruchia* claimed by the abbots of Inis-Cathaig.

Much curious and interesting matter is contained in the several texts.[231]

158. *Amra Senáin*

Senán sóer sidathair . . . ná bi sáethach sen. Senán s. s.

MSS: LBr 241. — TCD 1336 (H. 3. 17) s XV–XVI cols. 832–5. — Brussels Bibl. roy. 4190–200 s XVII f. 269. Ed: WS *ZCP* III (1901) 220–5 [text, trans. of preface and epilogue only: " The present ed. is made from a good photograph of the copy in H. 3. 17, the obvious inaccuracies of the *Lebor Brecc* facsimile rendering its reproduction inexpedient. It is to be hoped that some Continental Celtist will edit the Brussels copy with its gloss, and that some Dublin scholar will tell us what the *Lebor Brecc* copy really contains. It will then, perhaps, be possible to translate the text of this obscure *amra*."]

[228] The germ of the story is in *Vit. Trip.* 206; where, however, Senán is born 120 years later. Cf. *ibid.* 166.
[229] AU.
[230] Cf. p. 179 *supra.*
[231] The Irish Life has a poem on the destruction of the horses of Lugaid, king of Raithlenn, attributed, impossibly, to Colmán mac Léníne (d. 604): Aeinis Senán tes ind ailén Árda Neimidh . . . mór do ghrádhaibh doratad dhó daltaibh aine. 44 ll.

This eulogy of Senán is written in language of intentional difficulty and obscurity similar to that of the *Amra* of Colum-cille (no. 212) which it closely resembles. It too is ascribed to Dallán Forgaill.

159. *Míorbuile Senáin:* The Miracles of Senán s XIV

Beccán do sccélaib Senáin an ard-naoimh uasail. . . . [Verses] Án an cathair caomh so anocht. . . . Ar brú reilge na naomh nán. 48 stanzas.

MSS: Brussels Bibl. roy. 2324–40 ff. 241^V–8; 4190–200 ff. 277–9^V [O'Clery MSS; *cf.* pp. 38, 309 *supra*]. — RIA 23 L 11 s XVIII pp. 241 *sqq* [a poor copy of the version in Br. 4190–200]. ED: C. Plummer *ZCP* X (1915) 1–35 [text, trans.]. There is a partial Latin trans. in Colgan *AA. SS.* 537–8.

This is an account, written probably in the fourteenth century, of happenings during that and the preceding hundred years which the author considered to be due to the intervention of St. Senán. It has value for the history and social conditions of that age; and the information regarding Senán's churches and their inter-relationships can, doubtless, be used in part for earlier epochs. The text ends with a poem giving a long list of famous saints with whom Senán had made alliances, and who were bound to avenge any injury to his churches.[232]

VI. CELL-SLÉIBHE-CUILINN (KILLEEVY) AND ST. MONENNA

Cell-Sléibhe-Cuilinn — " the Church of the Mountain of Cuilenn " — is the present Killeevy, in the barony of Upper Orior, Armagh, at the foot of the mountain, the name of which is written in English Slieve Gullion. It was one of the more important monasteries for nuns in early mediaeval Ireland. In 923 it was plundered by the Norsemen,[233] and may thereafter have fallen into decay. Conchubran, writing probably in the eleventh century, speaks as though it had recently been restored.[234] In 1150 there is an annalistic record of the death of " Cailleach [a Nun?] of Cell Shléibhe, a pious, good senior." [235]

Killeevy was in the territory of the Conaille Muirthemne, who dwelt in southern Armagh and in Louth around Dundalk bay. This was one of the smaller states of the province of Ulidia, and the people, like the more important Dál Araidi to the east of them, were Picts, one of the scattered remnants of that race which may at one time have extended over much, if not the whole, of Ireland.

[232] The poem is given only by Brussels 2324–40. There it is followed by 9 other Irish poems, of which Plummer gives the incipits, *op. cit.* 3 n. O'Clery adds a note dated in the Donegal friary on the Drowse, Dec. 1, 1629, that he had copied the miracles and the poems at Limerick from a copy belonging to Conaire óg (" the younger "), son of Conaire, son of Muiris Ó Maol-Conaire, a copy which he had made from an old vellum book.

[233] AU.   [234] III xii.   [235] FM.

The foundation of Killeevy is ascribed to a certain Darerca, better known by a hypocoristic name of obscure origin, Mo-Ninna or Mo-Nennai She was of Pictish race, but whether of the Conaille or of the Dál Araid is not determined by the sources.[236]

The fame of Monenna extended further than her church of Killeevy could throw it. In England the monastery of Burton-on-Trent claimed as its patroness a certain Modwenna, whom tradition, seemingly, described as a lady of Irish origin. When the hagiographers searched the Irish calendars the only person of approximate name to be found was Monenna of Killeevy. So, with the help of some further accretions from Scottish story, our saint was embarked on a still more illustrious career in Great Britain. To her cult at Burton-on-Trent it is that we owe the preservation of the majority of the documents relating to Monenna.

160. The Lives of St. Monenna

(i) Virgo venerabilis, nomine Darerca, cognomento Monynne . . . cursuque feliciter consumato, migravit ad Christum, c. q. r. in s. s. Amen. Post tertium vero . . . sufficienter recreati sunt qui potaverunt. (ii) [Conchubran] Fuit inter Hibernenses gentes virgo vite venerabilis et morum sancta industria decorata, nomine Monenna . . . in mansionibus simul perfectorum cum Christo, q. r. in s. s. Amen. (iii) [*Nova Legenda Anglie*] Virgo quedam fuit in Hibernia nomine Modwenna . . . confractoque ergastulo liberatus est.

MSS: (i) Cod. S. ff. 79–82ᵛ. (ii) BM Cotton. Cleopatra A ii *s* XII ff. 3ᵛ–56ᵛ [Esposito thinks it probable this MS came from Burton-on-Trent]. (iii) BM Cotton. Tiberius E i *s* XIV ff. 199ᵛ–204ᵛ [this is an abridgment, by John of Tynemouth, of a " Sanctae Modvennae Vita et Tractatus de Miraculis eius," compiled by Geoffrey, abbot of Burton-on Trent 1114–1151, and to be found in BM Reg. 15 B IV *s* XIII ff. 76–88, and in MS no. 260 of Lord Mostyn's Library (4th *Report Historical MSS. Commission*, App. 361). According to Esposito, an ed. of this Life, by Prof. A. T. Baker, of Sheffield, was to have been published by the Literary Society of Stuttgart. Another abridgment of Geoffrey's work is found in BM Lansdowne 436 *s* XIV ff. 126ᵛ–31ᵛ.] EDS: (i) *AA. SS. ex Cod. S.* 165–88 [cf. HZ *Göttingische gelehrte Anzeigen* I (1891) 186]. (ii) *AA. SS. Boll.* Jul. II (1721) 297–312 [defective]. — Mario Esposito *Proc. RIA* XXVIII C (1910) 202–51 [excellent ed.: cf. *RC* XXXII (1911) 371–2]. (iii) Capgrave *Nova Legenda Anglie* (ed. Horstman, Oxford 1901) II 198–213. COMM: Hardy *Cat.* I pt. i (1862) 94–100. — Forbes *Kalendars of Scottish Saints* (1872) 404–7. — Skene *Celtic Scotland* II (1877) 37–8. — O'Hanlon *Lives of the Irish Saints* VII (1892) 55–63, 79–93. — M. Esposito " The Sources of Conchubranus' Life of St. Monenna " *EHR* XXXV (Jan. 1920) 71–8 [important].

---

[236] The notes and pedigrees in Fél. Oeng. July 6, represent her as grand-niece of Eochu, from whom sprang the Úi Echach Coba, the ruling family of Dál Araidi, and eighth in descent from Fiacha Araide, eponymous ancestor of the Dál Araidi. Moreover, Version I of her Life says that she was born in Magh-Coba, the seat of the Úi Echach in western Down, north-east of Newry. But the same version, the redactor of which evidently did not pay attention to his geography, says that she was born in the land of the Conaille, and several passages indicate that she was claimed as of that people.

Version I of the Life of Monenna is a purely Irish redaction, but is not older than the twelfth century, and quite possibly is not much older than the Codex Salmanticensis. It is an abridgment — to all appearances a faithful abridgment — of an earlier document which was used also by Conchubran. This earlier document was in turn the reproduction — perhaps with interpolations and editing, for Conchubran may have been not entirely responsible for the confusion of his work — of a primitive Life which was older than the ninth century. Some considerations will show that the primitive Life may even be as old as the first half of the seventh, and thus a contemporary of Cogitosus's Life of Brigit, Jonas's Life of Columbanus, and Cuimíne's Life of Columcille.[237]

Appended to the Life are three sections describing events that happened after the saint's death: a vision seen three days later by one of the sisters; a list of the first three abbesses who succeeded her, and an account of a miracle in the time of the third; and another narrative of a miracle during the rule of the same abbess, on the occasion of a visit to the monastery by a bishop Finbar who bore the second name Vinnian.[238]   The second of these sections reads as follows:

" After the death of St. Darerca, in accordance with her own directions Bia [daughter of Ailell] [239] was made abbess, then Indiu [Dognidui, daughter of Mo(c)tha, son of Lilac [240]] and then Derlasre [daughter of Daisrem, son of Buissid] who ruled over the monastery sixty [fifty] years. In her time a very famous miracle occurred. For she with skill and zeal was building in the monastery of blessed Darerca a church of smooth planks — as is the custom of the Irish people — and had it almost completed. There was still wanting that timber, called by the Latins the spine, which is placed on the top of a building to join together the two sides. The workmen searched through the woods for such a piece of wood, and at length found it in a spot high and difficult of access.[241]   But when they had cut it down they were unable by any device to remove it [they had thought at first that in some way by means of windlasses (*per trocleas*) they could drag it away; but no machine of men nor strength of oxen could move it even a little space] because of the roughness of the ground. The abbess, knowing this, and despairing of the bringing of the timber to the monastery, sought the patronage of St. Darerca, saying: ' St. Darerca dwells in heaven, and for her this house is being built on earth: she can help us if she will.' The next day the beam was found by the workmen in an open space near the monastery which could be reached without any harm to animals or men. The carpenters, moved by curiosity, went to see if there were any traces of the huge timber apparent along the way, and saw some few branches broken at the tops of the trees. [From this they came to the conclusion that the beam was carried through the air by angels.[242]   And now that the building has been restored, this spine of which we have been speaking is held in honor as a relic.[243]] "

237 *Cf.* nos. 147, 48, 213.
238 So in Conchubran. The form is an indication of antiquity. Undoubtedly Finnian of Magh-Bile (d. 579 AU). *Cf.* no. 183.
239 The words in brackets are taken from Conchubran's version.
240 This would make her Monenna's sister. Possibly one or two names have dropped out of the pedigree, which originally represented her as niece or grand-niece of the saint.
241 Doubtless Slieve Gullion was in the writer's mind.
242 Cod. S. adds some pious observations.
243 This comment is presumably due to Conchubran himself.

It is a reasonable inference that these sections represent a series of notes appended successively to the text of Monenna's Life in the manuscript preserved in the monastery of Killeevy. The second section, translated above, contains two such distinct entries, the first being — as it is in any case — a valuable old historical record of the first three abbesses who succeeded the foundress, and of their pedigrees. Such an entry would be made, naturally, during the administration of the fourth, who, according to a later list,[244] died about 624 after ruling twenty-four years. The conclusion would be that the Life itself was written before the end of the first quarter of the seventh century.[245]

Version II of the Life of Monenna, which dates in all probability [246] from the eleventh century, gives a fuller text than Version I, with many changes and much additional matter. Its author was an Irishman, Conchubranus — perhaps the Latinising of the common name Conchobhar — who had visited the monastery of Killeevy, had seen the relics of the saint that were preserved there, and had several times made the journey of five or six days (for the traveller on foot) between Killeevy and Kildare.[247] He may have been a cleric of Kildare.

Conchubran's sources consisted of (1) some redaction of Version I, which here is in fuller form; (2) certain local legends, as of the swineherd of mac Loithe,[248] king of Orior; of the wolves of Killeevy, who guard the cattle of the church; and, perhaps, of the robber Glunelath and St. Coemgen, and Coemgen's hot spring, though this may be taken from other hagiographic sources; (3) a modification of the historical accounts of the visit to Ireland of Aldfrid of Northumbria, of the plundering raids by tl e forces of Ecgfrid, and of the recovery of the plunder by Adamnán; [249] (4) English legends of a saint who founded churches in the forest of Arderne or Arden (in Warwickshire) and on Andredseye, in the river Trent; (5) Scottish legends of church foundations in the south of Scotland; [250] (6) stock miracle stories and similar matter as used in other *acta*. The older version was taken as the basis, and the additional material inserted by way of interpolation, often very clumsily. What is less comprehensible, the earlier sections were disarranged without apparent reason.[251]

Version III, by Geoffrey of Burton, is known through the published text of John of Tynemouth's abridgment. It is avowedly written in honor of the patroness of Burton-on-Trent. It appears to be based on Conchubran's work, which has, however, been treated with much editorial freedom — excision, modification and rearrangement being freely used to produce a fairly consistent narrative.

There is an Anglo-Norman poem of the twelfth century entitled "La Vie

---

[244] *Cf.* no. 161.

[245] If this be correct, the mention of Patrick is of especial interest. He is designated " episcopus " and " pontifex." A person who died in 517 might well have been baptized by him, and Magh-Coba in Down would be in one of the chief fields of his labors.

[246] *Cf.* Esposito *EHR loc. cit.*

[247] *Cf.* his text II vii, III i, xi, xii.

[248] An historical personage: *cf.* CS 518 and note; AU 520 and note.

[249] *Cf.* p. 284 *supra*.

[250] These seem to depend on an assimilation of the names Monenna or Moninna and Mo-Ninn, an Irish hypocoristic form of Ninian.

[251] See the analysis by Esposito, *EHR l. c.*

de Sainte Modwenne." It consists of about 10,360 lines, but has never been published.[252]

LL 371 c has a short anecdote of Monenna, in Irish; also in *Fél. Oeng.*[1] p. cxvi, *Fél. Oeng.*[2] 166, in briefer form. *Cf.* Plummer *Misc. hag. Hib.* Cat. no. 156.

161. The Successors of Monenna

Vixerat autem sancta Monenna . . . Medboc filia Midgasa abbatissa annis quindecim.

MS: BM Cotton. Cleopatra A. ii *s* XII ff. 58[v]-9. EDS: Mario Esposito *Proc. RIA* XXVIII C (1910) 244-5; *EHR* XXXV (Jan. 1920) 75-6.

This is a short note of some historical interest giving Monenna's genealogy and a list of her successors, from the fifth to the fifteenth abbess, with the years of their incumbency. It is found in the English manuscript which contains Conchubran's Life, and in all probability is the copy of a document obtained from Killeevy by the monks of Burton-on-Trent. It must have been drawn up to supplement the Life of the saint kept at Killeevy, which, we have seen reason to believe,[253] carried an added note giving the names of the second, third and fourth abbesses. It contains no dates, but from the periods assigned to the abbesses and from certain other information an approximate chronology can be constructed.[254] The annals mention only the sixth abbess, Conchen, who is said to have died about 653 x 658.[255] The eighth died, according to the list, sixteen [256] years later, in "the great mortality," which was in 664 and 665.[257] The thirteenth abbess, whose rule came to a close one hundred and seven years later, was the daughter of a certain Foidmenn, whose obit is placed in 752.[257] It can be deduced that the administration of the fifteenth superioress of Killeevy ended some time about 815 x 820. The inference follows that this record was drawn up during the first half of the ninth century.[258]

The Foidmenn just mentioned was king of Conaille-Muirthemne, within whose territory Killeevy lay. His sister and daughter were successively abbesses of the institution, and it is quite probable that at other periods also the office was controlled by the royal family of the Conaille. We learn that the eighth abbess was grandniece of the fifth, and the ninth and tenth were sisters, nieces of the eighth.

[252] Oez seignurs pur Deu nus pri. . . . Ceste vertu et terminee. Amen. Bodl. Digby 34 *s* XIII ff. 1-80. *Cf.* Hardy *op. cit.* 99; H. Suchier *Über die Vie de Saint Alban* (Halle 1877) 149; Gaston Paris *La Littérature Française au Moyen Âge* (Paris 1888) 215. Also Esposito *Proc. RIA l. c.*, who says that an ed. by Prof. A. T. Baker was in preparation for the Literary Society of Stuttgart.
[253] *Cf.* p. 368 *supra.*
[254] It is to be borne in mind that numerical entries in manuscripts are notoriously liable to corruption.
[255] CS 653; FM 654; TCD MS H. 1. 18 (quoted by Hogan *Onomasticon Goedelicum* 212) 658.
[256] Perhaps we should read "thirteen" — xiii for xui.
[257] AU.
[258] It is possible that Gnathat, ninth abbess, who ruled for thirty years after "the great mortality," was the same person as the Gnathnat, abbess of Kildare, who died, according to FM, in 687. Such plural dignities were not infrequent, and there seem to have been specially friendly relations between Killeevy and Kildare.

162. Hymns in honor of Monenna

(i)[Refrain?] Deum, deorum Dominum . . . 1 stanza. Audite sancta studia. . . . Collocasti in gloria. 23 stanzas.
(ii) Audite, fratres . . . tamquam aura limpida [MS aurea lampada] 23 stanzas. Gloria patri . . . [1 stanza in same metre, another different].

MS: BM Cotton. Cleopatra A. ii s XII ff. 1–3^v (i), 56^v–8 (ii). EDS: Blume *An. hymn.* LI (1908) 335–7 (i), 337–40 (ii). — Esposito *Proc. RIA* XXVIII C (1910) 239–42 (i), 242–4 (ii); *cf.* 246.

These two hymns are interesting specimens of Hiberno-Latin versification. It seems probable that they were composed at Killeevy, and in the eighth, or possibly seventh, century. The first alludes to a few miracles which are related at greater length in Monenna's Lives; the second has practically no biographical matter.

CHAPTER V

THE MONASTIC CHURCHES — PART II: CHURCHES OF THE SIXTH TO NINTH CENTURIES; GENERAL TREATISES

I. The Monastic Churches — Foundations of the Sixth Century

In the preceding chapter the theory has been advanced that something like a revolution took place in the Irish Church in the sixth century, as a result of which its organisation and administration became predominantly, if not exclusively, monastic. The earlier church-foundations seem to have been made, in the more important cases, either in pagan shrines which were thereby turned to Christian use, or in the fortified residences of princes converted to the new faith. By the sixth century the conversion of Ireland was an accomplished fact — even though a pagan minority may have lingered on for another hundred years or so — and a generation was arising which adopted with enthusiasm the Christian teaching and sought in the monastic life the most complete fulfilment of its precepts. To these men, gathering together in small groups under a spiritual leader and withdrawing to a secluded place where they might build their cells around a small oratory and lead the cœnobitical life without disturbance, was due the foundation of the monastic churches. The records and legends of these church founders will now be considered; two of them, Colum-cille of Iona and Brendan of Clonfert, have left such an important literature that they must be given separate sections.

(a) Mainister-Buite (Monasterboice), the Monastery of St. Buite

What seems to have been an old tradition declared that St. Columcille was born on the day on which St. Buite mac Brónaigh died. This was probably in 521[1]; the Annals of Ulster — in entries, however, not earlier than the eighth century — give the dates 519 and 523. Mainister-Buite (Monasterboice), " Buite's monastery," probably one of the oldest of the monasteries of Ireland, was in the modern Louth, near Drogheda, in

---

[1] Reeves *Ad.* pp. lxviii *sq.*

the midst of the territory of the Cianachta-Breg, to whom Buite was said to belong. It remained a church of some importance, at least from the eighth to the twelfth century, and interesting ecclesiastical monuments, including two high crosses and a round tower, still survive. One of the crosses was erected by a certain Muiredach, who has been identified with the "Muiredach son of Domnall, *tanase*-abbot [*i.e.*, holding the right of succession to the abbacy] of Árd-Macha, and *árd-maer* ['high steward,' apparently the person who collected its dues for the church of Armagh] of the Southern Úi-Néill, and *comarba* of Buite mac Brónaigh, head of counsel of all the men of Breg [eastern Meath], lay and clerical," who died, according to the Annals of Ulster, in 924. This would suggest that at this time Monasterboice was part of the *paruchia Patricii*, but there is no further evidence on the subject, and the church certainly maintained its independent succession of abbots.[2]

163. Life of St. Buite

Sanctus pater et electus Dei pontifex Boecius . . . panem latum preparauit, et butiro superficiem eius . . . [ends imperfect].

MSS: Bodl. Rawl. B 505 *s* XIV/XV ff. 154ᵛ–6ᵛ. — Dublin, Franciscan Convent A 24 A.D. 1627, pp. 178 *sqq.* — BM Add. 4788 (Cod. Clar. 39) ff. 73ᵛ *sq* [a Ware transcript]. — Brussels Bibl. roy. 8967 [a Ward transcript]. All the later MSS are copies, with more or less emendation, of Rawl. B 505, which in turn was copied from Rawl. B 485 *s* XIII/XIV, where the *Vita*, as shown by the table of contents, originally held the last place, but is now lost. Before the copy was made the end of the text was either lost or illegible. EDS: Wm. Skene *Chronicles of the Picts and Scots* (Edinburgh 1867) 410–11 [extracts]. — *VV. SS. Hib.* (1910) I pp. xxxiv–xxxvi, 87–97. *Cf.* E. W. B. Nicholson *ZCP* VI 448–53.

The extant Life of Buite is late: it is formed by the combination of two earlier texts, one a short *Vita* ending with his prophecy of the future greatness of Colum-cille, the other an account of the miracles of his boyhood. The whole is probably quite fabulous. Buite is made to visit Italy (or, perhaps, Wales), and the land of the Picts, modern Scotland.[3]

(b) Aran and St. Énda

Of the many ecclesiastical foundations established by Irish church-men on the islands around the coasts of Ireland and Scotland, perhaps

---

[2] See R. A. S. Macalister *Muiredach Abbot of Monasterboice 899–923 A.D. his life and surroundings* (Dublin 1914) for a description of the high cross, and a popular account of the Ireland of the tenth century.

[3] The Litany of Irish Saints in LL 373c (no. 586) seems to regard Buite as the leader of a band of pilgrims who crossed the sea. Legend said that he used as a pillow the brain-stone of Mesgegra with which Conchobar mac Nessa, king of Ulster in the heroic age, was slain. Apparently a stone on his grave was looked on as this identical missile.

the most famous, after that of Iona, was Ára-mór, the largest of the Aran islands, situated at the entrance to the Bay of Galway. Remains of several early monastic buildings are still to be seen there. The foundation of this religious establishment is attributed to St. Énda, of whom the annals have no record, but who seems to have lived in the first half of the sixth century. Óengus mac Nadfráich, king of Munster, who died in 490 or 491, according to the Annals of Ulster, is said to have made him a grant of Aran, but this is probably a late Munster legend.

164. Life of St. Énda

Mirabilis Deus omnipotens in sanctis suis hunc virum sanctissimum, scilicet Endeum . . . ad monasterium suum reddiens, in manus Dei omnipotentis animam suam commendans, exspirauit.

MSS: Bodl. Rawl. B 485 s XIII/XIV ff. 103–8; Rawl. B 505 s XIV/XV ff. 90 sqq. — Dublin, Franciscan Convent A 24 A.D. 1627 pp. 291 sqq. EDS: Colgan AA. SS. 704–10 [imperfect at beginning]. — AA. SS. Boll. Mart. III 267–74. — VV. SS. Hib. I pp. lxii–lxiv, II 60–75. COMM: Roderick O'Flaherty (ed. Jas. Hardiman) Description of West or H-Iar Connaught (Dublin 1845) 79 sqq [re topographical data]. — HZ "Keltische Beiträge II" Zs. f. deut. Alterthum XXXIII (1889) 206 sqq [explains the falsification of Énda's pedigree].

The existing Life of Énda is a late production, worked up from many different sources. Several of the sections are variants one of another. The text has little directly historical but considerable topographical interest. In legendary fame Énda was second only to Finnian of Clúain-Iráird as a monastic teacher. The Life gives as his pupils Finnian, Ciarán of Clúain-moccu-Nóis, Brendan of Clúain-ferta and Columba of Hii.[4]

(c) CLÚAIN-IRÁIRD (CLONARD) AND ST. FINNIAN

Clúain-Iráird or Clúain-Eráird (Clonard), "Erard's meadow," was on the upper Boyne, on the northern or Meath side where the river divides that county from Kildare. It was one of the most important of the ancient Irish churches. The surrounding territory had belonged to the Lagin, and was held, or claimed, by them until 515, when its conquest by the Úi Néill was completed. As Clonard must have been founded before, or not very long after, this event, it is natural that its early associations were with the churches of Leinster.

The founder was a Finnio moccu Telduib,[5] who died, according to the Annals of Ulster, in the great epidemic of 549. The

---

[4] Pedigrees of Énda are in LL 347h, LBr 14e, BB 217a (cf. 231a), Rawl. B 486 f. 35d, but they all make Énda the son of Conall Derc of Air-gíalla (d. 615). This, as HZ has noticed, is due to an attempt to identify him with one of the Úi Corra of Imram Curaig húa Corra (no. 618). The Martyrology of Tallaght (no. 273) offers a more consistent pedigree. Cf. also Fél. Oeng.[2] 70, 112.

[5] A century later one of Finnian's successors was Colmán moccu Delduib (AU 654). This indicates that the family remained associated with Clonard.

name, which may represent an earlier *Uindio* or *Uennio*, appears in later writings as Finnian, Findian, Findén, etc. It is, perhaps, probable, but no more, that this saint was identical with the Venniaus of whom Columbanus speaks and the Vinniaus,[6] author of the earliest Irish penitential. The Vinianus of Adamnán is more likely to be the bishop of Mag-Bile.[7] The *Catalogus sanctorum Hiberniae*[8] mentions our Finnian among the saints of the second order, and a note — doubtless posterior — gives "the names of the disciples of St. Finnian of Clúain-Iráird." Legend, perhaps of later development, made him "tutor of the saints of Ireland," and especially of "the twelve apostles of Ireland."[9] This became a fundamental idea of Irish hagiography, and almost every saint living within a century of his time is represented to have been a pupil of the founder of Clonard.

165. Life of St. Finnian of Clonard

(i) Vir erat de nepotibus Loscani nomine Fintanus . . . et mortuus est, sicut dixit Finnianus, eodem anno. (ii) Fuit uir nobilis in Hiberniae . . . [as (i)]. (iii) Atfiadar didiu, a cumair ferta 7 mírbuili in cráibh-dhigh-seo . . . isan aentaid is uaisli cech, n-aentaid, i n-aentaid na naeibh-Trinóidi, A. 7 M. 7 S. N. Ailim trócaire Dhé, roairiltnigem in aentaid sin. In s. s. Amen.

MSS: (i) Cod. S. ff. 83–6ᵛ. (ii) Bodl. Rawl. B 485 s XIII/XIV ff. 54–8ᵛ; Rawl. B 505 s XIV/XV ff. 156ᵛ *sqq.* — Dublin Franciscan convent A 24 pp. 1 *sqq.* (iii) Bk. Lis. s XV ff. 23–5ᵛ. — BM Addit. 30512 ff. 6–9.—Brussels Bibl. roy. 2324–40 f. 29; 4190–200 f. 196.[10] — RIA A. iv. 1 (Stowe 9) s XVII pp. 149–64. — TCD 1285 (H. 1. 11) A.D. 1752 ff. 111–3 [copy of Addit. 30512]. EDS: (i) Colgan *AA. SS.* (1645) 393 *sqq.* — *AA. SS. ex Cod. S.* (1888) 189–210. (iii) *Lis. Lives* (1890) 75–83, 222–30, 342–6. COMM: Baring-Gould and Fisher *Lives of the British Saints* III 30–7. — Paul Walsh " Place names in Vita Finniani " *ZCP* X (1915) 73–7.

Several versions of a Life of Finnian have been preserved. Of these, Versions I and II are abbreviations of the same original text,[11] somewhat modified for purposes of edification. Version II has a long addition from the Life of Columba of Terryglass.[12] Version III is an Irish translation which, though probably later in date, represents the original more fully and accurately. That original itself would not seem to have been an early document; but there is no means of assigning it even an approximate date. It bears no evidence of having been intended for lectionary or homiletic purposes; but has considerable secondary historical interest, and must have been based on the local records, pretensions and traditions of Clonard.[13] A special zeal for the

---

[6] *Cf.* pp. 240–1 *supra*.   [7] *Cf.* no. 183.   [8] No. 271.

[9] These were twelve of the principal saints of the sixth century, but there is disagreement among the sources as to just who made up the twelve.

[10] So WS gives the Brussels texts. Plummer *Misc. hag. Hib.* Cat. no. 37 lists only the second, ff. 203–10.

[11] " These things have been extracted from the first book of his Life " (*cap.* 12).

[12] No. 176.

[13] There are such local touches as the account of his crossing the Boyne to " Eiscir-Branain " " in which Ard-Relic [at Clonard] stands to-day," and of his founding a church at Ros-Findchuill (near Clonard) " which to-day is (called) Less-in-Memra."

supernatural importance of the saint and for the peculiar sanctity of Clonard is shown at least in the Book of Lismore version. After a bardic eulogy in which Finnian is compared with St. Paul, the text proceeds: "And even as the angel promised to Paul that no one who should go into the clay of Rome should after Doom become an inhabitant of hell, even so the angel promised to Findian that no one over whom the mould of Ard Relic [the burial ground at Clonard] should go would be an inhabitant of hell after the Judgment, and as Paul died in Rome for the sake of the Christian people, lest they should all perish in the pains and punishments of hell, even so Findian died in Clonard for sake of the people of the Gael, that they might not all perish of the Yellow Plague." [14]   Moreover Finnian, along with Patrick and Christ, is to judge the men and women of Ireland on Doomsday.

A large part of the Life consists of accounts of the many church-foundations made by Finnian. His *paruchia* must have been a league of Leinster churches, having relationships with a few institutions in north Connacht.

There was a strong tradition that Finnian was a disciple of the British saints David, Gildas and Cathmael (?). He was, probably, a representative of the same monastic movement that Gildas and David represented in Britain. He was sent back from Britain to "renew faith and belief in Ireland after Patrick," words similar to those that describe the mission of Gildas to the western island.[15] Two interesting passages support this view. Finnian, when founding churches in Leinster, was attacked by a certain Bresal, at the instigation of Cremthann, a bishop, a story which seems to point to a time of disagreement between monks and bishops.[16] There is also a curious story according to which Finnian, at the request of many saints, visited Rúadán of Lorrha, and, after a contest in miracle-working, induced him to have "a common mode of living" with the others. The story is confused with some folk-legend of a wonderful nectar-giving tree possessed by Rúadán, but it may preserve the memory of a struggle over questions of church discipline.

(d) Clúain-moccu-Nóis (Clonmacnois) and St. Ciarán

Bibliography

In addition to general works on archaeology and hagiography: "Notes on the architecture of Ireland: Clonmacnois" *Gentleman's Magazine* 1864 pt. i pp. 141 *sqq.* — Jas. Graves "Enumeration of the ancient Irish monumental stones at present existing at Clonmacnois" *Journ. Kilkenny Archaeol. Soc.* III (1854–5) 294 *sqq.* — Westropp *Journ. RSAI* XXXVII (1907) 277 *sqq;* 329 *sqq.* — R. A. S. Macalister *The memorial slabs of Clonmacnois, King's County: with an appendix on the materials for a history of the monastery* (RSAI: Dublin 1909); *The Latin and Irish Lives of Ciaran* (London, New York 1921). — L. Gougaud *Dict. d'archéol. chrét. et de liturgie* III pt. II (1914) 2014–24. Macalister has in preparation a history of the monastery.

---

[14] *Lis. Lives* 229. A conflicting record immediately follows to the effect that Finnian died at Inis-mac-nIndeirc on the river Shannon. Further testimony to the pre-eminence of Clonard is given by the angel's promise that a visit to Finnian's altar would be as efficacious as a visit to Rome. — *AA. SS. ex Cod. S.* 194.

[15] *Cf.* p. 177 *supra.*

[16] Any cause of scandal is removed from the Cod. S. version by making Cremthann a local princeling.

The river Shannon to the south of Athlone flows through a low-lying country where the meadows and pasture-lands that line the banks are frequently under water in flood time. In the sixth century, when Ireland was richly wooded and the amount of surface water was far greater than now, this must have been a wild fen country with few or no habitations. Here, the story goes, Diarmait mac Cerr-béil, great-grand-son of Níall *nói-gíallach*, was hiding, a fugitive from the enmity of the reigning *árd-rí*, Tuathal *moel-garb*, when St. Ciarán with eight companions came down the Shannon and obtained his assistance in building a little monastery at the place formerly known as Árd-Tiprat, "Height of the Well," but thereafter as Clúain-moccu-Nóis, "Meadow of the race of Nós," now Clonmacnois.[17]

Clonmacnois was, after Armagh, the greatest of the monastic churches of Ireland; perhaps it surpassed Armagh as a centre of learning and liter-ature. Its *paruchia*, the league of churches under its headship, may not have been as extensive or as well organised as those of Sts. Colum-cille and Patrick, but it laid claim to ecclesiastical rule over half of Ireland, and, according to Tírechán, already in the seventh century it had absorbed churches which, in his opinion, rightfully belonged to Patrick. The "Law" of Ciarán, which, no doubt, involved a tax paid to his church, is mentioned as imposed in Connacht in 744, 788 and 814.[18] Clonmacnois suffered much from the onslaughts of the Vikings, and from the internal anarchy of the tenth, eleventh and twelfth cen-turies, but its vigor was not permanently impaired until the coming of the Anglo-Normans. There is reason to believe that it played an important part in that amalgamation of secular and ecclesiastical, Gaelic and Latinist learning which characterised the post-Viking epoch, and that it did much for the preservation both of old Irish literature and of the records which formed the basis of the national annals. The Annals of Tigernach and the Annals of Clonmacnois were, it would seem, com-piled within its walls, and there were written the codices *Lebor na hUidre* and Rawlinson B. 502, oldest of manuscripts in the Irish language.

The sources for the history of the monastery, both archaeological and literary, are, comparatively, quite abundant. At its site, on the east side of the Shannon in Offaley, about eight miles from Athlone, are some of the most important of ancient Irish ecclesiastical ruins. The

---

[17] The story of the foundation of Clonmacnois, told at greater length than in the Lives of Ciarán, and other matter on the relations between that saint and Diarmait, can be found in the secular tale *Aided Diarmata maic Cerr-béil* (Death of Diarmait) — O'Grady *SG* I 72–82, II 76–88.

[18] AU. *Cf.* p. 336 *supra*.

THE MONASTIC CHURCHES—II

inscribed grave-slabs, although now the merest debris, still give some
indication of the fame of this Westminster Abbey of Gaelic Ireland.

> "In a quiet watered land, a land of roses,
> Stands St. Ciarán's city fair,
> And the warriors of Erin, in their famous generations,
> Slumber there."

166. Life of St. Ciarán of Clúain

(i) Sanctus abbas Kyaranus de plebe Latronensium . . . in sempiterna die sine nocte, in regno eterno
sine fine, ante tribunal Christi, Qui c. P. et S. S. v. et r. in s. s. Amen. (ii) Vir gloriosus, et uita sanctissimus abbas, Queranus, . . . quibus beneficia oportuno tempore impendit. Metrum de eo sic: Matre
Quiarani sedente in curru uolubili . . . Gloriosum in omnibus nouissimis temporibus. [This last is a collection of verses in various metres.] (iii) Beatus et venerabilis abbas Queranus nobili . . . fideles in
fide consolidarentur et infideles confunderentur. Finit. Amen. [Incomplete.] (iv) Omnia que cumque
uultis ut faciant . . . . .i. Cech maith as ail libh do dhénamh . . . i n-aentaid na noeib T. A. 7 M. 7 S.
N.. . . Ros-aitreabham in s. s. Amen.[19]

MSS: (i) Cod. K. ff. 144ᵛ-8. (ii) Bodl. Rawl. B 485 ff. 91–4; B 505 ff. 127–30.
(iii) Cod. S. ff. 77ᵛ-8ᵛ. (iv) Bk. Lis. ff. 35-9ᵛ. — Brussels Bibl. roy. 4190-200 s
XVII ff. 154–70 [copied by O'Clery from " the book of Aodh óg Úa Dálacháin of Les
Cluaine in Meath "]. Eds: (i) VV. SS. Hib. I pp. xlvii–li, 200–16. (ii) Macalister
Latin and Irish Lives of Ciaran 172–83. (iii) AA. SS. ex Cod. S. 155–60. (iv) Lis.
Lives 117–34, 262–80, 355–9 [text, trans., notes]. Trans: Macalister op. cit. [trans.
of the four versions]. Cf. AA. SS. Boll. Sept. III 370–83 [historical commentary].

The importance of Clonmacnois is reflected in the fame of her founder.
Ciarán (or, in earlier orthography, Cérán or Quérán), although he was
of humble origin — he is commonly designated mac in tsáir, "son of the
wright," or "carpenter," — and died apparently at an early age without
having played any very prominent part in contemporary affairs, became
one of the heroic figures of hagiography. His father's occupation [20]
probably was the point of origin of the legends which gave him a career
of thirty-three years paralleling in several respects that of Christ. The
chronological indications given by the annals and the Lives are various
and inconsistent, but it seems certain that Ciarán was born in the
decade 510–20 and founded Clonmacnois in that of 540–50.[21] There
was an ancient record known to Tírechán which stated that a certain
deacon Justus of Fidarte (Feurty, co. Roscommon), a disciple of Patrick,

---

[19] Appended in Bk. Lis. is a scribal note: " It is not I that am responsible for the meaningless words
that are in this Life, but the bad manuscript."
[20] If this, too, did not arise from the seeking after parallels.
[21] If Clonmacnois was founded in the year when Tuathal moel-garb died, and if Anscombe's chronology
(cf. p. 178 supra) is correct, the date is two decades earlier. — Macalister thinks Ciarán died in 556 (Latin
and Irish Lives of Ciaran 159).

had baptized Ciarán in the one-hundred-and-fortieth year of some unidentified era.[22]

The several versions of the Life of Ciarán contain much the same material, although they differ slightly in the arrangement and treatment of the episodes. They all seem to depend ultimately on a text or collection of texts compiled at Clonmacnois at an early date, probably not later than the ninth century. The matter is unusually interesting, and of considerable historical value.

The primitive Life was written at a time when various articles believed to be relics of Ciarán were still in existence. One was the hide of the cow which Ciarán had taken with him to Finnian's school at Clonard: " That cow was dun, and was called Odhur Kyarain, and its fame remains forever in Ireland. . . . So its skin remains in honor even to this day in the monastery of St. Ciarán; for through it, by the grace of God, miracles are performed. And above all it has this especial virtue, as holy old men, the disciples of St. Ciarán, have handed down to us, that it has been shown supernaturally that every man who shall have died [resting] on it, will possess eternal life with Christ."[23]

Another story tells of Ciarán's pet fox, which attempted to eat the leather cover of a book. It was hunted and fled to Ciarán. " That book is to-day called Pólaire Ciaráin (Ciarán's Tablets)." The hagiographer goes on to moralise: " That is most proper for these, the wicked men who dwell near to the Church, and who get the benefit of the Church, both communion, and baptism, and food, and teaching, and nevertheless they cease not persecuting the Church till a king's persecution, or a mortality, or an unknown illness comes to them; and then they must needs go under the protection of the Church, even as the fox went under Ciarán's cowl."[24]

Other relics still existing in the writer's day were Ciarán's stone cap; [25] the Cassal Senáin, Senán's Robe, which Ciarán had sent afloat down the Shannon to St. Senán at Inis-Cathaig, and Coemgen's Bobán, the bell of Ciarán which at his death he bequeathed to Coemgen of Glendalough.

Some other passages of particular interest may be noted: (1) The story of Ciarán's mother making blue dye-stuff, and ordering Ciarán away. " They did not deem it right or lucky to have men in the same house in which cloth was getting dyed."[26]   As Stokes points out, this indicates both the antiquity of dyeing and the probability that it was at some time regarded as a female rite or mystery, from presence at which males were excluded. (2) The story of the quern which ground corn for Ciarán, told in two different versions. (3) The leagues entered into by Ciarán with his namesake of Saigir and with Finnian of Clonard, legends which, no doubt, owe their existence to relationships between the churches in later years.[27]   (4) The reference to the merchants of the Gauls, who brought wine to Ciarán at Clonmacnois. This has

---

[22] Tírechán took it to mean that 140 years had elapsed between the death of Patrick and the birth of Ciarán (LA f. 12V), while the author of the Tripartite Life thought it meant the 140th year of Justus's own life (Vit. Trip. I 104).

[23] Cod. K. cap. xv.   Cf. " Leabhar na hUidhre," p. 15 supra.

[24] Lis. Lives.   Cf. Macalister op. cit. 115.   There must have been a special occasion for this " aside," but his suggestion as to what it was is not attractive.

[25] Cf. p. 380 infra.   [26] Lis. Lives 356.   [27] Cf. CS 838; AU 926, 1014.

interest for the history of early Irish trade relations.[28]   (5) The legend of Crichid, Ciarán's farmer, who went to Saigir, extinguished the sacred fire there, and afterwards was killed by wolves.   Ciarán brought down fire from heaven to renew the flame, and restored Crichid to life.   (6) The strange story of the jealousy of the other saints of Ireland towards Ciarán, which was the cause of his early death.

The account of Ciarán's death, as given in Version I, has a note of authenticity. " Our most holy patron Ciarán lived only one year in his monastery of Clúain.   When he knew that the day of his death was at hand, he prophesied bewailing the later evils which would be after him in his place.   Then the brothers said to him: ' What then shall we do in the time of those evils? Shall we stay here by your remains? Or shall we proceed to other places? '   To them St. Ciarán said: ' Hasten to other quiet places, and leave my remains just like the dry bones of the stag on the mountain; for it is better that you should be with my spirit in heaven, than to be alongside my bones on earth with scandal.'   St. Ciarán mortified his body much, and we set down an instance thereof.   He used to have a stone cap on his head, which even to this day remains in the monastery of St. Ciarán, and is venerated by all.   Now when he was becoming weak, he was unwilling that that stone should be removed from him, but ordered it to be placed on his shoulders, that he might have the labor even unto death for the sake of a perpetual reward in heaven.   When at length the hour of his death was at hand, he ordered that he be carried out of doors, and looking up towards heaven he said: ' Hard is that road, and this necessary.'   The brethren said to him: ' We know that nothing is difficult for you, father; but we poor people ought to fear this hour much.'   And having been brought back into the house he raised his hand and blessed his people and clergy, and having received the holy sacrament, on the 5th of the Ides of September he sent forth his spirit, in the thirty-third year of his age."

As noted above, the second *Vita* ends with a collection of verses in various metres: " Matre Querani sedente . . . "; " Mulieris regiae . . . "; " Cum puer oraret . . ."; " Alto et ineffabili . . . ."   They have been printed in *LH²* II 219 and *An. hymn.* LI 325–7.   Blume believes that they formed part of an office in honor of Ciarán. The fourth set of verses, " Alto et ineffabili . . . novissimis temporibus," 16 such ll., is also in LH(T) f. 31, and has been published by Dreves *An. hymn.* XIX 172 and in *LH²* I 157, II 218–20.   See also Macalister *op. cit.* 165.   This piece has been attributed to Columba of Iona.

167. Patrick's Prophecy of Ciarán

Rotairngeir dano Patraic tri fichit bliadan . . . i Cluain atá taisi Patraic, ut alii putant.

MSS: TCD 1319 (H. 2. 17) f. 397.   Also, as notes to Fél. Oeng., in Bodl. Rawl. B 512 f. 62 and Dublin Franciscan monastery A. 7.   ED: *Vit. Trip.* II 556–7.   *Cf. Fél. Oeng.²* 204–5.

Comlach, " Patrick's leper," brought relics from across the seas.   He was compelled to leave them in a cavity in a tree.   Patrick foretold that they were left for Ciarán,

---

[28] *Cf.* HZ " Über direkte Handelsverbindungen Westgalliens mit Irland in Altertum und frühen Mittelalter: 2.   Der Weinhandel Westgalliens nach Irland im 1. bis 7. Jahrhundert n. Chr." *Sitzungsb. d. k. preuss. Akad. d. Wissensch.* 1909 pp. 430 *sqq.*

who should be born sixty years later. And some say that Patrick's own relics are in Clonmacnois.[29]

168. The Miracle of Ciarán's Hand — *Echtra Ambacuc*

Ferthair oenach Tailten la Diarmait . . . Domnall mac Murchada oc ferthain ind oenaig. Finit.

MSS: LL 274. — Bodl. Rawl. B 512 *s* XV f. 140. — Dublin Franciscan convent MS A 9 (3) p. 32[b]. — Liber Flavus Fergusiorum *s* XV ff. 10[v], 37. — Edinburgh Nat. Lib. XXVI f. 2. EDS: O'Grady *SG* I 416, II 453 [LL text, trans.]. — J. Fraser *Ériu* VI ii (1912) 159–60 [LFF texts]. *Cf.* J. H. Todd (ed.) *The Irish Nennius* 206.

The present strange legend tells how Ciarán, as confessor to the *árd-rí*, Diarmait mac Cerr-béil, was with him at the *oenach* (assembly, or fair) of Tailtiu (Teltown, Meath).[30] A man, named in some versions Abacuc or Ambacuc,[31] took a false oath while holding his head under Ciarán's hand. As a result his head fell off, but he continued to live, and was brought by Ciarán to Clonmacnois. The story has some value for topography. It has found its way into the annals and forms an element of the secular tale *Aided Diarmata*.

169. Coirpre *crom* and St. Ciarán

Coirpre crom mac Feradhaig mic Lugdach . . . deamuin form. Conidh mairce bís de sin cen fháisittin dogrés.

MSS: BM Egerton 92 f. 30. — RIA Leabhar Úi Maini *s* XIV/XV f. 126[v]. — RIA Bk. of Fermoy *s* XIV/XV f. 51. — Bk. Lis. *s* XV f. 45. — Brussels Bibl. roy. 5100–4 *s* XVII f. 78. EDS: O'D *Journ. Kilkenny Archaeol. Soc.* 1858 pp. 453 *sq* [Eg. 92 text, trans.]. — WS *RC* XXVI (1905) 368–73 [text of Brussels MS, trans.]. — KM *ACL* III (1906) 224–6 [text of L. Úi Maini].

This legend tells how Ciarán replaced the head, rather unskilfully, on a wicked Coirpre, who had been decapitated for his evil deeds. Henceforth he was known as Coirpre *crom*, " the crooked." The *motif* is to show the benefit from confession and repentance, which saved Coirpre's head from the clutches of the demon, and also to exalt the claims of Ciarán's community over the Úi Maini of Connacht, of whom Coirpre became king.

170. Poems attributed to Ciarán

(i) An rim, a rí richid ráin . . . an rimm a rí richid ran.

MSS: LL 374. — BM Add. 30512 *s* XV f. 43[v]. — BM Egerton 175 p. 14. ED: Macalister *Latin and Irish Lives of Ciaran* (1921) 168–9 [text, trans.].

A metrical prayer on the subject of the shortness of his life, put into the mouth of Ciarán.

---

[29] The story is incorporated into *Vit. Trip.* (I 84), and into the Irish Life of Ciarán.

[30] One of the three " high gatherings of Ireland," or at least of the central plain, the other two being the *dál* of Uisnech and the *feis* of Tara.

[31] Doubtless the equivalent of the Vulgate name Habacuc (Septuagint 'Αμβακούμ), but how such a name found its way into the legend is not explained.

(ii) A fhir na heagna d'iarraidh . . . bur bhfreaga.

MS: Maynooth, Murphy MSS 70 p. 163, 72 p. 48; Renehan MSS 84 p. 151. ED: Thos. P. O'Nolan *IER* 4th ser. XXIV (1908) 393–4.

A moralising poem: the man who seeks wisdom or knowledge must seek it from God; all rewards are vain that do not come from Him.

For the so-called " Rule of Ciarán," see no. 268 (ii).

171. The Vision of Laisrén

Feachtas luid Laisren for slatrad . . . [ends imperfect].

MS: Bodl. Rawl. B 512 f. 44. ED: KM *Otia Merseiana* I (1899) 113–9 [with trans.].

This fragment contains the beginning of what was, no doubt, a complete vision of hell and heaven. It was seen by a certain Laisrén who went from the monastery of Clúain (the abbreviation almost always indicates Clúain-moccu-Nóis) to purify a church named Clúain-Chain in Connacht, and may have been the contribution made by the community of Ciarán to the vision literature of Ireland.

In LBr 259 and Brussels Bibl. roy. 5100–4 f. 76 there is a story of Cairbre *crom*, a bishop of Clonmacnois, and the ghost of a King Máel-Sechlainn. ED: WS *RC* XXVI 362–9. *Cf. Mart. Don.* Mar. 6. LAT. TRANS: Colgan *AA. SS.* 598–9.

In the Edinburgh National Library MS XXVI is a short legend of a ship sailing in the air, the anchor of which caught in the church of Clúain — doubtless Clúain-moccu-Nóis. Printed in *Anec.* III (1910) 8–9. *Cf. Ériu* IV 12; L. Gougaud *RC* XLI (1924) 354–8; and no. 602 iv. The episode is probably that noticed in the Annals of Ulster in 749.

We have a curious legend (called in Bk. Fer. *Scél saltrach na muice:* " Story of the pig's psalter ") of the disappearance of a bishop named Caencomrac, residing " on his pilgrimage" at Clonmacnois, who knew when everyone would die. MSS: Bk. Lis. f. 143ᵛ. — Bk. Fer. f. 42ᵛ. — RIA 23 M 50 (Hodges & Smith 150) p. 145. ED: O'Grady *SG* I 87–9, II 94–6 [with trans.]. Caencomrac was probably the historical personage of that name, bishop and abbot of Lugmad (Louth) who died in 903 (AU).

Dúnchad úa Bráin, *comarba* of Ciarán, died " on his pilgrimage " at Armagh Jan. 19, 989 (AU). A story of his sojourn in Armagh is in Bodl. Laud 610 f. 14, whence it has been published by KM *ZCP* III (1901) 35–6. The same story is in Liber Flavus Fergussiorum vol. I pt. iv f. 6; Brussels Bibl. roy. 2324–40 f. 113; and RIA Hodges & Smith 150 p. 164. *Cf.* Plummer *Misc. hag. Hib.* Cat. no. 132.

172. Poems on the Cemetery of Clonmacnois

(i) A reilec láech Leithe Cuinn . . . [19th stanza] ised dotriacht, a reilec! . . . [20th] áirem do rígh, a reilec! . . . [24th] isé is ríar do cach reilic!

MSS: Bodl. Rawl. B 512 *s* XV f. 121. — TCD 1378 (H. 5. 6) *s* XVII p. 150 [13 stanzas]. — TCD 1291 (H. 1. 17) A.D. 1755 f. 83 [17 stanzas]. EDS: W. M. Hennessy in Geo. Petrie (ed. M. Stokes) *Christian inscriptions in the Irish language* I (Dublin 1872) 79–82 [text of H. 1. 17, trans.]. — R. I. Best *Ériu* II (1905) 163–71 [text, trans.].

(ii) Hi ccathraig in toirnide . . . hi cathraig an toirnide. 17 stanzas.

MS: Transcription by O'C of a Brussels MS. ED: B. O'Looney in Geo. Petrie (ed. M. Stokes) *op. cit.* 76–8 [with trans.].

(iii) Cathír Chíarain Cluain mic nois . . . re rreibh na Suca. 19 quatrains.

MS: Bodl. Rawl. B 486 f. 29. ED: W. M. Hennessy in Geo. Petrie *op. cit.* 4–7 [with trans.].

These poems give lists of persons, chiefly kings, buried at Clonmacnois. Macalister declares that they are of little practical value for identifying the surviving slabs.[32] The first poem is attributed to Conaing *buidhe* Úa Máil-Conaire (d. 1314): the last five quatrains, an addition, say that it was written for the clergy of Clonmacnois, but, as they rejected it, it was presented to Cathal *crobh-derg* Úa Conchobhair, king of Connacht (d. 1224). There is an obvious anachronism of a century. The third poem, a late composition, was written, it is said, " by Enoch O'Gillan who lived on the borders of the River Suck," county Galway.

173. The Registry of Clonmacnois

MS: BM Addit. 4796 (Clarendon 51). ED: O'D *Journ. Kilkenny Archaeol. Soc.* 2nd ser. I ii (1858) 444–60.

We are told that this document was transcribed, by order of a certain Muirchertach O'Muiridhe, bishop of Clonmacnois, from the original entries which were in the Life of St. Ciarán (doubtless blank pages at the end of the Life used as a registry); and that Archbishop Ussher, in a report on the diocese of Meath, stated that this original transcription was in existence in his time, but " had lately been conveyed away." Copies of it were in the possession of Ussher and Sir James Ware, and Ware had a translation made by An Dubhaltach Mac Fir-Bhisigh, which is the present text. It contains an account of the various lands granted to the church of Clonmacnois by the several provincial kings and principal chieftains as a purchase for the right of them-selves and their descendants to be interred in a portion of the cemetery appropriated to their use, and for other privileges.

174. Life of St. Daig mac Cairill of Inis-Cáin-Dego (Inishkeen)

Vir venerabilis ac sanctus episcopus Daygeus . . . centesimo quadragessimo etatis sue anno feliciter obdormivit in Christo, q. c. P. et F. et S. s. v. ac r. D. per s. s. Amen.

MS: Cod. S. ff. 212–3ᵛ. EDS: *AA. SS. Boll.* Aug. III 656–62. — *AA. SS. ex Cod. S.* 891–902.

[32] *The memorial slabs of Clonmacnois* 96.

The obit of Dega or Daig mac Cairill is given by the Annals of Ulster in 587. He was of the Úi Néill family, and founder of Inis-Cáin-Dego (now Inishkeen, on the border of Louth and Monaghan), a church which is occasionally noticed in the annals down to the twelfth century. It must have belonged — at least for a time — to the *paruchia* of Clonmacnois, for Daig is represented to have been a disciple of Ciarán, and his artisan.[33]

The Life is a late abridgment. It is in the main a catalogue of the miracles performed by Daig, and of the monasteries which he founded, the lands which he obtained, and the saints with whom he was associated. The historical setting is quite fictitious, but it gives some information as to the scribal and handicraft work of the monasteries.

(e) INIS-CELTRA, TIR-DÁ-GLAS (TERRYGLASS) AND CLÚAIN-EDNECH (CLONENAGH)

R. A. S. Macalister " The history and antiquities of Inis Cealtra " *Proc. RIA* XXXIII C (1916) 93–174, 22 pls.

Inis-Celtra, " Church Island," sometimes spoken of as " Holy Island," is an island on the west side of the expansion of the Shannon river known as Loch Derg. It has some important church ruins, and many sepulchral slabs. Tír-dá-glas, " Field of two streams " (Terryglass), is near the eastern shore of Loch Derg, in the barony of Lower Ormond, Tipperary. It was, undoubtedly, the *ecclesia duorum agri rivorum* which, according to Adamnán,[34] was visited by Colum-cille. This district on the eastern side of Loch Derg had been Leinster territory in an earlier era, but must have passed under the dominion of Munster before the sixth century. Clúain-ednech, perhaps " Ivy meadow " (now Clonenagh, near Mountrath, in Leix), was, however, situated more than thirty miles due east in territory that remained permanently Lagenian. But these three churches, with others in the neighborhood of Loch Derg, and in Leinster and Connacht, are brought into association by the legends of their foundation, and by the records of their subsequent history.

The first name associated with Inis-Celtra is that of Mac Creiche,[35] a saint honored in the folk-lore of county Clare. Macalister may be right in seeing in him a pagan " incumbent " of the island — if, indeed, he was not a divinity.[36] There is a story of a nectar-giving tree, similar

---

[33] *Cf.* Fél. Oeng. Aug. 18, notes.

[34] *Vita Columbae* II xxxvi.

[35] Mac Creiche signifies literally " son of plunder." (An alternative is Mac Criche, " son of border " or " son of territory.") It is not a patronymic, but a nickname, or, perhaps, a name of pagan origin and significance to which we have no longer the clue.

[36] *Cf.* p. 314 *supra.*

to that at Lorrha,[37] which was probably a sacred tree of heathen times. Mac Creiche surrendered Inis-Celtra to Colum mac Crimthainn, or, as perhaps was the earlier form, " moccu Craumthannáin," [38] said to be of the royal line of the Lagin. He was the founder of the majority of these churches and of the community to which they belonged.

Colum died, according to the Annals of Ulster, in the year of the plague, 549. His first three successors were Nadcáem, Fintan (d. 603), and Colmán Stellan (d. 624).[39] Tír-dá-glas was founded, we are told, by Nadcáem, who, by entombing the body of Colum there, rendered it, in Irish law, the principal church of the *paruchia*.[40] Fintan, at the direction of Colum, who had lived there as a hermit, founded Clone-nagh.[41]

There is, however, another tradition which appears to know nothing of the activities of Mac Creiche and Colum at Inis-Celtra. According to it the church there was founded by St. Cáimín, who lived about a century after Colum: the Annals of Innisfallen give his death in 644.

175. Life of Mac Creiche

Incip[i]unt pauca de mirabilibus Mheic Creche .i. Mac Creche mac Pesslain . . . [Ends with a poem in 47 quatrains:] Maith an turus tangamar. . . . Gach ar fiad sa maith. [Last line is corrupt.] There follows the story of a cure wrought through the virtue of Mac Creiche's bell: Ro bái araile fer. . . . [Ends with a poem in 7 quatrains:] Mor na ferta sa dar lem. . . . Béraidh leis gach buaidh lán-mor.

MS: Brussels Bibl. roy. 2324-40 s XVII ff. 87-98 [transcribed by Michael O'Clery in June, 1634, from a copy made by Maelechlann Ó Callannáin in 1528 at Cell Mail-Odhráin (Killoran, barony Owney and Arra, co. Tipperary) for the *comarba* of Mac Creiche]. ED: Chas. Plummer *Misc. hag. Hib.* (Brussels 1925) 7-96 [with trans.]. *Cf.* O'C *MS Mat.* 630-2; Macalister *op. cit.* 135.

The life of Mac Creiche is late, fabulous, and of very little historical foundation. It is a combination of folk-lore, miracles, and monastic claims to tribute.

176. Life of St. Colum of Tír-dá-glas

Sanctus Columba de genere nobili Lagenensium de gente Chrauntanani . . . ubi cotidie per merita ipsius immensa beneficia a Domino praestantur per D. n. I. C., c. h. et g. in s. s. Amen.

MS: Cod. S. ff. 129-32[v].—Bodl. Rawl. B 485 ff. 139-42; Rawl. B 505 ff. 160-3. ED: *AA. SS. ex Cod. S.* 445-62. *Cf.* Colgan *AA. SS.* 356-7.

[37] *Cf.* p. 392 *infra.*

[38] AU has " nepos Craumthannain " and the Life, as below, " de gente Chrauntanani." The usual genealogy (*Fél. Oeng.*[1] p. clxxxii) makes him great-grandson of Cremthann and sixth in descent from Cremthannán, who was son of Cathair *mór*, one of the famous personages of the legendary history of the Lagin. Doubtless he was a member of the Úi Cremthannáin, who dwelt in the present Leix, in the neighborhood of Clúain-ednech.

[39] *Fél. Oeng.*[1] p. xc. The dates are from AU.

[40] *Cf.* p. 292 *supra.*

[41] For Oengus, author of the *Félire,* and his associations with Clonenagh, *cf.* pp. 471, 480 *infra.*

Colum's Life has some elements of antiquity — for example, the proper names — but as a whole must be a late production. It has value for social ideas and customs: the story of the saint's funeral is especially interesting. The text seems to have been expanded by borrowings from the tradition of the more famous Columba of Iona.

177. Life of St. Fintan

(i) Fintanus sanctus, filius Crumthini, genere Maccu Edagur, . . . inter choros angelorum suauia carmina canentium, ad eterna migrauit gaudia, r. D. n. I. C. simul cum P. et S. s. in s. s. Amen. (iii) Sanctus abbas Fintanus, uir uite uenerabilis, de prouinchia Laginensium . . . [as i].

MSS: (i) Cod. S. ff. 99ᵛ-103. (ii) Bodl. Rawl. B 485 ff. 148; B 505 f. 194. — Dublin Franciscan Convent A 24 pp. 285-91. (iii) Cod. K. ff. 74-6. Eds: (i) AA. SS. ex Cod. S. 289-304. (iii) Colgan AA. SS. 349 sqq.—AA. SS. Boll. Feb. III 16-21 [Colgan's text, with interpolations from S]. — VV. SS. Hib. I pp. lxx-lxxi, II 96-106.

Fintan moccu Echdach, or Edagur,[42] was, according to the genealogists, of the Fotharta, one of the branches of the Lagin. His Life is late, and not of special distinction. The earlier part is closely related to that of Colum mac Crimthainn.

178. Life of St. Cáimín

There is an unpublished metrical Life in Brussels Bibl. roy. 2324-40 ff. 264-73 (Caimin do dechad dar muir . . . lucht cráite mo primchille). Colgan had several texts, and has made a compilation from them in AA. SS. 746-7.

Cáimín is represented to have been half-brother to Gúaire of Aidne,[43] king of Connacht (d. 663 or 666), and a story of their relations is told in the secular tale Cath Cairn Chonaill. [44]

(f) Clúain-eóis (Clones) and St. Tigernach

Clúain-auiss, or Clúain-eóis, is the present Clones in Monaghan.

179. Life of St. Tigernach

(i) Venerabilis presul Tygernacus, regali ex progenie natus . . . signo crucis statim edito . . . [imperfect]. (ii) [As i] . . . secum perduxit, ubi perhenni perfruitur gloria in s. s. Amen. Ympnus ad Vesperas: Adest dies celebris sancti Tigernaci. . . . Et regno cum angelis celi confruamur. Amen. 21 ll. Ympnus ad Matutinum: Tigernach igne gratie . . . donet beata gloria. Amen. 32 ll.

MSS: (i) Cod. S. ff. 86ᵛ-7ᵛ [next folio, containing latter part of Life, has been removed]. (ii) Bodl. Rawl. B 485 s XIII/XIV ff. 116-8ᵛ; Rawl. B 505 s XIV/XV ff. 95ᵛ-7ᵛ. — Dublin Franciscan Convent A 24 A.D. 1627 pp. 21 sqq. Eds: AA. SS. Boll. April. I 402-4. — AA. SS. ex Cod. S. 211-20. — VV. SS. Hib. I pp. lxxxviii sq, II 262-9.

[42] MacN suggests that Dál Echdach, or Echach, which the moccu name points to, was a synonym of Fothairt, or Fotharta.
[43] Cf. pp. 421, 456 infra.
[44] ZCP III (1901) 203-19, and elsewhere. Cf. Plummer Misc. hag. Hib. Cat. no. 90. — For the psalter attributed to Cáimín, cf. no. 479 infra.

An entry in the Annals of Ulster, which, however, is of the ninth century or later, records the death of Tigernach of Clones in 549. An alternative date is 550. The Life of Tigernach, of which we have only slight variations of one version, is late, but has some appearance of being based on authentic traditions. His father is said to have been of the Leinstermen; [45] it was through his mother, Derfráich, that he was related to the Air-gíalla, in whose territory he built his church. He is said to have been baptised by Bishop Conlaed of Cell-dara at Brigit's orders, and to have been made a bishop himself at the command of Brigit. He was, we are told, bishop of Clochar (Clogher, co. Tyrone) before the founding of Clúain-auiss.

(g) Dam-Inis (Devenish) and St. Mo-Laisse

Dam-Inis, Daimh-Inis, "Ox Island," now Devenish, in Lower Loch Erne, about two miles from Enniskillen, contains a fine round tower and other remains of ecclesiastical architecture. There are many references in the annals to the church and to its abbots, the *comarbai* of St. Mo-Laisse. We still have the shrine which one of these, Cennfaelad (1001–1025), had made to contain Mo-Laisse's " Gospel " (*Soiscél Molaise*).[46]

180. Life of St. Mo-Laisse of Devenish

[Lat.] Postquam, diuina gratia operante, per sancti Patricii predicacionem. . . . Lasrianus feliciter in Domino obdormiuit; qui cum P. et S. S. u. et r. in s. s. Amen. [Ir.] Araile erlam [MS erum] uasal adamra somholta . . . ní deachaidh leo co buadach [last line of a passage in verse; there are several such passages in the Life].

MSS: (Lat.) Bodl. Rawl. B 485 ff. 94–7ᵛ; B 505 ff. 135–7ᵛ. — Dublin, Franciscan Convent A 24 pp. 31 *sqq.* (Ir.) BM Add. 18205 ff. 1–17 [" a well-written sixteenth century small quarto MS on vellum . . . , the remainder of which consists in a number of metrical pieces on the dues, privileges and rights of Molasius' successors. These, like all *memoria technica* productions, which is what they really are, have no literary merit. The Text, as though somewhat inattentively taken down from dictation (a common practice, responsible for much textual imperfection) is in places defective or obscure and, formally, altogether modernised; so also is the spelling, which is frequently incorrect to boot. The first page of the MS is much defaced; O'Curry renounced to make it out; but any errors in the pedigree as printed are of little consequence since, so far as Molasius is concerned, it is fictitious." — O'Grady *SG* II p. vii]. — RIA 23 A 43 [a poor paper copy of the preceding, made by O'Reilly]. — Brussels Bibl. roy. 4190–200 ff. 96 *sqq* [written by O'Clery in 1628–9]. EDS: (Lat.) *VV. SS. Hib.* I p. lxxiv, II 131–40. (Ir.) O'Grady *SG* I 17–37, II 18–34 [text of Addit. 18205, trans. of prose only].

Lasrén, or Lasrian, moccu Nechtai (i. e., of the Nechtraide, Nechtraigi, or Corcu Nechtae), who is usually referred to by the hypocoristic form Mo-Laisse, was among

---

[45] The pedigree is traced back through seven generations to Dáire *barrach*, son of Catháir *mór* — *Fél. Oeng.*² 110, 112.

[46] Geo. Coffey *Guide to the Celtic antiquities of the Christian period preserved in the National Museum, Dublin* (Dublin 1909) 44–5. The " Gospel " is lost.

the more famous of the saints of the sixth century. The Annals of Ulster enter his death under 564 and 571.

His Latin Life was compiled as a homily to be read on his festival, September 12. It is late in date, but appears to be an abbreviation of a longer treatise. The Irish Life is a curious compilation of the traditions and legends of Devenish and its neighborhood. It consists, in the main, of a series of poems on incidents in the saint's life, with paraphrases in prose. The poems may represent semi-popular compositions which gradually accumulated among the *littérateurs* of Devenish and the neighboring families. Then some person acting in the interests of that church collected and edited them, adding a prose accompaniment. His work was quite uncritical. He makes Mo-Laisse in old age go as a pupil to Finnian of Clonard (d. 549), and also by his prayers stay the great plague of 665. The annual payments due to Mo-Laisse's community from the people of Ireland because of this service are set forth. Other claims are based on the actions of Mo-Laisse at the time of the cursing of Tara and the *árd-rí* Diarmait by St. Rúadán.[47] He tried to make peace, and, failing in that, obtained salvation for the king's soul and the kingship for his descendants. " As for Molasius, however," the patriotic hagiographer proceeds, " after this he made no further stay at all at this contest with the saints by Tara; for in his eyes it was a lamentable thing that Tara must be abolished and the seat of Ireland's sovereignty put from her vigour: he knowing well as he did that in the end the saints must prove stronger than the king of Ireland."

Many other curious legends are associated with Molaise. The story of his birth is drawn from secular myth; it is also attached to Conchobar mac Nessa. He is said to have removed three times fifty Mananns out of hell in order to save the soul of a certain Manann, a jester.[48] Of his relics preserved at Devenish his missal (*soscéla beg* — little gospel) and his bell (*éloidhech*) were sent down from heaven while he was on pilgrimage to Rome, and his flagstone was that on which he sailed over the sea. A significant passage tells a story of his copying a " book of ways," or itinerary.

The Irish Life ends with a secular story of the exile of the Dartraige, a people whose name is preserved in that of the barony of Dartry, co. Monaghan. They are represented as originally of Munster, but banished because of the cruelties they practised on the Úi Conaill Gabra, and the assistance they gave foreigners and gentiles. It is probable that in some early exemplar a leaf or more was lost containing the conclusion of the Life of Molaise and the beginning of the story of the Dartraige.[49]

181. Mo-Laisse's Hymn

Abbas probata omnino. . . Dei prae participibus.   24 ll.

MS: LH(T) f. 31ᵛ.   EDS: *IER* V (1869) 224. — Dreves *An. Hymn.* XIX 222. — *LH²* I 158, II 220-1. — Blume *An. Hymn.* LI (1908) 327-8.

---

[47] *Cf.* no. 184.

[48] *Cf.* Aided Bresail: *Lis. Lives* p. xxvii.

[49] There may have been some association between the Dartraige and Devenish to cause the juxtaposition of the two narratives. In historical times the Dartraige seem to have been scattered through Monaghan, Leitrim, Sligo and Roscommon. In 869 Martan, abbot of Clonmacnois and Devenish, died. *CS* says he was of the " Dartraige Daiminnsi," Dartraige of Devenish. O'D thought this an error for D. Coininsi, the present barony of Dartry in Monaghan.

This alphabetical poem in praise of Mo-Laisse is found only in the later part of the Trinity College *Liber Hymnorum*, but is in Hiberno-Latin versification and probably dates from the early middle ages.

(h) Clúain-credal or Cell-Íte (Killeedy), the Church of St. Íte

The Úi Conaill Gabra were one of the branches of the Úi Fidgente [50] and occupied the western part of the plain of Limerick. The name is perpetuated in the present baronies of Upper and Lower Connello. Their patron saint was Deirdre, or Íte,[51] said to be by origin of the Dési, whose church was at Clúain-credal (perhaps " Meadow of devotion," " Holy Meadow "), later known as Cell-Íte. It is now Killeedy, in the barony of Glenquin, about five miles south of Newcastle and at the foot of the mountains of Slíab-Luachra, which formed the southern boundary of the Úi Conaill Gabra. The efficiency of her patronage is confirmed by an annalistic record of 552: " the battle of Cuilen, in which fell the Corcu Oche of Munster through the prayers of Ita of Clúain." [52] The Corcu Oche were a people of this same district, perhaps vassals of the Úi Conaill Gabra. The Annals of Ulster give two dates for her death, 570 and 577.[53] Her name is preserved in Rosmead (co. Westmeath) and in several churches of Cornwall. That her fame was wide-spread, even outside Ireland, is indicated by the mention of her in one of Alcuin's poems.[54]

As in the case of the majority of Munster monastic churches, little is known of the later history of Clúain-credal. It may have changed from a nunnery to a monastery for men, for we hear occasionally of abbots, and Íte is said to have prophesied that no nun would succeed her.[55] It was plundered at least twice by the Norsemen.[56]

---

[50] *Cf.* p. 364 *supra.*

[51] Mart. Don. preserves the tradition that " Deirdre was her first name," and the Life by John of Tynemouth gives this in the form " Derithea." The name Íte appears in many variations: Ita, Ida, Itha, Ithey, Issey, and, with the prefixes of affection *to*, thy, and *mo*, my, Teath, Mite and Mide.

[52] AU. *Cf.* Tig., FM, Keating (ed. ITS III 56).

[53] The obits of Gildas and Oenu of Clonmacnois, Ciarán's successor, are also entered under these two dates. Similar alternative entries with interval of seven years are found for other events.

[54] *Cf.* no. 340 ii.

[55] This is in connection with the disgusting story that, as one of her ascetic practices, she allowed her side to be eaten by a giant stag-beetle. *Cf.* Bk. Lec. f. 166ᵛ; *Fél. Oeng.*² 44. The legend is given as an annotation to the words of Fél. Oeng.: " she succoured many grievous diseases," so there is some basis for the hypothesis of Baring-Gould and Fisher, who rationalise the stag-beetle into a cancer.

[56] *Cf. CGG.*

182. Life of St. Íte

(i) De uita et miraculis beatissime uirginis Ite . . . secunda Brigida meritis et moribus, de agro, traditum est sepulture, regnante D. n. I. C., q. c. D. P. et S. S. u. et r., D. in s. s. Amen. (ii) Sacrosancta siquidem uirgo Ita . . . est terrae traditum, regnante, etc. (iii) Sancta uirgo Derithea, que alio nomine Itta . . . in Hibernia nata et conuersata, sancto fine quieuit in domino XVIII Kalend. februarii.[57]

MSS: (i) Cod. K. ff. 109ᵛ–12ᵛ. (ii) Bodl. Rawl. B 505 ff. 169ᵛ–72ᵛ. — Dublin Franciscan Convent A 24 pp. 212 sqq. (iii) Bodl. 240 s XIV p. 808. EDS: (i) Colgan AA. SS. 66 sqq [he " seems to have taken more than his usual liberties with the text " - Plummer]. — AA. SS. Boll. Jan. I 1062 sqq [3rd ed. (1863) II 344–50]. — VV. SS. Hib. I pp. lxxii sqq, II 116–30. (iii) Nova Legenda Anglie (ed. Horstman, Oxford 1901) II 543–4. Cf. Baring-Gould and Fisher Lives of the British Saints III 324–31.

Three recensions of Íte's Life are extant. Of these, Version iii is a short epitome made by John of Tynemouth in the fourteenth century. All versions probably go back to a very early original. Version i preserves a reference to an individual " whose son still lives."[58] This would place the original text of this passage not later than the middle of the seventh century — perhaps contemporary with Cogitosus.

In the annotations to Fél. Oeng., Jan. 15, in LBr and Laud 610 there is a poem in six quatrains, ascribed to Íte but obviously of much later date. It is based on the legend, told of many saints, that she received the Infant Jesus in her arms. Ísucán . . . cé beth am ucht Íssucán. EDS: Fél. Oeng.¹ p. xxxv; Fél. Oeng.² 44–5. TRANS: Geo. Sigerson Bards of the Gael and Gall 2nd ed. (London 1907) 165–6.

(i) MAG-BILE (MOVILLE) AND BISHOP FINNIAN

Mag-Bile, or Magh-Bile, " the plain of the old [and sacred?] tree," is the present Moville, about a mile north-east of Newtownards, in county Down. This was in the " fifth," or province, of the Ulaid and on the borders of their own túath, and became the site of their chief church. It was founded by a member of the Dál Fiatach find, the royal dynasty of the Ulaid. This was St. Vinnio, Finnio, or Finnian,[59] moccu Fiatach, who died, according to the Annals of Ulster, in 579. It would seem that ancient hagiographers have confused in some degree his acta with those of his namesake of Clonard, just as modern commentators have disputed as to which should be identified with the " Vennianus " of Columbanus and the " Venniaus " of the earliest Irish

---

[57] In An. Boll. XVII 50, 159, a fourth Life is cited " de Magno Legendario Austriaco ": Igitur secundum Pauli ap. preceptum . . . et ecclesia S. Brigide dicitur. Cf. Plummer Misc. hag. Hib. Cat. no. 267.

[58] It must be remembered, however, that the hagiographers are suspected of occasionally manufacturing, out of whole cloth, such touches of verisimilitude.

[59] The name has many variations: cf. p. 375 supra.

penitential.[60]   There is little doubt that the " episcopus Finnianus " of Cuimíne *ailbe* [61] and the " Findbarrus episcopus," "Vinnianus episcopus," and " episcopus Finnio " of Adamnán [62] was the saint of Mag-Bile. But the hagiographers went on to identify our Finnian with a Finnian of Druim-Finn [63] (perhaps Dromin, co. Louth), to whose quarrel with Colum-cille legend ascribed the exile of the latter from Ireland, and with Frediano, bishop of Lucca in Italy.[64] Incredible as is the last supposition, it had the result of incorporating into the Life of Frediano, and thereby preserving, *anecdota* from the Life of Finnian. One such is a reference to the bringing of " gospels " from Rome to Ireland, a tradition which presents itself also in *Félire Oengusso*.[65] Modern scholars have suggested that Finnian may have introduced into Ireland one of the first copies there known of St. Jerome's Vulgate.

183. Life of St. Finnian of Mag-Bile

Reuerentissimus pontifex Finanus, qui et Wallico nomine Winninus . . . in loco qui ab eius wallico nomine Kilwinin appellatur.

MSS: BM Cotton. Tiberius E i. A.D. 1325×1350. EDS: *Nova Legenda Anglie* (ed. Horstman, Oxford, 1901) I 444–7.

With the exception of a brief notice in the *Breviary of Aberdeen*,[66] the only Latin Life of Finnian is that which John of Tynemouth, in the first half of the fourteenth century, abridged from some text now lost. He obtained it from Welsh sources.[67]

On Colmán mac Mur-chon of Mag-Bile, see pp. 269, 332 *supra*.

(j) Lothra (Lorrha) and St. Rúadán

Lothra, now Lorrha, in northern Tipperary near Loch Derg, about five miles north-east of Terryglass, was one of the most important of the

[60] *Cf.* pp. 240, 375 *supra*. If the received chronology of the Finnians, Gildas and Columbanus is correct, it would favor the equating of Columbanus's Venniaus with this Finnian. Tradition, however, points to Finnian of Clonard.

[61] Cap. iii, iv. *Cf.* no. 213.

[62] *Vita Columbae* I i, II i, III iv. *Cf.* no. 214.

[63] If he is not a doublet of Finnian of Mag-Bile. *Cf.* pp. 435, 442.

[64] *Cf.* no. 40.

[65] Under Sept. 10 Finnian is said to have come over sea " with law," which the glossator interprets as meaning with the Law of Moses, or with the Gospel, " for it is Findia that first brought the whole gospel to Ireland." *Cf.* Todd *St. Patrick* 104 *sqq*; H. J. Lawlor " The Cathach of St. Columba " *Proc. RIA* XXXIII C (1916) no. xi.

[66] *Cf.* p. 484 *infra*.

[67] The sojourn of Finnian at Candida Casa, or Whitherne, is mentioned in the preface to Mugint's Hymn (no. 90), as well as in the Lives. — Finnian is a character in the legend of Túan mac Cairill (KM *Voyage of Bran* II (London 1897) 287 *sqq*).

monastic churches of Munster. Its founder, St. Rúadán, was said to be of the Eoghanacht of Cashel, the dominant race of the southern province from the fifth to the tenth century. His death is assigned to the year 584.[68]

184. Life of St. Rúadán

(i) Rodanus sanctus, filius Birri, ex nobili genere natus. . . . Ruodanus magnum honorem et premium habet in celis, in conspectu eterni regis omnipotentis D. et D. n. I. C., c. h. et g. in s. s.   Amen.   (ii) Sanctus Ruadanus de nobilioribus trahens originem . . . [as (i)].   (iii) Beatissimus abbas Ruadhanus de nobilissimo genere Hybernie . . . honorem et premium sempiternum in celis [habet] in conspectu eterni P., et I. C. F. eius, D. n., s. S. Paracliti, c. t. et u. D. est h. et g. in s. s.   Amen.   (iv) Ba soichenelach inti hisin d'fuil riograide Mumhan .i. Ruadhán finn . . . ar naen aird-ri, aga fil an sith suthain 7 comhlanas an uile maithesa, et reliqua. [Appendix] Fechtus dia ndeachaid anti naomh Rúadan . . . gur moradh ainm De 7 Ruadhain desin.

MSS: (i) Cod. S. ff. 106–8.   (ii) Bodl. Rawl. B 485 ff. 145–7ᵛ; B 505 ff. 97ᵛ–100. — Dublin Franciscan Convent A 24 pp. 14 *sqq.*   (iii) Cod. K. ff. 86–8ᵛ. — TCD 175 ff. 53 *sqq.*   (iv) [Irish] Brussels Bibl. roy. 2324–40 *s* XVII ff. 193–201ᵛ, 160ᵛ–1. — RIA A. 4. 1 (Stowe IX) pp. 287 *sqq.*   EDS: (i) *AA. SS. Boll.* Apr. II 382–6. — *AA. SS. ex Cod. S.* 319–32.   (iii) *VV. SS. Hib.* I pp. lxxxvi *sq,* II 240–52.   (iv) *BNE* I pp. xl, 317–29, II 308–20, 362–3.   *Cf.* Plummer *Misc. hag. Hib.* Cat. no. 173.

The different recensions of Rúadán's Life appear to go back to a common original, which, however, must have been of comparatively late date.[69] The first recension is probably a careful abbreviation of the original. The second varies only slightly from the first. The fourth seems to be an Irish translation from Latin, but not from any of the still surviving texts. The greater part of the Life forms a catalogue of churches founded and miracles wrought. There is here a story somewhat similar to that in the Life of Finnian of Clonard[70] regarding the wonderful food-giving tree at Rúadán's monastery, and the relations between Rúadán and Finnian.

Rúadán's name is associated in Irish tradition especially with the story of his cursing of Tara, the ancient residence of the kings of Ireland. The development of this story was, we may believe, the work of the secular story-tellers, from whom it was adopted, perhaps with modifications, by the hagiographer.[71] At its base there may have been a brief early record of a struggle between the saint and the *árd-rí* over the right of sanctuary, a fruitful source of trouble between Church and State. It was generally assumed that Tara was abandoned because of the curse of Rúadán. But, in addition to the probability that the whole story of the cursing is an invention of a much later age, it appears that Tara continued to be a royal residence for nearly a century. Dr. Norman Moore suggested that it was finally deserted as a result of the great epidemic of 664–5, in which the joint sovereigns, Diarmait and Blathmac, died.

---

[68] Tig.

[69] One passage in Version III preserves the formula " noster senex," pointing to composition in Rúadán's community. This must be a survival from an earlier stage in the development of the text. In its present form it certainly implies that the monastery of Lothra was a thing of the past. Under 1106 FM record the death of a *comharba* of Rúadán: he is probably to be classed with the erenaghs of Lothra of whom we hear from the middle of the tenth century.

[70] No. 165; *cf.* p. 384 *supra.*

[71] *Cf.* Stair ar Aed Baclám: O'Grady *SG* I 66–71, II 70–4.

(k) Bishop Aed mac Bricc

Aed, son of Brecc, is one of the few Irish saints the basis of whose fame is personal and general, rather than monastic. His principal churches were Cell-áir (" Church of slaughter," or " defeat "?), now Killare in Westmeath, and Slíab-liac (" Stony mountain "), at the promontory now called Slieve League, on the northern side of Donegal bay. They were not places of consequence, and contributed but little to the development and propagation of Aed's legend. But the fact that he was of the royal Úi Néill family, and his reputation for sanctity and especially as a patron through whose supernatural aid headaches might be cured, insured to him lasting fame. He was known as the *sui-liag*, the " master-physician."[72] His obit is given under 589 and 595.[73]

185. Life of St. Aed mac Bricc

(i) Aidus sanctus episcopus, qui vocatur filius Briccii, . . . hodie ad celum migravit: ubi sine merore in eternum gaudebit, r. D. n. J. C. c. P. et S. s. in s. s. Amen. (iii) Beatissimus Edus episcopus filius Bricht . . . migrauit ad celum. R. D. n. I. C., cui est magnificentia ab omni creatura cum eodem D. P. et S. s., qui sine fine u. et r. per o. s. s. Amen.

MSS: (i) Cod. S. ff. 108ᵛ-14. (ii) Bodl. Rawl. B 485 ff. 97ᵛ-103; B 505 ff. 149ᵛ-54. — Dublin Franciscan Convent A 24 pp. 165 *sqq.* (iii) Cod. K. ff. 134-5(2). — TCD 175 (E. 3. 11) ff. 110ᵛ *sqq.* Eds: (i) *AA. SS. ex Cod. S.* 333-60. (iii) Colgan *AA. SS.* 418 *sqq.* — *VV. SS. Hib.* I pp. xxvi-xxviii, 34-45. — All 3 in *AA. SS. Boll.* 10 Nov. IV 495-531. — *Cf. Journ. RSAI* VI 325 *sqq.*

The three recensions of this Life are not far removed from a common original, to which the text of *Codex Salmanticensis* is nearest. Version ii, and, to a greater degree, Version iii, have been toned down and curtailed. Versions i and ii were intended to serve as homilies for the saint's festival.

The Life on which our texts depend was compiled at a late date, probably the twelfth century, and not in Aed's own community. It is a composite production, drawn in part from genuine legends — in some cases several versions of the same story were incorporated — but consisting largely of matter taken over quite freely from secular sources or from the common stock of hagiographic material. Some of the anecdotes convey interesting information: *e.g.*, as to ploughing; as to the building of those earthen ramparts that surrounded most monasteries and well-to-do residences; as to hallucinations caused by druids.

186. Prayer against headache

O rex, O rector regminis. . . . Sanum, atque vigilat. 5 stanzas.

MS: Carlsruhe Landesbibl. Cod. Augiensis CCXXI s VIII f. 191. Eds: Mone *Lateinische Hymnen des Mittelalters* III (Freiburg 1855) 181-2. — *Lis. Lives* 324. — Blume *An. hymn.* LI (1908) 315-6. *Cf.* Reeves *Proc. RIA* VII (1858) 91.

[72] So in a fragmentary Life of Brigit, Rawlinson B 512 ff. 31-5ᵛ.   [73] AU.

St. Aed mac Bricc is invoked against headaches in this riming, jingling Latin hymn which is at least as old as the eighth, and might be of the seventh century. It has a resemblance to the *loricae.*

(l) ACHAD-BÓ (AGHABOE) AND ST. CAINNECH

Achad-bó, " the cow-field," is the present Aghaboe, barony of Upper Ossory, Leix. It became the principal church of the Osraige, surpassing their earlier religious capital of Saigir. It was not till after the coming of the Anglo-Normans that it was itself displaced by Cell-Cainnich (Kilkenny), which had probably once been a subordinate church of the *paruchia.* Cainnech founded other churches in both Ireland and Scotland. In Ireland we hear especially of Dromachose in his home-land, the Cianachta of what is now northern Derry, and of Clúain-Bronig in Offaley, near Birr. It is probable that in Scotland the majority of his churches were later dedications;[74] he came to be known there as Kenneth and was the most popular of Irish saints after Colum-cille and Brigit.[75]

187. Life of St. Cainnech

(i) Sanctus Kannechus de genere Corcodalann. . . . Et accipiens eukaristiam de manu ejus, migravit ad Dominum: cui h. et g. in s. s. Amen. (iii) Cainnicus, sanctus abbas, de genere Connath Dhuinne Gemhyn . . . in monasterio Achadh bó quinto Idus Octobris feliciter migrauit ad D. I. C., cui est h. et g. in s. s. Amen.

MSS: (i) Cod. S. ff. 114–110^V (*recte* 119^V). (ii) Bodl. Rawl. B 485 ff. 128^V–34^V; B 505 ff. 143–7^V [imperfect]. — MS of Franciscan Convent, Dublin, pp. 142 *sqq.* (iii) Cod. K. ff. 124–7.[76] EDS: (i) *Vita S. Kannechi* (Dublin 1853) [printed by the Marquess of Ormonde as extra vol. of Kilkenny Archaeol. Soc.]. — *AA. SS. ex Cod. S.* 361–92. (iii) *VV. SS. Hib.* I pp. xliii–xlv, 152–69. *Cf. AA. SS. Boll.* Oct. V 54–6, 642–6, and Suppl. 74*–76*.

Cainnech, or Caindech, moccu Dálon (that is, of the Corcu Dalann, a branch of the Cianachta Glinne Gaimen, who dwelt in the present barony of Keenaght, co. Derry) was a contemporary and apparently a companion of Colum-cille. He is mentioned several times by Adamnán.[77] It would seem that he spent part of his earlier life in the western isles of Scotland, but later removed to southern Ireland, where he founded Clúain-Bronig and Achad-bó. The Annals of Ulster record Cainnech's birth at 521 and 527, and his death at 599 and 600.

The Latin Life of Cainnech is preserved in three versions, all of which go back clearly to a common original. The text of *Codex Salmanticensis* is nearest to that original, which may, possibly, have been in Irish. The Life, although containing an abundance of wonderful anecdotes, has more of the historical note than the greater number of

[74] Reeves *Ad.* 417; Forbes *Kalendars of Scottish saints* 227.
[75] No. 220 (lii) is a poem attributed to Cainnech.
[76] BM Clarendon 39 contains Ware's extracts from Rawl. B 505; TCD 1100 transcripts by Bishop Reeves from Cod. S. and Cod. K. TCD 1059, also by Reeves, is a transcript of Cod. K, with notes.
[77] *Lib.* I *cap.* iv; II xiii, xiv; III xvii.

Irish *vitae sanctorum.* It is an exceedingly interesting document, although some passages are taken over directly from Adamnán's *Vita Columbae,* and others, especially accounts of miracles, are of the common subject-matter of hagiology. The value of the Life for topography is considerable, and it has several important references to social customs and institutions. Among these are preaching on Sunday; [78] writing; [79] libraries; [80] the evangeliarium, *Glass Kannechi,* written by the saint; [81] horse-back riding; [82] the door called *dorncleth;* [83] the oath-bound outlaws known as *dibergich.* [84] But the most noteworthy passage is, perhaps, that relating to the savage custom of *gialcherd,* or *gallcherd:* [85]

" On another day, when St. Cainnech, in the land of the South Leinstermen, came to a great assembly of the people around their king, Cormac mac Diarmait, a little boy was led forth by the people to a cruel and very pitiable death, the *gialcherd.* Seeing this horrible deed, Cainnech besought the king for the boy's liberty, but was refused. He prayed to God, and his prayer was heard. For the boy was thrown on the spears placed pointing upwards, but the spears could not kill nor harm him, — except that his eyes were always crossed as a result of looking on the horrible punishment. He is Dolue Lebdeic. The king gave him to Cainnech; afterwards he was an illustrious man, whose monastery is called Kell Tolue [Killaloe]." [86]

188. Legend of Cromm *dubh*

Araile laithi do Chaindech noem a n-oilen Rosa Cre . . . .

MSS: Bk. Lis. f. 68ᵛ. — Bk. of Fer. f. 62ᵛ.—RIA 24 L ɪɪ f. 21. Eᴅ: Thos. Roche *Irisleabhar Muighe Nuadhad* I (1910) pt. iii 76. *Cf.* J. P. Dalton " Cromm Cruaich of Magh Sleacht " *Proc. RIA* XXXVI (1922) C iv p. 51 and *passim.*

Anciently throughout Ireland — and even now, or quite recently, in some parts — the last Sunday in July was held in special honor under the name *Domnach Cruimm duibh,* " Black Cromm's Sunday." This must be the survival of a pagan festival of the god Cromm *dubh,* identical, doubtless, with Cromm *Cruaich.* But the legend here noted gives another explanation of the name: Cainnech heard from a demon how St. Patrick and his company had come from heaven to save the soul of a certain man named Cromm *dubh.*

For poems referring to Cainnech see pp. 437 *sqq infra.*

(m) Bᴇɴᴅ-ᴄʜᴏʀ (Bᴀɴɢᴏʀ) ᴀɴᴅ Sᴛ. Cᴏᴍɢᴀʟʟ

Bend-chor,[87] the modern Bangor, was situate on the southern shore of Belfast Loch. Scholars are familiar with this monastery because of

---

[78] *Cap.* xviii.   [79] xlii.   [80] xxxiii.   [81] lii.   [82] xlviii, li.   [83] xlvii.
[84] xlv. *Cf. Vita s. Albei* xxxvi: *AA. SS. ex Cod. S.* 251.
[85] *Gialcherd,* " treatment of hostages"; *gallcherd,* " foreign art." *Cf.* HZ *Göttingische gelehrte Anzeigen* 1891 pp. 187–8: he considers it a Viking custom; but *cf. RC* XII 393 *sqq.*
[86] xli. *Cf.* p. 404 *infra.*
[87] The name appears to signify a row of points or peaks. *Cf.* KM " Zur keltischen Wortkunde " iv no. 66: *Sitzungsb. d. k. preuss. Akad. d. Wissensch.* 1913 no. xlix pp. 952–3.

the association with it of the saints Columbanus of Bobbio and Malachy
of Armagh, and also of the liturgical manuscript known as the Antiphonary of Bangor. It was founded, according to the Annals of Ulster, in
555 or 559. In the seventh and eighth centuries Bend-chor was one of
the principal monastic churches, but its position exposed it to the attacks
of the Norsemen. Although the annals record what appears to be an
unbroken succession of *comarbai* of St. Comgall, the monastic body
declined and by the tenth century seems to have disappeared. In the
twelfth it was restored by the reforming St. Malachy.[88]

The founder of Bend-chor was Comgall moccu Aridi, of the Dál
Araide, the Pictish race whose territory lay but a short distance north
and west of Bend-chor. The Annals of Ulster date his life as from 515
or 519 to 601 or 602; the Annals of Tigernach, under 602, and the Martyrology of Tallaght say that he died on May 10, in the ninety-first
year of his age and the fiftieth year, third month and tenth day of his
abbacy. The hymns of Bend-chor, [89] composed in the seventh century,
testify to the honor accorded Comgall in his own monastery. From
Jonas of Bobbio,[90] writing about 640, we learn that he was the master
of Columbanus, and from Adamnán,[91] some forty years later, that he
was the close friend of Columba of Iona. He is called the sole heir of
Columba's virtues and merits in a notice of that saint's death, written,
in the opinion of Zimmer, when the news thereof arrived on the Continent.[92]

189. Life of Comgall

(i) De aquilonali Hybernie regione, nomine Dail n-Araidhe . . . in honore nostri patroni Comgalli con-
struxit, et in nomine sancte Trinitatis, P. et F. et S. S., cui est h. et p. in s. s. Amen. (ii) Beatus ac
venerabilis abbas Comgallus, nobilissimo Aradensium genere . . . Octagessimo autem etatis sue anno
vi° idus maii, migravit ad Christum: q. c. P. et F. et . S. s. v. et r. D. per o. s. s. Amen.

MSS: (i) Cod. K. ff. 90ᵛ-4. — TCD 175 ff. 57 *sqq.* (ii) Cod. S. 191ᵛ-2 [the folio
which followed 191 is missing]. — Bodl. Rawl. B 485 ff. 153 *sqq*; B 505 ff. 100 *sqq.* —
Dublin Franciscan Convent A 24 pp. 46 *sqq.* EDS: (i) Fleming *Collectanea sacra*
(Louvain 1667) 303-13 [text of Cod. K., with extracts from Cod. S.]. — *AA. SS. Boll.*
Mai. II 582-8. — *VV. SS. Hib.* I pp. lviii *sq*, II 3-21 [Cod. K. collated with TCD
175]. (ii) *AA. SS. Boll.* Mai. II 580-2. — *AA. SS. ex Cod. S.* 773-8.

Two versions of the Life of Comgall are available. The first, fairly extensive, seems
to be based on an Irish original.[93] Either the translation, or the original, or probably
both, were prepared at Bangor by a member of the community.[94] The date must

---

[88] *Cf.* pp. 766–7 *infra.*　　[89] No. 92.　　[90] I iv. *Cf.* no. 48.　　[91] I xlix; III xiii, xvii. *Cf.* no. 214.
[92] *Cf.* no. 413; also *Sitzungsb. d. k. preuss. Akad. d. Wissensch.* 1909 no. xxi pp. 584 *sqq.*
[93] *Cf. cap.* xxi.
[94] *Cf.* lviii " nostri patroni Comgalli "; xvii " peruenientes huc," altered by a second hand in Cod. K.
to " illic."

be either as early at least as the tenth century, or subsequent to about 1125, after the monastery of Bangor had been restored by Malachy. The second version, represented by several texts which, though not quite identical in form, are so in substance, is short and was prepared as a summary of a longer narrative — a narrative which differed, however, from Version i.

190. Story of Comgall and a foreign monk

Manach cráibdech táinic tairis anoir . . . .

MSS: Bodl. Rawl. B 512 *s* XIV/XV f. 141ᵛ. — Bk. Lis. f. 69ᵛ. — BM Egerton 92 *s* XVI f. 30. — Edinburgh Nat. Lib. of Scot. XXVI f. 2ᵛ. — TCD H. 3. 17 col. 678. ED: KM *Gaelic Journal* IV 229; *Anec.* III (1910) 9–10 [text only, from the Edin. MS.].

A curious story of a foreign monk who comes from the East to Bangor to vie in devotion with Comgall. A Latin version is given in *Vita Comgalli* I *cap.* xlvi.

On Comgall see also Plummer *Misc. hag. Hib.* Cat. nos. 124–6.

In the library of the monastery of Fulda there was, in the ninth century, a copy of a rule of Comgall, apparently in Latin. (G. Becker *Catalogi bibliothecarum antiqui* (Bonn 1885) 30.) This rule is no longer known: probably it formed the basis for the rule of Columbanus (no. 45). The Irish verses usually entitled *Ríaguil in Choimded*, the " Rule of the Lord " (no. 268 i), is in one MS attributed to Comgall, but this hardly justifies its inclusion among documents of Bend-chor.

(n) CLÚAIN-FERTA-MOLÚA (CLONFERTMULLOE OR KYLE) AND DRUIM-SNECHTA (DRUMSNAT), CHURCHES OF ST. MO-LÚA

Lugaid moccu Ochae, whose birth is recorded in 554 and death in 609,[95] was of the Corcu Oche, or Oiche.[96] People of this name dwelt in Fernmag (now Farney), in the present Monaghan, and among the Úi Fidgente, in the plain of Limerick. According to the Lives, Lugaid was of the southern Corcu Oche, who, the annals tell us, two years before his birth suffered a severe defeat " through the prayers of Ita of Clúain[-credail]," [97] patroness of their neighbors the Úi Conaill Gabra. But it may be noted that his first church-foundation, Druim-snechta, " Ridge of snows " (now Drumsnat, south-west of the town of

[95] AU.

[96] The Corcu Oche were, it would seem, an ancient race who, in the sixth century, either were already or became — perhaps as a result of the battle of 552 — vassals to the Úi Fidgente, a kindred sprung from the Eoganachta, the dominating people of Munster. But some genealogists and hagiographers attached the race, and the saint, to the Úi Fidgente line.

[97] *Cf.* no. 182.

Monaghan), was in the region of the northern race. His more famous monastery was Clúain-ferta-Molúa, "Molúa's Meadow of graves" (Clonfertmulloe, now Kyle, in Leix, northwest of Borris-in-Ossory), in the land of the Osraige, and he is represented as descending, on his mother's side, from the Dál Birn, a name which seems to have been a synonym for Osraige. He is also associated, either as inmate or founder, with several other churches.

The saint was popularly known by the hypocoristic form of his name, Mo-Lúa.

191. Life of St. Mo-Lúa of Clúain-ferta-Molúa

(i) Sanctus Lugidus de genere Corchode . . . et coronam vite eterne accepit a Domino. Cui h. et g. in s. (ii) Fuit vir vite venerabilis de provinchia Mumenie, de regione Hua Figenti, de plebe Corchoiche, nomine Molua . . . proinde coronam vite eterne accepit a D.D. n. I.C., cui c.D. P. et S.S. h. et g. manet in s. s.   Amen.   (iii) Beatissimus abbas Lugidius, generosis ortus parentibus . . . et collaudemus Filium Dei, qui c. P. et S. s. v. et r. D. per o. s. s.   Amen.

MSS: (i) Cod. S. ff. 94^v-9^v.   (ii) Cod. K. ff. 112^v-6. — TCD 175 f. 92 [last 11 cap. only].   (iii) Cod. S. ff. 202-12. — Bodl. Rawl. B 505 ff. 126-7^v. — Dublin Franciscan Convent A 24 pp. 99 sqq.   EDS: (i) AA. SS. Boll. Aug. I 342-52. — AA. SS. ex Cod. S. 261-88.   (ii) Fleming Collectanea sacra (Louvain 1667) 368 sqq. — VV. SS. Hib. I pp. lxxxiii sq, II 206-15.   (iii) AA. SS. ex Cod. S. 879-90.

Three versions of Mo-Lúa's Life have been handed down which, though differing in certain details, go back to a common origin.   The first two are quite full, the third very much abbreviated.   The contents of the third have the appearance of memoranda, to be expanded by the preacher, and the form of its conclusion shows that it was to be read, or preached, to "the brethren" on the saint's festival.   Moreover, while the first two versions represent the story as told at Clúain-ferta-Molúa, the third is a Druim-snechta composition.[98]   Version i is in some parts, and perhaps as a whole, a translation from the Irish.   None of the extant versions seems to be older than the twelfth century, but the greater part of the subject-matter may go back to a text or texts written when Bend-chor and Clúain-ferta-Molúa were still flourishing, that is, not later than the ninth century.

The Life of Mo-Lúa, particularly in its first version, is an interesting document.   It is especially valuable for place and personal names, and for many pictures of conditions and customs in secular and monastic life.   The following passages may be noted: the advice of the king to Mo-Lúa not to found a church in his own country;[99] the herding of lambs, pigs and especially calves, to keep them from their mothers, duties referred to repeatedly in the acta sanctorum, but nowhere more frequently than here; the (juridical?) distraint of cattle;[100] the making of butter;[101] the use of mills;[102] the custom of heating water for the table by putting a hot iron in it;[103] dice;[104] the ampu-

---

[98] The matter relating to Druim-snechta is relatively much fuller in iii: while in i we are told only that Mo-Lua remained there, in iii it is stated that he founded the church. In Cod. S. the heading of i is "Incipit vita sancti Lugidi Cluonaferta," of iii "Incipit vita Molua Droma-snecta."

[99] Cap. xxx.   The story, no doubt, was invented to explain why no church of Mo-Lúa existed in what was believed to be his home-land.

[100] ii.   [101] lix.   [102] xi, xxii.   [103] xvii.   [104] xxx.

tation of a foot; [105] the captive allowed to beg his ransom; [106] the body of criminals designated " scola diaboli," perhaps the " dibergich " of *Vita Cannechi*; [107] the royal demand for refection at a monastery; [108] the picture of the religious leader setting out on the road to found a church, " with a few monks and five cows "; [109] pilgrimage; [110] the exhortation to confession; [111] the monastic rule; [112] the office of *oeconimus*; [113] the poet at a monastery; the work of the monks in cutting down the forest; [114] the saint's aversion to women; [115] and the picture of the little house in which an inmate of the monastery dwelt, connected with which is a charming anecdote of the saint's stratagem to induce such a one to accept a companion.[116]

It should be observed that this Life has some features of real biography, and gives to its hero an individual personality.

(o) LAND-ELO (LYNALLY) AND ST. COLMÁN ELO

Land-, or Lann-Elo, the " house," or " monastery of Elo," is the modern Lynally, south-west of Tullamore, in Offalley. Its reputed founder was Colmán moccu Sailni (*i.e.*, of the Dál Sailne, an Ulster race, probably a branch of the Dál Araide),[117] who, from his church, is known as Colmán Elo. The annalists place his death in 611, being, according to Tigernach, the fifty-sixth year of his age.

192. Life of St. Colmán Elo

(i) Fuit vir vite venerabilis, nomine Colmanus, filius Beugne,[118] . . . cum magno honore et psalmis et ympnis et canticis spiritalibus laudantes et benedicentes Dominum: c. est h. et g. in s. s. Amen. (iii) Fuit vir vite venerabilis, Colmanus nomine, de nobili gente Hybernie, . . . multi in psalmis et ympnis et canticis spiritualibus laudantes et benedicentes sanctam Trinitatem, P. et F. et S. S., c. est h. et g. atque p. in s. s. Amen. (iv) Colman Eala immorro, do sliocht Eiremhoin . . . go mbia for nemh; et reliqua. [Ends imperfect. Contains five sets of verses: Treisi an ecclas na gach rígh, 96 ll.; Dá chích acc Colman Eala, 142 ll.; Tri haonaighe Erenn búdhéin, 24 ll.; Do bhainnib líontar lathrach, 28 ll.; Cluain da crand, 57 ll.]

MSS: (i) Cod. S. ff. 123ᵛ-9ᵛ. (ii) Bodl. Rawl. B 485 ff. 135-8ᵛ [imperfect]; B 505 ff.139ᵛ-43 [imperfect]. — Dublin Franciscan Convent A 24 pp. 130 *sqq.* (iii) Cod. K. ff. 129ᵛ-32ᵛ. — TCD 175 ff. 106 *sqq.* (iv) [Irish] Brussels Bibl. roy. 2324-40 s XVII ff. 219-26. EDS: (i) *AA. SS. ex Cod. S.* 415-44. (iii) *VV. SS. Hib.* I pp. lvii *sq*, 258-73. (iv) *BNE* I pp. xxxii *sq*, 168-82, II 162-76, 345-7.

From certain passages in Adamnán's Life of Colum-cille, and from church-dedications in Scotland,[119] we may infer that Colmán Elo spent part of his earlier life in that

[105] ix. [106] xli. [107] xliv; *cf.* p. 395. [108] li. [109] xxxi. [110] xlii; *cf.* Version III *cap.* xxxiii. [111] xxxvii. [112] lxiv. [113] xxii, xxiii, lvii. [114] xxxviii. [115] xxviii, xxxii. [116] xxxvi.

[117] The hagiographer, however, attached him to the Úi Néill. His origin from the Dál Araide may have a bearing on the close connection which existed between Land-Elo and Mac Nisse's church of Condere. Colmán's Lives say nothing on the subject, and Mac Nisse's record only his prophecy of Colmán. *Cf.* p. 352 *supra.*

[118] This spelling points to a very old record. It is older linguistically than Beogna, the form used by Adamnán.

[119] Forbes *Kalendars of Scottish saints* (1872) 305.

country, in association with the founder of Iona. Adamnán speaks of his returning to Ireland in the year of Columba's death.[120]

The Latin Life of Colmán is not as interesting as many others, but it seems to be of fairly early date. It is quite largely a monastic production, and is of some value for the routine life of the monks. The three recensions depend ultimately on a common source which may have been written at Lann-Elo when that church was still flourishing — not later than the tenth century.

The Irish text is not a Life but a collection of *anecdota* in prose and verse having only a slight connection with the matter found in the Latin *vitae*. It may be a compilation, made in the later middle ages, of legends in prose and verse current among the Fir Cell [121] (occupying the baronies of Eglish, Ballycowan and Ballyboy, Offalley), whose patron Colmán was and in whose territory stood his church.[122]

(p) Árd-sratha (Ardstraw) and St. Eogan

Árd-sratha, " High strand," now Ardstraw, near Strabane, Tyrone, was claimed as a Patrician foundation,[123] but its patron in later days was a Bishop Eogan, who seems to have lived in the sixth century. Eogan was of the Dál Meisi Corb, one of the branches of the ruling kindred of the Lagin. In Tírechán's time Ardstraw was independent of, and regarded by him as hostile to, the community of Patrick.[124] There is but little material for the history either of the church or of its founder.

193. Life of St. Eogan

Sanctus ac venerabilis pontifex Eugenius . . . anima sancta per manus angelorum redditur Christo, c. h. et g. in s. s. Amen.

MSS: Cod. S. ff. 215ᵛ-7. Eds: *AA. SS. Boll.* Aug. IV 624-7. — *AA. SS. ex Cod. S.* 915-24.

This Life is, like many of the texts in the latter part of *Codex Salmanticensis*, a very late and abridged version, and has not much historical interest. One curious passage describes a heathen rite for the consecration of a spear.

(q) Fidnacha (Fenagh), the Church of St. Caillín

Fidnacha (Fenagh), also known as Dún-Baile, Beran-in-brait, and Cnoc-na-ríg, is in Leitrim, about three miles south-west of Ballinamore.

---

[120] *Vita Columbae* I v, II xv. Adamnán at one place calls him a " holy bishop," at another a " priest."

[121] O' Clery copied his text from a book belonging to Eachraidhe Ó Siaghail (O'Shiel) of Fir Cell.

[122] KM has edited, with trans., a quatrain addressed to Colmán as patron of horse-back riding. — *ZCP* I (1897) 455. See also Plummer *Misc. hag. Hib.* Cat. no. 101.

[123] LA f. 15: Patrick " came into Ardd Sratho and ordained Macc Ercae bishop." From this arises a note in the Calendar of Oengus to the effect that Eogan was a son of Bishop Erc, of Slane. *Fél. Oeng.*[1] p. clxvii, and Aug. 23.

[124] LA f. 11ᵛ. .

Part of an ancient church and monastery is still standing. The patron saint was Caillín mac Niatach, who, according to one tradition, was a disciple of Benignus, but is also made a contemporary of Colum-cille. He was patron likewise of the local princely family of Úa Ruairc. In the later middle ages the family of O'Roddy [125] were hereditary *comarbai* of Caillín at Fenagh.

Leabar Fidnacha, the " Book of Fenagh," is a manuscript in the Royal Irish Academy acquired about 1886 from the bishop of Ardagh. It was written in 1516 by Muirghes Ó Máil-Chonaire at the request of Tadhg O'Roddy, and seems to have been copied, with some additions and prose expansions of the verse, from a work which the scribe calls " the Old Book of Fenagh," or " the Old Book of Caillín." It contains a list of the lands, privileges, honors and rights of sanctuary attaching to Fenagh, with references to St. Caillín, chiefly in explanation and justification of the church's claims. The book is, in fact, an example of a *lebar sochair*.[126] Much of the matter is in verse, attributed to Caillín, Colum-cille, and Flann *Mainistrech*, or anonymous.[127] A few of the poems are also found elsewhere. The bulk of the book is probably of the later middle ages, but doubtless was based on the traditions and customs of an earlier period.

The text has been published in full: W. M. Hennessy and D. H. Kelly *The Book of Fenagh in Irish and English, originally compiled by St. Caillin, archbishop, abbot, and founder of Fenagh, alias Dunbally of Moy-Rein tempore St. Patricii* (Dublin 1875).[128] *Cf.* Denis Murphy " On an ancient MS Life of St. Caillin of Fenagh, and on his shrine" *Proc. RIA* 3rd ser. I C 441–5 [read 28 June, 1886]. — The same Life of Caillín is in Brussels Bibl. roy. 2324–40 ff. 303–54, and, in part, in BM Cotton. Vesp. E. ii ff. 108-20·[A.D. 1535]. *Cf.* Plummer *Misc. hag. Hib.* Cat. no. 14; Flower *Cat.* 465-8.

(r) CORCACH (CORK) AND ST. BAIRRE

The city of Cork (in Irish *Corcagh*, " Marsh ") owes its origin to the monastery, probably at first a mere hermit's refuge, founded in early Christian times on an island in the midst of the marsh at the mouth of the river Lee. Of its reputed founder, St. Bairre, Barr (" Crest "), or Findbarr (" Fair-crest "), there is little trustworthy information — not even of the era in which he lived, although this seems to have been the sixth century. His Lives indicate that Cork was the head of a considerable *paruchia* of churches in southern Munster.

194. Life of St. Bairre

(Lat. i) Sanctus Dei electus atque dignus pontifex Barrus . . . episcopi Corcagie.   (Lat. ii) Sanctissimus Dei electus . . . ad caelum pertingere. Migrauit autem . . . regnaturus, &c.   (Ir. i) Mobarri dino do Connachtaibh . . . bail i ttaitne amail grein i naentaidh uasal-aithrech . . . A., M., 7 S. N.   Amen.

MSS: (Lat. i) Cod. K. ff. 132ᵛ-4. — TCD 175 (E. 3. 11) f. 109 *sqq.* (Lat. ii) Bodl. Rawl. B 485 ff. 118ᵛ-21; B 505 ff. 137ᵛ-9ᵛ. — Dublin Franciscan Convent A 24 pp.

125 *Cf.* p. 46 *supra.*   126 *Cf.* p. 300 *supra.*
127 They are entered under their incipits in R. I. Best's *Bibliography.*
128 Only a few copies were printed, and the work is now extremely rare.

124 *sqq.* (Ir. i) RIA Bk. Fer. *s* XV ff. 59ᵛ-60 [fragment]. — Brussels Bibl. roy. 2824-40 ff. 122ᵛ-8. — RIA A. 4. 1 (Stowe ix) pp. 1-17 [damaged]. (Ir. ii) RIA 23 B 1 *s* XIX pp. 506-28; 150 pp. 129-37 [imperfect]; 168 pp. 110-6. — Dublin King's Inns MS 19. EDS: (Lat. i) R. Caulfield *Life of St. Fin Barre* (1864). — *VV. SS. Hib.* I pp. xxxi *sq*, 65-74. (Lat. ii) Caulfield *op. cit.* (Ir. i) Patrick Stanton " The Life of St. Finbar of Cork " *Journ. Cork Hist. and Archaeol. Soc.* II (1893) 61-9, 87-94 [text, trans.]. — *BNE* I pp. xv *sq*, 11-22, II 11-21 [text, trans.]. *Cf. AA. SS. Boll.* Sept. VII 142-51; Baring-Gould and Fisher *Lives of the British Saints* III 20-4.

The Lives of Bairre are of the late middle ages, and quite fabulous. The Latin and first Irish recensions are not closely related, although they cover much the same ground. The second Irish recension seems an expansion, with variations, of the matter of the first. A legend in the second Latin version which tells how Bairre rode from Britain to Ireland on a horse loaned him by St. David is, doubtless, an old sea-myth which became attached to Bairre either because of his name or of the location of his church.

195. Old Irish Poem in praise of Bairre

Bairri bréo bithbúadach . . . barr broga Briúin. 2 stanzas.

MSS: Bodl. Laud 610. — BB. Quotation in the tract entitled " Duodecim partes poeticae." EDS: RTh *IT* III (1891) 57. — KM *Bruchstücke der alteren Lyrik Irlands* (*Abhandl. d. preuss. Akad. d. Wissensch.* 1919 phil.-hist. Kl. vii) (Berlin 1919) 23-4 [with Ger. trans.].

(s) CLÚAIN-COIRPTHE OR CELL-BERAIGH (KILBARRY) AND ST. BERACH

Clúain-coirpthe, " the polluted meadow," is the modern Kilbarry, on the Shannon river, in the parish of Termonbarry, barony of North Ballintober, Roscommon. It is said to have been founded by St. Berach, probably in the sixth century. Neither church nor saint holds a very prominent position in the literature, but in popular regard, especially in Connacht, they seem both to have stood high.

196. Life of St. Berach

(Ir.) Ego sitienti dabo [129] . . . naemh Beraigh . . . 7 co ro aitreabam in riced, in s. s. Amen. [Lat.] Inter cetera que Dei plena potentia, . . . et sic in pace dormiens, beatam animam suo reddidit Creatori. Oracio: Deus qui beatum Berachum . . . cum angelis adunari. Per Dominum.

MSS: (Ir.) Brussels Bibl. roy. 4190-200 ff. 71-87ᵛ. (Lat.) Bodl. Rawl. B 485 ff. 58ᵛ-62ᵛ; B 505 ff. 191ᵛ-4ᵛ. — Dublin Franciscan Convent A 24 pp. 275 *sqq.* EDS: Colgan *AA. SS.* 340 *sqq* [Lat. text, with extracts from Ir.]. — *AA. SS. Boll.* Feb. II 832-9 [reprint from Colgan]. — *VV. SS. Hib.* I pp. xxxiii *sq*, 75-86 [Lat.]. — *BNE* I pp. xvi, 23-43, II 22-43, 326-8 [Ir.].

Both versions of the Life of Berach are late, and do not offer evidence of having been based on early texts. The Irish appears to be earlier and more original than the

---

[129] The opening sections are the same as those of the Life of St. Caillín.

Latin. It is a homily for the saint's festival, and is concerned especially to set forth the history of his relics, of his blessings, and of the dues which should be paid to his church.

(t) St. Fintan of Dún-Blesci, or Duleng (Doon)

197. Acts of St. Fintan

Nimis honorati sunt amici tui, . . . scilicet Fintanus, . . . et ceteris similibus in magna gloria fulget in celis sicut sol.

MS: Cod. S. ff. 88ᵛ-90. Eds: Colgan *AA. SS.* 11 *sqq.* — *AA. SS. ex Cod. S.* 225-34.

Fintan of Duleng (otherwise Dún-Blesci, now Doon in bar. Coonagh, co. Limerick) was an obscure saint of whom little is known. His Life in *Codex Salmanticensis* is the first in that manuscript to take the form of a homily. The compiler seems to say — what the character of the text would suggest — that it is an abridgment of a longer work. It is probable that the exemplar used was imperfect, for there is nothing said of the saint's death, and the text seems to end abruptly. Fintan may have lived in the second half of the sixth century.

(u) Glenn-dá-locho (Glendalough) and St. Coemgen

Glenn-dá-locho, " Valley of two lakes " (Glendalough), a lonely and picturesque valley in the midst of the mountains of Wicklow, contains some of the most noteworthy monuments of pre-Norman ecclesiastical architecture in Ireland. These, and the many references in the annals and elsewhere, indicate that Glendalough was an important centre of Irish religious life from the sixth to the twelfth century.

The reputed founder of the monastery of Glendalough was Coemgen, or Coemghen (*anglice* Kevin), who was, we are told, of the royal race of Leinster. He retired to the glen to lead a hermit's life, and the disciples who gathered around him formed the monastery. The death of Coemgen is entered in the Annals of Ulster under 618 and 622, but the record is doubtful. He is given an age of one hundred and twenty or one hundred and thirty years, which may be a misunderstood chronological *datum*.

198. Life of St. Coemgen

(i) Vir erat in provinchia Laginensium, que est quinta pars Hybernie, in plebe videlicet Dal Machscorb . . . migrauit, tertio nonas Iunii, ad Ierusalem celestem, ad regnum sine fine, Dominum D. n. I. C. Cui est c. D. P. et S. S. g., h., et p., per o. s. s. Amen. (ii) Adest nobis, fratres, gloriosi abbatis Caymgini . . . Obiit autem vir Dei etatis sue .c.ᵐᵒ et. xxx.º anno, r. D. n. I. C., cui c. P. et S. s. h. et g. in s. s. Amen. (iii) Ro boi tra a bfioghair 7 a ffaistine . . . gan accra fiach do neoch fora ceile et cetera. (iv) Do sir Caoimhgin móran d'Eirinn . . . 's do diogail taccra na mban. (v) Erlam uasal oiregda . . . fuar Caoimhghin bas.

MSS: (i) Cod. K. ff. 64ᵛ-70ᵛ. (ii) Cod. S. ff. 203-5. — Bodl. Rawl. B 505 ff. 116ᵛ-7ᵛ. (iii) Brussels Bibl. roy. 2324-40 s XVII ff. 274-7ᵛ [Irish; prose; imperfect at end].

(iv) *Ibid.* ff. 278-86[v] [Irish; verse]. (v) TCD 1346 (H. iv. 4) pp. 146–65 [written by Hugh O'Daly, 1725]. — RIA 24 M 38 pp. 1 *sqq* [by Labhras Mac Anallaigh, 1765: these two MSS contain an Irish text, a mixture of prose and verse; in the second the order of chapters is somewhat different from that of the first, and the language is modernised]. EDS: (i) *AA. SS. Boll.* Jun. I 310–22. — *VV. SS. Hib.* I pp. liv–lvi, 234–57. (ii) *AA. SS. ex Cod. S.* 835–44. (iii, iv, v) *BNE* I pp. xxvii–xxxii, 125–67, II 121–61, 342–5. *Cf. Religionswissenschaftliche Bibliothek* II: Heinrich Günter *Die christliche Legende des Abendlandes* (Heidelberg 1910); *RC* XLII (1925) 172.

There are five versions of the Life of Coemgen. The first, in Latin, is quite extensive. The second is much shorter, being an abbreviated text prepared at a late date for lectionary or homiletic use in some monastery. The Irish texts are late, and are not closely related to the Latin. Plummer's conclusions regarding these documents may be summarised as follows: Version iii is an incomplete and somewhat careless summary of an earlier Life; Version iv is a composite production, based in part on material similar to that used by iii; Version v is derived mainly, but not entirely, from iv. The date of the first version seems to be the tenth or eleventh century. The reference to Dublin is interesting: " St. Garban dwelt near the city of Ath-Cliath, which is in the northern district of the Leinstermen, situated on a gulf of the sea. Its name [Duibh Linn] in Irish [*scotice*] is equivalent to the Latin *nigra terma;* and it is a powerful and warlike city, where ever dwell men fierce in battle, and skilful in handling fleets." [130]

The texts have little historical value, except for *Kulturgeschichte.* They illustrate the development of extreme ideas in asceticism, if not in the sixth and seventh, then in the tenth and later centuries. Version iv devotes considerable space to the alleged rights and privileges of the church of Glendalough.

(v) CELL-DA-LÚA (KILLALOE) AND ST. FLANNAN

Cell-Da-Lúa (Killaloe, Clare) takes its name from a Mo-Lúa, or Da-Lúa, who was its founder.[131] Its patron, however, was Flannan mac Toirdelbaig, whose father was said to be a pious king of the Dál gCais, the ruling race of North Munster. The chronological *data* are slight and fictitious, but it appears probable that the church was founded in the sixth century and that Flannan flourished in the seventh. There is no Life of Mo-Lúa, but Flannan owes his fame to his close association with the royal line of the Dál gCais, represented in the eleventh and twelfth centuries by the O'Briens.

On the rise to power of the O'Briens in the tenth and eleventh centuries, and the reorganisation of the Irish Church on the basis of a territorial episcopacy in the twelfth, Killaloe became an ecclesiastical centre of importance. According to Keating, Brian *bóroimhe* built a church here, but the cathedral church is attributed to Domnall Úa Briain, who died in 1194, after being king of North Munster for about thirty years.

[130] *Cap.* xxix. [131] *Cf.* p. 395 *supra*, probably a purely hypothetical identification.

A Donnchadh Úa Briain, bishop of Cell-Da-Lúa, died in 1164, and another O'Brien, Constantine, was bishop in 1179 and attended the Third Lateran Council.

199. Life of St. Flannan

(ii) [Prologue] Simillima proportione vite . . . [*Vita*] Flannanus itaque. . . . Flannani, que et quanta hic et in futuro pena debetur.

MSS: (i) Bodl. Rawl. B 485 ff. 157^v *sqq* [mutilated]; B 505 ff. 163 *sqq*. (ii) Cod. S. ff. 168–74^v. (iii) Cod. K. f. 35^v [frag.]. EDS: (ii) *AA. SS. ex Cod. S.* 643–80. *Cf. AA. SS. Boll.* VI 488–91; Malone *Life of St. Flannan* (Dublin 1902).

Two versions of the Life of Flannan are known. The shorter, and probably earlier, has not been published. The longer is a product of the times of Domnall Úa Briain. It is a document unique among the Lives of early Irish saints. Form, style, and in some degree subject-matter would suggest continental rather than Irish composition. The Irish Lives generally are condensed narratives with little of literary device. This is an expanded pseudo-literary production. Those touches of local topography which abound in so many Irish Lives are here wanting. The author puts in considerable ecclesiastical padding, parades his scriptural and classical learning, and writes in a verbose and rhetorical style. He was probably a foreign ecclesiastic who came to Killaloe under the patronage of the O'Briens: perhaps a member of one of those continental religious communities which established themselves in Ireland in the twelfth century, and to which Domnall Úa Briain was quite friendly.[132] The date is fixed by the report given of a prodigy which happened " lately " in Lismore, at the time when Frederic, " Romanorum imperator, rex invictus," captured and destroyed Milan (*i.e.*, A.D. 1162).

The text gives information on many interesting topics, as " the demon Albé " who was fabled to have helped Flannan's father — probably Aoibheall, the tutelary *bean sidh* of the O'Briens; the " abadactores," robbers, " with whom woody Hibernia always abounds; " the " iaculatores," perhaps wandering jugglers and rimers, whose chief characteristic was their irreverent audacity.

(w) ST. CRANAT OF FIR MUIGHE (FERMOY)

Of Cranat little is known. She was a patroness of the Fir Muighe (Fermoy, co. Cork), and in their district she is still remembered in popular tradition. Two of her churches were Cell-Cranatan, now Kilcranathan, parish of Ballyclogh, co. Cork, and Disert Cranatan, perhaps Hermitage, near Doneraile. It seems probable that she lived in the second half of the sixth century; but it is doubtful whether she should be identified with the St. Craebnat who is mentioned in some martyrologies at July 17.

---

[132] To eulogise the O'Briens is the author's particular aim. He compares them with the Romans in a misquotation of the famous passage of Vergil, *Aeneid* vi 853.

200. Life of St. Cranat

Feachtus do deachaidh Cairpre Crom. . . . [Ends with 9 quatrains:] Mo dherc sa, gidh dercc a dath . . . Nárab croch cir-dubh mo derc.

MSS: BM Egerton 92 A.D. 1453 f. 12ᵛ [imperfect; according to Robin Flower, this once formed part of Bk. Fer.]. — RIA A. iv. 1 (Stowe 9) pp. 90–3. — Brussels Bibl. roy. 2324–40 s XVII ff. 128ᵛ–9ᵛ. ED: Chas. Plummer *Misc. hag. Hib.* (Brussels 1925) 157–69 [with trans.].

Although bearing the title of Life, this text is merely a story of how the saint, to avoid matrimony, plucked out her eyes, and afterwards had them miraculously restored. The verse especially seems to be of some antiquity.

(x) St. Mo-Laga of Tulach-min-Molaga

Probably also of the sixth century was another patron of the royal race of Fir Muighe, Loichen or Mo-Laga. His church was Tulach-min-Molaga, not identified, but evidently near the modern Fermoy.

201. Life of St. Mo-Laga

Molaga dino d'feraib Muighi . . . 7 fria chomarbada tara eise. [Incomplete.]

MSS: Bk. Fer. ff. 60–1ᵛ. — Brussels Bibl. roy. 2324–40 ff. 130–4. — RIA A. iv. 1 (Stowe 9) pp. 41–52. ED: Fáinne Fionn *Irish Rosary* XV (1911). LAT. TRANS: Colgan *AA. SS.* 145–51.

II. The Churches and Legend of St. Brendan

Bibliography

See the general bibliographies, especially Hardy *Cat.* I 159–64; the Bollandists' *Bibl. hag. lat.* 214–6 and *Supp.* 59–60; Chevalier *Répertoire . . . Bio-bibliog.* I 694–5; Duine *Memento* 51–7, 110–4. Jos. Dunn gives an extensive bibliography in the article cited below.

EDS. of the early texts: Achille Jubinal *La légende latine de S. Brandaines, avec une traduction inédite en prose et en poésie romanes* (Paris 1836) [NB, with Old French trans. in prose and verse: good texts and an important introduction]. — Carl Schröder *Sanct Brandan Ein lateinischer und drei deutsche Texte* (Erlangen 1871) [NB: *cf.* *Germania* XVI 60; *Romanische Studien* I 553 *sqq.*]. — P. F. Moran *Acta Sancti Brendani Original Latin documents connected with the Life of Saint Brendan, Patron of Kerry and Clonfert* (Dublin 1872) [VB, NB, the *Oratio Brendani* (*cf.* no. 588), and other writings relating to the saint]. — Also *VV. SS. Hib.* and *BNE.* FOREIGN VERNACULAR TEXTS: D. Paul Jakob Bruns *Romantische und andere Gedichte in alt-plattdeutscher Sprache aus einer Handschrift der akademischen Bibliothek zu Helmstädt* (Berlin, Stettin 1798) 159–216: " Reisen des h. Brandanus." — Ph. Blommaert *Oud-*

vlaemsche Gedichten der XII XIII en XIV Eeuwen (Ghent 1838–41) I 91–120, II 1–28:
" Reis van sinte Brandaen." — Thos. Wright *Sanct Brandan, a mediaeval legend of the
sea, in English verse and prose* (Percy Society: London 1844). — Brill *Van Sinte
Brandane* (Gronningen 1871). — C. Horstmann *Archiv für das Studium der neur.
Sprachen u. Literaturen* LIII (1874) 16–48; *The early South-English Legendary* (Early
Eng. Texts Soc. 1887) 220–40. — H. Suchier " Brandans Seefahrt " Böhmer's *Romanische Studien* I (1875) 553–84. — Louis De Backer "La légende flamande de S. Brandon
et sa bibliographie," in Édouard Rosweyre and Oct. Uzanne *Miscellanées bibliographiques* (Paris 1878). — Th. Auracher " The Old French Brendan in the Arsenal Library " *Zs f. romanische Philologie* (1878) pp. 37–46. — Francesco Novati *La Navigatio s. Brendani in antico Veneziano* (Bergamo 1893). — E. Bonebakker *Van Sente
Brandane* (Amsterdam 1894). — Carl Wahlund *Die altfranzösische Prosaübersetzung
von Brendans Meerfahrt* (*Skrift. Humanist. Vetensk.-Samf.* IV) (Upsala 1900) [has
also a survey of the literature]; " Eine altprovenzalische Prosaübersetzung von
Brendans Meerfahrt " *Festgabe für Wendelin Foerster* (Halle 1902) 175–98. — H. Cal-
mund *Prolegomena zu einer krit. Ausgabe des ältesten franz. Brendanlebens*, Dissert.
(Bonn 1902). — A. Bayot " Le voyage de St. Brendan dans les légendiers français "
Mélanges Moeller I (1914) 456–67. — Wilhelm Meyer *Die Ueberlieferung der deutschen
Brandanlegende* (Göttingen 1918). — Mario Esposito *Mélanges philologiques* (Florence
1921) 22.

COMMENTARIES on the legend: O. F. Peschel " Der Ursprung und die Verbreitung
einiger geographischen Mythen im Mittelalter: Die Legende von den Schiffahrten
des heil. Brandan " *Deutsche Vierteljahrsschrift* 1852–4 no. lxvi pp. 242–50; also in
J. Löwenberg's *Abhandl. z. Erd- u. Völkerkunde* I (Leipsic 1877) 20–8.— " Notes on the
Life of St. Brendan " *IER* Oct. 1871–Jan. 1872; *cf.* 1912 pp. 173–4. — Gustav Schirmer
Zur Brendanus-Legende (Leipsic 1888) [an important study, especially for a comparison of NB with the Irish translation of VB]. — HZ "Keltische Beiträge II Brendans
Meerfahrt " *Zs. f. deut. Alterthum* XXXIII (1889) 129–220, 257–338; also " Die
frühesten Berührungen der Iren mit den Nordgermanen " *Sitzungsb. d. k. preuss.
Akad. d. Wissensch.* 1891 pp. 279–317 [the first is a very valuable study of the Irish
" voyage " literature, and of the relations therewith of the Brendan Legend; the conclusions are to be controlled by Plummer's studies]. — M. J. de Goeje " La légende
de St. Brandan " *Actes du huitième congrès international des orientalistes 1889*, Sect.
sémitique (Leyden 1891) [oriental influences and parallels]. — Denis O'Donoghue
Brendaniana St. Brendan the Voyager in story and legend (Dublin 1893; 2nd ed. 1895)
[*cf. An. Boll.* XIV 121]. — A. C. L. Brown " Barintus " *RC* XXII 339–44. — F. Lot
" Le curach et les pélerinages par mer " *Annales de Bretagne* XI 362–3. — J. M. Mac-
kinlay " In oceano desertum " *Proc. Soc. of Antiquaries of Scotland* XXXIII (1899)
129–33. — Chas. Plummer " Some new light on the Brendan Legend " *ZCP* V (1905)
124–41 [in the main, a study of VB, and of its relations to NB: in part to be modified
by reference to *VV. SS. Hib., BNE,* and Pfitzner's dissertation (*cf.* p. 416)]. — Alfred
Schulze " Zur Brendanlegende " *Zs. f. romanische Philologie* XXX (1906) 257–79. —
F. Nansen *In northern mists* 2 vols. (London 1911), especially chap. ix " Wineland the
Good, the Fortunate Isles, and the discovery of America " [an important examination
of the Brendan Legend in its relations both to the later Norse sagas and to the earlier
classical and oriental literatures; tends to over-strain the parallels]. — J. F. Kenney
" The Legend of St. Brendan " *Trans. Roy. Soc. of Canada* 1920, sect. ii 51–67 [*cf. RC*
XXXIX (1922) 393–5]. — Jos. Dunn " The Brendan problem " *Catholic Hist. Rev.*

VI (Jan. 1921) 395–477. — L. Gougaud RC XXXIX (1922) 210–1, 355–6; *Gaelic pioneers of Christianity* (Dublin 1923) 117–20. On the Judas episode: Seb. Merkle "Die Sabbatruhe in der Hölle" *Römische Quartalschrift* IX (1895) 484–509. — P. F. Baum " The mediaeval legend of Judas Iscariot " *Publications of the Modern Language Assoc. of America* XXXI (1916) 481–632; " Judas' Sunday rest " *Modern Language Review* XVIII (1923) 168–82.

GEOGRAPHICAL TREATISES bearing on St. Brendan's Island and its identification with America: M. P. d'Avezac *Les Iles fantastiques de l'océan occidental au moyen âge* (*Nouvelles annales des voyages et de science géographique* I) (Paris 1845) 293. — E. Beauvois " La Découverte du nouveau monde par les Irlandais " *Congrès des Américanistes de Nancy* 1875 pp. 41–93 [*cf. RC* III 101–5]; " La grande terre de l'ouest dans les documents celtiques du moyen âge " *Congrès des Américanistes de Madrid* 1881 pp. 45–74; " L'Élysée transatlantique et l'Éden occidental " *Rev. de l'hist. des religions* VIII (1883) 273–318, 673–727. — Paul Gaffarel " Les explorations maritimes des Irlandais au moyen âge " *Rev. politique et littéraire* Jan. 2, 1875; " Les voyages de St. Brandan et des papae dans l'Atlantique au moyen âge " *Bulletin de la Soc. géog. de Rochefort* II (1880–1); *Histoire de la découverte de l'Amérique* pt. I (Paris 1892) chaps. vi–vii [Beauvois and Gaffarel draw extravagant conclusions from the evidence]. — K. Kretschmer *Die Entdeckung Amerikas in ihre Bedeutung für die Geschichte des Weltbildes* (Berlin 1892) 186–95. — R. D. Benedict " The Hereford Map and the Legend of St. Brendan " *Bull. of the Amer. Geog. Soc.* XXIV (1892) iii. — T. J. Westropp " Brasil and the legendary islands of the North Atlantic " *Proc. RIA* XXX (1912) C 223–260. — W. H. Babcock " The so-called mythical islands of the Atlantic in mediaeval maps " *Scottish Geographical Magazine* May–Aug. 1915 pp. 261–9, 315–20, 360–77, 411–22; " St. Brendan's explorations and islands " *The Geographical Rev.* VIII (1919) 37–46.

CHURCHES OF BRENDAN IN BRITAIN: A. P. Forbes *Kalendars of Scottish saints* (Edinburgh 1871) 284–7. — Skene *Celtic Scotland* II (2nd ed. 1887) 77–8. — Baring-Gould and Fisher *Lives of the British saints* I (London 1907) 233–62.

The Ciarraige were an ancient people who by the time of written history had been broken up into a number of isolated groups scattered over the western part of Ireland, in Connacht and Munster. The best known of these branches is the Ciarraige Luachra, who dwelt west of Slíab-Luachra around Tralee bay in the northern part of the county which takes from them the name of Kerry. Their patron saint was Brénaind [133] moccu Alti, or Altai, who, his name indicates, was of the Altraige, the principal subdivision of the Ciarraige Luachra. The strength of the ancient devotion is indicated by the local place-nomenclature: Brandon Bay, Brandon Hill, Brandon Headland, Brandon Point, Brandon Well, are some of the place-names of the district around Tralee.

---

[133] Etymologists say the original form was *Brénfind*, " putridus capillus." There are many different forms. The Latin " Brendanus " or " Brendenus " and the English " Brendan " or " Brandon," come from a hypocoristic derivative, *Bréndán*. *Cf.* KM in *Sitzungsb. d. kgl. preuss. Akad. d. Wissensch.* 1912 pp. 436, 1148; also *RC* XXXIX (1922) 393; KM *Miscellanea Hibernica* (*Univ. Illinois Studies in Language and Literature* II iv) (Urbana Nov. 1916) 10 n. 2; *Cath. Hist. Rev.* IV (Jan. 1921) 399.

Brénaind, or Brendan, died, according to the Annals of Ulster, in 577 or 583. He had founded his chief monastery, Clúain-ferta-Brénaind, " Brendan's Meadow of graves," in 558 or 564. Clúain-ferta-Brénaind, now Clonfert, is in Connacht, barony Longford, county Galway, just west of the Shannon above Loch Derg. He had other foundations on islands in the Shannon river and in Loch Corrib. In his home-land his most important church was Árd-ferta, " Height of graves," now Ardfert, which was, we are told, of earlier foundation but donated to Brendan.

The fame of the saint was spread, we may believe, around the Irish coasts by the Ciarraige and other maritime peoples of the West, and perhaps carried to what is now Scotland, to Wales and to Brittany, in all of which the cult of Brendan became established. But it is reasonably certain that Brendan himself made a voyage to the Scottish isles, and perhaps to Strathclyde, Cumbria or Wales. His Lives speak of such a voyage, and, more important, Adamnán, in his Life of Columba,[134] testifies that Brendan, with Comgall of Bangor, Cainnech of Achad-bó and Cormac úa Liatháin, visited Columba in the island of Hinba.

His close associations with the western Irish coast and the Scottish islands would be sufficient to ensure the presence of a large maritime element in the traditions of the saint. It is not, then, surprising that, when the secular and the ecclesiastical literatures of Ireland began to fuse, Brendan became the hero of a Christianised tale of the *Immram*, " voyage," type, a type of pagan romance which itself must have sprung from the folk-lore of the maritime peoples of Ireland who for unknown ages had looked out upon the mystery of the broad Atlantic.

The substantial point of contact between the *immrama* of the *filid* and the *acta sanctorum* of the clerics was the actual over-seas movement of the Irish ascetics who went forth seeking in foreign or desert places abodes where they might lead an exalted religious life.[135] This movement had begun in Brendan's own time: the settlement of Colum-cille in Iona, of Columbanus in eastern Gaul, and perhaps his own journey to Britain, seem to have been inspired by such motives. But it was not till the seventh and eighth centuries that it reached its culmination: then the Irish monks occupied as hermitages the wild and often almost inaccessible islands of the Irish and Scottish coasts, the Hebrides,

[134] III xvii.
[135] *Cf.* pp. 487–8 *infra*. The " Island of the Family of Ailbe " of NB seems to be derived from a story, now lost, of a voyage made by monks of Ailbe's community seeking an island inthe ocean, perhaps " Thule."

Orkneys, Faroes, and even distant Iceland.[136]   In Adamnán's account of the unsuccessful voyages of Cormac úa Liatháin [137] in search of such a desert in the ocean we see a historical record just turning into legend.[138] It was not around the figure of Cormac, however, but around that of Brendan that the lore and the romance of this extraordinary phase of the history of the sea coalesced. Amalgamated therewith was, quite naturally, a considerable element of the Christian " vision " literature. In its final literary form the resulting tale is the chief single contribution of Ireland to the general literature of mediaeval Europe.

The bulk of the texts bearing on the Brendan Legend are derived from two documents, a *Vita Brendani* (VB) and a *Navigatio Brendani* (NB). The *Navigatio* has come to us practically intact, but the *Vita* is represented only by versions that are abbreviated, or mutilated, and contaminated by the *Navigatio*. Nevertheless these versions are sufficiently numerous to make practicable a fairly trustworthy reconstruction of the *Vita Brendani*.

The somewhat extrinsic character of the " ocean voyage " sections of the *Vita* makes it probable that they were not part of the original text, which included only the journey to Britain. Moreover, the fact that the *Félire* of Oengus [139] has no allusion to the voyage supports the view that when it was written, about A.D. 800, the legend of such an adventure either had not arisen, or had not attained wide currency. On the other hand the manuscript evidence shows that the *Navigatio Brendani*, which is manifestly the more developed form of the story, cannot be of later date than the first half of the tenth century. Could we be certain that the Brendan passages in the earliest Lives of St. Malo were part of the original texts we might with some confidence place the first phase in the development of the Legend within the period from about 800 A.D. to about 870; in any case there is a good presumption that it was a product of the ninth century.[140]

---

[136] *Cf.* pp. 545-8 *infra.*

[137] Possibly the name signifies, not " grandson of Liathan," but " member of the Úi Liatháin race," a people of whom one section dwelt on and to the east of Cobh harbor, and another in the Goidelic settlements in Wales.

[138] *Vita Columbae* I vi, II xlii; *cf.* I xx.

[139] No. 272.

[140] The Martyrology of Tallaght (no. 273), which may be of the ninth century, commemorates on March 22 the " going forth of the family of Brendan."   In the secular romance — with Christian accretions — *Immram curaig Máil-dúin* there is a solitary survivor of fifteen disciples of Brendan of Birr who had found a hermitage in the western ocean. Brendan of Birr was an older contemporary of the patron of Clonfert: in connection with his name there is in Fél. Oeng. an obscure allusion to the sea. HZ thought that the story of the voyage was originally attached to this Brendan, whose family it is that the Martyrology of Tallaght mentions. *Cf. BNE* II 330.

In the *Vita Brendani* two voyages are described, the first unsuccessful in attaining its object, the second successful. The object sought was an island in the ocean, of which, in response to his prayers to be shown a " secret land " whither he might withdraw " on pilgrimage," Brendan had been given a miraculous vision. The tale is thus directly linked up with that impulse to voluntary exile which had so great an influence in Irish religious history. When the goal is reached Brendan is directed not to remain, but to return and teach the way of life to the Irish.[141] It is clear that we have here a version of the legend adopted by Brendan's community, to promote both the fame of their patron and the authority of his monastic rule.

In the *Navigatio* Brendan's object is not the discovery of a retreat in which he may lead the anchorite's life, but of " the land of promise of the saints," described to him by a certain abbot Barinthus, who himself had visited it. *Tír tairngiri*, " Land of Promise," is the term used by early Irish scriptural glossators to designate the " Promised Land " of Canaan, and the " Kingdom of Heaven " of the new dispensation.[142] Evidently in the mind of the author of the *Navigatio* the phrase was associated with the Celtic Elysium of the West, described in secular romances, and it is actually used in this sense by later writers.[143] Accordingly the narrative is, in considerable part, composed of what seem to be stock incidents and descriptions drawn from the *immram* group of stories.[144] Nevertheless the tale is not written from the point of view of Brendan's community, or even, in any exclusive sense, from the point of view of the Irish Church: its tone is more cosmopolitan than that of any other Irish hagiographical document.

Into the Legend of St. Brendan in its several forms went many other ingredients besides Irish myths of the " happy otherworld " in the

---

[141] It may be noted that several elements of the VB narrative are found also in the litany no. 586, a text composed probably in the first half of the tenth century. *Cf.* HZ *Zs. f. deut. Alterthum* XXXIII 302.

[142] HZ *Zs. f. deut. Alterthum* XXXIII 287–8, refers to the Würzburg Glosses (*cf.* no. 461) on *Hebrews* iv 4, vi 15; I *Cor.* x 4.

[143] A clue to the transition in the Brendan Legend may possibly be found in VB. Brendan, after his vision of the island in the ocean, hears a voice which says: " Just as I promised the Land to the People of Israel, and was their support that they should reach it, so do I promise you the island which you have seen, and will make good My word in deed." — *AA. SS. ex Cod. S.* 764.

[144] In the *Immram curaig húa Corra, Immram Snedgusa agus maic Riagla*, and, still more, *Immram curaig Máile-dúin*, parallel passages of considerable extent are to be found. The relations between these four texts have not yet been fully elucidated. The first two mentioned are late compositions, but the " Voyage of Máel-dúin " is older than the Brendan Legend, for which HZ thought it served as model and quarry. It is probable, however, that in the text as we have it there has been re-borrowing by the Máel-dúin from the Brendan. The Legend of St. Brendan really belongs to the class of Christian *immrama*, voyage sagas, but its subject-matter and associations are such that, for the purposes of this introduction, it can best be treated in connection with the hagiographical documents.

western ocean and Christian " visions " of heaven and hell: much folk-lore that is common to all western Europe; the geographical knowledge and ideas of the time, including northern — perhaps Norse and Ice-landic — and very considerable oriental matter; [145] and many literary reminiscences, drawn from the Bible and from the classics, or at least the *Etymologies* of Isidore of Seville.

The Brendan Legend seems to have passed to the continent of Europe by way of " Britain " (*i.e.*, Wales-Cornwall) and Brittany. At latest by the early tenth century it had contributed, in both its chief forms, to the *acta* of St. Malo. An often-quoted passage in the old French *Roman du Renard* [146] suggests that there was also a Breton tale of Brendan.[147] Schröder thought that the centre of dissemination of the *Navigatio Brendani* over Europe was the lower Rhine valley, where Irish ecclesiastics were numerous in the ninth and early tenth centuries. The work was translated into many of the vernacular languages of Europe — Norman-French, Old French, Middle English, Flemish, Dutch, German, Provençal, Italian, Norse. The existence of St. Bren-dan's Isle became one of the fixed ideas of geography; it continued to appear on charts of the Atlantic until the eighteenth century. Even yet the Legend is sometimes offered as evidence of an Irish discovery of America antedating both Columbus and the Norsemen.

202. *Vita Brendani:* Life of Brendan

(VB1) Inter praeclara Ecclesie luminaria beatus abbas Brandanus . . . in claritate resurrecturum in adventu Domini n. J. C. qui c. P. et F. [*sic*] et S. s. v. et r. per o. s. s.   Amen.

MS: Cod. S. 189–91ᵛ.   ED: *AA. SS. ex Cod. S.* 759–72.

This is the only text derived from the original VB without any contamination from NB. Unfortunately it has been much abbreviated, for purposes, as the writer states, of reading, in church or refectory. He wrote at a late date, and not, so it appears, for Brendan's own community.

(VB2) Fuit uir uite uenerabilis, Brandanus nomine, qui tanquam . . . sepultum decimo septimo Kalendas Iunii, regnante D. n. I. C., q. c. P. et S. s. u. et r. D. in s. s.   Amen.

MSS: Bodl. Rawl. B. 485 ff. 72ᵛ–91; B. 505 ff. 101ᵛ–16. — Dublin Franciscan Con-vent, A 24, pp. 50 *sqq.*   ED: *VV. SS. Hib.* I 98–151.

---

[145] *Cf.* Beazley *Dawn of modern geography* II (1901) 230–40; E. Blochet *Les sources orientales de la Divine Comédie* (Paris 1901) 21 *sqq*, append.

[146] I 2389 *sqq.*

[147] Or, possibly, only that the verse translation of the " Voyage " was looked on as forming part of the Arthurian cycle of romances.

This text has been formed by a very crude conflation of VB with NB, consisting simply of the insertion of almost the whole of NB into VB. The clumsiness of the amalgamation has resulted in the preservation of much material sacrificed by other compilers.

(VB3) Natus est beatissimus Brendanus Abbas . . . Cluayn-ferta c. g. et h. cum psalmis et hympnis spiritualibus r. D. n. J. X. cœlum et terram et omnes creaturas c. P. et S. S. in s. s. Amen.

MS: Cod. K. ED: Moran *Acta S. Brendani* (1872) 1–26 [the editor has, unfortunately, removed the NB sections of the text; he prints NB separately].

The text of Brendan's Life preserved in the *Codex Kilkenniensis* has been formed by a simple, but not unskilful, conflation of VB and NB. The "voyage" sections of VB are omitted, and for them is substituted a nearly complete text of NB. The version of VB used runs closely parallel to that of VB1 and VB2, but it is a quite distinct text. Although, apparently, not written in a Brendan community, it belonged to a time when the *paruchia* of Brendan was still an active organisation.

(VB4) Fuit uir uite uenerabilis, Brandanus nomine, genere Momoiensis, . . . Que cuncta que uiderat, per ordinem narrauerat. Finit.

MS: Cod. S. ff. 69–77^v. ED: *AA. SS. ex Cod. S.* 113–54.

This is a very simple conflation of VB and NB. It would seem that some late hagiographer, preferring the narrative of NB to that of VB, but realising that it is not cast in the traditional form of *acta sanctorum*, substituted for the usual introduction a summary of the earlier portion of VB. In the NB narrative which forms the remainder of this Life there is one extensive lacuna.

(VB5) Sanctus enim Brendanus abbas in occidentali parte . . . plenus virtutibus et miraculis migrauit ad dominum, xvii kalendas iunii; et in Cluenarca sepelitur.

ED: *Nova Legenda Anglie:* ed. Horstman (Oxford 1901) I 136–53.

This is the most skilful of all the conflations of VB and NB. It " follows the VB up to and including Brendan's prayer for a ' terra secreta ' to which he might retire. It then makes the visit of Barrinthus the answer to this prayer, and so leads into the narrative of the NB which is followed to the end, after which a few of the incidents of Brendan's later life are added from VB." [148]

(VB6) Beatus uir qui timet Dominum, in mandatis eius uolet nimis. Is fechtnach 7 as firén foirbhthe . . . Ni ralaimset [immorro] ní do fhiarfaigi [7 no aemdais . . .]. Several poems, of which the following are the more important, are incorporated into the text: Brenuinn breo betha buadhaig . . . 5 quatrains. Ard reileac na n-aingel n-an . . . 10 quatrains. Tri longa seolais in saoi . . . 3 quatrains. Dia do betha, a Brenainn, sunn . . . 6 quatrains.

MSS: Bk. Lis. *s* XV ff. 30^v–4^v [*cf. ZCP* II 545, 548–9 *re* a modern fragmentary copy]. — BN Fonds celtique et basque 1 (Ancien fonds 8175^1) ff. 81^v–7 [a composite codex; this section written apparently in 1518]. — RIA A. 4. 1 (Stowe 9) pp. 175–204. — Cambridge Fitzwilliam Museum McClean 187 ff. 29 *sqq* [from the Black Book of Molaga; *cf.* Plummer *Misc. hag. Hib. Cat.* no. 9]. — BM Egerton 91 ff. 26–30^v. EDS:

[148] Plummer *ZCP* V 131–2.

Lis. Lives 99–115, 247–61, 349–54 [Lismore text, trans., notes]. — D. O'Donoghue *Brendaniana* (Dublin 1893) [Lismore text, trans.]. *Cf. BNE* I pp. xviii *sqq.*

In form, this document is a homily in the Irish language, intended for Brendan's feast day, May 16. Actually it is an Irish version of VB, perhaps based on a Latin original. There is considerable contamination from both NB₁ and NB₆. The narrative ends abruptly after the arrival in the Land of Promise, but the text continues without a break, giving the latter part of the Vision of Adamnán.[149] No doubt the common exemplar of our manuscripts had lost some leaves containing the end of the one and the beginning of the other text, but the copyist wrote on without noticing the *lacuna.* This Life may be assigned with probability to the twelfth century.

(VB7) Beatus uir qui timet, etc. [the opening section differs only slightly in verbal forms from VB6] . . . co cantaiccibh spiratalta i nonóir A. 7 M. 7 S. N. Ailim trocaire . . . in s. s. Amen.

MS: Brussels Bibl. roy. 4190–200 ff. 224–63ᵛ [the colophon says it was copied from a book written in 1536 by Siograid Úa Máel-Conaire for Rose, wife of Níall óg Úa Néill]. ED: *BNE* I pp. xvi–xxii, 44–95, II 44–92, 328–37. *Cf. VV. SS. Hib.* I p. xl.

This is the most composite of the Lives of Brendan, and constitutes the last stage in the conflation of VB and NB. The greater part consists of alternate extracts from Irish recensions of these two documents. The versions used are VB6 and a text of NB similar to that found in VB4. An attempt, far from exhaustive, was made to harmonise inconsistencies. The latter part of the text consists of extracts from other versions of NB and reproductions of the separate anecdota noticed below under no. 208.

203. *Navigatio Brendani:* The Voyage of Brendan

(NB1) Sanctus Brendanus, filius Finlocha, nepotis Alti . . . vite sue finivit in pace, r. D. n. J. C., cujus regnum et imperium sine fine permanet in s. s. Amen.

MSS: Very numerous; the following are some of the more important: BM Add. 36736 *s* X [formerly of the Abbey of St. Maxim at Trèves]. — BN lat. 3784 *s* XI ff. 93 *sqq*; 5572 *s* XI. — Rome Bibl. Sessoriana 114 *s* XIII. — Oxford Lincoln College 27 *s* XI/XII ff. 186ᵛ *sqq.* — Vat. Palat. lat. 217 *s* XII *in.* — BM Cotton. Tiberius D iii *s* XII ff. 107–18; Vespasian A xiv *s* XII ff. 101ᵛ *sqq.* — BN lat. 2333 A *s* XIII; 4887 *s* XII. — Bodl. Laud Misc. 410 *s* XII ff. 40ᵛ *sqq* [the 5 Laud Misc. MSS of NB belonged once to the Carthusian monastery of Mainz]. — Vat. Regin. 481 *s* XII ff. 28–42ᵛ. — BM Cotton. Vespasian B x *s* XIII ff. 11ᵛ–21; Harl. 3776 *s* XIV ff. 67–75ᵛ; 3958 *s* XIII ff.103ᵛ–21ᵛ; Reg. 8 E xvii *s* XIII ff. 128ᵛ–38ᵛ .— BN lat. 2444 *s* XIII; 5137 *s* XIII; 5284 *s* XIII; 5348 *s* XIII; 5371 *s* XIII. — Bodl. Laud Misc. 237 *s* XIII ff. 229 *sqq* [3 fol. missing]; 44 *s* XIII ff. 27ᵛ *sqq* [the latter part of the text is added in a 15th cent. hand]. — Oxford Balliol College 226 *s* XIII ff. 72–86. — Cambrai Bibl. pub. 735 *s* XIII. — Florence Bibl. Laurentiana I 362 cod. xii *s* XIII. — BM Harl. 108 *s* XIV ff. 42–59ᵛ. — Cambridge Corpus Christi College 275 *s* XIV ff. 46–58ᵛ. — BN lat. 2845 *s* XIV; 6041A *s* XIV. *Cf.* also the MSS of VB2, VB3, VB4, VB5, VB7. EDS: Jubinal *La légende latine de s. Brandaines* (1836) 1–55 [good text]. — W. J. Rees *Lives of the Cambro-British Saints* (Llandovery 1853) [incomplete and poor]. —Schröder *Sanct Brandan* (1871). — Moran *Acta Sancti Brendani* (1872) 85–131 [Jubi-

149 *Cf.* no. 226.

nal's text collated with other MSS]. Comm: C. Steinweg " Die handschriftlichen Gestaltungen der lateinischen Navigatio Brendani " *Romanische Forschungen* VII 1–48 [also as a Dissertation, Halle 1891]. For critical commentaries, *cf.* pp. 407–8 *supra*.[150]

The *Navigatio Sancti Brendani* is an elaborate and finished composition. If evidence to the contrary were not forthcoming, it would be natural to conclude that it was written at a comparatively late date. Zimmer expressed the opinion that it could not have been earlier than 1050. But after he wrote a tenth-century manuscript was acquired by the British Museum — and one which shows, by its mistakes, that it itself is a copy. This puts the *terminus ad quem* well back into the middle or first half of the tenth century. It was written by an Irishman, and, almost certainly, in Ireland.

The differences between this relation and the *Vita Brendani* are very striking. The *Navigatio* has, for one thing, come to us practically intact and in its original form. More important, while the topic is the same and many of the episodes are, at bottom, identical, the treatment, both in general and in particular, is quite different.

" The *Navigatio* is the work of a literary artist of high merit. The theme is the voyage only, not the life, of the saint, and the plot is much simpler and better worked out, while the narrative is enriched with an amplitude of incident and detail quite unknown to the other versions. Even yet the story has sufficient literary power to hold the reader's interest; in its own day this tale of the wonders of the sea — then to all minds the region of mystery and terror — told in a simple and free-flowing style, with its matter-of-fact tone and unfaltering resourcefulness of imagination, must have been most impressive. The author — or authors — drew freely from the resources which the geographical knowledge, the literature and the folk-lore of Ireland and of western Europe offered, and shaped all with care to his own purpose. But that purpose was not solely, nor indeed primarily, to describe the wonders of the ocean. As we note the meticulous care with which he elaborates the precepts of Brendan, and the rules of life, the devotions, the method of observing the canonical hours,[151] the psalms sung, the prayers said, the penances observed among the inhabitants, human and superhuman, of the oceanic islands, we come to realise that the author is painting a picture of the ideal monastic life. The *Navigatio Brendani* is the epic — shall we say the Odyssey? — of the old Irish Church." [152]

(NB2) Donna Aaliz la reine Par qui valdrat lei devine. . . . Par qui lui enuunt plusur que mil.

Eds: Suchier in Böhmer's *Romanische Studien* I (1875) 555 *sqq*. — Francisque Michel *Les voyages merveilleux de St. Brandan à la recherche du paradis terrestre* (Paris 1878).

[150] The " Legenda in Festo Sancti Brandani " published by Moran, pp. 132–9, " e codice MS. Bibliothecae Vallicellianae seculi xiii — Tom. vii Fol. 141–3 " is a poorly executed abbreviation of NB1.
[151] On this and some other liturgical subjects the *Navigatio* is an interesting source.
[152] I have borrowed from a paper in the *Trans. Roy. Soc. Canada*, noticed on p. 407 *supra*.

Comm: Max Wien *Das Verhältniss der Handschriften der anglonormannischen Brandanlegende* (Inaugural Dissertation) (Halle and Eisleben 1886). — Gaston Paris *La Littérature française au moyen âge* (Paris 1888) 214. — *ZCP* V 139–40. — Erich Pfitzner *Das anglonormannische Gedicht von Brendan als Quelle einer lateinischen Prosafassung* (Dissertation) (Halle 1910). — *BNE* I pp. xxii *sqq.*

This poem in Norman-French, written about 1121 for Alix of Louvain, second wife of Henry I of England, is the oldest extant version of the Brendan Legend in a vernacular other than Irish. It is derived from NB1, but with peculiar modifications, many of them un-Irish — such as the rampart of precious stones, the guardian dragons, and the supernatural sword surmounting the gate of paradise.

(NB3) [Prologue] Predecessorum sacra facta . . . [Vita] Fuit igitur uir iste Brendanus in insula occidentali . . . in intercessione Brendani possidere mereamur; per eundem, qui c. P. et F. et S. s. u. et r., D. per o. s. s. Amen.

MSS: Bodl. e Musaeo III *s* XII *ex* pp. 213–26 [formerly belonged to abbey of Valle Crucis in Denbighshire]. Ed: *VV. SS. Hib.* I pp. xlii *sqq*, II 270–92. Comm: *ZCP* V 138–41. — Pfitzner *op. cit.* under NB2. — *BNE* I pp. xxii *sq.*

This Latin text was regarded by Dr. Plummer as the original from which the Anglo-Norman poem, NB2, was derived; but Dr. Pfitzner has argued that it is the secondary text and NB2 the original, and he appears to have the better case.

(NB4) Vana vanis garriat pagina pagana . . . Vigeat et valeat Alexander meus. Amen. 311 quatrains.

MS: BM Cotton. Vespasian D ix *s* XIII ff. 1–9. Eds: Ernst Martin *Zs. f. deut. Alterthum* XVI (1873) 289 *sqq*. — Moran *Acta S. Brendani* 45–84. *Cf. ZCP* V 140.

This jingling Latin metrical Life of Brendan is based mainly on the Anglo-Norman poem on the subject, with some extracts from NB1.

(NB5) Brandainnes fu uns sains hom fils Synloca . . . et là fina-il les jors de se vie em pais. — Amen. Chi défine de sains Brandains et des merveilles k'il trouva en le mer d'Irlande.

MS: BN 7595 ff. 254 *sqq*. Ed: Jubinal *La Légende latine de S. Brandaines* 57–104.

This version of the legend, believed to date from the end of the twelfth century, is a translation into French of NB1.

(NB6) Bator da apstol decc na hErenn hi cCluain Iraird . . . [contains two poems; the second concludes the text] Batar ic foghlaim tréin treall, . . . 8 quatrains. Iudas Scarioth me indiu . . . 13 quatrains.

MSS: RIA Liber Flavus Fergusiorum *s* XV pt. ii ff. 50ᵛ–1 [or pt. ii sect. v ff. 7ᵛ–8]. — BM Egerton 1781 ff. 152ᵛ–3ᵛ [written in 1487 by Diarmaid *bacach* Mac Parthalain]. — Brussels Bibl. roy. 2324–40 ff. 70ᵛ–1ᵛ; 5100–4 ff. 12 *sq* [both copied by Michael O'Clery, in 1627 and 1634 respectively, from " the Red Book of Munster," written by Murchadh Ó Coinlis, probably early in the fifteenth century]. — BM Egerton 136 *s* XVII ff. 75–9. — TCD H. 1. 11 ff. 58 *sqq* [copy of preceding]. Eds: RTh *ZCP* X (1915) 408–20 [text, Germ. trans.]. — *BNE* I pp. xix *sq*, xxiv *sq*, 96–102, II 93–8, 337–8 [text, trans.].

We have here a distinct tradition as to the occasion of Brendan's voyage. A wonderful flower from the Land of Promise appeared to the twelve apostles of Ireland, who were then at Clúain-Iráird. Brendan of Birr was chosen by lot to go in search of that land, but as he was old Brendan of Clonfert went in his place. The text is incomplete: it resembles the Latin *Navigatio*, but the treatment of the episodes is quite original.

204. Satirical verses on the Brendan Legend

Hic poeta, qui Brendani uitam uult describere . . . Cunctis nobis quod concedat Rex celestis patrie. Amen.

MS: Oxford Lincoln College 27 s XI/XII f. 2ᵛ. Eds: Paul Meyer *Romania* XXXI (1902) 376. — *VV. SS. Hib.* II 293–4.

Verses, written probably in England in the eleventh or early twelfth century, which ridicule the legend of Brendan's voyage, and declare it to be positively heretical.

205. Life of St. Malo

(i) By Bili, clerk of Alet, second half s IX. (ii) Anonymous, s IX. (iii) By Sigebert of Gembloux, 1076 x 1099. (iv) Attributed to Baudry, bishop of Dol from 1107 to 1130. (v) Anonymous, in verse.

Eds: (i) F. Plaine *Bull.-mém. de la soc. archéol. d'Ille-et-Vilaine* XVI (Rennes 1884) 138–264. — F. Lot *Mélanges d'histoire bretonne* (Paris 1907) 331 *sqq*; also in *Annales de Bretagne* XXIV (1909). — There is an abridgment in *Nova Legenda Anglie* (ed. Horstman) (Oxford 1901) II 149–58. WS publishes the " whale incident " from Bili in *Lis. Lives* 352. (ii) Short recension: A. de La Borderie *Bull.-mém.*, etc., as *supra*, 265–312. Long recension: Joh. a Bosco (Dubois) *Bibliotheca Floriacensis* (Lyons 1605) 485 *sqq.* — Lot *op. cit.* 287 *sqq* and *Annales de Bretagne* XXIII. (iii) Surius *De probatis sanctorum historiis* VI (Cologne 1575) 341–51. — Migne *PL* CLX 729–46. (iv) Mabillon *AA. SS. o. s. B.* I 217–22. (v) Plaine *Rev. hist. de l'Ouest* XII (1896) 177–92, and separately [*cf. An. Boll.* XVI 103]. Comm: A. du Chêne *Étude sur les anciennes vies de S. Malo* (Nantes 1885) [extract from *Rev. hist. de l'Ouest* I (1885); *cf. Annales de Bretagne* April 1886 pp. 275–8]. — H. Gaidoz *RC* VI 384. — L. Duchesne *Bulletin critique* VI (Jan. 15, 1885) 26–8; *RC* XI (1890) 1–22. — F. Plaine *Vie de s. Malo* (Rennes 1886). — Lot *op. cit.* 97 *sqq.* — J. Loth *Les noms des saints bretons* (Paris 1910) 87. — Baring-Gould and Fisher *Lives of the British saints* III 411–34. — F. Duine *Saints de Domnonée* (Rennes 1912) 65–7; *Memento* 51–7, 110–4.

St. Maclovius, Machutus, or Malo is said to have been a native of Britain and to have founded the church of Alet in Brittany. There are two Lives of the ninth century, one by Bili, a cleric of Alet, thought to have been written about 869, and another, anonymous, which exists in two redactions. Lot regards the longer redaction as the earliest text of Malo's *vita*, placing it in the second quarter or middle of the ninth century, while Duine considered the short redaction to be of the second half of the ninth, though probably not earlier than Bili's, and the longer to be of the tenth century.

In both of these ninth-century Lives are passages giving the Brendan Legend, with variations. If they are not interpolations they constitute the earliest documentary records of the legend that can be approximately dated; in any case they are among its oldest products, for they are found in manuscripts of the tenth century. Brendan here becomes a Welshman, abbot of Llancarvan, and Malo his disciple.[153] The source seems to be oral tradition handed down at Llancarvan and transmitted to Brittany.[154] One, or two, voyages are made in quest of a wonderful island, and several of the adventures described have near parallels in the Irish documents.

The two later biographers of Malo, with hints at conscientious scruples, suppress the Brendan incidents.

206. Raoul Glaber's Five Books of Histories

EDS: Duchesne *Historiae Francorum SS.* IV (Paris 1641) 1–58. — Bouquet VIII (Paris 1752) 238–40, X (1760) 1–63. — Migne *PL* CXLII 611–98. — M. Prou *Collection de textes pour servir à l'étude et à l'enseignement de l'histoire* I (Paris 1886) [best ed.]. FR. TRANS: Guizot *Collection des mémoires* VI 169–355. *Cf. ZCP* V 136.

Rodulphus, or Raoul, Glaber was an erratic monk of eleventh-century France, born about 985, died about 1047. While at the abbey of Cluny, about 1031–3, he began his Histories, and continued the work until nearly his death. They are bizarre and untrustworthy, but preserve many of the curious and superstitious stories and beliefs of the time. In Book II, chapter ii, *à propos* of the appearance of a whale off the coast of Normandy, he gives a summary account of Brendan's voyage, drawn, with much inaccuracy, from NB1.

207. Poem on Brendan s XI

Mochen, mochen, a Brénaind, . . . rom chrideón is mochenón. 9 quatrains, some imperfect.

MS: LL f. 366. ED: KM " Ein mittelirisches Gedicht auf Brendan den Meerfahrer " *Sitzungsb. d. k. preuss. Akad. d. Wissensch.* 1912 pp. 436–43 [*cf. ZCP* IX 187; *RC* XXXIII 387–8].

Kuno Meyer, on linguistic grounds, assigns this Irish poem to the eleventh century. He thinks it probable that it once formed part of a Life, or Saga, of the saint, which would thus antedate the Irish Life, VB6, by at least half a century. In any case, it is the earliest known document in Irish devoted wholly to Brendan. The poem is an address of welcome to the saint, perhaps on his return from one of his voyages. It is based in part on traditions evidently of a different order from those to be found in either VB or NB. Neither the holy island of the one,[155] nor the land of promise of the other, is mentioned.[156] There are allusions to a few subjects mentioned in VB, and also to Letha,[157] Taprophane and the Sun-Tree,[158] Rome, Tours and Iona, pilgrimage to the Jordan and Mount Zion, and residence among the Greeks. It appears that by this author the " Voyage of Brendan " is rationalised into a pilgrimage to the East.

---

[153] By reflex action, the name of Machutus, as companion of Brendan, has been introduced into a few MSS of NB1.

[154] Lot's text, *lib.* I *cap.* xv: " ut fideles viri de generatione in generationem narrant."

[155] Unless, perhaps, in the mutilated quatrain 7.

[156] But see *ZCP* V 129 n.

[157] Here, no doubt, Brittany, where devotion to Brendan was well established.

[158] Taprophane = Ceylon. The Irish knew of it through *Togail Troi* and of the Sun-Tree through *Scéla Alexandir.*

208. Minor legends connected with Brendan [159]

(i) The Birth of Brendan

Brenaind mac Findloga maic Elchon . . . .

MS: LL 371. ED: H. Gaidoz *Recueil de textes étrangers* (Paris 1888). — *Lis. Lives* 349–50. — *Fél. Oeng.*² 132–3.

Wonders connected with the birth of Brendan, and the prophecies regarding him made by Bishop Erc and Becc mac Dé.

(ii) *Foscél ar Brennain:* Story of Brendan

Luid Brénainn do thabairt anma a máthar a hifern . . . ro isam, ro aitrebam, etc.

MSS: LL 371. — BN Fonds celtique et basque 1 s XV f. 29ᵛ. — TCD H. 3. 18 p. 40. ED: J. Vendryes " Trois historiettes irlandaises " *RC* XXXI (1910) 309–11 [text, Fr. trans.].

A conversation between Brendan and Bishop Moinenn of his church of Clonfert, on the subject of death. It is given in an abbreviated form in VB1, where the saint's interlocutor is his sister, Briga.

(iii) *Scéla an trír maccléirech:* Story of the three clerical students

Tríar maccléirech di fhearuibh Eirenn. . . . conad torruma aingel uasaibh dogrés ina n-indsi.

MSS: LL 283. — Bk. Lis. s XV f. 42ᵛ. EDS: Henri Gaidoz " Les trois clercs et le chat " *Mélusine* IV (1888) 6–11 [LL text, Fr. trans.]. — *Lis. Lives* pp. viii–x [text, trans.].

We have here the story of three clerical students, and a cat, who went " on their pilgrimage " over the ocean in a boat having neither oars nor provisions. It is the basis of one of the episodes in VB. The *motif* appears to be to proclaim the spiritual efficacy of the hymn *Hymnum dicat.*[160]

(iv) Story of Brendan and the bird angel

Feacht do Brenuinn mac hui Altai a Cluain Ferta . . . ocat aran air fitiud-sin, ol Brenainn. Cunad hi an dithramhacht Brenainn.

MSS: Bodl. Rawl. B 512 s XIV/XV f. 142. — Bk. Lis. s XV f. 43ᵛ. ED: *Lis. Lives* pp. xiii–xv [text, trans.].

A clerical student at Clonfert played on the harp for Brendan. The saint explained his want of appreciation by saying that he did not care for earthly music since he had heard the singing of the angel Michael, in form of a bird. The anecdote seems to hold no *arrière-pensée*.

---

[159] See also the prefaces to the hymns *Ní car Brigit* and *Brigit bé*, nos. 148, 95 (iii).
[160] P. 252. There is an allusion to this tale in the litany no. 586.

(v) *Scél Dobar-chon:* Story of Dobar-chú

Bai Brenainn mac Finnloghai a nDubh-dhoire . . . Contains poem: A Chú-cúan . . . Ma becc do sealbh, a Chú-cúan. 8 quatrains.

MS: Bk. Lis. f. 45ᵛ. — RIA Liber Flavus Fergusiorum vol. II pt. v f. 12 [almost illegible]. ED: S. H. O'Grady *Mélusine* IV 298–9. The story was incorporated into VB7.

It would appear that there was in North Munster, in the present Clare, a kindred called Úi Dobar-chon, " Descendants of Water-dog " (*i.e.*, Otter), who observed tabus against taking fish from the (neighboring) Loch Lír, burning bracken, and eating salmon warm off the spit. The story accounts for these peculiarities: the eponymous ancestor was turned into an otter by Brendan because he killed the saint's oxen.[161]

In the seventh century the most famous abbot of Clonfert and *comarba* of Brendan was St. Cuimíne *fota* ("long " or " tall ") (592–662),[162] who, according to the genealogists, was of the royal family of the Eoganacht of Loch-Léin, that is, the western branch of the ruling race of Munster, who dwelt around the Lakes of Killarney. There is a great amount of scattered legendary matter regarding Cuimíne:[163] some of it can be found in the notes to *Félire Oengusso*, November 12, and to his hymn in the *Liber Hymnorum*.[164] The following texts may, because of their association with him, be here considered.

209. Legends of Cuimíne *fota* and Mac-dá-cherda

(i) Cumáin foda mac Fiachna, sui ecna . . . [Ends with a poem of 24 quatrains:] An abrai rim, a Chomgain . . . is na dicheil an abair.
(ii) Mac Telene do feraib Muman . . . tíagait dia tir 7 a n-eneach leo.
(iii) In Mac Da Cherda imraiter sund . . . do co ndeachaid dochum nime.

MSS: (i) YBL col. 335, p. 326 facs. (ii) YBL col. 797, p. 133. — BM Harl. 5280 f. 25. (iii) YBL col. 798, p. 134. ED: J. G. O'Keeffe *Ériu* V (1911) 18–44 [text, trans., notes].

(i) A dialogue in verse, on moral and religious questions, between Cuimíne *fota* and Comgan, otherwise Mac-dá-cherda, " Son of two arts." [165] The name, we are told, arose from the fact that at times he was a lunatic, at other times a man of remarkable wisdom.

---

161 In Cod. S. f. 222 (cols. 945–6 of the ed.) there is an unintelligible fragment which seems to consist of an extract from a story of a search for a certain " Engus Liach Dana," and of the conclusion of a Life of Brendan. — On Brendan see also Plummer *Misc. hag. Hib.* Cat. nos. 79, 83, 84.
162 AU.
163 An unpublished Life is in Brussels Bibl. roy. 2324–40 ff. 47–53: Báoi rí amhra for Ciarraighe Luachra . . . . *Cf.* Plummer *Misc. hag. Hib.* Cat. no. 31.
164 *Cf.* nos. 272, 93. See especially *LH*¹ I 81–93.
165 *LH*¹ I 58.

(ii) This is one of a cycle of stories connected with Gúaire Aidne, king of Connacht (d. 663 or 666). At his court three Munstermen show their versatility: Cuimíne as a *segond*, " champion "; [166] the fool Mac-dá-cherda as a *fili*, " poet; " and the bishop Mo-Ron-óc as an *óinmit*, " fool." The editor calls attention to the possibility that this piece is a satire on those " hangers-on " of the Irish courts, the *fili*, the *segond* and the *óinmit*.

(iii) A series of anecdotes, some of them quite obscure, about Mac-dá-cherda, ending with his association with Cuimíne *fota*.[167]

210. Elegy for Cuimíne *fota*, attributed to Colmán moccu Clúasaig

Marb frimm andess, marb antúaid . . . ba hálaind mar adchoäs. 8 quatrains: the order is not certain.

Parts of the poem are found in *3 Frags.* p. 60, *FM s. a.* 661; Cormac's Glossary sects. 419 and 673 of KM's ed. in *Anec.* IV; and in the following MSS: Bodl. Rawl. B 503 f. 12; BM Harl. 5280 f. 46ᵛ; TCD 1337 (H. 3. 18) 19, 68, 634. Collected and published, with Germ. trans., in KM *Bruchstücke der älteren Lyrik Irlands* (*Abhandl. d. preuss. Akad. d. Wissensch.* 1919 phil.-hist. Kl. vii) (Berlin 1919) 41–3. It is not certain that all the stanzas belong to this poem, nor that the poem, as reconstructed, is complete. Cuimíne died in 662 (AU). The elegy professes to be written in that year by Colmán moccu Clúasaig,[168] but, although the language is early Old Irish, it is doubtful if the composition can be quite so ancient.

CENN-ETIG (KINNITTY) AND ST. FÍNÁN

Adjoining the Ciarraige Luachra, and occupying the southern part of the county Kerry, dwelt another ancient people, the Corco Duibne, whose name is preserved in that of the barony of Corcaguiny. Their patron saint was Fínán *cam* (the term usually means " crooked," but here " squinting "). He is represented to have been a disciple of Brénaind moccu Alti. The annals do not mention him, but his Lives make him a contemporary of Falbe Fland, king of Munster, who died in 637. Like his master, he founded his principal church at a considerable distance from his home-land, at Cenn-Etig, " Etec's Head," now Kinnitty, barony of Ballybrit, Offalley, about eighteen miles south-east of Clonfert. It is convenient to treat of Fínán and his church here, although it is not clear whether Kinnitty was ever a part of the *paruchia* of Brendan.

---

[166] The word is usually so translated: O'Keeffe suggests " sportsman."

[167] The most important text relating to Mac-dá-cherda is the unpublished *Imthechta na dá n-Óinbhide*, " Adventures of the two idiot saints," *i.e.*, Mac-dá-cherda and Conall Clogach. This is found in RIA Stowe B. iv. 1 A.D. 1671 pp. 149–78; also D. iv. 1 ff. 27 *sqq*, and 23 C 19 A.D. 1810 pp. 49–157. It contains another version of (i), and some of the incidents in (iii).

[168] *Cf.* pp. 726–7. FM give the death of Colmán in the same year, which they make 661. But there was a tradition that he lived at least till 664.

211. Life of St. Fínán

(i) Finanus sanctus de genere Corcoduibne . . . ad tribunal Christi, ubi fulget sicut sol in r. D. in s. s. Amen. (iii) Fionan Náomh do Chorca Dhuibhnne . . . le hainglibh Neimhe, agus do fíoradh sin uile. Finit. (iv) Fuit vir vite venerabilis, nomine Finanus, . . . Finanus patronus noster sicut sol fulget in eternum, in presencia gloriosissime sancte Trinitatis. C. est h. et g. in s. s. Amen.

MSS: (i) Cod. S. ff. 103-5^v. (ii) Bodl. Rawl. B 485 ff. 142 *sqq*; B 505 ff. 205^v *sqq*. — Dublin Franciscan Convent A 24 pp. 257 *sqq*. (iii) BM Egerton 112 ff. 510 *sqq*. — RIA 23 B 1; 23 M 50. — Dublin King's Inns Lib. 19. — MS of F. A. Mac-Collum of London *s* XIX *in* [all these MSS are late]. (iv) Cod. K. ff. 84^v-6. — TCD 175 ff. 51 *sq*. — RIA Stowe No. 9 ff. 53-64. — Brussels Bibl. roy. 2324-40 ff. 135-8 [the last 2 MSS contain an Irish trans. of this recension]. EDS: (i) *AA. SS. ex Cod. S.* 305-18. (iii) R.A.S. Macalister *ZCP* II 545-65 [text of Mac Collum's MS, trans.]. (iv) *VV. SS. Hib.* I pp. lxvii–lxx, II 87-95 [text of Cod. K.]. — Fáinne Fionn *Irish Rosary* XV (1911) [the Irish trans.].

The four recensions of the Life of St. Fínán depend on a common original, written at Cenn-Etig by a member of the community. The first recension represents an abbreviated version for general use; and the second is likewise an edition for general use, but somewhat farced with ecclesiastical padding. Recension iii seems to be a seventeenth century rendering into Irish of the second version. The fourth, though older, is farther removed from the original — yet it preserves the " pater noster," " patronus noster," which indicate the source in a composition of Fínán's community. A comparison of the different versions affords an interesting study of the way in which primitive ideas and customs which gave offence, or were not understood, in later times, were gradually obliterated in successive editions of saints' Lives.

III. St. Columba, or Colum-cille, and the *Paruchia Columbae* — The Irish Mission in North Britain

Bibliography

Colgan *Tr. Thaum.* 319-514. — Reeves *Ad.* [see p. 430 *infra;* the most important work on the whole field]. — Montalembert *Les moines d'occident* III (Paris 1868) 101-334 [also in Eng. trans.; elaborate but untrustworthy: *cf.* p. 288 *supra*]. — Skene *Celtic Scotland* II (Edinburgh 1877; 2nd ed. 1887) chaps. ii–iv [valuable]. — P. F. Moran *Irish saints in Great Britain* (Dublin 1879). — A. Bellesheim *Geschichte der katholischen Kirche in Schottland* I (Mayence 1883) 27-65 [also Eng. trans.]. — John Dowden *The Celtic Church in Scotland* (S. P. C. K.: London 1894). — Douglas Hyde *Literary History of Ireland* (London 1899) [of interest with regard to the Irish poems]. — L. Menzies *St. Columba of Iona* (London etc. 1920). — A. O. Anderson *Early sources of Scottish History* (Edinburgh and London 1922) I 17-117. On the chronology of Columba see A. Anscombe " The obit of St. Columba and the chronology of the early kings of Alban " *EHR* July 1892 pp. 510-31; *The date of the obit of St. Columba* (London 1893); and the controversy between him and B. MacCarthy in *The Academy* Sept. 10, Nov. 19, Dec. 3, 10, 24, 1892 [but see Reeves *Ad.* 309-12; Anderson *op. cit.* 103-6]. On the island of Iona: J. Drummond *Sculptured monuments in Iona and the West Highlands* (1881). — H. Dryden "Sculptured monuments in Iona" *Antiquary* 1881. — E. C. Trenholme *The story of Iona* (Edinburgh 1909) [has a good description of the island and its antiquities]. — F. M. McNeill *Iona: a history of the island* (London 1920). On Durrow: Sterling de Courcy Williams "The termon of Durrow" *Journ. RSAI* 5th ser. IX (1899). Legends of Columba in Europe: L. Gougaud *RC* XXXIX (1922) 207–9; Eng. trans. in *Gaelic pioneers of Christianity* (Dublin 1923) 113–6.

The most distinguished centre of Irish religious life at the end of the sixth and through the seventh century was not within the land of Ériu. It was the little island of I, Hii, or Iona,[169] to the west of modern Scotland, some eighty miles from the Irish coast. This is a rugged, windswept island — with, however, a few patches of fertile soil — about three and one-half miles long by one and one-half broad, facing the Atlantic on the west, but on the east separated by a channel of about a mile in width from the extensive island of Mull. Beyond Mull lay, to the east and south, the Irish colony of Dál Riada, sprung from the people of the same name in north-east Ireland; and, to the north, the kingdom of the Picts.

Thither came, in 563,[170] Columba — in Irish usually designated Colum-cille, "Dove of the church" — prince of the royal Úi Néill line and, so far as birth goes, most illustrious of the saints of Ireland. His great-grandfather was that Conall Gulban, son of Níall *nói-gíallach*, who, with his two brothers, had conquered north-western Ulster and set up the new provincial kingdom of Ailech. Three of his first cousins were monarchs of Ireland, and he himself might well have attained that dignity had he not chosen a different path.[171] Small wonder that his community became the most powerful religious body in the Irish world, and that his successors in the abbacy of Iona, usually his kinsmen of the Cenél Conaill blood, were spoken of as the heads of the Irish Church.

---

[169] *Cf.* A. Holder *Alt-Celtischer Sprachschatz* II 66–7. The form "Iona" is derived, by a misreading, from Adamnán's Latin adjective "Ioua." *Cf.* Reeves *Ad.* 258–62, 313–4. It is noteworthy that to Bede Hii is not part of Britannia. Adamnán, however, regards it as in Britain. *Cf.* Plummer *Baedae opera historica* II 186.

[170] Bede says 565. *Cf.* Plummer *op. cit.* II 130.

[171] The community of Clonmacnois, in their legends of their founder, Ciarán *mac in tsáir*, showed little regard for other saints, and even, though somewhat half-heartedly, impugned the reputation of the great Colum-cille. *Cf.* Macalister *The Latin and Irish Lives of Ciaran* 95, 166–7. The *savoir-faire* with which the aristocrats of the Columban *familia* crushed this plebeian effrontery is impressive: "It fell on a time that there was a quarrel, wherein was no great malice, between Colum-cille and Ciaran, the son of the wright. And an angel came to them and brought an axe, an adze and an augur with him. And he told Ciaran not to liken himself to Colum-cille as to quarrel with him, for whereas Ciaran had given up for God naught save his father's labouring suit, Colum-cille had given up the kingship of Ireland." — A. O'Kelleher and G. Schoepperle *Betha Colaim Chille* (Urbana 1918) 60–1. The same story is in Colgan *Tr. Thaum.* 396.

Columba, who, it would appear, had already played a rôle of importance in the ecclesiastical history of his native land, came to his new home " wishing to be an exile for Christ," [172] but found in the result that he had entered on a career of far wider influence. The Scots of North Britain recognised him as their ecclesiastical head,[173] the Picts accepted from him the Christian religion. More churches subject to his jurisdiction were founded in Scotland than in Ireland. With Ireland close relations were maintained by the occasional visits of himself to his native land and of some of his great contemporaries to Iona, and by the continual passing to and fro of the lesser brethren of the monasteries.

In Ireland Columba's principal foundations were Dair-mag, " Oak-plain," now Durrow, county Offaley, established in the territory of the Southern Úi Néill, and Daire-Calgaich, " Calgach's Oak-wood," now Derry, set up among the Northern Úi Néill in 546.[174] Reeves gives a list of forty other Irish churches, and fifty-six Scottish, exclusive of Iona, which formed part of the *paruchia* of Columba, or were associated with his cult.[175] Not all of these were founded by the saint; but it is possible that the records have been lost of other actual foundations.

Some forty years after the death of their patron the Columban community and the church of Iona undertook, and, within a quarter of a century more, carried to a successful conclusion, a still greater missionary enterprise than the conversion of the Picts. This was that mission to the English of Northumbria to which some notice has already been given.[176]

For a century, more or less, following Columba's death his clergy dominated the religious life of Ireland — or at least northern Ireland — Scotland [177] and Northumbria, until in all three their power was shattered or destroyed by the Easter Controversy. In Northumbria King Oswiu, at Whitby in 664, declared against the Celtic customs, and the Irish monks, who in thirty years had turned the land from paganism, went back to Iona or to distant Mayo.[178] In Ireland the Romanising party exalted Armagh and the Patrician communities at the expense, in prestige at least, of the Columban.[179] In what is now Scotland North-

---

172 Adamnán *Vita Columbae* 2nd preface.
173 This must be the meaning of Columba's ordination of King Aedán. Adamnán *Vita Columbae* III v.
174 So AU, but the date is uncertain.
175 Reeves *Ad.* 276–98, 461–2.
176 Chap. III sect. v *supra*.
177 " The island called Hii, whose monastery was for a long time the chief of almost all those of the northern Irish, and all those of the Picts, and had the direction of their people." Bede *Hist. Eccl.* III iii.
178 *Cf.* pp. 224, 463.   179 *Cf.* pp. 325, 329.

umbrian conquest of the Lowlands and Dál Riada restricted the sphere of influence of Iona; the Columban communities established in Pictland were driven out in 717 by the Romanising King Nectan; [180] and in the mother church itself a schism, continuing into the second half of the eighth century, seems to have followed the abbot Adamnán's acceptance of the Roman discipline in 688. [181] Iona, as the church where the saint's body reposed, held, until the ninth century, the primacy of all Columba's foundations both in Ireland and in Scotland. But necessity compelled a change when the sea-rovers from Scandinavia began to sweep down the west coast of Scotland. Henceforth Kells or some other Irish monastery was the usual seat of the *comarba* of Colum-cille. A fantastic legend tells how the saint's body was ultimately interred at Downpatrick, but this had no legal consequences. [182] In Scotland the jurisdiction of Columba's successor gradually passed away, in spite of the facts that a Columban community was maintained at Iona for two centuries more — with intervals of desolation — and that for a short time following Kenneth mac Alpin's accession to the Pictish throne about 844 Columban influences were in the ascendant throughout North Britain. In Ireland the league of Colum-cille's churches remained next to the Patrician in power and dignity until the end of the twelfth century.

Hence it is that Columba, although greatest of Irish missionaries, has always been looked upon as a saint of the homeland, where he takes rank in the pre-eminent trinity of " Patrick, Brigit and Colum-cille." In his own day no break in culture or social organisation, and almost none in political, separated the west of Scotland from the north of Ireland. In later ages it was in Ireland that his ecclesiastical *paruchia* persisted longest and his legends flourished most luxuriantly.

Columba died about 597. [183] We possess records of his life written by three eminent churchmen who flourished within a century of that date, two at least of whom possessed unusual facilities for acquiring information — Cuimíne *Ailbe*, abbot of Iona 657–669, Adamnán, abbot 679–704, and the Venerable Bede, who was born in 673 and died 735. [184] The result is that Columba stands out as a clear-cut historical personality

---

[180] AU: " Expulsion of the community of Ia across Dorsum Britanniae [the mountains separating Perthshire from Argyll] by King Nectan."

[181] Skene *Celtic Scotland* II 172–8, 278–88.

[182] Colgan *Tr. Thaum.* 446. *Cf.* Berchan's Prophecy, in W. F. Skene *Picts and Scots* 79 *sqq.*

[183] Reeves accepts June 9, 597, as the date, which seems to be most consonant with the traditions. The various Irish records are inconsistent. MacCarthy gives 596, and Anscombe 580.

[184] *Cf.* no. 67. Also no. 413, and p. 324.

against a background wherein his associates in sanctity, including the legend-encrusted Patrick and the half-mythical Brigit, move as shadows in a land of twilight.

But Columba too has his legend. As the "poet saint" and the "exile of Erin" he made a peculiar appeal to the mediaeval imagination. The development of mythical matter can be traced through the various late documents, especially the prefaces and annotations to *Amra Coluim-cille*. Peculiarly worthy of note were the results of the legend in the domain of literature: it produced, in the early Middle Irish period, a considerable mass of verse, some of it poetry of merit.[185]

For early Latin poems attributed to Columba see no. 91. *Cf* also. p. 380 *supra*.

212. Amra Coluim-cille

Día Día dorrugus re tías inna gnúis . . . de nemíath nél. (2 quats.) Ní discéoil d'uib Neil . . . Nimda huain. [. . . Ní discéoil.]

MSS: LH(T) ff. 33, 26-8ᵛ. — Bodl. Rawl. B 502 *s* XII ff. 54-9ᵛ. — LU *s* XII *in* 5-15 [imperfect]. — YBL *s* XIV cols. 680 *sqq*, facs. pp. 71 *sqq*. — LBr *s* XIV ff. 238-48 [imperfect]. — BM Egerton 1782 *s* XV/XVI ff. 1-14ᵛ [imperfect]. — RIA Stowe C. 3. 2 *s* XV [imperfect]. Extracts are in many MSS: *e.g.*, the old Irish Life of Columcille (no. 215) has the preface, and several fragments are in Bodl. Laud Misc. 615 *s* XIII/XIV. EDS: J. O'Beirne Crowe *The Amra Choluim Chilli* (Dublin 1871) [LU text and part of LBr; trans.; glosses omitted; of value only as a curiosity]. — WS *Goidelica*² (London 1872) 156-73 [text of LH(T), modified by LU; trans.]. — *LH*² I 162-83, II 53-80, 223-35 [text of LH(T), trans., notes; — severely criticised by WS. Notes on the release of Scandlán *mór* and on the death of Columba, from LH(T), are in *LH*² I 187-9, II 85-7; 236-8.]. — WS "The Bodleian Amra Choluimb Chille" *RC* XX (1899) 30-55, 132-83, 248-89, 400-37, XXI (1900) 133-6 [text of Rawl. B 502, trans., notes; best ed., but far from final; appendix contains following pieces, with trans., from the introductions in other MSS: *Scandlán mór's Captivity* [186] *and the Oppressiveness of the Poets* — Egerton 1782; *The Dispute about the Dalriadans* — YBL; *Conall's Rudeness and Domnall's Courtesy* — YBL; *Story of Labraid and Moriath's Harper* — YBL; *St. Columba's Battles* — Egerton 1782; *Dallan's Death and Burial* — Egerton 1782; several poems attributed to Columba, or referring to him, are to be found among these]. COMM: John Strachan "The Date of the Amra Choluimb Chille" *RC* XVII 41-4. — HZ "Über direkte Handelsverbindungen Westgalliens

---

[185] The saint's name became connected with the cycle of secular romances that centres around Mongan. *Cf.* KM and Alfred Nutt *The Voyage of Bran* I (1895) 87 *sqq*, II (1897) index under "Colum Cille"; *ZCP* II (1899) 313-20.

[186] A version of this tract occurs, as a note to the *Amra*, in LH(T). *Cf. LH*² I 187-8, II 85-6, 236-7.

mit Irland " iv: *Sitzungsb. d. k. preuss. Akad. d. Wissensch.* (1910) 1032–44 [studies the connection between this type of Irish literature and the works of the Latin grammarian Virgilius Maro: *cf.* no. 20]. — KM *Miscellanea Hibernica: University of Illinois Studies in Language and Literature* II no. iv (Urbana, Nov. 1916) 25–7 [with text, trans. of opening quatrains].

The *Amra Coluim-cille*, " Eulogy of Colum-cille," is a composition of extraordinary obscurity, partly because of the antiquity of the language, but mainly by reason of its intentionally artificial character. It is, indeed, the most famous example of *bérla na filid*, that pseudo-rhetorical, arbitrarily reconstructed phraseology and diction which was regarded as a distinct language, the use of which was the insignia and the prerogative of the *filid*. The character of the linguistic forms makes it impossible that the *Amra* as we have it is a composition of the sixth century. Nevertheless it may be that all our copies depend on a re-editing, perhaps in the eighth century, of an original text of the sixth. The character of the subject-matter and the persistence of a few archaic word-forms lend support to such an hypothesis.

There is, as yet, no satisfactory translation of the *Amra*, but the problem is probably not insoluble. The glosses in the manuscripts, on which the translations have largely depended, are the guesswork of late commentators to whom the language and the enigmatical allusions were almost as foreign as to the Irish scholar of to-day, and to whom the resources and the restraints of modern philology were alike wanting.

The several manuscripts have prefaces [187] to the text, varying considerably in character and extent, but all dealing, in the main, with the national convention, *mór-dál*, of Druim-Cetta and the occasion, arising therefrom, of the composition of this eulogy. The convention of Druim-Cetta (now The Mullagh, or Daisy Hill, near Newtownlimavady, co. Derry) [188] is mentioned by Adamnán, who, although he says nothing of the acts of the convention, speaks of Columba's presence there as of a well-known fact.[189] The legend given in the preface, with what historical basis we do not know, says that Columba sought three objects: to release Scandlán *mór*, prince of the Osraige, held prisoner by the *árd-rí;* to make peace between the men of Ireland and the Irish colony in North Britain; and to protect the *filid*, the members of the learned orders, from the banishment with which they were threatened. He was successful in all three. Then Dallán Forgaill, chief of the *filid*, began the *Amra*, but was ordered by Columba to desist until after his, the saint's, death.[190]

In any case a panegyric of a prince of the royal blood, as Columba was, would be an appropriate task for the " poet laureate " of Ireland.

---

[187] The LU preface is probably the earliest. In its present form this belongs to the period between 1008, when Fer-domnach, abbot of Kells and *comarba* of Colum Cille, — to whom reference is made — died, and 1106, the year of the death of Máel-Muire, one of the scribes of the MS (*cf.* p. 15). The passage in which appear the names of Fer-domnach and Máel-Suthain (perhaps Máel-Suthain úa Cerbhaill, who died 1010: *cf.* p. 743) may be, as HZ believed, an accretion: on linguistic grounds he assigned the text to the ninth century, but other philologists do not accept an earlier dating than the second half of the tenth. — One version of the preface is incorporated into the old Irish Life of Colum-cille in the National Library of Scotland MS XL. *Cf.* no. 215.

[188] *Cf.* Reeves *Ad.* 37 n. b.

[189] *Vita Columbae* I x, xlix, II vi.

[190] Many quotations from early Irish poems are included in the literary annotations that have been incorporated into the prefaces.

213. Life of Columba by Cuimíne *Ailbe*

Sanctus igitur Columba, Scotorum natione . . . quieverunt undae marinae: gloria tibi Domine. Amen. [*Cap.* xxv–xxvii:] Perpendat itaque lector . . . Dominus complevit ad l. et g. nominis sui, c. est h. et g. in s. Amen.

MSS: St. Omer Bibl. pub. 716 *s* XIII vol. v ff. 160–3 [formerly of S. Maria de Claromarisco — Clairmarais, St. Omer]. — Brussels Bibl. roy. 7460 *s* XIII ff. 167–9 [formerly of monastery of Vaucelle, Cambrai]. — Vienna, the former K. K. Privat-fideikomiss-Bibl. 9397a A.D. 1479 vol. iii ff. 802–4 [a Sanctilogium of John Gielemans: an abridged text; *cf. An. Boll.* XIV 21]. EDS: Colgan *Tr. Thaum.* 321–4. — Mabillon *AA. SS. o. s. B.* I (Paris 1668) 361–6; 2nd ed. (Venice 1733) 342–9 [from a MS of Compiègne, bearing title "auctore Cummeneo Albo"]. — Pinkerton *Vitae antiquae sanctorum* (London 1789) 27–45 [reprint from Mabillon]. — W. M. Metcalfe *Pinkerton's Lives of the Scottish saints* I (Paisley 1889) pp. xviii–xx, 51–69. — Gertrud Brüning ZCP XI ii (1917) 291–304, 260–72 [also printed separately (Halle a. S. 1916): *cf.* p. 431 *infra*. See review by Anton L. Mayer *Historisches Jahrbuch* XXXIX, Jahrgang 1918–9 (Munich 1919) 374–6]. COMM: Bruno Albers "Zu den beiden ersten Lebensbeschreibungen des Abtes Columba von Iona" *Studien u. Mitteilungen zur Geschichte des Benediktinerordens u. seiner Zweigen* XXXIII (1912) 405–20 [*cf.* W. L[evison] *NA* XXXVIII (1913) 331]. — J. F. Kenney "The earliest Life of St. Columcille" *Cath. Hist. Rev.* Jan. 1926 pp. 636–44.

Cuimíne *Ailbe*, or Cummeneus Albus, great-grandson of a first cousin of Columba, was the seventh abbot of Iona, ruling from 657 to 669. In the oldest copy of Adamnán's Life of Columba, apparently transcribed by the abbot Dorbéne, who died in 713, there is a passage said to be extracted from a work by Cuimíne on the miracles of Columba. It is probable, but not certain, that the use of this quotation, and its attribution to Cuimíne, are due to Adamnán himself.[191] The Life here under consideration contains the passage in question *verbatim*, and was, in at least one manuscript, attributed to Cuimíne *Ailbe*.[192]

This document is divided into twenty-seven chapters, but it is obvious that the original text ended with chapter twenty-four, and that the remainder is made up by later accessions. Practically the whole text is to be found, word for word, in Adamnán's *Vita Columbae*, but with the addition of words, phrases and sentences that greatly expand the narrative. The original twenty-four chapters (with two exceptions),[193]

---

191 *Cf.* p. 432 *infra*.

192 It was first published, as an anonymous text, by Colgan, from a transcript, made, some time after 1575, by Nicolaus Belfortius, a canon regular of Soissons, from a MS otherwise unknown. The same text, with many minor variations, was published by Mabillon in 1668 from a MS of Compiègne in which it was ascribed to "Cummeneus Albus." Mabillon's MS has since disappeared.

193 Of these, one — *cap.* iv, main portion — is, almost certainly, a later interpolation in the Cuimíne text. It comes in awkwardly, and is the kind of anecdote — the first miracle, the changing of water into wine — that a mediaeval copyist would be likely to add. The other, *cap.* xiv, may be genuine: if so, and if our text is that of Cuimíne which Adamnán knew, the reason why he did not incorporate it into his third book is because it alone — a story of a hunting weapon of miraculous powers — could not be strained into doing service under the general title of that book, "De angelicis visionibus."

so expanded, and reinforced by several independent sections, form Adamnán's Book III.[194]

It has long been a subject of dispute whether this Life is the genuine work of Cuimíne, afterwards adapted and expanded by Adamnán, or is in reality a later abridgment of Adamnán's own work, an abridgment which came to be identified with the lost Life by Cuimíne. Of recent critics who have declared against its authenticity the most noteworthy are Bruno Albers,[195] Wilhelm Levison and Gertrud Brüning. Miss Brüning has made a very important study of the question, but her arguments are hardly convincing.

If Cuimíne was the author, the Life must have been written before 669, when he died, and after 642, date of the death of Domnall *brecc*, king of the Irish colony of Dál Riada in the present Scotland, after which that kingdom passed under the control of the Angles of Northumbria, an event to which Cuimíne appears to allude.[196] It would then be, with the probable exception of the Life of Brigit by Cogitosus, the earliest product of Irish hagiography.

214. Adamnán's Life of Columba

[Preface I] Beati nostri Patroni, Christo suffragante. . . . [Preface II] Vir erat vitae venerabilis et beatae memoriae, monasteriorum pater . . . [Life] Vir itaque venerandus qualia virtutum . . . ab omni integer labe, ipso D. n. J. C. dignante: c. est c. P. h., v., l. et g., et i. sempiternum in unitate S. S., per o. s. s. [Epilogue] Post horum trinalium . . . sublimat honoribus, qui est benedictus in s. Amen.

MSS: The longer recension: Schaffhausen Stadtbibl. Msc. Generalia 1 [*cf.* Keller *Mittheilungen der antiquarischen Gesellschaft in Zürich* VII iii (1851) 85; Reeves *Ad.* pp. xiii–xxiv; *Anzeiger zur Schweizerische Geschichte und Altertumskunde* V–VI Jahrgang (Zürich 1859–60) 60 *sq*; Fowler *Adamnani Vita S. Columbae* (1894) pp. viii, 166; H. Boos *Verzeichnis der Inkunabeln und Handschriften der Schaffhauser Stadtbibliothek* (1903) i, 67; *Thes. Pal.* II (1903) p. xxxi; Mario Esposito *Proc. RIA* XXVIII C (1910) 71–2; W. M. Lindsay *Early Irish minuscule script* (*St. Andrew's Univ. Pub.* VI: Oxford 1910) 1–4. Folio codex, in Irish majuscule, with much ornamentation; has the appearance of being a special, probably an " official," transcript.[197] The scribe

[194] The following table indicates the parallel chapters of Cuimíne and Adamnán:

Cuimíne	Adamnán		Cuimíne	Adamnán
i	.....................III i		xiii	.....................III xviii
ii	.....................III ii		xiv	.... II xxxvii
iii	.....................III iv		xv	.....................III xix
iv	(first sentence).........III iv		xvi	.....................III xxii
	(remainder of chap.)..... II i		xvii	.....................III xxii, xxiii
v	.....................III v		xviii–xxiv.....................III xxiii
vi	.....................III vi			I i, viii
vii	.....................III xi		xxv	II xxi, xxvi, xxxii, xxxiii,
viii	.....................III xii			xxxv, xxxvi
ix	.....................III viii			III xxiii
x	.....................III xv		xxvi	.... II xliv
xi	.....................III xvi		xxvii	.... I iii
xii	.....................III xvii			

[195] He suggests that the work is an early draft made by Adamnán himself.
[196] *Cap.* v.
[197] Lindsay *loc. cit.*

writes his name " Dorbbeneus ": it is generally agreed that he was the Dorbéne who became abbot of Iona in June, 713, and died in October. The MS formerly belonged to Reichenau, where Stephen White found it, about 1625, and copied it for Colgan. In 1845 it was re-discovered by Keller at Schaffhausen, where it had been since before 1795.] — BM Cotton. Tiberius D. III s XII/XIII ff. 192–217 [damaged by fire]. — BM Addit. 35110 s XII (1154–65?) ff. 96ᵛ–143 [formerly Phillipps 26075: cf. Cat. of Additions to MSS in British Museum 1894–1899 (London 1901) 161; Liebermann NA X 592 — where the no. is given as 26074 — and H. Omont Catalogue des manuscrits latins et français de la collection Phillipps acquis en 1908 pour la Bibliothèque nationale (Paris 1909) 237]. — BM Reg. 8. D. IX s XVI in. ff. 1–70 [defective at beginning; cf. HZ Zs. f. vergl. Sprachf. XXXII 199]. The shorter recension: St. Gall Stiftsbibl. 555 s IX ff. 1–83 [apparently written in the time of Abbot Grimald (841–72): Ratpert's " Casus s. Galli " ed. Meyer von Knonau Mittheilungen zur vaterländischen Geschichte XIII (St. Gall 1872) 48; MGH SS. II 70; Becker Catalogi bibliothecarum antiqui (Bonn 1885) 56 no. 68]. — Munich Staatsbibl. 6341 s X ff. 1–51 [formerly Freising 141].— Heiligenkreuz (Austria) 12 s XII ex ff. 222ᵛ–6 [cf. Xenia Bernardina II i (Vienna 1891) 121; An. Boll. XVII 65]. — Zwettl 24 s XIII [cf. Xenia Bernardina II i 311; An. Boll. loc. cit.]. — Admont (Styria) 24 s XIII ff. 172ᵛ–85 [cf. An. Boll. loc. cit.]. — Vienna Nationalbibl. lat. 336 s XIII ff. 294ᵛ–310ᵛ [op. cit.]. — Melk M. 5 s XV ff. 151ᵛ–72ᵛ [op. cit.; these Austrian MSS form one family]. — Heidelberg Salem IX. 31 s XIII ff. 113ᵛ–35ᵛ. — Cod. K. ff. 39–51ᵛ. — Wolfenbüttel 357 (Helmstedt 322), s XV ff. 317ᵛ–38ᵛ [cf. O. von Heinemann Die Handschriften der herzoglichen Bibliothek zu Wolfenbüttel I i (1884) 268]. Other modified versions of Adamnán's text are in Metz Bibl. de la ville 523 s XI ff. 19–51; BN 5308 s XII ff. 287ᵛ–92ᵛ; BN 5278 s XIII ff. 393–9; Le Mans 217 s XII ff. 102ᵛ–6ᵛ; Florence Bibl. Laurenziana Ashburnham 58 (15) s XI/XII ff. 117–31. Unclassified texts in BM Addit. 19726 s XI f. 59 [Cat. of Additions 1854–1860 (London 1875) 2]; and BN 5323 s XIII ff. 133–40. EDS: Longer recension: Colgan Tr. Thaum. 336–72. — AA. SS. Boll. Jun. II (1698) 197–236. — J. Pinkerton Vitae antiquae sanctorum (London 1789) 47–187 [poor]. — Wm. Reeves The Life of St. Columba, founder of Hy, written by Adamnan ninth abbot of that monastery The text printed from a manuscript of the 8th century with the various readings of six other manuscripts preserved in different parts of Europe To which are added copious notes & dissertations illustrative of the early history of the Columbian institutions in Ireland and Scotland (Dublin The Irish Archaeological and Celtic Society; Edinburgh The Bannatine Club: 1857) [Best ed.   The text, based on the Schaffhausen MS, though good, is not perfectly accurate — "Reeves has . . . disregarded the peculiarities of Adamnan's orthography, which are often both curious and instructive.   In some instances, where the spelling of the MS is perfectly correct according to Brambach and the best Latin codices, it has been spoiled in the edition " (WS The Academy XXX (1886) 227; cf. Mario Esposito Proc. RIA XXVIII C (1910) 72).   The extent and scholarly character of the editorial matter renders this ed. one of the most valuable of Irish historical publications.   " It is doubtful whether in the annals of literature so much important information has ever before been so lavishly accumulated and so skilfully arranged within a few hundred pages, or whether any other editorial task has ever been more thoroughly executed " (F. E. Warren Liturgy and Ritual of the Celtic Church pref. p. xi)]. — W. F. Skene The Historians of Scotland VI (Edinburgh 1874) [Reeves's ed., re-arranged, somewhat abridged, but with additions and trans.]. — W. M. Metcalfe Pinkerton's Lives of the Scottish saints I (Paisley 1889) pp. xx–xxxi, 73–209 [good ed.]. — J. T. Fowler Adamnani Vita S. Columbae (Oxford

1894; 2nd ed. 1920) [based on Reeves]. Shorter recension: H. Canisius *Antiquae lectionis* V ii (Ingolstadt 1604) 559–621; 2nd ed. by J. Basnage I (Antwerp 1725) 674–709. — L. Surius *De probatis sanctorum historiis* (Cologne 1618) VI 144–61. — Messingham *Florilegium* (Paris 1624) 141–84 [from Canisius]. — B. Gonon *Vitae patrum Occidentis* (Lyons 1625) 420 *sqq* [based on Surius]. — Ussher *Sylloge* (Dublin 1632) 42–4; *Whole Works* IV 454–6 [prologue and epilogue only]. — Migne *PL* LXXXVIII 725–76. Cf. *Thes. Pal.* II (1903) pp. xxxi, 272–80 [passages containing Irish names]. TRANS: Daniel MacCarthy *Life of St. Columba or Columbkille* (Dublin 1889). — J. T. Fowler *Prophecies, Miracles and Visions of St. Columba* (London 1895) [a close and careful trans.]. — Wentworth Huyshe *The Life of Saint Columba* (*The New Universal Library*) (London n. d.) [serviceable and generally trustworthy]. COMM: The works of Thos. Wright, P. Geyer, and M. Manitius, cited p. 283 *supra*. — Roger *L'Enseignement* 261–3. — Bruno Albers *op. cit.* p. 428 *supra* [an attempt, not very successful, to prove that the authors of the early Lives of Columba were actuated by a desire to present their patron as the equal of St. Benedict in certain remarkable experiences]. — Pfister *Berliner philol. Wochenschrift* (1914) p. 1491 [on Adamnán as hagiographer]. — Gertrud Brüning " Adamnan's Vita Columbae und ihre Ableitungen " *ZCP* XI ii (1917); also separately (Halle a. S. 1916) [very important; *cf.* pp. 428–9 *supra*].

Adamnán (624–704), ninth abbot of Iona, of whose life and works something has been said above,[198] has given us in his *Vita s. Columbae* " perhaps the most valuable monument of the Irish Church which has escaped the ravages of time " (Reeves). His is the last, and much the most important, of the four historical sources of real worth that seventh-century Ireland has left us: the other three are the books of Cogitosus, Tírechán and Muir-chú.[199]

The Life was written in Iona,[200] and at the request of the brethren,[201] after 679, when Adamnán became abbot.[202] The lower limit is fixed by his death in 704. In the last chapter of the second book he alludes to two visits made by him to King Aldfrid of Northumbria: these, from the evidence of Bede and the annals, seem to have been in 686/687 and 688/689. Another passage bearing on this subject is that in which he refers to the misfortunes of the descendants of King Aedán of Dál Riada after the battle of Roth (Mag-Rath, 637): " from that day to this they are in decline through foreign pressure, a fact which fills one's breast with grievous sighs." The " foreign pressure " began about 642, when the Dál Riada of North Britain lost their independence under the attacks of Britons and Northumbrians, and ended with the death of the Northumbrian King Ecgfrid in 685.[203] This passage, which seems itself to be an addition of later date than the surrounding text, must,

---

[198] *Cf.* pp. 216, 245, 283.
[199] Nos. 147, 127, 128.   [200] I i, xxx, and *passim.*   [201] *Praef.* I.   [202] I i, iii, III xix.
[203] *Cf.* Bede *Hist. Eccl.* IV xxvi.

therefore, have been written before, or very soon after, 685.[204]   On the whole it seems probable that the Life was, for the most part, written before 685, but received its final form in, or soon after 688/689; [205] the last chapter of Book II, containing the references to Adamnán's visits to Aldfrid, may have been the last written, for it is probable that the third book, if it was an expansion of an older Life by Cuimíne Ailbe, was the first produced.[206]

Of his sources Adamnán speaks thus: " Let no one think that I lie about this famous man, or write things dubious or not determined; but be it known that I shall narrate what has been handed down in the consistent tradition of our elders, trustworthy and discerning men, setting down in all candor the facts I have been able to find written in books before my time, and those which, in response to my careful enquiries, have been related to me orally by certain well-informed, trustworthy old men, who spoke from personal knowledge and conviction." [207]   The written sources included the Life by Cuimíne Ailbe and, if the text which now bears that name is genuine, at least one other document.[208]   Some of the sources of oral tradition are named: Failbe (ruled 669–79), Adamnán's predecessor as abbot, who, in the time of the fifth abbot, Ségine (ruled 623–52), had heard the narratives of King Oswald of Northumbria and St. Ernene, or M-Ern-occ; [209] through the same Ségine came a story told by Columba's disciple, Silnan; [210] Oissene, disciple of St. Fintan, or Munnu; [211] Máel-Odrán moccu Rin, a priest, apparently of Derry; [212] old men who had received information from Lugbe moccu Blai, a disciple of Columba; [213] Finan, anchorite of Durrow; [214] Commán, nephew of Fergno, fourth abbot (ruled 605–23); [215] Virgno (Fergno), an anchorite in the islands of the Scottish coast, whose report came through certain old men; and a monk, Ernene moccu Fir-Roide, a contemporary of Columba who lived to talk with Adamnán.[216]   Perhaps in the category of orally transmitted sources should be placed

---

[204] In the Schaffhausen MS, which is in majuscule script, this passage is in minuscule, but was written by the same pen.   It would seem that the scribe left a blank space to be filled in, but when he came to make the entry found that he had underestimated the space required and was forced to reduce the size of his script.   Professor Lindsay suggests that Dorbéne was copying from Adamnán's autograph, and that the passage in question was an ' afterthought ' of the biographer, added on the margin or on an interposed slip of parchment in the autograph copy (Early Irish Minuscule Script 2–3). We can be certain that this passage was not in the original text of Adamnán; the fact that a recension, that of Cotton. Tiberius D III and Reg. 8 D IX, has come to us from which it is absent suggests that some considerable time elapsed before it was inserted.   Yet, as is shown above, its contents prove — unless the Schaffhausen MS was written long after 713 — that it goes back to a date prior to, or at least not much later than, 685.

[205] Adamnán joined the Roman party in the Easter controversy about 689–90, and attempted to win over Iona.   A schism seems to have resulted, in which only a minority of the monks followed their abbot. Adamnán came to Ireland in 692, and again in 697, when it would appear that he remained until the year of his death, 704.   The Life was not written in Ireland, and its tone favors the conclusion that it was not written after this controversy had become acute.   HZ, without offering any cogent reason, seems to say that our text is a second edition prepared by the author after he had accepted the Roman doctrine (" Über direkte Handelsverbindungen Westgalliens mit Irland " 3 A Sitzungsb. d. k. preuss. Akad. d. Wissensch. 1909 xx 544).   Reeves thought the date was 692 x 697, Skene, with better reason, 688 x 692.

[206] I am inclined to think that our text is such a second or later edition of a work which originally consisted of only one book.   Several superficial features suggest this: the two prefaces, the peculiar character of chapter i of Book I, the introductory section of Book III.

[207] Praef. II.

[208] The vision reported by Virgnous, III xxiii: this is not in the extant Cuimíne.   [209] I i, iii.

[210] II iv.   [211] I ii.   Cf. AU 687.   [212] I xx.   [213] I xliii.   [214] I xlix.   [215] III xix.   [216] III xxiii.

the hymns in Irish relating to Columba of which Adamnán speaks,[217] and which may possibly have included the *Amra*.

The traditions and legends which are embodied in Adamnán's compilation are, in the main, the product of the monastery. His *Vita Columbae* is the chief record of the old Celtic monastic Church of Ireland. As abbot of Iona, *comarba* of Colum-cille, and, in a sense, primate of the Church of Ireland,[218] he stands pre-eminent as a witness to its character and history. We may lament that his knowledge and talents were devoted to hagiography rather than to history, that he made himself a successor of Cogitosus and Cuimíne rather than a predecessor of Bede, but we must acknowledge that in his own way he has given a uniquely valuable picture of the external form and internal character of the ecclesiastical system in which he bore so prominent a part. That picture — as, indeed, likewise, his delineation of the character and career of his hero — differs markedly both from the representations of Irish hagiographers of four centuries and more later, and from the reconstructions of some modern historians. In all that concerns the Celtic Church of Ireland, its faith and devotions, its monastic life and ecclesiastical organisation, the student may still with profit scan the lines of Adamnán's *Vita Columbae*.

One other aspect of the Life should be signalised. It is the most considerable surviving literary production of the Celtic Church of Ireland. It shows, for its time, a quite respectable degree of culture. The Latinity is clear, concise, grammatical, and indicative of some feeling for literary finish. The dominating literary influence was the Bible; Miss Brüning has shown that to it are to be added the Latin Life of St. Antony, Sulpicius Severus's Life of Martin of Tours, the Dialogues of Gregory the Great, Constantius's Life of Germanus of Auxerre, the *Gesta Silvestri*, Vergil, Juvencus, and possibly Hegesippus and Dionysius Exiguus. There are also some few traces of the style of the *Hisperica Famina*.

A shorter recension of Adamnán's work, prepared by some later hagiographer, exists in several manuscripts and has been published by Canisius and others; and there seems to be at least one other abbreviated text not yet published. The Life in the Breviary of Aberdeen [219] is an abridgment of Adamnán, as is also that in the *Nova Legenda Anglie*,[220] where some matter from Bede is added.

215. The old Irish Life of Colum-cille

Exi de terra tua . . . .i. Facoibh do thir 7 do thalamh . . . . [Ends with a long series of conventional clauses.] Roissem, roaitreabhum, in s. s. Amen.

MSS: LBr pp. 29–34. — Bk. Lis. ff. 7ᵛ–11. — Edinburgh Nat. Lib. of Scot. Gael. XL *s* XV/XVI pp. 13–28. — BN Celt. et basq. 1 (Ancien fonds 8175¹) *s* XV ff. 53–6ᵛ. — RIA Reeves 42 pp. 71–80. — Dublin King's Inns 10 ff. 21ᵛ–6. EDS: WS *Three Middle-Irish homilies* (Calcutta 1877) [LBr text, trans.]. — *Lis. Lives* 20–33, 168–81, 299–317 [text, trans., notes]. TRANS: W. M. Hennessy " The Old Irish Life of St. Columba ": Skene *Celtic Scotland* II (Edinburgh 1877) 467–507 [based on LBr, Lismore and Nat. Lib. texts]. COMM: WS *RC* II (1874) 197 *sqq* no. x, V (1883) 393–4. — H. Gaidoz *Les gâteaux alphabétiques* (Paris 1886). — G. Brüning " Adamnans Vita Columbae und ihre Ableitungen " sect. viii *ZCP* XI ii (1917) 272–6.

²¹⁷ I i.   ²¹⁸ *Cf.* p. 423.   ²¹⁹ Under June 9. *Cf.* p. 484 *infra.*   ²²⁰ Ed. Horstman I (1901) 198–206.

This Life of Colum-cille in Irish, cast in the form of a homily, for the saint's feast, on the favorite Irish text, *Genesis* xii 1, is found in four recensions, each of which has its own peculiarities. The common exemplar was probably at least as old as the eleventh century, and seems to have been an abridgment of an earlier, perhaps tenth- or even ninth-century, Life. It was written in Ireland, doubtless in a Columban monastery, and is an Irish presentation of much of the matter of which Adamnán gave an earlier, and Ionan, version. However, although the author seems not to have used Adamnán directly, it may be that from that work came ultimately a large part of his material. There are several passages of great folk-lore interest.

216. Simeon's Lines on Columba A.D. 1107 X 1114

Sancte Columba pater, quem fudit Hibernia [ma] ter . . . . Hunc librum clare qui dignum duxit arare.
25 ll.

MS: BM Cotton. Tiber. D III *s* XII f. 217 [somewhat damaged in the fire of 1731]. EDS: Ussher *Brit. Eccles. Antiq.* XV (*Whole Works* VI 230, 239) [quotations from MS while still uninjured]. — Reeves *Ad.* Pref. p. xxix. — H&S I pt. I 276–7.

These somewhat crude Latin verses are found at the end of a Life of Columba in a series of Saints' Lives, transcribed, according to Reeves, in 1180. They were written, as appears from their contents, by a monk named Simeon, at the order of King Alexander I of Scotland (1107–1124), and before the death of his Queen, Sibylla (d. 1122). They were composed under the direction of a certain William, presumed to be William, bishop of Man, whose episcopate ended in the period 1109–1114. Consequently the date of composition would be within the years 1107 to 1114. Simeon was, possibly, a monk of Hii itself, although at this time the island was nominally subject politically to Norway and ecclesiastically to the See of Man.

The poem gives expression to a prayer that Columba may be a patron to the various persons mentioned above, and to the clergy and people of Scotland.

217. Life of Columba from *Codex Salmanticensis*

Venerabilis abbas et plurimorum pater cenobeorum Columba . . . claritas frequentare non cessat, ad l. et g. ejus qui c. P. et F. et S. s. v. et r. in s. s. Amen.

MS: Cod. S. ff. 205–10ᵛ. EDS: Colgan *Tr. Thaum.* 325–32. — *AA. SS. ex Cod. S.* 845–70. COMM: G. Brüning "Adamnans Vita Columbae und ihre Ableitungen" sect. ix *ZCP* XI ii (1917) 276–83.

The Life of Colum-cille found in the extant portion of the *Codex Salmanticensis*,[221] and published by Colgan as the Life by Cuimíne *Ailbe*, consists of two parts. The first nineteen chapters form a distinct Life, of composite character, the contents being drawn either from Adamnán — though in modified form and apparently not at first hand — or from the old Irish Life at an earlier stage in its history than that represented by the present texts. This portion must be old, for there is a quotation from it in the *Vita Brendani*.[222] It contains a few seemingly original passages. The

---

[221] It is probable that there was a Life of the saint in the first forty-seven folios, now lost.
[222] VB2 *cap.* civ: from *cap.* xiv *Vita Columbae.*

remaining eleven chapters are a later annex, made up of *verbatim* excerpts from Adamnán, which, however, differ considerably from the now received version.

218. Life of Columba from *Codex Insulensis*

MSS: Bodl. Rawl. B 485 ff. 37–43ᵛ; B 505 ff. 118 *sqq*. — Cod. S. f. 88 [a fragment of the passage *re* the cause of Columba's exile]. EDS: Ussher *Antiquities* xvii (*Whole Works* VI 466 *sqq*) [part of the passage *re* the cause of the saint's exile]. — Colgan *Tr. Thaum.* 332 [the fragment from Cod. S.]. — *AA. SS. ex Cod. S.* 221–4 [the same fragment]. — H. J. Lawlor " The Cathach of St. Columba " App. III *Proc. RIA* XXXIII C 408–12 [text of passage *de causa peregrinationis s. Columbae*]. *Cf. ZCP* V (1905) 435–6.

When the *Codex Salmanticensis* was compiled in the fourteenth century the scribe had access to a tract on " the cause of the ' pilgrimage ' of St. Columba," which he copied into his book between the lives of Tigernach of Clones and Fintan of Duleng. In the manuscript as it exists at present only a fragment of the tract remains, the first folio having been removed, perhaps because the story was not considered sufficiently edifying. Fortunately the full text has been preserved in a Life of Columba in the *Codex Insulensis*, a Life which is simply a second recension of that which has just been catalogued as the " Life from *Codex Salmanticensis*." The work of the reviser consisted, for the most part, of the insertion of the matter contained in the story as to how Colum-cille got his name, and of the tract *de causa peregrinationis s. Columbae*, and of a re-arrangement of the matter relating to the saint's death. The section " on the cause of exile " tells the story of Columba's quarrel with the *árd-rí*, Diarmait mac Cerr-béil, over this king's judgment on the rights to a copy of a manuscript, and of the synod of Tailtiu, at which Columba was threatened with excommunication.

219. Minor sources relating to Columba

(i) Columba's disciples and relatives

Haec sunt duodecim virorum . . . praesentem finivit vitam.

MSS: BM Reg. 8. D IX *s* XVI *in*. f. 70. EDS: Pinkerton *Vitae antiquae sanctorum* (London 1789) 187. — Reeves *Ad.* 245–7. — Metcalfe *Pinkerton's Lives* I 208–9. — *Thes. Pal.* II 281.

This short list of Columba's companions in the founding of Iona, and of his near relatives, seems to preserve a very old text.

(ii) Columba in Aran

MSS: Bodl. Rawl. B 512 f. 141. — BN Fonds celtique 1 f. 56ᵛ. EDS: KM *Gaelic Journ.* IV (Dec. 1892) 162 [Rawl. text, trans.]. — J. Vendryes *RC* XXXIII (1912) 354–6 [Paris text, Fr. trans.].

Columba discovered on the island of Aran the grave of Talgaeth, an abbot of Jerusalem.[223]

---

[223] Incorporated into O'Donnell's Life of Colum-cille, sect. 155.

(iii) Origin of the name Colum-cille

MS: LBr 236 b. ED: *Lis. Lives* 301–3 [text, trans.]. *Cf. Fél. Oeng.*[1] p. c; *Fél. Oeng.*[2] 146.

Why the saint was called Colum-cille, " Dove of the church." His virtues and his asceticism.

(iv) Prayer ascribed to Colum-cille

Dumfett Cristt cuntt cumhachta . . . spiratt naomh dom insorchughadh. amhein amhén.

MS: Bodl. Laud 615 p. 115. ED: KM *ZCP* VI (1908) 258.

In the secular historical tract on the *Bóroma* there is a passage of much interest regarding the relations of Columba with the *árd-rí* Aed mac Ainmerech. It is published separately in *Lis. Lives* 306–8. It contains the stories of the three kings who alone in his time, according to Columba, went to heaven. On this is based the poem by WS " King Ailill's Death."—The Life of St. Kentigern tells of the relations between him and Columba, and the exchange of staffs which they made. *Cf.* p. *173 supra*. Columba's staff was afterwards preserved at Ripon. *Cf.* p. *153 supra*.

220. Irish Poems relating to Colum-cille

The principal MS is Bodl. Laud 615 (=L) *s* XV, a vellum codex containing 150 [224] religious poems, the majority of which either refer to Colum-cille or are presented as his compositions. *Cf.* KM *Ériu* V (1911) 7–14, where a list of first lines is given, in alphabetical order. A number of poems of the Colum-cille cycle are not in this collection.

As it is impossible to give even an approximate chronology to these poems, they have been arranged in the alphabetical order of the incipits.

(i) A Brénaind, abair rium sin . . . 7 quatrains. MS: L p. 5. ED: KM *ZCP* VII 302. *Cf. Cath. Hist. Rev.* VI (Jan. 1921) 404. Dialogue between Colum-cille and Brendan.

(ii) A chléirigh an churraig cain . . . . 7 quatrains. MS: L 97. ED: KM *ZCP* X 341.

(iii) A Dhé dhil. . . . 7 quatrains. MSS: L 101. — TCD 1284 (H. 1. 10) A.D. 1742 f. 149ᵛ. ED: KM *ZCP* X 51. Poem in praise of hospitality, attributed to Colum-cille.

(iv) A Dia cid nach ndingbai dind . . . . MS: YBL 873. EDS: O'D in Petrie " Tara Hill " *Trans. RIA* XVIII (1837) 123; *FM s. a.* 555 [with trans.]. — *Tig.* in *RC* XVII 143–4. On the battle of Cuil Dremne; attributed to Colum-cille.

(v) A Éire, is duit is doraidh . . . . 8 quatrains. MS: L 118. ED: KM *ZCP* XII 392. Colum-cille.

[224] As KM suggests, this number was probably purposely fixed to equal the number of the psalms, and the volume, like several other old codices, bore the title *Saltair*.

(vi) A fir féil . . . . 3 quatrains. MSS: L 101. — TCD 1284 (H. 1. 10) f. 168. EDS: KM *ACL* III 222; *Ériu* IV (1908) 17 [with trans.]. Colum-cille on hospitality.

(vii) A gilla, glac do leabhar . . . . 13 quatrains. MS: L 10. ED: KM *ZCP* XII 385. Colum-cille.

(viii) Aibind beith ar Beind Edair . . . . 24 quatrains. MSS: Brussels Bibl. roy. 5100–4 p. 35. — Maynooth Murphy 72 p. 135. EDS: T. Connellan *Reidh-Leighin air ghnothuibh cearba* (1835) 60–1. — O'C in Reeves *Ad.* 285–9 [with trans.]. — T. P. O'Nolan *IER* 4th ser. XXIV (1908) 494–9 [with trans.]. TRANS: KM *Selections from ancient Irish poetry* (London 1911) 83–5; (2nd ed. 1913) 85–7. *Cf.* Douglas Hyde *Literary history of Ireland* (London 1899) 169–78. Colum-cille's address to Ireland. A composite poem: many of the stanzas, more or less modified, are found in other poems.

(ix) Aingil Dé dom dín . . . . 31 or more quatrains; originally ended at 19th. MSS: LBr p. 262. — L 25. — RIA 23 G 23 p. 118; 23 N 13 p. 277; F. II. 3 p. 1. — Maynooth Murphy 70 p. 94; Murphy 39 p. 212; O'Renehan 96 p. 234. ED: Thos. P. O'Nolan *Miscellany presented to Kuno Meyer* (Halle a. S. 1912) 253–7. Prayer to the angels and saints for protection; in one MS is designated " Sciath-lúirech Choluim Chille." *Cf.* no. lxvii *infra*.

(x) A Muire mín maithingen . . . . 16 quatrains. MSS: L 90. — RIA 23 N 10 p. 18; Stowe B. iv. 2 s XVII f. 137. EDS: J. Strachan *Ériu* I i (1904) 122. — P. Walsh *IER* 4th ser. XXIX (1911) 172–7 [with trans.]. — C. Plummer *Irish Litanies* (London 1925) pp. xxiii, 96–9 [with trans.]. TRANS: KM *Selections from ancient Irish poetry* (London 1911; 2nd ed. 1913) 32–3. Colum-cille: prayer to the B. V. M.

(xi) An echtrach-sa scíath mo sgol . . . . MS: L 102. ED: KM *ZCP* X 344–5. Colum-cille.

(xii) Aod mac Ainmerech na n-all . . . . 5 quatrains. MS: L 49. ED: KM *ZCP* XIII 8. *Cf. RC* XX 138. Colum-cille on the kings at the convention of Druim-cetta.

(xiii) Benaidh bhar cluig ar Conall . . . . 3 quatrains. MS: L 78. ED: KM *ZCP* X 48. Colum-cille curses the prince Conall at Druim-cetta.

(xiv) Cainnech coem comarbha . . . MS: Bodl. Rawl. B 502 f. 54. ED: WS *RC* XX 146–9 [with trans.]. Colum-cille in praise of Cainnech.

(xv) Cainnech mo chomarci . . . 7 stanzas. MS: RIA 23 N 10 p. 91. ED: KM *ACL* III 219–21. Colum-cille in praise of Cainnech.

(xvi) Caomh Colum cáidh . . . . MS: L 18. ED: KM *Voyage of Bran* I (London 1895) 88–90 [with trans.]. Mongan in praise of Colum-cille: connected with the Mongan cycle of secular texts.

(xvii) Ceileabrad úaim-si d'Árainn . . . . MSS: L 28. — TCD 1285 (H. 1. 11) A.D. 1752 f. 143. — BM Egerton 142 f. 84. ED: Th. O'Flanagan *Trans. Gaelic Soc.* I (Dublin 1808) 180–9. Colum-cille's farewell to Aran.

(xviii) Ceileabram, léighim, lubrum . . . . 5 quatrains. MS: L 138. ED: KM *ZCP* VIII 231. Colum-cille.

(xix) Celiubroim do Dun mBaili . . . . ED: W. M. Hennessy and D. H. Kelly *Book of Fenagh* (1875) 208–15 [with trans.]. Colum-cille's blessing of Fenagh.

(xx) Cethrar sagart, suairc in dám . . . . 5 stanzas. MS: L 19. ED: KM *ZCP* X 343. Báithín mac Cúanach, said to be of the sixth century, on Colum-cille and other saints.

(xxi) Cluig tolla . . . . 3 quatrains. MS: L 36. ED: KM *ZCP* XII 386. Colum-cille.

(xxii) Coinne Mongáin is Coluim cháim . . . . 3 stanzas [*Ériu* V 9 says 22]. MS: L 21. ED: KM *Voyage of Bran* I 87 [with trans.]. Muru of (F)Othan on the meeting of Colum-cille and Mongan.

(xxiii) Colum cáid cumachtach . . . . 5 stanzas. MSS: LU 15. — Bodl. Rawl. B 502 p. 107. — L 47. ED: Julius Pokorny *ZCP* VIII (1912) 285–8, 420. *Cf. RC* XX 146; *IT* III 56. An O-I prayer to Colum-cille, perhaps of ninth century.[225] It is ascribed in one place to Cainnech.

(xxiv) Colum-cille cend Alban . . . . . Mugrón, *comarba* of Colum-cille. *Cf.* p. 727 *infra*.

(xxv) Comhnaigh a Chríost im chroidhe. . . . MS: Maynooth Murphy 8 p. 334; 72 (3 F 20) p. 50. ED: C. Ward *Míl na mBeach* (Dublin 1911) 45–6, 94–5. Colum-cille.

(xxvi) Cormac cain buich neóit . . . . MSS: In the introduction to the Amra Coluim-cille; also L 49. ED: WS *RC* XX (1899) 44 [with trans.]. *Cf. LH²* I 163, II 55. Colum-cille.

(xxvii) Cormac húa Liatháin lf glan . . . . 24 quatrains. MSS: L 118. — Brussels Bibl. roy. 5100–4 p. 40. EDS: O'C in Reeves *Ad.* 270–5 [with trans.]. — KM *ZCP* XII 390–2. Dialogue between Colum-cille and Cormac.

(xxviii) Cros Críst tarsin gnúis-si . . . . Prayer attributed to Colum-cille. *Cf.* p. 727 *infra*.

(xxix) Cúghaire dochúalmar . . . . 3 quatrains. MS: L 129. ED: KM *ZCP* XII 396. Colum-cille.

(xxx) Déna a Ghúaire maith um ní . . . . 5 stanzas. MS: L 23. ED: KM *King and Hermit* (London 1901) 28 [with trans.]. Colum-cille's blessing, which produced the hospitable character of Gúaire Aidne.

(xxxi) Dena mo fhreisnes a meic . . . . MS: Bk. Lec. ED: O. Connellan *Trans. Ossianic Soc.* V (1860) 250–7. Colum-cille. On the mythical invasions of Ireland.

(xxxii) Día ard airleathar . . . . 3 quatrains. MSS: Bodl. Rawl. B 502 p. 106. — L 48. ED: KM *ZCP* X 345. Colum-cille.

(xxxiii) Día do betha a Chorbmaic cain . . . . 17 stanzas. MS: L 34. — Brussels Bibl. roy. 5100–4 p. 38. ED: O'C in Reeves *Ad.* 264–9 [with trans.]. Dialogue between Colum-cille and Cormac úa Liatháin, after the latter's ocean voyage.

(xxxiv) Día lim fri gech sním . . . . 18 quatrains. MSS: L p. 91. — RIA 23 N 10 p. 19. — RIA Stowe B. IV. 2 f. 137ᵛ. EDS: KM *ACL* III (1905) 6–7. — A. O'Kelleher *Ériu* IV (1910) 235–9 [with trans.]. TRANS: E. J. Gwynn *LH²* II 210–1 [partial]. A *lorica*. Colum-cille.

(xxxv) Día mór dom imdeghail . . . . 83 stanzas. MS: L 122–7. — Bk. Lec. f. 170ᵛ. ED: KM *ZCP* VIII 198–217, X 37–41, 444. Colum-cille, or an Úa hEmín.

(xxxvi) Día na ndúl dom dhídin . . . . 17 quatrains. MS: L 116. ED: KM *ZCP* X 347–8. Colum-cille.

(xxxvii) Do cluin Ísa guth an chluicc . . . . 3 quatrains. MS: L 120. ED: KM *ZCP* XII 395. Colum-cille.

(xxxviii) Dofed andes a ndáil Fiadhatt . . . . 25 quatrains. MS: L 114–5. ED: KM *ZCP* VIII 197–8. Bécán mac Luigdech to Colum-cille.

---

[225] Versification and to some extent vocabulary are imitated in no. xiv *supra*, and in the Life of Colmán mac Lúacháin (KM's ed. p. 11: see no. 238).

(xxxix) Donál chon cenduig co cert .... 7 stanzas. MS: L 138. Ed: S. H. O'Grady " Irish prognostications from the howling of dogs " *Mélusine* V (1890) 85–6 [with trans.]. — KM *ZCP* XIII 7–8. Colum-cille.

(xl) Dorala for mo menmuin .... 18 stanzas. MS: L 104. Ed: KM *ZCP* X 338–40. Colum-cille.

(xli) Druim-cetta cete na noem ... MSS: Bodl. Rawl. B 502 f. 55. — L 111. Ed: WS *RC* XX 136–41 [with trans.]. On the convention of Druim-cetta.

(xlii) Eineach úaisle ná gach dán .... 8 quatrains. MS: L 25. Ed: KM *ZCP* IX 486. Colum-cille.

(xliii) Éirigh cumm na híarmérghe .... 6 quatrains. MS: L 138. Ed: KM *ZCP* X 48. Colum-cille: on death.

(xliv) Éistea frim a Báithín búain .... MSS: L 82. — TCD 1284 (H. 1. 10) f. 157. — TCD 1354 (H. 4. 13) f. 210. Ed: N. O'Kearney *The prophecies of Sts. Columkille,* etc. (1856). *Cf.* O'C *MS Mat.* 400 *sqq.* Colum-cille: prophecy of events from his own time to the coming of the English; is sometimes designated " Mesca Coluim-cille." One stanza is quoted in the LL version of CGG, Todd's ed., p. 225.

(xlv) Fersaighecht an tempuil tall .... 34 stanzas. MS: L 7. Ed: KM *ZCP* IX 172–5. Colum-cille.

(xlvi) Fir usci .... MS: RIA Bk. of Húi Maine, f. 119. Ed: KM *ACL* II 141 [partial]. Colum-cille. Contrasting the clergy of the time with those of earlier ages.

(xlvii) Fort fhóisam, a Muire .... 5 quatrains. MS: L 113. Ed: KM *ZCP* VI 257; *Sitzungsb. d. k. preuss. Akad. d. Wissensch.* philol.-hist. Kl. 1917 pp. 442–4, 1918 p. 374 [with Germ. trans.]. Colum-cille.

(xlviii) Forlethan mo chádhus .... 24 quatrains. MS: L 67. Ed: KM *ZCP* XII 387–9. Colum-cille.

(xlix) Gabh mo thegasc, a Aodh na n-ech .... 4 quatrains. MS: L 78. Ed: KM *ZCP* X 48. Colum-cille.

(l) Gébaid a ainm dim anmaim-se .... 10 ll. MSS: L 132. — Brussels Bibl. roy. 5100–4 p. 41. Ed: KM *ACL* III 231. Colum-cille's prophecy of Adamnán.

(li) Gebé benus a dhubhthaig .... 3 quatrains. MS: L 79. Ed: KM *ZCP* X 50. Colum-cille.

(lii) Guidium mac Feidelmid .... 9 stanzas. MS: Bodl. Rawl. B 505 *s* XV *in* f. 60. Ed: KM *ACL* III 217–9. An eulogy of Colum-cille by Cainnech. *Cf.* nos. xiv, xv, xxiii *supra.*

(liii) Inmain áidhe ilbúadhach .... 8 stanzas. MS: L 37. Ed: KM *ZCP* X 340–1. Patrick's prophecy of Colum-cille.

(liv) Loch Febail Coluim-cille .... 17 quatrains. MS: L 15. Ed: KM *ZCP* VII 303–4. Báithín mac Cúanach.

(lv) Longas Inbir Domnann .... 27 quatrains. MS: L 130. Ed: KM *ZCP* X 343–4. Colum-cille.

(lvi) M'aonarán dam isan slíab .... 15 quatrains. MSS: YBL p. 318. — L 5. Eds: O'D *Miscellany IAS* I (1846) 1–15 [with trans.]. — KM *ZCP* VII 302–3. Colum-cille: an assertion of predestination, used as a *lorica* for travellers.

(lvii) Mairg doní peta dá cholainn .... 5 quatrains. MS: L 121. Ed: KM *ZCP* XII 395. Colum-cille.

(lviii) Mairg duine cáines cléirech .... 6 quatrains. MS: L 118. Ed: KM *ACL* III 222. Colum-cille: " He who abuses a priest, goes to hell."

(lix) Marbh anocht mo cholann-sa .... 37 quatrains. MS: L 88. Ed: KM *ZCP* XII 392–5. Colum-cille.

(lx) Mellach lem bith i n-ucht ailiuin . . . . 12 quatrains. MS: Brussels Bibl. roy. 5100–4 p. 34. ED: KM ZCP V 496–7. TRANS: O'C in Skene Celtic Scotland II 92–3. Colum-cille: describes his life in exile.

(lxi) Mithig dam-sa tairerad . . . . 10 quatrains. MSS: Bk. Lis. 53ᵛ. — L 108. — RIA 23 N 3 p. 175. EDS: O'D FM s. a. 926 [with trans.] — KM ACL III 311–2. Colum-cille or Céle Dabhaill mac Scannláin (d. 927).

(lxii) Mo chean Caillin caid . . . . ED: W. M. Hennessy and D. H. Kelly Book of Fenagh (Dublin 1875) 200–5 [with trans.]. Colum-cille's eulogy of Caillin.

(lxiii) Mo chean duit a chluicc blaith bind. See no. 141 (i) supra.

(lxiv) Ná sír fis do tsaegail shuail . . . . 13 quatrains. MS: L 5. ED: KM ZCP VII 300–1. Colum-cille.

(lxv) Ránag i Rachrainn na rígh . . . . 16 quatrains. MS: L 103. ED: KM ZCP X 53–4.

(lxvi) Robad mellach, a mic mo Dé . . . . 10 quatrains. MSS: RIA B. IV. 2 f. 141. — RIA 23. N. 10 p. 91. — Brussels Bibl. roy. 5100–4 p. 41. EDS: O'C in Reeves Ad. 274–5 [with trans.]. — KM ZCP VII 309–10. Metrical trans. in Geo. Sigerson Bards of the Gael and Gall. Colum-cille: an " exile " poem on the delights of Ireland.

(lxvii) Scíath Dé do nim umam . . . . 25 stanzas. MSS: LBr 262b. — L 27. — Brussels Bibl. roy. 2324 f. 67ᵛ; 4100–5 p. 3. ED: KM ZCP X 346–7. Called the " Lorica " or " Scíathlúirech " of Colum-cille. Cf. pp. 254, 271 supra.

(lxviii) Sgíth mo chrob ón scríbinn . . . . 3 quatrains. MS: L 55. EDS: KM Gaelic Journal VIII 49 [with trans.]; ZCP XIII 8. TRANS: KM Selections from ancient Irish poetry (1911) 87, (2nd ed. 1913) 89. Colum-cille.

(lxix) Sechnaidh ifern, a dháine . . . . 13 quatrains. MS: L 103. ED: KM ZCP XII 389–90. Colum-cille. Description of hell.

(lxx) Secht sailm sunn re haithrighe . . . . 6 quatrains. MS: L 120. ED: KM ZCP XIII 10. Colum-cille: on the seven penitential psalms.

(lxxi) Tarfas dam-sa dul for sét . . . . 3 quatrains. MS: TCD 1337 (H. 3. 18) p. 60. ED: KM ZCP VI 260. A dream of Colum-cille.

(lxxii) Tegh Mulling meic Faolain . . . . 5 stanzas. MS: Brussels Bibl. roy. 5100–4 p. 65. ED: WS Anec. II 39–40. Colum-cille.

(lxxiii) Temair Bregh gidh línmar libh lín a fer . . . . 9 stanzas. MS: L 128. EDS: N. O'Kearney The prophecies of sts. Columkille, etc. (1856) [with trans.]. — KM ZCP XIII 9. Colum-cille: the decline of Tara.

(lxxiv) Tiucfa aimser a Brénainn . . . . 6 stanzas. MS: L 139. — TCD 1284 (H. 1. 10) f. 160; 1289 (H. 1. 15) p. 925; 1354 (H. 4. 13) f. 207. ED: O'Kearney op. cit. Prophecy of Colum-cille.

(lxv) Tiucfa aimser dubach . . . . 28 quatrains. MS: L 79–80. ED: KM ZCP X 49–50. Colum-cille.

(lxxvi) Torach, aitreab nemnech naom . . . . 17 quatrains. MS: L 96. ED: KM ZCP X 341–2. Colum-cille.

(lxxvii) Treide as dile lem ro-fagbus . . . . 3 quatrains. MS: L 36. ED: KM ACL III 224. Colum-cille.

(lxxviii) Tríar as mesa tic a clí . . . . 5 quatrains. MS: L 36. ED: KM ZCP X 338. Colum-cille.

(lxxix) Trúag lem, a Báithín dil bías . . . . 28 quatrains. MS: L 77. ED: KM ZCP X 51–3. Colum-cille.

Many other poems, or fragments of poems, are to be found in the Irish Lives of Colum-cille, especially O'Donnell's, and in the prefaces to the Amra.

Attention has been called in the first chapter to the fact that, about the eleventh and twelfth centuries, a new Irish literary cycle arose, consisting of romances and poems relating to Find mac Cumaill and the *fianna*. The majority of the poems were dramatically put into the mouth of the legendary poet of the *fianna*, Oisín. There was a contemporary cycle of poems, less extensive and relating to a very different subject, but of a similar literary *genre*, which centred around St. Colum-cille.

Colum-cille was regarded as in a peculiar manner the saint of the *filid*. He had, it was believed, himself been trained as a *fili*, and at Druim-cetta he had saved his fellow-craftsmen from sentence of banishment. So in the eleventh, twelfth and thirteenth centuries many nameless poets combined to produce a literature in his renown. Some poems are eulogies of the saint, but the majority are represented as his own compositions. Of these, part are impersonal, chiefly devotional in character, and in some cases were, doubtless, written with no thought of being fathered on the founder of Iona; part are dramatic and biographical, monologues spoken by the saint, or in a few cases, dialogues with certain of his contemporaries. This biographical poetry is of considerable literary merit — it shows especially the Irish observation and appreciation of nature — and dramatic consistency. It presents the saint as he appealed to the imagination of his countrymen some five centuries after his death — particularly as the exile extolling the charms of his native land. It is the earliest Irish corpus of formally nationalist propaganda.

Although later ages accepted these compositions as genuine, it is probable that at the time of production they were no more forgeries than were, say, the monologues which Robert Browning put into the mouths of historical characters. This can scarcely be said, however, of the " prophecies " of Colum-cille, which really form a separate class of documents. They are numerous, and their concoction has gone on till quite recent times. A few that relate to pre-Norman history, and appear to have a respectable age, are included in the list given above, but the prophecies of Colum-cille have but little value, even as records of events which they profess to foretell.[226]

Of the poems as a whole, the earliest appear to be nos. xxiii and xlvii, of the ninth century. Nos. x, lxviii, parts of no. viii, and probably others, seem to be of the tenth century, and the great majority of the eleventh, or later.

[226] O'C *MS Mat.* 399–411.

221. Life of Colum-cille by Manus O'Donnell A.D. 1532

(T) innscantar beatha an ab[b]ad naemtha 7 an uasal-athar 7 primfaidh nimhe . . . 7 dogebsa flaithess De da anmain fa deoigh. Do fíradh sin uile; cor moradh ainm De 7 C. C. de sin.

MSS: Bodl. Rawl. B 514 A.D. 1532 ff. 1–60. — Dublin Franciscan monastery A 8 [copy of preceding]; A 23. — RIA 23 K 40 s XVII. EDS: Colgan *Tr. Thaum.* 389–446 [a copious abstract in Latin, but with omissions and expansions that make it not entirely trustworthy]. — Richard Henebry, Andrew Kelleher *ZCP* III (1901) 516–71, IV (1903) 276–331, V (1905) 26–87, IX (1913) 242–87, X (1915) 228–65, XI i (1916) 114–47 [text, trans.; incomplete]. — A. O'Kelleher and G. Schoepperle *Betha Colaim Chille Life of Columcille (Univ. of Illinois Bulletin* vol. XV no. 48) (Urbana, Ill. 1918) [*cf. ZCP* XIII iii (1921) 383–4]. Cf. *Facs. Nat. MSS. Ire.* pt. III pls. lxvi, lxvii. COMM: Gertrud Brüning " Adamnans Vita Columbae und ihre Ableitungen " sect. x *ZCP* XI ii (1917) 283–7. — *Cf.* Plummer *Misc. hag. Hib.* Cat. no. 27.

Maghnas Úa Domhnaill, or Manus O'Donnell, was one of the leading warrior princes of Ireland in the first half of the sixteenth century. Although he did not become " The O'Donnell " until the death of his father in 1537, his name is prominent in the annals from 1511. The castle of Port-na-trí-namat, or Lifford, where, he says, he completed the composition of this Life, was built by him in the summer of 1527.

The Life is a vast compilation from all sources available at the time. Although Adamnán's Life could not be found, use was made of the old Irish Life, the introduction to the *Amra*, sections of Adamnán indirectly preserved, poems, popular legends, and other saints' Lives in which Colum-cille is mentioned. Romances like *Imthecht na Tromdáime,* " Proceedings of the Bardic Institute," and *Echtra clerech Choluim Cille,* " Adventure of Colum-cille's clerics " [227] contributed to the whole. Several books not now known are named by the author as among his sources,[228] but, although the matter additional to that to be found in earlier Lives of the saint is very great, little of it has real biographical interest. The most important of these additions are the account of the conference of Druim-cetta (which agrees with the introduction to the *Amra*), and that of the battle of Cúl-dremne (which in an abbreviated form appeared in the tract *De causa peregrinationis s. Columbae* incorporated into the Life of the Rawlinson codices.[229]

There is an unpublished Life of Colum-cille in Dublin King's Inns 19 pp. 708–1083: Beatha an naoimh ghlormair. i. Colum-cille . . . 7 go ndeantur go siorruidhe. *Cf.* Plummer *Misc. hag. Hib.* Cat. no. 28. For various anecdotes related to Colum-cille, the majority unpublished, see *ibid.* nos. 104–5, 107–12, 114–5, 117–22.

On the " Rule of Colum-cille " see p. 474 *infra.*[230]

[227] *Cf.* no. 229.
[228] O'Kelleher and Schoepperle give a list of the sources quoted by O'Donnell—*op. cit.* pp. xlvi *sqq.*
[229] No. 218.
[230] In the library of the monastery of Fulda there was, in the ninth century, a " regula abbatis Columbicellae," no doubt an early monastic rule in Latin which claimed Colum-cille as its author. It is no longer known. *Cf.* G. Becker *Catalogi bibliothecarum antiqui* (Bonn 1885) 30.

222. Life of St. Baithín

Reverendus pater abbas Baithinus . . . patribus suis additus est. Hec pauca de vita sancti Baithini.

MS: Cod. S. ff. 210ᵛ–202 [wrong arrangement: 202 should occupy the place of 212]. — Bodl. Rawl. B 485 ff. 43–4; B 505 ff. 124–5. Eds: *AA. SS. Boll.* 237–8. — *AA. SS. ex Cod. S.* 871–8.

Baithín, or Baithene, the cousin, intimate friend, and fellow-worker of Colum-cille, succeeded his master as abbot, and died in 598. He is mentioned frequently by Adamnán. The Life is late, and is, in the main, only a short catalogue of miracles.

There is a short story of Baithín and Colum-cille (Baithin mac Brenainn . . . 7 ba hecnaidhi amra ée) in the following MSS: Bodl. Rawl. B 512 f. 142; Bk. Lis. f. 45ᵛ; Edinburgh Nat. Lib. I p. 15; RIA Liber Flavus Fergusiorum vol. II pt. iii f. 8; Brussels Bibl. roy. 2324–40 f. 112; RIA 23 G 25 p. 115 [imperfect]. Eds: KM *Gaelic Journal* IV (1893) 229 [with trans.]; Douglas Hyde *An teglaisech Gaedelach* Nov. 1920. *Cf. Mart. Don.* 162–4. — The story of Baithín's vision of three chairs in heaven, given in the account of the origin of Colum-cille's name (no. 219 iii) and in *Fél. Oeng.*[1] p. ci, *Fél. Oeng.*[2] 146, is found separately in TCD H. 3. 17 col. 677 and H. 3. 18 p. 417. *Cf.* Plummer *Misc. hag. Hib.* Cat. nos. 74–5.

223. Life of St. Farannán

Tiondsccantar annso betha Fharannain uasail . . . 7 ata marsin osin ille.

MS: Brussels Bibl. roy. 4190–200 ff. 91ᵛ–4ᵛ [by O'Clery 13 Feb. 1629; from a little book of the *comarba* of Farannán]. Ed: Chas. Plummer *Anec.* III (1910) 1–7 [text only]. Lat. trans: Colgan *AA. SS.* 336–9.

Farannán, who is associated with Columba in his short and very late Life, is represented to have been fifth in descent from Eoghan, son of Níall *nói-giallach.* He was founder of the church of Alt-Farannáin (now Alternan, in the north of bar. Tireragh, Sligo).

224. Life of St. Adamnán

Accinge sicut uir lumbos tuos. In spirut naem, an spiorat dorosce cech spiorut, in spirut roin-sorchaidh . . . . Ailim trocaire De tre impidhe Adhamnain co roisem ind áentaidh sin in s. s. Amen.

MS: Brussels Bibl. roy. 4190–200 ff. 29–33 [by O'Clery: "Finis 6 Maij 1628"]. Ed: Skene *Picts and Scots* (1867) 408–9 [extract with trans.]. — R. I. Best *Anec.* II (Halle 1908) 10–20 [text only]. Trans: M. Joynt *The Celtic Review* no. 18 (Oct. 15, 1908) 97–107. *Cf.* J. Vendryes "Une Correction au Texte du Betha Adamnáin " *RC* XXXIV (1913) 306; "L'Épisode du chien ressuscité dans l'hagiographie irlandaise " *RC* XXXV (1914) 357–60. — E. Maguire *Life of St. Adamnan* (Dublin 1917).

The Irish Life of Adamnán is a late composition, described by Dr. Reeves as "a miserable production, full of absurdities and anachronisms." This condemnation is, doubtless, deserved, if the document is to be tested as a record of the career of the historical Adamnán. But compared with other products of later Irish hagiography it is not peculiarly degenerate. It embodies some curious products of popular religion and folk-lore. The form is that of a homily for the saint's festival.[231]

225. Prayers and Poems attributed to Adamnán

(i) Colum Cille co Dia do-m-erail . . . . MSS: LH(T) f. 28^V. — Bodl. Rawl. B 502. — YBL. — RIA Stowe C. III. 2. [In all MSS it follows the *Amra Coluim-cille*.] EDS: WS *Goidelica* (1872). — *LH*[2] I 184, II 81–2, 235 [with trans.]. This short prayer resembles in obscurity the *Amra* of Colum-cille, with which it is associated in the manuscripts.

(ii) Indiu cia chenglaid chuacha . . . . 13 quatrains. MS: LL 307 b. ED: O'Grady *SG* I 387–8. In the Bóroma tract.

(iii) Noimh na cceithre raithe . . . . 7 stanzas. MSS: RIA 23 P. 3 A.D. 1467 f. 19. — Brussels Bibl. roy. 5100–4 f. 92^V. ED: Mary E. Byrne *Ériu* I 225–8 [with trans.]. Called *Féilire Adamnáin*, the " Calendar of Adamnán "; is a prayer addressed to the saints of the four seasons, that is, all the saints whose festivals are celebrated during the year. It is ascribed also to Ciarán, and to Cormac mac Cuilennáin.

(iv) Trí cémenn cindti do chách . . . . 3 quatrains. MSS: Bodl. Laud 610 f. 112 b. — Bk. Lis. f. 143 b. — RIA 23 G 25 p. 112; 23 C 19 p. 132. ED: KM *ACL* III (1906) 215.

(v) Trí fótáin nach sechainter . . . . ED: KM *Selections from early Irish poetry* (Dublin 1909). Also ascribed to Cormac.

These texts belong to the same general class as the poems of Colum-cille. All, except possibly no. i, are of a date some centuries later than Adamnán.

226. *Fis Adamnáin:* Adamnán's Vision

(Magnus dominus noster et magna virtus ejus et sapientiae ejus non est numerus.)[232] Is uasal ocus is adamraigthe . . . .

MSS: LU pp. 27–31. — Brussels Bibl. roy. 4190–200 ff. 39–46 [copy of preceding]. — LBr pp. 253–6. — RIA Liber Flavus Fergusiorum I pt. ii ff. 3^V–6^V. — BN Fonds celtique et basque 1 *c* A.D. 1518 ff. 95 *sqq.* — Bk. Lis. *s* XV ff. 34^V–5 [fragment attached to Life of Brendan VB6: *cf.* pp. 413-4 *supra*]. EDS: O'D *Grammar of the Irish language* (1845) [extracts]. — WS *Fis Adamnáin Slicht Libair na Huidre Adamnán's Vision* (Simla, privately printed, 1870) [LU text, trans.]. — EW *IT* I (1880) 165–96 [LU and LBr]. — Jos. Vendryes *RC* XXX (1909) 349–83 [BN text, trans.]. — G. Dottin *Manuel d'irlandais moyen* II (1913) 101–6 [extracts]. TRANS: " Mac dá Cherda " [= WS]

[231] An anecdote of Adamnán — found in a shorter form in the Life — is edited by KM, *ZCP* V (1905) 495-6, from TCD 1317 (H. 2. 15 pt. ii) p. 59. It is also in *Mart. Don.* (1864) 254. — There is a short Latin Life of Adamnán in the Breviary of Aberdeen (*cf.* p. 484), *Pars Aest. Prop. SS.* 114^V–15: S. Adamnanus praeclaris ortus parentibus de nobilissimi Conaldi regis progenie . . . . Cuius corpus in insula Yens. debito honore humatum est. — *AA. SS. Boll.* Sept. VI 642 gives an historical commentary on the saint. *Cf.* Mabillon *AA. SS. o. s. B.* III ii, 499 *sqq.* — For other texts related to Adamnán *cf.* Plummer *Misc. hag. Hib.* Cat. nos. 65, 67, 70–2.
[232] LBr.

Fraser's Mag. LXXXIII (1871) 184–94; also, with emendations, in Margaret Stokes *Three months in the forests of France* (London 1895) 265–79. COMM: Alfred Nutt in *The Voyage of Bran* (*Grimm Library* 4) I (London 1895) 219–23. — C. S. Boswell *An Irish precursor of Dante* (*Grimm Library* 18) (London 1908) [extensive study of the text, and of related literature, Irish and foreign; has trans.]. — St. John D. Seymour "The seven heavens in Irish literature" *ZCP* XIV (1923) 18–30; "The eschatology of the early Irish Church" *ibid.* 179–211.

An abridgment of this Vision was incorporated into one version of the Voyage of Columcille's clerics; *cf.* pp. 447–8.

The next most important of the Irish "vision" texts, after that of Fursa,[233] is the tenth- or eleventh-century[234] composition known as "Adamnán's Vision." It professes to give an account of a vision which Adamnán had at the time of the *mór-dál*, or national convention, at which *Cáin Adamnáin* was enacted. In reality it is a literary description of heaven and hell by some later ecclesiastic, presented as a vision of Adamnán possibly because of a tradition ascribing to him some such experience, possibly because the author was a member of the Columban community and specially devoted to Adamnán. The matter is derived in part from scriptural and apocryphal texts,[235] in part from the Irish "voyage" stories. Boswell and Seymour believe that there are extensive interpolations: the linguistic evidence, however, shows that these cannot be of much later date. The piece has considerable value as an exposition of eschatological ideas, and also some as a witness to social conditions.[236]

227. Life of St. Blathmac by Walahfrid Strabo

Si tantam meruere suo pro carmine famam . . . . Regnat, et aeterno pollet sine fine decore.

MSS: St. Gall Stiftsbibl. 899 *s* IX/X f. 49. EDS: Canisius *Lectionis antiquae* VI (new ed. II ii p. 201). — Messingham *Florilegium* 399. — *AA. SS. Boll.* 19 Jan. II 236–8. — Colgan *AA. SS.* I 128. — *Bibl. max. vet. patrum* XV (Leyden 1677) 210. — Mabillon *AA. SS. o. s. B.* III ii 439–41 (Venice ed. III ii 398). — Pinkerton *Vitae antiquae sanctorum* (London 1789) 459. — Migne *PL* CXIV 1043–6. — E. Dümmler *MGH Poet. lat. aevi Carol.* II 297–301 [best ed.]. — Metcalfe *Pinkerton's Lives of the Scottish saints* II (Paisley 1889) 293–7. TRANS: A. O. Anderson *Early sources of Scottish history* I (1922) 263–5 [partial]. COMM: Skene *Celtic Scotland* II 297–302. — HZ *NA* XVII (1892) 209–11. On Walahfrid Strabo see pp. 207, 550.

Iona was pillaged by the Norsemen in 795, 802, and 806. As a result the congregation of Columba obtained in 804 a grant of Cenannus, now Kells, in Meath, and by 814 had built a new church there, to serve as metropolis.[237] For a period, perhaps, Iona was deserted, but it was soon reoccupied under a prior or abbot named Blathmac, an

---

[233] No. 296.

[234] WS on linguistic grounds assigned it to the 11th cent.; EW to the 10th, or possibly 9th; Ó Máille (*Ériu* VI 102) to the first quarter of the 11th; and Seymour, from the subject-matter, to the tenth. A prose text may easily be older than its language, which may be due to the scribe.

[235] Notably a fragment published by Dom De Bruyne, from a Reichenau MS, in *Rev. Bénédictine* XXIV (1907) 311. *Cf.* M. R. James *JTS* XX 15, and Seymour, *op. cit.*

[236] There is a second Vision attached to Adamnán. It is, however, associated with the religious panic of 1096, and may best be considered in that connection. No. 627.

[237] See, for a summary of this history, Reeves *Ad.* 387–9.

Irishman. The head of the order, at this time a certain Diarmait, remained, for the most part, in Ireland. In 825 the Vikings again descended on Iona and slew Blathmac and his companions. The story of their martyrdom travelled as far as Reichenau, where Walahfrid Strabo wrote in hexameter verse this Life of Blathmac.[238]

228. Life of St. Indrechtach by William of Malmesbury

MS: Bodl. Digby 112 s XII f. 195. Abridgment in the *Sanctilogium* of John of Tynemouth (no. 117). EDS: *Nova Legenda Anglie*, new ed. by C. Horstman (Oxford 1901) II 56–8. — *AA. SS. Boll.* 5 Feb. I 689–90 (1863 ed.: 694–6) [from the *Nova Legenda*].

Diarmait, *comarba* of Columba at the time of the martyrdom of Blathmac, was succeeded by Indrechtach úa Finechta. Under 849 the Annals of Ulster record that he went to Ireland with the *minda* of Colum-cille (*i.e.*, sacred objects which had belonged to, or been otherwise associated with, the saint.)[239] These had already, since the appearance of the Norse danger, been taken back and forth between Scotland and Ireland several times. It was now the era when Kenneth mac Alpin, having united the crowns of the " Scots " and the " Picts " in North Britain, was attempting to consolidate his kingdom: one of his measures was the reorganisation of the Church, after the Irish model, with its center at Dunkeld, in the midst of his dominions. It would look as though an agreement was reached to divide the Columban churches into two jurisdictions, one with its centre at Kells or elsewhere in Ireland, the other at Dunkeld, and likewise to divide the reliquaries of the patron saint. For, according to the " Chronicle of the Kings of Scotland," or " Pictish Chronicle," Kenneth, in the seventh year of his reign, *i.e.*, 848–9, "transported the relics of Columba to the church which he had built [at Dunkeld]." [240]

Five years later Indrechtach was, according to the Annals of Ulster and of Innisfallen, martyred by Saxons while going to Rome. There can be little doubt that he is the Indract, son of an Irish king, murdered with his companions near Glastonbury while returning from Rome, whose Life was written by William of Malmesbury. It is evident, however, that William had little trustworthy *data:* he places the events in the time of Ine, king of Wessex (c 689–c 730).

The short legends of saints in the Breviary of Aberdeen (p. 484 *infra*) are occasionally to be associated with the establishment and early history of the Irish Church in the northern and western parts of what is now Scotland. — See also *Kalendars of Scottish Saints*, edited by Alexander Penrose Forbes, Bishop of Brechin (Edinburgh 1872); M. Barrett " Irish saints honored in Scotland " *Amer. Cath. Quarterly Rev.* XLIV (1919) 331–43.

In the Breviary of Aberdeen (*Prop. sanct. pro temp. hyem.* f. lxix; also Skene *Chronicles of the Picts and Scots* 421–3) is an unusually long legend of a St. Boniface who came

---

[238] There is a reference to Blathmac and Diarmait in the tract on Tallaght, *Proc. RIA* xxix (1911) C 153.

[239] *Cf.* Reeves *Ad.* 315 n.

[240] *Cf.* Skene *Chronicles of the Picts and Scots* 8; *Celtic Scotland* II 306–8; A. O. Anderson *Early sources of Scottish history* I 279, 288.

from Rome in the time of King Nectan and converted the Picts. The story evidently arose from the action of Nectan in accepting the Roman Easter and expelling the Columban clergy. Some late writers identify Boniface with a Curitan (Kiritinus in a Utrecht MS. used in *AA. SS. Boll.* Mart. II 444–5) who is honored in Irish martyrologies on March 16, which is Boniface's day. Curitan is mentioned in *Cáin Adamnáin* (no. 81), and was evidently an Irish, or more probably Pictish, member of the Columban community who followed Adamnán in accepting the Roman discipline. *Cf.* Skene *Celtic Scotland* I 277, II 229; A. O. Anderson *Early sources of Scottish history* I 205, 211.

229. The Adventures — or Wanderings — of Colum-cille's clerics (*Echtra*— or *Merugud* — *clérech Choluim Cille*); The Voyage of Snedgus and Mac Ríagla (*Immram Snedgusa ocus Maic Ríagla*).

(i) Snedgus 7 Mac Riaghuil . . . rom be nem co soillsi sneidhe. 76 quatrains. (ii) Bai dochraite mor for Feraib Rois . . . indisid bar scela uile d'fheraib Eirind [incorporates the preceding verse version]. (iii) Antan tanic derid rigi . . . [indisid bar scéla] co feraib Erenn [incorporates part of version i]. (iv) O thairnig trah deired rigi . . . 7 an cochall ar altoir Choluim Chille. Conadh merugad cleirech Coluim Chille ainm an sgeoil sin. [Contains 9 sets of verses.]

MSS: (i, ii) YBL cols. 391–5 (facs. pp. 11b–13b). (iii) YBL cols. 707–15 (facs. pp. 86b–90b). (iv) Bk. Fer. 86 (old f. 58). — BM Addit. 30,512 f. 1. EDS: (i) RTh *Zwei Versionen der mittelirischen Legende von Snedgus und Mac Riagla* (*Programm zur Feier des Geburtstags seiner k. Hoheit des Grossherzogs Friedrich . . .*) (Halle a. S. 1904) [with Germ. trans.; corrections and additions in *ZCP* V (1905) 418–21, VI (1908) 234–5]. (ii) WS *RC* IX (1888) 14–25 [with trans.]. (iii) RTh *op. cit.* [with Germ. trans.; omits the matter from Adamnán's Vision]. — WS *RC* XXVI (1905) 130–70 [with trans.]. — (iv) Tomás Ó Máille in *Miscellany presented to Kuno Meyer* (Halle a. S. 1912) 307–26 [text of Addit. 30,512, with variants of Bk. Fer.]. TRANS: Mod. Ir.: Eugene O'Growney *Gaelic Journ.* IV (1891) 85–8. Germ.: RTh *Sagen aus dem alten Irland* (Berlin 1901) 126–30. COMM: O'C *MS Mat.* 332–5; *M&C* III 385. — HZ *Zs. f. deut. Alterthum* XXXIII (1889) 211–20. — The story is incorporated into Manus O'Donnell's Life of Colum-cille (ed. O'Kelleher and Schoepperle 382–401).

The congregation of Columba came to have a " voyage " legend, but it did not, as might have been expected, develop from the story of Cormac úa Liatháin.[241] Its heroes were two otherwise unknown, perhaps fictitious, members of the community of Iona, Snedgus and Mac Ríagla. It seems to have been designed to explain, among other things, the origin of two relics, a cowl and a large leaf or fan, which, it is probable, had been at Iona. The leaf was identified with the *cuilebadh*, or *cuilefadh*, of Colum-cille, which seems to have been brought to Kells about the year 1090.[242]

The story told how the Fir Roiss and Mugdornai Maigen,[243] kindred and probably identical peoples who dwelt in parts of Monaghan, Louth and Meath, slew their ruler, Fiacha, brother of Donnchad, son of an *árd-rí* Domnall. Donnchad went against

---

[241] *Cf.* pp. 410, 438 *supra.*

[242] Tig., and O'C *MS Mat.* 334.

[243] The Mugdornai, or Mugdoirn, and Fir Roiss were, to judge from the evidence, a very old people who had been subject to the Ulaid, and then to the Dál Cuinn rulers of Airgíalla, and perhaps now, if any trust can be placed in this tale, were, with other parts of Airgíalla, passing under the Úi Néill; iii and iv say curiously, that they slew their own kings, possibly an echo of an ancient rite of human sacrifice.

them, and applied to Colum-cille (or his *comarba*) at Iona for judgment. Snedgus and Mac Ríagla brought his decision, which was that sixty couples of the guilty should be put into boats and sent afloat on the sea. Snedgus and Mac Ríagla, when returning to Iona, determine to make a voyage over the ocean. They have experiences similar to, or the same as, those of Máel-Dúin, Brendan, and the sons of Úa Corra, visit many islands, among them that where the victims of their sentence dwell, and return to Iona, bringing the cowl and the giant leaf. Some texts add a prophecy of the coming of foreigners, apparently the Northmen.

The legend may be fairly old, for the earliest version, which does not attempt to tell a complete story, implies the knowledge of such a story in the audience. But if it ever had a historical basis and chronological consistency these have been destroyed by the tamperings of both myth-maker and antiquarian. From linguistic and other evidence it appears that version i was composed in the tenth, or possibly ninth, century. The prose versions are all late: the oldest, no. ii, may be of the eleventh, but is more probably of the twelfth century.[244]

For the history of Kells in the eleventh and twelfth centuries, see Chap. VIII, sect. ii.

IV. The Monastic Churches — Foundations of the Seventh Century

(a) Ferna (Ferns) and associated churches: St. Maedóc

The Úi Cennselaig, descendants of Énda *cenn-salach*, king of Leinster about the beginning of the fifth century, were the most powerful family of southern Leinster. They ruled over what is now Wexford county, and parts of Carlow and Wicklow. Their favorite church was Ferna, or Ferns, which displaced Mag-Arnaide as the chief monastery of the Lagin of the South. The founder of Ferns had been a Bishop Aed, or Aed-án, usually designated by the hypocoristic form of his name, M'-Aed-óc, Maedóc or Moedhóg, Anglicised Mogue. Tradition said that several other churches in the neighborhood had been established by him, as well as Disert-nArbri (now Dysert, parish of Ardmore, Waterford) in the Dési and Clúain-Claidbaich (Clooncagh) in Úi Conaill Gabra. Maedóc was of Connacht birth, and churches in Breifne, in particular Druim-Lethan (Drumlane, bar. Loughtee, co. Cavan) and Ros-Inbir (Rossinver, bar. Rosclogher, co. Leitrim), claimed him as their founder, although they do not seem to have ever formed part of the *paruchia* of Ferns.[245]

---

[244] KM thought (*ZCP* XI 148) that version i and the poem on Máel-Dúin (*ibid.; Anec.* I 50) were by the same author, RTh (*ZCP* XII 278) that the second imitated the first. — Version iii includes a shorter redaction of Adamnán's Vision (no. 226).

[245] Maedóc of Ferns and Maedóc of Breifne were, perhaps, distinct persons.

Interesting are the relations, on chronological grounds improbable if not impossible, set up between our saint and David of Wales. They probably reflect associations of a later age between Ferns and Menevia. —Maedóc died in 626.[246]

230. Life of St. Maedóc

(i) Fuit vir quidam nobilis in regionibus Connactorum, nomine Sedia. . . . Sanctus enim Aidus . . . D. n. I. C., cui est h. et g. in s. s.   Amen.   (ii) Vir quidam in regione Connactorum, nomine Sedia . . . pridie kal. marcii.   Sanctus enim iste in vita sancti David . . . festum eius recolitur.   (iii) Fuit quidam uir nobilis in regionibus Connachtorum, nomine Sethna. . . . Sed sanctus et patronus noster, Moedhog, inter choros angelorum, etc.   (iv) Fuit vir quidam nobilis in regione Hybernie, nomine Sema, . . . pridie kal. februarii coronatur a Domino: cui est l. et h. per infinita s. s.   Amen.   (v) [As preceding.]   (vi) Gabhuis rí coigeadh Connacht dar bhó comainm Sena. . . . Andara lá do mi Febriairi docoidh Moeog a naontaigh aingel, etc.   Amen.   (vii) Do boi duine uasal saidbir hi cConnachtuibh darb ainm Sédna. . . . [Contains 22 poems, of which 5 are at the end; the last is in 29 stanzas:] Maircc dan comharsa naomh garcc. . . . Maircc do chách dan comarsa.

MSS: (i) BM Cotton. Vespasian A XIV c A.D. 1200 ff. 96ᵛ-104ᵛ. (ii) BM Cotton. Tiberius E I s XIV. (iii) Cod. K. ff. 51ᵛ-6ᵛ. (iv) Cod. S. ff. 133-7ᵛ. (v) Bodl. Rawl. B 485 ff. 154ᵛ-7ᵛ [imperfect]; B 505 ff. 180ᵛ-4. — Dublin Franciscan Convent A 24 pp. 264 sqq. (vi) RIA A. IV. 1 (Stowe 9) A.D. 1627 pp. 132-47. (vii) Brussels Bibl. roy. 2324-40 ff. 168-218ᵛ [O'Clery's colophon is dated Nov. 17, 1629]. — TCD 1297 (H. 2. 6) pt. II [written about 1715 by John Magauran for Brian Maguire]. — RIA 23 O 41 pp. 241-328 [in 1721 by James Maguire]. — TCD 1406 (H. 6. 3) [in 1737 by Hugh O'Daly]. — RIA Reeves MS 32. Eds: (i) Colgan AA. SS. 208 sqq. — AA. SS. Boll. Jan. II 1111-20. — W. J. Rees Cambro-British Saints (Llandovery 1853) 232-51. — VV. SS. Hib. II 295-311. (ii) Nova Legenda Anglie (ed. Horstman) (Oxford 1901) I 18-22. (iii) VV. SS. Hib. I pp. lxxv-lxxviii, II 141-63. (iv) AA. SS. ex Cod. S. 463-88. (vi) BNE I pp. xxxiii, 183-9, II 177-83, 347-9. (vii) BNE I pp. xxxiii-xxxvii, 190-290, II 184-281, 349-57 [last two with trans. and notes].

Recension (i) is an English abstract from an Irish original which, though not of great antiquity, seems to have been much the earliest redaction; (ii) is a summary of the preceding; (iii) is a development of the original matter of (i), prepared by a monk of Ferns; (iv) is an abridged version based on (iii); (v) closely resembles (iv), but is further abridged; (vi) is a condensed translation of (iii); and (vii) is a late mediaeval compilation, by a writer of Breifne, made from (iii) and from the legends and claims of the churches of Drumlane and Rossinver. All the redactions, but especially the last, are interesting sources for the social and intellectual conditions of the times when they were written.

(b) Tech-Munnu (Taghmon) and St. Fintan, or Munnu

Tech-Munnu, "Munnu's house," now Taghmon, and anciently Acheth-Liacc-Echdromma, was a monastic church of some importance situated south-west of the present town of Wexford. Its founder was Fintan moccu Moie, son of Tulchan or Tailchan, a saint who is better known by the name Munnu (i.e. Mo-Fhinnu). Munnu died in 635.[247]

[246] AU.   [247] AU.

231. Life of St. Fintan, or Munnu

(i) Fintanus sanctus, summi Dei . . . in conspectu eterni regis sine fine manet r. D. n. I. C. in s. s.   Amen.
(ii) Fuit vir vite venerabilis, nomine Munnu, . . . XII Kal. Nouembris emisit ad presentiam Christi
Iesu, q. c. D. P. et S. S. v. et r. in s. s.   Amen.   (iii) [*Incipit* as II] . . . celo reddidit XII° Kal. novem-
bris.   Ubi cum angelis et sanctis letatur in g. D. P.: c. c. F. s. et S. s. sit majestas et imperium per infinita
s. s.   Amen.

MSS: (i) Cod. S. ff. 110^v [*recte* 119]–123^v.   (ii) Cod. K. ff. 127–9^v.— TCD 175 f.
105 [imperfect].   (iii) Cod. S. 137^v–40^v.   (iv) Bodl. Rawl. B 485 ff. 121^v–4; B 505
ff. 148–9^v [imperfect].— Dublin Franciscan Convent A 24 pp. 157 *sqq.*   EDS: (i)
AA. SS. Boll. Oct. IX 325–41. — *AA. SS. ex Cod. S.* 393–414.   (ii) *VV. SS. Hib.* I
pp. lxxxiv–lxxxvi, II 226–39.   (iii) *AA. SS. ex Cod. S.* 489–504.

Of the four recensions of the Life of Munnu, the second and third are closely related
and the fourth is only a slight variation from the third.   All are derived from one
ultimate source which incorporated much primitive matter, but cannot be dated, even
approximately.   The *Vita Fintani* is one of the most interesting and valuable of Irish
acta sanctorum.   " Generally the historical element in this life is larger than in some
others, and we get an impression of Munnu as a real man, and not merely a peg to hang
miracles on; a man of somewhat harsh and hasty temper, but placable and conciliatory when the momentary irritation was over." [248]   Several illuminating pictures are
presented, drawn from monastic and secular life, and there are many references to
the political history of south Leinster.   The Life contains also a notable, but much
corrupted, narrative of the Easter Controversy in southern Ireland and of the synod
held in Mag-Ailbe.   Munnu was the spokesman of the old order, and Lasrian, of
Leighlin, of the Roman usage.

Adamnán tells us that Fintan went to Iona just after Columba's death, but was sent
back by Baithine to Ireland.   In the Life of Cainnech there is a curious story of an
earlier visit made by the saint and his father, the druid Tulchan, to Iona.[249]

(c) LETH-GLENN (LEIGHLIN) AND ST. LASRIAN, OR MO-LAISSE

Leth-glenn (Leighlin), which became one of the principal churches
of the Lagin, appears to have been an ancient establishment, of the sixth
century or perhaps earlier.   Its foundation is ascribed to a mythical
and ubiquitous St. Gobbán.   Its patron, however, was a later abbot,
Laisrén moccu Imde (*i.e.*, of the Dál nImde, a race living apparently in
the present co. Louth), who died in 639.[250]   He is better known by the
Latin name Lasrianus, or the hypocoristic Mo-Laisse, or Do-Laisse.

---

[248] Plummer *VV. SS.* Introd.
[249] An allusion to Fintan's journey to the Land of Promise indicates that there was a voyage legend
attached to his name
[250] AU.

232. Life of St. Lasrian, or Mo-Laisse, of Leighlin

(i) Inter supernae cives Hierusalem, . . . clementiam Salvatoris, I. C. D. n. cui c. P. et S. s. est h. et g. in s. s. Amen. (ii) Sanctus Lasrianus, apostolice sedis legatus. . . . Cui misericors pater ait: Ligneum [imperfect].

MSS: (ii) Cod. S. 194ᵛ-5ᵛ [the next folio is missing]. Eds: (i) *AA. SS. Boll.* April. II 544-7 [from a MS supplied by Henry FitzSimon]. (ii) *AA. SS. ex Cod. S.* 791-8.

The Life of Mo-Laisse is a late and unsatisfactory production — probably not earlier than the twelfth century. It alleges that he made two visits to Rome, on the first of which he was consecrated bishop by Pope Gregory, and on the second appointed apostolic delegate to Ireland. References to him in the Life of Munnu and elsewhere indicate that he was the principal advocate of the Roman Easter in southern Ireland in his time.

233. Story of Mo-Laisse and his sister *s* X

Boí síur Mo-Laissi Lethglinne . . . in bfait do tessarcain anma(e) ar demnaib.

MSS: LL *s* XII pp. 285-6. — Bk. Lis. f. 42ᵛ. Eds: Julius Pokorny *Miscellany presented to KM* (1912) 207-15 [text, Germ. trans.]; *ZCP* IX (1913) 235-41 [critically restored text]. *Cf. Lis. Lives* p. x.

This is one of several curious stories intended to inculcate a belief in the " virtue " of the recitation of the " *Beati*," the 118th (119th) Psalm. The language is of the beginning of the tenth century.

(d) The Churches of St. Carthach, or Mo-Chuta: Rathan, Liss-Mór

Rathan, now Rahan (about five miles from Tullamore, in the bar. Ballycowan, Offalley), was an ancient church of the territory of the southern Úi Néill, having been founded in the fifth century, according to tradition, by the bishop Camelacus.[251] The fame of the founder died out, and in later ages the name of Rathan was usually associated with that of St. Carthach, Mo-Chuta, Mo-Chutu, or Mo-Chuda, who was abbot there early in the seventh century. Carthach was of the Ciarraige Luachra, of modern Kerry, and local ecclesiastical and racial jealousy was responsible, according to the legends, for his expulsion by the secular and church rulers of the midlands. The annals, in recording the event under 636, say that it took place "in diebus paschae."[252] As there is some reason to believe that Mo-Chuta was an adherent of the Roman Easter,[253] Dr. Reeves may have been right in interpreting this as " in the time of the Easter controversy."[254] Mo-Chuta went to the land of the Dési and founded Liss-mór, " Great fort " (Lismore on the

[251] *Cf.* no. 88, pp. 260 *sq.* [252] AU; Tig. (*RC* XVII 183).
[253] See the Life of Colmán mac Lúacháin, no. 238. [254] *Cf. VV. SS. Hib.* I p. xlvi n.

Blackwater river), which became, especially towards the end of our period, one of the greatest monasteries in Munster. It contained a hospice for lepers,[255] and tradition assigned the establishment of such an institution at both Liss-mór and Rathan to Mo-Chuta. There seems to have been quite a group of churches subject to Liss-mór, of some of which mention is made in the Lives. Mo-Chuta died, according to the annals, in 637, but the legends would seem to require a longer sojourn than a year in Liss-mór and its neighborhood.

234. Life of Mo-Chuta

(ia) Gloriosus episcopus Carthagus, . . . pridie idus Maii migrauit ad Christum. C. est h. et g. atque p. c. D. P. in unitate S. S. in s. s. Amen. (ib) Gloriosus episcopus Carthagus . . . . An t-easbog glórmhar . . . do mí Mai a naonta na N. T., A. 7 M. 7 S. N. a saogal na saoghal. Amen. (ii) Cartaghus dino do clannaibh Fergusa . . . 7 dochuaidh i naentaidh aingeal i ffrecnairc na T., A., M., 7 S. N. (iii) Beatissimus Christi famulus Carthacus . . . cunctosque deosculans, pridie idus maii migrauit ad Christum. C. h. et p. in s. s. Amen. Antiphona de eo ad Magnificat. Gloriose presul, . . . culmine.

MSS: (ia) Cod. K. ff. 94-9ᵛ [imperfect]. — TCD 175 ff. 60ᵛ-6 [imperfect].[256] — (ib) RIA 23 M 50 A.D. 1741 [copied by John Murphy na Raheenach: cf. p. 55 supra]. — Dublin King's Inns Library MS 19. (ii) Brussels Bibl. roy. 2324-40 ff. 151-7ᵛ [written by O'Clery 1629]. — RIA Stowe A IV 1 s XVII [probably from same original; inserts the Indarba] (iii) Cod. S. ff. 192-4ᵛ. Eds: (ia) AA. SS. Boll. Mai. III 378-88. — VV. SS. Hib. I pp. xlv-xlviii, 170-99. (ib) P. Power ITS XVI (1914) [from 23 M 50]. (ii) Fáinne Fionn Irish Rosary XIV-XV (1910-1). — BNE I pp. xxxvii sq, 291-9, II 282-90, 357-8. (iii) AA. SS. Boll. Mai. III 375-8. — AA. SS. ex Cod. S. 779-90.

At Liss-mór in the twelfth, or perhaps eleventh, century a Latin Life of Mo-Chuta was written which is still extant. The other versions, Irish and Latin, are derived from it almost entirely. The Life in all its redactions contains exceedingly valuable material for ecclesiastical history and for topography, but of the twelfth century more than of the seventh. The historical setting given to Mo-Chuta's career is not very accurate.

235. The Expulsion of Mo-Chuta from Rathan (Indarba Mo-Chuda a rRaithin)

Mo-Chutta mac Finaill do Ciarraigibh Luachra . . . 7 for an ecclais fria reimes. Et hec omnia completa sunt, etc. [Here are added 4 quatrains of a poem:] Ro la an doman bacc ar bacc . . .

MSS: Bk. Fer. ff. 34ᵛ-6ᵛ [imperfect]. — Brussels Bibl. roy. 4190-200 ff. 266-70. — Bodl. Ashmole 1763 f. 58 [imperfect]. — RIA A. iv. 1 (Stowe 9) pp. 18 sqq. Ed: BNE I pp. xxxviii sq, 300-7, II 291-8. There is a somewhat different version in the notes to Fél. Oeng. Mar. 11.

This is a semi-secular, and quite dramatic, version of the record of Mo-Chuta's expulsion as found in the Lives. It also has some value as a source for social and ecclesiastical conditions.

[255] Cf. Colgan Tr. Thaum. 445. The leper colony is still remembered in local tradition around Lismore. — ITS XVI 191.

[256] A fragment, described in a hand which may be Colgan's as from Cod. K, is among the "sparsa folia" of the Franciscan Convent, Dublin.

236. Minor texts relating to Mo-Chuta

(i) Ind ecclas naemh nemdha . . . lenaid as in ecclass. 11 stanzas. MS: Brussels Bibl. roy. 4190–200 f. 270ᵛ.²⁵⁷ EDS: KM *ZCP* X (1915) 43–4 [text]. — *BNE* I pp. xxxviii *sq*, 308–9, II 299–300. Poem, attributed to Mo-Chuta, setting forth praises of, and men's obligations towards, the Church.

(ii) Mochudae Rathain cona coimhtional . . . nis fainic cuca doridhisi. MSS: Bodl. Rawl. B. 512 f. 142. — Brussels Bibl. roy. 4190–200 f. 271. ED: *BNE* I pp. xxxviii *sq*, 310, II 300–1. Story of the devil entering Rahan by reason of the distraction of a monk.

(iii) Mochuttae Rathain immorro dorinne roind da coimhtionol . . . . MSS: Bodl. Rawl. B 512 f. 142ᵛ. — Bk Lis. f. 44ᵛ. — Brussels Bibl. roy.'4190–200 f. 271. — RIA 23 M 50 *s* XVIII p. 166. EDS: KM *ZCP* III 32–3 [text]. — *BNE* I p. xxxix, 310–1, II 301–2, 360. Story of the devil inducing Mo-Chuta to go on pilgrimage.

For the " Rule " ascribed to Mo-Chuta see pp. 473–4 *infra*.

237. Tract on the sons of Úa Suanaig

Fiachra cettamus, mac Eachach . . .   Port in Geochaigh in bhail ro marbhadh é.

MS: Brussels Bibl. roy. 4190–200 ff. 272–4ᵛ. ED: *BNE* I p. xxxix, 312–6, II 303–7, 360–2.

Of the history of Rathan after the expulsion of Mo-Chuta nothing is known until the eighth century, when the deaths are recorded of Fidmuine Úa Suanaig, anchorite, and Fidairle Úa Suanaig, abbot.²⁵⁸ The present loose collection of notes treats of these men, and of various happenings at Rathan down to the year 1156. The object is to show the glory of Rathan, and the certain vengeance that followed if it were insulted.

(e) LANN (LYNN), CHURCH OF ST. COLMÁN MAC LÚACHÁIN

The church of Lann, or Lann meic Lúacháin (Lynn, an old parish three miles south of Mullingar in Westmeath) honored as its founder and patron St. Colmán mac Lúacháin. Neither church nor saint was prominent in the national story, but the church was located in the midst of the dominions of the powerful families of the southern Úi Néill, and the saint, unlike the patrons of more famous establishments in the neighborhood, was, according to the generally accepted genealogy, of the Clann Cholmáin *móir*, the chief branch of the same race.²⁵⁹

---

²⁵⁷ So Plummer, who says he knows no other copy. But KM attributes his copy, which agrees with Plummer's almost in every detail, to the Brussels MS 2324–40 f. 263ᵛ. Father Grosjean informs me that KM's number for the MS must be a slip; that the present f. 270 of 4190–200 was formerly 263.

²⁵⁸ AU 757, 763. We read of a " Law " of Úa Suanaig at 748.

²⁵⁹ In the Life he is called " the only patron saint of the race of Colmán *mór*."

Although not recognising superior jurisdiction in Liss-mór, the clergy of Lann maintained friendly relations with that church, and were accustomed, we are told, to go there " on their pilgrimage." The cause was that Colmán had been a disciple of Mo-Chuta. This tradition may be trustworthy, as also that which says that Colmán's first foundation was Cell-Uird (perhaps Kilworth), the " church of the order," in Fermoy, so called " because in it the order which Molaise had brought with him from Rome was first set up." The reference may be to the liturgy rather than to the church calendar, but it suggests that Mo-Chuta and Colmán were adherents of Mo-Laisse of Leighlin and the Romanising party in the paschal controversy.

238. Life of St. Colmán mac Lúacháin

Uiriliter agite 7 confortetur cor uestrum omnes qui speratis in Domino. An spirat nóem,[260] . . . cid hé sin bid drú[th] nó díbergach nó mac mallachta. Finit.

MS: Rennes Bibl. de la Ville 598/15489 s XIV/XV ff. 75–89ᵛ. Eds: C. P. Cooper [Appendices to a Report on Rymer's *Foedera*] Supplement to Appendix A Plate XIII (1869) [facs. specimen]. — KM *Betha Colmáin maic Lúacháin Life of Colmán son of Lúachan* (RIA Todd Lecture Ser. XVII) (Dublin 1911) [text, trans., notes, etc.]. Cf. J. Vendryes RC XXXIII (1912) 357–9; Paul Walsh ZCP VIII (1912) 590–3; J. C. MacErlean *Studies* I i (March 1912) 183–93 [reviews]. Also Paul Walsh " The Topography of Betha Colmáin " ZCP VIII (1912) 568–82.

The Life of Colmán mac Lúacháin seems to be of the twelfth century, and may have been inspired by the discovery of his relics in 1122: " The shrine of Colmán son of Lúachan was found in the burial-place of Lann, a man's cubit in the earth, on Spy Wednesday."[261] The author evidently had few or no trustworthy documents regarding the saint's career. " Happier than the Irish people, Colman had no history; his biographer undertook to supply him with one."[262]

All the ordinary devices of Irish hagiography appear here in the most extreme form. Story after story is told to justify the claims of Colmán's churches to lands, privileges, and honors, anachronism after anachronism cements the ties which unite them with other great ecclesiastical establishments of Ireland, miracle after miracle exalts their patron above all other saints. Summarising his work at its conclusion, the hagiographer declares: " Now it is evident from these stories about Colmán son of Lúachan that God thinks no cleric more wonderful than him. For what other cleric in Ireland has gone on a lake without a boat but he? Again, what cleric," etc., etc.

The biographer's freedom from the restrictions of recorded fact, and the comprehensive spirit in which he worked, have resulted in the production of a document which,

---

[260] Cf. the similar opening words of Vit. Trip. (no. 135) and of the Life of Adamnán (no. 224).
[261] AU. A note added to the Life says that they were buried in the time of the Danish marauder Turges (d. 845).
[262] Vendryes.

if of little value for the history of the seventh century,[263] has the greatest importance as a record of conditions and ideas in Ireland in the twelfth, and in particular for the topography and the ecclesiastical organisation of Westmeath. " Indeed, what with its wealth of varied and picturesque incidents taken from the life and customs of the people, its many instances of religious practices and information on ecclesiastical matters generally, its topographical details, and its folklore, it will always count, next to the Tripartite Life and the biographies of Colum Cille, as the richest and fullest among the Lives of Irish saints that have come down to us."[264]

(f) Líath-Mochoemóc (Leamakevoge), the Church of St. Mo-Choem-óc

Líath-mór, or Líath-Mo-Choem-óc (now Leamakevoge, east of Thurles, bar. Eliogarty, co. Tipperary), was one of the chief churches of the Éli, an ancient people who dwelt in northern Tipperary and southern Offalley.

239. Life of St. Mo-Choem-óc

Beatissimus abbas Mochoemog de prouincia Connactorum. . . . Lyath, ubi per eum a Christo multa miracula patrantur, C. est h. et g. c. D. P. et S. S. in s. s. Amen.

MSS: Cod. K. ff. 80ᵛ-4ᵛ. — TCD 175 (E. 3. 11) ff. 49 *sqq* [mutilated at beginning]. — Brussels Bibl. roy. 2324-40 ff. 289-302 [an Irish trans. of this text]. Eds: Colgan *AA. SS.* 589-96. — Fleming *Collectanea sacra* (1667) 380-91. — *AA. SS. Boll.* Mart. II 280-8. — *VV. SS. Hib.* I pp. lxxviii *sq*, II 164-83.

Of Mo-Choem-óc, or Mochoemog, the founder, little is known except what is to be derived from this evidently late and largely fictitious Life. The Annals of Ulster give his obit under the year 656.[265]

(g) Tech-Mochúa (Timahoe), the Church of St. Mo-Chúa

This Tech-Mochúa, the " house," or monastery, of St. Mo-Chúa, is to be identified with Timahoe village in Leix.

240. Life of St. Mo-Chúa of Tech-Mochúa

Clarus genere uir erat, nomine Mochua, . . . anno uite sue nonagesimo IX° Kal. Ianuarii feliciter quieuit, prestante D. n. I. C., c. est l. et i. per infinita s. Amen.

MSS: Bodl. Rawl. B 485 ff. 114-6; B 505 ff. 93ᵛ-6 [in these 2 MSS the Life is erroneously assigned to Mochúa of Balla]. — Dublin Franciscan Convent A 24 pp. 42 *sqq*. Eds: *AA. SS. Boll.* Jan. I 45-7. — *VV. SS. Hib.* I pp. lxxix-lxxxi, II 184-9.

---

[263] The chronology is hopeless, but events and personages of this century seem to have been chiefly in the compiler's mind.

[264] KM. — The Life contains a most interesting, though incomplete, description of one of the ceremonies at the inauguration of the high-king of Ireland at Tara.

[265] FM say that he was 413 years old, a statement which may conceal some annalistic record.

The Life is brief. Mo-Chúa is said to have been a Connachtman, and to have entered religion in mature life, hence being designated one of the three ex-laics, or ex-warriors (*athlaech*), of Erin. Anecdotes tell how he cured Colmán Elo (d. 611) of a sudden loss of memory, and Munnu (d. 635) of leprosy, and procured fine weather for an entire year while St. Cianan (d. 489) was building his stone church at Duleek,[266] the first of its kind in Ireland. The Chronicon Scotorum records his death at a date which has been equated with 654, but the other events of the same annal are found in the Annals of Ulster at 658.

(h) CELL-MAIC-DÚACH (KILMACDUAGH), THE CHURCH OF ST. COLMÁN MAC DÚACH

Gúaire of Aidne, king of Connacht, who died in 663 or 666, is one of the great personages of the literary tradition. There is a whole cycle of romances and poems grouped around him as the central figure.[267] His outstanding characteristic is usually hospitality, for which his name became proverbial. His family was the southern branch of the Úi Fiachrach,[268] known as Úi Fiachrach Aidne, and their territory, Aidne, corresponded with the barony of Kiltartan and diocese of Kilmacduagh in Galway. Cell-maic-Dúach was their principal church, and its founder, Colmán son of Dúa, or Dúach, is brought by the legends into association with Gúaire, although his pedigree, which makes him ninth in descent from the *árd-rí* Nath-Í (d. 428) would suggest that his *floruit* should come later by about fifty years.[269]

241. Story of Colmán mac Dúach and Gúaire Aidne

Colmán mac Dúach, diatá Cell meic Dúach, dochóid . . . clann Gúaire meic Colmáin óssin amach co bráth. Finit.

MS: YBL col. 796, p. 133 of facs. — Brussels Bibl. roy. 5100–4 f. 82. ED: J. G. O'Keeffe *Ériu* I i 43–8 [with trans.]. — WS *RC* XXVI 372–7. Versions of the same tale are in Keating, ITS ed. III 64 *sqq*, and *AA. SS. Boll.* 29 Oct. XII 880–92.

Gúaire's caldron is borne by angels to the hermitage of Colmán; Gúaire follows, and induces the saint to found the church of Cell-maic-Dúach, to which henceforth Gúaire's offspring and his territory are dedicated. The date of composition of the story is probably in the tenth century.

(i) ST. CELLACH OF CELL-ALAID (KILLALA)

The church of Cell-Alaid (Killala) is said to have been founded by Patrick. The story of its martyred bishop Cellach is a comparatively

---

[266] Dam-liag, *i.e.*, the " stone house," *par excellence*.   [267] *Cf.* nos. 209, 242.
[268] *Cf.* O'D *The genealogies, tribes, and customs of Hy-Fiachrach* (IAS: Dublin 1844).
[269] See also Fahy *History and antiquities of Kilmacduagh* (Dublin 1893).

late literary romance. For the sake of completeness it is included here, but that such a person as Cellach ever existed is very doubtful.

242. Life of Cellach

Rí ro gab for Connachtu i. Eogan *bél* . . . [Ends with a long poem:] Fás anocht áittreb Eogain . . . co bfuil a phort folam fás.

MSS: LBr pp. 272–7. — RIA Liber Flavus Fergusiorum vol. II pt. ii ff. 5ᵛ–8ᵛ. — Brussels Bibl. roy. 2324–40 ff. 53ᵛ–9 [a copy by O'Clery of the LBr text, but having value because that MS was then in a better state of preservation]. — RIA Hodges & Smith 224 p. 10. ED: O'Grady *SG* I 49–65, II 50–69 [with trans.]. — *AA. SS. Boll.* Mai. I 106–10 [1866 ed.] [Lat. version received from Thos. Sirinus: *cf.* pp. 41, 186].

The tale represents Cellach to have been successively a student at Clonmacnois, king of Connacht, bishop of Killala, and a refugee hermit. Finally he was murdered by his disciples at the instigation of Gúaire Aidne, who is here presented, quite exceptionally, as a thorough villain. The setting is unhistorical, the time varying from the first half of the sixth to the middle of the seventh century. The literary qualities of the composition, and especially of the nature poetry which it incorporates, are very high.[270]

(j) BRÍ-GOBANN (BRIGOWN), THE CHURCH OF ST. FIND-CHÚ

Brí-gobann, "Smiths' hill," is now represented by the parish of Brigown, co. Cork. The monastery was on the site of the present Mitchelstown, where there was a round tower that fell in 1720. It was one of the chief churches of the Fir-Muige (Fermoy), and, indeed, of southern Munster.

243. Life of St. Find-chú

Boi brugaidh amra a nUlltaib fecht n-aill do Mhughdhornaibh . . . 7 geinemain Finnchua, etc.

MSS: Bk. Lis. ff. 25ᵛ–30ᵛ [colophon: "It is the friar O'Buagachain who wrote this Life out of the Book of Monasterboice."]. — Brussels Bibl. roy. 2324–40 ff. 35–43, and 113–22 [this second adds "Out of the Book of MacCarthy Reagh this Life of Finnchu has been written in the convent of the Friars in the House of Mo-Laga (Timoleague) the 20th June 1629"]. — Dublin Franciscan Convent A 9 (3) pp. 17–24. — RIA A. iv. 1 (Stowe 9) pp. 65–89. ED: *Lis. Lives* 84–98, 231–46, 347–8 [text, trans., notes]. — Fáinne Fionn *Irish Rosary* XV–XVI (1911–2). *Cf.* Plummer *Misc. hag. Hib.* Cat. no. 36.

Find-chú, or Finn-chúa, died, according to the Four Masters, in 664, of the Yellow Plague. His figure is not prominent in church history, but in popular tradition he bore the character of a typical Irish saint, of irascible temper and having a *penchant*

---

[270] There is a curious parallel between the circumstances of Cellach's death, and the verses connected with it, on the one hand, and, on the other, Henry Newbolt's poem, "He fell among thieves," and the incident which that records. *Cf.* Col. Algernon Durand *The making of a frontier* chap. ii.

for extraordinary forms of self-torture. The *Félire* of Oengus [271] relates, among other matters, that he suspended himself on two hooks in his armpits, seeking the guerdon that whoever should call upon him in the hour of death, should be saved from hell. In the Life this is expanded into a story of seven smiths who made seven sickles on which he might abide seven years to obtain a place in heaven, having given that to which he was himself entitled to a king of the Dési. The place where the smiths worked was called Brí-gobann (Smiths' Hill).

The Life of Find-chú has more of a secular form and tone than the majority of saints' Lives in Irish. There is little of the monastic flavor about it except the record of tributes and honors due to the saint. It resembles the popular romances. A noteworthy feature is the explanation of place names by incidents in the saint's life. It was composed probably towards the end of the eleventh or beginning of the twelfth century, when the Norse inroads were still a vivid tradition, and the rivalry of North and South had become a recognised element in Irish polity. The references to gillies, to battle-banners, to nose-tax, etc., and to the victories achieved by Find-chú over foreign marauders, determine the date as post-Viking. The author was a patriotic Munsterman. After describing a victory achieved by his hero over invaders from the north, he adds: "Wherefore Find-chua left to Munstermen, from that time forward till Doomsday, to defeat foreigners and every host besides when charging down a height; and verily this is fulfilled."

The document has much interest as a source for popular customs and ideas.

The first four, at least, of the five copies of the Life listed above go back to the text of the now lost Book of Monasterboice.

(k) THE CHURCHES OF ST. FÉCHÍN OF FOBAR (FORE)

The name of St. Féchín is usually associated with that of his monastery of Fabar or Fobar,[272] now the village of Fore in Westmeath, where there are the ruins of a very old church. But his work seems to have been chiefly in the west of Connacht, where his most important foundation was the celebrated monastery of Cunga, or Cong.[273] To him were ascribed also the churches of Omey island and Árd-oilén, "High Island," off the most westerly coast of Galway.

244. Life of St. Féchín of Fore

(Ir. i) Fear aintech aibhinn almsanach . . . [Ir. ii is imperfect at both beginning and end.] [Lat.] Sanctus ac uenerabilis abbas Fechinus nobili parentum . . . "Transfer hinc, et transibit."... A puero Christus Fechinum mox benedixit . . . Frigore membra domans, in aquis uigilare solebat. 27 ll. Ymnus de eo. Festum diem celebremus . . . . Murus contra uicia. 16 ll. Ad laudes. Regem regum collaudemus . . . . Tibi sit laus, gloria. Amen. 69 ll.

MSS: (Ir.) Cheltenham Phillipps 9194 A.D. 1329 ff. 1–8ᵛ [*cf.* KM *Academy* May 10, 1890 p. 321]. — YBL cols. 1–2, 125–8, pp. 434–7 [fragments]. (Lat.) Bodl. Rawl.

[271] *Fél. Oeng.*[1] p. clxxii. It preserves an early and obscure poem regarding Find-chú, attributed as a prophecy to Find mac Cumaill: Ticfa sund oilithreach . . . gar cian coticfa. 21 ll.

[272] *Cf. FM, s. a.* 1176, n.

[273] *Cf.* O'Flaherty *Iar-Connaught* 106, 112–5, 120–1, 279.

B 485 ff. 111–4; B 505 ff. 178ᵛ *sqq.* — Dublin Franciscan Convent A 24 pp. 220 *sqq.*
EDS: Colgan *AA. SS.* 130–3 [Lat. text], 133–9 [compilation from 3 Ir. Lives]. — *AA.
SS. Boll.* Jan. II 329–32; (1863 ed.) 693–7. — WS *RC* XII (1891) 318–53, XIII (1892)
299 [Ir. text, trans. — poems omitted]. — *VV. SS. Hib.* I pp. lxiv–lxvii, II 76–86 [Lat.
text]. *Cf.* Paul Walsh *Place Names of Westmeath* (Dublin 1915) 69 *sqq*; J. Loth *RC*
XXXVII (1919) 306 *sqq* [re the name Fobar].

Of Féchín, or Moéca (=Mo-Fhéca), we have one Latin and two Irish Lives. The
Latin is a late mediaeval abbreviation of an older work, ending incomplete: to it are
added a short poem on the saint's miracles, and two hymns for his feast, none of
which is based on the preceding text. The two Irish Lives, of which the second is
quite imperfect, represent somewhat older versions. They are separated by a note,
referring to the first: " Nicholas junior, son of the abbot of Cong, put this Life of
Féchin out of Latin into Gaelic, and O'Duffy [274] took and wrote [it]; and this is the
year of the age of the Lord to-day, 1329, etc." Colgan had three Irish sources, one,
a translation from Latin, obtained from the monastery of the island of Omey (Imaid
Féichín), which Féchín was reputed to have converted from paganism; a second, in
antique style, wanting beginning and end; and a third, metrical, in 74 distichs. The
first and second may be those still preserved. Colgan ascribes our Latin Life to
Augustin Magradin, of Inis-na-náemh, or Saints' Island. [275]

Féchín died of the Yellow Plague in 665 or 668. [276] His legend emphasises especially
the extraordinary mortifications which he practised.

———

Gormgal (d. 1018), abbot of Féchín's foundation of Árd-oilén, was enrolled in the
lists of saints. [277] Corcran *clérech* (d. 1040) wrote for the monks of Árd-oilén a treatise
on the virtues and relics of St. Gormgal which Colgan saw, [278] but which, apparently,
no longer exists.

(1) EMÍNE *BÁN* OF ROS-GLAISI

Ros-glaisi was a church on the river Barrow, probably Ross in
Wexford.

245. Cáin Eimíne báin

Dolotar flaithi Laighen isin duinebath . . . ó Laignib co brath.

MSS: RIA 23 P 3 f. 16. — BM Addit. 30512 f. 27. — Brussels Bibl. roy. 2324–40 f. 99
[called ' Life of Emine ']. — TCD H. 1. 11 f. 133 [copy of Addit. 30512]. ED: J. G.
O'Keeffe *Anec.* I 40–5 [text only]. TRANS: Chas. Plummer *Ériu* IV 39–46.

———

[274] Several of the O'Duffy family are associated in the records with Cong: *cf.* FM 1150, 1168, 1223;
Proc. RIA VI 225.
[275] *Cf.* p. 19 *supra.* — The Latin and the second Irish Life say that his contemporary, Aileran the Wise
(no. 107), wrote a Life of Féchín.
[276] See the strange story told in the Life of St. Gerald of Mayo (no. 252).
[277] *Cf.* p. 482 *infra.*
[278] *AA. SS.* 206 n.

The story relates how Emíne *bán* and forty-nine of his monks vicariously sacrificed themselves by voluntary death in order to save Bran úa Faeláin, king of Leinster, and forty-nine princes of the Lagin, from pestilence. The narrator seems to have been thinking of the Yellow Plague of 664–5, but Bran, who died in 693, succeeded to the throne in 680 at the earliest.

In TCD 1336 (H. 3. 17) *s* XV–XVI col. 678 there is a short story of Emíne *bán* and Cormac mac Cuilennáin. ED: KM *ZCP* VII 299. TRANS: Plummer *Ériu* IV 40.

(m) Ros-Cré (Roscrea), the Church of St. Cronán

Ros-Cré, now Roscrea, in north-eastern Tipperary, was one of the principal churches of Élei,[279] and its founder, St. Cronán, was patron of the district. The annals do not offer any chronological *data* regarding Cronán, but his biographer appears to have placed him in the seventh century.

246. Life of St. Cronán of Ros-Cré

(i) Gloriosus abbas Cronanus de provinchia Mumenensium . . . Cronanus, inter choros angelorum cum gaudio inenarrabili et suauissimis carminibus migravit ad C., Cui est h. et g. cum D. P. et S. S., in s. s. Amen. (ii) The same *incipit*.

MSS: (i) Cod. K. ff. 88^v–90^v. — TCD 175 (E. 3. 11) ff. 55^v *sq.* (ii) Cod. S. ff. 147–9 [imperfect at end, but no *lacuna* in present MS]. EDS: (i) *VV. SS. Hib.* I pp. lix–lx, II 22–31. (ii) *AA. SS. Boll.* Apr. III 580–3 [ed. of 1866, 585–9: the last three sections, wanting in Cod. S., were supplied by Thomas O'Sheerin, ed. of Fleming's *Collectanea sacra;* they are practically identical with Version i]. — *AA. SS. ex Cod. S.* 541–50.

The two versions of the Life of Cronán are very closely related, and depend on a common source, from which neither is much removed. This original was written at Roscrea by a member of the community for the use of the brothers, probably in the eleventh or first half of the twelfth century. It was in the main a simple catalogue of miracles. The most noteworthy of these miracles is that of the copying of the book of Dimma, which, no doubt, was believed to be the codex which still bears that name: [280] the scribe did the work in one continuous effort of forty days and forty nights.

(n) Balla and St. Cronán, or Mo-Chúa

Balla, or Balna (now a village in bar. Clanmorris, co. Mayo), seems to have been an important monastery of north-western Connacht, although it is seldom mentioned in the annals. Its founder was another

279 *Cf.* p. 22 *supra.*
280 No. 458.

Cronán, also known by the hypocoristic name Mo-Chúa, who died, according to the Annals of Ulster, in 694.[281]

247. Life of St. Mo-Chúa of Balla

(i) Homo proficiscens uocauit seruos suos tradidit illis bona sua. O dhochuaidh in fer maith . . . a cholla ind oeine, ind apstanait, quia crucifixus est mundus illi, et ipse mundo. (ii) Vir sacer Cronanus, Mochua quoque dictus, . . . aetatis suae sexto et quinquagesimo in Caelitum coetum migrauit.

MSS: (i) Bk Lis. ff. 40–2ᵛ. — BM Egerton 91 s XV f. 56ᵛ [fragment]. — BN Fonds celt. et basq. 1 ff. 32–3.⁴— Brussels Bibl. roy. 2324–40 s XVII ff. 107–12. — RIA A. iv. 1 (Stowe 9) pp. 119–31. EDS: (i) Lis. Lives 137–46, 281–9, 360–1 [text, trans. notes]. (ii) Colgan AA. SS. 789–90 [Latin trans., by Philip O'Sullivan, from Irish]. — AA. SS. Boll. Jan. I 47–9. Cf. Plummer Misc. hag. Hib. Cat. no. 50.

The Irish Life of Mo-Chúa, in the form of a homily, is a very late and crude composition. It has many quotations of verse, which seem to have been, in part, the basis of the prose. It also sets forth the claims of Mo-Chúa's church from the north Connacht kindreds, the Úi Fiachrach and the Síl Muireadaigh.[282]

(o) THE CHURCH OF ST. MOLING: TECH-MOLING (ST. MULLINS)

St. Moling [283] was the last of the ancient patrons of Ireland whose fame was national more than local. He was, however, peculiarly a patron of the Lagin, for whom he is said to have obtained the remission of the bóroma tribute, which the high-kings had long claimed from Leinster. To his death various dates are assigned, from 692 to 697. The Cáin Adamnáin tract says that he was at Adamnán's synod, which is usually placed in 697. It is stated that he was a disciple of Máedóc of Ferns, and that he himself became bishop at Ferns, and also at Glendaloch. But his own church was Tech-Moling, or Ros-mBruic, now St. Mullins, in Carlow. This remained for centuries, and even to recent times, an important religious centre and place of pilgrimage.[284]

248. The Latin Lives of St. Moling

(i) De Australi Laginensium plaga que dicitur Kennselach . . . s. Molyng diuerso temporum cursu operatur gratia C. C. est h. et g. atque p., c. D. P. in unitate S. S. in s. s. Amen. (ii) Venerabilis presul ac propheta Dei Dayrchellus . . . ovans migrauit ad Christum, qui sine fine v. et r. in s. s. Amen.

MSS: (i) Cod. K. ff. 70ᵛ–4. — Brussels Bibl. roy. 4190–200 ff. 59–68 [a poor transcript of preceding]. (ii) Cod. S. ff. 199ᵛ–201. — Bodl. Rawl. B 485 f. 50; B 505 f. 124. —

---

[281] CS has the obit under 690, but also, with the name as Dachua (=Do-Chúa), under 637 (probably recte 638). This earlier date has generally been accepted by hagiologists, probably because Cronán is represented to have studied under Comgall of Bangor. The princes of Connacht with whom he is associated seem to be of the second half of the century.

[282] There are so many Mo-Chúas, and even so many Cronáns, that the patron of Balla is sometimes confused with his namesakes, especially with Mo-Chúa of Clúain-Dolcain. Cf. p. 702 infra.

[283] This is a hypocoristic name, but its origin is obscure. There are several inane stories connecting it with the Irish word meaning " to leap." " Moling" is sometimes followed by the epithet " Lúachair." His original name is given as Dairchell or Tarchell.

[284] Cf. R. Butler (ed.) John Clyn's Annals of Ireland (IAS: Dublin 1848) s. a. 1348; J. F. M. ffrench " St. Mullins, Co. Carlow " Journ. RSAI 5th ser., pt. IV, vol. II.

Dublin Franciscan Convent A 24 p. 39. EDS: (i) *VV. SS. Hib.* I pp. lxxxi *sqq*, II 190–205. — P. O'Leary *St. Mulling* (1887) [trans., notes]. (ii) *AA. SS. Boll.* Jun. III 406–10, 3rd ed. (1867) IV 331–4 [has also some inaccurate extracts from Version i]. — *AA. SS. ex Cod. S.* 819–26. *Cf.* Baring-Gould and Fisher *Lives of the British Saints* III 487–90.

The first version is not, in its present form, older than the middle of the twelfth century. It has several passages of considerable historical interest. The second version is much later, represents a different tradition, and is greatly condensed, being, in fact, only an uninteresting summary list of miracles.

249. Birth and Life of Moling (*Geinemain Molling ocus a Bhethae*)

Bai brughaidh cétach amra irdairc . . . isindara blíadain ochtmogat a áeisi. Finis.

MSS: RIA Liber Flavus Fergussiorum *s* XIV/XV I ff. 13–5. — Brussels Bibl. roy. 4190–200 ff. 43–65ᵛ. — Dublin Franciscan Convent A (9) p. 30 [a mere fragment]. — Edinburgh Nat. Lib. V f. 11 [frag.]. EDS: WS *RC* XXVII (1906) 257–312 [text, trans., glossary]; *The Birth and Life of St. Moling* (Paris 1906) [reprint of preceding; *cf.* " Notes on the Birth and Life of St. Moling " *RC* XXVIII (1907) 70–2 — *addenda* and *corrigenda*]; *Specimens of Middle-Irish Literature No. I The Birth and Life of St. Moling* (London 1907) [revised ed., privately printed; contains text and trans. of poems omitted in preceding ed.]. *Cf.* O'C *M&C* III 34–6 [a free rendering of the story of Gobbán *saer*].

The Irish Life of Moling is a composition entirely distinct from both the Latin Lives, which it parallels only remotely at a few points. Though there are touches showing editing by the community of Moling,[285] the subject-matter is, for the most part, pure legend and folk-lore direct from the people. It has much importance for the light it throws on social and moral conditions, beliefs and customs in the eleventh and twelfth centuries.

250. Minor texts relating to Moling

(i) Fechtus dosum ac irrnaighthi . . . Is 6r glan, is nem im gréin . . . is find-druine find, is 6r. 8 quatrains. MSS: Monastery of St. Paul, Carinthia MS 86.1b (XXV d. 86) [2 quatrains only; *cf.* no. 535]. — LL 284b. — BB 256. — Bk. Lis. f. 45. — Bodl. Laud 610 [note to Fél. Oeng.]. — Bodl. Rawl. B 512 f. 141ᵛ. EDS: The St. Paul verses: *IT* I 319. — HZ *Glossae Hibernicae* (Berlin 1881) 268. — *Thes. Pal.* II pp. xxxiii *sq*, 294. The entire poem: WS *Goidelica*² (1872) 180–2. — *Fél. Oeng.*¹ pp. cv *sq*. — *Fél. Oeng.*² 156–7. TRANS: In all except *IT* and HZ. Also KM *Ancient Irish Poetry* (London 1911) 39–40. The preface in Fél. Oeng. says that the devil sang this song in praise of the man who does God's will, after he had failed to circumvent Moling. The St. Paul codex seems to attribute it to Moling himself, and, although the present text is of the ninth century, it is quite possible that it is the modification of a composition of the end of the seventh.

(ii) Fecht do Moling issin Táidin conacca Máel-Dobur-chon . . . MSS: LL 283ᵛ. — Notes to Fél. Oeng. in Laud 610. — Bodl. Rawl. B 512 f. 64ᵛ. — TCD 1319

---

[285] As, for example, the tribute to be paid by the Húi Dega (of south central Leinster) to Moling — *cap.* xiv.

(H. 2. 17) p. 397b. Eds: KM *RC* XIV (1893) 188–90, 194 [with trans.; *cf. ibid.* XVII (1896) 319]. — *Fél. Oeng.*² 152–3. A certain Máel-Dobor-chon [286] demonstrates to Moling how he would have rescued Christ.

(iii) LL 285. Ed: KM *loc. cit.* 190–3. Moling, a captive to brigands, is released because of the verses he composes. — For other short texts related to Moling *cf.* Plummer *Misc. hag. Hib.* Cat. nos. 154–5.

251. Poems ascribed to Moling

(i) Rochúala . . . iss é do less, rochúala. 7 quatrains. MS: LL p. 149. Ed: KM *Miscellanea Hibernica (Univ. of Illinois Studies in Lang. and Lit.* II iv Nov. 1916) 17–8 [with trans.] Praise of King Móinach of Cashel, a contemporary of Moling, because he does his duty in severely punishing criminals. Old Irish, but can hardly be as early as Moling's time.

(ii) A collection of 24 poems. One is ascribed to Colum-cille [*cf.* no. 220 lxxii *supra*], the others to Moling. MS: Brussels Bibl. roy. 5100–4 *s* XVII pp. 50–67. Ed: WS *Anec.* II (1908) 20–41 [text only; *cf. ibid.* III 76–7 for textual emendations]. This is a cycle of Moling poems similar in character to, and of about the same date—eleventh century and later — as the Colum-cille cycle [no. 220]. One is found also in *Geine-main Molling ocus a Bhethae.*

(iii) The " Ecstasy," or Prophecy, of Moling (*Baile Moling*): Atberim libh a Laigh-niu . . . . 47 quatrains. MS: YBL col. 340. Synopsis, with texts and trans. of a few lines, in O'C *MS Mat.* 420–1, 628–9. A " prophecy," written about the middle of the twelfth century, relating chiefly to affairs of Leinster, and ending with prognostications of calamities, including the " Broom out of Fánad." [287]

Poems attributed to Moling are found also in the tract on the *Bóroma* and in the Annals of Ulster *s. a.* 695. On the Book of Mulling, see no. 456.

(p) Mag-nEo (Mayo) and St. Gerald

Bede gives at some length a narrative [288] of the career in Ireland of Bishop Colmán of Lindisfarne after his withdrawal from Northumbria as a result of the Synod of Whitby in 664. Taking with him his Irish and thirty English followers he returned by way of Iona to Ireland and established a monastery on an island off the west coast known as Inis-bó-finne, " Island of the white cow " (Inishbofin to the north of Clifden). A dispute arising between the two races — Bede says because the Irish wished to live on the labors of the English — Colmán separated them and gave the English an establishment of their own at Mag-nEo (Mayo) on the mainland. " This monastery," says Bede, " is to this day pos-

[286] *Cf.* p. 420 *supra.*   [287] *Cf.* pp. 749–53 *infra.*   [288] Bede *Hist. Eccl.* IV iv.

sessed by English inhabitants; being the same that, grown up from a small beginning to be very large, is generally called Mageo; and as all things have long since been brought under a better method, it contains an exemplary society of monks, who are gathered there from the province of the English, and live by the labor of their hands, after the example of the venerable fathers, under a rule and a canonical abbot, in much continency and singleness of life." Fifty years after Bede Alcuin's letters show that an important church of English monks still existed at Mayo.[289] And Mag-nEo na Sachsan, "Mayo of the Saxons," continued to be a place of note in Irish ecclesiastical records for many centuries.

252. Life of St. Gerald of Mayo

Fuit uir uite uenerabilis, Geraldus nomine, . . . Geraldum, cuius meritis et precibus dignetur pietas diuina misereri nostri. Amen.

MSS: Bodl. Rawl. B 485 ff. 108–111; B 505 ff. 203ᵛ–5ᵛ. — Dublin Franciscan Convent A 24 pp. 251 sqq. EDS: Colgan AA. SS. 599 sqq. — AA. SS. Boll. Mar. II 288–92 [extracts from Colgan]. — VV. SS. Hib. I pp. lxxi sq, II 107–15.

Under 732 the annals record the death of " Gerald, pontifex of Mayo of the Saxons." Of Gerald a very fabulous Life is extant. He is said to have been an Englishman who accompanied Colmán to Ireland, where he became the founder and first abbot of Mayo.[290] But he is also associated with events which had happened and personages who had died in Ireland before Colmán's arrival, and there are other equally curious historical aberrations. Many passages, however, have unusual interest — as those treating of the relations between the druids and the Christian teachers, and the story accounting for the claim of Gerald's successors to every tenth fish caught in the river Moy. Noteworthy is the remarkable explanation of the cause of the Great Plague of 664–5, a relic of some venerable propaganda for the Social Revolution. It is found in briefer version in the preface to Colmán's Hymn in Liber Hymnorum.[291] Diarmait and Blaithmac, joint high-kings, held an assembly at Tara to consider the problem of over-population in Ireland. The nobles proposed that God should be invoked to send a pestilence upon the lower orders and thus reduce their numbers. Féchín of Fore approved of the proposal, Gerald — so says his biographer — opposed it. Féchín and his party fasted on God to obtain their demand, the pestilence came, and multitudes died — notably Féchín and many nobles and ecclesiastics — but Gerald was spared.

(q) Clúain-Brónaig (Clonbroney) and St. Samthann

Clúain-Brónaig (Clonbroney, near Granard, co. Longford) was a monastery of women which enjoyed some renown. One tradition said that it was founded by Patrick, who placed there two daughters of his

---

[289] No. 340.
[290] If Gerald did accompany Colmán, he must have been then a mere boy.
[291] Cf. no. 582.

early master, Mil-chú.[292] The Brigitine community claimed it as one of the monasteries founded by disciples of Brigit.[293] But in later times Samthann, whose obit is given under 739, was honored as its patroness. She was said to have been also for a time prioress of Urnaidhe (now Urney, on the borders of Tyrone and Donegal, near Lifford).

253. Life of St. Samthann

Sancta et uenerabilis uirgo Samthana . . . ascendens in celum, ubi uita fruitur eterna in s. s. Amen.

MSS: Bodl. Rawl. B 485 ff. 150–3; B 505 ff. 167^v–9^v. — Dublin Franciscan Convent A 24 pp. 206 sqq. EDS: VV. SS. Hib. I pp. lxxxvii sq, II 253–61.

The Life, in its present form, is late and brief, but it seems free from glaring historical inaccuracies, and may go back to an early and good text.

V. CHURCH FOUNDATIONS OF UNCERTAIN DATE

The chronology of the Irish acta sanctorum is notoriously fantastic. Nevertheless for the greater number of these ancient founders of churches there is sufficient evidence to enable us with some confidence to assign the floruit of each to an era of fairly wide limits, as the fifth, sixth or seventh century. But in a few cases the material is either so scanty or so unsatisfactory that it is impossible to say more than that the founders of these churches lived at some time in the heroic age of the old Irish Christianity. Such are St. Naile, of Inber-Naile (Inver, off Donegal Bay), and Cell-Naile (Kinawley, south-west of Upper Loch Erne, on the borders of Fermanagh and Cavan); St. Colmán, or Mo-Cholm-óc, founder of Druim-mór, in Mag-Coba (now Dromore, co. Down); St. Magniu, of Cell-Maignenn (Kilmainham, south of Dublin); St. Grellan, of Craeb-mór or Craeb-Ghrelláin (Creeve, in northern Roscommon) and Cell-clúaine (Kilclooney at Ballinasloe); St. Lasair, of Cell-Ronáin (Kilronan, bar. Boyle, co. Roscommon), and several other churches; St. Cuanna, or Cuannatheus, of Cell-Cuanna (Kilcoona, east of Loch Corrib and south-east of Headford, in Galway); and St. Mochulleus, perhaps of Innsnat.

254. Life of St. Naile

Rí ro gabhastair flaithes . . . 7 dá cloicc-mionnaibh. [Incomplete.] Contains 8 sets of verses.

MS: Brussels Bibl. roy. 4190–200 ff. 129–42. ED: Chas. Plummer Misc. hag. Hib. (Brussels 1925) 97–155 [with trans.].

[292] Cf. Vit. Trip. I 20, 90, 168.   [293] No. 150.

A very late piece of hagiography, and a very poor one, whether from the literary, the historical, or the religious point of view.

255. Life of St. Colmán, or Mo-Cholm-óc, of Druim-mór (Dromore)

Beatissimus vir Colmanus, Drumorensis episcopus . . . inter verba orationis spiritum Deo reddidit: cui h. et g. in s. s. Amen.

MSS: Cod. S. ff. 201-3. — Bodl. Rawl. B 485 ff. 50-1; B 505 f. 210 [imperfect]. Eds: *AA. SS. Boll.* Jun. II 25-9. — *AA. SS. ex Cod. S.* 827-34. *Cf.* Baring-Gould and Fisher *British Saints* II 162-4.

Short and fabulous: in the main an abbreviated catalogue of miracles.

256. Life of St. Magniu of Cell-Maignenn (Kilmainham)

Maignenn 7 Toa 7 Cobthach 7 Libréan . . . [ends imperfect].

MSS: BN Fonds celt. et basq. 1 ff. 30-2. — BM Egerton 91 ff. 49 – 51^v [written by Uilliam Mac an Legha, from whom we have other MSS dated 1463 and 1467]. Ed: O'Grady *SG* I 37-49, II 35-49 [text, trans., notes]. *Cf.* Baring-Gould and Fisher *British Saints* III 453-7.

Late and very fabulous: largely taken up with the saint's miracles, the tributes due to him, and his blessings, curses and prophecies.

257. Life of St. Grellan of Craeb-Grelláin (Creeve)

I naimsir Lughdach meic Laeghaire . . . 7 betha Grellain gonuicce sin.

MSS: Brussels Bibl. roy. 4190-200 ff. 88-91. — RIA 23 O 41. Ed: O'D *Tribes and customs of Hy-Many* (IAS: Dublin 1843) 8-14 [extract, including poem attributed to the saint beginning: Mor mo chain ar cloinn Maine . . .]. — *AA. SS. Boll.* 10 Nov. IV 483-95.

For services rendered to Maine *mór*, ancestor of the Úi Maini (who dwelt in southern Roscommon, eastern Galway, and some small sections of Clare and Offalley), Grellan is to receive certain tributes from that race.

258. Life of St. Lasair

Bái ri amhra oireadha a nEoghanacht. . . . [Ends imperfectly with the verses] Dobhennaigh Lasair an aig . . . is leo drumchla gacha ráithe. 4 quatrains.[294]

MSS: Brussels Bibl. roy. 4190-200 ff. 117-28 [by O'Clery, Jan. 26, 1629]. — RIA Stowe B. IV. 1 pp. 97-103 [by David O'Duigenan in 1670]. Ed: L. Gwynn *Ériu* V (1911) 73-109.

Lasair, " Flame," was the daughter of Ronán, whose name is preserved in Cell-Ronáin, of which she is patroness. She is also associated with Achad-Beithe (Aghavea in Fermanagh), Cell-Laisre of Loch-Mac-nÉn (Killassery in south-west Fermanagh),

[294] The Life contains six other sets of verses.

and Cell-Laisre of Gailenga (Killasser, bar. Gallen, Mayo). Both texts were derived from the O'Duigenans,[295] who were hereditary *comarbai* of Lasair at Cell-Ronáin. The editor believes the Life to be a modernisation of a late Middle-Irish composition.

259. Acts of St. Cuanna, or Cuannatheus

MS: Cod. S. ff. 218-9 [imperfect]. Eds: Colgan *AA. SS.* 250 *sq.* — *AA. SS. ex Cod. S.* 931-8.

Late and fragmentary, but much padded, Life of an obscure saint.

260. Life of St. Mochulleus

MS: Cod. S. f. 220 [fragment: folios preceding and following probably lost]. Ed: *AA. SS. ex Cod. S.* 939-44. *Cf. RC* XIX 352-3.

Another obscure saint, here made a contemporary of Gúaire of Aidne (d. 663 or 666). His identification with a Mochuille of Innsnat has been suggested. In style this fragment resembles that on Cuannatheus but differs from almost all others in the codex.[296]

261. Story of Cáirech *dergáin* of Clúain-Boirenn and Ricinn, daughter of Crimthann mac Lugdach

Crimthann mac Lughdhach diatá Crimthann . . . do Dia et di Cháirich.

MS: RIA B. iv. 2 (Stowe 23) A.D. 1628 f. 145 [written by Michael O'Clery]. Ed: KM *ACL* III iv (1907) 308-9 [text only].

This curious story is connected with Cáirech *dergáin*, reputed foundress of the community of nuns at Clúain-Boirenn (Clonburren, bar. Moycarn, Roscommon) and one of the patron saints of the Úi Maine. She is said to have been a sister of a certain Ronán of Druim-Inasclainn, and also of Énda of Aran,[297] but at least this last relationship is fictitious.

262. Life of St. Attracta of Cell-Saile

MS: Dublin Franciscan Convent A 24 ad init. Eds: Colgan *AA. SS.* pp. 278-81. — *AA. SS. Boll.* 9 Feb. II 297-300. *Cf.* the Boll. *Bibl. hag. lat.* II 1156; Plummer *Misc. hag. Hib.* Cat. no. 210.

Neither the time at which Attracta lived nor the place where her church of Cell-Saile (said to be in Crich-Conaill) was located, is certain.

[295] *Cf.* p. 20 *supra.*

[296] A " Teodricus " is mentioned as King of Ireland in " modern times ": probably either Toirdelbach Úa Briain (1073-86) or Toirdelbach Úa Conchobuir (1120-1156). — A *Vita Mochullei* is to be found in the following continental MSS: Holy Cross Monastery, Lower Austria, 11 *s* XII; Admont Stiftsbibl. 25 *s* XIII; Melk Stiftsbibl. F 8 *s* XIII. It has not been published. It contains, however, an account of the *Triumphus s. Lamberti de castro Bullonio*, by an eye-witness. This was the name given to the capture in 1141, by the Bishop of Liége, of which St. Lambert was patron, of the castle of Bouillon. Bouillon had been pledged to the Bishop by the famous Godfroi de Bouillon in 1096, and seized by a secular count in 1134. The *Triumphus* has been extracted and published by Pertz *MGH SS* XX 512-4.

[297] No. 164.

VI. The Reform Movement of the Eighth and Ninth Centuries —
The *Céli Dé* (Culdees)

Bibliography

W. Reeves " On the Céli-Dé, commonly called Culdees " *Trans. RIA* XXIV (1873)
Sect. " Antiquities " pp. 119–263. Also separately, *The Culdees of the British Islands*
(Dublin 1864) [the principal work on its subject]. — W. F. Skene *Celtic Scotland* II
chap. vi. — L. Gougaud " Culdées " *Dict. d'archéol. chrét. et de liturgie* III pt. II
(1914) 3186–90.

Those who are familiar with the ecclesiastical history of Europe in
the middle ages know that it is a story of continually recurring reform
movements aimed at the restoration of the spirituality and the energy
of clergy and monks who were as continually slipping back into worldli-
ness and laxity. Very similar is the contemporary history of the Church
in Ireland. It seems probable that the great monastic movement of the
sixth and seventh centuries, and the eremetical of the seventh and eighth,
were in part at least an attack on what was considered the degeneracy of
the older religious establishments. By the eighth century the beginnings were apparent of that secularisation which overwhelmed the
monastic churches in the tenth and eleventh centuries. That there was
a re-action against this decay several facts indicate: (1) the development of the *dísert*, attached or in close proximity to the monastic church,
where the more devout monks, and the " pilgrims " from other establishments, might lead the life of recluses and at the same time share in the
religious work of the church; (2) the change in religious ideals, which
were becoming more rigorous and more Puritanical; (3) the appearance
of a number of leaders who sought to promote and organise these reform
tendencies; (4) the rise of the *Céli Dé*.

A few of the reformers may be named: Fer-dá-chrích [298] (" Man
of two districts "), abbot of Dair-inis [299] (d. 747 [300]); the Úi Suanaig of
Rathan [301] (d. 757 and 763), the bishops Caencomrac (d. 791) and
Dub-littir (d. 796), of Finn-glas; Elair (d. 807), who was head of a body
of anchorites on an island in Loch-Cré, about two miles south-east of
Ros-Cré; Fothad *na canóine* (" of the canon "), of Othan, or Rathan

---

[298] *Cf.* p. 352 *supra.*
[299] " Oak-island," probably in the Blackwater river, near Youghal: *cf.* p. 249 *supra.* There was another
Dair-inis in Wexford harbor: *cf.* p. 312 *supra.*
[300] All these dates are from AU.
[301] *Cf.* no. 237.

(in Donegal), whose obit is under 819; Euchu úa Tuathail, abbot of Lugmad (Louth), who died in 822. Certain churches — some of them founded under its influence — became peculiar strongholds of the new movement: among these were Liss-mór;[302] Finn-glas, about two and one-half miles north of the Liffey river where Dublin now stands; Loch-Cré, apparently an anchorites' establishment, subsidiary to Ros-Cré;[303] Tír-dá-glas;[304] and probably Disert-Diarmuta, now Castledermot, Kildare.

But the chief apostle of the eighth-century reform movement seems to have been Máel-Rúain, and its most important centre was his monastery of Tamlachta, now Tallaght, just south of Dublin. There is no Life of Máel-Rúain,[305] and we know little of his career, but it is evident that he made a deep impression on the religious circles of his time. His name, " Tonsured " *i.e.*, devotee, " of Rúadán," suggests that he came from Lothra [306] or its neighborhood, and there seems to have been a tradition that he was a student under Fer-dá-crích. Tamlachta was founded probably in the third quarter of the century, and Máel-Rúain died in 792. Many of his disciples attained to eminence in religion, as Bishop Echaidh (d. 812), his second successor in the abbacy; Oengus mac Oengobann, author of the well-known martyrology; Máel-Dithruib, anchorite of Tír-dá-glas (d. 840);[307] Comgan *fota*, " the tall," (d. 870), anchorite of Tamlachta, called *dalta*, " foster-son," of Máel-Rúain.

To Máel-Rúain is ascribed the authorship of a religious rule, and, very doubtfully, of a hymn and a penitential. From his church of Tamlachta, or Tallaght, come three famous documents, the Martyrology of Oengus, the Martyrology of Tallaght, and the Stowe Missal.[308] It should be added that it seems to be to this epoch, and to the reforming clergy, either directly, as of their composition, or indirectly, as a result of the impulse given by them, that we owe the extant Irish religious rules. With the exception of the rule of Columbanus,[309] written on the continent of Europe, all the Irish rules are of the eighth or ninth century, or later. Many of them bear the names of famous early saints, but these either are the guess-work of redactors, or perhaps in some cases indicate that the rule was derived from the community of which the saint in question was the founder.[310]

---

[302] *Cf.* p. 451 *supra*.   [303] *Cf.* p. 460 *supra*.   [304] *Cf.* p. 384 *supra*.
[305] *Cf.* Plummer *Misc. hag. Hib.* Cat. nos. 46, 147–8.
[306] *Cf.* p. 391 *supra*.   [307] FM.
[308] Nos. 272, 273, 555.   [309] No. 45.
[310] In the " Notes on the customs of Tallaght " references are made to the Rules of Comgall and Columcille, but the matter noticed is not to be found in the rules which to-day bear the names of those saints.

Had events followed their hitherto normal course it is possible that Tallaght would have become as famous in church history as Clonmacnois or Armagh. But three years after Máel-Rúain's death the Norse Vikings appeared on the Irish coasts. In or about 840 they made a permanent settlement at Dublin, and thereafter the existence of Tallaght must have been on sufferance of the pagan stronghold only five miles distant. Finn-glas was even nearer the enemy. And in general the churches of all parts of Ireland became so often the victims of disturbance and plundering that their decline and secularisation proceeded much more rapidly, and the reform movement succumbed. By the eleventh century the only trace of it left was the existence of ecclesiastical bodies called *Céli Dé* (anglicised " Culdees ") at a few of the churches.[311]

Who the *Céli Dé* were is not very clear.[312] But it seems certain that they owed their origin as a distinct institution to the reform movement of the eighth century. The term " *céle* of God " had, no doubt, a general sense of perhaps long standing,[313] but its technical application to a special spiritual association dates, on our evidence, from the first half of the ninth century. In the " Notes on the customs of Tallaght " it seems to designate all who were leading a strict monastic life under spiritual direction and in accordance with the ideals of Máel-Rúain, Elair, Máel-Dithruib, etc.; but the Rule of Fothad *na canôine* has distinct sections for *Céli Dé* and for monks. The most satisfying hypothesis seems to be that the *Céli Dé* were the communities of religious who gathered around the reform leaders as the monks of an earlier age had gathered around the primitive church-founders; that their aim was to revive the ancient zeal and discipline of the monastic churches; and that the method followed was to combine the austere life of the recluses or anchorites, already an element in the majority of the larger churches, with a community organisation and the close and strict supervision of a spiritual superior. It is probable that in some churches, as Tallaght, they formed the whole monastic body; in others, as at Ros-cré, a distinct community set up in the neighborhood of the old church; and in

---

[311] *E.g.*, *cf.* the mention Giraldus Cambrensis makes of those of Loch-Cré. — *Topographia Hibernica* II iv.

[312] The supposition of Reeves, Skene, HZ and others that the *Céli Dé* were modeled on the " regular canons " whom Chrodegang, bishop of Metz, organised in 747, seems to be quite gratuitous. However, in this, as in much else, events took a somewhat parallel course in Ireland and on the Continent.

[313] Such is its earliest manuscript occurrence, in the Milan glosses (*cf.* p. *202*): *Thes. Pal.* I 65 l. 29; HZ *Celtic Church* 100. The word *céle* (plur. *céli*) had the general significance of " companion," and more particularly the companion of lower *status* who was attached by a sense of love and duty. There were many derived meanings. In the social organisation as described in the brehon tracts the word designates a person of a quite definite class, a class as well defined as, and roughly approximating to, that of the *cliens* in Latin and the vassal in English treaties. The ecclesiastical use of the word as a technical term was, no doubt, influenced by this secular usage.

others, as at Armagh,[314] a group residing within the monastic bounds, perhaps performing most of the sacerdotal and eleemosynary duties, and constituting a community of " stricter observance " in the midst of the older, larger, and laxer organisation.

For a hymn in honor of St. Michael, attributed to Máel-Rúain of Tamlachta, see no. 581.

263. Poem on Oengus mac Oengobann

Aibind suide sund amne . . alt re n-abar [alt] aibind.   13 quatrains.

MS: LBr 106ᵛ [following his *Félire*].   ED: *Fél. Oeng.*[2] pp. xxiv–xxvii [with trans.]. TRANS: KM *Selections from ancient Irish poetry* (London 1911; 2nd ed. 1913) 86 (88) [partial].

Oengus, son of Oengoba and grandson of Oiblén, was a monk at Clúain-Édnech (Clonenagh in Leix) who became a disciple of Máel-Rúain at Tamlachta.   It is probable that he afterwards brought the institutions of Máel-Rúain to the church which he founded, Dísert-Oengusa (now Dysartenos, in Leix).   By modern writers he is generally referred to as Oengus " the Culdee."   What we know of him is derived principally from this poem, and from the prose prefaces added to his Martyrology.   The opening verses of the poem have a simplicity and dignity that won the favorable comment of Matthew Arnold [315] many years ago, but, as often happens in Irish compositions, the effect is marred by the grotesque and, from the literary point of view, irrelevant details introduced in the later stanzas.

264. Notes on the customs of Tallaght

Athlaoch bói hi comaidecht . . . indruth nad cobradar.

MS: RIA 3 B 23 pp. 33–52 [316] [by Tadg úa Rig-bardan, who was writing another MS in 1473].   There is a 17th cent. paraphrase of this and parts of the Rule of the *Céli Dé* in the Dublin Franciscan MS G 36: *cf.* Gwynn in his ed. as *infra*, p. 123 n.   Also excerpts in BM Addit. 30512 f. 33ᵛ.   ED: E. J. Gwynn and W. J. Purton "The Monastery of Tallaght" *Proc. RIA* XXIX (1911) C 115–79 [*cf. RC* XXXII (1911) 481–4].

This is a copy of the commonplace book of some unknown observer of monastic customs in the ninth century.   The bulk of it seems to have been written at different times not long before 840, though perhaps some sections were added after that date. The greater part consists of statements as to what " they " believe and practise, and what " he " thinks and teaches: " they " are the followers of Máel-Rúain and his friends, and are probably identical with the *Céli Dé* who are twice mentioned, and " he " seems to be Máel-Dithruib of Tír-dá-glas, who is repeatedly quoted by name.

---

[314] *Cf.* AU 821.   [315] *On the Study of Celtic literature.*
[316] A scribe interpolates the text of the *Abgitir Crábaid* (no. 265) and of two anecdotes, all of which formed no part of the original Notes.   The two anecdotes, in fragmentary condition, are in RIA Stowe C. i. 2 f. 38, and have been published, with trans., by O. J. Bergin *Ériu* II 221–6.

In fact, the notes have the appearance of being due to a monastic Boswell whose Johnson was Máel-Dithruib. The phraseology suggests that the compiler was not writing at Tamlachta, but perhaps at Tír-dá-glas; it was, however, the rules and customs of Tamlachta as established by Máel-Rúain and transmitted by Máel-Dithruib that were the chief object of his interest. To expound or illustrate the rules many anecdotes and sayings of saints and ecclesiastics are given, as well as a few legends. The majority of these personages seem to have been leaders in the religious movement of the eighth century. Almost all the phases of monastic life are covered, in a haphazard way; much of the matter is closely related to that of the Prose Rule of the *Céli Dé*.

265. The *Apgitir Crábaid*, "Alphabet of Devotion," of Colmán moccu Béognae

Hiris co ngním, acobur co feidli . . . dál fri hesérgi al-laithiu bráthae. Finis. Amen.

MSS: YBL cols. 228-9 p. 410, and 570-2, pp. 252-3. — Bodl. Rawl. B. 512 ff. 37-9. — BM Harl. 5280 ff. 38^V-41. — The following are incomplete: RIA 23 P 3 ff. 15^V-8^V; Bk. Lis. f. 39^V [*cf. Lis. Lives* 135]; TCD 1337 (H. 3. 18) p. 40; Cheltenham Phillipps MS pp. 46, 48 [*cf. Fél. Oeng.*^{2} pp. ix *sqq*]; Brussels Bibl. roy. 2324-40 f. 67; 5100-4 p. 1. EDS: T. Hudson Williams *Modern Language Notes* I 29-31 [partial]. — KM *ZCP* III (1910) 447-55 [text only].

This composition is usually ascribed to Colmán, or Mo-Cholm-óc, moccu Béognae, but sometimes to St. Fursa.[317] Colmán is a personage of whom little is known; he is described as of Liss-mór, and, in places, as a disciple of Mo-Chuta. The text, a catechetical instruction on piety and morality, can hardly be as old as Fursa, and perhaps not as old as Colmán, but it may be of the eighth century.

266. The Rule of the *Céli Dé*

Riagail na celed nde ó Moelruain cecinit. Biait prointge acas magníficat . . . flatha nime cen forcend. Roisam uile . . . in s. s. Amen. Finit.

MS: LBr ff. 9^V-12^V. ED: O'D in Reeves "On the Céli Dé" *Trans. RIA* XXIV (1873) 202-15 [with trans.]. *Cf.* J. Strachan's paper on "The Deponent Verb" *Trans. Philol. Soc.* 1892 p. 517 n.

The title to this document seems to say that it is a paraphrase — in prose — of a verse composition of Máel-Rúain. It is commonly designated "the Prose Rule of the Culdees," to distinguish it from the section which treats of them in the versified Rule of Mo-Chuta, or Fothad *na canóine*. Reeves had assigned it to the twelfth or thirteenth century, but Strachan declares it to be in substance an early composition, probably of the ninth century. The statement in the heading, therefore, may well be correct.

The Rule consists of a long and miscellaneous collection of regulations for a religious community. These do not throw any light, except in one respect, on the distinction between the *Céli Dé* and the older monks: they might have been written for any of the monastic communities founded in the sixth or seventh century. The one possible

---

[317] *Cf.* no. 296.

distinction is that the *Céli Dé* appear to have been all clergy: the monks, of course, included laymen as well as clerics.[318]   The regulations cover such subjects as devotions, especially the canonical hours, food (there is very interesting information regarding the various foods of the time), confession, penance, abstinence and fasting, emigration to foreign lands (here condemned), works to be performed, education, the manner of taking tithes, and, in general, the relations between the church and the secular population which it served.   A considerable number of rules are based on superstitious, generally magical, ideas.[319]

267. The Rule of Fothad *na canóine*, or the Rule of Mo-Chuta

His 6 ascnam na flatha . . . The no. of quatrains vary, 105 to 145.

MSS: LBr pp. 261-2. — YBL col. 221 p. 407. — BM Addit. 30,512 f. 20. — RIA 23 N 10 p. 82. — TCD 1285 (H. I. 11) A.D. 1752 f. 125^v.   EDS: O'D in Reeves " On the Céli-Dé " *Trans. RIA* XXIV (1864) 200–1 [the sect. on the *Céli Dé*, " Dia mbem fo mám cleirchechta " from YBL, with trans.]. — EW *Kurzgefasste irische Grammatik* (1879) [same section]. — KM *Gaelic Journ.* V (1895) 187–8 [part, from LBr, with trans.]; *ACL* III (1907) 312–20 [text from Addit. 30,512 and 23 N 10]; *ZCP* XIII (1919) 27–30 [the section on the refectory, from 23 N 10, LBr and YBL]. — MacEclaise *IER* 4th ser. XXVII (1910) 495–517 [from LBr, with variants; has trans.]. TRANS: O'C *IER* I (1864) 112–8, 172–80. — Fr., of sect. on *Céli Dé*, by Gaidoz, in art. by Gougaud *Rev. Bénédictine* Jan. 1911 pp. 86–9.   COMM: J. Strachan *Trans. Philol. Soc.* 1892 p. 516 [also as separate paper, *History of the deponent verb in Irish* p. 73]. — Gougaud *Rev. Bénédictine* July 1908 p. 322.

This metrical composition consists of a set of regulations for the Christian life, divided into nine sections, which treat respectively of the duties of all believers, of the bishop, the priest, the abbot, the confessor, the monk, the *Céli Dé*, the king, and of the order to be observed in regard to the refectory, to devotions, and to the observance of feasts and fasts.   The arrangement and extent of these sections varies considerably in the several versions.   The rule is ascribed traditionally to Mo-Chuta of Rathan and Liss-mór,[320] but manifestly is not of his era.   One manuscript attaches it to Fothad *na canóine*, a famous ecclesiastic who in 804 obtained the approval of a decision exempting the clergy from military service,[321] and who died in 819.[322]   Fothad's authorship is quite possible, for the language of the composition belongs to the beginning of the ninth century.[323]   In any case the rule seems to be a product of that reform move-

[318] This may be in part the occasion for the general opinion that the *Céli Dé* were " canons regular " introduced into Ireland.   But the main reason seems to be a failure to grasp the full significance of the monastic character of the Irish church: in Europe the normal monastery was more or less withdrawn from the world, and the normal parish church was not a monastery; in Ireland the normal parish church (to adopt a term which is only roughly applicable to the situation) was a monastery, and the first duty of the normal monastery was to serve as parish church to the surrounding people.
[319] *Cf.* no. 264.
[320] Pp. 451-3 *supra.*
[321] The preface to the Martyrology of Oengus professes to give the poetical terms of this decision: *Fél. Oeng.*1 pp. vi, viii, x; *Fél. Oeng.*2 4–5, 10–1. As regards exemption of the clergy from actual fighting, this seems merely to re-enact the terms of *Cáin Pátraic* and of *Cáin Adamnáin;* but apparently Fothad's judgment exempted all inmates of churches, lay monks as well as clerics, and not only from fighting but from attendance or service of any kind on military hostings.
[322] AU.   [323] Strachan *loc. cit.*

ment of which the most important result was the development of the *Céli Dé*.[324] The section on the king may have been originally an independent composition, of the *tecosca*, or "mirrors for princes," type. (*Cf. Speculum* Oct. 1927 p. 435 n. 2.)

The Rule of Ailbe of Imblech-ibair, although probably, in its original form, of the eighth century, does not seem to have any connection with the *Céli Dé*, and was written at Imblech-ibair. It has, therefore, been included among the records of that church (no. *123*).

268. Miscellaneous monastic rules

GENERAL COMM: L. Gougaud *Rev. Bénédictine* XXV April 1908 pp. 167–84, July pp. 321–33; *Dict. d'archéol. chrét. et de liturgie* II pt. II (Paris 1910) 2969 *sqq*: sect. ix on " Monastic Rules and Penitentials."

(i) The Rule of the Lord (*Ríagul in Choimded*); Rule of Comgall

Comae ríaguil in Choimded . . . buith fo riaguil mo chomae. The no. of quatrains varies from 29 to 36.

MSS: Brussels Bibl. roy. 5100–4 pp. 31–3. — RIA 23 N 10 pp. 88, 17. — RIA 23 P 3 A.D. 1467 f. 13. — TCD 1285 (H. I. 11) A.D. 1752 p. 157. ED: J. Strachan *Ériu* I pt. II (1904) 191–208.

(ii) Rule of Ciarán

Ma asbera a dheoraidh . . . ma asbera dho deorach. 16 stanzas.

MS: RIA 23 P 3 f. 14. ED: J. Strachan *Ériu* II (1905) 227–8 [text only].

(iii) Rule of Colum-cille

Bith ind uathad illucc fo leith . . . manabat solma do derae.

MSS: Bodl. Rawl. B. 512 ff. 40ᵛ–1. — Brussels Bibl. roy. 5100–4 p. 23. EDS: O'C in W. Reeves (ed.) *Primate Colton's visitation of the diocese of Derry* (Dublin 1850) 109–12 [with trans.; reprinted in H&S II i 119–21; and trans. only in Skene *Celtic Scotland* II 508–9 and *Dict. Christ. Antiq. s. v.* " Monastery "]. — KM *ZCP* III (1901) 28–30 [text of Rawlinson]. *Cf.* Reeves *Ad.* 336–9.

(iv) Rule of the Grey Monks (*Ríagul na manach líath*)

Coram liath lethet baisi . . . feghaidh sein arna sinaib. 10 quatrains.

MS: RIA 23 P 3 f. 13ᵛ. ED: J. Strachan *Ériu* III (1905) 228 [text only].

---

[324] If Fothad was the author, it is possible that the attribution to Mo-Chuta came about in this way: Fothad belonged to the church of Fathan in Inishowen, about 6 miles from Derry. A confusion of the names " Fathan " and " Rathan " might result in the " rule of Fathan " becoming the " rule of Rathan," and, therefore, of the great saint of Rathan.

(v) Rule of Cormac mac Cuilennáin

Samud búain briathar isel . . . is inmainsé samadh samud. 14 quatrains.

MSS: Brussels Bibl. roy. 5100–4 pp. 29 *sq.* — RIA 23 N 10 pp. 78–9. — RIA 23 P 3 f. 14b. ED: J. Strachan *Ériu* II (1905) 62–8 [with trans.].

(vi) Rule of Echtgus úa Cúanáin of Ros-cré

A dhuine nach creit iar coir . . . derlaiccet dona dáoinibh. 86 quatrains. There are marks of endings at the 30th and 38th quatrains.

MS: Brussels Bibl. roy. 5100–4 p. 16. ED: A. G. van Hamel *RC* XXXVII iv (1919) 345–9.

These religious rules in verse are of the era here under consideration: the *Rule of the Lord* may be of the end of the eighth, the others are of the ninth century. Of the various attributions of authorship that to Cormac mac Cuilennáin alone may be authentic. The contents are for the most part moral exhortations: such specific regulations as there are — and these, frequently, interpolated — relate chiefly to the devotions at the canonical hours, to penance, and to personal austerities. They are designed for ascetics, and the so-called Rule of Colum-cille refers specifically to the recluses attached to a church.[325]

The *Ordo monasticus de Kil-ros* (Holsten (ed. Brockie) *Codex regularum* II 64–6; Migne *PL* LIX 563–8) gives interesting information regarding a community of *Céli Dé* in Scotland.[326] The Celtic monastic Church in the two countries was still the same in spirit and organisation.

269. The Testimony of Coeman (*Teist Choemáin*) as to Sinchell's school

Teist Choemain Cluana . . . Iss iat so cinte. . . . A maigistir amodh. Finid.

MSS: LL p. 371 c. — Bodl. Rawl. B 512 f. 39. ED: KM *Hibernica Minora (Anec. Oxon.* Med. & Mod. Ser. VIII) (Oxford 1894) 41–2 [with trans.].

The full title is: " Testimony of Coeman of Clúain-mac-Treoin [a church in Leinster] as to the school of Sinchell the younger of Cell-achid " [Cell-achid-drommo-foto, " the church of the field of the long ridge," now Killeigh in Offalley, three and three-quarter miles s. e. of Tullamore]. [327] Cell-achid was an important church of the Úi Failgi (who occupied portions of the present Offalley and Leix) and, indeed, one of the famous monasteries of Ireland. Its records, however, have largely perished. Its patrons were the two Sinchells, Sen-Sinchell, *i.e.*, " the elder," who died in 549,[328]

---

[325] The *Ainmchairdes Manchain Leith* in RIA 23 N 10 p. 89 and Stowe B. IV. 2 f. 139a, ed. by KM in *ZCP* VII 310, is a text of similar character. It is attributed to Manchán of Líath-Mancháin [now Lemanaghan, Offalley] who died in 665 (AU), but is said to be in the linguistic forms of the ninth century.

[326] *Cf.* Reeves *Ad.* 338; H. Dumaine art. " Bains " sect. v " Immersions celtiques " *Dict. d'archéol. chrét. et de liturgie* II pt. I (1910) 93–7 [based on information given by Dom Gougaud].

[327] *Cf.* p. 22 *supra.*   [328] AU.

and Óc-Sinchell, or Sinchell-óc, " the younger," said to be his disciple. The present brief outline of good monastic customs seems to be a work of the eighth or ninth century which was put into the form of a description of the rules of Cell-achid at the time of the younger Sinchell.

270. The Law of Sunday (*Cáin Domnaig*)

Consists of 3 parts: (a) the epistle of Jesus concerning Sunday; (b) three examples of supernatural punishment for the transgression of Sunday; (c) the *Cáin Domnaig* proper, a highly technical law tract on the observance of Sunday and the punishments for its violation. — (a) Intinscana eipistil int Shlánícceda . . . flaith nime cen forcend. Finit. (b) Alaili céli Dé . . . (c) De corus cana in domnaich budesta. Soiri domnaig o trad . . . cumsanadh indi dogress.

MSS: LBr pp. 202-4 [a, pt. of c]. — BM Harl. 5280 ff. 36-9 [a, b, c]. — RIA 23 N 10 pp. 103 *sqq* [pt. of a, b, c]. — YBL cols. 217-20, pp. 405-6 of facs. [a, partly illegible]; cols. 957 *sq*, p. 215 of facs. [contains most of what is illegible in preceding]. — Edinburgh Nat. Lib. Gael. XL pp. 71-5 [c]. — RIA Liber Flavus Fergusiorum I f. 45 [a], II f. 41 [b]. — BM Addit. 4783 f. 5ᵛ. Eds: (a) J. G. O'Keeffe *Ériu* II (1905) 189-214 [with trans., etc.]. — (b) KM *ZCP* III 228 [text only]. — (c) O'Keeffe *Anec.* III (1910) 21-7 [text only]. Comm: H. Delehaye " Note sur la légende de la lettre du Christ tombée du ciel " *Bull. de l'Acad. roy. de Belgique*, Cl. des lettres, 1899 pp. 171-213. — Maximilian Bittner " Der vom Himmel gefallene Brief Christi in seinem morgendländischen Versionen und Rezensionen " *Denkschriften d. k. Akad. d. Wissensch. z. Wien* philos.-hist. Kl. 1906 vol. LI pt. I 236 *sqq.* — R. Priebsch "Quelle und Abfassungszeit der Sonntagsepistel in der irischen ' Cáin Domnaig ' " *Modern Language Rev.* II (1907) 138-54. — W. Köhler " Himmels- und Teufelsbrief " in Gunkel and Scheel's *Religion in Geschichte und Gegenwart* III (Tübingen 1910) 31-3. — E. Renoir " Christ (Lettre du) tombée du ciel " *Dict. d'archéol. chrêt. et de liturgie* III pt. I (1913) 1534-6. — L. Gougaud *RHE* XX ii (1924) 213-5.

One of the most remarkable of Christian myths is that of the letter of Christ which fell from heaven. It has been current from the sixth century to the present day, and — at one time or another — in all Christian lands from Abyssinia to Iceland and from Ireland to Russia. The date, place and circumstances of its origin have not been determined: [329] all known versions, however, seem to go back to a Latin original which is at least as old as about 581, when flourished Licinianus, bishop of Carthagena, by whom it is mentioned and condemned.

The letter was written by Christ and fell at Rome, or Jerusalem, or Bethlehem, etc. It orders the religious observance of Sunday and the strict suspension of all labor. Ecclesiastical regulations on a few other

[329] There is a fragment of a letter attributed to Peter, bishop of Alexandria (who died a martyr in 311), which resembles the "epistle from heaven." However, though early, it is of uncertain date and later than Peter. *Cf.* Carl Schmidt *Fragment einer Schrift des Märtyrer-Bischofs Petrus von Alexandrien* (*Texte u. Untersuchungen z. Geschichte d. altchristl. Literatur* new ser. V fasc. 4) (Leipsic 1901); *An. Boll.* XX (1901) 101-3.

subjects are appended. Dire anathemas are set forth against those who do not obey the letter or doubt its authenticity.

Ireland received this epistle probably from the Frankish dominions, where it was spreading in the eighth century.[330] The Irish text itself declares that it was brought from Rome by Conall mac Coel-maine, abbot of Inis-coel (Inishkeel, on the south side of Gweebara bay, Donegal), who lived towards the end of the sixth century.[331] But under 887 the annals have the entry: " An epistle came with the pilgrim to Ireland, with the *Cáin Domnaigh* and other good instructions."[332] But while the sixth century seems too early, this seems too late a date. Perhaps a notice in the *Chronicon Scotorum* under 811 may be related to the introduction of the same myth: " This was a year of prodigies. It was in it the *Céle Dé* came over the sea from the south, dry-footed, without a boat, and a written roll used to be given him from heaven, out of which he would give instruction to the Irish, and it used to be taken up again when the instruction was delivered; and the *Céle Dé* was wont to go each day across the sea, southwards, after imparting the instruction." The time accords better with that from which, on grounds of probability, the vogue of the letter in Ireland may be dated; and the development of a stricter Sabbatarianism appears to coincide with the institution of *Céli Dé*.

The *Cáin Domnaig*, in the strict sense, is not the epistle but the brehon law tract based on it, by which provision was made for the secular enforcement of Sunday observance. Both the translation of the epistle and this law seem to be of the ninth century.

The Sunday Letter reached Anglo-Saxon England by way of Ireland as well as directly from the Continent. Among the texts which make use of some version of the letter, no. xliv of the collection [333] of Anglo-Saxon homilies which is put under the name of Wulfstan, archbishop of York (1003–23), appears to be based on an Irish source. This homily tells also of an Irishman, a deacon named Nial, who, not many years before, had risen from the dead and related wondrous things which he had seen in the other world. Now we have a letter of Egfred, bishop of Lindisfarne, to Wulfsige, archbishop of York, written c 830×837, referring to the errors of a certain Pehtred, who had written a book in which were set forth the story of the deacon Nial, and of the letter that fell from heaven, and other suspected matter. Dr. Priebsch concludes [334] that the so-called Wulfstan homily no. xliv was derived from Pehtred's book. It is to be noted that the " deacon Nial " is a Niall mac Ialláin, or Gialláin, who, according to the Irish annals,[335] was stricken with paralysis about 825, but lived to about 855×860, seeing many visions " as well false as true."[336]

---

[330] The use of such a letter was one of the charges brought by St. Boniface against Bishop Adelbert or Aldebert in 745 (Hefele-Leclercq *Histoire des conciles* III 878; *cf.* pp. 521 *sqq infra*); and in 789 Charlemagne condemned the dissemination of a letter alleged to have fallen from heaven (*MGH Capitularia* I ed. Boretius, 60).

[331] Archdall's *Monasticon*, I 100, says that he was killed about 590. The source is not apparent, but the date agrees with the genealogies which make him fifth in descent from Niall *nói-giallach*.

[332] AU, CS. FM has a similar record under 884. The departure of the " pilgrim " is given by CS under 898, FM under 893.

[333] A. [S.] Napier *Wulfstan: Sammlung der ihm zugeschriebenen Homilien* (Berlin 1883).

[334] R. Priebsch " The chief sources of some Anglo-Saxon homilies" *Otia Merseiana* I (1899) 129–47, where the whole subject is examined.

[335] AU 860; FM 854, 858; 3F 852.

[336] So AU. *Cf.* p. 560 *infra*

VII. GENERAL TREATISES ON THE SAINTS

It seems most convenient to consider here a number of general treatises on the early Irish saints. Prominent among these are the calendars and martyrologies, which were primarily liturgical documents for practical use as tables of the festivals of the year. But they also served as historical catalogues, or as epitomes of hagiography. This is especially the case with the Irish metrical martyrologies, which were intended to be memorised and recited by the devout Christian as the honor-roll of the history of the Church. It is from this point of view that they have the greater interest to-day, and are therefore catalogued here, rather than with the liturgical documents to which, in one sense, they more properly belong.[337]

271. The Catalogue of the Saints of Ireland s VIII (?)

Primus ordo sanctorum erat in tempore Patricii . . . postea lucernas ardere in vallibus conspexit. [Ussher's older MS: . . . tertius sicut stella.] Cod. S. adds: Hec extracta sunt de antiqua vita Patricii. Nota. Hec sunt nomina discipulorum sancti Finniani Cluana Hyrard . . . et episcopus Senach.

MS: Cod. S. ff. 78ᵛ–9. Ussher used 2 MSS not now known. EDS: Ussher *Brit. Eccl. Antiq.* XVI (1639) 913 (*Whole Works* VI 477–9). — Fleming *Collectanea sacra* (Louvain 1667) 430–1. — *Rer. Hib. SS.* II (1825) 162–5. — H&S II ii (1878) 292–4 [from Ussher]. — *AA. SS. ex Cod. S.* 161–4. TRANS: Todd *St. Patrick* (1864) 88–9. *Cf.* Bury *St. Patrick* (1905) 285–7. The Ussher text is better than that of Cod. S.

This " Catalogue of the Saints of Ireland," written probably in the first half of the eighth century, is an attempt to summarise the religious history of Ireland down to the Great Plague of 664–5. This history is divided chronologically into three epochs, each having its order of saints of a descending degree of sanctity. It is clear that the author has consciously sacrificed historical truth to a symmetrical arrangement, but, after allowance is made therefor, the document supports a conclusion to be drawn from other evidence, that the ecclesiastics of the reorganized Celtic Church in Ireland after the Great Plague and the Paschal Controversy had but a hazy notion of the early history of Irish Christianity.

The following is a summary of this classification of saints:

(1) *Ordo sanctissimus* A.D. 432–544. 350 holy bishops, Franks,[338] Romans, Britons, and Irish, founders of churches, all under the leadership of Patrick, using the same tonsure,

---

[337] On the early history of martyrologies in western Europe see Dom H. Quentin *Les martyrologes historiques du moyen âge. Étude sur la formation du martyrologe romain* (Paris 1908). There is a short catalogue of Irish, and Celtic, martyrologies in the sect. " Sources vii " of L. Gougaud's art. " Celtiques (Liturgies)," *Dict. d'archéol. chrét. et de liturgie* II pt. II (1910) 2969–3032.

[338] *I.e.*, Gauls. Already in Tírechán the designation "Franci" is applied to Patrick's Gallic companions. *Cf.* LA f. 9ᵛ.

the same liturgy of the mass, keeping the same Easter, and receiving women as " consortes."³³⁹ (2) *Ordo sanctior* 544–598. 300 saints — a few of them bishops but many priests — using different liturgies (one was received from the British saints David, Gildas and Docco) and different rules of life, but one tonsure and one date for Easter, and refusing the ministrations of women. (3) *Ordo sanctus* 598–665. 100 saints — a few bishops, but many priests — who lived as hermits, using different liturgies, different tonsures, and different dates for Easter. The names are given of several saints of the second and third orders.

Certain foreign martyrologies of early date have some Irish interest, though this is usually more liturgical than hagiological: (a) The Martyrology of Bede. *Cf.* p. 232 *supra*, and references there given. The best MS of the primitive recension, St. Gall Stiftsbibl. 451, is said to be in an Irish hand of *s* IX. *Cf.* G. Scherrer *Verzeichniss der Handschriften der Stiftsbibliothek von St. Gallen* (Halle 1875) 147. (b) The Calendar and Martyrology of Willibrord. *Cf.* no. 69. (c) The martyrology in the Sacramentary of Rheinau. *Cf.* p. 704 *infra*. EDS: Gerbert *Monumenta vet. lit. alem.* I 455–63; Delisle *Mémoire sur d'anciens sacramentaires* append. *Cf.* H. A. Wilson *The Calendar of St. Willibrord* (Henry Bradshaw Soc. LV) (1918) p. xvi.

272. The Martyrology of Oengus (*Félire Oengusso*) c. A.D. 800

[Prologue] Sén a Christ mo labrai . . . ind rígrad im-rordus. 5 quatrains, apparently a later addition. Imrordus in rígraid . . . tóided ré síl dóine. 80 quatrains. [Calendar] Re síl dálach dóine . . . ascnam céim for caland. 365 quatrains; the notes of some MSS give an extra stanza for leap-year. [Epilogue] Ón chalaind co araili . . . ind rígrad imrordus. 141 quatrains.

MSS: LBr pp. 75–106 (of facs.) *s* XV *in* [the oldest copy, but deviates most from the archetype]. — Bodl. Rawl. B 505 ff. 211–20 *s* XV [was originally distinct from the rest of this codex; preface, prologue and epilogue missing; has best text]. — Bodl. Laud 610 ff. 59–75 A.D. 1453. — RIA 23 P. 3 ff. 1–12 A.D. 1467 [written by Uilliam Mac an Legha: see *Ériu* VII ii (1914) 126]. — Dublin, Franciscan Convent, Merchants' Quay, MS *s* XV [written by Ruaidri Úa Luinín (d. 1528) for Cathal Mac Maghnusa Mag Uidhir (d. 1498): cf. p. 23 *supra*]. — Cheltenham, Phillipps MS pp. 20–45 *s* XV (?) [imperfect. Formerly belonged to Edward O'Reilly. When examined by WS it was in the library of the Rev. John E. A. Fenwick, Thirlstane House, Cheltenham — *Fél. Oeng.*² pp. ix *sq*]. — Bodl. Rawl. B 512 ff. 53ᵛ–64 A.D. 1500 [the calendar proper is missing, although the notes are given]. — Brussels Bibl. roy. 5100–4 pp. 68–119 A.D. 1630 [copied by Michael O'Clery from a book written by Siodrach Úa Máel-Conaire in 1533; cf. no. 275]. — O'Davoren's Glossary in BM Egerton 88 ff. 80–93

---

³³⁹ The allusion is believed to be to the " spiritual marriage," an institution which existed in the primitive Irish Church as well as in other parts of Christendom. On the general subject see: H. Achelis *Virgines subintroductae Ein Beitrag zu I Kor. vii* (Leipsic 1902); " Subintroductae " *Realencykl. f. prot. Theol. u. Kirche* (Leipsic 1907); " Agapetae " Hastings' *Encyclopaedia of religion and ethics*. — Ad. Jülicher " Die geistlichen Ehen in der alten Kirche " *Archiv. f. Religionswissenschaft* VII (1904) 373–86. — Pierre de Labriolle " Le ' mariage spirituel ' dans l'antiquité chretienne " *RH* CXXXVII (1921) 204–25. For the Irish evidence: T. Olden " On the *consortia* of the first order of Irish saints" *Proc. RIA* 3rd ser. III 415–20. — KM *op. cit.* p. 735 *infra*. — L. Gougaud " Mulierum consortia: Étude sur le syneisaktisme chez les ascètes celtiques " *Ériu* IX (1923) 147–56. For a tradition of a strange aberration of the custom see *Fél. Oeng.*² 41.

[of which there is an imperfect copy by Duald Mac Firbis in TCD 1317 (H. 2. 15b) pp. 43–59] [ed. WS *Three Irish glossaries* (London 1862); *ACL* II (1903–4) 197–504] contains extracts from the calendar. — There is a glossary to Fél. Oeng. in TCD 1337 (H. 3. 18) pp. 616–22, in which 112 quatrains are cited. EDS: O'C " Patron saints of Ireland, from Ænghus Ceile De " in Kelly *Martyrology of Tallagh* (Dublin [1857]) 153–61 [extracts with trans.; *cf.* WS *RC* VI (1885) 358–70]. — WS *On the Calendar of Oengus* (*Trans. RIA: Irish MS Ser.* I) (Dublin 1880) [read Nov. 13, 1871: contains prefaces of LBr, Laud 610 and Rawl. B 512; texts of these and Rawl. B 505; and glosses and notes of LBr; with trans. *Cf. RC* V (1883) 339–80; Strachan *Contributions to the history of the deponent verb in Irish* (1894) 110; RTh *ZCP* I (1897) 345]. — WS *Félire Óengusso Céli Dé The Martyrology of Oengus the Culdee* (Henry Bradshaw Soc. XXIX) (London 1905) [prefaces of LBr and Laud 610; critical text of the verse; notes from the several MSS; with trans. *Cf. ZCP* VI (1908) 235–42. There is an ill-founded criticism by Cardinal Moran *Irish Theological Quarterly* 1906 pp. 259–73]. — The glossary in H. 3. 18 is published in WS *Three Irish glossaries* (London 1862) pp. lxvi–lxxv, 125–40. COMM: J. Strachan " Final vowels in the Félire Oenguso " *RC* XX (1899) 191–8, 295–305. — WS " Notes on the Martyrology of Oengus " *RC* XXIII (1902) 83–7. — RTh " Die Abfassung des Félire von Oengus " *ZCP* VI (1908) 6–8; *ibid.* XI ii (1917) 309–10. — KM " The rules of assonance in Irish poetry " *Ériu* VI i (1911) 103–11, esp. 108–10; *RC* XXXIII i (1912) 96–8.

Of Oengus mac Oengobann something has already been said.[340] The tradition which ascribes to him this earliest of extant Irish martyrologies is generally accepted:[341] the linguistic characteristics agree with a date about A.D. 800. The latest saint commemorated is the author's *aite*, or tutor, Máel-Rúain of Tamlachta, who died in 792. The dead kings Donnchad and Bran who are mentioned in the prologue are probably the high-king Donnchad, who died in 797, and Bran *árd-chenn* (" high-head "), king of the Lagin, who was slain in 795. Their respective successors were Aed *oirnide* (" the dignified "), who reigned till 819, and Finsnechta *cethar-derc* (" four eyes "), who was deposed in 805 and died in 808. It is reasonably probable that the *félire* was composed within the period 797 x 808. Though in all likelihood a pure invention, the story in the prose prefaces to the effect that Oengus read the work to Fothad *na canóine* in 805 is not impossible. Likewise improbable but not impossible is the statement of the preface that the composition was begun in the church of Cúl-bend-chuir (Coolbanagher, bar. Portnahinch, Leix), carried on in large part at Clúain-Eidnech, and completed at Tamlachta.

The prologue and epilogue contain eulogies of the saints in general, proclamation of the triumph of God's people in Ireland as elsewhere, explanation of the method of composing the calendar,[342] and of its merits, and prayers for the author's salvation.

---

[340] *Cf.* no. 263.

[341] So WS in his 2nd ed.; in the first he had argued for the tenth or eleventh century.

[342] The author uses with remarkable skill the very difficult *rindaird* metre. The object is, of course, mnemonic and devotional, and the result is not to be judged as poetry in the restricted sense. — The sources mentioned are, in addition to " the host of the books of Ireland," four works whose Irish designations WS equates with " the vast tome of Ambrose, the *Sensus* of Hilary, the *Antigraph* of Jerome, the *Martyrology* of Eusebius." The *Antigraph* is, no doubt, the so-called *Martyrologium Hieronymianum*, but the identity of the others is uncertain. *Cf. Fél. Oeng.*² p. xliv. It appears probable that the insular type of the *Martyrologium Hieronymianum*, represented now by the Echternach Martyrology, or Martyrology of Willibrord (no. 69), formed the basis on which Oengus worked. *Cf.* Bishop *Liturgica historica* (1918) 252.

The calendar proper consists of a quatrain for each day of the year, beginning January 1, in which are given respectively the names of the chief saints to be commemorated on such day, usually with a conventional phrase or epithet attached, but sometimes with allusion to historical or legendary matter. Although many foreigners, especially martyrs, are commemorated — sometimes not very accurately — the majority of the saints are Irish: the work is, indeed, a witness to the unified national character of the old Irish Church.

To the *Félire Oengusso*, as to certain other ancient and venerated texts, like the early law tracts and several of the hymns, a mass of glosses and notes has been attached. The bulk of these are probably of the eleventh century or later, and as commentaries on the text of Oengus are, at times, neither trustworthy nor edifying; but taken for what they are, a vast and heterogeneous mass of myth, legend, folk-lore, and the debris of history and of literature, they form a rich quarry for the scientific investigator.

In the Carlsruhe Bede, Codex Augiensis CLXVII, ff. 16^v-17^v, there is a calendar, written by an Irish hand, it would seem in the second quarter of the ninth century. The Irish names, very few, are published in *Thes. Pal.* II 283; see also HZ *Glossae hibernicae* 229, *Supplement* 12. *Cf.* no. 525.

There is a metrical Latin calendar, found in three English manuscripts, which has Irish symptoms. MSS: BM Cotton. Galba A XVIII [*cf.* E. M. Thompson *Ancient manuscripts in the British Museum* Pt. II *Latin* 12–3; Bishop *Liturgica historica* (1918) 140–1: a psalter, written on the Continent in the ninth century, which, perhaps, belonged to King Athelstan and was given by him to Winchester cathedral; the additional matter, including the calendar, was added in England in the tenth century]. — BM Cotton. Tiberius B V; and Julius A VI [in which the text is considerably modified]. ED: E. Hampson *Medii aevi kalendarium* (London 1841) I 397–420. COMM: WS *Academy* 29 June 1895 p. 545; *Martyrology of Gorman* p. xlvi. — J. H. Hessels *Academy* 6 July 1895 p. 12. — The Rev. H. Thurston " The Irish origins of Our Lady's conception feast " *The Month* May 1904 pp. 453 *sqq*; " England and the Immaculate Conception " *ibid*. Dec. 1904. — Bishop *op. cit.* 254–6. The calendar, which may have been written about the end of the ninth century, commemorates ten Irish saints and mentions fourteen other feasts apparently derived from Irish sources. WS and Thurston considered it Irish, Hessels thought it might equally be Anglo-Saxon. Bishop advanced the theory that it was composed by an Irishman in England, perhaps one of the " Scotti " at the court of Alfred the Great, who used as his basis a practical church calendar of Winchester.

273. The Martyrology of Tamlachta (Tallaght)

MSS: LL pp. 355–65 (of facs.). — Brussels Bibl. roy. 5100-4 ff. 182–97^v.[343] ED: Matthew Kelly *Calendar of Irish saints, the Martyrology of Tallagh; with notices of the patron saints of Ireland and select poems and hymns* (Dublin [1857]) [poor ed.].

[343] So J. Van den Gheyn's *Catalogue* I (Brussels 1901) 321. WS (*cf.* p. 482 *infra*) and Plummer *Misc. hag. Hib.* Cat. no. 182 give ff. 209–24^v.

Until an edition of this work consonant with modern scholarship appears,[344] what is said regarding it must be purely tentative. It is a prose calendar of saints, probably prepared at Tamlachta early in the tenth century: the last personage commemorated is Coirpre *cam*, a bishop, of Clúain-moccu-Nóis, who died, according to different sources, in 899 [345] or 904.[346] In the text itself its composition is ascribed to Máel-Rúain and Oengus, which may, or may not, mean that it has grown out of a compilation which they began. Unlike the *Félire Oengusso*, this martyrology begins on December 25. In both copies there is a gap from November 1 to December 16.

Colgan [347] made use of a document which he called the " Calendar of Cashel," believing it to have been compiled for the service of that church. He states that the latest saint noticed was Gormgal, abbot of Árd-oilén,[348] who died in 1018,[349] and that it contained but few names not found in the *Félire Oengusso*. According to Gougaud,[350] the beginning of a list of the saints mentioned in this calendar is in Brussels Bibl. roy. 5100–4.

The Martyrology of Ricemarch (ed. H. J. Lawlor, Henry Bradshaw Soc., 1914), of the second half of the eleventh century — which will be considered later — has some Irish associations and interest.

274. Cuimmín's Poem on the Saints of Ireland

Cuimin Condeire cecinit. Carais Pattraicc phuirt Macha . . . itche na naomh ro charus. 37 quatrains.

MSS: Brussels Bibl. roy. 2324–40 f. 44–6; 5100–4 f. 238 [fragment; both this and the preceding are in Michael O'Clery's hand]. — TCD 1284 (H. 1.10) A.D. 1742 p. 150. — RIA 23 E 16 p. 346 [25 stanzas]. EDS: M. Kelly *Martyrology of Tallagh* (Dublin [1857]) 160–71 [poor text, trans. by O'C]. — WS *ZCP* I (1897) 59–73 [text, trans., notes, etc.]. *Cf.* Plummer *Misc. hag. Hib.* Cat. no. 199.

This versified catalogue of Irish saints was composed, if we may judge from the linguistic evidence, in the eleventh or twelfth century. It is attributed, however, to a Cuimmín of Condere, identified with an ecclesiastic who died, according to the annals, in 659. One quatrain is assigned to each saint, and describes his virtues, or, frequently, his extraordinary ascetic practices. It has interest as a compendium of the opinions held five centuries later regarding the heroes of the early Irish Church.

275. The Martyrology of úa Gormáin (*Félire húi Gormáin*) A.D. 1166 x 1174.

[Preface] Is he inad i ndernad in felerese. . . . [Calendar] IHS. Ianuarius. For kalaind aird Enair, fo recht Isu ergna . . . adíu ceim for kallaind. [Epilogue] Cech noeb ro búi, bias . . . cech noeb ro búi, bias. In all, 2796 lines.

MS: Brussels Bibl. roy. 5100–4 ff. 124–97[V] [351] [preceded by a testimonial as to the trustworthiness of this copy, by Michael O'Clery, dated Aug. 18, 1633. WS gives a full description and catalogue of the MS.] ED: WS *Félire Húi Gormáin The Martyrology of Gorman* (Henry Bradshaw Soc. IX) (London 1895) [text, trans., etc.]. *Cf. Academy* 28 Dec. 1895 p. 569 [*addenda* and *corrigenda*].

Our information regarding the *Félire húi Gormáin* is derived chiefly from the preface, which is itself a document of some interest:

" This is the place wherein this martyrology was composed, Cnoc-na-nApstol (the Hill of the Apostles) in Louth.   At the time of its composition Ruaidhri Úa Conchobhair was king of Ireland,[352] Gilasius was *comharpa* of Patrick,[353] and Aedh Úa Cáillaidhe was bishop of Airghialla.[354]   Máel-Maire úa Gormáin, abbot of the aforesaid Cnoc, composed it.   And besides the seeking of heaven for himself and for everyone who should sing it through, it is this that impelled him to make it, the fewness of the saints of Ireland whom Oengus brought into his martyrology and the multitude of the saints of the rest of the world for whom the Church has appointed festival and mass, (but whom) Oengus has left out, and (lastly, because) a great number of those whom he brought in were not arranged on the days on which the Church celebrates their festivals.   And this, surely, as we have ascertained, was the reason why Oengus did so, because it was thus in the Martyrology of Tamlachta, out of which he composed his martyrology. . . ."

The above text would indicate that the martyrology was composed within the period A.D. 1166-1174.   Gilla-maic-Liac, or Gilasius, who died on March 27, 1174, and Gilla-Mo-Chaidbeo, " abbot of the Monastery of Peter and Paul in Árd-Macha," who died four days later, are commemorated in the work, although, as has been seen, it is described as composed within the term of the former's bishopric.   The two names occur at the end of stanzas, and may well be additions by úa Gormáin himself, or by another.   Colgan [355] identified Máel-Maire húa Gormáin with the Máel-Muire hÚa Dunáin, [356] abbot of Cnoc-na-sengán, " Hill of the ants," who died in 1181: [357] no doubt correctly, for Cnoc-na-sengán and Cnoc-na-nApstol designate the same place, in English known as the abbey of Knock, a little east of the town of Louth.

The foundation of Máel-Muire's church is thus recorded by the Four Masters, under 1148: " The church of Cnoc-na-sengán was finished by the bishop Úa Caellaidhe and Donnchadh Úa Cearbhaill, and was consecrated by Úa Morghair, a successor of Patrick; and a *neimeadh* [*i.e.*, ecclesiastical lands] was assigned to it in Lughmadh." [358] This monastery seems to have been one of canons regular of St. Augustine, and its establishment an important step in the reform movement of the twelfth century, of which Máel-Maidhóg Úa Morgair (St. Malachy) was the great leader, and Donnchad Úa Cerbaill, king of Air-gíalla, one of the most prominent lay supporters.[359]   Máel-

---

[352] *I.e.*, 1166-1183, or, perhaps, 1186.

[353] Gilla-maic-Liac was archbishop of Armagh from about 1137 to 1174. *Cf.* p. 766 *infra*.

[354] He died in 1182 (ALC) and had been bishop since 1138 or 1139. *Cf. Proc. RIA* XXXII (1913) C 29-30.

[355] *AA. SS.* 737.

[356] WS comments that he knew of no sure instance where an Irishman was called at one time by the name of his paternal, at another by that of his maternal grandfather.   But by this time *úa*, which may mean grandson, was well established as the formula for a family name, being followed by the designation of the founder of the family, however remote; and it is probable that one of Máel-Muire's descriptions indicates his family, the other his grandfather.

[357] FM.

[358] The founding of this monastery is mentioned in a notice of Úa Cerbaill's death. *Cf.* p. 770 *infra*. See also the *County Louth Archaeological Journal* IV 239.

[359] *Cf.* pp. 776, 770 *infra*.

Muire's *Félire* may be regarded as a product of the same movement, designed to bring the Irish calendar and Irish hagiology into greater association and harmony with those of the rest of Christendom.

Like the *Félire Oengusso*, this calendar is in metre,[360] and begins on January 1. It commemorates about 3450 persons, biblical, continental, English, British and Irish.

276. List of Double Names of Irish Saints

Crimthand ainm Coluim cille, ...

MS: LL 354d. ED: *Lis. Lives* 300–1.

Many of the saints of Ireland were known, each by two or more names. Some of the alternative designations are distinct names, some are only hypocoristic forms. A few of these aliases are given in the present list.

277. Comparisons of Irish and Foreign Saints

Hic incipiunt sancti qui erant bini unius moris: Johannes baptiza — Epscop Ibar, ...

MSS: LL 370 c, d. — Brussels Bibl. roy. 5100–4 f. 208. EDS: *LH*[1] I 69–70. — M. Kelly *Martyrology of Tallagh* (Dublin [1857]) pp. xli *sq*. — *Lis. Lives* 298–9.

One of the conceits of Irish hagiographers was the equation, because of some real or fancied resemblance, of the heroes of their own native *sanctilogium* with the famous personalities of world Christianity. Some of these comparisons are here gathered into a list.

278. Lists of Irish Saints of the same name (*Comainmniugad naem hÉrenn*). Lists of Irish virgin Saints of the same name (*Comanmand naeb uag hÉrenn*)

MSS: LL 366e *sqq*. — Bodl. Rawl. B 502 ff. 52[v] *sq*. — BB 225d *sqq*. — Bk. Lec. ff. 56 *sqq*. — BM Addit. 30512 ff. 48 *sqq*. — RIA 23 D 9 pp. 352 *sqq* [has first tract only]. ED: D. T. Brosnan *AH* I (Maynooth 1912) 314–65.

A late Scottish work which nevertheless is of considerable interest to the Irish student is the Breviary of Aberdeen, compiled chiefly by William Elphinstone, who was bishop of Aberdeen 1483–1514, and printed at Edinburgh in 1509–10. It was reprinted at London in 1854, and also as one of the publications of the Bannatyne Club.[361] The lessons contain extracts from or synopses of the legends of many Irish saints, and of Scottish saints of the period when Irish ecclesiastical influence was predominant in Scotland. These are of much historical value, and in some cases have been drawn from sources which no longer exist.

---

[360] *Rinnaird mór.*
[361] The calendar of the Breviary is printed in A. P. Forbes *Kalendars of Scottish Saints* 111–24.

279. The Martyrology of Donegal

MSS: Brussels Bibl. roy. 5095–6 [autograph of Michael O'Clery, dated April 19, 1630: has six testimonials by Irish scholars and bishops, dated in 1636–7]; 4639 [another autograph of O'Clery, but shorter than preceding; the title is dated at Douai, 1629, but the work itself at the monastery of Donegal, 1628: it is probably the first fair copy]. ED: *The Martyrology of Donegal A Calendar of the saints of Ireland Translated from the original Irish by the late* John O'Donovan. . . . *Edited, with the Irish text, by* James Henthorn Todd . . . *and* William Reeves (IA&CS: Dublin 1864). *Cf. Proc. RIA* IV 557.

Of the work of Michael O'Clery, and of the compilation of this, the last and largest of the calendars of Irish saints, some account has been given in the first chapter.[362] Its title is *Félire na naomh nÉrennach*, "Calendar of the Irish Saints," but because it was written in the home on the river Drowse of the Franciscan friars of Donegal it has always been known as the Martyrology of Donegal.

In the Stowe Missal (no. 555), and in certain litanies (nos. 586,590), there are important lists of Irish saints. The pedigrees of the saints are also sources of considerable extent, but the treatment of them will be reserved till that of the secular genealogies is reached. For these and other similar documents see Plummer *Misc. hag. Hib.* 225–31.

[362] Pp. 40 *sqq supra.*

CHAPTER VI

THE EXPANSION OF IRISH CHRISTIANITY

From the Seventh to the Twelfth Century

Bibliography

The guides provided by Potthast, Chevalier, Monod, Molinier, Wattenbach, Manitius, and the Bollandists [*cf.* pp. 91, 289 *supra*].[1] Also works by Ebrard [p. 520], Hauck [p. 106], Margaret Stokes [p. 183], Roger [p. 106], and Boissonade [p. 157]. — Gabriel Monod *Études critiques sur les sources de l'histoire mérovingienne* 2 vols. (Paris 1872–85); *Études critiques sur les sources de l'histoire carolingienne* (Paris 1898). — L. Van der Essen *Étude critique et littéraire sur les vitae des saints mérovingiens de l'ancienne Belgique* (Louvain and Paris 1907) [very important]. — W. Levison " Conspectus codicum hagiographicorum " *MGH SS. rer. merov.* VII pt. II (1920) 529–706. — Nicolaus Vernulaeus *De propagatione fidei christianae in Belgio per sanctos ex Hibernia viros* (Louvain 1639). — A. F. Ozanam *Études germaniques* 2 vols. (Paris 1872) [contains an enthusiastic but somewhat uncritical account of Irish influences on the Continent]. — HZ " Über die Bedeutung des irischen Elements für die mittelalterliche Cultur " *Preussische Jahrbücher* LIX (Jan. 1887): trans. by Jane Loring Edmonds *The Irish element in mediaeval culture* (New York 1891) [good introductory sketch, but over-enthusiastic]. — Walther Schultze " Die Bedeutung der iroschottischen Mönche für die Erhaltung und Fortflanzung der mittelalterlichen Wissenschaft (mit besonderer Rücksicht auf die noch vorhandenen irischen Handschriften in Bibliotheken des Continents) " *Centralblatt für Bibliothekswesen* VI Jahrg. (1889) 185–98, 233–41, 281–98. — J. von Pflugk-Harttung " The Old Irish on the Continent " *Trans. Roy. Hist. Soc.* new ser. V (1891) 75–102. — T. A. Walsh " Irish saints in Belgium " *Ecclesiastical Rev.* XXXIX (1908) 122–40 [treats of the cult of saints of Ireland, but this is important testimony to the former influence of Irish *émigrés*]. — L. Gougaud "L'oeuvre des Scotti dans l'Europe continentale (fin v^e–fin xie siècles)" *RHE* IX (1908) 21–37, 255–77; " Les saints irlandais dans les traditions populaires des pays continentaux " *RC* XXXIX (1922) 199–226, 355–8. These two arts. have been published in translation, with slight expansion, chiefly in the notes: L. Gougaud (trans. V. Collins) *Gaelic pioneers of Christianity The work and influence of Irish monks and saints in continental Europe VIth–XIIth cent.* (Dublin 1923). See also his *Chrétientés celtiques* (Paris 1911) 134–74, 285–94, and *passim.* [These studies by Dom Louis Gougaud are the most useful in the field.] — W. Levison " Die Iren und die Fränkische Kirche " *Hist. Zs.* CIX (1912) 1–22. — A. Mayer " Die Iren auf dem Kontinent im Mittelalter " *Hochland* XIII ii (Munich and Kempten 1915–16) 605–14. — Paul Grosjean " Un poème

1 Some or all of these, as well as the principal church histories, should be consulted by the student who wishes to make an intensive study of any of the subjects touched on in this chapter.

486

latin du xviie siècle sur les saints irlandais honorés en Belgique " *An. Boll.* XLIII i-ii (1925) [the poem was written by an Irish Jesuit, possibly Father Henry Fitz-Simon [2]].

One of the most striking features of Irish history as a whole, from the earliest records to the present day, has been the continual stream of emigration which has passed from the shores of the western isle. Whether as warriors, as adventurers, as " pilgrims," as refugees, or as home-seekers, every age has known its Irish emigrants. The Irish emigrants of the early middle ages were those religious men and women, pilgrims, hermits, missionaries, whose names are found associated with every country, almost every country-side, of western Europe.

The two most famous of early Irish exiles were St. Columba, founder of Hii, or Iona, off the west of Scotland, and St. Columbanus, founder of Luxeuil in eastern France and Bobbio in northern Italy. There were, however, many lesser men whose names have been handed down to us by more or less trustworthy records as followers of the same paths, and hundreds of others, we may be sure, all traces of whom have long been lost in the *debris* of history. On the other hand, so usual a thing was it for the man of peculiar sanctity in Merovingian Gaul to be either an Irishman or a disciple of the community of Columbanus, that one or the other attribute was assigned at times without just cause by the early Gallic hagiographers. The modern student should be on his guard against this source of error: it may well be that some of the names which appear in the following pages are present as a result of such a misrepresentation.

The most important among the motives that sent Irishmen to foreign lands during the period considered in the present work was the ascetic spirit of Irish Christianity. Something has been said of this in previous pages.[3] The same ideal which led to those acts of personal mortification, sometimes heroic to the modern eye, sometimes repulsive, which form so prominent a feature of the religious life of ancient Ireland, drove crowds of devotees to abandon their homes and seek abodes in the islands around the Irish and Scottish coasts, in far-off Iceland, in Cornwall and Brittany and the lands of western Europe.

A well-known entry in the Anglo-Saxon Chronicle, under the year 891 or 892, may be quoted here, because of its concrete illustration of this phase of Irish religious life:

[2] *Cf.* p. 37 *supra.*
[3] *Cf.* especially pp. 303, 458, 459 *supra.*

"Three Irishmen came to king Alfred in a boat without any oars, from Ireland, whence they had stolen away, because they desired, for love of God, to be in a state of pilgrimage, they recked not where. The boat in which they came was wrought of two hides and a half, and they took with them food sufficient for seven nights; and on the seventh night they came to land in Cornwall, and then went straightways to king Alfred. Thus they were named: Dubslane, and Macbethu, and Maelinmun."

The motive is recorded in various phrases by the writers of the *Acta Sanctorum:* "Peregrinatio pro Dei amore," "propter nomen Domini," "ob amorem Christi," etc. The command to Abraham, "Egredere de terra tua et de cognatione tua," seems, as a call to the sacrifice of the dearest associations, to have appealed in a peculiar manner to the Irish people.[4] It should be noted that in this usage "peregrinatio" did not mean pilgrimage in the usual modern signification of the word: in fact, through all the early middle ages the Latin word "peregrinus," as used in Ireland, and the Irish "deórad," meant, not the man who went on a definite journey to a definite shrine, from which it was his intention, after paying his devotions, to return, but the man who, for his soul's good, departed from his home-land to dwell for a space of years, or for the rest of his life, in strange countries.

However, many of the Irish of whom we hear in continental Europe, especially from the ninth century on, were pilgrims in the modern sense. The journey to the tombs of the apostles in Rome was the favorite pilgrimage, but occasionally that was undertaken to the Holy Sepulchre in Jerusalem. Another motive of this expansion movement — probably at first a result thereof, and then by reaction a contributing cause — was the spirit of evangelisation. Columba sailed from Ireland to Britain "pro Christo peregrinari volens," but he became the Apostle of the Picts, and the monastery he founded the base for the conversion of Northumbria. In Gaul and Germany likewise the Irish monks and hermits soon found themselves impelled to preach the Gospel to their pagan or semi-pagan neighbors. As disciples gathered around to benefit from the spiritual wisdom and grace of the stranger hermit whose reputation for holiness was enhanced by his origin, appearance, and mode of life, the cell became a monastery, a centre for the diffusion of Irish Christianity in the surrounding districts. So Irish monastic discipline, Irish ecclesiastical law, Irish penitential rules and customs, Irish biblical texts, even a certain amount of Irish learning passed into the life of Europe.

The main contribution of exiles of Erin to European learning came, however, as a result of other forces. The ninth century is the one era

4 *Cf.* Gougaud *Chrétientés Celtiques* 134–6.

when the typical Irishman in mediaeval Europe was the "scholar," not the "saint." Now the ninth century was the age when the Norse Vikings were dealing their heaviest blows at the Irish monasteries. Then the men whose chief interest was in scholarship, who, had the Irish schools remained what they were in the time of Bede, might have been expected to find ample employment in their native land, became refugees in foreign countries. The enlightened policy of Charles the Great, Louis the Pious and Charles the Bald gave a warm welcome to these evicted savants, and thereby encouraged their fellow-sufferers at home to follow in their footsteps.

In the present chapter the records of this expansion of Irish Christianity will be considered, beginning in the seventh century. The work and career of Columba and his companions in North Britain, of his successors in Northumbria and in England further south, and of Columbanus and his monks in Gaul and Germany and Italy, either are so intimately bound up with the history of the home-land, or have such importance for the story of the ancient Irish Church before it accepted the Roman discipline, that it has seemed desirable to treat of them in the preceding chapters. So too has it been with those vague legends of early Irish hermits and church-founders in Wales and Cornwall and Brittany, which, if based on actual events, belong to the beginnings of the Irish Church.

I. Irish Influences in the Merovingian Dominions in the Seventh Century

Bibliography

In addition to the works cited at the beginning of the chap., see the art. of G. Bonet-Maury [p. 186 *supra*]. On the chronology of the Merovingian monarchy, see the following: Bruno Krusch " Zur Chronologie der merowingischen Könige " *Forschungen zur deutschen Geschichte* XXII (1882). — Joseph Tardif *Les chartes mérovingiennes de l'abbaye de Noirmoutier avec une étude sur la chronologie du règne de Dagobert II* (Paris 1899). — W. Levison " Das Nekrologium von Dom Racine und die Chronologie der Merowinger " *NA* XXV (1909). — Paul Edmond Martin *Études critiques sur la Suisse à l'époque mérovingienne* (Geneva and Paris 1910). — L. Levillain " La succession d'Austrasie au viie siècle " *RH* CXII (1913) 62–93. — Krusch " Chronologica regum Francorum stirpis Merowingicae " *MGH SS. rer. merov.* VII pt. II (1920) 468–516.

The struggles between the several sections of the Frankish dominions — Neustria, comprising central and western Gaul; Austrasia, northern and eastern Gaul and western Germany; and Burgundy, south-eastern

Gaul — and their kings, which had troubled the career of Columbanus, came to a lull about the time of that saint's death. Under Clothair II (d. 629) and his son Dagobert I (d. 639) unity and peace were maintained in a quite exceptional degree, and the Merovingian monarchy attained the zenith of its power. At the same time the religious influences which Columbanus had planted at Luxeuil made themselves felt throughout Gaul, and with them went a welcome to all religious exiles from Ireland.

The work of several of the immediate disciples of Columbanus has been already noticed: St. Gall in Switzerland; his alleged companion, St. Magnus; St. Deicolus of Lure, in Burgundy; St. Roding of Beaulieu, in the Argonne; St. Valery of Leucone, in Picardy; St. Salaberga of Laon; and St. Omer, of Thérouanne.[5]   At least as important as any of these was Donatus, bishop of Besançon (d. 660), of whom, however, there is no ancient Life. At the same time the spirit of Columbanus was affecting many of the leading Frankish nobles and officials of the court. Richarius, or Riquier (d. c 645), a noble of Picardy, rescued two Irish priests from the attack of the populace, was by them turned to the religious life, and founded the monastery of Centula, now St.-Riquier (dept. of Somme). — Chagneric, a noble who dwelt near Meaux, east of Paris, had a son Chagnoald, a disciple of Columbanus at Luxeuil, and afterwards bishop of Laon, and a daughter, Burgundofara, or Fara, who, then a young girl, was specially blessed by that saint when he stopped with the family after his expulsion from Burgundy.[6] She afterwards founded the convent of Faremoutiers [7] in the same region. Another son of Chagneric, Burgundofaro or Faro (d. c 672),[8] became bishop of Meaux and showed himself a friend of ecclesiastics from Ireland, two of whom, Killian and Fiacre, he induced to settle in northern Gaul. — Desiderius, Didier, or Géry (d. 654), treasurer of Clothair II, became bishop of Cahors, on the river Lot, a tributary of the Garonne, where he became the friend of an Irish recluse named Arnanus. — Sigiramnus, or Cyran (d. c 655), an officer of Clothair II and Dagobert I, who became abbot of Longrey in Berry (dept. of Indre), owed his conversion in part to an Irish bishop, Falvius,[9] who took him on a pilgrimage to Rome. — Eligius, or Eloi (d. 660), was one of the most famous personages of

  5 See pp. 205–9 *supra*.
  6 Jonas *Vita Columbani* I xxvi.
  7 *Cf.* Bede *Ecclesiastical History* III viii.
  8 Strictly, Jonas does not say that Burgundofaro was son of Chagneric, although he speaks of him as bishop of Meaux.
  9 The Aquitaine recension of the *Martyrologium Hieronymianum* gives the name of Falbeus on 15 kl. Aug. (Migne *PL* XXX 482. *Cf. NA* XXIV 543.)

seventh-century Gaul. Educated as a goldsmith, he became in time master of the royal mint and counsellor of Dagobert I. He founded many churches and monasteries,[10] and did much to spread the Irish monastic rule and customs. He became bishop of Noyon in 640, and, in association with the mayor of the palace Erchinoald, assisted in the transfer of the remains of St. Fursa about 654.[11] — Wandregisil, or Vandrille (d. 667 or 668), a count of the palace and said to be of royal blood, was carried in spirit by an angel to Bobbio and given a view of the monastery, as a result of which he renounced the world; he practised austerities similar to those of the Irish saints, and wished to pay a visit to Ireland;[12] and about 648 he founded the abbey of Fontenelle, near Caudebec below Rouen. — Another influential officer of the court of Dagobert I, and a friend of Eloi and Vandrille, was Dado, Audoen, or Ouen (d. c 683). He and his brothers had, as boys, been blessed by Columbanus when the Irish abbot was journeying through Austrasia.[13] About 635 they founded the Columban monastery of Rebais (east of Paris, between the Grand Morin and Petit Morin rivers), and in 640 Dado became bishop of Rouen. — A young friend of Ouen, named Philibert (d. 684), who had been brought up at court, entered this monastery of Rebais when twenty years old, and afterwards went to Luxeuil and Bobbio. About 655 he founded the famous abbey of Jumièges, on the Seine below Rouen, on land granted by King Clovis II and his queen Bathild. Later he erected, on an island near the mouth of the Loire, the monastery afterwards known as Noirmoutier. We are told that at Jumièges he dedicated an altar to Columbanus, and that among his disciples was an Irishman named Sidonius, or Saëns.

280. St. Richarius, or Riquier

(i) The oldest Life

EDS: *An. Boll.* XXII 186–94. — Br. Krusch *MGH SS. rer. merov.* VII (1920) 438–53. COMM: *An. Boll.* XXVI 45–51. — Krusch *NA* XXIX (1904) 42-8. — B. Sepp in L. Helmling's *Hagiographischer Jahresbericht für das Jahr 1903* (Kempten 1904) 122–3.

[10] In the charter granted by him in 632 to his monastic foundation at Solignac he requires that it follow the path of Luxeuil and maintain the rule of Benedict and Columbanus; that no bishop or other outside person shall have power in the monastery; but that, in case of defection or insubordination, the abbot of Luxeuil may intervene. — *MGH SS. rer. Merov.* IV 746-8; *cf. ibid.* V 88. — He built the church of St. Quentin, to receive the body of that saint, at a place apparently already occupied by Irish monks. *Cf. ibid.* IV 424.

[11] *Cf.* p. 501 *infra.* Eloi was succeeded as bishop of Noyon by Mommelin, a monk of Luxeuil who had been abbot of a monastery at Sithiu, afterwards St. Bertin, at St. Omer (dept. of Pas-de-Calais), and died about 686. On the basis of a miniature of the twelfth century it has been claimed that Mommelin wore the Irish tonsure. *Cf.* Krusch *NA* XXX 502; Van der Essen *Étude critique* [p. 486 *supra*] 375 n. 3; Gougaud *Gaelic pioneers* 15.

[12] *Vita* cap. ix: Krusch's ed. pp. 17-8.

[13] *Vita Columbani* by Jonas, I xv.

(ii) Life by Alcuin s VIII ex

EDS: Surius *De probatis sanctorum historiis* (Cologne 1571) II 865-70. — Duchesne *Alchuini opera* (Paris 1617) pt. II cols. 1419-32. — Mabillon *AA. SS. o. s. B.* II (1669) 187-97. — *AA. SS. Boll.* April. III 442-7. — Frobenius *Alcuini opera* tom. II vol. I (Ratisbon 1777) 175-82. — Migne *PL* CI 681-94. — Krusch *MGH SS rer. merov.* IV (1902) 381-401.

(iii) Chronicle of the abbey of Centula, or St.-Riquier, by Hariulf, s XII

EDS: D'Achéry *Spicilegium* IV 419 *sqq* (2nd ed. II 291-356). — Migne *PL* CLXXIV 1211 *sqq*. — F. Lot *Hariulf Chronique de l'Abbaye de Saint-Riquier* (Paris 1894: *Collection de textes pour servir à l'étude et à l'enseignement de l'histoire*). — E. Dümmler *MGH Poet. lat. aevi Carol.* I (1881) 365-6 [Angilbert's epitaphs]. *Cf.* Roger *L'Enseignement* 404 n. 1; M. Stokes *Three months in the forests of France* 75-7.

The story of the relations of St. Riquier with the two Irish priests, Caidocus [14] and Fricorius, is told in Alcuin's Life and also, with some additional details, in the *Chronicle of the abbey of Centula* (St.-Riquier) written by Hariulf, a monk of that establishment who died in 1143. According to him, Fricor adopted the name Hadrian because of the uncouthness of his native designation to continental ears. Hariulf also preserves the epitaphs written for these two Irishmen. They were composed by Angilbert (d. 814), abbot of Centula and friend of Charles the Great, who was the author of several poems and prose works.

281. Life of St. Faro, bishop of Meaux, by Hildegaire A.D. 869

EDS: Duchesne *Historiae Francorum SS.* (Paris 1636) I 567-71 [excerpts]. — Mabillon *AA. SS. o. s. B.* II (Paris 1669) 607-25. — *AA. SS. Boll.* Oct. XII 609-16 [a different text]. — Krusch *MGH SS. rer. merov.* V (1910) 171-203. *Cf.* G. Gröber in *Raccolta di studii critici dedicata ad Alessandro d'Ancona festeggiandosi il XL anniversario del suo insegnamento* (Florence 1901) 589-94; Joseph Bédier *Les Légendes épiques* IV (Paris 1913, 2nd ed. 1921) 290-335.

This Life of St. Faro, or Burgundofaro, was written by Hildegaire, one of his successors in the see of Meaux (855-76). It was based on an older Life, and has considerable historical value. Hildegaire also had a Life of St. Killian, and refers to him several times. He likewise refers frequently to Columbanus. He speaks of the large numbers of " Scoti " who come to Gaul — no doubt a ninth-century touch.

282. Life of St. Killian of Aubigny

Fuit vir venerabilis vitae in Ibernia, vocabulo Cillianus. . . . Deo soli famulatum reddentibus, cui. . . . Amen.

MSS: Douai 857 *s* X ff. 105-14; 840 *s* XII ff. 153-5. ED: A. Poncelet *An. Boll.* XX (1901) 432-44. COMM: A. Cuvillier *Histoire de st. Kilien, évêque missionaire de l'Artois* (Lille 1861). — AdeJ *RC* XXIII 110-1. — B. Krusch *MGH SS. rer. merov.* V (1910) 173-4.

[14] From his name we might infer that Caidoc was a Briton, but all the sources are specific in declaring his Irish origin.

The extant Life of St. Killian, or Chillen, the Irish anchorite who was induced by St. Faro of Meaux to settle at Aubigny, near Arras, contains much that is absurd. Hildegaire refers in his Life of St. Faro [15] to a Life of Killian in his possession. It must have represented a very old tradition, since it preserved the name in the form Chillenus. This form, philologists believe, cannot be much, if any, later than the seventh century.

283. Life of St. Fiacra s XII/XIII

[Prologue] Egregius Christi confessor Fiacrius. . . . [Vita] Beatus Fiacrius eremita . . . ad lucem immarcescibilem, quam solus inhabitat J. C. D. n., qui cum P. et S. s. v. et r. D. per infinita s. s. Amen.

EDS: *AA. SS. Boll.* Aug. VI 598–616. Abridgments in the Breviary of Aberdeen; Capgrave *Nova Legenda Anglie* (ed. Horstman, Oxford, 1901) I 441–4; Messingham *Florilegium* 390–2 [Capgrave's text]; and Surius *De probatis sanctorum historiis* VII (Cologne 1581) 651–3. COMM: Mabillon *AA. SS. o. s. B.* II 598 *sqq. — Hist. litt. de la France* XIV (1817) 633. — Ricard *La vie et les miracles de s. Fiacre, patron de la Brie, d'après les Bollandistes, avec pièces justificatives* (Paris 1865). — Joseph Casimir O'Meagher "Saint Fiacre de la Brie" *Proc. RIA* 3rd ser. II 173–6. — Bollandists' *Cat. cod. hagiog. lat. in Bibl. nat. Parisiensi* II 349–54. — *Mélanges Havet* (Paris 1895) 211 *sqq. — An. Boll.* XXIII 209.

Of the Irish churchmen who settled in Brie, the most famous was St. Fiacra (d. c 670), whose hermit's cell became the monastery of Breuil. His legendary reputation stood very high in mediaeval France, but the historical remains of the saint are unsatisfactory. The only available Life is not earlier than the twelfth century. Mabillon refers to an eleventh-century Life by the poet Faulcoie, but this would seem never to have been published.

284. Life of St. Didier, bishop of Cahors s VIII

EDS: *Gallia Christiana* II (1656) ff. 460–6ᵛ. — Labbe *Novae bibliothecae* I (Paris 1657) 699–716 [poor]. — Migne *PL* LXXXVII 219–46 [reprint]. — R. Poupardin *La vie de st. Didier* (Paris 1900). — Krusch *MGH SS. rer. merov.* IV (1902) 547–602.

This Life was composed from good sources and is a valuable historical document.

285. Life of St. Cyran of Longrey s X

EDS: Labbe *Novae bibl.* II (Paris 1657) 439–44. — Mabillon *AA. SS. o. s. B.* II 432–8, 2nd ed. 414–9 [both incomplete]. — *An. Boll.* III (1884) 379–407. — Krusch *MGH SS. rer. merov.* IV (1902) 603–25.

This work, a tenth-century redaction of an older Life, is filled with errors and has but little value.

286. Life of St. Eloi, bishop of Noyon s VIII

EDS: Surius *De probatis sanctorum historiis* VI (Cologne 1575) 629–85; 2nd ed. 709–65. — Labbe *Novae bibl.* (Paris 1657) II 517 *sqq.* — D'Achéry *Spicilegium* (Paris 1661)

[15] *Cf.* no. 281.

V 147–302; 2nd ed. (Paris 1723) II 76–123 [*cf. An. Boll.* XVIII 44]. — Ghesquière
AA. SS. Belgii (Brussels 1785) II 198–310. — Migne *PL* LXXXVII 479–594. —
Bruno Krusch *MGH SS. rer. merov.* IV (1902) 634–761, VII pt. II (1920) 842–4. Comm:
Reich *Über Audoens Lebensbeschreibung des h. Eligius* (Halle 1872: Dissertation).
— Roth *Geschichte des Benefizialwesens* 299. — Hauck *Kirchengeschichte Deutschlands* I
[*vid.* Index]. — Wattenbach *DGQ.* — Van der Essen *Étude critique* [p. 486 *supra*] 324–
36. — Parsy *Saint Eloi* (*Les Saints*) (Paris 1907).

Our Life of St. Eloi is a farced production of the first half of the eighth century. It
may have made use of a Life by St. Dado, or Ouen, of Rouen, but only a small fragment of that composition can now be identified. The author of our redaction was
an enemy of the Irish emigrants and their customs in the controversies of the eighth
century, and represents Eloi and the Irish bishop Failbe, or Falvius,[16] as champions
of Roman observances and opponents of the " transmarine heretics," to whose party
they, in reality, adhered.

287. Life of St. Wandregisilus, or Vandrille

(i) By a contemporary. Eds: Labbe *Novae bibl.* I (Paris 1657) 784–91. — Mabillon
AA. SS. o. s. B. 526–34. — *AA. SS. Boll.* Jul. V 265–71. — W. Arndt *Kleine Denk-
mäler aus der Merowingerzeit* (Hanover 1874) 22–47. — Krusch *MGH SS. rer. merov.*
V (1910). (ii) Dedicated to Vandrille's successor, Lambert (who was bishop of Lyons,
680–90), but has come to us farced with extracts from other works, including the Life
of Columbanus. Eds: Mabillon 534–46. — *AA. SS. Boll.* 272–81. *Cf. An. Boll.*
XVII 297–306; XIX 235. Comm: F. Lot *Études critiques sur l'abbaye de St-Wandrille*
(Paris 1913).

288. Life of St. Dado, Audoenus, or Ouen, bishop of Rouen

(i) Written shortly after his death. Ed: *AA. SS. Boll.* 24 Aug. IV 805–10. *Cf. NA*
XII 603. — *MGH SS. rer. merov.* V 536–67 [*cf.* VII 847]. (ii) Ascribed to a certain
Fridegodus *s* IX/X. Ed: *AA. SS. Boll. loc. cit.* 810–9. (iii) Redaction of preceding,
s XI (?). Ed: *An. Boll.* V (1886) 67–146. (iv) Verse, by Thierry, monk of St. Ouen,
s XI. Eds: Moustier *Neustria pia* 23, 72, 346. — Migne *PL* CL 1189–92. (v) Poem
in his honor, probably by his successor Ansbert. Ed: Wattenbach *NA* XIV (1889)
171–2. — *MGH SS. rer. Merov.* V 542. Comm: Sauvage *An. Boll.* V 67–75. — Vacandard *Rev. des quest. hist.* Jan. 1898 pp. 5–50, Jan. 1901 pp. 5–58; *Vie de s. Ouen, évêque
de Rouen* (Paris 1902)

289. Life of St. Agile of Rebais *s* VII (?)

Eds: Mabillon *AA. SS. o. s. B.* II 316–26. — *AA. SS. Boll.* Aug. VI 574–87. Comm:
Hist. lit. de la France III (1735) 635–6. — M. Büdinger *Sitzungsb. d. Wiener Akad. d.
Wissensch.* XXIII (1857) 372–83. — *An. Boll.* XXIII 151.

St. Agilus, or Ayeul, a disciple of Eustasius of Luxeuil, was the first abbot of the Columban monastery which Dado founded at Rebais. His Life, which dates from the ninth

---

16 *Cf.* p. 490 *supra.*

century, is in part extracted from Jonas's account of Eustasius. It testifies [17] to the fact that Rebais became a favorite stopping place for Irish pilgrims on the road to or from Rome.

290. Life of St. Filibert, or Philibert, abbot of Jumièges s VIII, IX

EDS: Duchesne *Historiae Francorum SS.* I (Paris 1636) 658. — Mabillon *AA. SS. o. s. B.* II (Paris 1669) 818-25. — *AA. SS. Boll.* Aug. IV (1739) 75-80. — R. Poupardin *Monuments de l'histoire des abbayes de St-Philibert* (Paris 1905). — W. Levison *MGH SS. rer. merov.* V (1910) 568-604, VII pt. II (1920) 847-8. COMM: J. Tardif *Les Chartes Mérovingiennes de Noirmoutier* [*cf.* no. 295]. — E. Vacandard *Vie de s. Ouen, évêque de Rouen* (Paris 1902).

The Life of St. Philibert was written about the middle of the eighth century, and re-edited in the ninth. It contains an incidental allusion to Irish commerce with the district of the Loire: " Not much later an Irish ship filled with various merchandise came to shore, and supplied the brothers with an abundance of shoes and clothing."[18]

291. Life of St. Sidonius

EDS: (i) *S* X/XI. Ménard *Martyrologium sanctorum ordinis Divi Benedicti* (Paris 1629) 747-50. — *An. Boll.* X (1891) 438-40. (ii) *S* XII. *An. Boll. ibid.* 406, 425-38. COMM: E. Vacandard *Vie de s. Ouen, évêque de Rouen* (Paris 1902) 202-245.

Sidonius, or Saëns, is said to have been an Irishman who became a disciple of St. Philibert, and afterwards abbot of a monastery in the diocese of Rouen (Saint-Saëns, dept. Seine-Inférieure, arr. Neufchâtel).[19]

With the death of Dagobert I the Merovingian monarchy began to decline. The spirit of sectionalism increased, the nobles became more insubordinate, and the officials known as " mayors of the palace " gradually usurped the royal power. This disintegration was largely due to the succession of a series of minors to the throne. Dagobert's kingdom was divided between his two young sons, Clovis II receiving Neustria, Sigebert III Austrasia. Administration fell to the mayors of the palace, Erchinoald in Neustria and Grimoald in Austrasia. Grimoald's father, who died in 640, was Pippin the Elder, of Landen, founder of the famous line later known as the Karlings, or Carolingians.

[17] *Cap.* xxiv.
[18] Ed. Levison p. 603.
[19] Sidonius is mentioned in the Life of Ouen no. ii (no. 288). *Cf. MGH SS. rer. merov.* V (1910) 560. There are also some passages relating to him in the tenth-century Life of Leutfredus, or Leufroy (d. *c* 738), " abbas Madriacensis," *i.e.*, of the place later known as Croix-St-Leufroy, near Evreux. EDS: Mabillon *AA. SS o. s. B.* III i 583-92. — *AA. SS. Boll.* Jan. IV 105-12. — W. Levison *MGH SS. rer. merov.* VII (1920) 1-16. See *cap.* vii *sqq.*

Echinoald's friendship for the Irish clergy is shown by his devotion to St. Fursa, of which something will be said in the following section. Clovis also, and his queen, St. Bathild,[20] who had been a slave in Erchinoald's household, supported the monastic movement sprung from Ireland and Luxeuil. After the death of Clovis in 657, Bathild, while acting as regent for the boy Clothair III, built the abbey of Corbie, and the convent of Chelles, near Paris, both under the rules, or at least the inspiration, of Luxeuil.

Meanwhile in Austrasia Sigebert III had died in 656 and his young son, Dagobert II, was seized by Grimoald, forcibly tonsured, and given to Dido, or Dodo, bishop of Poitiers, to be taken to Ireland, where, doubtless, he was placed in a monastery. What the circumstances were which made Dido the ready tool of Grimoald we do not know, but his position at Poitiers was most favorable for communication with Ireland. It seems probable that it was under him that the Irishman who is known as St. Fridolin established himself in Poitiers.

The story of Dagobert II reads like a romance. For about twenty years he remained hidden in Ireland. Meanwhile Grimoald had died, about 662; Childeric II, second son of Clovis, had become king of Austrasia and, after the death of Clothair III in 673, of Neustria also; and the murder of Childeric in 675 had been followed by an outbreak of anarchy. Ebroin, the strong man of Neustria, who had succeeded Erchinoald as mayor of the palace in 659, but whom Childeric had shut up in the monastery of Luxeuil, escaped, killed the new mayor of the palace, Leudesius, Erchinoald's son — there was a tradition that he had been baptised by Fursa — and seemed about to play the rôle of Grimoald for the whole Frankish dominions. It was probably the friends of Childeric who then, to strengthen themselves against the vengeance of Ebroin, recalled Dagobert from Ireland: but Eddi, in his Life of Wilfrid of York, puts it that Dagobert's friends and relatives, hearing from sailors that he was alive, communicated with Wilfrid, who effected the exile's return to Austrasia[21] in 676. Ebroin countered by putting forward Theuderic, or Thierry III, youngest son of Clovis, whom he had been holding a prisoner. The war between Ebroin and Dagobert ended in 677, but in 679 Dagobert was murdered by some Austrasians, perhaps partisans of Ebroin.

---

20 There are two Lives of this saint: (i) by a contemporary at Chelles, where she spent the last years of her life; (ii) an expanded version, of the end of the 8th or beginning of the 9th century. EDS: (i) *AA. SS. Boll.* Jan. II 739–42. — Mabillon *AA. SS. o. s. B.* II 775–84.   (i, ii) Krusch *MGH SS. rer. merov.* II 482–508.

21 It probably was not safe to attempt to bring him back by the direct route to the Loire and then across Gaul.

To complete the story: Ebroin was assassinated in 680, and the new representative of Austrasia, Pippin the Younger, grandson of Pippin the Elder and nephew of Grimoald, became in 689 mayor of the palace for all the Frankish territories. For him and his descendants the road now led direct to the sovereignty of the Franks and the empire of the West.

In the struggle between Ebroin and Dagobert the names of a few personages appear in whom we are interested. Among the partisans of Ebroin were Dado, or Ouen, bishop of Rouen, and Ultán, abbot of Péronne; [22] among those of Dagobert, Philibert of Jumièges and Ansoald, seemingly a relative of bishop Dido of Poitiers, whom he succeeded in that see in or before 675. Philibert was thrown into prison by his former friend Ouen, and, when released, fled to Ansoald, by whom he was granted the island of Herio, on which he built his monastery of Noirmoutier. Ansoald, like his predecessor, had associations with the Irish: he had as a friend Tomianus, Irish bishop of Angoulême, and he reconstructed for Irish " pilgrims " the church of Mazerolles (dept. Vienne, cant. Lussac-les-Châteaux).

292. St. Fridolin of Säckingen — Life by Balther s X ex

Beatus Fridolinus ab extremis partibus . . . cum eo pondere nequeant abire.

MSS: Carlsruhe Landesarchiv MS 429 s XII. — Basel Univ. Bibl. E. II 4 s XV. EDS: Colgan *AA. SS.* 479–92 [from a St. Gall MS now lost].—*AA. SS. Boll.* Mart. I 430–41 [the prologue contains interesting bibliographical information: a portion of the Life was incorporated into a sermon on the translation of the body of St. Hilary by Peter Damian in the eleventh century, published here, Jan. II 81–3]. — F. J. Mone *Quellensammlung der badischen Landesgeschichte* I (Carlsruhe 1848) 1–17, 99–111. — Krusch *MGH SS. rer. merov.* III 350–69 [best; introduction valuable]. — Goldast *Rerum Alamannicarum SS* I (1606) 384 [epitome; also in later eds.]. COMM: Hefele *Geschichte der Einführung des Christenthums in Südwest-Deutschland* (Tübingen 1837) 243–60. — Alois Lütolf *Die Glaubensboten der Schweiz vor S. Gallus* (Lucerne 1871) 267–300. — Herm. Leo *Der heilige Fridolin* (Freiburg i. Br. 1886). — A. Burckhardt " Die Heiligen des Bistums Basel " *Basler Jahrbuch* 1889 pp. 144–71. — Gottfr. Heer *St. Fridolin der Apostel Alämanniens* (Zürich 1889). — Meyer von Knonau " Nochmals die Frage von St. Fridolin " *Anzeiger für schweizer Geschichte* XX (1889) 377–81 [criticism of Heer]. — Schulte " Beiträge zur Kritik der Vita Fridolini des Balther " *Jahrbuch für Schweizergeschichte* XVIII (1893) 134–52. — G. Kurth *Clovis* (Tours 1896; Paris 1901) II 254. — Wattenbach *DGQ* (7th ed. Berlin 1904) I 155. — J. P. Kirsch *Cath. Encycl.* VI (1909).

The Life of St. Fridolin, founder of the monastery of Säckingen (in Baden on the Upper Rhine), was composed by a certain Balther, monk of Säckingen, who, having studied at St. Gall, dedicated the Life to Notker Labeo, a teacher in the monastery of St. Gall

---

[22] *Cf.* no. 300.

who died in 1001. He tells us that he wrote it from memory after having read a Life of the saint at a monastery named Helera. Such a Life had formerly been at Säckingen, but was carried away at the time of a barbarian inroad; still there were many people who remembered having read it and who, apparently, helped out Balther's story with their own recollections. Thus on his own testimony Balther's version must be regarded as untrustworthy: his credibility becomes still more doubtful in view of the fabulous character of much of the Life, the historical improbability of its pictures of conditions and events in the early sixth century, and the absence of all reference to Fridolin in earlier writers. There has been much discussion of this problem, but the conclusion may be summarily stated as being that the whole Life is suspect. It represents Fridolin as an Irishman who came to Poitiers and, under the protection of Clovis I, who had conquered that region in 507, restored the church of St. Hilary and collected his relics. Later he travelled to the river Rhine, founding monasteries in honor of St. Hilary on the way, and, finally, Säckingen, a monastery which by the ninth century had become of much importance. He also labored as a missionary in the surrounding country. The legend is extravagant, and the setting in the reign of the first Clovis quite improbable. If there is a germ of truth in the traditions, it seems probable that Fridolin was at Poitiers during the reign of Clovis II, and perhaps during the episcopate of Dido.[23]

Fridolin became the patron saint of the canton of Glarus, Switzerland, and devotion to him is wide-spread in southern Germany, Switzerland and Austria.[24]

293. *Liber historiae Francorum; Gesta regum Francorum* A.D. 726-7, 736

EDS: [Freher] *Corpus Francicae historiae* (1613) I 55-86. — Duchesne *Historiae Francorum SS.* I (1636) 690-722. — Bouquet II (1739; 2nd ed. 1869) 539-71. — Migne *PL* XCVI 1421-66. — Krusch *MGH SS. rer. merov.* II (1888) 238-328, VII pt. II (1920) 772-5.

The fullest account of the exile and restoration of Dagobert II is in this source, which exists in two editions, the first prepared by a monk of Paris — or of Rouen — in 726 or 727, the second by some dweller in Austrasia in 736. It is a chronicle of considerable importance for the middle and end of the seventh century.[25]

294. Council of Bordeaux A.D. 663 x 675

ED: F. Maassen *MGH Concilia aevi merovingici* I (Hanover 1893) 215-6 [cf. 216 l.19]. Cf. Gams *Series episcoporum* 490; AdeJ *RC* XX 105-6.

One of the subscribers to the acts of this council held at " Modogarnomo castro " on the river Garonne was " Tomianus Aequilesiminus urbis episcopus." This Tomianus,

[23] O. D. Watkin's *History of penance* II (London etc. 1920) 622 points out that the statement that Fridolin was visited by two relatives, priests lately engaged on the mission in Northumbria, suggests a date about 650.

[24] Cf. Gougaud *Gaelic pioneers of Christianity* 141.

[25] The Life of Wilfrid of York by Æddi, or Eddius (no. 66), may be a slightly earlier record of the exile of Dagobert: see cap. xxvi–xxvii (xxvii–xxviii), xxxi (xxxiii). As a result of his share in Dagobert's restoration, Wilfrid suffered much annoyance from Ebroin and his faction when travelling to Rome in 678 and returning in 680.

bishop of Angoulême, is regarded by Celticists as an Irishman, having a name identical with that of his contemporary, Tommene mac Ronain, bishop of Armagh, who died in 661.

295. Ansoald, bishop of Poitiers

(i) *Donatio* of Ansoald to the abbot Philibert, 1 July A.D. 677.   (ii) *Mandatum* of Ansoald to the deacon Launegisel 1 April A.D. 678.

EDS: Léon Maître " Cunauld, son prieuré et ses archives " *Bibl. de l'École des chartes* LIX (1898) 233–61. — J. Tardif "Les Chartes mérovingiennes de Noirmoutier " *Nouvelle Rev. de droit français et étranger* XXIIᵉ année (Paris 1898) 763–90 [text 783–6; also published separately as *Études mérovingiennes* (Paris 1899)]. *Cf.* Antoine Thomas *Annales du Midi* I 51, 394, XI (Jan. 1899) 68–9; AdeJ *RC* XX 105–6.

The original grant of Heri or Herio from Ansoald to Philibert [26] is lost, but a subsidiary charter making certain additional grants, the order for the execution of this instrument, and the record thereof made by the contemporary officials of the municipality of Poitiers, have been preserved in copies of the eleventh century at the château of Cunauld on the Loire. Cunauld was the site of a monastery belonging to Noirmoutier, and was one of the stopping places where the monks of that abbey remained for some years when in the ninth century they abandoned their mother-house before the menace of the Northmen and retired by short stages into Bourgogne.

The subscriptions to the *Donatio* include the following: " Thomeneus, episcoporum minimus, iubente Ansoaldo presule, subscripsi. Romanus, indignus tamen episcopus, subscripsi." The same names are found attached to the *Mandatum*. Thomeneus and Romanus are to be identified with Tomene of Angoulême and Roman, or Ronan, of Mazerolles.[27]

(iii) Ansoald's Will

EDS: Pardessus *Diplomata* II 239. — J. Tardif "Les Chartes mérovingiennes de Noirmoutier " *Nouv. Rev. de droit fr. et étr.* XXIIᵉ année (Paris 1898) 763–90 [text 789–90]. *Cf.* L. Levillain " Les origines du monastère de Nouaillé " *Bibl. de l'École des chartes* LXXI (1910) 281.

In the surviving fragment of his will Ansoald tells of his restoration of Mazerolles: " I found the monastic house of Mazerolles on the river Vienne deserted, without worshippers or services. I completely restored it, and placed over it a holy pilgrim of God of Irish race, Bishop Romanus,[28] with his fellow pilgrims, directing that the pilgrims should abide there permanently." After the death of Romanus, as no suitable successor could be found among its inmates, the community was placed under a certain Chroscelmus, who seems to have been abbot of Nouaillé.

[26] *Cf.* p. 491 *supra.*
[27] *Cf.* no. 294, and *infra.*
[28] It is just possible that this was the Ronan who took part in the Council of Whitby, 664. *Cf.* Bede, *Hist. Eccles.* III xxv.

II. Perrona Scottorum, and the Irish in Picardy and Flanders

Bibliography

Ludwig Traube *Perrona Scottorum, ein Beitrag zur Ueberlieferungsgeschichte und zur Palaeographie des Mittelalters (Sitzungsb. d. philos.-philol. u. d. histor. Cl. d. kgl. bayer. Akad. d. Wissensch.* (Munich 1900) IV 469-538); also in Franz Boll (ed.) *Vorlesungen und Abhandlungen von Ludwig Traube* III (Munich 1920) 95-119 [a brilliant investigation of the hitherto obscure history of the Irish colony at Péronne, and of some questions of Irish palaeography]. — N. Friart *Histoire de St. Fursy et de ses deux frères* (Paris, Brussels, etc. 1913). — Of the works listed at the beginning of the chapter see especially those by Gougaud and Van der Essen, and Margaret Stokes *Three months in the forests of France* 81 *sqq.*

The Irish associations with the northern corner of France and with Belgium under the Merovings seem sufficiently important and self-contained to demand integral treatment. Early in the seventh century Irish religious ideals and customs were introduced here by Columban's disciple, Valery of Leucone; [29] by the Irish (or perhaps British) Caidoc and Fricor, and their disciple Riquier; [30] by St. Amand, a native of Aquitaine, who, we are told, was one of the first to join the Irish movement; [31] and by St. Bathild's monastery of Corbie. [32] But it was with the coming of Fursa and the settlement of an Irish colony at Péronne that the heyday of Irish influence in Picardy and Flanders was inaugurated.

St. Fursa, who was of the next generation after Columbanus, had not the direct influence on European history of the founder of Luxeuil and Bobbio, but in one respect attained an even greater fame. The story of his visions seems to have made a profound impression on the mediaeval mind, both in his native land and throughout the rest of Europe. The incorporation of an abridged account of his career and supernatural experiences into Bede's *Ecclesiastical History* must have contributed much to the dissemination of his renown.

After establishing the monastery of Cnoberesburgh in East Anglia (now Burgh Castle in Suffolk) Fursa journeyed on to France, attracted, it may be, by the spreading influence of the disciples of Columbanus. Of his life in France we know little, except that he won the high regard of Erchinoald, mayor of the palace in Neustria. [33] On the death of the

---

[29] *Cf.* p. 209 *supra.*
[30] *Cf.* no. 280.
[31] *MGH SS. rer. merov.* V 395. For the Lives of Amand, see Molinier *Sources de l'histoire de France* I no. 427; *MGH SS. rer. merov.* V [*cf. ibid.* VII 846-7].
[32] *Cf.* p. 495 *supra.*
[33] *Cf.* p. 496 *supra.*

saint, his body was at once taken possession of by Erchinoald as a sacred treasure for the new church he was just completing at Péronne. This fact, and the uncorrupted state in which the holy man's body was preserved, insured the importance of Péronne as an object of pilgrimage, especially for the men of Ireland.

Within a short time after Fursa's death, his brother Foillan, who had succeeded him at Cnoberesburgh, was driven from East Anglia, and brought his monks to settle at the tomb of their founder. Although the oldest Life of Foillan says that the strangers were, after a short time, expelled — and we know that Foillan himself passed to other spheres of activity [34] — yet another brother, Ultán, is found as abbot there some years later, he is followed by the Irishman Cellan, and various references (collected by Traube) to " Perrona Scottorum " indicate that it continued a peculiarly Irish institution until the end of the eighth century,[35] it may be until its destruction by the Norsemen in 880.

An interesting relationship has been established between the Abbot Cellan and the Anglo-Saxon scholar Aldhelm,[36] and Traube offers evidence suggesting that Péronne constituted, with the neighboring monasteries of Corbie and St.-Riquier, which also have Irish associations, an *entrepôt* on the Continent for Anglo-Saxon manuscripts.

When Foillan left Péronne he went into what is now Belgium, where he received the support of Sts. Ita and Gertrude, of the church of Nivelles, and also of Grimoald, mayor of the palace in Austrasia. Ita was the widow and Gertrude the daughter of Pippin the Elder, of Landen, after whose death, in 640, they had, on the advice of St. Amand, founded at Nivelles a double monastery under Irish discipline. Ita was the first abbess; she was succeeded, in 652, by Gertrude; and she, in 659, by her niece, Vulfetrude, daughter of Grimoald.

Many other Irish monks besides Foillan and his brother Ultán were laboring, then and later, among the Belgic peoples. In the cases of the majority, however, the traditions are obscure and fabulous.

296. St. Fursa

(i) *Vita prima Fursei s* VII   (ii) *Virtutes Fursei s* IX *in*

(i) Fuit vir vitae venerabilis . . . adjuvante d. n. J. C. qui c. P. et S. s. v. et r. in s. s.   Amen.   (ii) Rem actam adque gestam . . . praestante d. n. J. C. qui v. et r. per o. s. s.   Amen.

MSS: Very numerous.   See the *MGH* eds. and *An. Boll.* XVII 28 *sqq.*   With some exceptions they fall into three classes, those having the *Vita prima* only, those which

---

[34] *Cf.* no. 298 *infra.*
[35] AU 779: " Moinan mac Cormaic, abbot of Fursa's monastery in France, died."
[36] *Cf.* no. 306.

add the *Virtutes*, and those which add the *Additamentum Nivialense de Fuilano* (no. 298 *infra*). Eds: Capgrave *Nova Legenda Anglie* (ed. Horstman, Oxford 1901) I 461-8 [epitome]. — Surius *De probatis sanctorum historiis* I (Cologne 1576) 381-8; (Cologne 1617) I 259 *sqq* [*Vita*]. — *AA. SS. Boll.* Jan. II 36-44; 401-8 of 1863 ed. [*Vita, Virtutes*]. — Colgan *AA. SS.* (Louvain 1645) 75 *sqq.* — Mabillon *AA. SS. o. s. B.* II (Paris 1669) 299-315; 2nd ed. 287-96. — *AA. SS. ex Cod. S.* 77-112 [poor text]. — Krusch *MGH SS. rer. merov.* IV (Hanover and Leipsic 1902) 423-49 [best ed.; *cf.* *ibid.* VII pt. II 837 *sqq*]. Comm: Grützmacher *ZK* XIX (1898) 190-6 [important]. — C. Plummer *Baedae opera historica* II 169-74. — C. S. Boswell *An Irish precursor of Dante* (London 1908) 166-9.

(iii) *Vita secunda s* XI/XII

[Prologue] Considerans, reverende frater. . . . [Vita] Igitur tempore . . . divinis virtutibus, adiuvante d. n. J. C. qui cum P. et S. s. v. et r. in s. s. Amen. [Miracula] Gloriosi confessoris. . . . Egregius itaque Christi . . . trino in unitate Deo, qui v. et r. in s. s. Amen. [Epilogue] Elimatis, carissime frater . . . fideliter proferantur.

Ed: *AA. SS. Boll.* Jan. II 44-54 (408-18 of 1863 ed.).

(iv) Irish Life

In tan ro bái Sigbert hi rrighe Saxan . . . feghadh Bethaid Fursa 7 fogheba iatt.

MSS: Brussels Bibl. roy. 2324-40 ff. 158-60. — RIA A. iv. 1 (Stowe 9) pp. 165-74 [*Cf.* pp. 40, 309 *supra*.] Ed: WS *RC* XXV (1904) 385-404 [with trans.].

Bede in his *Ecclesiastical History* [37] gives an account of the career of St. Fursa and of his visions, derived mainly from a " little book " of the saint's Life to which he refers. The story of his visions of heaven and hell is the earliest example of this kind of Irish literature, which was to have so great an influence on the imagination of Ireland and of Europe in later centuries.

The *Vita prima* is evidently a close reproduction of the text used by Bede. It tells of Fursa's journey to England, after A.D. 630, and founding of a monastery in the dominions of King Sigbert (King of East Anglia, who, after retiring to a monastery, was killed, not later than 644). About 640 x 644 Fursa crossed to France, established a monastery at Lagny, on the Marne river a few miles from Paris, and performed wonderful miracles, of which we are told in the *Virtutes*. He was on intimate terms with Erchinoald, and, perhaps, with Clovis II and St. Bathild. He died probably in 649,[38] and, as has been stated above, was buried at Péronne.[39] The *Vita prima* and the *Virtutes*, though containing much that is fabulous, are of substantial historical value. Krusch thinks that the *Vita prima* was written in the seventh century, not

---

[37] III xix.

[38] AU.

[39] He set out to visit his brothers in " Saxonia," *i.e.*, England, but died on the way at Maceriae (Mézerolles, in Ponthieu on the Authie: *cf.* Mabillon *op. cit.* II 310). The *Annales Laubienses* (Martène *Thesaurus anecdotorum* III 1410-31; *MGH SS* IV 9-20) refer to his pilgrimage to Gaul, and the coming of Foillan and Ultán, under the year 649.

long after Fursa's death, and the *Virtutes* about the beginning of the ninth century. The *Vita secunda* is attributed to two monks, Serlo and Rotbertus, but has as preface an epistle by Arnulf, abbot of Lagny, who died in 1106.[40]

297. Life of St. Eloquius

EDS: (i) Surius *De probatis SS. hist.* 3 Dec. VII (1581) 977-8; 3rd ed. XII (1618) 120. (ii) *Analectes pour servir à l'hist. ecclés. de la Belgique* V (1868) 344-54. *Cf.* Boll. *Bibl. hag. lat.* no. 377. COMM: E. Sackur *Deutsche Zs. f. Geschichtswissensch.* II (Freiburg i. Br. 1889) 376-81.

Eloquius or Éloque, said to be an Irishman, was Fursa's successor as abbot of Lagny. The oldest version of his Life was written at the monastery of Waulsort not earlier than the tenth century.

298. St. Foillan

(i) *Additamentum Nivialense de Fuilano s* VII

Post discessu vero . . . beneficia orationum, adiuvante d. n. J. C., qui cum P. et S. s. v. et r. per o. s. s. Amen.

MSS: See under Fursa, and Krusch's introd. to his ed. ED: Krusch *MGH SS. rer. merov.* IV (1902) 449-51 [*cf.* VII pt. II 837 *sqq*]. COMM: Berlière " La plus ancienne vie de St. Foillan " *Rev. Bénédictine* IX (1892) 137-9.

(ii) *Vita prima*, by Paul

In nomine Domini incipit descriptio beati Foillani . . . a devotis percipitur, praestante D. n. J. C., qui v. et r. cum D. P. in unitate eiusdem S. s. per o. s. s. Amen.

MSS: Brussels Bibl. roy. 9742 *s* XII; 7483 *s* XIII; 18654 *s* XII. ED: *AA. SS. Boll.* Oct. XIII (1883) 381-5.

(iii) *Vita altera*

Benignum Dominum Deum nostrum. . . . Plurimorum quidem sanctorum . . . quae salutifera sunt, poscentium, praestante D. n. I. C., qui cum D. P. et S. s. v. et r. D. per o. s. s. Amen.

MSS: Berlin 791 *s* XI. — Namur Séminaire 45 *s* XI/XII f. 110ᵛ-3ᵛ. — Metz 395 *s* XI. — Brussels Bibl. roy. 18653-7 *s* XII f. 73ᵛ-9ᵛ; 7460 *s* XIII f. 940-3. — Trèves 1151 IV (olim 965) *s* XIII. EDS: *AA. SS. Boll.* Oct. XIII 385-90. *Cf.* Colgan *AA. SS.* 90-100. — *Nova Legenda Anglie* has an abridgment of this Life (ed. Horstman, Oxford 1901 pp. 447-50).

(iv) *Vita tertia*

Circa tempora quibus in Francia . . . velut inter ignes luna minores.

MSS: Brussels Bibl. roy. 8928 *s* XVII; 18654; 10850. ED: *AA. SS. Boll.* Oct. XIII 391-5.

[40] Hymns in honor of St. Fursa, " Laudes almi confessoris " and " Laeta plaude Hibernia," are published in *AA. SS. Boll.* Jan. II 36 (400-1 of the 1863 ed.). *Cf.* also *Bibl. hagiog. lat.* I (Brussels 1898-9), and the *Supplementum* (1911); Plummer *Misc. hag. Hib.* Cat. nos. 141-2; and no. 233 *supra.*

(v) *Vita quarta*, in verse, by Hillin *s* XII *in*

[Introductory Acrostic] His ita literulis libet insinuare notatis . . . 9 ll. [The acrostic reads: Hillinus Cantor Levita Fossensis Cenobii.] [Prologue] Quo dicante mihi lenis fuit ira magistri . . . 46 ll. [Vita] Praesul Foillanus, martyrque Dei venerandus. . . . Flamine cum sancto tempore perpetuo. A very long poem. Followed by a 4 ll. prayer: O Foillane, Dei martyr, civis paradisi. . . . Ecclesiae sanctus, detque pius Dominus.

MS: Brussels Bibl. roy. 8928. ED: *AA. SS. Boll.* Oct. XIII 395–408.

(vi) *Vita quinta* by Philippe de Harvengt *s* XII

[Prologue] Rogatus, et instanter rogatus. . . . [Vita] Ut vita martyris . . . aeternaliter glorietur, qui est super omnia Deus benedictus in s. s. Amen.

MSS: Mons 8439 *s* XIII. — BN 5371 *s* XIII. EDS: Migne *PL* CCIII 1325–38. — *AA. SS. Boll.* Oct. XIII 408–16. *Cf.* Colgan *AA. SS.* 100–2. On St. Foillan *cf.* J. Rousseau *Vie de s. Feuillien, évêque et martyr, patron de la ville de Fosses* (Liége 1739). — Corblet *Hagiographie du diocèse d'Amiens* IV (Paris 1874) 277, V 75. — Margaret Stokes *Three months in the forests of France* (London 1895) 127 *sqq.* — Van der Essen *Études d'hagiographie médiévale* II (*Analectes pour servir à l'histoire ecclési-astique de la Belgique* 1906); *Étude* [p. 486 *supra*] 149–61.

Foillan (Faelan, Faolan, Foelan) was St. Fursa's brother and succeeded him as abbot of Cnoberesburgh.[41] Compelled by the outbreak of war to abandon that institution, he journeyed to his brother's tomb at Péronne, where he was well received by Erchin-oald, mayor of the palace. Later he resided for a time at Nivelles, the monastery of St. Ita and St. Gertrude, and finally founded a monastery of his own at Fosses [42] (near Namur). He is said to have been murdered by robbers, apparently about 655.[43] The *Vita prima* of Fursa, and the so-called *Additamentum Nivialense*, an appendix to that text written by a monk of Nivelles not long after Foillan's death, are the earliest sources. The other Lives of Foillan seem to be of the eleventh century or later.[44]

299. St. Gertrude

(i) *Vita prima c* A.D. 670. (ii) *Virtutes c* A.D. 700. (iii) Appendix to the *Virtutes c* A.D. 783. (iv) Expansion of the *Vita prima*, sometimes called the *Vita tertia s* XI. (v) *Vita tripartita c* A.D. 1100.

EDS: (i) Surius *De probatis sanctorum historiis* II (Cologne 1578) 302–6; 2nd ed. 197. — J. G. a Ryckel *Vitae S. Gertrudis* (Louvain 1632); *Historia sanctae Gertrudis* (Brussels 1637). — *AA. SS. Boll.* Mar. II (1668) 594-600. — Mabillon *AA. SS. o. s. B.* II (1669) 463-72, 2nd ed. 445 *sqq.* — Krusch *MGH SS. rer. merov.* II (1888) 447–74 [also

---

[41] *Cf.* Bede *Hist. Eccl.* III xix.

[42] Fosses was still a " Monasterium Scottorum " in the ninth century: Einhard *Translatio SS. Mar-cellini et Petri* IX 86 (composed in 830) in *AA. SS. Boll.* Jun. I 198.

[43] The *Additamentum Nivialense* says that the mayor of the palace, Grimoald, and his friend, Dido, bishop of Poitiers, arrived at Nivelles the day the body of Foillan was brought there, and helped to carry it into the monastery.

[44] Hymns in honor of St. Foillan are published by the Bollandists, and by Moran *Essays* (Dublin 1864) 327–8.

ii, iii; *cf.* VII pt. II 791–7]. (iv, v) J. G. a Ryckel *op. cit.* COMM: Van der Essen *Étude* 1 *sqq* [he points out the imperfections of Ryckel's ed.].

The *Vita prima* is a valuable source for the careers of St. Foillan and St. Ultán, and for the history of the Irish religious influences in Belgium. It was written by a contemporary, a monk of Nivelles, and, it appears, an Irishman. If this last is correct, he was one of the earliest of Irish hagiographers, being about coeval with Tírechán, the writer on St. Patrick.

300. Texts relating to St. Ultán

(i) Life of St. Rictrude, abbess of Marchiennes, by Hucbald of St.-Amand A.D. 907

EDS: *AA. SS. Boll.* Mai. III 79–89. — Mabillon *AA. SS. o. s. B.* II 937–50. — Ghesquière *AA. SS. Belgii* IV 488 *sqq.* — Migne *PL* CXXXII 829–48. — *MGH SS. rer. merov.* VI (1913).

(ii) Life of St. Eusebia, abbess of Hamay *s* X *ex* (?)

EDS: *AA. SS. Boll.* Mar. II 450–7. — Mabillon *op. cit.* II 984–90.

(iii) Life of St. Amatus, or Amé, bishop of Sens *s* XI

EDS: *AA. SS. Boll.* Sept. IV 120–31. — Ghesquière *op. cit.* IV 589–93. On the relation of these three *vitae* to Ultán see Traube *op. cit.* (p. 500 *supra*) 481–2; also works by Martin and Levillain noted on p. 489 *supra*.

St. Rictrude (d. 687), widow of a Frankish nobleman Adalbald, entered the double monastery of Marchiennes, originally founded by St. Amand, and became abbess. Her daughter Eusebia became abbess of the neighboring house of Hamay, and her son Mauront founded the monastery of Breuil near St.-Amand. Marchiennes was destroyed by Norsemen in 879, and the older Life of Rictrude perished. In 907 a well-known hagiographer, Hucbald of St.-Amand,[45] wrote a new Life. He was a historian of honesty and good sense, and seems to have used the surviving traditions and various scattered sources with care. His text [46] is the authority for the statement that King Thierry III (which means the mayor of the palace Ebroin) had St. Amatus, or Amé, bishop of Sens, confined in the monastery of Péronne under the abbot Ultán. The similar statements in the Lives of Eusebia [47] and Amé [48] seem to be copied, or amplified, from Hucbald's work. The story comes into the Rictrude cycle because Amé was, we are told, transferred to the care of Mauront at Breuil after the death of Ultán.

301. Life of St. Goban

Mundi Salvator, humanae calamitati . . . mirabilia post mortem, ad laudem Dei et Domini n. J. C., quem praedicaverat per vitam, qui v. et r. cum P. et S. s. in s. s. Amen.

ED: *AA. SS. Boll.* Jun. IV 21–5 (ed. 1867 V 19–22).

45 *Cf.* p. 592 *infra.*   46 II xxiv.   47 *Cap.* i.   48 *Cap.* iv *sqq.*

Goban (the name is familiar to students of Irish legend) was a disciple of St. Fursa. His existence is vouched for by Bede,[49] otherwise it might be called in doubt, for the *Vita* is worthy of little trust. He is said to have been killed in Gaul about 670.

302. Life of St. Madelgisil, or Mauguille, by Hariulf *c* A.D. 1090

[Prologue] Domino dilectissimo Patrique. . . . [Vita] Francorum regnum tenente Lodoveo . . . aegritudinem continuo deposuit, adiuvante merito sancti per gratiam D. n. J. C., cui est h. et g. in s.   Amen.

EDS: Mabillon *AA. SS. o. s. B.* IV ii 537-44, 2nd ed. 548-55. — *AA. SS. Boll.* Mai. VII 265-9, 3rd ed. 260-4. — Migne *PL* CLXXIV 1441-50. *Cf.* Corblet *Hagiographie du diocèse d'Amiens* III (1873) 226-35; F. Lot *Hariulf: Chronique de l'abbaye de Saint-Riquier* (Paris 1894) pp. x-xi.

Madelgisil, or Mauguille, was, according to tradition, a companion of Fursa who became a hermit in Ponthieu and died *c* 685. His Life was written by Hariulf of Saint-Riquier,[50] and dedicated to Gervin II, bishop of Amiens (d. 1102). Little reliance can be placed on it.

303. The Acts of St. Adalgisus, or Algéis

ED: *AA. SS. Boll.* Jun. I 223-7 (3rd ed. 217-22). *Cf. Hist. lit. de la France* VII (1746) 190.

This saint was, we are told, a priest of Thiérache in Picardy who lived in the middle of the seventh century. According to his Life, found in a manuscript from a monastery of St. Foillan, he was of Irish origin. The Life, however, is probably fictitious, being plagiarised from the accounts of Fursa given in Bede and elsewhere.

304. Life of St. Etton, or Zé

ED: *AA. SS. Boll.* Jul. III 48-62. *Cf.* A. Delobelle *Saint Etton, évêque patron de Dompierre* (Dompierre 1892). — Van der Essen *Étude* 282-4.

Etton is represented to have been an Irishman who settled at a place called Fescau,[51] near Dompierre (Nord). The Life is late, probably eleventh century, and legendary. Etton is brought into association with the saints Amand, Vincent Madelgaire, Gertrude, Foillan and Ultán.

305. Life of St. Vincent Madelgaire

EDS: (i) Poncelet *An. Boll.* XII 422 *sqq.* (ii) *AA. SS. Boll.* 14 Jul. III 657-77. COMM: Van der Essen *Étude* 284-8.

Madelgaire, a native of Hainault, became a monk, adopting the name Vincent, and founded a monastery on his estate at Soignies. His Life, which in the oldest extant

[49] *H'st. Eccl.* III xix.
[50] *Cf.* no. 280 (iii).
[51] The Irishman Hetto of Fescau is mentioned in the *Gesta episcoporum Cameracensium* (II xxxiv). a work compiled in A.D. 1041-4. Ed: Pertz *MGH SS* VII 393 *sqq.*

form is probably of the beginning of the eleventh century, and also the Life of Etton, makes Vincent go on a journey to Ireland, whence he brought back Fursa, Foillan, Ultán, Éloque, Algéis and Etton. But Van der Essen has shown that this story must be a late accretion.

306. Cellanus

(i) Cellanus to Aldhelm

Domino lectricibus ditato . . . integro pausat corpore.

(ii) Aldhelm to Cellanus

Miror, quod me tantillum . . . [a single sentence].

In William of Malmesbury *De gestis pontificum Anglorum* V cxci, clxxxviii. Eds: N. E. S. A. Hamilton *Willelmi Malmesbiriensis De gestis* etc. (RS: London 1870) 333, 337. — Traube *Perrona Scottorum* 477–9.

(iii) Verses by Cellanus

Istam Patricius sanctus sibi vindicat aulam. . . Ambo stelligeri capientes praemia caeli. 8 ll. Quid Vermendensis memorem tot milia plebis. . . . Haec modo Cellanus, venerandi nominis abbas, Iussit dactilico discrivi carmina versu. 10 ll.

MS: Florence Bibl. Laurenziana Cod. lat. plut. LXVI 40 *s* IX ff. 61–2. Eds: Bandini *Cat. cod. lat. Bibl. Mediceae* II 812. — Traube *Perrona Scottorum* 484–9. — KM *Ériu* V (1911) 110–1. *Cf.* Roger *L'Enseignement* 260; Levison *ZCP* XX (1936) 382–90.

William of Malmesbury,[52] in his *De gestis pontificum Anglorum*, completed in A.D. 1125, has saved for us part of a correspondence between Cellanus, abbot of *Perrona Scottorum*, and the English scholar Aldhelm.[53]   Moreover there is, in a Florentine manuscript of the ninth century, a collection of short sets of distichs on various subjects, of which the two longest, in hexameters, seem to be an inscription for a chapel dedicated to St. Patrick, and an inscription for another church in Picardy.[54]   The second contains the name of Cellanus, and Traube makes it almost certain that all were written by, or under the direction or influence of, Cellanus of Péronne, who died in 706.[55]   The Patrick verses are important evidence for the history of devotion to that saint.[56]

307. *Fundatio monasterii Blandiniensis*

Eds: F. Van de Putte *Annales abbatiae s. Petri Blandiniensis* (Ghent 1841) 65–9; *Annales de la Soc. d'émulation pour l'hist. et les antiquités de la Flandre occid.* 1st ser.

[52] *Cf.* p. 608 *infra.*   [53] *Cf.* no. 62.
[54] Some of the briefer texts also have the appearance of being inscriptions.
[55] If the Cellanus of the Lorscher Annals (no. 308), and the Cellan mac Sechnusaigh of AU, are the same man as Cellanus of Péronne.
[56] It may be noted that Patrick is mentioned in the *Vita s. Gertrudis* (no. 299), written by an Irishman at Nivelles *c* A.D. 670.— In the Leningrad (Petersburg) Codex Q.I. 15 *s* VIII (Ir. script?) f. 63ᵛ (published in facs. by A. E. Burn, *Facsimiles of the Creeds* (London 1909) pl. XIX) there is a curious acrostic in 32 ll., *Iohannis celsi rimans misteria caeli.*   It is found also in the Leningrad Codex F. XIV. 1 *s* VIII/IX, a MS written in the Corbie script but, Traube thinks, probably at the monastery of St. Riquier, near Corbie and Péronne.   The acrostic has been published by E. Miller, *Journal des Savants* 1876, p. 117.   Burn suggests that Cellanus may be the author.

III 200. — Holder-Egger *MGH SS.* XV ii 621-4. *Cf. AA. SS. Boll.* Nov. I 358, 375; Wattenbach *DGQ* I⁶ (1893) 384.

This account of the foundation of the monastery of St. Peter of Mount Blandin, in Ghent, gives some information regarding St. Celestinus, an Irishman who became abbot there *c* 682.

308. The Lorscher Annals

Eds: Ussermann *Germaniae sacrae prodromus* I (1790) p. xxxv. — *MGH SS.* I (1826) 22-30. — Eberhard Katz *Jahresbericht des öffentl. Stiftsuntergymnasiums der Benedictiner zu St. Paul in Kärnten* (St. Paul 1889). *Cf.* Wattenbach I⁶ 145. — Monod *Études critiques sur les sources de l'histoire carolingienne* I *Annales carolingiennes* (*Bibl. de l'École des Hautes Études* fasc. CXIX) (Paris 1898) 84-5.

The " Lorscher Annals," ⁵⁷ so named from the abbey of Lorsch, in the Grand Duchy of Hesse, near Worms, cover the years 703 to 768. Among their obituary notices are several distinctively Irish names: 704 Conan, bishop; 705 Domnan, abbot; 706 Cellan, abbot; 707 Tigermal; 726 Dubdecris,⁵⁸ abbot; 729 Macflatheus; perhaps 727 Daniel of Lagny.

The following personages, whose legends describe them as Irish, are not connected with the Fursa group. The texts have little solid basis, and the Irish origin, and in some cases perhaps the existence, of the several saints is dubious.

309. St. Monon

Eds: (The shorter Life) Surius *De prob. SS. historiis* 18 Oct. VII (1581) 783-5. — *AA. SS. Boll.* Oct. VIII 367-9. — Barbier *Analectes pour servir à l'hist. ecclés. de la Belgique* V (1868) 410-4. (The longer Life) Poncelet *An. Boll.* V (1886) 193-206 [207-8 hymns]. *Cf.* Van der Essen *Étude* 144-9.

This saint is presented to us as an Irishman who, in the time of Bishop John of Tongres (d. 646/647), settled as a hermit in the forest of Ardenne, and was there murdered by robbers. The extant Lives were written at the end of the tenth or in the first half of the eleventh century.⁵⁹

---

⁵⁷ It is necessary to distinguish carefully between the several sets of annals associated with the name of Lorsch.

⁵⁸ *I.e.,* " Dub-dá-chrich."

⁵⁹ Monon is mentioned by Hériger, abbot of Lobbes (d. 1007), in his *Gesta episcoporum Tungrensium* xxxi (ed. in *MGH SS* VII 161 *sqq*; Migne *PL* CXXXIX 957 *sqq*).

310. Life of St. Livinus

EDS: (i) Serarius *Epistolae s. Bonifacii* (Munich 1605) 233–52 [poor]. — Mabillon *AA. SS. o. s. B.* II 449–61. — Ghesquière *AA. SS. Belgii* III 96. — Migne *PL* LXXXVII 327–44, LXXXIX 871–88. (ii) Surius *De prob. SS. hist.* VII (Cologne 1581) 825–6. COMM: Nurnberger *NA* VIII (1883) 325. — O. Holder-Egger " Zu den Heiligengeschichten des Genter St. Bavoskloster" *Historische Aufsätze dem Andenken an G. Waitz gewidmet* (Hanover 1886) 622–65 [an important piece of destructive criticism]. — Descamps *Vie de s. Liévin* (Tournai 1891). — Wattenbach *DGQ⁶* I 132, 387; II 493.

St. Livinus, Livin, or Liévin, apostle of Brabant, was, his biographer informs us, a native of Ireland. It is related that he suffered martyrdom about 660. The biographer calls himself " Bonifacius peccator," and was once thought to have been the great St. Boniface. Holder-Egger has shown that the Life is a fictitious production, posterior to 1007, and that even the existence of Livinus is doubtful. It is probable that he is a doublet of the English St. Liafwin, or Lebuin, (d. 773), of Deventer in Holland. In any case, its testimony is of more value for the fame of Irish missionaries in the mind of a hagiographer of the eleventh century than for the authenticity of an Irish Livinus in the seventh.[60]

311. Saints Wiro, Odger and Plechelm

(i) Life of St. Wiro

EDS: *AA. SS. Boll.* Mai. II 309–20, VII 654–5. — Willemsen *Publications de la soc. hist. et archéol. dans le duché de Limbourg* XXII (1885). *Cf. Nova Legenda Anglie* (ed. Horstman, Oxford 1901) II 444–6.

(ii) Life of St. Odger

EDS: *AA. SS. Boll.* Sept. III 612–5. — Ghesquière *AA. SS. Belgii* VI 219–25. — Willemsen *loc. cit.*

(iii) Life of St. Plechelm

EDS: *AA. SS. Boll.* Jul. IV 50–60. — Ghesquière *loc. cit.* 199–218. — Willemsen *loc. cit.* COMM: A. Wolters *De heil. Wiro, Plechelmus en Odgerus en het Kapittel van Sint-Odilienberg* (Roermonde 1862). — Willemsen *Limburgsch Jaarboek* V (1897–8) 159–83 [re the nationality of the saints]. — Van der Essen *Étude* 105–9.

These three saints are honored at Roermonde, in the province of Limburg, Holland. There, at Mont-Sainte-Odile, they founded a monastery on land given them by Pippin of Heristal. They died about the end of the seventh century. Wiro and Plechelm are said to have been Irish, Odger British or English. The Life of Wiro seems to be of the ninth century: the other two are later than, and dependent on, it. They have not much value as historical sources.

---

[60] There is extant a set of verses which purport to be an epistle from Livinus to a certain abbot Florbert of Ghent. They are actually of the eleventh century. Ussher *Sylloge* (Dublin 1632) 19, *Whole Works* IV 423–6. — Mabillon *AA. SS. o. s. B. s.* II 404. — Migne *PL* LXXXVII 345–6. *Cf.* Holder-Egger *op. cit.*

312. Life of Sts. Lugle and Luglian

Post gloriosissimam Domini . . . glorificat in terris: ad l. et g. nominis sui, quod est benedictum in s. Amen.

EDS: A. Herbi *Vita ss. fratrum Luglii et Lugliani* (Atrebati 1579) 7–31. — Ghesquière *et al. Acta Sanctorum Belgii* VI (Tongerloae 1794) 1–19. — *AA. SS. Boll.* Oct. X 108–22. COMM: Dangez *La vie des s. frères martyrs Lugle et Luglien* (Montdidier 1862). — V. de Beauville *Examen de quelques passages d'une dissertation de M. l'abbé Dangez sur la vérité du fait de la translation des reliques de s. Lugle et Luglien à Montdidier* (Amiens 1862). — Van der Essen *Étude* 418–20.

Saints Lugle and Luglian were two brothers, pilgrims from Ireland, who suffered martyrdom in northern France, in a forest near the town of Thérouanne, towards the end of the seventh century. This Life, which is quite fabulous, was written, at the earliest, in the tenth century.

313. Life of St. Oda

ED: Thysius in Ghesquière *AA. SS. Belgii* VI 587–631. COMM: Van der Essen *Étude* 192–7.

Nothing is known of Oda except that she was the patroness of Sint-Oden-Roey, near Bommel, in N. Brabant. Her Life was written in the second half of the twelfth century by Guetzelo, a priest of Rolduc. It seems to have been based on the local legend and some arbitrary borrowings from other *vitae*. It gives an Irish origin to Oda, and places her about the beginning of the eighth century.

314. Life of St. Dympna

Suave redolentis . . . communiter cum gaudio referentes Domino n. J. C., qui v. et r. per o. s. s.   Amen.

EDS: Surius *De probatis sanctorum historiis* II (Cologne 1617) 216. — *AA. SS. Boll.* Mai. III 479–89 [475–84 ed. 1866]. COMM: Messingham *Florilegium* (Paris 1624) 343–9 [epitome]. — Bogaerts *Dympne d'Irlande: légende du VIIe siècle* (Antwerp 1840). — Kuyl *Legende der martelaaren van Gheel, ss. Dymphna en Gerebernus* (Antwerp 1860); *Gheel vermaerd door den eerdienst der heilige Dymphna* (Antwerp 1863).—*Hist. litt. de la France* XXVII (1877) 404. — Heuckenkamp *Die heilige Dimphna* (Halle, Saxony, 1887) [dissertation]. — Janssens *Ste. Dimphne, patronne de Gheel* (Lierre 1894). — Van der Essen *Étude* 313–20.

In the thirteenth century a certain Pierre, canon of the church of St. Aubert of Cambrai, wrote a *Vita* of St. Dympna, or Dymphna, who had long been venerated at the town of Gheel near Antwerp. The Life was written at the request of Guido, bishop of Cambrai (probably Guiardus or Guido de Lauduno 1234–47), and is said to be based on oral traditions. It has no historical value, but considerable folk-lore interest. It is, of course, possible that the popular tradition was accurate as to the Irish nationality of the saint. She is venerated as a patroness against insanity, and Gheel is famous as a sanatorium for the treatment of lunatics.

Irish hagiologists have sometimes identified Dympna with Damnat, patroness of the monastery for women called Tech-Damnata, " Damnat's house " (Tedavnet, Monaghan).[61]

[61] *Cf.* Margaret Stokes *Early Christian art in Ireland* (1887) 97–9.

III. The Irish Missionaries in South-Western Germany

While some Irish clerics were promoting monasticism and Christian faith and morals in seventh-century Gaul, others, towards the eastern frontiers of the Frankish empire, were converting to the religion of Christ the pagan, or semi-pagan, Germanic peoples. Christianity had survived here since Roman times, but Christians were, relatively to Gaul, few and feeble. In the central districts, Thuringia and Franconia, and more particularly in the southern, Alemannia or Suabia and Bavaria, the main work of evangelisation was done by Celtic, or Celtic-trained, monks and hermits during the seventh and early eighth centuries. We know that Columbanus and Gall, perhaps a disciple of Gall named Magnus, and Fridolin of Säckingen, had labored here, and also that the monastery of Luxeuil exercised an influence to the east of the Rhine as well as to the west. Columbanus had brought both Irish and Britons to Luxeuil, and in later days Irish and Britons shared in the conversion of Suabians and Bavarians. The written records of their work, however, have almost entirely perished.[62]

315. Life of St. Wendelinus

ED: *AA. SS. Boll.* 21 Oct. IX 342–51. *Cf.* Boll. *Bibl. hag. lat.* no. 1275. COMM: Ph. Heber *Die vorkarolingischen christl. Glaubensboten am Rhein* (Frankfort a. M. 1858) 172–5. — Lesker *St. Wendelinus* (Donauwörth 1898). — Zürcher *St. Wendelinus-Buch* (Menzingen 1903).

Wendelin was a hermit in the district of Trèves from whose cell the abbey of Tholey developed. The date of his death is usually given as 607 or 617, but it seems probable that his *floruit* was really later in the seventh century. His Life, written in the later middle ages, says that he was " exortus Scotorum regione," which may enshrine an old tradition that he was of Irish birth. Such a tradition, however, might have no value for the historical fact.

316. *Acta* of Sts. Marinus and Annianus, apostles of Bavaria

(i) *Vita*   (ii) Legend in verse   (iii, iv) Sermons

EDS: Johannes à Via *Vita ss. Marini . . . et Aniani* (Munich 1579) [iv]. — *Monumenta Boica* I (1763) 343–50 [ii]. — Holder-Egger *NA* XIII (1888) 22–8, 585 [i, part of ii, iii]. — Bern. Sepp *Vita ss. Marini et Anniani* (Ratisbon 1892) [i, ii, iii, iv]. COMM:

---

[62] Thaddaeus, abbot at Ratisbon about the middle of the fifteenth century, wrote a *Chronica fundationis Scotorum* relating to Kilian, Virgilius, and other Irish missionaries in Germany. Extracts are given in Canisius *Antiq. lect.* IV ii 473–4; ed. Basnage IV (Antwerp 1725) 752. *Cf.* Ussher *Works* IV 462. Little attention has been paid to it, but it probably has no special historical value.

Raderus *Bavaria sancta* I (1704) 87–92. — Wm. Reeves *Proc. RIA* VIII 295–300. — Riezler *Forschungen z. deut. Gesch.* XVIII (1878) 540. — Wattenbach *DGQ* II⁶ 378. — Boll. *Bibl. hag. lat.* 813–4.

The monastery of Rot on the river Inn, in south-eastern Bavaria, held in especial honor the saints Marinus and Annianus, whose remains rested within its walls. They had been removed thither from the village of Aurisium, where, according to the legend, they had been exhumed in the first half of the eighth century. This, we are further told, was about a century after their death, which on this testimony would have taken place in the earlier part of the seventh century. They were Irishmen who, returning from Rome, settled in Bavaria, where they taught the people until Marinus was martyred by invading barbarians and, on the same day, Annianus died a natural death. Manifestly, this is all legendary matter of indeterminate historical value.

317. St. Kilian of Würzburg and his companions

(i) *Passio prima c* A.D. 840

Fuit vir vitae venerabilis . . . sublevati sunt, regnante Pippino primo orientalium Francorum rege feliciter [sublevati sunt, qui etiam . . . per s. s. Amen.]

For the MSS of the two Passions, which are numerous, see the classified lists in the *MGH* eds. Eds: H. Canisius *Antiquae lectionis* tom. IV ii (Ingoldstadt 1603) 642–7 [ed. J. Basnage (Amsterdam 1725) III i 180–2]. — Mabillon *AA. SS. o. s. B.* II (Paris 1669) 991–3, 2nd ed. 951–3 [text of Canisius]. — *AA. SS. Boll.* Jul. II (Antwerp 1721) 612–4. — Franz Emmerich *Der heilige Kilian, Regionarbischof und Märtyrer historisch-kritisch dargestellt* (Würzburg 1896) 3–10 [good critical ed.; the work is a valuable collection of *monumenta Kiliana*]. — W. Levison *MGH SS. rer. merov.* V (Hanover and Leipsic 1910) 711–28 [best ed.]. Comm: Göpfert *St. Kilianus-Büchlein* (Würzburg 1877, 2nd ed. 1902). — Stamminger *Franconia sancta* I (Würzburg 1881) 58–133. — Hauck *Kirchengeschichte Deutschlands*² I (1898) 370–2 [3rd and 4th eds. 386 *sqq*]; *s. v.* in *Realencyklopädie f. prot. Theologie u. Kirche.* — Wattenbach *DGQ*⁶ (1893) I 124, II 386, 504. — S. Riezler " Die Vita Kiliani " *NA* XXVIII (1903) 232–4. — Hefner " Das Leben des heiligen Burchard " *Archiv des historischen Vereins von Unter-franken und Aschaffenburg* XLV [also published separately: Würzburg 1904]. — *An. Boll.* XX 434.

(ii) *Passio secunda s* IX

[Prologue] Sanctorum Martyrum certamina. . . . [Passio] Beatus Kylianus Scotorum . . . manifestare curabimus, ad l. et g. D. n. J. C., qui c. P. et S. s. v. et r. D. per infinita s. s. Amen.

Eds: Surius *De probatis sanctorum historiis* IV (Cologne 1573) 131–5 [incomplete]. — Serarius *S. Kiliani Franciae orientalis quae et Franconia dicitur apostoli gesta* (Würzburg 1598) [text of Surius]; *Opuscula theologica* I (1611) 318–21 [reprint]. — J. P. Ludewig *Geschichtschreiber von dem Bischofthum Würtzburg* (Frankfort 1713) 966–93 [text of Surius]. — Canisius *loc. cit.* 628–41 [ed. Basnage III i 174–9]. — Messingham *Florilegium* (1624) 318–24 [text of Canisius]. — *AA. SS. Boll.* Jul. II 614–9 [text of Canisius]. — Franz Emmerich *op. cit.* 11–25 [best ed.]. An abridgment is in *Nova Legenda Anglie* (ed. Horstman, Oxford, 1901) II 128–9.

Cillianus, or Kilian, is reputed to have been an Irish bishop who went to the continent with eleven companions and became the apostle of Thuringia and Eastern Franconia. At Würzburg, in or about the year 689, he and his co-workers Colman and Totman were murdered. Burchard, first bishop of Würzburg under St. Boniface, transferred their relics in 752 to the cathedral.

Levison thinks that the older " Passion " of St. Kilian was written about 840 — not earlier than 833.[63] Its trustworthiness has been strongly impeached, and no doubt it contains much that is fabulous. But the missionary labors and violent death of the saint can hardly be questioned. The second " Passion " is also of the ninth century, but later than the first. It has been expanded with matter which does not seem to have additional value.

There are several allusions to Kilian of earlier date than either " Passion ":

(1) In a description of the Würzburg March c 779: Chroust *Monumenta palaeographica* I 5 *tab.* 10; Müllenhóff and Scherer *Denkmäler Deutscher Poesie und Prosa*[3] I 226, II 361. (2) In a calendar written in 781 by a certain Gottschalk for Charles the Great: F. Piper *Karls der Grosses Kalendarium und Ostertafel* (1858) 26. (3) *Annales Maximiniani* X a. 787 (788): *MGH SS* XIII 21. (4) *Annales Einhardi a.* 793: *MGH SS* I 179; Migne *PL* CIV 444; Kurze *SS. Rer. Ger. in usum Scholarum* (1895) 94-5. (5) *Annales Mosellani a.* 792/3: *MGH SS* XVI 498. (6) A royal confirmation of A.D. 807: *MGH Diplomata Karol.* I 275 no. 206. (7) Hrabanus Maurus *Martyrologium* A.D. 842 x 854: Canisius *Antiquae lectionis tom.* VI [ed. Basnage II ii 333]; Migne *PL* CX 1155. [A short but interesting notice of Kilian.] (8) *Cf.* also the reference in the Würzburg necrology, a marginal entry in a copy of Bede's Martyrology, published by Dümmler, *Forschungen zur deutschen Geschichte* VI (1866) 116.

318. Life of St. Disibod, by Hildegard A.D. 1170

In mystica visione ut Deus . . . me a lecto erigere, si sibi placuerit. Amen.

EDS: *AA. SS. Boll.* Jul. II 581-97. — Migne *PL* CXCVII 1095-1116. COMM: Mabillon *AA. SS. o. s. B.* III ii 496-8. — J. B. Cardinal Pitra *Analecta sacra* VIII 352 -7. — Falk " Der heilige Disibod, sein Leben und seine Verehrung " *Der Katholik* LX Jahrg. (Mainz 1880) I 541-7. — Wattenbach *DGQ* I[6] 40. — Hauck *Kirchengeschichte Deutschlands* I (1898) 292, (1904) 304. — Gougaud *Les chrétientés celtiques* (Paris 1911) 80-1.

Disibod is one of those Irish saints who stand out in high relief in continental ecclesiastical tradition but of whom history can accept hardly the existence.[64] The author of his Life was an extraordinary mediaeval mystic, Hildegard, abbess of Rupertsberg, known as the Sibyl of the Rhine,[65] who spent her early years on the Disenberg. She asserts that she wrote from supernatural revelation, but it seems probable that her

---

[63] Emmerich and Hefner assign it to c 752.

[64] The earliest record of him seems to be a notice in the *Martyrologium* of Hrabanus Maurus, VI Id. Sept.: Migne *PL* CX 1167.

[65] There is an extensive literature on Hildegard. *Cf. An. Boll.* XXXIX i-ii (April 1921) for reviews. Chas. Singer (ed.) *Studies in the history and method of science* (Oxford 1917) has a paper on " The scientific views and visions of St. Hildegard."

real source of information was the local legends. Disibod is said to have come from Ireland in the second half of the seventh century, and settled as an anchorite on the Nahe, not far from where it flows into the Rhine at Bingen. His retreat became in time the monastery of Mount Disibod, Disibodenberg, or Disenberg.

319. Life of St. Corbinian, bishop of Freising, by Aribo, or Arbeo *c* A.D. 768

Domino Virgilio sacrae. . . . Isdem venerandus vir Dei. . . .

MSS: BM Addit. 11880 *s* IX ff. 186ᵛ–214ᵛ. — Carlsruhe Cod. Augiensis XXXII *s* IX ff. 124–8ᵛ. Eds: S. Riezler *Abhandl. d. k. bayer. Akad. d. Wissenschaft.* hist. Kl. XVIII i (Munich 1888) 219–74 [also separately]. — Krusch *MGH SS. rer. merov.* VI (1913) 497-635; *Arbeonis Vitae sanctorum Haimhrammi et Corbiniani* (*SS. rer. Germ. in usum scholarum*) (Hanover 1920) [with a valuable introd.; *cf.* G. Morin " À propos des préliminaires de B. Krusch à la Vita Corbiniani " *Rev. Bénédictine* XXXI (1914) 178–84, and Krusch's reply, *NA* XXXIX (1914) 550–2]. — The letter of dedication to Virgilius of Salzburg is ed. by Dümmler *MGH Epistolae Karolini aevi* II (1895) 498. — There is a later redaction of this *Vita*, as to which see Potthast, and Krusch as above. Comm: L. Steinberger " Zu Arbeos *Vita Corbiniani* " *NA* XL (1915-6) 245-8. — Widemann " Die Herkunft des hl. Korbinian " *Altbayr. Monatschrift* XIII (1915-6) 16 *sqq* [*cf. NA* XLI (1917) 332-3]. — R. Bauerreiss " Irische Frühmissionäre in Südbayern " *Wissenschaftliche Festgabe zum zwölfhundertjährigen Jubiläum des heiligen Korbinian* (Munich 1924) 43–60 [collects traces, some hitherto unnoticed, of Irish missionaries in southern Bavaria, one of whom Corbinian is believed to have been].

Arbeo, Aribo, or Heres, fourth bishop of Freising (north-east of Munich), ruled that diocese from 764 to 783. In 765 he transferred the remains of the first bishop, Corbinian, from his grave in the Vintsgau in the Rhaetian Alps to the church of St. Mary in Freising. Not long after this — Krusch believes before 20 January, 769 — he wrote the Life of Corbinian at the request of his Irish neighbor, Virgilius of Salzburg,[66] to whom it is dedicated.

Corbinian, who died in or about 725, was one of the apostles of Bavaria, and his Life, although written from a different point of view, has interest as a source for the history of the Celtic missions. Corbinian's name is Celtic, and, as the author inadvertently discloses, he was regarded as of British origin. He may have been Irish, British, or sprung from some continental Celtic population.[67]

320. Life of St. Alto, by Othlon *c* A.D. 1060

Beatus igitur Alto . . . forsitan sunt abicienda.

MS: Munich Staats-Bibl. 21707 *s* XV ff. 21 *sqq.* Eds: *AA. SS. Boll.* Feb. II 359–6ᴸ. — Mabillon *AA. SS. o. s. B.* III ii 217–20, 2nd ed. 196–8. — Waitz *MGH SS* XV ii 843–6 [only complete ed.]. Comm: Wattenbach *DGQ* II (1894) 66. — Hauck *Kirchengeschichte Deutschlands* I (1904) 541.

---

[66] No. 329.

[67] Krusch suggests that he may have been a native of the Alpine valley where he was buried.

St. Alto was one of the Irish missionaries in Bavaria in the eighth century the facts of whose career can be perceived only dimly behind the haze of later traditions. He was honored as the founder of the monastery of Altenmünster, in the diocese of Freising. His Life was written by Othlon, a monk of St. Emmeramus in Ratisbon, and afterwards of Fulda, who died in 1072.

IV. THE ABBEY OF BOBBIO

Bibliography

See the works listed on pp. 86, 186–7 *supra*. Also C. Cipolla and G. Buzzi *Codice diplomatico del monastero di San Colombano di Bobbio fino all' Anno MCCVIII* 3 vols. (Rome 1918). — G. Buzzi *Studi Bobbiesi* (Rome 1918) [corrections to first two vols. of preceding work]. — W. M. Lindsay "The Bobbio Scriptorium "*Centralblatt f. Bibliothekswesen* XXVI (1909) 293–306.

Of the Irish origin of the abbey of Bobbio something has been said above in connection with St. Columbanus. From the beginning Bobbio was an Italian, not an Irish, monastery, but it is certain that Irish influence was quite strong there throughout the seventh century, and that in later years Irish monks occasionally visited or settled in this foundation of their famous countryman. But precise documentary evidence of the presence of Irishmen at Bobbio after the passing of Columban's companions is very slight. The proof of their presence and influence at least till the end of the seventh century is derived chiefly from the character of the writing in the earliest manuscripts surviving from the Bobbio scriptorium. These are sometimes in Irish, sometimes in North Italian script, but the abbreviation forms are strongly Irish.

Best known of these early Bobbio codices are: Naples Biblioteca Nazionale IV A 8, containing the Grammar of Charisius and the Liber Pontificalis, this last written A.D. 687 x 701, and the former Vienna Hofbibl. MSS nos. 16 and 17. *Cf.* W. M. Lindsay *Early Irish minuscule script* (Oxford 1910) 30–6; Rudolf Beer "Bemerkungen über den ältesten Handschriftenbestand des Klosters Bobbio " *Sitzungsb. d. k. Akad. d. Wissensch. in Wien*, Philos.-hist. Cl. 1911, no. xi; and *Monumenta palaeographica Vindobonensia* II (Leipsic 1910) [facsimiles and description of Vienna 16].[68] IV A 8 contains a few O-I glosses which have been published by RTh *ZCP* XV (1925) 300–1. O–I Glosses on Eutyches in Vienna 16, ff. 57–68, have been published by Nigra *RC* I 58 *sq*; WS *Goidelica²* 51; HZ *Glossae Hibernicae* 228, *Suppl.* 12; *Thes. Pal.* II pp. xii, 42.

[68] Many of the leaves of the early Bobbio MSS are palimpsest, derived from much older codices. Beer has advanced the theory that they are remnants of the library which Cassiodorus placed in the monastery he founded at Vivarium or Squillace, in southern Italy (*cf.* p. 662 *infra*), which library, on this theory, must have been acquired, at least in part, by Bobbio.

321. Epitaph of Cummian of Bobbio

Hic sacra beati membra Cumiani solvuntur . . . ubi tegitur corpus. [16 ll.] . . . fecit Iohannes magister.

MSS: Vat. Palat. 833 [from Lorsch]; and others. Eds: Muratori *Antiquitates Italicae* III (Milan 1740) 680. — Rossetti *Bobbio illustrato* (Turin 1795). — Dümmler *MGH Poet. lat. aevi Carol.* I (1881) 107. — Strecker *ibid.* IV fasc. ii–iii 723 no. 138. — Margaret Stokes *Six months in the Apennines* (London 1892) 171–3 [with trans.]. — C. Cipolla and G. Buzzi *Codice diplomatico del monastero di San Colombano di Bobbio* I (Rome 1918) 118–23.

L. A. Muratori (1672–1750), the celebrated Italian scholar, copied from a stone in the monastery of Bobbio the epitaph of an Irish bishop Cumianus, erected by Liutprand, king of the Lombards, who reigned 712-744. Cummian spent, we are informed, the last seventeen years of his life at Bobbio, and died there at an advanced age. The inscription, as well as all other record of its subject, has disappeared, but copies of it exist in several mediaeval manuscripts.

One, or two, poems written by an Irish monk of the ninth century who, after being an inmate of Bobbio, abandoned the monastery, are noticed p. 604 *infra.* — Also, at p. 602, a grant made to Bobbio by Donatus of Fiesole in 850.

322. Catalogues of the Library of Bobbio

(i) Catalogue of *s* XI: Eds: Muratori *Antiquitates Italicae* III (Milan 1740) 817–24. — Becker *Catalogi bibliothecarum antiqui* (Bonn 1885) xxxii pp. 64–73. The list of Dungal's books is translated in Margaret Stokes *Six months in the Apennines* 296-7, and commented on in Traube *O Roma nobilis* [*cf.* p. 530 *infra*] 40. *Cf.* also *MGH Poet. lat. aevi Carol.* I 394; *Centralblatt f. Bibliothekswesen* IV (1887) 443; *NA* XXXII (1907) 663.

(ii) Catalogue of A.D. 1461. Ed: A. Peyron *M. Tulli Ciceronis orationum . . . fragmenta* [*cf.* p. 85 n. 360 and p. 201 *supra*].

(iii) Catalogue of A.D. 1494. Ed: Raphael Maffeus Volaterranus *Commentariorum rerum urbanarum* IV 140.

The oldest catalogue of the Bobbio library does not indicate which of its manuscripts were written in Irish script. It does, however, include a list of twenty-nine works which were presented to the monastery by Dungal, " principal of the Irish." Formerly it was thought that he was one of the Dungals of the age of Charles the Great and Louis the Pious.[69] But Gottlieb has shown that he must have lived in the eleventh century. — Undoubtedly many other books in the library, besides Dungal's, were of Irish origin [*cf.* nos. 484, 485 *infra*].

[69] *Cf.* pp. 538 *sqq infra.*

V. Irish Influences in Continental Europe in the Eighth Century

Pippin the Younger, or Pippin of Heristal, died in 714 and was succeeded in the office of mayor of the palace and virtual ruler of the Frankish empire by his son Charles, called *Martel*, " the Hammer." Charles Martel was succeeded in 741 by his sons Carloman and Pippin the Short, who ruled jointly till 747, when Carloman retired to a monastery. In 751 Pippin deposed the last Merovingian king and seized the throne: in 754 he was crowned at St.-Denis by Pope Stephen II. In consideration of the Pope's support Pippin led an army into Italy against the Lombards, and began the long and close association between the Carolingian monarchy and Rome. On his death in 768 he was succeeded by his two sons, Charles and Carloman, but Carloman died in 771. Charles, known to the two great nations that sprang from his empire as " Karl der Grosse " and " Charlemagne," was, on Christmas Day, 800, crowned by Pope Leo III as Roman Emperor.

The Karlings were more interested in religious affairs than were the Merovings, and far more effective in controlling them. But a change had come over the religious situation. When Columbanus and his contemporaries re-established fairly close ecclesiastical associations between Ireland and the Continent they found in Gaul a moribund episcopal hierarchy and a population in large part only nominally Christian, and in the lands to the east of the river Rhine peoples almost wholly pagan. The great religious movement of the seventh century was of Irish, and especially of Columban, inspiration, and took the form, as was natural, of the establishment of monasteries, usually exempt from external episcopal jurisdiction either because of special provision or because the abbot was also bishop, monasteries that became centres from which, in Gaul, the lax Christians were galvanised into piety, in Germany the heathens were converted to Christianity. Into this situation the emigration of Irish anchorites fitted without difficulty: the hermit's cell became the nucleus of the monastery.

In the meanwhile, by a curious chance, England became the field of conflict of two missionary enterprises, the one directed from the Irish Iona, the other from Rome. The Roman triumphed, and although the new English clergy owed much to Ireland, they became zealous advocates of the Roman system of church government and discipline. Under Irish influence, it seems certain, they undertook a mission to the pagans

of Frisia.   Thence they spread out over the adjoining districts of what
is now Germany, including those which had been, or were being evan-
gelised by Irishmen and Britons.   They received the warm support of
the Karlings and the greatest of the English missionaries, St. Boniface, became finally the organiser of the Church in Germany and the
reformer of the Church in Gaul.

As a result, the revival on the Continent of hostility towards the Irish
was not unnatural.   The wandering Irish bishop or priest who to the eyes
of Merovingian Gaul had been a saint became to Boniface and the reorganised hierarchy an insubordinate cleric and possibly a heretic.
From this time on the continental ecclesiastical authorities found it
necessary to legislate repeatedly for the control of unattached priests
and wandering bishops, " episcopi vagantes," [70] who are sometimes
described specifically as " Scotti."   No doubt such legislation was
necessary: in the monastic Church of their native land the bishops
might normally exercise their functions apart from any administrative
position in the ecclesiastical organisation, but in a diocesan Church such
action, obviously, would be anomalous, and might become a serious
abuse.   This, however, was only one feature of the distrust, contempt, or
jealousy, open or latent, towards the Irish, which we discover here and
there during the next two centuries.[71]

Nevertheless the Irish exiles continued to come in large numbers to
the Continent, and, on the whole, to fare very well.   The Carolingian
princes in particular, although reviving and enforcing the Roman ideals
of organisation and discipline, showed themselves constant friends to all
" holy pilgrims " from Ireland.

322a. St. Pirmin and the monasteries of Reichenau and Murbach

Another of the shadowy, and ubiquitous, missionary saints of the eighth century was
Pirminius, Pirminus, or Priminius, whose death is placed about 753/754.   He was
the founder of the important monasteries of Reichenau (Augia dives), on an island in
Lake Constance, and Murbach, in Alsace; one of the apostles of what are now Baden,
Wurtemberg and Switzerland; in addition, according to what was possibly a
false tradition, bishop of Meaux. There are several Lives, but none is very trustworthy
as a source for the saint's career: (1) By a monk of Hornbach, in the 9th cent.   EDS:

[70] *Cf.* Bruno Krusch " Zur Eptadius- und Eparchius-Legende " *NA* XXV (1900) 138 *sqq.*

[71] One of the earliest displays of this hostility may be that of the author of the treatise on chronology
usually designated the *Laterculus Malalianus*, because based on a work of Johannes Malala Antiochenus,
who wrote in A.D. 573.   The *Laterculus Malalianus* is believed to have been composed in the eighth
century, and in Italy, probably Rome.   The author warns his readers against the verbose deception of
the Irish, who believe themselves to possess wisdom but have lost knowledge.   ED: Mommsen *MGH
Auct. antiq.* XIII (*Chronica minora* III) (1898) 424–34.

Mone *Quellensammlung der badischen Landesgeschichte* I (Carlsruhe 1848) 30–6, 526. — Holder-Egger *MGH SS* XV i (1887) 21–31. — *AA. SS. Boll.* 3 Nov. II i (1894) 33–47. (2) Of the 11th cent.; attributed to Garemann, abbot of Hornbach (d. 1008), to Warmann, bishop of Constance (d. 1034), to Othlon of Ratisbon and Fulda (d. 1072), and to others. EDS: Mabillon *AA. SS. o. s. B.* III ii 140–53. — *AA. SS. Boll. loc. cit.* Cf. Manitius *Lat. Lit.* II 446–9. (3) Of the 13th cent., attributed to Henry, abbot of Reichenau (d. 1234). EDS: Mone *op. cit.* 39–45. — *AA. SS. Boll.* Nov. II i 47–50. Cf. Breitenbach *NA* II 170–4; Zapf " Der Ursprung von Pirmasens " *Mittheilungen d. histor. Vereins d. Pfalz* XI (Speier 1883); Wattenbach *DGQ* I (1893) 275–6, 374. Pirmin is described as a " peregrinus," and from this it has been assumed that he was Irish or English, more probably the former. We have a work of which he is believed to be the author, a student's compilation from various canonical works, *Dicta abbatis Priminii de singulis libris canonicis scarapsus.* MS: Einsiedeln Stiftsbibl. 199 *s* VIII/IX. EDS: Mabillon *Vetera analecta* IV (Paris 1675) app. 569 *sqq.* — Gallandius *Bibl. vet. patrum* XIII (Venice 1779) 277–85. — Migne *PL* LXXXIX 1030 *sqq.* — C. P. Caspari *Kirchenhistorische Anecdota* I (1883) 150–93. It contains what is believed to be the earliest copy of the Apostles' Creed as now known. This has been reproduced in Burn *Facsimiles of the Creeds* (Henry Bradshaw Soc. XXXVI) (London 1909). In the palaeographical notes by Ludwig Traube, pp. 33–4, 49–51, attention is called to certain orthographical peculiarities in the MS which may be either Irish or Spanish, and one purely Spanish form. Traube suggests that these may be derived from the autograph, and, if so, that Pirmin may have been a Spaniard. See also Dom J. Perez " De Patrologia española: San Pimerio " *Boletin de la Real Acad. de la Historia* LXXVII (1920) 132–50; F. Flaskamp " Zur Pirminforschung " *ZK* 1925 pp. 199–202.—For later Irish associations with Reichenau, see pp. 550, 668 *sqq.*

See *Addenda*.

323. Life of St. Odilia *s* IX/X

EDS: Mabillon *AA. SS. o. s. B.* III ii 488–96. — Pfister *An. Boll.* XIII 9–32. — Levison *MGH SS. rer. merov.* VI 24–50. Cf. *NA* XVIII 702.

Odilia (d. *c* 720) was abbess of Hohenburg in Alsace. It was her custom, says her Life, to receive in her monastery women pilgrims both from Ireland and from Britain, and also religious men coming from various provinces. The Life, however, has little original value, being in large part an adaptation of that of St. Salaberga of Laon.[72]

324. St. Boniface

(i) Correspondence

The following are the principal eds.: (S) Nicolaus Serarius *Epistolae S. Bonifaci* (Mainz 1605). — *Nova bibl. vet. patrum* II (Paris 1639) 48–121. — *Bibl. magna vet. patrum* XVI (Paris 1654) 48–121. — *Bibl. maxima vet. patrum* XIII (Leyden 1677) 70–140 [the order and texts of these 3 eds. agree with S]. — (W) S. A. Würdtwein *Epistolae S. Bonifacii* (Mainz 1789). — (G) J. A. Giles *S. Bonifacii opera* 2 vols. (London 1844). — Migne *PL* LXXXIX 687–804 [texts of G]. — (J) Philip Jaffé *Bibl. rerum Germanicarum* III (Berlin 1866) 8–315 [selection]. — (D) Ernst Dümmler *MGH Epistolae* III (Berlin

[72] Cf. p. 209 *supra*

1892) 231–431 [best]. — (T) M. Tangl *Die Briefe d. hh. Bonifatius u. Lullus* (*Epistolae selectae in usum scholarum* I) (Berlin 1916) [*cf. NA* XL (1916) 641–790]. GER. TRANS: Ph. H. Külb *Sämmtliche Schriften des heiligen Bonifaz* 2 vols. (Ratisbon 1859). — Tangl *Geschichtschreiber d. deut. Vorzeit* XCII (Leipsic [1912]).

(ii) Life by Willibald A.D. 755 x 768 (?)

EDS: Canisius *Lect. antiq.* IV ii (1603) 341–86, 742–5. — Serarius *op. cit.* 253–84 [re-edited in Giles *op. cit.* II 143–82]. — Mabillon *AA. SS. o. s. B.* III ii 1–27 [reprint in Migne *PL* LXXXIX 603–34]. — *AA. SS. Boll.* 5 Jun. I 460–73, 3rd ed. 452–65. — *MGH SS* II 331–53. — Jaffé *Bibl. rer. Ger.* III 422–71. — A. Nürnberger *XXVII Bericht der Philomathie zu Neisse* (Breslau 1895). — W. Levison *Vitae s. Bonifatii* (*MGH SS in usum scholarum*) (1905). TRANS: Geo. W. Robinson (Cambridge, Mass. 1916). — Germ.: Külb *op. cit.* II 213–70. — M. Tangl *Geschichtschreiber d. deut. Vorzeit* XVI (3rd ed. Leipsic 1920). — There are other German trans. For later Lives, which are almost entirely dependent on Willibald and the correspondence, and for other material on Boniface, see Potthast, Wattenbach, Molinier, the Bollandists' *Bibl. hag. lat.*, and Levison's ed. COMM: The literature is very extensive. See the guides just mentioned and the principal church histories; also Gross *Sources and literature of English history.* — [J. H.] A. Ebrard *Bonifatius: ein Nachtrag zu dem Werke 'Die iroschottische Missionskirche'* (Gütersloh 1882. — Hauck *Kirchengeschichte Deutschlands* I. — F. C. Conybeare " The character of the heresy of the early British Church " *Trans. Hon. Soc. Cymmrodorion* 1897–8 (London 1899) 84–117. — G. Kurth *St. Boniface* (Collection *Les Saints*) (Paris 1902) [brief and scholarly; gives some attention to the disputes with Celtic ecclesiastics]. — Walther Koehler *Mitteilungen d. oberhessischen Geschichtsvereins* N. F. X [gives some space to the Irish Church in Germany]. — F. S. Serland " The controversy concerning baptism under St. Boniface " *Amer. Cath. Quart. Rev.* XLII (1917) 270–5.

Bonifacius, or Bonifatius — the Latin name of Wynfrith, a West-Saxon priest — was born about 675 and in 716 joined the English mission in Frisia. Disturbances compelled him to return to England, but in 718 he was again on the Continent, where he remained for the rest of his life. He labored as a missionary in Frisia, Hessia, Thuringia, and other parts of Germany, but his chief work was that of organisation and reform, and of the promotion of the spiritual power of the Pope. He visited Rome in 718–9, when he received papal authorisation for his mission; in 722, when he was consecrated bishop; and in 738, when he was appointed papal legate. Already in 732 he had received the pallium; and in 748 he was appointed archbishop of Mainz and primate of Germany. In 744 his disciple, Sturmi, under his direction, founded the monastery of Fulda (in Hesse-Cassel), the most important of several monastic foundations due to him. Finally, in 754, he resigned his dignities and returned to missionary work in Frisia, where he died a martyr.

The letters to and from Boniface are important historical documents. So also is the earliest Life, written by his companion Willibald, who was bishop of Eichstätt in Bavaria, c 741–786. Both offer some information regarding the difficulties that arose between Boniface and his Irish contemporaries.[73]

In 716 Theodo, duke of Bavaria, visited Rome. Pope Gregory II sent back with him three legates with instructions to reform abuses (*MGH Leges* III 451 *sqq*). Theodo, however, died in the following year; war broke out soon after between the Bavarians and Charles Martel; and it was not till Boniface's visit to Rome in 738 that a good opportunity offered to renew the attempt at introducing the Roman discipline into southern Germany. Gregory III wrote to the bishops of Bavaria and Alemannia directing them to reject the teaching and rites of paganism, as well as of the Britons who came thither and of other false priests and heretics. (The specific mention of Britons is perhaps due to the fact that the Church of Wales had not yet accepted the Roman Easter.) (Migne *PL* LXXXIX 580; H&S I 203; S cxxix; WG xlv; J xxxvii; DT xliv.) Another letter to Boniface directed him to set up four bishoprics and ordain three bishops in Bavaria. (Bishop Vivilo of Passau, previously ordained by the Pope, was recognised as in good standing.) (S cxxx; WG xlvi; J xxxviii; DT xlv p. 293). On his return Boniface stopped in Bavaria and, with the support of Duke Odilo, coerced the false bishops and heretical priests who had seduced the people, and appointed three new bishops, John of Salzburg, Erembert of Freising (he was said to be the brother of Corbinian[74] and, if so, may have been a Celt who went over to the Roman side), and Gaibald of Ratisbon. (Willibald's Life of Boniface vii.)

On April 21, 742, the first general council of the Church in Germany was assembled by the prince Carloman and Boniface, at what place we do not know. It ordered that unknown bishops or priests should be allowed to exercise their ministry only after being examined in synod. (Mansi XII 367).

Two years later, having taken up the task of reforming the Church of Gaul, Boniface held a council at Soissons.

325. Acts of the Council of Soissons A.D. 744

EDS: Labbe *Concilia* VI 1552–5. — Bouquet IV 110. — *MGH Leges* I 20–1. — Verminghoff *Concilia aevi Karolini* (1906) 33–6.

This council provided for the establishment of a certain Abel in the archiepiscopal see of Reims. Other enactments condemned the Gaul Adelbert (who is associated by Boniface with the Irishman Clement as a heretical disturber of religious order), and directed that wandering priests and bishops must secure the approbation of the diocesan bishop within whose jurisdiction they wished to officiate.[75]

---

[73] Boniface describes his troubles, but without specifically naming his opponents, in a letter to Daniel, bishop of Winchester 742 to 746: S iii, WG xii, J lv, DT lxiii.

[74] See Krusch's ed. of the Life of Corbinian (no. 319 *supra*) 586 and notes.

[75] The Council of Ver, held in 755, the year of Boniface's death, has a similar enactment: Canon xiii (Mansi XII 583): " As regards wandering bishops, who have no dioceses, and as to the validity of whose ordination we have no knowledge, it is decreed, in accordance with the regulations of the holy Fathers, that they must not minister in another's diocese, nor perform any ordination, except by command of the bishop to whom the diocese belongs." For legislation to the same effect in the ninth century *cf.* p. 529 *infra*.

326. Flodoard: History of the Church of Reims A.D. 948

Cf. no. 39 *supra.*

Flodoard gives a very full account,[76] supported by excerpts from documents, of the appointment of Abel, a priest from the abbey of Lobbes, to the archiepiscopal see of Reims about 744. He says that Pope Zachary made the appointment on the suggestion of St. Boniface, but does not specifically state, as does Folcuin of Lobbes, that Abel was an Irishman. — It may be added here that from the following century Flodoard preserves the record of an Irish pilgrim who, whilst on the road to Rome, was attacked on the banks of the Aisne by robbers and killed.[77]

327. Folcuin: History of the Abbots of Lobbes (*Gesta abbatum Lobiensium*) *c* A.D. 980

EDS: D'Achéry *Spicilegium* VI 541–88 [*ed. nov.* II 730–59]. — *MGH SS.* IV 52–74. — Migne *PL* CXXXVII 545–82. COMM: *AA. SS. Boll.* Aug. II 111–7 [valuable]. — Hauck *Kirchengeschichte Deutschlands* I (Leipsic 1898) 526, 529, 551; (ed. 1904) 543, 567. — Duine *Memento* 23.

Folcuin, abbot of Lobbes (in Hainault, Belgium) from 965 to 990, based this work mainly on the archives of his monastery. He relates how an Irishman named Abel was summoned from Lobbes to the archiepiscopal see of Reims to replace Melo, deposed by the Council of Soissons in 744. The appointment was made by Pippin on the advice of Boniface, and received the approval of Pope Zachary, but Abel met with opposition in his new office and returned to Lobbes, where he became abbot.[78]

328. Acts of a Roman Synod Oct. 25, A.D. 745

EDS: [*Cf.* p. 519] G II 40. — D 316–22. — Mansi XII 373 *sqq*, and the other collections of Councils. *Cf. NA* XXIV (1899) 466–7. Also Hefele (trans. Leclercq) *Histoire des Conciles* vol. III pt. II pp. 873 *sqq*.

This synod, held by Pope Zacharias in Rome, formally anathematised Adelbert and Clement. Its acts contain some interesting statements as to the teachings of the two men.[79]

Five of the letters in the Boniface collection refer to the case against the Gaul Adelbert and the Irishman Clement: S cxliv, addit. to cxxxiv–cxxxv, cxxxvii, cxlviii, cxxxix; W lix, addit. to lxvi–lxvii, lxx, lxviii, lxxiv; G liv, II p. 40, lx, lxviii, lxiv; J xlviii, l, li, liii, lxiii; DT lvii, lix, lx, lxii, lxxvii; *cf.* Ussher *Sylloge* no. xv. The second of these

---

[76] II xvi.   [77] IV xlviii.

[78] In letters to Boniface dated 22 June and 5 November, 744 (S cxliv, cxliii; W lix, lx; G liv, lv; J xlviii, xlix; DT lvii, lviii) Zachary states that he is sending the pallium to Abel. In 746/747 Abel is one of several " coepiscopi " who join with Boniface in an exhortation to Ethelbald, king of Mercia (S xix; W lxxii; G lxii; J lix; DT lxxiii).

[79] It may be noted that one of the devices used by Adelbert, who would seem to have been a religious mountebank, was the " Letter of Christ fallen from Heaven " (*cf.* no. 270).

is the acts of the Roman synod of 745. However in no. lxxvii, dated 5 Jan. 747, Pope Zachary asks that the case of the deprived bishops Adelbert, Godalsac and Clement be once more considered in council. We have nothing further on the subject.

329. Texts relating to St. Virgilius of Salzburg

GEN. COMM: Olden *DNB s. v.* "Fergil." — Ph. Gilbert "Le pape Zacharie et les antipodes" *Rev. des questions scientifiques* XII (1882) 478–503. — Kretschmer *Die physiche Erdkunde* (Vienna 1889). — HZ *NA* XVII (1892) 211. — Fasching "Zur Bischofsweihe des hl. Virgilius von Salzburg" *Jahresbericht d. k. k. Staats-Oberrealschule in Marburg* 1894 pp. 1 *sqq.* — Hermann Krabbo "Bischof Virgil von Salzburg u. seine kosmologischen Ideen" *Mittheilungen d. Instituts f. österreichische Geschichtsforschung* XXIV (Innsbruck 1903) 1–28 [valuable]. — M. R. James *Cambridge medieval history* III 513. — Br. Krusch *MGH SS. rer. merov.* VI (1913) 517–20, 545 [excellent summary]. — H. Van der Linden "Virgile de Salzbourg et les théories cosmographiques au VIII° siècle" *Bull. de l'Acad. roy. de Belgique, Cl. des lettres* 1914 pp. 163–87. — G. Metlake (pseud.) "St. Virgil the Geometer" *Eccles. Rev.* LXIII (1920) 13 *sqq.*

Ferghil, abbot of the monastery of Achadh-bó-Cainnigh [80] in Osraige, whose obit is given by the Annals of the Four Masters in 784,[81] has been identified with a certain Virgilius whom St. Boniface denounced for his cosmological ideas; and he in turn with Virgilius, bishop of Salzburg. These identifications, especially the second, are probable, though not entirely certain. It would appear that he left Ireland about 742 "pro amore Christi," and that in Gaul he attracted the favor of Pippin the Short by his learning and ability. In 743 Pippin put down an insurrection led by Duke Odilo of Bavaria, and, apparently soon after, sent Virgilius to Bavaria, recommending him strongly to Odilo. The situation has the appearance of being delicate, but Virgilius won the support of his new patron.[82] Bishop John, whom Boniface had appointed to the diocese of Salzburg, had died, and Virgilius was placed in charge of the diocese. He was not ordained bishop, but administered the diocese as abbot of the monastery of St. Peter which St. Hrodbert, or Rupert, the first bishop, had founded in Salzburg.[83] The sacramental functions of the episcopate were performed for him by a bishop "Dobdagrecus," no doubt an Irishman named Dub-dá-chrich. This, we are told, was because of the humility of Virgilius; the true cause, we may presume,

---

[80] P. 394 *supra.*

[81] AU, however, assign it to 789.

[82] The relations between Virgilius and Pippin are not well authenticated, and may be mythical.

[83] Hrodbert was abbot and bishop, and died, it would appear, in 718. Some late texts say he was an Irishman, but the only basis for this in the earliest Life seems to be a mistaken emendation of an illegible word in one MS. It is quite likely, however, that he was an adherent of the Irish ecclesiastical customs. The best ed. of the earliest Life is by W. Levison *MGH SS. rer. merov.* VI (1913) 140–62; see especially 157. *Cf. Cath. Encycl. s. v.* "Rupert, Saint." On the translation of his body by Virgilius in 773 *cf. MGH SS* XI 8 n. 32.

was that St. Boniface would not permit his consecration. That took place in 755, the year after Boniface's death.[84]

Modern interest has attached itself to Virgilius because of his alleged doctrine of antipodes. The idea, although generally repudiated by Christian writers, was not new; he might have obtained it from Isidore, or Bede, or Martianus Capella. The text in question testifies rather to the zeal of St. Boniface as a heresy-hunter than to the originality or profundity of the Irishman's cosmological theories.

(i) Letter of Pope Zachary to Boniface, July 1, A.D. 744 or 746

EDS: [Cf. p. 519] S cxxxiv. — W lxii. — G lvi. — J lviii. — DT lxviii. Also Ussher *Sylloge* no. xvi. — Mansi XII 325.

Boniface had ordered the re-baptizing of certain persons who had received the sacrament from a priest who used an illiterate formula. The facts were reported to the Pope by "Virgilius and Sedonius, religious men dwelling in the province of the Bavarians," and he now instructs Boniface that the repetition of the ceremony is not necessary. Sidonius seems to have accompanied Virgilius from Gaul, and later to have become bishop of Passau on the Danube, north of Salzburg.

(ii) Pope Zachary to Boniface, May 1, A.D. 748 [85] (?)

EDS: S no. cxl. — W lxxxii. — G lxxi. — J lxvi. — DT lxxx. Also Ussher *Sylloge* xvii; Mansi XII 339.

The Pope, among many other matters, orders the excommunication of an Irish priest named Samson, whom Boniface had reported as teaching that the imposition of the bishop's hands was sufficient, without baptism, to admit to the Church. With regard to Virgilius, who is sowing hatred between Boniface and Duke Odilo, his assertion that he had the Pope's authority to receive a vacant Bavarian bishopric is false. If he be convicted of having professed the perverse doctrine "that there are another world and other men under the earth, and another sun and moon," let him be excommunicated. But Virgilius has been summoned, by letters to the Duke, to appear before the Pope for trial, and in the meanwhile Boniface is to exercise patience with reference to both Virgilius and Sidonius.

The position of Virgilius in Bavaria was probably too strong to be shaken, for we hear nothing further of the accusation.

(iii) *Indiculus Arnonis; Notitia Arnonis* A.D. 798

EDS: There are several. Canisius *Lect. antiq.* 2nd ed. III ii 452. — De Rozière *Rev. hist. de droit français et étranger* 1859. — F. Keinz *Indiculus Arnonis et breves notitiae*

---

[84] The *Annales Salisburgenses* place his consecration in 767. — *MGH SS* I 89. But see Krusch *MGH SS. rer. merov.* VI 519.

[85] This is indicated by the dating *formulae* of the letter: but it speaks of Duke Odilo of Bavaria as though he were still living, whose death Hundt, approved by Krusch, places on Jan. 18, 748. — Hundt " Über die Bayerischen Urkunden aus der Zeit der Agilofinger " *Abhandl. d. k. bayer. Akad. d. Wissensch.*, hist. Kl., XII (Munich 1873) 168; *MGH SS. rer. merov.* VI 509.

Salzburgenses (Munich 1869). — W. Hauthaler *Salzburger Urkundenbuch* I (1910) 16, 28–9. *Cf. NA* XII 69.

Arno, a pupil of Alcuin, succeeded Virgilius as bishop of Salzburg in 785, and became archbishop, 798–821. This list which he prepared of the possessions of the cathedral church is our evidence for a struggle between Virgilius and Duke Odilo over certain property which the latter wrested from the monastery and gave to his chaplain, Ursus.

Sometime in 748–50 Virgilius was witness to a confirmation by Duke Tassilo of a grant by Odilo to the church of Freising. (Theodorus Bitterauf *Die Traditionem des Hochstifts Freising* I (*Quellen u. Eröterungen z. bayer. u. deut. Gesch.* N.F. IV) (Munich 1905) 29.) He was associated also with official acts connected with the church of Freising in 776, and apparently at other times. (*Ibid.* 99; *MGH SS. rer. merov.* VI 519–20). For his connection with the writing of a Life of St. Corbinian by Bishop Arbeo of Freising *c* 668 see no. 319.

(iv) Letter of Abbot Adalbert to Virgilius A.D. 770 x 784

EDS: *Monumenta Boica* XIV (Munich 1784) 351. — Dümmler *MGH Epist. Karol. aevi* II (Berlin 1895) 497.

A letter, probably from the abbot Adalbert who is known to have been in charge of the monastery of Tegernsee (south-east of Munich) in 770, informing Virgilius of the death of one of the monks.[86]

(v) *Liber Confraternitatum ecclesiae S. Petri Salisburgensis*

ED: S. Herzberg-Fränkel *MGH Necrologia* II i (1890). [See Potthast *s. v.* " Necr. Salz."] COMM: Herzberg-Fränkel " Über das älteste Verbrüderungsbuch von St. Peter in Salzburg" *NA* XII 63. — A. Ebner *Die klösterlichen Gebets-Verbrüderungen bis zum Ausgange des karolingischen Zeitalters* (Ratisbon 1890) 39.

This is the earliest record-book of the names of persons connected with the cathedral-monastery of St. Peter at Salzburg. It has some interest for early Irish associations with Bavaria. The name of Virgilius has been erased from among those of the living, at the beginning of the book, and entered, in another hand, among the dead. Critics are agreed that the book was begun by, or under the direction of, that bishop.

Melchior Goldastus in his notes on Columbanus cites a glossary attributed to Virgilius: *Paraeneticorum veterum* I (1604) 82, 83, 152, 155; *cf.* Ussher *Sylloge* [*Whole Works* IV 465].

(vi) Epitaph of Virgilius

Hic pater et pastor humilis, doctusque sacerdos. . . . Pro quo, quisque legis versus, orare memento.   10 ll.

ED: Dümmler *MGH Poet. lat. aevi Karol.* II (1884) 639. *Cf. MGH SS. rer. merov.* VI (1913) 520.

[86] Krusch suggests that this arose from an agreement among the bishops and abbots of Bavaria to hold services for any of their associates who should die. *MGH Concilia* II 96 *sq*; *cf. SS. rer. merov.* VI 519.

(vii) Alcuin's poem on Virgilius

Quae cernis veniens, lector, haec inclita tecta. . . . Praesentis necnon aeterni et gaudia regni.   18 ll.

The various eds. of Alcuin's poems: as Dümmler *MGH Poet. lat. aevi Karol.* I (1881) 340 no. CIX xxiv.   On Alcuin, *cf.* no. 340.

The testimony of his epitaph, and of Alcuin, a younger contemporary, regarding Virgilius is, in the absence of any early biography, of especial importance. They put his Irish origin beyond doubt. He died on November 27, 784.[87]

(viii) *Libellus de conversione Bagoariorum et Carantanorum c* A.D. 871

Eds: Canisius *Antiq. lect.* II 248 [poor]. — Frehner *Scriptores rerum Bohemicarum* (Hanover 1602) 15-20. — Wattenbach *MGH SS.* XI (Hanover 1854) 4-14.

(ix) Life of Virgilius.   After A.D. 1181

Eds: Canisius *ibid.* 1139. — Mabillon *AA. SS. o. s. B.* III ii 309-18. — Wattenbach *op. cit.* 86-95. *Cf.* Wattenbach *DGQ* II (1894) 303.

The *Libellus* is a valuable little treatise on the conversion of the Bavarians and Carinthians, extending from the time of St. Rupert to 871. It offers the earliest narrative account of the continental career of Virgilius. The Life is an expansion of the matter in the *Libellus*, and is of little if any independent worth. After becoming bishop of Salzburg, Virgilius initiated the conversion of the Carinthians by sending to them a bishop, Modestus.

330. Sources relating to Bishop Dub-dá-chrich

Dub-dá-chrich (the name appears as "Dobdagrecus" and even " Tuti Graecus") became, it would seem, abbot of the monastery of Chiemsee, and obtained for that house property which was claimed by the church of Freising. By an agreement of 804 part of this was restored. (Bitterauf *op. cit.* [p. 525 *supra*] 183; *cf.* 313.) But by a charter of Oct. 25, 788, Charles the Great had granted to the church of St. Stephen at Metz the monastery of Chiemsee "quod Doddogrecus peregrinus habuit." (E. Mühlbacher *MGH Diplomat. Karol.* I (1906) no. clxii pp. 219-20.) *Cf. MGH SS. rer. merov.* VI 514.

331. Clement: Letter to Duke Tassilo II of Bavaria *c* A.D. 772

In nomine Patris, etc.   Haec pauca scribere incipio ego Clemens amicus vester peregrinus . . . et dilectantur in letitia.

Eds: E. Zierngibl *Neue histor. Abhandl. d. baier. Akad. d. Wissensch.* I (Munich 1779) 246-8. — E. Dümmler *MGH Epistolarum* IV (1895) 496-7.

This is a letter written to Duke Tassilo (the successor of Odilo and friend of Virgilius) and the Bavarian people expressing hopes for their victory over their enemies.   Its

---

[87] His death is recorded in the *Annales Juvavenses maiores* (*MGH SS* I 87) and the *Annales Salisburgenses* (*ibid.* 89), and, under 785, in the *Annales s. Emmerami Ratisponenses maiores* (*ibid.* 92).

date seems too late to allow identification of the writer with the heretic Clement who troubled St. Boniface,[88] and it is probably too early for the teacher in the palace school [89] — though some turns in the phraseology are reminiscent of the latter's style.

332. The Legend of St. Erhard of Bavaria

(i) Life of Erhard, by Paul A.D. 1054 x 1073

EDS: *AA. SS. Boll.* Jan. I (Antwerp 1643) 535–9. — Colgan *AA. SS.* (Louvain 1645) 22–32. — Levison *MGH SS. rer. merov.* VI (1913) 1–21.

We know little more of Erhard than that he held the rank of bishop, and died in Bavaria before 784. This Life was written at the suggestion of Heilica, abbess of the Lower Monastery of Ratisbon. The *Vita* proper opens with the sentence "Herhardus,[90] qui gloria fortis interpretari potest, Narbonensis gentilitate, Nervus civilitate, genere Scoticus fuit." Perhaps for "Scoticus" we should read "Gothicus." He may have been Irish, but it does not seem probable.[91]

(ii) Life of St. Albart c A.D. 1152 x 1181

EDS: Bernard Pez *Thesaurus anecdotorum novissimus* II pt. iii (Augsburg 1721) 181–4. — Levison *MGH SS. rer. merov.* VI (1913) 21–3. COMM: S. Riezler *Forschungen zur deutschen Geschichte* XVIII (1878) 541–5.

This very fabulous *Vita* was written by a monk of the Irish monastery at Ratisbon. Its chief value is as an illustration of the ideas prevalent there in the twelfth century. Albart is represented to have been an Englishman who was induced by Erhard, bishop of Artinacha (Artmacha, Árd-Macha?) to come to Ireland. There he became Archbishop of Cashel. Later he and Erhard set out from Ireland as pilgrims and visited Pope Formosus (891–896). Albart went on to the Holy Sepulchre, buried a companion, Gillipatrick, there, and, returning, buried another, John, at Salzburg. In Ratisbon, where he found the tomb of his friend Erhard, he remained until his own death.

333. St. Rumold, or Rombaut, of Malines

(i) Life by Thierry of St.-Trond c A.D. 1100

EDS: Surius *De probatis sanctorum historiis* VII (Cologne 1581) 563–8. — Hugh Ward (ed. Th. Sirinus) *Acta, martyrium, liturgia antiqua et patria s. Rumoldi* (Louvain 1662) [there is said to have been an earlier edition at Malines, 1634]. — *AA. SS. Boll.* Jul. I 241–9 (215–22 of 3rd ed. 1867).

(ii) Anonymous Life s XIII, XIV or XV

EDS: Hugh Ward *op. cit.* — *AA. SS. Boll.* Jul. I 253–66 (225–34 of ed. 1867). On St. Rumold *cf.* P. Claessens *Vie de s. Rombaut, apôtre de Malines* (Malines 1875); *An.*

---

[88] *Cf.* pp. 521–3 *supra.*   [89] *Cf.* no. 344.

[90] KM suggested to me that this might be the Germanised form of the Irish *Erard.*

[91] There are later Lives of Erhard, but they have no independent value.

Boll. III 193, XIV 54, 249; J. Laenen *Histoire de l'église métropolitaine de St. Rombaut à Malines* 2 vols. (Malines 1919–20) [important; *cf. RHE* XIX (1923) 411–4].

Rumold, or Rombaut, honored as the apostle of Malines (Mechlin), Belgium, was, according to the early traditions, a stranger who lived there as a hermit and was murdered. The Life, written by a certain Thierry, abbot of St.-Trond in the diocese of Liége, is quite fabulous. It makes Rumold to have been a bishop of Dublin. The Irish origin of the saint must be regarded as doubtful. His death is assigned to about 775.

334. Life of St. Maxentia

ED: *Nova Legenda Anglie* (ed. Horstman, Oxford 1901) II 175–6.

John of Tynemouth's abridgment is all that remains of the *Vita* of this saint, whose nationality, and, indeed, existence, are dubious. Her father was "a certain king of the Irish." She crossed the sea, came to Beauvais, where she founded a convent, and was there murdered. Her tomb was the scene of many miracles, and was held in especial honor by " Carolus, who was at that time reigning."

335. The monastery of Honau

COMM: W. Reeves *Proc. RIA* VI (1853–7) 452–61. — Hauck *Kirchengeschichte Deutschlands* I (Leipsic 1898) 294, (ed. 1904) 305.

On an island called Honau, then situated in the Rhine near Strasburg but now no longer existing, there was about A.D. 772 a *monasterium Scottorum* which had been Irish probably from its foundation. Honau, Péronne, Fosses and Mazerolles are the only religious houses of this period as to which we have precise statements that they were peculiarly Irish in character, but the first document noticed below, as well as some other texts, indicates that such Irish monasteries on the Continent were already numerous.[92]

(i) Decree of Charles the Great A.D. 772 × 774

Carolus gratia Dei rex Francorum vir illuster commendat . . . gratiam nostram vultis habere.

ED: E. Mühlbacher *MGH Diplomata Karol.* I (Hanover 1906) no. lxxvii pp. 110–1.

The king directs the restitution of certain property stolen from the monks of Honau. " The illustrious Charles, by the grace of God king of the Franks, gives orders to all who have taken anything from the church of the Irish which is in the island of Honau that each restore again everything that he has received or carried off without the authorisation of the abbot Beatus. And if any one retains even a little, he orders all the magistrates of that region to search for all the goods of the church as per schedule, in accordance with the law of the Franks, for the goods of the pilgrims are the property of the king.[93] Therefore let all those things we have spoken of be restored

[92] See *Addenda.*
[93] " quia res peregrinorum propriae sunt regis."

to the church of the Irish without any let or hindrance,—whether land or vine or stock or vassals or silver or gold. But if any one will not do this, let him know that he is disobeying a royal command, for the kings of the Franks have given freedom to all Irish pilgrims, to the end that no one shall carry off anything of their property, and that no generation except their generation shall occupy their churches. So act from henceforth, as you may wish to experience our favor."

This is the earliest extant official confirmation of the privileges of distinctively Irish monasteries.

(ii) Donation of the abbot Beatus

ED: Mabillon *Annales ord. s. Benedicti* II (1704) 699 no. xix. The Irish names subscribed are in Z² p. xiv; *Supplement to Thes. Pal.* (Halle a. S. 1910) 76–7. *Cf. The Academy* no. 955 (Aug. 23, 1890) 229.

(iii) *Necrologium Honauense*

ED: Mone *Zs. f. d. Gesch. des Oberrheins.* IV 251.

336. Charles the Great: Letter to Offa, king of the Mercians A.D. 784 x 796

EDS: Baluze *Capitularia regum Francorum* I (Paris 1677) 198 [also later eds.]. — Jaffé *Bibl. rer. Germ.* IV (Berlin 1867) 351. — H&S III 486–7. — *MGH Epistolarum* IV 131.

An Irish priest in the diocese of Cologne had been accused of eating meat in Lent, and was being sent home to his own bishop for judgment. This letter requests Offa, king of Mercia, to forward him on his way.

337. The Second Council of Châlon-sur-Saône A.D. 813

EDS: Labbe VII (1672) 1281. — Mansi XIV (1769) 91–108. — *MGH Concilia* II 282. *Cf.* E. Bishop *Liturgica historica* (Oxford 1918) 172.

It is convenient to consider this document here, although it dates from the ninth century. The council, held by order of Charles the Great, at Châlon-sur-Saône, is explicit in condemning Irish *episcopi vagantes:* Canon xliii.[94] — " In some places there are Irishmen who say that they are bishops and ordain many irresponsible persons as priests and deacons without having any authorisation from their lords or the magistrates. The ordination of these men, since it very frequently results in the heresy of simony, and is liable to many abuses, we have all unanimously decreed ought to be regarded as null and void."[95]

[94] See also canons xli, xliv, xlv.

[95] The Council of Mayence, held in this same year 813, indulged in very picturesque denunciation of " clerici vagi," "habentes signum religionis, non religionis officium, hippocentauris similes, nec equi, nec homines," but does not specify them as *Scotti.* — *Concilium Moguntiacum* can. xxii: Mansi XIV 71; *MGH Concilia* II 267. — In 813 also the Third Council of Tours adopted decrees against these wandering, unattached ecclesiastics. — *Conc. Turonense* III can. xiii: Mansi XIV 85; *MGH ibid.* 288. (The same council, however, enjoined bishops to receive at their tables foreigners and the poor. — Can. vi *ibid.*)
A capitulare, likewise of 813, directed each bishop to enquire if there were any such foreign clerics in his diocese, and, if so, to send them home. — *Capitul. Aquisgranense* xxiii: Migne *PL* XCVII 364; *MGH Capitularia* I 174.

VI. Irish Scholars in the Carolingian Empire under Charles the Great and Louis the Pious

Bibliography

The following, out of many works, may be mentioned as of special application to this and the following sections dealing with the ninth century: E. Lavisse *Histoire de France* II pt. I. — Louis Halphen *Études critiques sur l'histoire de Charlemagne* (Paris 1921) [has little bearing on the subjects here considered, but is an important re-examination of the history of Charles the Great]. — B. Hauréau *Singularités historiques et littéraires* (Paris 1861) [gives some attention to the Irish schools and teachers]. — L. Maître *Les écoles épiscopales et monastiques de l'Occident depuis Charlemagne jusqu'à Philippe-Auguste* (Paris 1866). — J. B. Mullinger *The schools of Charles the Great* (London 1877) [an important study, but the author develops his story of a controversy between the party of the Irish teachers and that of Alcuin and his followers more elaborately than the texts warrant]. — Clerval *Les écoles de Chartres au moyen âge* (Chartres 1895) [includes a general survey of the Carolingian schools]. — Manitius *Lat. Lit.* I 243 *sqq* [important]. — Sir John Edwin Sandys *A history of classical scholarship from the sixth century B.C. to the end of the middle ages* 3rd ed. I (Cambridge 1921) chap. xxv. — L. Traube *O Roma nobilis Philologische Untersuchungen aus dem Mittelalter* (*Abhandl. d. k. bayer. Akad. d. Wissensch.* I Cl. XIX ii) (Munich 1891) [contains, among other studies, several of great importance for the history of the Irish on the Continent in the 9th cent.]. — Wm. Turner " Irish teachers in the Carolingian revival of learning" *Cath. Univ. Bull.* XIII (July, Oct. 1907) 382–99, 562–81. — Two works on mediaeval Latin culture which will be found of interest to the student of the share of the Irish therein are L. Traube *Einleitung in die lateinische Philologie des Mittelalters* (*Vorlesungen u. Abhandlungen* II) (Munich 1911) [*cf.* esp. 39 *sqq*]; and P. Lehmann "Aufgaben u. Anregungen d. lat. Philologie d. Mittelalters" *Sitzungsb. d. k. Bay. Akad. d. Wissensch.* Philos.-philol. u. hist. Kl. 1918 (Munich 1918).

The energy and good fortune of the Karling line had turned the dissolving Merovingian kingdom into a powerful Romano-German empire, the material basis on which learning and literature might revive. Charles the Great, by reason of his intellectual curiosity, his sense of responsibility, his respect for learning and dislike of ignorance and slovenliness, gave the impulse which inaugurated that revival. The two great movements, sprung from Ireland and England, which had affected the Church in the Frankish dominions during the seventh and eighth centuries had been religious and moral in character, and had promoted or preserved scholarship only as a necessary appanage. But the monasteries that Columbanus had inspired, and the diocesan organisations that had been galvanised by Boniface, were the instruments available to the hand of Charles in his work for a higher civilisation. In a series of *capitularia* issued from 787 to 789 he gave orders and laid down regulations for the maintenance of schools of letters in all bishoprics and monasteries of the empire.   The palace school,[96] which under the Merovingians seems to have been a training-ground in deportment for the children of the nobility, became now the chief centre of letters and scholarship.   But, although Charles promoted, both directly and indirectly, what may be designated the higher branches of learning and literature, and in particular seems to have been interested in the emendation of the biblical text and in the reform of the liturgy, his principal aim was the creation of a body of men who could read intelligently and use grammatically the Latin language, and who could copy a document or a book in a script readily readable. It seems clear that the great majority of Irish exiles who found employment in continental Europe during the ninth century did so as scribes or as teachers of grammar.

Many of the scholars whom the new policy brought into prominence were from outside the Frankish territory.   Most noteworthy was Alcuin, who came from York in Northumbria, where a tradition of learning had been maintained since the days of Bede, and where one of the finest libraries of the early middle ages had been collected.   When returning from a journey to Rome, in 780-1, on ecclesiastical business, he met Charles at Parma and was induced to enter his service.   From 782 to 796 he was, with some intermissions, master of the palace school, and practically minister of education, and from 796 to 804 abbot of the monastery of St. Martin at Tours.   With the palace school were associated, it would appear, the Irishmen Clemens and Dicuil; at Pavia an Irishman named Dungal taught, who in 825 became a kind of supervisor of education in northern Italy; and there were other teachers from the western isle as to whose spheres of activity we have little knowledge. As the century progressed the Norse attacks drove Irish scholars in increasing numbers to the Continent, but that some had been already attracted to the service of the Carolingian Empire before the breaking of that storm is certain.

Charles the Great died in 814 [97] and was succeeded as emperor by his son, called Louis the Pious (d. 840).   Historians have commonly deplored his weakness in the administration of secular affairs, but there was no break from the tradition of his father in the promotion of religion

---

[96] See Vacandard in *Rev. des quest. hist.* LXI (1897) 490, LXII (1897) 546, LXXVI (1904) 549.

[97] The author of the *Planctus Caroli*, a lament for the great emperor written shortly after his death by a monk of Bobbio, has been classed by some as an Irishman, but this is not probable.   The poem is found in Bouquet V (Paris 1744: 2nd ed. 1869) 407-8, where it is wrongly ascribed to Columban of St. Trond; in Migne *PL* CVI 1257 *sqq*; Dümmler *MGH Poet. lat. aevi Carol.* I (1881) 434-6, II (1884) 694; Waitz (ed. Holder-Egger) *Einhardi Vita Karoli Magni* (*MGH SS. rer. Germ. in usum scholarum*) (1911) 48-50. *Cf.* Dümmler *NA* IV (1879) 151.

and learning and the patronage of foreign pilgrims and scholars. He
and his second queen, Judith, entrusted the education of their son, afterwards known as Charles the Bald, to Walahfrid Strabo, a brilliant disciple of Hraban Maur (himself Alcuin's chief successor as a teacher),
and to his training, as well as to the general tone of culture in the court,
was due the important patronage which learning and letters received
in later years from this prince.

338. Life of Charles the Great, by Einhard A.D. 817 x 836

Eds: Duchesne *Hist. Franc. SS.* II (Paris 1636) 93–106. — *AA. SS. Boll.* Jan. II
877–88 (3rd ed. III 493–503). — Bouquet V (Paris 1744; 2nd ed. 1869) 88–103.
— *MGH SS* II (1829) 443–63. — Waitz *MGH SS. rer. Germ. in usum schol.* (1880);
6th ed. by O. Holder-Egger (1911) [good]. — Migne *PL* XCVII 9–62. — Jaffé *Bibl.
rer. Germ.* IV (Berlin 1867) 507–41. — H. W. Garrod and R. B. Mowat *Einhard's
Life of Charlemagne* (Oxford 1915) [*cf. Le Moyen Âge* XIX (1915) 149–52; *RH* CXXI
(1916) 316–7]. — Louis Halphen (*Les classiques de l'histoire de France au moyen âge* I)
(Paris 1923) [with Fr. trans.]. Trans: Eng.: Wm. Glaister (London 1877). — A. J.
Grant *Eginhard and the Monk of St. Gall — Early Lives of Charlemagne* (*Medieval
library* XIV) (London 1922). Fr.: Guizot *Collect. des mém. rel. à l'hist. de France* III
119–61. Germ.: O. Abel *Geschichtschreiber d. deut. Vorzeit* (Berlin 1850; 2nd ed.
by Wattenbach, Leipsic 1880; 3rd ed. 1893; 4th ed. by Tangl, 1912, 1920). Comm:
For the older bibliog. and criticism see the guides by Potthast *s. v.*; Molinier I 197–200;
Wattenbach *DGQ* I⁷ 210 *sqq*; and Monod *Études critiques sur les sources de l'histoire
carolingienne* 155 *sqq*. — Mlle. Bondois *La translation des saints Marcellin et Pierre*
(Paris 1907) [mainly a study of Einhard and his times]. — Manitius *Lat. Lit.* I 639–
46. — L. Halphen *op. cit.* [p. 530 *supra*] 60–103 [first appeared in *RH* CXXVI (1917)
271–314; a very important piece of destructive criticism]. — Buchner *Einhards
Künstler- und Gelehrtenleben* (*Bücherei d. Kultur u. Geschichte* XXII) (Bonn and Leipsic
1922) [takes the pre-Halphen view of Einhard, but is a good study of the era].

Einhard, or Eginhard, was born in the district of the river Main, in Franconia,
probably about 775, and studied at the monastery of Fulda. The abbot sent him to
the palace school, apparently in 791–2, where he became the pupil of Alcuin. He
remained attached to the court, but held no position of prominence until the accession
of Louis the Pious, who made him one of his chief ministers. Losing the imperial
favor about 830, he retired to his native country, founded the monastery of Seligenstadt,
and died there as abbot in 840.

His Life of Charles the Great was written between 817 and 836, probably after his
retirement in 830. It is one of the famous biographies of the middle ages, but its
value as historical material is not placed as high now, especially since the appearance
of Halphen's studies, as formerly. It is tendencious and panegyrical, and influenced
by the model of Suetonius. Einhard seems neither to have had much " inside knowledge," nor to have been accurate in the use of his sources. But the book has interest
and value—among other things, for the story of the revival of learning. It tells [98] of
the emperor's friendship for " peregrini," which was so great that they became a

[98] *Cap.* xxi.

burden to the palace and the kingdom, a statement in which Halphen suspects some personal malice of long-standing towards the Irish.[99] The only specific mention of the Irish is in the following peculiar passage:

" By his munificence he [Charles] had the kings of the Irish so disposed to court his favor that they never spoke of him otherwise than as ' Lord ' and themselves as his subjects and servants. Letters are in existence sent by them to him in which they express in this manner their regard for him."[100]

Nothing similar is to be found in any other source, Irish or continental—except such as are obviously derived from Einhard—and the only explanation suggested is that the writer has confused English with Irish, and then strained his matter quite recklessly— as, indeed, he seems to have done throughout this chapter—to serve his panegyric.[101]

A metrical version of Einhard's Life, with additions from some other sources, was composed by a Saxon clerk c A.D. 888 x 891. EDS: Duchesne II 136 sqq. — Bouquet V 136-84.—MGH SS I 227-79. — Migne PL XCIX 683-736. — Jaffé IV 544-627. — P. von Winterfeld MGH Poet. lat. aevi Carol. IV fasc. i (1899) 1-71.

339. The History of Charles the Great (De gestis Karoli Magni) by the Monk of St. Gall A.D. 883 x 887

EDS: Duchesne II 107-35. — Bouquet V 106-35. — MGH SS II 731-63. — Migne PL XCVIII 1371-1410. — Jaffé IV 628-700. GERM. TRANS: Wattenbach in Geschicht-schreiber d. deut. Vorzeit (3rd ed. 1890). [Cf. bibliog. to no. 338]. COMM: For the older literature see Potthast s. v.; Wattenbach DGQ I⁷ 307; Molinier I 200-1. — L. Halphen Études critiques sur l'histoire de Charlemagne (Paris 1921) 104-42 [appeared first in RH CXXVIII (1918) 260-98]. See also Margaret Stokes Six months in the Apennines (London 1892) 202-3.

In December, 883, the Emperor Charles the Fat stopped at the monastery of St. Gall when returning north from Italy.[102] In response to his request then made, one of the monks wrote this anecdotal account of the great emperor. The author is usually identified with Notker Balbulus.[103] The work professes to be based on oral tradition, but this element does not seem to have been large. For the greater part it is literary legend manufactured from the written sources and from general folk-lore motifs, and has but little historical value.

The work opens with a bizarre account of the beginning of the revival of learning in the dominions of Charles through the arrival of two Irishmen who proclaimed that they had wisdom for sale. The author appears to have in mind Clement of the palace school and Dungal of Pavia, but as a narrative of events the story is pure fiction.

[99] Halphen op. cit. Cf. p. 537 infra, n. 115.
[100] Cap. xvi.
[101] Halphen op. cit. 96-7. " Il est difficile d'expliquer les dires étranges d'Einhard autrement que par toute une série de confusions."
[102] Cf. p. 595 infra.
[103] Cf. nos. 412, 413.

340. Correspondence and Poems of Alcuin

Comm: Th. Sickel "Alcuinstudien" *Sitzungsb. d. k. k. Akad. d. Wissensch. z. Wien* LXXIX (Vienna 1875) 461–550. — K. Werner *Alcuin und sein Jahrhundert* (Paderborn 1876). — E. Dümmler in *Allgemeine deutsche Biographie* I 343–8; "Alchuinstudien" *Sitzungsb. d. k. preuss. Akad. d. Wissensch.* XXVII 495–523; "Zur Lebengeschichte Alcuins" *NA* XVIII (1893) 53–70. — A. F. West *Alcuin and the rise of the Christian schools* (New York, London 1892, 1893). — C. J. B. Gaskoin *Alcuin, his life and his work* (London 1904). — Manitius *Lat. Lit.* I 273–88. — Moncelle in *Dict. d'hist. et de géogr. ecclés.* fasc. vii (1912) 30 *sqq.* The literature is very extensive, and may be traced through the usual guides.

(i) The Letters of Alcuin

Eds: (F) Froben *Alcuini opera* (Ratisbon 1776) I 1–297. — (M) Migne *PL* C 139–512, CI 1317–20. — (J) Jaffé *Bibl. rer. Germ.* VI (Berlin 1873) 144–897. — (D) Dümmler *MGH Epistolarum* IV (1895) [best].

These are very important historical sources. The following are the most interesting to the Irish student:

Ad Leutfredum episcopum coenobii Mugensis in Hibernia. A.D. 773 x 786 Eds: F ccviii. — J vii. — M 493. — D ii p. 19. Letter written to Leuthfriht, bishop of the Anglo-Saxon monastery of Mayo which Colmán established in Ireland when he withdrew from Lindisfarne after the Council of Whitby, 664. *Cf.* pp. 216, 463 *supra.*

Georgii episcopi Ostiensis ad Hadrianum Papam A.D. 786. Eds: J x. — D iii 19–29. — H&S III 447–61. Report of the papal legate, the bishop of Ostia, on two councils held in England this year. At the first council "Alduulfus, Myiensis ecclesie episcopus," that is, bishop of Mayo, was present and signed sixth.

Ad Colcu A.D. 790. Eds: F iii. — J xiv. — M CI 142. — D vii 31–3. — Ussher *Sylloge* 37–8 [*Whole Works* IV 466–7]. — Colgan *AA. SS.* 20 Feb. Alcuin writes to the "magister" Colcu concerning the news of the world, in particular the victories of Charles, and sends alms and gifts, partly his own, partly from the king. "I thy son, and Joseph thy fellow-countryman, are by the mercy of God in good health; and all thy friends who are with us continue prosperously in the service of God." Colcu—the name is Irish— would appear to have been a teacher in Britain, doubtless at York.[104] As will be seen, Joseph also was an Irishman.

Ad Josephum A.D. 790. Eds: J xvi. — D viii pp. 33–4. Alcuin, who is now in Britain, writes to his "son" Joseph, giving him various directions about matters of business. "Your master Colcu is well, and so are your friends who are with us."

Ad Josephum A.D. 790 x 793. Eds: F cxxxi. — J xx. — M 444. — D xiv 40. Alcuin writes to his "son" Joseph, consoling him in his ill-health.

[104] He has been identified with Colcu úa Duinechda (no. 580), who died in 796 (AU), and who was, according to FM, a member of the community of Clúain-moccu-Nóis. The identification has little more value than a guess, for the name Colcu was quite common. It is, of course, not impossible that a teacher from Clonmacnois should be at York at this time. The assumption that Alcuin's letter was directed to Clonmacnois gives a forced and improbable meaning to the texts in which he mentions Colcu.

Ad Remedium episcopum A.D. 791 x 796. EDS: F cxxxii. — M 445. — J ccxiii. — D lxxvii. Alcuin to Remedius, bishop of Chur, with, *inter alia*, the request " Direct prayers, I beseech you, for the soul of Joseph my disciple."

Ad Domnum Regem A.D. 798. EDS: F lxvii. — J xcviii. — M 266. — D cxlv pp. 231–5. *Cf.* Hauréau *Singularités historiques et littéraires* 26; C.J.B. Gaskoin *Alcuin*: *his life and work* (London 1904) 102–6, 253–8. Alcuin had written to Charles the Great in regard to certain changes in the calendar for the year 797. The king replied sending him some criticisms on his suggestions made by certain inmates of the palace school, and thus brought on a heavy astronomical correspondence of which this is the first letter. " In my innocence and ignorance I did not know that a school of the Egyptians was carrying on its work in the famous palace of David: [105] when I went away [106] I left Latins there; I know not who has slipped in Egyptians. Nor have I been as ignorant of the Memphritic computation as well-disposed towards the Roman usage," etc. Some have seen in this an attack on Clemens Scottus or other Irish scholars at the palace school,[107] part of a wide-spread controversy then raging. The suggestion is plausible, but there is no conclusive evidence in its support.

Nobilissimis Sanctae Ecclesiae filiis, qui per latitudinem Hiberniensis insulae Deo Christo religioso conversatione et sapientiae studiis servire videntur c A.D. 792 x 800. EDS: F ccxxi. — M 500. — J ccxvii. — D cclxxx 437–8. Alcuin congratulates the monks of Ireland on the good reports of them he has heard from Bishop Dungal: [108] " In ancient times very learned teachers were accustomed to come from Ireland to Britain, Gaul, and Italy."

Ad Patres Mugensis Ecclesiae A.D. 793 x 804. EDS: J cclxxvi. — D cclxxxvii 445–6. A friendly letter to the monks of Mayo, urging devotion to study. " Let your light shine in the midst of a most barbarous people." [109]

(ii) Poems by Alcuin

EDS: Froben *Alcuini opera* (Ratisbon 1776) II 219. — Migne *PL* CI 761. — Dümmler *MGH Poet. lat. aevi Carol.* I (Berlin 1881) 342. — *Vit. Trip.* II 503.

Among Alcuin's poems are two short stanzas[110] commemorative of Irish saints, the one of " Patricius," " Cheranus," " Columbanus," " Congallus " and "Adomnanus," the other of " Brigida " and " Ita." [111]

---

[105] All this is an echo of the pedantry of the scholars and courtiers who gathered around Charles and formed a make-believe academy — somewhat after the manner of Virgilius *grammaticus* (no. 20) and his friends — in which they adopted scriptural or classical names: Charles was " David, " Alcuin " Flaccus " (*i.e.*, Quintus Horatius Flaccus), Einhard " Beseleel," etc.

[106] *I.e.*, when he became abbot of Tours in 796.

[107] *Cf.* no. 344. AdeJ suggests that Clement had spoken of the Irish descent from Scotta, daughter of Pharaoh. Apparently this fable was in existence in the eighth century.

[108] *Cf.* pp. 538 *sqq.* None of the Dungals with whom we meet is elsewhere referred to as a bishop.

[109] Alcuin makes several other references to Ireland and the Irish. In his *Versus de sanctis Euboricensis ecclesiae* vv. 455 *sqq.* he speaks of a learned but irreligious Irishman who, having fallen sick of the plague, was cured and converted by a relic of the Northumbrian king Oswald; and in the same poem, vv. 835 *sqq.* refers to the raid made on the Irish, — " the peoples of the Irish . . . always friendly to the English " (gentes Scotorum . . . Anglis et semper amicas) — by Egfrid of Northumbria in 684. (Froben II 246, 250; Migne *PL* CI 822–3, 829–30; Dümmler 180, 188.) These two passages are probably based directly on Bede.

[110] Ed. Dümmler CX xv, xvi.

[111] For other texts by Alcuin see nos. 68, 280 (ii), 329 (vii).

341. Josephus Scottus: Poems A.D. 782 x 796

(i) [Ad Sanctum Liudgerum] Frater amore dei cognato dulcior omni. . . . Concordat modico. Felix sine fine valeto! 16 ll. (ii) [Ad Albinum] Isaiae brevibus, lector, mysteria verbis. . . . Sic placet Albino talem nos ferre laborem. 7 ll. Hieronimus monuit postremi in fronte libelli. . . . Care magister ave, dominus te salvet ubique. 11 ll. [Prose] Haec brevi, prout . . . clemens dominus Iesus. (iii) [Ad Carolum Regem] Primus avus vivens, en, nos in morte redegit. . . . Hinc genetrix verae tu sumis semina vitae. 35 ll. [Forms a peculiar acrostic, fully illustrated in Dümmler's ed.] (iv) [Ad Carolum Regem] Dic, o Carle, putas quae verae signa salutis. . . . Carmina, si iubeas sed plus, superaddo camenas. 41 ll. [First 35 ll. contain another peculiar acrostic.] (v) [Ad Carolum Regem] Vita, salus, virtus, verbum, sapientia, sponsus, . . . Tuque memento mei dicor qui nomine Ioseph. 39 ll. [Acrostic.] (vi) [Ad Carolum Regem] Inclyta si cupias sancti sub culmina templi. . . . Frugifero cispes: laudant modo sidera caeli. 36 ll. [Acrostic.]

MSS: (i) [From the *Vita Liudgeri*]. (ii) [From the Commentary on Isaias: cf. *infra*]. (iii-vi) Berne Stadtbibl. 212 *s* IX/X ff. 123-6. EDS: *AA. SS. Boll.* Mar. III 645 [i]. — *MGH SS* II 409 [i]. — Migne *PL* XCIX 821-2 [ii, part]. — H. Hagen *Carmina medii aevi* (Berne 1877) 116-24, 216-20 [iii-vi]. — Dümmler *MGH Poet. lat. aevi Carol.* I (Berlin 1881) 149-59 [i-vi]. COMM: Dümmler *NA* IV 139. — Manitius *ibid.* XI (1886) 558, XXXII (1907) 663, XXXVI (1911) 765; *Lat. Lit.* I (1911) 547-9. — Wattenbach *DGQ* I (1904) 171. — Riese *Anthologia Latina* I ii (1906) 6, 383. — K. Strecker *NA* XLIV (1924) 220.

There can be little reasonable doubt that the " Ioseph abbas Scottus genere," author of these Latin poems, is the same man as the pupil of Colcu and friend of Alcuin.[112] It is possible, as Colgan suggested, that he is identical with the " Joseph nepos Cernae abbas Clúana maccu Nóis " whose obit is given in the Annals of Ulster as of 794. The metrical epistle addressed to Liudger, bishop of Münster (d. 809), was incorporated into the Life of that prelate written by his successor, Altfrid (d. 859). No. ii of the above list includes the verses which open and close Joseph's *Commentary on Isaias*,[113] and the concluding prose epistle. The remaining four sets of verses are ingenious acrostics dealing with religious subjects, written for the edification of the great Charles.[114]

342. Theodulf, bishop of Orleans: Poem to Charles the Great
A.D. 796

EDS: Sirmondi *Opera* II (Paris 1696). — Migne *PL* CV 322. — Dümmler *MGH Poet. lat. aevi Carol.* I (1881) 483-9 (carm. 25); see also p. 492 (carm. 27). *Cf.* Mullinger *Schools of Charles the Great*; Halphen *Études critiques sur l'historire de Charlemagne* 69-70,

Theodulf, bishop of Orleans, was born in Spain about 760, and died in 821. With the exception of Alcuin he was the most distinguished man of letters in the dominions of Charles the Great, and became famous both as a poet and as a theologian. He made himself a virulent opponent of the Irish. In this poem addressed to Charles he denounces the " Scottellus " as

" Res dira, hostis atrox, hebes horror, pestis acerba,
    Litigiosa lues, res fera, grande nefas " etc., etc.

---

[112] *Cf.* no. 340 (i).

[113] The *Commentary* has never been printed. It was compiled from St. Jerome at the request of Alcuin. In Scherrer *Verzeichnis der Handschriften der Stiftsbibliothek von St. Gallen* (1875) 95 it is wrongly attributed to Bede. MSS: BN 12154 *s* IX ff. 1-192. — St. Gall Stiftsbibl. 254 *s* IX ff. 2-252.

[114] Joseph may have been the author of some riddles now lost: *cf.* G. Becker *Catalogi bibliothecarum antiqui* (1885) 28, 37. Turner (" Irish Teachers in the Carolingian Revival " 390) proposes him as the author of one of the sets of glosses on the *Isagoge* of Porphyry.

The poem mentions as of the party of Theodulf against the Irishman several disciples of Alcuin,[115] and some historians have regarded it as an episode of an Alcuin-Clement controversy.[116]

343. Letter from Benedict of Aniane to Gisarnarius

Baluze *Miscellaneorum* V 54. — Migne *PL* CIII 1413.

Benedict, abbot of Aniane (d. 821),[117] was one of the most influential churchmen in the reigns of Charles the Great and Louis the Pious. In this letter, written to a disciple, he warns against the " syllogism of deceit " which was in favor " with modern scholastics, especially with the Irish." This is one of several evidences to the distrust felt by more conservative ecclesiastics towards the Irish and their dialectic methods.

344. Texts related to Clemens Scottus

(i) His *Ars grammatica* A.D. 815 x 831

(a) [*Ars grammatica* proper] In dei nomine pauca incipiunt de philosophia et de partibus eius. M. Omnibus divina stimulante . . . aut positione longae fiunt. Finit de partibus orationis. Then follow some abbreviations which Steinmeyer (*Die Althochdeutschen Glossen* IV 539) interprets: Clemens grammaticus principi augustissimo Hlotario filio domni Hludowici imperatoris. (b) [Treatise on metre] Pes est syllabarum . . . et constantinopolitanorum. (c) [Treatise *de barbarismo*] Incipiunt pauca de barbarismo collecta de multis. . . . Troia capta fuit. (d) [Dedicatory verses addressed to Lothair] Pauca tibi, Caesar, de multis, magne Hlothari. . . . Floribus hinc redolent, post sua liba ferunt. 18 ll. Manitius and Tolkichn believe that (d), the original dedication of (a) to Lothair, was misplaced by the editor.

MSS: Bamberg M. V. 18 *s* X ff. 1–70 [complete]. — Vat. Reg. 1442 *s* XI ff. 1 *sqq*[a, multilated at end]. — BN 13026 *s* IX ff. 131–60 [parts of a]. — Leyden Voss. 4to 33 *s* X ff. 75–81, 159–70 [part of a, c]. — Munich Staatsbibl. 14401 *s* XI ff. 154–68 [parts of a]; 17210 *s* XII ff. 98–100 [b]. — Berne Stadtbibl. 123 *s* X ff. 1–31ᵛ [a, incomplete]. — Valenciennes Bibl. publ. M. 7. 3 *s* IX/X [c]. EDS: H. Keil *Grammatici latini* I (Leipsic 1857) pp. xix–xxi [d]; *De grammaticis quibusdam latinis infimae aetais commentatio* (*Programm*, Erlangen 1868) 9–15 [preface of a, d]. — E. Dümmler *MGH Poet lat. aevi Carol.* II (1884) 670 [d]. — M. Esposito "Hiberno-Latin MSS in the libraries of Switzerland" II *Proc. RIA* XXXC (1912) 8–14 [part of a]. COMM: B. Hauréau *Singularités hist. et litt.* (Paris 1861) 19–24. — Müller *Neue Jahrbücher f. Philologie u. Paedagogik* XCIII (1866) 385, 389, 557–9. — H. Hagen *Anecdota Helvetica* [supplement to Keil's *Grammatici latini*] (Leipsic 1870) [discusses the value of the texts of older grammarians preserved by Clement, and publishes some of these]. — B. Simson *Jahrbücher des fränkischen Reichs unter Ludwig dem Frommen* II (Leipsic 1876) 255–61 [account of the palace school during this period]. — Dümmler *Geschichte d. ostfränk. Reichs* II (Berlin 1865) 649 [good]. — *NA* IV (1879) 258. — Wattenbach *DGQ* I⁷ (1904) 227, 253. — Manitius *Lat. Lit.* I (1911) 456-8 [excellent: see also *NA* XXXII (1907) 673].

[115] There is a half-contemptuous allusion to Einhard — " Nardulus " — as preparing arrows to slay the " Scottus," who is better described as " sottus." — *Vv.* 155 *sqq.* This last witticism seems to have been a favorite in the early middle ages. *Cf.* p. 589 *infra.*

[116] *Cf.* p. 535 *supra.*

[117] *Cf.* p. 199 *supra.*

The Clement who was one of the heroes of the story told by the monk of St. Gall [118] may be identified with the " Clemens Scottus," " Clemens Hibernicus," master of the palace school and author of the *Ars grammatica*, without accepting that picturesque narrative as a historical record of his arrival in the Frankish Empire. He would appear to have been the successor,—perhaps the immediate successor,—of Alcuin in the palace school,[119] and was still at court in 826.[120] The future emperor Lothair seems to have been one of his pupils. From an entry in the Würzburg necrology [121] it is believed that he ended his life in that favorite resort of Irish " pilgrims." His grammatical works, of which only some fragments have been published, are valuable as indications of the character of the instruction in his time, and as aids for the textual criticism of the earlier authors whom he quotes. These quotations are numerous and extensive, but may testify to the extent of the palace library rather than to that of Clement's unknown home in Ireland.

(ii) Catalogue of the abbots of Fulda

EDS: J. F. Böhmer *Fontes rerum Germanicarum* III (Stuttgart 1863) 161-4. — Waitz *MGH SS.* XIII 272-4.

This catalogue (A.D. 744–916) relates of Abbot Ratgar (802–817): "At that time also he sent Hrabanus and Hatton to Tours to Master Albinus to learn the liberal arts ... Modestus and others to Clemens Scottus to learn grammar." Modestus, or Reccheo, was a monk of Fulda whose name has been preserved as a friend of Candidus, a *savant* of that monastery in the ninth century.

DUNGAL OF ST.-DENIS

Bibliography

L. A. Muratori *Antiquitates Italicae medii aevi* III diss. xliii 815-8. — E. Dümmler *NA* IV (1879) 142-4, 254-6. — M. Manitius *ibid.* XI (1886) 561; *Lat. Lit.* I 370-4 [good]. — L. Traube *O Roma nobilis* (1891) 332-7 [a brief but important study on the identification of the several Dungals and their writings]. — A. Hauck *Kirchengeschichte Deutschlands* II (1900) 154 *sq.* — Wattenbach *DGQ* I⁷ 170. — K. Strecker *NA* XLIV (1922) 222.

The name of Dungal was common in mediaeval Ireland, and common, it would appear, among the Irish exiles in the Carolingian empire. Several documentary and literary references to a man of this name, and

---

[118] *Cf.* no. 339.

[119] *Cf.* pp. 535, 537. However, we do not meet with decisive evidence of Clement's presence in the palace school until the reign of Louis the Pious.

[120] A ninth-century poet known as Ermoldus Nigellus wrote a lengthy metrical panegyric of Louis the Pious in which he mentions Clement among those present at the court when the Danish king Harold was baptized in 826: *MGH Poet. lat. aevi Carol.* II 69. Clement is also mentioned in some verses written before 817 to the young Prudentius, afterwards bishop of Troyes (*cf.* no. 382; also p. 576 *infra*), who was educated at the palace school: *ibid.* I 581.

[121] " IV Kal. Junii Clementis Magistri Palatini ": Dümmler in *Forschungen zur deutschen Geschichte* VI (Göttingen 1866) 115-9.

several works ascribed to him, have been preserved to us. Formerly it was assumed that all were to be assigned to one man, who began his career in the palace school or in the famous monastery of St.-Denis, a few miles north of Paris, later was transferred to Pavia, and died at Bobbio. Traube, however, has shown that it is probable there were at least four Dungals, — the recluse at St.-Denis, the teacher in Pavia, a companion of Sedulius Scottus, and a monk of Bobbio in the eleventh century. It is possible that the first two were identical, although chronological considerations are against such a theory. A considerable number of pieces in prose and verse is available which in some cases are attributed by the manuscripts to an author of the name Dungal, in others are manifestly associated with those so attributed. Traube has assorted this material with much skill and shown that nearly all that was due to a Dungal should be assigned to the recluse of St.-Denis. If Traube is right, Dungal must have come to St.-Denis about 784 and have been still living there in 827.

345. Charles the Great: Letter to Dungal c A.D. 804 x 814

Sententias sive rationes . . . post tenebras spero lucem.

MS: Brussels Bibl. roy. 9587 s IX ex f. 51. ED: Dümmler *MGH Epist. Karol. aevi* II (Berlin 1895) 552. *Cf.* Manitius *Lat. Lit.* I 461.

A request for information as to the nature of darkness and nothingness, à propos of a treatise " de nihilo et tenebris " sent to the Emperor by Fridugis, pupil of Alcuin and afterwards abbot of Tours.

346. Dungal: Letters

(i) [To the Emperor Charles] In nomine Patris. . . . Audivi ergo, domine dilectissime, ego Dungalus, . . . amantissime pater. A.D. 811. (ii) [To a bishop] In nomine Patris. . . . Dungalus devotus. . . . Vestra copiosissima . . . protegat alarum. *C* A.D. 800 x 814. (iii) [To an abbot] Domino honoratissimo . . . Memor nostri . . . sicut modo sum. *C* A.D. 800 x 814. (iv) [To Abbot Adam] Domino veneratissimo. . . . Vestra beneficia . . . beatissime valeatis. *C* A.D. 800 x 814. (v) [To a priest] Domino sancto. . . . Sagacissima vestra. . . . Presbitero claro moribus et merito. *C* A.D. 800 x 814. (vi) [To an abbot] *C* A.D. 800 x 814. (vii) [To Theodrada, daughter of the Emperor Charles] In nomine. . . . Theodradae Dungalus peregrinus. . . . Saepe volui. . . . Moribus et specie ornatam, Theodrada, salutat. After A.D. 814. (viii) [To an abbot] Domino reverentissimo. . . . Modo vobis. . . . Veras ac validas opto salutis opes. *C* A.D. 814.

MSS: Berlin Staatsbibl. Phillipps MS 1784 s IX ff. 1–13 [i]. — BM Harl. 208 s IX ff. 113–7 [ii-viii]. EDS: D'Achéry *Spicilegium* X 143 (2nd ed. III 324) [i]. — Migne *PL* CV 447–58 [i]. — Jaffé *Bibl. rer. Germ.* IV (Berlin 1867) 396–400, 430–6. — Dümmler *MGH Epist. Karol. aevi* II (Berlin 1895) 570–83.

The first of these letters was written by Dugal of St.-Denis in 811, in reply to a request made by the Emperor through Waldo, abbot of that monastery from 806 to 813, for an explanation of the occurrence of two solar eclipses in the preceding year. Dungal gave a scientific explanation, adopting, of course, the Ptolemaic system. His reply contains extensive quotations from Macrobius.[122] The seventh letter conveys his good wishes, on her entrance into the convent, to Theodrada, daughter of Charlemagne, whom we know from other sources to have been abbess of a convent near Paris in 824. The remaining six epistles are more personal and throw some light on Dungal's character and circumstances: ii and iii are begging letters; iv asks Abbot Adam of Jumièges for a horse that he may visit the king, as his own has become lame and blind; [123] he also recommends to the abbot a needy Saxon (doubtless an Englishman); vi accompanies a consignment of silver to be made into altar-vessels.

347. Dungal's Reply to Claudius, bishop of Turin A.D. 827

Hunc itaque libellum. . . . Ego ambiguitas . . . ipse dederit, adjuncturus.

MS: Vat. Reg. 200 s XI/XII ff. 7-10 [formerly of St.-Denis. There were two MSS in Bobbio: Becker *Catalogi bibliothecarum antiqui* (Bonn 1885) 507; *NA* XXXII 663.] EDS: *Bibl. max. vet. patrum* (Leyden 1677) XIV 199-200. — Migne *PL* CV 465-530. — Dümmler *Epist. Karol. aevi* II (1895) 583-5 [prologue only].

The Iconoclastic controversy had spread to the West in the reign of Charles the Great, especially as a result of a faulty translation of the Greek Acts of the Second Council of Nicaea (787) which Pope Hadrian I sent to the Frankish ruler. This translation represented the Council as declaring that the same adoration was due to sacred images as to the Holy Trinity. The bishops of the West promptly repudiated such a doctrine. Some went further, among them Claudius, a Spaniard who had been appointed bishop of Turin in 816. Claudius destroyed the crosses and other religious representations in his diocese, and, when remonstrated with by his friend Abbot Theutmir, issued, in 824, an "Apologeticum" condemning the invocation of saints, veneration of relics and images, pilgrimages, etc.[124] At the request of Louis the Pious and his son Lothair, Dungal undertook to reply. His arguments are for the most part based on Patristics. A notable feature is the extensive use he makes of the Christian poets, quoting from Prudentius, Paulinus of Nola, Fortunatus and Sedulius. He thereby has preserved some fragments of their works which otherwise would have been lost. Because of similarity of style, mainly, the author of this tract has been identified with the inmate of St.-Denis. It is possible, however, that he was Dungal of Pavia.[125]

348. Poems of Dungal of St.-Denis

(i) Poems attributed to Dungal

(i) Hos versus in honorem Hildoardi episcopi Dungalus peregrinus. . . . Hanc tibi victricem, dux inclite sume. . . . Exiguum et famulum commemorare tuum.   20 ll.   The initial letters form the legend " Hildoardo Dungalus tue."   *C* A.D. 800 x 816.
(ii) Dungalus magister: Martyribus venerandis busta ut trina coruscant. . . . Praemia cuique Deus est non peritura daturus.   8 ll.   A.D. 815 x c 830.

[122] Dungal adds " For Pliny Secundus and other books by which I believe I could supplement this information we have not with us in these parts "; but this need not necessarily mean that he had used the desired books in Ireland. *Cf.* Manitius *Lat. Lit.* I 373.
[123] He admits here that his countrymen are a burden to the Franks: " We poor pilgrims, it may well be, appear a disagreeable burden to you because of our numbers and our noisy importunity."
[124] Migne *PL* CV 459-64; Dümmler *op. cit.* 610-3.
[125] No. 357.

MSS: Leningrad (Petersburg) λ. Q. V. Otd. II. 5 s IX ff. 44ᵛ-5 [i]. — BN lat. 7520
s IX f. 73ᵛ [ii].   EDS: Dümmler *NA* IV (1879) 255-6 [i]; *MGH Poet. lat. aevi Carol.*
I (1881) 411-2 [i], II (1884) 664-5 [ii]. — Dom A. Staerk *Les manuscrits latins du
Vᵉ au XIIIᵉ siècle conservés à la Bibliothèque Impériale de St. Pétersbourg* I (1910) 200.

These poems were written by Dungal in honor of two of his ecclesiastical friends.
The first is to Hildoard, bishop of Cambrai (790-816), a locality where Irish influences
seem to have been especially strong.[126] The second refers to Hilduin, who was
appointed abbot of St.-Denis in 815, was banished by Louis the Pious in 830, restored
in 831, and died in 840.[127] It was evidently written at St.-Denis, and resembles in
style the verses of the " Hibernicus exul " collection.

(ii) Poems attributed to " Hibernicus exul "

(i) O deus omnipotens, convexae conditor arcis. . . . Munera, quaeso tui devoti sumere servi.   28 ll.
His ego litterulis domini deposco salutem. . . . Gundradae egregiae moribus et facie.   6 ll.   (ii) Hos
Karolo regi versus Hibernicus exul. . . . Sic fatus, regis cum dono ad castra recessit.   103 ll.   [2 folia
have been cut out of the MS.]   C A.D. 787.   Three poems addressed to Charles follow, apparently written
at St.-Denis and forming one collection with the preceding, but by other authors.

MS: Vat. Reg. 2078 s IX/X ff. 123 *sqq* [this MS once belonged to Petau of Paris].
EDS: Martène and Durand *Veterum scriptorum amplissima collectio* VI (Paris 1729)
811 *sqq.* — Angelo Mai *Classicorum auctorum e Vaticanis codicibus editorum* V (1833)
405 *sqq.* — Migne *PL* XCVIII 1443-5. — Dümmler *MGH Poet. lat. aevi Carol.* I
(1881) 395-9.   Cf. *Hist. lit. de la France* IV 497.

The poem by the anonymous " Hibernicus exul," addressed to Charles the Great
on the occasion of the surrender of the dominion of Bavaria to the Frankish king by
Duke Tassilo in 787, has long been known as one of the earliest examples of the Carolingian panegyrics.   It was early suggested, and is now generally accepted, that the
author is identical with Dungal of St.-Denis.   The same man was the author of another
poem in the same collection, addressed to Gundrada, cousin of Charlemagne.

349. Verses from St.-Denis

(i) Epitafium Folradi.   Felix illa hominum est mors et preciosa bonorum. . . . Pro peregrino me, posco,
precare tuo.   16 ll.   A.D. 784 (?)   (ii) Item aliud Epitafium.   Qui pietate pater, pastor cura, ore magister. . . . Aeternis meruit laudibus et precibus.   6 ll.   A.D. 806 (?)   (iii) Item alii versus.   Egregii pro-
ceres Clotharius ac Dagobertus. . . . 4 ll.   Item alii versus.   Effigies regum hic et nomina clara reful-
gent. . . . 4 ll.   A.D. 811 (?).   (iv) [Epitaphium Pippini] Hoc iacet in tumulo Pippinus, rex venerandus
. . . raptus ab orbe fuit.   20 ll.   A.D. 810 (?).   (v-a) Qui manibus librum, lector, comprenderis istum,
. . . Det sibi, dic, dominus perpetuam requiem.   10 ll.   (b) Item aliud.   Hoc recubat tumulo Motharius ille sacerdos. . . . Ante fuit humilis, plenus amore dei.   6 ll.   (vi) Item.   Quisquis es hunc
cernens titulum, dic pectore puro: Sit requies illi, lector opime, precor.   Te precor, omnipotens quadrati
conditor orbis, . . . De mortis nullus lege solutus adest.   36 ll.   (vii) Item.   Authelmi monachi busto
sunt membra sub isto. . . . Perpetuam requiem det sibi, posce, deus.   10 ll.

MS: Vat. Reg. 2078 s IX/X.   EDS: Martène and Durand *Veterum scriptorum amplissima collectio* VI (Paris 1729) 816 *sqq.* — Migne *PL* CV 530-2. — Dümmler *MGH
Poet. lat. aevi Carol.* I (1881) 404-7 [nos. xii-xviii].

---

[126] Cf. pp. 247, 283 and Gougaud, *Gaelic Pioneers of Christianity* 47-8.
[127] Cf. p. 580 *infra.*

These seven sets of verses were composed at St.-Denis, probably either by Dungal or under his supervision and influence: (i) epitaph of Fulradus, abbot of St.-Denis (d. 784), by Dungal; (ii) epitaph of Fardulf, abbot of St.-Denis (d. 806), probably by Dungal; (iii) epitaphs of the royal princes Lothair and Dagobert, Pippin and Charles; (iv) epitaph of Pippin (d. 810); (v) preface to a book written by a priest named Motharius, and epitaph of Motharius; (vi) a poem on Dungal, written by one of his pupils; (vii) epitaph of a monk named Authelm. The poems show some strivings after style, and reminiscences of the sixth-century Christian poet, Fortunatus of Poitiers, but are, at least in parts, quite vapid.

350. Verses addressed to an abbot named Dungal

. . . [128] praesulis Dungalo abbati. O venerande pie frater mihi semper amande. . . . Aurea his iunxit pocula larga . . . [last word missing]. 56 ll.

MS: Carlsruhe Cod. Augiensis CXCV f. 1ᵛ [this fol. was originally distinct from the rest of the codex, but is of about the same date, s IX *in*; the *recto* is in Irish script, the *verso* in Continental]. EDS: K. Strecker *Zs. f. rom. Philol.* XLI 566 *sq* [corrected from the MS by K. Preisendanz]; *MGH Poet. lat. aevi Carol.* IV fasc. ii–iii (1923) 1124–7.

The text of this poem has been made out from the faded and defaced manuscript only with great difficulty. It is an address to an Irish abbot named Dungal who was residing on the Continent, but whether he is to be identified with any of the Dungals otherwise known is not certain.

SMARAGDUS OF ST.-MIHIEL

Bibliography

Histoire littéraire de la France IV 439–47. — Hauréau *Singularités historiques et littéraires* (1861) 100–28. — Dümmler *NA* IV (1879) 250–3. — Ebert *Allgemeine Geschichte der Literatur des Mittelalters im Abendlande* II (1880) 108–12, Fr. trans. 123–8. — H. Robas " Étude sur Smaragde " *Annales de l'Est* XII (1898) 266–80. — Wattenbach *DGQ* I⁷ 227. — Manitius *Lat. Lit.* I 461–8, II 806; *NA* XXXII 670 *sq*.

Smaragdus (the word is Greek: σμάραγδος, a precious stone of green color; σμαραγέω, to roar, especially used of the sea) was abbot of a monastery at Castellio which in 819 he removed to the neighboring St.-Mihiel on the Meuse. Little is known of his personal history. Manitius suggests that he was " perhaps of Irish origin," and several slight clues favor the hypothesis. One of these is the knowledge he shows of Pelagius; [129] another the character of his grammatical studies. One ninth-century copy of his commentary on Donatus [130] has glosses described

---

[128] This word, probably the name of the author, has not been deciphered.
[129] *Cf.* p. 662 *infra.*
[130] BN 13029, from Corbie. *Cf.* J. Loth *ACL* III iv (1907) 249–56.

variously as Breton, Cornish, Welsh: the fact indicates familiarity in Celtic circles with his writings. Even the adoption of a Greek name supports the theory of Irish nationality. His Gaelic designation, it might be expected, would be one of those containing the root *muir*, " sea," [131] of which the most likely would be *Muiredach*. Now it is noteworthy that the catalogue, made in 993, of the library of the abbot Adso of Montier-en-Der, lists a work "Moridach super Donatum";[132] an eleventh-century catalogue of Toul gives " Uuidrae super Donatum,"[133] perhaps a corrupted form; and the same work was, it is said, in St. Oyan.[134]

Such observations fall short of being proofs of the Irish, or even insular, origin of Smaragdus, but they require that some attention be given here to his life and works.

The principal source for his history, outside his own writings and his epitaph, is the *Chronicon monasterii s. Michaelis Virdunensis*, which covers the period 722–1034 and was written soon after the last date. Besides several incomplete eds., including Waitz *MGH SS* IV 78–86, there is a full ed. by L. Tross (Hammone 1857) [see pp. 8 *sqq*]. His epitaph, beginning " Cum pius imperii," is in Tross *op. cit.* 9; Mabillon *Vetera analecta* II 386; Bouquet VI 271; Dümmler *MGH Poetae lat. aevi Carol.* I 605. His writings were to be found in many mediaeval libraries — see G. Becker *Catalogi bibliothecarum antiqui*, index — and he is mentioned in their works on ecclesiastical writers by the twelfth-century authors Sigebert of Gembloux, Honorius of Autun, and the Anonymous Mellicensis.[135]

351. Writings of Smaragdus

(i) *Expositio Libri Comitis:* Commentary on the epistles and gospels of the Sundays

MSS: BN 2341, written before 843. — Einsiedeln Klosterbibl. 39 *s* IX. — Munich Staatsbibl. 6210 *s* IX; 6214 *s* X. ED: Migne *PL* CII 13–594. *Cf.* A. Souter *JTS* IX 584 *sqq*, XXIII 73 *sqq*.

(ii) *Via regia:* Instructions for the king

MSS: Vat. Reg. 190 *s* X. — Vienna National-Bibl. 956 *s* X. ED: Migne *PL* CII 933–70. — Dümmler *MGH Epistolarum* IV 533 [the dedicatory epistle]. *Cf.* A. Werminghoff *Hist. Zs.* LIII 193.

(iii) *Diadema monachorum:* Manual of monastic life

MSS: Valence 292 *s* XI. — Munich Staatsbibl. 2539 *s* XII; 12104 *s* XII. ED: Migne *PL* CII 593–690.

---

[131] *Cf.* HZ *Sitzungsber. d. k. preuss. Akad. d. Wissensch.* 1891 p. 310.
[132] G. Becker *Catalogi bibliothecarum antiqui* no. xli 12.
[133] *Ibid.* no. lxviii 226.
[134] Manitius *Lat. Lit.* I 462.
[135] *Cf.* Manitius *op. cit.* 462, and see Potthast for bibliographies.

(iv) *Expositio in regula s. Benedicti:* Explanation of the Rule of St. Benedict

MSS: BN 4210 s IX. — Kórnik (Poland) Bibl. Akademii Nauk 124 s IX. — Valence 275 s IX. — BM Addit. 16961 s X. — Vat. Reg. 1025 s X. — BN 12638 s XIII. ED: Migne *PL* CII 689–932. *Cf.* E. Bishop *Liturgica historica* (Oxford 1918) 214–5.

(v) *Liber in partibus Donati:* Commentary on Donatus

MSS: BN 13029 (from Corbie); 7551; 14089, all of s IX; 7533; 11275; 18520; nouv. acq. 1832, all of s X. — Carlsruhe Cod. Augiensis ccxli s IX ff. 48ᵛ–71ᵛ [incomplete]. — Berne Stadtbibl. A 92 no. 22 s XII/XIII [fragment]. *Cf.* L. Traube *Abhandlungen d. k. bay. Akad. d. Wissensch.* XXI 718 [*re* Spanish MSS]. EDS [partial]: Mabillon *Vetera analecta*² 358. — H. Keil *De grammaticis quibusdam latinis infimae aetatis commentatio* (Erlangen 1868) 19 *sqq.* — H. Hagen *Anecdota Helvetica* (Leipsic 1870) pp. ccxxxix *sqq.* — E. Kalinka *Wiener Studien* XVI 113–5. — Manitius *NA* XXXVI 60. Several poems found in the preceding treatises have been collected and edited by Dümmler *MGH Poet. lat. aevi Carol.* I 604–19, II 698. *Cf.* Manitius *NA* XI 563.

Of the above-mentioned works, the commentary on the epistles and gospels is drawn from the Fathers of the Church and certain other writers, as Pelagius,[136] Pseudo-Primasius, and Victor of Capua. There was a copy of it in Cologne in 833 and another in Reichenau about the same time. The *Via regia,* a kind of " Mirror for Princes," seems to have been addressed to Charles the Great, before whom it held up examples extracted from the Old Testament. The *Diadema monachorum* was for the instruction of his own monks, to whom it was to be read each evening. Manitius thinks that it was written after the death of Charles the Great. The Explanation of the Rule of St. Benedict was, it appears probable, connected with the monastic reform movement which the Emperor Louis the Pious and his friend, St. Benedict of Aniane, inaugurated after the accession of the former in 814. Smaragdus seems to have used the *Codex regularum* of Benedict of Aniane.[137] The Commentary on Donatus also was composed for the use of his monks. It is one of the most remarkable of such works produced in the early middle ages, but has been published only in small part.

Other works attributed to Smaragdus [138] in old records but not now known are *De generibus metrorum, De VII plagis,* and *Super partem psalterii.* An anonymous treatise giving advice to a prince, probably one of the sons of Louis the Pious, which is preserved in BM Reg. 12. C. XXIII s IX, with some verses found also in Cambridge Univ. Lib. Gg. 5. 35 s XI ff. 378–81; Madrid Bibl. Nacional 14, 22 s X ff. 69 *sqq,* may also, in the opinion of Manitius,[139] be due to Smaragdus.

[136] *Cf.* A. Souter " Character and history of Pelagius' Commentary " (*Proc. Brit. Acad.* VII) (1916) 34–6.
[137] *Cf.* p. 199 *supra.*
[138] Ardo, abbot of Aniane (d. 843) was also known as Smaragdus, and some of these compositions may have been by him. *Cf.* L. Traube *Abhandlungen d. k. bay. Akad. d. Wissensch.* XXI 718.
[139] *Op. cit.* 467–8.

DICUIL

Bibliography

T. Wright *Biographia Britannica literaria* I (1842) 372–6. — E. Dümmler *NA* IV (1879) 256–8. — W. Meyer " Der Ludus de Antichristo " *Sitzungsb. d. k. bay. Akad. d. Wissensch.*, Philos.-philol. Cl. (Munich 1882) I 68n., 91, 94, 97; *Gesammelte Abhandl. zur mittellateinischen Rythmik* I (1905) 193–6, 216, 220, 222 [studies the rhythm of Dicuil's verse]. — A. Ebert *Allgemeine Geschichte der Literatur des Mittelalters im Abendlande* II (1880) 392–4. — M. Esposito " Dicuil, an Irish Monk in the ninth century " *Dublin Rev.* 1905 pp. 327–37; " An Irish teacher at the Carolingian court: Dicuil " *Studies* III (March 1914) 651–76 [the second of these arts., which differs much in tone from the first, is the most important study on the subject in English]. — Manitius *Lat. Lit.* I 647–53 [very valuable].

Of Dicuil nothing more is known than what can be derived from his own writings. From these we gather that he was an Irish monk who already in 814 was on terms of intimacy with the Carolingian court, and who was still living in 825. The name of his Irish teacher was Suibne, and he had been present when this man received a monk who had visited the Holy Land before 767. He himself had known Irish anchorites who sailed to the islands in the northern seas before the beginning of the Viking raids, that is, before the close of the eighth century, and, it would appear, had himself visited some of those island hermitages. From the evidence of this kind the suggestions may be hazarded that Dicuil, or Dichull, was a native of Ireland who entered the abbey of Hii during the life-time of Suibne, abbot who died in 772;[140] that he came to the Continent between 795 and 810,[141] perhaps as a fugitive from the Norse sack of Hii in 806; that he became a teacher in the palace school; and that he died soon after 825.

352. Verses *De arte grammatica*

Hic codex pueris plus quam sapientibus aptus. . . . Dicuil hos fecit titulos aperire libellos.

MSS: Valenciennes Bibl. publ. 394 (formerly 377, and N. 2. 23) *s* IX/X f. 54ᵛ [from St.-Amand]. — Leyden Voss. Lat. Q. 33 f. 111. EDS: H. Keil *Grammatici latini* III (Leipsic 1859) 390 [Priscian's *Partitiones* is published pp. 459–515]. — Dümmler *MGH Poet. lat. aevi Carol.* II (1884) 667–8. *Cf.* Riese *Anthologia latina* II p. xxvi; L. Müller *Rheinisches Museum* N. F. XX 359.

These verses are appended to a tract entitled *Prisciani Partitiones duodecim versuum Aeneidos principalium*, apparently an edition of that text prepared by Dicuil. His

---

140 It must be borne in mind that Suibne was a common Irish name.

141 His account implies that he had seen the elephant which died at Aix-la-chapelle in that year, but he does not actually say that he did.

astronomical treatise gives plentiful evidence that Dicuil was interested in grammatical studies. The present poem refers to a work on the subject in prose, and the prologue to the *Mensura orbis terrae* speaks of a *congregata epistola de quaestionibus decem artis grammaticae* which, it would seem, he had just completed. These works are not now known.

353. Treatise on Astronomy A.D. 814–816

Nunc genitum Carolo. . . . De Mense Apreli. Si quotus mensis . . . deinde per metrum nuntiavi. Prosa tacet, claudens dicet retantia metrum. . . . Ante diem clauso componet vesper Olympo.

MS: Valenciennes Bibl. publ. 404 (formerly 386 and N. 4. 43) *s* IX*ex* ff. 66–118 [from the monastery of St.-Amand in Flanders: belonged to, and possibly was written by Hucbald].[142] EDS: E. Dümmler *NA* IV (1879) 256–8 [metrical extracts only]. — M. Esposito " An unpublished astronomical treatise by the Irish monk Dicuil " *Proc. RIA* XXVI C (1907) 378–446 (*cf. ZCP* VII 506–7). — K. Strecker *MGH Poet. lat. aevi Carol.* IV fasc. ii–iii (1923) 659–60, 917 [the poems]. COMM: On astronomy in the 9th century see Cantor *Vorlesungen über Geschichte der Mathematik* I (1894) 781–90.

This is a treatise in four books, dedicated to the Emperor Louis the Pious. It is written in a peculiar mixture of prose and verse, and is of considerable interest to the student of mediaeval versification and the development of rhythmical poetry. Its composition was begun in the year 814 — one of the early pages was written on April 18 — and was continued during the next two years. Astronomical and especially computistical matter form the main theme, but there are considerable digressions on grammatical and metrical subjects. At the end of the first book is a rhythmical poem entitled " De ymno per rythmum facto " in which he defends his metrical usage. The astronomical information given is for the most part practical — rules for finding the month and the day of the month, the moon's age, the date of Easter and of the beginning of Lent, discussions of the length of the lunar and solar year, of the lunar cycle of nineteen years, of the great cycle of the sun and moon, and of the bissextile or leap year. There are, however, speculations on such subjects as the distances between heaven and earth and between the several planets, etc., the existence of a south polar star, the revolutions of the planets. Much of this, as of all early mediaeval scientific studies, now seems puerile or absurd, but, as in his geographical work, Dicuil displays a broad interest in his subject and an openness of mind that deserve recognition. He makes no reference to sources; apparently the work was based on his personal knowledge of the calculations used by the church authorities in Ireland,[143] England and the Frankish empire in regulating the calendar. As a summary of the astronomical knowledge of the early ninth century it has peculiar value.

354. Treatise on Geography (*Liber de mensura orbis terrae*) A.D. 825

Post congregatam epistolam de quaestionibus decem artis grammaticae cogitavi ut liber de mensura provintiarum orbis terrae sequeretur. . . . De Europa. Principium ergo erit . . montibus solus altior videatur. [Verses:] Dicuil accipiens ego tracta auctoribus ista. . . . Nocte bobus requies largitur fine laboris. 31 ll.

MSS: Class I: BN lat. 4806 *s* IX ff. 25–40. Class II: Dresden Dc 182 *s* IX *ex.* ff.

142 *Cf.* pp. 505, 592.
143 He speaks of the usage of his countrymen in placing the intercalary day at March 22: " according to the rule of the Greeks and Latins which my people in Ireland in this calculation always observe."

50ᵛ-62 [belonged to Reims, and afterwards to Michelsberg, near Bamberg]. Class III:
All these MSS derived from a book which was formerly in the cathedral lib. of Speyer
[*cf.* Seeck *Hermes* IX (1875) 218 *sqq*; *Notitia dignitatum* (Berlin 1876) pp. ix-xi;
Mommsen *MGH Auct. ant.* IX *Chron. min.* I (1892) 527-31]. Bodl. Canonic. Misc.
378 A.D. 1436 ff. 47-62ᵛ [copied from the Speyer MS for Petrus Donatus, bishop of
Padua: there are copies of this in Munich Staatsbibl. lat. 794 *s* XV pp. 93-125; BN
Nouv. acq. lat. 1424*s*XVI ff. 49 *sqq*]. — Vienna Nationalbibl. 3103 'A.D. 1484' ff. 36-50ᵛ;
Vienna 3102 A.D. 1529 ff. 36ᵛ-51 [both now in Trent]. — Vienna 12825 *s* XV ff. 87ᵛ-
113ᵛ. — BN lat. 9661 *s* XV ff. 37-50ᵛ. — Florence Bibl. Mediceo-Laurenziana Plut. 89
sup. cod. 68 *s* XV ff 77ᵛ-102ᵛ. — Venice Bibl. s. Marci 3329 (Lat. X. 88) *s* XV. —
Madrid Bibl. nacional Res. 36 (Q. 129) *s* XV ff. 48-64 [described in the *Archiv* VIII 791-
2 in 1843]. — Munich Staatsbibl. lat. 10291 A.D. 1544 x 1551 ff. 47-62 [copy in Vat. Barberini 809 *s* XVI]. — Munich lat. 4013 *s* XVI ff. 49ᵛ-66. — Munich lat. 1607 *s*
XVI/XVII ff. 41-70. — BM Cotton. Vesp. E. VI *s* XVII ff. 18ᵛ-22 [extracts]. All
these codices contain chiefly works on geography and probably go back to one or two
collections of such made in the ninth or early tenth century. That representing
Class II stands between Classes I and III, but seems to be more closely related to
the former. EDS: C. A. Walckenaer *Dicuili liber de mensura orbis terrae* (Paris 1807).
— Letronne *Récherches géographiques et critiques sur le livre de mensura orbis terrae*
(Paris 1814). — G. Parthey *Dicuili liber de mensura orbis terrae* (Berlin 1870) [best].
— E. Dümmler *MGH Poet. lat. aevi Carol.* II (1884) 666-7 [concluding verses only].
COMM: K. Müllenhoff *Hermes* IX (1875) 182-95; *Deutsche Altertumskunde* III (1892)
230-50.— HZ *Sitzungsb. d. k. preuss. Akad. d. Wissensch.* 1891 philos.-hist. Kl. 279-317.
— *Rev. Bénédictine* XV (1898) 145. — Beazley *Dawn of Modern Geography* II (1901)
162-4, 227-9, 317-27. — Wattenbach *DGQ* I⁷ (1904) 171. — Detlefsen *Erdkarte
Agrippas* (*Quellen u. Forschungen z. alten Geschichte u. Geographie* XIII) (Berlin 1906)
11 *sqq*. — Esposito *Hermathena* XVII (1910-11) 63. — Fridtjof Nansen *In northern
mists* (London 1911) I 162-7. See also Manitius and especially Esposito, *op. cit.*
p. 545 *supra.*

Dicuil's geographical compendium, the earliest of its kind written in the Frankish
Empire, was completed in the year 825 and is his last and most important work. It
is divided into nine chapters, dealing with Europe, Asia, Africa, Egypt, longitude and
latitude, certain rivers, islands, the Tyrrhenian Sea, and mountains. The information
is drawn almost entirely from ancient writers, and represents the geography of the
Roman Empire, not of the Carolingian world. From the prologue it would seem that
the immediate occasion of Dicuil's work was his becoming acquainted with a *Mensuratio* or *Divisio orbis terrae* [144] prepared under the orders of the Emperor Theodosius II
in 435, a copy of which was probably in the library of Charles the Great and had been
used by Godescalc between 781 and 783 in the composition of his *Evangelistarium*.[145]
Dicuil bases his first four chapters on this treatise, and in the fifth quotes the verses
attached by the scribe to the copy he employed. As the work of Theodosius depends
largely on that of Augustus and Agrippa, Dicuil's treatise becomes important for the
geography of the Augustan age. Dicuil had unusual facilities for his time: he seems
to have had several copies of Pliny, one of Julius Honorius and of the so-called cos-

---

[144] Discovered, and published, by Schweder: *Beiträge zur Kritik der Chorographie des Augustus* I (Kiel
1876): also Riese *Geographi latini minores* (1878) 15-20, and xviii-xix.

[145] *Cf.* L. Traube " Zur Chorographie des Augustus " *Sitzungsb. d. k. bay. Akad. d. Wissensch.* phil.-hist.
Cl. 1891 (Munich 1892) pp. 406-9; and in Franz Boll (ed.) *Vorlesungen u. Abhandl. v. L. Traube* III (Munich
1920) 17-20.

mography of Aethicus, of Solinus, of Priscian's *Periegesis*, of Isidore, works some of which, according to the evidence we possess, must have been very rare in the ninth century. Many other authorities are mentioned, some of them mythical. But fully half the text consists of excerpts from Pliny, taken either directly or through Solinus. Though much that he accepts would be thought to strain credulity, it is more remarkable that he occasionally questions and even contradicts his sources. Of greater importance are his personal contributions — unfortunately very few. He speaks of the elephant sent by Harún al Raschid to Charlemagne in 804, which died in 810; of a monk Fidelis whose narration of his pilgrimage from Ireland to the Holy Land by way of Egypt and the canal between the Nile and the Red Sea Dicuil himself had heard; of the Irish solitaries who frequented the islands around Great Britain and Ireland, and even journeyed to the Faroes, for nearly one hundred years, but were now driven out by the northern sea-robbers; of the account of Thile (Iceland) given him by certain religious men who resided there from February to August in 795.

---

355. Puzzle Problems of the schools

(i) [Problem I] Ludus inest pulcher, si quis bene noverit illum Quadam nocte niger Dub nomine, Candidus alter. . . . Ut me velle viros viros fallere nemot putet.   14 ll.   (ii) [Solution I] Ita sederunt: Quattuor eximii candoris, quinque nigelli. . . . Candidus ingenio praeditus atque sui.   14 ll.   (iii) [Solution II] Bis duo nam nivei praesunt et quinque nigelli. . . . Orbem tunc furvus demum determinat unus.   9 ll. BN 2772 adds 3 ll. ending:] Quam clari vitam perdant corporibus aptam.   (iv) [Solution III] Albi bis bini praecedunt ordinis arcem. . . . Albi ter quini glomerantur terque nigelli.   13 ll.   (v) [Solution IV] Egregius lector, qui vult recitare Camenas. . . . Unius et fusci concludit orbita cursum.   (vi) [Solution V] Versus de ludo qui fit cum xxx tesselis.   Ordine fit primus regali nomine functus. . . . Iam niger accedens variatum terminet orbem.   14 ll.   (vii) [Problem II] Idem forte [vigens] dux quadam mane rubente. . . . Ingenio cuncta quaeque gerenda bona . . . [ends imperfect].   36 ll.

MSS: BN 13029 [formerly of Corbie] *s* IX f. 11^v [i], f. 4 [ii], f. 2 [iv]. — Einsiedeln Klosterbibl. 326 *s* IX [i, ii]. — BN 7899 *s* IX f. 176^v [ii]. — Wolfenbüttel 4161 [Weissenburg 77] *s* X*in* [i, ii]. — Valenciennes Bibl. publ. 394 [*cf.* p. 545 *supra*] *s* IX/X f. 47 [i, iii twice]. —Madrid Bibl. nacional Ca. 14 n. 22 [formerly of Toledo] *s* X f. 140 [i, ii, vii]. — Ivrea Bibl. capitolare 27 (? 37) *s* X [iii]. — Boulogne Bibl. publ. 40 [formerly of St. Bertin] *s* X last fol. [v]. — BN 2772 *s* X/XI f. 57 [iii]. — Wolfenbüttel 4642 *s* XI f. 41 [i, ii]. — Vat. Palat. lat. 235 *s* XI f. 36 [i, ii]. — Trèves Stadtbibl. 1093 (1694) *s* XI f. 116 [i, ii]. — Leyden Universiteitsbibl. Voss. Q. 15 *s* XI [ii]. — BN Nouv. acq. lat. 1630 frag. *s* XI f. 22^v [ii; i missing probably because of lacuna], f. 4 [iii]. — BN 8091 *s* XII f. 127 [i, ii, iii, vii]. — Leyden Universiteitsbibl. Voss. Q. 33 *s* XII f. 58 [ii]. — Rouen Bibl. de la ville 1409 [formerly Jumièges 27] *s* XII f. 131^v [ii]. — Douai Bibl. publ. 318 [formerly of Marchiennes] *s* XII f. 171^v [iii]. — Douai 320 *s* XII f. 164 [variant of iii]. — Berne Stadtbibl. 704 *s* XII [variant of iii]. — Berlin Staatsbibl. Phillipps 1694 (formerly of St. Arnulf of Metz) *s* XII/XIII f. 77^v [i, vi]. — Basel Universitätsbibl. AN IV 11 *s* XIII p. 76 [ii]. — Bodl. F. 1. 17 *s* XIV f. 45 [i, ii, iii, vii]. Eds: Riese *Anthologia latina* II no. 727 [i, ii]. — Baehrens *Poetae latini minores* V (Leipsic 1883) 370-2 [i, ii, vii]. — Goetz and Loewe *Leipziger Studien* I [vii]. — Wattenbach *NA* XVII 355 [vi]. — Manitius *NA* XXXVI (1910-1) 68-72 [i, ii, iv; has valuable commentary]. — Karl Strecker *MGH Poet. lat. aevi Carol.* IV fasc. ii, iii 1118-24. Comm: L. Müller " Über ein heutiges Kinderspiel " *Fleckeisens Jahrb.* 1865 pp. 217-23. — Strecker *NA* XLIV (1922) 235-6.

These are curious and interesting little poems, though not of great historical importance. They consist of catch-problems in arithmetic and their solutions, evidently products of Carolingian scholastic circles, perhaps in part of the palace school. The first problem is of Irish composition — it may have had its origin in the Irish schools, and have been put in verse by some Irish teacher on the Continent — and so, too, seem some at least of the other poems.

The manuscripts have only three notes as to authorship: the ninth-century BN 7899 attributes Solution I to a " Berno," otherwise unknown; the twelfth-century Rouen 1409 assigns Solution I to Clemens Scottus; and the twelfth-century BN 8091 gives Solution II to " Thomas Scottus."

There are several references to a Thomas, teacher in the palace school: (1) in a poem, written before 817, addressed to Prudentius,[146] who afterwards became bishop of Troyes: *MGH Poet. lat. aevi Carol.* I 581 v. 55. (2) an eulogistic poem addressed to Thomas by Walahfrid Strabo:[147] " Culmen apostolici coepisti nominis heres . . . Unius siquidem membra sumus capitis " (14 ll.): *ibid.* II 387. (3) a poem to Thomas by Florus of Lyons (d. *c* 859) thanking him for poems received: MS. Vat. Reg. 598 *s* IX f. 61. ED: Fed. Patetta *Atti della R. Accadem. delle Scienze di Torino* XXVII 123 *sqq.* *Cf.* Manitius *Berlin. philol. Wochenschrift* 1892, p. 749; *Lat. Lit.* I 566. (4) Sigebert of Gembloux (d. 1112) attributes to Thomas a " book of enigmas, brief, it is true, but full of truth and elegance, in which he presents a mother and her seven daughters, which are the seven liberal arts . . . ." The book was written for Hilduin.[148] Migne *PL* CLX 576.

Manitius assigns at least the first four poems to Thomas Scottus, whom he identifies with the " praeceptor palatii." Strecker considers that the versification of Solution II, which alone bears the name of Thomas, indicates a date later than the first half of the ninth century.

356. Texts relating to the Irish monk Macarius

(i) Hraban Maur: *De computo*

ED: Migne *PL* CVII 669. COMM: E. Köhler *Hrabanus Maurus und die Schule zu Fulda* (Dissert. Leipsic 1869; Progr. Chemnitz 1870) 21, 25. — Ebert *Allgem. Geschichte d. Lit. d. Mittelalters* II (1880) 127. — Manitius *Lat. Lit.* I 288-302, esp. 290, 298.

(ii) Ratramnus of Corbie: Letter to Odo, bishop of Beauvais

EDS: Mabillon *AA. SS. o. s. B.* IV ii pp. lxxvii *sq* (*cf. Annal. o. s. B.* III 139-40). — Dümmler *MGH Epistolarum* VI [*Aevi Carolini* IV] (1902) 153-4. *Cf.* E. Renan *Averroès et l'Averroïsme* (Paris 1882) 131; Manitius *Lat. Lit.* I (1911) 412-7.

Hraban Maur, or Hrabanus Maurus Magnentius, was born at Mainz about 776 x 784. He entered the monastery of Fulda at an early age and in 802 was sent to Tours to study under Alcuin. In 822 he became abbot of Fulda, and in 842 resigned, apparently because of his support of the Emperor Lothair and opposition to Louis the German. In 847 he became archbishop of Mainz, and died in 856. He was the

---

[146] *Cf.* p. 577 *infra.*   [147] *Cf.* pp. 532, 550.   [148] *Cf.* p. 580 *infra.*

most learned man of his day and Alcuin's greatest successor as a teacher. Under him Fulda became the leading monastic school in the Carolingian empire. He has left very extensive writings on both religious and secular subjects. His treatise on the computus was written in 820. It is dedicated to a " Marcharius," at whose request it was written. He is believed to be the same as the Irish monk, Macarius, against whom Ratramnus wrote.

Ratramnus (d. after 868) was a monk of Corbie who compiled several theological treatises. One of these, *De quantitate animae*, was a refutation of the doctrine of monopsychism expounded by an Irishman named Macarius, who, on the basis of a passage in St. Augustine, taught that each man's mind was only a part of a single universal mind. The work was undertaken at the request of Odo, abbot of Corbie and afterwards (861-881) bishop of Beauvais. The treatise itself has never been published, but we have here the introductory letter to bishop Odo.

357. Lothair: *Constitutiones Olonnenses* A. D. 825

EDS: Muratori *Rer. Italic. SS.* I ii (Milan 1723) 151-3. — *MGH Leges* I (Hanover 1835) 248-53. — Boretius *MGH Capitularia regum Francorum* I (Hanover 1883) 327. TRANS: Margaret Stokes *Six months in the Apennines* (London 1892) 205.

In 821 Lothair, eldest son of the Emperor Louis the Pious, was crowned king of Lombardy. As such he issued, in 825, a decree reorganising education in northern Italy. The foremost place in the new system was given to one Dungal, teacher at Pavia. We have no further evidence by which to identify this Dungal.[149]

358. Irish associations of Walahfrid Strabo

EDS. OF HIS WORKS: Migne *PL* CXIII–CXIV. *Poems:* Dümmler *MGH Poet. lat. aevi Carol.* II (1884) 267–423. *De rebus ecclesiasticis:* A. Knöpfler (Munich 1890; 2nd ed. 1899). On the Lives of St. Gall and St. Blathmac *cf.* nos. 50 (iii), 227. COMM: See the guides by Potthast, Wattenbach and Chevalier. Dümmler *NA* IV (1879) 270–86. — Ebert *Allgem. Geschichte der Literatur des Mittelalters* II (1880) 145–66. — A. Jundt *Walahfrid Strabon, l'homme et le théologien* (Cahors 1907). — P. Eigl *Walahfrid Strabo* (*Stud. u. Mitteil. aus d. kirchengeschichtl. Seminar d. theol. Fakultät*, Vienna 1908). — E. Madeja *Stud. u. Mitteil. z. Gesch. d. Benediktinerordens* XL 251 *sqq.* — Manitius *Lat. Lit.* I 302–14. — F. von Bezold in *Hist. Zs.* 3rd ser. XXXIV.

Walahfrid Strabo was born in Suabia in 808 or 809, at an early age entered the monastery of Reichenau under the abbot Haito (who had visited Constantinople as the envoy of Charles the Great), and there studied under Erlebald, Wetti (who wrote a Life of St. Gall[150]), Tatto and Grimald (afterwards arch-chaplain to Louis the German). About 827 he went to Fulda, St. Boniface's establishment, where he had as teacher Hraban Maur.[151] In 829 the arch-chaplain Hilduin [152] summoned him to the imperial court, where, as stated above,[153] he won the favor of Louis the Pious and the Empress Judith, and became preceptor to their son Charles. In 838 he succeeded Erlebald as abbot of Reichenau, and died in 849 while on a journey to the court of Charles. Within a comparatively short life-time he had acquired a brilliant renown as theologian, poet, and man of letters.

---

[149] *Cf.* pp. 538-9 *supra.*   [150] No. 50 (ii).   [151] *Cf.* no. 356 (i).   [152] *Cf.* p. 541, 580.
[153] P. 532 *supra.*

Both at Reichenau and at the imperial court Walahfrid must have met many Irish exiles, and it was, doubtless, from personal experience that he wrote the often-quoted passage regarding " the Irish people, with whom the custom of travelling into foreign lands has now become almost second nature."[154] He wrote Lives of the martyr Blathmac and of St. Gall, and there are several passages in his other works that are of Irish interest. His *Libellus de exordiis et incrementis quarundam in rebus ecclesiasticis rerum*, or *De rebus ecclesiasticis*, a valuable source for liturgical antiquities, contains a noteworthy passage regarding the Irish custom of repeated prayers and genuflection.[155] One of his poems [156] is addressed to an Irish priest named Probus to whom he was sending copies of the poems of Fortunatus and of that *Mensuratio orbis terrae* which Dicuil had used.[157] Probus had sent him a request for these through an Irishman, Chronmal. The same poem has references to the Irish at Reichenau.

There are other texts relating to Probus. He was a friend of Lupus, or Loup, abbot of Ferrières (*c* 805– *c* 862), who also was a pupil of Hraban Maur and a leading man of letters. Lupus in two of his epistles speaks of the works of Probus. (Nos. xx, xxxiv. The letters of Lupus are published in Migne *PL* CXIX 431–60; G. Desdevises du Dézert *Lettres de Servat Loup* (Paris 1888); Dümmler *MGH Epistolarum* VI 7–107. *Cf.* the usual guides and Manitius *Lat. Lit.* I 483–90.) The death of Probus is recorded in an eulogistic notice under the year 859 in the Annals of Fulda (*Annales Fuldenses*), which in this part were written by Rudolf of Fulda, another disciple of Hraban Maur. (For eds. see Potthast, Wattenbach or Molinier. The best is by F. Kurze in *SS. rer. Germ. in usum scholarum ex MGH* (Hanover 1891).)

359. Verses by Colmán to Colmán

Colmano versus in Colmanum perheriles Scottigena ficti patriae cupidum et remeantem. Dum subito properas dulces invisere terras. . . . Ut tibi perpetuae contingant gaudia vitae. 37 ll.

MS: BM Reg. 15 B XIX *s* IX. Ed: KM *Ériu* III (1907) 186–9.

These verses were composed on the Continent by an Irishman named Colmán and addressed to another of the same name who was about to return to Ireland. There is no internal evidence as to the date, but the manuscript is of the ninth century, written, it would appear, at Reims. Colmán was one of the most common of Irish names, and gives us no clue as to author or recipient.[158] The Latinity is very good: there are many reminiscences of Vergil, and some, perhaps, of Lucan and other authors.

360. *Ars Malsachani* s VIII/IX

Verbum est pars orationis . . . huc usque sufficiat. Finit congregatio Salcani filii de verbo.

MS: BN lat. 13026 [formerly of Corbie] *s* IX ff. 161–81. Ed: M. Roger *Ars Malsachani Traité du verbe publié d'après le ms. lat. 13026 de la Bibliothèque Nationale* (Paris

---

[154] " De natione Scotorum, quibus consuetudo peregrinandi iam paene in naturam conversa est." — *Vita s. Galli* II xlvii.
[155] Migne *PL* CXIV 952–3. *Cf.* Herbert Thurston *Studies* XIII Dec. 1923 p. 584.
[156] *MGH* ed. no. xlv p. 393.   [157] *Cf.* p. 547 *supra*.
[158] As a mere possibility, reference may be made to the " Colmán son of Ailell, abbot of Slane and of other monasteries in France and in Ireland," who died in 825 (AU).

1905). Comm: B. Hauréau *Singularités historiques et littéraires* (Paris 1861) 18. — Hoefer *Nouvelle biographie générale* XXXIII (Paris 1863) 103-4. — H. Keil *De grammaticis quibusdam latinis infimae aetatis commentatio* (Programm, Erlangen 1868) 17-8. — Ch. Thurot " Extraits de divers manuscrits latins pour servir à l'histoire des doctrines grammaticales au moyen âge " *Notices et Extraits des mss. de la Bibl. impériale* XXII pt. ii (Paris 1869) 4. — Manitius *Lat. Lit.* I (1911) 521-3, II 809.

The title given this work in the manuscript (in a different hand) would suggest the name Mael-Sachan, or perhaps Mael-Sechlainn, but the *explicit* of the text itself shows that the author's name was Mac Salchann. Beyond this, and that he lived not later than the ninth century, nothing is known of his personality. It may be that he lived and wrote in Ireland, and that his work was carried to the Continent by one of his countrymen. The probability, however, is that he was himself a teacher in some of the Carolingian schools. His book is a grammatical compilation on the Latin verb, based in the main on Donatus, but using also Consentius, Eutyches, Charisius, Diomedes, Probus, Priscian, the grammarian Virgilius Maro, and various commentators and glossators. He cites several classical authors, especially Vergil, but apparently always at second hand. His work does not present the purest Latin standards even of the eighth century, and Hauréau's assertion that he knew Greek seems to be without foundation.

361. Cruindmel: On metre

Haec, dulces iuvenes, prompti servate, rogamus, . . . vobiscum faciat talia noster amor. 18 ll. In dei nomine de metrica ratione pauca incipiunt ex multis grammaticorum libris excerpta. Discite, me, pueri, versus si scribere vultis Nam veterum rite carmina prisca sequor. Omnibus metrice artis . . . meruit de exilio liberari.

MSS: BN 13026 *s* IX ff. 41-56 [formerly of Corbie]. — Munich Staatsbibl. 6411 *s* IX ff. 82ᵛ-95ᵛ, 68 [formerly of Freising]; 14420 *s* IX ff. 21-36 [from St. Emmeramus, Ratisbon]. Eds: H. Keil *De grammaticis quibusdam latinis infimae aetatis commentatio* (Programm, Erlangen 1868) 17-18 [verses, and beginning and end of treatise]. — J. Huemer *Cruindmeli sive Fulcharii Ars Metrica Beitrag zur Geschichte der karolingischen Gelehrsamkeit* (Vienna 1883). — Dümmler *MGH Poet. lat. aevi Carol.* II (1884) 681 [verses only]. Comm: B. Hauréau *Singularités hist. et litt.* (Paris 1861) 19 *sqq.* — Ch. Thurot " Extraits de divers manuscrits pour servir à l'histoire des doctrines grammaticales au moyen âge " *Notices et extraits des manuscrits de la Bibliothèque impériale* XXII pt. ii (Paris 1869) 4. — Dümmler *NA* IV (1879) 258-9. — Manitius *Lat. Lit.* I (1911) 523-5.

Cruindmel was an Irish schoolmaster living probably in some part of the Frankish empire [159] in the first half of the ninth century. We have no certain knowledge as to his date. The name, in the form Crunnmael, occurs frequently in the Irish annals in the eighth and ninth centuries. The Annals of Ulster, for example, have the entry under 821 " Crunnmael mac Odhrain, abbas Cluana Irairrd, obiit." The treatise on metre which bears the name of Cruindmel [160] is of considerable importance because of the number of extracts it contains from pagan and early Christian

---

[159] Cruindmel, like Mac Salchann, may never have left Ireland.
[160] Munich MS. 6411 adds to the text a few lines ending " Cavete filiole botrate Fulcharium Nec non suum socium sic sane Sedulium," which led Huemer to suggest that Fulchar might be the author. More probably he was the scribe of the Freising copy.

writers. Bede's *De metrica arte* was, apparently, his chief source, but this is expanded by the use of Donatus, Servius and Sergius, Aldhelm, the grammarian Virgilius Maro, Isidore of Seville, and many others. Quotations from Vergil and Sedulius are very numerous; he also quotes Plautus, Terence, Lucretius, Horace, Lucan, Fortunatus, Ambrose, Paulinus of Nola, etc., etc. The exact relationship between Cruindmel and his many ultimate sources has not been fully determined.

362. Anonymous Commentary on Donatus

MS: Milan Bibl. Ambrosiana L 22 sup. *s* X. COMM: R. Sabbadini " Spogli Ambrosiani Latini " *Studi Italiani di filologia classica* XI (1903) 165–85. — Manitius *Lat. Lit.* I 519–21. — KM *Sitzungsb. d. k. preuss. Akad. d. Wissensch.* philos.-hist. Cl. 1914 no. xxi p. 640 [O–I gloss].

This interesting commentary on the work of the Latin grammarian Donatus, which has importance especially because it preserves other early grammatical matter otherwise lost, is believed by its discoverer to be of Irish authorship.

VII. The Circle of Sedulius

Bibliography

See bibliog. at the beginning of this chapter, and of section v: especially L. Traube *O Roma Nobilis* and Manitius *Lat. Lit.* I 315–23. — F. Keller " Bilder und Schriftzüge " etc. [*cf.* p. 98 *supra*]. — E. Dümmler *NA* IV (1879) 315–20. — H. Pirenne *Sedulius de Liége* (*Mém. couronnés et autres mém. pub. par l'Acad. roy. de Belgique* XXXIII) (Brussels 1882). — Ebert *Allgem. Gesch. d. Lit. d. Mittelalters* II (1880) 191–202; Fr. trans. II 214–26. — Schlosser *Sitzungsb. d. k. Akad. in Wien*, philos.-hist. Cl. CXXIII (Vienna 1891) 101 *sqq.* — Balau *Sources hist. de Liége* (1903) 70–2. — S. Hellmann *Sedulius Scottus* (*Quellen u. Untersuchungen z. lat. Philologie d. Mittelalters* I i) (Munich 1906) [important]. — *NA* XXXII 677; XXXVI 769; XLIV 230.

After the death of Louis the Pious the Carolingian monarchy went the way of the Merovingian, and from much the same causes. The history of these later Carolingians may be here sketched briefly, as a setting to the matter that follows. After a series of wars which began long before their father's death in 840, the sons of Louis the Pious, by the treaty of Verdun in 843, divided the empire between them. The eldest, Lothair I, who had succeeded to the title of emperor, received Italy and a long strip of territory northward to the North Sea, including the capital of Aix-la-Chapelle. The second son, Louis " the German," received the predominantly Germanic lands to the east, and the youngest, Charles " the Bald," the Gallic territories to the west. Lothair died in 855; of his three sons, the Emperor Louis II, Lothair, and Charles of

Provence, the last survivor, Louis, died in 875. In the east, or Germany, Louis the German died in 876, one of his sons in 880 and another in 882. The third, Charles " the Fat," became emperor in 881, and ruler of all the Carolingian dominions in 885, and was deposed in 887. His illegitimate nephew, Arnulf, ruled Germany from 887 to 899, and the eastern branch of the Carolingians came to an end with the death of Arnulf's son, Louis " the Child," in 911. In the west Charles the Bald maintained his kingdom through stormy times till his death in 877. He had been crowned emperor at Rome in 875. After Charles the Great, he was the best patron of learning among the Carolingians. His descendants, amid Norse inroads and feudal uprisings, kept up a precarious royal succession until 987.

It was during the middle and later part of the ninth century that Irish influences in European scholastic circles reached their zenith. The refugees from the pillaged monasteries at home were probably then most numerous, the ideal of religious exile still persisted, and " pilgrims," in the modern sense of the word, were appearing in considerable numbers. An instance of the development of the idea of pilgrimage is seen in the embassy which Máel-Sechlainn, high-king of Ireland, sent to Charles the Bald in 848 announcing a victory over the Norsemen and requesting a free passage on a pilgrimage to Rome.[161] Some of these pilgrims remained on the Continent, as, for example, the two known as Marcus and Moengal at the monastery of St. Gall.[162]

Several ninth-century manuscripts in Irish script, preserved in various European libraries, have common features in their marginal annotations which indicate that they were written by, or belonged to, a group of these Irish scholars who were more or less closely associated with each other. The chief evidence is in the list of proper names found in the *marginalia*, names some of which are well known from other sources. The most famous is Sedulius, sometimes Sedulius Scottus, or Sedulius Scottigena. From him Professor Traube designated the whole group " the Circle of Sedulius." The manuscripts which we owe to Sedulius and his friends are of very great importance both for Irish history and linguistics and for the general history of European culture.

Sedulius arrived at Liége about 848 and was warmly welcomed by the bishop of that diocese, Hartgar. Of his earlier life we know nothing. It has been suggested that he was a member or companion of the embassy

---

[161] *Annales Bertiniani* in Migne *PL* CXV CXXV; also ed. C. Dehaisnes (*Soc. de l'hist. de France*) (Paris 1871) and Wirtz (1881).
[162] *Cf.* p. 596 *infra*.

which arrived on the Continent in 848 from Máel-Sechlainn. This, however, is pure supposition. The mention of Ruadri, king of Wales 844–878, suggests that Sedulius may have spent some time in that country on his way to the Continent. At Liége he seems to have settled down to the life of a *littérateur* and a *savant.* His literary abilities, and, no doubt, pleasing personality, kept him in friendly relationships with the bishops not only of Liége but also of the neighboring dioceses of Cologne,[163] Münster, and Metz. He took care also to send eulogistic verses to various members of the royal family and of the nobility. Sedulius, in fact, seems to have been a good early-mediaeval type of the scholar-courtier. Of his scholarship there can be no doubt. He was one of the most learned men of his time,— not an especially high standard. He was at once scribe, poet, grammarian, philosopher, theologian. How far his very considerable acquaintance with classical authors, and substantial — even if quite limited — knowledge of Greek may have been acquired in Ireland is matter of doubt. Hellmann has maintained that most of the classical lore of Sedulius was obtained by him after coming to the Continent. It would seem reasonable to believe that at least the fundamentals of his knowledge and proficiency had been acquired in his native land. But the evidence is so slight as necessarily to leave the question open.

Of the end of his life we know no more than of its beginning: after about 860, or perhaps 874, he disappears.

Among his companions Sedulius speaks with especial eulogy of Fergus, Blandus, Marcus and Beuchell, " the fourspan of the Lord, the glory of the Irish race." [164] Fergus, whose name is of frequent occurrence, seems to have been the author of an epic eulogistic of King Charles the Bald.[165] Dubthach, a name occasionally found associated with the Circle, is to be regarded, if some rather precarious identifications be accepted, as an earlier arrival in the Carolingian dominions. He, too, sojourned for a time at the Welsh court. Although Liége seems to have been the centre of this Irish colony, its members wandered from place to place: some of them appear to have gone to Milan in northern Italy, and either founded, or associated themselves with, another Irish colony in that city.

---

[163] We have no precise information as to earlier Irish associations with Cologne, but evidence thereof is provided by the marks of Irish influence in Cologne MSS from the time of Archbishop Hildebald (791–819). *Cf.* Hans Foerster *Die Abkürzungen in den Kölner Handschriften der Karolingerzeit* (Tübingen 1916).
[164] " Quadrigae domini, Scottensis gloria gentis " (*carmen* xxxiv).
[165] *Carmen* xxxv.

363. The Bamberg cryptogram A.D. 818 x 844

Haec est inscriptio, quam Dubthach . . . termino bene sonat.

MS: Bamberg H. J. IV s X f. 106ᵛ. Eds: WS " On a mediaeval cryptogram " *The Academy* XLII (July 23, 1892) 71–2. — J. Loth *Annales de Bretagne* VIII (1892) 289–93; " Étude sur le cryptogramme de Bamberg " *RC* XIV (1893) 91. Comm: J. L. Heiberg *Bull. de l'Acad. roy. de Copenhague* (Oct.–Dec., 1889) 199–201. — Gougaud *Les Chrétientés celtiques* (Paris 1911) 244–5.

The Irish had even more than the normal mediaeval taste for the obscure, the enigmatical, and the esoteric. A good example of their love for secret writing is given by a cryptogram preserved in a Bamberg manuscript. Attached to the cryptogram is a letter from certain Irishmen on the Continent to their teacher Colgu in Ireland.

" This is the inscription which was offered as an ordeal by Dubthach to the learned Irishmen at the castle of Mermin King of the Britons. For he so far thought himself the best of all the Irish and the Britons as to believe that no Irish scholar, much less British, would be able to interpret that writing before King Mermin. But to us, Caunchobrach, Fergus, Dominnach and Suadbar, by the help of God it did not remain insoluble." Then follows the interpretation of the cryptogram — " Mermin rex Conchen salutem " — and the explanation of the method by which it was composed, that of substituting, in accordance with a fixed table, Greek letters for Latin. " Please understand, wise and estimable Colgu, our very learned teacher, that we are not transmitting this exposition to you as to one needing such enlightenment; but we humbly ask that in your kindness you would give this information to such of our simple and unsophisticated Irish brethren as may think of sailing across the British sea, lest perchance otherwise they might be made to blush in the presence of Mermin, the glorious king of the Britons, not being able to understand that inscription."

Mermin has been identified with Mervyn Vrych, king of Wales (d. 844). It is noteworthy that Sedulius Scottus had relations with his successor, Ruadri. Colgu can hardly be the same as the friend of Alcuin; [166] the name, however, was fairly common in early mediaeval Ireland.[167]

364. Manuscripts from the Circle of Sedulius

(i) The Leyden Priscian

MS: Leyden Universiteitsbibl. F. 67, A.D. 838 [formerly of Egmont Abbey]. Facs: New Palaeographical Soc. pls. xxxii, xxxiii [ff. 7ᵛ, 166]. Fds: of O–I Glosses: Pott *Intelligenzblatt zur allgemeinen Litteraturzeitung* (1846) 28, 89. — WS *Goidelica* (1872) 56. — HZ *Glossae Hibernicae* (1881) pp. xxi *sqq*, 226–7. — *Thes. Pal.* II (1903) pp. xxiv, 231, 419. Cf. *ZCP* I 17. Comm: Hertz in Keil's *Grammatici latini* II (1855) pp. xiii–xvii. — E. Dümmler *Zs. f. deut. Alterthum* XIX (1876) 147 [with ed. of some marginal verses]; *NA* IV (1879) 569. — B. MacCarthy *Codex Palatino-Vaticanus 830 (RIA Todd Lect. Ser.* III) (1892) 351; *AU* IV (1901) pp. xcv *sq.* — Traube *O Roma nobilis* 352. — Lindsay *Early Irish minuscule script* (Oxford 1910) 36–40.

---

166 *Cf.* p. 534 *supra*.
167 The key set forth in this text is found to decipher a marginal entry in the eighth or ninth century MS of Juvencus in the Cambridge University Library. *Cf.* WS *The Academy* Sept. 10, 1892.

CONTENTS: Ff. 1-7 Priscian's interpretation of the *Periegesis* of Dionysius; 9-207 his *Artis grammaticae libri XVIII;* 208-18 his *De nominibus et pronominibus.* In the margins and elsewhere are some Latin poems [*cf.* no. 366] and a few Latin and Irish glosses. The text of the first two sections is of the type found also in *Sangallensis* 904, *Augiensis* 132, and *Fragmentum Ambrosianum* A 138 *sup.*, and is, no doubt, of Irish tradition. Both text and glosses of *Leidensis* are very closely related to those of *Sangallensis.* SCRIPT: For the first two sections, Irish, ninth century, but with a few continental abbreviations that suggest that the transcription was done on the Continent. (The last section is of the twelfth century, and not Irish.) At the end of the *Periegesis* (f. 7ᵛ) is the entry: " Dubthach copied these verses in a brief space of time; pardon, reader, the errors you may notice," followed by some minute computistical *data* which give the date April 11, 838.[168] It is probable that Dubthach is the man whose name occurs in the *marginalia* of manuscripts from the Circle of Sedulius, and he may also be identical with the author of the Bamberg cryptogram and with the scholar whose death is recorded by the Annals of Ulster in 869: " Dubthach mac Máel-Tuile, doctissimus Latinorum totius Europae, in Christo dormiuit."

(ii) The St. Gall Priscian

Cf. nos. 367, 533 *infra.* There can be little doubt that this codex was in the hands of members of the Circle of Sedulius; but it was, almost certainly, written in Ireland and, with a possible slight exception, not by persons of whom we hear in the Sedulian texts. It has, therefore, been noticed in a later section.

(iii) The Greek Psalter of Sedulius

MS: Paris Bibl. de l'Arsenal 8407 (2 of Greek ser.) *s* IX [formerly of the monastery of St.-Nicholas-du-Pré, at Verdun]. FACS: Bernard de Montfaucon *Palaeographia graeca* (Paris 1708) III 7, 235 *sqq* [ps. c, ci]. — Omont " Inventaire sommaire des mss. grecs " *Mélanges Charles Graux* (Paris 1884) 313 [f. 55]. COMM: Gardthausen *Griech-ische Paläographie* (1879) 427. — Brandt's ed. of Lactantius pp. civ *sqq* [*cf.* p. 567 *infra*]. — AdeJ *CLC* I (1883) 380. — Traube *O Roma nobilis* 344-5, 359. — S. Berger *Histoire de la Vulgate* (Paris 1893) 116, 411. — Gregory *Textkritik des neuen Testamentes* I (1900) 61.

CONTENTS: All in Greek, with Latin interlinear trans.: ff. 1-53 the psalter; ff. 54-64 biblical *cantica*, the Our Father, the Nicene Creed; ff. 65-6 fragment of the *Divinae Institutiones* of Lactantius. The text of the psalms closely resembles that of the Basel Psalter. SCRIPT: Irish. Both Greek and Latin may have been found in the *Vorlage*, but it seems certain that the scribe had some knowledge of Greek. The subscription, on f. 53 at the end of the psalter, runs: CHΆΤΛΙΟC. CKΌΤΤΟC. ΕΙΩ. ΕΓΡΑΨΑ. He is generally, though not universǎlly, identified with Sedulius of Liége.[169]

(iv) The Basel Psalter

MS: Basel Universitätsbibl. A. vii. 3 *s* IX. FACS: Aug. Baumeister *Denkmäler des klassischen Altertums* (Munich 1885-8) II 1132-3 [ps. xxix 10 - xxx 6]. COMM: H. C.

---

[168] Pub. by Hertz *Priscian.* I 13; HZ *Glossae hibernicae* p. xxii; Traube *MGH Poet. lat. aevi Carol.* III (1896) 685; also in MacCarthy *op. cit.*

[169] HZ *The Celtic Element in Mediaeval Culture*, speaks of a MS of Sedulius at Vienna, containing the *Vita Columbae.* I know nothing more of the MS.

M. Rettig *Antiquissimus quatuor evangeliorum canonicorum codex Sangallensis graeco-latinus* (Zürich 1836) 43. — F. Keller *op. cit.* [p. 98 *supra*] 86 pl. xii, 5 (Reeves's trans. 29 pl. iii). — H. Omont *Cat. des mss. grecs des bibl. de Suisse* (Leipsic 1886) [extract from *Centralblatt f. Bibliothekswesen* III 389. — S. Berger *Histoire de la Vulgate* (Paris 1893) 115-6, 376. — W. M. Lindsay *Early Irish minuscule script* (Oxford 1910) 47 *sqq.*

CONTENTS: (1) What appears to be a liturgical office (no. 571) and some other later additions; (2) the psalter, in Greek with Latin interlinear trans. In all, 99 ff. Textually, it is closely related to the Psalter of Sedulius. SCRIPT: Irish, beautifully written. Palaeographically it resembles very markedly *Codex Sangallensis* 48 and *Codex Boernerianus;* indeed, it is possible that originally the three formed parts of one large bible codex.[170] One of the scribes was, apparently, a Marcellus who has sometimes been identified with the Marcellus or Moengal of St. Gall (*cf.* no. 411). On spaces left blank entries were subsequently made by a hand which has been identified with that of the copyist of the greater part of *Codex Bernensis* 363. It must have passed into his possession along with *Codex Sangallensis* 48 and the exemplar from which he copied his own codex.

(v) *Codex Sangallensis* 48

MS: St. Gall Stiftsbibl. 48 *s* IX. FACS: H. C. M. Rettig *Antiquissimus quatuor evangeliorum canonicorum codex Sangallensis graeco-latinus* (Zürich 1836) [complete, with good description]. — *Palaeographical Soc.* ser. I pl. 179 [Luke i 1-8; better facs. but assigns to wrong date]. — F. Steffens *Lateinische Paläographie* (Fribourg 1903-6) pl. xlvii 1 [John i 1-]. COMM: G. Scherrer *Verzeichniss d. Hss. d. Stiftsbibl. v. St. Gallen* (Halle 1875) 20 *sq.* — H. Rönsch in Vollmöller's *Romanische Forschungen* I (1883) 419 *sqq* [re Latin trans.]. — Omont *Cat. des mss. des bibl. de Suisse* (Leipsic 1886) 56. — S. Berger " De la tradition grecque " *Mém. de la soc. nat. des antiquaries de France* LII (Paris 1891) 144-54, esp. 148. — J. Rendel Harris *The Codex Sangallensis* (Cambridge 1891). — Traube *O Roma nobilis* (1891) 347-8. — Berger *Hist. de la Vulgate* (1893) 114. — F. H. A. Scrivener (ed. E. Miller) *Plain introd. to the criticism of the New Testament* 4th ed. (London etc. 1894) I 156-8, II 51. — Lindsay *Early Irish minuscule script* (1910) 47 *sqq.*

CONTENTS: (1) Poem of pseudo-Hilarius; (2) prologues to the gospels, Eusebian canons, etc.; (3) the four gospels in Greek, with Latin interlinear trans.; (4) a poem addressed to Christ (no. 368). In all, 119 ff. The Latin text is mixed Old Latin and Vulgate, the whole modified in some degree to accord with the accompanying Greek.[171] SCRIPT: Of the above divisions, (3) is Irish, resembling the Psalter of Sedulius, the Basel Psalter and the *Codex Boernerianus;*[172] (2) is in a contemporary Carolingian minuscule hand; (1) and (4) are later, by an Irish hand which Traube identifies with that of *Codex Bernensis* 363. MARGINALIA: The following names are found: Gottschalk (*cf.* pp. 576-7 *infra*); Aganon (perhaps the bishop of Bergamo, Italy, 837-867[173]); Adal[hard?]; and the Irish Sedul[ius], Dub[thach], Kat[hasach], and Don[gus].

170 Traube, however, was of the contrary opinion: *O Roma nobilis* 52 n. 1.

171 In the apparatus of biblical criticism the texts are usually denoted by Δ and δ.

172 Traube suggests that the scribe may have been the Fergus whose name is met with occasionally in other MSS, but this is only a guess.

173 Traube thought that the MS might have been carried to Milan.

(vi) *Codex Boernerianus* [174]

MS: Dresden (former königliche) Bibl. Msc. A 145 b s IX. FACS: *Der Codex Boernerianus . . . in Lichtdruck nachgebildet mit einem Vorwort von* Dr. Alexander Reichardt (Leipsic 1909) [text of the epistles]. ED: Ch. F. Matthaei *XIII Epistolarum Pauli codex graecus cum versione latina veteri vulgo antehieronymiana olim Boernerianus* (Meissen 1791). COMM: H. Rönsch in Hilgenfeld's *Zs. f. wissenschaftliche Theologie* XXV (1882) 488, XXVI (1883) 73, 308 [*re* the Latin trans.]. — HZ *Glossae Hibernicae* (1881) pp. xxxiii *sqq*; *Supplementum* (1886) 14. — Traube *O Roma nobilis* 348. — Berger *Hist. de la Vulgate* (1893) 114. — F. H. A. Scrivener (ed. E. Miller) *Plain introd. to the criticism of the New Testament* 4th ed. I (London etc. 1894) 179–82. — Gregory *Textkritik des neuen Testamentes* I (Leipsic 1900) 111-4, II 612. — *Thes. Pal.* II (1903) p. xxxiv. — Hellmann *Sedulius Scottus* (1906) 148 n. 5. — Lindsay *Early Irish minuscule script* (1910) 47 *sqq*. Reichardt in his preface calls attention to many other authors that have used or commented on this text.

CONTENTS: (1) First fol., unnumbered, and ff. 100–11^v: interpretation of St. Matthew's gospel to v 22; (2) ff. 1–99^v: Greek text of the epistles of St. Paul (except Hebrews), with interlinear trans.; (3) f. 111^v: fragment of a Greek treatise περὶ νόμου πνευματικοῦ, with Latin interlinear trans. — it is ascribed to a " Marcus monachus." Textually, the Greek is very nearly related to the *Codex Augiensis* of the Pauline epistles (no. 500 *infra*). The Latin was based on an Old Latin version, modified to bring it into conformity with the Greek.[175] SCRIPT: Irish; (2) and (3) by the same hand, (1) different. Traube thought it was written and used by Sedulius, Hellmann is of the contrary opinion.[176] The script resembles *Sangallensis* 48 and the Basel Psalter, and, like them, has indications of having been written on the Continent. MARGINALIA: Two quatrains in O–I (*Addenda infra*). The following names are found: Don[gus]; Dub[thach]; Fergus; Comgan; Aganon (*cf.* p. 558 *supra*); Angelbert (perhaps the bishop of Milan 824-860); Godiscalcus (*i.e.*, Gottschalk: *cf.* p. 576 *infra*); Gonthar (bishop of Cologne 850–869); Hartgar (bishop of Liége 840–854); Hilduin (bishop of Cologne 842–849); Mar [perhaps Marcus, perhaps Martianus Capella]; Ioh[annes] (doubtless Eriugena).

(vii) *Codex Bernensis* 363

MS: Berne Stadtbibl. 363 s IX [sometimes designated *Cod. Bongarsianus*[177]]. FACS: H. Hagen *Codex Bernensis 363* (*Codices graeci et latini photographice depicti duce Scatone de Vries* II, Leyden 1897) [complete; good facs.; commentary, etc., unsatisfactory]. — Chatelain *Paléographie des classiques latins* pl. lxxvi *sq* [pls. of 2 pages]. — F. Steffens *Proben aus griechischen Hss. u. Urkunden* (Trèves 1912). EDS. OF O–I GLOSSES: WS *Goidelica*² (1872) 54. — Constantino Nigra *RC* II (1875) 446-52. — HZ *Glossae Hibernicae* (1881) pp. xxxi *sqq*, 263. — *Thes. Pal.* II (1903) pp. xxv, 235. *Cf.* WS *Academy* XXX (1886) 227-8. COMM: H. Hagen *Catalogus codicum Bernen-*

---

174 In the early eighteenth century the MS belonged to C. F. Boerner, of Leipsic.
175 The texts are denoted in biblical criticism by the symbols G and g.
176 *Cf. ZCP* VI 551 n.
177 This MS once belonged to the abbey of St. Benoît-sur-Loire, at Fleury, near Orleans. In 1562, during the wars of religion, the Huguenots sacked the abbey; the MSS were saved and retained by Pierre Daniel, of Orleans. At his death they were divided between his friends, Paul Petau and Jacques Bongars. Bongars died in 1612 and left his MSS to René de Graviset of Strasburg, who subsequently went to Switzerland. His son founded a public library in Berne, and donated to it his books, including this MS.

sium (Berne 1875) 347–50. — Gottlieb *Wiener Studien* IX 151 *sqq.* — A. Reuter *Hermes* XXIV (1889) 161. — Traube *O Roma nobilis* 348–50. — L. C. Stern *ZCP* IV (1903) 178–86. — *Album palaeographicum duce Scatone de Vries* (Leyden 1909) pp. xxv *sqq.* — Lindsay *Early Irish minuscule script* (1910) 50–4. — A. C. Clark *The descent of manuscripts* (Oxford 1918) 27–31. Also the chief critical editions of Horace.

CONTENTS: Ff. 1^V, 195–7: extracts from Dioscorides; (2) ff. 2–143: commentary by Servius on the Bucolics, Georgics and Aeneid of Vergil; (3) ff. 143–53^V: the Rhetoric of Chirius Fortunatianus; (4) ff. 153^V–65^V: the Dialectic and Rhetoric of St. Augustine; (5) ff. 165^V–6^V: the " ars rhetorica Clodiani de Statibus "; (6) ff. 167–86^V: poems of Horace (odes, epodes, *carmen saeculare, ars poetica*, part of satires), with a Life of Horace prefixed; (7) ff. 187–8^V: extracts from Ovid's *Metamorphoses* I, II; (8) ff. 188^V–94: fragment of Bede's History; (9) f. 194^V: 3 poems to Tado, archbishop of Milan (no. 369); (10) f. 195: a short extract from Priscian; (11) ff. 196^V–7^V: 6 poems on various subjects (no. 369). All this forms important evidence for the interests and activities of Irish scholars in Europe about the year 900, and earlier. The texts of Servius and Horace are very valuable; that of Horace is the most extensive and perhaps the oldest known, but the poems are curiously mutilated by omissions. SCRIPT: Several scribes, one predominating; all Irish. Apparently written in northern Italy, perhaps at Milan, towards the end of the ninth or early in the tenth century. The *marginalia* would suggest a date about the middle of the ninth century, contemporary with the other books of the Circle of Sedulius. Traube believed that this codex is a copy of one or more older Irish MSS which had belonged to the Circle of Sedulius, and from which the annotations in question were here transcribed. It has been noticed above that the Basel Psalter and *Codex Sangallensis* 48, MSS of the Sedulian group, also passed through the hands of the chief scribe of Bernensis 363. MARGINALIA: In Latin and Irish, some of considerable interest: " concerning genuflection as practised by the Irish," " concerning the Irish who die in the stranger's land," etc. The following Irish names are found in the margins or glosses: Sed[ulius] (many times), Fergus, Dub[thach], Suadbar, Cathasach, Johannes, Comgan,[178] Dungal,[179] Colgu,[180] Cormac, Macc Longáin, Mac Ciallláin,[181] Taircheltach,[182] Robartaich,[183] [St.] Brigit. Among continental names are Gottschalk, Agano, Queen Angelberga,[184] Hincmar (" Higmarus "),[185] Bishop Adventius,[186] Ratramnus.[187] Older authors to whom references are made are Donatus, Fulgentius, Hadrian, Honoratus, Isidore, Martianus Capella, Priscian, Sergius and Virgilius.

Traube thought that an uncial MS of Juvencus — Cambridge, Corpus Christi Coll. 304 s VII/VIII — had been in the hands of the companions of Sedulius. Seemingly the only reason was the occurrence in f. 75^V of the name " Engelberga," which he identified with that of Queen Angelberga. — *O Roma nobilis* 353.

[178] *Cf.* p. 559.   [179] *Cf.* p. 538.   [180] *Cf.* p. 556.
[181] Glosses a reference to the long life granted the Sybil. *Cf.* p. 477 *supra*.
[182] Glosses " magica ars." The magician Taircheltach mac na Cearda, of whose display of supernatural power in the year 858 an account is given in *3 Frags.* 136.
[183] " Lege hic librum fabularum Robartaich," annotating a reference to the stories of Castor and Pollux, Theseus and Hercules.
[184] Wife of the Emperor Louis II. *Cf.* pp. 553–4.
[185] *Cf.* pp. 576, 588, 600.   [186] Of Metz, 855–875.   [187] *Cf.* no. 356 (ii).

365. The Poems of Sedulius Scottus c A.D. 848–858

MSS: Brussels Bibl. roy. 10615–729 s XII ff. 214–23 [formerly of Cues]. — Metz Bibl. de la ville 500 s XI [no. x only].[188] EDS: De Reiffenberg *Annuaire de la bibl. roy. de Belgique* IV (1843) 87 [i, ii]. — E. Dümmler *Jahrbücher f. vaterland. Geschichte* I (Vienna 1861) 167–88 [5 poems to Eberhard]. — E. Grosse (Programm des Friedrichs-Gymnasiums, Königsberg 1868) 2–13 [14 poems]. — E. Dümmler *Sedulii Scotti carmina quadraginta* (Halle 1869); *Geschichte des ostfrankisches Reichs* II 682 [iv]; *Forschungen z. deut. Geschichte* V 394 [lxxi]. — Nolte *Rev. des sciences ecclés.* 1877 pp. 279–80 [lxviii, lxix]. — Pirenne *Sedulius de Liége* [partial]. — Traube *MGH Poet. lat. aevi Carol.* III (1886) 151–237 [complete]. — G. M. Dreves *An. hymn.* L (1907) 229–36 [7 poems, after Traube]. COMM: Dümmler *NA* IV (1879) 315–20. — Traube *O Roma nobilis* 341–3, 358 [valuable classification and analysis]. — K. Strecker *NA* XLIV (1922) 230.

A collection of 83 poems, the majority of them written during the episcopate of Hartgar, bishop of Liége 840–854. Many were written for Hartgar. The following is a brief summary of Traube's classification:

i–xix c 848–855 (874?): miscellaneous: i–xi are addressed to Hartgar; xii and xiv to Charles the Bald; xv is on a meeting of Charles the Bald and Louis the German (855 or 874); xvi is addressed to Wulfing, an officer of the Emperor Lothair; xvii is on the death of Hartgar; xviii, xix on the accession of his successor, Franco, bishop of Liége 855–901.

xx–xxvi c 848: poems addressed to royalty, the Emperor Lothair, his Empress Ermingard, and their sons Louis and Charles.

xxvii: A prayer for a fellow-countryman: Christe, tuo clipeo Dermoth defende, precamur. . . .

xxviii–xxxv c 854–858: addressed to Charles the Bald, Louis II, Franco, etc.; xxxiv Ad Suos: Egregios fratres, Fergum Blandumque saluta, Marcum, Beuchellem,[189] cartula, dulce sonans . . . ; xxxv Ferge, decus vatum . . . .

xxxvi–xliv c 848: addressed to various persons, including King Charles the Bald; Duke Eberhard of Friuli in Italy (a successful warrior against the Saracens); the Abbess Berta, daughter of the Emperor Lothair; and a certain Count Rotbert.

xlv: De strage Normannorum: Gaudeant caeli, mare. . . . xlvi: Contra plagam: Libera plebem tibi. . . . xlvii: De quodam altari: In hoc altari. . . . These three poems may have been written before Sedulius came to the Continent. The first celebrates a victory over the Norsemen, gained probably by the Irish; the third apparently refers to an altar set up by King Ruadri of Wales.

xlviii–lxv c 848–858: To Lothair, Hartgar, Berta, Leutbert, bishop of Münster (849–871), Eberhard,[190] Rotbert.

---

[188] There were two codices of poems of Sedulius at Toul in the 11th cent.: Becker *Catalogi bibliothecarum antiqui* (Bonn 1885) 152.

[189] *Cf.* p. 555 *supra.*

[190] No. liii accompanied a copy of Vegetius *De re militari* sent by Hartgar to Eberhard. *Cf.* p. 567.

lxvi–lxxv c 855–8: poems addressed to various patrons with whom he maintained
friendly relations after the death of Hartgar — Franco; Duke Eberhard; Gunthar,
bishop of Cologne (850–869); Addo or Hatto, abbot of Fulda (842–856); Adventius,
bishop of Metz (858-875).

lxxvi–lxxxiii c 848–858: to Hilduin, bishop of Cologne (842-849); Charles, third son
of Lothair; Berta. lxxxi: De rosae liliique certamine: Cyclica quadrificis curre-
bant. . . .

Scattered through the collection are several poems of a general character, not written
for a special personage or occasion.

366. Verses from the Leyden Priscian

MS: Leyden Universiteitsbibl. F. 67 ff. 1^v–3 [cf. no. 364 (i); these verses were added
in the 2nd half of the 9th cent.]. Eds: E. Dümmler Zs f. deut. Alterthum XIX (1876)
146 sqq. — L. Traube MGH Poet. lat. aevi Carol. III 687–8, 690.

Five short sets of verses: (i) Title, or rather two titles, for a pallium which Charles the
Bald and his queen Irmintrud, or Irmindrud (m. 842, d. 869), sent to Rome to be
placed on the altar of St. Paul the apostle, in the time of Pope Nicholas I (858–867).
(ii, iii) Couplets to, or about, Bacchus. (iv) The author appeals to Wulfad for heat,
contrasting his condition, suffering from the cold, with that of his fellow-monk, Carloman, warmed by a good fire. Carloman (d. 877) was the son of Charles the Bald,
who was tonsured in 854 and became abbot of Soissons in 860. Wulfad, a friend of
Johannes Eriugena,[191] was his tutor, abbot of Montier-en-Der (856) and Soissons (858),
afterwards archbishop of Bourges. (v) Fragment, the opening lines of a poem. —
Traube, from the evidence of style, considered these verses to be of Irish composition.
They were probably written about 858–9 by the Irish monk who then owned the manuscript, and who was, no doubt, stopping at Soissons in the kingdom of Charles the
Bald.

367. Poems from Codex Sangallensis 904 A.D. 850 x 863

(i) Lex mala menbra. . . . 4 ll. [Imperfect.] (ii) Umbrifera quadam nocte. . . 50 ll. [Imperfect.]

MS: St. Gall Stiftsbibl. 904 s IX pp. 88–9 [= f. 40; cf. no. 533]. Eds: E. Dümmler
Anzeiger f. Kunde d. deut. Vorzeit XVIII (1871) 10 sq. — Nigra Reliquie Celtiche (Turin
1872) 6 sqq. — Traube MGH Poet. lat. aevi Carol. III (1886) 238–40. Comm: Nolte
Rev. des sciences ecclés. IVe sér. (1877) 281 sqq. — Traube O Roma nobilis (1891) 347.

These two poems were written by some Irishman, probably of the Circle of Sedulius.
The first is the beginning of a metrical treatise on morals; the second an eulogy of
Gunthar, bishop of Cologne 850–869, which, no doubt, was composed during his episcopate. The script is continental, not Irish, and the poem to Gunthar appears to be
a mere rough draft, written by the owner of the codex on a leaf left blank by the original
scribe.

191 Cf. p. 585 infra.

368. Verses from *Codex Sangallensis* 48 *s* IX/X

γραμματα γραινγενων κατα σκηματα σοφε γυνοσκεις Cerne: labore meo lingua Pelasga patet. . . .
Des mihi perpetui, te rogo, regna poli. 22 ll.

MS: St. Gall Stiftsbibl. 48 [*cf.* no. 364 (v)]. Eds: Rettig 395 [*cf. ibid.*]. — Traube
MGH Poet. lat. aevi Carol. III 686–7. *Cf.* Clark *The Abbey of St. Gall* (Cambridge
1926) 110.

This poem, in Irish script, forms a prayer to Christ. Traube conjectured that the
scribe (and possible author) was one of the writers who produced *Codex Bernensis* 363.

369. Poems from *Codex Bernensis* 363 *c* A.D. 850 x 868

MS: Berne Stadtbibl. 363 *s* IX/X ff. 194ᵛ, 196ᵛ-7ᵛ [*cf.* no. 364 (vii)]. Eds: Traube
MGH Poet. lat. aevi Carol. III (1886) 232–7 [i–v, vii–ix]. — Daniel *Thesaurus hymnologicus* I 209, IV 163, 370 [vi].

These anonymous verses seem to have been written by a member of the Circle of
Sedulius into the *Vorlage* of *Bernensis* 363, and were copied by the scribe of that codex.
It would appear that the author lived at Milan. The style resembles that of Sedulius,
but Traube thought there was sufficient distinction to indicate a different poet. Summary: (i) Easter poem, addressed to Tado, archbishop of Milan (860–868); (ii) another address to Tado; (iii) to a Sofridus; (iv, v) to the Emperor Lothair; (vi) on
St. John the Baptist; (vii) verses to be inscribed on a chalice belonging to Angelbert,
archbishop of Milan (824–860); (viii) to Tado; (ix) to Leofrid, or Liutfrid, brother-
in-law of the Emperor Lothair.

370. Poem by Dungal

Baldo, dei famule, clare magister, . . . Et virtute dei vive valeque. 34 ll.

MS: Munich Staatsbibl. 14743 *s* IX f. 160. Eds: Dümmler *Archiv für österreich.
Gesch.* XXII 289. — *MGH Poet. lat. aevi Carol.* I (1881) 412–3. *Cf.* Foltz *Geschichte
der Salzburger Bibliotheken* 14. — Traube *O Roma nobilis* 336–7. — M. Manitius *Lat.
Lit.* 374.

It would be tempting in this poem to read Waldo for Baldo and regard it as addressed
by Dungal of St. Denis to his abbot.[192] But the consensus of opinion is that Baldo
was a scribe of Salzburg and the author the Dungal, companion of Sedulius, whose
name appears in *Codex Bernensis* 363 f. 54. The metre, which is unusual, was used
by the Circle of Sedulius.

371. The grammatical works of Sedulius: Commentary on Eutyches

Quoniam in arte Euticis grammatici . . . de nominibus sint traducta.

MSS: Zürich Zentralbibl. C. 99 *s* IX [31 ff., this text only]. — BN lat. 7830 *s* XII ff.
17–50. — Munich Staatsbibl. 6411 *s* X [excerpt only: *cf.* Keil *Halle Ind. Lect.*, 1875,

192 *Cf.* p. 539.

p. v [193]]. ED: H. Hagen *Anecdota Helvetica* (Leipsic 1870) pp. lxxiii–lxxix, 1–38
[introd., text, notes]. *Cf.* Ch. Thurot " Documents relatifs à l'histoire de la grammaire
au moyen âge " *Comptes-rendus de l'Acad. des Inscriptions et Belles-Lettres* 2nd ser.
VI (1870) [extract in *RC* I 264–5].— Hagen in Bursian's *Jahresbericht* I ii (1873)
1420.— *Rev. critique* XIII (1873) 86.— Z^2 p. xlii [also HZ *Glossae Hibernicae* 228].
— Traube *O Roma nobilis* 357.— E. Dümmler *MGH Epistolarum* VI pt. I (1902)
206 n. — M. Roger " Le 'commentariolum in artem Eutychii' de Sedulius Scottus "
Rev. de philologie 1906 pp. 122–3.— Manitius *Lat. Lit.* I 318.

Hagen assigned this commentary on the *Ars de discernendis coniugationibus* of Eutyches
to the time of Charles the Great, but there is no reason to doubt that it was by Sedulius
Scottus. The author seems to have made use of Priscian, the *De differentiis et societati-
bus Graeci Latinique verbi* of Macrobius, and other works, among them perhaps the
grammarian Virgilius Maro. Traube and Manitius believe that the work was written
by Sedulius before leaving Ireland: he introduces an Irish word casually into the text,
and he says that he wrote " rogatu fratrum."

Sedulius also wrote commentaries on Priscian, on the *Ars minor* of Donatus, and
perhaps also on the *Ars major*. See Manitius *Lat. Lit.* I 319, II 802 and the references
there given. It is reported that an ed. of the commentary on Priscian is being prepared by Paul Lehmann.

372. Sedulius: On Christian Rulers (*Liber de rectoribus christianis*)

[Preface] Omne ministerium, trifido quod praeminet orbe. . . . Postquam regale sceptrum . . . insuper
vero regnum caelorum, praestante g. s. et d. n. I. C., cui est perpes g. et p. cum P. et S. S. in s. s. Amen.

MSS: Bremen Stadtbibl. C 36 *s* IX ff. 17^v *sqq.* — Berlin Staatsbibl. Theol. fol. 368
s XII ff. 77^v–96^v.— Vat. Palat. 591 A.D. 1472 ff. 99–130. EDS: Marquard Freher,
G. Voegelin (1619). — Mai *Spicilegium Romanum* VIII 1–69. — Migne *PL* CIII 291–
332. — Traube *MGH Poet. lat. aevi Carol.* III (1896) 154–66 [the 21 poems only]. —
Hellmann *Sedulius Scottus* (Munich 1906) 1–91. COMM: R. W. Carlyle and A. J.
Carlyle *A History of mediaeval political theory in the West* I [by A. J. Carlyle]' (Edinburgh and London, etc. 1903) 215–62 *passim* [one of the very few books in this field
that have noticed Sedulius]. — H. Tiralla *Das augustinische Idealbild d. christl.
Obrigkeit als Quelle d. Fürstenspiegel d. Sedulius Scottus u. Hincmar v. Reims* (Dissertation) (Greisswald 1916).

This work, of which the fuller title runs *Liber Sedulii de rectoribus christianis et conven-
ientibus regulis quibus est res publica rite gubernanda*, has the greatest general historical
interest of any of the writings of Sedulius. It is one of a small group of ninth-century
works [194] which began that long series of " Mirrors for Princes " produced by the political thinkers of mediaeval and early modern times. The Christian ruler to whom the
work refers was probably Louis II, emperor after 855, but he may be Lothair II,
brother of Louis. The work shows no special traces of the influence of the author's life
in Ireland. He bases his system on Christian ethics as established by the Fathers of the
Church, and also makes use of several books of the late Roman Empire, as the *Scrip-*

---

[193] Hagen also used a copy by Büchler of a copy made by Cornelius Bock from an unidentified MS,
supposed to be from Bobbio.
[194] Hellmann *op. cit.* 1.

tores Historiae Augustae,[195] the *Historia Tripartita* of Cassiodorus, the *Mitologiae* of Fulgentius. Although there is some incoherence of detail, the author's theory is presented as a fairly consistent whole. It is that the state is a religious institution, but not in the sense in which the Church is so described: rather the ruler's sacred character consists in that he is appointed by God to protect and help the Church in its work. The most insistent practical admonition is that the ruler should hold frequent synods and give his assent and support to what is there decreed by the holy bishops.

373. The theological writings of Sedulius

(i) *Collectaneum in omnes beati Pauli epistolas*

Antiquam ad apostolica . . . epistolam Romae scripserit.

MSS: Munich Staatsbibl. 9545 [from Oberaltaich] *s* X 2nd part ff. 77–166 [partial]; 6238 [formerly of Freising *s* X *ex* [incomplete]. — Zürich Zentralbibl. Rh. 72 [formerly of Rheinau] *s* X pp. 1–411 [nearly complete]. — Fulda Aa 30 [formerly Weingarten 27] *s* XI/XII ff. 1–99 [incomplete]. — Bamberg B. V. 24 [formerly of Michelsberg] *s* XII ff. 2–104 [incomplete]. — Hamburg theol: 1046 *s* XIII/XIV. The orthography in the MSS shows traces of Irish origin. EDS: Migne *PL* CIII 9–270. COMM: R. Simon *Histoire critique des principaux commentateurs du nouveau testament* (1693) 379–82. — A. Resch *s. v.* " Agrapha," Harnack's *Texte und Untersuchungen* IV 422. — Hellmann *Sedulius Scottus* 147–97. — A. Souter " The sources of Sedulius Scottus' collectaneum on the epistles of St. Paul " *JTS* XVIII (1917) 184–228. See also the works by HZ and Souter cited p. 661 *infra*.

This, and the analogous treatise *Collectaneum in Mattheum*, as yet unpublished, are the two most elaborate of the works of Sedulius, and indicate the character of his scriptural studies. The present work has a peculiar significance because of its relationship to the commentary by Pelagius on St. Paul. The text of Sedulius belongs to a little group of Pauline commentaries, all but one of which are of direct Irish origin. This makes it probable that he either wrote his *Collectaneum* in Ireland, or used books brought from Ireland.[196]

(ii) *Collectaneum in Mattheum*

MSS: Berlin Staatsbibl. Meerm. 56 (= Phillipps 1660, formerly Meerm. 426) *s* X ff. 1–190 [*cf.* Rose *Verzeichnis d. lat. Hss.* I 104 *sqq*]. — Vienna National-Bibl. 740 [*cf.* Denis *Codices manuscripti theologici bibl. palat. Vindob.* I i 294; *Tabulae cod. mss. bibl. pal. Vindob.* I 124]. *Cf.* Manitius *Lat. Lit.* I 317, II 802. Not published.

(iii) Explanations of the arguments and other matter prefixed to the gospels

MSS: Basel Universitätsbibl. F. v. 33 *s* X ff. 1–43[v]. — Einsiedeln Stiftsbibl. 132 *s* X pp. 2–112. — Vat. Palat. 242 *s* X/XI. — Berlin Staatsbibl. Meermann 56. EDS: Angelo Mai *Scriptorum vet. nova collectio* IX (1837) 159 *sqq*; *Spicilegium Romanum*

---

195 *Cf.* Mommsen *Hermes* XIII 298–301.
196 *Cf.* pp. 661 *sqq infra*.

IX (1843) 29 sqq. — Migne PL CIII [Mai's texts]. Comm: Wordsworth Evangelium secundum Matthaeum I. — Traube O Roma nobilis 357. — Esposito Proc. RIA XXVIII C iii (1910) 63–5.

(a) Epistolae Hieronimi ad Damasum papam explanatio. Migne 331–48. (b) Commentary on the prologue to the four gospels. Migne 348–52. (c) Explanatiuncula in argumentum secundum Matthaeum, Marcum, Lucam. Migne 274–90. (d) Commentary on the system of canons for a harmony of the Gospels by Eusebius.[197] Esposito 83–91. (e) Explanatiuncula de breviariorum et capitulorum canonumque differentia et connexione deque eorum aequalitate atque inaequalitate speculatio. Migne 271–2; Esposito 91–5.

374. The miscellaneous *Kollektaneum* of Sedulius

MS: Cues (on the Moselle) Hospitals-Bibl. 52 (C 14) s XII ff. 246–73[V]. Comm: Jos. Klein *Über eine Hs. des Nicolaus von Cues nebst ungedruckten Fragmenten Ciceronischer Reden* (Berlin 1866). — Traube O Roma nobilis 364–73. — S. Hellmann *Sedulius Scottus* (1906) 92–146. — Manitius *Lat. Lit.* I 320–3. — E. Hohl *Rhein. Mus.* LXIX 580 sqq.

This *Kollektaneum* is a collection of notes of various kinds, chiefly excerpts from classical authors, which is found in a manuscript that probably derived its origin from Liége. The text is clearly a copy of an earlier exemplar written by an Irishman. Traube has made it certain that the original collection belonged to Sedulius Scottus, and Hellmann has shown how extensively he made use of it in preparing his *De rectoribus Christianis*. It appears, in fact, to have been his common-place note-book. Hellmann (p. 96, 137 sqq) further points out that similar material is found in the *Hibernensis* Collection of Canons, in the Cologne MS 2178 s VIII, and in the Corpus Christi College, Cambridge, MS 279 s IX/X, and believes that all were drawn from one large collection of moralising sentences. The truth of the supposition, and the extent to which, if true, it applies to the material in the *Kollektaneum*, are obviously important topics for the investigator either of the extent of the scholarship of Sedulius or of the character of the learning of Ireland in the ninth and earlier centuries. Circumstantial evidence, at least, points to Sedulius having obtained the greater part of his notes from Irish, not continental, sources.

(i) *Proverbia Grecorum*

Haec vero de Grecorum prudentia . . . militare possimus. Vale in Christo. Sapiens sapientem adiuvat . . . stultissime utitur. Deo gratias.

EDS: Klein *op. cit.* 25–6. — E. Dümmler *MGH Epistolarum* VI pt. i (1902) 206 [these give the dedicatory epistle]. — Hellmann *op. cit.* 121–35. Cf. KM *Triads of Ireland* (*RIA Todd Lect.* XIII) (Dublin 1906) pp. xiv–xv. Cf. no. 522.

This collection of sayings, professedly translated from the Greek, is known also through references in other sources.[198] It is now generally regarded as an actual adaptation made in Ireland in the sixth century from Greek originals.

---

[197] Sedulius uses the Latin version attributed to Jerome.
[198] Cambridge Corp. Christ. Coll. MS. 388 (415); the *Hibernensis* collection of canons *lib.* XXV; a letter of a certain Kathvulf of the 8th century: *MGH Epistolarum* IV 502 (cf. p. 282 supra).

(ii) Miscellaneous pieces, which often correspond to Bede's *Kollekta-neum* [199]

(iii) *Senex et adolescens*

Senex dixit contra adolescentem: Si vis fieri meus discipulus . . . dulcia pendant poma.

ED: Hellmann 120.

A short dialogue between Age and Youth which seems to be based on a passage in the *Liber de moribus* attributed to Seneca.

(iv) *Proverbia Senecae*

Cf. Klein 27–31.

Extracts from the *Liber de moribus*.

(v) Extract from Vegetius *De re militari* [200]

Cf. Klein 39 *sqq*; Traube 365–7.

(vi) Extracts from Orosius

Cf. Klein 40–5.

(vii) Extracts from Valerius Maximus

Cf. Hellmann 145.

(viii) Extracts from Macrobius

Cf. Klein 47–8.

(ix) Fragments of Cicero

Cf. Klein 49–58, 80–6; Traube 365, 367–9; Hellmann 106, 144–5.

Extracts and fragments of the following works: *In Pisonem, Pro Fonteio, De Inventione, Auctor ad Herennium, Pro Flacco, Philippicae, Paradoxa, Tusculanae.* Some of these compositions, *e.g. In Pisonem,* were almost unknown in the middle ages, and a few passages are preserved for us only in this collection. The only scholars of the ninth century who equalled or surpassed Sedulius in knowledge of Cicero were Lupus, abbot of Ferrières,[201] and a certain Hadoard who also made a collection of extracts from the Roman orators, but, unlike Sedulius, was careful to insert Christian emendations in his texts.

(x) Extracts from Lactantius *Divinae Institutiones*

Cf. Klein 92n.; Traube 365; S. Brandt and G. Laubmann *Lactanti opera omnia* pars I (*Corp. SS. Eccles. Lat.* XIX) (Vienna 1890) pp. civ *sqq*.

The works of Lactantius were uncommon in the middle ages, but Sedulius undoubtedly was familiar with them. He makes a citation also in his Greek psalter.[202]

[199] *Cf.* no. 541.   [200] *Cf.* p. 561 *supra.*   [201] *Cf.* p. 551 *supra.*   [202] No. 364 (iii).

(xi) Fragments of the grammarian Rufinus Antiochenus

Cf. Klein 93–4.

(xii) Extracts from Frontinus

Cf. Klein 87–91.

(xiii) Extracts from the *Scriptores historiae Augustae*

Cf. Klein 95 *sqq*; Mommsen *Hermes* XIII 298–301.

(xiv) A large collection of sentences in 27 chapters

Cf. Klein 100 *sqq*; Traube 369–71.

This is another important collection which includes considerable extracts from the so-called Caecilius Balbus, Publilius Syrus, Porphyrio's Commentary on Horace, Terence, the Epitome of Aurelius Victor, Cicero, Seneca, Charisius, Jerome *Adversus Rufinum*, Augustine *De civitate Dei*, Fastidius *De vita Christiana*. The collection as a whole may have been made by Sedulius on the Continent, or may have been brought from Ireland. Some of the sources from which it is drawn have peculiarly Irish associations. " Caecilius Balbus " is the name attached to a work which seems to have had the following history: a Greek collection of sayings was, at a fairly early date, translated into Latin; the translation was then interpolated with extracts from Publilius Syrus; from the resulting text two sets of excerpts were made, a longer and a shorter version.[203] The shorter version has been incorporated almost entirely into the present anthology, and also, with the title "sententiae philosophorum," into a similar gathering by Heiric of Auxerre.[204] Porphyrio's Commentary on Horace, of which Sedulius here makes considerable use, was almost unknown in the middle ages.[205] The work of Charisius was likewise very rare, and apparently preserved to us only by way of Ireland.

375. Sedulius: *De graeca*

MSS: St. Gall Stiftsbibl. 292; also a Carlsruhe MS. ED: Steinmeyer *Die althochdeutschen Glossen* II 623 [Steinmeyer and Sievers IV (1898) 409, 447]. *Cf.* Traube *O Roma nobilis* 344; Manitius *Lat. Lit.* I 322.

A small collection of Latin *lemmata* with Old High German glosses, which in the Carlsruhe MS bears the title " Sedulius de greca." Traube believes that the text was a revision by Sedulius of a recension of the *Hermeneumata* of the Pseudo-Dositheus. Dositheus was one of the texts preserved by the Irish,[206] and probably one of the means of retaining some little knowledge of Greek in the schools of Ireland.

203 Wölffin *Caecilii Balbi de nugis philosophorum quae supersunt* (Basel 1855). — W. Meyer *Die Sammlungen der Spruchverse des Publius Syrus* (Leipsic 1877) 44. — J. Scheibmaier *De sententiis quas dicunt Caecilii Balbi* (Munich 1879).

204 *Cf.* no. 407. Heiric had an Irish teacher, Elias, afterwards bishop of Angoulême (no. 404). In the eleventh century the library of Bobbio contained a book, " Liberum I de sententiis philosophorum": G. Becker *Catalogi bibliothecarum antiqui* xxxii, 433.

205 On Sedulius's knowledge of Horace *cf.* Manitius *Analekten zur Geschichte des Horaz im Mittelalter.*

206 *Cf.* the Bobbio catalogue in Becker *Catalogi bibliothecarum antiqui* 414.

376. Letter on the translation of the Psalter into Latin

Scottus quidam in territorio Mediolanensi commorans Graecae linguae gnarus de psalterio in linguam Latinam transferendo atque emendando disserit. Ut reprobare superflua . . . videntur, favente Domino emendavi.

MSS: Munich Staatsbibl. 343 *s* IX ff. 1^v–9^v. — Vat. 82 *s* IX ff. 2^v–12^v; 83 *s* IX ff. 1–9^v. [All are of Milanese origin.] Eds: Vezzosi in J. M. Thomasius *Opera omnia* II (Rome 1747) pp. xx–xxvi. — E. Dümmler *MGH Epistolae* VI i (Berlin 1902) 201–5. *Cf.* G. Morin *Rev. bénédictine* X (1893) 193–7. — Hellmann *Sedulius Scottus* 95 n. 2.

This very interesting letter or tract was attributed by Dom Morin to Sedulius, on what Hellmann thinks insufficient ground. Manitius favors Morin's opinion. The anonymous character of the text is peculiar, in view of the early date of the manuscripts, and suggests that the copyists knew little about their exemplar. It is possible, though improbable, that Sedulius visited Italy. But it is certain that there was an Irish colony in Milan, and that some of his companions found their way thither. The letter discusses the problem of translating the Psalms from Greek into Latin and indicates in some measure the character of the scholarship and the literary customs of the time.

VIII. Johannes Eriugena and the Irish colony of Laon and Reims

Bibliography

See bibliog. to the chapter, and to the preceding two sections. F. A. Staudenmaier *Johannes Scotus Erigena und die Wissenschaft seiner Zeit* (Frankfort-am-Main 1834). — A. Hellferich *Die christliche Mystik* II (Gotha 1842). — Saint-René Taillandier *Scot Erigène et la philosophie scolastique* (Strasburg 1843). — François Monnier *De Gottescalci et Johannis Scoti Erigenae controversia* (Paris 1852). — F. Christlieb *Leben und Lehre des Johannes Scotus Erigena* (Gotha 1860). — Johannes Huber *Johannes Scotus Erigena Ein Beitrag zur Geschichte der Philosophie und Theologie im Mittelalter* (Munich 1861) [useful]. — A. Stöckl *Geschichte der Philosophie und Theologie im Mittelalter* I (Mainz 1864) 31-128; *De Johannes Scotus Erigena* (Münster 1867). — H. J. Floss *Joannis Scoti opera quae supersunt omnia* in Migne *PL* CXXII (Paris 1865) [the only ed. of Johannes approaching completeness; it was, for its time, a very creditable work]. — O. Hermens *Das Leben des Scotus Erigena* (Jena 1868). — Barthélemy Hauréau *Histoire de la philosophie scolastique* pt. I (2nd ed. 1872) 148–75. — Ersch und Gruber's *Encyclopädie* XXXVII (Leipsic 1872) 82–99. — H. Rähse *Des Johannes Erigenas Stellung zur mittelalterlichen Scholastik und Mystik* (Rostock 1874). — L. Noack *Über Leben und Schriften des Johannes Scotus Erigena: die Wissenschaft und Bildung seiner Zeit* (Leipsic 1876). — F. J. Hoffmann *Der Gottes- und Schöpfungsbegriff des Johannes Scotus Erigena* (Jena 1876). — J. Bass Mullinger *The schools of Charles the Great and the restoration of education in the ninth century* (London 1877) [*cf.* p. 530 *supra*: gives a good survey of the intellectual life of the 9th century]. — P. Hoffmann *De Johannis Scoti Erigenae vita et doctrina* (Halle 1877). — G. Anders *Darstellung und Kritik der Ansicht von Johannes Scotus Erigena, dass die Kategorien nicht auf Gott anwendbar seien* (Jena 1877). — A. Ebert *Allgemeine Geschichte der Literatur des Mittelalters im Abend-*

lande II (Leipsic 1880) 257–67 [useful]. — R. L. Poole *Illustrations of the history of medieval thought* (London 1884; 2nd ed. 1920) [an appreciation of Eriugena's position in the history of philosophy and religion]. — G. Buchwald *Der Logosbegriff des Johannes Scotus Erigena* (Leipsic 1884). — Schrörs *Hinkmar, Erzbischof von Reims, sein Leben und seine Schriften* (Freiburg i. Br. 1884) [useful for the predestination controversy]. — P. Gabriel Meier *Die sieben freien Künste im Mittelalter* Heft II (Programm: Einsiedeln 1887) 24 [a study of Eriugena's astronomical knowledge]. — Schwenke *Philologus* Suppl. V (1889) 404 [a study of his knowledge of Cicero]. — Traube *O Roma nobilis* 355, 360, 362–3; *Prooemium* to his ed. of the poems in *MGH Poet. lat. aevi Carol.* III (1896) [an excellent summary of the facts regarding Eriugena]. — Bäumker *Jahrbuch für Philosophie und spekulative Theologie* VII (Paderborn 1893) 346, VIII 222 [on the name of Johannes]. — T. Wotschke *Fichte und Erigena* (Halle 1896). — F. Picavet " Les discussions sur la liberté au temps de Gottschalk, de Raban Maur, d'Hincmar et de Jean Scot " *Rev. internationale de l'enseignement* 1896. — Mandonnet *Rev. Thomiste* V (Fribourg en Suisse 1897) 383–94. — A. Brilliantoff *The influence of oriental theology on occidental in the works of Johannes Scotus Erigena* (St. Petersburg 1898) [an important study in Russian; see *Zs f. wissensch. Theol.* XLVII (Leipsic 1904) 126 *sq*]. — Alice Gardiner *Studies in John the Scot (Erigena) a philosopher of the Dark Ages* (London 1900) [a fairly good introductory treatise]. — Astier " Mémoire sur Scot Erigène au Congrès des Sociétés Savantes à Paris, Séance du 4 avril 1902 de la section d'histoire et de philologie " *Bibl. de l'École des Chartes* LXII. — J. Dräseke *Johannes Scotus Erigena und dessen Gewährsmänner* (Leipsic 1902) [valuable]; *Zs f. wissensch. Theologie* XLVI (1903) 563; *Theologische Literatur-Zeitung* 1906 pp. 435–6; *ZK* XXXIII (1912) 73–84. — Thomas *Rev. internationale de l'enseignement* 1903 p. 193. — Turner *History of Philosophy* (1903) 246–57. — Wattenbach *DGQ* I (1904) 323–4. — James Mark Baldwin *Dictionary of Philosophy and Psychology* III pt. I: Benjamin Rand *Bibliography of philosophy, psychology, and cognate subjects* (London and New York 1905) 197–8 [a long bibliographical list]. — E. K. Rand *Johannes Scottus: Quellen und Untersuchungen zur lateinischen Philologie des Mittelalters herausgegeben von Ludwig Traube* Bd. I Heft II (Munich 1906) [very important: *cf. Bibl. de l'École des Chartes* LXIX (1908) 423–7]. — C. M. Deutsch in the Hauck-Herzog *Realencykl. f. prot. Theologie u. Kirche* XVIII (1906) 86–100 [good]. — J. E. Sandys *A History of classical scholarship from the sixth century B.C. to the end of the middle ages* (2nd ed. Cambridge 1906; 3rd ed. 1921) 491–6; " Notes on mediaeval Latin authors " *Hermathena* XII (Dublin 1908) 428 *sqq* [suggestive remarks on the classical knowledge of Johannes]. — Whittaker *Apollonius of Tyana* (1906) 123–64. — M. Manitius *NA* XXXII (1907) 678–9. — Jacquin " Le Néo-Platonisme de Jean Scot " *Rev. des sciences philosophiques et théologiques* I (Kain, Belgium, 1907) 674–85 [contains an investigation into the knowledge of Greek possessed by Eriugena]. — Grabmann *Geschichte der scholastischen Methode* I (1909) 202–10. — Maurice De Wulf (trans. P. Coffey) *History of Mediaeval Philosophy* (London 1909) 167–73 [a brief statement of his philosophical teachings. 5th ed. of French original published at Louvain and Paris 1925, and trans. of vol. I, by E. Messenger, at London]. — M. Manitius " On Johannes Scottus and the library of Fulda " *NA* XXXIV (1909) iii; *Lat. Lit.* I (1911) 323–39 [very valuable].—M. Esposito *Hermathena* XV 362 [list of writings, and bibliography]; *Studies* I iv (Dublin Dec. 1912) 678–81 [an examination into the attainments in Greek of Johannes, Martinus, etc.]; *Studies* II viii (Dec. 1913) 505–7 [valuable bibliography]. — Friedrich Überweg *Grundriss der Geschichte der Philosophie* II: *Die mittlere oder die patristische und scholastische Zeit* (10th ed. by Matthias Baumgartner, Berlin 1915) 221–33 [excellent]. —

F. Overbeck (ed. C. A. Bernoulli) *Vorgeschichte u. Jugend d. mittelalt. Scholastik* (Basel 1917) 133 *sqq.* — P. Lehmann *Hermes* LII 113 *sqq*]important]. — A. Schneider *Die Erkenntnislehre des Johannes Eriugena im Rahmen ihrer metaphysischen und anthropologischen Voraussetzungen nach den Quellen dargestellt* I, II (*Schriften d. Strassburger wissenschaftl. Gesellschaft in Heidelberg* N. F. III, VII) (Berlin and Leipsic 1921, 1923). — M. L. W. Laistner " The survival of Greek in western Europe in the Carolingian age " *History* Oct. 1924 pp. 177–87; " Martianus Capella and his ninth century commentators " *Bull. of the John Rylands Library* IX i (Jan. 1925) 130–8. — H. Bett *Johannes Scotus Erigena* (Cambridge 1925). — H. Doerries *Zur Geschichte der Mystik — Erigena und der Neoplatonismus* (Tübingen 1925).

Contemporary with the group of Irish scholars whose central figure was Sedulius of Liége and whose sphere of action was chiefly, though not exclusively, the central kingdom of the Emperor Lothair, another little colony of exiles gathered in the West-Frankish kingdom of Charles the Bald, especially at Laon. Here the dominating personality was that of the famous Johannes Scottus Eriugena, as he is somewhat tautologically described. Johannes lived as a teacher — probably master — in the palace school of Charles the Bald. Other members of the group were Martinus Hiberniensis, after Johannes and Sedulius the most important Greek scholar of the age, Aldelmus, called the brother of Johannes Scottus, Helias, bishop of Angoulême, and perhaps Dunchat of Reims and that unnamed inmate of the monastery of Soissons who wrote verses that are to be found in the Leyden Priscian.[207]

With the exception of St. Columbanus, Johannes Scottus, or Eriugena,[208] was the most important individual that Ireland gave to continental Europe in the middle ages. Some slight evidence points to his being a layman, but this supposition, remarkable if true, remains doubtful. He must have arrived at the palace school at least as early as 845, and seems to have remained there until 870 or later. Of the end of his life we know nothing.[209]

Eriugena's writings divide themselves into several classes. Probably the earliest compositions were some of his works for the school-room: a commentary on Martianus Capella, extracts from Macrobius, a translation of the *Solutiones* of Priscianus Lydus (if really his work), perhaps a commentary on the grammarian Priscian. Hincmar of Reims drew him into the field of philosophy and theology, where he produced his *De praedestinatione*. Next Charles the Bald made use of his knowledge of Greek to obtain translations of Pseudo-Dionysius, and of a treatise

---

[207] No. 366.

[208] The MSS seem to show that he called himself Johannes Eriugena — from Ériu, the word now better known in its oblique-case form, Érinn, or Erin — but was designated by his contemporaries Scottus, or Scottigena.

[209] *Cf.* p. 588 *infra.*

by Maximus Confessor. Then came his philosophical and theological *magnum opus*, the *De divisione naturae*. Other theological writings and several curious Greco-Latin poems accompanied or followed these more famous works. While some productions not his own have been attributed to him, it is probable that others of genuine character have been lost.[210]   But what remain are ample for an appreciation of his style and thought.

He had a good mastery of the Latin language, and wrote a pithy and fairly clear and elegant style. He was very proud of his attainments in Greek, which were unique among his continental contemporaries. But he did not unduly over-rate them: in the dedications of the two translations made for Charles the Bald he insists that he is only a beginner in Greek studies. His Greek composition is poor, but it is certain that he could wrestle the meaning from even quite difficult Greek texts.

The question of the source of his knowledge is interesting. It has been represented on the one hand that it was merely the normal Hellenic learning preserved in the schools of Ireland, on the other that it was acquired entirely after his arrival on the Continent. A good case has been made out for the contention that the Greek texts with which he shows familiarity were met with by him only after leaving his native land.[211]   On the other side Traube points out that all knowledge of Greek in the Frankish dominions in the middle of the ninth century appears to have had an Irish source.[212]   It should be remembered that Eriugena was a man of quite unusual mental powers: it may well have been possible for him, by applying a very moderate knowledge of gram-

---

[210] A treatise *De corpore et sanguine Domini*, which has been assigned to Johannes, is regarded by some critics as the work of Gerbert. Raoul Heurtevant, *Durand de Troarn et les origines de l'hérésie bérengarienne* (Paris 1912) Append., concludes that it was written by Ratramnus (p. 550 *supra*). The *Integumenta*, a poem explaining allegorically Ovid's *Metamorphoses*, regarded by Gaston Paris (*Hist. litt. de la France* XXIX 504, 512, 516) as by Johannes, is classed by Traube (*op. cit.* 526 n. 8) as of the 13th century; and the verses beginning " Nobilibus quondam fueras," appended to some copies of the translation of Pseudo–Dionysius, are assigned by the same authority to Italian authorship (*ibid.* 554). In an eleventh-century catalogue of the monastery of St. Evre at Toul there is the entry " Johannes Scotus de compoto et natura canum et Hincmarus de fonte vitae vol. I " (Becker *Catalogi bibliothecarum antiqui* lxviii, 192; *cf.* Manitius *op. cit.* 339). In the fifteenth century there was in Michelsberg a MS entitled " Disputatio Theodori Graeci cum Johanne Scoto." It is now identified with the *Clavis physicae* of Honorius Augustodunensis (Grabmann *Geschichte d. scholast. Methode* II 136; J. A. Endres *Honorius* 64 *sqq*, 140 *sqq*). And the existence of a gloss on Priscian quoting Johannes may be evidence that he left a commentary on that author. Munich Staatsbibl. 561 *s* XIII contains " Priscianus minor cum expositione Johannis." *Cf.* Manitius *ibid.* 331, II 803.

[211] Jacquin *op. cit.*

[212] " Whoever on the continent in the days of Charles the Bald knew Greek, was an Irishman, or at least his knowledge was transmitted to him through an Irishman, or the report which endows him with this glory is false." — *O Roma nobilis* 354. In the same work, pp. 353–6, 361, Traube investigates the knowledge of Greek possessed by the Irish exiles at this time, and the means by which it was obtained, and gives a bibliography of the subject. *Cf.*, however, M. Esposito " Greek in Ireland during the Middle Ages " *Studies* I iv (Dublin Dec. 1912) 665–83; Manitius *Lat. Lit.* II 802–3.

mar and vocabulary acquired in his native schools to Greek texts found in European libraries, to attain a proficiency impossible to the average of his fellows.

In the intellectual field Eriugena's achievements can hardly — in a comparative estimation — be too highly appreciated. " While his contemporaries were only lisping in philosophy, and even his successors for centuries did no more than discuss a small number of disconnected philosophical questions, Eriugena in the ninth century worked out a complete philosophical synthesis. Apart from those incredibly daring speculations which made him the *enfant terrible* of his time, he reads like a pantheistic contemporary of St. Thomas." [213] But this very fact that he was several centuries in advance of his time, coupled with the easy discovery of heretical tendencies in his writings — although he himself, fortified no doubt by the Neo-Platonism of Pseudo-Dionysius, which he and his contemporaries looked on as the teaching of the Apostle to the Gentiles, never doubted of his own thorough orthodoxy — prevented his influence on intellectual development being at all commensurate with his genius. Perhaps for the same reasons his works have hardly yet received due investigation.

377. Dunchad

(i) Computistical notes, with title: *Commentum Duncaht pontificis Hiberniensis quod contulit suis discipulis in monasteri[o] sancti Remigii docens super astrologia Capellae Varronis Martiani*

MS: BM Reg. 15 A. XXXIII f. 3 *s* IX [a distinct leaf inserted in the codex]. Ed: M. Esposito *ZCP* IX (1913) 161-2; *cf.* 159-63.

(ii) Commentary on Martianus Capella

MSS: BN 12960 *s* IX/X ff. 25-30; 8786 *s* X; 14754 *s* XII. Ed: Manitius *Didaskaleion* (Turin 1912) 139-56 [not complete]. Comm: Narducci *Bollettino di Bibliografia e di Storia delle Scienze Matematiche e Fisiche* XV (Rome 1882) 553-8. — Traube *NA* XVIII (1893) 103-5. — Manitius *ibid.* XXXVI (1910) 57-60; *Lat. Lit.* I 525-6, II 803, 809. — M. Esposito *ZCP* VII (1910) 499-506; *Studies* II (Dec. 1913) 508; *Didaskaleion* III (1914) 172-81. — M. L. W. Laistner " Martianus Capella and his ninth century commentators " *Bull. of the John Rylands Library* IX i (Jan. 1925) 130-8.

In the British Museum manuscript Reg. 15 A XXXIII, which came from Reims, there is a single folio, inserted from some other codex, which contains computistical matter ascribed to a " Duncaht " who, we are told, taught in the monastery of St. Remi, expounding Martianus Capella. Manitius has identified as the work of this Duncaht,

[213] De Wulf (trans. Coffey) *History of medieval philosophy* (1909) 167.

or Dunchad, the fragments (covering books II, IV, V) of a commentary on the *Satyricon*, or *De nuptiis Philologiae et Mercurii*, of Martianus Capella,[214] in three Paris manuscripts. Traube had suggested that he might be the author of a commentary on the translation by Boethius of the *Isagoge* of Porphyry which is found in another manuscript in Paris; [215] and also that he was one of the teachers of Remigius of Auxerre.[216] But the whole subject of Dunchad's career and writings is quite obscure.[217]   It seems probable, but is not certain, that his commentary on Martianus Capella was written before that by Johannes Eriugena.

378. Johannes Eriugena: Extracts from Macrobius (*Excerpta Macrobii de differentiis et societatibus graeci latinique verbi*)

EDS: L. von Jan *Macrobii opera* I (Leipsic 1848) pp. lxxix, 229 *sqq.*—H. Keil *Grammatici latini* V: *Artium scriptores minores* (Leipsic 1868) 595–630 [see also introd.]. *Cf.* Teuffel-Schwabe *Geschichte der römischen Literatur* (5th ed. 1890) no. 444, 9; Manitius *Lat. Lit.* I (1911) 338.

Ambrosius Theodosius Macrobius, a Roman philosopher and grammarian, flourished about the beginning of the fifth century.   He has left two works of some importance, — the *Saturnalia*, ostensibly a record of discussions among a group of friends which took place during the feast of that name, valuable for the many quotations given from earlier authors; and a commentary on the *Somnium Scipionis*, a passage in Cicero's *De Republica*, which has importance because of its testimony to the physical, and especially the astronomical, knowledge and beliefs of the time.   Of a third work, comparing the Greek and the Latin verb, we have only excerpts.   The manuscript text ends with the note: " End of the selections from the book of Ambrosius Macrobius Theodosius which Johannes culled for the purpose of teaching the rules of the Greek verbs . . . since Macrobius Theodosius composed a book on the subject of the differences and agreements of the verbs of both languages, namely, Greek and Latin, it seemed to me right to make a selection from his work, following the same order." Little doubt is entertained that the excerpts were made by Johannes Eriugena.

379. Johannes Eriugena: Commentary on Martianus Capella

MS: BN 12960 *s* IX ff. 47–115ᵛ [this was a MS of Corbie, where it is mentioned in a catalogue of the 12th century: G. Becker *Catalogi bibliothecarum antiqui* lxxix 224; Hauréau *Notices et extraits des mss. de la bibl. impériale et autres bibl.* XX (Paris 1862) ii 1 *sqq* – some extracts]. EDS: M. Manitius *Didaskaleion* I (Turin 1912) 139–72, II 43–61 [extracts]. COMM: E. Narducci *Bollettino di Bibliografia e di Storia delle Scienze Matematiche e Fisiche* XV 505–80 [*cf.* esp. 523–7, 552]. — L. Traube *NA* XVIII (1893) 103–4. — E. K. Rand *Johannes Scottus* (Munich 1906) 11, 81–2. — M. Manitius *NA* XXXVI (1911) 57–60; *Lat. Lit.* I 335–7; II 803–4. — M. L. W.

---

[214] Martianus Capella wrote this exposition — in an allegorical setting — of the " seven liberal arts" in north Africa, probably early in the fifth century.   The work was edited by Eyssenhardt, 1866.   On Martianus see Sandys *History of classical scholarship* I³ (1921) 241–3.

[215] BN 12949 f. 46.

[216] *NA* XVIII 103. *Cf.* Manitius *Lat. Lit.* I 504–5.

[217] A commentary on the first book of Pomponius Mela in BN 4854 has been ascribed to Dunchad, but incorrectly. — Henri Omont, as reported by M. Esposito *Studies* March 1914.

Laistner " Martianus Capella and his ninth century commentators " *Bull. of the John Rylands Library* IX i (Jan. 1925) 130–8.

The commentary by Eriugena on Martianus Capella has not been published, nor has an adequate study yet been made of the relationships between the various commentaries on this work which were prepared in the ninth century.[218] Such publication and study would be important for the investigator of the origin, character, and transmission of the encyclopaedic knowledge of the time. Narducci gives some information on the mathematical lore of the work, and Manitius some examples of John's rationalising tendencies, and of his etymological ventures.[219] It seems probable that this is one of his earlier compositions.

380. Translation of the *Solutiones* of Lydius Priscus

Cum sint multae et uariae . . . commouent proprio motu.

MSS: BN lat. 13386 ff. 160 *sqq s* IX [the text follows that of *De Praedestinatione*]. — BM Harl. 3969 *s* XIV ff. 139ᵛ–60. — Mantua A. IV. 25 *s* XIV (?). — BM Cotton. Vesp. A. II. 13 *s* XIV ff. 148–57. EDS: Duebner (Paris 1855). — I. Bywater *Prisciani Lydi quae extant (Supplementum Aristotelicum* I ii) (Berlin 1886) 41–104. COMM: J. Quicherat *Bibl. de l'École des chartes* sér. III tome IV 248 *sqq.* — Traube *MGH Poet. lat. aevi Carol.* III 522 n. 3. — Rand *Johannes Scottus* p. ix n. 1.—Manitius *Lat. Lit.* I 331, 338. — M. Esposito " Priscianus Lydus and Johannes Scottus " *Classical Rev.* XXXII (1918) 21–3.

Chosroes king of Persia sent, it is said, a series of questions on scientific subjects to a certain Lydius Priscus who lived in the time of Justinian. Lydius prepared a collection of answers, which, in the ninth century, were translated from the Greek into Latin by some scholar of the Carolingian dominions. Quicherat and others have suggested Eriugena as the probable translator, though there is no conclusive proof. Traube gives the name of Fergus (the friend of Sedulius) as a possible alternative. The translation seems to be poorly done, but may have been based on a poor text.[220]

381. Johannes Eriugena: On predestination A.D. 851

[Dedicatory Epistle] Johannes Scottus Hincmaro Remensi et Parthulo [Pardulo] Laudunensi episcopis librum de divina praedestinatione rogatu eorum compositum mittit. Dominis illustribus et merito. . . . Fari non possum, . . . Pax Christi abundet in cordibus vestris. Caesare sub Karolo Francorum gloria pollet, Litora ceu pelagi piscibus atque salo: Secta diabolici damnatur dogmatis atque Pastorum cura splendet amoena fides.[221] [Main Text] Cum omnis piae . . . aeterna miseria luctaturos. [Epilogue] Quae cum ita sint, ecce . . . nullo modo pertinere.

MS: BN 13386 [formerly of Corbie] ff. 103–59 [this part *s* IX *ex*]. EDS: Gilbert Mauguin *Veterum auctorum qui IX saeculo de praedestinatione et gratia scripserunt opera et fragmenta* I (Paris 1650) 103 *sqq.* — H. I. Floss in Migne *PL* CXXII 347–440. — E. Dümmler *MGH Epistolarum* V (1899) 630–1 [the dedicatory epistle]. *Cf.* no.

---

[218] For the beginning of such an investigation, see Laistner's paper.

[219] Manitius *Lat. Lit.* I 335 calls attention to a contemporary reference to the philological teachings of John in an anonymous epistle published in *MGH Epistolarum* VI 184.

[220] It was used by Vincent of Beauvais (*c* 1190—*c* 1264). *Cf.* Manitius *Lat. Lit.* II 803.

[221] Traube was doubtful of the authenticity of these verses.

397 for eds. of the verses. COMM: J. Bass Mullinger *The schools of Charles the Great* [p. 569 *supra*] 171 *sqq.* — Schrörs *Hinkmar* [p. 570 *supra*] 117 and *passim.* — Freysted " Über den Prädestinations-streit " *Zs f. wissenschaftlich Theologie* 1893. — Jacquin " Le néo-platonisme de Jean Scot " [p. 570 *supra*] 674–85 [contains a study of the sources of *De Praedestinatione*]. And, in general, the works mentioned pp. 530, 569 *supra*.

Early in the ninth century a certain Saxon count named Berno dedicated his son Gottschalk, still a child, to the monastery which had been founded under the auspices of St. Boniface at Fulda. When Gottschalk came of age, feeling no vocation to the monastic life, he asked permission to leave, but Hrabanus Maurus,[222] then abbot, declared that he could not be excused from his vows. Nevertheless Gottschalk departed, and obtained, from a synod at Mainz in 829, the dispensation sought. Hrabanus, however, prevailed on the Emperor Louis the Pious to quash this action, and Gottschalk was sent back to the religious life, but allowed to transfer himself to the monastery of Orbais in the diocese of Soissons. Here the Saxon devoted himself to the study of St. Augustine, and was peculiarly attracted by the question of predestination. Leaving his monastery on the pretext of a pilgrimage to Rome, he spent the greater part of several years in northern Italy, where he was patronised by Eberhard of Friuli, the warrior count to whom Sedulius Scottus dedicated some poems,[223] and obtained many adherents to his doctrines. Being still pursued by Hraban Maur, who denounced him as a heretic because of his tendency towards rigid predestinarianism, he appeared in 848 before the Council of Mainz (where Hraban had become archbishop in 847) and attempted to confute his persecutor. The council, however, condemned Gottschalk's teachings, and handed him over to his own metropolitan, Hincmar, archbishop of Reims (845–882), for punishment. Charles the Bald held a council at Quierzy next year, and Gottschalk was condemned to burn his writings, to be scourged, and to be confined for life in the monastery of Hautvilliers.

The predestination controversy had aroused great interest. In the scriptural manuscripts of the Circle of Sedulius we find the name of Gottschalk repeatedly entered opposite passages having a bearing on his argument. The severity of his punishment helped, doubtless, to win sympathisers for his cause, which was espoused by such scholars as Ratramnus of Corbie, Prudentius, bishop of Troyes, and Lupus Servatus, abbot of Ferrières.[224] Hincmar himself wrote extensively on the subject, and, as he doubtless wished to gain all the support possible, he and his suffragan, Pardul, bishop of Laon (847–857), invited Johannes

222 *Cf.* no. 356 (i).   223 *Cf.* p. 561 *supra.*   224 *Cf.* p. 551 *supra.*

Eriugena, master of the palace school, to enter the lists on behalf of free will.

Eriugena's contribution must have been somewhat startling to his expectant allies. He proposed to attack the problem with the weapons of dialectics — division, definition, demonstration, and analysis.[225] He strove to establish the principle of predestination only to good, and based his arguments on St. Augustine and the Greek Fathers, whom, however, he seems to have known as yet only in translations. He referred with approval to the secular and suspect Martianus Capella. Among his fundamental principles he seems to have held the Neo-Platonic doctrine of the non-existence of evil.

382. Prudentius: On predestination, in reply to Johannes Scottus
A.D. 851

[Dedicatory Epistle] Ad Wenilonem Senonensem archiepiscopum. Reverentissimo Patri et Beatissimo Pontifici. . . . Accensus, prout decet . . . sospitem servare dignetur. [Text] Blasphemias tuas, Joannes, atque impudentias . . . memoriae tenacius valeat commendare.

EDS: Mauguin *Veterum auctorum qui IX saeculo de praedestinatione et gratia scripserunt opera et fragmenta* I (Paris 1650) 194 sqq. — *Bibl. max. vet. patrum* XV (Leyden 1677) 467 sqq. — Migne *PL* CXV 1009–1366. — E. Dümmler *MGH Epistolarum* V (1899) 631–3 [dedicatory epistle]. *Cf.* Schrörs *Hinkmar, Erzbischof von Reims* 117.

On the appearance of the *De Praedestinatione* of Johannes Eriugena it was sent by Wenilo, archbishop of Sens (836–855), to Prudentius, bishop of Troyes (846(?)–861), with a request for a refutation. Prudentius — which was the name adopted by Galindo, a Spaniard by birth — had been educated at the palace school, where he became an admirer of Eriugena.[226] Afterwards he attained prominence as a poet, theologian and historian: he has left a valuable continuation of the *Annales Bertiniani*.[227] Shoitly befoie the appearance of John's work he had, in a letter to Hincmar, defended the doctrine of a double predestination, and was now the obvious protagonist to be pitted against the Irishman. His reply is an absolute condemnation both of John's conclusions and of his methods: " use is to be made, not at all of the illusions of sophistry, but of the manifest statements of Holy Writ." [228] One incivility suggests the inference that John was a layman: " you, a barbarian, and a man honored with no grade of ecclesiastical dignity, and never so to be honored by Catholics."[229] Another passage should be conclusive as to his Irish origin: " You, the one surpassing all in cleverness, Ireland has sent to Gaul in order that those things which no one could know without your help might be discovered by means of your scholarship." [230]

[225] διαιρετική, ὁριστική, ἀποδεικτική, ἀναλυτική. This passage was apparently obtained from the *Prolegomena* by David the Armenian to Porphyry's *Eisagoge*. By what intermediaries it reached John we do not know.
[226] " I read your shameless and blasphemous words with the greater grief, John, because I formerly regarded you with such intimate personal affection and esteem " (Opening of the text).
[227] *Cf.* p. 554 *supra*.
[228] Migne *PL* CXV 1014.
[229] *Ibid.* 1043.   [230] *Ibid.* 1194.

383. Florus: Book against Johannes Scottus A.D. 852

[Preface] Venerunt ad nos cuiusdam vaniloqui et garruli hominis scripta. . . . [Text] Primo namque capitulo . . . in Apocalypsi comminantem pariter et pollicentem: Qui vicerit . . . haec in ecclesiis. [*Apoc.* XXI 7, 8, 25-27, XXII 14-16.]

ED: Migne *PL* CXIX 101-250.   *Cf.* Schrörs *Hinkmar* 117.

Florus was a deacon of the church of Lyons and a learned ecclesiastical writer of the first half of the ninth century. In the controversy aroused by Gottschalk he had written in support of the doctrine of a double predestination. When the book of Johannes Eriugena arrived at Lyons Florus was asked to prepare a refutation, a task which resulted in the present work.

384. Remigius of Lyons: Book on the three epistles c A.D. 853 x 855

EDS: *Bibl. max. vet. patrum* (Leyden 1677) XV 666 *sqq.* — Migne *PL* CXXI 985-1068.   *Cf.* Schrörs *Hinkmar* 122.

Hincmar of Reims and Pardul of Laon sent letters to the church of Lyons in regard to the predestination controversy. A treatise, discussing these two letters and a third epistle by Hraban Maur, was written at Lyons, probably by Remigius, archbishop of that city (852-875). It is characterised by an absence of the bitterness which is found in so many of the other controversial writings of the time. The letter by Pardul of Laon here quoted explains the way in which Eriugena was brought into the contest: " because there was such great disagreement on these questions we induced that Irishman, John by name, who is in the royal palace, to write."[231] This must be regarded as reasonably conclusive evidence that, at the date of the letter by Pardulus, Johannes was teaching in the palace school.

385. Council of Valence A.D. 855;   Council of Langres A.D. 859

ED: Mansi XV (Venice 1770) 1-13, 537-40.

It was not long until the authorities of the Gallic Church put forth as unrestrained a condemnation of Eriugena's theses as of those of Gottschalk which he had under- taken to refute. Canons iv and vi of the Council of Valence and iv of the Council of Langres denounced his methods of reasoning as " diabolical inventions," " old women's stories," and, borrowing the crowning insult from St. Jerome, " Irish porridge."[232]

386. Johannes Eriugena: Translation of the works of Dionysius the Areopagite A.D. 858 x 860

[Versus] Hanc libam sacro Graecorum nectare fartam. . . . Nodosae vitis sumitur uva ferax. 24 ll. [Dedicatory Epistle] Gloriosissimo Katholicorum regum Karolo Johannes extremus sophyae studentium salutem. Valde quidem admiranda . . . excellentiam essentiae recurrere. [Versus] Lumine sidereo Dionysius auxit Athenas. . . . Praedicti patris mystica dicta docent. 24 ll. [Libri quattuor de caelesti ierarchia, de ecclesiastica ierarchia, de divinis nominibus, de mystica theologia.] " Omne datum optimum,"

[231] Migne *PL* CXXI 1052.
[232] " Scotorumque pultes." *Cf.* p. 162 *supra.*

etc. Sed et omnis Patre . . . perfectione, et summitas omnium. [Epistolae diversae X] i Tenebrae quidem obscurae. . . . ii Quomodo omnium summitas. . . . iii Ex occulto est. . . . iv Quomodo, inquis, Jesus. . . . v Divina caligo est. . . . vi Noli hoc aestimare. . . . vii Ego quidem nescio. . . . viii Hebraeorum historiae aiunt. . . . ix Sanctus quidem Timotheus. . . . x Appellans sacram animam . . . ecum sunt, trades.

MSS: Very numerous. Traube (*MGH Poet. lat. aevi Carol.* III 525) distinguishes 3 families: I Francogallic. These go back to the copy, corrected and annotated by the papal librarian Anastasius, which Pope Nicholas I returned to Charles the Bald in 861 or 862. [*Cf.* Valentine Rose *Die lateinische Meermann-Handschriften d. kgl. Bibl. zu Berlin* 67 *sqq.*] Berlin Staatsbibl. Phillipps 46 *s* X [*cf.* Rose *op. cit.* 66]. — Florence Bibl. Laurentiana Plut. 89 sup. 15 *s* XI *ex* [*cf.* Bandini *Catalogus* III 259]. — Berne Stadtbibl. 19 *s* X/XI [*cf.* Herman Hagen *Catalogus codicum Bernensium* (Berne 1875) 12]. — BN nouv. acq. 1490 *s* X. — Basel Universitätsbibl. O iii 5·*s* XII [*cf.* Esposito *Proc. RIA* XXVIII C (1910) 66]. There are also MSS of *s* XII in Avranches and Darmstadt. II Italic. These are believed to be derived from a copy transcribed in the 10th century by John, Duke of Campania, from an exemplar of Family I. [*Cf.* Otto Hartwig *Centralblatt für Bibliothekswesen* III (1886) 165; Leitschuh *Führer durch die k. Bibl. zu Bamberg*[2] 39.] Cassino 221 *s* XI. — Bamberg B IV 8 *s* XI/XII. III Germanic. These are derived from a copy made in the 11th century from an Italic exemplar by Othloh, monk of St. Emmeramus in Ratisbon. Munich Staatsbibl. 14137 *s* XI [Othloh's autograph]. There are copies in Munich, Vienna and the Vatican. EDS:[233] Floss in Migne *PL* CXXII 1023–1194. — Ussher *Sylloge* 40–44 [*Whole Works* IV 476–82: the epistle and verses "Lumine sidereo" from a MS of Trinity College, Cambridge]. — Félix Ravaisson *Rapports sur les bibliothèques des départements de l'ouest* (Paris 1841) 559–60 [the poem "Lumine sidereo"]. — E. Dümmler *MGH Epistolarum* VI i (1902) 158–61 [the dedicatory epistle]. *Cf.* also no. 397. COMM: Jacquin "Le néo-platonisme de Jean Scot" [p. 570 *supra*] 674–85. — Otto Bardenhewer (trans. Thos. J. Shahan) *Patrology The Lives and Works of the Fathers of the Church* (Freiburg i. Br. and St. Louis Mo. 1908) 535–41. — Manitius *Lat. Lit.* I 333. — M. Grabmann "Ps.-Dionysius Areopagita in lateinischer Übersetzungen des Mittelalters" *Beiträge zur Geschichte des christlichen Altertums und der byzantinischen Literatur — Festgabe Ehrhard* (Bonn 1922) 181 *sqq.* — P. Lehmann "Zur Kentniss der Schriften des Dionysius Areopagita im Mittelalter" *Rev. Bénédictine* III (1923) 81–97 [this and the preceding assume that the trans. by Hilduin is lost]. — See also the works mentioned *supra*, pp. 569–71 and the articles on Dionysius in the *Realencykl. f. prot. Theologie u. Kirche* and the *Cath. Encycl.*

In the second half of the fifth century some unknown Greek writer, probably a Syrian of heretical sympathies, composed a number of works which professed to have been written by Dionysius the Areopagite, the convert of St. Paul at Athens.[234] Although used at first chiefly by the Monophysite heretics — in a conference at Constantinople in 533 the orthodox Hypatius, bishop of Ephesus, flatly refused to accept their authenticity — they gradually were adopted by Catholic theologians until the Lateran Council of 649 and the sixth Ecumenical Council of Constantinople in 680, by quoting them as evidence against heretical doctrines, seemed to put the final seal on their genuineness. Henceforth throughout the middle ages they were to be among the most popular of religious writings. This was especially the case in the East. In the

---

[233] An edition was published in 1503: *cf.* Strauss *Opera rariora* I 77; Graesse *Trésor des livres rares* II 399.

[234] *Acts* xvii 34.

West the language remained for a time a bar to their popularity, though in Rome the presence of many Greek monks and other sojourners from the Orient insured their preservation. In 757, as one of the results of the close association between the Papacy and the Carolingian rulers of the Frankish empire, a copy of the Dionysiac writings was, along with other books, sent by Pope Paul I to Pippin the Short.[235] This codex may have still been in the palace library in the time of Johannes Eriugena, or it may have disappeared. Its coming had no immediate consequence in the Gauls. But a different result followed on the gift of another copy, made in 827 by the Byzantine Emperor Michael II to the Frankish Emperor Louis the Pious.[236]

Just north of Paris an important monastery had grown up [237] at the shrine of an obscure early Christian martyr, Dionysius, or Denis.[238] Through Merovingian and Carolingian times this St. Denis had increased in fame until he became the peculiar patron of the West Franks. Hilduin,[239] abbot of the monastery from 815 — the man to whom Dungal, Irish inmate of that cloister, addressed one of his poems [240] — was from about 820 arch-chaplain and confidential adviser to Louis the Pious. It would seem that, at the request of Louis, he, with several collaborators, produced, some time between 831 and 835, a translation of the writings of Pseudo-Dionysius.[241] In 835 Louis commissioned him to write a Life of St. Denis.[242] The resulting work [243] amalgamated into one person the convert of St. Paul, the martyr of Paris, and the author of the theological treatises.[244] The identification continued to be accepted for many centuries.

Probably about 858 [245] Charles the Bald called upon the Irishman Johannes, the teacher in his palace school, to make a new translation of the writings of this great Father of the Church, so intimately connected on the one hand with the foundations of Christianity, and on the other with the Empire of the Franks. John seems to have worked resolutely to produce an independent version. His knowledge of Greek was sufficient to enable him not only to make a fairly accurate literal translation of the obscure original, but also to grasp quite fully its general significance.[246] For this he

[235] MGH Epistolarum III 529.

[236] MGH Epistolarum V 330. The MS is now BN Grec. 437.

[237] Cf. Léon Levillain " Les plus anciennes églises abbatiales de St. Denis" Mémoires de la Soc. de l'hist. de Paris et de l'Ile-de-France XXXVI (1909); " Études sur l'abbaye de St. Denis à l'époque mérovingienne " Bibl. de l'École des chartes LXXXII (1921) 5–116.

[238] Cf. G. Kurth Études franques (Paris 1919) II 297–317.

[239] Cf. F. Lot " De quelques personnages du IXᵉ siècle qui ont porté le nom de Hilduin" Le Moyen Âge XVI (1903) iv, XVII (1904) iv; " Les abbés Hilduin au IXᵉ siècle " Bibl. de l'École des Chartes March-June 1905.

[240] Cf. p. 541 supra.

[241] Cf. P. G. Théry " Hilduin et la première traduction des écrits du Pseudo-Denis ' Rev. d'hist. de l'Église de France IX (1923) 23–40 [see also RH July 1923 p. 297]; " Le texte intégral de la traduction du Pseudo-Denis par Hilduin " RHE XXI (1925) 33–50, 197–214. He identifies the text as still surviving.

[242] MGH Epistolarum V 326.   [243] Migne PL CVI 23–50.

[244] Cf. R. Foss Über den Abt Hilduin von St. Denis und Dionysius Areopagita (Berlin 1886); P. G. Théry " Contribution à l'histoire de l'aréopagitisme au IXᵉ siècle " Moyen Âge 2nd ser. XXV (May-Aug. 1923) 111–53.

[245] Cf. Traube MGH Poet. lat. aevi Carol. III 520. Traube thought that Hincmar of Reims, writing on the predestination controversy in 859/860, had quoted from the work of Johannes (Migne PL CXXV 313). Théry, however, has shown (RHE XXI 39 sqq.) that Hincmar's quotations are from the translation by Hilduin.

[246] In ironical mock-humility he requests any person who may doubt the fidelity of his version to " refer to the Greek codex from which I made my translation: there, perchance, he will find whether it is so or not." Ep. ad Karolum.

had been prepared by the Neo-Platonic studies of which his *De praedestinatione* had given evidence. It was principally on John's translation, as amended by the papal librarian Anastasius, that the very extensive knowledge and use of Pseudo-Dionysius in the West during the middle ages depended.

The writings of Pseudo-Dionysius consist of four treatises, on the " celestial hierarchy " — the nine angelic choirs, — the " ecclesiastical hierarchy " — the various grades in the Church, — the " divine names " — the nature of God and His relationship to created things — and " mystical theology " — the means of mystic union between the soul and God; and ten letters, four to a monk Caius, one each to a deacon, Dorotheus, a priest, Sopater, the bishop Polycarp, a monk, Demophilus, the bishop Titus, and the Evangelist John. The whole forms a body of vague, mystical, allegorical, and somewhat theosophical doctrines cast in a Christian mould but manifestly much influenced by Neo-Platonism, especially the teachings of Proclus (411–485). To John, whose mind was already inclining towards such a *Weltanschauung*, the discovery of such complete confirmation in so sacred an authority must have been conclusive. He accepted the veiled pantheism of Dionysius not as a thing to be explained away by orthodox subterfuges, but to be drawn forth as the vital principle of true Christian philosophy.

337. Pope Nicholas I: Letter to King Charles the Bald A.D. 858 x 860

[Fragment] Relatum est apostolatui . . . acceptius habeatur.

EDS: The *Decretum* of Ivo of Chartres IV civ in Migne *PL* CLXI 289–90; *ibid.* CXIX 1119. — Floss *ibid.* CXXII 1025–6. — Ernst Perels *MGH Epistolarum* VI pt. II fasc. I (Berlin 1912) 651–2. COMM: T. Christlieb *Leben und Lehre des Johannes Scotus Erigena* (Gotha 1860) 27. — Lapôtre *De Anastasio bibliothecario* p. 278. — Traube *MGH Poet. lat. aevi Carol.* III 519. — Perels *NA* XXXIX 43–153.

St. Ivo, or Yves, of Chartres, the first great canonist of the West, has preserved in his *Decretum* a letter written by Pope Nicholas I to Charles the Bald requiring that the translation of the works of Dionysius the Areopagite, lately made by " a certain man John, of Irish race," should be sent to Rome for examination. Reports had evidently reached the Pope which made him suspect the orthodoxy of the new translation. There is a later interpolated version which makes John a teacher at Paris and directs that he himself should proceed to Rome.

388. Anastasius: Letter to Charles the Bald

Inter cetera studia . . . regnum transferat quandoque. Explicit. Data X Kal. April. indict. VIII.

MS: Florence Bibl. Laurentiana Plut. 89 sup. 15 s XI/XII. EDS: Ussher *Sylloge* 45 sqq [*Whole Works* IV 483–7]. — Floss in Migne *PL* CXXII 1025–30. *Cf.* Manitius *Lat. Lit.* I 678 sqq; Ernst Perels *Papst Nikolaus I und Anastasius Bibliothekarius* (Berlin 1920).

To Anastasius, the Papal librarian, was assigned the task of examining and correcting the text of John's translation of Pseudo-Dionysius. The manuscript which he returned with his corrections and marginal annotations, said to be taken mainly from

Greek commentators, seems to be the exemplar from which all extant copies were ultimately derived. John's original text has disappeared, but it is not probable that any very extensive changes were made in it. Accompanying the codex Anastasius sent a letter, dated 23 March, 860, to Charles the Bald which gives high praise to the work of Eriugena.

" It is a wonderful thing how that barbarian, living at the ends of the earth, who might be supposed to be as far removed from the knowledge of this other language as he is from the familiar use of it, has been able to comprehend such ideas and translate them into another tongue: I refer to John Scotigena, whom I have learned by report to be in all things a holy man." He makes the criticism, however, that the translator, because of a modest desire to adhere closely to the exact words of the original, left much which still required an interpretation.

389. Johannes Eriugena: Commentary on Dionysius the Areopagite

(i) On the " Hierarchies "

Sancti Dionysii Areopagitae primus liber . . . nisi in animo. [There is a considerable gap in the middle of all known texts.]

MSS: Vat. 652 s XI. — Munich Staatsbibl. 380 s XII. — Basel Universitätsbibl. O iv 34 s XII. — Bruges 160 s XIV/XV. ED: Floss in Migne PL CXXII 125–266.

(ii) On the " Ecclesiastical Hierarchy "

Secundus vero liber, cui est inscriptio . . . eodem modo de ceteris [ends imperfect].

MSS: Leipsic Universitätsbibl. 188 s XIII. — BN 15630 s XIII. — Vat. 177 s XIV. ED: Floss loc. cit. 265–8. COMM: Grabmann op. cit. [p. 570 supra] 183. — Brilliantoff, Dräseke, op. cit. [p. 570 supra]. — Théry RHE XXI 205 sqq.

(iii) On the " Mystical Theology "

[Prologue] In prologo super librum de divinis nominibus. . . . " Trinitas supersubstantialis " etc. Titulus huius libri . . . super omnia absolutus. (Explicit opus multum utile, et obscurum valde.)

MS: Vienna Nationalbibl. hist. eccl. 136 s XIV. ED: Floss loc. cit. 267–84. COMM: P. G. Théry Vie Spirituelle, Mar. 1925 Supp. [as noted in RHE XXI 206].

Doubtless Eriugena himself realised that his close adherence to the original left obscure much of his translation of Pseudo-Dionysius. To elucidate it he provided a commentary, extant only in part, which is remarkable among early mediaeval commentaries because of the effort it makes to set forth the literal meaning of the text. To do this Johannes draws on his knowledge of the Greek language. He also makes use, but with more than usual appositiveness, of the familiar allegorical methods of explanation.

His editor, Floss, attributed to Johannes also two short commentaries on the " Celestial Hierarchy " and the " Mystical Theology," but the criticism of Théry and others has shown that the identification is erroneous.

390. Johannes Eriugena: Translation of the *Ambigua* of Maximus Confessor A.D. 860 x 867

[Dedicatory epistle] Domino gloriossissimo piissimoque Divina Providente atque adiuvante gratia Regi Karolo Johannes extremus servorum vestrorum perpetuam in Christo salutem. Hoc opus Maximi . . sympliciter transtulisse. [Verses] Kyrrie, caeligenae cui pollet gratia formae. . . . 24 ll. Quisquis rhetorico verborum syrmate gaudet. . . . 12 ll. Quisquis amat formam pulchrae laudare sophiae. . . . 20 ll. [Text] Sanctissimo ac beatissimo archiepiscopo Cyzici Joanni Maximus humilis monachus. Laudantur quidem, et fortassis . . . pertransierunt vestigiis.

MSS: Paris Bibl. Mazarine 561 *s* IX *ex* [*cf. Cat. des mss. de la bibl. Mazarine* I 226]. — Bibl. de l' Arsenal 237 *s* IX/X [*cf. Cat. des mss. de la bibl. de l'Arsenal* I 128]. — Vat. Regin. 569 *s* IX f.9 [one leaf only].[247]— BN 2203 *s* XIV. EDS: Thos. Gale *Joannis Erigenae De divisione naturae libri V* (Oxford 1681) appendix [MS. not now known]. — Floss in Migne *PL* CXXII 1193-1222. — Félix Ravaisson *Rapports sur les bibl. des dép. de l'ouest* (Paris 1841) 556-8 [poems only]. — E. Dümmler *MGH Epistolarum* VI (1902) 161-2 [dedicatory epistle only]. COMM: J. Dräseke *Stud. z. Gesch. d. Theol. u. Kirche* IX (1902) 52 *sqq*; *Zs. f. wiss. Theol.* XLVI (1903) 563, XLVII (1904) 250 *sqq*; *Theologische Studien u. Kritiken* 1910 pp. 530 *sqq*, 1911 pp. 20 *sqq*, 204 *sqq*. — Manitius *Lat. Lit.* I 334.

Maximus Confessor (*c* 580–662) was one of the most famous of Greek theological writers and champions of Catholic doctrine. His use and interpretation of Pseudo-Dionysius did much to bring that author into repute among the orthodox. A codex of one of his treatises, an explanation of ambiguous passages in the sermons of St. Gregory Nazianzen (ἄπορα εἰς Γρηγόριον), must have been preserved in the palace library or some monastery of France in the time of Charles the Bald. Soon after the completion of his version of Pseudo-Dionysius Charles called upon Johannes Eriugena to render the same service for this text of Maximus. The resulting translation is similar in character to its predecessor. It has some importance in illustrating John's ideas.

It is believed that John also made a translation, for his own use, of the *De hominis opificio* of Gregory of Nyssa. *Cf.* Dräseke " Gregorios von Nyssa in den Anführungen des Johannes Scottus Erigena " *Theol. Studien u. Kritiken* LXXXII (Gotha 1909).

391. Johannes Eriugena: Περὶ Φύσεων Μερισμοῦ, *id est, De divisione naturae c* A.D. 867

Magister. Saepe mihi cogitanti . . . convertit in lucem.

MSS: Bamberg H. J. IV 5 and 6 *s* IX. — Reims 875 *s* IX. [These MSS contain notes and corrections said to be in John's own hand: the Bamberg MS seems to have been once in Reims: possibly both belonged to Hincmar.] — BN 12964 *s* IX. — Avranches 230. — BM Harl. 2506 *s* X [excerpts: *cf.* Turner *Catholic University Bulletin* XIII 566 n. 4]. — BN 12960 *s* X [beginning only]. — Floss made use of three St.-Germain

---

[247] This passage, thought to be from a work by Johannes, *Liber de egressu et regressu animae ad Deum*, has been published by Carl Greith *Spicilegium Vaticanum* (Frauenfeld 1838) 30 *sq*, and by Floss in Migne *PL* CXXII 1023-4. P. Lehmann has shown that it is really an extract from the trans. of Maximus Confessor (*Hermes* LII 116-8). *Cf.* Manitius *Lat. Lit.* II 803.

MSS: 309 *s* XI, 830 *s* XI, 280 *s* XII in BN, and BN 1764 *s* XII.[248] ED: Floss in Migne *PL* CXXII 439–1022. GERM. TRANS: Ludwig Noack *Johannes Scotus Erigena über die Eintheilung der Natur* (*Philosophische Bibl.* Bds. LXXXVI–LXXXVII) (Leipsic 1870, 1874).[249] COMM: Manitius *Lat. Lit.* I (1911) 328–30, 334–5.—The works mentioned *supra.* pp. 569–71. — Delisle *Le cabinet des mss* II 125. — A. Schmitt *Zwei noch unbenutzte Hss des Johannes Scotus Erigena* (Bamberg 1900). — J. Dräseke " Johannes Scotus Erigena und dessen Gewährsmänner in seinem Werke De Divisione Naturae Libri V " *Studien z. Geschichte d. Theologie u. d. Kirche* IX ii (Leipsic 1902) 10–63 [study of the use of earlier Greek and Latin authors by Johannes]. — Manitius *NA* XXXII 678 *sqq.* — Ludwig Traube (ed. E. K. Rand) " Palaeographische Forschungen Vter Teil: Autographa des Iohannes Scottus " *Abhandl. d. k. bay. Akad. d. Wissensch.* I Cl. Bd. XXVI Abt. I (Munich 1912) [*cf. Bibl. de l'École des Chartes* LXXIII (1912) 301 *sqq.* But Rand in *University of California Publications in Classical Philology* V viii (1920) advances reasons for doubting the genuineness of these alleged autographs].

The most important work of Johannes Eriugena, and the first great philosophical production of western Europe, is the *De Divisione Naturae*. Unfortunately no adequate study of it has yet been made, at least in the English language. It is a philosophico-theological discussion, in the form of a dialogue, of the constitution of the universe, or " Nature ": " Nature " is analyzed, " divided," into four aspects: " Nature creating but not created," the Neo-Platonic ἕν, God as the origin of all things; " Nature creating and created," the world of Platonic ideas; " Nature created but not creating," the world of sense-phenomena; " Nature neither created nor creating," God the end, the destination, of all things. The Neo-Platonic mysticism which he imbibed from Pseudo-Dionysius, Maximus Confessor, Chalcidius,[250] and others, permeates the whole, and has been developed into a quite thorough-going pantheism. Rationalism, too, is one of its cardinal doctrines, but a rationalism most incongruous with the usual modern conception thereof, for it is based on the principle that the intellect is God Himself speaking in man. All this body of teaching is reconciled in full sincerity with the dogmas of Catholic Christianity.

The older authors whom Johannes certainly made use of in preparing his *magnum opus* are Vergil, Pliny, Augustine, Boethius, Martianus Capella, Hilary, Jerome and Ambrose, of the Latins, and Pseudo-

---

248 A brief extract from the *De divisione naturae*, treating of the Aristotelian categories, is found in St. Gall Stiftsbibl. 274 *s* IX p. 4, and has been edited by M. Esposito, *Proc. RIA* XXXVIII (1910) C 75. *Cf.* P. Lehmann " Johannes Scottus über die Kategorien " *Berliner philologische Wochenschrift* XLI (1921) 670-2.

249 An Eng. trans., in MS, by the Irish poet, William Larminie, is said to be in the National Library. Dublin; *cf.* M. Esposito *Studies* II (Dec. 1913) 506, who says it should be used only with caution.

250 Sandys (*Hermathena* XII 428 *sqq*) says that John's quotation from Plato's *Timaeus*, in *De Div. Nat.* I xxxi, is entirely independent of the translation by Chalcidius.

Dionysius, Epiphanius, Gregory of Nyssa, and Maximus Confessor of the Greeks.

The work is dedicated to his fellow-student Wulfad, afterwards bishop of Bourges.[251]

392. Johannes Eriugena: Commentary on the *Opuscula sacra* of Boethius *c* A.D. 868 x 870

Commentum Boethii De Trinitate. Quinti dicebantur . . . commendat.

MSS: In the following codices the commentary appears as a complete work: BN lat. 12957 *s* IX f. 2 *sqq.* — Bern Stadtbibl. 265 *s* X/XI ff. 68 *sqq.* — Einsiedeln Stiftsbibl. 235 *s* X/XI pp. 96-164. — BN lat. 2788 *s* XI ff. 29 *sqq.* — St. Gall Stiftsbibl. 134 pp. 134 *sqq* s XI. — Munich Staatsbibl. 11314 *s* XI/XII ff. 26 *sqq.* — St. Gall Stiftsbibl. 768 *s* XII pp. 9 *sqq.* In the following the commentary forms an interlinear and marginal gloss: Vat. Urb. 532 *s* IX ff. 1 *sqq.* — Bern Stadtbibl. 510 (f. 1), 517 (f. 22^v) *s* IX/X. — Bamberg Q VI 32 *s* IX/X ff. 1^v *sqq.* — Munich Staatsbibl. 18765 *s* X ff. 2 *sqq.* — Vat. lat. 567 *s* XI ff. 66^v *sqq*; Reg. 592 *s* XI ff. 77^v *sqq.* ED: E. K. Rand *Johannes Scottus* (Munich 1906) 3-80. COMM: Manitius *Lat. Lit.* I (1911) 337-8.

This Commentary was written soon after the death of Pope Nicholas I in 867. It is another example of the — for his time — superior exegetical work of Johannes. According to the editor it shows in places a toning down of the strongly heretical tendencies of the *De Divisione Naturae*.

393. Life of Boethius

MSS: Oxford Corpus Christi Coll. 74 *s* XI. — Florence Bibl. Laurentiana Plut. 78, 19 *s* XII f. 3^v. ED: Peiper *Boethii De Consolatione Philosophiae* (Leipsic 1871). *Cf.* M. Esposito *Hermathena* XVII (1912) 109-11.

A short Life of the Christian scholar and philosopher Boethius (d. 524/525) which the manuscript attributes to Johannes Scottus.

394. Homily on the prologue to the Gospel of St. John, attributed to Johannes Eriugena

Vox spiritualis aquilae . . . prophetalium visionum, cui gloria c. P. et s. S. per o. s. s. Amen.

MSS: Alençon 149. — Vienna 679. — BN lat. 2950 *s* XII ff. 179-89 [the first attributes it to Johannes Scottus, the other two texts are anonymous]. EDS: Félix Ravaisson

---

[251] *Cf.* p. 562 *supra.* In the Paris MS Bibl. Mazarine 561 *s* IX f. 219^v there is a library cat. which has been published by Petit-Radel, *Recherches sur les bibliothèques* 95-6, and by G. Becker, *Catalogi bibliothecarum antiqui* (Bonn 1885) 42 no. xxi. As published the first item reads " biblia Vulfadi," but, as Lehmann has noted, *Hermes* LII 113 *sqq,* and as the facs. in L. Traube (ed. E. K. Rand) *Palaeographische Forschungen* V [see p. 584 *supra*] pl. xii clearly shows, it is " Bibli Vulfadi." Evidently this was the list of Wulfad's books; among them are " Sti Dyonisii ariopagitae," " litterae eiusdem," " libri perifiseon II, " " Scoliarum Maximi."

Rapports sur les bibl. des dép. de l'ouest (Paris 1841) 334–55. — Saint-René Taillandier *Scot Érigène et la philosophie scolastique* (Strasburg 1843) 299 *sqq.* — Floss in Migne *PL* CXXII 283–96. *Cf.* Hauréau *Notices et extraits des mss. de la bibl. nationale* XXXVIII 410–4.

This homily is of very considerable interest even to the modern reader. The opening sections of the Gospel of St. John must have made an especial appeal to a man of Eriugena's peculiar philosophical conceptions. Its treatment here has a comprehensiveness, ease, and felicity which seem to argue a date of composition when his opinions had reached maturity. He uses his knowledge of Greek occasionally in order to elucidate passages by means of the original text.

395. Johannes Eriugena: Commentary on the Gospel of St. John. Four Fragments

MS: Laon 81 *s* IX [either John's autograph, or a copy revised by him: *cf.* Traube in Rand *Johannes Scottus* pp. viii–ix.[252] There is a facs. of a page in Traube (ed. Rand) *Palaeographische Forschungen* V (p. 584 *supra*).] ED: Floss in Migne *PL* CXXII 297–348, 1241–4. *Cf.* Manitius *Lat. Lit.* I 327.

These considerable fragments of a commentary by Johannes on the Gospel of St. John are of great importance. He had the advantage over his contemporaries of being able to develop a textual criticism by use of the Greek text, of which he had one or two manuscripts. His textual criticism served as an instrument for his exegesis, an exegesis bound down by the allegorical methods of his time yet showing on the one hand a laudable insistence on the determination of the literal meaning, and on the other originality and profundity in the paraphrastic comment.

396. Commentary on the Old Testament attributed to Johannes Eriugena

MSS: Vat. Reg. lat. 215 A.D. 876/7 ff. 88–106. — Berne Stadtbibl. 258 *s* IX [*cf.* H. Hagen *Catalogus codicum Bernensium* (Berne 1875) 288–9; G. Löwe *Prodromus corporis glossariorum latinorum* (Leipsic 1876) 174]. EDS [of O–I glosses]: HZ *Glossarum Hibernicarum Supplementum* (Berlin 1886) 1–2. — WS " Notes of a philological tour " *Academy* XXX (Oct. 2, 1886) 228; " The Old-Irish glosses in Regina Nr. 215 " *Zs. f. vergleichende Sprachforschung* XXX (1889) 555–61; " Glosses from Turin and the Vatican 1 Old-Irish " *Academy* XXXVII (Jan. 18, 1890) 46–7; " Glosses from Turin and Rome 2 The Old-Irish glosses in Rome " *Beiträge z. Kunde d. indogermanischen Sprachen* XVII (1891) 138. — Bruno Güterbock " Aus irischen Handschriften in Turin und Rome " *Zs. f. vergleichende Sprachforschung* XXXIII (1893) 103–5 [with important commentary]. — *Thes. Pal.* I (1901) pp. xiii, 1–2.

In a manuscript now in the Vatican, written in 876 or 877, there is a glossary to the books of the Old Testament compiled by taking alternate extracts from two other glossaries. The one set of extracts is distinguished by the marginal entry " AI " or " HAI," the other by " IO " or " IOH." In this last set are found several Old Irish glosses,

[252] But see Rand *op. cit.* [p. 584 *supra*].

which, however, have no very great intrinsic interest. The same compilation is preserved in a Berne codex, also of the ninth century, but evidently further removed from the originals than the Vatican text. Both manuscripts are by continental scribes who apparently did not understand Irish, but the glosses in that language are more corrupt in the Berne version. Moreover, in that text the " IO " extracts are not continued after the first three books of the Pentateuch. Güterbock has shown that it is quite probable that the " HAI'" passages are from a commentary prepared by Haimo of St.-Vaast, one of the teachers of Heiric of Auxerre, and that those marked " IO " are due to Iohannes Eriugena.

397. The Poems of Johannes Eriugena

MSS: See below. *Cf.* Dümmler *NA* IV (1879) 531–4; Strecker *ibid.* XLIV (1922) 231; Traube *Prooemium* to his ed. Eds: Angelo Mai *Classicorum auctorum* V 426–48 [poems from the Reginae codices]. — Floss in Migne *PL* CXXII 1221–34, 1237–40 [poems from the Reginae and Laon codices]. — Miller *Notices et extraits des mss. de la bibl. nat.* XXIX pt. ii (Paris 1880) 194-8 [the Greek words collected by Martinus in Laon codex 444; *cf.* pp. 23–4]. — Traube *MGH Poet. lat. aevi Carol.* III (Berlin 1896) 518–56 [excellent ed. with very valuable introd.].

Summary of Traube's classification: I Caesare sub Karolo, etc. *Cf.* no. 381.

II MS: Vat. Reg. 1587 *s* X ff. 57–64ᵛ. (i) Hellinas Troasque suos. . . . 82 ll. A.D. 859. (ii) Aspice praeclarum radiis. . . . 72 ll. (iii) Auribus Aebraicis notum. . . . 74 ll. (iv) Haec nostram dominam Yrmindrudis. . . 52 ll. (v) Mystica sanctorum panduntur. . . . 50 ll. (vi) Emicat ex Erebo lux. . . . 40 ll. (vii) στίχοι τοῦ Ιωαννοῦ τῷ βασιλεῖ Καρολῷ. Lux superans animas. . . . 24 ll. (viii) οἱ στίχοι τοῦ Ιωαννοῦ τῷ κυρίῳ αὐτοῦ τῷ ἄνακτι Καρολῷ· Si vis ουρανίας. . . . 84 ll.

III MS: Laon 444 *s* IX ff. 296–7. *Cf.* no. 400. This part, as also V, consists of extracts of Greek words and verses made by Martinus from poems by John, including those in II and IV.

IV MS: Vat. Reg. 1709 *s* X ff. 16ᵛ-8. (i) Versus ιωηαννις σκωθθι. Postquam nostra salus. . . . 82 ll. (ii) Item stichos eiusdem. Graculus Iudaeus iam . . . [imperfect]. 20 ll.

V MS: Laon 444 *s* IX ff. 296ᵛ-8. *Cf.* III *supra*.

VI Σήμερον, αὐτοκράτωρ φρόνιμος. . . . 8 ll. [Greek in Latin characters]. MS: Brussels Bibl. roy. 10078-84 *s* XI/XII *fol. addit.* [written by an unlearned scribe].

VII (i) Hanc libam, etc. (ii) Lumine sidereo, etc. *Cf.* no. 386.

VIII (i) Kyrrie, caeligenae, etc. (ii) Quisquis rhetorico, etc. (iii) Quisquis amat, etc. *Cf.* no. 390.

IX Versus Iohannis Scotti ad Karolum Regem. Aulae sidereae paralelos undique circos. . . . 101 ll. MS: Cambridge Corpus Christi Coll. 223 *s* X.

X Hic iacet Hincmarus cleptes vehementer avarus: Hoc solum gessit nobile, quod periit.²⁵³ MSS: Vat. Reg. 240 *s* X. — Munich Staatsbibl. 14569 [once of St. Emmeramus, Ratisbon] *s* XI f. 72ᵛ.

²⁵³ *Cf.* Traube *O Roma nobilis* 363.

XI Ornat [acus mi] ro sabanum molimine fulta. . . . 12 ll. MS: BN 1764 f. 145ᵛ [Traube thought not by John].

It is probable that all, or almost all, the poems of Johannes Eriugena were written after 858. They indicate his religious feelings and interests, his esteem for the Pseudo-Dionysius, and his relationship with Charles the Bald. One set of poems was dedicated to that king between 859 and 869: of these, one poem (II iv) refers to Irmintrud, Queen of Charles the Bald (842–869); another (II i) congratulates Charles on a victory over Louis the German in 859; a third (II ii) describes the angelic hierarchies according to the scheme of Dionysius. Some verses (IX) relate to a church dedicated to Mary which Charles the Bald had enlarged and adorned. One poem (VI) is an eulogy of Dionysius. A couplet (X) forms an ironical epitaph for John's early friend and, apparently, later enemy, Hincmar, archbishop of Reims, written while that famous churchman was still living. The poems are noteworthy because of the large number of Greek words, phrases, lines, whole passages, found scattered through them. The Greek is usually bad both in orthography and syntax, but it is evidence that Johannes must have had some rough fluency in the use of the language. Many of the mistakes, doubtless, are due to the copyists.

398. Psilotrum

MS: Avranches 2940 s XI. Cf. Félix Ravaisson Rapports sur les bibl. des dép. de l'ouest (Paris 1841) 131–3; Traube MGH Poet. lat. aevi Carol. III 518.

This curious little tract is found in a manuscript containing treatises on various pseudo-scientific subjects.²⁵⁴ It contains a description of a medicament said to have been used and recommended by Bishop Pardulus and the grammarian Fregus. The author adds: "Moreover the learned Greeks, as I have heard from Johannes, make very great use of this medicine."²⁵⁵ There can be little doubt that the Johannes here referred to is Eriugena, and Pardulus the bishop of Laon. Traube suggests that Fregus is Fergus, the friend of Sedulius Scottus.

To Johannes is attributed a fragment on the Life of Vergil, found in a contemporary manuscript. Cf. J. Brummer Philol. LXXII 288 sq; Manitius Lat. Lit. II 803.

William of Malmesbury,²⁵⁶ in his Gesta pontificum Anglorum (lib. v: ed. N. E. S. A. Hamilton (RS: London 1870) 392–4), completed in 1125, and Gesta regum Anglorum (II cxxii: ed. W. Stubbs I (RS: London 1887) 131–2), of which the first edition was finished about 1125, gives an account of Johannes Scottus who, he says, came to

---

²⁵⁴ The title is "Psilotrum ad noxios quosque humores extrinsecus dissicandos [desiccandos] et pilos qui displicent extirpandos."

²⁵⁵ "Non solum autem, ut superius dictum est, pilos delet verum etiam noxium humorum impetum reprimit; quo et frequenter Pardulus utebatur episcopus, et Fregus grammaticus, qui et dicebant: Quicumque hoc tertio usus fuerit in Martio, non opus ei febrium molestiam timere in anno illo. Graeci quoque sapientes, ut audivi a Johanne, hoc maxime utuntur medicamine. Nec aliquando fortassis alteram pro dessicandis humoribus curavit accipere potionem."

²⁵⁶ Cf. p. 608 infra.

England in the time of Alfred the Great and settled at Malmesbury, and was there murdered by his pupils. There is, however, no trustworthy support for this legend, which perhaps rests on a confusion of names. (*Cf.* Traube *MGH Poet. lat. aevi Carol.* III 522 n. 1.) In the *Gesta pontificum* William relates an anecdote embodying what has been called the best *bon mot* of the middle ages: Charles the Bald, entertaining his Irish guest Johannes, enquired over the cups: " Quid distat inter sottum et Scottum? " and received the reply " Tabula tantum."

MARTINUS HIBERNIENSIS

After Johannes Eriugena the most important member of the group of Irish exiles in the kingdom of Charles the Bald was Martinus Hiberniensis, a teacher at Laon. Of him, however, we know very little.

399. Annales Laudunenses et S. Vincentii Mettensis breves

ED: Holder-Egger *MGH SS* XV 1293-5.

These annals contain contemporary records made at Laon in the ninth and tenth centuries. The following entries are believed to refer to Martinus:
" 819 [Martinu]s Hiberniensis born, who was afterwards to be an exile, and a teacher at Laon." " 875 [Mar]tinus Hiberniensis slept in Christ." Entries under the years 892 and 903 mention ecclesiastics at Laon named Adelelmus and Bernardus, doubtless those so designated in Codex 444.[257] Perhaps Adelelmus may be identified with the " brother " of Johannes Eriugena.[258]

400. Codex Laudunensis 444 A.D. 858 x 869

MS: Laon Bibl. publ. 444. COMM: F. Ravaisson in *Cat. gén. des mss. des bibl. publ. des dép.* I (Paris 1849) 234 *sqq.* — E.Miller *Glosscire grec-latin de la bibl. de Laon* (*Notices et extraits des mss. de la bibl. nationale et autres bibl.* XXIX pt. ii) (Paris 1880) 1-230 [a valuable study of the contents, with publication of extensive extracts]. — H. Omont *Album paléographique* (Paris 1887) tab. xxiii. — G. Goetz in G. Loewe's *Corpus glossariorum latinorum* II (Leipsic 1888) pp. xxvi *sqq*, 487-506 [the Greco-Latin idioms]. — L. Traube *O Roma nobilis* 355, 362-3; *MGH Poet. lat. aevi Carol.* III (1896) 523, 686-97 *passim*, 821. — J. Vendryes " Les mots vieil-irlandais du manuscrit de Laon " *RC* XXV 377-81. — AdeJ " Un fragment grec transcrit en lettres latines par un irlandais au VIIIe ou IXe siècle " *RC* XXVI 384-7. — F. N. Robinson *ibid.* 378-9. — WS *Suppl. to Thes. Pal.* (Halle 1910) 81. — Lindsay *Classical Rev.* XXXI 128.

PRINCIPAL CONTENTS: (i) F. 2: Verses on the eight vices: Labitur heu nimium . . . 16 ll. EDS: Bernard de Montfaucon *Palaeographia graeca* (1708) 249. — Ravaisson *op. cit.* 235. — G. F. Hildebrand *Glossar. lat. bibl. Paris.* (Göttingen 1854) p. x; *Zs. f. d. Gymnasialwesen* VII 117. — Traube *MGH Poet. lat. aevi Carol.* III 692-3. (ii)

[257] *Cf.* no. 400. [258] *Cf.* no. 402.

F. 2^V: Extract from a homily attributed to St. John Chrysostom. ED: Miller *op. cit.*
11. (iii) F. 3: Dedicatory epistle to the abbot of St. M[aria at Laon]: Dilectissimo
abbati S. M. fidissimus amicus veram in Christo salutem: Lectis epistolae. . . . ED:
Du Cange *Glossarium mediae et infimae Latinitatis* I (new ed. Paris 1840) 27. *Cf.*
Montfaucon *loc. cit.* (iv) F. 4: Examples of Greek idioms, drawn from Macrobius.
Cf. Miller 13-4. (v) F. 4^V: Greek and Latin alphabets. *Cf.* Ravaisson 234 [facs.].
(vi) Ff. 5-255: Greco-Latin glossary. ED: Miller 25-112. [Found also in BM
Harl. 5792 *s* VII, which once belonged to Nicholas Cusa.] (vii) Ff. 255^V-74: List
of pairs of Greek and Latin words, similar in meaning but differing in gender. ED:
Miller 112-8. (viii) F. 275^V: Verses written in Tironian notes (the ancient short-
hand) and probably addressed to Hincmar,[259] bishop of Laon (858-69): Graecarum
glossas domino. . . . 6 ll. EDS: Ravaisson 234 [facs.]. — W. Schmitz *NA* XV (1890)
197-8 [reporting the solution of the script by the abbé J. C. Gauthey of Marseilles].
— Traube *MGH Poet. lat. aevi Carol.* III 686. (ix) Ff. 276-87^V: Greek words used
by Priscian, with Latin equivalents. ED: Miller 118-75. (x) Ff. 294-7: Glossary
of Greek words used by Johannes Eriugena, and Greek poems by him. *Cf.* no. 397. (xi)
F. 297^V: Verses in Greek written by Martin at the conclusion of his notes on Johannes
Eriugena; a bilingual epigram in praise of "Iohannes" and "Liuddo"; a Greek
prayer for Queen Irmindrud — φύλαξον, ὤ θεός, τὴν βασίλισσαν . . . ; and another
for Charles the Bald — ὤ κύριε, βοήθησον . . . . ED: Traube *loc. cit.* 697. (xii) Ff.
300-6: Greek paradigms. ED: Miller 202-5 [only those showing peculiar orthogra-
phy]. (xiii) Ff. 306-9: Greco-Latin glossary. ED: Miller 206-9. (xiv) Ff. 288-93,
309-18: Miscellaneous scraps of information on Greek subjects, lists of words, prayers,
explanations of the alphabet, remarks on pronunciation, etc.

This codex bears the old entry " Bernard and Adelelm gave this book to God and
to St. Maria of Laon," which points to a dedication made at Laon about the end of the
ninth century. It is written in continental script by Martinus Hiberniensis — who
is here described as διδάσκαλος [260] — and two or more of his fellow-students. The
three Irish glosses found in it, which seem to have been entries in the exemplar to guide
the binder, were copied by a scribe who was ignorant of Irish. They occur in the portion containing the principal Greco-Latin glossary, and perhaps indicate that the exemplar of the glossary was derived from Ireland. The manuscript is an important witness to the character of the knowledge of Greek possessed by Irish teachers on the
Continent in the ninth century. It seems to have been a collection of all the information available to the writers which would be useful for Greek studies. If we remember
that Greek was a sealed subject to almost all the scholars of western Europe at the
time, we can have considerable respect for the amount of rough working knowledge
here made available. But judged by strict standards the Greek of the manuscript
is poor. Inaccuracies in orthography, grammar and interpretation abound throughout. The teacher-scribe Martinus, a contemporary and admirer — doubtless friend —
of Johannes Eriugena, makes some attempts to follow that erudite in Greek poetical
composition, but is even less successful.

---

[259] His uncle, Hincmar of Reims, wrote of him: " You who not only cannot speak, but cannot even
understand, without the help of an interpreter, the language in which you were born, have made use of
mongrel and corrupt terms, Greek and sometimes Irish and other barbarities, according to your whim,
where Latin words would have amply sufficed." *Hincmari opera,* ed. J. Sirmond II 547; also Du Cange
op. cit. I 26.
[260] F. 297^V.

A fragment of the Greek text of the Gospel of St. John,[261] written in this codex in Latin characters apparently from an exemplar of Irish provenance, was accepted by d'Arbois de Jubainville as evidence that the Greek text of that Gospel, perhaps of the whole New Testament, had been preserved in Ireland.

401. Scholica graecarum glossarum

MSS: Vat. reg. 215 s IX ff. 112–22. — BM Reg. 15 A XVI ff. 74 sqq. — Barcelona Ripoll. 74 s X. — BN lat. 4883 s X/XI. — Bodl. Barlow 35 s X/XI. ED: Goetz Corpus glossariorum latinorum V 583–6 [extracts]. — M. L. W. Laistner " Notes on Greek from the lectures of a ninth century monastery teacher " Bull. of the John Rylands Library VII iii (Aug. 1923) 421–56 [cf. Studies XIII (Mar. 1924) pp. 163–5]. Cf. Goetz op. cit. I 148, 294, 302; Laistner " Martianus Capella and his ninth century commentators " op. cit. IX i (Jan. 1925) 130–8.

Laistner has identified this collection of Greek words, with explanations and observations in Latin, as notes from the lectures of Martin of Laon. He shows also that there is some reason to believe that Martin was the author of a commentary on Martianus Capella.

402. Aldelmus c A.D. 850–900

MS: BN 12929 f. 42. Cf. Cousin Fragments de philosophie du moyen âge (1855) 259; Traube NA XVIII (1893) 104; MGH Poet. lat. aevi Carol. III (1896) 518–19, 711 n.

One page of a manuscript in the Bibliothèque Nationale, Paris, contains a table of dominical letters written — no doubt copied — by " Aldelmus frater Johannis Scotti." The term " brother of Johannes Scottus " need not necessarily mean blood-relationship. On the other hand the form of the name, which obviously is not Irish, need not preclude Irish birth. Many of the Irish exiles adopted new names: this was probably done by John himself. Aldelmus may be identical with the ecclesiastic of Laon mentioned by the Annales Laudunenses.[262]

403. Adhelmus philosophus: Fragments

MSS: Liége 77 s XIV. — Paris Bibl. Mazarine 861 (1274) s XIV. ED: J. B. Pitra Spicilegium Solesmense III (Paris 1855) pp. iv, xxvi, 425–7.

Thomas Cantipratanus in his De Naturis Rerum has preserved a number of fragments attributed to an " Adhelmus Philosophus." They are, for the most part, mythical stories of real or mythical animals, conceived in the spirit of mediaeval natural history. Cardinal Pitra, who edited these fragments, believed that the author should be identified with the Aldelmus who was " brother of Johannes Scottus."

404. Gautbertus: Grammaticorum διαδοχή s X ex

EDS: Archiv d. Gesellschaft f. ält. deut. Geschichtskunde X 333. — L. Müller Rheinisches Museum NF XXII (1867) 635–6. — Léopold Delisle Notices et extraits des mss. de la *bibl. nat. et autres bibl.* XXXV (Paris 1896) 311–2.   Comm: L. Traube *O Roma nobilis* (1891) 373; *MGH Poet. lat. aevi Carol.* III 422. — Wattenbach *DGQ* I⁵ 282 n.

This obscure writer Gautbert gives us what purports to be a record of the transmission of learning from the seventh century to the tenth, a kind of genealogy of scholarship beginning with Venerable Bede. John Eriugena, Helias [263] of Angoulême, and the Laon school evidently entered into the scheme.

" Theodulf of Orleans through Johannes Scottigena completed the philosophic training of Helias, a man of the same nation, very learned in all subjects. Now Helias, after instructing Heiric, was given, as a reward for his wisdom, the see of Angoulême.[264] Then Heiric taught Remigius, a monk of St. Germanus of Auxerre, and another monk of St. Amandus, Hucbald,[265] giving the one mastery in letters, the other in music."

Gautbert mentions also as famous scholars, apparently of the group which may loosely be called the Laon colony, two men of " British " origin, Daoch and Egroal, and a third, Hisrael, whose nationality is not specified. Any or all of these may have been Irish.

405. Sacramentary of the church of Angoulême

MS: BN lat. 816 *s* VIII/IX.   *Cf.* Léopold Delisle " Mémoire sur d'anciens sacramentaires " *Mémoires de l'Institut National de France, Académie des Inscriptions et Belles-Lettres* XXXII (Paris 1886) 91–6.

This sacramentary, which formerly belonged to the church of Angoulême, consists of two parts, the first containing the collects and prefaces of the masses of the year, the second a mixed collection of collects and prefaces for various masses, and other prayers and ceremonies.   On fol. 146 [266] is found " ordo de sacris ordinibus benedicendis," to which the following marginal note has been added in a hand of the eleventh century: " Helias Scotigena acted according to this rule, and bishop Ugo according to the Roman order.   First is said the Introit, then *Kirri eleison*.   Then the bishop says *Oremus*, and the deacon *Flectamus genua*.   Collect of the day . . . ."   Hugues I was bishop of Angoulême *c* 988.

406. History of the bishops of Auxerre

Eds: Labbe *Novae bibl.* I (Paris 1657) 411–526. — *Bibl. hist. de l'Yonne* I (Auxerre 1850) 309–509. — Migne *PL* CXXXVIII 219–394. — Waitz *MGH SS* XIII (1881) 393–400 [extracts].

This chronicle of the bishops of Auxerre relates that, in the latter part of the ninth century, Wibald or Wicbald, after serving for some time in the royal palace (teaching in the palace school?) was elevated to the see of Auxerre.   He had been educated by

---

[263] Marianus Scottus the Chronicler uses this name as the equivalent of the Irish Ailill.

[264] In the *Annals of Angoulême* (*Annales Engolismenses*) there is an entry under the year 860 in a hand of the twelfth century: " Bishop Helias died September 22: he removed the body of the martyr St. Benignus from the city of Angoulême." *MGH SS* XVI 486.

[265] *Cf.* p. 505 *supra.*

[266] Delisle, 94–5.

Johannes Scottus " who at that time spread the rays of wisdom through the Gauls."[267] This part of the chronicle was prepared in the twelfth century, but it is based on a composition of Eriugena's contemporary, Heiric of Auxerre.

407. Heiric of Auxerre: Life of St. Germanus A.D. 859 x 876

EDS: *AA. SS. Boll.* Jul. VII 221–5. — Migne *PL* CXXIV 1131–1208. — Traube *MGH Poet. lat. aevi Carol.* III pt. ii fasc. i (1892) 428–517. *Cf.* HZ *Nennius Vindicatus* (Berlin 1893) 169. Also pp. 163, 592 *supra*.

Heiric of Auxerre was born in 841 and entered the monastery of St. Germanus at Auxerre when seven years old. He received a good education; it is possible that one of his teachers was the Irishman Elias, afterwards bishop of Angoulême. He died soon after 876. One of his most notable compositions was a metrical version of the Life of St. Germanus, the famous bishop of Auxerre in the fifth century. The writing of the Life must have spread over several years, but the dedicatory epistle to Charles the Bald which is prefixed to it seems to have been written about 876. Among his sources of information Heiric mentions an aged British bishop named Marcus, who had studied in Ireland, and, after a long incumbency of the episcopal office, had come to France as a pilgrim and lived the life of an anchorite at Soissons. This Marcus has, without any conclusive reason, been identified with the uncle of Moengal who settled at St. Gall.[268] It is possible that he was the Marcus who was a friend of Sedulius Scottus,[269] and there is some reason to believe that he was the man to whom the Vatican version of the *Historia Britonum* was at least attributed.[270]

Heiric's work contains one passage of special interest to the student of the fortunes of the Irish abroad. Amid his fulsome tributes to Charles the Bald, he speaks of the great numbers of Irishmen coming to the dominions of that king. Greece, we are told, grieves in jealousy at the way her glory is drawn away to the Frankish dominions. " Why should I mention Ireland, of which almost the whole people, despising the dangers of the sea, migrate, with their crowd of philosophers, to our shores. The more learned a man is the more likely is he to sentence himself to exile that he may serve the wishes of our most wise Solomon."

Remigius of Auxerre (d. *c* 908), who was a pupil, according to Gautbert (no. 404), of Heiric of Auxerre, and perhaps also of Dunchad (no. 377), seems to have been an heir of Irish learning. He wrote commentaries on biblical books, and on several of the chief secular school-texts. His commentary on Martianus Capella is closely related to those of Dunchad and Johannes Eriugena (*cf.* Laistner *Bulletin of the John Rylands Library* IX i (Jan. 1925) 130–8). On Remigius see Manitius *Lat. Lit.* I 504–19, II 808–9.

A commentary on the *Ars maior* of Donatus, published by H. Hagen *Anecdota Helvetica* 219–66 from Einsiedeln 172 *s* X pp. 138–95, probably comes, directly or with modifications, from Remigius. It has a short passage — Hagen's ed. 221; also in Traube *Perrona Scottorum* [*cf.* p. 500 *supra*] 532–7, where a copy in Munich Staatsbibl. lat. 17210 *s* XIII ff. 15–20ᵛ is also used — setting forth the different varieties of script.

[267] There appears to be a connection with the statement of Gautbert (no. 404).
[268] *Cf.* no. 411. · [269] *Cf.* pp. 555, 561 *supra*. [270] *Cf.* p. 154 *supra*.

One was " [litterae] tunsae, quas Scotti in usu habent," apparently the Irish minuscule, perhaps so named originally in contrast to the elongated Merovingian writing.[271]

IX. THE ABBEY OF ST. GALL

Bibliography

Cf. p. 10 *supra.* Ildefons von Arx *Geschichte des Kantons St Gallen* (St. Gall 1810–3); *Berichtigungen und Zusätze* (St. Gall 1830). — F. Weidmann *Geschichte der Bibliothek von St Gallen* (St. Gall 1841). — Ferdinand Keller *op. cit.* [p. 98 *supra*]. — Hermann Wartmann *Das Kloster St Gallen* (*Neujahrsblatt* I–II) (St. Gall 1863–4); *Urkundenbuch der Abtei St Gallen* I–V (Zürich 1863–1904). — Gabriel Meier " Geschichte der Schule von St Gallen im Mittelalter " *Jahrbuch f. schweiz. Geschichte* X (Zürich 1885). — Hogan " The monastery and library of St. Gall " *IER* XV (1894). — G. Meyer von Knonau " St Gallen " *Realencyklopädie f. prot. Theologie u. Kirche* VI (1899) 344–53. — M. Esposito *Proc. RIA* XXVIII C iii (1910) 72–9. — Traugott Schiess *Geschichte der Stadt St Gallen* (St. Gall 1917). — J. M. Clark *The Abbey of St. Gall as a centre of literature & art* (Cambridge 1926) [gives special attention to Irish influences]. — Gustav Scherrer *Verzeichniss der Handschriften der Stiftsbibliothek von St Gallen* (Halle 1875). — Paul Lehmann *Mittelalterliche Bibliothekskataloge Deutschlands und der Schweiz* I (Munich 1918) 55–148.

After the death of St. Gall [272] a church or chapel was, it seems probable, maintained at the site of his hermitage and tomb, and it is quite possible that a few anchorites, perhaps some of them Irish " pilgrims," had their cells in the neighborhood. But that an organised monastery, even of the Celtic type, existed before A.D. 720 is unlikely. In that year the church was placed in charge of a priest named Othmar, who became the first abbot. There is no evidence of direct Irish participation in the foundation of the monastery, but its organisation seems to have followed in the main the ideals of Columbanus. But Irish ecclesiasticism was on the decline in south-western Germany, and under Othmar's successor, Johannes, in 760, the Benedictine Rule was adopted in its entirety by the abbey of St. Gall.

St. Gall was one of the important centres of Irish influence in continental Europe, but it never was an Irish monastery. Indeed, so far as the sources show, only a very small number of Irishmen became permanent members of the community. But it would appear that many more were temporary inmates, for a few days or months or years, being induced by the fame of the founder either to make his church the terminus

[271] But see G. Gundermann *Berl. phil. Wochenschr.* 1903 pp. 1454 *sq*, noticed by Manitius *Lat. Lit.* II 792.

[272] *Cf.* no. 50.

of a pilgrimage or to turn aside thereto when going to or returning from Rome; that some few of the Gaels who became monks of St. Gall possessed remarkable talents as scholars and as teachers, and exercised an abiding influence on the intellectual life of the abbey; and that a peculiarly large collection of Irish manuscripts was accumulated in the library.

408. Ermenrich of Ellwangen: Letter to the Abbot Grimald c A.D. 854

MS: St. Gall Stiftsbibl. 265 s X p. 72. EDS: Dümmler (Halle 1873) [in the university Programm, and separately]; *MGH Epistolarum* V (1899) 536-80. — Traube *MGH Poet. lat. aevi Carol.* III (1896) 701 [the poem " Hoc ipse " only: a poem of mixed Greek and Latin lines added to the text, and believed to be of Irish authorship]. COMM: Dümmler " Über Ermenrich von Ellwangen und seine Schriften " *Forschungen z. deut. Geschichte* XIII (1873) 473-85, XIV 403-4; " Ermenricus " *NA* IV (1879) 321-2. — Ebert *Allgemeine Geschichte der Litteratur des Mittelalters* II (1880) 179-84. — Wattenbach *DGQ⁶* (1893) I 282-4, 290. — Manitius *Lat. Lit.* I (1911) 493-9.

Ermenrich (d. 874) was a monk of Ellwangen (in Württemberg, east of Stuttgart) and afterwards bishop of Passau, but he had also spent some time in the monasteries of Fulda, Reichenau and St. Gall. Grimald, to whom this epistle is addressed, was the abbot of St. Gall (841-872) who developed the monastic library which Gozbert [273] had begun. The letter is of considerable importance as a source for the state of learning in the ninth century. Ermenrich speaks in the warmest terms of the services rendered to learning by scholars coming from Ireland. There are references to Sts. Columban and Gall, and incidentally to the controversy over predestination.

409. Charles III (the Fat): Charter Sept. 23, 882

EDS: T. Neugart *Codex diplomaticus Alemanniae et Burgundiae Transjuranae intra fines dioecesis Constantiensis* I (1791) 436. — H. Wartmann *Urkundenbuch der Abtei St. Gallen* II 323. *Cf. Wiener Sitzungsb.* XCII 403; J. F. Böhmer (ed. E. Mühlbacher) *Regesta Imperii* I: *Die Regesten des Kaiserreichs unter den Karolingern* (Innsbruck 1889) p. 627 no. 1597.

By this charter Charles the Fat granted to the monastery of St. Gall the Irish monastic establishment on Mount St. Victor, with the church and some additional property.[274]

410. Ratpert: *Casus S. Galli*

EDS: M. Goldast *Scriptores rerum alamannicarum* I i (Frankfort 1616, 1661) 19 *sqq.* — Ildefons von Arx *MGH SS.* II (1829) 59-74. — Migne *PL* CXXVI 1057-80. — Meyer von Knonau *Mittheil. z. vaterländ. Geschichte herausg. vom hist. Verein d. Kantons*

---

273 *Cf.* p. 206 *supra.*
274 Another charter by the same emperor granted a villa called Rötis to the monastery of St. Gall for the maintenance on Mount St. Victor of a hospice for twelve pilgrims making the journey to Rome. Neugart 451; Wartmann 247. *Cf. Wiener Sitzungsb.* XCII 388, 394; Böhmer-Mühlbacher p. 638 no. 1650.

St. Gallen XIII [also as *St. Gallische Geschichtsquellen* II (St. Gall 1872) 1–64]. COMM: Wattenbach *DGQ⁶* I (1893) 269, 272–3. — Manitius *Lat. Lit.* I 607–8.

Ratpert (d. before 895) was a monk of St. Gall, famous in his age for his learning and literary skill. His *Casus S. Galli* is an account of the foundation of the monastery and of its fortunes up to his own time. It is our source for the story of an Irishman named Eusebius who came to St. Gall about the middle of the ninth century, but soon retired to the neighboring Mount St. Victor, where he led the life of a hermit for thirty years, dying in 884. According to Ratpert it was at the request of Eusebius that Charles the Fat granted Mount St. Victor to the monastery of St. Gall.²⁷⁵

411. Ekkehard IV: First Continuation of the *Casus S. Galli* c A.D. 1030

EDS: Goldast *SS. rer. Alamannicarum* I i (Frankfort 1616, 1661) 35 *sqq* (ed. 1730) 11–64. — Ildefons von Arx *MGH SS.* II 74–147. — Meyer von Knonau *Mittheil. d. hist. Vereins f. St. Gallen* XV, XVI (1877) [reprint in *St. Gallische Geschichtsquellen* III (1877) 1–450]. GERM. TRANS: *Geschichtschreiber d. deut. Vorzeit* LIV (Jahrg. X Bd. II) (Leipsic 1878). COMM: *Mittheil. d. antiquar. Gesellsch. in Zürich* Bd. XII Heft VI (1859) 260. — Wattenbach *DGQ⁶* I (1893) 269, 393–5. — HZ " Über die Bedeutung des irischen Elements für die mittelalterliche Kultur " *Preussische Jahrbücher* LIX (Berlin 1887) [Eng. trans: J. E. Edmonds *The Irish element in mediaeval culture* (New York 1891)]; *NA* XVII (1892) 210–1; *Pelagius in Irland* (Berlin 1901) 221–4, 449. — Manitius *Lat. Lit.* II 561–9.

The *Casus S. Galli* of Ratpert was continued from 891 to 971 by Ekkehard IV, a monk of St. Gall who died after 1057. In the opening sections he gives some account of the monastery before 891. One passage is of peculiar interest:

" In the time when Grimaldus was canonical abbot [841–72], and Hartmotus serving as his pro-abbot, so to speak, a certain Irish bishop Marcus returning from Rome came to visit St. Gall — as it were to his compatriot. He was accompanied by his sister's son Moengal, afterwards called by us Marcellus, a diminutive from his uncle's name Marcus. This man was exceedingly learned in sacred and in secular knowledge. The nephew was elected to our body and the bishop was asked to remain in our place for some time. After long deliberation they reluctantly consented. On the day appointed Marcellus distributed much of his uncle's money through a window, because he was afraid that his fellow-travellers might assault and mangle him. For they were furious at him as though it were at his persuasion that the bishop was remaining. The bishop gave his horses and mules to such persons as he chose by name; his books, his gold and his clothes he kept for himself and for St. Gall. At last, clad in his stole, he blessed his departing companions. So with many tears on both sides they separated. The bishop with his nephew and a few servants of his own tongue remained. After a time Marcellus was given charge of the cloister schools, with Notker — afterwards called Balbulus — and other boys who had entered the monastic life."

Fellow pupils of Notker Balbulus who doubtless passed under the instruction of Moengal were Tuotilo,²⁷⁶ poet, musician, painter and sculptor; Ratpert, first compiler of

---

²⁷⁵ *Cf.* no. 409. Ekkehard IV, in his *Liber benedictionum* (ed. J. Egli *Der Liber benedictionum Ekkeharts* (St. Gall 1909)), eulogises St. Eusebius.
²⁷⁶ *Cf.* Clark *Abbey of St. Gall* 296–7.

the *Casus S. Galli;* Waldramm the monastic librarian; and perhaps abbot Hartmann (d. 925). All these men contributed to the development of mediaeval hymnody, and some historians have seen the influence of Moengal's Irish musical tastes in the fame thus acquired by St. Gall. Of Moengal's skill as a scribe we still have evidence in the St. Gall charters written by him in 853, 854, 855, and 860.[277] These are written in continental script, not in the Irish calligraphy which, doubtless, was to be found in the books brought by Marcus.

The death of Moengal is recorded in the Necrology of St. Gall: " II Kal. Oct. obitus Moengal cognomento Marcelli viri doctissimi et optimi." [278] Zimmer identifies him with a Moengal whose obit is given in the Annals of Ulster under 871: " Moengal the pilgrim, abbot of Bangor, brought his old age to a happy close."

412. Notker Balbulus: Letter to Liutward, archbishop of Vercelli
c A.D. 885

EDS: Migne *PL* CXXXI 1003–4. — Dümmler *St. Gallische Denkmale aus der karolingischen Zeit* (Zürich 1859) 223–4. *Cf.* Clark *The Abbey of St Gall* (1926) 177–8. On Notker see G. Meyer von Knonau *Lebensbild des heiligen Notker von St Gallen* (Zürich 1877); Manitius *Lat. Lit.* I 354–67.

This is an account by Notker Balbulus (*c* 840–912) of the beginnings of his work at St. Gall in composing musical sequences for the church services. In it he refers to his teacher Marcellus. Liutward was a Swabian, and chancellor to Charles the Fat.

413. Notker Balbulus: Martyrology A.D. 891 x 896

EDS: H. Canisius *Antiquae lectionis* (Ingolstadt 1601–4) VI; 2nd ed. by Basnage (Antwerp 1725) II iii 89–184. — Migne *PL* CXXXI 1025–1164. *Cf.* HZ " Über direkte Handelsverbindungen Westgalliens mit Irland " 3 B: *Sitzungsb. d. k. preuss. Akad. d. Wissensch.* Philos.-hist. Cl. 1909 no. xxi 583–94.

Notker's Martyrology contains several notices of Irish saints, in particular a long section on Columba of Iona which is of considerable importance, since it does not seem to be based directly on any extant source.[279]

In St. Gall Stiftsbibl. 381 *s* XI there is a collection of St. Gall poems written for the most part, it would seem, in the ninth century. Several of them are in praise of the Irish forerunners, Columban and Gall, but they have no biographical value. Others are connected with events in the history of the Abbey, such as the visit of Charles the

[277] Wartmann *Urkundenbuch der Abtei St. Gallen* II 44, 48, 60, 87. He is mentioned in two charters of 865, *ibid.* 123–4. Some have thought that he was one of the scribes of Basel Universitätsbibl. A. vii. 3 (no. 364 iv) and Zürich Stadtbibl. C 79. *Cf.* Clark *op. cit.* 38.
[278] *MGH Necrologia* I (1888) 481. Moengal is mentioned as a monk of St. Gall in the Liber Confraternitatum Augiensis (Reichenau) *MGH Libri Confraternitatum* (Berlin 1884) 169, 123. — C. P. Cooper in *Appendix A, Supplement,* p. 7 (to unpublished Report on Rymer's *Foedera*) gives a reference to a homily by Moengal said to be in a MS of the library of Bremen. *Cf.* Clark *op. cit.* 39.
[279] *Cf.* p. 324 *supra.*

Fat. ED: Paul von Winterfeld *MGH Poet. lat. aevi Carol.* IV i (1899) 315–49. *Cf.* Anselm Schubinger *Die Sängerschule St Gallens* (Einsiedeln 1858) [Fr. trans. by Briffod]; Dümmler *Mitteil. d. antiq. Gesellsch. in Zürich* XII pp. vii *sq*, 255 *sqq*; Manitius *Lat. Lit.* I 605–7.

414. Dubduin: Verses *s* X/XI

Hic sunt insignes sancti, quos insula nostra. . . . Bessibus labrisque canens quod dixit amice. 16 ll.

MS: St. Gall Stiftsbibl. 10 *s* X/XI p. 3. EDS: Ildefons von Arx *Berichtigungen u. Zusätze z. d. Geschichten d. Kantons S. Gallen* I (1830) 20 [incomplete]. — C. P. Cooper *Appendix A* [to a Report on Rymer's *Foedera*] (London 1835?: issued by the Master of the Rolls 1869) 92–3. — F. Keller *op. cit.* [p. 98 *supra*] 59 *sq* [trans: Reeves *UJA* VIII (1860) 215]. — E. Dümmler *NA* X (1885) 341–2. *Cf.* Wattenbach *DGQ* (1904) 270 n.; J. M. Clark *The Abbey of St Gall* (1926) 29–30.

In these very barbarous hexameter verses — some of the errors of which may, however, be due to the copyist — an otherwise unknown Irishman named Dubduin, residing in the monastery of St. Gall, extols the holy men sent forth by his native isle, who, however, we are told, are despised by the haughty dignitaries of the world. Two of those buried at St. Gall are mentioned by name, " Dubslane " and " Faelan." We are made acquainted with these names by the Necrology of St. Gall: " Sept. 12 Obit of Dubsalan, Irish monk and priest "; " June 3 Obit of Faillan the Irishman, a very learned and kindly teacher."[280] A contemporary Dubslan is mentioned in the Anglo-Saxon Chronicle.[281] Although the author's knowledge of grammar and versification is very much limited, he makes what has the appearance of being a *bona fide* quotation from Vergil, *Aeneid* X 543.

The second Life of St. Wiborada, who received special veneration at St. Gall,[282] was written in 1072 by an Irish monk of the abbey whose name is given as Hepidan. MS: St. Gall Stiftsbibl. 761. EDS: *AA. SS. Boll.* 2 Mai. I 293–308. — Mabillon *AA. SS. o. s. B.* V 61–6. *Cf.* Scherrer *op. cit.* [p. 594 *supra*] 178; Von Arx *Geschichte* I 279; Clark *Abbey of St Gall* 44.

415. Registers of St. Gall

(i) *Liber confraternitatum* and *Liber promissionum*

EDS: E. Arbenz *Das St. Gallische Verbrüderungsbuch und das St. Gallische Buch der Gelübde* (*Mitteil. z. vaterländ. Geschichte von St. Gallen* XIX, N. F. IX) (1884) [also separately]. — P. Piper *MGH Libri confrat.* (1884) 9–143.

[280] *Mitteil. z. vaterländ. Geschichte herausg. vom hist. Verein z. St. Gallen* XI (N. F. I) 52, 43. In the Annales Sangallenses Maiores the death of Faillan is given under 991 (*MGH SS* I 72–85); Carl Henking " Die annalistichen Aufzeichnungen des Klosters St Gallen " *Mitteil. z. väterland. Geschichte* XIX (St. Gall 1884) 195–368.

[281] *Cf.* p. 488 *supra*.

[282] She was a recluse who lived near the monastery, where her brother was attending school, and was murdered by the Hungarian raiders in 925 or 926.

(ii) *Necrologium*

Eds: Goldast *SS. rer. Alamann.* I (1616) 155–65, 2nd ed. 94–100. — E. Dümmler and H. Wartmann " St Galler Todtenbuch und Verbrüderungen " (*Mittheilungen*, etc. N. F. I) (1869) 1–124; H. Wartmann " Das zweite St Galler Todtenbuch " *ibid.* XIX (1884) 369–463. — Fr. L. Baumann *MGH Necrologia* I (1888) 462–87. *Cf. NA* VIII 440. *Cf.* Clark *Abbey of St Gall* (1926) 31 and *passim* [see index].

The Book of Professions at St. Gall was begun about A.D. 808; earlier records back to about 720 were copied into it, and it was continued to the eleventh century. The Confraternity Book — the lists of persons from outside the monastery, secular ecclesiastics, inmates of other monasteries, and laymen, who were admitted to " fraternity " with the monks [283] — was begun about 810 and continued into the tenth century. The Necrology seems to cover the greater part of the ninth and tenth centuries. There are two exemplars, of which the second (Cod. 453) was copied from the first (Cod. 915) about A.D. 1190. These records contain a small number of Irish names, but not so many as might be expected. Probably others are disguised under Latin or continental forms.

416. Catalogues of the library of St. Gall

Cf. the works (cited elsewhere) by Becker (cited p. 516), Gottlieb (p. 620), Lehmann (p. 594), Scherrer (p. 594). Also Clark *The Abbey of St Gall* (Cambridge 1926) 280 *sqq.*

(i) MS: St. Gall Stiftsbibl. 728 *s* IX; copy in 267 *s* IX. Eds: G. Haenel *Serapei* II 8–23. — Weidmann 364–96. — Becker no. xxii pp. 43–53. — Gottlieb no. clxxxv. — Lehmann no. xvi pp. 66–82. *Cf.* Richard Stettiner *Die illustrierten Prudentiushandschriften* (Strasburg dissertation) (Berlin 1895) 94–6, 111–7.

(ii) MS: *Ibid.* 267. Eds: Haenel *loc. cit.* 22–3. — Weidmann 396–400. — Becker no. xxiii pp. 53–4. — Gottlieb no. cmx. — Lehmann no. 20 pp. 87–9.

(iii) In Ratpert's *Casus S. Galli*, p. 70 of ed. Ildephonsus von Arx, pp. 47–8 of ed. Meyer von Knonau. — Becker no. xxiv pp. 54–6. — Gottlieb no. cmxi. — Lehmann no. xvii pp. 82–4.

(iv) Catalogue of A.D. 1461. Ed: Weidmann 401–22. — Gottlieb no. mccclxxxvii. — Lehmann no. xxiii pp. 101–18.[284]

The library of St. Gall was built up, for the greater part, in the ninth century under the abbots Gozbert (816–836), Grimald (841–872) and Hartmuot (872–883). Of the catalogues noted above, no. i is a general list prepared the greater portion during Grimald's rule, but part under Hartmuot, no. ii a list of books which Grimald gave to the monastery, and no. iii books which Hartmuot wrote—or, more probably, which were copied in the scriptorium under Hartmuot's supervision—while Grimald was abbot. No. iv was prepared as one of the measures to check the raids made on the library by the scholars of the Renaissance. St. Gall was an important depository of Irish books: thirty items " Scottice scripti " and one, " Sermones in volumine

---

[283] *Cf.* E. Bishop *Liturgica historica* (Oxford 1918) 344 *sqq.*
[284] A catalogue published by Haenel, *Serapei* 1 81–4, and Becker, no. xv pp. 32–5, was regarded by the latter and by Ildephonsus von Arx as of St. Gall. A. Holder declared it to be of Reichenau — *Die Reichenauer Handschriften* 1 (Leipsic 1906) p. viii.

scottico veteri," are entered in the first of the above catalogues. Perhaps some of these came from the Irishman Marcus,[285] to whom, according to the second list, Grimald gave a psalter.

X. Other Records of the Irish in Continental Europe in the Ninth Century

417. Council of Meaux June 17, A.D. 845

Mansi XIV 815-42. — Harduin *Conc.* IV 1490 *sqq.*

The acts of this Council of Meaux contain the earliest explicit reference to " hospitalia Scottorum," hospices, it would seem, which had long been established in the Frankish dominions for the temporary succour or permanent shelter of Irish pilgrims and refugees. According to can. xl, these had already been alienated from the designs of their founders: " Moreover the hospices of the Irish, which holy men of that race built in this kingdom and endowed with property obtained because of their sanctity, have been entirely alienated from that service of hospitality; and not only are new-comers not received in those hospices, but even the very men who from infancy have in the same places been serving the Lord in religion are sent forth and compelled to beg from door to door." The Council directs that these institutions be restored to their original uses, and requests the intervention of the king, Charles the Bald, to effect this restoration.

418. Capitulare of Charles II A.D. 846

MGH Leges I (Hanover 1835) 388-93.

Some of the canons of the Council of Meaux, including can. xl, were approved by Charles the Bald at a " Conventus " held at Epernay in the following year.

419. Letter from the bishops of the dioceses of Reims and Rouen to Louis, king of Germany A.D. 858

EDS: F. Walter *Corpus Iuris Germanici Antiqui* III (1824) 79-96. — Migne *PL* CXXVI 9-25, in especial 17. COMM: E. Dümmler *Geschichte des ostfränkischen Reichs* I (Berlin 1862; vol. VII pt. I of *Jahrbücher der deutschen Geschichte*) 406-25. — E. Lavisse *Histoire de France* II (Paris 1903) 380. — L. Lallemand *Histoire de la charité* III (Paris 1906) 183.

In 858 Louis the German attacked and almost overthrew his brother, Charles the Bald, whose dominions lay within what is now France. It would seem that it was during Louis's temporary occupation of their territories that the bishops of the dioceses of Reims and Rouen, probably at the instigation of the celebrated Archbishop Hincmar of Reims, addressed a letter to him in which, among many other subjects, the *hospitalia Scottorum* are considered. Louis is here urged to see that these hospices are properly

[285] *Cf.* no 411.

administered, in accordance with the objects for which they were founded in the times of his predecessors, and — what also, no doubt, was a recommendation of significance — that they be made subject to the paternal jurisdiction of the diocesan bishops.

420. Liége Letters A.D. 854 x 901

(i) Domino venerabili episcopo. . . . Notum sit vestrae pietatis . . . praestantia in Christo. [Verses] Christe, fave votis, salvator maxime mundi. . . . In cuius pennis flagrat odore salus. (ii) Vestrae nobili caritati . . . istis, michi fecistis. Omnia Christus habet, per Christum cuncta reguntur; Mentior haud vobis: omnia Christus habet. (iii) Cum vestrae caritatis . . . et religione praedictus. Sumite Scottigenam devota mente benigni; O vos Francigenae, sumite Scottigenam. (iv) Domino venerabili multisque modis laudabili Franconi episcopo ego nomine Electus Scottigena, presbyter dignitate, misericordiam semper et felicitatem et gloriam in Christo. Notum sit vestrae pietatis . . . per multa saecula conservet.

MS: Leyden Universiteitsbibl. Voss. O. 92 ff. 122–3 [this part of MS is of *s* X *in*; *cf.* Gundlach *NA* XII (1887) 486–7]. EDS: E. Dümmler " Lütticher Briefe " *NA* XIII (1888) 360–3; *MGH Epistolarum* VI (1902) 195–7. — Traube *MGH Poet. lat. aevi Carol.* III (1896) 690–1 [verses only].

In the ninth and tenth centuries the usual route for pilgrims from Ireland to Rome was across Wales and England to the Straits of Dover, through the Low Countries to the Rhine, and up the Rhine to Switzerland and the passes of the Alps. Liége was a convenient stopping-place on this road, and during the residence there of Sedulius Scottus and the administrations of his friends Bishops Hartgar (840–854) and Franco (854–901) we may believe it became a favorite resort for Irish pilgrims and exiles. By some chance six letters have been preserved to us from the papers of Bishop Franco, four of which were written to him by Irish pilgrims. They all have a certain formal resemblance which may mean nothing more than that they followed the style locally adopted. The first two, however, are so similar to each other as to suggest that they were written by the same man, while the fourth is noticeably different in style and tone from the other three. The writer of the first seeks for help from the bishop in his indigent, almost starving condition, and asks that provision be made for him among the brethren in accordance with the directions of the emperor. In the second the writer asks assistance for himself " a poor Irish pilgrim returning wearied from Rome ": he explains that he is neither a grammarian nor skilled in Latin speech, testimony to the usual occupation of Irishmen in Europe. The recipient of the third epistle is asked to receive an old Irish priest who, because of the infirmity of his feet, cannot continue the journey to Rome with his brothers: he will say masses and prayers for his benefactors. In the fourth letter Electus Scottigena, a priest, asks Bishop Franco to restore his property, which was stolen from him by certain persons of Franco's diocese who were on the same boat with him returning from Rome. He states the number and value of the articles, chiefly clerical vestments and clothing, among them " iv osas Scotticae vestis."

421. Life of St. Donatus, bishop of Fiesole

(i) Beatissimus Christi sacerdos . . . inveniamus solatia. Praestante d. n. J. C., etc. The Life contains a famous poem on Ireland, attributed to the saint: Finibus occiduis describitur optima tellus, . . . Inclita gens hominum milite, pace, fide. 12 ll. Another poem, said to have been composed by him on his death-bed, is undoubtedly by a hagiographer: Christe Dei virtus, splendor, sapientia Patris. . . . Spiritus et sanctus, Numero Deus impare gaudet. 27 ll. His epitaph was perhaps written by himself: Hic ego Donatus, Scotorum sanguine cretus, . . . Ut mihi concedat regna beata sua. 12 ll. (ii) Litterarum luce perfusa. . . . In nomine igitur Patris . . . ut pervenire mereamur ad aeterna, ipso praestante etc. (iii) Donatus ex Scotia . . . honore maximo tumulavit.

MSS: Florence Bibl. Laurentiana Plut. XXVII. 1. s XI ff. 46ᵛ sqq [cf. Dümmler NA IV (1879) 515]; Cod. Strozzianus II s XI f. 82. [Cf. on these 2 MSS: Bandini Catalogus codicum lat. bibl. Laurentianae I 617, 779–84, II 272–80.] EDS: AA. SS. Boll. Oct. IX 648–62. — Traube MGH Poet. lat. aevi Carol. III (1896) 691–2 [poem on Ireland, and epitaph]. COMM: Colgan AA. SS. 237. — Scipio Ammirato Vescovi di Fiesole, di Volterra e d'Arezzo (Florence 1637). — F. Ughelli Italia sacra III 274; 2nd ed. 213. — Ozanam Documents inédits pour servir à l'histoire d'Italie depuis le VIIIᵉ siècle jusqu'au XIIᵉ (Paris 1850) 49–56. — E. Dümmler NA IV (1879) 515.— Margaret Stokes Six months in the Apennines (1892) 227–53.

According to the Vita Donatus was an Irishman who decided to become a pilgrim abroad because of the ravages of evil men — probably the Vikings. On his return from Rome he stopped at Fiesole and was chosen bishop by the inhabitants. His epitaph, which, it is thought, was written by himself, declares that he ruled in Fiesole for more than forty-seven years, and lays emphasis on his teaching of metrics and grammar. It also speaks of his services to the kings Lothair and Louis, suggesting that it must have been composed either before or very soon after the death of Louis II in 873. Other names are borne by the bishops who represented Fiesole at the Roman Council of 826 and the Council of Florence in 877. We would be thus forced to conclude that Donatus obtained the see about 826 x 829 and died about 874 x 877. According to the Life he was still living in February, 876, when he met the Emperor Charles the Bald in Italy and obtained certain favors for his church.[286] He is mentioned in other sources as being at Rome in 844 when Pope Sergius II consecrated Louis as King of the Lombards,[287] and in 861 at the Lateran Council.[288] On August 20, 850, he granted to the monastery of Bobbio a church in the district of Piacenza, to which was afterwards added a hospice for Irish pilgrims.[289]

422. Life of St. Findan, of Rheinau s IX/X

Cum Deus omnipotens electos. . . . Vir igitur quidam nomine Findan . . cum cautela exaratae.

MSS: St. Gall Stiftsbibl. C. 23 s X/XI. — Carlsruhe Landesbibl. Cod. Augiensis 84 s XI ff. 20–4. — Engelberg Stiftsbibl. I¼ s XII ff. 225ᵛ sqq. EDS: M. Goldast Rerum alamannicarum scriptores aliquot vetusti I (Frankfort 1616) 318–22; 2nd ed. (1661) 204–7, 3rd ed. (1730) X 203–6. — Mabillon AA. SS. o. s. B. IV i 377–82, 2nd ed. 356–60. — Mone Quellensammlung der badischen Landesgeschichte I (Carlsruhe 1848) 54–61. — Holder-Egger MGH SS XV i (Hanover 1887) 502–6. Cf. AA. SS. Boll. Feb. I 336, 3rd ed. 340. — HZ Glossae Hibernicae (1881) pp. xli sq, 272–4. — Thes. Pal. II (1903) pp. xxx sq, 258, 422 [these 2 give the passages containing Irish notes]. — Zapf Monumenta anecdota historiam Germaniae illustrantia I 446. — Reeves Trans. RIA XXIV ii (1873) 263.

286 Cf. Traube loc. cit. 692.

287 Liber Pontificalis: Migne PL CXXVIII 1298; L. Duchesne's ed. (Bibl. des écoles françaises d'Athènes et de Rome 2nd ser. III) II 90.

288 Mansi XV 603–4.

289 Gougaud Gaelic pioneers of Christianity 82; G. Tononi Ospizio pei pellegrini irlandesi (Strenna Piacentina 1891); RH XLVIII (1892) 123–4.

St. Findan, or Fintan, was an Irishman who is said in his Life to have been captured by the Vikings and carried to the Orkneys. There he escaped, and then made his way to the Continent. He went on pilgrimage to Rome, and on his return stopped with certain anchorites dwelling on the island of Rheinau [290] in the Rhine near Schaffhausen, where, after four years devoted to clerical duties, he spent the last twenty-two years of his life as a recluse. It is believed that he died in 878. The *Vita*, though written apparently soon after his death, contains much fabulous matter. It has one of the earliest references to the *Céli Dé*, or Culdees,[291] and portions of a religious rule said to have been received from heaven. The text contains a few Old Irish sentences and phrases.[292]

Manitius *Lat. Lit.* II 800 suggests that a certain Grimlaic, a priest of the diocese of Reims who lived towards the end of the ninth century, may have been an Irishman. It does not seem probable. His Rule for *inclusi* is in Berlin Staatsbibl. Meerm. 110 s X/XI [from Reims]. *Cf.* also *Histoire lit. de la France* V (1740) 685-7; Migne *PL* CXXIX 863; *MGH SS* XIII 560; and other references in Chevalier *Bio-Bibliographie.*

423. Anonymous poems written by Irishmen

EDS: L. Traube " Carmina Scottorum latina et graecanica " *MGH Poet. lat. aevi Carol.* III pt. II ii (1896) 685-701. — Karl Strecker "Versus Scottorum " *ibid.* IV fasc. ii-iii (1923).

(i) Poem on the death of the Emperor Lothair A.D. 855

Cf. L. Traube *Wochenschrift f. klass. Philologie* 1891 N. 12; *O Roma nobilis (Abhandl. d. k. bay. Akad. d. Wissensch.* I Cl. XIX ii) (Munich 1891) 336.

(ii) Poem to Charles the Bald A.D. 870 x 873

Biblorum seriem. . . . O miranda nimis domini sapientia summi . . . prae regibus extat. . . . perproba proprietas. 108 ll. Contains one line in Greek.

MS: BN 2 s IX ff. 1^v- 3 [formerly of St.-Denis, a bible written, it is said, by an Irishman, for Charles the Bald; *cf.* p. 658 *infra*]. ED: Traube *MGH Poet. lat. aevi Carol.* III (1886) 255-7; *cf.* 700.

(iii) Poem on Adalhard, bishop of Verona A.D. 877/878

Siderum factor dominusque caeli. . . . Glorificetur. Amen. 80 ll.

MS: Vat. 5751 s X f. 62^v [formerly of Bobbio]. EDS: Baronius *Annales ecclesiastici* XV, 8th ed. (Lucca 1744) 480; 9th ed. by Theiner (Paris 1868) 449. — Biancolinus

---

[290] *Cf.* E. Rothenhäusler in *Zs. d. Gesellsch. f. Beförderung d. Geschichts-, Altertums- und Volkskunde v. Freiburg-i.-Br.* XIX i-ii [rev. in *RH* Sept.-Dec. 1904 p. 184].

[291] *Cf.* pp. 470 *sqq supra*.

[292] A Rheinau MS, no. 30 of the Universitätsbibl., Zürich — a MS of considerable importance in liturgical studies — contains a fragment of a calendar which, it has been thought, was brought to Rheinau by Fintan. *Cf.* E. Egli " Das sogen. Fintan-Martyrologium " *Anzeiger f. schweiz. Geschichte* new ser. VI (1890-3) 136-41; Em. Munding *Das Verzeichnis der St. Galler Heiligenleben und ihrer Handschriften* (Beuron 1918) 119.

Dei vescovi e governatori di Verona (Lucca 1757) 35–7. — E. Dümmler *Gesta Berengarii imperatoris* (Halle 1871) 61–5, 134–6. — L. Traube *loc. cit.* 693–5.

(iv) Verses written by a fugitive from Bobbio *s* IX second half

Nocte dieque gemo, quia sum peregrinus et egens . . . sed [faci]e[nt,] faci . . . [vivere] sic pot[eris]. 48 ll.

MS: Vat. 5751 *s* X f. 71ᵛ [formerly of Bobbio: the page is much defaced]. Eps: Mai *Classici auctores* V 458. — Traube *loc. cit.* 688–9. *Cf.* Gougaud *Les Chrétientés celtiques* (1911) 165.

(v) Verses referring to Guido, king of Italy (889) and emperor (891–4)

MS: BN 3877 *s* X f. 3ᵛ. Eps: F. Monnier *De Gothescalci et Ioh. Scotti controversia* (Paris 1853) 95. — Traube *loc. cit.* 701.

(vi) Verses on Porphyry's *Isagoge*

Scripturae finem sibi. . . . 4 ll.

MS: BN 12949 *s* IX f. 52ᵛ. Eps: Cousin *Ouvrages inédits d'Abélard* (Paris 1836) 625. — L. Traube *NA* XVIII (1893) 105; and *loc. cit.* 685.

(vii) Prayer to God, in Greek

ὑψηλὸς κύριος, δυνατός, φιλοεργός, ἄμωμος . . . διαπαντός διατηρήσῃς.

MS: Gotha I 17 *s* IX f. 3 [formerly of Murbach]. Eps: Montfaucon *Palaeograph. graec.* (Paris 1708) 220. — Traube *loc. cit.* 698.

(viii) Verses on the alphabets

(a) ὁροθεσία καὶ ἔκθεσις γραμμάτων ‘Εβραϊκῶν. Adam primus homo, doctrinam commonet aleph. . . . Quo baptizari voluit sine πτεγματε [? πταισματε] Christus. 30 ll. (b) κατάλογος γραμμάτων ἑλλήνων. Quattuor his nunc versiculis perpende, magister, . . . ω finis perfecta iugans et iuncta resolvens. 26 ll.

MSS: Gotha I 17 *s* IX ff. 3ᵛ–4. — Vat. Reg. 339 *s* X f. 49. Eps: Montfaucon *loc. cit.* [partial]. — Traube *loc. cit.* III 698–700.

Some of these poems profess to be of Irish authorship; others are so classed because of their style and their manuscript relations.

(iv): The author was an Irish monk of Bobbio who, to avoid some punishment, fled to the monastery of St. Zeno at Verona, where he was employed in teaching boys. Poor and sick, he laments his condition and longs to return to the shelter of St. Columbanus. The facts that the two poems are found in the same manuscript, and that the author of each must have been living in Verona towards the end of the ninth century, makes attractive the identification of the refugee with the eulogist of Adalhard (no. iii).

(viii) This is a versified presentation of the commentary of St. Jerome on the Hebrew and Greek alphabets.[293]

[293] Migne *PL* XXII 442, XXIII 1305.

XI. The Irish Abroad in the Tenth, Eleventh and Twelfth
Centuries

Bibliography

W. Wattenbach " Die Congregation der Schottenklöster in Deutschlands ": Otte and Quast *Zs. f. christliche Archäologie u. Kunst* I 21–30, 49–58. — Renz " Beiträge zur Geschichte der Schottenabtei St. Jacob " *Studien und Mittheilungen aus dem Benedictiner und Cistercienserorden* 1895 pp. 64–84, 250–9, 418–25, 574–81; 1896 pp. 29–40, 229–39. — Hogan " Irish Monasteries in Germany " *IER* 1895. — Wolfsgruber *s.v.* " Schottenklöster " in Wetzer and Welte's *Kirchenlexikon oder Encyklopädie der katholischen Theologie und ihrer Hülfswissenschaften* X (Freiburg i. Br. 1897) 1905-7.

The eastern, or German, portion of the Frankish dominions recovered first from the anarchy into which later Carolingian rule had degenerated. With the disappearance of the eastern branch of the Karlings a Saxon family won the throne: Henry I, 919–936; Otto I, 936–973, who in 962 was crowned emperor at Rome; Otto II, 973–83; Otto III, 983–1002; Henry II, known as St. Henry, 1002–1024. These men showed a vigor in the organisation of both State and Church which resembled that of the early Carolingians, and they too were helped in their works of reform by Irish exiles.

Towards the close of the ninth century the character and direction of Irish emigration changed. Men whose chief interest was in scholarship disappeared from the movement, and the religious became again the dominating impulse. The route turned aside from France to the valley of the Rhine, Lorraine, and Upper Germany, the domain of the new imperial line. A few, but not many, Irishmen contributed to the revival of religion and learning in England begun by Alfred the Great and continued by St. Dunstan.

The persistence of asceticism is shown by the considerable number of Irish monks who became " inclusi " in German religious houses, that is, had themselves solemnly interned in cells where, walled up from his fellows, each spent the rest of his life in a penitential regimen beside his open grave. The incluse's cell had some resemblance to the " desert " of the monasteries in Ireland. That such penitents were not so isolated from the active world as might at first thought be supposed is shown by the fact that the great Chronicle of Marianus Scottus was written while its author was leading such a life of confinement.

In Lorraine in the tenth and eleventh centuries Irish churchmen played an auxiliary part in the ecclesiastical reform movement carried out by the bishops of Metz and Verdun. In Germany in the eleventh and twelfth centuries a long series of monasteries — *Schottenklöster* — were founded, at Ratisbon, Würzburg, Nürnberg, Constance, Vienna, Memmingen, Eichstätt, Erfurt, Kelheim (1231), drawing their inmates continuously from the western isle, but administered under the Benedictine rule. They were organised by Innocent III into a congregation with periodical chapters. The influence of this Irish monastic body was felt even in the remote dominions of Poland and Russia. Ireland not only contributed recruits to the ranks of the monks, but also, for the first time in recorded history, sent pecuniary contributions to support these establishments abroad — at Cologne and at Ratisbon.

In the thirteenth century the Irish monastery at Ratisbon either itself produced, or through its influence was the occasion of the composition of, a romance which is one of the off-shoots of the epic cycle of Charles the Great and which gives a fabulous and extravagant account of the activities of Irish missionaries on the Continent in the early middle ages. ED: A. Dürwaechter *Die Gesta Caroli Magni der Regensburger Schottenlegende* (Bonn 1897).

424. The Irish at Glastonbury

See *Cath. Encycl.* and Chevalier *Topo-Bibliographie s. v.* " Glastonbury." Also J. Armitage Robinson *The times of St. Dunstan* (Oxford 1923).

(i) Asser: Life of King Alfred (*Annales rerum gestarum Ælfredi magni regis*) c 894

EDS: F. Wise (Oxford 1722). — *MHB* (1848) 467–98. — W. H. Stevenson *Asser's Life of King Alfred* (Oxford 1904). TRANS: J. A. Giles *Bohn's Antiquarian Library* IV (1848) 43–86 [reprint 1908]. — J. Stevenson *Church historians of England* II pt. II (1854). — E. Conybeare *Alfred in the chroniclers* (London 1900). — A. B. Cook (Boston [1906]). — L. C. Jane (London 1908).

(ii) Life of St. Dunstan, by B [294] s X *ex*

EDS: *AA. SS. Boll.* Mai. IV 346–59. — Migne *PL* CXXXIX 1423–56. — Wm. Stubbs *Memorials of St. Dunstan* (RS: London 1874) pp. x *sqq*; 3–52; 458–72.

(iii) Life of St. Dunstan by William of Malmesbury c A.D. 1126

ED: Stubbs *op. cit.* pp. xxxv *sqq*, 250–324.

[294] So the author designates himself.

(iv) The Antiquity of Glastonbury (*De antiquitate Glastoniensis ecclesiae*) by William of Malmesbury *c* A.D. 1130–8

EDS: Gale *Historiae Britannicae SS* (Oxford 1691) 291–335. — Hearne *Adam of Domerham* I (Oxford 1727) 1–122. — Migne *PL* CLXXIX 1681–1734. *Cf.* W. W. Newell *Pub. Mod. Lang. Assoc. of Amer.* XVIII (1903) 459–512; J. Armitage Robinson *Somerset historical essays* (London 1921).

Glastonbury, in Somerset, on a hill in the midst of meadows which, in ancient and mediaeval times, were wide marshes, was an ancient village-site dating back far beyond written history. When in the fourth century the Irish were making settlements in western Britain, this, it would seem, was one of the places which they occupied.[295] Perhaps while the population was still Goidelic, certainly at a very early date, a Celtic monastery was founded, and when, towards the end of the seventh century, the district was conquered by the West Saxons, these, already Christians, respected its religious character. Glastonbury remained an important monastic church all through the middle ages.

Around the church of Glastonbury an elaborate legendary history developed. We are concerned here only with its Irish aspects, which were probably based on genuine associations with Ireland. As so often happens, the associations produced the legend, and then the legend maintained the associations. The saints Patrick, Benignus, Brigit, and, perhaps with more truth, Indract,[296] were made to visit Glastonbury. One of the two Patricks into whom hagiography split the apostle of Ireland was buried there, but the records differ as to whether it was the elder or the younger Patrick. To visit his tomb, and a church having for them so many other interests, pilgrims came from Ireland, and occasionally passed on to settle in other parts of England. At Glastonbury many Lives of Irish saints were collected or written, and from these, doubtless, were derived the majority of the texts which were used by John of Tynemouth.[297]

After the denunciations of the Council of Celchyth,[298] the next evidence of the presence of Irish ecclesiastics in England is the statement of Asser, monk of St. David's in Wales who became helper and biographer of Alfred the Great, that certain " Scotti " came to that king's court.[299] In the following century, as we learn from the contem-

---

[295] *Cf.* p. 149 *supra.*

[296] *Cf.* no. 228.—The calendars in the *Leofric Missal* (ed. F. E. Warren, 1883) and the *Bosworth Psalter* (ed. E. Bishop, 1908) — this written, it is believed, for the use of the church of Canterbury in Dunstan's time — were derived from the calendar of Glastonbury. Two Patricks and Brigit were commemorated. *Cf.* Robinson *The times of St. Dunstan* 98 *sqq.*

[297] *Cf.* no. 117.

[298] No. 71.

[299] Stevenson's ed. p. 60. They probably were from Glastonbury, and were distinct from the three men mentioned by the Anglo-Saxon Chronicle (*cf.* p. 487 *supra*). See also the Chronicle of Ethelwerd

porary biographer of St. Dunstan, abbot of Glastonbury and archbishop of Canterbury(c 909?–988), there were Irish pilgrims at Glastonbury whose books were read by Dunstan when a youthful inmate of that monastery. The twelfth-century Life by William of Malmesbury gives a more developed account of this Irish education of Dunstan.

William (c 1075–c 1143), a man of mixed Norman and English blood, was brought up from childhood in the abbey of Malmesbury — which also had its Irish associations [300] — and spent most of his life either there or in the neighboring Glastonbury. The excellent libraries of these two monasteries enabled him to indulge his studious disposition. A long series of works issued from his pen, almost all of a religious or historical character. He was favorably situated for an acquaintance with Irish, Welsh and Breton traditions. He was especially inspired by the motive of recording the fame of Glastonbury, and his treatise on the antiquities of that church is the chief source for its legendary history, and also for its relations with Ireland.[301]

425. History of the monastery of Waulsort s XII–XIII

EDS: D'Achery Spicilegium VII 565 sqq; new ed. II 709–29. — Waitz MGH SS. XIV 505–41. COMM: AA. SS. Boll. Jan. II 385–7, 749–51, April. III 814–22 (ed. 1866 pp. 823–31). — Hist. litt. de la France XIII 515–7, XXI 703. — Schultze Forschungen zur Geschichte der Klosterreform im 10. Jahrhundert (Dissertation, Halle 1883) 55. — L. Lahaye Étude sur l'abbaye de Waulsort (Liége 1890). — Dom U. Berlière Monasticon belge I (Bruges 1890) 40. — A. Bellesheim " Über einige Beziehungen Irlands zu Reichsstadt Aachen und Diözese Lüttich " Zs. des Aachener Geschichtsvereins XIV (1892) 50. — Joseph Bédier Les Légendes épiques, recherches sur la formation des chansons de geste II (Paris 1908) 403 sqq, 2nd ed. (1917) 415–38.

The monastery of Waulsort was situated in the Ardennes, between Dinant and Givet. Its History is the work of two authors. The first, writing about the middle of the twelfth century, carried the narrative down to 1101; the second continued it into the second quarter of the thirteenth century. It is a legendary and not very trustworthy record.[302] The story of the foundation of Waulsort and of its fortunes under its early Irish abbots is told in some detail. The first three abbots were Maccalan,[303] Cadroe and Forannan.

(d. c 998) in MHB 517-8. E. Bishop suggests that to them was due the metrical calendar in the Cotton. MSS Galba A XVIII, Tiberius B V, and Julius A VI. — Liturgica historica (1918) 256 (cf. p. 481 supra).

[300] Cf. p. 226 supra.

[301] William's Gesta regum Anglorum and Gesta pontificum Anglorum have their main value, with regard to Irish history, as records of relations between England and Ireland. The former has some Glastonbury material paralleling the De antiquitate; the second the fragments relating to Cellanus of Péronne noticed p. 507 supra; and both some anecdotes regarding Johannes Eriugena (cf. p. 588 supra).

[302] The foundation of Waulsort is attributed to a Count Eilbert, who is clearly the same personage as the Count Ybert de Ribemont of the chanson de geste of " Raoul de Cambrai," composed about the end of the twelfth century. The chronicle of Waulsort and the author of the chanson made use of similar, if not identical, legends relating to the counts of Vermandois. Now Eilbert, the actual founder of Waulsort (no. 426) was the vassal of Count Adalbert of Vermandois. The two personages have been merged into one. There is a fictitious charter bearing the date 976 which professes to make or confirm certain grants and privileges to Waulsort by Count Eilbert and others. The story of the foundation of the monastery as given in the charter is in agreement with that in the Historia. — Abbé Joseph Barbier in Analectes pour servir à l'histoire ecclésiastique de la Belgique II 266; Waitz MGH SS. XIV 516-17.

[303] The continuation of the Annals of Flodoard records the death of " Malcallanus, natione Hibernicus,"

426. Otto I: Charter to the monastery of Waulsort Sept. 19, A.D. 946

Ed: *MGH Diplomatum regum et imperatorum Germaniae* I (Hanover 1884) 160–1. *Cf.* Lahaye *Étude sur l'abbaye de Waulsort* (Liége 1890) 11; Carl von Kalckstein *Geschichte des französischen Königsthums unter den ersten Kapetingern* (Leipzig 1877) 257.

Otto I, king of Germany (after 962, Holy Roman Emperor), by this charter gave official recognition to the monastery of Waulsort, which, we are here told, had been founded and endowed by a nobleman Eilbertus and his wife Heresuindis for the benefit of certain servants of God " coming from Ireland ' on pilgrimage ' and wishing to live under the rule of St. Benedict." It directed that the institution was to be for the use of the Irish, and that the abbot should be an Irishman, so long as such might be found among the inmates. The monastery was to devote itself especially to the care of foreign pilgrims.

427. Life of St. John Gorzien, by John of Metz A.D. 980

Eds: Labbe *Novae bibl.* I (Paris 1657) 741–76. — *AA. SS. Boll.* Feb. III 690–715. — Mabillon *AA. SS. o. s. B.* V 365–412. — *MGH SS* IV 337–77. — Migne *PL* CXXXVII 241–310. *Cf.* Wattenbach *DGQ* I⁶ (1893) 370.

The Life of St. John Gorzien, abbot of Tübingen (d. 974), was written by his friend John, abbot of the monastery of St. Arnulf at Metz. It gives some slight information regarding St. Cadroe.

428. Life of St. Cadroe, by Reimann or Ousmann *c* A.D. 995

Dedicatio operis. Venerabili in Christo Patri Immoni. . . . Prologus. Pietas omnipotentis Dei. . . . Regii igitur sanguinis . . . sepultus in B. Felicis ecclesia, vivit c. C. in aet. s. Amen.

Eds: Colgan *AA. SS.* 494–501. — *AA. SS. Boll.* Mart. I 468–81. — Mabillon *AA. SS. o. s. B.* V 487–501. Comm. etc.: *MGH SS* IV 483–4, XV ii 689–92 [extracts]. — W. F. Skene *Chronicles of the Picts and Scots* (Edinburgh 1867) pp. xli *sq*, 106–16 [extract]. — Wattenbach *DGQ* I⁶ (1893) 372. — Manitius *Lat. Lit.* II 236–9.

Of Reimann, or Ousmann, reputed author of the *Vita Cadroae*, there is no information. The Immon to whom it was dedicated was probably abbot of Waulsort (991–5), but there were several important ecclesiastics of the name in the second half of the tenth century. The author did not know the saint personally, but seems to have written soon after his death. Cadroe is said to have been a native of the Irish colony in what is now Scotland. He was educated at Armagh, we are told, and all his companions were Irish. Setting out " on his pilgrimage " he came to the monastery of Waulsort, where he was made abbot. About 953 Bishop Adalbero of Metz summoned him to that city to take charge of the monastery of St. Clement. From that position he

abbot of St. Michael, in Thiérache, under the year 978. *Cf.* also *AA. SS. Boll.* Jan. II 749–51. There is a charter of 945 by which the bishop of Laon, with the consent of the archdeacon Herbert, who held it as a benefice, granted to a lady named Hersent (no doubt the wife of Eilbert was in mind) the oratory of St. Michael in Thiérache for the use of men who had come from Ireland on pilgrimage (A. Piette *Cartulaire de l'abbaye de St.-Michel-en-Thiérache* (Vervins 1883) II no. i). But this charter also is probably fictitious (Bédier *op. cit.* 2nd ed. 428 n.).

institued important monastic reforms throughout Lorraine. His death has been placed in 978.

Prefixed to the Life is a version of the mythical history of the origins of the Irish people.

429. Life of St. Forannan, by Robert of Waulsort A.D. 1130 X 1145

Prologus. Quoniam in culmine. . . . Gloriosus igitur Domini sacerdos Forannanus . . . ad regna illius perveniamus, qui v. et r. per s. s. D. Amen.

EDS: *AA. SS. Boll.* April. III 807-14 (ed. 1866: 816-23). — Mabillon *AA. SS. o. s. B.* V 588-95, 2nd ed. 575-83. *Cf.* Wattenbach *DGQ* II⁶ (1894) 153.

Robert, the author of this *Vita*, was an abbot of Waulsort in the twelfth century. His subject, Forannan, was an Irishman who succeeded Cadroe as abbot of Waulsort, and died in 982. Under Forannan's administration the monastery flourished; another house, that of Hastières, was attached to it by Thierry, bishop of Metz.

430. Life of St. Bruno, by Ruotger A.D. 966 x 967

EDS: Surius *De probatis sanctorum historiis* V (1574) 701-22; (1580) 785-806; X (1618) 163-75; III (1875) 664-87. — Leibnitz *SS. rer. Brunsv.* I 273-90. — *AA. SS. Boll.* Oct. V 765-90.— *MGH SS* IV 254-75. — Migne *PL* CXXXIV 941-81. *Cf.* Wattenbach *NA* VIII 191; Manitius *Lat. Lit.* II 175-9.

This Life of St. Bruno, brother of the Emperor Otto I, and archbishop of Cologne from 953 to 965, was written by Ruotger, an inmate of the monastery of St. Pantaleon which Bruno founded at Cologne. Bruno, who came to be regarded as one of the most scholarly men of his time, received his education from many different sources. One of his teachers was an Irish bishop, Israel,[304] to an eulogy of whose learning Ruotger devotes some space.

———

There are several other texts which may relate to this bishop. Flodoard speaks of an " Israhele Brittone " as at the Council of Verdun in 947 (Flodoard *Annales*: *MGH SS* III 394; ed. Ph. Lauer (Paris 1906) 107, 205; *cf.* p. 183 *supra*), and Richer of " Israhele Brittigena " (*Historiarum* II lxvi: *MGH SS* III 602). Bruno also was at this council. In the *Necrologium* of St. Maximin of Trèves there is an entry: " VI. Kal. Mai. Israhel episcopus nostrae congregationis monachus " (Hontheim *Prodrom. hist. Trevir.* II 975; there is a note " In libro mortuali Epternacensi ad hunc diem notatur: Israel episcopus conversus s. Maximini "); and in the *Necrologium Merseber-gense·* " VIII. Kal. Mai. Israhel episcopus " (E. Dümmler *Neue Mittheilungen des thüring.-sächs. Geschichtsvereins* XI 233). In a 10th-century catalogue (no. 404 *supra*) Hisrael is mentioned as the pupil of an otherwise unknown Ambrosius (Leyden Universiteitsbibl. Voss. O. 15 f. 147ᵛ: L. Delisle *Notices et extraits des mss. de la bibl. nat.* XXXV i 312). An Israhel is quoted in an addition to the commentary by Remigius of Auxerre on the *Ars minor* of Donatus in Munich Staatsbibl. 17209 *s* XII/XIII (ed. Fox (Leipsic 1902) 11). Finally in Vat. Regin. 421 *s* XI is a poem beginning " Rotbertum salvere iubent preconia metri " which has the title " Versus Israhelis de arte metrica super nomen et verbum." There was a Rotbert archbishop of Trèves 930-56.

304 *Cap.* vii.

431. Life of St. Gérard of Toul, by Widric A.D. 1027 x 1049

EDS: *AA. SS. Boll.* April. III 206–13. — Martène and Durand *Thesaurus novus anecdotorum* III 1048–74. — Calmet *Histoire de la Lorraine* I " Preuves " 132–53, 2nd ed. (Nancy 1748) 174–96. — Waitz *MGH SS* IV 490–505 [incomplete].

Gérard was bishop of Toul 963–994. The author of his Life, Abbot Widric of Toul, describes his friendship for Irish clerics.

" Moreover he collected no small crowd of Greeks and Irish, and fed this mixed body of many tongues at his own expense. It was their custom to assemble daily at the different altars in the chapel, where they offered the services of supplication and praise to God after the manner of their countries " (" more patrio ").[305] The phrase seems to imply that there were still some peculiarities in the Irish liturgy.

A strange story is told in connection with the death of Gérard, which occurred on April 23, 994. " A certain man of good character, one of the Irish whom he maintained, rose at the break of dawn and passed through the streets of the city, declaring with lamentations and outcries that his father and lord, the holy bishop, was about to be removed from this world, and that the Lord had given him definite warning of this in a vision. The hearts of all were shocked at this mournful decree, and the sad outcome testified to the Irishman's truthfulness."[306] For the bishop died the same day.

432. Life of Adalbero II, bishop of Metz, by Constantine c A.D. 1012 x 1017

EDS: Labbe *Novae bibl.* I (Paris 1657) 670–82. — *MGH SS* IV 658–72. — Migne *PL* CXXXIX 1553–76.

Adalbero II was bishop of Metz 984–1005. His Life was written by his devoted friend Constantine, abbot of St. Symphorian at Metz 1004–1024. Constantine says of him: " Irish and other holy pilgrims he always held in very dear regard." Adalbero was a friend of the Irishman Fingen, abbot of St. Clement in Metz, to whom he entrusted also the then ruined monastery of St. Symphorian.

433. Otto III: Charter to the monastery of St. Symphorian at Metz Jan. 25, A.D. 992

EDS: Calmet *Histoire de la Lorraine* II (2nd ed. Nancy 1748) " Preuves " 247. — T. Sickel *MGH Diplomatum Regum et Imperatorum Germaniae* II pt. ii (1893) 493.

Otto III, Holy Roman Emperor from 983 to 1002, granted a charter in 992 to the monastery of St. Symphorian at Metz. The gist of the text is as follows:

Adalbero, bishop of Metz, has come to us saying that, for the love of God and of the martyr St. Symphorian, he has begun to rebuild a certain abbey outside the walls of the city of Metz, and asking for a confirmation of that abbey. We hereby confirm all gifts made thereto, or to be made. It is directed that the first abbot, an Irishman named Fingenius, who has now been installed there by the above-mentioned bishop,

---

[305] Ed. Waitz p. 501.   [306] *Ibid.* 503.

and his successors, shall receive Irish monks, so long as such is possible. Should monks from Ireland fail there, the number of inmates is always to be maintained by recruits of other nationalities. Our memory and that of our parents, and of the present bishop and his successors, must be retained there forever.[307]

434. History of the bishops of Verdun (*Gesta episcoporum Virdunensium*) c A.D. 918 x 923 and 1047

EDS: D'Achery *Spicilegium* XII 251 *sqq* (new ed. II 233–62). — Calmet *Histoire de la Lorraine* I " Preuves " 193–206, 2nd ed. II (1748) " Preuves " pp. i *sqq*. — Waitz *MGH SS* IV 36–51 [*cf*. 501, 503]. — Migne *PL* CXXXII 501–28.

This ecclesiastical history of Verdun, begun by a certain Bertarius in the early part of the tenth century and continued from 925 to 1047 by a monk of St. Vannes, gives us further information regarding St. Fingen, the Irishman who became a reformer and restorer of monasteries in Metz. He is said to have ended his life at the monastery of St. Vannes in Verdun. St. Vannes was a very poor church: he had " only seven Irish monks under his abbacy." Fingen was buried " in the church of St. Felix outside the walls of the city of Metz."[308]

435. Life of Richard, abbot of St. Vannes in Verdun s XII *in*

EDS: Mabillon *AA. SS. o. s. B.* VI pt. i 519–65. — Wattenbach *MGH SS* XI 280–90.

Richard, a monk from Reims, succeeded Fingen as abbot of St. Vannes in Verdun in 1004 and died in 1046. His Life was written by an anonymous monk of St. Vannes about the beginning of the twelfth century. It gives an account at some length (*cap*. iv–vi) of the career of Fingen.

436. Hugh of Flavigny: *Chronicon Virdunense seu Flaviniacense* s XII *in*

EDS: Labbe *Novae bibl.* I (1657) 75–272. — *MGH SS* VIII 288–502. — Migne *PL.* CLIV 21–404.

Hugh, the author of this chronicle, was born in or near Verdun about 1065. He was educated at the monastery of St. Vannes, and seems to have accompanied the abbot Raoul to Flavigny when that ecclesiastic was expelled from Verdun by the imperialist party in one of the contests between the Emperors and the Papacy. In 1096 he became abbot of Flavigny, and later, going over to the imperialist side, returned to St. Vannes as abbot. His chronicle, which comes down to the year 1102, contains much valuable information. It gives a rather full account of Fingen, and of his career, first in the monastery of St. Felix at Metz, afterwards as abbot at St. Vannes.[309]

---

[307] In the *Carmen Mettense* (no. 437) mention is made of a charter from the Pope. This does not seem now to be in existence.

[308] In the annals of St. Vannes (*Annales S. Vitoni Virdunensis*) the death of Fingen is recorded in 1005 (4). — *MGH SS* X 526.

[309] We are told that a longer record of Fingen can be obtained " in vita Teoderici eximii Mettensis episcopi." The Life of Theoderic, or Thierry, is not now known: it is supposed to have been included in Alpert's *De Episcopis Mettensibus*, of which a fragment is published in *MGH SS* IV 697. *Cf*. p. 610 *supra*.

437. Carmen Mettense

MS: Brussels Bibl. roy. 10615–10729 s XII, cod. 10710 ff. 175-8ᵛ. Ed: E. Dümmler *NA* V (1880) 433–7 [partial]. *Cf.* Pertz *Archiv* VII 1006.

The *Carmen Mettense* is a poem or series of poems beginning with a general summary of sacred history and ending with a more particular account of the founding of the church of Metz and of the saints of that church. It was probably written by an Irishman at Metz in the eleventh century. Dümmler has published the later part dealing with the history of Metz in the tenth century. It speaks at some length of Cadroe and Fingen, and of the two bishops of the name of Adalbero.

438. Moriuht, Irish poet of Rouen s X

Ed: H. Omont " Satire de Garnier de Rouen contre le poète Moriuht " *Annuaire-bulletin de la soc. de l'hist. de France* XXXI (1894) 193–210.

Garnier was a monk of the monastery of St. Ouen at Rouen and a favorite of Robert, archbishop of Rouen (989–1037). This piece is a rude satire against an Irish poet, whose name is given as Moriuht, who had been a friend of the preceding archbishop, Hugh (942–989).

439. Catalogue of the abbots of St. Martin of Cologne

Eds: *MGH SS* II 214–5. — J. F. Böhmer *Fontes rerum Germanicarum* III (Stuttgart 1853) 344–6. — J. H. Kessel *Monumenta historica ecclesiae Coloniensis* (Cologne 1862) pp. i–xii. *Cf.* Oppermann " Kritische Studien zur älteren Kölner Geschichte " *Westdeutsche Zs. f. Geschichte u. Kunst* XIX (1900) 271–344 [*re* authenticity: *cf.* Dom U. Berlière in *Archives belges* April, 1901, pp. 89–91; *Rev. Bénédictine* XVIII (1901) 424–7].

The celebrated monastery of St. Martin at Cologne was, according to Marianus Scottus, assigned to the Irish in 975, and became one of the most important of their continental establishments in the eleventh century. The Catalogue gives an account of the early history of the monastery, but it is under grave suspicion of having been seriously falsified in the eighteenth century.

440. Life of St. Colmán s XI

Praefatio: Princeps apostolorum Petrus. . . . Vita: Regnante gloriosissimo imperatore Heinrico, qui tertio Ottone mortuo. . . . Dei virtus et Dei sapientia, quae cum D. P. et S. s. v. et r. per o. s. s. Amen.

MSS: Admont Stiftsbibl. 25 s XIII ff. 115ᵛ–116ʳ. — Bonn Universitätsbibl. 5314 s XIII. Eds: P. Lambecius *Commentariorum de bibliotheca caesarea Vindobonensi* II viii 611–8. — A. F. Kollar *Analecta monumentorum omnis aevi Vindobonensia* I (Vienna 1761) 843–55. — H. Pez *Scriptores rerum Austriacarum* I (Leipsic 1721) 94–109. — *AA. SS. Boll.* Oct. VI 357–62 (*cf.* Suppl. 13 Oct. 149*–152*). — Waitz *MGH SS* IV (1841) 674–81. Comm: J. Urwalek *Der königliche Pilger St. Colomann* (Programm, Vienna 1880). — Wattenbach *DGQ* II⁶ (1894) 318. — Gougaud *RC* XXXIX (1922) 223–4, and *Gaelic Pioneers of Christianity* (1923) 143–5.

Colmán, or Colomann, was an Irish saint who, going on a pilgrimage to Jerusalem, was murdered at Stockerau near Vienna in 1012. His tomb at Melk was erected by the Emperor Henry II. He is one of the patrons of Austria. The Life is of some value for Austrian history.

441. Life of St. Anatolius

ED: *AA. SS. Boll.* Feb. I 355–60 (1863 ed. 359–64). COMM: H. Zinzins *ZKG* XLVI (1928) 394.
Anatolius was a bishop who flourished in Burgundy about 1029. He was, according to report, of Irish origin.

442. Bishop John of Ireland

Adam of Bremen: History of the bishops of Hamburg (*Gesta Hamma-burgensis ecclesiae pontificum*)

EDS: J. M. Lappenberg *MGH SS* VII (1845) 267–389. — Same text in *SS. rer. germ. in usum scholarum* (1846); 2nd ed. by L. Weiland (1876); 3rd ed. by B. Schmeidler (1917). — Migne *PL* CXLVI (1853) 434–62. GERM. TRANS: J. C. M. Laurent in *Geschichtschreiber der deutschen Vorzeit* (1850); 2nd ed. by Wattenbach (1888). COMM: J. Fischer " Kann Bischof Johannes aus Irland mit Recht als erster Martyrer Amerikas bezeichnet werden " *Zs. f. kath. Theologie* XXIV (1900) 756-8.

Adam was a *protégé* of Archbishop Adalbert of Bremen, and master of the cathedral school in that city, where he died probably in 1076. His work is of great importance for the history and geography of northern Europe. He gives an account [310] of a Bishop John from Ireland who preached to the pagans in northern Germany, probably Mecklenburg, and there suffered martyrdom about 1066. Through a misunderstanding it has sometimes been stated that John died in America.

For Irish influences in the city of Trèves in the eleventh century see Marx *Geschichte des Erzstiftes Trier* II ii (Trèves 1860) 329, 339; Beissel *Geschichte der Trierer Kirchen* (Trèves 1887) 205; *Geschichte der Evangelienbücher in der ersten Hälfte des Mittelalters* (Freiburg i. B. 1906) 122.

443. Chronicle of Marianus Scottus *c* A.D. 1072–1082

MSS: Vat. Palat.[311] 830 *s* XI. — BM Cotton. Nero. C. V. *s* XI *ex.* — Frankfort 104 *s* XIV. — Liége 242 *s* XV.[312] EDS: Herold (Basel 1559). — Pistorius *Veteres*

---

[310] III xx, 1, lxx.

[311] The Palatine collection of MSS was sent in 1623 to Rome from Heidelberg, the capital of the Palatinate, when that city was captured by the forces of Maximilian of Bavaria. The greater part was returned in 1816, but some MSS are still in the Vatican. An entry in this codex indicates that in 1479 it was still in the monastery of St. Martin at Mainz, where it must have remained from the time when it was written. *Cf. MGH SS* XVI 480.

[312] Certain computistical works by a Marianus Scottus, said to be in MS at Ratisbon, may be parts of this chronicle. *Cf.* Houzeau-Lancaster *Bibliographie de l'astronomie* I (1889) 1448; M. Esposito *Hermathena* XV 364.

Scriptores rerum Germanicarum I (Frankfort 1613) 266 *sqq* [2nd ed. by Struvius I (1726) 448–656] [all these eds. are very poor]. — Waitz *MGH SS* V (Hanover 1884) 481–564 [*lib.* III only]. — Migne *PL* CXLVII 623–796 [reprint: *cf.* 601 *sqq*]. COMM: Reeves *Proc. RIA* VII 290–2. — HZ *Glossae Hibernicae* (Berlin 1881) pp. xlii *sq*, 274–82. — WS *The Academy* XXXV (1889) 26–7; "Hibernica" *Zs. f. ver. Sprach.* XXXI (1890) 247 *sq*. — B. MacCarthy *The Codex Palatino-Vaticanus 830* (RIA Todd Lect. Ser. III) (Dublin 1892) [an elaborate study of the chronicle, with much extraneous matter added]. — Wattenbach *DGQ* II⁶ (1894) 114–6, 382. — Manitius *NA* XXXII (1907) 694; *Lat. Lit.* II 388–94.

Marianus Scottus the chronicler, whose Irish name was Moel-Brigte,[313] was born in 1028 and entered the monastery of Magh-bile, or Moville, co. Down, in 1052. In 1056, for some trifling offense, the abbot, Tigernach Bairrcech, sentenced him to banishment from Ireland.[314] On August 1 he arrived at Cologne, where now for three-fourths of a century the monastery of St. Martin had been in Irish hands. In 1058 he went to Fulda, in 1059 was ordained priest in the church of St. Kilian, the Irish martyr, at Würzburg, and immediately afterward had himself walled up as an incluse at Fulda. In 1069 he was removed to a similar position in the monastery of St. Martin at Mainz. There he died in 1082 or 1083.[315]

The *Codex Palatino-Vaticanus* 830 seems to be in part Moel-Brigte's own autograph, but mainly from the hand of a fellow-countryman — he too an exile by sentence of his ecclesiastical superior — who served as amanuensis.[316] The whole was corrected, apparently by Moel-Brigte. The codex contains 170 folios. Of these, the first twenty-four are occupied by miscellaneous chronological matter, tables, lists, etc. On fol. 15 is a list of kings of Leth Chuinn or the northern half of Ireland from the semi-mythical Conn *cet-chatach* to Flann son of Máel-Sechnaill (d. 916).[317] It does not seem to be strictly accurate even in the historical period. The remaining folios are taken up by the chronicle. A number of Irish poems are copied into the margins.

The *Chronicon* consists of a prologue and three books, of which the first extends from the Creation to the Incarnation, the second from the Incarnation to the Ascension, the third from the Ascension to 1082. There are also some later entries. The prologue

---

[313] An acrostic on f. 165ᵛ gives this form. *Cf.* MacCarthy *op. cit.* 9.

[314] Anmchad, a monk of Inis-Celtra, was banished by his superior Corcram [Corcran?]. He went to the monastery of Fulda in Germany, where he became an *inclusus* and died in 1043. Marianus, after telling his story, adds: " Ita Tigernach . . . mihi culpabili in aliqua levi culpa pronuntiavit." This has generally been interpreted as above, but Macalister points out that it need mean only that Tigernach held up to Marianus the case of Anmchad as an example. — *Proc. RIA* XXXIII (1916) C 105.

[315] " Marianus inclusus " is entered on 11 Kal. Jan. in the *Necrologium* of Metz. — Jaffé *Bibl. rer. Germ.* III 728. On inclusion see L. Gougaud " Étude sur la réclusion religieuse " *Rev. Mabillon* Jan. 1923 pp. 26–39, April pp. 77–102.

[316] This marginal note, in Irish and Latin, is found on fol. 33: " It is pleasant for us to-day, O incluse Moelbrigte, in the incluse's cell in Mainz, on the Thursday before the feast of Peter, in the first year of my sentence, that is, in the year of the killing of Diarmait, king of Leinster; and this is the first year I came from Scotland [Albain] in perigrinitate mea. Et scripsi hunc librum pro caritate tibi et Scotis omnibus, id est Hibernensibus, quia sum ipse Hibernensis."

[317] This list is published by HZ *op. cit.* 281–2, and by MacCarthy 93–8, 335–6.

and first and second books contain some computistical documents and studies. By a misconception Marianus adopted a chronology of his own in which the numbers of the years exceed those of the vulgar era by 22. His work has some importance in the history of chronicle-writing both in Ireland and on the Continent. It was used extensively by Sigebert of Gembloux, Florence of Worcester and other later chroniclers. A considerable number of Irish items are to be found in it, but not so many as might be expected. Those relating to Patrick, Brigit, Colum-cille and Columbanus have been gathered by MacCarthy. The work is, however, of very great value for the history of the Irish in Germany in the tenth and eleventh centuries.

444. Life of Marianus, abbot of Ratisbon A.D. 1184/1185

Sanctorum patrum illustriumque . . . videbunt in Sion Deum deorum, cui est h. et g. in s. s.

MS: Boll. used a MS. in the Carthusian monastery of Gaming (Kemnick, Gemnikho) in Lower Austria. Ed: *AA. SS. Boll.* Feb. II 361–72 [the introduction is of much interest]. Comm: Raderus *Bavaria sancta* II 227–8. — Reeves *Proc. RIA* VII 292–301 [gives an account of the life and works of Marianus]. — Graf von Walderdorff "Die Heiligen Mercherdach und Marian und der Ursprung der Schotten-Convente in Regensburg" *Verhandlungen des histor. Vereins von Oberpfalz und Regensburg* N. F. XXVI (1879). — Wattenbach "Die Congregation der Schottenklöster in Deutschlands" Otte und Quast's *Archäolog. Zs.* I. — G. A. Renz "Beiträge zur Geschichte der Schottenabtei St. Jakob und des Priorates Weih St. Peter in Regensburg" *Studien und Mittheilungen aus dem Benedictiner- und dem Cistercienser-Orden* XVI (1895) 64 *sqq* and "Regesten" 250 *sqq.* — John Lynch (ed. Matthew Kelly) *Cambrensis Eversus* II 397 *sqq* [re alms from Ireland sent to Ratisbon]. — L. Abraham "Mnisi irlandzcy w Kijowie" *Bulletin international de l'Acad. des sciences de Cracovie-Cl. de philol. d'hist. et de philos.* (1901) 137 *sqq* [a study of the Irish mission to Kieff]. — A. Parczewski "Początki chrystjanismu w Polsce i Misya Irlandska" *Annuaire de la Soc. des sciences de Posen* 1902 ["Beginnings of Christianity in Poland and the Irish mission": *cf.* L. Léger in *RC* XXVI (1905) 389].

The Life of Muiredach Macc Robartaig, or Marianus Scottus, — who is to be carefully distinguished from his namesake the chronicler, — was written about a century after his death by an Irish monk of Ratisbon. It is of very great importance for the history of the Irish monasteries in central Europe in the eleventh and twelfth centuries.

The Maic Robartaig (Maic Robhartaigh), Maic Roarty, or Raffertys, were a family of some prominence in Donegal. They were the hereditary custodians of the *Cathach* of the O'Donnells, and the name of a contemporary and perhaps a kinsman of Marianus, Domnall Mac Robartaig, *comharb* of Colum-cille at Kells 1062–1098, is to be seen on the silver case of that psalter.[318]

Muiredach Mac Robartaig, with two companions who are named John and Candidus, set out on a pilgrimage to Rome in 1067. Arriving

[318] *Cf.* no. 454.

at Bamberg, they stopped for a year at the monastery of Michelsberg. Passing on to Ratisbon, they intended to make that, too, only a resting place in the journey, but were induced by a fellow-countryman, an incluse named Muirchertach, to remain permanently. Later John became an incluse at Göttweich in Lower Austria.[319] In 1076, we are told, Muiredach built the Irish monastery of St. Peter at Ratisbon, commonly known as Weih-Sanct-Peter. He died in 1088.

Muiredach was the ideal scribe of an Irish monastery. The author of the *Vita* gives an account of his labours " as his contemporary, the father Isaac, a man of one hundred and twenty years who had lived under his rule, often related: — Such great talent for writing did Divine Providence confer on Blessed Marianus, that with his speedy pen he completed many extensive volumes. To tell the truth without any dissimulation, among all the achievements which the Divine Mercy deigned to work through the instrumentality of that man, I deem worthy of most praise and admiration, and I myself admire most, the fact that, with scanty food and clothing, assisted by his brothers who prepared the parchment, he, for the sake of an eternal reward, wrote through with his own hand, not once or twice but innumerable times, the Old and New Testament with its expository comments. Moreover during the same time he had written many little books and many manuals of the Psalter for poor widows and clerks of the same city, for the benefit of his soul, without any hope of earthly reward. Moreover many monastic congregations which, recruited from Ireland through faith and charity and the desire to imitate Blessed Marianus, inhabit Bavaria and Franconia ' on pilgrimage,' are supplied for the most part with the writings of Blessed Marianus." [320]

The *Vita* goes on to narrate the fortunes of the Irish monks in Germany — the founding of the monastery of St. James of Ratisbon in 1090, and of monasteries at Würzburg (1134), Nuremberg (1140), Constance (1142), Vienna (1155), and Eichstätt (1183). Many Irish ecclesiastics followed Muiredach to Ratisbon: his six immediate successors were from the north of Ireland, the seventh, Domnus, from the south. Christianus succeeded Domnus, and was the first abbot recorded to have sought alms in Ireland for the Irish foundations abroad:

" On the completion of these matters, and the placing of the monastery on a free and firm basis, the happy father and abbot Christianus revisited his paternal country,

[319] He is mentioned in a *Vita s. Altmanni*, the founder of Göttweich: *MGH SS* XII 226–43.

[320] Of these many MSS only one, the Vienna Codex 1247, is known certainly still to exist. Aventinus, the Bavarian annalist, who was at Ratisbon before the destruction of the monastery, speaks of a psalter with commentary written by Marianus. " There are extant in the Lower Monastery at Ratisbon the Psalms of holy David, with commentaries, written on parchment, the work of Marianus. I add his preface, carefully transcribed word for word: In the year of the Incarnation of Our Lord 1074, the youth Henry being Emperor, the abbess Machtylda ruling the abbey of St. Mary and St. Herhard, the eleventh year of the decemnovennal cycle, indiction 12, Marianus Scotus, in the seventh year of his pilgrimage, collected these small billows from the deep sea of the holy Fathers, namely Jerome, Augustine, Cassiodorus, Arnobius and St. Gregory; and for his soul's salvation, to the honor of Our Lord and Saviour Jesus Christ, and of his Mother Mary, ever Virgin, and of St. Herhard, has written them out and arranged them in one book . . . " *Annales Boiorum lib.* V.

Ireland, and was received with very great honor by the kings and princes of that land. Two hundred silver marks were collected for him, and he returned joyful to his home. With this money the father Christianus did not erect the walls or buildings of a monastery; but, what was far better, wisely looking into the future, he obtained, through Henry, Burchgrave of Ratisbon, and Otto, Landgrave, lands and property for the use both of the present and of future brothers."

But his predecessor, Domnus, had sent envoys to Ireland who had brought back rich presents; he himself made a second visit, and died there; and his successor, Gregory, also journeyed to the home-land soon after his consecration. In the thirteenth century the congregation of the Schottenklöster held one or more houses in Ireland.

A more remarkable undertaking was that of a monk named Mauricius who, a little earlier, visited Kieff in Russia,[321] established a mission there, and returned with a consignment of furs, from the proceeds of the sale of which the monastery of St. James at Ratisbon was completed.

The Irish monasteries in Germany, after a brilliant history, gradually declined and were taken over by Germans. At Ratisbon the last Irish monks were ejected in 1515 as usurpers and their monastery of St. James was entrusted to Scottish ecclesiastics whose national name proved to the sixteenth century their title to the heritage of the ancient " Scotti."

445. Copy of the Epistles of St. Paul, by Marianus Scottus (Codex Vindobonensis 1247) A.D. 1079

MS: Vienna lat. 1247 (former Hofbibl. VIII D 26; Theol. 287). FACS: *Palaeographica Soc.* I 191 and H. Smith Williams *Manuscripts, Inscriptions and Muniments* Med. ser. pl. 107 [end of Hebrews]. — Chroust *Monumenta palaeographica* ser. I, pt. x, pl. 1 [ff. 9ᵛ–10ʳ]. COMM: Lambecius *Comment. de Bibl. Caes. Vindob.* (1679) 749. — Denis *Codices manuscripti theologici bibl. palatinae Vindob.* I 127–31. — Reeves *Proc. RIA* VII 294–300. — W. Wattenbach " Un autographe de Marianus Scottus " *RC* I 262–4. — Z¹ p. xxiv, Z² p. xviii. — HZ *Glossae Hibernicae* (Berlin 1881) pp. xliii–xlv, 283–4; *The Irish Element in Mediaeval Culture* [cf. p. 486]; *Pelagius in Irland* (Berlin 1901) 12, 119, and *passim*. — Hellmann *Sedulius Scottus* (Munich 1906) 147–97. — Alexander Souter " The Commentary of Pelagius on the Epistles of Paul " *Proc. Brit. Acad.* 1905–6 pp. 409–39. *Cf.* p. 661 *infra*.

This large quarto vellum codex of 160 folios, beautifully written in continental minuscule,[322] is an autograph of Marianus Scottus, begun on or shortly before March 23, 1079, and completed May 17 of the same year. It contains the epistles of St. Paul according to the Vulgate text, and the spurious Epistle to the Laodiceans, introduced, with a marginal note casting doubt on its authenticity, between Colossaeans and Thessalonians, the position it holds in *Liber Armachanus*. The authentic epistles

---

[321] For a letter written to Wratislaw, king of Bohemia, in connection with this mission see Pez *Thesaurus anecdotorum* (Augsburg 1721–9) VI i 291.

[322] According to HZ the marginal notes, though certainly by the same pen, are in the Irish script.

have extensive marginal comments and interlinear gloss. The commentary is said to be drawn from St. Gregory, Pseudo-Ambrosius, St. Jerome, St. Augustine, Fulgentius, Origen, Cassian, Haimo, Leo, Pelagius, Alcuin, the *Liber Pastoralis* and Petrus Diaconus. The text of Pelagius found here has been shown by Hellmann to be very closely related to that used by Sedulius Scottus. The marginalia contain a few Irish words. The colophon at the end of the manuscript reads: " In honor of the undivided Trinity Marianus Scottus wrote this book for his pilgrim brothers. May he rest in peace. For the love of God say devoutly Amen. To-day is Saturday, May 17, A.D. 1079." Over the scribe's name is the gloss: " i. muredach tróg [the unfortunate] macc robartaig." [323]

446. Life of Bishop Silaus of Lucca

Cum Deus in sanctis suis. . . . Hic namque confessor egregius alta progenie . . . iterum miracula coeperunt coruscare.

ED: *AA. SS. Boll.* 21 Mai. V 62–7, VII 825. COMM: F. M. Fiorentini *Vita miracoli e memorie di s. Silao vescovo Irlandese* (Lucca 1662). — O'Hanlon *Lives of Irish saints* V 528. — Margaret Stokes *Six months in the Apennines* (1892) 99–104.

Silaus, Silao, or Sillan was an Irish bishop who, returning from a pilgrimage to Rome, stopped at Lucca, where he died. The date is sometimes given as 1094. The Life, thought to have been written towards the end of the twelfth century, is quite fabulous: it brings the saint into association with Patrick, and says that he was preceded in his visit to Lucca by his sister Mingarda.

447. Sermon by Dermatius A.D. 1117

Ego Dermatius, natione Hyberniensis, omnibus qui manentem . . . in pauperes Christi beneficentissimi fueritis. Valete. Et cum, annuente Deo, vestram hanc sensero beneficentiam, etiam pro Raimbaldo, quaeso, Leodiensi orate, qui proficiscenti mihi hanc pro viatico providit et conscripsit epistolam.

EDS: Martène and Durand *Thesaurus novus anecdotorum* I (Paris 1717) 340–1. — Migne *PL* CLV 485–90.

Dermatius, or Diarmait, an Irishman, but evidently addressing an audience in a foreign land, urges them to depart from Babylon and go to Jerusalem. He states specifically that by Babylon he means the world, by Jerusalem the heavenly Jerusalem. Nevertheless the work has been classed as a description of a pilgrimage to Palestine. The date is given as 1117, and the author alludes to various alarming natural phenomena of that year. If the final sentence of the published text belongs to this document, it would seem to indicate that the scribe of this particular copy obtained his exemplar from Raimbaud, canon at Liége in 1117, dean 1141–9.

448. David Scottus

Cf. Ekkehard *Chronicon Universale: MGH SS* VI 243; William of Malmesbury *Gesta regum Anglorum*: Migne *PL* CLXXIX 1375; Johannes Trithemius (ed. Mabillon)

---

[323] There was, it is said, a copy of a work by Marianus Scottus entitled " Liber excerptus de evangelistarum voluminibus sive doctoribus " in BM Cotton. Tib. E. IV 26 s XII ff. 162–78. This codex has been almost entirely destroyed by fire. Esposito believes that certain works of his said to be at Ratisbon should be ascribed to Marianus the Chronicler (*Hermathena* XV 364). *Cf.* no. 443.

Annales Hirsaugienses (St. Gall 1690) I 349, 403–4; Hardy *Cat.* II 207–8; Tout in *Dict. Nat. Biog. s.v.*; M. Esposito *Hermathena* XIV 527; J. M. Clark *The Abbey of St. Gall* (Cambridge 1926) 31, 45, 51, 93.

According to Ekkehard the Chronicler, who flourished in the first quarter of the twelfth century, and William of Malmesbury, David Scottus [324] was in charge of the cathedral school at Würzburg when he attracted the attention of the Emperor Henry V, who took him to Italy as historiographer in 1110. Of his historical work only a few fragments are preserved by these writers. William, who should have had accurate information on such a matter, says that he was identical with the David who was bishop of Bangor in Wales 1120–39. This, and his name, suggest that he may have been a Welshman, however in that case the epithet " Scottus " is to be explained. But according to the Würzburg chronicler Trithemius, writing at the beginning of the sixteenth century, he was in Würzburg in 1137; if so, he was probably the David who, with other Irishmen of Würzburg, has his name in the first *Necrologium* of the abbey of St. Gall [325] under November 27.

For an Irish monk Marcus who was at Ratisbon in 1149 see no. 619.

449. Irish books in mediaeval libraries

EDS. of catalogues: G. Becker *Catalogi bibliothecarum antiqui* (Bonn 1885). — Th. Gottlieb *Über mittelalterliche Bibliotheken* (Leipsic 1890). Various German and Austrian learned societies are cooperating in bringing out a new series, of which one volume has appeared: *Mittelalterliche Bibliothekskataloge — Deutschlands und der Schweiz* I *Die Bistümer Konstanz und Chur* ed. Paul Lehmann (Munich 1918). On Irish MSS: L. Traube *Perrona Scottorum* [*cf.* p. 500 *supra*] esp. pp. 529–32.

In one form or another a very large number of catalogues of mediaeval libraries have been transmitted to modern times. Occasionally in these catalogues the Irish origin of a book is indicated. The more important of such lists are for the monasteries of Bobbio and St. Gall, and have been noticed among their records.[326] Traube [327] collected the entries from other sources, and his compilation may be repeated here in brief: Catalogue of St. Riquier, A.D. 831: " collectarium scotaicum . . . ." Becker *op. cit.* no. xi 175. Catalogue of the monastery of St. Peter at Rebais, *s* X/XI: " unus textus Scotticus." Becker no. cxxxii 1; Gottlieb *op. cit.* p. 260 no. 719. Catalogue of the same monastery, *s* XII: " duo texta Scotica." Becker no. cxxxiii 1–2. Catalogue of the monastery of St. Peter at Chartres, *s* XI: " de partibus orationis tractatus Scottisca littera." Becker no. lix 55. Catalogue of the monastery of St. Évre at Toul, A.D. 1049 x 1083: " Hier[onymi] epistolae Scoticum volumen I "; " liber Effrem Scotticum vol. I." Becker lxviii 16, 103. Catalogue of the monastery of St. Remacle at Stavelot, A.D. 1105: " psalterium Scottum." Gottlieb p. 290 no. 280. Catalogue of St. Maximin at Trèves, *s* XII: " Augustinus de karitate scotice, in quo habetur

---

[324] C. P. Cooper, in *Supplement to Appendix A* [to Report on Rymer's *Foedera* projected but never published] (issued 1869) 84, refers to a MS at Würzburg containing " David Scottus de Purgatorio Patritii." *Cf.* p. 355 *supra*.

[325] St. Gall Stiftsbibl. 915.

[326] Pp. 516, 599 *supra*.   [327] *Op. cit.*

passio vii dormientium "; " unus scottice scriptus "; " expositio psalterii scottice conscripta." Becker no. lxxvi 41, 95, 151. Catalogue of St. Vaast at Arras, s XII: " sentencie.patrum Scotice." Becker no. cxxv 106. Traube adds an extract from Eberhard, written 1152 x 1155, which speaks of the difficulty of reading certain old schedules of Fulda in Irish script.[328] Dronke *Traditiones et antiquitates Fuldenses* (Fulda 1844).

[328] Nec poterat quaeque schedula leviter legi prae nimia vetustate et inexperientia scotticae scripturae.

CHAPTER VII

RELIGIOUS LITERATURE AND ECCLESIASTICAL CULTURE

Seventh to Twelfth Century

In the present chapter an examination will be made of the direct sources for the history of the spiritual and intellectual life of the Irish Church down to the second half of the twelfth century, in so far as these have not already received sufficient notice. In a broad sense, it is true, every text that emanated from the Church is a record of its religion or its culture; but here the title will be restricted to the documents that bear directly on these topics, that is, to works of devotion and to works of ecclesiastical literature and learning. Such a classification will include the Bible and works of biblical exegesis; the writings of the Fathers and Doctors of the Church and other foreign ecclesiastics, and commentaries thereon; any original productions in theology, philosophy and Church history; the texts, with annotations, of secular Latin and Greek literature and learning that were studied and copied in the Irish monasteries; liturgical *formulae*, prayers and hymns, and similar texts for private devotions, whether of Irish or of foreign origin; homilies and didactic documents; and the apocryphal and other imaginative compositions of a religious character; but it will not include those texts of secular Gaelic scholarship and literature which, as has been seen, were, especially in the later part of our period, frequently transcribed or even composed by churchmen.

Also omitted from consideration here are, as has just been said, those sources that, for one reason or another, are treated elsewhere. The most important of these are (1) original works composed in Ireland up to the early years of the eighth century and illustrative of the general history of the Irish Church for the period ending with the completion of conformity with the Continent on the Easter question, the period to which chapter III is devoted; (2) hagiographical texts and legends and other documents connected with local churches, to be found in chapters IV and V; (3) the writings of Irishmen abroad — the most important surviving evidence of their scholarship — in chapter VI; and (4) certain sources which seem to be closely associated with the reform movement of the twelfth century and are reserved for chapter VIII.

N.B.: Throughout this chapter only the larger or more important facsimiles of MSS will be mentioned in the bibliographies. For further references see L. Gougaud " Répertoire des fac-similés des manuscrits irlandais " *RC* XXXIV (1913) 14–37; XXXV (1914) 415–30; XXXVIII (1920) 1–14.

A. BIBLICAL AND INTELLECTUAL

I. The Bible

Bibliography

M. Roger *L'Enseignement* (1905) 228 *sqq* [the study of the Scriptures in the monastic schools]. — Gougaud *Les Chrétientés celtiques* (1911) chap. viii " La culture intellectuelle et les doctrines théologiques " [useful, but not exactly covering the field]. — The following may be consulted on the character and relationships of Irish biblical texts: Abbé Fulcran Vigouroux (ed.) *Dictionnaire de la Bible* 5 vols. (Paris 1895–1912). — Jas. Hastings (ed.) *A Dictionary of the Bible* (New York and Edinburgh 1903) [see the arts. " Latin Versions, The Old," by H. A. A. Kennedy, III 47–62; " Vulgate," by H. J. White, IV 873–90]. — E. Nestle in *Realencyklopädie f. prot. Theol. u. Kirche* 3rd ed. III 36 *sqq.* — F. H. A. Scrivener (ed. E. Miller) *A plain introduction to the criticism of the New Testament* 4th ed. 2 vols. (London etc. 1894) [esp. the art. " Latin Versions " by H. J. White]. — C. R. Gregory's " Prolegomena " to Tischendorf's *Novum Testamentum Graece*, 8th ed., III (Leipsic 1894) 971–1108; and *Textkritik des Neuen Testaments* (1900). — J. Wordsworth and H. J. White *Novum Testamentum Latine sec. ed. s. Hieronymi* (Oxford 1889–) [in progress; the Gospels and Acts have been published; has a careful critical examination of the Irish family of Vulgate texts]. — J. Gwynn *LA* (1913) pp. cxxxv *sqq* [further careful study of the Irish texts, based on preceding]. — H&S I (1869) sect. ii append. G: A. W. Haddan " Latin versions of the Holy Scriptures in use in the Scoto-Britannic Churches " [studies the evidence left by Irish and British writers as to the character of the biblical texts used by them; and also in some degree the MSS]. — Samuel Berger *Histoire de la Vulgate pendant les premiers siècles du moyen âge* (Paris 1893) [esp. pt. I chap. iii " Les textes irlandais et anglo-saxons," chap. iv " Les Irlandais en Europe ": the best historical study of the modifications of the Vulgate text; devotes much attention to the Irish MSS, but does not always distinguish with sufficient precision between those of Irish and those of English origin or affiliation]. — Dom John Chapman *Early History of the Vulgate Gospels* (Oxford 1908) [holds that the " Irish " type of gospel text is fundamentally Old Latin, modified by the Vulgate]. — H. C. Hoskier *Concerning the genesis of the versions of the New Testament* 2 vols. (London 1910) [an important study in which particular attention is given to Irish MSS; the presentation of the results is not always as clear as might be]. — The best critical ed. of the Vulgate is, so far as it has gone, that of Wordsworth and White; and, before them, for the New Testament, that of C. Tischendorf (Leipsic 1864). Since 1907 a commission at the Vatican has been carrying out elaborate preparations for a revised edition.[1] (*Cf. Cath. Encycl. s. v.* " Vulgate,

[1] In this connection a discussion of principles of textual criticism has arisen which is interesting to all students of the subject, although having little direct connection with the Irish texts: Dom Henri Quentin

Revision of "). See also the works on palaeography noticed on pp. 97–9 *supra*, especially J.A. Bruun *An enquiry into the art of the illuminated manuscripts of the middle ages* pt. I *Celtic illuminated manuscripts* (Edinburgh 1897). — Stephan Beissel *Geschichte der Evangelienbücher in der ersten Hälfte des Mittelalters* (Freiburg i. Br. 1906).

The chief subject of study in the monastic schools of early Christian Ireland was the Bible. With the exception of such instruction as was of practical necessity for carrying on the services of the Church, all other studies, including that of the Fathers of the Church, were ancillary to the reading, comprehension, and exposition of the Scriptures. The predominance thereof is witnessed to by the whole literary remains of the early Irish Church. The monastic traditions as set down by a later age in almost innumerable Lives of saints tell the same story: the important element in an ecclesiastic's education was the reading of the Scriptures, and — it may be remarked — in especial the reading of the Psalms. Nor, even if other evidence were lacking, could it be said that these represented the ideas of the twelfth century reflected onto the sixth and seventh: the seventh-century texts offer identical testimony.

In the *scriptorium* as well as in the master's cell the Bible was pre-eminent. Copies of the Gospels, of the Psalms, and of the other books of Holy Writ were the most numerous products of scribal activity. On them were lavished the treasures of the illuminator's art. Of the output during more than four centuries of some hundreds of monastic *scriptoria* only a scanty remnant of codices and fragments of codices survive to-day, and of these a majority are scriptural texts. This result has been due in part to the reverence in which these texts were held, giving them a better chance of preservation, but there can be little doubt that it also represents real preponderance in numbers in the original production.

With Irish saints and Irish scholars, Irish copies of the Bible passed to Britain and the Continent. They are found to-day scattered through many foreign libraries and museums, further records of the early mediae-val emigration movement from Ireland. Much more extensive evidence is given by the large number of foreign biblical manuscripts in which traces more or less numerous are to be found of the peculiar Irish text of the Scriptures. The more important foreign manuscripts showing this Irish influence are noticed in the following pages, but there are many others noted by Berger in which, though attenuated, it is still present.

Mémoire sur l'établissement du texte de la Vulgate (Paris 1922); *Essais de critique textuelle* (1926). — De Bruyne *Rev. Bénédictine* April 1923. — Burkitt *JTS* Oct. 1923. — E. K. Rand " Dom Quentin's Memoir on the text of the Vulgate " *Harvard Theological Rev.* 1924 pp. 197–264.

Scholars are hampered, in spite of the vast amount of study that has been expended on biblical texts, by the fact that accurate information is not at their disposal regarding much of this Irish, or semi-Irish, material: only a small number of the manuscripts have been described by persons having modern expert knowledge either of Irish palaeography or of Irish biblical texts. Without such descriptions it is often impossible for the student who cannot see the manuscripts themselves to know which is Irish, which " Anglo-Saxon"; which the work of an Irish scribe on the Continent, which a continental copy of an Irish original; which shows direct Irish influence, which that influence working through English intermediaries. And it must further be remembered that neither in palaeography nor in textual criticism has the Irish field yet been as well tilled as those of other European countries.

The following may serve as an introductory summary of our present knowledge of the versions of the Scriptures in use in Ireland: (1) There is not the slightest reason to believe that the Irish ever in our period were acquainted with the Hebrew text. (2) The case is a little better for knowledge of Greek texts. There is a considerable amount of scattered and indecisive evidence favoring the hypothesis of a genuine, though limited, familiarity with the Greek language, in early Christian Ireland, and such would almost certainly involve study of the Greek Bible. Also, as stated below, the theory has been advanced that the " Irish " type of mixed Latin biblical texts shows traces of corrections from Greek originals. All this is quite inconclusive. Certain it is that in the ninth century several Irishmen, as Sedulius Scottus, prepared and used Greek copies of parts of the Bible, but whether they brought these texts from Ireland or found them in European libraries is not determined. (3) But there is not the slightest doubt that the Old Latin version was long known and extensively used. In fact, it is not impossible that the Irish were the most important of the agents who have transmitted to us Old Latin texts. The manuscripts to be considered under this heading are of two kinds: first, a few, generally very early, which offer little external evidence of Irish origin but of which the textual relationships show that they, or the texts they represent, existed on Irish soil, perhaps as part of the original Christian inheritance from Europe: such are the Codex Claromontanus, Codex Bobbiensis, and Fragmenta Sangallensia; and others undoubtedly Irish, as Codex Usserianus I, Codex Usserianus II, a St. Gall liturgical fragment,[2] the Book of Mulling and the Book of Dimma, of which the last two are much contaminated by

Vulgate readings. (4) The Vulgate manuscripts also are to be divided into two classes, those containing a very pure text, as the Book of Durrow, the *Cathach* Psalter, and, if it is Irish, the Book of Lindisfarne; and those showing extensive admixture of Old Latin. These last — at least so far as the gospels are concerned — constitute a well-recognized family commonly designated " Irish." As regards the other parts of the Bible, neither is the same amount of material at hand, nor has an equally thorough examination been made of what we have: but in general they seem to be differentiated from non-Irish texts, perhaps not so sharply but in much the same way as the Gospels. Although the manuscripts of this family contain many interesting and peculiar readings, it is not chiefly by the presence of any fixed set of readings running through them all that they are distinguished. Their distinctive characteristics are of a more general nature. The first of these is that the basic Vulgate is of sound and early type: that is, it is quite pure and free from corruptions other than those characteristic variations presently to be noted. Secondly, the Old Latin element is abnormally large even among " mixed " texts. It is irregular in its distribution: the readings sometimes succeed each other in quick succession, sometimes are almost entirely absent for many pages. Moreover, when the several manuscripts of the " Irish " family are compared among themselves in these respects, they are found to vary as much as each does within itself. " No two of the members agree with anything of consistency or continuousness, yet no one of them is without something of special affinity here and there to each of the others; each and all share in this common characteristic of the group." [3] It is to be added that conflate readings and dittographs are, as would be expected in texts so composed, numerous, and their occurrence is equally variable with the other elements. Thirdly, there are many small and unimportant variations of the text, chiefly in the Gospels, insertions, omissions, changes in the order of words. A few of these result from the harmonising, or perhaps marginal comparison, of the texts of two or more Gospels, but the great majority have no bearing on the meaning and have but one object — rendering the text easy to follow by persons not perfectly familiar with the Latin language. The constant reading aloud of the Scriptures, especially the Gospels, to the inmates of the monastic churches, many of whom must have had but a slight acquaintance with Latin, would naturally lead to the insertion here and there of small conjunctions and pronouns, the occasional alteration of the order of words,

---

[3] Hoskier, *op. cit.*, differing from the majority of the critics, seems to think that the actual elements entering into each of the Irish texts can be determined with some precision. — *Cf. LA* p. clxxiv.

which form the bulk of these aberrations. A fourth characteristic of the " Irish " family has been said to be the indications it offers of corrections made directly from the Greek. These are neither very numerous nor very important, and may be due to Old Latin readings which have not survived in our comparatively few Old Latin manuscripts.

It seems probable that it was during the sixth century that St. Jerome's version was accepted in Ireland as the standard text of the Scriptures, and that its adoption was very gradual both as regards the several divisions of the Bible and as regards the different churches. There was a tradition that Finnian of Mag-Bile [4] (d. 579) was the first to introduce the Gospels into Ireland, bringing them from Italy. The statement as it stands is obviously false, but it is possible that Finnian really was associated with the introduction of the new, Hieronymian, text of the Gospels. And the textual evidence suggests that the Vulgate came to Ireland directly from Italy.

(a) VERY EARLY BIBLICAL TEXTS OF IRISH ORIGIN OR RELATIONSHIP

450. *Fragmenta Sangallensia* and *Fragmenta Curiensia*

MSS: St. Gall Stiftsbibl. 1394 part. — St. Gall Stadtbibl. 70 part. — Chur Rhaeisches Museum MS [formerly in the episcopal archives]. All are of *s* V. EDS: Frag. Sangall.: Batiffol *Note sur un évangéliaire de St-Gall* (Paris 1884); " Fragmenta Sangallensia " *Rev. archéologique* 1885 pp. 305–21. — H. J. White *Old Latin Biblical Texts* II (Oxford 1886). Frag. Cur.: E. Ranke *Curiensia Evangelii Lucani fragmenta latina* (Vienna 1874) [also described by him in *Theol. Studien u. Kritiken* 1872 pp. 505–20]. COMM: P. Corssen *Göttingische gelehrte Anzeigen* 1889 p. 316 [*re* the original unity of the two sets of fragments]. — Hoskier *op. cit.* [p. 623 *supra*] I 10–4 and *passim* [see index].

SYMBOL: Frag. Sangall. *n*; Frag. Cur. *a2*. SCRIPT: Uncial; according to Hoskier, has palaeographical evidences of Irish origin. CONTENTS: St. Gall Stiftsbibl. frags.: Matt. xvii 1–xviii 20, xix 20–xxi 3, xxvi 56–60, 69–74, xxvii 62–xxviii 3, 8–20; Mark vii 13–31, viii 32–ix 10, xiii 2–20, xv 22–xvi 13. St. Gall Stadtbibl.: John xix 28–42, and part of xix 13–27. Chur: Luke xi 11–29, xiii 16–34. TEXT and COMMENT: It has been practically established that all these fragments are the debris of a single evangeliarium. This was, textually, very closely related to a celebrated Old Latin MS, the Codex Vercellensis, which, a doubtful tradition says, was written by Eusebius, bishop of Vercellae (d. A.D. 370). The location of these fragments suggests Irish origin, a suggestion which is strengthened by the strong influence that their text has exercised on known Irish biblical documents, especially on Codex Usserianus I (no. 453).

[4] *Cf.* no. 183.

451. Codex Bobbiensis

MS: Turin Bibl. nazionale G. VII. 15 s IV/V. Eds: F. F. Fleck (1837) [poor]. — Tischendorf (1847–9). — Sanday and Wordsworth in *Old Latin Biblical Texts* No. 2 (Oxford 1886). Comm: Gregory *Textkritik des Neuen Testaments* (1900) 605. — *JTS* V (1903) 88 *sqq.* — Hoskier *op. cit.* [p. 623 *supra*] I 35 *sqq* and *passim* [see index].

Symbol: *k*. Script: Uncial; provenance not determined on palaeographical grounds. Hoskier declares it was written in Ireland. The scribe was careless. Contents: Mark viii 8–11, 14–16, 19–xvi 9; Matthew i 1–iii 10, iv 2–xiv 17, xv 20–36. Text: Old Latin — with some Vulgate additions — of what is usually designated the African type. Hoskier finds in it a Greek and, notably, a very old Syriac base. As stated below, it is closely related to Codex Usserianus II (no. 477). History: This was a Bobbio MS which, tradition said, had belonged to Columbanus. The possibility of Irish origin has generally been disregarded, but the close Irish textual relationships that Hoskier brings out make it highly probable.

452. Codex Claromontanus

MS: Vat. lat. 7223 s V *ex* [formerly of Clermont]. Eds: Mai *SS. vet. nova collectio Vaticana* III (Rome 1828) 257 *sqq.* — Belsheim *Evangelium sec. Matthaeum . . . e codice olim Claromontano nunc Vaticano* (Christiania 1892). Comm: Hoskier *Concerning the genesis of the versions of the New Testament* (1910–1) I 10–4, and *passim*, II 1 *sqq.*

Symbol: *h*. Script: Uncial. Hoskier is quite certain that it is Irish, and adds that it is, " in all probability, the oldest codex which has Irish decoration." Usually it has been assigned to the fourth or fifth century, but he places it in the early sixth. Contents and Text: The four gospels, with some *lacunae*. St. Matthew is Old Latin, the other three Vulgate. The Vulgate is described as of normal type. This MS is closely related textually to BM Harl. 1775 s VI/VII. In its Old Latin it has strong affiliations with Codex Usserianus I and other Irish texts.

453. Codex Usserianus I

MS: TCD 55 (A. 4. 15) s VI *ex.*—Facs: Cf. Gougaud *RC* XXXIV 22, 37. Ed: T. K. Abbott *Evangeliorum versio antehieronymiana ex codice Usseriano, accedit versio vulgata secundum codicem Amiatinum* 2 vols. (Dublin 1884). Cf. H. J. Lawlor *Book of Mulling* (1897) 43 *sqq* [partial collation]. Comm: *RC* VI 350. — Berger *op. cit.* 31, 381. — Hoskier *op. cit.* [p. 623 *supra*] (1910–1) I *passim* [see index]. — *LA* pp. cxli *sq.*

Symbol: *r* or *r₁*. Script: Irish semi-uncial. Ff. 180. Contents: The four gospels, much mutilated, arranged in the order Matthew, John, Luke, Mark. The text is Old Latin, and is usually described as of the " European " family. Hoskier, however, classifies it as " an accommodated *a d h*," where *a* represents a text similar to that of the *Fragmenta Sangallensia* (no. 450), *d* the Latin text of the Codex Bezae,[5] and *h* the text of Codex Claromontanus (no. 452).

[5] Codex Bezae — Cambridge Univ. Lib. Nn. II. 41 s V/VI — is a famous biblical MS containing Gospels and Acts in both Greek and Latin. The Latin text is Old Latin, of which it presents one of the impor-

454. The *Cathach* of Colum-cille

MS deposited in RIA library: *s* VI/VII. Facs: *Cf*. Gougaud *RC* XXXIV 35. Ed: H. J. Lawlor " The Cathach of St. Columba " *Proc. RIA* XXXIII (1916) C 241–443 [text reproduced as exactly as print permitted; with valuable commentary, including palaeographical notes by W. M. Lindsay]. Comm: Sir Wm. Betham *Irish antiquarian researches* (Dublin 1827) I 110–2 [inaccurate]. — Reeves *Ad*. 233, 249, 319. — O'C *MSS Mat*. 327–32. — *4 th Report Hist. MSS. Commission* (1874) Append. 584 *sqq*. — M. Esposito " The so-called Psalter of St. Columba " *Notes and Queries* ser. XI (1915) nos. 286, 301 (XI 466, XII 253).

Script: Irish semi-uncial. Ff. 58, consecutive but all more or less mutilated. Contents: Vulgate text of psalms, xxx 10–cv 13: according to Jerome's second, or " Gallican," trans. The text is remarkably pure, but with a large number of unimportant slips of the pen, many of them corrected by the original hand, and a very few Old Latin variations. The rubric headings were added by the same hand but subsequently to the text: Lawlor has made a study of them which leads to the conclusion that they were derived from the original from which descended, ultimately, the similar matter in certain Northumbrian texts of *s* VII/VIII: the Codex Amiatinus; [6] the *De psalmorum libro exegesis* attributed to Bede (Migne *PL* XCIII 477 *sqq*); the Paris Anglo-Saxon psalter [7] (ed. B. Thorpe *Libri psalmorum versio antiqua latina cum paraphrasi anglo-saxonica* (Oxford 1835); the first fifty, with all the headings, in J. W. Wright and R. L. Ramsay *Liber psalmorum The Anglo-Saxon psalms* (Boston and London 1907)); and the Carlsruhe psalter, Codex Augiensis 107 (ed. Lagarde *Psalterium iuxta Hebraeos Hieronymi* (Leipsic 1874) 1–152). One result is that these Northumbrian texts depend on a work which came from Ireland by way of Iona. Lawlor shows also that this evidence makes it probable that the *Cathach* was written not later than 650. It is not impossible that it is, as tradition states, the actual writing of St. Columba (d. 597). History: In the eleventh century this manuscript was enclosed in a *cumdach* or shrine, still preserved, bearing the inscription, in Irish: " Pray for Cathbarr Úa Domnaill by whom this reliquary was made and for Sitric son of Mac Aedha who made it and for Domnall Mac Robartaigh [8] *comarba* of Kells by whom it was made." Cathbarr Úa Domnaill died in 1106, his father Gillachrist in 1038. Domnall Mac Robartaigh was *comarba* of Colum-cille and abbot of Kells [9] from about 1062 to 1098. Property of Mac Aedha, " artificer," Sitric's father, is the subject of a Kells charter [10] of the twelfth century. In the fourteenth century, it would seem, the present lid was put on the shrine and it was permanently closed. Whether when first enshrined it was the property of the Columban clergy or of the Úa Domnaill family — who became the dominating branch of the Cenél Conaill, Columba's relatives — in the later

tant exemplars. It has interesting associations with certain Irish texts, and Hoskier believes that " *d*, or the parent of *d*, or a copy of *d*, found its way to Ireland in the sixth century " (*op. cit*. I p. xii; see also index). The Codex Bezae has been published by Kipling (Cambridge 1793) and Scrivener (1864). See also Scrivener and Miller *op. cit*. [p. 623 *supra*] I 124–30, II 45; J. Rendel Harris *A study of Codex Bezae* (Cambridge 1891); and F. H. Chase *The Syriac element in Codex Bezae* (London 1893).

[6] As is well known, this text was derived from an Italian exemplar; but the rubrics of the psalms are clearly of a different provenance.

[7] BN lat. 8824 *s* XI.

[8] The family Mac Robartaigh of Tory Island were, at a later date, official custodians of the *cathach* under the O'Donnells, but it is not certain that this Domnall was of the same kindred.

[9] *Cf*. p. 755 *infra*.

[10] No. 632.

middle ages it became the *cathach*, " battler," of the O'Donnells, that is, a relic to be borne to battle as a talisman of victory. The O'Donnell tradition is set forth in Manus O'Donnell's Life of Colum-cille: [11] it was the very book the surreptitious writing of which by Columba led to his quarrel with Finnian, the battle of Cúl-Dremne, and the saint's exile to Scotland.[12] " If it be borne thrice sunwise round the host of Cenél Conaill when about to engage in battle they return safe in triumph." [13]   After the Treaty of Limerick Daniel O'Donel, in whose possession it then was, carried it to France, where in 1723 he had a silver case made for its protection.   O'Donel, who had risen to the rank of brigadier-general in the French service, died without heirs in 1735. By his will he directed that the relic should be given to the head of the O'Donel family: apparently he left it deposited in a monastery in Paris.   From there it was brought back to Ireland in 1802 by Sir Capel Molyneux and delivered to his father-in-law, Sir Neal O'Donel, of Newport, Mayo.   In 1813 Sir William Betham, Ulster King of Arms, to whom the shrine had been loaned, opened it and found within a decayed wooden box containing the manuscript of the psalter.[14]   Since 1843 both shrine and codex have been deposited in the Library of the Royal Irish Academy.

The MS BM Addit. 37518 has at the end two fly-leaves, ff. 116-7, forming a single sheet. The first has certain " morning prayers " of Gelasian origin, the second John xiv 7-14, Luke xxiv 49-53 in medium uncials, and, on the verso, Mark xiv 15-20, in very large uncials. The Catalogue classes these as in 8th century English script. E. S. Buchanan, however, has published the Mark fragment as Irish of the sixth century: *JTS* April, 1912.

(b) Biblical Texts written in Ireland in the Seventh Century
and Later

455. The Book of Durrow

MS: TCD 57 (A. 4. 5) s VII². Facs: *Examples of Celtic ornament from the Books of Kells and Durrow* (Dublin 1892). — Stanford F. N. Robinson *Celtic illuminative art in the Gospel Books of Durrow, Lindisfarne and Kells* (Dublin 1908). *Cf.* Gougaud *RC* XXXIV 20-1. Collation of text: T. K. Abbott *op. cit.* [p. 628 *supra*]. — Lawlor *Book of Mulling* (1897) 15-68 [partial]. — *LA* pp. cxxxvii *sqq* [partial; — these three works have valuable descriptions]. — Comm: Reeves *Ad.* 242, 327. — *RC* VI 555. — Abbott " On the colophon of the Book of Durrow " *Hermathena* VIII (1893) 199 *sqq.* — Berger *op. cit.* 41, 381. — Bruun *op. cit.* 45-7. — Gregory *Textkritik* 712. — Beissel *op. cit.* 106 *sqq.* — H. J. Lawlor *Proc. RIA* XXXIII (1916) C 317-22, 403-7 [*cf.* p. 629 *supra*; includes a note by Lindsay on the colophon].

---

[11] No. 221.

[12] *Cf.* pp. 391, 435, 442, *supra.*

[13] Ed. O'Kelleher and Schoepperle 182.

[14] This was done without the consent of the owner and in defiance of the O'Donnell tradition that the opening of the shrine was unlawful.   An action in chancery resulted, and some interesting information is preserved in the statements of the rival parties.

SYMBOL: dur or durm. SCRIPT: Irish semi-uncial. Gwynn thought not later than A.D. 650, Lindsay about 700. Elaborately illuminated: ranks next to the Books of Kells and Lindisfarne. Ff. 250. CONTENTS: The four gospels, complete. The text is Vulgate, of a remarkably pure type, resembling those of the *Codex Amiatinus* and the Lindisfarne Gospels. There are many errors, but they are for the most part superficial.[15] COLOPHON: On what is now f. 12^V, but originally towards the end of the codex: " I ask thy blessing, holy priest Patricius,[16] that whoever shall hold this little book in his hand may remember the scribe Columba who have written this gospel-book for myself in the space of twelve days by the grace of our Lord I have written." After a blank space, in the same hand: " Pray for me my brother the Lord be with you." Abbott's theory, as developed by Lawlor and Lindsay, is that the volume we have is a richly ornamented copy of the " little book " which Columba — no doubt the saint who founded Durrow and Iona — wrote in twelve days; and that the first colophon is Columba's and the second, addressed to him, is due to the scribe of our copy. HISTORY: On the monastery of Dair-mag, or Durrow, see p. 424 *supra.* The book was formerly enclosed in a silver shrine, or *cumdach;* this is now lost, but a copy of the inscription has been entered — by O'Flaherty, author of *Ogygia* —in the manuscript. "Prayer and blessing of Colum-cille on Flann macc Mail-Sechnaill king of Ireland by whom this shrine was made." The annals record the reign of this Flann with unusual precision. He died about 1 p.m. on Saturday, May 25, 916, having reigned 36 years, 6 months and 5 days.[17] The shrine, therefore, was made within the period 879 x 916. In the first half of the seventeenth century, although the monastery had long passed away, the book and its shrine were still preserved at Durrow. An entry in the Martyrology of Donegal says that the " Book of Columcille, called the Book of Durrow, a copy of the New Testament in Irish letters " was then at Durrow, in the district of the Mac Geoghegans, " with gems and silver on its cover." Connell Mac Geoghegan, in his translation of the *Annals of Clonmacnois*, completed in 1627, mentions the book in his account of Colum-cille. " He wrote 300 bookes wth his one hand. They were all new Testaments, left a book to each of his Churches in the Kingdome, which Bookes have a strange property which is that if they or any of them had sunck to the bottom of the Deepest waters they would not lose one letter, signe, or character of them, wch I have seen partly myselfe of that book of them which is at Dorow in the K^s County, for I saw the Ignorant man that had the same in his Custody, when sickness came upon cattle, for their Remedy putt water on the booke & suffered it to rest there a while & saw alsoe cattle returne thereby to their former or pristin state & the book to receave no loss." [18] It was examined by Ussher,[19] and probably also by Ware.[20] Finally Henry Jones, who had been Scout Master to Cromwell's army in Ireland, and became bishop of Meath in 1661, obtained possession of the manuscript and donated it to Trinity College, Dublin, of which institution he was vice-chancellor.

---

[15] On f. 13 ^{V} there is a long Irish entry that has not been deciphered. It may be a charter or convenant, similar to those in the Book of Kells. *Cf.* pp. 753–6.

[16] An interesting invocation of this saint. But why is he termed " presbyter," not " episcopus "?

[17] AU 916.

[18] *Annals of Clonmacnois* (ed. Murphy) 95–6. Fortunately the custodian, in spite of his faith, applied the water to the back of the book, where it filtered through a number of leaves, leaving them seriously stained. But the greater part of the codex, including all the finer specimens of illumination, escaped and is in a good state of preservation. — On f. 116^V there is an entry made by Connell Mac Geoghegan, dated 1633.

[19] *Britannicarum Ecclesiarum primordia* (Dublin 1639) *cap.* xv, *Whole Works* VI 232.

[20] *De Hibernia et antiquitatibus ejus* (London 1658) 186.

456. The Book of Mulling [21]

MS: TCD 60 s VII/VIII. FACS: *Cf.* Gougaud *RC* XXXIV 28-9. ED: H. J. Lawlor *Chapters on the Book of Mulling* (Edinburgh 1897) [text of certain Old Latin sections, partial collation of remainder, and an extensive critical examination of the whole]. — Hoskier *op. cit. passim* and especially II 278-378 [partial collation]. COMM: Palaeography, etc.: Abbott "Note on the Book of Mulling" *Hermathena* VIII 89 *sqq.* — Bruun *op. cit.* 61-2. — W. M. Lindsay *Early Irish minuscule script* (Oxford 1910) 16-24, pls. vii, viii. Text: H & S I (1869) Append. G 170-98. — John Stuart *The Book of Deer* (Spalding Club: Edinburgh 1869) pp. 34 *sqq.* — Berger *op. cit.* 33-4, 380. — Gregory *Textkritik* 711. — *LA* pp. cxlii *sqq.* *Cf.* also WS "A note on the Book of Mulling " *The Academy* L (1896) 82.

SYMBOL: mull and μ. SCRIPT: Irish minuscule, pointed. At least four scribes of the original texts: [22] (1) St. John: writing and abbreviations both very old; (2) the other three gospels; (3) two folios in St. Luke; (4) the introductory documents: script and abbreviations later, perhaps much later, than the others. According to Lindsay, the hand of the scribe of St. John is found occasionally in the other gospels, which, if correct, makes the writing of at least the four gospels contemporary. CONTENTS: All the leaves found in the shrine, or *cumdach*, of Moling have been bound into one volume, of 99 folios, but it is certain that some of these (see next item) did not form part of the original Book of Mulling, that several leaves of that codex are missing, and that the present arrangement is not correct. Lawlor has determined the original arrangement to have been in five gatherings: (1) the epistle to Damasus, arguments to the gospels, and Eusebian canons; now imperfect: ff. 18-28; (2) St. Matthew, and at the end, in a space originally left blank, an office for the sick: [23] ff. 29-50; (3) St. Mark: ff. 1-17; (4) St. Luke: ff. 54-81; (5) St. John, the colophon, some liturgical notes, [24] and a kind of map or plan: [25] ff. 82-94; (6) three single leaves, each having a miniature of an evangelist, which may, or may not, have formed part of the original Book. TEXT: Each gospel has a distinct tradition. Matthew and Luke are divided into sections similar to those of the Old Latin; Mark according to the Eusebian sections used with the Vulgate; and John was copied from a text written *per cola et commata, i.e.*, in short stichometric lines. The amount of Old Latin varies, but it would seem that, whatever be the case in later *evangeliaria*, all the gospels of Mulling are basically Old Latin, with Vulgate modifications. The whole has been emended quite extensively, possibly by the scribe of the introductory documents. COLOPHON: By the scribe of St. John: asks for the reader's prayers, and concludes: " Now the name of the writer is called Mulling. End of the four gospels." The form is peculiar, and could hardly have been written by the St. Daircell to whom was given the popular *sobriquet* of " Moling Luachra." Lindsay, however, was willing to accept it as his autograph. Lawlor thought it a copy of the saint's work. HISTORY: The Book was the property of the Kavanaghs of Borris Idrone, near St. Mullins, the ancient Tech-Moling, [26] in Carlow. There it was seen by Gen. Vallancey about 1783. [27] Soon after it was deposited in Trinity College, Dublin. At the beginning of the fifteenth century

---

[21] This is the usual spelling in English in this connection, although the saint's name is more correctly given as " Moling."

[22] That is, exclusive of later entries such as the corrections, the office for the sick, the liturgical notes, and the plan.

[23] No. 562.   [24] No. 562.   [25] Lawlor *Book of Mulling* chap. viii.

[26] *Cf.* p. 461 *supra*.   [27] *Cf.* p. 58 *supra*.

it had been in the possession of the famous Art Kavanagh, or Art McMurrough, whose name is on the *cumdach*.[28] We may be certain that it came originally from Tech-Moling.

457. Gospel fragment attached to the Book of Mulling

COMM: Lawlor *op. cit.* 12–3. — Lindsay *op. cit.* 23–4.

SCRIPT: Irish minuscule, *s* VIII, or possibly VII. CONTENTS: Ff. 95–8, gospel fragments: Matt. xxvi 42–xxvii 35; Mark i 1–iv 8; v 18–vi 35. Also three miniatures, ff. 51–3, which may, however, have belonged to the Book of Mulling.

458. The Book of Dimma

MS: TCD 59 (A. 4. 23) *s* VII/VIII. FACS: *Cf.* Gougaud *RC* XXXIV 23–4. EDS of O–I passages: *Thes. Pal.* II (1903) pp. xxix, 257. COLLATION: Hoskier *op. cit.* append. ii; see also append. iii and *passim* [partial]. — *LA* pp. cxxxvi *sqq* [partial collation of text by Dr. Bernard]. COMM: Palaeography: Lindsay *Early Irish minuscule script* (1910) 12–6, pls. v, vi; " Irish cursive script " *ZCP* IX (1913) 301–8. Text: Berger *op. cit.* 43, 381. — Gregory *Textkritik* 712.

SYMBOL: dim. SCRIPT: Irish cursive for the first three gospels, minuscule for John. Probably three scribes: one wrote the first three pages, second continued to end of Luke, third transcribed the fourth gospel. Script and abbreviations seem to indicate a date between Book of Mulling and Book of Armagh. The ornamentation is slight and of, comparatively, inferior character. CONTENTS: The four gospels, with slight *lacunae* in those of Mark and Luke. The blank space between Luke and John is filled, by a hand of much later date, with prayers for the sick.[29] TEXT: Apparently Old Latin base, with extensive revision from the Vulgate. COLOPHON: One of the scribes, by name Dimma,[30] has added a note after each gospel; that at the end of Luke, in a mixture of Latin and Irish, reads: " finit. amen. I give thanks to God. pray for Dianchride (?) for whom this book has been written and for Dimma the writer. amen." At the end of John is the entry, in a different script and apparently of later date, " dimma mac nathi," followed by a half-illegible scribal prayer in Irish. HISTORY: The book belonged to the monastery of Ros-Cré. A legend regarding the writing of this, or some other *evangeliarium*, attributed to a scribe Dimma, is told in the Life of Cronan of Ros-Cré.[31] Its shrine, or *cumdach*, was made by O'Carroll of Éle[32] about 1150, and repaired by a bishop of Limerick about a century later.[33] Both book and shrine remained in the neighborhood of Ros-Cré (Roscrea) until the beginning of the nineteenth century.

459. The Maihingen Gospels

MS: Harburg (Bavaria) Öttingen-Wallersteinische Bibl. I. 2. 4⁰ 2 *s* VIII¹. COMM: Wattenbach *Anzeiger f. Kunde d. deut. Vorzeit* XVII (1869) 289–93 [Fr. trans: *RC* I

---

28 " Arthurus rex dominus lagenie." 29 No. 563. 30 *Cf. RC* XXXVI (1915–6) 360–1.
31 *Cf.* p. 460 *supra.* 32 *Cf.* p. 22 *supra.*
33 For a description of the *cumdach* see M. I. Monck Mason " Description of a rich and ancient box containing a Latin copy of the Gospels " *Trans. RIA* XIII; Petrie (ed. M. Stokes) *Christian Inscriptions in the Irish language* II. 100-2.

(1870) 27–31; with facs.]. — Dümmler *ibid.* XXVI (1879) 80 *sqq.* — Wattenbach *NA* XII 234. — Bartsch *Zs. f. roman. Philol.* II (1878) 216. — Berger *op. cit.* 52. — Lawlor *Book of Mulling* 27–8. — Esposito *Proc. RIA* XXX (1912) C 2.

SCRIPT: Insular semi-uncial, usually described as Irish, but Lindsay says Anglo-Saxon. Extensive ornamentation in the Irish style; said to resemble that of *Codex Epternacensis.* CONTENTS: The four gospels, apparently of the " Irish " mixed type, but the text does not seem to have been carefully examined. Also Aileran's poem on the evangelical canons (no. 107 ii) and an acrostic poem at the end giving the name of the author, and, apparently, the scribe of the MS, as Laurentius. HISTORY AND COMMENT: Formerly belonged to the church of St. Arnulf at Metz. Wattenbach, whose opinion is favored by Berger, Lindsay and others, suggested that it came from Echternach and that the scribe was the Laurentius who, in the first quarter of the 8th century, wrote the Martyrology of Echternach, or, of St. Willibrord (no. 69). Irish influences, of course, must have been very strong at Echternach.

460. Gospels of Willibrord: *Codex Epternacensis*

MS: BN 9389 *s* VII/VIII. FACS: Silvestre *Paléographie universelle* (Paris 1839–41) pl. ccxxvi. — J. O. Westwood *Palaeographia sacra pictoria* (London 1843) " Anglo-Saxon MSS " pl. xxi. — Le Comte de Bastard *Peintures et ornements des mss.* pls. lxxiv–lxxx. — L. Delisle *Le cabinet des mss.* (Paris 1868–81) pl. xix 8. COLLATION: Wordsworth and White *op. cit.* — *LA* pp. cxliv *sqq* [partial]. COMM: A. Reiners " Les mss. anciens d'Echternach conservés à la Bibl. nat." *Publications de l'Institut de Luxembourg* XL (Luxemburg 1889) 25 *sqq.* — Bellesheim *Geschichte der katholischen Kirche in Irland* I (Mainz 1890) 623. — Berger *op. cit.* 52, 406. — Scrivener *op. cit.* II 80. — Gregory *Textkritik* 683.

SYMBOL: ЭP or ept. SCRIPT: Insular semi-uncial or large minuscule, classed by some as Irish, by others as Anglo-Saxon. The ornamentation, considerable in amount, is Irish. CONTENTS: The four gospels. TEXT: Of the " Irish " mixed type. The Vulgate is of a very good class, resembling that of the Book of Durrow and the Gospels of Lindisfarne. A few of the variations are regarded by some critics as continental. There are extensive marginal and interlinear emendations, in a second hand, which are even more markedly Irish than the primary text. HISTORY: A note on the second last folio, bearing date 558, says that the text has been corrected according to a book from the library of the priest Eugippius, which was said to have belonged to St. Jerome. Eugippius, author of the Life of St. Severinus of Austria, lived at Naples in the beginning of the sixth century. Those who favor an English origin for this *evangeliarium* advance the same hypothesis as for the Gospels of Lindisfarne,[34] — that the Abbot Hadrian brought the prototype to England from Naples. But it seems certain that, whatever be the explanation of the note, and whether this MS was written in Ireland, in England, or at Echternach, the immediate forerunners of the text were Irish. The Book of Durrow and the *Cathach* of Colum-cille are evidence that good — and, doubtless, Italian — texts had come to Ireland. — The *Codex Epternacensis* came from St. Willibrord's monastery of Echternach,[35] where tradition said that it had belonged to that saint.

[34] *Cf.* p. 651 *infra.*   [35] *Cf.* p. 233 *supra.*

461. The Würzburg St. Paul: *Codex Paulinus Wirziburgensis*

MSS: Würzburg Universitätsbibl. M. p. th. f. 12 *s* VIII *ex.* FACS: L. C. Stern *Epistolae Beati Pauli glosatae glosa interlineali Irisch-lateinischer Codex der Würzburger Universitätsbibliothek in Lichtdruck herausgegeben und mit Einleitung und Inhaltsübersicht versehen* (Halle 1910) [with 72 plates; complete]. — *Cf.* Gougaud *RC* XXXVIII 4. EDS: Lat. glosses: HZ *Pelagius in Irland* (Berlin 1901) 39–137. O–I glosses: Z¹ 1039–63; Z² pp. xvi *sqq*, 1026–42 [partial]. — HZ *Glossae Hibernicae* (Berlin 1881) pp. ix–xvii, 1–198, pl. [text; *cf. Supplementum* (Berlin 1886) 6–10; also WS in *Literarische Centralblatt* 24 Nov. 1883]. — WS *The Old-Irish Glosses at Würzburg and Carlsruhe* pt. I (London, Philological Society, 1887) [text, trans.; *cf. Academy* XXXII (1887) 340, *RC* IX (1888) 104–8, 364–70]. — *Thes. Pal.* I (1901) pp. xxiii–xxv, 499–712 [text, trans.]. TRANS: T. Olden *The Holy Scriptures in Ireland one thousand years ago; selections from the Würzburg Glosses* (Dublin 1888) [ignores the Latin glosses]. COMM: On text: Berger *op. cit.* 54. On Lat. glosses: S. Hellmann *Sedulius Scottus* (Munich 1906) 147–97 [*cf.* p. 553 *supra*]. — A. Souter "The Commentary of Pelagius on the Epistles of Paul" *Proc. Brit. Acad.* 1905–1906 pp. 409–39. On O–I glosses: RTh *RC* VI (1885) 318 *sqq*; "Das Alter der Würzburger Glossen" *ZCP* III (1901) 47–54. — Chr. Sarauw *Irske Studier* (Copenhagen 1900) 136 *sqq.* — J. Strachan "Some Notes on the Irish Glosses of Würzburg and St. Gall" *ZCP* III (1901) 55–60. — HZ "Zu den Würzburger Glossen" *ZCP* VI (1908) 454–530, VII (1910) 271–87 [chiefly a discussion of divergencies in readings between his and WS's eds. of the glosses]. — L. Chr. Stern "Bemerkungen zu dem Würzburger Glossencodex" *ZCP* VI 531–45. — J. Fraser "The Prepositions in the Würzburg Glosses" *ZCP* VIII (1912) 1–63 [of grammatical interest almost solely]. — J. Pokorny *ZCP* X (1915) 36, 68.

SCRIPT: Irish minuscule. French palaeographers of the last century assigned it to the 9th or 10th century, HZ to the 8th or 9th, Z to the 8th; Traube also inclined to the 8th, and Stern thought it only a little older than LA. It is now generally assigned to the 8th century. Orthography, abbreviations and illumination are Irish. The glosses are by three hands: 1 the so-called *prima manus*, possibly that of the scribe of the text, to which is due a small number of glosses distributed through the MS; 2 the chief glossator to f. 32ᵛ; 3 the chief glossator, f. 33 to end. Some have considered the writing of the glosses to be contemporary with the text; Lindsay declares that they are, for the greater part, manifestly much later. Ff. 36; one missing at beginning, another at end. CONTENTS: Epistles of St. Paul, complete except for latter portion of Hebrews, lost with last folio. This volume has very great interest as one of the few surviving Irish biblical MSS which were produced, not for liturgical, devotional or artistic purposes, but for use in the study and the lecture-room. GLOSSES: A great mass, interlinear and marginal, Latin, Irish, and mixed. The Irish glosses form the earliest considerable *corpus* of Old Irish extant in a practically contemporary MS, and are of great philological importance. Those of the *prima manus* are assigned to the end of the 7th or beginning of the 8th century, and were transcribed from an older exemplar; those of the chief glossators are of the 8th, Pokorny thinks of its third quarter. The Latin glosses are of much greater value than the Irish in showing the character of biblical exegesis in the Irish schools. They consist in the main of extracts from older commentaries. The annotations are attributed as follows: Origen (in the translation by Rufinus) 21 times, and apparently once besides, where by a slip of the pen the scribe wrote *aur* for *ori*; Hilary (by which is designated the author of the

" Ambrosiaster " commentary on St. Paul [36]) 29 times — to correct errors arising from a confusing of *Hl* and *Pl*, one of these passages should be assigned to Pelagius, while eight credited to him should be added to the Hilary citations; Jerome 116 times — four of these extracts are actually from Pelagius; Augustine 11 times — one is from Pelagius; Gregory the Great 50 times — eight are Pelagian; Isidore 5 times. But the great source of this Irish commentary was Pelagius, and consequently it has become in turn a most valuable source for the reconstruction of Pelagius's Exposition of the Epistles of St. Paul. Pelagius is quoted 957 times, in ten of which the attribution is erroneous; moreover, 16 extracts attributed to other authorities were really derived from Pelagius, as well as 348 anonymous quotations. Thus there are in all 1311 glosses of Pelagian origin. Other anonymous glosses are due to Origen, " Hilary," and Jerome, and especially to the " Pseudo-Primasius " (the orthodox edition of Pelagius prepared by Cassiodorus [37]), to which no title is ever given in this manuscript. Two passages erroneously ascribed to Pelagius were derived from this last work, which may also have been the medium to which were due some of the anonymous quotations from Pelagius. The exemplar of Pelagius used appears to have been pure and unmutilated. The text thereof is closely related to that used by Smaragdus of St. Mihiel [38] and Sedulius Scottus [39] in the ninth; and by Marianus Scottus in the eleventh century.[40] HISTORY: It is probable that the MS, which formerly belonged to the cathedral at Würzburg, was brought thither in the early middle ages: the place was frequented by Irishmen from the time of St. Killian, and from 1134 to 1497 it had an Irish monastery.

462. The Würzburg Gospel of St. Matthew

MS: Würzburg Universitätsbibl. M. p. th. f. 61 *s* VIII². ED: G. Schepps *Die ältesten Evangelienhandschriften der Würzburger Universitätsbibliothek* (Würzburg 1887). COMM: K. Köberlin *Eine Würzb. Evangelienhandschrift* (Programm) (Augsburg 1891). — Berger *op. cit.* 54.

SYMBOL: Würzburg J. SCRIPT: Semi-uncial, Irish or Anglo-Saxon: the text of the 8th, the glosses of the 9th century. CONTENTS: The Gospel of St. Matthew, with extensive commentary. TEXT: Irish, of the mixed type. It shows strong influence of the Codex Bobbiensis and Codex Usserianus II text. COMM: Is usually described as Anglo-Saxon, but may be Irish. Has a note on the introduction of the Greek computus into Ireland by Mo-Sinu maccu Min.[41]

463. The Cambridge Irish Gospels

MS: Cambridge Univ. Lib. Kk. 1. 24 *s* VIII.

SYMBOL: Bentley, the great English scholar of the early 18th century, cited it as χ. SCRIPT: Irish semi-uncial, resembling the Book of Kells and the Gospels of St. Chad. Ff. 118. CONTENTS: Luke and John, incomplete. TEXT: The first eight chapters of Luke form a curious medley of Old Latin and Vulgate versions, the remainder is of the usual Irish type, Vulgate with an admixture of Old Latin. — Full information regarding this MS is not available.

[36] *Cf.* p. 661 *infra.*   [37] *Cf.* p. 662 *infra.*   [38] *Cf.* pp. 542 *sqq supra.*
[39] *Cf.* p. 565 *supra.*   [40] *Cf.* pp. 618 9.   [41] *Cf.* no. 55.

464. Cottonian fragments of Gospels

MS: BM Cotton Otho C. V. s VIII (?). Facs: Thomas Astle *The origin and progress of writing* (London 1784) pl. xv no. 1 p. 98. — Jos. B. Silvestre *Paléographie universelle* IV (Paris 1841) pl. I, 1. *Cf.* Scrivener and Miller *op. cit.* II 76.

Script: Insular — probably Irish — semi-uncial. Damaged in the fire of 1731: 64 fols. survive but are illegible.

465. Codex Palatino-Vaticanus 68

MS: Vat. Palat. lat. 68 s VIII. Eds of Irish glosses: WS " The Old-Irish Glosses in Palatine 68 " *The Academy* XXXV (1889) 361–2; " Glosses from Turin and the Vatican, Old-Irish " *ibid.* XXXVII (1890) 46–7. — WS " Hibernica 1 The Glosses in Palatine 68 with commentary " *Zs. f. vergl. Sprachf.* XXXI (1890) 232–6. — Bruno Güterbock " Aus irischen Hss. in Turin und Rome " *ibid.* XXXIII (1893) 100–5. — *Thes. Pal.* I (1901) pp. xiv, 3. Comm: W. M. Lindsay *Early Irish minuscule script* (Oxford 1910) 67–70 [palaeography]. — A. S. Napier *Old English glosses* (Oxford 1900) p. xxxii [on the A–S glosses]. — R. L. Ramsay *ZCP* VIII (1912) 428, 453 [on the biblical commentary].

Script: Insular minuscule, but in every way it seems difficult to determine whether this MS is immediately of Irish or of English provenance. The abbreviations show both Irish and English characteristics, and some peculiar to itself. Ff. 46. Contents: An incomplete copy of the psalter, and of a Latin commentary thereon, with a few Irish and Northumbrian glosses. The commentary consists of a series of extracts, especially from Hilary, Jerome, and Theodore of Mopsuestia. The Theodoran matter seems to be derived from the Latin summary attributed to Columbanus.[42] The glosses are written continuously with the text — although distinguished from it by *apices* [43] — a fact which makes it fairly certain that the whole is a copy of an earlier exemplar. The Northumbrian glosses are not later than the early 8th century, the Irish of the same date or perhaps the middle of the century. Colophon: Runs continuously with the text, suggesting that it too was copied from the original.[44] The name is English—Edilberict son of Berictfrid. Comment: The hypothesis may be advanced that this is a close copy, made by an Irish scribe in the second half of the 8th century, of a book written in the first half thereof by an Englishman who was in close association with the Irish, perhaps one of those students who were so numerous in Ireland early in the century.[45] But any opinion must remain tentative until a more adequate study of the MS and its contents has been made.

466. The Stowe Gospel of St. John

MS: RIA D. II. 3 ff. 1–11 s VIII/IX. Collation: J. H. Bernard " On the Stowe St. John " *Trans. RIA* XXX (1893) 313–21 [with *Cod. Amiatinus*]. Comm: B. Mac-

---

[42] *Cf.* no. 47.

[43] So are marked the Irish names of places in the Schaffhausen Adamnán (p. 429 *supra*) and LA.

[44] " Sicut portus oportunus navigantibus, ita vorsus novissimus scribentibus. Edilberict filius berictfridi scripsit hanc glosam [*i.e.*, commentary]. Quicumque hoc legat, oret pro scriptore; et ipse similiter omnibus populis et tribubus et linguis et universo generi humano aeternam salutem optat in Christo. Amen. Amen. Amen."

[45] *Cf.* p. 231 *supra*.

Carthy " On the Stowe Missal " *Trans.* RIA XXVII (1886) 135 *sqq.* — Berger *op. cit.*
42-3, 381. — Lindsay " Irish cursive script " *ZCP* IX (1913) 301-8. — Sir Geo. F.
Warner *The Stowe Missal* II (Henry Bradshaw Soc. XXXII) (London 1915) pp. xxxix-
xliii, pls. vii–ix. *Cf.* no. 555.

SCRIPT: Irish cursive, approaching minuscule; resembles the Book of Dimma cursive.
A crude miniature of St. John on the last page, and some ornamentation on the first.
Ff. 11. A gathering of 12, of which the first has been cut away. Now bound with the
Stowe Missal. CONTENTS: Extracts from the Gospel of St. John.[46] Bernard supports
the hypothesis that the gaps were due to a mutilated condition of the exemplar, which,
in that case, must have had some peculiar interest or sanctity. TEXT: The normal
" Irish " mixed type. COLOPHON: " I give thanks to God. Amen. Finit. Amen.
I ask whomsoever may read this book to remember me, the scribe, a sinner, namely
[here follow several characters in ogam], the pilgrim. Amen. May he be well who
has written, and he for whom it has been written. Amen." The ogams yield the word
Sonid, but some further crypticism may be involved, for this would be a very unusual
personal name.[47] HISTORY: The known history is that of the Stowe Missal. Their
presence in the same *cumdach,* shrine, may imply that they came from the same
monastery.

467. The *Domnach Airgid* manuscript

MS: RIA 24 Q 23 *s* VIII/IX. FACS: *Cf.* Gougaud *RC* XXXIV 33. COMM: Geo.
Petrie *Trans.* RIA XVIII 1 *Antiq.* (1838) 14–24 [treats mainly of the shrine]. — O'C
MS Mat. 322–7 [extracts from Petrie]. — J. H. Bernard " On the Domnach Airgid
MS " *Trans.* RIA XXX (1893) 303–12. — Bruun *op. cit.* 38–41.

SCRIPT: Irish semi-uncial, resembling that of Cod. Usserianus II. Ornamentation
Irish. 39 leaves, in dilapidated condition. CONTENTS: Sections of the gospels: Matthew i 1–v 25, Mark i 1–iv 12, Luke i 6–ii 35, John i 1–iv 14; evidently the
remnants of an *evangeliarium.* The text seems to be of the normal " Irish "
mixed type. HISTORY: The *Domnach Airgid,* " silver shrine," is a receptacle
consisting of an inner case of yew covered with bronze and plated with silver,
and an outer of silver with plates of gold and enamelling.[48] The outer was made
by John O'Barrdan at the order of John O'Carbry, *comarba* of Tigernach of Clones,[49]
who died in 1353. It was preserved in the neighborhood of Enniskillen until the early
part of the last century, and was said to have belonged to the Maguires of Fermanagh.
Tradition declared that the inner box was the reliquary called *Domnach Airgit* which,
according to the Vit. Trip.,[50] Patrick had given to Mac Cairthinn of Clochar.[51] When
opened it was found to contain four sections of parchment, coalesced through age and
dampness, which, when separated, yielded the present membranes. As their original
size was larger than the box, they had to be folded when placed in it. Moreover, both

---

[46] John i–vi 30; vii 45–viii 14; viii 19–33 (umquam); viii 53 (qui)–59; xii 9–39 (credere); xvii 11
(Pater sancte)–xviii 1; xviii 4–13; xviii 15 (discipulus)–23; xix 40–xx 23; xx 26–xxi 6; xxi 9–end.

[47] However, it looks as though there was a play between this word and the Latin *sanus* with which the
following clause begins, in sound and also in meaning, a connection being assumed between *sonid* and
Irish *son, sona, sonad,* " happy."

[48] *Cf., e.g.,* Coffey *Guide to the Celtic antiquities of the Christian period preserved in the National Museum,
Dublin* (Dublin 1909) 45–6, 78–9.

[49] No. 179.   [50] *Vit. Trip.* I 176–7.   [51] *Cf.* p. 351 *supra.*

from tradition and from its appearance, the shrine was a depository for relics, not for a manuscript. It would seem, therefore, that, while the shrine may be that mentioned in the Vit. Trip., the MS was not originally part of its contents but was placed there at some unknown time for safe-keeping.

468. The Gospels of St. Chad

MS: Lichfield Cathedral Lib. *s* VIII[1]. FACS: *Cf.* Gougaud *RC* XXXV 418–9. COLLATION: F. H. A. Scrivener *Codex s. Ceaddae latinus* (Cambridge 1887) [with *Cod. Amiatinus* in the 1857 ed. of Tregelles]. — Wordsworth and White *op. cit.* — *LA* pp. cxxxvii *sqq* [partial]. EDS. of Welsh entries: W. J. Rees *Liber Landavensis* (Llandovery 1850). — J. G. Evans *The text of the Book of Llan Dâv* (Oxford 1893). COMM: *Collected papers of Henry Bradshaw* (Cambridge 1889) 458–61. — Gregory *Textkritik* 642. — W. M. Lindsay *Early Welsh script* (Oxford 1912) 1–7. — H. E. Savage " The story of St. Chad's Gospels " *Trans. Birmingham Archaeol. Soc.* XLI (1915) [also separately].

SYMBOL: L. SCRIPT: Semi-uncial, Irish, or, in the opinion of some, Welsh: resembles that of the Book of Kells, but is slightly coarser. The ornamentation is Irish. Ff. 110; a large section at the end has been lost. CONTENTS: Matthew, Mark, and Luke to iii 9. Text is of the " Irish " mixed type; the percentage of scribal errors seems larger than usual. The Old Latin element comes largely from a text of the type of Codex Usserianus II (no. 477). There are many marginal notes in Old Welsh and Anglo-Saxon, by which the history of the MS can be partially traced. HISTORY: An entry, thought to be of the early 9th century, records that the book was purchased from one Cingal by Gelki, son of Apihtiud, and donated to St. Teliau, *i.e.*, to the monastic church of Llandaff in southern Wales, close to the Bristol Channel. Other notes show that it remained there at least till the middle of the 10th century. In the second half of that century it was in the cathedral church of Lichfield, which had been founded by St. Ceadda, or Chad.[52] There it has since remained.

469. The Turin Fragment of Second Peter

MS: Turin Bibl. nazionale F. IV. 24, last page. EDS. of O–I glosses: WS " Glosses from Turin and the Vatican 1 Old-Irish " *Academy* XXXVII Jan. 18, 1890 pp. 46–7, 65; " Glosses from Turin and Rome 1 The Old-Irish glosses in Turin " *Beiträge z. Kunde d. indogerm. Sprachen* XVII (1891) 134 *sq.* — Bruno Güterbock " Aus irischen Hss. in Turin u. Rome " *Zs. f. vergl. Sprachforschung* XXXIII (1893) 87 *sq.* — *Thes. Pal.* I (1901) pp. xxvi, 713–4. *Cf. ZCP* I (1897) 349.

This MS, which formerly belonged to Bobbio, contains a copy of Walahfrid Strabo's Life of St. Gall,[53] written *s* XI. The last page is a palimpsest, with the original text of which we have here to do. SCRIPT: Irish minuscule, *s* VIII. Interlinear and marginal O-I glosses by same hand. CONTENTS: Beginning of second epistle of St. Peter. GLOSSES: Copied from an earlier exemplar. On linguistic grounds are assigned to the end of the 7th or the early part of the 8th century.

[52] Ceadda, according to Bede (*cf.* p. 231 *supra*), had been educated in Ireland. He became bishop of Mercia, 669–672. Quite naturally, a tradition grew up that the book had belonged to him.

[53] No. 50 (iii).

470. Codex Sangallensis LX

MS: St. Gall Stiftsbibl. 60 s VIII/IX. Facs: *Cf.* Gougaud *RC* XXXVIII 13. Comm: Keller *op. cit.* [p. 98 *supra*] and Reeves's trans. — J. Ebersolt *Rev. archéol.* 5th ser. XIII (1921) 1–6. — Berger *op. cit.* 56, 416.

Script: Irish semi-uncial. Irish illumination. Pp. 70. Contents: Gospel of St. John, of the " Irish " type. Tischendorf made some use of this MS, but otherwise it is not well known. It is generally identified as one of the volumes " Scottice scripti " mentioned in the oldest catalogue of St. Gall.[54]

471. The Book of Kells: Codex Cenannensis

MS: TCD 58 (A. 1. 6) s VIII/IX. Facs: There are many reproductions of pages or letters from this famous MS, as well as descriptions of it. *Cf.* Gougaud *RC* XXXIV 16–20, 37. — J. O. Westwood *Palaeographia sacra pictoria* (London 1843); *Facsimiles of miniatures and ornaments in Anglo-Saxon and Irish MSS* (London 1868). — J. H. Todd "Remarks on illuminations in some Irish biblical MSS" *Soc. of Antiq. of London: Vetusta Monumenta* VI (1869). — *Palaeographical Soc. Facs.* pls. 55–8, 88–9. — *Facs. Nat. MSS. Ire.* I (1874) pp. ix–xii, " Description " 12–21, pls. vii–xvii. — *Examples of Celtic ornament from the Books of Kells and Durrow* (Dublin 1892). — S. F. N. Robinson *Celtic illuminative art in the Gospel Books of Durrow, Lindisfarne and Kells* (Dublin 1908). — *The Book of Kells described by Sir Edward Sullivan, Bart., and illustrated with twenty-four plates in colours* (London etc. 1914). Collation: T. K. Abbott *Evangeliorum versio antehieronymiana* (Dublin 1884). — Wordsworth and White *op. cit.* — H. J. Lawlor *Book of Mulling* (1897) 43 *sqq* [partial]. — *LA* pp. cxxxvi *sqq.* Comm: On art and palaeography: Margaret Stokes *Early Christian art in Ireland* (London 1875). — Hartley *Proc. Roy. Dub. Soc. Science* N. S. IV (1885) 485 *sqq* [re pigments used by illuminators]. — Middleton *Illuminated MSS in classical and mediaeval times* (Cambridge 1892). — Bruun *op. cit.* 77–81. — Romilly Allen *Celtic art in pagan and Christian times* (London 1905). — L. Gougaud " L'art celtique chrétien " *Rev. de l'art chrétien* 1911. See also the usual works on palaeography. Text: Berger *op. cit.* 41–2, 381. — Gregory *Textkritik* 711.

Symbol: ken or Q. Script, etc.: Irish semi-uncial; and Irish ornamentation. Represents the highest attainment of Irish writing and Irish illumination, and is one of the world's finest illuminated MSS. The decoration is incomplete. Ff. 339: a considerable number have been lost, at the end, within the codex, and perhaps at the beginning. Contents: The Eusebian canons, *breves causae, argumenta,* and the four gospels.[55] On pages originally left blank records have been entered of grants of land made at Kells in the 11th and 12th centuries.[56] Text: A somewhat inferior example of the normal " Irish " mixed type; marred especially by a large number of conflate readings, or doublets. History and Comment: Came to TCD in 1661 with part of Ussher's library. He had obtained it, apparently, from one Gerald Plunket, of Dublin, in whose possession it was in 1568, and to whom it may have come from Richard Plunket, last abbot of Kells, by whom that abbey was surrendered

---

[54] *Cf.* p. 599 *supra.* Becker *Catalogi bibliothecarum antiqui* (Bonn 1885) xxii 7.
[55] The *lacunae* are Luke xii 6–18, John xii 27–xiii 20, xvii 19–end.
[56] *Cf.* pp. 754–6 *infra.*

to the Crown on Nov. 18, 1539. As the entries mentioned above show, the book had been at Kells in the 11th century. Moreover it is, there can be little doubt, the book mentioned in the Annals of Ulster under the year 1007: " The great gospel of Columcille was wickedly stolen in the night out of the western sacristy of the large stonechurch of Kells — the chief relic (*mind*) [57] of the western world on account of its wrought shrine. That gospel was found after two months and twenty nights, its gold having been taken off, and a sod over it." The discoloration of some of the leaves may be due to this period of inhumation. Of the earlier history of the MS we know nothing: the colophon, if it had one, was lost with the last leaves. Cenondas, later Cenannus, now Kells, is mentioned by Tírechán,[58] but did not become ecclesiastically important until the headquarters of the Columban *paruchia* were established there in 807–14.[59] If the book was written at Kells, it must have been very soon after 814; and possibly to replace a volume lost when the Vikings plundered Iona in 802 and 806; if at Iona, it may be that the incomplete character of the decoration is a result of the break caused by the removal to Kells. Critics have ranged from the 6th to the 9th century in dating the MS, but from our present knowledge of Irish art and of Irish biblical texts it may reasonably be assigned to the 8th — and preferably the second half — or to the early 9th century.

472. Gospels of mac Regol: Rushworth Gospels

MS: Bodl. Auct. D. ii. 19 *s* VIII/IX. Facs: *Palaeographical Soc. Facs.* pls. xc, xci [with analysis of the script, by Thompson]. — *Cf.* Gougaud *RC* XXXV 427–8. Collation: Jos. Stevenson and Geo. Waring *The Lindisfarne and Rushworth Gospels* (*Publications of the Surtees Soc.* XXVIII, XXXIX, XLIII, XLVIII) (Durham etc. 1854–61–63–65) [collated with Lindisfarne Gospels; Anglo-Saxon gloss in full; not accurate]. — Wordsworth and White *op. cit.* — *LA* pp. cxxxvi *sqq* [partial]. Comm: Art and palaeography: *Rer. Hib. SS.* I p. ccxxxi. — Bruun *op. cit.* 64–5. — Samuel Hemphill " The Gospels of Mac Regol of Birr: a study in Celtic illumination " *Proc. RIA* XXIX (1911) C i 1–10. Text: Berger *op. cit.* 43, 398. — Lawlor *Book of Mulling* 23. — Gregory *Textkritik* 654.

Symbol: rush or R. Script: Irish semi-uncial, resembling the Gospels of St. Chad, but more irregular. Ornamentation, both drawing and coloring, very elaborate and of purely Irish character; resembles that of the Gospels of Lindisfarne, but is cruder. Nevertheless is a wonderfully rich and beautiful example of illumination. Ff. 169, about 14 × 10½ inches in size, the largest of the Irish gospel books. Some leaves lost at the beginning, and the volume is much weather-beaten, but the text is complete except for three small *lacunae* in Luke. Contents: The four gospels, in the " Irish " type of text. Hoskier (*op. cit.* 9) seems to think that it has Syriac elements additional to those of the older Irish texts. Scribal errors are numerous, and those inversions in the order of words which are found in all Irish redactions are here more frequent than is usual. An interlinear Anglo-Saxon version of the gospels has been added, that of Matthew in Mercian, of the others in Northumbrian. The volume has thus become

[57] The word is of some interest. As Reeves has shown, *mind* or *mion*, pl. *minda*, *mionna*, signifies various personal articles associated with a saint, his crozier, his books, etc., as distinct from *martra*, relics in the sense of remains of his body.

[58] *LA* 24a, 454a; *Vit. Trip.* II 318.

[59] *Cf.* p. 445 *supra*.

one of the most valuable of Anglo-Saxon linguistic records. Colophon: " Mac Regol illuminated [perhaps ' wrote and illuminated '] this gospel book: whoever reads and understands the story let him pray for mac Regol the scribe." [60] It is commonly accepted that he is the mac Riaghoil úa Magleni, scribe and bishop, abbot of Birr, who died, according to AU, in 822. History: Towards the end of the tenth century the book was at the monastery of Harewood in England, when two scribes, Farman and Owun, wrote the interlinear Anglo-Saxon gloss. Nothing further is known of its history until 1665, when it was in the hands of John Rushworth, Deputy Clerk to the House of Commons during the Long Parliament. By him it was presented to the Bodleian Library.

473. The ancient *Codex Sangermanensis* 108

MS: Leningrad (Petersburg) former imperial Library F. I. 8 *s* VIII/IX (once St. Germain 108). Facs: *Cf.* Gougaud *RC* XXXVIII 11. Comm: A. Staerk *Les mss. latins du Ve au XIIIe siècle conservés à la bibl. de Saint-Pétersbourg* (Petersburg 1910). — Gregory *Textkritik* 721.

Script: Insular — Irish or English — semi-uncial. Ornamentation of Irish type. Ff. 214, of which the last belongs elsewhere. Contents: The gospels. It is said that the volume at one time belonged to St. Maur-les-Fossés; but its place of origin — Ireland, England, or on the Continent at the hands of Irish or English scribes — is uncertain.

474. The Book of Armagh: *Liber Ardmachanus*

Cf. nos. 131, 523, 560. Ed: *LA*. Collation: Wordsworth and White *op. cit.* Comm: HZ *Pelagius in Irland* (Berlin 1901) 10, 25–39, and *passim* (*cf.* p. 661 *infra*). — Gregory *Textkritik* 711.

Symbol: arm or D. Contents: The second section of the Book of Armagh, following the Patrician documents, contains the only manuscript copy of the complete New Testament, of Irish origin, still surviving. The order of the books is: Gospels, Pauline Epistles, Catholic Epistles, Apocalypse, and Acts. Each of these divisions forms a separate section of the codex, and may have been at one time an independent volume. The only section, however, showing evidence thereof is that of the Pauline Epistles, the first page of which is defaced. To the text of St. Paul, the Catholic Epistles and the Apocalypse may, or may not, have been attached when it had this separate existence. These different divisions will be considered in what appears to be the order

[60] F. 169^V.

Macregol dipin	Etintelligerit
cxit hoc euange	istam narratio
lium: Quicum	nem orat pro
que legerit	macreguil scripto
	ri.

The form of the name is noteworthy, even though we allow for the fact that mac Regol might preserve the spelling in use when he was young. It is usually said that the change from ē to ia took place at the end of the seventh or the beginning of the eighth century. *Cf.* T. Ó Máille *The language of the Annals of Ulster* (Manchester 1910) 71–2. This difficulty, however, can hardly prevent the identification with the abbot and scribe of Birr, which is on other grounds satisfactory. The name is not common.

in which they were written. It is to be noted that the Gospels, at least in part, and probably the other books, except Acts, were prepared under the supervision of the abbot and scribe Torbach (d. 808). The Pauline writings, in the opinion of Gwynn, are in the main Vulgate of a good type, but with many and important variations, chiefly Old Latin readings; but, according to Chapman, are Old Latin with Vulgate modifications. In these affinity is shown with the *Codex Boernerianus*,[61] the Old Latin passages cited by Sedulius Scottus,[62] and the Balliol codex.[63] The text probably came from an exemplar separate from that of the Gospels and a distinct branch of the general Irish tradition — a statement which seems true also of the Catholic Epistles and the Apocalypse.[64] It is to be noted that the Epistle to Colossians follows the two Thessalonians, and is followed by the apocryphal Laodiceans, which bears a warning that it is rejected by Jerome. A peculiar interest attaches to the *prologi* and *argumenta* which are prefixed to these epistles. Of the five such treatises which precede the opening text — Romans — the first is designated " Prologue of Hilary on the Apostle," and is in reality the outline of the Epistle to the Romans in the " Ambrosiaster " commentary;[65] the second, found also in many foreign manuscripts, is here, almost uniquely, described as " Prologue of Pilagius on all the Epistles ";[66] the third, on Romans, is also in many other Pauline manuscripts, but here alone is attributed to " Pilagius " or Pelagius;[67] the fourth, without heading, is a general preface, also found elsewhere; and the fifth is a brief *argumentum* to Romans, attributed to Pelagius.[68] A short *argumentum* of like character is prefixed to each of the other Pauline letters, and designated, except in four cases, as Pelagian.[69] Thus the Book of Armagh is perhaps the most important witness to the continued regard paid to Pelagius by the old Irish Church, and also a valuable source for the reconstruction of his Commentary on the writings of Paul.[70] The Catholic Epistles can be studied only under limitations, for there is no other Irish exemplar, and only a few fragments of the Old Latin versions. It would seem, however, that the fundamental text is Vulgate, resembling that of *Codex Amiatinus* — which in this portion is of somewhat inferior character — with Old Latin modifications which, though of considerable number, are generally merely verbal. — The examination of the text of the Apocalypse is limited by much the same difficulties, but here we can use the evidence of complete Old Latin versions. The basic Vulgate text is good — better, it would appear, than that of the preceding section — and the infiltration of Old Latin not of great importance and not peculiarly Irish, being found, for the most part, also in foreign exemplars. — Next to be considered are the Gospels, at which we know the scribe to have been working in the year 807. The

---

[61] *Cf.* no. 364 (vi).   [62] *Cf.* pp. 564 *sqq supra.*   [63] *Cf.* pp. 657–8.

[64] The, relatively, much more frequent use of abbreviations in the epistles than in the gospels tends to the same conclusion.

[65] *Cf.* p. 661 *infra.* This is further evidence that the author was known in Ireland from early times as Hilary.

[66] So also in the MS of Marianus Scottus (no. 445) and in Berne A 73 s XIII, a copy of the whole bible. Perhaps Würzburg th. f. 12 (no. 461) would have to be added to these if the first leaf of that codex were not missing.

[67] Marianus ascribes it to Jerome, and it has been lost in St. Gall 73 and in Würzburg th. f. 12. The testimony of the Reichenau MS CXIX, however, makes its Pelagian origin probable. *Cf.* p. 663 *infra.*

[68] This is found in other MSS, including that by Marianus and Würzburg th. f. 12, but not St. Gall 73 (where it is probably lost with the first leaf) or Reichenau CXIX, but only in LA is it assigned to Pelagius.

[69] The exceptions are 1 and 2 Corinthians, 2 Timothy, and Hebrews. This last seems to be of a different character from the others. These Arguments, with modifications, are found in the Marianus and Würzburg and other texts of Paul, in St. Gall 73 (except Colossians), and in the Reichenau CXIX (except 1 and 2 Corinthians). To Galatians LA prefixes also another *argumentum*, from Jerome.

[70] *Cf.* pp. 661–4.

prefatory matter usual to Vulgate *evangeliaria* is inserted at the beginning of this section and before each separate gospel. At the end of Matthew is entered the collect for that saint's feast, on which day this page was written, and at the end of John are extracts from the *Moralia* of Gregory the Great, arranged in a geometrical design around the concluding lines of the evangelist. The text agrees in its general characteristics with those of the other manuscripts of the " Irish " family. It is worthy of note that it is an edited text, not a faithful copy of a single exemplar, and that the editing gives evidence of a knowledge, insight, and good judgment which redound to the credit of Fer-domnach, or, more probably, of his superviser, the abbot Torbach.[71] The redaction of the Acts of the Apostles [72] seems to have been removed by a considerable interval from that of the other sections, and probably was latest in date.[73] Also, it was derived from a different source. The other sections have few glosses: here they are comparatively numerous and sometimes of considerable length, are both marginal and interlinear, and are in Latin and Irish. Textually also the Armagh Acts are peculiar. The Vulgate is even purer than that of the Gospels; moreover, it is not disfigured by those many little unimportant variations which characterise the Irish family of Vulgate Gospels. But, on the other hand, the variations due to Old Latin influence are both more numerous and intrinsically more important than in the Gospels, and they come from a text of a different type.[74] Gwynn conjectured that the following was the process by which such a result was produced: " (1) A MS. of the Vulgate Acts in a substantially pure form; (2) enriched by a careful hand by the insertion on its margin of a large collection of Old-Latin additions or enlargements of the text as presented by the Vulgate; (3) transcribed by a copyist who endeavoured with imperfect skill to work these marginalia, or as many of them as he thought fit, into the body of his transcript. A copy produced by such a process, acquired by our scribe or the director of his work and carefully reproduced by him, would present just such a text." [75] It would seem that, while the other books of scripture were transcribed from, or given the form of, devotional or service books, this has retained the marks of its origin in the student's cell. If the conjecture as to date be correct, the more careless calligraphy, inferior editorship, and unusual character of the text may result from the removal of the guiding hand of the abbot Torbach.

475. Gospels of mac Durnan

MS: London, Lambeth Palace MS *s* IX/X. There are many descriptions of the illumination, and reproductions of pages, but there is little description of the text. FACS: *Cf.* Gougaud *RC* XXXV 419–20. EDS of O-I gloss: WS *Goidelica*[2] (1872) 54. — HZ *Glossae Hibernicae* (1881) pp. xxxiii, 264. — *Thes. Pal.* I (1901) pp. xxii, 484. COMM: Art and palaeography: J. H. Todd " Account of a MS of the four gospels in the

[71] The question of the use of Greek texts is interesting: Gwynn can find no substantial evidence of such use; on the other hand, H. J. White " cannot help thinking that it has been to a certain extent corrected from the Greek."

[72] Just before the Acts the MS has the heads of a homily on the promise of the coming of the Holy Ghost.

[73] Gwynn's conclusion that the delay was due to difficulty in obtaining an exemplar (*LA* p. cxxxii) does not seem well founded. That the first church of Ireland should, at the beginning of the ninth century, have to wait for a long period, probably several years, in order to obtain a copy of the Acts of the Apostles, is highly improbable.

[74] *Cf.* p. 628 *supra*. In the Gospels there is but little relationship between the Old Latin readings of LA and those of Codex Bezae, but in the Acts they show a marked resemblance to each other.

[75] *LA* p. ccxii.

library at Lambeth " *Proc. RIA* I (1836-40) 40-1. — S. W. Kershaw *Art treasures of the Lambeth Library* (London 1873) 27-9. — Middleton *Illuminated MSS in classical and mediaeval times* (Cambridge 1892). — Bruun *op. cit.* 65-7. — L. Gougaud " L'art celtique chrétien " *Rev. de l'art chrétien* 1911. Text: Berger *op. cit.* 43, 390. — H. J. Lawlor *Book of Mulling* 24. — Gregory *Textkritik* 642. General: AdeJ *Cat.* pp. xcvii *sqq.* — J. Armitage Robinson *The times of St. Dunstan* (Oxford 1923) 55-9.

SCRIPT: Irish minuscule — of *s* X, declared HZ, but this is not certain. The decoration, very rich and carefully executed, is Irish; it resembles the Book of Lindisfarne. If produced in the time of mac Durnan it is our latest example of the best Irish illuminating art.[76] CONTENTS: The four gospels, it would seem of the usual " Irish " mixed type. RECORD OF GIFT: On f. 3[v], by an English scribe, in rhythmical, alliterative Latin: " Maeielbrithus mac Durnan teaches this Gospel through the tripartite world in a manner worthy of God. But Aethelstan Anglo-Saxon king and ruler gives it to the metropolitan church of Canterbury for ever." This testifies that this Irish *evangeliarium* was donated to Christ Church, Canterbury, by the English king Athelstan (*c* 924-939), and at least implies that it had been associated with mac Durnan. We may guess that it was a gift from him to Athelstan. But there is no support for the usual assumption that mac Durnan was the scribe, or even that the codex was written in his time. — Máel-Brigte mac Tornáin, or Dornáin, who died, according to the Annals of Ulster, in 927, " at a happy old age," was the foremost clergyman of Ireland in his day — " head of the piety of all Ireland and of the greater part of Europe " he is called.[77] He was *comarba* of Patrick, apparently from the death of the abbot Máel-Coba in 888, and *comarba* of Colum-cille from 891, thus uniting in his own person the two most important dignities of the Irish Church. He was also *comarba* of Adamnán, that is, head of a group of churches founded by that saint, a kind of off-shoot of the Columban community. In 913 he went into Munster " to ransom a pilgrim of the Britons." [78] That he was a man of vigor may be inferred from the annalistic report of an event of 893. On Whitsunday there was a fight in the monastic city of Árd-Macha between the Cenél Eogain (rulers of the modern Inishowen and Tyrone) and the Ulaid (of Down). Máel-Brigte suppressed the disturbance, had four of the Ulaid hanged, and exacted a fine of 210 *cumals* [79] and other payments from each party.

476. The Psalter of Southampton

MS: Cambridge St. John's Coll. 59 *s* X/XI. FACS: *Cf.* Gougaud *RC* XXXV 416. EDS of Irish glosses: WS *Goidelica*[2] (1872) 58-60. — HZ *Glossae Hibernicae* (1881) pp. xviii *sq*, 209-12. — *Thes. Pal.* I (1901) pp. xiv, 4-6. COMM: *LH*[2] II 240. — R. L. Ramsay *ZCP* VIII (1912) 471 *sqq* [the Latin glosses and their relationship].

SCRIPT: Irish semi-uncial: HZ thought of *s* X *ex.*; with Irish illumination. CONTENTS: The psalter was either itself intended for liturgical use, or derived from such a source. It has the psalms divided into the three fifties according to Irish custom, and has the following canticles inserted after these several divisions: After the first division: F. 35[v] Riming prayer " Deus altissime rex angelorum " etc. [also in AB f. 25[v]]. [The

---

[76] An artist of the 13th or 14th century has added four illustrations of the life of Christ.
[77] FM.   [78] AU.
[79] The term originally signified a female slave. As a unit of exchange it came to be used as the equivalent of three cows.

Song of the three Children:] " Benedicite omnia opera . . . " (Dan. iii 57–88). F. 36ᵛ
Canticle of Jesus [son of Sirach]: " Confitebor tibi domine . . . " (Ecclesiasticus li).
F. 37 Canticle of Ezechiel: " Ego dixi in dimidio . . . " After the second division:
F. 69ᵛ Riming prayer " Deus quem exercitus canit angelorum " etc. [also in AB f. 26ᵛ].
Canticle of Anna, mother of Samuel: " Exultavit cor meum . . . " (I Kings or
I Samuel ii). F. 70 Canticle of Mary the sister of Moses [sic]: " Cantemus domino
gloriose . . . " (Exodus xv 1–19). F. 70ᵛ Canticle of Habacuc the prophet: " Domine
audiui . . . " (Habacuc iii). After the third division: F. 99ᵛ Riming prayer " Te
dominum de coelis laudamus " etc. [cf. AB II 24, 67]. [Canticle of Moses]: " Audite
caeli . . . " (Deut. xxxii 1–43). GLOSSES: In several hands: of the Irish, some seem
contemporary with the MS, others of considerable antiquity. The Latin glosses, much
more numerous, are derived, apparently, from the Old Irish treatise on the psalter
(no. 516), and reproduce many passages from the work on the psalm titles ascribed
to Bede.[80]

477. The Garland of Howth: *Codex Usserianus* II

MS: TCD 56 (A. 4. 6) s VIII/IX. FACS: J. H. Todd "Remarks on illuminations in
some Irish biblical MSS " Soc. of Antiq. of London: Vetusta Monumenta VI (1869).
Cf. Gougaud RC XXXIV 21–2. ED: H. C. Hoskier The text of Codex Usserianus 2
(London 1919). COLLATION: T. K. Abbott Evangeliorum versio antehieronymiana
(Dublin 1884) [quite imperfect; see Hoskier's ed.]. COMM: Berger op. cit. 42, 381.
— Robt. Cochrane " The ecclesiastical antiquities in the parish of Howth " Journ.
RSAI 5th ser. III (1893). — Hoskier Concerning the genesis of the versions of the New
Testament (1910–1) passim [used Abbott's collation].

SYMBOL: r 2. SCRIPT: Irish semi-uncial; Irish illumination: although fairly elabo-
rate, the ornamentation, compared with the better examples of Irish art, is crude.
Ff. 86. CONTENTS: The four gospels with many lacunae. TEXT: Old Latin, with
Vulgate modifications varying in amount in different parts. The Old Latin text is
very important: Hoskier has shown that it is practically the same as that of Codex
Bobbiensis (no. 451). HISTORY: This MS came to Trinity College with Archbishop
Ussher's library. Up to his time it had been kept in the island near Howth known
as Ireland's Eye, or Inis-mac-Nesáin.[81] Of its origin nothing is known.

478. Psalter (Vitellius F. xi)

MS: BM Cotton. Vitellius F. xi s X/XI. FACS: Cf. Gougaud RC XXXV 423–4.
COMM: Romilly Allen Proc. Soc. Antiq. Scotland XXXI 326.

SCRIPT: Irish semi-uncial. Irish illumination of debased type. Ff. 59, some illegible.
Badly damaged by the fire at Ashburnham House in 1731. CONTENTS: The psalms,
in the three fifties, with canticles and collects at the end of each division.

479. Psalter of St. Caimín

MS: Dublin Franciscan convent A 1 s XI ex. FACS: Facs. Nat. MSS. Ire. IV
pt. ii (1884) p. cxii, pl. xxi. EDS of Irish glosses: AdeJ Bibl. de l'École des chartes

---

[80] Cf. p. 666 infra. [81] Cf. Ussher Britannicarum ecclesiarum antiquitates cap. xvii: Whole Works VI 531.

XLVI (1885) 345; *RC* VII (1886) 96. — *Thes. Pal.* I (1901) pp. xiv, 6. — Gwynn *Ériu* IV (1910) 182. Comm: Hennessy *IER* IX (1873) 241–7. — Bruun *op. cit.* 83. — M. Esposito " On the so-called Psalter of St. Caimin " *Proc. RIA* XXXII (1915) C v 78–86.

Script: Irish semi-uncial (resembling that of Vat. Codex palatinus 65,[82] which was probably written in Scotland *s* XII/XIII) and, for the scholia, apparently by the same hand, minuscule. A good example of the later, and poorer, Irish script. Several illuminated capitals resembling those of the Psalter of Ricemarch. Ff. 6. Contents: An imperfect copy of that favorite psalm of the old Irish Church, *Beati immaculati*, no. cxviii (cix); doubtless the remnant of an once complete psalter. There are considerable marginal and interlinear scholia, drawn from older commentaries, and a few Irish glosses. History: The MS has a note by Michael O'Clery to the effect that he obtained it from Flann and Bernard Mac Bruaidedha,[83] or Mac Brody, of a family who dwelt in the *termonn* of St. Caimín, and from Diarmait O'Duibhceartaigh. The tradition received by them was that the book had been written by St. Caimín.

480. Psalter (Galba A. v)

MS: BM Cotton. Galba A. v *s* XII[1]. Facs: *Facs. Nat. MSS. Ire.* II p. xxiv, " Description " 39, pl. xlix.

Script: Irish minuscule, angular. Irish illumination. Writing and ornamentation late. Damaged by the fire in the Cottonian library in 1731. Contents: The psalms, divided into the three fifties, with canticles and collects after each division.

481. The Corpus Christi College Gospels

MS: Oxford Corpus Christi Coll. 122 after A.D. 1140. Facs: *Cf.* Gougaud *RC* XXXV 430. Comm: Berger *op. cit.* 43, 399. — J. Armitage Robinson *The times of St. Dunstan* (Oxford 1923) 69–71, 171–81 [with facs. of the *alea evangelii*, and text and paraphrase of description thereof].

Symbol: C (Bentley); CCC (Westcott). Script: Irish minuscule. Contents: The four gospels (missing is John i 1–33, vii 33–xviii 20), with the usual prefaces, Eusebian canons, and reference tables. Text is of the " Irish " type. On f. 5[V] there is a curious diagram known as the *Alea Evangelii*, or " Gospel Dice." This is a square table containing 324 small squares of equal size, divided by red lines, and having playing pieces marked thereon. There is an explanation of the diagram which, however, leaves the reader no wiser as to how the game was played. A note calls it the " Gospel dice which Dubinsi bishop of Bangor brought from the king of the English, that is, from the house of Athelstan of the English, drawn by a certain Frank and by a learned Roman, that is, an Israelite." Dubinnsi, bishop of Bangor, died, according to the Annals of Ulster, in 953, and Athelstan ruled in England from about 924 to 939. — There are one or more entries in Irish. History: The MS was presented to Corpus Christi College on April 23, 1619, by one of its fellows, Henry Parry. The family

---

[82] *Cf.* ZCP VIII 246 *sqq.*

[83] They were, it seems likely, the sons of the Connor Mac Brody whose testimonials are attached to the Martyrology of Donegal (*cf.* pp. 43, 485 *supra*) and to the Annals of the Four Masters.

probably had associations with Ireland: an Edward Parry was bishop of Killaloe, 1647–50, and friend of Sir James Ware.

482. Codex Harleianus 1023

MS: BM Harl. 1023 *s* XII. FACS: See Gougaud *RC* XXXV 425. ED: E. S. Buchanan *The Four Gospels from the Irish Codex Harleianus (Sacred Latin Texts* III) (London 1914). TRANS: Buchanan *The Four Gospels from the Latin Text of the Irish Codex Harleianus* (London 1914). *Cf. AB* II 40.

SCRIPT: Irish minuscule. CONTENTS: The four gospels, defective at the beginning of Matthew, with prefaces and other miscellaneous matter. The text is Vulgate, modified to a considerable extent by " Irish " readings.

483. The Gospels of Máel-Brigte

MS: BM Harl. 1802 A.D. 1138. FACS: *Cf.* Gougaud *RC* XXXV 425–6. Also *Recueil de facs. à l'usage de l'École des chartes* no. 351. EDS of Irish matter: W. Reeves *Proc. RIA* V 45–67 [paper read Jan. 13, 1851: contains text and trans. (by O'C) of many Irish verses and notes, not wholly accurate; also description of codex]. — WS " The Irish verses, notes and glosses in Harl. 1802 " *RC* VIII (1887) 346–69. COMM: Berger *op. cit.* 44, 287, 387. — Gregory *Textkritik* 644.

SYMBOL: Bentley's W. SCRIPT: Irish minuscule: very beautiful, especially that of the minute glosses. On a small slip introduced after f. 49 the scribe has added, in extremely small characters, the boast, in Irish: " Had I wished, I could have written the whole commentary like this." Ff. 156. CONTENTS: The four gospels, with the usual introductory matter; an extensive interlinear and marginal commentary, covering Matthew to chap. xxvii, and parts of Mark and Luke; and a considerable number of quatrains in Irish. The scriptural text is Vulgate, with some " Irish " modifications. The commentary, part of which seems to be of later date than the text, is said to be drawn from Origen, Cyprian, Eusebius, Jerome, Leo, Gregory, Gennadius, Priscian, Bede, Man[chén].[84] COLOPHON: A lengthy entry in Irish, which gives the scribe's name as Máel-Brigte húa Máel-Úanaigh, the place of writing as Armagh, and the date as 1138, and adds a list of the kings of the chief divisions of Ireland.[85] HISTORY: We know nothing further of the MS until the beginning of the 18th century, when it was in the royal library, Paris. Thence it was stolen by Jean Aymon, who carried it to Holland, where it was sold, about 1718, to Humphrey Wanley, agent of Robert Harley.

In the Bodleian Library, Oxford, there is a copy of the gospels — Rawlinson G. 167 *s* VIII — which is in large Insular majuscule.

[84] *Cf.* p. 276 *supra.*

[85] Other notes by the scribe indicate that he was writing in the twenty-eighth year of his age, and in the " second year after the great storm " (*cf.* ALC 1137), and that his tutor was Mac in-tacairt of Tuignetha (Tynan, near Armagh, where the family MacIntagairt were still established in the time of James I). He also asks favor for the soul of Máel-Issu, who was probably Máel-Issu Mac Máel-Coluim, " chief keeper of the calendar of Armagh, its chief antiquary and librarian," who died, according to FM, in 1136.

(c) BIBLICAL TEXTS WRITTEN BY IRISH SCRIBES ABROAD

484. Codex Ambrosianus I 61 sup.

MS: Milan Bibl. Ambrosiana I 61 sup. *s* VII. COMM: Berger *op. cit.* 58–9.

SCRIPT: Irish semi-uncial, a good script. Corrections in several hands, one of them Irish, another Merovingian cursive. CONTENTS: The four gospels. TEXT: " Irish" mixed type, but lacking some of the more noteworthy passages. The corrections are remarkable, containing many interesting Old Latin readings. PALIMPSEST: Ff. 90–1 are palimpsest leaves from a copy of the Gothic Bible of Ulphilas. From Bobbio — where the present MS was written — came many of our palimpsests.

485. Codex Taurinensis O. iv. 20

MS: Turin Bibl. nazionale O. iv. 20 *s* VIII. FACS: *Cf.* Gougaud *RC* XXXVIII 10–1. COMM: A. Kingsley Porter *op. cit.* 80.

An *evangeliarium* from Bobbio, and probably written in that monastery, which has rich Irish ornamentation.

486. Codex Sangallensis LI

MS: St. Gall Stiftsbibl. 51 *s* VIII/IX. FACS: *Cf.* Gougaud *RC* XXXVIII 12–3. COMM: On art and palaeography: F. Keller *op. cit.* [p. 98 *supra*]; also trans. by Reeves. — G. Scherrer *Verzeichniss d. Hss. d. Stiftsbibl. v. St. Gallen* (Halle 1875). — Jean Ebersolt " Miniatures irlandaises à sujets iconographiques " *Rev. archéol.* 5th ser. XIII (Jan.–March 1921) 1–6. — J. M. Clark *The Abbey of St Gall* (Cambridge 1926) 126 *sqq.* On text: Berger *op. cit.* 56, 416. — Gregory *Textkritik* 708.

SCRIPT: Irish semi-uncial; at the very end it changes to continental minuscule,[86] although having the appearance of being by the same hand. If this be the case, the MS was, almost certainly, written on the Continent,[87] for there is no trace of the use of continental script in Ireland at so early a date. It is, of course, possible that the book was carried from Ireland in an unfinished state. The ornamentation is Irish and very elaborate and beautiful. In both calligraphy and illumination this MS deserves to be ranked with the Books of Kells, Lindisfarne, Durrow, St. Chad, Mac Regol and Mac Durnan. CONTENTS: The four gospels, in a text of the "Irish" mixed family; Old Latin readings are particularly numerous in Matthew.

487. The Trèves Gospels

MS: Trèves Domschatzkammer 134 *s* VIII. FACS: *Cf.* Gougaud *RC* XXXVIII 4. COMM: Kugler *Kleine Schriften* II (Stuttgart 1854) 341. — Schnaase *Geschichte*

---

[86] *Cf. ZCP* IX 304.

[87] But perhaps not at St. Gall, for the volume is not mentioned among the " Libri Scottice scripti " of the ninth-century catalogue (p. 599 *supra*). This, however, is not conclusive proof.

der bildenden Künste III² (Düsseldorf 1896) 616 *sqq.* — Braun " Trierer Buchmalerei " *Westdeutsche Zs.* Supplementary vol. IX 65 *sqq.* — Beissel *op. cit.* 122-4.

SCRIPT: Lindsay: " Partly insular half-uncial, partly uncial. The scribes seem to pass from one script to the other. Some of the uncial resembles the thick Merovingian minuscule of the apparently contemporary marginalia and corrections. The illuminations have no Irish and no Anglosaxon features." [88] But Beissel, who should be well acquainted with the MS, declares it to be written by two scribes, a continental who wrote the introductory matter and the St. John, and an Irishman named Thomas to whom are due the other three gospels and the miniatures; and he places the date well on in the Carolingian ninth century, and thinks the place may have been Echternach. Others have guessed that the scribe Thomas was the abbot of that name who ruled Honau [89] 750-770. CONTENTS: The four gospels. The present writer has no information as to the type of text.

488. Codex Sangallensis X

MS: St. Gall Stiftsbibl. 10 *s* X. *Cf.* G. Scherrer *Verzeichniss d. Hss. d. Stiftsbibl. v. St. Gallen* (Halle 1875) 3.

This codex of 478 pages was written at St. Gall in the tenth, or possibly eleventh, century, apparently by an Irish scribe. It begins with a short hexameter poem by an Irishman named Dubduin.[9C] The remainder of the manuscript is occupied by the following books of the Old Testament: Job, Proverbs, Ecclesiastes, Canticle of Canticles, Wisdom, and Ecclesiasticus. Accompanying their respective books are the prologues of St. Jerome to Job, Proverbs, and Ecclesiasticus. Little information regarding it is available.

489. The Double Psalter of St. Ouen

MS: Rouen Bibl. publ. 24 *s* X. FACS: *Cf.* Gougaud *RC* XXXVIII 8. COMM: *Cat. gén. des mss. des bibl. des dép.* I (Paris 1886) 7. — Schultze *Centralblatt f. Bibliothekswesen* VI (1889) 292. — Berger *op. cit.* 51.

This codex is classed as an Irish manuscript of the tenth century. It contains the Psalter according to two of the versions of Jerome, the " Gallican " and the translation from the Hebrew. It formerly belonged to the church of St. Ouen, and at an earlier date to that of St. Evreult.

See also nos. 364 (iii), (iv), (v), (vi), 445.

[88] *Notae latinae* 488.
[89] *Cf.* p. 528 *supra.*
[90] *Cf.* no. 414.

490. Gospels of Lindisfarne: St. Cuthbert's Gospels: Book of Durham

MS: BM Cotton. Nero D. iv s VIII *in.* FACS: Very numerous: *cf.* Gougaud *RC* XXXV 421–3. Stanford F. N. Robinson *Celtic illuminative art in the Gospel Books of Durrow, Lindisfarne and Kells* (Dublin 1908). — *The Lindisfarne Gospels Three plates in colour and thirty-six in monochrome . . . with introduction by* E. G. Millar (BM: London 1923). COLLATION: Wordsworth and White *op. cit.* ED: Jos. Stevenson and Geo. Waring *op. cit.* [p. 641 *supra*]. COMM: Art and palaeography: Bruun *op. cit.* 48–60. — G. F. Warner *Illuminated MSS in the British Museum* (London 1903). — Beissel *op. cit.* III *sqq.* Text: Berger *op. cit.* 39–41, 385. — G. Morin *Rev. Bénédictine* Nov.-Dec. 1891 pp. 481 *sqq*, 529 *sqq* [liturgical aspects, and Italian and Byzantine relations]. — F. G. Kenyon *Our Bible and the ancient MSS* (London 1895); *Handbook to textual criticism of the New Testament* (London 1901; 2nd ed. 1912). — Gregory *Textkritik* 642. — Chapman *op. cit.* [p. 623 supra]. HISTORY: R. A. S. Macalister "The colophon in the Lindisfarne Gospels" *Essays and studies presented to William Ridgeway* (Cambridge 1913) 299–305 [argument for the Irish origin of the MS]. — G. Baldwin Brown *The arts in early England* V (1921) 337–41 [in opposition to Macalister].

SYMBOL: Y. SCRIPT: Insular semi-uncial; illumination is of the Irish type, of which, with the single exception of the Book of Kells, it is the most magnificent example in existence. It is, however, a purer specimen of that type than the Book of Kells, which contains certain late or extraneous elements. Lindsay finds in the abbreviations some features which he considers English rather than Irish. CONTENTS: The four gospels with the usual preliminary matter of Vulgate copies — the epistle to Damasus, prefaces, Eusebian canons, arguments and *capitula*. In addition, there are lists of feasts prefixed to the gospels giving the particular texts to be read on each; these lists seem to be derived from the liturgy of the church of Naples about the beginning of the seventh century. It is an obvious inference that the exemplar of the Gospels of Lindisfarne was a MS that came from Naples or its vicinity. TEXT: Vulgate, a very pure text; resembles the English Codex Amiatinus and the Irish Book of Durrow. There are, however, some variations, chiefly, it would seem, from a text of the type of Codex Claromontanus (no. 452). In the tenth century a priest named Aldred added an Anglo-Saxon version as an interlinear gloss, which he did not scruple to write across the finest illuminated pages. It gives the MS a linguistic value similar to that of the Gospels of Mac Regol. COLOPHON and HISTORY: " Eadfrith, bishop of the church of Lindisfarne, first wrote this book for God and St. Cuthbert and all the saints in general who are in the island. And Ethiluald, bishop of the people of Lindisfarne, bound and covered it on the outside, as he well knew how to do. And Billfrith, the hermit, worked the ornaments of metal that are on it outside . . . and Aldred, an unworthy and very wretched priest, with God's help and St. Cuthbert's, glossed it in English. . . . Eadfrith, Oethiluald, Billfrith, Aldred made this gospel book for God and Cuthbert, and adorned it." Eadfrith was bishop of Lindisfarne from 698 to 721, Ethilwald from 724 to 740. This story of their partnership in producing the codex represents the traditions of two hundred years or so later, after vicissitudes which must have been very damaging to the historical records and memory of the community of Lindisfarne. The monastery there was pillaged by the Vikings in 793, and the inmates slaughtered. Through the next three-quarters of a century of Norse terror Lindisfarne church maintained a precarious existence; about 878 it was abandoned by the remnant of the monks, who, according to a curious story, attempted to flee to Ireland, lost the " Gospels of St. Cuthbert " in the sea, recovered the book miraculously after four days,[91] and finally found refuge in the north of England. Of the fortunes of the book during the next hundred years we know nothing; it was at Durham at the end of the tenth century, and was returned to Lindisfarne towards the end of the eleventh. Of Aldred and his relations with Lindisfarne there is no information. COMMENT: The majority of critics have accepted the statements of the colophon, and have pointed out that Hadrian, who had been abbot of a monastery on the island of Nisita in the Bay of Naples, seems to have visited Lindisfarne with Archbishop Theodore, and may have left there a Neapolitan *evangeliarium*. On the other hand Macalister calls attention to the weakness of the tradition and the improbability that English scribes, pupils of the Irish, and pupils who had some time before repudiated their teachers, should have, in this single case, brought Irish art to its highest development some one hundred years before the date at which, as is to be inferred from the available evidence, it attained a similar stage in Ireland, and emphatically declares that Eadfrith not only did not write, but never even saw, the Book of Lindisfarne.

491. The Gospels of St. Boniface

MS: Fulda Landesbibl. Cod. Bonifatianus III *s* VIII. FACS: *Cf.* Gougaud *RC* XXXVIII 2. COMM: Carl Scherer *Die Codices Bonifatiani in der Landesbibl. zu Fulda* (Fulda 1905). — W. M. Lindsay *Early Irish minuscule script* (Oxford 1910) 4–12; " Irish cursive script " *ZCP* IX (1913) 301–8; *Proc. RIA* XXXIII (1916) C 399 n. 2. — KM *ZCP* VIII (1912) 173–5 [the Irish glosses].

SCRIPT: Insular — apparently Irish — cursive; it might be Cornish, of which little is known. Some pages show fantastic arrangements of text and variations of script such as were occasionally indulged in by Irish scribes. Abbreviations are in general Irish, but Lindsay considers two or three to be Welsh or English. The miniatures are of poor execution, but of Irish type, and the vellum is of the coarse kind found usually in Irish MSS. Ff. 65. CONTENTS: The four gospels. There are a few O-I glosses in the original hand, but apparently copied from the exemplar. One has a form which has been considered not older than the ninth century. COLOPHON AND NOTE: At the end, written continuously with the text and without any distinction from it: " Amen. I give thanks to God. Cadmug wrote it." It, too, was probably copied from the exemplar. Cad-mug was a not uncommon O-I name. On the last leaf is a note in golden Carolingian minuscules to the effect that Abbot Huoggi of Fulda (elected 891) obtained from King Arnulf [92] (d. 899) the restitution of this MS, which St. Boniface " as we have learned from the report of our elders, wrote with his own hands." COMM: Boniface was born at Crediton and studied as a youth at Adescancastre (Exeter?). It is not impossible that he made this copy of an Irish *evangeliarium* at this time,

[91] Symeon of Durham *History of the Church of Durham* II xii.
[92] *Cf.* p. 554 *supra*.

although the script differs much from other alleged examples of his writings. Or the book may have been written by a Cornish or an Irish scribe, and afterwards came into Boniface's possession. But no hypothesis fully satisfies the conditions.

492. Codex Beneventanus

MS: BM Addit. 5463 s VIII *med.* FACS: Palaeog. Soc. 1st ser. pl. 236. COMM: Berger *op. cit.* 91 *sq.* — Scrivener and Miller *op. cit.* II 77. — Lawlor *Book of Mulling* 26 n.

SYMBOL: Bentley's F, Wordsworth's ჇF. SCRIPT: Uncial, with Beneventan minuscule additions and corrections. CONTENTS: The four gospels, in a text closely resembling those of Irish origin. HISTORY: It formerly belonged to the monastery of St. Peter at Beneventum. On the strength of an inscription which it contains it has usually been regarded as written for Ato, abbot of S. Vincenzo al Volturno, near Beneventum, 739–760. However, Berger thought that it was written in Gaul.

493. Codex Paulinus Wirziburgensis II

MS: Würzburg Universitätsbibl. M. p. th. f. 69 s VIII². COMM: Oegg *Korographie von Würzburg* 391. — Schepps *op. cit.* [p. 636 *supra*] 37. — Berger *op. cit.* 54. — *ZCP* VI 543 n.

SCRIPT: Minuscule; the beginning of each epistle is in uncial, with Greek letters occasionally substituted for Roman. English, but showing Irish influence in both script and illumination. Ff. 60. CONTENTS: The Pauline epistles. It is to be expected that the text also contains an Irish element, but our knowledge of the Irish features of these epistles is not great.

494. The Gospels of St. Gatien

MS: BN nouv. acq. lat. 1587 s VIII/IX. FACS: *Cf.* Gougaud *RC* XXXVIII 7. ED: J. M. Heer. COLLATION: Wordsworth and White *op. cit.* — *LA* pp. cxliv *sqq* [partial]. COMM: Berger *op. cit.* 46–7, 410. — Hoskier *op. cit.* I 436 and *passim.*

SYMBOL: gat. SCRIPT: " In rude imitation of Insular half-uncial " (Lindsay). Ff. 109. CONTENTS: The four gospels. TEXT: Closely related to the " Irish " mixed type — so closely that it may, with caution, be accepted as a witness thereto. COLOPHON: In a mixture of Latin and debased Greek gives the scribe's name as Holcundus. HISTORY: Belonged to St. Gatien's, Tours, and may have been written at Tours.

495. The Codex Bigotianus

MS: BN 281 and 298 s VIII *ex.* FACS: Delisle *Le cabinet des mss.* III pl. x 1, 2, p. 214. COLLATION: Wordsworth and White *op. cit.* COMM: Berger *op. cit.* 50, 403. — Scrivener and Miller *op. cit.* II 80. — Gregory *Textkritik* 682.

SYMBOL: B or big. SCRIPT: Uncial; shows Irish influence, and much more so does the ornamentation. Ff. 216 and 49. CONTENTS: The four gospels in a text having strongly Irish affinities. HISTORY: In the fifteenth century it belonged to the abbey of Fécamp, on the English Channel.

496. The Gospels of Marmoutier

MS: BM Egerton 609 s IX *in.* COLLATION: Wordsworth and White *op. cit.* — *LA* pp. cxxxviii *sqq* [partial]. COMM: Delisle *Notices et extraits des mss. de la bibl. nat.* XXXI i 178. — Berger *op. cit.* 47, 388.

SYMBOL: E and mm. SCRIPT: Continental minuscule; the ornamentation shows Irish influence, but is of a somewhat grotesque type. Ff. 102. CONTENTS: The four gospels (with *lacunae*, Matthew xv (in part), Mark vii–end, Luke i–vii 23) in a text closely related to the "Irish" family. HISTORY: The codex came from the abbey of Marmoutier at Tours. It is probable that it was copied from an Irish book.

497. The Gospels of St. Martin

MS: Tours Bibl. publ. 22 s IX. FACS: *Nouveau traité de diplomatique* III 50, 161, pls. xxxv, xlv. COLLATION: Wordsworth and White *op. cit.* — *LA* pp. cxliv [partial]. COMM: L. Delisle *Mémoire sur l'école calligraphique de Tours au IXe siècle* (Paris 1885). — Berger *op. cit.* 47–8, 420.

SYMBOL: MT, mt, mrt. SCRIPT: Carolingian uncials, in gold. Ff. 279. CONTENTS: The four gospels, in a text resembling those of Marmoutier and St. Gatien and closely related to the "Irish" family, although probably not copied at first hand from an Irish exemplar. HISTORY: It was, almost certainly, a product of the school of calligraphy which Alcuin established at Tours about A.D. 800, and the scribe was probably English or Irish. It was the volume on which the kings and princes of France took the oath as canons of the church of St. Martin of Tours.

498. The Confraternity Book of Pfäffers: *Liber Confraternitatum Fabariensis*

MS: St. Gall Stiftsarchiv 1 s IX *in.* COMM: Berger *op. cit.* 57–8, 419. — Beissel *op. cit.* 127. The confraternity entries have been published by A. Birlinger, *Alemannia* IX 57–71; and by P. Piper *MGH Libri confrat.* (1884) 358–94.

SYMBOL: fab. SCRIPT: Continental; sometimes designated "Rheto-Roman." The ornamentation is a curious mixture of Irish and native designs. CONTENTS: This was a copy of the gospels, on the blank pages of which the confraternity records [93] of the monastery of Pfäffers were entered. The earliest seems to be of about 830, and it is probable that the gospels were written before this. It is stated that the text is purely of the "Irish" type. Pfäffers, in eastern Switzerland, south of St. Gall and not far from the upper Rhine, was an independent abbey till about 891 x 920, when it passed under the jurisdiction of St. Gall. We do not know of it as specially a resort for Irish "pilgrims," but this whole region was permeated by Irish influences in the eighth and ninth centuries.[94]

[93] *Cf.* p. 599 *supra.*   [94] *Cf.* pp. 511 *sqq supra.*

499. Codex Sangermanensis 86

MS: BN lat. 11553 s IX *in.* ED: Wordsworth *Old Latin Biblical Texts* I (Oxford 1883) [St. Matthew only]. COLLATION: Wordsworth and White *op. cit.* COMM: Berger *op. cit.* 65–72. — Scrivener and Miller *op. cit.* II 47, 69–70. — Lawlor *Book of Mulling* 25–6.

SYMBOL: *g* 1 [for Matthew], G [remaining gospels]. SCRIPT: Continental. CONTENTS: New Testament. TEXT: Usually given as being Old Latin in Matthew, Vulgate with Old Latin admixture in the other gospels. Hoskier (*op. cit.* I 115) claims that the basis is Old Latin throughout, with close affinities to the Codex Claromontanus (no. 452). HISTORY: According to Berger, it came from the neighborhood of Lyons. Later it was in the monastery of St. Germain-des-Prés, where it was first numbered 15 and later 86.

500. Codex Paulinus Augiensis

MS: Cambridge Trin. Coll. B. 17. 1 s IX. ED: F. H. Scrivener *An exact transcript of the Codex Augiensis* (Cambridge and London 1859). COMM: Scrivener and Miller *op. cit.* I 177–82.

SYMBOLS: For Greek, F paul.; for Latin, f. SCRIPT: Greek, uncial; Latin, continental minuscule. Abbreviations and orthography show some traces of insular influence. The scribe of the prototype was probably Irish or English. Ff. 136 of two columns each page, the inner having the Greek, the outer the Latin. CONTENTS: The Pauline Epistles in parallel texts, Greek and Latin; imperfect at the beginning, both texts opening at Romans iii 19; at the end the Greek breaks off at Philemon 20, while the Latin continues to the conclusion of Hebrews. Evidently the Greek exemplar — which, however, may never have included Hebrews — was incomplete; it contained three considerable *hiatus* at which, in this MS, the Greek column is left blank while the Latin runs on continuously. There are some interlinear Latin glosses inserted in the Greek text. TEXT: The Greek text is so closely related to that of *Codex Boernerianus* (no. 364 vi) that it seems probable they were copied from the same *Vorlage.* The interlinear glosses, too, come from the Latin of *Codex Boernerianus* or its prototype. But the Latin text of *Codex Augiensis* is entirely independent. It is Vulgate, with a mixture of Old Latin and many peculiarities; also with, apparently, a few modifications due to the accompanying Greek, and some slight traces of Irish influence. HISTORY: The MS belonged to Reichenau. Whether or not it had Irish antecedents, it must have been linked with the history of the *Codex Boernerianus* and, in general, with that of Irish biblical influences in Europe.

501. Codex Augiensis CCXI

MS: Carlsruhe Landesbibl. Cod. Augiensis ccxi s IX *ex.* COMM: Berger *op. cit.* 56, 383.

SCRIPT: Continental. Ff. 169. CONTENTS: The four gospels, with introductory matter, (imperfect at beginning and end), in a Vulgate text with many Irish readings. It is a Reichenau MS.

502. The Book of Deer

MS: Cambridge Univ. Lib. I. i. 6. 32 *s* IX/X. Facs: *Cf.* Gougaud *RC* XXXV 416–7. Ed: John Stuart *The Book of Deer* (Spalding Club: Edinburgh 1869). Eds of Gaelic passages: WS *Goidelica*[2] 106–11. — *Thes. Pal.* II pp. xxix *sq*, 257. Comm: Scrivener and Miller *op. cit.* II 77. — F. O. Russell " The Book of Deer " *Celtia* Mar. 1901. — Gregory *Textkritik* 639.

Contents: Ff. 86, imperfect. Contains Matt. i 1–vii 23; Mark i 1–v 36; Luke i 1–iv 12; John complete. Also a fragment of an office for the visitation of the sick. In the 12th century there were added, in Gaelic, the legend of the foundation of the monastery of Deer, and the records of certain grants and a charter. Text of gospels: Vulgate, but with many old and peculiar readings. History: This book belonged to the monastery of Deer in Aberdeenshire, which, according to tradition, was founded by St. Columba, who placed over it St. Drostan. It was the last of the Columban institutions to survive in Scotland. In 1697 the Book of Deer was in the possession of Bishop Moore, of Norwich and Ely, and with the rest of his library was purchased in 1715 for the University of Cambridge.

503. The Angers Gospels

MS: Angers Bibl. pub. 20 *s* IX/X. Comm: Berger *op. cit.* 48–9, 375.

Script: Continental. The decoration shows Irish influence. It was written by a French or, possibly, Breton, scribe. Ff. 125. Contents: The four gospels in a text showing evidences of an at least partial Irish ancestry. It seems to be of the same general character as that of the Tours group of MSS and the *Codex Bigotianus*.

504. The Gospels of Athelstan

MS: BM Reg. I. A. xviii *s* X *in.* Comm: E. M. Thompson *Catalogue of ancient MSS in the British Museum* (London 1884) 37. — Berger *op. cit.* 49–50, 386.

Script: Continental. There are some traces of Irish ornamentation. Ff. 199 (193–9 belong to another *evangeliarium* of about the same age as the bulk of the MS). Contents: The four gospels in a text resembling the Tours group of codices (pp. 653–4 *supra*) and having Irish characteristics. Note: In English script, perhaps of the 13th century: states that the book was given by King Athelstan (reigned 924–39) to the church of St. Augustine at Canterbury.

505. *Codex Laud. latinus* 102

MS: Bodl. Laud. lat. 102 *s* X *in.* Comm: Berger *op. cit.* 54–5, 398.

Symbol: laud. Script: English — possibly Irish — minuscule. Ff. 210. Contents: The four gospels, in a composite text, showing some Irish influence. There are entries by a second hand, also of the tenth century, in which the Irish element is more pronounced than in the primary text. History: It was a Würzburg MS, one of those which Archbishop Laud had purchased and removed to England when, in 1631, the Swedes captured that city from the Imperial forces.

506. *Codex Sangermanensis* 1199

MS: BN lat. 13169 (St. Germain 1199) *s* X. COMM: Berger *op. cit.* 48, 408–9. — Scrivener and Miller *op. cit.* II 47. — Gregory *Textkritik* 604.

SYMBOL: *g2.* SCRIPT: Continental minuscule; some traces of Irish influence in its ornamentation. Ff. 116. CONTENTS: The gospels. TEXT: Old Latin and Vulgate; appears to have some Irish elements. HISTORY: In the 12th century or earlier was at Le Mans, and at a still earlier date seems to have been at Angers.

507. *Codex latinus Monacensis* 9545

MS: Munich Staatsbibl. 9545 *s* X ff. 1–76. ED of glosses, and COMM: S. Hellmann *Sedulius Scottus* (Munich 1906) 186–90.

This MS of the Pauline and Catholic Epistles was transcribed on the Continent but, it is thought, descends from an Irish text. It contains the arguments of Pelagius and, in the interlinear notes, extracts from his commentary. The codex formerly belonged to Altaich, with which we do not hear of Irish associations; but Hellmann suggests that the original came from Würzburg, where Gozbald, abbot of Altaich, was bishop 842–55.

508. The Psalter of Ricemarch

MS: TCD 50 (A. 4. 20) *s* XI. FACS: *Cf.* Gougaud *RC* XXXIV 22–3. ED: H. J. Lawlor *The Psalter and Martyrology of Ricemarch* 2 vols. (Henry Bradshaw Soc.: London 1914). COMM: J. O. Westwood " Notice on a MS of the Latin psalter written by John brother of Rhyddmarch " *Archaeologia Cambrensis* I (1846). — Bruun *op. cit.* 82–3. — W. M. Lindsay *Early Welsh script* (Oxford 1912).

SCRIPT: Minuscule of Irish appearance. The decoration is also of the later type of Irish illumination. Ff. 158. CONTENTS: The psalms in the Vulgate text, divided into the three fifties, but without canticles or collects. Also a martyrology and other pieces in Latin. COLOPHON: At the end are verses giving the names of those employed in writing and decorating the volume: among them are Ricemarch and John, sons of Sulgen. Ricemarch is identified with the bishop of St. David's who succeeded his father Sulgen in 1089 and died in 1096. He has been already mentioned as author of a Life of St. David.[95] The family of Sulgen is known to have had close relations with Ireland. It is probable that this psalter is the copy of an Irish exemplar.

509. The Balliol Epistles of St. Paul

MS: Oxford Balliol Coll. Lib. 157 (arch. E. 5. 2) *s* XV *med.* *Cf. Theologische Literaturzeitung* XXVIII xiv (5 July 1913) 442. COMM: Alex. Souter " The character and history of Pelagius' Commentary on the Epistles of St. Paul " *Proc. Brit. Acad.* VII (1916); *Pelagius' Expositions of thirteen Epistles of St. Paul* I, II (Cambridge 1923–6).

SYMBOL: *ball.* SCRIPT: Italian minuscule: appears to be copied from an early MS in insular script, probably Irish and not later than the 9th century. It is a reasonable

[95] *Cf.* no. 35.

inference that this came from Bobbio, but whether written there or in Ireland is not determined. CONTENTS (of portion here considered): The Pauline epistles, in an Old Latin text resembling LA, with the uninterpolated commentary by Pelagius, here attributed to Jerome.[96]

Several other biblical MSS have been classed as Irish: Würzburg Universitätsbibl. Mp.th.q.1a s VII has been identified — the evidence is only for modern times — with a gospel book which, according to tradition, was taken from the tomb of St. Killian. There seems to be no good reason for supposing that the MS had any association either with Killian or with Ireland. (Cf. Berger op. cit. 54; Beissel op. cit. 120.) — Milan Bibl. Ambrosiana E 53 inf. s VIII x X and E 26 inf. s IX/X each contains remnants of a bible. They were Bobbio MSS, but perhaps not of Irish association. (Cf. Scrivener and Miller op. cit. II 71; Gregory Textkritik 716; Beissel op. cit. 129.) — The very fine " Second Bible of Charles the Bald ": BN 2, written c 870 x 873, was, according to some, the work, at least in part, of an Irish scribe. (Cf. no. 423 ii; Berger op. cit. 287, 399; Traube MGH Poet. lat. aevi Carol. III 242, 700; also Scrivener and Miller op. cit. II 68 and references there given.) Textually, however, it springs from the revision of the Vulgate made by Theodulf of Orleans (no. 342). — The following codices are either certainly, or probably, English, but showing Irish influence in decoration, script or text. Several of them have, however, been classed by some investigators as Irish: The "Gospels of St. Augustine": Bodl. Auct. D. II. 14 (Bodley 857) s VII (bodl. and O), formerly of Canterbury, and regarded as having been brought there by St. Augustine, but certainly written in England, and showing some slight Irish elements. (Cf. Berger op. cit. 35; Scrivener and Miller op. cit. II 79; Gregory Textkritik 654; Beissel op. cit. 90.) — Durham Cathedral Lib. A. II. 16 and A. II. 17, s VIII, evangeliaria, the second incomplete. The ornamentation of one resembles that of the Gospels of Lindisfarne, and both have Irish features. (Cf. Gregory Textkritik 640; Beissel op. cit. 115; Gougaud RC XXXV 418). — Maaseik (Belgium) Église Ste. Catherine MS s VIII[1], an evangeliarium said to have been written in 728. (Cf. Gougaud RC XXXVIII 6.) — Cambridge Corpus Christi Coll. 197 s VIII: part of Luke and John; has Irish textual elements. (ÉD. of John: J. Goodwin Pub. Cambridge Antiq. Soc. XIII (1847). Cf. Gregory Textkritik 646; Beissel op. cit. 91.) — The "Selden Acts": Bodl. Selden supra 30 (3418) s VIII first half, (O₂): an English copy of the Acts of the Apostles in a text showing some relationship with that of LA. — The " Psalter of St. Salaberga ": Berlin Staatsbibl. Hamilton Collection 553 s VIII[1] contains the psalms, Nicene Creed and certain canticles. The script and ornamentation, which are well executed, may be English or Irish. In the 17th century the book was in the monastery of St. John at Laon, and was believed to have belonged to the foundress, St. Salaberga (cf. p. 209 supra). This is hardly possible. (Cf. Wattenbach NA VIII 241; Stern ZCP III 444–6; Gougaud RC XXXVIII 2; Lindsay Notae Latinae 446.) — The " Gospels of Canterbury ": BM Reg. 1. E. vi s VIII ex. (Bentley's P), an imperfect copy of the gospels from the monastery of St. Augustine, Canterbury, which was formerly looked upon as the property of that saint, part of a bible given him by Gregory the Great. It is an English MS of much later date: the text has some Irish readings and the ornamentation a mixture of Irish and Italian motifs. (Cf. Scrivener and Miller op. cit. II 75–6; Gregory

[96] Cf. pp. 661–4 infra.

Textkritik 646; Beissel *op. cit.* 130 *sqq.*) — Essen Münsterkirchenschatz MS *s* VIII/IX, an *evangeliarium* which has in its ornamentation a curious mixture of Irish and English with Visigothic, Langobard and Frankish *motifs.* (*Cf.* Beissel *op. cit.* 161; Gougaud *RC* XXXVIII 2.) — Vat. Barberini lat. 570 *s* VIII is an *evangeliarium.* (*Cf.* Gougaud *RC* XXXVIII 10). — BM Harl. 1772 *s* VIII/IX (Z₂ and hrl) is a copy of the Epistles and Apocalypse, written probably in northern England, although Berger thought it was French. The decoration shows considerable Irish influence, and the text, which is related also to those of Codex Amiatinus and Codex Fuldensis, may have similar associations. (ED: E. S. Buchanan *The Epistles and Apocalypse from the Codex Harleianus (Sacred Latin Texts* I) (London 1912). *Cf.* Berger *op. cit.* 50.) — Berne Stadtbibl. 671 *s* IX/X is an *evangeliarium* in 78 ff. which has been usually classed in both script and text as Irish, but which Lindsay considers to be Cornish. (*Cf.* Berger *op. cit.* 56-7, 377-8; Lindsay *Notae Latinae* 448.)

Many liturgical documents contain short scriptural extracts, some of which have value for biblical textual criticism. *Cf.* pp. 689 *sqq infra.*

II. Books of the Monastic Schools

Bibliography

See preceding section. Also, or especially: *Thes. Pal.* — Roger *L'Enseignement.* — Manitius *Lat. Lit.* — Lindsay *Early Irish minuscule script* and *Notae Latinae* [*cf.* pp 97-8 *supra*]. — Gougaud *Les Chrétientés celtiques* [p. 107 *supra*]. — Sir John E. Sandys *A history of classical scholarship* I 3rd ed. (Cambridge 1921).

Holy Writ, it has been said, was the main subject of study in the Irish monastic schools and the main object of reproduction in the *scriptoria.* Its importance has demanded that a section, the preceding, should be devoted to the Irish copies of biblical texts and to the evidences of their distribution and influence in other lands. In the present section consideration will be given to the remaining literature of the schools — which, indeed, for the most part, gathers around the study of the bible and has its different parts more or less closely linked together. This literature includes the works of the Fathers of the Church and other early Christian writers, commentaries on the Scriptures derived more or less directly from those writers, other compositions of Irish moralists and exegetes, text-books on the Latin and Greek languages and literatures and commentaries on the text-books, and geographical, historical and computistical treatises. It might seem that a sharp division should be made between the personal compositions of the Irish teachers and the copies which they used of patristic and other foreign writings. But actually the works of Irish origin are so largely extracted from or based on the others that the line of division is not very clear. Some of the Irish compositions have been noticed above when a survey was being made of the records of the early " Celtic " Church.[97]

Those older Christian writings which were known and studied in Ireland are revealed to us also in part by allusions, extracts, or adaptations in other branches of Irish Christian literature, such as the canonical and penitential collections and the devotional compositions. But we have not the help of the catalogues of monastic libraries which are so important for the study of the intellectual life of continental Europe. No Irish monastic catalogue has survived, and the lists of " libri scottice scripti " in European libraries [98] are, of course, quite limited.

(a) BIBLICAL COMMENTARIES: COMMENTARIES ON THE GOSPELS

510. Turin fragment of Commentary on Matthew

MS: Turin Bibl. nazionale F. vi. 2 (no. 4) s IX [from Bobbio]. EDS of O-I gloss: WS Goidelica[2] (1872) 2; " Glosses from Turin and the Vatican 1 Old-Irish " Academy XXXVII (Jan. 18, 1890) 46–7; " Glosses from Turin and Rome 1 The Old-Irish glosses in Turin " Beiträge z. Kunde d. indogerm. Sprachen XVII (1891) 134. — Br. Güterbock " Aus irischen Hss. in Turin u. Rome" Zs. f. vergl. Sprachforschung XXXIII (1893) 86. — Thes. Pal. I pp. xxi, 484.

A single folio, in Irish minuscule, from a Commentary on St. Matthew. The extant portion treats of chap. xxvii. There is one Irish gloss.

511. Turin fragments of Commentary on Mark

MS: Turin Bibl. nazionale F. IV. 1 (no. 7) s IX. Cf. A. Peyron Ciceronis fragmenta inedita I (Stuttgart and Tübingen 1824) 192. EDS: WS Goidilica (1866); 2nd ed. (1872) 54. — Constantino Nigra Glossae hibernicae veteres Codicis Taurinensis (Paris 1869) [text and glosses, with extensive introduction and notes, chiefly of linguistic interest; cf. H. Ebel Beiträge z. vergl. Sprachforschung VI (1870) 234–7]. — HZ Glossae Hibernicae (Berlin 1881) pp. xvii sq, 199–208. — Thes. Pal. I (1901) pp. xxii, 484–94 [with trans. of O-I glosses; cf. Supplement (1910) 35].

Two small folia written in Irish minuscule script, which he, in accordance with the usage of the time, called Saxon, were discovered by the classical scholar Peyron among some Bobbio manuscripts and placed by him in the library of the university of Turin. This little codex has been found to contain one of the important collections of Old Irish glosses. The main text was a commentary on the Gospel of Mark, which has been ascribed to St. Jerome,[99] but only two small fragments survive on these pages:

[97] Chap. iii.   [98] Cf. pp. 516, 599, 620 supra.
[99] Jerome's authorship is denied by Vallarsi, probably rightly.

i 1-7, xiv 52-xvi 22. The glosses were quite extensive, partly in Latin but mainly in Irish. Text and glosses are in different hands, both Irish, of the early ninth or possibly eighth century. On linguistic grounds the Irish glosses are considered to be of about the same age as those of the famous Milan collection.[100] Whether the codex was brought to Bobbio from Ireland, or written in Bobbio or some other continental monastery, has not been determined.

512. Commentary on Luke

MS: Milan Bibl. Ambrosiana H. 78 sup. + Turin Bibl. naz. G. v. 15 s VI. FACS: *Palaeographical Soc. facs.* pl. 137.

This copy of a commentary by St. Ambrose on the Gospel of Luke is said to be in early Irish minuscule, possibly of the seventh century. Perhaps it was written at Bobbio.

Sedulius Scottus and Johannes Eriugena: see pp. 565, 586.

(b) COMMENTARIES ON THE EPISTLES OF ST. PAUL — THE COMMENTARY OF PELAGIUS

Bibliography

Cf. no. 26. HZ *Pelagius in Irland Texte und Untersuchungen zur patristischen Litteratur* (Berlin 1901) [*cf.* C. H. Turner *JTS* Oct. 1902 pp. 132-41]. — Ed. Riggenbach " Unbeachtet gebliebene Fragmente des Pelagius-Kommentars zu den Paulinischen Briefen" *Beiträge zur Förderung christlicher Theologie* IX i (Gütersloh 1905). — S. Hellmann *Sedulius Scottus* (Munich 1906) 147 *sqq* [*cf.* p. 553 *supra*]. — Alex. Souter *JTS* July 1906; " The Commentary of Pelagius on the Epistles of Paul: the problem of its restoration " *Proc. Brit. Acad.* 1905-6 pp. 409-39. — *JTS* VIII (1906-7) 526-36. — Souter " The character and history of Pelagius' Commentary on the Epistles of St. Paul " *Proc. Brit. Acad.* VII (1916). — G. Morin " Fragments pélagiens inédits du ms. 954 de Vienne " *Rev. bénédictine* XXXIV (1922) 265-75. — Souter *Pelagius' Expositions of thirteen Epistles of St. Paul* I *Introduction* (Cambridge 1922), II *Text*, etc. (1926) [*cf.* *RHE* XIX (1923) 556-9]. — H. J. Chapman " Pélage et le texte de s. Paul " *RHE* XVIII (1922) 469-81, XIX (1923) 25-42.

It has been seen that, in the eighth-century Irish *Codex Paulinus Wirziburgensis*,[101] the patristic authorities drawn on for the glosses to the epistles of St. Paul were Origen (in the translation by Rufinus), the so-called " Ambrosiaster " [102] (whom the Irish knew as Hilary), Jerome, Augustine, Cassiodorus, Gregory the Great, Isidore (slightly), and, above

---

[100] Pp. 202-3.   [101] No. 461.
[102] *Cf.* Alex. Souter *A study of Ambrosiaster* (Cambridge 1905); *The Expositor* 8th ser. VII (London 1914) 224-32.

all, the heretic Pelagius. This interesting preference for the work of Pelagius is indicated by the other available sources.

Of the career of Pelagius and of the certainty that he was of insular, and the possibility that he was of Irish origin, something has already been said.[103] His Commentary on the Epistles of St. Paul was written before A.D. 410, and was not seriously anti-orthodox except in one passage.[104] It seems to have circulated in anonymous copies, if not from the time of composition at least from a very early date. One of these anonymous copies was in the library which the Italian statesman Cassiodorus placed in the monastery he founded at Vivarium in southern Italy before 540, and was revised by him and his monks. The revision, it seems certain, is the same as a text published in 1537 as the work of a certain Primasius, and now commonly designated Pseudo-Primasius. Apparently in the same sixth century some unknown student took another anonymous copy of the Pelagian commentary, added considerable matter to it, and issued it under the name of St. Jerome. It is now designated Pseudo-Jerome. By additions and modifications Pseudo-Jerome developed into two chief versions and several minor variations; insular redactors played a considerable part in its history, but, seemingly, the majority of them were Welsh or English rather than Irish. Throughout the middle ages Pseudo-Primasius, Pseudo-Jerome, and even the original Pelagius survived, but it was chiefly if not exclusively the Irish who preserved the knowledge that the primary author was Pelagius. He is quoted by name not only by the *Codex Paulinus Wirziburgensis* but also by the *Hibernensis* collection of canons, the Book of Armagh, Smaragdus of St. Mihiel, Sedulius Scottus and Marianus Scottus.[105]

Heinrich Zimmer was led by the many Irish associations of the Pelagian text to publish an extensive study in which he advanced the theory that Pelagius, an Irishman, had sent his commentary to his homeland and that there only it had been kept intact. Later investigations do not support the contention either that the Irish Pelagian matter was a legacy handed down within the shores of the western isle from the days of the heresiarch, or that the unadulterated texts were exclusively Irish, the contaminated continental. But Zimmer made an effective beginning of the work of restoring the original commentary, a work which has been carried to a successful issue by Souter. A bye-product of

[103] P. 161 *supra.*   [104] On Romans v 15.
[105] *Cf.* pp. 636, 249, 643, 544, 565, 619.

, this achievement has been the throwing of considerable light on old Irish exegesis.[106]

The *Codex Vindobonensis* 954 (former Hofbibliothek, Vienna) contains some Pelagian matter. *Cf.* Morin *op. cit.* [p. 661 *supra*]. It is from Bobbio, and is thought to have been written by the corrector of Codex 16 [p. 515 *supra*].

Codex Paulinus Wirziburgensis I *s* VIII.   See no. 461.

513. *Codex Augiensis* CXIX

MS: Carlsruhe Landesbibl. Cod. Augiensis CXIX *s* IX [the commentary on Hebrews, which is not Pelagian, was added *s* X].   Comm: A. Holder *Die Reichenauer Handschriften* I (Leipsic 1906) 303-4. — Souter *opp. cit.*

According to Holder and Souter this MS was written at Reichenau in the ninth century, probably the first half, by five scribes, of whom one was Irish.   It contains the original text of Pelagius's commentary, copied from an exemplar which seems to have been of not later date than the sixth century.   Whether that exemplar came from Ireland or not we cannot determine.[107]

514. *Codex Sangallensis* LXXIII

MS: St. Gall Stiftsbibl. 73 *s* IX.   Comm: HZ *op. cit.* 217-350 [description and collation; this last not of much value: " what he gives is on the whole to be relied upon, but there are literally thousands of omissions." — Souter]. — Souter *opp. cit.*

This is a manuscript of the ninth century, probably of the first half, consisting of 131 folios in continental script, written by two chief scribes, with occasional intervention of a third, and of a fourth, a corrector.   The orthography and abbreviations have Irish characteristics: Zimmer and Souter have inferred that the *Vorlage* was an Irish book, and Souter believes that it in turn was copied from a Spanish exemplar.   The codex contains an anonymous commentary on the Pauline epistles, which Zimmer considered to be the original composition of Pelagius — with additions due to an Irish scribe — but which in reality is closely related to Pseudo-Jerome and may descend from a common ancestor with the various versions of that compilation. Zimmer and Souter have accepted — not on very strong grounds — the identification of this book with the *Expositio pelagii super omnes epistolas pauli in vol. I* of the ninth century (about 850) catalogue of the St. Gall library.[108]

---

[106] Chapman has studied the question of the biblical text used by Pelagius and concludes that it was Old Latin of the same type as that which was quoted by Gildas.

[107] The fact that the nearest related text seems to be that quoted by Sedulius Scottus slightly favors an Irish origin.

[108] Becker *Catalogi bibliothecarum antiqui* (Bonn 1885) 47, no. xxii 218.   Becker gave this item as an addition to the catalogue, and from that HZ inferred that the book was one of those brought by Marcus and Moengal (*cf.* no. 411); but Souter states that it is one of the original entries. — HZ suggested that the present codex no. 73 had lost its first folio, carrying the old title.

Sedulius Scottus: see p. 565 *supra*.
Codex latinus Monacensis 9545: *cf.* no. 507.
Marianus Scottus: *cf.* no. 445.
The Balliol Epistles of St. Paul: *cf.* no. 509.

(c) COMMENTARY ON THE CATHOLIC EPISTLES

See no. 105.

(d) COMMENTARIES ON THE PSALMS — THE COMMENTARY OF THEODORE OF MOPSUESTIA

Bibliography

R. L. Ramsay " Theodore of Mopsuestia and St. Columban on the Psalms "; " Theodore of Mopsuestia in England and Ireland " *ZCP* VIII (1912) 421–51, 452–97. Also the bibliography there given. — L. Pirot *L'oeuvre exégétique de Théodore de Mopsueste* (*Scripta pontificii Instituti Biblici*) (Rome 1915). — De Bruyne " Le commentaire de Théodore de Mopsueste aux épîtres de s. Paul " *Rev. Bénédictine* XXXIII (1921) 53–4.

With the probable exceptions of the Gospels and the Pauline Epistles the Psalter was studied in the Irish monastic schools more than any other book of the Old or New Testament. Almost all the Latin patristic commentaries seem to have been known and used. What is of peculiar interest, however, both for Irish and for general church history, is the fact that the commentary of the Syrian heretic Theodore of Mopsuestia was preserved, in more or less modified versions, and exercised an influence greater than any other on the Irish exegetes.

Theodore was born at Antioch about A.D. 350, and held the post of bishop of Mopsuestia, in south-eastern Asia Minor, from 392 to 428. Throughout his life he remained in good standing in the Church. The commentary on the psalms is said to have been his earliest exegetical work; it shows clearly his chief characteristics, his preference for realistic and pseudo-historical explanations, and aversion from the allegorical interpretations of the Alexandrian school which came to be generally accepted by orthodox Christianity. The original Greek text is lost, perhaps as a result of its author's condemnation as a heretic by the Fifth General Council, at Constantinople, in 553, but fragments, translations and adaptations are so extensive that its content can be quite fully restored.

From the available evidence it would appear that the Latin versions have all descended through Irish channels.

515. Latin translation of Theodore's Commentary

MSS: Turin Bibl. Nazionale F. IV. 1, fascs. 5, 6 s VIII/IX [surviving fragments of two MSS, both of Bobbio origin].— Milan Bibl. Ambrosiana C. 301 inf. s VIII/IX ff. 4-13 [also a Bobbio MS; *cf.* p. 202]. COMM: G. Ottino *I Codici Bobbiesi nella Biblioteca Nazionale di Torino indicati e descritti* (1890). — C. Cipolla *Codici Bobbiesi della Biblioteca Nazionale Universitaria di Torino* (1907). — W. M. Lindsay " The Bobbio Scriptorium: its early minuscule abbreviations " *Centralblatt für Bibliothekswesen* XXVI (1909) 392-6 [these treat of the MSS]. — G. Mercati *Atti di R. Acad. di Scienze di Torino* XXXI (1896) 655-76 [reprinted in " Varia Sacra " fasc. iii pp. 91 *sqq: Studi e Testi* no. 11 (Rome 1903)]. — R. L. Ramsay *op. cit.* 428, 441-51 [these treat of the text].

In certain manuscripts of the eighth or ninth century which belonged to, and probably were written in, the Irish monastery of Bobbio in northern Italy, are to be found extracts, ranging from psalm xvi to psalm xl, from an early Latin translation of Theodore's treatise. Whether the translation was made in Ireland or not cannot be determined, but if, as seems certain, it is the source of the Columbanus commentary,[109] and if that is really due to Columbanus, then this Latin translation must have been introduced into Ireland, or prepared there, as early as the sixth century. It is a free and somewhat abbreviated, but fairly accurate, version. No attempt is made to excise or palliate the unorthodox tendencies of the original.

Abridgment of Theodore's Commentary, ascribed to Columbanus: See no. 47.

516. Treatise on the Psalter, in Old Irish

Is hé titul fil i n-dreich ind libuir se. . . . Ab eo didiu, úád immthiag. [Ends imperfect.]

MSS: Bodl. Rawl. B. 512 s XV ff. 45-7. — BM Harl. 5280 s XVI ff. 21-4. ED: KM *Hibernica Minora, being a fragment of an Old-Irish treatise on the Psalter [Anec. Oxon. Med. & Mod. Ser. pt. VIII]* (Oxford 1894) [text, trans. etc.; *cf. ZCP* I 171-2]. COMM: HZ " Anzeige der Hibernica Minora " *Göttingische Gelehrte Anzeigen* 1896 pp. 376-409 [some valuable comments and suggestions; *cf. ZCP* I 496-7]. — R. L. Ramsay *op. cit.* 421-97, *cf.* especially 465-74 [a study of the relations of the treatise as a carrier of Theodoran matter].

In two well known Irish manuscripts of the fifteenth and sixteenth centuries we have copies of a fragmentary Irish commentary on the psalms. The text of the two copies is the same, both end abruptly at the same word, and both evidently are derived from the same source. That source was itself a copy made at a comparatively late date. The original composition, the linguistic evidence shows, was written well back in the Old Irish period, at least as early as A.D. 850. The fragment surviving contains only the introduction and part of the comment on the first psalm. If the work was completed in accordance with the plan on which it was inaugurated — and there is some reason to believe that it was so completed [110] — it must have formed a book of

109 *Cf.* no. 47.
110 The Latin glosses in the Southampton Psalter (*cf.* no. 476) appear to be based on this treatise. As they are continued through the psalter, the inference is that the compiler had our treatise in complete form before him. See also what is said below regarding the West-Saxon Psalms.

considerable magnitude. Kuno Meyer suggests that what has escaped destruction is only the first quaternion of the original codex.

The treatise took the favorite Irish form of a catechism, or series of questions and answers. It seems to have been, for its time, a fairly exhaustive study. The following passage, characteristically Irish in its schematic formalism, gives the author's proposed method of treatment:

" There are four things that are necessary in the psalms, to wit, the first story (*stoir*), and the second story, the sense (*siens*) and the morality (*morolus*). The first story refers to David and to Solomon and to the above-mentioned persons, to Saul, to Absalom, to the persecutors besides. The second story to Hezekiah, to the people, to the Maccabees. The meaning (*siens*) to Christ, to the earthly and heavenly church. The morality to every saint."

Here, in this fourfold system of interpretation set forth by an unknown Irish writer of the eighth century, is found the final fusion of two great streams of Christian exegesis, the Alexandrian, represented by Origen, Jerome, Cassiodorus, and other orthodox commentators, and the Antiochean, of which the chief exponent was Theodore of Mopsuestia. The immediate source of the Theodoran matter seems to have been, for the most part, the *argumenta* and *explanationes* of the *In psalmorum librum exegesis*, ascribed — probably correctly as regards these parts — to Bede, which in turn had as its source the abridgment of which Columbanus was reputed to be author. The compiler used also another source, probably the early Latin translation, and the works of many other commentators, of whom he mentions Hilary, Ambrose, Jerome, Augustine, Cassiodorus, Gregory and Isidore.

The Psalter of Southampton: See no. 476.

Poem of Airbertach mac Coisse: See no. 545.

According to Ramsay, the O-I treatise described above was used, perhaps in a Latin form, by the author of the tenth-century West-Saxon version of the first fifty psalms in the so-called Paris Psalter (ed. J. W. Bright and R. L. Ramsay *Liber Psalmorum The West-Saxon Psalms* (Boston and London 1907)).

517. Commentary on the Psalms by Cassiodorus

MS: Laon Bibl. de la Ville 26 s IX *in.* Cf. *ZCP* VIII (1912) 175–6 [text of glosses].

Cassiodorus was the author of a commentary on the psalms, based on the *Enarrationes* of Augustine. A copy of the commentary, written by an Irish scribe in the early ninth century, is in Laon. Whether it was written in Ireland or on the Continent is not certain. It contains a series of Old Irish marginal glosses, of the irrelevant, " aside " character common to many such notes in Irish manuscripts.

(e) Commentaries on other Books of the Old Testament

518. Commentary on Job

MS: Bodl. Laud Misc. 460 s XI/XII. Ed (of Irish glosses): WS " Hibernica VII The notes in Laud 460 " Zs. f. vergl. Sprachforschung XXXI (1890) 254-5.

Copy of a Latin commentary on the Book of Job, written in an Irish hand and containing glosses in Irish.

519. Commentary on Isaias

MS: BN lat. 9526 s VIII. Facs: Silvestre Paléographie universelle IV pl. xii.

The script of this copy of St. Jerome's Commentary on Isaias has been classed as Irish.

(f) Other Patristic and related Studies

520. Codex Ambrosianus O. 212 sup.

MS: Milan Bibl. Ambrosiana O. 212 sup. c A.D. 700. Facs: A. E. Burn Facsimiles of the creeds (Henry Bradshaw Soc. XXXVI) (London 1909) 22-3, pls. XXII–XXIV.

Script: Irish, a mixture of semi-uncial and minuscule. It is a Bobbio MS, and may have been written there; but, in the absence of evidence to the contrary, the natural inference is that it came originally from Ireland. Ff. 18. Part of codex lost. Contents: (i) The De ecclesiasticis dogmatibus of Gennadius, a Semipelagian of Marseilles who lived towards the end of the fifth century (ed. Migne PL LVIII 979-1054). (ii) The Faith of Bachiarius (cf. p. 351 supra). (iii) The Quicumque vult, or Athanasian Creed.[111] (iv) A sermon on the Ascension. (v) The Creed of Damasus under the title " Faith of Jerome." This is in a later 8th century hand.

521. Codex latinus Monacensis 6298

MS: Munich Staatsbibl. lat. 6298 (olim Freising 98) s VIII ex. Facs: Silvestre Paléographie universelle IV (Paris 1841) pl. vi [f. 71ᵛ]. — A. E. Burn Facsimiles of the creeds (Henry Bradshaw Soc. XXXVI) (London 1909) 7, 21-2, pls. xx, xxi [ff. 1ᵛ-2]. Cf. W. M. Lindsay Early Irish minuscule script (Oxford 1910) 11.

Script, etc.: Large minuscule, described as Anglo-Saxon. Lindsay (Notae Latinae 467) accepts this classification. It may, however, be Irish. Ff. 114. Contents: A collection of sermons attributed to St. Augustine. The collection was probably made by Caesarius of Arles (d. 542), who wrote the prologue. Immediately following this prologue is the Quicumque vult, or Athanasian Creed. A modern note says that the MS belonged to St. Corbinian (cf. p. 514 supra).

---

[111] This seems to be the oldest extant copy.

522. *Codex Ambrosianus* F. 60 *sup.*

MS: Milan Bibl. Ambrosiana F. 60 sup. *s* VIII. EDS of O-I glosses: HZ *Gloss. hib. supplementum* (Berlin 1886) 4. — *Thes. Pal.* II pp. xxiv, 234. — W. M. Lindsay *ZCP* VII (1910) 266-7.

SCRIPT: Irish minuscule. CONTENTS: " Sententiae sanctorum doctorum et patrum." At the end are some " scraps of monastery lore," distinct from the bulk of the volume but also Irish and perhaps equally old. Among these are glosses, taken from a copy of the *Proverbia Graeca*,[112] which include a few Irish words. The MS came from Bobbio.

523. The Armagh copy of Sulpicius Severus's Memoirs of St. Martin

Cf. nos. 131, 474, 560, and pp. 158-9 *supra.* The received text is ed. by C. Halm *Corp. SS. eccles. lat.* I (Vienna 1866); a poorer ed. in Migne *PL* XX 159-76. *Cf.* also Zellerer *Palaeographicae et criticae de Sulpicio Severo Aquitano commentationes* (Munich 1912).

The last of the three large divisions of the Book of Armagh contains the greater part of the writings of Sulpicius Severus on St. Martin of Tours. These include the Life, the Dialogue of Postumianus (usually, but not here, divided into two dialogues), the Dialogue of Gallus (these two documents are in this manuscript reckoned as the second and third books of the Life), and the Epistles to Eusebius and Aurelius, but not that to Bassula.

Sulpicius Severus, Martin's biographer, was his younger contemporary, having been born, it would seem, after 350, and living until later than 410. He was an Aquitanian of noble birth and good literary training, and his writings on St. Martin, as they were among the earliest, so also were among the most popular of mediaeval biographies of saints. This popularity alone might account for their presence in the Book of Armagh, but it seems certain that in Ireland there was a peculiar veneration for Martin as a kind of national apostle. The Armagh text had, in the opinion of Babut, who made a special study of the subject, come to Ireland from Gaul before 460 and, in its broader aspects, was the most faithful heir of the original composition. Others have not fully accepted his arguments, but the Irish version certainly represents a distinct and very old manuscript tradition.

This portion of the Book of Armagh appears to have been one of the last written — though possibly not as late as the Acts of the Apostles. Part of the decorative work on initial letters for which space was left has never been finished. Also the last few leaves are of that peculiarly fine vellum which otherwise was reserved for the Gospel of St. John — a fact which probably indicates at least that the Martin memoirs were transcribed at a later date than the gospels.

———————

Among the manuscripts of Irish provenance formerly the property of the monastery of Reichenau but now in the library of Carlsruhe are three students' note-books which resemble each other in script and seem

[112] *Cf.* no. 374 (i).

to be of about the same date. One of these is a collection of theological and liturgical texts known as the Carlsruhe Augustine; another is a text-book in Latin grammar, the Carlsruhe Priscian; and the third a compilation of chronological and computistical matter which, from the documents occupying the bulk of its folios, is designated the Carlsruhe Bede. At the monastery of St. Paul in Carinthia there is another Irish manuscript from Reichenau containing miscellaneous matter, which, from its contents, seems to belong to the same group, although a comparison of the script has not, apparently, been made. These four codices are of great value to the investigator of the intellectual and devotional interests of Irish ecclesiastics in the ninth century. In the present subsection the Augustine and the Bede will be examined, and also several other manuscripts and texts which illustrate Irish patristic and related studies.

524. The Carlsruhe Augustine

MS: Carlsruhe Landesbibl. Cod. Augiensis CXCV s IX in. FACS: J. B. Silvestre (trans. Madden) *Universal palaeography* (London 1850) 609 II pl. 220. EDS of O-I glosses: *IT* II i (1884) 143-63. — WS *The Old-Irish glosses at Würzburg and Carlsruhe* (London 1887) 195-204, 338-40. — *Thes. Pal.* II (1903) pp. ix, 1-9. COMM: A. Holder *Die Reichenauer Handschriften* I (Leipsic 1906) 438-44. — W. M. Lindsay *Early Irish minuscule script* (Oxford 1910) 57-60, pl. XI.

SCRIPT: Irish minuscule, resembling those of the Carlsruhe Bede and the Carlsruhe Priscian. On spaces originally left vacant entries have been made in Carolingian minuscule of the ninth century (but with insular abbreviations, indicating that the writer was probably an Irishman dwelling on the Continent). Thirteen leaves are palimpsest (the first text a psalter), a fact which suggests that the MS was written on the Continent. The liturgical section at the end has different palaeographical characteristics and was probably of independent origin; it is this part that is connected by its contents with the codex of St. Paul in Carinthia. — Ff. 47, of which the first and last, although Irish, did not belong to this volume. They have been attached to it, however, from a very early date. CONTENTS: Ff. 2-17ᵛ, 18-37ᵛ: Augustine's *Soliloquiae* (Migne *PL* XXXII 869-904, 1035-80). Ff. 17ᵛ-18: Augustine's *Retractationes cap.* iv (ed. Knöll *Corp. SS. eccl. lat.* XXXVI 22-5). Ff. 37ᵛ-8: Various brief notes.[113] Ff. 38ᵛ-42: Augustine's *De praesentia dei ad Dardanum* (Migne *PL* XXXIII 832-42). F. 42: On the eight chief sins (from Eutropius of Valencia: Migne *PL* LXXX 80). Ff. 42ᵛ-4ᵛ: Excerpts from Augustine, Bede, Jerome, Gregory. Ff. 45-6ᵛ: Hymns (*cf.* pp. 714-5 *infra*). F. 46ᵛ: The Apostles' Creed, followed by a paragraph begin-

[113] Including the following verses:

Aspice marmoreas superantes astra columnas
quas híc sanctigeri fulcit arena soli
Felix famosus Heleranus Finnia Fergi
fulgida donifero lumina sacra [facta] deo.

O magnum Scotiae misit Pictonia diues
munus relliquias quas uelit esse suas.
Unde uenit Tytan et nox ubi sidera condit
quaque dies medius flagrantibus aestuat horis.

Ed. by K. Strecker, among "Versus Scottorum," *MGH Poet. lat. aevi Carol.* IV ii-iii (1923) 1124.

ning " Maioris culpae manifeste quam occulte peccare." Of the covering sheets f. 1 has theological notes, some from Augustine, on the *recto* in Irish script, on the *verso* in continental; f. 47^r the hymns *Cantemus in omni die* (no. 98) and *Sanctus Petrus, apostolus* (no. 94 i); the *verso* is illegible. O-I GLOSSES: To the notes on the first page, and to the texts from Augustine. Windisch believed that they were by the same hand as the text. Linguistically they are assigned to the ninth century, but some, if not all, seem to have been copied from another MS.

525. The Carlsruhe Bede

MS: Carlsruhe Landesbibl. Cod. Augiensis CLXVII *c* A.D. 836 x 848. FACS: C. P. Cooper *Appendix A to a Report on Rymer's Foedera* p. 60. — J. B. Silvestre (trans. Madden) *Universal palaeography* (London 1850) p. 609 II pl. 220. — *New Palaeographical Soc. Facs.* pl. 34. EDS: Of O-I glosses and calendar: HZ *Glossae Hibernicae* (Berlin 1881) pp. xxiv-xxix, 229-52; *Supplementum* (Berlin 1886) 12. — WS *The Old Irish Glosses at Würzburg and Carlsruhe* (London 1887) 210-37, 344-50; " Hibernica IV. The fragments found in the Reichenau Baeda " *Zs. f. vergl. Sprachf.* XXXI (1890) 246-7. — *Thes. Pal.* II (1903) pp. x-xi, 10-30, 283; *Supplement* (1910) 66-7. — *The Academy* Dec. 29, 1883 p. 435 [the saints' names mentioned in the calendar]. Of the Annales Augienses brevissimi: F. J. Mone *Anzeiger f. Kunde d. teutschen Vorzeit* IV (1835) 16-7. — *MGH SS* III (1839) 136-7. — Migne *PL* CXLII 1213-4. *Cf.* F. Kurze *NA* XXIV (1899) 444. COMM: A. Holder *Die Reichenauer Handschriften* I (1906) 393-8. — B. MacCarthy " The Carlsruhe Bede " *Academy* XXXVIII (1890) 176; *Codex Palatino-Vaticanus No. 830 (RIA Todd Lect. Ser.* III) (1892) 351-2; *AU* IV pp. xciv *sq* [these treat of chronology]. — H. M. Bannister *JTS* V (1903) 51-2 [date and place of origin]. — W. M. Lindsay *Early Irish minuscule script* (Oxford 1910) 54-7.

SCRIPT: Irish minuscule, with occasional entries in continental script. The marginal notes are also in both Irish and continental hands. Ff. 5-12, which did not originally form part of this codex, are in Caroline minuscule of the 9th century, but the abbreviations are much the same as in the other sections: they were probably either written by an Irish scribe or copied from an Irish exemplar. CONTENTS: Ff. 1-4: Computistical and astronomical notes, tables and verses. Ff. 13-4: Zodiacal signs, tables of years, and various sets of verses relating to the calendar. Ff. 14-6: The Dionysian cycles from A.D. 532 to 1063. Ff. 16^v-7^v: An ecclesiastical calendar (*cf.* p. 481 *supra*); also another set of verses on the calendar. Ff. 18-21: Bede's *De rerum natura* (ed. Giles VI 99-122). Ff. 21-3: *De temporibus liber* II (*ibid.* 123-38). Ff. 23-45^v: *De temporum ratione* (*ibid.* 139-270). Ff. 45^v-6: *De sex huius saeculi aetatibus* (*ibid.* 270-2). Ff. 46-7^v: From the *Chronicon* of Isidorus junior (ed. Mommsen *MGH Auct. antiq.* XI 426-81). Ff. 47^v-8^v: Letter from Proterius, bishop of Alexandria, to Pope Leo the Great on the paschal question (Ballerini's ed. of the letters of Pope Leo I (Venice 1753) 1264-74; Migne *PL* LXVII 507-14). Ff. 48^v-9: Letter of Pope Leo the Great on the paschal celebration (Ballerini I 1283-4). F. 49: Notes on the calendar (ed. A. Holder *Rhein. Museum* new ser. XXIX (1874) 167-9). — Ff. 5-12 have miscellaneous matter, including the *Gloria in excelsis* in Greek and Latin, computistical rules, and the Dionysian cycles for the years A.D. 1-531. ANNOTATIONS AND GLOSSES: The O-I glosses are on the opening notes and on the Bedan texts; they seem to be by a contemporary hand, and, linguistically, to be of the 9th century.

But in part they correspond with glosses in the Vienna Bede (no. 526), and both evidently descend from a common exemplar. Two entries refer to recent events in Irish history: f. 15 " Aed king of Ireland dies " (the commentators say that this is attached to the year 817; it is given in AU under 819); f. 17 " Death of Mur-chad, son of Máel-dúin, in Clúain-maccu-Nóis, on the bed of Ciarán, in the tenth year " (*i.e.*, of the decemnovennal cycle beginning 817 = 826: he was king of the Cenél Eogain, and was deposed, according to AU, in 823). On ff. 14–5, by a hand different from those of the text and the Irish glosses, are a few annalistic records of Frankish history, known as the *Annales Augienses brevissimi*, from A.D. 687 to 848. HZ concludes that the main text was written not later than 848. It has been inferred that it is not earlier than 836 because the calendar includes the feast of All Saints, which was established in France and Germany in 835. The addition of St. Quentin to the calendar led Bannister to suggest that the volume was produced at Peronna Scottorum.

526. The Vienna fragment of Bede

MS: Vienna Nationalbibl. 15298 (suppl. 2698) *s* VIII/IX. Eds of O–I glosses: WS *Goidelica*[2] (1872) 51 *sqq.* — HZ *Glossae Hibernicae* (1881) pp. xxix–xxx, 253–8 [*cf.* *Supplementum* (1886) 13]. — Strachan " The Vienna Fragments of Bede " RC XXIII (1902) 40–9. — *Thes. Pal.* II (1903) pp. xi, 31–7.

This remnant of a codex consists of four badly damaged leaves, parts of which are lost and parts so abrased as to be very difficult of deciphering. They contain a section of Bede's *De Temporum Ratione* (*cap.* vii–xxii, otherwise v–xx), with many interlinear and marginal notes and glosses, Irish and Latin, in several hands. The text is of the same recension as the Carlsruhe Bede, and some of the glosses are the same, indicating a common source; the majority of the glosses, however, are independent.

527. The Cologne fragments of Bede

MS: Cologne Stadt-Archiv GB–A no. 82 and 85 *s* X. Ed (of O-I glosses): RTh ZCP XV (1925) 297–301.

These two leaves contain part of Bede's *De arte metrica*, with glosses in Latin and in Irish. They are in continental script, of the tenth century, it is said, but were probably copied from an Irish exemplar of the ninth.

528. The Vatican Computus

MS: Vat. 5755 ff. 2–3, 63–73. Eds of O-I glosses: O. Dziobek " Altirische Glossen " *Beiträge z. Kunde d. indogerm. Sprachen* V (1880) 63–7 [poor; *cf.* B. Güterbock *ibid.* VII (1883) 342–3]. — HZ *Glossae Hibernicae* (1881) pp. xxx, 259–61 [*cf.* WS " Spicilegium Vaticanum " *Academy* XXXV (Jan. 12, 1889) 26–7]. — *Thes. Pal.* II (1903) pp. xii, 39–41. On the Dionysian paschal writings *cf.* p. 214 *supra*.

Among a number of manuscripts from Bobbio which are now in the Vatican is one, said to be of the eleventh century, containing a copy of Augustine's *De Trinitate*. Bound up with it are several folios from another codex, a computus written in old

Irish script. The date of this has not been determined, but Stokes and Strachan considered the language of the Irish glosses to be as old as the eighth century, and declared that there was no clear evidence that they were copies. Part of the computistical matter consists of the Paschal Arguments of Dionysius viii, ix, x, and xiv, and it is to these that the Irish glosses, together with a wealth of Latin annotations, are attached.

529. The Nancy Computus

MS: Nancy Bibl. de la Ville 59.[114] Eds (O-I glosses): AdeJ *Bibl. de l'École des Chartes* 6e sér. II (1866) 509–10, III (1867) 471–5. — Henri Gaidoz " On Irish glosses recently found in the library of Nancy " *Proc. RIA* X (1867) 70–1. — WS *Goidelica*² (1872) 54. — HZ *Glossae Hibernicae* (1881) pp. xxx sq, 262. — *Thes. Pal.* II (1903) pp. xii, 41.

In the library of Nancy is to be found one small fragment of the *disiecta membra* of old Irish scholarship in the shape of a single piece of parchment which has been used as a binding on one of the codices. It is a leaf from a computus, written in an Irish hand of the eighth or ninth century. The text consists of the Paschal Arguments xii and xiii attributed to Dionysius, to which are added a large number of marginal and interlinear Latin notes and a few Irish glosses.

530. The Cambridge Juvencus

MS: Cambridge Univ. Lib. Ff. iv. 42 s IX. Eds (glosses): WS "Die Glossen und Verse in dem Codex des Juvencus zu Cambridge " *Beitr. zur. vergl. Sprachf.* IV (1865) 385–423, VII (1873) 410–6 [Welsh and O-I]. — *Thes. Pal.* II (1903) pp. xiii, 44 [O-I]. Comm: Skene and Bradshaw *Archaeologia Cambrensis* 3rd ser. X 153–6. — H&S I 198, 622–3. — WS *Academy* Sept. 10, 1892 [application of key of Bamberg cryptogram; cf. no. 363]. Eds. of Juvencus: Migne *PL* XIX. — Marold (Leipsic 1886) (in *Bibliotheca Teubneriana*). — Hümer (Vienna 1891) (in *Corpus SS. eccles. lat.*). Comm: RTh *RC* XI 91. — T. H. Parry-Williams *Univ. of Wales Bulletin of the Board of Celtic Studies* I ii (May 1922) 120–3.

Juvencus was a Spanish priest and poet of the fourth century, whose principal composition was a rendering into dactylic hexameters of the story of the life of Christ, drawn from the gospels, especially that of Matthew. This work was regarded with much favor during the middle ages; the fact that it was known to Columbanus makes it probable that it had reached Ireland by his time.[115]

The manuscript here considered was written in Wales, probably at the abbey of Llan-Carvan, in the first half of the ninth century. It contains a large number of Welsh and a small number of Irish glosses; also, on a fly-leaf at the end of the codex, two hymns, apparently in an Irish hand of the latter part of the ninth century, and some corrupt Latin entries in a Welsh script of later date. There are allusions to two abbots of Armagh, Nuadu (d. 812) and Fethgna (d. 874). Finally, a marginal entry in cypher proves to be written in the same code as that expounded in the Bamberg cryptogram (no. 363) by certain Irishmen who visited the court of " Mermin, King of the Britons," identified with Mervyn Vrech, king of Wales, who died in 844. Skene and Bradshaw believed that the manuscript was carried to Ireland in the second half of the ninth century, and afterwards returned to Wales.

---

[114] Lindsay, *Notae Latinae* 469, gives this as codex 317 (356), a Bobbio MS.   [115] *Cf.* p. 191.

531. The Trèves Enchiridion of St. Augustine

MS: Berlin Staatsbibl. Joseph von Görres Collection 87 *s* IX/X. ED (O-I glosses and relevant text): L. C. Stern *ZCP* VII (1910) 475-97.

HISTORY: The library of the ancient Abbey of St. Maximin at Trèves contained many valuable mediaeval manuscripts. During the disturbances which followed the French Revolution the abbey was sequestrated and the manuscripts scattered. A considerable number were obtained by Johann Joseph von Görres, at this time a warm admirer of the Revolution, but later one of the leading champions of Catholicity in the intellectual and political circles of Germany. In 1902 his collection was offered for sale, and purchased by various libraries. Among the manuscripts acquired by the Royal Library at Berlin is one entitled " S. Augustini Opera Varia " which has interest for Irish students. It consists of two codices bound together in 1750, the second only of which is here considered. SCRIPT: Caroline minuscule of the second half of the 9th century; has certain additions — including the Latin and Irish glosses — written in another hand, possibly of later date, the end of the ninth or beginning of the tenth century. Neither scribe was Irish, but one at least of the texts was copied from an Irish original. CONTENTS: F. 65: Augustine's " Enchiridion," or handbook, on Faith, Hope and Charity. (Migne *PL* XL 231.) F. 116: The abbot Cherimon on Free Will (*ibid*. XLIX 915). F. 117: Defence of Catholic Faith against heretics, attributed to St. Jerome. (In the so-called *Sacramentarium Leonianum*,[116] of which the best ed. is by C. L. Feltoe, Cambridge, 1896.) F. 129ᵛ: Extracts from Basil and Gregory Nazianzen. F. 135ᵛ: Letter of Pope Celestine regarding the falsehood of Adam, original sin, and the grace of God. (Migne *PL* L 531.) F. 140: Sermon by Augustine on the text that through Adam death and through Christ life have come to all men. (Extract from the treatise " Against Julian.") F. 141: Book of Augustine on Eighty Questions. (Migne *PL* XL 9.) F. 175ᵛ: On the conversation of Epicureans and Stoics with the Apostle Paul. (*Ibid*. XXXVIII 808.) F. 180: Sermon on the text: What was said by God to Moses, I am Who I am. (*Ibid*. 63.) GLOSSES: The first fifty-one chapters of the Enchiridion carry a large number of Old Irish and Latin glosses, the majority Latin. They are absent from the rest of this treatise — probably because the copyist for some reason ceased transcribing them at this point — and from the remainder of the codex. Peculiarities in the Latin orthography indicate that the text as well as the glosses of the Enchiridion was drawn from an Irish exemplar. That work, at least, was known and studied in the Irish schools. It is not stated whether there is similar evidence for the Irish origin of any of the other texts found here. The Irish glosses are of interest chiefly to students of linguistics. They seem to vary in date, being the product, doubtless, of several generations of scholars. They approach most closely to the Milan glosses in language forms, and in the present collection are thought to date from the ninth century.

532. The Hohenfurt Manuscript of the Dialogues of Gregory the Great

MS: Hohenfurt Stiftsbibl. 71 *s* XI. ED (glosses): KM *ZCP* VIII (1912) 176-7.

In the Cistercian Monastery of Hohenfurt, near Budweis, Bohemia, there is a manuscript copy of the " Dialogues " of Pope Gregory the Great, written in a modified

[116] *Cf*. p. 686 *infra*.

Irish script. On the margins are a few notes in Irish — others have probably been lost. They were entered on certain saints' festivals in the years 1081 and 1082. The scribe's name was Eoin — John. It would seem that the manuscript was written on the Continent.

Mention should be made here of the MS Boulogne Bibl. publ. 58 (63–64) s VIII², which formerly belonged to the monastery of St. Bertin. It contains the Letters of St. Augustine, and is noteworthy for the very primitive abbreviations found in it, indicating that the *Vorlage* was of the seventh century or earlier. The script is insular minuscule, and Lindsay gives a notice of it in *Early Irish minuscule script* (Oxford 1910) 70–4; but in *Notae Latinae* (Cambridge 1915) 448 he classes it as " probably Anglosaxon."

Of the use of the works of Isidore of Seville in Ireland there is ample evidence. It is doubtful, however, whether any MS copy, written in Ireland, survives. Beeson, in his catalogue of the MSS, notices a considerable number of codices showing " insular " influences; he does not attempt to distinguish between Irish and English. — C. H. Beeson *Isidor-Studien* (*Quellen u. Untersuchungen z. lat. Philologie d. Mittelalters* IV ii) (Munich 1913): see esp. 120 *sqq*, 129 *sqq*.

(g) LATIN AND GREEK GRAMMATICAL AND LITERARY STUDIES

533. Irish Copies of Priscian

(i) The Leyden Priscian (no. 364 i)
(ii) The St. Gall Priscian

MS: St. Gall Stiftsbibl. 904 s IX. EDS (of O-I glosses): C. Nigra *Reliquie Celtiche* I *Il manoscritto irlandese di S. Gallo* (Turin 1872) [selection]. — G. I. Ascoli *Il Codice irlandese dell' Ambrosiana* II *Appendici e illustrazioni Le chiose irlandesi del codice di San Gallo* (*Archivio Glottologico Italiano* VI) (Rome 1879) [complete text of glosses; trans. unfinished; *cf.* WS " The Old Irish Glosses on the St. Gall Priscian " *Academy* XXVII 370 (May 23, 1885); " A Collation of Ascoli's edition of the Old-Irish Glosses at St. Gall " *Kgl. Sächs. Gesellschaft der Wissenschaften, Berichte, Philol.-Hist. Cl.* 1885 pp. 175–88]. — *Thes. Pal.* II (1903) pp. xviii–xxiii, 49–224 [best ed. and trans.]. COMM: On the glosses: WS " Notes on the St. Gallen Glosses " *ZCP* II (1899) 472–9.— J. Strachan " Some Notes on the St. Gall Glosses " *ibid.* III (1901) 60; " On the Language of the St. Gall Glosses " *ibid.* IV (1903) 470–92.— RTh *RC* VI 318; *Zs. f. vergl. Sprachforschung* XXXVII 55. — H. Pedersen *ibid.* XXXV 316. — HZ *ibid.* XXXVI 471. — J. Strachan *Trans. Philological Soc.* 1899–1901 pp. 47, 57; *RC* XX 304.— L. Traube *O Roma nobilis* (Munich 1891) 50 (346) *sqq* [the association of this MS with the Circle of Sedulius]. — B. G. Güterbock *Zs. f. vergl. Sprachforschung* XXXIII 92n. [date of MS]. — W. M. Lindsay *Early Irish minuscule script* (Oxford 1910) 40–7; *Hermathena* XVIII (1914) 44.

(iii) The Ambrosian fragment

MS: Milan Bibl. Ambrosiana A 138 sup. *s* IX f. 3. EDS of O-I glosses: HZ *Glossarum Hibernicarum Supplementum* (Berlin 1886) 3. — *Thes. Pal.* II (1903) pp. xxiv, 232.

(iv) The Carlsruhe Priscian

MS: Carlsruhe Landesbibl. Cod. Augiensis CXXXII *s* IX first half. FACS: C. P. Cooper *Appendix A to Report on Rymer's Foedera* pl. II. — Silvestre *Paléographie universelle* (Paris 1841) IV pl. 10; trans. Madden (London 1850) II pl. 221. EDS of O-I glosses: Z^1 pp. xxxii *sq*; Z^2 pp. xxiii, 1022–6. — HZ *Glossae Hibernicae* (Berlin 1881) pp. xxi, 219–25; *Preussische Jahrbücher* LIX (1887) 42 *sqq*. — WS *Old-Irish glosses at Würzburg and Carlsruhe* (London 1887) 205–9, 341–3. — *Thes. Pal.* II (1903) pp. xxiv, 225–30. COMM: W. M. Lindsay *Early Irish minuscule script* (Oxford 1910) 60–4. — The text of Priscian was edited by Hertz in Keil's *Grammatici latini* (1855–9). He used, *inter al.*, the Leyden, St. Gall and Carlsruhe MSS.

Priscian, who flourished at Constantinople about A.D. 500, wrote a treatise in eighteen books on Latin grammar (*Institutio de arte grammatica*), which became one of the principal grammatical text-books of the middle ages. It was studied and esteemed in Ireland [117] as elsewhere, and there are at least four manuscripts which are of Irish origin.[118]

The St. Gall Priscian, which is well known to Celtic scholars as containing one of the three most important collections of Old Irish glosses, is a volume of 240 pages.[119] The script is Irish minuscule, and abbreviations and orthography are Irish. It contains the text of the first sixteen books of Priscian's work, and of the seventeenth down to " naturaliter " (Hertz's ed. II 147 l. 18). The book was transcribed about the middle of the ninth century, probably either in 845 or in 856. The principal scribes were Máel-Patricc and, probably, Coirbbre; short sections were written by Finguine and Donngus; and the master of the scriptorium seems to have been Máel-Brigte. Allusions are made to Cobthach, Fergus, Máel-Lecán and Ruadri (perhaps Ruadri, son of Mermin, king of Wales [120] 844–78). On a page originally left blank a later hand has written a poem in honor of Gunthar, bishop of Cologne 850–69.[121] From these names it is inferred that the codex belonged to members of the Circle of Sedulius.[122] It was, no doubt, written in Ireland, but where we do not know. One of the scribes, probably Donngus, declares in a marginal note that he and Coirbbre were from Inis-Maddoc, but that place has not been satisfactorily located.[123]

The *marginalia* of this codex — little prayers and scraps of conversation, some of them perhaps circumventions of the rule of silence — have an enduring interest as affording glimpses of the life of these monastic scribes. " A blessing on the soul of Fergus. Amen. I am very cold." " It is dark to me." " Oh! my hand." " The parchment is rough, and the writing." " This page has not been written very slowly."

---

[117] " Er ist gewissermassen der irische Nationalgrammatiker." — Hellmann *Sedulius Scottus* 100.
[118] *Cf.* Manitius *Lat. Lit.* I 319.
[119] The pagination reaches 249, but after 79 it jumps to 88.
[120] *Cf.* p. 555 *supra*.
[121] *Cf.* no. 367.
[122] *Cf.* pp. 554 *sqq supra*.
[123] From the preface to Sanctán's Hymn (no. 583) it was west of Clonard. O'C (*MS Mat.* 27) identifies it with Inch, in Templeport lake, co. Leitrim.

"Love remains as long as property remains, O Máellecán." "New parchment, bad ink. O I say nothing more." "Nightfall and time for supper." Coirbbre especially "was a most regular observer of the pious Irish habit of beginning his day's task with a prayer, entered in the top margin, e.g. *fave Brigitta, adiuva Brigitta, fave Patricie.*" [124]. With the marginal notes should be noticed three little Irish poems.

The text carries as commentary a great mass of interlinear and marginal glosses in Latin and Irish. The Latin glosses have not as yet been published, but the Irish have been much studied for linguistic purposes. They seem to vary in date from the early ninth to the first half of the eighth century, and even occasionally the seventh. It is probable that they are not homogeneous, but come from different sources of varying antiquity.[125] Even the glosses in one *Vorlage* might have been added thereto at various epochs. Strachan has made an analysis [126] of the linguistic features of the Irish which bear on the problem of date; his results are not definitive, but they show that the proportion of older to later forms varies quite markedly in different sections of the codex. The glosses were penned by three or more writers — none of whom appears to be identical with any of the scribes of the main text — and at the same time as, or very soon after, the writing of that text.

The authority most frequently cited in the commentary is Isidore of Seville; among others are the grammarians Cicero and Vergilius, Bede, Orosius, Ambrose, Boethius, Cassian, Jerome, Lactantius, Dionysius Thrax, Gaudentius, Maximianus, Papirinus, Polibius Medicus, Probus, and several whose names are given in abbreviated forms, among them two Irish "blunderers," "Mael- " and "Cua-." The Máel-Gaimrid who is also mentioned is perhaps the same as he whose name is found in the Milan Commentary on the Psalms,[127] and as the "excellent scribe and anchorite, abbot of Bangor " who died in 839. Reference is made to two manuscripts, a "liber Niciae " and a "liber Romanus."

The Ambrosian Fragment is a single leaf, originally independent of, but apparently attached for a very long time to, a copy of the commentary on the Pauline Epistles by Haymon of Auxerre.[128] As this codex came from Bobbio doubtless the Priscian also belonged to that monastery. It is written in Irish minuscule, and carries Irish glosses. The Carlsruhe Priscian is a volume of 107 folios in Irish minuscule of probably the first half of the ninth century. F. 1 is nearly illegible: it may have contained some extracts from Isidore's *Etymologiae*; ff. 2–106 have the first sixteen books of Priscian. There are many marginal and interlinear glosses, Irish and Latin, added by several hands; of which the Irish at least were, for the most part, copied from an older manuscript. The Latin glosses have not been published.[129]

---

[124] Lindsay. Other saints and scriptural personages mentioned are Aaron, the Holy Virgin, St. Paul, Julius, Martin, "Sanctus Diormitius," Mochoe of Noen-druim.

For an interesting study of these Irish *marginalia* see a paper on " Colophons and Marginalia of Irish Scribes " by Charles Plummer in *Proc. British Academy* 1925.

[125] Lindsay (*op. cit.* 42) has called attention to evidence which makes it probable that the scribes of the main text had access to at least two exemplars.

[126] *ZCP* IV 470 *sqq.*

[127] *Cf.* p. 202. It is of interest that a Coirbre is there alluded to as an authority along with Máel-Gaimrid.

[128] *Cf.* Manitius *Lat. Lit.* I 516–7.

[129] Possibly this is the MS which was given to Reichenau by a priest named " Uragrat " apparently in A.D. 823 x 838. *Cf.* Becker *Catalogi bibliothecarum antiqui* viii 27. — Whether it was written in Ireland or abroad is not certain; its apparent relationship with the Carlsruhe Augustine suggests the latter.

These four manuscripts represent a common, and, no doubt, Irish, recension of Priscian, but no one of the four is derived from another. The Leyden codex and the Ambrosian fragment are very closely related. The Carlsruhe text stands a little apart from the others; nevertheless it is clear that a considerable portion of the Irish glosses here and in the St. Gall volume had, ultimately, the same origin.

534. Irish copies of Eutyches

(i) The Vienna Eutyches (p. 515 *supra*)
(ii) The Paris fragments

MSS: BN 10400 ff. 109–10 *s* IX; 11411 ff. 123–4 *s* IX. EDS of O-I glosses: J. Loth *RC* V (1883) 470. — WS " Notes of a philological tour I " *Academy* XXX (Sept. 25, 1886) 209; " Hibernica XVI The glosses on Eutychius de discernendis coniugationibus " *Zs. f. vergl. Sprachforschung* XXXV (1898) 587 *sqq.* — *Thes. Pal.* II (1903) pp. xiii, 42. COMM: L. Delisle *Bibl. de l'École des chartes* 5th ser. III (1862) 510, IV (1863) 233. — *Mém. de la Soc. de linguistique de Paris* V 161.

Eutyches or Eutychius, a disciple of Priscian who flourished in the first half of the sixth century, was, like his master, studied extensively in the early middle ages. Of Irish copies of his work, that from Bobbio now in Vienna has been described.

In two codices of the Bibliothèque Nationale, Paris, which are made up of fragments of old manuscripts, are found a few leaves containing portions of the same treatise. They had been used as book-bindings, and the text is very difficult to decipher. That they all came from a single codex is not improbable. The script is Irish, apparently of the ninth century, and there are a few Old Irish glosses, copied, and in a different ink from the main text.

535. The St. Paul Irish Codex

MS: Unterdrauberg, Carinthia, Kloster St. Paul 25. 2. 31, formerly 25. d. 86 (Codex Sanblasianus 86) *s* IX *in.* DESCRIPTIONS: *IT* I (1880) 312 *sqq.* — HZ *Glossae Hibernicae* (1881) pp. xxviii *sqq* [inaccurate; *cf.* also *Supplementum* (1886) 14]. — *Thes. Pal.* II (1903) pp. xxxii *sqq.* — L. Chr. Stern " Über die irische Handschrift in St. Paul " *ZCP* VI (1908) 546–55, VII 290–1 [careful description, with excerpts from Latin text].

Since 1809 there has been in the monastery of St. Paul, at Unterdrauberg in Carinthia, an Irish manuscript which formerly formed part of the rich collection of Irish material at the monastery of Reichenau. It is a codex of eight folios, about $8\frac{1}{2} \times 6$ inches in size.[130] Originally it was a quinio, the usual Irish gathering of five sheets, but the owner removed one sheet before he had finished his writing, with the result that there is a textual break between folios 1 and 2, though none between 7 and 8. The script is minuscule, by one hand throughout, though varying in character; is somewhat careless; and, with the exception of a small part in which continental writing is used, is Irish. Linguistic forms in some of the Irish texts make it certain that the book is not earlier than the first years of the ninth century.

---

[130] It has as binding a sheet of smaller size, an ancient biblical fragment (Matt. xxii).

It is clear that we have here the commonplace book of an Irish student monk of the ninth century who, after attaining at least to maturity in his native land, went to the Continent. As such it has unusual interest. The interest would be greater had it been written in Ireland, for then we would have an unique example of a note-book from an Irish monastic school. But if written at St. Gall or some other resort of Irish "pilgrims" in southern Germany or northern Italy — as seems certain [131] — it contains nothing, in the Latin sections, unusual or such as we might not expect to find. It does, however, testify clearly to one fact, the intimate association that could exist between the native Gaelic culture of Ireland and the Latin ecclesiasticism of the monk. It offers us some most valuable fragments of old Irish literature and folk-lore. It testifies also to the Irish interest in Greek studies.

The following is a summary of the contents: F. 1: Introduction to a Commentary on the Æneid. F. 1^v 4: Miscellaneous extracts on grammar, biblical geography, and animal lore, of the curious mediaeval type (cf. ZCP VI 548). F. 1^v 20: Irish incantation: "Adgúisiu fid nallabrach." F. 1^v 25: Irish poem: "Messe ocus Pangur bán." F. 2: Fragment of scholia on Æneid I 28-39 (cf. ZCP VI 549). — An astronomical table (in the Pseudo–Bedan Ephemeris: Migne PL XC 753). F. 2^v: Notes on grammar, logic and astronomy (based on Charisius, Boethius, Hyginus), and the elements of Greek (cf. ZCP VI 550). Ff. 3-4: Further notes on Greek vocabulary, grammar, etc. (ibid.). Ff. 4^v-5^v: Miscellaneous notes and extracts on metaphysics, metrics, etymology, exegesis, astronomy (ibid. 551-2). Ff. 6-8: Twenty-nine hymns for the canonical hours (ibid. 552-3; cf.p. 714 infra). F. 8^v: Two Irish poems: "M'airiuclan hi Tuaim Inbir," "Is én immo niada sás." — Declension of the Greek ὁ κιθαριστής. — Theological passage regarding angels.— Æneid II 659. — Irish poem "Aed oll fri andud nane." [132]

536. Manuscripts of the "Short Exposition of Vergil's Georgics"

MSS: BN Lat. 11308 s IX; 7960 s X. — Leyden Universiteitsbibl. B. P. L. 135 s XI. EDS: H. Hagen Servii Grammatici qui feruntur in Vergilii carmina commentarii III fasc. ii Appendix Serviana (Leipsic 1902) [text and glosses]. — Thes. Pal. II 48, 418 [O-I glosses]. Cf. p. 286 supra.

This grammatical treatise is found with Irish glosses in three manuscripts, two of which contain portions of the Vergilian commentary of the seventh-century Irishman Adananus (or Adamnán?). Although all three are in continental script, they all go back to a common Irish Vorlage.

537. The Munich Glossary

MS: Munich Staatsbibl. lat. 14429 s IX ff. 222-6^v (cf. Graff Althochdeutscher Sprachschatz I xli). EDS (of O-I glosses): HZ Zs.f. vergl. Sprachforschung XXXIII (1893) 274-94. — Thes. Pal. II (1903) pp. xiii, 43.

An alphabetical Latin glossary forming part of a codex which is assigned to the ninth century. To many of the items have been added glosses, written in various hands. Among these are a few Old Irish entries, in the same hand as the main text.

---

[131] The earlier part might possibly be of Irish origin. The continental script is found in one of the hymns on f. 7^v and in the theological note on 8^v.

[132] These poems will be considered in Vol. II.

538. *Codex Bernensis* 207

MS: Berne Stadtbibl. 207 *s* IX/X. Comm: Hagen *Anecdota Helvetica* (Leipsic 1870) pp. xv *sqq.* — Lindsay *Early Irish minuscule script* (Oxford 1910) 64–7.

This collection of *miscellanea*, chiefly grammatical works, formerly belonged to the monastery of Fleury.[133]. The script is continental minuscule, with some insular features, and the abbreviations are almost entirely insular. That the connection, and, indeed, the origin of the contents, are Irish is made probable by the presence of the ogam among various alphabets described. It may be the work of a continental scribe copying Irish exemplars; or of an Irishman who, residing in continental Europe, had adopted the current script; or — this is Lindsay's opinion — of the scriptorium of an Irish monastery on the Continent.

The contents of the volume are almost entirely grammatical (ff. 80^V–1 have an excerpt from a panegyric on " Constantinus Augustus "), and the most extensive items are the works of Donatus (ff. 2^V–17, 18^V–77, 101–12) and commentaries thereon (ff. 81^V–101, 140^V–8 — this last by Sergius). Other treatises included are by Servius (ff. 77^V–80^V — the original title gave the author's name as Mars Erulus *grammaticus*), Asper (ff. 130–40), Petrus (ff. 148–68) and Isidore (ff. 168 to end — excerpts), besides three that are anonymous (ff. 17–8^V, 112–27^V, 127^V–9^V).

539. The Bodleian Chalcidius

MS: Bodl. Auct. F. 3. 15 *s* XII. Eds of Irish glosses: WS " The Irish glosses and notes in the Bodleian Chalcidius " *Academy* XXXI (April 16, 1887) 275–6; " Irish glosses and notes on Chalcidius " *Zs. f. vergl. Sprachforschung* XXIX (1887) 372–8 [complete ed.]. Comm: Rev. Chas. O'Conor *Bibliotheca MS. Stowensis* I (Buckingham 1818) 399. — Hauréau *Histoire de la philosophie scolastique* I (Paris 1872) 76, 81–2 [on Chalcidius in mediaeval philosophy]. — Wrobel *Platonis Timaeus interprete Chalcidio* (Leipsic 1876) [ed. of C. with ref. to this MS. in pref. p. xix]. — Switalski " Des Chalcidius Kommentar zu Plato's Timaeus " *Beitr. z. Gesch. d. Phil. d. Mittelalters* 1902 III 6 [the sources of C.].

The chief source of a knowledge of Plato in western Europe in the early middle ages was the work of a certain Chalcidius who had written in the fourth or fifth century — he is sometimes said to have been a Spanish contemporary of Orosius. His writings consisted of a Latin translation of a part of the *Timaeus*, with a commentary thereon in which contributions were levied from other works of Plato and from those of many later and some earlier Greek philosophers. They thus formed a source also for knowledge of ancient Greek thought. In the twelfth century Chalcidius seems to have had considerable influence on West-European philosophy. That he was studied in Ireland at this time the present codex gives evidence. It is written in an Irish hand of the twelfth century and contains some contemporary, or nearly contemporary, Irish glosses and notes.

Nearly three hundred years before this the work of Chalcidius had been known and used by Johannes Eriugena,[134] but whether his acquaintance therewith was prior to his arrival on the Continent or not is not certain.

---

[133] *Cf.* p. 559 *supra.*
[134] In his *Exposition of Martianus Capella* (no. 379). *Cf.* Manitius *Lat. Lit.* I 336.

The remainder of this codex, following the copy of Chalcidius, is said to contain an astronomical treatise and a tract on the Aristotelian categories, all in an Irish hand.

540. The Laon fragment of a school dialogue

MS: Laon Bibl. de la ville 55 s IX. Eds of O-I glosses: WS *RC* XXIX 269-70. — *Thes. Pal. Suppl.* 82. Comm: KM *Sitzungsberichte d. k. preuss. Akad. d. Wissensch.* 1914 pp. 480-1 [*cf. RC* XXXV iii (1914) 399-400].

The Laon codex 55 is a ninth-century copy of Bede's Commentary on the Book of Proverbs. The fly-leaves, attached to it no doubt at a later but still ancient date, are cuttings from a MS written in Irish minuscule probably of the ninth century. They contain part of a catechism on grammar, a dialogue between M (Magister) and Δ (Discipulus). The *marginalia* include a few Irish glosses and some Latin verses which give time and place to the relic:

> " What is the glory and fortune of the world, what the pomps of the crowd,
> When Cathasach has not had power to escape the fate of death?
> For he has forsaken us, the wise and learned master,
> The dutiful, virtuous youth, the decorous superior." [135]

Kuno Meyer has shown that this eulogy was of an ecclesiastic who is mentioned in AU under 897: " Cathusach mac Fergusa, *tanase* abbot [136] of Árd-Macha, a pious young man, died." It is a warrantable inference that the manuscript was written at Armagh towards the end of the ninth century. Meyer suggests that it may be due to the " Bishop Mochta, pupil of Fethgna, an anchorite and excellent scribe of Árd-Macha," who died in 893. This, however, is purely a guess.

541. *Kollektaneum Bedae*

Ed: Migne *PL* XCIV 539 *sqq.* Comm: S. Hellmann *Sedulius Scottus* (Munich 1906) 100; *Pseudo-Cyprianus de xii abusivis saeculi* (Leipsic 1909) 16.

This collection of excerpts and abstracts from many sources, some now unknown, forms a remarkable mine of curious mediaeval lore. It is attributed, falsely, to the Venerable Bede; but was, it seems most likely, compiled by an Irishman in the eighth century.

542. Life of Vergil

MS: Unterdrauberg in Carinthia Kloster St. Paul 25 d. 65 s VIII/IX. Ed: J. Brummer *Vitae Vergilianae* (Leipsic 1912) 54 *sqq.* Comm: M. Petscheni*g Wiener Studien* IV 168.

[135] gloria quid mundi felix quid pompaue turbae
dum Cathasach potuit non sortem euadere mortis
nam nos deseruit sapiens prudensque magister
atque pius iuuenis castus custosque decorus.

[136] *I.e.*, the person having the right of succession to the abbacy.

It is believed that this short Life of the Roman poet Vergil, which probably goes back at least to the eighth century, was composed by an Irishman.[137]

543. Florence copy of Boethius

MS: Florence Bibl. Laurentiana 78, 19 s XII. FACS: G. Vitelli and C. Paoli *Collezione florentina di facsimili paleografici greci e latini* (Florence 1886) pl. 4 [one fol.].

This copy of the *De consolatione philosophiae* of the Italian statesman and philosopher Boethius [138] (c 480-524) has been classed as of Irish writing.

544. Fragments from Fulda

MS: Basel Universitätsbibl. F. iii. 15 s VIII-IX. FACS: *Cf.* Gougaud *RC* XXXVIII 11-2. COMM: Lindsay *Notae Latinae* 445-6.

A considerable number of MSS from St. Boniface's monastery of Fulda are now in the library of the university at Basel. As would be expected, many of the MSS of Fulda were of English origin or script; but a few seem to have been Irish. The codex at Basel marked F. iii. 15 is made up from several originally independent volumes, all from Fulda. Some of these Lindsay classes as continental or Anglo-Saxon in script; one — F. iii. 15d, s VIII — containing "Isidorus Junior" *De vitiis*, the fifth-century Gallic grammarian Consentius, and other matter, as "insular [Irish?] minuscule"; another — F. iii. 15f s VIII — containing Isidore *De natura rerum*, as "insular halfuncial or large minuscule"; and a third — F. iii. 15l s VIII — containing Isidore *Liber differentiarum*, as "insular minuscule."

(h) THE SCHOOL OF ROS-AILITHIR

In the first chapter attention has been called to the fact that after the ninth century a shifting took place in the Irish ecclesiastical schools from Latinist to Gaelic culture, from the Latin to the Irish language. By some chance several texts composed by the head of one of these schools have been preserved.

Under the year 1016 the Annals of Ulster record the death of Airbertach mac Coisi-dobráin, *airchinnech* of Ros-Ailithir. According to O'Conor's Annals of Inisfallen, in the year 972, which seems to correspond with 991 of the correct chronology, the Northmen from Waterford destroyed Ros-Ailithir and took prisoner the *fer légind*, mac Cossedobráin, who was afterwards ransomed by the great Brian at Scattery Island. This undoubtedly is the same man as the mac Cosse, *fer légind* of Ros-Ailithir, to whom the Book of Leinster attributes a versified geography, and the Bodleian codex Rawlinson B. 502 the same work and some religious and scriptural poems.

[137] *Cf.* p. 286 *supra.* [138] *Cf.* p. 585 *supra.*

Ros-Ailithir — Headland of the Pilgrim — is the present Roscarbery, on the south-west coast of county Cork, between Clonakilty and Glandore. It is said to have derived its designation from a saint known as Colmán the Pilgrim. It was the principal monastery of the Corcu Loegde.[139]

545. Religious Poems by Airbertach mac Coisse A.D. 982

(i) A Dé dúlig adateoch . . . nímfargba dott' éis, a Dé. A. 3 quatrains. (ii) Cethrur doraega, ní dalb, . . . ní fitir acht Día dúlech. A dé. 36 quatrains or sextets. This section is broken into several sub-sections. (iii) Cenn ard Ádaim, étrocht rád, . . . is lais cach fáth, cach forcenn. C. 3 quatrains. (iv) Airbertach roraith cen ail . . . is Mac Cosse rochaemchind. C. 1 quatrain. (v) In rí rodelb nem im gréin . . . ocus talam a forcenn. Cenn ard. 1 quatrain. (vi) Innocht féil Tómais cen tláis, . . . feib assebert in fáith Dé. A. Dé dúlig. 5 quatrains.

MSS: Bodl. Rawl. B. 502 s XII f. 46. — Vat. Palat. 830 A.D. 1072 f. 38 marg. [iii]. EDS: B. MacCarthy *Codex Palatino-Vaticanus 830* [*RIA Todd Lect. Ser.* III] (1892) 24 [iii: text, trans.]. — WS *Zs.f. vergl. Sprachforschung* XXXI (1890) 249–50 [iii: text, trans.]. — KM *ZCP* I (1897) 496–7; III (1901) 20–3 [complete, text only]. COMM: R. L. Ramsay *ibid*. VIII (1912) 474–6 [with trans. of four quatrains, by Eleanor Hull].

These poems consist of an opening invocation of God, an account of the composition of the Psalms, three quatrains on the creation of Adam, two quatrains attached thereto, from which we learn the name of the author, and five quatrains on St. Thomas. The main part of these verses, that treating of the Psalms, is drawn directly from the Old Irish prose treatise on the Psalter of which only the opening sections have survived.[140] The verses were, doubtless, written by Airbertach with the design that they should be committed to memory by his pupils in Ros-Ailithir as a compact summary of his teaching on that portion of Holy Writ. At the close of this section of the work are some chronological references which indicate that the year in which he was writing was 982. From the last section, that on St. Thomas, we learn that the day was that saint's feast, December 21. The legendary matter regarding the creation was, we are expressly told, translated by Airbertach from Latin into Irish. Nearly a century later the penitential exile from Ireland who was acting as an amanuensis to Marianus the Chronicler, at Mainz,[141] entered these three verses in the margin of his manuscript. Kuno Meyer believed that this scribe was a Southerner, and probably educated at Ros-Ailithir. But by his time, doubtless, the little poem had become the common property of the schools. Similar matter is to be found in the tracts on the creation in *Leabar Breac* and the Book of Ballymote.[142] The concluding verses, dedicated to St. Thomas the Apostle, are based on the fabulous " Acts of Thomas."

546. Geography of Ros-Ailithir

Mac Cosse Fer Legind Ruis Ailithir cecinit. Ro fessa i-curp domuin dúir. . . tir is tarbach ro fess on. 68 quatrains.

MSS: LL s XII pp. 135–6. — Bodl. Rawl. B. 502 s XII p. 66. ED: T. Olden " On the Geography of Ros Ailithir " *Proc. RIA* 2nd ser. II (1884) 219–52 [text, trans., notes; *cf*. KM *RC* VI 192].

139 *Cf*. p. 310 *supra*.   140 *Cf*. no. 516.   141 *Cf*. pp. 614–6.
142 *Cf*. no. 616 and *Todd Lecture Series* III 24–5.

This versified compendium of geography in the Irish language is ascribed to Mac Coisse. It was evidently intended to serve as a text to be memorised by the students. Like many other text-books of the middle ages it makes no use of contemporary practical knowledge, but is a compilation from late classical sources, especially from Pomponius Mela.[143] The geography set forth is that of the Roman Empire, not of the tenth century of the Christian era. Within these limitations the author's work is not discreditable. He begins by describing the five zones into which the earth is divided, two frigid, two temperate, and one torrid. The north temperate zone is the habitat of the human race. He then proceeds to a description of the known lands and peoples of the three divisions of the inhabited world, Europe, Asia and Africa. Apparently he had some slight knowledge of Greek, a knowledge, it may be noted, which was entirely wanting to at least one of his copyists.[144]

547. Poem on the War with the Midianites

Rochúala crecha is tír thair . . . is mo maith rochúala-sa. 25 quatrains.

MS: Bodl. Rawl. B. 502 s XII f. 46ᵛ. ED: KM ZCP III (1901) 23-4 [text only].

The authorship of this poem is not stated, but it is possibly the composition of Air-bertach mac Coisse-dobráin, with whose known works it is placed in the single codex in which it has come to us. The subject is the conquest of the Midianites by the people of Israel, as related in the thirty-first chapter of the Book of Numbers.

———

In BM Cotton. Tiberius B. v f. 58 there is a tenth-century map of the world attached to a copy of Priscian's Latin version of the *Periegesis* of Dionysius, which, it is stated, was copied from a map in the scribe's exemplar of Priscian. It is one of the best maps of the early middle ages. There is reason to believe that it was drawn by an Irishman. EDS: Cartembert (1830) for the BN. — Bevan and Phillot *Mediaeval Geography* (1874) p. xxxiv. *Cf.* Beazley *Dawn of modern geography* II (1901) 559-63, 608-12; also p. 132 *supra*.

B. LITURGICAL AND DEVOTIONAL

Bibliography

A good general introduction is Mgr. L. Duchesne's *Origines du culte chrétien* (Paris 1888; 5th ed. 1920), of which there is a trans. by McLure, *Christian Worship* (S. P. C. K.: London 1919). Several books by Dom Fernand Cabrol also serve as good preliminary studies: *Le livre de la prière antique* (Paris 1900), and in trans. *Liturgical prayer: its history and spirit* (London 1922); *Origines liturgiques* (Paris 1906); and *Introduction aux études liturgiques* (Paris 1907). Daniel Rock's *The Church of Our Fathers*, originally published in 1849, re-edited by G. W. Hart and W. H. Frere in 4 vols. (London 1905), although treating primarily of English customs, contains an immense amount of liturgical information of general interest.

[143] *Cf.* no. 6.   [144] The scribe of Rawlinson B. 502.

Adrian Fortescue " Liturgical Books," in *Cath. Encycl.*, is a compact and useful art. Other works deserving mention are: Suitbert Bäumer *Geschichte des Breviers* (Freiburg i. Br. 1895), and trans. by R. Biron *Histoire du bréviaire* (Paris 1895). — Ferdinand Probst *Die abendländische Messe vom fünften bis zum achten Jahrhundert* (Münster 1896) [gives much attention to the Irish material]. — P. Batiffol *Histoire du bréviaire romain* 3rd ed. (Paris 1911); *Études de liturgie et d'archéologie chrétienne* (Paris 1919). — Edmund Bishop *Liturgica historica Papers on the liturgy and religious life of the Western Church* (Oxford 1918) [a collection of remarkable essays by a man who was perhaps the foremost English student of liturgy in his time,[145] and one who was keenly interested in the Irish sources]. — Richard Stapper *Grundriss der Liturgik* 3rd ed. (Münster 1922). — Ildefonso Schuster (trans. Arthur Levelis-Marke) *The Sacramentary (Liber Sacramentorum) Historical and liturgical notes on the Roman Missal* I (London 1924). — The chief work of reference on liturgy will be, when completed, the *Dictionnaire d'archéologie chrétienne et de liturgie* [cf. p. 105 supra]. There is one periodical devoted to the subject, the *Jahrbuch für Liturgiewissenschaft*, ed. by O. Casel, O. S. B. (Münster 1921–). For the Irish liturgical sources the best guide and commentary is the excellent article by Dom Louis Gougaud " Celtiques (Liturgies) " in the *Dict. d'archéol. chrét. et de liturgie* II ii (1910) 2969–3032. He presents the subject in much briefer form in *Les Chrétientés celtiques* (Paris 1911) 295–313: " La liturgie et la dévotion privée." Another very good summary is Henry Jenner's " Celtic Rite " in *Cath. Encycl.* The most important collection of sources in one vol. is F. E. Warren's *The liturgy and ritual of the Celtic Church* (Oxford 1881) [see reviews by Duchesne and Gaidoz *RC* V 139–45]. There is also an interesting gathering of documents in the preface to A. P. Forbes *Liber Ecclesie Beati Terrenani de Arbuthnott* (Burntisland 1864).

The origin of Christian liturgy is a subject to which has been given in recent years much historical investigation, but it is not one that directly interests the student of Irish history, for by the fourth and fifth centuries, when Christianity was establishing itself in that land, the public official services of the Church had already passed from the period of beginnings to that of well-defined forms and *formulae*. The interest of the Irish liturgical remains, after that which is naturally inherent in the discovery of actual facts, consists chiefly in tracing the relationships between the Irish and the other principal variations of the Christian liturgy, and determining how much of the former is borrowed, how much independent. Undoubtedly also liturgical affiliations may testify to other associations; but deductions of this kind are restricted by the consideration that the Irish appear to have been eclectics in liturgical matters, drawing texts from many sources solely because of the appeal made to their somewhat exuberant religious fancy.

By the beginning of our period Christian liturgy had grown into two main divisions, Eastern and Western. Although Christianity had

---

[145] See the obituary notice by W. H. Frere " Edmund Bishop, liturgist " *Church Quarterly Review* LXXXVII (1918) 145–9.

come to the West from the East, brought by Syriac and Greek colonists and missionaries, by the end of the fourth century it was using Latin as its official language, and in several other respects its western ritual was distinct from that of the East. Noteworthy is it that the chief ceremony of the Church, that of the Eucharist, known in the East as " the liturgy " and in the West as " the mass," had in the East a limited number of fixed *formulae* for the whole year, but in the West, while maintaining an immutable basis, allowed extensive changes from Sunday to Sunday and from feast to feast in the superstructure of prayers.[146] To this especially is due the development in the West, from the fourth to the eighth century, of a very rich liturgical literature.

The chief subdivisions of western liturgy were the Roman, the Ambrosian (of the diocese of Milan), the Gallican, the Mozarabic (of the Visigothic dominions in Spain and for a time in Aquitaine), and the Irish or Celtic.[147] It is usually said that the Irish was merely an off-shoot of the Gallican: doubtless the faith and the ritual came together from Gaul to Ireland, immediately from the western Gallic coast and mediately through the British Church. The very considerable Mozarabic and oriental elements in the Irish liturgy may also result in part from early Irish communications with Aquitaine, southern Gaul, and Spain. But, as has been suggested, an equally important factor may have been Irish eclecticism. Furthermore, a quite appreciable part of the Irish liturgy appears to be indigenous.

Only a few Irish texts of earlier date than the end of the eighth century survive, and in those of later date there is a large and increasing Roman element. Communications with Rome were reopened in the sixth century and must have become much more frequent after the adoption of the continental Easter-reckoning in the seventh. Roman influence in the liturgical texts may have roughly paralleled Italian influence in the biblical texts of Ireland. However, not only in Ireland but throughout western Europe there was a movement towards liturgical uniformity on the basis of the Roman model.

Some indication of this movement can be obtained from a brief account of the principal sacramentaries of the early Roman rite, the names of which should, moreover, for other reasons, be familiar to the student of the Irish or any other western liturgy. The earliest is the

[146] This distinction belongs only to the part taken by the celebrant: the scriptural lessons read by his assistants varied in the East as well as in the West.

[147] It is now generally assumed that there was a Celtic rite common to British and Irish Churches, but it must be remembered that the surviving documents are practically all Irish.

" Leonine," variously ascribed to the fifth, sixth, or seventh century. It is quite purely Italian, but, in the opinion of some scholars, was written in Gaul to aid in the introduction of the Roman rite. The next, the " Gelasian," exists in several redactions of the seventh and eighth centuries: the earliest has a slight, the later a large Gallican admixture. All were compiled in the Frankish empire, and those of the eighth century seem to represent the liturgy contemporarily in use in northern France and in Germany at a time when the true Gallican rite was falling back to the south and south-west and disappearing. Finally, the " Gregorian " is the Roman sacramentary which Pope Adrian I sent to Charles the Great between 784 and 791, and which that monarch ordered to be used throughout his dominions. It had been in use in Rome at least one hundred years earlier, and probably, as tradition said, represented a revision effected by Pope Gregory the Great. But almost all the manuscripts now known contain extensive additions from the Gelasian, and some from Gallican sources, made, it seems probable, chiefly by Alcuin.

What were the services for which collections of liturgical *formulae* were required? (1) The administration of the sacraments, for some of which the minister must be a bishop, for others he might be either priest or bishop. To some of these might be attached other services, as the blessing of the font and water to baptism, the visitation and communion of the sick to extreme unction. The most important ceremony was that of the eucharistic consecration, the mass, in which, besides the celebrant, two other sets of persons took part, his assistants, who read the scriptural lessons, and the choir, which sang various parts of the service, either independently or as responses to the celebrant. A priest celebrating alone had to take all for himself except a few responses. (2) The psalms, canticles, lessons, hymns, chants and prayers prescribed for the canonical hours, together making up the divine office; normally sung by all the monks in common, but in the case of isolated ecclesiastics recited in private. (3) Miscellaneous ceremonies, such as the consecration of nuns, various kinds of blessings, the burial service.

In the earlier middle ages the books in which the texts for these services were entered were not sharply fixed either as to number or as to extent of contents. There seems, however, to have been a broad attempt to provide for each person or class a book or books which would contain all the matter which he or they required, and nothing more. The earliest and most important of such books was the *sacramentary*, containing the words uttered by the minister in administering all the sacraments, including the mass service, but not the lessons or the parts sung by the choir. Out of the sacramentary grew the *missal*, the mass-book, which contained the entire text of the mass, including lessons and chants, but, if of the type accurately represented by its title, nothing more. However, as the usual object of a missal was the service of an isolated priest, it was frequently made still more valuable for him by adding texts for the other sacraments he might be called on to administer.

The Bibles and biblical books from which the lessons were read, and the martyrologies and *computus* by which the feasts of the year were known, have already been described.[148]

Although a considerable amount of liturgical matter must have been composed in Ireland, a larger and a more illuminating manifestation of Irish religious thought is given by the extra-liturgical and private devotional exercises — prayers, hymns, etc. Very remarkable is the extent to which the language of the people, Irish, was used in these compositions.[149]

I. TREATISES ON LITURGICAL SUBJECTS

Catalogue of the saints of Ireland: *cf.* no. 271.

548. Treatise on the different orders for the Divine Office

Ratio de cursus qui fuerunt ex auctores. Si sedulo inspiciamus cursus . . . beatus Benedictus vixit.

MS: BM Cotton. Nero A. II ff. 37–42 [according to Lindsay *Notae Latinae* 461 " written, perhaps at Verona, in 767; or transcribed, somewhat later, from an original of 767 "]; Cleopatra E. I ff. 5–7 [said to be a 17th cent. copy of preceding]. EDS: H. Spelman *Concilia* I (London 1639) 176. — D. Wilkins *Concilia* IV (London 1737) 741–2. — Moran *Essays* 243–6 [with trans.]. — H&S I 138–40. — Warren *Lit.* 77–80. — *Vit. Trip.* I p. cxx, II 502–3. — *AB* II pp. xxv *sq* [these two have only the part *re* the *Cursus Scottorum*]. — J. Wickham Legg in *Miscellanea Ceriani* (Milan 1910) 151–61 [best ed.].

A somewhat obscure document which professes to give an account of the origins of six *cursus* or orders for the celebration of the canonical hours — *Cursus Romanus, Cursus Gallorum, Cursus Scottorum, Cursus alius orientalis, Cursus S. Ambrosii, Cursus S. Benedicti.* The Irish (with which is joined the British) is traced from St. Mark through eastern transmitters to John Cassian, the monks of Lérins, Caesarius of Arles, Sts. Lupus and Germanus, their disciple St. Patrick, Comgall and Waldolenus

---

[148] Pp. 623 *sqq*, 479 *sqq*, 223.

[149] The occasional occurrence of rubrics in Irish in the liturgical books is another extraordinary phenomenon.

and Columbanus, by whom this *cursus* was established at Luxeuil. It is usually assumed that the author was a seventh- or eighth-century Irish monk residing on the Continent.

549. Tract on the Mass

[Stowe] Indaltoir fiugor [LBr: Conid hesin fotha . . .] . . . forberther heres nhoco.

MSS: Stowe Missal (no. 555) *s* IX ff. 65^v-7.— LBr f. 126 (facs. p. 251). EDS: O'C *MS Mat.* 376-7, 613-4 [extract from LBr]; *IER* II (1865) 170-9 [complete, with trans.] — WS *The Irish passages in the Stowe Missal* (privately printed: Calcutta 1881); revised ed. in *Zs. f. vergl. Sprachforschung* XXVI (1882) 497-519 [both have trans.]. — B. Mac Carthy " On the Stowe Missal " *Trans. RIA* XXVII Antiq. (1886) 245-65 [text, trans. of both texts].— *Thes. Pal.* II (1903) pp. xxvii *sq*, 252-5 [text, trans. of Stowe].— Facs., text, trans. in Warner's ed. of Stowe [*cf.* p. 692]. TRANS: D. Macgregor *Trans. Aberdeen Ecclesiological Soc.* III ii (1898) 293-340 [based on both texts]. COMM: Chas. Plummer *Zs. f. vergl. Sprachforschung* XXVII (1885) 441-8.

This explanation of the mass, in Irish, is entered at the end of the Stowe Missal in a script which appears to be distinctive but may, in the opinion of Warner, be by one of the original scribes. He thinks that in any case it is not later than the ninth century. The linguistic features are not inconsistent with ninth- or late eighth-century composition. The same tract, with many variations of text and considerable additional matter at the beginning, is in *Lebar Breac*.

550. Tract on the canonical hours

[Prose] Cid ara ndentar celebrad . . . [Verse] Tanic teirt dénamm tarbai . . . dia cobair co trén tanic. 40 quatrains; the Stowe copy has one more, ending: ic aes rechta cen imrall.

MSS: RIA 23 N 10 [Stowe] pp. 96-7 [verse only].— LBr p. 247. ED: R. I. Best in *Miscellany presented to Kuno Meyer* (Halle a. S. 1912) 142-66 [text, trans., notes].

Best assigns the verse to the eleventh or twelfth century; the prose, which serves as an introduction, is later than the verse. Both set forth the historical reasons for the observation of the eight [150] canonical hours.

551. Tract on the consecration of a church

MS: LBr pp. 277-8. EDS: Thos. Olden *Trans. St. Paul's Ecclesiological Soc.* IV (London 1897) 98-104, 177-80 [with trans.].— WS in *Miscellanea Linguistica in onore di Graziadio Ascoli* (Turin 1901) 363-87 [with trans.]. COMM: Gougaud " Celtiques (liturgies) " *Dict. d'archéol. chrét. et de liturgie.*

This treatise was dated by Olden as prior to 1186, but for reasons which may be not well founded; however, it probably belongs to our period.

---

[150] In a brief note in TCD 1336 (H. 3. 17) col. 675, published, with trans., by Best in *Ériu* III i (1907) 116, the more primitive six hours are explained. Eight hours are named in a poem published by KM, *ZCP* VI (1908) 271, from TCD 1337 (H. 3. 18) p. 44: Ocht n-airich go ngolaige . . . na trí tráth da hocht. 6 quatrains.

552. Tract on the liturgical colors

Cachtt [r. Ceist] cia lasa tucait . . . 7 ina thairmthechtus.

MS: LBr p. 108. — Liber Flavus Fergusiorum II f. 41. ED: *Vit. Trip.* I pp. clxxxvii-cxci [with trans.]. TRANS: Moran *Essays* 171-2.

This explanation of the mystical significance of the colors used in the priestly vestments may be later than our period.

553. Poem on twenty maledictive psalms

Sreth a salmaib suad slan . . . for oen insint srethugud.   10 quatrains;   . . . gabad seis na srethi si. 3 quatrains.

MS: Bodl. Rawl. B 512 f. 51ᵛ. ED: KM *Hibernica minora* (Oxford 1894) 44-6.

Presumably these twenty psalms were to be sung by the clergy in malediction, as at the cursing of Tara.[151] According to the poem they were arranged by Adamnán. They are nos. 2, 3, 5, 7, 13, 21, 34, 35, 37, 38, 49, 51, 52, 67, 68, 78, 82, 93, 108, and the canticle of Moses, Deut. xxxii, " Audite caeli quae loquor." The added stanzas give the names of twenty apostles and saints to be invoked at the same time.

II. BOOKS FOR THE USE OF PRIESTS AND BISHOPS AT THE MASS AND
OTHER SERVICES

554. The Bobbio Missal

MS: BN lat. 13246 (formerly St. Germain 1488) s VIII. EDS: Mabillon *Museum Italicum* I pt. ii (1687) 278-397 [a good ed. in some ways, but orthography not preserved, only one of additions by second hand given, and many inaccuracies in text; — the discovery of the MS is described in " Iter Italicum litterarium " *ibid.* pt. i 217]; 2nd ed. (1724). — Muratori *Liturgia romana vetus* II pt. iii (Venice 1748) 775-968; *Opere minori* (Naples 1760) 370-469; *Opera omnia* XIII (Arezzo 1773) 607-926 [reprint of Mabillon]. — Migne *PL* LXXII (1849; and reimpression by Garnier, 1878) 451-574 [from Mabillon, but ascribed to Muratori]. — George Hay Forbes " Missale Vesontionense " in Neale and Forbes *The ancient liturgies of the Gallican Church* II (Burntisland 1858) 205-56, III (1867) 257-368 [based on preceding eds., and incomplete, but with editorial matter of considerable value].— J. O'Laverty *An historical account of the diocese of Down and Connor* II (Dublin 1880) append. ii-vii [the *Missa Romensis cottidiana*]. — *The Bobbio Missal* 3 vols. (Henry Bradshaw Soc. LIII, LVIII, LXI) (London 1917; 1920; 1924) [1st vol. contains facs. complete, published by J. Wickham Legg; 2nd has text, ed. by E. A. Lowe; 3rd has notes by Dom André Wilmart, E. A. Lowe, and H. A. Wilson]. — A critical ed. of the missal was promised by Dom Cagin. — The following eds. of some special sections may be noted: (1) The catechism of sacred history ff. 7-8: Paul Meyer " Ioca mona-

151 *Cf.* pp. 388, 392 *supra.*

chorum Texte du VI⁰ siècle écrit au VIII⁰'" *Romania* I (1872) 483-90; *Recueil d'anciens textes bas-latins, provençaux et français* I (1874) " Bas-latin " no. 20, " Ioca monachorum " p. 16 [the attribution to *s* VI is not well founded].   (2) The rhythmical prayers in the mass of Holy Saturday f. 105^V *sq*: W. Meyer *Nachrichten d. k. Gesellsch. d. Wissensch. z. Göttingen*, philol.-hist.   Cl. 1913 pp. 218 *sqq*; *Abhandlungen* etc. new ser. XV iii (1914) 86 *sqq*.   (3) The incantation ff. 253^V-4: Aug. Boucherie *Revue des langues romanes* V (1874) 103-13; *cf.* his *Mélanges latins et bas-latins* (Montpellier 1875).   (4). The blessings of water f. 273 *sq*: Ad. Franz *Die kirchlichen Benediktionen in Mittelalter* I (Freiburg 1909) 140 *sq*.   (5) The blessing of the oil added on f. 286: Paul Meyer *Recueil* etc. p. 15.   (6) The penitential ff. 286^V-91: Wasserschleben *Die Bussordnungen der abendländischen Kirche* (Halle 1851) 407-12. — Schmitz II (1898) 322-6.   (7) The rule for celebrating mass f. 292^V-3: Wilmart *Revue Charlemagne* II (1912) 1-16.   (8) The establishment of the seven grades of holy orders f. 293: Wilmart *Rev. des sciences relig.* III (Strasburg 1923) 305-27.   (9) The biblical canon f. 299: Zahn *Geschichte des neutestamentlichen Kanons* (1890) II 284-8. — In A. E. Burn *Facsimiles of the creeds* (Henry Bradshaw Soc. XXXVI) (London 1909) pl. IV there is a facs., with letterpress, of f. 88 containing the Apostles' Creed.   COMM: L. Delisle *Le Cabinet des manuscrits de la Bibliothèque impériale* III (Paris 1881) 224-5 [good description of MS]; *Mémoire sur d'anciens sacramentaires* (Paris 1886) 78-80. — Warren *Lit.* (1881) 272-3. — Bäumer *Zs. f. kath. Theologie* XVI (1892) 485 *sq*. — Probst *Die abendländische Messe* (1896) 35-9, 359-65. — Dom Paul Cagin *Paléographie musicale* V (1896-9) 10, 96-184, 195-8 [valuable analysis]. — F. Kattenbusch *Das apostolische Symbol* I (Leipsic 1894) 186-8. — Duchesne " Sur l'origine de la liturgie gallicane " *Rev. d'hist. et de litt. relig.* V (1900) 38-43; *Origines du culte chrétien* 5th ed. (1920) 166-8 [also in earlier eds.]. — Bishop " Liturgical Note " in Kuypers *The Book of Cerne* (Cambridge 1902) 234 *sqq passim*, esp. 239, 244, 276-7; " On the early texts of the Roman Canon " *JTS* IV (July 1903) 555-78, reprinted, with some additions, in *Liturgica historica* (1918) 77-115 — see also 190-1. — A. E. Burn *op. cit.* (1909) 4-6, 28-30, 44-7 [including palaeographical note by Traube]. — A. Wilmart " Bobbio (Missel de) " *Dict. d'archéol. chrét. et de liturgie* II i 939-62 [excellent analysis and bibliography, with facs. of 4 pp.; reprinted, with considerable additions, in the 3rd vol. of the Henry Bradshaw Soc. ed.]; " Le palimpseste du Missel de Bobbio " *Rev. Bénédictine* XXXIII (1921) 1-18. — G. Morin *Rev. Bénédictine* XXXI (1914) 326-32. — F. C. Burkitt " The Bobbio Missal " *JTS* XXVI (Jan. 1925).

In the year 1685 Louis XIV of France directed the celebrated Jean Mabillon, Benedictine of the Congregation of St. Maur, to make a tour through Italy for the purpose of acquiring books and manuscripts for the libraries of France.   While on this journey Mabillon spent three days — June 5-8, 1686 — at the ancient Hiberno-Italian monastery of Bobbio, where he found the codex since generally known as the Missal of Bobbio.   It was taken back by him to France and placed in the library of his own monastery of St. Germain-des-Prés, whence it has passed to the Bibliothèque Nationale.

The book has been variously designated *Sacramentarium Gallicanum, Missale Vesontionense, Bobiense*.   It forms one of the outstanding and hitherto insoluble problems for the historical critic in the fields both of palaeography and of liturgy. Its palaeographical features have but little that is insular, and there is practical certainty that it was written on the Continent: the difficulty is to assign it a locality and a date. The liturgical contents include matter of Gallican, Irish, Roman, Spanish, perhaps even Milanese provenance. Here the problem resolves itself into the question whether the volume is in origin an Irish service-book which has been copied and revised by Gallican scribes, or a Gallican book which has been modified by Irish influences. The enquiry is complicated by the character of the Irish liturgy, in its basis Gallican, in its superstructure eclectic.

SCRIPT, etc.: The volume contains 300 ff., each about 7 × 3½ in., in 36 gatherings of varying size. It was probably designed to be easily portable. The parchment is not uniform, but in some parts fine, in others coarse. The last gathering, ff. 296–300, is palimpsest. A partial gathering formed by ff. 251–4 seems to be an insertion: script and parchment have a distinct character. The body of the missal is by one hand in a peculiar mixture of uncial, semi-uncial and minuscule forms, which, however, was evidently regarded by the scribe as a majuscule script. It does not belong to any recognised school, and does not seem to have been the work of a trained penman. *Additamenta* have been made to the missal on the first gathering of 8 ff., doubtless an addition, and on pages apparently left blank at the first writing; they are in two different but both very unpleasing, scraggy scripts. Lowe declares that they are by the same hand, and, although not accepting it, indicates the evidence supporting identification with that of the chief scribe. The abbreviations may be described as Merovingian, with slight insular and Spanish elements. The orthography shows the marked influence of Low Latin speech, chiefly in the *additamenta*, which were written quite carelessly. There is some reason to believe that the body of the missal was copied conscientiously, page for page, from an exemplar. THE PALIMPSEST: The primary text was of St. Ambrose's commentary on Luke, in semi-uncials of the fifth or sixth century. CONTENTS: I Ff. 1–8. A separate gathering, containing *additamenta:* notes on Matthew; fragment of a sermon; catechism of sacred history. II Ff. 9–272ᵛ. The Missal proper: The *Missa Romensis* [152] *cottidiana* comes first and forms the basis of the whole series of masses, to which it supplies the prayers of the canon and some other elements. The subject-matter is Roman, set in a Gallican framework. It bears a close resemblance to the ordinary of the mass in the Stowe Missal. Bobbio, Stowe and the *Missale Francorum* (Vat. Regin. 257) offer us, indeed, one early, and probably Irish, recension of the Roman canon. There are sixty other masses, with one interpolated, as noted above : they also show affinities with Irish documents, but less markedly, and in general would be classed as Gallican. In the cases of certain special texts, however — as the ceremonies of Easter, including the " Order of Baptism," and perhaps the mass for the dead — the Irish elements are quite considerable.—Each mass is, as a rule, preceded by a double or triple lesson (they belong to the " Irish " mixed family of biblical texts); the book is, therefore, a true missal — the earliest

---

[152] On "Romensis" = Romanus (a "Spanish symptom"), see L. Traube *Textgeschichte der Regula s. Benedicti* (Munich 1898) 129–30 [also in *Abh. d. k. bayer. Akad. d. Wiss.* III Cl. XXI iii].

of its kind — which could be used without bible or lectionary. III Ff. 273–86. What might be called a ritual or a pontifical: *formulae* for blessing water, for the consecration of virgins and widows, for the nuptial and other benedictions, for evening and morning prayers, and for the blessing of oil. IV Ff. 286ᵛ–91: Penitential (*cf.* pp. 243–4): It is of mixed Irish and Gallic origin, and seems to have been already in its present form when the compiler put it in this codex. V Ff. 291ᵛ–300ᵛ. *Additamenta:* an exorcism; a rule on the hours for saying mass; an account of Christ's establishment of the grades of holy orders; the causes of damnation and salvation; important dates in the life of Christ; *formulae* for the reconciliation of penitents; blessings of bread; explanation of the hours of the Divine Office (*cf.* no. 550); the Apostles' Creed; the biblical canon; a few miscellaneous prayers at mass. COMMENT: Appearances suggest that the missal was not a monastic book, but was written for, and probably by, a secular priest or bishop who lived in a place removed from the chief centres of culture and intellect. The majority of critics have thought, chiefly because of the character of the Low Latin forms, that the book was written in Gaul, and, because of the Irish features, in Luxeuil or its neighborhood. Wilmart at one time suggested Rhaetia, on the north side of the Alps, and Morin Septimania, around Narbonne. Edmund Bishop and, in his later publications, Wilmart, because of his conclusion that the palimpsest leaves came from northern Italy, prefer Bobbio or its neighborhood. The date has been generally given as the seventh century, but Lowe declares for the eighth. Finally, Bäumer, Probst, Cagin and especially Bishop have regarded the Missal as derived from an Irish service-book, an opinion to which Wilmart seems to incline. Other liturgists have, for the most part, classed it as fundamentally Gallican.

555. The Stowe Missal

MS: RIA Stowe D. II. 3 s VIII/IX. EDS: D. Fitzgerald " Irish Missals " *The Academy* XVII (1880) 48. — W. H. Hennessy " Irish Missals " *ibid.* 86 [this and the preceding give extracts, with trans., from the Irish passages]. — Warren *Lit.* (1881) 198–268 [text of Order of Baptism, Order of the Visitation of the Sick, etc., and the Mass, with introduction and notes: the text, copied under difficulties, is not accurate, and much progress has since been made in liturgical scholarship]. — WS *The Irish passages in the Stowe Missal, with some notes on the Orleans glosses* (Calcutta 1881) [50 copies privately printed]; " The Irish passages in the Stowe Missal " *Zs. f. vergl. Sprachforschung* XXVI (1882) 497–519 [reprint, with revision, of preceding]. — H. Grisar " Der gelasianische Messcanon " *Zs. f. kathol. Theologie* X (Innsbruck 1885) [text of the Stowe canon, based on Warren]. — B. MacCarthy " On the Stowe Missal " *Trans. RIA* XXVII (1886) 135–268 [introduction, text of mass and order of baptism, text and trans. of Irish treatise on the mass, litany from St. Gall (p. 700); read 8 June, 1885; included a criticism of WS, and led to a long controversy in the *Academy* (see below); text, although better than Warren's, not perfect, conclusions as to age not well founded, but descriptive and liturgical matter of much value]. — Suitbert Bäumer " Das Stowe-Missale neue untersucht" *Zs. f. kathol. Theologie* XVI (Innsbruck 1892) 446–90 [text of mass, based on MacCarthy, and comment]. — Ferdinand Probst *op. cit.* p. 684 *supra* (1896) 40–99 [text of mass, based on Grisar and Bäumer, and extensive commentary]. — *Thes. Pal.* II (1903) pp. xxvii *sq*, 250–5 [text, trans. of spells, rubrics and tract on the mass; criticises MacCarthy's ed.]. — Geo. F. Warner *The Stowe Missal* [Henry Bradshaw Soc. XXXI, XXXII] (London 1906, 1915) [best ed.; vol. I facs., vol. II introd., transcription, translation of Irish passages (from *Thes. Pal.*), and notes; includes whole MS except Gospel of St. John; liturgical questions are treated very briefly]. TRANS: J. Charleson *Trans. of the Glasgow Ecclesiological Soc.* 1898 [ordinary and canon of mass]. COMM: Chas. O'Conor *Bibliotheca MS. Stowensis A descriptive catalogue of the MSS. in the Stowe Library* I (Buckingham 1818) App. [long, but not wholly trustworthy, description]. — Sotheby & Co. *Catalogue of the important collection of Manuscripts from Stowe* (London 1849) lot 996 [the sale cat.]. — Jas. H. Todd " On the ancient Irish missal and its silver box, described by Dr. O'Conor in his Catalogue of the Stowe MSS. and now the property of the Earl of Ashburnham " *Trans. RIA* XXIII (1856) 3–37 [Todd's opportunity for examining the MS was quite inadequate, and his description suffers thereby]. — F. E. Warren *The Academy* XV (1879) 124–5; XVI (1879) 393–4, 465; XVIII (1880) 278; XIX (1881) 10–1; XXXI (1887) 290–1, 311, 327–8; XXXII (1887) 27, 57; XLVI (1894) 304–5. — WS *ibid.* XXXI 237–9; XXXII 26–7, 41–2, 204–5. — B. MacCarthy *ibid.* XXXI 450–2; XXXII 42–3, 185–6, 425–6 [the greater part of these letters to the *Academy* consist of the criticisms and *corrigenda* by Warren and WS to MacCarthy's ed., and the resulting controversy]. — Chas. Plummer " Notes on the Stowe Missal" *Zs.f.vergl.Sprachforschung* XXVII (1885) 441–8. — HZ " Zum Stowe Missal " *ibid.* XXVII 376–81. — J. Wordsworth *The Mystery of Grace* (London 1901) 92. — Bishop "٭On the early texts of the Roman Canon " *JTS* IV (1903) 555–78; " The Litany of Saints in the Stowe Missal " *ibid.* VII (1906) 122–36; these articles are reprinted, with additions, in his *Liturgica historica* (1918) 77–115, 137–64. — In both of the encyclopaedia articles, by Jenner and Gougaud, noted p. 684 *supra*, there is a valuable analysis of the Irish mass, order of baptism, and order of visitation of the sick, based mainly on Stowe; see also Gougaud *Les Chrétientés celtiques* (1911) 302–7. — E. Gwynn *Irish Church Quarterly* IX (1916) no. xxxiv 119–33 [*résumé* of discussions to date, with acceptance of Warner's conclusions; *cf. RC* XXXVII (1917–9) iv 403–5].

Our information as to the early history of the old Irish missal which forms part of the Stowe collection is very meagre. Dr. Charles O'Conor did not mention it in the body of his catalogue of the Stowe manuscripts, but devoted a long article to it in the appendix, facts which suggest that it was a recent acquisition and not part of the library of Charles O'Conor of Belanagare. He says that it was found on the Continent by " the late John Grace, Esquire, of Nenagh in Ireland, who was formerly an officer in the German service." This John Grace has not been positively identified, but as the second Marquess of Buckingham (afterwards Duke of Buckingham and Chandos), who inherited the title and, *inter alia*, the Stowe Library, in 1813, was connected through his wife with the Grace family, and was on friendly terms with Sheffield Grace (author of *Memorials of the Family of Grace*, privately printed in 1823) it is probable that the codex was obtained by him directly from that family. For its previous history we are dependent on such evidence as can be extracted from the text, and from the inscriptions on the *cumdach*, or case, in which it is enclosed. The approximate date of construction is indicated by the inscriptions on the lower, and older, of the two larger surfaces of the casket. They mention Donnchadh, son of Brian, who was joint-king of the Dál gCais and, to a greater or less degree, over southern Ireland from 1014 to 1023, and sole king from 1023 until he went on pilgrimage to Rome, where he died in 1064; and Mac Raith, king of the Eoghanacht of Cashel from 1045, who died in 1052. It is probable that the casket was made within the years 1045 x 1052, and that the missal was then at some place in north-eastern Munster. That it was in the same region three centuries later, when the upper face of the *cumdach* was replaced or re-decorated, we learn from the inscriptions it carries. They attribute this new work to Philip O'Kennedy, king of Ormond, and Aine his wife, and to the *comharba* Gilla-Rúadán Ó Macán. Philip O'Kennedy died in 1381,[153] having succeeded to his kingdom probably in 1371. Of Ó Macán we know nothing, but his Christian name — " Servant of Rúadán " — and his title make it probable that he was the *comharba* [154] — which at this time signified the hereditary holder of the church lands — of St. Rúadán of Lorrha.[155] Lorrha is in the barony of Lower Ormond, northern Tipperary, which in the second half of the fourteenth century formed part of the dominion of the O'Kennedys.

It is a reasonable inference that the Stowe Missal was, in the first half of the eleventh century, preserved as an ancient heirloom in some church of northern Tipperary, as Lorrha or Terryglass, and that it remained in the same place or neighborhood at least till the end of the fourteenth century. Moreover, when next the book can be definitely located, apparently about the beginning of the nineteenth century, it was at Nenagh, less than twenty miles from Lorrha. Although there is no strong reason to doubt O'Conor's statement that Grace had discovered the missal on the Continent, it is possible that this was an unfounded inference from the fact of his Continental service, and that in reality the codex never left north-eastern Munster until it passed to the library at Stowe House, Buckinghamshire, some time before 1818.

It is clear that two distinct codices have been bound together to make the volume as it stands to-day: one, consisting of the first eleven leaves, contains extracts from the Gospel of St. John;[156] the other, which alone is considered here, was the original missal. It seems possible that the two may have been in close association from an early date, if not from their origin.

Of the Irish character of the Stowe Missal there is no doubt; but in other respects it has been the subject of almost as much disagreement among scholars as has the Missal of Bobbio.

---

[153] FM.   [154] *Cf.* pp. 747-9 *infra.*   [155] *Cf.* pp. 637-8 *supra.*   [156] No. 466.

SCRIPT, etc.: Contains 57 leaves (*i.e.*, ff. 12-[68]), each about 5⅝ × 4½ in., of which the last, plain and unnumbered, is pasted to the cover. The vellum is of the coarse type usual in Irish MSS, and in places is much darkened. There are four gatherings: ff. 12-28, 29-46, 47-58, 59-[68]. These were not all part of the original codex: the first two gatherings, containing the missal proper, were drastically revised at a very early date, partly by removing some leaves and inserting others, partly by erasing and writing over some of the leaves retained. Of the original parchment in these gatherings there remain ff. 12, 13, 15 to 17, 20, 21, 26 to 28, 29, 32 to 34, 37 to 46. The reviser's signature is at the bottom of f. 37, where his work on the text of the mass ends:[157] " Móel cáich [158] scripsit." In the original text Warner distinguishes at least five hands: A¹ the first gathering; A² the second gathering; A³ ff. 47-51ᵛ; A¹ (?) 52; A⁴ 53-64; A⁵ 64ᵛ-5. (The Irish tract on 65ᵛ-7 may be by one of these scribes; the spells on 67ᵛ are by different, but perhaps not much later, hands.) The writing of all these shows a marked similarity, indicating that they belonged to the same scriptorium: it is Irish minuscule of a peculiar angular type. The script and the abbreviations point to the early ninth century, about A.D. 800-15, as the probable date of writing. Móel-cáich's script is a rounded minuscule, of an appearance more familiar to students of Irish MSS. He must have been trained in a different school. Authorities of the last century concluded that he worked a century or more after the original scribes, but the present opinion is that he was very little later. The Irish language forms of the treatise on the mass and of the Irish rubrics [159] are also in accord with a date in the first half of the ninth century.

CONTENTS: I Ff. 12-46: The missal proper. (a) The preparation for mass: Prayers of the class known as *apologiae sacerdotis*.[160] The longest is a confession and intercession, " Peccavimus, Domine,[161] . . . ," to which is integrally attached a litany of saints,[162] beginning with *Kyrie eleison*,[163] Móel-cáich has added the names of continental saints of special Irish veneration, and of many Irish saints.[164] (b) The beginning of mass: The tract at the end of the codex (no. 549 *supra*) indicates that the chalice was prepared before mass, as in the Gallican and Mozarabic and still in Eastern rites, and that an *introit* was sung. Neither is mentioned here: the first was a ceremony for which written directions were not required, and the second was of the part, not

---

[157] On f. 46ᵛ he has made an addition to the order of baptism.

[158] The first element signifies " bald," or " tonsured," the second " blind," " squinting," or " one-eyed." If the name is peculiarly Christian in composition it may mean " Servant of the blind [saint]," but it is possible that it is of pagan origin, " Servant of the blind," or " one-eyed [god]."

[159] The Stowe Missal is the most notable example of the use of the Irish language in liturgical rubrics.

[160] *Cf.* Cabrol " Apologies " *Dict. d'archéol. chrêt. et de liturgie* I ii (1907) 2591-601.

[161] Such confessions were favorite prayers in the Irish Church. *Cf.* Cabrol *Les origines liturgiques* (1906) 227-42. That here given is also in St. Gall 1395 (no. 557 ii), and seems to be peculiarly Irish.

[162] The original list of saints of this litany, before Móel-cáich's additions, is in St. Gall 1395. The saints invoked are the Blessed Virgin, the twelve apostles in the order given by Matthew, and Paul, Mark, Luke and Stephen. Some of these were omitted in Stowe. A litany resembling the expanded Stowe text is in Witzel's Fulda Missal (no. 556). Bishop points out (*op. cit.* p. 693 *supra*) that the frame-work of the litanies of Stowe, Witzel, and BM Reg. 2 A xx (no. 576) is the same as that of a Greek litany in BM Cotton. Galba A XVIII (the " Athelstan Psalter ") f. 200 and Titus D XVIII f. 12, and that there are grounds for believing that this Greek litany came to England from Rome in the time of the Syrian Pope Sergius (687-701).

[163] On the *Kyrie eleison* and its probable introduction into Ireland by the Romanising party of the seventh century see p. 334 *supra*.

[164] The list of Irish saints is general, without local significance. The latest named is Samthann (d. 739). — It should be noticed that ff. 30-31 of the Stowe codex have been misplaced: they should come between ff. 12 and 13.

of the priest but of the choir. Our MS has four collects — two added by Móel-cáich — and the *Gloria in excelsis*. (c) Epistle and gospel: The epistle — here, as in other early liturgies, designated the " apostle " — is I Cor. xi 26–32, the gospel John vi 51–7. No provision is made for other readings, a feature curious and almost unique. Possibly the texts here are given *exempli gratia*, or for circumstances when extra service-books would not be available. It seems a good presumption that in Ireland, as elsewhere, all important churches had, if not lectionaries, collections of gospels and epistles with *capitularia* or indices assigning the proper lessons to the various days. — Between epistle and gospel are a series of prayers and psalms, the gradual and accretions thereto; a " bidding prayer " in which intercession is made for various classes of the Christian clergy and people, including " the most pious emperors and the whole Roman army"; [165] and other prayers. The introduction of many prayers between epistle and gospel was an Irish peculiarity; it would seem that the Stowe had still more before Móel-cáich's revision. — Just before the gospel is a direction for the " half uncovering " of the chalice. (d) Creed to preface: The Nicene Creed with some interlinear emendations, notably the addition of the *filioque;* prayers at the offertory, of which one is introductory to the reading of the diptychs of the dead;[166] the *Sursum corda* responses; and the preface. This last consists of that prescribed in the present Roman Missal (as in the Bobbio) for common ferias, with a long interpolation just before the " per quem " clause, an interpolation which, though containing passages resembling the present Sunday preface, is in the main unique. Rubrics in Irish indicate that there were also proper prefaces (doubtless those in the special masses on ff. 38–45 are meant) to be substituted for this, some of which had the " per quem " ending, but others continued with their own proper text to the *Sanctus*. The *Sanctus* is nearly as in the Roman Missal, but with a post-sanctus addition, the wording of which suggests that originally, as in the first of the special masses of Stowe, in those of the Carlsruhe and Piacenza fragments (nos. 558, 559), and in the Gallican usage, it was followed immediately by the *Qui pridie* prayer of consecration. But the present missal, as also the *Hanc igitur* of LA (no. 560), testify to the use of the Roman canon in Ireland at the beginning of the ninth century. (e) The canon: This, which the rubric heading designates " Sunday Canon of Pope Gelasius," consists of the usual prayers of the Gelasian (and modern Roman) canon, but with some interesting variations and additions.[167] As has been stated above,[168] Stowe, Bobbio, and the *Missale Francorum* have a common recension of the Roman canon, although they differ considerably among themselves. To *Memento etiam Domine famulorum* is attached the rubric " Here the names of the living are recited," while to *Memento etiam Domine et eorum nomina* is added a long series of names of biblical personages and of saints, foreign and Irish.[169] The last column is left blank for further entries. Móel-cáich's

---

[165] This prayer, with but slight variations, was in Witzel's Fulda Missal, and somewhat similar texts are in the Gallican and Ambrosian liturgies, though not at this part of the mass. They are all of Greek origin: there is no doubt that this is a translation from the Greek. *Cf.* L. Duchesne *Origines du culte chrétien* 5th ed. (1920) 210-3.

[166] What follows to the Canon is by Móel-cáich.

[167] In the *Te igitur* prayer intercession is made for " our abbot [and] bishop N." The *Hanc igitur* has the curious addition: " Which we offer Thee in honor of Our Lord Jesus Christ and in commemoration of Thy blessed martyrs in this church which Thy servant built for the honor of Thy name and Thy glory . . . him and all the people snatch from the worship of idols and convert to Thee, the true God, Father Almighty." Some have seen in this evidence that the Stowe mass dated back to the days when Christianity was still laboring for the conversion of a pagan Irish people.

[168] P. 691.

[169] The latest person commemorated is Máel-rúain of Tallaght (d. 792). — MacCarthy's theory that

additions to the canon include an extensive interpolation in *Memento etiam Domine famulorum*, of continental origin but preserved only in Irish documents;[170] variants to *Communicantes* for Christmas, New Year's, Epiphany, Holy Thursday,[171] Easter, Low Sunday, Ascension Day and Pentecost; and an ending to *Qui pridie* resembling those of the Apostolic Constitutions and the Syriac, Coptic, Ambrosian and Mozarabic liturgies.[172] At the end of the canon are the ceremonies of intinction and fraction. (f) From the *Pater Noster* to the end of the mass: The *Pater Noster*, with introduction and embolism differing only slightly from the present Roman; the *Pax* in two *formulae;* the commixture; the communion, with the *Agnus Dei* and a series of antiphons and alleluias [173] — similar series are in the Communion of the Sick in Stowe and in the Books of Dimma, Mulling and Deer, in the St. Gall fragment and in AB (*cf.* pp. 700–4, 710); post-communion as in Bobbio and the St. Gall fragment; and a concluding thanksgiving and dismissal. (g) Special masses: The Stowe Missal has no proper for saints' days and other festivals, and only three special masses: for saints, for living penitents, and for the dead. It is, as MacCarthy has remarked, the smallest known volume that ever passed under the title of missal.[174] The application of the several prayers that make up this supplement of three masses is not certain: there are no rubrics and the commentators have for the most part avoided the problem. The second and third of these masses have each five sections, of which the first and second appear to be collects, the third a prayer connected with the offertory, the fourth is a preface and the fifth may be a post-communion. Now in the ordinary outlined above there are two obscure rubrics: just before the epistle, " the augment here," and at the offertory, " the second part of the augment here over the oblations." We may infer that of the special mass prayers just enumerated the first and second form the augment, the third is the second part of the augment, the fourth is the variation of the preface for which the rubrics make provision (p. 696 *supra*), and the fifth is to be either added to or substituted for one of the last two in the ordinary. The texts of the first special mass, however, do not accord so well with this explanation: there are seven sections, of which the fifth is a preface, the sixth a post-sanctus, and

two persons were designated, Bishop Mél (*cf.* p. 172) and Rúadán of Lorrha, has no support. — The next latest names are the Canterbury bishops Laurentius, Mellitus and Justus, of the early seventh century. The list, although it includes most of the famous old Irish saints, is not of the conventional type of Móel-cáich's litany in the preparation for mass: it includes too many obscure and unusual names. Nor is it a copy of the local diptychs in any of the older and larger churches: in that case it would have included the succession of abbots. The addition of these lists of names to the Memento of the Dead grew, doubt-less, out of the custom of reading at mass the names of the dead from the diptychs. In early times these were read at the offertory, and the practice was continued in the Gallican rite. As has been seen, Stowe has prayers at the offertory designed to accompany this reading. But in the Roman usage the reading of the diptychs was transferred to the canon; the Memento of the Dead is the prayer which was attached to it. At Rome this was omitted on Sundays and festivals, possibly on all occasions except at masses for the dead; but when the Roman liturgy was introduced into Ireland and Gaul the Memento was retained at all masses. Whether the list of names attached to it in Stowe took the place of the diptychs, or whether the diptychs were also read at the offertory, we do not know. It seems certain that at Armagh the names of the deceased abbots were read at some place in the mass until a comparatively late date. *Cf.* pp. 352–3 *supra.* — This prayer in Stowe is printed in Duchesne *Origines du culte chrétien* 5th ed. (1920) 221–3.

[170] It is in the Fulda Missal (no. 556) and the second fragment of Carlsruhe (no. 558).

[171] By an oversight the scribe has omitted portions of the texts for Epiphany and Holy Thursday.

[172] *Cf.* Paul Lejay " Ambrosien (Rit) " *Dict. d'archéol. chrét. et de liturgie* I 1417. Móel-cáich's text agrees almost word for word with that of the Biasca Sacramentary, a 9th or 10th century Ambrosian MS. *Cf.* E. Renaudot *Liturgiarum orientalium collectio* (Frankfort 1847) II 111.

[173] Here Móel-cáich's emendations end.

[174] That it may not have been unique is suggested by the fact that the original text of the first Carlsruhe fragment (no. 558) seems to be of the same three masses.

the seventh a post-communion. The first section appears to be the augment at the offertory, the second and third may be collects, and the fourth is a curious text, seemingly a combination of one or two collects and part of a preface. II Ff. 46ᵛ–60: The order of baptism. The Order of Baptism, as originally transcribed, begins on f. 47 and ends on f. 60, where without any indication of a break or a change of subject the Order of Visitation of the Sick commences. Subsequently Móel-cáich or a scribe of his school added a prayer on f. 46ᵛ, which had previously been left blank. This part of the codex, although written with some care, seems to have been copied from a *Vorlage* in which the texts were in confusion — perhaps from a private notebook where matter relating to baptism had been written down at haphazard from many different sources. Two sections may, however, be differentiated; the first, relating to the catechumenate and the preparation for baptism, in which this confusion is rampant; the second, the blessing of the font and baptism itself, where a certain order is discernible.[175] III Ff. 60–65: Order of visitation of the sick, etc. This is the longest of the four surviving versions of this service as in use in the Irish Church, of which the other three are in the Book of Dimma,[176] the Book of Mulling,[177] and the Book of Deer.[178] In the last only the communion service is given. All four bear a close resemblance to each other, and are evidently but variations of one liturgy. The contents of the Stowe version are as follows: A preface or bidding prayer,[179] six collects;[180] lessons drawn from Matt. xxii 23, 29–33, and xxiv 29–31;[181] the unction;[182] the Our Father, with introduction and embolism;[183] three prayers for the sick man;[184] the pax;[185] the communion;[186] two post-communions;[187] six communion anthems;[188] the thanksgiving;[189] the blessing;[190] the signing with the cross; and a second pax.[191] IV Ff. 65ᵛ–7: Treatise in Irish on the mass (no. 549). V F. 67ᵛ: Three spells in Irish.

COMMENT: Todd assigned the original text of the missal to the sixth century, Bäumer to about 627–40, MacCarthy to 625–50, Duchesne to the eighth century, Warren to the ninth, and Sir F. Kenyon (*Thes. Pal.* II p. xxvii) to the beginning of the tenth or end of the ninth. Móel-cáich's work was dated by Bäumer about 740–50, by MacCarthy about the middle of the eighth century, and by others in the tenth. As stated above, the general opinion now is that the script is of the early ninth century, and Warner has established fairly conclusively that the MS must have been originally

[175] In order to show the extent of this derangement, the Stowe texts may be compared with the outline of the Roman and Gallican services as given by Duchesne, *Origines du culte chrétien* (5th ed. 1920) 311–46.

[176] No. 563.   [177] No. 562.   [178] No. 564.

[179] Dimma has the same prayer, and Mulling one closely resembling it.

[180] Five of these are also in Dimma.

[181] The first of these is also in Dimma.

[182] The *formulae* of Dimma and Mulling are essentially the same as this though there are verbal differences between all three texts.

[183] With verbal variations, and in some cases additional prayers, this introduction is found also in Dimma, and the embolism in all the versions.

[184] Only in this version.

[185] Almost as in the mass. It is a combination of two *formulae* given in Dimma.

[186] There are variations in the communion *formula* in all four, and also in the Stowe mass and the Stowe order of baptism.

[187] One of these also in Dimma.

[188] *Cf.* p. 697 sect. (f). Of these six, four are in Dimma, two in Mulling, three in Deer.

[189] In all four versions with variations.

[190] Also in Dimma and Mulling: in the latter at the beginning of the service.

[191] The signing and the second pax are in Dimma.

written about 792 x 815, and that Móel-cáich's revision took place very soon after. Warner further argues with considerable force that the presence of the name of Máel-rúain, founder of Tallaght, who died in 792, as last of the bishops commemorated in the list of saints attached to the Memento of the Dead, saints none other of whom was later than the early seventh century, makes it probable that the missal was written at Tallaght after 792. Máel-rúain was succeeded by Air-fhinnan (d. 803) and Bishop Echaidh (d. 812), of whom the second at least was commemorated as a saint. The absence of his name would give 812 as a *terminus ad quem*. But, although the case for Tallaght is attractive, some considerations of a different tenor should be noticed. It is by no means certain that the local diptychs are represented by the list of saints attached to the Memento of the Dead; they may have been a distinct document, read at the offertory. And Máel-rúain acquired such a high reputation, especially among the followers of what has been called above [192] the reform movement of the eighth century, that his name might naturally be added to the Memento at many other churches besides Tallaght. Warner's further conjecture that the primary object of the missal was to provide Tallaght with an authoritative ritual, does not persuade. Its small size, poverty of ornamentation, fixed lections and paucity of proper readings and special masses — as well as the inconsiderate manner in which it was treated by the reviser — indicate that the book was not produced as the official missal of an important church, or high ecclesiastic, but rather as a private service-book which a priest could easily carry with him and find therein the minimum ritual necessary for the performance of his functions. That its contents were drawn from the books of the monastery where it was transcribed may be assumed. The most probable explanation of the revision it underwent is that it soon passed to another monastery where a somewhat different ritual prevailed, and was emended to suit the usage of its new home.[193] With regard to the liturgical contents, the close agreement of the Fulda Missal (no. 556), the St. Gall and Carlsruhe fragments (nos. 557, 558), and the canon of the Bobbio Missal (no. 554) make it probable that we have in the original text of Stowe a mass of wide though not universal acceptance in Ireland. It may well represent approximately the mass which was evolved by the Romanising churches of southern — or perhaps more particularly of central — Ireland in the seventh century. In the matter due to Móel-cáich the Gallican element seems greater; perhaps his church was one where the old Irish liturgy had been less affected by Roman influence.[194]

556. The Missal of Fulda

ED: Georg Witzel (Vuicelius) *Exercitamenta syncerae pietatis* (Mainz 1555) [extracts only]. COMM: Paul Lejay *Rev. d'hist. et de litt. relig.* VII (1902) 561.

Georg Witzel (1501–1573), a native of Hesse, became a writer of some prominence in the controversies of the German Reformation. In 1554 he settled in Mainz and

---

[192] *Cf.* pp. 468 *sqq supra.*

[193] Warner, who thinks — against the probabilities, as it seems to the present writer — that the revision as well as the original writing took place at Tallaght, suggests that the missal may have been brought to northern Munster by Donnchadh mac Briain as part of the pledges he took from Leinster in 1026.

[194] To the present writer it seems an acceptable hypothesis — nothing more — that the Stowe Missal was transcribed at Tallaght, within the period 792 x 812, from the liturgy of that church; was carried to Lorrha within, at most, the next twenty-five years (there may have been close associations between Lorrha and Tallaght: *cf.* p. 469 *supra*); and was there revised by Móel-cáich in accordance with the liturgy of Lorrha.

devoted the remainder of his life to literature and scholarship, publishing a great number of works. One of the earliest of these was his *Exercitamenta syncerae pietatis*, in which he gave extracts from an old missal of the monastery of Fulda.[195] This missal is not now known, but Witzel's extracts show that it was of Irish provenance, and that its text was very nearly related to, though not identical with, that of the Stowe Missal.

557. The St. Gall fragments

Codices 1394 and 1395 in the monastic library of St. Gall are gatherings of remnants of ancient manuscripts, bound together by the historian von Arx when he was librarian. They include the following interesting fragments of Irish sacramentaries, missals or rituals.

(i) Fragment of a requiem mass

MS: St. Gall Stiftsbibl. 1395 pp. 430–3 *s* VIII. FACS: F. Keller " Bilder u. Schriftzüge " [p. 98 *supra*], and Reeves's trans. — C. P. Cooper *Appendix A* [p. 99 *supra*] pl. xxxi. EDS: A. P. Forbes *Liber Ecclesie Beati Terrenani de Arbuthnott* (Burntisland 1864) pp. xlviii–l. — H&S I (1869) 197 [gospel]. — Warren *Lit.* (1881) 180–2. — H. J. White in J. Wordsworth *Old Latin Biblical Texts* II (1886) [gospel]. COMM: G. Scherrer *Verzeichniss d. Hss. d. Stiftsbibl. v. St. Gallen* (Halle 1875) 463. — S. Berger *RC* VI 350–1; *Histoire de la Vulgate* (Paris 1893) 31, 418. — F. H. A. Scrivener and E. Miller *Plain introduction to the criticism of the New Testament* (London 1894) II 49–50.

This remnant — two leaves — contains apparently the introit [196] and gospel of a mass for the dead. The gospel is the story of the raising of Lazarus, taken from John xi 14–44. The text is not Vulgate but Old Latin, with many peculiar characteristics which seem to be Irish. It is closely related to Codex Usserianus I and to Codex Bezae. Symbol in textual criticism: p.

(ii) Intercessory prayer and litany

MS: St. Gall Stiftsbibl. 1395 p. 179 *s* VIII/IX. FACS: Cooper *op. cit.* pls. xxiii, xxiv. EDS: A. P. Forbes *op. cit.* p. xlviii. — Warren *Lit.* (1881) 179–80. — B. MacCarthy " On the Stowe Missal " *Trans. RIA* XXVII (1885) 233–7. *Cf.* p. 695 *supra*.

This single richly ornamented leaf contains the same confession, intercession and litany of saints as that with which the Stowe Missal opens. The concluding clauses are missing, but doubtless would have been found on the next leaf.

(iii) Fragments of the mass service

MS: St. Gall Stiftsbibl. 1394 iv pp. 95–8 *s* IX (?). FACS: Keller *op. cit.* pl. xi 6. — Cooper *op. cit.* pls. vi, xxix, xxx. EDS: A. P. Forbes *op. cit.* pp. xlv–xlvii. — C. J. Greith *Geschichte der altirischen Kirche* (Freiburg i. B. 1867) 440–2. — Warren *Lit.* 175–9. — MacCarthy *op. cit.* 234–7 [partial]. *Cf.* Scherrer *op. cit.* 459.

---

[195] See p. 520 *supra*.   [196] Ps. lxv 2–3: " Te decet, domine."

These two leaves contain portions of masses apparently proper to the feasts of the Circumcision and Epiphany, and the ordinary of the mass from the *Pater noster* to the post-communion. This latter part resembles closely the text of the Stowe Missal.— Scherrer and others have suggested that we have here the remains of the missal in Irish script which is mentioned in the oldest catalogue of St. Gall.[197]

(iv) Office for the visitation of the sick

MS: St. Gall Stiftsbibl. 1395 pp. 444–7 *s* VIII/IX. FACS: Cooper *op. cit.* pls. xxv–xxvii. EDS: A. P. Forbes *op. cit.* pp. l–li. — Warren *Lit.* 182–3. *Cf.* pp. 697–8 *supra*.

These leaves contain a section of a prayer (known in its complete form from several continental sources) [198] which formed part of an old Irish office for the visitation of the sick.

(v) Blessings of water

(a) Benedictio aquae et salis ad spergendum in dom[ibus]: Domine sancte pater omnipotens instaurator. . . . (b) Item benedictio aquae spargendum in domo: Deus, qui ad salutem humani generis. . . . (c) Item alia: Exorcizo te, creatura aquae . . . .

MS: St. Gall Stiftsbibl. 1395 pp. 444–7 *s* VIII. FACS: Cooper *op. cit.* pls. xxv– Forbes *op. cit.* p. li. — Warren *Lit.* 183–4.

These three prayers are on the reverse of a finely illuminated page. They are to be found, sometimes with considerable variations, in several continental liturgical collections; [199] the three are also in the Bobbio and the second and third in the Stowe Missal.

558. The Carlsruhe fragments

MSS: Carlsruhe Landesbibl. App. Aug. CLXVII [fragments of vellum formerly used in binding Aug. CLXVII] *s* VIII/IX. EDS: H. M. Bannister *JTS* V (1903) 49–75 [includes valuable commentary]. O–I passages: WS *Zs. f. vergl. Sprachforschung* XXXI (1889) 246 *sq.* — *Thes. Pal.* II (1903) pp. xxix, 256 [*cf. Supplement* (1910) 76].

Among the Reichenau manuscripts at Carlsruhe Dr. Holder identified as Irish two strips of vellum which had been used as binding for the codex known as the Carlsruhe Bede (no. 525). They were found to be fragments from two old sacramentaries or missals. (1) A mutilated sheet, forming originally two leaves of a codex, written in part in an insular Irish hand of the late eighth or early ninth century. F. 1 contains what seem to be portions of a mass for penitents and a mass for the dead. F. 2 has part of the preface and the post-sanctus (with variations) of the Stowe mass for apostles and other saints. The first scribe left the greater part of f. 2 blank: it was filled in by an Irishman writing on the Continent, who inserted the epistle, gradual, gospel and *ordo* of a mass for captives, five collects, and part of a preface. This

---

[197] *Cf.* no. 416.

[198] " The same prayer occurs in the Sacram. Gelas. p. 747, in a ninth-century French (Fleury) Ritual, printed by Martene (lib. III. cap. 13, vol. II. p. 381), and in a twelfth-century Salzburg Pontifical (ib. p. 387), where it opens thus, ' Omnipotens sempiterne Deus qui humano corpori animam,' &c." Warren *loc. cit.*

[199] *Cf.* Warren *loc. cit.*

arrangement of the lections is reminiscent of the Bobbio Missal. In two places here Bannister believed he found allusions to the Northmen. (2) Another mutilated sheet, now in two parts, written in an insular Irish hand of apparently about the same epoch as the preceding. In an upper margin is the entry " sancte trinitatis et sancti cronáni filii lugaedón." Cronán or Mo-Chúa of Clondalkin was son of Lugaed, according to the notes to the Calendar of Oengus, August 6.[200] There is, therefore, some grounds for conjecturing, with Bannister, that the service-book of which this sheet had formed part belonged originally to the monastic church of Clondalkin. There are some Irish passages, badly mutilated. One apparently prays for preservation " from a flood of foreigners and foes and pagans and tribulations; from plagues of fire and famine and hunger and many diverse diseases." This suggests that when it was written the raids of the Norsemen had become familiar. The liturgical text seems to be a considerable but much mutilated part of a mass in commemoration of saints. — The close relationship of both these fragments with the Stowe and Bobbio Missals is noteworthy.

559. The Piacenza fragment

MS: Piacenza, Archivio of St. Antonino MS s IX/X (?). ED: H. M. Bannister *JTS* V (1903) 49–75.

Among the documents belonging to the church of St. Antonino at Piacenza [201] there was discovered a sheet of parchment containing four pages written in Irish minuscule, but with some continental traits. The date of the script has been assigned variously from the ninth to the fourteenth century, but the text can hardly be later than the ninth. The two outer pages are illegible; the two inner contain parts of three masses, one of which is headed " ordo missae sanctae mariae," while the other two contain prefaces which are found also in the Bobbio Missal. There are rubrics in Irish.

560. Liturgical sections of the Book of Armagh

MS: LA ff. 19, 53ᵛ. EDS: Warren *Lit.* — *Vit. Trip.* II 350–1 [f. 19]. — *LA* pp. lxxv, 37, 100, 464–5. *Cf.* nos. 131, 474, 523.

F. 19. At the end of the additions to Tírechán [*cf.* p. 335 *supra*] are two groups of catch-words and abbreviations, similar in form but having no connection in matter with the Patrician notes which precede. The first group has not been satisfactorily interpreted; the second consists of a number of allusions to the life of Pope Gregory the Great, with the text in full of the *Hanc igitur* prayer of the Roman canon. — F. 53ᵛ. At the end of the Gospel of St. Matthew is a collect in his honor (Deus inmensae clementiae . . .), doubtless to be recited on his feast day, on which this page was written.

[200] The " comotatio " (*cf.* p. 335 *supra*) of the relics of " Mochua mac U Lugedon " is given in AU 790, that is, about the beginning of the epoch to which the present MS is assigned. MacN has consequently included " moccu Lugedon " in his list of *mocu* eponyms, *Proc. RIA* XXIX C 79. The evidence of the present MS, however, makes it possible that we should read mac Lugedon, and that the " mic U Lugedon " of AU is an error, perhaps resulting in some way from the facts that abbots of Clondalkin designated Ua Lugedon are mentioned under the years 781 and 801.

[201] There were close relations between Piacenza and Bobbio.

561. Ritual for penance

MS: Basel Universitätsbibl. F. iii. 15. EDS: A. P. Forbes *Liber Ecclesie Beati Terrenani de Arbuthnott* (Burntisland 1864) pp. xliv *sq.* — Warren *Lit.* 151–2 [here described as of St. Gall].

Formulae for confession and the assignment of penance. No person since Forbes seems to have examined the text in the manuscript, which contains many sections, some Irish, some English.[202]

562. Liturgical sections of the Book of Mulling

MS: TCD 60 [*cf.* no. 456]: ff. 49^v–50 *s* VIII/IX; f. 94^v *s* VIII (?). EDS: A. P. Forbes *Liber Ecclesie Beati Terrenani de Arbuthnott* (Burntisland 1864) pp. x–xi. xx–xxii. — Warren *Lit.* 171–3 [these two give the office for the visitation of the sick]. — H. J. Lawlor *Chapters on the Book of Mulling* (Edinburgh 1897) 9–10 [description of ff. 49^v–50^r], 145–66 [study and reconstruction of the liturgical notes on f. 94^v]. *Cf.* also *The Academy* Jan. 26, 1895, p. 83, Feb. 2, 1895, p. 106; *LH* I (1898) pp. xxi–xxvi; H. Jenner " Celtic Rite " sec. vi, *Cath. Encycl.*

The Book of Mulling contains two liturgical passages, an Office for the Visitation of the Sick, entered on a space originally left blank at the end of the Gospel of St. Matthew, and a collection of notes giving the outline of some ecclesiastical office, written on what was the last page of the codex following the Gospel of St. John. (1) The first of these was written some time after the bulk of the manuscript had been finished: the script is of a manifestly later period. The text resembles the similar rituals in the Stowe Missal, the Book of Dimma, and the Book of Deer. (2) The second is so faded as to be almost undecipherable, and all that can be said of the script is that it seems to be due to a different hand from that which wrote the Gospel of St. John immediately preceding. Lawlor with great patience and ingenuity elucidated these obscure lines, and reconstructed the office of which they were the headings. He believed it to be a daily office at the monastery of Tech-Moling (St. Mullins) and thought it possible that it was said by each monk in his cell before all assembled for the service of Matins. Dr. Bernard, however, noticing its close resemblance to the service prescribed in the Second Vision of Adamnán[203] as an intercession against the pestilence which, legend and prophecy said, was to arise in Ireland on the feast of the Decollation of St. John, is of the opinion that the two were identical, and quotes evidence[204] that Tech-Moling was a place of such intercession against plague.

563. Liturgical sections of the Book of Dimma

MS: TCD 59 (A. 4. 23) ff. 52–54 *s* VIII/IX [*cf.* no. 458]. EDS: A. P. Forbes *Liber Ecclesie Beati Terrenani de Arbuthnott* (Burntisland 1864) pp. xii–xiv, xvii–xx. — Warren *Lit.* 167–71. See also nos. 555, 562, 564.

The scribes of the gospel texts in the Book of Dimma left some folios blank between those of Luke and John, and thereon a later hand entered a ritual which constitutes, doubtless, the office of visitation of the sick as used in the monastery of Roscrea in

[202] *Cf.* p. 681 *supra.*   [203] No. 627. *Cf.* pp. 750 *sqq.*   [204] *Cambrensis Eversus* (ed. Kelly) I 132.

the second half of the eighth or first half of the ninth century. The service, which closely resembles those of the Stowe Missal, the Book of Mulling and the Book of Deer, consists of the anointing and the communion of the sick person, with the accompanying prayers.

564. Liturgical sections of the Book of Deer

MS: Cambridge Univ. Lib. I i. 6. 32 ff. 28^v-9 s XI [cf. p. 656]. EDS: Paley Home and Foreign Review I (1862) 487-8. — A. P. Forbes Liber Ecclesie Beati Terrenani de Arbuthnott (Burntisland 1864) pp. xiv-xv, xxii-xxiii. — John Stuart The Book of Deer (The Spalding Club: Edinburgh 1869). — H&S II pt. I (1873) 275. — Warren Lit. (1881) 164-5.

The tenth-century Scottish manuscript known as the Book of Deer contains a liturgical office, of Irish type, entered, apparently towards the end of the eleventh century, on two pages originally left blank. It is a ritual for the visitation and communion of the sick, closely related to those of the Stowe Missal, the Book of Dimma and the Book of Mulling,[205] but does not include, as they do, the prayers for the administration of extreme unction.

565. The Zürich fragments

MS: In the library of the Antiquarian Society of Zürich, deposited in the Stadtbibl. FACS: Keller " Bilder u. Schriftzüge " [p. 98 supra] 88, pl. xiii no. 3. EDS: A. P. Forbes Liber Ecclesie Beati Terrenani de Arbuthnott (Burntisland 1864) p. xlv. — Archaeological Journal XXXI (1874) 85-6. — Warren Lit. 23.

This is a sheet, two leaves, from an old Irish manuscript, which has been used as a book-binding. The script is Irish, of the tenth century or earlier. The first page is illegible, the second has the order of consecration of a virgin, the third part of the commendation of a departing soul, and the fourth the debris of an unidentified service.

Mention should be made of certain documents which, though apparently not containing Irish liturgical texts, either had, or were believed to have, Irish associations: (1) Zürich Zentralbibl. Rh. 30 c A.D. 800. This is one of the MSS used in H. A. Wilson The Gelasian Sacramentary (Oxford 1894). Cf. also Gerbert Monumenta veteris liturgiae alemannicae I (1777) 362; UJA VIII (1860) 304; L. Delisle Mémoire sur d'anciens sacramentaires (Paris 1886) 84 no. ix; E. Bishop Liturgica historica (Oxford 1918) 77 sqq. It has been identified with the " very old missal " mentioned in Codex 1305 of the St. Gall Stiftsbibliothek as at the monastery of Rheinau: " This missal, written by some Irishman, our St. Fintan, coming from Ireland, either himself wrote or brought, written, with him to our monastery of Rheinau." — G. Haenel Catalogi librorum manuscriptorum qui in bibl. Galliae, Helvetiae, etc. asservantur (Leipsic 1830) 734. On St. Fintan see pp. 602-3 supra; on the calendar in this codex p. 479. The book may have belonged to Fintan, but it did not have its origin in Ireland. The script is continental. Delisle thought it was written in northern Gaul. It is a

[205] Nos. 555, 563, 562.

Gelasian sacramentary of the type known as " the Gelasian of the eighth century." [206]
(2) St. Gall Stiftsbibl. 348 c A.D. 800. Also used in Wilson op. cit. Cf. G. Scherrer
Verzeichniss d. Hss. d. Stiftsbibl. v. St. Gallen (Halle 1875) 122; Delisle op. cit. no. x;
Bishop loc. cit. This codex belonged to Remedius, bishop of Chur (800–20), and
may have been written at Chur. It shows, according to report, strong marks of
Irish palaeographical influence. The contents form a sacramentary of the " Gelasian
of the eighth century " type. If Edmund Bishop was right in his conjecture that the
Irish were concerned in the modifications which the Roman liturgy underwent in
Gaul and northern Italy in the eighth century [207] it may be that this and the preceding
sacramentary are more or less products of their work. (3) Cambrai Bibl. publ. 164
(formerly 159) A.D. 790 x 816. Cf. Cat. des bibl. des départements XVII (1891) 44–5;
Bishop op. cit. (see index of MSS), and JTS IV (1903) 414–5; H. A. Wilson The Gregorian Sacramentary under Charles the Great (Henry Bradshaw Soc. XLIX) (London
1915). This was written for that Bishop Hildoard of Cambrai who was a friend of
the Irishman Dungal.[208] According to some it shows evidence of Irish influence in
its production; but the contents are the original Gregorian sacramentary as sent to
Charles the Great by Pope Adrian, without the Carolingian additions. (4) Ibid.
162–3 (formerly 158) s IX. Cf. Cat. des bibl. loc. cit.; Bishop loc. cit. This also is
said to show Irish influence. The text is the Gregorian sacramentary fused with
Carolingian additions. (5) Vat. lat. 3325 (s XI) cover s X/XI. ED: H. M. Bannister
JTS IX (1908) 414–21. This eleventh-century copy of Sallust has as binding two
leaves of a missal or sacramentary in Irish-continental handwriting, apparently of
the tenth or eleventh century. The Sallust, possibly with its binding, once belonged
to the abbey of St. Blandin near Tournai. The two leaves contain masses for the
feast of Holy Innocents, incomplete; the Circumcision, complete; and the vigil of
the Epiphany, incomplete. The gospel of the second is from a Gospel of " James
son of Alphaeus," hitherto unknown, but possibly derived from the apocryphal pseudo-
Matthew. The contents as a whole show no evidence of Irish origin.

566. The Drummond Missal

MS of Drummond Castle, s XI. ED: A. P. Forbes Kalendars of Scottish Saints (Edinburgh 1872) pp. xv–xviii, 1–32 [calendar only]. — G. H. Forbes Missale Drummon-
diense the ancient Irish missal in the possession of the Baroness Willoughby de Eresby
(Burntisland 1882) [cf. J. Dowden The Academy 15 Dec. 1883 p. 393]. — COMM:
A. P. Forbes Liber Ecclesie Beati Terrenani de Arbuthnott (Burntisland 1864) pp. xxxviii–
xxxvi. — F. E. Warren The manuscript Irish missal belonging to the President and
Fellows of Corpus Christi College Oxford (London 1879) pp. 1–13 [collation of the canon].

SCRIPT, etc.: Irish minuscule, classed as of s XI. A small volume containing 109 ff.
of about 6 × 4½ in. Initial letters generally are ornamented with yellow. CONTENTS:
F. 1: Blessing of water. — Calendar. This is a continental calendar, with names of
the more famous Irish saints inserted. By the loss of a folio the entries from Sept. 22
to Oct. 10 inclusive are missing. F. 18: Exorcisms of salt and water, and prayers
"for every ecclesiastical grade." At f. 22 the missal proper begins with a votive mass of
the Holy Trinity. There are many votive masses, a considerable number common
of saints, and very few proper of saints or of the season. No Irish saints are commemorated by masses. The preface and canon are given at f. 37. In the canon at

[206] Cf. p. 686 supra.   [207] Op. cit. 84n.   [208] Cf. p. 541 supra.

the prayer *Communicantes* there are added to the usual text the names of Sts. Martin, Gregory, Augustine, Jerome, Benedict and Patrick, and at the *Nobis quoque peccatoribus* those of Sts. Eugenia and Brigit. The volume is, however, purely a Roman missal of the post-Carolingian type. — Three quatrains in Irish are written on the upper margins of ff. 43^v-4, 89^v-90, and 90^v-1, and at the end of the missal there is a short dialogue in Irish verse between St. Coemgen and St. Ciarán of Saigir (*cf.* nos. 198, 124), beginning " Is mochen a noeb chlerig."

567. The Corpus Missal

Oxford Corpus Christi Coll. 282 *s* XII^1. ED: F. E. Warren *The manuscript Irish missal belonging to the President and Fellows of Corpus Christi College Oxford* (London 1879).

SCRIPT: Irish, usually classed as of the 12th century. It is a portable volume, about 6½ × 5 inches, and quite thick, containing now 212 leaves, but imperfect at the end. There is very considerable ornamentation of the usual Irish character. CONTENTS: Opens (like the Gregorian) with the canon; the ordinary is missing. Then follows a long series of votive masses, ending with the order of marriage and the nuptial mass. A limited number of masses of the season come next, beginning with the first Sunday of Advent and ending with Pentecost. The masses proper of saints follow, of which only two are for Irish saints — Brigit and Patrick. Concluding the missal portion are thirteen masses common of saints. Then follow the order of baptism and of blessing water; the blessing of homes; the visitation, anointing and communion of the sick; and the commendation of the departing soul. The texts are essentially those of the Roman rite. Quite a number of readings agree with the Sarum usage. There are also many minor variations, some of which seem peculiarly Irish. In a litany appointed for Holy Saturday supplication is made that God may preserve the King of the Irish and his army, and grant them life, health and victory. In an earlier intercession of the same day mention is made together of " our most blessed Pope, our venerable Bishop, our most glorious King N., and his most noble offspring N." [209] Various expressions indicate that the book was for the use of a male religious community. COMMENT: It is a reasonable inference that the missal was a product of the reform movement of the twelfth century [210] and belonged to one of the houses of the continental religious orders established in Ireland before the Norman invasion. Warren guessed that the time was the reign of Toirdelbach Ûa Conchobuir (*c* 1136-1157), and the place the church of Clones.

III. BOOKS FOR THE DIVINE OFFICE AND COLLECTIONS OF SIMILAR LITURGICAL TEXTS

568. The Antiphonary of Bangor

MS: Milan Bibl. Ambrosiana C. 5 inf. *s* VII. FACS: F. Steffens *Lateinische Paläographie* I (Fribourg 1903) pl. xxiv no. 3; Fr. ed. pl. xxvi [f. 30]. See also Henry Bradshaw Soc. ed., *infra.* EDS: L. A. Muratori *Anecdota ex Ambrosianae Bibliothecae*

209 Warren's ed. pp. 133, 128.   210 *Cf.* pp. 745 *sqq infra.*

codicibus . . . [usually quoted as *Anecdota Ambrosiana*] IV (Padua 1713) 119–59 [some omissions, chiefly of well known texts, and many errors, probably due to the copyist; all subsequent eds., till that of the Henry Bradshaw Soc., are based on this]; *Opera omnia* XI pt. III (Arezzo 1770) 217–51. — Migne *PL* LXXII 579–606. — Warren *Lit.* (1881) 187–94 [selections]. — J. O'Laverty *An historical account of the diocese of Down and Connor* II (Dublin 1884) App. pp. ix–xlv [more nearly complete than Muratori's ed., but not accurate]. — F. E. Warren *The Antiphonary of Bangor* 2 vols. (Henry Bradshaw Soc. IV, X) (London 1893, 1895) [I: descriptive introd., complete facs., and letter-press; II: liturgical introd., emended text, valuable notes and appendices]. There are various eds. of individual texts: see analysis of contents *infra*. Comm: *Rer. Hib. SS* I (1814) " Epist. nuncup." pp. clxiii–clxxvi. — W. Reeves *UJA* I (1853) 168–79. — Otto Seebass *Über Columba von Luxeuils Klosterregel und Bussbuch* (Dresden 1883) 25 *sqq.* — Ebert *Allgemeine Geschichte der Literatur des Mittelalters im Abendlande* I (1889) 621 *sq.* — Manitius *Geschichte der christlich-lateinischen Poesie* (Stuttgart 1891) 482 *sqq.* — *The Tablet* 16 Dec. 1893 p. 972. — W. C. Bishop " A service book of the seventh century " *Church Quarterly Rev.* XXXVII (1893–4) 337–63 [interesting and ingenious suggestions]. — B. Zimmerman *IER* XVI (June 1895) 635 *sqq.* — G. Morin " Explication d'un passage de la règle de s. Colomban relatif à l'office des moines celtiques; destination de la formule 'ad pacem celebrandam' dans l'Antiphonaire de Bangor " *Rev. Bénédictine* XII (1895) 200–2. — S. Bäumer (trans. R. Biron) *Histoire du bréviaire romain* I (Paris 1895) 239 *sqq*, 263 *sq* [includes some adverse criticism of Warren's work]. — F. Cabrol " Bangor (Antiphonaire de) " *Dict. d'archéol. chrêt. et de liturgie* II pt. I (1910) 183–91 [very important]. — L. Gougaud " Celtiques (Liturgies) " *ibid.* II pt. II (1910) 2969 *sqq* [especially sects. on " Sources " and " The Divine Office "]. — W. M. Lindsay *Early Irish minuscule script* (Oxford 1910) 1. — Manitius *Lat. Lit.* (1911) 160–2.

Of the ancient monastery of Bend-chor, or Bangor,[211] the only important surviving relic is a small manuscript service-book in the Ambrosian Library at Milan, whither it was brought by the founder, Cardinal Federico Borromeo, from the abbey of Bobbio. It was designated *Antiphonarium Benchorense*, " the Antiphonary of Bangor," by its first editor, the Italian scholar Muratori, and the name, though inappropriate, has become permanent.

Script, etc.: A codex of 36 leaves, about 9 × 7 inches in size, of coarse vellum; in three gatherings, of 5 (ff. 1–6, 10–13), 4 (ff. 14–21), and 7 (ff. 22–8, 30–6) sheets. In the centre of the third gathering a narrow slip (f. 29) was inserted to carry the last few lines of the text on the preceding page; and three single leaves (ff. 7–9) have been bound into the first gathering, forming an interpolation in the midst of another text. The script is semi-uncial, passing into minuscule, and resembles somewhat that of the Schaffhausen Adamnán (*cf.* p. 429 *supra*). Script, ornamentation, abbreviations and orthography are Irish, and are not inconsistent with a seventh-century date.

Contents: First Part: ff. 1–17ᵛ b 14. This consists, according to the primary plan, of three canticles drawn from the Sacred Scriptures and ten metrical hymns or poems: " Canticle of Moses " (*Deut.* xxxii 1–43); [212] " St. Hilary's Hymn " (p. 252); " Apos-

---

[211] *Cf.* pp. 395–7 *supra*.   [212] *Cf.* p. 689 *supra*.

tles' Hymn " (no. 89 iv); " Blessing of Holy Zachary " (*Luke* i 68-80); " Hymn for the Lord's Day " (" Te Deum laudamus," having the anthem " Laudate pueri " — *Ps.* cxii 1 — prefixed); " Hymn at the Communion of the Clergy " (no. 89 v); " Hymn at the Blessing of the Candle " (no. 89 i); " Midnight Hymn " (" Mediae noctis tempus est "); " Hymn for the Natal Day of Martyrs or for the Sabbath at Matins " (no. 89 iii); " Hymn at Matins on Sunday " (no. 89 ii); " St. Patrick's Hymn " (no. 87); " St. Comgall's Hymn " (no. 92 i); [213] " St. Camelacus's Hymn" (no. 88). — But, as has been noticed above, three extra folios (7-9) have been interpolated into this part of the codex, on which are written two more scriptural canticles, one designated simply " Canticle " (" Cantemus Domino " *Exodus* xv 1-19), and the other " Blessing of the Children " (" Benedicite " *Dan.* iii 57-88). Where now placed, they break into the " Blessing of Zachary." The script of these leaves is that of the hand which wrote ff. 26ᵛ-30ᵛ, but neither there nor elsewhere is there any break in the MS into which we could believe that they once fitted. Warren advanced the theory " that they were originally intended to be loose, and to be shifted backwards or forwards to that part of the MS. where the collect or anthem occurs which was to be used in connection with them." [214] It is more probable that when the scribe of ff. 26ᵛ-30ᵛ took over the MS he, or his superior, decided that these two texts should be included in the collection of scriptural canticles which the volume was to contain, and he accordingly wrote them out on loose sheets of vellum to be attached to the first part of the codex. Possibly from the first they were inserted at what must have seemed an appropriate place, the text of the " Blessing of Zachary." — Throughout this Part the script of the text is by the same hand, with the exceptions of these three interpolated leaves and of the last stanza of the " Hymn at the Blessing of the Candle," a kind of doxology, which has a distinct character but may, perhaps, not be from a different scribe.

Second Part: ff. 17ᵛ b 16-29. This Part forms a repertory of sets of collects, divided into two groups: (1) those to be recited at the various hours of the Divine Office; and (2) those to be appended to certain canticles, psalms and hymns. It was designed — as will be seen presently — to extend from f. 18 to f. 28ᵛ, that is, from the middle of the second gathering to the middle of the third. The first of the two sections into which it falls contains collects for the hours of " secunda " (corresponding with that which is now designated prime), terce, sext, none, vespers, " initium noctis " (corresponding with compline),[215] nocturn (vigils or matins), and matins (the present lauds). Three different sets of collects for these hours are given, beginning at the top of f. 18, and also a single collect " at secunda," entered on f. 17ᵛ, apparently to fill space left at the end of the collection of canticles and hymns. Of the three sets, the first consists of short riming prayers, one for each of the hours beginning with " secunda," except the last, matins, which has three. This series differs both in content and in form,[216] from the bulk of the other matter in the Antiphonary. The second set [217] appears to have

<hr>

[213] It should be noted that the ornamentation of the initial letters of these two hymns is more elaborate than that of any others in the MS.

[214] Such collects and anthems are found scattered through the latter part of the volume, from f. 22 to the end.

[215] Warren equates " initium noctis," nocturn and matins with what he designates first nocturn, second nocturn, and third nocturn combined with lauds, respectively.

[216] Warren calls attention to the fact that the dotted ornamentation of capital letters which prevails generally in the book is discontinued throughout this set of collects.

[217] A cross placed in the margin calls attention to the beginning of this series; the same mark seems to be frequently used for a like purpose throughout the rest of the MS. Possibly it indicates a new exemplar, or a new part of an exemplar, rather than editorial divisions of the present collection.

been that in most frequent use at Bangor: it consists of single collects for each of the day hours from " secunda " to vespers, two for " initium noctis," followed by prayers at the giving of the " pax," by the symbol or creed,[218] and by the " Our Father "; then one collect for nocturn and two for matins. After these come a long series of intercessions for special classes of persons: the common prayer of the brethren,[219] the dominating thought of which is supplication for the forgiveness of sins; prayers for the baptized, the clergy, the abbot,[220] the monks, for peace of peoples and kings, for blasphemers, the impious, those going on a journey, those giving thanks, those doing alms-deeds, the infirm, captives (?), those in tribulation (?), and penitents (?). (Two commemorations of martyrs and one collect of a general character are included in this group of special petitions, possibly because of some misunderstanding on the part of the scribe or confusion in his *Vorlage*.) In these collects we may see, no doubt, the development of the scheme of prayers which was prescribed — for the day hours — by Columbanus, who carried the discipline of Bangor to the continent of Europe just about one hundred years before the date usually assigned to the Antiphonary: " With the augment of the intervening versicles, first for our sins, then for the whole Christian people, then for priests, and the other consecrated grades of holy orders, next for those doing alms-deeds, after that for the peace of kings, finally for our enemies,[221] that God may not reckon it as a sin to them that they harass us and rob us, for they know not what they do." (*Regula Coenobialis* vii.)[222] The last of the three sets consists of a collect for nocturn and three for matins. If, as the passage quoted from Columbanus suggests, the long series of prayers for special classes of persons really belongs to the day hours, it probably forms part of that set; otherwise it is a series in which all but the last two hours are missing. The second of the two groups into which this Part is divided is made up of eight or nine sets of collects for the following occasions: (a) after the canticle " Cantemus Domino "; (b) after the " Benedicite," or Blessing of the Three Children; (c) after the " Three Psalms," *i.e.*, Psalms cxlviii– cl; (d) after the " Evangelium," which, seemingly, designates the gospel canticle " Benedictus," the Blessing of Zachary; (e) after " the Hymn " (the particular hymn used probably varied from day to day or from season to season);[223] and (f) a collect " of the martyrs."[224] The collects in each set are arranged in this order, but the number in a set varies from the entire six to only one.[225] — The handwriting in this Second Part continues the same as in the first to f. 25^v, where, at the third collect of the fifth set in the group just mentioned, there is a slight change of style. On the next page, at the " post hymnum " of the sixth set, another and larger script begins, and on f. 26^v, at the beginning of the eighth series, we meet with a very notable script

---

[218] An interesting text: *cf.* p. 722 *infra*.

[219] Perhaps this title applies to the whole series, not merely to the first prayer.

[220] Cabrol calls attention to the fact that here alone, among all these litanic prayers, there are only the anthems, no " oratio." This has significance for his theory that the Antiphonary was the abbot's book.

[221] Columban's intercession " for our enemies " is replaced by those for blasphemers and the impious, of which the first contains the passage quoted by the saint and based on *Acts* vii 59.

[222] Cabrol is of the opinion that this series of prayers and versicles constitutes the series of litanic prayers which is recited ordinarily at the end of the great offices.

[223] *Cf.* pp. 714–5 *infra*.

[224] Jenner (" Celtic Rite," *Cath. Encycl.*) suggests that we have here an outline of the Bangor office of Lauds.

[225] Several of these texts are met with also in the Turin Fragment (no. 569); but elsewhere very few (with the exception, of course, of the *Pater noster*) have been discovered — one collect and an anthem from another in the Stowe Missal (no. 555), one in LH (no. 574), two in the Southampton Psalter (no. 476), and, of these two, one also in the psalters Vitellius F. XI and Palatinus 65 (*cf.* p. 646).

— that in which the interpolated folios 7–9 are written — which continues to the end of this part. It is to be noted that the last few lines of the last collect are on a narrow strip of vellum (f. 29) inserted in the middle of the third gathering. This makes it probable that the next page (beginning what is here distinguished as the Third Part) had already been written, and — as a deduction therefrom — that in the original design there was to be a division point in the book at this place.

Third Part: ff. 30–36. The last of the three main divisions of the codex contains a heterogeneous collection of texts written down by many different scribes. It opens with the " Verses of the Community of Bangor " (no. 92 ii), having its own distinct script. The last scribe of the Second Part, passing over this text, inserted after it a form of exorcism, found also in the Stowe Missal and elsewhere. Then another scribe wrote a prayer " de martyribus," probably to fill space, for on the following page, in another handwriting, begins a long series of anthems, constituting the only part of the MS (ff. 31^v–3^v) to which its accepted title can logically be applied. Anthems are given for Psalm lxxxix, for the " Three Psalms," for the canticles " Cantemus Domino," " Benedicite " and " Gloria in excelsis " — the text of this last is transcribed in full, — for the communion, and " de martyribus." The bulk of this series seems to have been written by one scribe,[226] but the final page is in a new handwriting. After a blank half column, indicating the end of a division, there follow several prayers or collects for the Divine Office, set down more or less at haphazard, it would appear, by various scribes. On f. 34^r one of them has written a " common prayer for the day hours," a " prayer for our abbot," and a " common prayer for ourselves,"[227] ending with the " Our Father," the whole perhaps to serve as a short substitute for the series of intercessions for special classes of persons given on ff. 20–22: the second and third are identical with collects of that set. A second [228] has inscribed collects for matins and nones on f. 34^v; and on f. 35^r others " ad secundam " and " de martyribus " were entered by a third, whilst a fourth, at some later time, added a collect — to follow " Te Deum " on Sundays — on the lower part of this page, originally left vacant. The script of this last contributor is markedly different from any other in the codex. Two more " Te Deum " collects, one of them merely an expansion of the above, are transcribed on f. 35^v by three different hands. On f. 36^r another penman wrote a collect " for the blessing of the candle," and one for " Te Deum ": the latter was subsequently partially erased when it was discovered that it had already been twice recorded on the preceding folio. Finally we come to the last page and, in a new script, the interesting and important poem " In Memory of Our Abbots " (no. 92 iii).

It will be seen that the manuscript has in some degree the appearance of a liturgical common-place book. As it now stands it can hardly be the publication of the monastic *scriptorium* in the sense in which the majority of the other early codices may be so described. Probably it was begun as such — the existence of the Turin fragment [229] shows that

---

[226] Warren thought there were two, but the differences might be attributable to a change of pen. Several of these anthems are also in the Stowe Missal, St. Gall MS 1394, Book of Mulling, Book of Dimma, Book of Deer, and LH.

[227] " Common oroit dún," another example of the use of the Irish language in liturgical books. *Cf.* pp. 687, 695. The titles of this page seem to be by the writer of the text.

[228] Warren thought this might be the same scribe as he who wrote the last page of the series of anthems.

[229] No. 569.

it was not unique — but the sporadic character of script and contents in the later part of the volume points rather to its possession or use by many successive holders, who each made his own addition to the collection. The rubrical titles, we may note, are by the same hand throughout, and evidently were added after the book was completed. Furthermore, it is clear that when the texts were written the insertion of the present titles was not contemplated: in fact, it is very doubtful whether the adding of rubrics in any form was part of the original design. This constitutes presumptive evidence that our book was a special compilation, not a transcript or new edition of a kind of service-book already in common use; also that in the primary plan it either was not intended for practical use in the choir, or, if for such use, was to be in the hands of some person whose knowledge of the liturgy was such that no rubrical guidance would be required.

Many attempts have been made to classify the Antiphonary of Bangor. O'Laverty thought it a service-book proper to Bangor, containing only, or chiefly, such matter as was peculiar to the usage of that church in the observance of the Divine Office, and serving as a local supplement to the service-book in general use. Another suggestion was that it was a fragment of a larger codex which had contained also the entire psalter. Still another was that it was an abbreviated breviary, a portable service-book for the use of travellers. Edmund Bishop was of the opinion that it had been formed by the combination of four or five small service-books, which, after the loss of some leaves and the interpolation of others, resulted in the present manuscript. None of these solutions has commended itself to later liturgists. Only two theories remain to be seriously considered: Warren's, " that it is a companion volume to the Psalterium and Lectionarium for use in the Divine Office, either (1) on Easter Eve and Easter Day; or (2) on Saturdays and Sundays in Easter-tide; or (3) on Saturdays and Sundays throughout the year, and also on Feasts of Martyrs . . . and that the preponderance of evidence is in favour of " the last; and Cabrol's, that it was the book either of the hebdomadarian — the priest who, according to the custom — at least of Benedictine monasteries — was appointed each week and had, among other duties, that of commencing the devotions at the various canonical hours; or, more probably, of the president of the choir, who would be the abbot or the prior. With this book, the " book of hymns of the week," and the Bible,[230] the abbot would be

---

[230] The abbot, it is assumed, directed the lector where to begin and to end the readings, and would have a Bible beside him for this purpose. Our MS, however, with its scriptural canticles, has the appearance of being a companion to the psalter rather than to the whole Bible; indeed, as the abbot would un-

in a position to direct all the offices and devotions, habitual or special, of the monastery.

Cabrol's hypothesis meets the difficulties of the problem better than any other. It does not seem, however, to give due emphasis to the peculiar manner in which the codex was compiled. That manner of compilation points to its being to a considerable degree a personal and chance production: priest's or prior's or abbot's liturgical handbook it doubtless was, but it appears to have been at the same time his commonplace book.

It is generally agreed that the date of the manuscript is fixed within the era 680 x 691 by the last item, the hymn " In Memory of our Abbots." It is possible, however, that this is an addition later than the bulk of the codex; and, on the other hand, not impossible that the codex is of later date and the hymn a copy of an older exemplar.[231]

Of the importance of the Antiphonary of Bangor there is no question. It may be the oldest extant Irish manuscript: it is the oldest to which precise dates can — with probability — be assigned. Apart from some fragments it is the only record surviving of the old Irish church services unaffected by the Romanising movement of the seventh and eighth centuries, and is one of the very few western liturgical books of the seventh century which we possess. The Antiphonary of Bangor and the " Orationale Gothicum " are the only two liturgical books, other than mass books, written in western Europe in the seventh century and still available for study. In it the specialists find their primary sources for the Gallican, Ambrosian, Mozarabic and oriental elements of the old Irish liturgy, for the curiously vigorous cult of martyrs, for the details of the divine office, for the Irish versions of Holy Scripture; [232] and through its pages the general student can receive the voice of the daily worship of God carried across twelve centuries from those famous, but shadowy, monasteries of ancient Ireland.

569. The Turin liturgical fragment

MS: Turin Bibl. nazionale F. IV. 1 [233] s VII. Facs: C. Cipolla *Codici Bobiesi* (1907) pl. xxxiv. Ed: Wilhelm Meyer " Das turiner Bruchstück der ältesten irischen Litur-

doubtedly know his psalter and the weekly *cursus hymnorum* by heart, he could direct the chants and litanical prayers by the help only of the present book.

[231] Under ordinary circumstances it would be brought up to date by the addition of lines commemorating the later abbots, but this was made impossible by its alphabetical character.

[232] The scriptural readings have been analyzed by Warren, vol. II pp. xxxi–xxxix. They give the interesting result that the " Irish " type of text — at any rate in the gospels — was already established when the Antiphonary was written.

[233] This volume has other Irish sections: *cf*. nos. 511 and 515.

gie " *Nachrichten v. d. k. Gesellsch. d. Wissensch. z. Göttingen* philol.-hist. Kl. 1903 pp. 163–214 [with dissertation making a comparison with AB; *cf.* F. E. Warren *JTS* IV (1903) 610–3; P. Lejay *Rev. d'hist. et de litt. relig.* IX (1904) 169 *sq:* each of these reviews gives a good account of the document].

Among the remains of the library of Bobbio is this fragment of six leaves now bound with various other pieces to form a codex at Turin. It is a fragment of an Irish service-book resembling the Antiphonary of Bangor, but, in the opinion of its editor, Meyer, is of earlier date. He also thought that it was written at Bobbio. Script, abbreviations and contents, however, are Irish.

CONTENTS: " Canticle of Moses " (Exod. XV 8–19) [the beginning lost]; 2 collects thereto; " Canticle of the three children " (Dan. iii 57–88); [234] 2 collects thereto; 3 collects to the " Three Psalms " (cxlviii–cl); *Ymnum dicat turba fratrum* (p. 252 *supra*); 2 collects " post evangelium "; *Spiritus diuinae lucis* (no. 89 ii); 2 collects " de martyribus "; *Te Deum laudamus;* 2 collects thereto; 2 collects for sext. All these items are in AB, except four collects, of which one is in the Southampton Psalter (no. 476).

570. The Paris fragments of an Antiphonary

MS: BN nouv. acquis. lat. 1628 *s* VIII/IX. ED: G. Morin *Rev. Bénédictine* XXII (1905) 329–56.

This codex contains fragments of an antiphonary written in an Irish, or at least insular, hand. It belongs to the Gallican liturgical family, and does not seem to have any close relationship with the Antiphonary of Bangor.

571. Liturgical sections of the Basel Psalter

MS: Basel Universitätsbibl. A. vii. 3 *s* IX ff. 1–3 [no. 364 (iv)]. ED: A. P. Forbes *Liber Ecclesie Beati Terrenani de Arbuthnott* (Burntisland 1864) pp. xli–xliv. *Cf.* Warren *Lit.* (1881) 185; Lawlor *Book of Mulling* (1897) 164–5; *LH*[2] I (1898) pp. xxvi–xxviii.

The first three leaves of the Irish psalter at Basel contain liturgical notes written by several Irish hands of somewhat later date than that of the bulk of the manuscript. The following are the liturgical articles: Hymn *Cantemus in omni die* (no. 98); collect thereto (*LH*[2] I p. xxvii); hymn *Alta audite* τὰ ἔργα (no. 95 ii); hymn *Christus in nostra insula* (no. 95 i) [first line only]; intercession to B. V. M.; epistle of Christ to Abgarus [235] [title only]; prayer of St. John *Deus meus et Pater* [opening words]; prayer entitled *De conscientiae reatu ante altare;* [236] invocations of B. V. M., saints and

---

[234] These are the canticles on the inserted leaves in AB: *cf.* p. 708 *supra*.

[235] *Cf.* H. Leclercq " Abgar (La légende de)" *Dict. d'archéol. chrét. et de liturgie* I i 87–97; L. Gougaud *RHE* XX ii (1924) 212–3.

[236] Also in Angers Bibl. de la ville 18 (formerly 14) *s* IX/X f. 180[v], where it has the title *Confessio sancti Patricii episcopi*, and in the Bk. of Cerne ff. 48–50, with title *Alma confessio*. In the Bk. of Nunnaminster the latter part of the prayer is on f. 34: what precedes is missing through the loss of a leaf. The texts of the several MSS differ considerably: the *incipit* of the Basel Psalter is " Domine Deus omnipotens ego humiliter te adoro "; of the Angers MS " Deus, Deus meus, rex omnipotens ego " etc.; of the Bk. of Cerne "Deus Deus meus omnipotens ego " etc. It is either an *apologia sacerdotis* (*cf.* p. 695 *supra*)

angels (*Atlantis* V 76). It is possible that part of the above was the outline of some office.

572. The *Cursus hymnorum*

MSS: Unterdrauberg, Carinthia, Kloster St. Paul 25. 2. 31 *s* IX *in*. ff. 6–8 [no. 535]. — Carlsruhe Landesbibl. Cod. Aug. CXCV *s* IX *in* ff. 45–6ᵛ [no. 524]. — Cologne Kapitelsbibl. 106 (formerly Darmstadt 2106) *s* IX [*cf*. Jaffé and Wattenbach *Ecclesiae metropolitanae Coloniensis codices manuscripti* (Berlin 1874) 43 *sq*; Blume thought this of Irish origin, but Lindsay (*Notae Latinae* 453) says " it seems to be the MS prepared at Tours in a hurry by Alcuin in 802 for Bishop Arno of Salzburg " (*cf*. p. 525 *supra*). Alcuin's Irish affiliations in liturgical and devotional matters are well known.] — For later MSS, none of which is Irish, see the list in Blume *An. hymn.* LI pp. xvii–xix. Comm: Clemens Blume *Der Cursus s. Benedicti Nursini und die liturgischen Hymnen des 6.–9. Jahrhunderts* (*Hymnologische Beiträge* III) (Leipsic 1908); " Gregor der Grosse als Hymnendichter " *Stimmen aus Maria-Laach* LXXIV (1908) pp. 269 *sqq; An. hymn.* LI (1908) Einleitung. — A. S. Walpole *Early Latin hymns* (Cambridge 1922) introd.

On the continent of Europe under the Benedictine rule there was prescribed, in the early middle ages, a certain number of hymns to be sung in fixed order at the canonical hours. Except for a few assigned to special occasions, the cycle of these hymns was completed each week. What this early *cursus hymnorum* was has been determined, after careful investigation, by Clemens Blume.

That a similar weekly rotation of hymns was used at the divine office in Ireland, and that hymnaries, books containing the order of hymns for the week, were issued by the Irish *scriptoria*, is to be inferred from several allusions in ancient texts. The following passage from Adamnán's Life of Columba [237] is pertinent:

" At another time, a book of hymns for the week,[238] written by the hand of St. Columba, together with the leather satchel in which it was enclosed, fell from the shoulders of a boy who, slipping off a bridge, was drowned in a certain river in the country of the Leinstermen. This little book, after remaining in the water from the Feast of the Nativity of the Lord till the end of the Paschal season, was found on the bank of the river by some women walking there, and carried to a certain priest, Iogenan, a Pict by race, whose property it formerly was, being still in the same satchel, which was not only water-soaked, but badly decayed. Yet when this Iogenan opened the satchel, he found his little book sound, and as clean and dry as if it had remained all that time in a case, and had never fallen into the water. . . . Concerning the above-

or a penitential confession, or, quite probably, was used as both. There can be no doubt that it was composed long after Patrick's time, but the name doubtless testifies to its Irish origin. In the Angers copy a separate prayer beginning " Ante oculos tuos, Domine " has been interpolated into this text. *Cf.* p. 721 *infra*. Eds: Basel text: A. P. Forbes *Liber Ecclesie Beati Terrenani de Arbuthnott* (Burntisland 1864) pp. xlii–xliv. — Warren *Lit.* 185–7. Angers text: S. Berger *RC* XV (1894) 155–9. — *LH²* II 213–6. Cerne text: A. B. Kuypers *The Book of Cerne* (Cambridge 1902) 95–9.

[237] No. 214. *Lib*. II *cap*. ix.   [238] " hymnorum liber septimaniorum."

mentioned book of Iogenan, we received the account in unequivocal terms from several truthful and worthy men of good repute, who examined the same little book, which, after its submersion for the many days above stated, was perfectly white and clean."

Of prior date to the ninth century we have no such Irish *cursus hymnorum* surviving. But from the beginning of that century there are two Irish manuscripts — which in these sections, however, may possibly have been written on the Continent — that together contain a complete order of hymns. In the Irish St. Paul Codex are twenty-eight hymns, assigned to the several canonical hours of the week, and one for Easter; and in the Carlsruhe Augustine is a supplementary collection of nine, of which one seems to be for Easter, seven are for saints' festivals, and one is an extra hymn for terce. Moreover the contemporary Cologne codex 106, written on the Continent but of Irish, or more probably English, origin, gives eight of these hymns in the same order. Two things are noteworthy: (1) this new *cursus hymnorum*, appearing first in these Irish manuscripts, differed almost entirely from the older Benedictine *cursus;* and (2) from the tenth century onward it completely displaced the older collection throughout Latin Christendom, and, with modifications, persists to-day in the Roman Breviary.

Blume assumes that this new collection represents the *cursus* of the Irish Church, and that its introduction, and successful propagation, on the Continent were due to Irish and English ecclesiastics in the ninth century.

The fact that the collection is made up of individual hymns of continental, not Irish, origin Blume would explain by the theory that this *cursus* really is one drawn up by Pope Gregory the Great, which was adopted in Ireland from a " book of hymns of the week " which he sent to St. Columba.[239]

Militating against Blume's theory are the facts that, except in these two or three ninth-century codices, the hymns in question are scarcely either quoted or mentioned in early Irish literature; and that such scanty information as we possess regarding the constitution of the divine office in the Irish Church before the ninth century is of quite different tenor.

For the liturgical matter in the Southampton Psalter, *s* IX/X, see no. 476.

[239] *LH*[2] II 24. — On the other hand Thomas of Elmham in his *Historia monasterii S. Augustini Cantuariensis* (ed. C. Hardwick, RS 1858), compiled in 1414, professes to give (p. 97) a list of hymns for the canonical hours which Gregory sent to Augustine of Canterbury. It has nothing in common with our alleged old Irish *cursus*, but is the Benedictine collection with considerable variations.

573. The Paris fragment of an Irish hymnal

MS: BN lat. 9488 ff. 75-6 *s* XI(?). COMM: H. M. Bannister *JTS* IX (April 1908) 422-7 [gives a collation of the texts].

The Paris codex 9488 is made up of fragments from many old manuscripts which had been used as book-bindings. Two leaves are in a script which is described as being continental Irish, probably of the eleventh century, and evidently form a fragment of an Irish hymnal or other service-book. The contents are the *Hymnum dicat* (cf. pp. 252, 419), wanting the first three verses, *Spiritus divinae lucis* (no. 89 ii), and *Te Deum laudamus* (cf. pp. 717, 722). These texts occur in the same order, but with accompanying collects, in the Turin liturgical fragment (no. 569).

574. The *Liber Hymnorum* — Book of Hymns

MSS: TCD 1441 (E. 4. 2) *s* XI. — Franciscan Convent, Merchants' Quay, Dublin, MS *s* XI. FACS: *Facs. Nat. MSS Ire.* I (1874) pls. xxxii–xxxvi [pages and ornamental letters from TCD copy], xxi [from Franciscan copy]. EDS: J. H. Todd *Leabhar Imuinn The Book of Hymns of the ancient Church of Ireland* fasc. I (IA&CS: Dublin 1855),II (1869) [contains the first 18 texts of the TCD copy, with introductory matter relating to the 19th]. — J. H. Bernard and R. Atkinson *The Irish Liber Hymnorum* I *Text and introduction*,II *Translations and notes* (Henry Bradshaw Soc. XIII, XIV: London 1898) [complete text drawn from both MSS]. Of Irish texts only: WS *Goidilica* (Calcutta 1866); 2nd ed. *Goidelica* (London 1872). — *IT* I (1880) 3-58. — *Thes. Pal.* II (1903) pp. xxxv–xl, 298-359. There are many eds. of one or more of the hymns, as indicated in the special bibliographies.

We have two codices of the eleventh century, containing similar and largely identical matter, which are usually referred to jointly as the Irish *Liber Hymnorum*, " Book of Hymns." Little is known of the history of either: one has been in Trinity College, Dublin, since the seventeenth century; the other, which has come to the Franciscan monastery in Dublin by way of Louvain and St. Isidore's, Rome, was once the property of the Franciscan friars of Donegal, with whom it was consulted by Michael O'Clery in 1630. The first folio of the Trinity College copy is missing, but that of the Franciscan volume has the title " Book of hymns which the saints of Ireland composed." Though inaccurate as a title it indicates the character of these collections: they are antiquarian, not liturgical, compilations; — products, like much else of our literature, of that movement for gathering and annotating the relics of the national past which developed in the centuries following the Norse invasions. Though the two volumes differ in arrangement, and to some extent in contents, it is clear that for the majority of their texts they go back to a common *Vorlage*, a gathering, or group of gatherings, of hymns and other devotional compositions, with commentaries, put together in the tenth or early eleventh century. The ultimate sources must have been religious service-books, in many of which, it is quite probable, marginal annotations had been from time to time entered. The use of such sources explains the presence of scriptural, apocryphal and other non-Irish documents, and also of the antiphons which frequently are attached to the hymns.

Script, etc.: The TCD MS (T) is now of 34 ff., about $10\frac{1}{2}\times 7$ in., with three scraps of vellum bound in at the end. The folios from 25 to the end have been wrongly arranged by the binder. The writing, to f. 31, is a beautiful script, with illuminated initials. After f. 31 it is of inferior character and probably later date. In the main portion the script of the Latin texts is a square semi-uncial, that of the Irish an angular minuscule, that of the prefaces a similar but smaller script, and that of the glosses, and of the notes on the top margins, a still smaller hand. The Franciscan codex (F) consists of 23 ff., smaller in size than T. The main texts are in a large and pleasing minuscule, while the prefaces and marginal and interlinear notes are in a similar but much smaller hand. Palaeographically it seems as old as T, but some of its linguistic forms seem later.

Contents: The treatment of each document (except the later additions) includes the following: (1) The preface. This, in a mixture of Irish and Latin, sets forth (in accordance with a well-known convention of Irish commentators) the author, place, time and occasion of the composition of the following text. Alternative explanations and other accretions are frequently found. In the majority of cases the T and F prefaces are practically identical, and in almost all they are closely related. (2) The text. (3) The interlinear and marginal glosses. In T these are attached to all the texts to the end of the hymn *Ateoch ríg*, and appear occasionally on later folios; in F they are added only to the Irish documents, except that the *Altus prosator* has a few. The T and F glosses frequently agree, but as a whole they are not as closely related as are the prefaces. (4) The antiphons and collects which are attached to many of the texts. (5) In T only there are, to f. 22, many entries in the upper margins which appear to have been added at a later date and to have no direct connection with the principal text. They are difficult to decipher, but consist for the most part of extracts from Holy Writ and from patristic and mediaeval authors.—With regard to the arrangement of the texts, it should be noted that those common to both codices fall into certain groups: the order of the groups differs in the two, but the order of the texts within each group is the same. A partial exception to this rule is the fact that one of the T groups forms, with additions, two groups in F. These features have importance for the investigation of the genesis of the two collections, but that is too difficult a task to be attempted here. List of Contents of T: [Group A] The original first folio, which must have had the preface to the opening hymn, is missing. F. 1 " Hymn of St. Patrick bishop of the Irish " *Audite omnes amantes* (no. 87); f. 2 *Christus in nostra insula* (no. 95 i); f. 3 *Celebra Iuda* (no. 93); f. 4 *Parce Domine* (no. 90). [B] F. 4^v *Sén Dé* (no. 582); f. 6 *Cantemus in omni die* (no. 98). [C] F. 6^v *Ymnum dicat* (*cf.* pp. 252, 419); f. 8 *In Trinitate spes mea* (no. 97); f. 8^v *Martine te deprecor* (no. 99). [D] F. 9 *Gloria in excelsis*; f. 9^v *Magnificat*; *Benedictus*; f. 10 *Te Deum laudamus* (*cf.* pp. 716, 722). [E] F. 11 *Altus prosator* (no. 91 i) [a folio is missing between ff. 12 and 13, on which were stanzas 14–21 of the *Altus*];

f. 13 *In te Christe* (no. 91 ii); f. 13ᵛ *Noli Pater* (no. 91 iii); *Deus meus et Pater* (*cf.* p. 713); f. 14ᵛ the epistle of Christ to Abgarus (*cf.* p. 719 *infra*). [F] F. 15 *Genair Patraicc* (no. 132); f. 16 *Admuinemmair noeb-Patraicc* (no. 102); *Brigit bé* (no. 95 iii); f. 17 *Ní car Brigit* (no. 148); f. 19 *Ateoch ríg* (no. 583). The remaining items of T are not found in F: F. 19ᵛ Patrick's *Lorica* (no. 101); f. 20 " Lamentation of Ambrose " *Adonai Domine sabaoth*; f. 22ᵛ an abbreviation of the psalter (*cf.* p. 721) [there is a gap between ff. 24 and 25, as a result of which part of this text is missing]. From f. 31 the texts seem to be later additions: F. 31 *Alto et ineffabile* (p. 380); f. 31ᵛ *Abbas probatus omnino* (no. 181); *In spirut nóeb* (no. 585 vi); names of the apostles, in a quatrain; f. 32 *Ecce fulget clarissima* (no. 141 vii); *Phoebi diem* (no. 155 i); ff. 33, 26 the *Amra Coluim-cille* (no. 212); f. 28ᵛ *Colum-cille co Dia* (no. 225 i); pedigree of St. Mobi. Attached to the back of the codex are three fragments: (i) Hymn *Pilip apstal apstal cáidh*,[240] and five short and faded paragraphs, apparently notes on preceding texts; (ii) the release of Scandlan *mór* and the death of Columba (*cf.* pp. 426–7); (iii) poem on the five divisions of Munster, *Coig Mumain*. Contents of F: P. 1: Paragraph in praise of hymnody *Noem papa uasal oiregda*, and hymn *Triur ríg tainic do thig Dé*;[241] these are later additions. P. 2: Group E of T. P. 12: Group A. P. 20: Group C. P. 24: Group D1 — this consists of the *Gloria in excelsis* from T's Group D, preceded by *Benedicite* (*cf.* p. 708) and *Christe qui lux es* (in no. 572), and followed by *Christi Patris in dextera* (no. 587). P. 27: Group B. P. 31: Group D2 — the remainder of Group D, with *Cantemus Domino gloriose* inserted between the *Magnificat* and the *Benedictus*. P. 36: Group F. P. 45: The *Quicunque vult* (*cf.* p. 667), not in T.

It should be observed that many hymns and liturgical offices for the festivals or other commemorations of saints are either incorporated in or attached to many of the *vitae sanctorum*. Some of these have been noted above in chaps. IV and V.

IV. Books for Private Devotions

575. The Harleian Prayer-Book

MS: BM Harl. 7653 *s* VIII/IX. Ed: *AB* (1895) App. 83–97. Comm: E. M. Thompson *Catalogue of ancient manuscripts in the British Museum* pt. II *Latin* (London 1884) 61. — Walter de Gray Birch *Book of Nunnaminster* (1889) 114–9.

This is probably the only surviving fragment of an old Irish private prayer-book. It was compiled for a woman, doubtless a nun, in the eighth or perhaps ninth century. On the first page there is an Anglo-Saxon gloss of the tenth or eleventh century, indicating that the book

[240] Eleven quatrains giving an account, said to be due to the apostle Philip, of immortal birds that dwell in east Africa. Also in RIA Stowe C 3. 2 *s* XV. Ed. with trans. *LH*² I 185–6, II 83–4, 236.

[241] Poem on the three kings at Bethlehem, in 10 quatrains, of which the last two are a still later addition. Also in RIA 23 G 23 p. 307. Ed. with trans. *LH*² I 194, II 90–1, 239.

was then in England. There is, indeed, the possibility that it was written in England by an Irish scribe or one of Irish training.

SCRIPT, etc.: Seven leaves of coarse vellum, written in Anglo-Saxon semi-uncial, with Irish ornamentation and orthography. CONTENTS: A litany, imperfect at the beginning, in which many scriptural and early continental but no Irish saints are invoked; *Te Deum laudamus*, with prefatory collect; the hymn *In pace Christi dormiam* (no. 96); and five prayers, the last a fragment, of which two are also in the prayer-book Reg. **2** A.xx (no. 576), two in the Book of Cerne (no. 578), and two in the Fleury *Libellus precum* (p. 722 *infra*). No Irish saint except Patrick is mentioned in the book.

576. The Royal Library Prayer-Book

MS: BM Reg. 2. A. XX *s* VIII². FACS: C. P. Cooper *Appendix A to a Report on Rymer's Foedera* pl. xxiv [ff. 11ᵛ, 23]. ED: A. B. Kuypers *Book of Cerne* (Cambridge 1902) 201–25. COMM: E. M. Thompson *Catalogue of ancient manuscripts in the British Museum* pt. II *Latin* (London 1884) 60. — W. de Gray Birch *Book of Nunnaminster* (London 1889) 101–13. — *AB* II (1895) 89–102 [complete table of contents, and texts of several extracts]. — W. Meyer " Poetische Nachlese aus dem sogenannten Book of Cerne in Cambridge und aus dem Londoner Codex Regius **2** A xx " *Nachrichten v. d. k. Gesellsch. d. Wissensch. z. Göttingen* philol.-hist. Kl. 1917 iv 597–625.

This is a prayer-book written in the north of England, possibly at Lindisfarne, in the eighth century. It forms, with the Book of Nunnaminster, the Book of Cerne, and the Irish Harleian Prayer-Book, a group of closely related books of devotion, all of which were immediately or ultimately products of the Irish Church. That the first three were written in England is testimony to the persistence there of Irish influence.

SCRIPT, etc.: Northumbrian semi-uncial and large minuscule, in several hands. Ornamentation shows Irish influence. Marginal and interlinear additions by an English hand of about A.D. 1000. Ff. 52. CONTENTS: Ff. 1–11ᵛ: Extracts from the Gospels, to serve as lections for various feasts. The text is of the mixed " Irish " type. Ff. 11ᵛ–3ᵛ: The Lord's Prayer, Apostles' Creed, Epistle to Abgarus (*cf.* p. 718), and a prayer for protection. Ff. 13ᵛ–6: The *Magnificat*, Canticle of Zachary, and Canticle of the Three Children (*cf.* pp. 708, 717). F. 16ᵛ: A charm against bleeding. Ff. 17–25ᵛ: A collection of prayers, with eight headings;[242] one of these is in the Harleian Prayer-Book (no. 575) and the Fleury *Libellus precum* (*cf.* p. 722 *infra*). Ff. 26–7ᵛ: Litany having resemblances to the Stowe litany,[243] followed by praises of God. F. 28: The *Gloria in excelsis*, a creed, and a prayer. Ff. 29–38ᵛ: A series of 23 prayers beginning with the successive letters of the alphabet. F. 39: A prayer, followed by a paraphrase of the 83rd psalm, both thought to be by Bede (*cf.* Meyer *op. cit.*). F. 40: A metrical creed ascribed to Cuth[bert] or Cuth[rad],[244] followed by a formula of con-

---

[242] The first is ascribed to " Abbot Hygbald." Bede (*Hist. Eccles.* IV iii) mentions an abbot of the name " in the province of Lindsey," and there was a bishop of the same name, never called abbot, at Lindisfarne 780–803.

[243] *Cf.* p. 695 *supra*; also Bishop *Liturgica historica* 139 *sqq.*

[244] Cuthbert would be, no doubt, the saint, and Cuthrad or Cudrad a priest of Lindisfarne to whom Alcuin addressed a letter in 793–4 (Migne *PL* C 144).

fession. Ff. 40ᵛ-1: A kind of litany addressed to the B. V. M., apostles and angels. Ff. 41ᵛ-2: An intercession to God. Ff. 42–5: A collection of nine related prayers, attributed to a " Moucanus," which is probably a British name (*cf.* Meyer *op. cit.*). Ff. 45–9ᵛ: Five prayers, of which the first is penitential and the second a variety of *lorica*, with an exorcism in Greek. At the end of the fifth is another form of the charm against bleeding. F. 50: Hymn of Sedulius on the birth of Christ, a well-known alphabetical hymn in 23 stanzas. F. 51: Another alphabetical hymn in 23 stanzas, describing the New Jerusalem: " Alma fulget in caelesti," [245] etc.

577. The Book of Nunnaminster

MS: BM Harl. 2965 *s* VIII/IX. ED: Walter de Gray Birch *An ancient manuscript of the eighth or ninth century; formerly belonging to St. Mary's Abbey, or Nunnaminster, Winchester* (Hampshire Record Soc.: London 1889). COMM: E. M. Thompson *Catalogue of ancient manuscripts in the British Museum* pt. II *Latin* (London 1884).

The Book of Nunnaminster is a manuscript prayer-book which at one time belonged to Nunnaminster, that is, St. Mary's Abbey, Winchester, England, originally founded, it would seem, in the time of Alfred the Great, and probably by his Queen, Eahlswith. The book, however, antedates the monastery: the script is generally classed as of the eighth century, although its editor expresses the opinion that it may be by a ninth-century scribe who, in the earlier leaves especially, imitated the writing of an older exemplar from which he was copying. It was designed for the use of an abbess or other head of a community of nuns. In its contents it belongs to the Irish family of devotional compilations.

SCRIPT, etc.: English semi-uncial or large minuscule. Writing, ornamentation, abbreviations and orthography show Irish affinities. Ff. 41: the first gathering is lost, and there are gaps at ff. 32–33 and 33–34. Some additions have been made in the tenth century. CONTENTS: Ff. 1–16: The passion according to Mark (acephalous), Luke and John. Ff. 16ᵛ-20: Four prayers, of which the first [246] is ascribed to Pope Gregory the Great and the second to St. Augustine. Ff. 20–32ᵛ: A series of 44 short prayers related to events in the life of Christ.[247] F. 33: A communion hymn *Domine Deus, Iesu* (no. 579 vi) in 16 quatrains, and a rhythmical morning salutation, *Te deprecamur, Domine*. Ff. 34–7: Eleven miscellaneous prayers, the first a fragment of the so-called *Confessio s. Patricii* (*cf.* p. 713 *supra*), the last a prayer against poison. Ff. 37ᵛ-40: The *Lorica* of Laid-cend [no. 100]. F. 40ᵛ: A prayer for the cure of disease of the eyes, followed by what seems to be a magical *formula*.

578. The Book of Cerne

MS: Cambridge Univ. Lib. Ll. 1. 10 *s* VIII/IX. EDS: F. A. Paley "Liturgical manuscripts at Cambridge " *Home and Foreign Review* I (1862) 473–84 [extracts]. — A. B. Kuypers *The Prayer Book of Aedeluald the Bishop commonly called the Book of Cerne* (Cambridge 1902) [has a valuable liturgical note by E. Bishop. *Cf.* Paul Drews

---

[245] Published by E. Dümmler *Rhythmorum ecclesiasticorum aevi Carolini specimen* (Berlin 1881) no. ix p. 14.
[246] Also in the Bk. of Cerne (no. 578).
[247] These prayers are Roman rather than Irish in character. Four of them are in the Bk. of Cerne.

Literarisches Centralblatt 17 Jan. 1903.] Comm: H. A. Wilson " On a rhythmical prayer in the Book of Cerne " *JTS* Jan. 1904 p. 263. — F. Cabrol " Le Book of Cerne et les liturgies celtiques " *Rev. des quest. hist.* LXXVI (1904) 210–22, and his *Les origines liturgiques* (Paris 1906) 227–42. — W. Meyer " Poetische Nachlese aus dem sogenannten Book of Cerne in Cambridge und aus dem Londoner Codex Regius 2 A. xx " *Nachrichten v. d. k. Gesellschaft d. Wissensch. z. Göttingen* philol.-hist. Kl. 1917 iv 597–625. — E. Bishop *Liturgica historica* (Oxford 1918) 192–7.

The Book of Cerne is a manuscript volume which, it would seem, at one time belonged to the abbey of Cerne, in Dorset, England. It is divided into three parts, originally independent codices, of which we have here to do only with the second. This is a prayer-book for private devotions, chiefly of the Irish type: it is, indeed, used by Dom Fernand Cabrol to illustrate his description of the characteristics of the Celtic liturgy. He points out, however, that the book is actually a kind of liturgical mosaic where is found ancient debris of many origins. Edmund Bishop made a recondite investigation of these origins, showing that the Irish, the Mozarabic and the Roman elements preponderate. Mozarabic and even Roman may have come, in whole or in part, through Irish channels.

Script, etc.: English large minuscule. Ornamentation shows Irish influence. Ff. 98 [given as 2–99: the first folio is missing, and perhaps there is a loss at the end]. Contents: Ff. 1–40: The passion and resurrection of the Lord according to the four evangelists. The text is Vulgate of the " Irish " type. Ff. 40ᵛ–83ᵛ: 69 prayers, of which the first 52 are addressed to God,[248] the last 17 to the angels, B. V. M. and apostles. Some of these are rhythmical and riming compositions which might be classed as hymns. Several are combinations of two or more distinct documents. No. lxix is the same version of the same prayer as no. xxx; in some other cases the prayers seem to be fundamentally the same, but in quite different versions. The following should be particularly noticed: f. 43: the *Lorica* of Laid-cend (no. 100); f. 44ᵛ: *Te Deum laudamus* (*cf.* p. 722); f. 48: *Ante oculos tuos Domine* and *Deus, Deus meus omnipotens*;[249] f. 53ᵛ: *Deus Pater omnipotens, Domine caeli et terrae* (*cf.* p. 724); f. 66: *Sancte sator suffragator* (no. 579 xii). The Canticle of the Three Children, the *Gloria in excelsis*, and several psalms or parts thereof, are indicated by the opening words only. Ff. 84–7ᵛ: The following hymns: *Ymnum dicat turba fratrum* (*cf.* pp. 252, 419); *Luce uidet Christum; Pro peccatis amare; Domine Deus Iesu; Amici nobiles Christe* (*cf.* pp. 724–5). Ff. 87ᵛ–98: A collection of versicles from the psalms, forming a kind of abridged psalter (*cf.* p. 718 *supra*). Ff. 98ᵛ–9ᵛ: An apocryphal *Descensus ad inferna.* — Of the prayers and hymns, one is also in AB (no. 568), one in the Stowe Missal (no. 555), one in the Basel Psalter (no. 364 iv), 4 in the Harleian Prayer-Book (no. 575), 6 in the Royal Prayer-Book (no. 576), 17 in the Book of Nunnaminster (no. 577), 3 and fragments in Alcuin's *De psalmorum usu liber* and 10 and fragments in his *Officia per ferias* (*cf.* p. 722), 4 in the *Collectanea et flores* attributed to Bede (vol. III p. 499 of the Cologne, 1612, ed. of his works), 3 and a fragment in the Prayer-Book of Charles the Bald (pub. Ingolstadt 1583), 6 and a fragment in the Fleury *Libellus precum* (*cf.* p. 722), 3 in LH. — The MS has a few passages in the Mercian dialect of Anglo-Saxon: some of these seem to be contemporary and the rest

---

[248] A quite considerable number of these are *apologiae* or penitential confessions. *Cf.* p. 695 *supra*.

[249] *Cf.* p. 713 n. 236 *supra*. *Ante oculos tuos Domine* is also in the Stowe Missal (no. 555), and interpolated into the Angers copy of *Deus, Deus meus omnipotens.* It is also in several continental missals. *Cf* Kuypers *The Book of Cerne* p. xxxiii.

not later than the ninth century. HISTORY: On f. 21 are some verses giving the acrostic " Aedeluald episcopus," and the title of the abridgment of the psalter attributes it to " Oethelwald episcopus." Dom Kuypers therefore designated the codex " the Book of Aedeluald the Bishop." He is usually identified with Aethelwold who was bishop of the Mercian see of Lichfield A.D. 818–30. Drews and Edmund Bishop, however, thought that Bishop Aedeluald's book [250] was only one of the sources of the Book of Cerne; and, because of the " Irish " character of his work, inconsistent, runs the argument, with a ninth-century English date, Bishop contended that he must be the only other personage of the name known to have held episcopal rank at an early date, Aedeluald, bishop [251] from 721 to 740 of Lindisfarne, where Irish influences probably still lingered.

There are three continental prayer-books in which the Irish element, if not predominating, as it seems to do in the English books just noticed, plays an important rôle. Two of these are works the authorship of which is attributed to Alcuin: *De psalmorum usu liber cum variis formulis ad res quotidianas accomodatis*, in Migne *PL* CI 465–508; and *Officia per ferias, ibid.* 509–612. On Alcuin's liturgical work see Cabrol " Alcuin " *Dict. d'archéol. chrét. et de liturgie* I i 1072–92, and " Les écrits liturgiques d'Alcuin " *RHE* XIX (1923) 507–21, and the references there given. The Irish matters that entered into these compilations for private devotion were probably part of his Northumbrian inheritance, though they may have been due in part to his Irish associates, such as Colcu and Joseph (*cf.* pp. 534–6 *supra*), or to Irish influences on the Continent. Even stronger than in Alcuin are the Irish features in a so-called Fleury Prayer-Book of unknown authorship. It is a tenth-century MS in the Bibl. de la ville of Orleans, and was published by Martène in his *De antiquis Ecclesiae ritibus* IV xxxiv, reprinted in Migne *PL* CI 1490 *sqq*, under the title *Libellus sacrarum precum ex MS Floriacensi annorum circiter 900*. *Cf. AB* II 96.

V. IRISH TEXTS OF CERTAIN CHRISTIAN RELIGIOUS DOCUMENTS

Attention has been given (pp. 623 *sqq supra*) to the development of an Irish type of text of the Scriptures, or at least of large portions of the New Testament. In a somewhat similar way there were Irish modifications of those Latin texts of external origin which the Irish Church adopted for public and private devotions, such as the scriptural and other canticles, sacramentary prayers, hymns, litanies. In the case of *Te Deum laudamus* a special study of the Irish versions has been made in *AB* II (1895) 93–4. *Cf.* also Julian's *Dictionary of hymnology* and the *Cath. Encycl. s. v.* " Te Deum "; the references there given; *JTS* IX (April 1908) 425 *sqq;* and the *Church Quarterly Review* CII no. cciii (April 1926). — For that favorite hymn of the Irish, *Hymnum dicat*, see pp.252–3 *supra*. — In the history of the creeds an important rôle is taken by manuscripts of Irish origin or relationship. Of the Apostles' Creed

---

[250] Bishop would identify this with a " Hymnar of Edilwald " which was at one time in the library of Fulda.

[251] His argument is supported by the fact that the acrostic verses apparently contain errors due to transcription.

the Irish manuscripts offer some interesting and unique variations. See the articles on the several creeds in the *Realencykl. f. prot. Theologie u. Kirche* and the *Dictionnaire de théologie catholique;* A. and G. L. Hahn *Bibliothek der Symbole* 3rd ed. (1897); F. Kattenbusch *Das apostolische Symbol* 2 vols. (Leipsic 1894–1900); A. E. Burn *Introduction to the creeds* (London 1897) and *Facsimiles of the creeds* (Henry Bradshaw Soc. XXXVI) (London 1909). Kattenbusch and especially Burn are important for the Irish part of the history.

VI. HYMNS, PRAYERS AND OTHER DEVOTIONAL COMPOSITIONS OF IRISH ORIGIN OR CHARACTER

In the preceding pages some account has been given of the surviving liturgical and devotional books or collections, belonging to the period prior to A.D. 1170, that were of Irish origin or inspiration. It would obviously be impossible to list here all the individual liturgical *formulae* which were, or may have been, composed in Ireland. Even less possible is it to enumerate all the private prayers and hymns, all the literary pieces of a devotional cast, which the Christian Ireland of our period produced. In chap. III sect. vii some description has been given of such documents the date of which can, with good probability, be placed not later than the early years of the eighth century. The attempt is now made only to notice what seem to be the better known, the more important, or the more significant of those of later date.

Attention should be called to certain types of compositions which were especially popular with the Irish: (1) rhythmical prayers, often classed as hymns but probably intended for mnemonic recitation rather than for singing; (2) confessions and *apologiae;* [252] (3) litanies; [253] (4) *loricae.* [254] Sometimes the one document belongs to two or three classes.

579. Hiberno-English hymns and prayers

It has been seen that the English manuscripts, Regius 2 A. xx, the Book of Nunnaminster, and the Book of Cerne, are made up of material which is chiefly of Irish origin or inspiration. In these volumes and in certain continental codices of English (or in one case possibly Irish)

---

[252] *Cf.* p. 695 *supra.*

[253] The chief litanies and litany-like prayers in Irish have been published by the Rev. Dr. Charles Plummer *Irish Litanies* (Henry Bradshaw Soc. LXII) (London 1925).

[254] *Cf.* p. 254 *supra.* In connection with what follows the article of Dom Louis Gougaud " Étude sur les *loricae* celtiques " *Bull. d'ancienne littérature et d'archéologie chrétienne* I (1911) 265–81, II (1912) 33–41, 101–27, should be consulted.

provenance there are several hymns or rhythmical prayers which both in their subject-matter and in their verse-form have the marks of an Irish origin. As there is, perhaps, no Irish manuscript tradition of these texts, this Irish origin cannot be asserted without qualification: it remains possible that some of them were composed by English writers of Irish training. If they are of Irish composition it is quite probable, as has been stated previously,[255] that many of them are of the seventh century.

(i) Ad Dominum clamaveram ... possidere eximia. 17 quatrains. MSS: Cologne Kapitelsbibl. 106 (formerly Darmstadt 2106) s IX.— Munich Staatsbibl. 14447 s IX. — Carlsruhe Landesbibl. Cod. Augiensis CXXXV pt. iii s X f. 159. [These last 2 MSS contain Alcuin's exposition of the psalms, addressed to Bishop Arno of Salzburg, and it has been noted — p. 714 supra — that Lindsay thinks the first MS was prepared under Alcuin's direction for Arno.] Eds: [Cf. Chevalier Repertorium hymnologicum no. cxxii.] Froben Alcuini opera I i 389-90.— Migne PL XCIV 528.— Mone Lateinische Hymnen des Mittelalters I (Freiburg i. Br. 1853) 393-5.— Blume An. hymn. LI (1908) 293-4. A versified prayer, of which the first 15 stanzas consist of adaptations of the opening words of the 15 gradual psalms, or " songs of degrees," ps. cxix–cxxxiii.

(ii) Ambulemus in prosperis ... sempiternum in gaudium. 8 quatrains. MSS: BM Reg. 2 A. xx s VIII f. 25.— Bk. of Cerne s IX f. 46. Eds: Kuypers The Book of Cerne (1902) 91-2, 211. Cf. W. Meyer Nachrichten v. d. k. Gesellsch. d. Wissensch. z. Göttingen philol.-hist. Kl. 1917 pp. 598-9. A morning prayer.

(iii) Amici nobiles ... norunt florescere. 14 quatrains. MS: Bk. of Cerne f. 87. Eds: Kuypers op. cit. 173-4.— Blume op. cit. 314-5. Cf. Meyer op. cit. 614. An alphabetical poem in praise of virgins, apparently incomplete.

(iv) Christum peto, Christum preco ... terras atque aequora. 18 ll. MS: Bk. of Cerne f. 66ᵛ. Eds: Kuypers op. cit. 132.— Blume op. cit. 301.

(v) Deus Pater omnipotens, Domine caeli ac terrae ... ubi regnum regnorum saeculorum in saecula. Meyer arranges it in 52 ll., but the actual text is less. MS: Bk. of Cerne ff. 53ᵛ-4ᵛ. Eds: Kuypers op. cit. 106-8.— Meyer op. cit. 600-5.

(vi) Domine Deus, Iesu ... in sempiterna saecula. 16 quatrains. MSS: Bk. of Nunnaminster (no. 577) s VIII f. 33.— Bk. of Cerne ff. 86ᵛ-7. Eds: W. de Gray Birch An ancient manuscript ... formerly belonging to ... Nunnaminster (London 1889) 81-3.— Kuypers op. cit. 172-3.— Blume op. cit. 297-8. Apparently a communion hymn. It is doubtful whether this is a product of the Irish school of verse.

(vii) Heli, Heli, Domine mi ... ut sim sanus hic et in saecula. 11 ll. MS: Bk. of Cerne f. 62ᵛ. Eds: Kuypers op. cit. 124.— Blume op. cit. 301-2. Cf. Meyer op. cit. 6c6-7.

(viii) [Refrain] O Andreas sancte ... , followed by 11 stanzas: Te nunc peto, care ... regum sine fine. MS: Bk. of Cerne f. 81. Eds: Kuypers op. cit. 161-2.— Blume op. cit. 316-7. Cf. Meyer op. cit. 607.

255 P. 255 supra.

(ix) Peto [*MS* Teto] Petri . . . saeculorum in saecula. 11 stanzas. MS: Bk. of Cerne ff. 81^v-2. EDS: F. A. Paley *Home and Foreign Review* I (1862) 478. — Kuypers *op. cit.* 162-3. — Blume *op. cit.* 312-3. — Meyer *op. cit.* 1916 pp. 625-6. A prayer to the apostles.

(x) Pro peccatis amare . . . requiescam in pace. 12 stanzas. MS: Bk. of Cerne f. 86. EDS: Kuypers *op. cit.* 171-2. — Blume *op. cit.* 351-2.

(xi) Sancte Petre, apostole . . . in trinitate Dominus. 8 quatrains. MS: Bk. of Cerne ff. 79^v-80. EDS: Kuypers *op. cit.* 158-9. — Blume *op. cit.* 349-50. This may not be of the Irish school.

(xii) Sancte sator, suffragator . . . Sicque beo me ab eo. 29 ll. MSS: Bk. of Cerne f. 66. — Cologne Kapitelsbibl. 106. — Munich Staatsbibl. 14447. — Carlsruhe Landesbibl. Cod. Augiensis CXXXV pt. iii f. 159. [*Cf.* no. i *supra re* these 3 MSS.] — Munich Staatsbibl. 19410 *s* IX. — BN 8779 *s* IX. — Cambridge Univ. Lib. Gg. V. 35 *s* XI. EDS: [*Cf.* Chevalier *op. cit.* no. 18506.] Mone *op. cit.* 365-6. — Müllenhoff and Scherer *Denkmäler deutscher Poesie u. Prosa*³ (Berlin 1892) I 221, II 353-4. — Kuypers *op. cit.* 131-2. — Blume *op. cit.* 299-301.

(xiii) Te deprecamur Domine . . . in sempiterna secula. 5 stanzas. MS: Bk. of Nunnaminster f. 33^v. ED: Birch *op. cit.* 83-4.

(xiv) Te deprecor, Pater sancte . . . magni regis et potestas. 16 ll. MS: BM Reg. 2 A. xx f. 46^v. EDS: Kuypers *op. cit.* 221. — Meyer *op. cit.* 1917 pp. 624-5.[256]

580. *Scúap Chrábaid,* or Broom of Devotion, of Colcu úa Duinechda

[Part I] Ateoch frit, a Ísu nóib . . . 7 ina menmannaib [7 ina nindib]. [Part II] A Ísu noeb, a chara coem . . . Poil apstail ro raide: Quis me liberauit, etc. Amen.

MSS: YBL col. 336 (facs. p. 326) [this portion written by Murchad Ó Cuindlis in 1398-9]. — LBr p. 74 [pt. II and a frag. of pt. I]. — Brussels Bibl. roy. 2324 f. 71; 4190 f. 212; 5100 p. 9 [these 3 MSS are by Michael O'Clery; the 1st and 3rd from the *Lebar ruad Muimnech*, " Red Book of Munster," which also was written by Murchad Ó Cuindlis, the 2nd from a MS written by Giolla-glas Úa hUiginn in 1471]. EDS: B. Mac Carthy "On the Stowe Missal" *Trans. RIA* XXVII Antiq. (1886) 178-81 [pt. I with trans.] — KM *Otia Merseiana* II (1900-1) 92-8, 100-3 [with trans.]. — C. Plummer *Irish Litanies* (London 1925) pp. xvii-xix, 30-45, 111-2 [with trans.]. TRANS: O'C *IER* I (1864) 4-12. *Cf.* O'C *MS Mat.* 379-80.

The *Scúap Chrábaid,* or " Broom of Devotion," of Colcu úa Duinechda of Clonmacnois (d. 796) [257] seems to have been one of the most famous of old Irish prayers. The present text [258] is identified with it by O'Clery, apparently on the authority of the " Red Book of Munster," written in the fourteenth century. O'Clery, however, copied another *Vorlage* in which our document was attributed, without title, to Aireran *ind ecna, i.e.* Aileran the Wise (d. 665).[259] The language is not incon-

---

[256] The verses beginning *Altus auctor omnium,* which Blume publishes, *op. cit.* 302, are, it seems clear, not of Irish origin.

[257] *Cf.* p. 534 *supra.*

[258] It is not certain whether the two parts form one whole. O'Clery apparently thought so, and they are in immediate association in all the MSS.

[259] *Cf.* pp. 279-81 *supra.*

sistent with Colcu's authorship, but if due to Aileran must have been carefully modernised. There is also some slight reason to believe that our texts are derived from Clonmacnois.

In the " Notes on the Customs of Tallaght " [260] respectful reference is made several times to a Colcu. If, as is not improbable, he was Colcu úa Duinechda, evidence is thereby given that the latter was one of the leaders of the reform movement of the eighth century.

The prayer, especially in its first part, has the form of a *lorica*.

581. Hymn in honor of St. Michael

Archangelum mirum magnum . . . in regali culmine. 23 stanzas.

MS: Carlsruhe Landesbibl. Cod. Augiensis CCXXI *s* VIII/IX ff. 191-2 (*s* IX *in.*). ED: Blume *An. hymn.* LI (1908) 333-5.

At the close of the hymn is a collect, followed by: " Benedicat De[us] te et Michael for [= says] Moilrum. Amen." The person intended is, doubtless, Máel-Rúain of Tallaght (d. 792).[261] That Máel-Rúain had special devotion for the archangel Michael is implied in the preface to the Martyrology of Oengus.[262] It is, therefore, a fair inference that this hymn was in use at Tallaght, and quite possible that it was composed there, but Blume's ascription of its composition to Máel-Rúain is hypothetical.

It is a good example of Hiberno-Latin versification.

582. Hymn ascribed to Colmán moccu Clúasaig

Sén Dé donfé fordonté . . . sén Dé donfé fordonté. [19 quatrains] . . . ria slúag ndemnae diar sénad. [3½ quatrains] . . . Críst ronsóera ronséna. [4 quatrains].

MSS: LH(T) ff. 4ᵛ-5. — LH(F) pp. 28-30. EDS: WS *Goidilica* (Calcutta 1866); *Goidelica* (London 1872) 121 *sqq.* — B. MacCarthy (?) *IER* IV (1868) 402-9. — *LH*¹ II 122-36. — *IT* I 5, 321. — *LH*² I 25-31,II pp. xxxv-xl, 12-6, 113-22. — *Thes. Pal.* II pp. xxxvi *sq*, 298-306. Trans. in all except *IT*. COMM: H. Gaidoz *RC* V 94-103 [with Fr. trans.].

This hymn is a prayer for protection against evil, resembling the *loricae*. It falls obviously into three parts, of which the first seems to have been based on a Latin prayer similar to the " Commendation of a soul in its last moments " in the Roman Breviary. The Irish introduction and notes ascribe the first two parts, which they treat as one, to Colmán moccu Clúasaig, called *fer légind* of Corcaige (Cork),[263] or to him and his pupils, and the last to Diarmait úa Tigernáin, who was *comarba* of Patrick at Armagh, with interruptions, from 835 to 853, or to him and to Mugrón, *comarba* of Colum-cille from 964 to 980.[264] The Irish annotations say that the hymn was composed as a protection against the Yellow Plague of 664-5; but the annalists place the death of Colmán, whom they call úa Clúasaig, in 662, and the wording of the hymn does not

---

[260] No. 264. [261] *Cf.* p. 469 *supra.* [262] *Fél. Oeng.*² 12-3.
[263] *Cf.* p. 421 *supra.* [264] *Cf.* p. 727 *infra.*

suggest composition for such a special occasion. Moreover, it is generally agreed that the language forms demand a date not much before 800 nor, at least for the bulk of the piece, later than 850.[265]

583. Sanctán's Hymn

Ateoch ríg namra naingel . . . ateoch in ríg adróethach. 10 quatrains. Epscop Sanctán sancta sruith . . . macc rogénair i mBethil. 3 quatrains.

MSS: LH(T) f. 19. — LH(F) p. 43. EDS: WS *Goidilica* (Calcutta 1866); *Goidelica* (London 1872). — *IT* I 49-52, 324. — *LH*[2] I 129-32, II pp. lvi *sq*, 47-8, 206-8. Trans. in all except *IT*.

This is another of those old Irish hymns asking protection against dangers, physical and diabolical, which really belong to the same class of prayers as the *loricae*. The word *lurech*, Irish derivative from *lorica*, is used in the present text. Its author was, we are told, a Bishop Sanctán, who is commemorated in the calendars but of whom little else is known. According to the preface he was a Briton. The language seems to be of the ninth century.

584. Prayers attributed to Mugrón

(i) Litany of the Trinity: [Rawl.: Mugrón comarba Coluim Cille haec verba composuit de Trinitate.] Airchis dín a Dé athair . . . on ordnigther cech n-uasal. [Addit.: . . . onoir 7 inocbail in s. s. Amen.] (ii) Mugrón's *Lorica*: Cros Críst tarsin gnúis-si . . . cros Críst tar mo gnúis-si. 12 quatrains. (iii) Colum Cille cend Alban . . . trebhand treibhi Cuind Colum. 3 quatrains.

(i) MSS: LBr p. 74 [frag.]. — YBL col. 338, facs. p. 327. — Bodl. Rawl. B 512 f. 42. — BM Addit. 30512 *s* XV f. 37 [a longer recension]. ED: KM *Hibernica minora* (Oxford 1894) 42-3 [text from LBr and Rawl., with trans.]. — C. Plummer *Irish Litanies* (London 1925) pp. xxi, 78-85 [with trans.]. (ii) MSS: Bodl. Laud 615 p. 55. — RIA 23 G 4 and 23 G 5. ED: KM *ZCP* XII iii (1918) 387. TRANS: *LH*[2] II 212, 244 [partial]. (iii) MS: Bodl. Laud 615 p. 105. ED: KM *ZCP* X (1915) 340.

Mugrón, " *comarba* of Colum-cille in both Ireland and Scotland " since 964, died in 980.[266] Of the pieces ascribed to him, the first is a litany composed of three series of invocations addressed respectively to the three Persons of the Trinity; the second is a *lorica* in which the cross of Christ is invoked for protection; and the third a little poem in praise of Colum-cille. The second is also attributed to that saint,[267] but while Mugrón's authorship is linguistically possible, that of Columba is impossible.

585. Poems by Máel-Ísu Úa Brolcháin

(i) A aingil, beir, a Michil mórfhertaig . . . a marbad Anchrist ainglig. 9 stanzas. (ii) A Choimdhe baidh . . . non-geibh fot comm! 4 quatrains. (iii) A Choimdiu, nom-chomét . . . nom-chomét, a Choimdiu. 13 quatrains. (iv) Búaidh crábuidh, búaidh n-ailithre . . . tuc damh na ceithre búadha. 4 quatrains. (v) Deus meus adiuua me Tuc dam do sheirc . . . Deus meus adiuua me. 7 stanzas. (vi) In spirut nóeb immun . . . ronsóera do spirut. (vii) Dia háine ní longud . . . ifern ocus garseclae. 13 quatrains.

(i) MSS: YBL col. 336. — Bodl. Laud 610 p. 118. EDS: WS *Goidelica*[2] (1872) 175 [2 stanzas]. — KM *The Cath Finntrága or Battle of Ventry* (Oxford 1885) 88-9 [YBL

---

[265] MacN, however, apparently accepts Colmán's authorship. *Cf. Studies* Sept. 1922 p. 438.
[266] AU. [267] *Cf.* p. 438 *supra*.

text, with variants from Laud]; *Gaelic Journal* IV (1890) 56–7 [YBL text, trans.]. — C. Plummer *Irish Litanies* (London 1925) pp. xxii *sq*, 88–9 [with trans.]. TRANS: KM *Selections from ancient Irish poetry* (London 1911) 41. (ii) MS: Brussels Bibl. roy. 2324 p. 56. ED: KM *ACL* III iii (1906) 231. (iii) MS: BM Egerton 111 p. 15; Addit. 30512 f. 44. — TCD 1285 (H. 1. 11) f. 154ᵛ [copy of Addit.]. ED: KM *ZCP* VI (1908) 259–60. (iv) MS: Brussels Bibl. roy. 5100 ²⁶⁸ p. 56. ED: KM *ACL* III iii (1906) 230–1. (v) MS: LBr p. 101. ED: *Fél. Oeng.*¹ p. clxxxv [text, trans.]. — KM *Selections from early Irish poetry* [Dublin 1909] 8–9. TRANS: Geo. Sigerson *Bards of the Gael and Gall* 2nd ed. (London 1907) 207–8. (vi) MS: LH(T) f. 31ᵛ [this is in the later portion of the MS]. EDS: WS *Goidilica*¹ (1866), *Goidelica*² (1872) [text, trans.].—*LH*² I 159, II 52, 221 [text, trans.]. — *Thes. Pal.* II pp. xl, 359 [text, trans.]. (vii) MS: TCD 1285 (H. 1. 11) A.D. 1752 f. 140. ED: KM *ZCP* XII (1918) 296–7; *cf.* 454.²⁶⁹

Máel-Ísu ²⁷⁰ Úa Brolcháin died on Jan. 16, 1086, according to the Annals of Ulster, which describe him as " master of wisdom and of piety and in *filidecht* ²⁷¹ in both languages," *i.e.* Irish and Latin. His address to the archangel Michael, bilingual intercessory prayer, and invocation of the Holy Spirit are among the most famous of the religious poems of the later portion of our period.

586. Litany of Irish Saints

[Part I] Secht noeb epscoip déc ar secht cétaib di aes. . . . [Part II] Trí choicait curach di ailithrib Roman . . . [Part III] Secht noeb epscoip Dromma Urchailli. . . .

MSS: LL p. 373 of facs. — Leabhar Úi Maine f. 53 (formerly 109). — BM Addit. 30512 f. 23 [incomplete]. — TCD 1285 (H. 1. 11) f. 130 [incomplete]. — LBr p. 23 [pts. II and III]. EDS: B. Mac Carthy *IER* III (1867) 385–97, 468–77 [with trans.]. — C. Plummer *Irish Litanies* (London 1925) pp. xix *sq*, 54–75, 112–21 [with trans. and notes].

In this litany a vast number of Irish holy ones are invoked, some by name, some by place of origin, but the majority by the name of the saint or the church with which they were associated. It has the appearance of being an antiquarian rather than a devotional composition, but this is in part due to the incorporation of annotations into the text. The attribution of the authorship to Oengus " the Culdee " originated, in the opinion of Plummer, with Colgan. The earliest manuscript is of the middle of the twelfth century, and the document is probably a product of the ecclesiastical antiquarianism of the tenth and eleventh centuries. We cannot be certain whether the three parts into which the litany falls should be regarded as separate texts or not: they are all of a similar type, and have much value for topography and hagiology.

587. Hymn in praise of Sts. Peter and Paul

Christi patris in dextera . . . dominantem infinita. 50 ll.

MS: LH(F) f. 14. EDS: Dreves *An. hymn.* XIX 236 [*cf.* LI 350]. — *LH*² I 198–9 II 241–2.

Probably of Irish composition. The text may be imperfect.

²⁶⁸ *Cf.* C. Plummer *Irish Litanies* p. xxiii.
²⁶⁹ In Bk. Lis. f. 52ᵛ there is a poem by him, in 66 quatrains, on the eight principal vices: Ocht n-aerich na ndualuch . . . . *Cf. Lis. Lives* p. xviii.
²⁷⁰ The name means " Tonsured (*i.e.*, Devotee) of Jesus."
²⁷¹ *Cf.* pp. 3–4 *supra*.

588. Prayer of St. Brendan

In nomine P. et F. et S. S. Amen. Per sanctam Annunciationem . . . magnam misericordiam et sempiternam gratiam. Amen.

MSS: Rome Bibl. Sessoriana B. CXXVII. — Munich Staatsbibl. 13067 *s* XI/XII ff. 9–16ᵛ. — St. Gall Stiftsbibl. 321 *s* XIV. — BM Reg. 7. D. xxvi *s* XIV/XV. — Cambridge Corpus Christi Coll. 275 *s* XV. — Milan Bibl. Ambrosiana D. 158 inf. *s* XV ff. 37ᵛ-8. — BM Addit. 37787 *s* XV f. 165. ED: P. F. Moran *Acta sancti Brendani* (Dublin 1872) 27–44. COMM: G. Schirmer *Zur Brendanus-Legende* (Leipsic 1888) 11–2.—D. O'Donoghue *Brendaniana* (Dublin 1893) 97–103.

A long, litany-like prayer, addressed to God and the saints, containing a large number of allusions to events of scriptural history. It probably should be classed as a *lorica* of Irish origin, but its association with Brendan seems to be one of the developments of his legend.

589. Prayer to the Saviour and the Saints

[Part I] A Sláinicidh in ciniuda daona . . . i frecnarcus na Trinoti, in s. s. Amen. [Part II] Impide Maire 7 Eoin macain . . . hi frecnarcus na Trinoite, in s. s. Amen.

MSS: Bodl. Rawl. B 512 f. 41. — BM Addit. 30512 *s* XV f. 38. — BM Egerton 92 *s* XV f. 29 [pt. I].—Brussels Bibl. roy. 4190 f. 215 [copy by O'Clery of MS by Giolla-glas Úa hUiginn, 1471]. EDS: KM *Otia Merseiana* II (1900–1) 98–100, 103–5 [with trans.]. — C. Plummer *Irish Litanies* (London 1925) pp. xvi *sq*, 20–7, 111 [with trans.].

Whether the two parts of this fine prayer are distinct texts is not certain. The manuscripts, except in the case of the fragmentary Egerton 92, unite them, but, as Plummer notices, the first part is composed in the singular number, the second part in the plural. This second part seems designed for a community of nuns. The two parts, however, appear to be complementary to each other. The language is not inconsistent with an Old Irish date.

590. *Lorica* of Virgins

[No]m churim ar commairge . . . co nilur a phian.

MS: LL p. 360 of facs. ED: C. Plummer *Irish Litanies* (London 1925) pp. xxiii, 92–3, 121–3 [with trans. and notes].

In this metrical *lorica*, of which the manuscript is of the twelfth century, protection is sought of the Trinity and of various classes of saints, and, by name, of Mary and of twenty-eight Irish virgin saints.

591. *Lorica*

Ateoch friut an dechmad . . . atteoch friutsa a Athair. The original poem ended at l. 50; there are two additions, of 28 and 14 ll., respectively, with verbally similar endings.

MSS: RIA 23 N 10 p. 92. EDS: KM *ZCP* VIII (1912) 231–2; *Selections from early Irish poetry* [Dublin 1909] 3 [first part only]. — C. Plummer *Irish Litanies* (London 1925) pp. xxiii *sq*, 102–7 [with trans.].

This piece seems to be modeled on the *Scúap Chrábaid*,[272] and, indeed, is itself so designated in the first set of additional stanzas. The author also imitates the older *loricae*, such as Patrick's,[273] by naming many of the objects of nature, but the tone here is much more learned and academic.

592. Litany of the Blessed Virgin Mary

A Muire mór . . . ros aittrebam, in s. s. Amen.

MS: LBr p. 74. EDS: *Vit. Trip.* I pp. clxv–clxviii [with trans.]. — C. Plummer *Irish Litanies* (London 1925) 48–51 [with trans.]. TRANS: Moran *Essays* 224–5 [by O'C]. COMM: A. de Santi (Fr. trans. A. Boudinhon) *Les litanies de la sainte Vierge* (Paris [1900]) 105–7.

Stokes assigned this litany, or litany-like prayer, to the twelfth century. It is an interesting document for the history of devotion to Mary.[274]

593. The Penitential Litany of St. Ciarán

Omne malum feci coram te. . . . A Athair, a Meic, a Spirut Noim, dilguid. . . . A fir-Dia, tibi soli peccaui. Dilaig, dilaig, dilaig. Amen.

MSS: Bodl. Laud 610 *s* XV ff. 5ᵛ–6ᵛ. — BM Addit. 30512 *s* XV f. 36. — Brussels Bibl. roy. 2324 f. 69; 5100 p. 6 [both copied by Michael O'Clery from "the Red Book of Munster"]. ED: C. Plummer *Irish Litanies* (London 1925) pp. xvi, 2–17 [with trans.].

This litany, which is a lengthy confession of sins, is attributed in the O'Clery manuscripts to a Ciarán, and there is some slight reason to believe that it came from Clonmacnois. But it is far later than the time of Ciarán of Clúain; indeed, we cannot be quite certain that it is not later than our period. It is in Irish, but with some passages in Latin.

594. Poem asking three wishes of God

Mo theora ucse forsín Ríg . . in tan dobretha mo theora. 14 ll.

MSS: RIA Stowe B. IV. 2 [by Michael O'Clery]. — TCD 1285 (H. 1. 11) A.D. 1752 f. 151. ED: KM *Ériu* VI (1911) 116 [with trans.].

Described by Meyer as an "undoubtedly Old-Irish poem."

595. Blessing the road before a journey

Rop soraid in sét-sa . . . rop sóinmech, rop soraid. 3 quatrains.

MS: Bodl. Laud 615 p. 55. EDS: KM *ACL* III iii (1906) 221; *Ériu* VI (1911) 112 [with trans.].

A Middle-Irish poem which Meyer suggested might have been composed by Máel-Ísu Úa Brolcháin.

---

[272] No. 580.   [273] No. 101.
[274] In *ZCP* XII (1918) 379–83 KM has published a poem in honor of Mary from RIA 23 N 27 f. 23ᵛ — "Gabh ar h'ionchaibh mé, a Mhuire . . . bíodh 'sna dernannuibh derccá: 37 quatrains.

596. A Prayer for tears

Tuc dam, a Dé móir . . cía dobéra acht tú. 8 quatrains.

MS: BM Addit. 30512 f. 30ᵛ. ED: KM *ACL* III iii (1906) 232; *Ériu* VI (1911) 113–4 [with trans.].

Another Middle-Irish poem which, Meyer suggests, may be by Máel-Ísu Úa Brolcháin.

597. A Prayer to Christ for help

A Chríst cobra, tair chucum . . . bí 'com chobair, a chride. 8 quatrains.

MSS: BM Addit. 30512 f. 44.— TCD 1285 (H. 1. 11) p. 155 [from preceding]. ED: KM *Ériu* VI (1911) 114–5.

Meyer described it as a " late Old-Irish or early Middle-Irish poem," which probably means that it was composed within, as outside limits, A.D. 850 to 1050.

598. Prayer attributed to St. Fursa

Robé mainrechta Dé forsind fhormna-sa . . . in duine-sea.

MS: BM Addit. 30512 *s* XV f. 35ᵛ. ED: KM *ACL* III iii (1906) 232.

A litany-like short prayer attributed, quite impossibly, to Fursa.[275]

599. Prayer to the seven archangels for the days of the week

Gabriel lim i nDomhnaighibh . . . ar gach ngabud. 8 quatrains.

MSS: BM Addit. 30512 f. 22ᵛ.— RIA 23 P 3 f. 19. EDS: KM *ACL* II iii (1903) 138 [incomplete]. — Thos. P. O'Nolan *Ériu* II (1905) 92–4 [with trans.]. *Cf. ibid.* V 112. TRANS: *Celtic Review* Oct. 16, 1905, p. 200. — Ernest Rhys in Eleanor Hull *Poem-Book of the Gael* (London 1912) 134–5.

600. *Comad Croiche Críst*: Poem of the Cross of Christ

Creidim-si Críst israeracht . . . a tudhacht cóir a creitim. 7 quatrains.

MS: RIA 23 N 10 p. 94. ED: KM *Ériu* I (1904) 41–2 [with trans.].

A poetical act of faith in Christ.

601. A Hymn of praise to the Trinity

Bennocht ocus édrochta. . . .

MSS: BM Addit. 30512 *s* XV f. 30.— TCD 1285 (H. 1. 11) A.D. 1752 f. 137 [copy of preceding]. ED: R. I. Best *Ériu* IV (1908) 120 [with trans.].

The Litany of the Culdees of Dunkeld has been published by J. G. F. Gordon, from a Ratisbon MS, in *Notes and Queries* 3rd ser. IX 406–9; and reprinted in A. P. Forbes

[275] *Cf.* pp. 500 *sqq.*

Kalendars of Scottish Saints (Edinburgh 1872) pp. xxxiv *sq*, lvi–lxv, and H&S II pt. I 278–85. It is a Scottish litany of the late middle ages, which probably received its final form in the sixteenth century, but it may have its ultimate origin in an old Irish litany.

There are many short devotional pieces, in prose and in verse, of unknown authorship and uncertain date, the majority untranslated, which have been published in various periodicals and other collections, especially in *ACL*, *ZCP*, *IER*, *RC*, *Ériu*, and the *Gaelic Journal*. These do not seem to be of sufficient importance to demand individual notice here; some of them are listed in R. I. Best's *Bibliography of Irish philology and of printed Irish literature* (Dublin 1913) and in his " Bibliography of the publications of Kuno Meyer " *ZCP* XV (1925) 1–65.

C. HOMILETICAL, APOCRYPHAL AND IMAGINATIVE

Bibliography

Georges Dottin " Notes bibliographiques sur l'ancienne littérature chrétienne de l'Irlande " *Rev. d'hist. et de litt. religieuses* V (1900) 162–7 [*cf*. p. 92 *supra*]; *Manuel d'irlandais moyen* 2 vols. (Paris 1913) [especially vol. II].— Kuno Meyer and Alfred Nutt *The Voyage of Bran son of Febal . . . with an essay upon the Irish vision of the happy otherworld and the Celtic doctrine of rebirth* 2 vols. (Grimm Library IV, VI) (London 1895, 1897) [gives some consideration to the Christian eschatological literature of Ireland, which is treated more fully in the following work].— C. S. Boswell *An Irish precursor of Dante* (Grimm Library XVIII) (London 1908) [*cf*. p. 502 *supra*]. — L. Gougaud *Les chrétientés celtiques* (Paris 1911) 260–6: " Les Apocryphes." — St. John D. Seymour " The seven heavens in Irish literature " *ZCP* XIV (1923) 18–30; " The eschatology of the early Irish Church " *ibid*. 179–211.

In addition to the exegetical and scholastic, the liturgical and devotional, there is a considerable amount of exhortatory, imaginative and miscellaneous literature of a religious and ecclesiastical character. Earlier works of this kind, up to the beginning of the eighth century, have been noticed in chapter III. The great bulk of this literature, however, is later than the ninth century. In fact, about the beginning of the tenth century, almost contemporaneously with those linguistic changes which modern philologists have selected as marking the transition from Old to Middle Irish, a change came over Irish ecclesiastical literature and culture. To the predominantly Latin, or Hiberno-Latin, culture of the earlier period succeeded the predominantly Gaelic of the later.[276] The new age is distinguished not only by partially original works in Irish, but also by extensive translations from Latin into Irish.

[276] *Cf*. pp. 10 *sqq supra*.

And the greater part of this literature, although falling into several different classes, has its own common and distinctive note.

Chief among the classes of this later literature are: (1) antiquarian compilations, especially annotations on ancient texts, compiled, doubtless, in the schools [277] and imitating the earlier Latin *scholia*, but composed chiefly of extraordinary stories culled from popular legend and folk-lore; [278] (2) Lives of the saints and other hagiographical matter, usually adaptations or translations from earlier Latin documents and showing the strong influence of secular literature:[279] many of these Lives are in the form of homilies; (3) connected with the preceding is the very considerable amount of semi-dramatic poetry put in the mouths of the famous ancient saints but embodying late ideas and legends; (4) the voyage and vision literature, which had its greatest development, within a religious setting, during this period; (5) homilies, chiefly translations, more or less modified, of well-known Latin texts; and (6), what sometimes can scarcely be distinguished from the homilies, imaginative expositions of biblical and church history, of cosmic and eschatological ideas, based partly on the scriptures but mainly on Latin apocrypha and legends of continental origin. Although little of it has been preserved in its original form through Irish media,[280] a vast amount of this Christian mythical lore must have been circulating in Ireland in the tenth, eleventh and twelfth centuries, some of it very curious and unusual and but little known elsewhere in Europe. It was all used freely and fully by what we may call popular writers in Irish on religious subjects. Indeed, all this later Irish ecclesiastical literature of which an outline has just been given is characterised by an intense interest in the supernatural and the eschatological, and a constant delight in the wonderful and the bizarre.

602. Latin poems of Irish composition

(i) Vere nouo florebat humus, satus aethere sudo. . . Testentur fixum foedus thalamumque coronent. [Ends imperfect.] 92 ll. (ii) Perge carina: Per mare longum. . . .Mille coronas Posce salutis. 78 ll. (iii) Rauco sonora Languida voce. . . . Psallere voto Larga potestas. 27 ll. (iv) Incipit de signis et prodigiis et de quibusdam Hyberniae admirandis. Plurima mira malum signantia signa futurum. . . . Ends imperfect in the 133rd line.

(i) ED: A. Riese *Anthologia Latina* I fasc. ii (1870) 355–7 no. 941; 2nd ed. (1906) I pt. ii 361. (ii) ED: Pitra *Spicilegium Solesmense* III (1855) 399–400. *Cf.* Traube

277 The work of one of these later schools is illustrated on pp. 681-3 *supra*. Part of the texts there noticed are of the same character as those considered here.
278 As the notes to Fél. Oeng. and LH. 279 Chaps. IV and V *supra*.
280 Certain apocalyptic fragments published by Dom De Bruyne in *Rev. Bénédictine* XXIV (1907) from Reichenau CCLIV s VIII /IX were probably derived immediately from Ireland. Their significance for Irish literature is pointed out by M. R. James *JTS* XX 14 *sqq. Cf.* also *ZCP* XIV 22, 181.

MGH Poet. lat. aevi Carol. III 274 n.   (iii) MS: BN 8069 *s* X/XI f. 1ᵛ [a Vergil, preceded by some epigrams from Martial]. Eds: J. Quicherat *Bibl. de l'École des Chartes* 4th ser. III (Paris 1857) 352–3. — Riese *op. cit.* I ii 205–6 no. 739. *Cf.* Traube *loc. cit.* (iv) This is one of the sections added to Nennius: *cf.* pp. 152–5 *supra.* MSS: BN 11108 *s* XII; 4126 *s* XIII f. 12. — BM Cotton. Titus D. xxiv *s* XII *ex.* f. 74. Eds: Wright and Halliwell *Reliquiae antiquae* II (1845) 103–7. — Riese *op. cit.* I ii 257–8 no. 791; 2nd ed. I ii 269 [the first 31 ll.]. — Mommsen *MGH Auct. antiq* XIII (*Chron. min.* III) (1894, 1898) 219–22 [*cf.* p. 152 *supra*]. Comm: M. Manitius *Geschichte der christlich-lateinischen Poesie bis zur Mitte des 8. Jahrhunderts* (Stuttgart 1891) 240–1.—KM *Ériu* IV (1908) 3. — L. Gougaud *RC* XLI (1924) 355. — A version in Irish in BB f. 256 is published by Todd *The Irish version of the Historia Britonum of Nennius* 192 *sqq;* and another in Leabhar Húi Maine f. 115ᵛ by KM *ZCP* V 23–4.

These poems are of Irish origin but uncertain date. The first, second and fourth were ascribed to a Patricius who was commonly identified with St. Patrick. The second is a boat song, and the third, which is in the same Adonic metre, was classed by Traube as Irish, chiefly, it would seem, because of the character of the versification. The fourth poem consists of an opening section on wonders in general, followed by a particular account of the wonders of Ireland. Kuno Meyer would date it about A.D. 1000.

603. Old Irish Homily

[Restored text] Atluchammar buidi do Día . . . atarothrebam in s. s.   Amen.

MSS: YBL coll. 397 *sqq*, facs. 15–6. — RIA 23 P 2 ff. 17ᵛ–8 [written by William Mac an Legha in 1467]. Eds: KM *ZCP* IV (1903) 241–3 [text of 23 P 2]. — J. Strachan *Ériu* III (1907) 1–10 [text of YBL, restored text, and trans.].

A homily on the duties of thanksgiving to God and a life of virtue, which belongs to the later Old-Irish period, probably to about the middle of the ninth century.

604. Daniel úa Liathaide's advice to a woman

A ben, bennacht fort! ná ráid . . . ná ro lámur tríst, a ben.   7 quatrains.

MS: LL 278. — TCD 1337 (H. 3. 18) p. 731. Eds: EW *Berichte d. k. sächs. Gesellsch. d. Wissensch.* XLII (1890) 86–8 [with Germ. trans.]. — AdeJ "Documents irlandais publiés par M. Windisch " *RC* XII (1891) 158–60 [reprint of text, Fr. trans.]. — KM *Ériu* I (1904) 67–71 [with trans.].

This moral exhortation is attributed to a Daniel úa Liathaide, *airchinnech* of Liss-mór. The Four Masters, who call him abbot of Corcaige (Cork) and Liss-mór, say that he was mortally wounded in 861. In the opinion of Kuno Meyer the language may be of the ninth century.

605. Religious poems ascribed to Cormac mac Cuilennáin

(i) Dia comalltis réimm ndligid. . . . (ii) Eochair chéille coistecht. . . . (iii) In roghso, a Rí na rún . . . (iv) Is imdha eccla ar mh'anmain. . . .

(i) Ed: KM *Selections from early Irish poetry* [Dublin 1909]. (ii) MSS: YBL p. 420. — TCD 1337 (H. 3. 18) p. 37. — RIA 23 G 3 p. 37. — RIA 23 N 11 p. 179. Eds:

KM *ZCP* VI (1908) 270–1. — T. P. O'Nolan *IER* 4th ser. XXIV (1908) 395–7, 500–1 [with trans.]. (iii) MS: RIA 23 N 10 p. 17. ED: KM *ZCP* X (1915) 45–7. (iv) MS: Brussels Bibl. roy. 2324 p. 47. ED: KM *ACL* III (1906) 216.

Cormac mac Cuilennáin, bishop-king of Munster, was slain in 908. If his episcopal character was in anything more than the name he might be pointed to as marking the transition from the predominantly Latinist culture of the Irish Church in the earlier part of our period to the predominantly Gaelic in the later. He is best known by his secular compositions, Cormac's Glossary and the Book of Rights, but several religious poems are attributed to him. It is doubtful if any of the attributions are correct, although the third text noted above was an old and famous poem which was quoted in several of the treatises on grammar and metrics.[281]

606. Poem to Crínóg

A Chrínóc, cubáid do cheól . . . tan ragat íar céin ón chríaid. 11 quatrains.

MSS: Dublin Franciscan Convent A (9) *s* XV p. 40.—TCD 1363 (H. 4. 22) *s* XV. EDS: KM *ZCP* VI 266; *Sitzungsb. d. k. preuss. Akad. d. Wissensch.* Philos.-hist. Kl. 1918 pp. 362–71 [with Germ. trans.]. TRANS: KM *Selections from ancient Irish poetry* (London 1911) 37–8.

This tenth-century poem seems to be an address to one of those *virgines subintroductae* or *conhospitae* who, we have reason to believe, existed in the primitive Irish as well as continental Church.[282] But if this poem is not purely a work of historical imagination it leads to the remarkable conclusion that the custom persisted in Ireland till the tenth century.

607. Thanksgiving hymn of a sick man

Atlochar duit, a mo Rí . . . mór lemm a fot, at int at. 11 quatrains.

MS: Dublin Franciscan Convent A (9) *s* XV p. 40. EDS: KM *ZCP* VI (1908) 263; *Sitzungsb. d. k. preuss. Akad. d. Wissensch.* Philos.-hist. Kl. 1918 pp. 371–4 [with Germ. trans.].

Kuno Meyer believed that this tenth-century poem by a northern man who was sick in Munster was by the same author as the address to Crínóg.

608. Poem on the flightiness of thought

Is mebul dom imrádud . . . ní hinand is mé. 12 quatrains.

MS: LBr 262. ED: KM *Ériu* III 13–5 [with trans.]. TRANS: KM *Selections from ancient Irish poetry* (London 1911) 35–6.

A religious poem assigned by its editor to the tenth century.

---

[281] Two quatrains from LL, attributed to Cormac, are published in O'C *M&C* III 388 and translated by KM *Selections from ancient Irish poetry* 94.

[282] *Cf.* p. 479 *supra.*

609. The *Saltair na Rann*

MSS: Bodl. Rawl. B 502 ff. 19-40. — LBr p. 111 [poem no. x; also has, at p. 109, a prose paraphrase of parts of poems ii, iv, vi, viii, ix, xi]. — RIA 23 G 25 [corrupt modernised copies of poems iv–vi]. EDS: WS *Saltair na Rann (Anec. Oxon.* Mediaeval and modern ser. I iii) (Oxford 1883) [text only but with a *précis* of poems i, xi, xii. *Cf.* his emendations in *Academy* XXIV (1883) 31-2, and note, *ibid.* 114. Also RTh *RC* VI (1883) 96–109]. — B. MacCarthy *The Codex Palatino-Vaticanus no. 830* (RIA Todd Lect. Ser. III) (Dublin 1892) [text, trans. of the LBr paraphrase; *cf. RC* XXIV 243 *sqq*]. TRANS: Eleanor Hull *The Poem-Book of the Gael* (London 1912) 1–50 [parts of poems i, ii, vii, viii, xi, xii]. COMM: J. Strachan " The verbal system of the Saltair na Rann " *Philological Soc. Trans.* 1895 pp. 1–76 [*cf.* RTh *ZCP* I (1897) 342–56; KM *Sitzungsb. d. k. preuss. Akad. d. Wissensch.* 1914 pp. 947–52; *Miscellanea Hibernica* (Urbana, Ill, 1916) 37–8]. — KM " Zur Metrik von Saltair na Rann " *Sitzungsb. d. k. preuss. Akad. d. Wissensch.* philos.-hist. Kl. 1918 pp. 874–87. — St. John D. Seymour " The Book of Adam and Eve in Ireland " *Proc. RIA* XXXVI (1922) C 121–33; " The Signs of Doomsday in the Saltair na Rann " *ibid.* (1923) 154–63.

The *Saltair na Rann*, "Psalter of the Staves, or Quatrains," is a poetical composition in 162 cantos, of which the first 150 formed the original work — hence the name — and the last twelve are an addition, though probably of not much later date.   In the edition by Stokes there are in all 8393 lines.   The subject is sacred history from the creation, based on the Scriptures and, in some parts, on *apocrypha*.   The first poem gives a description of the universe; and, of the additions, nos. cli and clii express repentance and ignorance of God, and the others, in which the sacrifice of sense to metre makes interpretation difficult, set forth the signs and events of the nine days leading up to the last judgment.

Seymour points out that for the story of Adam and Eve [283] the author uses not only the apocryphon *Vita Adae et Evae* [284] but also the Greek *Apocalypsis Mosis*,[285] probably in a Latin version. He also shows that for the signs of Doomsday use was made of one of the Anglo-Saxon Blickling Homilies,[286] or of the matter on which it was based, and of the Apocalypse of Thomas.[287]   In l. 8009 the author professes to give his name: " I am Oengus *céle Dé*."   If by this is meant the Oengus mac Oengobann to whom is

---

[283] A legend giving the eight things from which Adam was created is in BM Addit. 4783: pub. with trans. by WS *Three Irish glossaries* (London etc. 1862) pp. xl *sq.* He gives a metrical trans. in *Academy* XXVI (1884) 236; *cf.* Brooke and Rolleston *Treasury of Irish poetry* (London 1900) 348–50. For the Latin original see Max Förster *Archiv f. Religionswissensch.* XI (1908) 479 *sqq*; *ZCP* VII (1910) 511, XII (1919) 47–8. — In the margins of Vat. Palat. 830 (no. 443) are several poems relating to Old Testament history. One, " Cenn ard Adaim . . . ," naming the different countries from which God took earth to make Adam's body, has been published by WS *Zs f. vergl. Sprachforschung* XXXI (1890) 249–50, and by B. MacCarthy *The Codex Palatino-Vaticanus No. 830* (Dublin 1892) 24; another " Cethror coic [fh]ichit . . . ," giving the number of the children of Adam, by MacCarthy, *ibid.* 26. — Another version of *Peannaid Adaim*, " The Penance of Adam," is in YBL facs. pp. 158–9 and Edinburgh Nat. Lib. XL pp. 45–8.   It has been published by A. O. Anderson *RC* XXIV (1903) 243–53, with trans.

[284] W. Meyer *Abhandl. d. k. bay. Akad. d. Wissensch.* 1879 (Munich); trans. Charles *Apocrypha and Pseudepigrapha of Old Testament* II.

[285] Tischendorf *Apocalypses Apocryphae*; trans. in *Ante-Nicene Library* XVI.

[286] R. Morris *Blickling Homilies (Early Eng. Texts Soc. Pub.)* pp. v, 90.

[287] Bihlmeyer *Rev. Bénédictine* July–Oct. 1911 pp. 270–82.   An Old-Irish poem on the end of the world, " Dofil aimser laithe mbratha," from Bodl. Laud 615 pp. 132–4, is published by KM *ZCP* VIII (1912) 195–6.

attributed the Félire Oengusso written about A.D. 800,[288] the passage must be a falsifying interpolation. The linguistic forms are those of Middle Irish, and must be more than a century later than the time of Oengus mac Oengobann. Moreover in poem xii the author gives certain chronological records and allusions to contemporary rulers which make it fairly certain that he was writing in the year of " the cattle-plague," 987. With this date the philological and other evidence agrees.[289]

In Rawl. B 502 the *Saltair na Rann* is followed by some chronological matter with the heading " According to the Seventy." With this is a poem on Babylon: Babilóin roclos hi céin . . . rocumthacht in Babilóin. 22 quatrains. All this is published by KM *ZCP* III (1901) 17–9.

610. Eve's Lament

Mé Eba ben Adaim uill . . .

MS: RIA Stowe B. IV. 2 f. 146ᵛ. ED: KM *Ériu* III (1907) 148 [with trans.; trans. also in *Selections from ancient Irish poetry* (1911) 34].

This dramatic monologue in verse is dated by Meyer as probably of the late tenth or early eleventh century.

611. Poem on the Day of Judgment

Bráth ní ba beg a brisim . . . tall i mbroscur in brátha. 24 quatrains.

MSS: Bk. Lis. f. 53. — Dublin Franciscan Convent A (9) p. 38. — RIA 23 G 27. ED: J. G. O'Keeffe *Ériu* III (1907) 29–33 [with trans.].

According to its editor this text is " possibly as old as the tenth century."

612. *Tenga Bith-núa:* The evernew Tongue

In principio fecit Deus caelum et terram et reliqua. Airdri domain as treisi cach righ . . . in Tenga Bithnua tosach in creidim.

MSS: Bk. Lis. ff. 46–52. — There are several abridgments, none older than *s* XIV, and none of much value for the restoration of the corrupt Lismore text: YBL cols. 700–7, facs. 81–6. — BN Fonds celtique 1 ff. 24–7. — Cheltenham Phillipps MS 9754 ff. 7–8. — BM Egerton 171 *s* XVIII 44–65. — Liber Flavus Fergusiorum. — Rennes 598/15489 ff. 70–4ᵛ. EDS: G. Dottin *RC* XXIV (1903) 365–403 [Rennes text, with Fr. trans.; *cf.* XXVIII (1907) 278–307, where a 19th-cent. version is given]; *Annales de Bretagne* XXXIV 190–207, 278–97 [the Paris text, with trans.]. — WS *Ériu* II (1905) 96–162, III (1907) 34–5 [Lismore text, with trans.].

The story tells how the bishops and kings of the East held an assembly at Mount Sion, where the spirit of the Apostle Philip, called the Evernew Tongue, addressed them. He received the name because his tongue was nine times cut out by the heathen, and

---

[288] *Cf.* pp. 471, 480 *supra.*
[289] MacCarthy argued that all this matter was a later accretion; but MacCarthy, although possessing a good working knowledge of the Irish language, had little understanding of philological science.

nine times miraculously restored. " In answer to questions put by the sages, the Evernew Tongue tells them about the creation of the universe, and treats especially of the seven heavens; of the seas, wells, rivers, precious stones and trees of the earth; of the sun and stars; of birds, men and beasts. The order of the six days in Genesis, chap. 1, is here followed. Lastly, the Evernew Tongue describes hell, doomsday, and heaven."

It was composed, probably on the basis of a Latin original, in the tenth or eleventh century.

613. Scéla Lái Brátha: Tidings of Doomsday

Dia dobennachad nanéstidi uli. Tabrad . . . Athar 7 Maic 7 Spirta Náim.

MS: LU 31–4. EDS: WS RC IV (1880) 245–57, 479 [with trans.]. — P. Walsh Mil na mBeach (Dublin 1911) 62–8. COMM: Alfred Nutt in KM The voyage of Bran son of Febal I (London 1895) 223–8. — C. S. Boswell An Irish precursor of Dante (London 1908) 171 sqq.

This description of the last judgment, set in the form of a homily, and composed, it seems probable, in the eleventh century, has considerable value as an exposition of contemporary Irish ideas on the other world.

614. Dá Brón Flatha Nime: The two sorrows of the Kingdom of Heaven

Cid aran apar brón in nim? Ninsa. Eli 7 Enóc. . . .

MSS: [Type I] LU 17–8 [wanting beginning]. [Type II] LL 280–1. — YBL 120–1. — BN Fonds celtique 1 ff. 27ᵛ–8. — Bk. of Fermoy 114–5. ED: G. Dottin RC XXI (1900) 349–87 [with Fr. trans.].

The two sorrows of the kingdom of heaven are the prophets Enoch and Elias, who have passed thither with their mortal bodies and are awaiting the end of time when they may die. The piece has much value as a source for the religious ideas of the time, especially the idea of Anti-Christ. As in the other writings of this class, the author worked from the basis of certain European Latin works: here probably the pseudo-Hippolyte De consummatione mundi, the pseudo-Augustine De Antichristo, and the Libellus de Antichristo of Adso of Montiér-en-Der, sometimes attributed to Alcuin. The text, apparently, was written in the eleventh century.

615. Scéla na hEsérgi: Tidings of the Resurrection

Tabrad cach día airi . . . Athar 7 Maic 7 Spirta Náim.

MS: LU 34–7. EDS: J. O'B. Crowe Scéla na Esérgi A treatise on the resurrection (Dublin 1865) [with trans.; of little value]. — WS RC XXV (1904) 232–59 [with trans.]. — P. Walsh Mil na mBeach (Dublin 1911) 69–78.

This account of the resurrection of the dead, written in the eleventh century and more probably in the second than in the first half, is, after the Vision of Adamnán and the Tidings of Doomsday, the most important source for mediaeval Irish eschatology.

616. Biblical stories and legends in *Leabhar Breac*

The early fifteenth-century codex *Leabhar Breac* (see p. 25 *supra*) contains chiefly religious matter. The contents are given in the introduction to the RIA facs. and, more briefly and usefully, in *PH* 36–40. Biblical history occupies ff. 109–60, 194–8. Part of this, ff. 133ᵛ–41, containing " Stories of the Gospels " and allied matter [290] in Irish, has been edited, with trans., by Edmund Hogan *The Irish Nennius from L. na Huidre and homilies and legends from L. Brecc* (RIA Todd Lect. Ser. VI) (Dublin 1895). This contains the well-known Lament of the Mothers of Bethlehem, " Cid ima n-delige mo mac grádach frim . . . ," which Hogan had published in *The Latin Lives of the saints as aids towards the translation of Irish texts and the production of an Irish dictionary* (RIA Todd Lect. Ser. V) (1894). It was also published, with trans., by KM in *Gaelic Journal* IV (1891) 89–90. There are verse trans. in Geo. Sigerson *Bards of the Gael and Gall*. 2nd ed. (London 1907) 178–9; KM *Selections from ancient Irish poetry* (London 1911) 42–3; Eleanor Hull *Poem-Book of the Gael* (London 1912) 154–5 [by A. P. Graves]. This piece has been ascribed to the eleventh century. The " Stories " as a whole are later, but most of the matter in LBr seems to go back at least to the twelfth century.[291] — WS has published in *RC* VIII (1887) 360–1 certain notes on the Magi from LBr 137, 199, and *ibid.*, with trans., a poem " Aurilius humilis árd . . . " from BM Harl. 1802 f. 5ᵛ. Another ed. of this poem, by O'C, was published by W. Reeves *Proc. RIA* 1st ser. V 47–50.—Notes on the apostles from LBr 180, with similar matter from YBL col. 332, BB f. 14ᵛ, and BM Harl. 1802 f. 9ᵛ, have been published by WS *RC* VIII 352 *sqq*, IX (1888) 364; and from Bodl. Laud 610 ff. 9ᵛ,38, by KM *ZCP* VIII (1912) 107, XII (1918) 397. [292] — On pp. 221–36 LBr has an account of the true cross, its discovery, events at the crucifixion, etc. Part of this has been published, with German trans., by Gustav Schirmer *Die Kreuzeslegenden im Leabhar Breac* (St. Gallen 1886).[293] — At p. 187 of LBr there is an account of the origin of All Saints' Day, the Irish *Samain:* it is published, with Germ. trans., by EW *IT* II 215–6; and, from LBr and Maynooth MSS, by P. O'Neill and T. Roche *Míl na mBeach* (Dublin 1911) 57 *sqq*.

617. The Passions and the Homilies in *Leabhar Breac*

A large portion of Leabhar Breac is taken up with passions — accounts of the sufferings of Christ and the apostles and martyrs — and homilies, sermons. These seem to have been composed towards the end of our period: in the opinion of Tomás Ó Máille, in the second half of the eleventh century. *Cf. Ériu* VI (1911) 1. They are in Irish, but have passages in Latin, sometimes very extensive. As they are all based more or less closely on Latin texts received from the continent of Europe they are not sources of the first importance for Irish history, but have interest as witnesses to the kinds of Latin literature circulating in Ireland, to the ways in which that litera-

---

[290] In Leabhar Húi Maine ff. 115, 116 there are poems on the childhood of Jesus (*'Sa ráith-sea rucadh Muiri*) and on the seventeen wonders at his birth *Inn-aidchi geini Chríst cain:* these have been published by KM *ZCP* VIII (1912) 561–3, V (1905) 24–5.

[291] Hogan, *ibid.* publishes from LBr 256 some notes on the creed, and from 257 instruction on the sacraments.

[292] A poem on the mission of the apostles (Ídail ó rohairgidsom . . . bríg anbfine cech ídail, 24 quatrains) from RIA Stowe B. IV. 2 p. 140 and RIA 23 N 10 p. 90 is published by KM *ZCP* XIII (1919) 15–6.

[293] In *ZCP* VIII (1912) 107 KM publishes two quatrains from TCD H. 3. 18 on the four woods in the cross.

ture was assimilated and modified, and, in connection with both these aspects, to the Irish religious ideas of the time.

These passions and homilies — with two exceptions noted below — have been published, with trans., by Robt. Atkinson, *The passions and the homilies from Leabhar Breac* (RIA Todd Lect. Ser. II) (Dublin 1887) [*cf.* the criticisms and observations by AdeJ *RC* IX (1888) 127–36;[294] H. Gaidoz *RC* X (1889) 463–70; WS *Philol. Soc. Trans.* 1890 pp. 203–4, reprinted, with additions, in *Beiträge z. Kunde d. indogerm. Sprachen* XVI (1890) 29–64]. The following is a list of these texts: P. 1 Passion of Christ's image; 4 history of Pope Sylvester [incomplete];[295] 7 meeting of the monks Paphnutius and Onophrius [incomplete];[296] 7 passion of Pope Marcellinus; 34 passion of Stephen, and finding of his body; 35 homily addressed to kings; 40 homily for Palm Sunday; 44 for Wednesday of the Betrayal; 45 on the fast of the Lord in the desert; 48 on the Lord's Supper; 52 for Pentecost; 56 on the circumcision of Christ; 59 on the Life of St. Martin [not published in *PH*, but by WS in *RC* II 381–402, with trans.]; 66 on charity; 68 on alms; 72 on St. Michael and the orders of angels; 107 on the transfiguration; 107 on penance; 160 passion of Christ; 170 the descent of Christ into hell;[297] 172 passion of Peter and Paul;[298] 175 of Bartholomew; 177 of James; 178 of Andrew; 179 of Philip; 181 of Longinus;[299] 183 homily on the Macchabees; 187 passion of John the Baptist;[300] 189 of the Seven Sleepers of Ephesus; 190 of St. George; 194 homily on the manifestation to Thomas; 198 on the Epiphany; 201 a second on St. Michael; 243 on the Ten Commandments; 248 on the Lord's Prayer; 251 on death (the debate of body and soul); 258 on fasting; 278 passion of St. Christopher [not published in *PH*, but by J. Fraser from this and Liber Flavus Fergusiorum I f. 16 (68), in *RC* XXXIV (1913) 307–27, with trans.].

The LBr Lives of Patrick, Colum-cille and Brigit are in the form of homilies. They have been noticed above, nos. 136, 215, 152.

618. The Voyage of the Úi Corra (*Immram curaig húa Corra*)

Flaithbhrúghaidh ceadach comramach . . . do Mo-Colm-oc mac Colmain i nAr[ain], conid de sin aspert in t-escop na b[riathra so:] Hua-Corro do Condachtuib . . . in clanna-sa hua-Corra. 16 ll.

MSS: Bk. Fer. f. 105 [*cf. Proc. RIA* Ir. MS ser. I pt. I (1870) 44–5]. — RIA 23 M 50 A.D. 1744 pp. 187–200. — RIA 23 N 15 A.D. 1760 x 1816 pp. 1 *sqq.* — RIA 23 C 19 s XIX pp. 158 *sqq.* ED: WS *RC* XIV (1893) 22–69 [with trans.]. TRANS: P. W.

---

[294] He calls attention to the fact that the homilies on death, fasting, the Lord's Prayer, penance and the Lord's Supper are also in BN Fonds celtique 1.

[295] A poem on the legend of the curing of Constantine by Sylvester is in *Fél. Oeng.*[1] p. xxxvi, *Fél. Oeng.*[2] 46. Another text on the same subject, from BM Harl. 5280 f. 26[V], is published by KM *ZCP* III (1900) 226–7.

[296] There is another version of this and the following in BM Egerton 91 f. 60; Bodl. Laud 610 f. 25; BN Fonds celt. 1 f. 112[V].

[297] This and the preceding are based in part on the apocryphal Gospel of Nicodemus. Another version of that Gospel is in YBL 812. A poem " Eiséirgi do éirigh Dia," on the " Harrowing of Hell," is published by O. J. Bergin, *Ériu* IV (1908) 112–9, from Bk. Fer. pp. 193–4.

[298] Also in BM Egerton 91 p. 14.

[299] Imperfect versions in BM Eg. 91 f. 13, and 136 p. 85.

[300] The same version is in YBL 849, and another in BM Eg. 91 p. 46. *Cf.* pp. 751 *sqq infra.*

Joyce *Old Celtic romances* 2nd ed. 1894; 3rd ed. 1907 pp. 400–26. COMM: O'C *MS Mat.* 289–94.— HZ *Zs. f. deut. Alterthum* XXXIII (1889) 182–211. — C. S. Boswell *An Irish precursor of Dante* (London 1908) 157–62.

The principal texts which form the Christian " voyage " literature of Ireland are the Voyage of Máel-dúin (which is really a pagan legend given a slight Christian setting), the Voyage of Brendan,[301] the Voyage of Snedgus and Mac Ríagla,[302] and the Voyage of the Úi Corra. This last as we have it is the latest of these romances, but the matter which enters into it is old, much of it being used also in the Voyage of Máel-dúin and the Voyage of Brendan. Unlike the other compositions which make up the Christian voyage and vision literature, it is not connected with any of the famous churches or saints.

Conall *derg* úa Corra *finn*, a *brugaid*[303] of Connacht, and his wife, the daughter of the *airchinnech* of Clochar,[304] had three sons, Lochán, Enna and Silvester,[305] who were consecrated to the devil from their origin. They destroyed half the churches of Connacht, and were about to destroy that of Clochar and kill their grandfather when they were stricken with repentance. They went to Finnian of Clonard, who directed them to rebuild the churches they had destroyed. Returning, they said that they had rebuilt all but one, Cenn-mara, "Head of the Sea" (Kinvara, on Galway bay). He answered that this above all must be reconstructed, for it was the church of Comman, the oldest of Ireland's saints. The Úi Corra accordingly erected the church of Cenn-mara, and then had a *curach* built, in which they set forth over the ocean. The wonders seen are recorded at considerable length: the purgatorial element is extensive, and is used to enforce the author's moral, and especially Sabbatarian, ideas. From a bishop who accompanied the adventurers the story came to St. Mo-Cholm-6c of Aran, by whom was written the versified summary at the close.

The setting of the legend is undoubtedly very late. Stokes thought the verse might be of the eleventh century. Zimmer believed that the tale is a recasting, in the thirteenth century, of a text of the eighth, the oldest of the "voyages," of which a small section at the beginning is preserved.[306]

619. The Vision of Tundale

[Prologue] Venerabili ac Deo devote domne G., Dei dono abbatisse, frater Marcus . . . adjuvante properemus. [Vision] Hybernia igitur insula est . . . qui superest cunctis, que ante diximus, J. C., d. n., cui h. est et g. per i. s. s. Amen. Explicit visio cujusdam militis nomine Tnugdali.

MSS: 54 are given by Wagner, who classes the following as of *s* XII: Vienna National Bibl. 815 ff. 76–103; 1321 ff. 95–100; Munich Staatsbibl. 4569 ff. 99ᵛ sqq; 18523 ff. 14–29; Berlin Staatsbibl. 100 ff. 1–66; Erlangen 403 ff. 156ᵛ–94. EDS: *Libellus de raptu animae Tundali et eius visione* [Cologne *c* 1470]. — O. Schade *Visio Tnugdali*

---

[301] Pp. 406–18 *supra*. [302] No. *229 supra*. [303] Rent-paying farmer. [304] *Cf.* p. 351 *supra*.
[305] The names were extracted from a martyrology, probably that of Oengus, for Dec. 31, on which date were commemorated Pope Sylvester I and two obscure Irish saints, Lochán and Enna, of Cell-na-manach (Kilnamanagh near Tallaght).
[306] The title is given in the list of tales in the twelfth-century LL: *cf.* O'C *MS Mat.* 587.

(Halle 1869).— Albrecht Wagner *Visio Tnugdali Lateinisch und altdeutsch* (Erlangen 1882). Of the eds. of vernacular versions, see esp. V. H. Friedel and KM *La vision de Tondale (Tnudgal) Textes français, anglo-normand et irlandais* (Paris 1907).[307] Comm: A. Mussafia *Sulla visione di Tundalo (Sitzungsb. d. k. Akad. d. Wissensch. philos. hist. Cl. LVII)* (Vienna 1871). — Alessandro d'Ancona *I Precursori di Dante* (Florence 1874).— Emil Peters *Die Vision des Tnugdalus, ein Beitrag z. Kulturgeschichte des Mittelalters* (Programm) (Berlin 1895). — C. S. Boswell *An Irish Precursor of Dante* (London 1908) 212–29. — H. J. Lawlor *St. Bernard of Clairvaux's Life of St. Malachy of Armagh* (London, New York 1920) notes *passim*. — St. John D. Seymour *ZCP XIV* (1923) 24, 182. — H. J. Lawlor " The biblical text in Tundal's Vision " *Proc. RIA XXXVI* (1924) 351–75.

The Vision of Tundale (Tnúthgal or Tnúdgal) was written by a monk named Marcus, according to some of the manuscripts at Ratisbon in southern Germany, where there was an Irish monastery. The historical *data* which the author provides indicate that the vision was seen in 1148 and that he wrote probably in 1149. He was evidently a Munster man, and a partisan of that ecclesiastical reform movement of which St. Malachy,[308] who died in 1148, was the leader.

The theme was, no doubt, Irish. The story is another contribution to the Christian Irish vision literature, of which earlier examples were the Vision of Fursa and the Vision of Adamnán.[309] The setting also was Irish. Tundale, or Tnúdgal, was a soldier of Cashel who had served under Cormac Mac Carthaigh, king of Desmond (d. 1138). While on a visit to Cork he fell into a trance and was taken by an angel through the other world, where he saw, and in part experienced, the sufferings of the bad and the rewards of the good. The author anticipates Dante in making Tundale meet with many of his contemporaries and friends. Among those whom he encountered were St. Patrick, St. Rúadán,[310] St. Malachy, King Cormac, Donnchad, brother of Cormac (d. 1144), Conchobar Úa Briain, king of Munster (d. 1142), Celestine, or Cellach, archbishop of Armagh (d. 1129),[311] Christian Úa Morgair, bishop of Clogher and Louth (d. 1138), and Nehemiah Úa Moriertach, bishop of Clúain-uama (Cloyne), who according to this text died in 1148.[312]

The eschatology of the piece resembles that of the first Vision of Adamnán, and there are many evidences of the influence of that apocryphal literature which was translated into Irish quite extensively in the eleventh century. But, apart from this, the description of the other world does not contain much that is peculiarly Irish. It is, in the main, an elaborate, but crude, compilation of cosmopolitan horrors.

With the exception of the Voyage of St. Brendan [313] — to which, as a literary production, it is far inferior — the Vision of Tundale became the most widely popular of all the stories of mediaeval Ireland. It spread out over Europe from Ratisbon, and was translated into German, French, Italian, Anglo-Norman, Middle English, and Norse. Finally in the second decade of the sixteenth century Muirges mac Paidin úi Maoil-Chonaire, compiler of the Book of Fenagh,[314] translated the tale into the language in which, it is pretended, Tundale originally told it to the monk Marcus.[315]

---

[307] For other vernacular eds. see Potthast's *Wegweiser*.   [308] *Cf.* no. 652.
[309] *Cf.* nos. 296, 226.   [310] *Cf.* no. 184.   [311] *Cf.* pp. 765–6 *infra*.   [312] FM 1149.
[313] *Cf.* pp. 414–7 *supra*.   [314] P. 401 *supra*.
[315] Found in TCD 1337 (H. 3. 18) pp. 771–6, 792–809.

620. Story of Máel-Suthain úa Cerbhaill

[O'C] Triar foglainntig tainicudar . . . in Innis Faithlenn isin eclais fos.

MS: RIA Liber Flavus Fergusiorum pt. i f. 11. — BN Fonds celt. 1 f. 44ᵛ. EDS: O'C *MS Mat.* 76-9, 529-31 [text, trans.; reprint in *LH¹* 249-50]. — J. Vendryes *RC* XXXV (1914) 203-11 [with Fr. trans.].

One of the objects to which the Irish story-teller turned his narrative of intercourse with the world beyond the grave was the exaltation of his favorite prayer. So we have supernatural testimony to the spiritual value of the *Beati* psalm and the hymn *Hymnum dicat.*³¹⁶ The present tale witnesses to the importance of the *Altus Prosator* hymn of Colum-cille.³¹⁷ It is attached to the figure of Máel-Suthain úa Cerbhaill (d. 1010), who is identified with the *anmchara* or confessor to Brian *bóroimhe.*³¹⁸

621. Description of the two deaths

Is c[oir] a fhis . . . thogus Dia neoch.

MS: Liber Flavus Fergusiorum I f. 25. ED: Carl Marstrander *Ériu* V 120-5.

It is a story of a holy monk who sees a vision of the death of the just man and of the wicked. In substance and style it resembles the homilies of Leabhar Breac. "The language gives evidence of considerable age."

622. Story of two young clerical students

Dias macclérech batar . . . as dech fil ann.

MSS: LL 278. — Bodl. Rawl. B 512 f. 140ᵛ. — Bk. Lis. f. 43. ED: *Lis. Lives* pp. x-xii [with trans.].

The familiar theme of the compact by which the first who dies is to return with tidings from the other world. It is here used to exalt the merits of the recitation of the *Beati* psalm.³¹⁹

623. Story of four young clerical students

Cethrur macclérech. . . .

MS: LL 281. ED: KM *Gaelic Journal* V (1894) 64, 79-80 [with trans.].

A story of four young clerics who went on a pilgrimage to Rome.

---

³¹⁶ *Cf.* pp. 451, 419 *supra.*   ³¹⁷ *Cf.* no. 91 (i).

³¹⁸ *Cf.* no. 144. — In *ZCP* V (1905) 498 KM publishes from Bodl. Laud 610 f. 92ᵛ a poem attributed to Máel-Suthain úa Cerbhaill: Cóictach, descipul, foglaintid . . . filed, fían for cóe [9 quatrains; the 10th, giving the author's name, ends:] bas certu atá cóe. This gives lists of seven grades or divisions of various ecclesiastical and secular matters, but is more a secular than a religious text.

³¹⁹ *Cf.* no. 233.

624. *Foscél ar Bannscail*—Story of the temptation of a confessor

Araile sruith noemda bói. . . .

MSS: LBr 242. — Bodl. Rawl. B 512 f. 140ᵛ. — BM Egerton 92 f. 27. — BN Fonds celtique 1 f. 28ᵛ. Ed: H. Gaidoz Κρυπτάδια IV (Heilbronn 1888) 262–81 [with Fr. trans.].

One of several stories, mostly incorporated into the *vitae sanctorum*, of the temptation of saints by amorous women.

As stated on p. 732 *supra* with regard to devotional pieces, many other minor religious compositions have been passed over here without individual notice. — Consideration of a certain number of Irish poems on secular subjects, but written by ecclesiastics or given an ecclesiastical setting, has been postponed in order that they may be described in association with the purely secular poetry to which they are closely related. Some of these, such as " The monk and his pet cat," " The black-bird's song," " The hermit's song," throw an interesting and pleasing light on the ancient monastic life.

CHAPTER VIII

THE REFORM MOVEMENT OF THE TWELFTH CENTURY

In the year 909 William, Duke of Aquitaine, founded the monastery of Cluny, in Burgundy, about fifteen miles north-west of Mâcon. It was designed to be an innovation in continental monasticism at a time when European religious life was in the ebb. The success of the project was extraordinary: Cluny itself became the most famous of abbeys, while by the twelfth century more than three hundred religious houses, scattered over Europe, were subject to its rule. On a principle well known to Irish monasticism but hitherto rejected by Benedictine, all these formed one congregation under the supreme dominion of the abbot of Cluny. The promotion of Cluniac ideals was almost equally successful, and the Cluniac reform movement became one of the greatest forces operating in western Europe in the eleventh century. Its influence extended far beyond the limits of the cloisters of the congregation, and when Lanfranc, first archbishop of Canterbury appointed after the Norman conquest of England, reorganised the English Church according to continental models, and his successor, St. Anselm, opposed William Rufus on the investiture question, they were merely applying the principles that Cluny had been teaching for nearly two hundred years. Finally, at the end of the eleventh and in the first half of the twelfth century, the ripples from the pebble that William of Aquitaine had dropped in Burgundy in 909 were lapping on the shores of Ireland.

The Cluniac movement, while having as its object the advancement of morality and devotion, was more directly practical than perhaps the majority of similar religious movements in the middle ages, including some which may be said to have derived from it their origin. It sought its ends by increasing the efficiency of the ecclesiastical body, both secular and regular. Education, independence, organisation, discipline constituted its prescription for the ills which afflicted the Church in the dark days of the tenth century. In particular, the Cluniac reformers are remembered for the struggle they inaugurated to free the clergy from the control, or even the influence, of secular society. One line of this struggle was against the marriage — the reformers called it concubinage — of the clergy. Another was against the absorption of the Church into the feudal system. From centuries of donations by the faithful to churches and monasteries it had resulted that abbots and bishops were holders of vast estates. With the evolution of feudalism it was natural that nobles and kings should claim and exercise similar rights over these as over other landed property, the right of investing the new incumbent and of exacting from him homage and service. From the right of investiture sprang inevitably the claim of appointment and from this the practice of using such appointments as gifts or rewards to relatives, favorites, partisans, servitors or, frequently, those who would pay the highest cash price, with little or no regard to the moral and ecclesiastical qualifications of the nominees. The cleansing of the Augaean stables which such conditions produced was a task that even Cluny, boldly though she undertook it, could scarcely accomplish.

Ireland in the eleventh century must have presented to the eyes of a continental reformer a spectacle far worse than that of countries with which he was more familiar. Actually, there was a fundamental unity in the life of western Christendom, and religious conditions in Ireland in the eleventh century, on the eve of reform, did not differ very essentially from those of the Continent in the tenth. But the external forms and circumstances were different, and to those inspired by the Cluniac ideals of organisation, uniformity and discipline — such men as Lanfranc, St. Anselm and St. Bernard — these strange external forms were among the worst evidences of depravity.

It must be remembered that what we call the Cluniac movement, like other similar developments in history, accomplished what it did because it found everywhere large numbers in a frame of mind prepared to act on its suggestions. So it was in Ireland. Inspiration, advice, example may have come from abroad, but the driving force which effected the ecclesiastical revolution of the twelfth century came from within the Irish Church. These Irish reformers had three tasks before them, the relative importance of which doubtless seemed different to different persons: the first was to bring the organisation and external form of the Church into uniformity with that of the Continent; the second was to abolish the abuses — evils from both the Irish and the foreign point of view — which had grown up; and the third was to improve the morality and spirituality of the people.

From at least the end of the sixth to the end of the eleventh century the most outstanding distinction between the Church in continental Europe and the Church in Ireland was, as has already been set forth, that the first was diocesan in organisation and episcopal in administration, the second monastic in organisation and abbatial in administration. There were, consequently, no archbishops in Ireland, and no primate, although the *comarba* of Patrick at Armagh exercised some jurisdiction over the whole island, based on the belief that the entire people owed their conversion from paganism to Patrick. Of the distinctive liturgy of the Irish Church and its gradual disappearance before that of Rome notice has been taken in the preceding chapter: it is evident from statements by Gilla-espuic of Limerick [1] and from other allusions that the old peculiarities still lingered to a greater or less degree in various local churches.

The general evil afflicting the Church in Ireland, as elsewhere, was laicisation, the absorption of the ecclesiastical by the worldly. In Ireland it took the form of decay of the monastic churches until they became, under their monastic form, largely secular institutions. The marriage of ecclesiastics, both clergy and lay monks, and the attraction of the church property, were secularising forces at work in Ireland as on the Continent. Of the earlier stages of decline some notice has been given in connection with the reform movement of the eighth century.[2] There can be no doubt that this decline was greatly accentuated by the attacks of the Northmen in the following two hundred years. By the eleventh century it would seem that in the average church the abbot, generally known as the *comarba*, " heir," of the saintly founder, or, if it were not the saint's principal establishment, the *aircinnech*, " head," had become a lay lord, whose family held the office and the church property from generation to generation; the monk, *manach*, had become a tenant of church-lands under the *aircinnech;* and the student, *scológ*,[3] had become a farm laborer. In some cases, apparently, all trace of a church-establishment had disappeared, except that the incumbent claimed for his lands, the *termonn* of the ancient monastery, those privileges and exemptions which had from of old been accorded to ecclesiastical property; but generally the *comarba* or *aircinnech* maintained a priest, and, in the more important churches, one or more bishops and several priests, to administer the sacraments and perform other sacerdotal duties. The larger churches were still extensive ecclesiastical institutions, with a numerous clergy, a school

[1] *Cf.* no. 651.   [2] *Cf.* pp. 468 *sqq supra*.
[3] *Cf. Sitzungsb. d. k. preuss. Akad. d. Wissensch.* philos.-hist. Cl. 1914 pp. 944–5.

presided over by a *fer légind* with his assistants and scribes, hospitals, sometimes attended by *Céli Dé*, who likewise had been secularised, and especially a hermitage or *disert*, where " pilgrims," *deôraid*, from other districts or churches lived in seclusion and maintained the ancient traditions of piety and asceticism. Moreover, these lay incumbents of the abbatial office seem to have been for the most part men of religion and learning who worked conscientiously for the good of the Church. But the exceptions must have been many and serious, and the whole situation, in which at least the greater part of the revenues and the greater part of the administrative power of the Church were in the hands of laymen who transmitted their positions by hereditary succession — of the Irish type — while the clergy were practically their hired servants, was obviously anomalous when not positively evil.

The laicisation of abbacies in Ireland and the feudalisation of bishoprics and abbacies in Europe had the same origin, the wish of the local ruling families to obtain and retain control of the rich property of the churches, and their manipulation of law and custom to effect that end. The established rule of succession to an Irish abbacy was that the abbot should be selected from the kindred of the founder; if they could not provide a qualified person, the selection was to be made from the kindred of the secular king or prince who had granted the land on which the monastery was built; next from among the monks of the church; and then in order from various other classes which were duly specified. But in practice the local ruling family usually got, sooner or later, complete control of the office and, by a lax interpretation of the qualifications required, converted it into their permanent possession.

Another source of trouble for the Irish churches was the attempt of the kings to exact from them dues and services similar to those imposed on other property-holders, just as in continental Europe difficulties arose over the feudal obligations which it was sought to impose on church lands. From the time of our earliest sources we find the churchmen claiming exemption from such impositions, and, it would seem, having a guarantee of " freedom " attached to all grants of land made to them. But in the tenth and eleventh centuries the secular powers became increasingly insistent on these claims, particularly that of *coindmed* — what English writers of a later age called " coigny " — the free billetting of troops and retainers for a certain period of time. In resistance to this " abuse " clerics and lay incumbents, reformers and anti-reformers alike were united.

Foreign critics of the Irish, then and subsequently, have had much to say as to the immorality into which the people had sunk. The chief specific charge was of looseness in sexual relations and disregard of the Christian law of matrimony; and the Brehon law tracts offer apparent testimony as to the justice of the indictment from the Christian point of view. But whether conditions as a whole were really worse than those of earlier times which have been described as the golden age of saints and scholars, or even than those of other countries of Europe, is undetermined. To estimate the morality of a people, either positively or relatively, without extensive and trustworthy records, is impossible. That religious sentiment, of a kind, was deeply planted in the Irish people is indicated by the story of the panic of the year 1096, an event that may, perhaps, be regarded as inaugurating the twelfth-century revival.

In the ecclesiastical revolution which was effected in this century the decisive movement was that of the hitherto dependent bishops, who, under foreign inspiration and that of certain of their own number who held diocesan administrative powers in the Danish towns of Dublin, Wexford, Waterford and Limerick, met together, organised, and assumed executive power in disregard or defiance of the *comarbai*. They set up dioceses and archiepiscopal provinces, selected cathedral churches, established diocesan chapters, and founded new monasteries occupied by branches of foreign religious orders. Of the local adjustments with *comarba* or *aircinnech* we know but little: probably the reform obtained important support here by winning several of the new dynastic families who in this era of civil as well as ecclesiastical revolution were rising into prominence. *Comarbai* and *aircinnig*, however, retained their lands and persisted till the seventeenth century, forming, under the designations "corbes" and "erenaghs," problems for English lawyers and historians. By customs doubtless dating from the arrangements of the twelfth century they rendered fixed contributions and services to the dioceses and parishes.

I. The " Broom out of Fánad "

Bibliography

O'C *MS Mat.* 399–430, and appendices. — R. A. S. Macalister " Temair Breg: a study of the remains and traditions of Tara 5. The Voice of Fál " *Proc. RIA* XXXIV (1919) C 344–61. — Käte Müller-Lisowski " Texte zur Mog Ruith Sage " *ZCP* XIV (1923) 145–63.

Students of mediaeval history are familiar with the " legend of the year 1000," the modern historians' myth of a panic which seized the people of Europe as the year A.D. 1000 approached, drove them in vastly increased numbers on pilgrimage to the holy places of Palestine, and thereby had as an ultimate result the Crusades and all that followed in their wake. Like those of other European countries, the Irish records know of no peculiar alarm produced by the year 1000, but they have much to say about a panic of the year 1096.

The Annals of Ulster read: " Great fear upon the men of Ireland before the feast of John of this year, until God spared [them] through the fastings of the *comarba* of Patrick and of the clergy of Ireland besides." The Annals of the Four Masters give more details: " The festival of John fell on Friday this year; the men of Ireland were seized with great fear, and the counsel taken by the clergy of Ireland, with the *comarba* of St. Patrick at their head, in order to save them from the mortality which had been predicted to them from a remote period, was to command all in general to observe a three days total fast, from Wednesday to Sunday, every month, and an [ordinary?] fast every day till the end of a year, except on Sundays and great festivals; and they also gave alms and many offerings to God, and many lands were granted to churches and the clergy by kings and princes. And so the men of Ireland were saved for that time from the fire of vengeance." The Annals of Clonmacnois add to the measures taken by the clergy " they also appointed certain prayers to be dayly said."

Obviously there can have been no occasion for such extraordinary alarm in the fact that in 1096 the feast of the decollation of John the Baptist, August 29, fell on a Friday. The production known as the Second Vision of Adamnán [4] informs us that the time of danger was when this occurred in a bissextile (*i.e.*, leap) and embolismal (*i.e.*, having an extra lunar month) year at the end of a cycle. The first two of these conditions were fulfilled in 1096, but as it was the fourteenth of the then universally used nineteen-year cycle the conjunction of the third is not so evident. Moreover, there seem to have been rival prognostications in which different chronological coincidences were given as the marks of the fatal year. But, no doubt, in 1096 men's nerves had been unstrung by a great epidemic which had raged from the first of the preceding August to the beginning of May.[5]

Various names were given to this threatened visitation of death: " the fiery dragon "; the *Roth Ramach*, " paddle-wheel " or " rowing wheel "; the *Scúap a Fánait*, " Broom from Fánad," *i.e.*, from the north, for Fánad was a district on the northern coast, in the present Donegal. They were to come " in vengeance for the killing of John," [6]

[4] No. 627.
[5] See the annals. Those of Clonmacnois, which show pseudo-rationalistic editing, make no mention of the panic but represent the special religious measures as designed to stay the plague.
[6] *Cf. Fél. Oeng.*, notes to Aug. 29.

and there is a whole cycle of stories which explain why this vengeance was to fall with peculiar force on Ireland.

After the crucifixion of Christ the greatest horror in human history, to the mediaeval Irish mind, was the decapitation of John the Baptist. But whereas the Irish had no more than the common human responsibility for the former — and perhaps not even that, for legend said that their pagan king, Conchobar mac Nessa, had died in a fit of righteous indignation on receiving knowledge of the crucifixion — they did carry a special national guilt in connection with the second named event, for it was an Irish druid, Mog Ruith, who actually executed the sentence on the Baptist.   Mog Ruith had the further culpability of being the chief assistant of Simon Magus in his contest with the apostles.[7]

Evidently, as Macalister has indicated, we have here the remains of ancient pagan cult and myth, only half understood, or completely misunderstood, by Christians of the tenth and eleventh centuries, but adapted by them to the purposes of the apocalyptic and eschatological literature then in such vogue.   Names of the form Mog Ruith, literally " Slave of Wheel," are pagan in significance: the second term is the name of a god or of something partaking of divinity.   An ogam inscription at Drumloghan in Waterford,[8] and perhaps another at Lamogue in Kilkenny,[9] give, as the name of an eponymous and, doubtless, divine ancestor, " Rottais " (in a peculiar genitive form).   The people represented were probably the Roithrige or Rothraige, a branch, it would seem, of the Dési:[10] later notices represented them as sprung from Mog Roith [11] — which was to substitute the priest for the god.   This primitive name *Rott-* is identical, so far as form goes, with the Irish word for " wheel."

The interpretation proffered by Macalister for these particular echoes of heathenism is at least ingenious: The *Roth*, " wheel," or *Roth Ramach*, " paddle-wheel," was the bull-roarer,— in Ireland, on this hypothesis, as among certain other peoples a sacred instrument used at secret religious services — and *Mog Ruith* was the priest who used it.   Precept and myth told of the calamities that would befall if the taboos connected with the sacred " wheel " were violated.   Fragments of this lore it was that writers of the tenth century turned into Christian apocrypha and prophecy.

---

[7] There may have been some connection between this invention and that of the seventh-century controversialists who declared that the Irish tonsure was the tonsure of Simon Magus.

[8] No. 218 in Macalister's *Studies in Irish epigraphy.*   [9] *Cf. Proc. RIA* XXXIV C 345.

[10] *Ibid.* XXIX C 74.   [11] Hogan *Onomasticon Goedelicum s. v.*

Be this as it may, it seems certain that in the year 1096 the apocalyptic and similar tendencies of ecclesiastical thought, noticed in the preceding chapter, which had been developing for two centuries or so, secured for a time complete domination over the whole population. From the records it may be inferred that the result was an increase of popular piety and of the influence of the clergy.

Certain secular texts, the general examination of which must be reserved for Part II of the present work, are in part involved in the aggregation of legends here being considered: (i) The genealogies: *cf.* ZCP VIII 332, 334, XIV 162–3; *Proc. RIA* XXXIV C 349. (ii) The *Dindsenchas Érenn*, " Antiquities of Ireland ": sections on Tlachtga: *RC* XVI 61; *ZCP* XIV 158–61; E. Gwynn *The metrical Dindsenchas* IV (RIA Todd Lecture Ser. XI) (Dublin 1924) 186–91; and on Crotta Cliach: O'C *MS Mat.* 426–8, 632–4 [includes a metrical prophecy ascribed to Moling, beginning: A Dé mair —]; *RC* XV 440. (iii) *Immacallam in dá Thuarad*, " Colloquy of the Two Sages ": *RC* XXVI 47. Of these, the first two contain early matter related to the legend of Mog Ruith, the third an allusion which a gloss explains by reference to the *Roth Ramach*.[12] (iv) *Forbhuis Droma-Damhgaire*: O'C *M&C* II 279–83 [extract];—professes to tell how Mog Ruith acquired the territory of Fir-Muige (Fermoy).

Of the texts already noticed the Life of Adamnán (no. 224) has a brief statement that Adamnán foretold a calamity following St. John's day, supposed to have been fulfilled in his own death; while one of Colum-cille's prophecies (no. 220 xliv) and the *Baile Moling* (no. 251 iii) give accounts of the threatened disaster in considerable detail.

625. *Imtheachta Moighi Ruith:* Adventures of Mog Ruith

Cacht ingen Catmaind do Breathnaib . . . oc forbus Droma Damgaire.

MSS: BB 265.— YBL 190. ED: Käte Müller-Lisowski *ZCP* XIV (1923) 154–6 [with Germ. trans.].

This text tells of Mog Ruith's training under Scáthach and Simon Magus.

626. Poems on the death of John the Baptist

(i) [Mackinnon] Apsalon baile in righ . . . Fa'n cenn toir an Apsolon. 6 quatrains. (ii) Clanna Israél uli . . . do tsíl Adhaim is da chland. 43 quatrains.

(i) MSS: Leabhar Úi Máine f. 152ᵛ.— Edinburgh Nat. Lib. Scot. Gaelic I pp. 14–5 [has version in prose, with the poem added in an abbreviated form]. ED: Mackinnon *Celtic Review* VIII (Oct. 1912) 168–70; *Descriptive catalogue of Gaelic manuscripts in Scotland* (Edinburg 1912) 76–7. [the Edinburgh verse, with trans.]. *Cf. Proc. RIA* XXXIV C 352. (ii) MS: Leabhar Húi Máine f. 123. ED: A. M. Scarre *Ériu* IV (1910) 173–81 [with trans.].

12 Mention is made of Mog Ruith in a twelfth-century poem by Gilla-in-Choimded úa Cormaic: LL 144; *ZCP* XIV 157.

These two poems are based on the passion of St. John the Baptist as given in Leabhar Breac,[13] but the second has other apocryphal matter, and both relate that the headsman was the Irish Mog Ruith. The second is attributed, quite impossibly, to Flann Fína mac Ossu, *i.e.*, Aldfrid, king of Northumbria, who died in 705.

627. The Second Vision of Adamnán

Uisio quam uidit Adamnanus. . . . Uae, uae, uae uiris Hiberniae. . . .

MS: LBr 258-9. — Liber Flavus Fergusiorum vol. II pt. ii f. 10. — TCD H. 2. 15 pt. ii p. 59. ED: WS *RC* XII (1891) 420-42 [with trans.]. COMM: O'C *MS Mat.* 424-5. — *LH²* I pp. xxi-xxvi.

The document known as the Second Vision of Adamnán [14] professes to be a prophetic vision seen by that saint, but in reality was, it would seem, composed in connection with the alarm of 1096. It warns against the chronological peculiarities which made that year portentous, describes the sins of the people, and sets forth the conditions of penance, good works and prayers by which the threatened calamity might be averted. Bernard has shown that the order of devotions here prescribed resembles very closely a liturgical office in the Book of Mulling.[15]

II. THE CHURCH OF CENANNAS (KELLS) IN THE ELEVENTH AND TWELFTH CENTURIES

Bibliography

O'D " The Irish Charters in the Book of Kells " *Miscellany IAS* (Dublin 1846) 127-58 [gives text, trans., and commentary].

It has been noticed already [16] that at the beginning of the ninth century the headquarters of the Columban community were transferred from Iona to Ireland and established in a new church built at Cenannas (Kells, in Meath) between 804 and 814. This seems to have remained the metropolis of the Columban monasteries in Ireland until some time in the twelfth century, when that position was taken by Doire (Derry).

To the church of Kells belonged the celebrated evangeliarium known as the Book of Kells. On blank spaces [17] in this codex there was copied, for safe-keeping, a series of records regarding the property of the church which are usually designated the Charters of the Book of Kells. The entries were all made at the same time — the second half of the twelfth century, O'Donovan thought — but it is evident that the original docu-

---

13 *Cf.* no. 617. 14 For the first vision *cf.* no. 226.
15 *Cf.* p. 703 *supra.* 16 *Cf.* p. 445 *supra.* 17 Ff. 6, 7, 27.

ments were drawn up at dates separated by considerable intervals. They are the chief records of this kind which have been preserved from the old Irish churches, though it can be inferred from many allusions in the *acta sanctorum* and other sources that similar registrations were made quite frequently.

From these documents considerable information can be drawn as to the organisation and polity of one of the principal of the monastic churches at the time of the decline of the old monastic order and the rise of the new episcopal and diocesan system.

628. Charter No. IV A.D. 1033 X 1049

Do saire cille delga inso. Fechtas tanic Conchobor . . . is brathair hé do colum cille.

EDS: O'D *op. cit.* 136–41. — *Facs. Nat. MSS. Ire.* II (1878) pl. lx [facs., letterpress, trans.].

This is a record of the grant of a church to the Columban community, and of its exemption from secular dues. The circumstances leading to the grant are first related: Conchobar Úa Máel-Shechlaind (of whom we hear in the annals from 1033 to his death in 1073; he is the first king of the Southern Úi Néill, or of the central province of Mide, or Meath, to be designated by the chroniclers " king of Tara," that title having signified hitherto the *árd rí* of all Ireland) held a conference with a man who evidently had been his enemy, an otherwise unknown " Gilla-Coloim, grandson of Aed." This one was associated in some way with Cenannas — probably he had been fostered, or at least educated, there — and the meeting was held under the protection of the *comarba* of Columba, Máel-Muire Úa hUchtain (who held the office at least from 1025 to his death in 1040),[18] but Conchobor violated the guarantee, carried off the unfortunate Gilla-Coloim " from the altar of Colum-cille," and put out his eyes. In atonement for the outrage a grant was made of Cell Delga (now Kildalkey), a church about ten miles south of Kells. The character of the grant is briefly stated: " with its territory and lands " (*co na chrích 7 co na ferund*), " to God and to Colum-cille forever " (*do dia 7 do colum cille co brath:* this type of *formula* continually recurs), " without tax, without tribute, without military service in battle or hosting, without billeting " (*cen cis cen chobach cen fecht cen [sh]luaged cen choinnim*) " to king or prince " (*rig na toisig*). Next follows a list of the " sureties and guarantees " (*commairche, slána*) for the observation of these conditions: of the clergy, Amalgaid *comarba* of Patrick [19] (his term was from 1020 to 1049) with the " Staff of Jesus " (*bachall Ísu*); the *comarba* of Finnian [of Clúain-Iráird] (probably Cellach Úa Cleircein, who died in 1043 after succeeding, it would seem, in 1019, or Fer-domnach Úa Innascaidh, 1043–1048); and the *comarba* of Ciarán [of Clúain-maccu-Nóis] (probably Loingsech Úa Flaithen, 1030–1042, or Echtigern Úa hAghrain, 1042–1052) with his *minna;* and, of the laity, the kings

18 *Cf.* Reeves *Ad.* 398–9.
19 He was a married man who received and transmitted his position by hereditary succession, and may not have been in holy orders. The term " clergy " was used in a wide sense as applying to all connected officially with the Church.

of four local *tuatha* in Mide, Oengus Úa Cainelbain [20] (O'Quinlan), king of Telach-árdd (the name is represented by Tullyard, two miles north-east of Trim, but the principality approximately by the baronies of Upper and Lower Navan, extending south and south-east of Kells); Máel-Ísu Mac Coirthen, king of Telach-cail (location not known); Gilla-Griguir Úa Dummaig, king of Mag-Lacha (the name is preserved in Moylagh, in the barony of Fore, west of Kells); Laidgnen Mac Maelan, king of Túath Luigne (the barony of Lune, south-west of Kells, but the ancient territory was of greater extent); and Queen Mor, granddaughter of Conchobar.[21] Thus the sureties were the heads of the chief church of Ireland and the two principal older churches of the midlands, and the rulers of the small states around Cenannas. Their guarantees were given " in the presence of the men of Mide, both laity and clergy " (*i.e.*, doubtless, at a *dál*, or assembly), and the whole matter was confirmed by all present giving their blessing to every king that should respect the exemptions granted, and their curse to any king by whom they should be violated. The document is thus a record of the most solemn kind of agreement known to Irish usage. The date must lie between 1033 and 1049.

629. Charter No. II A.D. 1073 x 1084

Ro edpair rí Temhrach . . . ocus dia chraidbechaib.

EDS: O'D *op. cit.* 130–3. — *Facs. Nat. MSS. Ire.* II p. lix.

Record of a grant made by the king of Tara, Máel-Sechnaill, son of Conchobar Úa Máil-Sechnaill, [22] and by the community of Kells, of the *Disert* of Colum-cille at Kells, to "pilgrims" (*deóraid*).[23] The *comarba* of Colum-cille was Domnall Mac [24] Robartaig, who ruled from 1062 to 1098, and for whom the *cumdach* of the *Cathach* of Colum-cille was made.[25] Among the securities and witnesses were Donnchad son of Art Úa Ruairc, king of Connacht, who was killed in 1084, and Donnchad mac Carthaich, king of Cashel, who fell in 1093. The date of the grant would thus be between 1073 and 1084.[26]

630. Charter No. III c A.D. 1092

Ferand do rúagell . . . iar na luaigh.

EDS: O'D *op. cit.* 132–7. — *Facs. Nat. MSS. Ire.* II pls. lix–lx.

Record of the purchase of land by the priest of Cenannas and his kinsmen. The boundaries are described, and a long list of the sureties given, among them " the four

---

[20] He died in 1085, and the last preceding king of whom we hear in 1033 (AU). He was head of the Úi Loeghaire, the senior, but not the dominant, branch of the southern Úi Néill. They were the descendants of Loeguire, king of Ireland in Patrick's time.

[21] This cannot be the same man as the Conchobar who was making the grant. His granddaughter would hardly be accepted as a surety for him, even if such an one could have been of sufficient age at this time.

[22] *I.e.*, son of the king of the preceding document. He reigned, it would seem, from 1073 to 1087 (AU).

[23] *Cf.* pp. 488, 748 *supra*.

[24] Elsewhere also " Úa."

[25] *Cf.* p. 629 *supra*.

[26] At the end of the " charter " is a request for a prayer for the scribe, Mac Maras *tróg*. This may be the " Mac Marais of Cairbre," whose death is recorded by AU in 1098.

strangers from the four cardinal points." The date seems to have been shortly before 1094.[27]

631. Charter No. VII A.D. 1114 x 1117 (?)

Dorogill gilla crist mac manchan . . . dhon leith aile.

EDS: O'D *op. cit.* 146–9. — *Facs. Nat. MSS. Ire.* II pl. lxi.

This is a record of a purchase of land for the community of Cenannas. The probability is that it dates from the rule of Máel-Brigte Mac Ronáin, who was *comarba* from 1114 to 1117.[28]

632. Charter No. V A.D. 1128 x 1138 (?)

Land ro chennaig . . .

EDS: O'D *op. cit.* 140–1. — *Facs. Nat. MSS. Ire.* II (1878) pl. lx.

This document, partly illegible, is a record of a purchase of property. It contains the names and dignities of several of the officials of Cenannas, in the first half of the twelfth century, perhaps *c* 1128 x 1138.[29]

633. Charter No. I A.D. 1128 x 1140

Muinter cennansa erraid . . . . .i. Luigne connacht.

EDS: O'D *op. cit.* 128–9. — *Facs. Nat. MSS. Ire.* II p. xliv n.

A grant by the community of Cenannas of two townlands (*baile*) in Luigne to the *Disert* of Cenannas for the support of " pilgrims."

634. Charter No. VI A.D. 1157 x 1166

Sochur arda brecan . . . do cach midiuch ar chena.

EDS: O'D *op. cit.* 142–7. — *Facs. Nat. MSS. Ire.* II pl. lxi.

The Úi Loeghaire [30] claimed the right of one night's billeting (*coinnmed*) every quarter of a year from the church of Árd-Brecáin.[31] Muirchertach Úa Lochlaind, king of Ireland (about 1157–1166) and Diarmait Úa Máil-Sechlainn, king of Meath (1157–1169) induced Aed, son of Cú-Ulad Úa Chaennulbán, to sell this claim: " the church, therefore, with its territory and lands, is free, for two reasons, viz.: on account of the general freedom of all churches and on account of this purchase."

---

[27] In this year Domnall son of Flann Úa Máil-Sechnaill, king of Tara, was slain. A difficulty arises from the fact that Fer-domnach Úa Clucáin is called *comarba*, although Domnall Mac Robartaig, who, as stated in the preceding text, held that position, did not die until 1098. It may be that Fer-domnach was abbot of Cenannas under Domnall, who, it is likely, was of Doire, but the transcriber of the document thought that he was *comarba* from the first; or perhaps there was a break between Cenannas and Doire.

[28] *Cf.* Reeves *Ad.* 403. [29] So Reeves *Ad.* 404.

[30] *Cf.* p. 755 *supra*. [31] *Cf.* p. 329 *supra*.

III. Anglo-Norman Ecclesiastical Intrusion in Ireland

Bibliography

The principal documents are in Ussher's *Sylloge* (*cf.* p. 104). A new and original investigation of this whole theme is a *desideratum.*

Anti-Irish prejudices had occasionally shown themselves in the old English Church, notably at the Council of Celchyth, and perhaps some suspicion of the absolute soundness of Irish Catholicity may have lingered till the end of Anglo-Saxon independence. But on the whole, from the end of the Easter Controversy to the Norman Conquest, ecclesiastical relations between Ireland and England were friendly. In particular, no spirit of aggression towards their brethren beyond St. George's Channel was displayed by English churchmen.

But with the Norman conquest of England in 1066 came a change. Englishmen disappeared from positions of leadership and were replaced by continental ecclesiastics whose fidelity to the new order could be trusted. The last English archbishop of Canterbury was deposed in 1070 and William the Conqueror nominated in his place Lanfranc, abbot of Bec, an Italian by birth but long a resident of Normandy, who seems to have been the chief agent in giving to William's predatory invasion the character of a holy war. As archbishop of Canterbury Lanfranc effected an energetic and fruitful, though unsympathetic, reorganisation of the English Church, and, further, proceeded to assert his supremacy, not only over the rival English see of York,[32] but also over the whole of Britain and Ireland. His pretensions were put forward in English controversies in 1072, and can be read in the letter which he wrote in that year to his former pupil, by then become Pope Alexander II.[33]

Opportune for the application of these theories was the circumstance that just at this period episcopal sees were being erected in the recently Christianized Hiberno-Scandinavian towns of Dublin, Wexford, Waterford and Limerick. From 1074 to 1140 a succession of bishops-elect from these new sees were consecrated at Canterbury. The explanation commonly offered is that these Scandinavian colonists preferred to form their ecclesiastical connections with their kinsmen in England rather

[32] There is reason to suspect Lanfranc of personal responsibility for a series of forgeries in support of his claims over York. *Cf.* H. Böhmer *Die Falschungen Erzbischof Lanfrancs von Canterbury* (Leipsic 1902), and, in defense of Lanfranc, Saltet in *Rev. des sciences ecclésiastiques* 1907, and A. J. MacDonald *Lanfranc, a study of his life, work and writing* (London, New York 1926).

[33] J. A. Giles *Beati Lanfranci . . . opera omnia* I (Oxford 1844) 24.

than with their Irish enemies; but the facts that almost all these early bishops were Irish in blood, although trained abroad, that the towns were generally under the dominion of one or other of the Irish kings, who sometimes joined in the recommendation of the episcopal candidate, and that there is no evidence of close association or sympathy between the Northmen of Ireland and the Gallicised Normans of England, render such a hypothesis dubious. More probably the townsmen wished partly to regularise their position in the universal Church, partly to insure their independence of the neighboring Irish *comarbai*. They made no objection to entering the Irish Church as soon as that had adopted a diocesan organisation in which their position was recognised. In the meanwhile the archbishops of Canterbury assumed the position of metropolitans over these sees, and exacted, and carefully preserved, declarations of submission and fidelity from all candidates who came seeking consecration.

Towards the Irish Church itself more circumspection was shown, but the Irish reputation for canonical irregularity and moral laxity gave occasion for admonitions having the tone, if not the form, of metropolitan charges. Anglo-Norman influences, we may be sure, helped on the Irish reform movement, especially through the friendship between Anselm, Lanfranc's successor in Canterbury, and Gilla-espuic, or Gillebert, bishop of Limerick, papal legate, and reform leader.

But the whole history of Ireland made it natural that the Irish Church would, in this crisis, seek inspiration and help on the Continent rather than in England. Rome and Clairvaux were the predominating external forces in effecting an ecclesiastical revolution, and under Roman direction a diocesan episcopacy was set up, with four archbishops, and the Hiberno-Danish sees were incorporated into the Irish ecclesiastical polity. The imperialism of Canterbury had the ground cut from beneath its feet, but Norman aggression was not thereby checkmated; the secular power stepped in, and, following the example of William I and Lanfranc, applied solemnly to the Pope for authorisation to conquer Ireland and restore religion and morality. Of this application something will be said in the succeeding volume.

635. Letter from the people of Dublin to Lanfranc, archbishop of Canterbury A.D. 1074 (?)

Venerando sanctae Cantuariensis. . . . Vestrae paternitati est cognitum . . . est forma doctrinae.

ED: Ussher *Sylloge* no. xxv; *Whole Works* IV 488–9 [from a Cottonian MS].

They state that, as the church of Dublin, " which is the metropolis of the island of Ireland," has lost its pastor, they have selected a worthy priest, Patricius,[34] whom they wish to be ordained as their bishop. The date was probably 1074, when died " Dunan, archbishop of the Foreigners."[35]

According to a late and at least partly legendary story in the Black Book of Christ Church, Dublin,[36] a site and endowment for that church were granted to Donatus (Dunan), the first bishop, by Sitric, Danish king of Dublin who died in 1042.[37] If it could be trusted, this would indicate that Bishop Dunan had established himself in Dublin before that date.

636. Letter of Lanfranc to Gothric (Godred?) king of Dublin A.D. 1074

Lanfrancus non suis meritis. . . . Venerabilem fratrem ac coepiscopum . . . feliciter vos perducat.

EDS: Ussher *Sylloge* no. xxvi; *Whole Works* IV 490–1.

This letter was carried back to Dublin by Patrick, who, sent over by the king and people, had been consecrated bishop by Lanfranc in 1074. Lanfranc announces the consecration, urges the king to reform the laxity in marital relations and other evils of his dominion, and advises him to hearken to the new bishop.

637. Letter of Lanfranc to Terdelvac (Toirdelbach) king of Ireland A.D. 1074 (?)

Lanfrancus peccator et indignus. . . . Nullam Deus majorem . . . vitam aeternam concedat.

ED: Ussher *Sylloge* no. xxvii; *Whole Works* IV 492–4.

Bishop Patrick of Dublin, it is probable, also carried back this epistle to Toirdelbach úa Briain, king of Ireland from 1072 to 1086, in which Lanfranc pointed out the evils prevailing in his kingdom and urged their extirpation.

638. Letter of Lanfranc to Bishop Domnald A.D. 1081/1082 (?)

Lanfrancus indignus sanctae. . . . In itinere positi . . . eis decrevimus.

ED: Ussher *Sylloge* no. xxviii; *Whole Works* IV 495–7.

In the text published by Ussher the letter is addressed to the Irish bishop " D "; but in an extract which that editor quotes from what he calls the annals of Canterbury there is a passage to the effect that Lanfranc, in the eleventh year of his episcopate, wrote an epistle on sacred doctrine to Bishop Domnald in Ireland. Lanigan [38] identifies the recipient with the Domnall Úa hEnna who died, according to the annals, in 1098, and who is sometimes called archbishop of Cashel. The letter is a reply to a request for information as to the necessity of the communion of children. A request

---

[34] No doubt, Gilla-Patraic.   [35] AU.

[36] Dugdale's *Monasticon Anglicanum* (ed. Caley, Ellis and Bandinel) VI 1148. *Cf.* Todd *War of the Gaedhil with the Gaill* 290.

[37] Tig., FM.   [38] *Ecclesiastical History* 2nd ed. III (1829) 455.

was also made for the solution of some problems in secular letters, but Lanfranc has renounced such subjects since undertaking pastoral duties.

639. Letter from Anselm to the bishops of Ireland A.D. 1095 (?)

Anselmus Cantuariensis ecclesiae metropolitanus. . . . . Odorem religionis vestrae . . . opere compleatis.

ED: Ussher *Sylloge* no. xxxiii; *Whole Works* IV 515–7.

This letter is addressed to " seniori Domnaldo " (Domnall Úa hEnna: *cf. supra*) and " Donato " (Donatus, or Donngus, bishop of Dublin, d. 1095), and the other bishops of Ireland. Anselm relates how he was forced against his will to accept the pontifical office, and what troubles he has since suffered. He asks for the prayers of the Irish bishops and urges that they consult him in difficulties. The date was probably early in 1095.

640. Letter from the people of Waterford to Anselm, archbishop of Canterbury A.D. 1096 (?)

Anselmo, Dei gratia Anglorum archiepiscopo. . . . . Pater sancte, caecitas . . . subscripsimus. . . . . episcopus subscripsi, &c.

ED: Ussher *Sylloge* no. xxxiv; *Whole Works* IV 518–9. The letter is also in Eadmer's *Historia novorum* (no. 650), ed. Rule, pp. 76–7.

The people of Waterford, wishing to have a bishop, chose Malchus,[39] of Irish birth but a monk of Winchester, and sent him, with this letter, to Anselm for consecration. The date was probably 1096, and the signatures are those of " Murchertachus rex Hiberniae " (Muircertach Úa Briain, king of the southern half, and claimant of the sovereignty of the whole of Ireland from about 1090 to 1119); " Dermeth dux frater regis " (Diarmait, his brother, who died in 1118); " Domnaldus episcopus " (*cf.* no. 638); " Idunan episcopus Midiae " (Máel-Muire Úa Dunáin, who died in 1117; he is mentioned in no. III of the Kells charters); " Samuel Dublinensis episcopus " (*cf.* pp. 761–2); " Ferdomnachus Laginiensium episcopus " (of Kildare, d. 1101).

641. Letters from Anselm to King Muirchertach A.D. 1095/1096 (?)

(i) Muriardacho glorioso gratia. . . . . Gratias ago Deo . . . regnum coeleste transeatis. Amen. (ii) Muriardacho gloriosos regi. . . . . Quoniam multa de vestra . . . coeleste regnum veniatis. Amen. . . . . ullatenus ducere.

EDS: Ussher *Sylloge* nos. xxxv, xxxvi; *Whole Works* IV 520–5.

Anselm. while praising the king's good government, urges that evils be extirpated, especially those connected with marriage and with the consecration of bishops. The two letters cover much the same ground, and Lanigan [40] thought they might be different recensions of one original. The letter or letters may have been brought to Ireland by Bishop Samuel of Dublin or Bishop Malchus of Waterford, whom Anselm consecrated in 1095 and 1096 respectively, or by both.

[39] Máel-Ísu Úa hAinmire, who died in 1135 (FM). *Cf.* H. J. Lawlor *St. Bernard's Life of St. Malachy* (1920) 18–9.

[40] *Eccles. Hist.* 2nd ed. IV 21.

642. Letter from Anselm to Malchus, bishop of Waterford

Anselmus archiepiscopus Cantuariae, amico. . . . Audivi, quod dominus Samuel . . . consulendo moneatis. Valete.

ED: Ussher *Sylloge* no. xxxviii; *Whole Works* IV 528–9.

A covering letter, transmitting that addressed to Samuel of Dublin.

643. Letter from Anselm to Samuel, bishop of Dublin

Anselmus archiepiscopus Cantuariae, venerabili. . . Audivi, quod libros . . . hominibus ostendas. Vale.

ED: Ussher *Sylloge* no. xxxix; *Whole Works* IV 530–1.

Reprimands him for having, as is reported, disposed of the books, vestments and other church ornaments — which Lanfranc gave to his uncle, Bishop Donatus — as though they were his private property; for having expelled the monks from his church; and for the practice of having a cross carried before him on the highway, a prerogative which belongs only to archbishops who have received the pallium from the Pope.

644. Letter from King Muirchertach to Anselm

Murchardachus rex Hiberniae, Anselmo. . . . Quam magnas vobis . . . mandaveris famulaturum. Vale.

ED: Ussher *Sylloge* no. xxxvii; *Whole Works* IV 526–7.

Muirchertach thanks Anselm for remembering him in his prayers, and also for succouring his son-in-law, Ernulf. This was Arnulph de Montgomery, lord of Pembroke, who with his brother, Robert de Belesme, earl of Shrewsbury, revolted in 1102 against Henry I of England, and found refuge, and perhaps obtained aid, in Ireland.

645. Letter from Gillebert, or Gilla-easpuic, bishop of Limerick, to Anselm *c* A.D. 1107

Anselmo Dei gratia Anglorum . . . Audieno, pater . . . . largitatem confido.

ED: Ussher *Sylloge* no. xxxi; *Whole Works* IV 511–2.

Congratulates Anselm on subduing the Normans to ecclesiastical discipline, and sends a gift of pearls. Written probably in or after 1107, when the settlement of the English investiture struggle was reached.

646. A Letter from Anselm to Gillebert

Anselmus servus ecclesiae Cantuariensis. . . . . Gratias ago reverentiae . . . misistis. Orate pro me.

ED: Ussher *Sylloge* no. xxxii; *Whole Works* IV 513–4.

Anselm returns thanks for the congratulations and gift; refers to their former acquaintanceship at Rouen; and urges that Gillebert act with vigor in his episcopal position, of his elevation to which he, Anselm, has just heard.

647. Letter from the people of Dublin to Ralph, archbishop of Canterbury c A.D. 1121

Domino reverentissimo ac religiosissimo, Radulpho. . . . Cum te, sancte pater, . . . retinere volueritis. Vale.

ED: Ussher *Sylloge* no. xl; *Whole Works* IV 532–3. Also in Eadmer *Historia novorum* (no. 650) ed. Rule 297–8.

Samuel Úa hAnglí, bishop of Dublin, died in 1121, and, according to the annals, Cellach, *comarba* of Patrick, " took the episcopacy of Ath-Cliath [Dublin] by choice of the Foreigners and of the Gaidhil." It is probable that this means " assumed the administration of the diocese," and that there was nothing disreputable in the transaction: Cellach seems, from the scanty information we have of him, to have been a man of high character and ability. Apparently there were two parties within the city, one of which sent a certain Gregory to England to be consecrated, while the other, in his absence, admitted Cellach.

The letter professes to be from all the citizens of Dublin, and the convention of the clergy, and requests the consecration of their bishop-elect, Gregory. They inform Ralph " that the bishops of Ireland are very jealous of us, and especially that bishop who dwells in Armagh, because we are unwilling to submit to their ordination, but wish always to be under your rule." The combination of flattery and threat which the document offers perhaps indicates anxiety as to whether their request would be granted, an anxiety which may have been due to the fact that Gregory was a layman, or, according to Eadmer, a subdeacon. Eadmer and the continuator of Florence of Worcester, who tell of the coming of Gregory to England, state that he was first ordained deacon and priest, and afterwards bishop.[41] According to Eadmer, when Gregory found Cellach in occupation of his see he returned again to England and took refuge with Anselm. A few years later, however, he was in peaceful possession of Dublin.

648. Letter from Henry I of England to Archbishop Ralph c A.D. 1121

Henricus rex Angliae. . . . Mandavit mihi . . . dilatione expleas. Teste Ranulpho cancellario apud Windelsor.

ED: Ussher *Sylloge* no. xli; *Whole Works* IV 534.

On the word of the king of Ireland and the citizens of Dublin, directs the consecration of Gregory. The king of Ireland was probably Toirdelbach Úa Conchobuir of Connacht, who in 1118 had obtained the submission of Dublin. His approval shows that the election of Gregory was not entirely a lining up of Gall against Gael.

649. Professions of obedience to the archbishops of Canterbury, made by the bishops of the Scandinavians, or Ostmen, in Ireland

ED: Ussher *Sylloge; Whole Works* IV 564–8.

The texts of the professions of Patrick, Donatus and Samuel of Dublin, Malchus of Waterford, Gregory of Dublin, and Patrick of Limerick (this last in 1140).

41 J. R. H. Weaver (ed.) *Chronicle of John of Worcester* (Oxford 1908) 16.

650. Eadmer: *Historia novorum in Anglia*

EDS: John Selden (London 1623). — Gabriel Gerberon (Paris 1675; later eds. 1721; Venice 1744) [attached to the works of Anselm]. — Migne *PL* CLIX 346–588. — Martin Rule (RS: London 1884). COMM: F. Liebermann *Anglo-normännische Geschichtsquellen* (Strasburg 1879) 284–302. — Rule *Cambridge Antiq. Soc. Communications* 1888 VI 195–304. — Ragey *Eadmer* (Paris [1892]).

Eadmer was a monk of Christ Church, Canterbury, and friend and confidant of Anselm. His *Historia novorum* is a history of England, and especially of the see of Canterbury, from about 960 to 1122, which is regarded by critics as a historical work of high value. It is our principal narrative source for the visits of episcopal nominees from Ireland to obtain consecration at Canterbury, and for other relations between that see and Ireland.[42]

In H&S I 357 there is a record (extracted from Cambridge Corp. Christi Coll. 111 f. 54) of an indulgence granted by Nicholaus, bishop of Llandaff, to those who should visit the church of Bath on the feast of the Exaltation of the Holy Cross. Similar indulgences were issued by several other bishops, among them " Mark bishop of Cloyne." This last was, doubtless, an Irishman, as to whose identity several conjectures have been advanced.

IV. THE ORGANISATION OF THE EPISCOPATE AND THE INTRODUCTION OF FOREIGN RELIGIOUS ORDERS

Bibliography

In addition to the sources mentioned below, the annals, especially FM, and Keating's History of Ireland (pp. 44, 81 *supra*), in which matter is drawn from the now lost Annals of Clonenagh, are important. Of secondary works, the church histories generally treat the period at considerable length, though not with full understanding. What is probably the best study, though admittedly incomplete, is by H. J. Lawlor in his trans. of *St. Bernard's Life of St. Malachy* (no. 652). For the struggle at Armagh see King *The early history of the primacy of Armagh* (1854) [*cf.* p. 319 *supra*] and Lawlor and Best " The ancient list of the Coarbs of Patrick " (1919) [*cf.* p. 353]. On the early Cistercian monasteries see Leopold Janauschek *Originum Cisterciensium tom.* I (Vienna 1877), which contains a catalogue of houses (index *s.v.* " Hibernia ") with a bibliography for each and a brief account of its foundation.

651. Gilla-easpuic, or Gillebert: *De statu Ecclesiae*

[Introductory epistle] Episcopis [et] presbyteris totius Hiberniae. . . . Rogatu, necnon et praecepto . . . valere merear. Amen. [Main text] Imago generalis Ecclesiae . . . martyrio paratus probetur.

MSS: Cambridge Univ. Lib. Ff. 1. 27 pp. 239–42.— Durham Chapter Lib. B. ii. 35. — Cambridge Corpus Christi Coll. 66 pp. 98–9 [prologue only]. EDS: Ussher *Sylloge*

---

[42] He tells us that in 1115 Gillebert, bishop of Limerick, assisted the archbishop of Canterbury and various English prelates in consecrating a bishop of St. David's. — *Historia novorum*, ed. Rule, pp. 235–6.

no. xxx; *Whole Works* IV 500–10. — Migne *PL* CLIX 995–1004. COMM: H. J. Lawlor *St. Bernard of Clairvaux's Life of St. Malachy of Armagh* (London, New York 1920) pp. xxx–xxxiii.

In the epistle, addressed to the bishops and priests of Ireland, Gilla-easpuic states that at their command he has attempted to write down the canonical customs in the observation of the hours and in carrying out the whole ecclesiastical order. It is a plea for liturgical uniformity rather than for that of hierarchical organisation, and some have thought that it accompanied a treatise on liturgical usage, now lost.

The treatise *De statu Ecclesiae* accompanied and explained a graphic representation of the Church, its members and officials, and their interrelations. It was designed to set forth to the Irish clergy the proper organisation of the Church under priests, bishops, archbishops, primates, and the Pope, and may be regarded as the programme of the reforming party. Obviously it was based on European conditions, and from the Irish point of view some of the statements must have been curiously incongruous.

The date is uncertain, but it was probably before the synod of Rath-Breasail, held in 1110 or 1111,[43] at which an episcopal organisation was drawn up for the whole of Ireland, and after Gilla-easpuic's correspondence with Anselm, which may be assigned to 1107.

652. Documents by St. Bernard of Clairvaux, relating to St. Máel-Máedóc Úa Morgair, or Malachy

(i) [Letter from Bernard to Malachy, A.D. 1141] Venerabili Domino et beatissimo patri Malachiae. . . . Inter multiplices aestus et curas . . . peccatoris oratio. In Domino valete. (ii) [Letter from Bernard to Malachy, A.D. 1141/1142] Malachiae Dei gratia episcopo. . . . Fecimus quod praecipit . . . orationibus commendantes. Valete. (iii) [Letter from Bernard to Malachy, A.D. 1143/1144] Amantissimo patri et domino. . . . Quam dulcia faucibus. . . memor in Christo. (iv) [Letter from Bernard to the Cistercian brethren in Ireland, November A.D. 1148] Religiosis fratribus qui in Hibernia. . . . Si haberemus hic . . . Christus custodiat. (v) [Sermon by Bernard on the death of Malachy, November 2, A.D. 1148] De coelo vobis hodie . . . suffragia non deesse. (vi) [Another, November 2, A.D. 1149 (?)] Liquet, dilectissimi, quod dum corpore . . . suaviter ardes, praestante D. n. J. C., qui c. P. et S. s. r. D. per o. s. s. Amen. (vii) [Life of Malachy by Bernard, January (?) A.D. 1149] [Prologue] Semper quidem operae . . . comperta sunt vobis. [Life] Malachias noster, ortus Hibernia . . . tecum et cum ipso pariter regnaturi in s. s. Amen.

MSS: Numerous; see Hardy *Cat.* II 236. EDS: *Cf.* Boll. *Bibl. hag. lat.* 770, 1368. The various eds. of Bernard's works, as that by Mabillon (Paris 1667; later eds. 1690, 1719, 1839), reprinted in Migne *PL* CLXXXII 545–6 [i], 558 [ii], 558–9 [iii], 578–80 [iv], 1073–1118 [vii], CLXXXIII 481–90 [v, vi]. The epistles are nos. 341, 356, 357 and 374 of Mabillon. Also the following partial eds.: i–iv: Ussher *Sylloge* nos. xlii–xlv, *Whole Works* IV 535–45. vii: Surius *De probatis sanctorum historiis* 3[44] Nov. VI (Cologne 1575) 88–115, 2nd ed. IV (1617) 27–41. — Messingham *Florilegium insulae sanctorum* (Paris 1624) 350–76. — *AA. SS. ex Cod. S.* 551–640. — *AA. SS. Boll.* 3 Nov. II i (1894) 135–66. TRANS: H. J. Lawlor *St. Bernard of Clairvaux's Life of St. Malachy of Armagh* (S. P. C. K.: London, New York 1920) [complete, with valuable commentary]. COMM: E. Vacandard " Un évêque d'Irlande au 12. siècle, Saint Malachie O'Morgair " *Rev. des quest. hist.* LII (1892) 1–57 [reproduced in condensed form

---

[43] *Cf.* Lawlor *op. cit.* pp. xxxvii *sqq.*
[44] Malachy died Nov. 2, but as this is All Souls' Day the feast is transferred to Nov. 3.

as chap. xxix of his *Vie de s. Bernard* 2nd ed. II (Paris 1897), 4th ed. (1910). — O'Laverty *Life of St. Malachy* (Belfast 1899). — H. J. Lawlor " Notes on St. Bernard's Life of St. Malachy " *Proc. RIA* XXXV (1919) C 230–64. — W. J. Ferrar " St. Malachy of Armagh: a twelfth-century saint " *Church Quarterly Rev.* XCI (1921) 247–59. — Jas. Wilson " The passages of St. Malachy through Scotland " *Scottish Hist. Rev.* XVIII (1921) 69–82. — H. Maxwell " St. Malachy in Scotland " *ibid.* 228–9.

There is an abridgment of St. Bernard's Life in the *Nova Legenda Anglie*, ed. C. Horstman II (Oxford 1901) 158–67, and an Irish trans. in the MS RIA 23 O 35 pp. 197–248. — A hymn in honor of Malachy is published in Martène *Amplissima collectio* I 746 and Migne *PL* CLXXXII 1117–8.

Domnall, *comarba* of Patrick, who with the clergy of Ireland had prescribed the measures by which to avert the calamity prophesied for A.D. 1096, was taken sick while at Dublin, in 1105, attempting to make peace between Muirchertach Úa Briain and Domnall Ua Lochlainn, king of the north of Ireland. He died at Damliac (Duleek) on the way home, and his body was brought to Armagh on August 12. He was the last of a series of eight members of the Úi Sinaich family who had held the comarbship in succession without taking holy orders. Cellach, grandson of Domnall's brother and immediate predecessor Móel-Ísu, was chosen for the office, and he, probably already influenced by the stirrings of reform, had himself ordained on September 23. In the following year he made an official visitation first of the Cenél Eoghain in the north and then of Munster. In Munster the reform movement was getting under way, and while there Cellach was consecrated archbishop. This seems to have been determined on by a national synod, and it is probable that at the same time Malchus, or Máel-Ísu Úa hAinmire, whom St. Anselm had consecrated bishop of Waterford in 1095, was made archbishop of Cashel.[45]

In 1120 Cellach made his next visit to Munster, and on this occasion, it would seem, he appointed as his vicar at Armagh a young man named Máel-Máedóc Úa Morgair, who had been born at Armagh in 1095, probably son of the *árd fer légind*, or chief professor, Mughrón Úa Morgair,[46] and had been educated there by Imar Úa hAedhagáin, a recluse, doubtless a *deórad*, and a promoter of reform.[47] Máel-Máedóc showed

---

[45] Cashel, the ancient residence of the kings of Munster, had been granted to the Church by Muirchertach Úa Briain, probably with the design that it should become an archbishop's see. FM give the date 1101, while Keating (ITS ed. III 296–7), who, however, is confused in his chronology, puts it in this year 1106.

[46] He died at the monastic church of Mangarit (Mungret), in Munster, probably " on pilgrimage," in 1102 (AU).

[47] He built the church of Sts. Peter and Paul in Armagh, probably for Augustinian Canons. It was consecrated in 1126. In 1148 he died on pilgrimage at Rome.

such zeal and vigor in this office that, it seems probable, he was already selected as the ideal leader to carry on the new movement, and was sent south to receive further training under the aged Máel-Muire, or Malchus, of Waterford and Cashel, who had now retired to the old monastery of Liss-mór. In 1123 there died at Liss-mór while " on his pilgrimage " Oengus Úa Gormain, *comarba* of Comgall of Benn-chor (Bangor), one of the famous monastic churches which had been entirely abandoned as a result of the Viking wars.[48] Either he or his successor was Máel-Máedóc's maternal uncle, and an arrangement was made, similar to the final settlement between bishops and *comarbai*, whereby a lay represen-tative retained the property while Máel-Máedóc received the site of the church, and, no doubt, the ecclesiastical rights and privileges. An opportunity was thus given to introduce the diocesan organisation into the north-east, and Máel-Máedóc, recalled from Liss-mór and conse-crated, became bishop of Coindire (Connor) and also abbot of Benn-chor, where he founded a new monastery in accord with continental ideas. About 1127 a political disturbance compelled him to leave Benn-chor and return to Munster, where he founded the monastery of Iveragh in what is now Kerry. On April 1, 1129, Cellach of Armagh died at Árd-Patraic [49] in Munster, and three days later was buried at Liss-mór. On April 5 Muirchertach, son of his predecessor Domnall, was instituted as *comarba*, in accordance with the old custom, and on his death in 1134 Cellach's brother, Níall, was appointed. But Cellach before his death had nominated Máel-Máedóc to be his successor, and in 1132 the reforming clergy, led by Máel-Muire of Liss-mór and Gilla-espuic of Limerick, the papal legate, insisted on Máel-Máedóc making the attempt to take possession of the primatial see. The struggle con-tinued five years, and seems to have ended with the triumph of Máel-Máedóc, perhaps by the help of Donnchad Úa Cerbhaill, a friend of the reformers, who became king of Air-gíalla, in which is Armagh, probably in 1136.[50] But as Máel-Máedóc immediately resigned the primacy in favor of Gilla-meic-Liag, or Gelasius, *comarba* of Colum-cille at Doire (Derry), and returned to Benn-chor, it is possible that some agreement was reached by which the victory of the reformers was made more acceptable to their opponents.

From Bangor Máel-Máedóc practically dominated the Irish Church for the remainder of his life. In 1139 he travelled to Rome to ask Pope

48 *Cf*. pp. 8–9 *supra*.
49 This church was the seat of the *maor*, or steward, of Patrick for Munster, who collected the contribu-tions to the Patrician community.
50 *Cf*. p. 770 *infra*.

Innocent II for the palls for the two Irish archbishops. The Pope answered that the request must come from a national synod; but he appointed Máel-Máedóc his legate in Ireland in place of Gilla-espuic, who was resigning because of old age. Going and coming the Irish bishop visited St. Bernard at Clairvaux, where was the most famous abbey of the new Cistercian order, an outgrowth of, and in some respects an ascetic reaction against, the Cluniac monastic movement. He left there four of his followers to be trained as Cistercian monks, and later sent others from Ireland. In 1142 these, with some continental brothers, founded the first Cistercian abbey in Ireland, Mellifont, near Drogheda. Before Máel-Máedóc's death five other houses had been established. In 1148 a synod was held at Inis-Patraic (off Skerries on the eastern coast), at which formal application was made for the palls. With this Máel-Máedóc set out, hoping to meet the Pope, Eugenius III, in France; but he went no further than Clairvaux, where on November 2, 1148, he died in the arms of St. Bernard.

Máel-Máedóc was the greatest of the leaders of the ecclesiastical revolution, and his Life by St. Bernard is our most important document for its history. It was written within three or four months of the saint's death, at the request of Abbot Congan, of the Cistercian monastery of the Suir, or Inislounaght, and other members of the order in Ireland, who also supplied information. On a careful examination the Life appears to be a trustworthy source, except that allowance must be made for Bernard's ignorance of Irish customs and circumstances, and for his unrestrained denunciation of what he did not understand, but believed to be evil.

Marcus, author of the Vision of Tundale (no. 619), itself a source of some importance for the reform movement of the twelfth century, visited Clairvaux, it seems certain, very soon after the death of Máel-Máedóc, and, doubtless, gave some assistance in the compilation of the Life. (Cf. Seymour Proc. RIA XXXVII (1926) C 90–1.)

The letters relate to the beginnings of the Cistercian order in Ireland.

St. Malachy is best known at the present day as the reputed author of a prophecy regarding the succession to the papal throne. The document has no bearing on Irish history, and Malachy's authorship is quite improbable. It was first published by Arnold Wion Lignum vitae I (Venice 1595) lib. II cap. xl pp. 307–11; other eds. in Gfrörer Prophetiae veteres pseudepigraphi (1840) 433; O'Brien Prophecy of St. Malachy (Dublin 1880). There is an extensive literature, of which the following may be noted: Adolf Harnack " Über den Verfasser und den Zweck der Prophetia Malachiae de summis pontificibus (1590) " ZK III (Gotha 1879) 315–24; H. Thurston The War and the Prophets (London 1915); E. Vacandard " La prophétie de Malachie sur la succession des Papes " Revue apologétique XXXIII (1922) 657–71, and in his Études de critique et d'histoire religieuses (Paris 1923) [cf. Studies Sept. 1923 pp. 509–11]. — There is also an alleged prophecy of Malachy regarding English domination in Ireland which is quite obviously a modern concoction.

653. The Council of Kells A.D. 1152

(i) List of bishoprics established by the Council of Kells

(a) The Liber Censuum of Cencius the Chamberlain, A.D. 1192. MS: Vat. lat. 8486. ED: Paul Fabre, L. Duchesne, *Le Liber Censuum de l'Église Romaine* (Paris 1889—): the Irish list is in vol. I pp. 232 *sqq.* This list was used by Ware in his *De Hibernia et Antiquitatibus ejus Disquisitiones* 2nd ed. (London 1658) 83–7; Harris (ed.) *Whole Works of James Ware: Antiquities of Ireland* 285 *sq.* (b) The Provinciale of Albinus, Cardinal Bishop of Albano, A.D. 1188/1189. MS: Vat. Ottob. lat. 3057. ED: Duchesne in *op. cit.* II 85 *sqq.* (c) MS: Montpellier Bibl. de l'École de médecine 92 *s*XII. ED: H. J. Lawlor " A fresh authority for the Synod of Kells, 1152 " *Proc. RIA* XXXVI (1922) C 16–22.

(ii) Ordinance of Cardinal John Paparo, papal legate

Quoted by Simon Rochfort, bishop of Meath, at a synod held at the monastery of Sts. Peter and Paul, Newtown, near Trim, 1216. ED: David Wilkins *Concilia Magnae Britanniae et Hiberniae* (London 1737) I 547. COMM: Lawlor *St. Bernard of Clairvaux's Life of St. Malachy of Armagh* (London, New York 1920) pp. xxvii *sqq.*

We have no records of the beginning of papal intervention in the Irish ecclesiastical revolution,[51] but the first papal legate, Gilla-easpuic of Limerick, was appointed, it seems certain, between 1107 and 1110. In 1110 or 1111 he held a synod at Ráith-Bresail, which is probably the same as Fiadh-mac-nAenghusa, at which the country, exclusive of Dublin, was divided into twenty-four dioceses, and their boundaries defined. In general principle this represented what the reformers were working for, but the exact letter of the decrees was not closely observed. In particular in Mide (Meath) a number of small dioceses had, apparently, already been created, and these persisted in spite of the provisions of Ráith-Bresail. According to certain of the annals a synod was held at Uisnech in 1111, at which still another diocesan arrangement for Mide was decreed. Of the work of Máel-Máedóc Úa Morgair as papal legate, and of his unfinished journey to ask that the Pope grant the pallium to two Irish archbishops, something has been said. Apparently another deputation was sent to Rome after the death of Malachy, and Pope Eugenius III commissioned Cardinal Johannes Paparo to bring the palls to Ireland. He reached England in 1150, but was held there for several months by King Stephen.[52] Finally he arrived in Ireland and held a Council at Kells, at which four palls were granted, giving recognition as archbishoprics to Dublin and Tuam as well as to Armagh and Cashel. The dioceses were organised into four provinces, and various other ordinances were enacted. Our information regarding the council is derived chiefly from Keating and the annals,[53] but we have also the scheme of diocesan organisation, preserved in three recensions: (1) the list of Irish bishoprics in the Liber Censuum, a schedule of dioceses and religious houses

---

[51] Ussher in his *Sylloge*, no. xxix, *Whole Works* IV 498-9, prints a letter from Pope Gregory VII to King Toirdelbach and the clergy and people of Ireland (Gregorius episcopus, servus servorum Dei, Terdelvacho. . . . Per orbem universum . . . VI. Kal. Mart.). It is now generally considered that the letter is a forgery. *Cf.* H. J. Lawlor in Stokes *Ireland and the Celtic Church* 6th ed. (London etc. 1907) 371.

[52] See John of Hexham in Arnold's ed. of *Symeonis monachi Dunelmensis opera omnia* (RS) I 326, and the Historia Pontificalis attributed to John of Salisbury in *MGH SS* XX 539 *sq.*

[53] FM do not mention Kells or the palls, but say that Paparo held a synod at Drogheda in 1152.

from which the Pope claimed revenue, compiled in 1192 by Cencius the Chamberlain, afterwards Pope Honorius III, and based, as regards this part, on a pastorale of 1164 x 1167; [54] (2) that in the provinciale of Cardinal Albinus of Albano, of 1188/1189; and (3) that in a manuscript of the Medical School of Montpellier, which its editor guesses may have come from Clairvaux. Moreover, in the acts of a synod held in Meath in 1216 an ordinance of Paparo at the Council of Kells is cited to the effect that as the bishops of the weaker dioceses died off they should be replaced by arch-priests.[55]

654. Foundation Charter of the Cistercian Monastery of Newry *c* A.D. 1156 x 1160

EDS: Dugdale *Monasticon Anglicanum* 1st ed. II 1031. — *Rer. Hib. SS* I 2nd proleg. 158. — O'D *Dublin Penny Journal* I (1832) 102-4.

By this document Muirchertach Úa Lochlainn, king of Ireland, granted his protection and certain lands to the monks at Ibar-cind-trachta (" the yew-tree of the head of the strand "), known in Cistercian records as *Viride lignum* and in modern times as Newry. There is an important list of witnesses. The date seems to be about 1156 x 1160.

655. Foundation Charter of the Augustinian monastery of Ferns A.D. 1160/1161 (?)

ED: Dugdale *Monasticon Anglicanum* II 1040, 2nd ed. 1141.

By this charter Diarmait Mac Murchadha, king of Leinster, granted lands to the new monastery of Ferna (Ferns). The date was probably 1160 or 1161.

656. Confirmation of the Foundation Charter of the Cistercian monastery of Killenny A.D. 1162 x 1165

MS: In Kilkenny Castle. EDS: *Facs. Nat. MSS. Ire.* II pl. lxii [facs. and letterpress; by a misreading the editor makes it apply to the abbey of Duiske]. — Constance Mary Butler and John Henry Bernard " The Charters of the Abbey of Duiske " *Proc. RIA* XXXV (1918) C no. i 4-8.

Diarmait Úa Riain, lord of Idrone, had granted [56] to the Cistercian abbey of Jerpoint, in what is now county Kilkenny, an abbey recently founded from Mellifont, certain lands as an endowment for a daughter-house at Cell-Lainne (Killenny). By the present instrument the grant was confirmed by the king of Leinster, Diarmait MacMurchadha.

---

[54] R. L. Poole *The Papal Chancery* (1915) 193 *sq.*

[55] In a letter from the Pope Honorius III mentioned above to Henry of London, archbishop of Dublin, dated 6 Oct. 1216, Paparo's orders for the incorporation of the diocese of Glenn-dá-locho into that of Dublin are noticed. — Gilbert (ed.) *Crede Mihi* (Dublin 1897) 11.

[56] This document is lost. There is a registration of a confirmation by Henry Úa Riain in 1424 (Butler and Bernard *op. cit.* 139-40).

657. Grant of Baile Dubgaill (Ballydoyle) to Aedán Úa Caellaighi, bishop of Louth, for a community of canons c A.D. 1162 x 1166

MS: TCD 525 s XV. ED: R. Butler *Registrum Prioratus Omnium Sanctorum juxta Dublin* (IAS: Dublin 1845) 50–1.

Diarmait MacMurchadha executed this grant about 1162 x 1166. Although made to the bishop of Louth it appears to have been for the benefit of the establishment afterwards known as the Priory of All Saints, Dublin.

658. Obituary notice of Donnchad Úa Cerbhaill, king of Air-ghíalla

MS: TCD 77 (B. I. 1) s XV/XVI. ED: Geo. Petrie *Origin and history of the Round Towers of Ireland* (Dublin 1845) 391 [with trans.]. The trans., revised, is also in WS *Félire Húi Gormáin The Martyrology of Gorman* (London 1895) p. xx, and H. J. Lawlor *St. Bernard of Clairvaux's Life of St. Malachy of Armagh* (1920) 170.

In a breviary of the late middle ages which belonged to the church of Árd-Macha and has sometimes been designated the " Antiphonary of Armagh " there is a notice of the year 1170, copied from some older manuscript. It asks a prayer for Donnchad Úa Cerbhaill, the king of Air-ghíalla who has been mentioned above [57] as a friend of Archbishop Máel-Máedóc and the reformers, and gives a brief account of his activities in reforming matters ecclesiastical in his kingdom and in founding and equipping churches and monasteries. — The Annals of Ulster state that Donnchad Úa Cerbhaill died as a result of a murderous assault by one of his servants committed in 1168.

659. Life and Miracles of St. Lorcan Úa Tuathail, or Laurence O'Toole

[Plummer's text. Prologue:] Benedictio et claritas et sapientia. . . . [Vita:] Dilectus igitur Deo et hominibus. . . . Rex regum, et Dominus dominancium, c. est g., h., et i, in sempiternum. Amen. [Translation and canonisation:] Igitur cum per annos quinque . . . fuere presentata [includes the letter of Pope Honorius authorising the canonisation]. [Epilogue to the miracles:] Huc usque miracula . . . perstringenda sunt. [Miracles:] Fuit autem apud Blangeium . . . ueritas iurata est.

(i. Panegyric by Jean Halgrin, or Jean d'Abbeville [58]): MSS: BN 14364 s XIII. — Rouen Bibl. municipale A 575 ff. 288–92 [extracts]. ED: The Bollandists *Catal. codd. hagiogr. lat. Bibl. nat.* III 236–48. (ii. Life by a canon of Eu): MS: Paris Bibl. Ste.-Geneviève 1833 s XVIII pp. 205 *sqq* [copied from a MS of Eu, since lost]. (iii. New ed. of preceding, by another canon of Eu): MSS: Cod. K ff. 116ᵛ — 24. — TCD 175 (E. 3. 11) ff. 92ᵛ *sqq.* — Brussels Bibl. roy. 8943 ff. 2–26ᵛ; 11987 ff. 167–74. EDS. Surius *Vitae SS.* 14 Nov. VII 310–24, 2nd ed. 331. — Messingham *Florilegium* (1624) 379–89. — Chas. Plummer *An. Boll.* XXXIII ii (1914) 121–82. (iv) MSS: Bodl. Rawl. B 485 f. 124ᵛ; B. 505 f. 207ᵛ. — For other MSS of the miracles see Plummer's ed. and Legris, *op. cit. infra* 133 *sqq*; also Cod. S. f. 167. COMM: O'Hanlon *The Life of St. Laurence O'Toole, archbishop of Dublin* (Dublin 1877). — A. Legris *Saint Laurent O'Toole* (*Saint Laurent d'Eu*) *Archevêque de Dublin* (Rouen, Eu 1914) [valuable].

[57] P. 766.
[58] Bishop of Besançon from 1225 to his death in 1237.

Lorcan Úa Tuathail, best known of the men on whom fell the task, after the success of the ecclesiastical revolution, of making the new religious machinery work effectively, was the son of the head of one of the principal families of northern Leinster, at this time rulers of the southern part of what is now Kildare. He was born about 1128, and for a time as a child was a hostage with Diarmait Mac Murchadha. About 1140 he was placed in the monastery of Glenn-dá-locha, and about 1153 became abbot. In 1162 he was consecrated archbishop of Dublin to succeed Gregory, who had died Oct. 8, 1161. Lorcan, who was above all a man of peace, became deeply involved in all the difficulties and horrors resulting from the Anglo-Norman invasion. While attempting to negotiate with Henry II of England on behalf of Ruadri Úa Conchobair he died at Eu, in Normandy, on November 14, 1180.

His tomb became a place of pilgrimage for many of the leading ecclesiastics of Ireland, his contemporaries. From them the canons of Eu must have learned much regarding Lorcan's history. In 1191 application was made for his canonisation, an application which was finally granted on December 11, 1225.

All the Lives seem to have been written shortly after canonisation, and to have been based chiefly on material collected for that process.

ADDENDA

PAGE

5   l. 16. *Cf. add.* to p. *756 infra.—Anc. Laws Ire.* V 450, 498, *re* juridical recognition of the written record (MacN).

9   n. 9. Perhaps Stowe Missal. *Cf.* pp. 693–4 *infra,* and *add.*

15   l. 7. Probably a copy (MacN).

15   n. 29. New ed. by Best and Gwynn in preparation.

22   n. 57. Prefix may be hypocoristic *do,* not numeral *dá.*

24   n. 72. BM Eg. 92 *s* XV, 32 ff., was part of Bk. Fer. (Flower *Cat.* 505–6).

25   l. 26. *Cf. add.* to p. 308 *infra.*

25   n. 74. TCD 1319 (H.2.17) p. 172 has 9 leaves (Abbott and Gwynn *Cat. Ir. MSS TCD* 112). *Cf. Proc. RIA* XXXVIII (1928) C 31–50.

25   n. 79. Maynooth College has other copies by the O'Longans.

25   n. 80. *Cf. ZCP* XVII (1928) 389–402.

30   n. 91. *Cf.* p. 37 n. 123.

37   n. 122. *Cf.* Sommervogel *Bibliothèque des écrivains de la Compagnie de Jésus* 10 vols. (Brussels 1890–1910).

52   l. 13. *Cf.* Coimisiún na Gaeltachta *Report* (Dublin 1926); *RC* XLIII (1926) 461–4.

56   l. 18. "Ó Cearbhalláin": *cf.* Ó Máille *ITS* XVII (1916).

63–7   *Cf.* P. M. MacSweeney *A group of nation-builders* (Dublin 1913).

68   n. 281. *London Times Lit. Supp.* Oct. 29, 1915, p. 381.

72   l. 5. In 1926 the School amalgamated with RIA; *Ériu* now pub. by RIA.

73   l. 14. E. Hogan *Outlines of the grammar of Old-Irish* (Dublin 1900).

74   l. 7. RTh, Pokorny and F. N. Robinson are preparing an O–I dictionary based on published glossaries.

82   l. 9. Georges Dottin died Jan. 10/11, 1928. *Cf. RC* XLV 435–9.

83   l. 10. Charles Plummer died Sept. 8, 1927. *Cf. ibid.* 431–5.

87   l. 32. *Cf.* M. R. James *EHR* April 1927 pp. 261–7.

87   n. 367. *Hist. MSS Commission Report on Franciscan MSS at the Convent, Merchants' Quay, Dublin* (Dublin 1906); T. A. O'Reilly "Franciscan MSS in the Convent, Merchants' Quay, Dublin" *Archivum Franciscanum Historicum* VIII (1914) 749–59; Paul Grosjean "Cat. hag. lat. bibl. Dubl." *An. Boll.* XLVI i–ii (1928).

93   l. 41. *Zs. f. vergl. Sprachf.* now pub. at Göttingen.

94   sub-sect. (d). *Scottish Gaelic Studies* (Oxford, Aberdeen 1926–).

94   l. 16. Table of contents, 1865–1922, by T. D. Shaw (London 1925).

95   l. 7. Trans: Vendryes *Language* (London 1925).

96   l. 37. Dinneen *Foclóir* new ed. (Dublin 1927).

97   sub-sect. (a). W. Wattenbach *Anleitung zur lateinischen Palaeographie* 4th ed. (Leipsic 1886). — W. M. Lindsay *Contraction in early Latin minuscule MSS*

(*St. Andrews Univ. pub.* V) (Oxford 1908). — C. G. Crump, E. F. Jacob (eds.) *The Legacy of the middle ages* (Oxford 1926) 197–226: E. A. Lowe "Handwriting" [excellent brief introd.]. — E. K. Rand "On the symbols of abbreviations for *-tur*" *Speculum* Jan. 1927 pp. 52–65; "A nest of ancient *notae*" *ibid.* April 1927 pp. 160–76. Sub-sect. (b). Fr. Steffens "Über die Abkurzungsmethoden der Schreibschule von Bobbio" *Mélanges offerts à M. E. Chatelain* (Paris 1910) 244–54. — Chas. Plummer "On the colophons and marginalia of Irish scribes" *Proc. Brit. Acad.* 1926.

98   sub-sect. (c). E. H. Zimmermann *Vorkarolingische Miniaturen* (Berlin 1916–18). — R. A. S. Macalister *The Archaeology of Ireland* (London 1928) 285–303.

99   sect. 5. E. Cavaignac *Chronologie* (Paris 1925).

100   sect. 6. M. Besnier *Lexique de géographie ancienne* (Paris 1914). — Lists of place-names in Irish census reports, esp. 1851, and in town-land index to ordnance maps.

101   sub-sect. (a). E. Pittard *Les races et l'histoire* (Paris 1924); trans. *Race and history* (London 1925). Sub-sect. (b). M. Ebert (ed.) *Reallexikon der Vorgeschichte* (Berlin 1924–) [to be completed in 15 vols.]. — V. Gordon Childe *The dawn of European civilization* (London 1925; 2nd ed. 1927). Sub-sect. (c). S. Feist *Kultur, Ausbreitung und Herkunft der Indogermanen* (Berlin 1913). — Childe *The Aryans* (London 1926).

102   sub-sect. (d). R. A. S. Macalister *op. cit.* (*add.* to p. 98) [important]; *Proc. RIA* XXXVII (1927) C 245–62.

103   sub-sect. (e). H. S. Crawford *Handbook of carved ornament from Irish monuments of the Christian period* (RSAI: Dublin 1926).

104   sub-sect. (b). O. Jones, E. Williams, W. O. Pughe *The Myvyrian archaiology of Wales* 3 vols. (London 1801–7), 2nd ed. 1 vol. (Denbigh 1870).

108   sub-sect. (f). R. W. Chambers *England before the Norman Conquest* (London etc. 1926) [extracts from sources, with well-informed commentary]. Sub-sect. (g). Eleanor Hull *A history of Ireland and her people to the close of the Tudor period* (London etc. 1926) [treats pre-Norman period briefly].

110   sect. I. *Bibliog.* W. Bremer in *Festschrift zu Feier des LXV-Jährigen Bestehens des römisch-germanischen Central-Museums* (Mainz 1927); trans. *Ireland in . . . Europe* (Dublin 1928).—G. Kraft *Antiquity* Mar. 1929 pp. 33–44.

112   n. 4. J. Loth *Mem. de la Soc. d'hist. et d'archéol. de Bretagne* VI (1925) 137 *sqq*, VII (1926) 1 *sqq*; Bosch Gimpera "La migration des types hispaniques à l'énéolithique et au début de bronze" *Rev. archéologique* 1925 ii 191 *sqq*.

114   n. 8. Attention was called to the Mitani names first by Hugo Winckler, *Mitteilungen d. deut. Orient-Gesellsch.* XXX (Berlin 1907) 51. Some associated Hittite documents at Boghaz-Keui show Aryan affinities, and several petty rulers in Syria of the same epoch seem to have Aryan names. *Cf.* Childe *The Aryans* (London 1926) 16–30.

116   n. 19. L. Siret *Questions de chronologie et d'ethnographie ibériques* (Paris 1913). — A. Schulten *Numantia* I (Munich 1914). — L. Pericot *La prehistoria de la peninsula Iberica* (Barcelona 1923). — P. Bosch Gimpera "Los Celtas y la arqueologia celtica en la peninsula iberica" *Boletin de la Sociedad española de Excursiones* XXIX (1923); "Ensayo de una reconstruction de la etnologia prehistorica de la peninsula iberica" *Boletin de la biblioteca Menendez Pelayo* (San-

PAGE

tander 1923); "Die Vorgeschichte der iberischen Halbinsel seit dem Neolitikum" *Prähistorische Zs.* 1924 pp. 81–130.

116 n. 21. Recent discoveries tend to put the Celtic invasion of Spain and of Italy in Hallstatt II. *Cf. supra*; H. Hubert *RC* XXXIV (1913) 424 *sqq;* XLIV (1927) 78–89.

122 n. 37 l. 4. After "(1924)": pp. 166–79. *Cf.* H. Obermaier *Boletin de la comision provincial de monumentos historicos e artisticos de Orense* VII (1923) 1 *sqq.—Bol. de la Real Acad. de la hist.* LXVII 164 *sqq.*

125 n. 51. Loth "Les Pictes d'après des travaux récents" *Ann. de Bretagne* VI 111–6. — J. Fraser *History and Etymology* (Oxford 1923); "The question of the Picts" *Scottish Gaelic Studies* II ii (Feb. 1928) 172–201.

128 l. 19. P. Charlesworth *Trade routes and commerce of the Roman Empire* (Cambridge 1924).

132 no. 10. *Proc. RIA* XXXII C iii 41–57. — Dinse *Centralblatt f. Bibliothekswesen* XXX (1913) 379.

132 n. 70. R. K. McElderry "Juvenal in Ireland" *Classical Quarterly* XVI 151.

136 l. 20. *"Chronicon imperiale"*: Wrongly attributed to Prosper of Aquitaine; written in southern Gaul, perhaps at Marseilles, and completed A.D. 452.

137 l. 35. The Vulgate psalter is a revised text, not the translation.

143 no. 20. D. Tardi "Sur le vocabulaire de Virgile le Grammairien" *Bulletin Du Cange* 1927 i.

147 l. 21. R. E. M. Wheeler *Prehistoric and Roman Wales* (Oxford 1925). — MacN "The native place of St. Patrick" *Proc. RIA* XXXVII (1926) C 118–40. — M. Cary *RH* CLIX (Sept.–Oct. 1928) 1–22 [summary of recent work].

148 n. 131. For the other side, Wheeler *op. cit.*

150 no. 23. F. Lot "De la valeur historique du 'De excidio et conquestu Britanniae' de Gildas" *Medieval Studies in memory of Gertrude Schoepperle Loomis* (New York, Paris 1927) 229–64. — *ZCP* XVII (1925) 401–6.

151 n. 140. *Cf.* G. H. Wheeler *EHR* Oct. 1926 pp. 497–503.

155 n. 151. In 14th-century pedigrees (*Y Cymmrodor* VIII (1887) 83 *sqq*) his descent is: "Brachan [= Broccán] son of Chormuc [= Cormac] son of Eurbre [= Coirbre] *Gwydel o Iwerdon"* [*i.e.*, "the Irishman from Ireland"].

166 l. 40. MacN *op. cit.* (*add.* to p. 147).

168 n. 53. MacN *op. cit.* 134 *sqq.*

171 l. 13. C. H. Slover "Early literary channels between Britain and Ireland" *Univ. of Texas Bulletin* no. 2648 (1926) (*Studies in Eng.* VI) 5–52; no. 2743 (1927) (*ibid.* VII) 5–111.

172 n. 63. P. Grosjean "Cyngar Sant" *An. Boll.* 1923.

175 l. 4. "of Wales": the Goidelic district Demet, or Dyfed. *Cf.* no. 35.

178 no. 35. COMM: *Cf. add.* to p. 475 *infra.—RC* XLV 141–72.

179 l. 4. See, however, Wade–Evans *Life* (1923) 57.—L. 21. *Del.* "to . . . *siddi."*

180 l. 2. *Scottish Gaelic Studies* II i (June 1927) 1–12.

180 no. 37 (1). G. H. Doble *St. Carantoc* (*Cornish Saints* XIV) (Shipston-on-Stour 1928). (7) *St. Petroc* (*ibid.* XI) (1927).

187 l. 4. Mériot "Colomban ou le Christianisme dans l'Est" *Mém. de la Soc. d'Ému- lation de Montbéliard* 1922–3 pp. 113–264. — S. B. Curti-Pasini *Il culto di San Colombano in San-Colombano al Gambro* (Lodi 1923). — M. V. Hay *A chain of*

PAGE

error in Scottish history (London etc. 1927) 78 *sqq* [controverts anti-papal interpretation].

191   l. 13. F. W. Kellett "Pope Gregory the Great and his relations with Gaul" *Cambridge Hist. Essays* (Cambridge 1889).

191   n. 107. In 594 Gregory sent a copy of his *Liber regulae pastoralis* (which Columbanus mentions here) to "the priest Columbus." — Epist. v 17: *MGH Epist.* I 299.

192   l. 21. Eds: Hay *op. cit.* 208–31 [Gundlach's text, trans.].

194   no. 42 (ix). L. Traube *Anzeiger f. deut. Altertum* XVIII (1892) 208 *sq*; *Vorlesungen u. Abhandlungen* III (1920) 168–9.

197   l. 35. Krusch *NA* XLVI (1925) 148–57.

199   n. 121. *Cf.* H. Plenkers *Untersuchungen zur Überlieferungsgeschichte der ältesten lateinischen Mönchsregeln* (*Quellen u. Untersuch. z. lat. Philol. d. Mittelalters* I iii) (Munich 1906).

201   l. 12. G. Morin *Rev. bénédictine* XXXVIII (1926) 164–77.

205   no. 49. M. Baudot *Le moyen âge* XXIX (1928) 120–70.

207   l. 7. Trans: Maud Joynt *The Life of St. Gall* (S. P. C. K.: London 1927).

207   l. 36. Some think by Walahfrid himself, unrevised.

208   l. 24. After "7569": ff. 176–83 [by Bollandus from MS of Nicolas Belfort, date unknown].

208   l. 31. Said to be a brother of Gall.

210   *Bibliog.* Gen: J. C. MacNaught *The Celtic Church and the See of Peter* (Oxford 1927). Time Reckoning, etc.: A. Giry *Manuel de diplomatique* (Paris 1894; reprint 1925) bk. II chap. iii sect. v. — R. Steele (ed.) *Compotus* (*Opera inedita Rogeri Baconi* VI) (Oxford 1926) introd. Tonsure: M. Joynt *Ériu* X (1928) 130–4.

213   n. 142. The Julian was the true year based on the heliacal rising of Sirius; our "true astronomical year" is from mean equinox (or solstice) to mean equinox (or solstice). *Cf.* Fotheringham *Ériu* X i (1926) 66.

223   l. 31. "Scotia" might include Iona (*cf.* Plummer *Baedae op. hist.* II 186) or even the Irish settlements in north Britain.

223   n. 193. L. Duchesne "La question de la Pâque au Concile de Nicée" *Rev. des quest. hist.* XXVIII (1880) 5–42; F. Daunoy *Echos d'Orient* XXVIII (Paris 1925) 424–44.

224   l. 6. H. Pierquin *Les annales et conciles de l'église d'Angleterre pendant la période anglo-saxonne* (Paris 1913).

226   l. 22. A. S. Cook "Sources of the biography of Aldhelm" *Trans. Conn. Acad. of Arts and Sciences* XXVIII; "Who was the Ehfrid of Aldhelm's letter?" *Speculum* Oct. 1927 pp. 363–73.

229   l. 19. Eds: B. Colgrave (Cambridge 1927) [with trans.].

230   l. 21. G. K. Fortescue *Subject index of modern works added to the library of the British Museum 1906–10* (London 1911) 401–2.

242   l. 14. E. Gwynn *The Rule of Tallaght* (*Hermathena* xliv 2nd suppl. vol.) (Dublin, London 1927) pp. xvii–xx.

242   l. 34. Perhaps written at Tamlachta under Máel-Rúain.

251   l. 4. F. J. E. Raby *A history of Christian-Latin poetry from the beginnings to the close of the middle ages* (Oxford 1927).

PAGE

253 n. 285. "The Pyrrhic accent and rhythm" *Virginia Univ. Alumni Bulletin* April 1923 [*cf. ZCP* XV (1925) 391–2].

263 l. 41. Trenholme *Story of Iona* (Edinburgh 1909) 156–61 [Mitchell's trans.].

264 l. 1. After "434": W. M. Lindsay "Columba's Altus and the Abstrusa glossary" *Classical Quarterly* XVII (1923) 175–99.

267 l. 35. After "323–6.": T. de R. [the Rev. Thos. Roche] *Irisleabhar Muighe Nuadhad* 1910 pp. 75–6.

275 After l. 3: No. 186 *infra* may be of *s* VII; it has affiliations with the *loricae*, and Hisperic reminiscences.

276 n. 373. Perhaps the monasteries of St. Carthach (Latinised Carthagus), *i.e.*, Rathan and Liss-mór (Grosjean). *Cf.* p. 451.

277 l. 27. "sesquivoli": Grosjean suggests "squirrels."

282 l. 24. Possibly Irish, the name modified from one with Celtic root *Catu.*

285 l. 15. "gloss." *Cf. Hermathena* xliv (1926) p. 67.

286 no. 113. *Cf. ZCP* XVII (1928) 371–2.

286 l. 33. After "472, 13": (6th ed.) 472, 9.

286 n. 421. Middle-Irish version LBr pp. 157–9: ed. and trans. V. Hull *ZCP* XVII (1928) 225–40.

288 l. 12. After "1921": 3rd ed. 1924.

289 l. 8. Vol. XLVI i–ii (1928) has the important "Catalogus codicum hagiographicorum latinorum bibliothecarum Dubliniensium," by Paul Grosjean.

290 l. 30. After "1906": 3rd ed. 1927.

290 l. 38. After "no. 2": expanded as *Sanctus Essai sur le culte des saints dans l'antiquité* (Brussels 1927).

290 l. 45. After "(Paris 1912)": Delehaye *Les origines du culte des martyrs* (Brussels 1912).

291 l. 4. Irène Snieders (posthum.) "L'influence de l'hagiographie irlandaise sur les vitae des saints irlandais de Belgique" *RHE* XXIV (July, Oct. 1928) 596–627, 827–67.

303 n. 48. Eng. trans. G. C. Bateman, additions by author (London 1927).

305 l. 30. Grosjean *op. cit.* (*add.* to p. 289) 98–100, 109–11.

306 l. 22. Grosjean *loc. cit.* 112–5.

306 n. 56. *Cf.* Grosjean *loc. cit.* 116–8. Maynooth 3 G 1 belonged to the Chandos collection, and, later, to Charles O'Connor of Belanagare. Grosjean found passages where Colgan's texts agree with it rather than with either Marsh's or the TCD MS. — Among hagiologists these two MSS are commonly designated "M" and "T" respectively. But in the present work "Cod. K" designates Marsh's MS, without prejudice to the question whether it is actually the vol. originally so named.

307 After l. 29: Cambridge Corp. Christ. Coll. 405 (from the Hospitallers, Waterford: see M. R. James's *Cat.* II) has interesting lessons drawn from Lives of Irish saints.

308 l. 40. Ó Buagachain, or Ó Buadachain, was not a scribe of Bk. Lis., but of "the short Book of Úa Buadachain," whence Life of Find-chú was copied into Bk. Lis. O'Buadachain took it from Bk. Monasterboice. *Cf.* Plummer *Misc. hag. Hib.* Cat. no. 36; Grosjean *Ériu* X ii 162.

309 no. 120. BM Eg. 180 is copy of Stowe A. 4. 1, by Muiris Ó Gormáin *c* 1780–1.

313 l. 11. Maynooth 3 G 1 pp. 35–47.

778 ADDENDA

PAGE
314 l. 12. (ii) Helueus episcopus beatissimus Hybernie insule alter Patritius . . . [as (i)].

314 l. 17. After "132–5": Maynooth 3 G 1 pp. 62–9.

314 n. 83. *MGH Auct. antiq.* XIII (*Chron. min.* III) 221–2.

316 no. 124. MSS: (i) BM Eg. 91 *s* XV ff. 42–4 [*cf.* Flower *Cat.* 444].

320 l. 44. After "1911": Eng. trans. 1912.

321 l. 18. Grosjean "Patriciana" *An. Boll.* XLIII iii–iv (1925) 241–60.—MacN *Journ. RSAI* LVII (1928) 1–21.

329 l. 30. Grosjean *loc. cit.* 241–50.

334 l. 14. Grosjean *loc. cit.* 255–6.

337 no. 131. Zimmermann *Vorkarolingische Miniaturen* (Berlin 1916) pls. 206–7. — Grosjean *op. cit.* (*add.* to p. 289) 82–3.

340 l. 15. Grosjean *op. cit.* (*add.* to p. 321) 250–5. — MacN *Proc. RIA* XXXVII (1926) C 123 [suggests that author was Aed of Slébte].

341 l. 4. MSS: Brussels Bibl. roy. sér. II 1124 (Phillipps 4705) [Grosjean's collation — incomplete — makes it almost certain that this is Colgan's Aulne MS]. — Cambrai 816 (721) *s* XV f. 145ᵛ.

344 l. 29. *Cf.* Ifor Williams *Bull. of the Board of Celtic Studies* IV (1927) 58–60.

345 l. 19. After "important]" : ; "Die Verbalformen der Vita Tripartita" *ibid.* XVI iii (1927) 411–52. *Cf. RC* XLV 100.

347 no. 140. *Cf.* Bollandists' *Bibl. hag. lat.* no. 6513. Date: 1181 x 1185. Cistercians came from Furnes, Benedictines from Chester.

348 l. 7. R. Flower "A Glastonbury fragment from West Pennard" *Notes and Queries for Somerset and Dorset* XVII pt. cxxxvi (1923) has part of an Anglo-Norman poem on Patrick, Benignus and Brigit from a MS of *s* XIII. *An. Boll.* XLIII iii–iv (1925) 355–6 lists an unidentified Life in Novare MS LXXVII (73) *s* XIII pt. ii ff. 1–8ᵛ, and Grosjean mentions another in Paris Arsenal 300 *s* XII f. 224ᵛ.

348 l. 22. Patrick O'Neill *Mil na mBeach* 34–5 [from Maynooth copies of Bk. Lis.].

348 l. 25. BM Add. 30512 *s* XV f. 17ᵛ [*cf.* Flower *Cat.* pp. xxxiv, 477]. — TCD 1285 (H. 1. 11) A.D. 1752 f. 118ᵛ [copy of preceding].

350 no. 142 (i). *Cf. Studies* Dec. 1926 pp. 660–1.

351 l. 15. Ir. Life has Lat. passage, perhaps fragment of an ancient text, claiming certain places near Tuam for the *paruchia Patricii.* — On Anglo-Norman poem, *cf. add.* to p. 348 l. 7 *supra,* and *An. Boll.* XLIII iii–iv (1925) 258–60.

351 n. 181. *Cf.* J. Duhr "Le De Fide of Bachiarius" *RHE* XXIV (1928) i 5–40, ii 301–31 [*cf. Rev. bénédictine* XL (1928): "Bull. d'anc. litt. chrét." p. [286]].

353 l. 7. *Cf.* Grosjean *AA. SS. Boll.* 9 Nov. IV 167–8; *An. Boll.* XLIII iii–iv (1925) 256–8.

354 l. 24. BM Eg. 92 f. 29ᵛ.

354 no. 146. G. Waterhouse *Hermathena* xliv (1926) 30–51.

356 l. 1 *sqq.* Roger of Wendover gives date, and statement that Owen was a follower of Stephen. Neither follows from Henry's narrative. (Waterhouse).

356 l. 3. "Louth": in Lincolnshire.

360 n. 218. After "123": and other MSS of no. 152 (i) *infra.*

361 l. 32. Cambridge Corp. Christ. Coll. 405 [frag.]. — TCD 1104 [transcript by Reeves of a MS — Bradshaw thought not later than *s* IX — which in 1875 was

PAGE

in the possession of the Rev. T. W. Carson; original in a continental hand, and having in one place "praecones" for "Britones," suggesting the ancient "Pretones." (Grosjean, who expects to edit the *Vita* in *An. Boll.*)] — TCD 179 (E. 4. 10) *s* XVII [Ussher's copy of a Cottonian MS — now lost — with variants from Stephen White's transcript of a Ratisbon MS used by Colgan and the Bollandists — also lost]. — Dublin Marsh's Lib. Z 4. 5. 12 *s* XVII *ex* [Marsh's copy of preceding].

362 l. 30. MSS: BM Eg. 91 ff. 58–62ᵛ [imperfect]; Eg. 136 A.D. 1630 f. 79 [frag.].

362 l. 37. After "31–6": [Grosjean believes from *Vorlage* of *s* VIII/IX].

362 l. 37, at end. Other extracts in *AA. SS. Boll.* 10 Nov. IV 502.

364 l. 36. After "201 *sqq*": — Dublin Fran. Con. A. 24 pp. 244–50. — Maynooth 3 G 1 pp. 69–78 [all MSS imperfect].

365 l. 5. After "769–78": [Colgan's abbrev. trans. of Brussels 2324–40 (Grosjean)].

365 l. 8. *Cf.* Flower *Cat.* pp. xxxiv, 447.

366 l. 7. MSS: BM Add. 19995 *s* XV f. 2 [frag., 11 stanzas].

378 l. 16 end. Dublin Fran. Con. A 24 pp. 104–11.

381 l. 7. MSS: BM Eg. 92 *s* XV f. 17ᵛ.

381 l. 8. *FM s. a.* 539.

381 l. 23. *Cf.* RTh *Ir. Sage* 282 n. 2; *ZCP* XIV 306.

381 l. 31. MSS: Brussels Bibl. roy. 2324–40 f. 84.

382 l. 15. After "259": BM Eg. 92 f. 26ᵛ.

382 l. 16. G. Dottin *Manuel d'irlandais moyen* II (Paris 1913) 119–23.

385 l. 32. Dublin Fran. Con. A 24 pp. 187–94.

386 After l. 4. Early poem on Colum: Ní bu cráeb crínfhedo . . . úas chiunn chuiri chráeb. 11 ll. MSS: Bodl. Rawl. B 502 f. 122ᵛ. — LL 315. ED: KM *Learning in Ireland in the fifth century* (Dublin 1913) 18–19, 29. Ascribed to a Mongán *éces* mac Echach.

386 l. 10. After "74–6": Maynooth 3 G 1 pp. 219–23.

387 l. 37. *Cf.* Flower *Cat.* 462–5.

388 n. 49. *Cf.* Flower *Cat.* 464.

390 l. 6. After "12ᵛ": Maynooth 3 G 1 pp. 152–9.

392 l. 16. After "53 *sqq*": Maynooth 3 G 1 pp. 129–34.

392 l. 19. After "173": *AA. SS. Boll.* Nov. IV 500.

393 l. 16. After "Amen.": (ii) almost as (i).

393 l. 19. Cod. S ff. 108–9ᵛ, 119, 111, 113–4.

393 l. 21. After "110ᵛ *sqq*.": Maynooth 3 G 1 pp. 171–5.

393 l. 23. *Cf. Studies* Dec. 1926 pp. 662–4.

393 no. 186. EDS: O. B. Schlutter *Amer. Journ. of Philol.* XX (1899) 71–4. — *AA. SS. Boll.* Nov. IV 503.

394 l. 23. (iii): Maynooth 3 G 1 pp. 175–82.

395 l. 21. MSS: RIA Hodges & Smith 150 p. 168. — Cambridge Univ. Lib. Add. 4183 pp. 165–6.

395 n. 85. KM "Zur keltische Wortkunde" II *Sitzungsb. d. k. preuss. Akad. d. Wissensch.* philos.-hist. Cl. 1912 pp. 1144 *sqq* no. 36; E. Gwynn *RIA Todd Lect. Ser.* XI (1924) 417.

396 l. 29. MSS (i): Maynooth 3 G 1 pp. 138–45.

397 l. 11. After "East": (*i.e.*, as Plummer suggests — Cat. no. 123 — Britain).

398 l. 17. MSS (ii): Maynooth 3 G 1 pp. 159–67.

780 ADDENDA

399   l. 30.   MSS (iii): Maynooth 3 G 1 pp. 182–90.

400   n. 122.   To Plummer's MS add: BM Eg. 92 ff. 16, 30^V.

401   After l. 17: Transcripts of present Bk. Fen.: RIA 23 P 8 [by O'D]; BM Eg. 186 [of certain poems, by Richard Plunket, c 1777]. Copies of poems from "the Old Book of Fenagh" are in Bodl. Rawl. B 514 [cf. E. C. Quiggin "Prolegomena to the study of the later Irish bards" Proc. Brit. Acad. V (1911) 46 sqq]; the Book of the O'Conor Don [cf. Douglas Hyde Ériu VIII i (1915) 78 sqq]; and a MacClean MS in Fitzwilliam Museum, Cambridge. Part of poem "Enna dalta Cairpri cruaid" (Bk. Fen. 330 sqq) in Todd Irish version of Nennius (IAS: Dublin 1868) append. pp. civ sqq.

401   l. 38.   MSS (Lat. i): Maynooth 3 G 1 pp. 167–71. Unidentified Lat. Life in Cambridge Corp. Christ. Coll. 405.

402   l. 4.   MSS: (Ir. ii) BM Add. 39665 A.D. 1807 ff. 107–12; 18948 A.D. 1829–35 ff. 32–8.

403   l. 37.   MSS: (i) Maynooth 3 G 1 pp. 103–13.   (ii) Dublin Fran. Con. A. 24 pp. 95–9,

405   ll. 7 sqq.   MSS: (i) Dublin Fran. Con. A. 24 pp. 194–206. — (iii) Maynooth 3 G 1 21–3 [frag.]. EDS: Grosjean An. Boll. XLVI i–ii (1928) 122–3 [Cod. K]: 124–141 [(i)].

407   COMMENTARIES: H. L. D. Ward Catalogue of romances in the British Museum II (London 1893) 516. — W. F. Thrall "Vergil's Aeneid and the Irish imrama: Zimmer's theory" Modern Philology XV (Dec. 1917) 65–90; "Clerical sea pilgrimages and the imrama" Manly anniversary studies (Chicago 1923) 276–83.

408   l. 6.   A. Cabassut "La mitigation des peines de l'enfer d'après les livres liturgiques" RHE (Jan. 1927) 65–70; L. Gougaud "La croyance au répit périodique des damnés dans les légendes irlandaises" Ann. de Bretagne: Mélanges bretons et celtiques offerts à M. J. Loth (Rennes 1927).

413   l. 6.   After "K": ff. 56^V–64^V; Maynooth 3 G 1 pp. 83–100.

413   l. 39.   After "9": by Donnell, son of Teigue junior, O'Sullivan, A.D. 1640; careless; Black Book derived from Bk. Lis. (Grosjean, from Plummer's papers).

415   (NB2).   EDS: E. G. R. Waters The Anglo-Norman Voyage of St. Brendan by Benedeit (Oxford 1928).

416   (NB3).   EDS: Waters op. cit.

416   l. 35.   After "MacParthalain": this part by anonymous scribe c 1484 (Flower Cat. 526).

416   l. 41.   Cf. A. C. L. Brown "The wonderful flower that came to Brendan" Manly anniversary studies (Chicago 1923) 295 sqq.

418   no. 207.   EDS: D. T. Brosnan AH I 362–3.

419   no. 208 (ii).   Modern copy recently added to TCD. — Part of matter in no. 603 infra.

419   no. 208 (iv).   EDS: T. de Roiste Mil na mBeach 33–4.

420   no. 208 (v).   Ed. by de Roiste, ibid. pp. 32–3.

422   l. 3.   (ii): As (i).

422   l. 8.   After "19": pp. 542–53.

422   no. 211.   MSS: (iii) BM Add. 18948 ff. 46–9^V. — Cambridge Univ. Lib. Add. 4183 pp. 178–84.   (iv) Maynooth 3 G 1 pp. 100–3.

422   sect. III Bibliog.   W. Douglas Simpson The origins of Christianity in Aberdeenshire (Aberdeen 1925) [cf. RHE July–Oct. 1925 p. 666]; The historical Saint

ADDENDA 781

Columba (Aberdeen 1927) [*cf. The Month* CL (1927) 312–20; *Scottish Gaelic Studies* II i (June 1927) 106–8; *An. Boll.* XLVI i–ii (1928) 197–9: argues that the northern Picts received Christianity from Candida Casa, Bangor and Glasgow, not at the hands of Columba]. — Leclercq "Iona" *Dict. d'archéol. chrét. et de liturgie.* — Wm. J. Watson *The history of the Celtic place-names of Scotland* (Edinburgh 1926).

426 l. 17. BM Eg. 1782: *cf.* Flower *Cat.* 263–6.

431 l. 19. Watson *op. cit.* (*add.* to p. 422).

433 no. 215. MSS: BM Eg. 91 ff. 22–6^V. Eds: Grosjean *Scottish Gaelic Studies* II ii (Feb. 1928) 111–71 (Nat. Lib. text, trans.)

435 no. 219 (ii). MSS: BM Eg. 91 f. 26.

436 l. 17. By Eoghan *carrach* O'Siaghail (Flower *Cat.* 543).

437 (ix). MSS: BM Eg. 2899 *c* A.D. 1500 f. iii. — Dublin Fran. Con. A 35 pp. 442–3 ["Sgiathluireach Choluim Cille"]. — (xvii). BM Add. 30512 f. 34.

439 (xliv). New ed. of O'Kearney, Dublin 1925. — (xlvi). BM Add. 30512 f. 41^V; 33993 f. 16^V. — Brussels Bibl. roy. 5100–4 f. 26^V.

440 (lx). Edinburgh Nat. Lib. Scot. Gael. V f. 10: Mackinnon *Catalogue* 81–2. — (lxix). MSS: BM Add. 30512 f. 42.

442 no. 221. J. Vendryes "À propos d'un quatrain annonçant la naissance de Colum Cille" *RC* XLV (1928) 93–101.

442 l. 33. *Expl.* uncertain: order of leaves wrong.

443 no. 222. MSS: Dublin Fran. Con. A 24 pp. 27–31.

444 no. 226. Seymour *Proc. RIA* XXXVII (1927) C 304–12.

445 After l. 21: The relics of Adamnán were deposited ultimately at the place thence called Scrín Adamnáin [A.'s shrine], Skreen, co. Sligo. Poem "A maccáin na sruith . . . " 19 quatrains. MSS: LL 370^V; BM Harl. 5280 f. 42; Brussels Bibl. roy. 2324–40 f. 83, 4190–200 f. 31 [probably from LL]. Ed: L. Gwynn *AH* IV 199–214. *Cf. IER* 1914 p. 457. Describes contents of reliquary.

447 no. 229. Eds: (i) *Cf. Hermathena* xliv (1926) 67–8. Comm: W. F. Thrall "The Legend of Snedgus and Mac Riagla, clerics of Colum Cille" *Univ. of Chicago abstracts of theses* Humanistic ser. vol. I 409–14; "Clerical sea pilgrimages and the *imrama*" *Manly anniversary studies* (Chicago 1923) 276–83; "The historical setting of the legend of Snedgus and Mac Riagla" *Studies in Philology* XXII iii (Chapel Hill, N. C. July 1925) 347–82.

447 l. 29. After "–20": *Sitzungsb. d. k. preuss. Akad. d. Wiss.* XVI (1891) 295–9.

449 no. 230. MSS: (iii) Maynooth 3 G 1 pp. 209–14. Eds: (vii) *An tEaglaiseach Gaedhealach* Mar. 1919 p. 8 [extract].

451 no. 232. MSS: (iii) Maynooth 3 G 1 pp. 256–8.

452 no. 234. MSS: (ia) Maynooth 3 G 1 pp. 23–35.

455 no. 239. MSS: Maynooth 3 G 1 pp. 120–9.

457 no. 243. MSS: *Cf. add.* to p. 308. — Edinburgh Nat. Lib. Scot. Gael. XXIV ff. 1–8.—Cambridge Univ. Lib. Add. 4183 pp. 187–8 [one poem].

460 no. 246. MSS: (i) Maynooth 3 G 1 pp. 134–8.

461 no. 248. MSS: (i) Maynooth 3 G 1 pp. 113–20.

463 no. 251 (i). *Cf.* R. M. Smith "The *Speculum Principum* in early Irish literature" *Speculum* Oct. 1927 pp. 411–45, esp. 435–6.

465 l. 9. After "206 *sqq*": also p. x, beginning only.

465 l. 34. *Cf.* Flower *Cat.* 571–2.

PAGE

466　l. 20.　After "23 O 41": pp. 236–40.

467　no. 262.　MSS: Maynooth 3 G 1 pp. 78–82 [frag.].

469　n. 307.　A modern, or modernised, dialogue between Mael-Rúain and Mael-Dithruib is in BM Eg. 187 A.D. 1686 f. 13 ; 146 s XIX f. 92^V; and other MSS. EDS: O'Kearney *op. cit.* [p. 439 xliv: *cf. add.*]. — J. H. Lloyd *Gaelic Journ.* XIV (1905) 838–9.

471　no. 264.　Fran. G 36 has 10 ff., *c* A.D. 1635; by an Irish Franciscan of Louvain, probably Colgan: Mod. Ir. rendering of a more extensive redaction of the "Notes"; ends imperfect. ED: E. Gwynn "The Rule of Tallaght" *Hermathena* no. xliv (2nd suppl. vol.) (Dublin, London 1927) [pp. 104–9: emendations to ed. in *Proc. RIA* XXIX].

472　no. 266.　ED: E. Gwynn *op. cit.* [preceding *add.*] 65–87, 97–103. — Almost all earlier part is in one or both redactions of no. 264; latter part resembles "Ríagail Pátraic" (*Ériu* I 216–24).

473　no. 267.　*Speculum* Oct. 1927 p. 435 n. 2.

473　n. 321.　To Fothad are ascribed 2 quatrains on repentance, of later date. MSS: BM Harl. 5280 f. 35^V. — RIA 23 N 10. ED: KM *ZCP* VII 299.

474　no. 268 (i).　MSS: BM Add. 30512 ff. 45^V–6.

475　After l. 17: An unallotted rule for clerics: Cid is dech do clerech . . . . MSS: LBr 260; TCD 1336 (H. 3. 17) s XV–XVI cols. 837–9; Dublin Fran. Con. A 9 s XV pp. 27–8. ED: Mac Eclaise *IER* 4th ser. XXVIII (1910) 475–9, XXIX (1911) 289–93.

475　l. 21.　L. Gougaud "Étude sur l'*Ordo monasticus* de Culross" *RHE* XXIII iv (Oct. 1927) 764–78 [relationship with Rhygyfarch's Life of St. David (no. 35); *ordo* a late derivative from *vita*].

475　no. 269.　MSS: BM Eg. 92 f. 17. — Lib. Flav. Ferg. pt. I f. 20^V.

476　no. 270.　TRANS: D. MacLean *The Law of the Lord's Day in the Celtic Church* (Edinburgh 1926) [(c); with comm.; *cf. RC* XLIII (1926) 448–51; *An. Boll.* XLVI i–ii (1928) 206–9]. COMM: H. Dumaine "Dimanche" *Dict. d'archéol. chrét. et de liturgie* IV i 858–994. — Flower *Cat.* 307–10. — W. R. Halliday *Speculum* Jan. 1927 pp. 73–8. — H. Delehaye "Un exemplaire de la lettre tombée du ciel" *Recherches de science religieuse* XVIII (Num. extraord. i–ii) (Feb.–April 1928) 164–9.

477　After l. 34: Late metrical version of *Cáin:* Dénaid cáin domnaig Dé dil . . . . MSS: Dublin Fran. Con. A 9 p. 39; BM Add. 4783 f. 7. ED: J. G. O'Keefe *Ériu* III (1907) 143–7 [from Fran. MS].

482　After l. 16: *Baile Bricín.* Bái Bricíni Túama Drecan . . . ol int aingiul. MSS: BM Harl. 5280 ff. 46–8; Eg. 1782 ff. 17–9. ED: KM *ZCP* IX 449–57. O–I text; revelation to St. Bricín, abbot of Túaim-Drecain (Toomregan, on borders of Cavan and Fermanagh?) of the nicknames, monasteries, and periods of abbatial rule of the saints of Ireland.

484　no. 276.　*Cf.* Flower *Cat.* 512 *re* list in BM Eg. 92 f. 17.

484　no. 278.　Attached is a poem on the patron saints of the chief divisions of Ireland: Hú Néill uile ar cul Coluim . . . 4 quatrains. LL 367. ED: Brosnan 361–2. *Cf. ZCP* XVI (1927) 453–7.

486–7　*Bibliog.* J. H. A. Ebrard *Die iroschottische Missionskirche* (Gütersloh 1875) [tendencious]. — Helen Waddell *The wandering scholars* (London 1927) 28–63 [*haut vulgarisation*]. — Jos. P. Fuhrmann *Irish mediaeval monasteries on the*

ADDENDA 783

Continent (Washington, D. C. 1927). — Gerard Murphy "Scotti Peregrini" *Studies* XVII (Mar., June, 1928) 39–50, 228–44. — P. W. Finsterwalder "Wege und Ziele der irischen und angelsächsischen Mission im fränkischen Reich" *ZK* XLVII ii. — Snieders *op. cit.* (*add.* to p. 291).

490   n. 9. *Cf. AA. SS. Boll.* Nov. II i p. [93].

500   l. 10. Snieders *op. cit.*

500   n. 31. E. de Moreau *St. Amand* (Louvain 1927) [*cf.* Van der Essen *RHE* XXIV (Jan. 1928) 155–9].

502   l. 5. After "75 *sqq*": [*cf. ZCP* V 434 n. 6].

502   l. 11. Kirwan *IER* 1912 pp. 170–87.

503   l. 23. [*Comm. praev.* by De Buck, pp. 380–1, has summary *re* Irish in Belgium, and relations with Karlings].

509   no. 310. *Cf.* M. Coens *An. Boll.* XXXIV–XXXV 306–30; A. Hofmeister *MGH SS* XXX pt. II fasc. i (1926).

510   no. 312. COMM: J. Corblet *Hagiographie du diocèse d'Amiens* IV (Paris 1874) 417–25 [bibliog.]. — J. Vendryes *RC* XLIV (1927) 101–8.

510   no. 314. COMM: A. Stracke "De oud-dietsche legende der H. Dimphna" *Bijdragen tot de geschiedenis* XVI (1926) 1–27.

511   sect. III. *Bibliog. Cf.* p. 486. — J. D. Schöpflin *Alsatia illustrata* 2 vols. (Colmar 1751–61). — P. A. Grandidier *Histoire ecclésiastique . . . d'Alsace* (Strasburg 1787). — C. I. Hefele *Geschichte der Einführung des Christenthums in südwestlichen Deutschland* (Tübingen 1837). — P. Heber *Die vorkarolingischen christlichen Glaubensboten am Rhein* (Frankfort 1858). — Falk "Schottenklöster im Elsass" *Katholik* 1868 pp. 309 *sqq.* — Also the works of Greith and Hauck (pp. 109, 106 *supra*).

514   After l. 4: St. Arbogast, bishop of Strasburg (d. 21 July 678?), and his successor, St. Florentius (d. 7 Nov. 687?), reputed Irish: Life of A. by Utho, b. of Strasburg 950–65. EDS: *AA. SS. Boll.* Jul. V 168–79. — Grandidier *Hist. de l'église et des évêques de Strasbourg* I (Strasburg 1776) pièces justif. — Migne *PL* CXXXIV 1003–8. EDS: Surius *De probatis SS. historiis* VI 136–7. — Grandidier *loc. cit.* — *AA. SS. Boll.* Nov. III 395 *sqq.* COMM: *Hist. lit. de la France* III (1735) 621–2. — Tanner *Bibl. Brit.-Hib.* (1748) 47, 288. — Wattenbach *DGQ*⁷ I 135. — Postina *Römische Quartalschrift* XII (1898) 299–305 (*cf. An. Boll.* XVIII 191). — Hogan *IER* 1902 pp. 481–90.

514   no. 319. TRANS: Jos. Schlecht *Die Korbinians-Legende nach der Handschrift des Klosters Weihenstephan* (Freising 1924). COMM: B. Sepp *Zehntes Sammelblatt des Historischen Vereins Freising* (Freising 1915) 22–9. — B. Arnold *Das Leben des hl. Korbinian* (Freising 1924). — A. M. Zimmerman *III Jahresbericht d. bay. Benedikt.-Akad.* 1924 (Metten 1925) 1–20.

514   no. 320. COMM: M. Huber "Der hl. Otto und seine Klosterstiftung Altomünster" in J. Schlecht (ed.) *Wissenschaftl. Festgabe z. zwölfhundertjährigen Jubiläum d. hl. Korbinian* (Munich 1924) 209–44.

518   no. 322a. COMMENTARY: M. Görringer *Pirminius Geschichte des linken Rheinufers* (Zweibrücken 1841). — Hogan *IER* 1894 pp. 405 *sqq.* — Fink *Dritter Jahresbericht der bayer. Benedikt.-Akad.* 1924 pp. 22 *sqq.* — K. Beyerle (ed.) *Die Kultur der Abtei Reichenau* 2 pts. (Munich 1925). — Fuhrmann *op. cit.* (*add.* to pp. 486–7) 41–53 [valuable]. — Gall Jecker *Die Heimat des hl. Pirmin* (*Beitr. z. Gesch. d. alt. Mönchtums u. d. Benediktinerordens* XIII) (Münster-in-W. 1927) [in-

cludes ed. of *Scarapsus*; Pirmin from Spain or south-western France — probably
near Narbonne]. — Four charters *re* the beginnings of Murbach — officially
known as "Vivarius Peregrinorum," and traditionally a colony of "Scotti"
(Murbacher Annals — compiled *s* XVI: *Anzeiger f. schweiz. Geschichte* IV
(1882–5) 167; Schöpflin *Alsatia illustrata* I (Colmar 1751) 737): (1) May 13, 728:
Privilege from Bishop Widegern of Strasburg: Schöpflin *Alsatia diplomatica* I
(Mannheim 1772) 10–3 [defective]; P. A. Grandidier *Histoire de l'église* . . .
de Strasbourg I (Strasburg 1776) pièces justif. 39; Pardessus *Diplomata* II
(Paris 1849) 352–5; *AA. SS. Boll.* Nov. II i 16; *cf.* Fuhrmann 50. (2) July 12,
728: Charter from King Theodoric IV: Schöpflin I 7 *sq;* Grandidier I Pièces
justif. 37; Pardessus II 351; *MGH Dipl. reg. Franc.* I 84 no. 95; *AA. SS. Boll.*
Nov. II i 15. (3) 731/732: Charter from Eberhard, count of Alsace: Schöpflin
I 8, 14; Pardessus II 363 *sq*; *AA. SS. Boll.* Nov. II i 18. (4) 735 × 737:
Charter from Eberhard: Schöpflin I 8–10; Pardessus II 255–7; *AA. SS. Boll.*
Nov. II i 17 *sq*. [*Cf.* W. Levison "Die Urkunden des Elsassischen Grafen
Eberhard" *NA* XXVII (1902) 368–88.] Murbach exempted from diocesan
control; occupied by "peregrini monachi"; one of a community of "monasteries
of Bishop Pirmin" containing such monks: — facts suggesting an Irish, or at
least Celtic, character. — Arnulfsau (Schwarzach, Bavaria) was of same class:
cf. charter of 748 from Bishop Heddo: Schöpflin I 17–9; Pardessus II 408–11;
Gallia Christiana V 458; Wasserschleben *Die irische Kanonensammlung* (Leipsic
1885) pp. xlvi *sq*. Heddo also endowed the monastery of Ettenheim (in Baden);
— the founder, St. Landelin, was regarded as Irish: Grandidier *op. cit.*; Migne
PL XCVI 1547; Hefele *Geschichte d. Einführung d. Christenthums i. s.-w.
Deutschland* (1837) 333; *Bibl. hag. lat.* no. 701–2. The word "peregrini," in
the Frankish dominions in the 8th cent., may have had the special connotation
of "Irish missionary monks": J. Friedrich *Kirchengeschichte Deutschlands*
II (Bamberg 1869) 602; *cf.* Fuhrmann *op. cit.* 49. — This movement, especially
the foundations of Pirmin and that at Honau (no. 335), was helped by the
family of Erchinoald (*cf.* pp. 496, 500 *supra*). His son Leudesius (*cf.* p. 496)
left a son, Adalric, or Ettico, duke of Alsace. Adalric's children were Duke
Adelbert of Alsace, Bothelo, Haicho, Bleon, St. Odilia, abbess of Hohenburg
(no. 323), and Eugenia, her successor. Of the next generation were Duke
Luitfrid, Count Eberhard, and Bishop Heddo of Strasburg (previously abbot of
Reichenau in succession to Pirmin), sons of Adelbert; Boronus, son of Bothelo;
Hugo, son of Haicho; and Hugo, son of Bleon.

519 no. 324 (i). TRANS: E. Kylie *The English correspondence of St. Boniface: The
King's Classics* (London 1911); reprint in *Medieval Library* XIX (London 1924) [part.].

523 no. 329. Lynn Thorndike *Isis* VI iii (1924) 369–70.

528–9 no. 335 (i). EDS: Mabillon *Annales ordinis s. Benedicti* II 699 no. xvii. —
J. G. Eccard *Origines familiae Habsburgo* (Leipsic 1721) 105 no. xii. — Grandidier *Hist. de l'église de Strasbourg* II (Strasburg 1778) 108 no. lxiv. — Migne *PL*
XCVII 927. — (ii). EDS: Schöpflin *Alsatia diplomatica* I (Mannheim 1772)
49 no. li. The following charters also relate to Honau while it was an Irish
establishment: (1) June 21, 723: Grant from Boronus (*cf. add.* to p. 518).
(2) Sept. 17, 723: Grant from Haicho. (3) Dec. 11, 723: Grant from Duke
Luitfrid and Eberhard. (4) 748: Grant from Boronus. (5) May 29, 748:
Grant from Hugo, son of Bleon. (6) Oct. 22, 749: Grant from Bodolus. (7)

PAGE

Sept. 15, 758: Grant of immunity, by Pippin the Short. (8) 758/759: Confirmation of possessions and privileges, by Pippin. (9) March, 770: Grant of immunity, by Carloman; similar to no. 7. (10) June 9, 775: Confirmation of earlier grants, by Charles the Great. (11) Dec., 775: Award to Honau, by Charles the Great, of property claimed by Corbie. (12) Jan., 778: Grant of immunity, by Charles the Great: similar to no. 7. (13) Oct. 17, 781: Grant of freedom from tolls, by Charles the Great. MSS: Only relatively modern copies exist. Mabillon's texts were from a codex of the church of Old St. Peter's, Strasburg (to which the ecclesiastical establishment of Honau had been transferred), copied in 1079 by Leo, canon of Honau (*loc. cit.* 59). EDS: Mabillon 695–700 [nos. 1–6, 8–13]. — Eccard 102–5 [nos. 8–13]. — Bouquet V 705, 720, 739, 745 [nos. 8, 9, 12, 13]. — Schöpflin 35, 43, 49–52 [nos. 8–13]. — Grandidier 88–9, 101, 121, 129, 140 [nos. 7–10, 12, 13]. — Migne *PL* XCVI 1531; 1533, 1545; 1577 (also XCVII 919); XCVII 957; 954; 961; 967 [nos. 7–13]. — Mühlbacher *MGH Dipl. Karol.* I (1906) 14–7, 69–70 143–4, 155–6, 187–8 [nos. 7–12].

529 After l. 14: Tradition said that Charles the Great placed an Irishman, Patto (d. 788?), over a monastery at "Amarbic;" that Patto became bishop of Verden (Hanover); and that he was succeeded in each by another Irishman, Tanco (d. 808?). *Cf.* Colgan *AA. SS.* 794–5, 348–9; *AA. SS. Boll.* Mar. III 844 (3rd ed. 840–1), Feb. II 889 (890).

532 no. 338. TRANS: S. E. Turner (New York 1880). COMM: F. Ganshof "Notes critiques sur Éginhard" *Rev. belge de philol. et d'hist.* 1924 pp. 725–58 [*contra* Halphen].

542 no. 350. *Cf. ZCP* XIV (1923) 426.

543 no. 351 (ii). *Cf.* M. L. W. Laistner *Speculum* July 1928 pp. 392–7.

551 l. 17. New ed. by L. Levillain: I (Paris 1927) (*Classiques de l'hist. de Fr. au m. â.* X).

553 sect. VII. *Bibliog.:* Waddell *op. cit.* (*add.* to pp. 486–7) 60 *sqq.*

555 n. 163. E. K. Rand *Speculum* Jan. 1927 pp. 58 *sqq.*

559 l. 25. Téicht do Róim .... 2 quatrains. F. 23 marg. inf. EDS: WS *Goidelica* ² (1872) 18. — HZ *Glossae hib.* (1881) 264. — EW *Berichte d. kgl. sächs. Gesellsch. d. Wissensch.* 1890 p. 84 [*RC* XII 153–4]. — *Thes. Pal.* II 296. *Cf.* LH ² II 191.

561 no. 365. COMM: E. K. Rand "Mediaeval gloom and mediaeval uniformity" *Speculum* July 1926 pp. 253–68 [with trans. of no. lxxxi].

563 no. 370. *Cf.* E. Munding *Abt-Bischof Waldo* (Beuron 1924) app.

569 sect. VIII. *Bibliog.:* Vernet *Dict. de théologie catholique* V (1913) 401–34 [valuable; good bibliog.]. — É. Gilson *Études de philosophie médiévale* (*Pub. de la fac. des lettres de l'univ. de Strasbourg* III) (Strasbourg 1921) 1–14. — C. R. S. Harris in Crump and Jacob (eds.) *Legacy of the middle ages* (Oxford 1926) 229–34. — L. J. Walker "The theistic philosophy of Erigena and Anselm" *Dublin Rev.* CLXXIX (Oct.–Dec. 1926).

571 l. 9. After "1925)": *Cf. History* July 1927 pp. 152–3, April 1928 p. 32.

572 n. 212. Hilduin of St. Denis, Walahfrid Strabo, Christian of Stavelot and Heiric of Auxerre show some knowledge of Greek. Possibly all had undergone Irish influence. On Christian *cf.* M. L. W. Laistner "A 9th-century commentator on the gospel according to Matthew" *Harvard Theological Rev.* XX (Cam-

bridge, Mass. 1927) 129–49. Stavelot, founded by St. Remacle c 645, may have had Irish connections. *Cf.* Fr. Baix *Étude sur l'abbaye de Stavelot-Malmédy* I (Charleroi, Paris, 1924).

574 n. 214. After "1866": and by Dick, 1925.

574 n. 215. ED: Cl. Bäumker and B. S. von Waltershausen *Frühmittelalterliche Glossen des angeblichen Jepa zur Isagoge des Porphyrius (Beitr. z. Gesch. d. Philos. d. Mittelalters* XXIV i) (Münster 1924). Eds. conclude author was not Dunchad, but belonged to *s* IX and to school of Auxerre.

580 n. 241. *Cf. Le moyen âge* 2nd ser. XXV 111–53.

582 no. 389 (iii). COMM: P. G. Théry "Inauthenticité du commentaire de la théologie mystique attribué à Jean Scot Erigène" *La vie spirituelle* III (1922) pp. [137]–[153].

591 l. 12. *Cf.* Laistner "Abbo of St. Germain-des-Prés" *Bulletin Du Cange* I (1924) 27–31.

594 sect. IX. *Bibliog.*: Rombaut Van Doren *Étude sur l'influence musicale de l'abbaye de Saint-Gall* (Louvain 1925). — Leclercq "Gall, Saint-, Abbaye de" *Dict. d'archéol. chrét. et de liturgie.* — Joynt *op. cit.* (*add.* to p. 207) introd.

594 l. 15. After "influences": *Cf. Speculum* 1927 pp. 354–6.

596 l. 15. After "1878": 2nd ed. by P. Butler, 1925.

597 no. 413. *Cf.* Krusch *NA* XXXV 275.

598 l. 28. E. Schlumpf *Zs. f. schweiz. Kirchengeschichte* July 1927 pp. 142–51.

600 no. 417. *Cf.* Fuhrmann *op. cit.* (*add.* to pp. 486–7) 54 *sqq.*

605 sect. XI. *Bibliog.*: E. Hauswirth *Abriss einer Geschichte der Benedictiner-Abtei U. L. F. zu den Schotten in Wien* (Vienna 1858). — M. Wieland "Das Schottenkloster zu St. Jakob in Würzburg" *Archiv d. hist. Vereins v. Unterfranken u. Aschaffenburg* XVI (1863) ii 1–182. — Johann Meier *Das ehemalige Schottenkloster St. Jakob in Regensburg und dessen Grundherrschaft* (Stadtamhof 1910). — Fuhrmann *op. cit.* 73 *sqq.*

605 l. 5. After "58": (Leipsic 1856) [trans. Reeves *UJA* 1859 pp. 227–47, 295–313].

606 no. 424. *Cf.* Robinson *Two Glastonbury legends* (Cambridge 1926); C. H. Slover "William of Malmesbury and the Irish" *Speculum* July 1927 pp. 268–83.

607 n. 296. *Cf. AA. SS. Boll.* 9 Nov. IV 169–70.

608 l. 3. After "monastery": Also in Life by Osbern of Canterbury, c 1090. EDS: Mabillon *AA. SS. o. s. B.* V 659–88. — Wharton *Anglia sacra* II 88–120. — *AA. SS. Boll.* Mai. IV 359–84. — Migne *PL* CXXXVII 407–56. — Stubbs *op. cit.* pp. xxxi, 69–161.

608 n. 303. Maccalan's first monastery was St.-Michel-en-Thiérache: he afterwards returned, leaving Cadroe in charge of Waulsort.

613 l. 21. After "344": XX (1901) 163 *sqq.*

614 l. 15. After "(1888)": 3rd ed. by Steinberg and Schmeidler (1926).

614 l. 17. *Cf. AA. SS. Boll.* 10 Nov. IV 564–6.

614 After l. 27: On the legend of the foundation, in *s* XI, of Schotten, Hesse, by two Irish princesses *cf.* Decker *Archiv f. hessische Geschichte u. Altertumskunde* I (1837) 134; Heber *ibid.* IX (1861) 319; Scott "Schotten in Hesse" *The Ancestor* July 1904 pp. 70–3; Fuhrmann *op. cit.* 103.

616 no. 444. COMM: Thom. Ried *Historische Nachrichten von den Schottenkloster Weih-St.-Peter zu Regensburg* (Ratisbon 1813). — Hogan "The Irish monas-

teries of Ratisbon" *IER* 1894 pp. 1015–29. — Meier *op. cit.* (*add.* to p. 605). — B. Leib *Rome, Kiev et Byzance à la fin du XIe siècle* (Paris 1924).

617 l. 28. Note after "(1183)": Würzburg: Trithemius "Chronicon monasterii s. Jacobi in suburbio Herbipolensi" *Opera spiritualia* (Mainz 1605) 1 *sqq*, and in Ludewig *SS. rer. Würzburg.* 993 *sqq.* — Wieland *op. cit.* (*add.* to p. 605). — Nuremberg: A. F. Oefele *Rer. Boicarum SS.* I (Augsburg 1763) 340 *sqq*, 348 *sqq.* Constance: K. Rieder "Beitr. z. Gesch. d. Schottenklosters z. Konstanz" *Freiburger Diöcesen-Archiv* N. F. II (1910) 309 *sqq.* Vienna: Hauswirth *op. cit.* (*add.* to p. 605); "Urkunden d. Benediktiner Abtei U. L. F. z. d. Schotten i. Wien" (*Fontes rer. Austriac.* XVIII) (Vienna 1859). — B. Pez *Thesaurus anecdotorum novissimus* VI (Augsburg 1729) 384, 436. Late necrological notes: *MGH Necrol. Germ.* V (Berlin 1913) 303–18.

618 l. 15. A new foundation at Kieff *s* XII *ex*, by Irish monks from Vienna, was abandoned because of a Mongol invasion in 1241. — There are many *diplomata* relating to the *Schottenklöster*, but the majority are later than 1170. Letters of protection from Emperors and Popes in *s* XII will be found in Paricius *Allerneueste und bewährte Nachricht von der römischen Reiches freien stadt Regensburg* (Ratisbon 1753).

623 l. 6. Zimmermann *op. cit.* (*add.* to p. 98).

624 l. 1. After "Revision of": E. Tobac *RHE* April 1927 pp. 242–53. — Vol. I (Genesis) of the new ed. has appeared (Rome 1926).

633 no. 458. R. I. Best "On the *subscriptiones* in the 'Book of Dimma'" *Hermathena* no. xliv (1926) 84–100: "Dimma" substituted for name of real scribe, perhaps by the writer of the office for the sick (no. 563); *cumdach* may be of *s* XII, but repaired by Tadhg Ó Cearbaill of Éle, probably him who died in 1407.

635 no. 461. O–I glosses: *ZCP* XVII (1928) 223–4.

638 no. 467. *Cf.* E. C. R. Armstrong and H. J. Lawlor *Proc. RIA* XXXIV (1918) C 96–126; Macalister *op. cit.* (*add.* to p. 98) 290–2.

648 l. 34. Ff. v + 109 — 13⅜″ × 10⅛″; 20–22 ll. to page. Luke ii–xxiv 47; John (f. 63) v 2–xxi 16. Illuminated.

651 no. 490. *RC* XLI (1924) 268–71. — Geo. Taylor *London Times Lit. Supp.* 11 Nov. 1926 p. 797. — Macalister *op. cit.* (*add.* to p. 98) 300–2.

652 l. 14. "Nisita": *Cf. EHR* XXXVI (Oct. 1921) 540–5.

654 After l. 2. Amiens Bibl. mun. 6–9, 11, 12. A.D. 772 x 781. *Cf.* Berger *op. cit.* 102–3, 374. Sections of a bible written at Corbie in the time of, and partly by, Abbot Maurdramnus. — Tours Bibl. publ. 10 *s* VIII *ex. Cf.* Berger *op. cit.* 204, 246, 419. Octateuch. — Dom J. Chapman believes that Amiens 6–7 (*Mo*) is a revised copy of an Irish, and Tours 10 (*Mar*) of an Anglo-Irish, Pentateuch (*Rev. bénédictine* XXXVII (1925) 5 *sqq*, esp. 13–20). E. K. Rand considers it more probable that the *Vorlage* of Tours 10 was Irish (*Speculum* Jan. 1927 pp. 61–5).

656 no. 502. Comm: Simpson *The historical St. Columba* 34 *sqq*.

657 After no. 508: Vat. Palat. lat. 65 *s* XI: Irish psalter.

661 After l. 12: St. Gall Stiftsbibl. 258: Commentary on John. *Cf. Hermathena* xliv (1926) 67.

661 sub-sect. (b). *Bibliog.:* F. C. Burkitt *JTS* XXVIII (1926–7) 97–101. — A. Souter *The earliest Latin commentaries on the Epistles of St. Paul* (Oxford 1927).

666 no. 517. *Cf. Hermathena* xliv (1926) 66.

667 no. 519. E. K. Rand says copy in BM Eg. 2831 *s* VIII (from Tours) has Irish associations: *Speculum* Jan. 1927 p. 62.

668 no. 523. FR. TRANS: Paul Monceaux *Saint Martin Récits de Sulpice-Sévère* (Paris 1926) [has valuable introd.]; Eng. trans. from Fr.: M. C. Watt (London 1928),

672 n. 114. So *Cat. gén. des mss. des bibl. pub. de France — Départements* IV (Paris 1886) 176–7. Collection of grammatical treatises; *s* IX.

678 l. 12. EDS: Petschenig *Wiener Studien* IV 168 *sq*; Tangl in W. Arndt's *Schrifttafeln* no. 42.

678 l. 23. After "sás": [part of no. 250 (i)].

678 no. 537. *Cf. ZCP* XVII (1928) 102–6.

680 no. 541. *Cf.* Flower *Cat.* 487–9.

683 After l. 19: BM Eg. 1782 ff. 49^v–50: 23 quatrains of school-questions, chiefly on Old-Testament history; ed. KM *ZCP* IV 234–7.

684 l. 25. G. H. Forbes co-operated with his brother.

688 n. 150. Note also in BM Eg. 92 f. 17; 1782 f. 45.

693 l. 27. T. F. O'Rahilly "The history of the Stowe Missal" *Ériu* X i (1926) 95–109 [Missal not on the Continent, but found, shortly before 1735, by O'Kennedy of Lackeen, near Lorrha, in the walls of an old castle, and given to the first Marquess of Buckingham by Sir Richard Grace, M.P. (d. 1801)].

699 n. 194. O'Rahilly's hypothesis is that the MS was taken to Terryglass from Tallaght by Máel-Dithruib (*cf.* pp. 469 *sqq supra*) or one of his comrades, and passed to Lorrha *c s* XII *ex.*

702 no. 560. *Cf.* A. P. Forbes *Missale de Arbuthnot* pp. lxxxix *sq.*

702 n. 200. There is a suspicion that "moccu" was sometimes translated "filius" (Grosjean).

714 no. 572. Cod. Aug. CXCV. *Cf.* P. Siffrin *Rev. bénédictine* XXXIX (1927) 135–6, XL (1928) 137–8. L. W. Jones, *Speculum* Jan. 1929, pp. 27–61, concludes that Cologne 106 was written at Cologne *c* 805. *Cf.* Rand *ibid.* Jan. 1927 p. 57.

718 n. 240. Derived from *Tenga Bith-núa* (no. 612).

724 (i) *Cf. add.* to no. 572.

728 no. 585 (vi). MSS: BM Add. 30512 f. 30^v. (vii) MSS: *Ibid.* f. 32^v.

731 no. 596. MSS: YBL p. 16 [frag.]. — BM Eg. 92 f. 6^v.

732 Division C. *Bibliog.:* Seymour "Notes on apocrypha in Ireland" *Proc. RIA* XXXVII (1926) C 107–17.

734 no. 602 (iv). COMM: *Studies* XIII (1924) 376.

736 l. 3. After "xi": Similar paraphrases in BM Eg. 92 f. 31; 1782 f. 44^v.

736 l. 17. *Cf. ZCP* XVI (1927) 453–7.

736 n. 283 l. 1. After "4783": f. 7; RIA Stowe D. IV f. 53^v; BM Eg. 1782 f. 45^v; 136 f. 74^v [*cf.* Flower *Cat.* 522].

736 n. 287 l. 1. After "270–82": M. R. James *The apocryphal New Testament* (Oxford 1924) 556. — At end: "The fifteen tokens of Doomsday" (WS *RC* XXVIII (1907) 308–26, 432, from BM Add. 30512 ff. 95–8); probably later than A.D. 1170: a variation of the theme, of which earliest Irish example may be in *Kollektaneum Bedae* (no. 541). The author seems to have known the *Saltair na Rann* additions. *Cf.* Seymour *loc. cit.*; Flower *Cat.* 501–2; R. Peiper *Archiv f. Literaturgesch.* IX (1880) 117 *sqq.*

737 no. 612. MSS: Lib. Fl. Ferg. pt. II ff. 35 *sqq.* — BM Eg. 136 A.D. 1630 ff. 53 *sqq*;
174 *s* XVIII ff. 1–12 [all Eg. texts are incomplete]. — Edinburgh Nat. Lib. Scot.
Gael. XLVII [frag.]; LV. — TCD 1287 (H. 1. 13) A.D. 1746 pp. 89 *sqq*; 1414
(H. 6. 10) *s* XVIII pp. 91 *sqq.* — RIA 23 L 29 *s* XVIII(?). COMM: James
JTS XX 9 *sqq.* — Flower *Cat.* 556–9.

739 l. 8. After "1895)": *Cf.* Flower *Cat.* 534–7 *re* frag. in BM Eg. 1781 ff. 76–86;
James *Latin infancy gospels . . . with a parallel version from Irish* (Cambridge
1927).

739 ll. 23 *sqq. Cf.* LBr 159, *Speculum* Jan. 1928 pp. 98–101.

739 l. 29. Similar matter in Bk. Lis. f. 67, BM Eg. 92 f. 31^V, BN Celt. et basq. 1 f.
15^V.

739 n. 293. Same theme in BM Add. 30512 f. 33, Lib. Fl. Ferg. I f. 10, and elsewhere. *Cf.* Flower *Cat.* 484.

740 l. 11. After "kings": Note: Another version in Nat. Lib. Scot. Gael. I pp. 3–4;
VII ff. 10^V–11^V. The story of David and Solomon (*cf. RC* II 382) also in YBL
p. 122, Bodl. Rawl. B 512 f. 144, Bk. Lis. f. 69, BM Eg. 92 f. 26. Another story
of David — *ibid.* and in Bk. Fer. f. 57, Eg. 1781 f. 150 — pub. S. H. O'Grady
Mélusine IV 163–6.

740 l. 15. After "trans.": Also Eg. 91 f. 44^V.

740 l. 18. After "Philip": (Closely related versions of passions of Philip, Andrew
and James in Nat. Lib. Scot. Gael. I pp. 3–4, 4–5, 5–6.)

740 l. 21. After "Commandments": (Also Nat. Lib. Scot. Gael. XXV ff. 6^V–15^V.)

740 l. 22. After "soul": (*Cf.* Gaidoz *loc. cit.*; Seymour *JTS* XXII 16 *sqq.*)

740 After l. 26: There are many other Lives and anecdotes of foreign saints (Plummer *Misc. hag. Hib.* 255 *sqq*), but generally late and unimportant. Noteworthy
is the Life (homily) of Gregory the Great (represented as of Irish birth and
buried in Aran) of which matter and perhaps text is of *s* XI/XII: Tunc dicet
rex his qui a dextris eius sunt. Atbera hÍsu Crist . . . . MSS: YBL cols.
858–63, pp.164–6. — BN Celt. et basq. 1 ff. 41–2^V. — TCD H. 2. 17 pp. 423–8.
— BM Eg. 91 ff. 30^V–2^V. — Bodl. Laud 610 f. 14^V [frag.]. — Edinburgh Nat. Lib.
Scot. Gael. V f. 5 [anecdotes]. EDS: KM *ZCP* III 36 [Laud]; XII 367–74
[YBL]. — Vendryes *RC* XLII 119–53 [BN; *cf. An. Boll.* XLV (1927) 167–8].
Grosjean is to edit several texts in next issue of *RC*.

740 n. 295. Another version BM Eg. 91 f. 67^V; Lib. Fl. Ferg. I ff. 10, 37^V.

740 n. 296. Story of Paphnutius also in Nat. Lib. Scot. Gael. I pp. 16–18.

740 n. 298. For other MSS, *cf.* Flower *Cat.* pp. xxxiii, 440; Mackinnon *Cat. of
Gaelic MSS in Scotland* (Edinburgh 1912) 80.

740 n. 299. *Cf.* LBr 159, *Speculum* Jan. 1928 pp. 101–3.

740 n. 300. After "849": (whence pub. *ZCP* XIV 144–53, with Germ. trans.),
Lib. Fl. Ferg. I f. 33^V, and Nat. Lib. Scot. Gael. I pp. 14–5 [*cf.* Mackinnon *op. cit.*
76–7, 80].

741 no. 618. COMM: W. F. Thrall "Vergil's *Aeneid* and the Irish *imrama*" *Modern
Philology* XV (Dec. 1917) 65–90.

742 l. 10. After "182": *Proc. RIA* XXXVII (1926) C 87–106.

743 no. 621. COMM: Seymour "The bringing forth of the soul in Irish literature"
JTS XXII 16 *sqq.*

750 l. 6. A slight peculiarity of the calendar in 1065 produced alarm in central
Europe. *Cf.* E. Joranson "The great German pilgrimage of 1064–1065" in

PAGE

L. J. Paetow (ed.) *The Crusades and other historical essays presented to Dana C. Munro* (New York 1928) 3 *sqq.*

756 After l. 28: Bk. Durrow f. 13ᵛ (*cf.* p. 631 n. 15 *supra*) deciphered by R. I. Best, "An early monastic grant in the Book of Durrow" *Ériu* X ii 135–42, facs.: Ostende nobis . . . Óentu mór eter Comgan . . . 7 dia tuccad. Flannchad filius filii scientis scripsit. Grant by Glenn-Uissen (Killeshin, 2½ miles w. of Carlow) to Durrow, A.D. 1086 x 1119. Contains interesting names, among them Gilla-na-nóem húa hÉnlúain, abbot of Durrow; Gilla-Adamnáin húa Cortén, priest of Durrow (mentioned in Kells Charter V (no. 632) as *comarba* of Columcille); Cathasach húa Corcráin, *airchinnech* of Glenn-Uissen (FM obit, erroneous, 1045); and Dublittir húa hÚadgaile, *fer légind*, known as author of a tract on *Sex aetates mundi* (in Bodl. Rawl. B 502, BB, Bk. Lec., and LU — imperfect). *Cf.* pp. 153–4.

763 sect. IV. *Bibliog.*: J. MacErlean *AH* III 1–33.

768 no. 653 (i). *Cf.* Flower *Cat.* 524–5.

771 end. *Cf.* M. V. Ronan *IER* 5th ser. XXVII 347–64, XXVIII 247–56, 467–80, 596–612.

ADDENDA, 1966

PAGE

25   n. 79. *The Book of Lismore* is now in Chatsworth Castle, Derbyshire.

87   n. 367. The Franciscan Library is now housed at Dun Mhuire, Killiney, co. Dublin.

96   l. 16. J. Loth "Les mots latins dans les langues brittoniques" *Annales de Bretagne* VII (1892) 205–42. — H. Pedersen *Vergleichende Grammatik der keltischen Sprachen* I (1909) 189–242.

145   l. 24. M. R. James *Cambridge Medieval History* III (1922) 500.

149   l. 4. For literature on Cormac's *Glossary* see J. Loth in *Le Moyen Âge* 3rd ser. XL (1930) 260 n. 1.

152   l. 36. J. Loth *Le Moyen Âge* 3rd ser. XL (1930) 261 (sides with Thurneysen; gives also additional bibliographical references).

154   l. 34. Footnote to *De sex aetatibus mundi*: Cf. pp. 670, 790.

159   n. 9. M. Varin "Mémoire sur les causes de dissidence entre l'Eglise bretonne et l'Eglise romaine" *Mémoires de l'Académie des Inscriptions et Belles Lettres* 1. sér. IV. 2 (1858) 117–20. — J. Loth *op. cit.* 266 *sq.*

160   n. 14. L. Mühlhausen "Die lateinischen, germanischen, romanischen lehnwörter im Cymrischen" *Festschrift Ernst Windisch* (Leipzig 1914) 249–348.

169   l. 12. J. Hardouin *Conciliorum collectio ragia* I (1715) 1789–93. — Mansi *Sacrorum conciliorum nova . . . collectio* VI (1761) 513–20. — Wilkins *Concilia Magnae Britanniae* I (1737) 2–3.

171   l.11. C. H. Slover "Early literary channels between Britain and Ireland" *Univ. of Texas Studies in English* no. 6 (1926).

175   l. 27. W. Levison *NA* XXXV (1910) 228; *Miscellanea Ehrle* II=*Studi e Testi* 38 (1924) 213 *sq.* [Wrdisten's use of *Actus Silvestri*].

192   l. 23. Jean Rivière "Saint Colomban et le jugement du pape hérétique" *Revue des sciences religieuses* III (1923) 277–82.

201   l. 12. A. Vaccari "Il salterio ascoliano e Giulio eclanese" *Biblica* IV (1923) 337–55. — R. Devreesse "Le commentaire de Théodore de Mopsueste sur les psaumes" *Revue Biblique* XXXVII (1928) 340–66; xxxviii (1929) 35–62.

209   l. 7. W. Levison *Histor. Aufsätze Aloys Schulte gewidmet* (Düsseldorf 1927) 67.

228   l. 16. P. W. Finsterwalder *Die Canones Theodori Cantuarensis und ihre Überlieferungsformen* (Weimar 1929) and the review by W. Levison *Zs. der Savigny-Stiftung für Rechtsgeschichte* L, Kanonist. Abt. XIX (1930) 699 *sqq.*

240   l. 20. J. Loth *Le Moyen Âge* XL (1930) 273 would write "Venniavus."

245   l. 3. Hardouin *Conciliorum collectio regia* I (1715) 1793–6. — Mansi *Sacrorum conciliorum nova . . . collectio* VI (1761) 522–8.

261   l. 4. But surely it would be impossible to point out Rathan in Offaly from Granard. But Hogan in *Doc. de S. P.* pt. II 195 and Warren in *AB* II 57 accept it. Hogan *Onomasticon* under Mag Cuini doubtfully identifies the last with

PAGE

617   l. 28.   P. J. Barry *Die Zustände im Wiener Schottenkloster vor der Reform des Jahres 1418* (Aichbach 1927).

619   no. 445.   Aegidius Gelenius *De admiranda sacra et civili magnitudine Coloniae* (Cologne 1645) 646 mentions Book II of *itineris sive periegesios S. Petri* by a Marianus Scottus, who is possibly identical with either the chronicler or the abbot.

628   l. 5.   A. Kingsley Porter *The crosses and culture of Ireland* (Yale 1931) 79.

633   l. 36.   The Öttingen-Wallersteinische Bibl. was formerly at Maihingen.

679   l. 2.   For a description of the MS, see H. Hagen *Catalogus codicum Bernensium* (Berne 1875) under its number.

702   l. 18.   Comm: E. Nasalli Rocca "L'Archivio capitolare di S. Antonino in Piacenza" *Archivio storico italiano* XV (1931) 290–6.

712   l. 22.   Was the Orationale Gothicum (Verona) really of the seventh century? (Pencilled note by J. F. K. in the margin of his hand copy.)

742   l. 11.   E. H. van Heurck *Les livres populaires flamands* (Antwerp 1931) 94–6.

743   l. 5.   Gougaud in *Modern Research* p. 13 refers to A de J *RC* XI 492–3. (Pencilled note by J. F. K. in the margin of his hand copy.)

CORRIGENDA

796 CORRIGENDA

798   CORRIGENDA

PAGE
675   l. 6.   For, *Foedera*, read, *Foedera, Suppl.*
677   l. 25.   For, Unterdrauberg, Carinthia, Kloster St. Paul 25. 2. 31, formerly 25. d. 86 (Codex, read, Kloster St. Paul, Carinthia, 86. 1b (25. 2. 31b; xxv. d. 86; Codex
680   l. 31.   For, Unterdrauberg in Carinthia Kloster St. Paul 25, read, Kloster St. Paul, Carinthia, xxv.
682   l. 12.   For, Vat. Palat., read, Vat. Palat. lat.
682   l. 39.   For, p. 66, read, f. 45^{r-v}
687   l. 20.   For, II ff., read, II s VIII/IX ff.
688   l 24.   For, N 10 [Stowe], read, N 10
704   l. 18.   For, Stadtbibl., read, Staatsarchiv (A. G. 19 no. XXXVI f. 57 = pp. 117/118)
705   l. 30.   For, s XI, read, now New York Pierpont Morgan Lib. M. 627 s XI ex.
712   l. 32.   For, 1^{233} s VII, read, 1 fasc. 9^{233} s VIII in.
714   l. 4.   For, Unterdrauberg, Carinthia, Kloster St. Paul, read, Kloster St. Paul, Carinthia,
720   l. 23.   For, semi-uncial or large minuscule, read, semi-uncial
737   l. 27.   For, celtique, read, celtique et basq.
737   l. 27.   For, Cheltenham Phillipps MS 9754, read, Dublin Nat. Lib. Gael. 9 (Phillipps 9754)
738   l. 22.   For, celtique, read, celtique et basq.
743   l. 3.   For, celt., read, celt. et basq.
744   l. 4.   For, celtique, read, celtique et basq.
753   l. 7. For, H. 2. 15, read, 1317 (H. 2. 15b)
753   l. 8.   For, p. 59, read, ff. 59–66
763   l. 14.   For, f. 54, read, s XII p. 54
765   l. 8.   For, 35 pp., read, 35 s XVIII pp.
765   l. 34.   For, *deórad*, read, *deórad Dé*
770   l. 3.   For, 525 s, read, 525 (F. 4. 29) s
770   l. 29.   For, A 575, read, 193 (A. 575)
770   l. 33.   For, 8943 ff. 2–26^v; 11987 ff., read, 8943 s XVII ff. 2–26^v; 11987 s XVI ff.

INDEX[1]

[1] This summary index to the sources and to a selected number of proper names and technical terms has been added for the assistance of the reader until more adequate aids can be provided at the end of Volume II.